Handbook of International
Economics

Handbook of International
Economics

VOLUME 4

Edited by

GITA GOPINATH
Harvard University, Cambridge, MA, USA
National Bureau of Economic Research, Cambridge, MA, USA

ELHANAN HELPMAN
Harvard University, Cambridge, MA, USA
Canadian Institute for Advanced Research
National Bureau of Economic Research, Cambridge, MA, USA

KENNETH ROGOFF
Harvard University, Cambridge, MA, USA
National Bureau of Economic Research, Cambridge, MA, USA

Amsterdam • Boston • Heidelberg • London • New York • Oxford
Paris • San Diego • San Francisco • Singapore • Sydney • Tokyo
North-Holland is an imprint of Elsevier

North-Holland is an imprint of Elsevier
The Boulevard, Langford Lane, Kidlington, Oxford OX5 1GB, UK
Radarweg 29, PO Box 211, 1000 AE Amsterdam, The Netherlands

British Library Cataloguing in Publication Data
A catalogue record for this book is available from the British Library

Library of Congress Cataloging-in-Publication Data
A catalog record for this book is available from the Library of Congress

ISBN–13: 978-0-444-54314-1

For information on all North-Holland publications
visit our website at http://store.elsevier.com/

Printed and bound in Poland
14 15 16 17 18   10 9 8 7 6 5 4 3 2 1

CONTENTS

CONTRIBUTORS

Mark Aguiar
Princeton University, Princeton, NJ, USA

Manuel Amador
Federal Reserve Bank of Minneapolis, Minneapolis, MN, USA

Pol Antràs
Harvard University, Cambridge, MA, USA
National Bureau of Economic Research, Cambridge, MA, USA
Centre for Economic Policy Research, London, UK

Ariel Burstein
University of California, Los Angeles, CA, USA
National Bureau of Economic Research, Cambridge, MA, USA

Arnaud Costinot
Massachusetts Institute of Technology, Cambridge, MA, USA
National Bureau of Economic Research, Cambridge, MA, USA

Charles Engel
University of Wisconsin, Madison, WI, USA
National Bureau of Economic Research, Cambridge, MA, USA

Gita Gopinath
Harvard University, Cambridge, MA, USA
National Bureau of Economic Research, Cambridge, MA, USA

Pierre-Olivier Gourinchas
University of California, Berkeley, CA, USA
National Bureau of Economic Research, Cambridge, MA, USA
Centre for Economic Policy Research, London, UK

Keith Head
Sauder School of Business, University of British Columbia, Canada
Centre for Economic Policy Research, London, UK

Jonathan Heathcote
Federal Reserve Bank of Minneapolis, Minneapolis, MN, USA
Centre for Economic Policy Research, London, UK

Guido Lorenzoni
Northwestern University, Evanston, IL, USA
National Bureau of Economic Research, Cambridge, MA, USA

Giovanni Maggi
Yale University, New Haven, CT, USA
Graduate School of Economics, Getulio Vargas Foundation, Brasil
National Bureau of Economic Research, Cambridge, MA, USA

Thierry Mayer
Sciences-Po, Paris, France
Centre d'études prospectives et d'informations internationales, France
Centre for Economic Policy Research, London, UK

Marc J. Melitz
Harvard University, Cambridge, MA, USA
National Bureau of Economic Research, Cambridge, MA, USA
Centre for Economic Policy Research, London, UK

Nathan Nunn
Harvard University, Cambridge, MA, USA
National Bureau of Economic Research, Cambridge, MA, USA

Fabrizio Perri
Federal Reserve Bank of Minneapolis, Minneapolis, MN, USA
National Bureau of Economic Research, Cambridge, MA, USA
Centre for Economic Policy Research, London, UK

Stephen J. Redding
Princeton University, Princeton, NJ, USA
National Bureau of Economic Research, Cambridge, MA, USA
Centre for Economic Policy Research, London, UK

Hélène Rey
London Business School, London, UK
National Bureau of Economic Research, Cambridge, MA, USA
Centre for Economic Policy Research, London, UK

Daniel Trefler
University of Toronto, Toronto, ON, Canada
National Bureau of Economic Research, Cambridge, MA, USA

Andrés Rodríguez-Clare
University of California, Berkeley, CA, USA
National Bureau of Economic Research, Cambridge, MA, USA

Stephen R. Yeaple
Pennsylvania State University, University Park, PA, USA
National Bureau of Economic Research, Cambridge, MA, USA

The aim of the Handbooks in Economics series is to produce Handbooks for various branches of economics, each of which is a definitive source, reference, and teaching supplement for use by professional researchers and advanced graduate students. Each Handbook provides self-contained surveys of the current state of a branch of economics in the form of chapters prepared by leading specialists on various aspects of this branch of economics. These surveys summarize not only received results but also newer developments, from recent journal articles and discussion papers. Some original material is also included, but the main goal is to provide comprehensive and accessible surveys. The Handbooks are intended to provide not only useful reference volumes for professional collections but also possible supplementary readings for advanced courses for graduate students in economics.

Kenneth J. Arrow and Michael D. Intriligator

Almost twenty years have passed since the publication of Volume 3 of the *Handbook of International Economics* in 1995. Much has changed since then, both in international trade and international macroeconomics. The changes are fourfold: (a) new questions have arisen as the world trade and payment system has evolved; (b) new data sets have become available; (c) new theoretical models have been designed to address new issues, but they have also enabled sharper and deeper analyses of older issues; and (d) new empirical studies have greatly enriched our understanding of the global economy.

The chapters in this handbook review, illuminate, and interpret these developments in a systematic way, making this material—which is technical at times—accessible to professional economists and graduate students alike. Trade is covered in the first six chapters, and international macroeconomics is covered in the subsequent six chapters.

1. INTERNATIONAL TRADE

Neoclassical analysis of foreign trade focused on comparative advantage at the sectoral level, be it due to variation in productivity or factor endowments. Firms as suppliers of unique brands of differentiated products and monopolistic competition were integrated into trade theory in the 1980s (see Krugman 1995 for a review). Yet as much as these improvements have been important, they focused on sectoral outcomes by treating firms within industries as symmetric entities. Given the aim of that research, which was to expand the neoclassical framework to accommodate intraindustry trade and large volumes of trade between similar countries, the symmetry assumption was a reasonable simplification. Except that it proved to be inadequate for interpreting evidence that emerged in the 1990s concerning the participation of firms in foreign trade, as new firm-level data sets became available. In these data, exporting firms differ systematically from nonexporters. Scholars responded with the development of new models in which firms are heterogeneous, and these models guided empirical studies with the new rich data sets.

Melitz and Redding review these developments in Chapter 1. After describing the patterns of firm heterogeneity in the data, they develop an integrated multisector analytical framework for discussing many issues that have been analyzed in the recent literature. In the data, exporters differ from nonexporters in a number of dimensions; e.g., exporters are bigger and more productive than nonexporters and they pay higher wages.

*We thank the National Science Foundation for financial support.

Studies of trade liberalization show that it leads to substantial reallocation within industries; low-productivity firms exit while market shares are reallocated to more productive firms, and especially to exporters. In addition, firms and product margins are important determinants of trade flows, because variation in the number of products explains a large fraction of the variation in trade volumes. These are some of the findings that motivated the original theoretical analysis that Melitz and Redding review in this chapter.

The analytical framework consists of sectors that have the features developed in Melitz (2003), as well as a homogeneous good sector (although the latter is shut down in some applications). Firms enter an industry in anticipation of a productivity draw. After the entry cost is sunk and a firm's productivity revealed, the firm has to decide whether to stay in the industry or exit. If it stays, it has to decide whether to serve only the domestic market or also export. There is a fixed cost of operation and a fixed cost of exporting, as well as variable trade costs. In the now familiar manner, firms choose among these strategies based on productivity: the least productive firms exit, the most productive become exporters, and intermediate-productivity firms serve only the domestic market.

Although these results are not new, the exposition is new and intuitive, making the analysis accessible to many readers. This useful feature characterizes the entire chapter. It is especially helpful in the discussion of within-sectoral reallocations in response to declining trade costs and the home market effect.

Melitz and Redding also explain how these models have guided estimation of trade flows and quantitative analysis. Some of these issues are discussed in more detail in Chapter 3 on gravity equations and in Chapter 4 on trade theory with numbers. They also discuss the integration of factor proportions into the multisector framework and some of its consequences, such as the relationship between factor endowments and endogenous sectoral productivity levels.

Up to this point preferences for variety were assumed to be of the constant-elasticity-of-substitution type, resulting in constant markups in percentage terms. In Section 8, Melitz and Redding replace those preferences with a generalized quadratic system that yields linear demand functions with an intercept that depends on sectoral conditions. Under these circumstances markups vary across firms and they respond to demand and supply shocks. Since trade is costly, international markets are not fully integrated and market size impacts markups and average sectoral productivity levels. As a result, productivity is higher and markups are lower in larger economies.

In this case multilateral trade liberalization leads to exit of low-productivity firms and market share reallocation toward more productive firms, including exporters, but in addition it reduces markups. The result is that prices are lower because of both higher productivity and lower markups.

Section 9 then examines endogenous firm-specific productivity levels, by allowing firms to engage in innovation or technology adoption that augments their productivity draws. Choice of product scope for multiproduct firms is also considered, which provides another endogenous source of productivity variation across firms. In a dynamic context this generates a complementarity between exports and productivity-enhancing investments, because the payoff to productivity improvements is higher for exporting firms.

A number of empirical studies have shown that key predictions of these models are consistent with the data. As a rule, exporters invest more than nonexporters in new technologies. And in the face of trade liberalization, multiproduct firms shed their worst products while nonexporters who switch to exporting invest the most in technology upgrading.

Finally, Melitz and Redding review the recent literature on the impact of trade on wage inequity in the presence of labor market frictions. Unlike the neoclassical writings that discussed wage inequality across workers with different characteristics, such as differences in human capital, the new literature emphasizes residual wage inequality—wage inequality between workers with similar characteristics—that has become a large contributor to the inequality of earnings. Firm heterogeneity plays an important role in this relationship, both theoretically and empirically, because firms with varying attributes within sectors pay different wages to workers with similar characteristics.

In Chapter 2, Antràs and Yeaple review the evolution of ideas about the role of multinational firms in the world's trading system. Much has happened on this front since the publication of the previous volume of the *Handbook of International Economics*. On the theoretical side the internalization decision has been afforded new foundations and within-industry firm heterogeneity has been extended to cover multinationals. On the empirical side new hypotheses emanating from the novel theory have been examined with rich new data sets.

Antràs and Yeaple first review some stylized facts about the operation of multinational corporations. Some of these are similar to stylized facts about trade flows; e.g., foreign direct investment (FDI) is concentrated within the group of rich countries and it exhibits large two-way flows (intraindustry FDI). There are, however, substantial differences across sectors; e.g., multinationals operate primarily in capital-intensive and R&D-intensive sectors. Within sectors, both the parents of multinationals and their affiliates tend to be larger, more productive, more R&D intensive, and more export oriented than nonmultinational corporations. And moreover, parents tend to specialize in R&D while affiliates tend to sell goods primarily in the host countries.

After presenting this evidence, Antràs and Yeaple develop a simple analytical framework of trade with monopolistic competition that includes multinational corporations (MNCs), but no within-industry heterogeneity. They apply it to horizontal FDI, driven by the proximity-concentration tradeoff. In this view a firm can serve a foreign market via export or subsidiary sales. The former entails variable trade costs—such as tariffs or freight—that are saved by the latter mode of operation, while FDI entails fixed costs of acquiring and operating a production unit in the foreign country, which are saved by exporting. The evidence, based on U.S. data, supports this tradeoff: export relative to subsidiary sales is lower in sectors with high variable trade costs and higher in sectors with high plant-level fixed costs.

Following this discussion, the theory is extended to include heterogeneous firms. Now the most productive firms become multinational corporations while the least productive (that remain in the industry) serve only the domestic market. Firms with intermediate productivity levels serve foreign markets via export sales. This sorting pattern holds in several data sets. The model also predicts a proximity-concentration trade-off, and it adds to it an impact of the degree of sectoral heterogeneity. That is, export relative to subsidiary sales is expected to be smaller in sectors with more productivity dispersion.

Vertical FDI is next examined. In this case firms choose to fragment their production process, locate some activities—such as R&D or design—in the headquarters and therefore in the home country, and other activities—such as production of intermediate inputs or assembly—in host countries of subsidiaries. Since this motive for FDI is primarily driven by cost considerations, differences in factor prices play a key role in these decisions. But firm heterogeneity is also important, and the models predict, consistent with the data, that within sectors more productive firms source their inputs from foreign countries. In the U.S. data, imports of inputs from foreign subsidiaries are highly concentrated among a small number of very large multinationals, and these subsidiaries are located in a small number of countries that include Canada, Mexico, and Ireland. There is, however, substantial variation across sectors and countries in export relative to subsidiary sales. In particular, U.S. firms export less relative to subsidiary sales in skill-intensive sectors to countries that are skill abundant.

Next, Antràs and Yeaple provide a detailed discussion of theories of the boundaries of firms, including their implications for multinational corporations. These include the transaction costs and property rights approaches to firms' boundaries. In addition to clearly explaining the insights from this literature, they develop several generalizations of key results. Here too firm heterogeneity plays center stage as do new features such as the role of incomplete contracts, the degree of contractibility of various activities, and the varying ability to contract in different countries. As in previous models, offshoring is concentrated among high-productivity firms, and the most productive among them engage in foreign direct investment. In addition, the property rights model predicts more integration in headquarter-intensive sectors, leading to larger shares of intrafirm trade, and subtle differences between the impact of better contractibility of headquarter and nonheadquarter activities. The latter predictions contrast with predictions of the transactions cost approach to boundaries of the firm, which are the same for all improvements in contractibility. A review of the evidence suggests that it is in line with several implications of the property rights approach.

We have chosen to devote an entire chapter to the use of gravity equations for the estimation of trade flows. Although these equations have been widely used for empirical analysis since Tinbergen introduced them in 1962, the theoretical foundations of these equations had been sketchy and only recent work has provided satisfactory formulations. As a result, empirical analysis of trade flows relies now more than ever before on theoretical foundations, and these foundations have also helped to develop estimation methods that are rooted in theory. This important literature is reviewed by Head and Mayer in Chapter 3.

The chapter starts with a historical review of the fundamental equation, developing three related definitions. It then proceeds to describe a sequence of theoretical models that yield gravity equations. Some are based on demand conditions, others on supply conditions. Some are competitive, others use monopolistic competition. Some have symmetric firms, others have heterogeneous firms. This part shows clearly the broad and wide reach of Tinbergen's original idea.

After reviewing the theory, Head and Mayer discuss theory-consistent estimation, covering a number of techniques. This section is more than useful, because it includes a very clear discussion of the advantages and limitations of alternative methods, including a Monte Carlo study of the main estimators.

Among the uses of gravity equations, estimates of the effects of policies—such as free trade agreements and currency areas—on trade promotion have been prominent. The chapter discusses these estimates, distinguishing between partial and general equilibrium effects, as well as broader issues of quantitative analysis based on gravity equations. It also covers recent research on estimation procedures that account for the presence of zero trade flows in data sets with many countries, and the separation of the intensive from the extensive margin of trade flows.

In Chapter 4, Costinot and Rodríguez-Clare discuss the use of structural gravity equations for quantitative assessments of the consequence of globalization. After reviewing a variety of models that yield gravity equations, they show that a number of them share a similar formula for the gains from trade. The ingredients of this formula are the proportional decline of the share of spending on a country's own goods and the elasticity of trade with respect to variable trade costs. This characterization applies to models of perfect competition and models of monopolistic competition, including models with firm heterogeneity, that satisfy certain "macro" restrictions.

Calibrated versions of these models can be used to compute in a simple way gains from trade. Such computations shed light on the role of various ingredients in the theory, serving as a "theory with numbers." For example, the gains are sensitive to the inclusion of many sectors and intermediate inputs.

In addition to gains from trade, structural gravity models can be used to evaluate the impact of trade policies, such as tariffs, by performing counterfactual exercises. These include the computation of optimal unilateral tariffs and comparisons of uniform versus nonuniform tariffs with the same average rate of protection. The chapter closes with a discussion of quantitative approaches that do not rely on gravity models.

In Chapter 5, Nunn and Trefler discuss an entirely new line of research, concerning the role of domestic institutions in shaping comparative advantage. This topic was not covered in previous volumes of the *Handbook of International Economics*, simply because the relevant literature has developed only recently.

The chapter begins with a discussion of contracting institutions. One view is that in two countries with similar technologies and factor prices, unit costs may differ due to differences in the quality of the legal systems, and that the cost differences vary across industries if the reliance on contracts is not the same in all of them. To evaluate this hypothesis it is necessary to develop sectoral measures of contract intensity and country measures of the quality of the legal systems. Scholars have indeed developed such indexes and the empirical studies show that countries with better legal systems tend to export relatively more in contract-intensive sectors. Moreover, the contribution of this source of comparative advantage to trade flows is quite large. There are, of course, significant methodological issues involved in this analysis, and they are clearly laid out in the chapter.

Other institutional features that have been studied include financial development and labor market institutions. Nunn and Trefler review the empirical literature and provide comparable joint estimates of various measures of product market, financial market, and labor market institutions on comparative advantage. Similarly to previous studies, they find that the impact of these institutional features on comparative advantage is comparable in size to the impact of factor endowments.

The chapter then proceeds to discuss informal institutions and cultural beliefs in shaping trade flows, and Nunn and Trefler relate the analysis of contracting institutions to outsourcing and integration covered in greater detail in Chapter 2. Finally, they discuss the historical evidence on reverse causality, from international trade to the formation of domestic institutions. These include episodes from the commercial revolution and the African slave trade.

The final chapter of those concerning trade, written by Giovanni Maggi, is devoted to international trade agreements. Although similar topics are covered in Volume 3 of the *Handbook of International Economics*, significant progress has been made since its publication in 1995. The chapter starts with a discussion of motives for trade agreements, using simple models to illustrate them. Importantly, the models include political economy considerations.

One motive for trade agreements is based on the terms-of-trade theory, which argues that a trade agreement avoids a Prisoners' Dilemma inherent in trade wars, and thereby leads to a more efficient outcome. This is an old argument that has received much attention and has been greatly refined over the years. A second motive concerns commitments. In this view trade agreements commit the government vis à vis domestic interest groups, thereby eliminating the implementation of some undesirable trade policies. This argument has also been refined in important ways in recent years. Finally, arguments that build on the "new" trade theory have been further developed. In this view of the world, trade policies impact firm entry and exit and reallocate profits across firms and countries. As a result, governments have incentives to engage in trade policies that take advantage of these responses, often at the expense of other countries. Trade agreements can mitigate some of these concerns. New empirical studies have addressed these motives and the chapter reviews the evidence.

Next comes a discussion of the design of trade agreements. The developments in this area are particularly novel. Naturally, in the absence of design costs this issue would not be challenging. In practice, however, these costs can be substantial. Maggi discusses two types of costs: contracting frictions, such as contract incompleteness, and imperfect enforcement. These shed light on the roles of various World Trade Organization (WTO) rules, such as the presence of binding trade instruments but nonbinding domestic policy instruments, the principle of reciprocity, or the most favored nation clause. They also shed light on the dispute settlement mechanism that was introduced with the formation of the WTO (which replaced the General Agreement on Tariffs and Trade (GATT) in 1995) after the completion of the Uruguay Round of trade negotiations.

In the final section Maggi discusses the formation of regional trade agreements that have proliferated since the formation of the WTO. The discussion includes the economic and political determinants of such agreements and the impact of these agreements on multilateral trade negotiations.

2. INTERNATIONAL MACROECONOMICS

As with international trade, international macroeconomics has seen major advances over the past two decades, driven both by new data sets and new theory. New databases have allowed researchers to explore nuances in classic questions such as the law of one price and the financial significance of current account deficits in novel ways with surprising results. Early models of financial market integration based on trade in bonds and a limited set of financial instruments have been supplanted by models with a much richer range of instruments. These range from models with complete asset markets to those with very specific frictions in goods and/or finanical markets. One very specific friction, resulting from the inability of sovereign nations to legally commit to international debt repayments was taken up in the previous handbook. However, there have been major advances in both theoretical sophistication and empirical foundations in this central area of research, so we revisit the issue here in a separate chapter. The reader may note that this volume does not include a separate chapter on New Open Economy Macroeconomic Models (following Obstfeld and Rogoff, 1996). We decided that this topic had already been covered recently by Corsetti, Dedola, and Leduc (2010) in the *Handbook of Monetary Economics*. We now turn to the individual chapters on international macroeconomics.

One of the fundamental issues explored in international macroeconomics is the relation between exchange rates and other macroeconomic variables. The first two chapters survey the progress made in understanding this relation with a focus on developments since the last handbook was published in 1995.

The first chapter by Burstein and Gopinath, "International Prices and Exchange Rates", surveys recent empirical and theoretical developments on the relation between exchange rates and prices. Empirical research on the extent of convergence in prices, in a common currency, across locations has been ongoing for several decades. This literature on purchasing power parity and exchange rate pass-through received a major boost as an increasing number of micro data sets on prices became available over the last decade. This has meant that we now know facts about price dispersion down to the level of a universal product code (UPC) sold by the same firm across locations within and across country borders. Similarly we have information on the sensitivity of prices to exchange rate changes at various stages of the retail chain, from at-the-dock prices, to wholesale prices and to retail prices with prices observed at high frequencies and for long periods of time.

Burstein and Gopinath first organize a large number of recent empirical results under the heading of five empirical findings and then provide a simple theoretical framework to interpret the facts. They do so by nesting in reduced form the various theoretical channels that can dampen the response of prices to exchange rates and that can generate price dispersion. They then describe recent developments in the literature that endogenously generate variable markups and pricing to market. These models add many realistic features to the pricing decisions of firms such as firm heterogeneity, consumer search, inventories, and distribution costs and complement the arrival of rich micro data in enhancing our understanding of the link between exchange rates and prices.

While the first of the international macro chapters focuses on the impact of nominal exchange rates on prices the second chapter by Engel, "Exchange Rates and Interest Parity", surveys advances in research on the topic of what determines nominal exchange rates. Engel provides an organizing framework around an interest parity condition for the large literature that investigates the connect or disconnect between exchange rates and macro fundamentals. This interest parity condition ties the current value of the nominal exchange rate to nominal interest rate differentials, the expected future value of the exchange rate, and a residual term that captures deviations from uncovered interest parity (UIP). He first surveys the traditional monetary approach to exchange rate determination that assumes UIP holds. Unlike the discussion in the previous handbook chapter on this same topic this chapter surveys the monetary approach through the lens of the dynamic and stochastic New Keynesian literature. This analysis highlights the implications for exchange rates, both from a theoretical perspective and for empirical testing, of the endogeneity of monetary rate setting and of more empirically motivated assumptions of price setting such as the distinction between producer and local currency pricing. Recent empirical tests of the ability of the monetary approach to explain and forecast exchange rates, both in and out of sample are described.

Then the chapter takes up recent developments on the residual term that captures deviations from UIP. There have been several recent developments in understanding this residual, including finance-based models of foreign exchange risk premia, heterogeneous private information, deviations from strict rational expectations, and other imperfections in capital markets. Engel provides a teachable framework for several of the insights of these models, discusses the empirical success of these newer approaches, and concludes with suggestions for future research that will help to improve our understanding of what determines nominal exchange rates.

The next two chapters survey the literature on international risk sharing, allocation of capital across countries, and current account dynamics. Are resources efficiently allocated across countries, and if not, what are the welfare gains from increasing efficiency? This important question and the research therein is the subject of the chapter by Heathcote and Perri titled "Assessing International Efficiency". The previous handbook did contain an excellent chapter on real business cycle models by Marianne Baxter, however, Heathcote and Perri provide some novel perspectives on the considerable literature that has evolved since then. In particular, there exists a long tradition in international macroeconomics of enumerating so-called puzzles related to, among others, cross-country co-movements in consumption, in investment, and co-movement between consumption and the real exchange rate. Heathcote and Perri depart from the language of puzzles and instead provide a unified framework to assess international efficiency both at business cycle frequencies and over the long-run. By doing so, they highlight the inter-connectedness between the various puzzles and discuss the relative merits of using quantities, such as relative consumption, versus prices, such as the real exchange rate, versus asset portfolio choices in assessing efficiency. The main analysis is performed in a neoclassical environment with symmetric countries but allowing for departures from asset market completeness. This provides a useful benchmark to measure disagreements between theory and data.

The chapter by Gourinchas and Rey, "External Adjustment, Global Imbalances, Valuation Effects", begins with a summary of recent empirical facts on capital flows, including those related to "global imbalances" and potential inefficiencies in resource allocation across countries. These facts have given rise to new models on the direction of capital flows that emphasize asymmetries across countries at various stages of development. This focus on asymmetries distinguishes the analysis in this chapter from the preceding chapter. The literature provides explanations for global imbalances based on cross-country differences in the ability of domestic agents to insure within-country idiosyncratic risk and cross-country differences in the ability of countries to supply stores of value/financial assets. Differences in demographic trends and the interaction between trade and finance frictions are also shown to generate capital movements that differ from the predictions of a neoclassical model. Gourinchas and Rey provide a valuable common framework within which to understand the different models. They highlight that the models share the feature that advanced economies can exhibit higher autarky real returns as compared to emerging economies thus rationalizing capital flows from emerging to advanced markets.

Another important development in the literature on external adjustment is the role of asset valuations in understanding changes in a country's net foreign asset position. These "valuation effects" can arise from capital gains/losses on a country's external portfolio including those from exchange rate movements when a country's assets and liabilities are denominated in different currencies. This channel of external adjustment is separate from the traditional "trade channel" which was the focus of the previous handbook chapter on this topic. Gourinchas and Rey survey this new literature on "valuation effects," the role it plays in understanding changes in a country's net foreign asset position and its quantitative importance for long-run solvency. The chapter concludes with a discussion of the differences across countries in the composition of their external balance sheets and its implications for the functioning of the international monetary and financial system.

The last two chapters survey the literature on sovereign debt and on financial crises. Aguiar and Amador, in their chapter "Sovereign Debt" review major developments in the literature on sovereign debt, default, debt overhang, and debt crises. The chapter first provides a quick summary of the leading empirical facts on sovereign debt. A distinguishing feature of sovereign debt is the limited mechanisms that exist for enforcing repayment. Accordingly, Aguiar and Amador provide a benchmark framework for debt and repayment decisions in an environment of limited commitment toward repayment. Their benchmark environment is a novel organizing framework that clarifies the main mechanisms of several seminal papers in the literature and highlights the negative consequences of limited commitment on risk-sharing, investment, and growth. The constrained efficient contracts they describe require state-contingency, but as they point out even with non-state contingent debt in reality there exists ex post state-contingency with renegotiations and haircuts. They use the benchmark framework and extensions such as unobservable shocks to clarify concepts of equilibrium default, renegotiation, excusable default, and inexcusable default. They also provide a description of self-fulfilling debt crises that results from coordination failures across foreign lenders.

Over the past decade there has been a growth in research that aims to quantify models of sovereign debt and match features of the data including the frequency of default and observed levels of debt to GDP in countries. Aguiar and Amador survey this literature and clarify the central features required by these models to match the empirical facts, including describing the dimensions along which the quantitative models perform poorly. Needless to say, in a world where many advanced countries, particularly in the periphery of Europe, are struggling with very high debt levels and low growth, the topic of sovereign defaults is likely to continue to remain a very active area of research.

The final chapter by Lorenzoni on "International Financial Crises" provides an overview of the theoretical developments in our understanding of international crises over the last thirty years. With the globalization of capital flows, a typical crisis combines features of sudden stops in capital flows, banking crises, and sovereign debt crises along with currency crises. While the previous handbook chapter focused exclusively on currency crises this chapter covers both the monetary and financial aspects of crises. Today, of course, we better understand the profound empirical and theoretical linkages across different types of crises. Lorenzoni starts with a description of the earlier models of currency crises and highlights the implications for capital flows when countries follow policies that are inconsistent with the maintenance of a fixed exchange rate regime. Similarly, he describes speculative attack models of currency crises. Next, he describes crises that originate with shocks to the current account, that is when there is a sudden stop in capital inflows for exogenous reasons and traces out the implications for the real economy, as a function of the exchange rate regime. He demonstrates the possible contractionary effects of exchange rate devaluations through the weakening of the country and firms' balance sheets, when assets and liabilities are denominated in different currencies.

Lastly the chapter surveys the literature that tries to explain why countries may end up with vulnerabilities to crises such as too large a current account deficit or an overvalued exchange rate or large sovereign debt. Here he describes the various approaches taken in the literature such as the impact of externalities that arise from the possibility of future government bailouts and the impact of pecuniary externalities when borrowers do not internalize the effect of their decisions on the real exchange rate that in turn affects their borrowing constraints. Lorenzoni then concludes with suggestions for future research especially those arising from the ongoing euro zone crises.

In conclusion, we would like thank a number of people who have helped us with this book. We are very grateful to James Anderson, Philippe Bacchetta, Fernando Broner, Arnaud Costinot, Dave Donaldson, Jonathan Eaton, Robert Feenstra, Fabio Ghironi, Gene Grossman, Olivier Jeanne, Andrei Levchenko, Karen Lewis, Rachel McCulloch, John McLaren, Virgiliu Midrigan, Maurice Obstfeld, Paolo Pesenti, Vincenzo Quadrini, Esteban Rossi-Hansberg, Robert Staiger, Jón Steinsson, Daniel Trefler, and Mark Wright who were discussants for the various chapters at a conference organized in September 2012 where the chapters were presented. Their comments were very influential in shaping the chapters. We would also like to thank Raluca Dragusanu, Wenxin Du, Rohan Kekre, Mikkel Plagborg-Moller, Ran Shorrer, and Vania Stavrakeva, who took very helpful notes during the conference. A very special thanks is owed to our assistant at Harvard, Jane Trahan, who aided the project at every stage of the process, and who played a central role in organizing the September 2012 conference.

Gita Gopinath and Kenneth Rogoff
Harvard University and NBER
Elhanan Helpman
Harvard University, CIFAR and NBER

REFERENCES

Corsetti, G., Dedola, L., Leduc, S., 2010. Optimal monetary policy in open economies. In: Friedman, B.M., Woodford, M. (Eds.), Handbook of Monetary Economics, vol. 3. Elsevier, pp. 861–933.

Krugman, P.R., 1995. Increasing returns, imperfect competition and the positive theory of international trade. In: Grossman, G.M., Rogoff, K. (Eds.), Handbook of International Economics. Elsevier, pp. 1243–1277.

Melitz, M.J., 2003. The impact of trade on intra-industry reallocations and aggregate industry productivity. Econometrica 71, 1695–1725.

Obstfeld, M., Rogoff, K.S., 1996. Foundations of International Macroeconomics, MIT Press Books. The MIT Press.

CHAPTER 1

Heterogeneous Firms and Trade*

Marc J. Melitz*[,†,‡] and Stephen J. Redding[†,‡,§]

*Harvard University, Cambridge, MA, USA
[†]National Bureau of Economic Research, Cambridge, MA, USA
[‡]Centre for Economic Policy Research, London, UK
[§]Princeton University, Princeton, NJ, USA

Abstract

This chapter reviews the new approach to international trade based on firm heterogeneity in differentiated product markets. This approach explains a variety of features exhibited in disaggregated trade data, including the higher productivity of exporters relative to non-exporters, within-industry reallocations of resources following trade liberalization, and patterns of trade participation across firms and destination markets. Accounting for these empirical patterns reveals new mechanisms through which the aggregate economy is affected by trade liberalization, including endogenous increases in average industry and firm productivity.

Keywords

Firm heterogeneity, International trade, Productivity

JEL classification codes

F10, F12, F14

1. INTRODUCTION

Theoretical research in international trade increasingly emphasizes firm-level decisions in understanding the causes and consequences of aggregate trade. Motivated by empirical findings using micro-level data on plants and firms, this theoretical literature emphasizes heterogeneity in productivity, size, and other characteristics even within narrowly defined industries. This heterogeneity is systematically related to trade participation, with exporters larger and more productive than non-exporters even prior to entering export markets. Trade liberalization leads to within-industry reallocations of resources, which raise average industry productivity, as low-productivity firms exit and high-productivity firms expand to enter export markets. The increase in firm scale induced by export market

---

* We are grateful to Treb Allen, Costas Arkolakis, Ariel Burstein, Davin Chor, Arnaud Costinot, Swati Dhingra, Gene Grossman, Keith Head, Elhanan Helpman, Andrei Levchenko, Thierry Mayer, Gianmarco Ottaviano, Esteban Rossi-Hansberg and participants at the *Handbook of International Economics* conference in Cambridge, MA in September 2012 for helpful comments and suggestions. We are also grateful to Cheng Chen for research assistance. The authors are responsible for any remaining limitations.

entry enhances the return to complementary productivity-enhancing investments in technology adoption and innovation, with the result that trade liberalization also raises firm productivity.

Models of firm heterogeneity provide a natural explanation for these and other features of disaggregated trade data that cannot be directly interpreted using representative firm models (whether based on comparative advantage or love of variety). From a positive perspective, accounting for these features of disaggregated trade enhances the predictive power of our models for patterns of trade and production. More broadly, theories of firm heterogeneity and trade have improved our understanding of the mechanisms through which an economy responds to trade. This is especially important from a policy perspective: for example, identifying potential winners and losers from trade liberalization, and generating counterfactual predictions for changes in policies related to trade. Finally, from a normative view, understanding all of the margins along which an economy adjusts to trade can be important for evaluating the overall welfare gains from trade. As we show more formally below, it is only under strong conditions that aggregate outcomes (at the sector or country level) are sufficient statistics for the overall welfare gains from trade. Even when these strong conditions hold, heterogeneous and homogeneous firm models can have quite different distributional implications for wage inequality, unemployment, and the political economy of trade protection.

The remainder of this chapter is structured as follows. Section 2 reviews empirical evidence from micro data that motivates theories of heterogeneous firms and trade. Section 3 introduces a general theoretical framework for modeling firm heterogeneity in differentiated product markets. Section 4 characterizes the model's closed economy equilibrium, while Section 5 examines the implications of opening to trade. In Section 6 we parameterize the firm productivity distribution and examine the model's quantitative predictions. Section 7 embeds this model of firm heterogeneity within the integrated equilibrium framework of neoclassical trade theory. Section 8 relaxes the assumption of constant elasticity of substitution (CES) preferences to introduce variable mark-ups and examine the effects of market size on the selection of firms into production and exporting. Section 9 explores a variety of extensions, where firm productivity is also endogenous. Section 10 discusses factor markets and the income distributional consequences of trade liberalization. Section 11 concludes.

2. EMPIRICAL EVIDENCE

The theoretical literature on firm heterogeneity and trade has been influenced by a number of empirical findings from micro data. One first set of empirical findings showed that firms participating in trade perform better along a number of dimensions. Using US Census data, Bernard and Jensen (1995, 1999) find that exporters are larger, more productive, more capital intensive, more skill intensive, and pay higher wages than non-exporters within the same industry. While the early empirical literature using plant and firm data focused on exports, more recent research using customs transactions data has shown that importers display many of the same characteristics as exporters. Indeed, firms that simultaneously export and import typically exhibit the highest levels of performance (see for example Bernard et al., 2007a,b, 2009).[1]

A second set of empirical results highlights the prominence of compositional effects across firms (within sectors). Dunne et al. (1989) show that around one third of US manufacturing plants enter and exit every five years. Exitors are smaller on average than incumbents and new entrants have higher average employment growth rates conditional on survival than incumbents, consistent with a Darwinian process of selection operating across plants and firms. Davis and Haltiwanger (1992) find that gross job creation and destruction across plants are much larger than would be needed to achieve the observed net changes in employment between industries, implying substantial reallocations within rather than across industries. Evidence that such compositional changes are important for the effects of trade liberalizations comes from a number of large-scale liberalization reforms. In the aftermath of the Chilean trade liberalization, Pavcnik (2002) finds that roughly two thirds of the 19% increase in aggregate productivity is the result of the real-location of resources from less to more efficient producers. While early empirical studies focused on documenting these compositional effects and contrasting export-orientated, import-competing, and non-traded industries, more recent research has connected intra-industry reallocation to direct policy measures of trade liberalization such as import tariffs. Following the Canada–US Free Trade Agreement (CUSFTA), Trefler (2004) finds that industries experiencing the deepest Canadian tariff cuts reduced employment by 12% but increased labor productivity by 15%.[2]

While the above empirical studies focus on reallocation in production, other related research emphasizes the role of firm and product margins in understanding patterns of trade. Using French export data by firm and destination market, Eaton et al. (2004) find that more than 60% of the variation in exports across markets of different size is explained by the extensive margin of the number of exporting firms. Using US export data by firm, product and destination market, Bernard et al. (2011) show that all of the negative effect of distance on bilateral trade flows is accounted for by the extensive margins of the number of exporting firms and exported products. Therefore, larger aggregate trade flows are not achieved by a simple scaling up of trade at the disaggregated level, but rather involve sub-stantial entry, exit, and reallocations of market shares across suppliers to different markets.

---

[1] These findings have been replicated for many countries, as discussed for example in Mayer and Ottaviano (2007) and World Trade Organization (2008). Following Bernard and Jensen (1999) a large empirical literature has sought to disentangle whether good firm performance causes exporting (selection into exporting) or exporting causes good firm performance (learning by exporting). The consensus from this literature is that there is strong evidence of selection into exporting. More recently, a number of studies have found evidence suggesting that exporting influences firm performance, as discussed below.

[2] For evidence from trade reforms in Colombia, India, and the US, see respectively Fernandes (2007), Khandelwal and Topalova (2011), and Bernard et al. (2006).

A third set of empirical findings provides evidence that plant or firm performance responds to the trading environment along a number of dimensions including overall productivity, technology adoption, the number and type of products supplied, and mark-ups of price over marginal cost. In Pavcnik (2002), one third of the increase in aggregate productivity following Chilean trade liberalization is attributed to increases in productivity within plants. Bustos (2011) and Lileeva and Trefler (2010) find that the entry into export markets induced by foreign trade liberalization stimulates the adoption of new technologies. Baldwin and Gu (2009) and Bernard et al. (2011) show that Canadian plants and US firms respectively rationalize product scope following CUSFTA. Levinsohn (1993) and Harrison (1994) find pro-competitive effects of trade liberalization in reducing mark-ups in Turkey and Cote d'Ivoire respectively. De Loecker and Warzynski (2012) uncover differences in mark-ups between exporters and non-exporters.

In the next section, we introduce a general theoretical framework for modeling firm heterogeneity in differentiated product markets that accounts for many of the empirical features outlined above. In particular, the model rationalizes performance differences between exporters and non-exporters, the contribution of exit and reallocation to aggregate productivity growth following trade liberalization, and the role of compositional changes in patterns of bilateral trade. Naturally, the model is an abstraction and does not capture all of the features of the data. For example, the baseline version of the model assumes constant mark-ups, and hence abstracts from pro-competitive effects of trade liberalization, although we relax this assumption in a later section. Furthermore, much of our analysis concentrates on heterogeneity in productivity and size across firms, and hence does not capture the rich range of dimensions along which trading and non-trading firms can differ. Additionally, the baseline version of the model yields sharp predictions such as a single productivity threshold above which all firms export and a stable ranking of the sales of exporting firms across all destination markets. Although these sharp predictions are unlikely to be literally satisfied in the data, they capture systematic relationships or average tendencies in the data, such as the higher average productivity of exporters and the correlation of relative exporter sales across destination markets.

3. GENERAL SETUP

We begin by outlining a general framework for modeling firm heterogeneity following Melitz (2003).[3] Throughout this chapter, we rely on models of monopolistic competition that emphasize product differentiation and increasing returns to scale at the level of the firm. Although this framework provides a tractable platform for analyzing a host of firm decisions in general equilibrium, it neglects strategic interactions between firms. Bernard et al. (2003) develop a heterogeneous firm framework that features head to head competition between firms, while Neary (2010) surveys the literature on oligopoly and

---

[3] An accompanying web appendix contains the technical derivations of results reported in this chapter.

trade in general equilibrium. In our monopolistic competition framework, all interactions between firms operate through market indices such as the mass of competing firms, and statistics of the price distribution. We begin by developing the industry equilibrium with heterogeneous firms, before embedding the sectors in general equilibrium. We start with a closed economy and then examine the implications of opening to international trade. To highlight the implications of firm heterogeneity as starkly as possible, we begin by considering a static (one-period) model, before turning to consider dynamics in a later section.[4]

3.1. Preferences

Consumer preferences are defined over the consumption of goods produced in a number of sectors $j \in \{0, 1, \ldots, J\}$:

$$U = \sum_{j=0}^{J} \beta_j \log Q_j, \quad \sum_{j=0}^{J} \beta_j = 1, \; \beta_j \geq 0. \tag{1}$$

Sector $j = 0$ is a homogeneous good, which is produced with a unit input requirement and is chosen as the numeraire. In some cases, we will require that β_0 is large enough that all countries produce this good in the open economy equilibrium. Within each of the remaining $j \geq 1$ sectors, there is a continuum of horizontally differentiated varieties, and preferences are assumed to take the Constant Elasticity of Substitution (CES) Dixit and Sitlitz (1977) form:

$$Q_j = \left[\int_{\omega \in \Omega_j} q_j(\omega)^{(\sigma_j-1)/\sigma_j} d\omega \right]^{\sigma_j/(\sigma_j-1)}, \quad \sigma_j > 1, \; j \geq 1. \tag{2}$$

This representation of consumer preferences, in which varieties enter utility symmetrically, implicitly imposes a choice of units in which to measure the quantity of each variety. There is no necessary relationship between this normalization and the units in which physical quantities of output are measured for each product in the data. Mapping physical quantities of output back to utility requires taking a stand on the relative weight of products in utility, which depends (among other things) on product quality.[5]

Using Y to denote aggregate income, the Cobb-Douglas upper tier of utility implies that consumers spend $X_j = \beta_j Y$ on goods produced by sector j. The demand for each differentiated variety within sector j is given by:

$$q_j(\omega) = A_j p_j(\omega)^{-\sigma_j}, \quad A_j = X_j P_j^{\sigma_j-1},$$

---

[4] For another review of the theoretical literature on firm heterogeneity and trade see Redding (2011), while Bernard et al. (2012) survey the empirical evidence.

[5] In some cases quality can be directly measured as for wine (see Crozet et al., 2012) or inferred from input use such as in Kugler and Verhoogen (2012). Alternatively, functional form assumptions can be made about the mapping between physical and utility units as in Baldwin and Harrigan (2011) and Johnson (2012).

where P_j is the price index dual to (2):

$$P_j = \left[\int_{\omega \in \Omega_j} p(\omega)^{1-\sigma_j} d\omega \right]^{1/(1-\sigma_j)}.$$

A_j is an index of market demand that proportionally scales every firm's residual demand. This market demand index, in turn, is determined by sector spending and a statistic of the price distribution (the CES price index). With a continuum of firms, each firm is of measure zero relative to the market as a whole, and hence takes A_j as given.[6]

3.2. Technology

Varieties are produced using a composite factor of production L_j with unit cost w_j in sector j. This composite factor, for example, can be a Cobb-Douglas function of skilled labor (S) and unskilled labor (U): $L_j = \bar{\eta}_j S_j^{\eta_j} U_j^{1-\eta_j}$; $\bar{\eta}_j$ is a constant such that unit cost is $w_j = w_S^{\eta_j} w_U^{1-\eta_j}$, where w_S and w_U are the skilled and unskilled wage. We index the unit cost by sector j, because even if factor prices are equalized across sectors in competitive factor markets, unit costs will still in general differ across sectors due to differences in factor intensity. The composite factor (with the same aggregation of labor inputs) is used for all productive activities within the industry, including both variable and fixed costs (incurred for overhead production as well as for entry and market access).[7] Thus, we can define a sector's aggregate supply L_j for this composite factor. In our multi-sector setting, the input supply L_j to each sector is determined endogenously. In several instances where we wish to characterize how inputs are allocated across sectors, we will assume a single homogeneous labor factor, in which case the input supplies L_j can be summed across sectors and set equal to the country's aggregate labor endowment.

Within each industry, each firm chooses to supply a distinct horizontally-differentiated variety. Production of each variety involves a fixed production cost of f_j units of the composite input and a constant marginal cost that is inversely proportional to firm productivity φ. The total amount of the composite input required to produce q_j units of a variety is therefore:

$$l_j = f_j + \frac{q_j}{\varphi}.$$

Since all firms with the same productivity within a given sector behave symmetrically, we index firms within a sector from now onwards by φ alone. The homogeneous numeraire

[6] While most of the firm heterogeneity literature assumes monopolistic competition with a continuum of firms, the case of a finite number of firms introduces a number of additional issues. If firms are large relative to the market ("granular"), idiosyncratic shocks to individual firms influence aggregate volatility, as in di Giovanni and Levchenko (2012). If granular firms internalize the effects of their price choices on the aggregate price index, they charge variable mark-ups even under CES preferences, as in Atkeson and Burstein (2008) and Edmund et al. (2012).
[7] See Flam and Helpman (1987) for an analysis of non-homothetic production technologies where fixed and variable costs can have different factor intensities.

sector is characterized by perfect competition and is produced one for one with the composite factor, so that $w_0 = 1$.

3.3. Firm Behavior

We now focus on equilibrium in a given sector and drop the sector j subscript to avoid notational clutter. The market structure is monopolistic competition. Each firm chooses its price to maximize its profits subject to a downward-sloping residual demand curve with constant elasticity σ. From the first-order condition for profit maximization, the equilibrium price for each variety is a constant mark-up over marginal cost:

$$p(\varphi) = \frac{\sigma}{\sigma - 1} \frac{w}{\varphi},$$

which implies an equilibrium firm revenue of:

$$r(\varphi) = Ap(\varphi)^{1-\sigma} = A \left(\frac{\sigma - 1}{\sigma} \right)^{\sigma - 1} w^{1-\sigma} \varphi^{\sigma - 1},$$

and an equilibrium firm profit of:

$$\pi(\varphi) = \frac{r(\varphi)}{\sigma} - wf = B\varphi^{\sigma - 1} - wf, \quad B = \frac{(\sigma - 1)^{\sigma - 1}}{\sigma^{\sigma}} w^{1-\sigma} A.$$

This constant mark-up of price over marginal cost is an implication of CES preferences and monopolistic competition, and ensures that higher firm productivity is passed on fully to consumers in the form of a lower price. Since demand is elastic, this lower price implies higher revenue for more productive firms. While we focus on productivity as the source of revenue heterogeneity across firms, heterogeneity in product quality across firms can be captured by relaxing the assumption that varieties enter preferences symmetrically in (2) and introducing a CES weighting parameter for each variety. Under our assumption of CES preferences and monopolistic competition, productivity and product quality are isomorphic in the sense that they both enter equilibrium firm revenue in exactly the same way.[8] Together constant mark-ups and the homothetic production technology (the ratio of average to marginal cost depends solely on firm output) imply that "variable" or "gross" profits are a constant proportion of firm revenue. Therefore the market demand index A proportionally scales both revenues and gross profits.

---

[8] While more productive, larger firms charge lower prices in the model, care should be taken in interpreting this prediction in the data, since as noted above the choice of units imposed by the symmetric representation of preferences (2) does not necessarily correspond to the units in which physical quantities are measured in the data. One potential explanation for more productive, larger firms charging higher prices in the data is that they produce higher quality varieties and producing higher quality involves higher marginal costs, as in Baldwin and Harrigan (2011), Johnson (2012), Kugler and Verhoogen (2012), and Manova and Zhang (2012).

3.4. Firm Performance Measures and Productivity

A key implication of the CES demand structure is that the relative outputs and revenues of firms depend solely on their relative productivities:

$$\frac{q(\varphi_1)}{q(\varphi_2)} = \left(\frac{\varphi_1}{\varphi_2}\right)^{\sigma}, \quad \frac{r(\varphi_1)}{r(\varphi_2)} = \left(\frac{\varphi_1}{\varphi_2}\right)^{\sigma-1}, \quad \varphi_1, \varphi_2 > 0.$$

where a higher elasticity of substitution implies greater differences in size and profitability between firms for a given difference in relative productivity.

Empirical measures of firm or plant revenue-based productivity (e.g. based on deflating sales or value-added with firm-specific price deflators) are monotonically related to the firm productivity draw φ. Since prices are inversely related to the firm productivity draw φ, revenue per variable input is constant across firms. Revenue-based productivity, however, varies because of the fixed production cost:

$$\frac{r(\varphi)}{l(\varphi)} = \frac{w\sigma}{\sigma - 1}\left[1 - \frac{f}{l(\varphi)}\right],$$

where input use $l(\varphi)$ increases monotonically with φ. A higher productivity draw increases variable input use and revenue, with the result that the fixed input requirement is spread over more units of revenue.[9]

Productivity φ is a catch-all that includes all sources of heterogeneity in revenue relative to factor inputs across firms, including differences in technical efficiency, management practice, firm organization, and product quality. For most of our analysis, we take firm productivity as exogenously determined upon entry. In later sections, we consider several extensions of our general framework that introduce an endogenous component to firm productivity and model its evolution over time. Opening further the black box of the firm remains an interesting area for further research, including the microfoundations of heterogeneity in firm productivity and the dynamics of firm productivity over time. While CES preferences and monopolistic competition imply that productivity and product quality enter equilibrium firm revenue in exactly the same way, different sources of revenue heterogeneity could have different implications in other frameworks. Furthermore, there are many other dimensions along which firms can be heterogeneous besides revenue per unit of input (e.g. factor intensity and product attributes).

3.5. Firm Entry and Exit

There is a competitive fringe of potential firms that can enter the sector by paying a sunk entry cost of f_E units of the composite input. Potential entrants face uncertainty

---

[9] In Section 8, we introduce endogenous mark-ups. This generates another channel for variations in revenue-based productivity. More productive firms set higher mark-ups, which raises their measured revenue-based productivity relative to less productive firms.

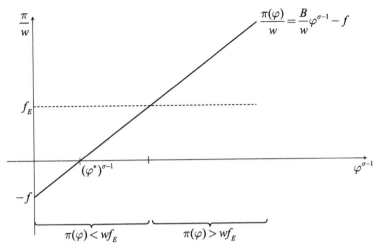

Figure 1.1 Closed Economy Equilibrium $\{\varphi^*, B/w\}$

about their productivity in the sector. Once the sunk entry cost is paid, a firm draws its productivity φ from a fixed distribution $g(\varphi)$, with cumulative distribution $G(\varphi)$.

After observing its productivity, a firm decides whether to exit the sector or to produce. This decision yields a survival cutoff productivity φ^* at which a firm makes zero profits:

$$\pi(\varphi^*) = \frac{r(\varphi^*)}{\sigma} - wf = B(\varphi^*)^{\sigma-1} - wf = 0. \tag{3}$$

The relationship between profits and productivity is shown graphically in Figure 1.1. Firms drawing a productivity $\varphi < \varphi^*$ would incur losses if they produced. Therefore these firms exit immediately, receiving $\pi(\varphi) = 0$, and cannot cover any portion of their sunk entry cost. Among the active firms, a subset of them with $\pi(\varphi) > wf_E$ make positive profits net of the sunk entry cost. Free entry implies that in equilibrium, this expected measure of *ex-ante* profits (inclusive of the entry cost) must be equal to zero:

$$\int_0^\infty \pi(\varphi)dG(\varphi) = \int_{\varphi^*}^\infty \left[B\varphi^{\sigma-1} - wf\right]dG(\varphi) = wf_E. \tag{4}$$

This framework captures a number of the features of micro data discussed above. Heterogeneity in firm productivity generates the systematic differences in firm employment, revenue, and profits observed in micro data (see for example Bartelsman and Doms, 2000). Selection into production (only firms with productivity $\varphi \geq \varphi^*$ produce) delivers the empirical regularity that exiting firms are less productive than surviving firms (as in Dunne et al., 1989).

4. CLOSED ECONOMY EQUILIBRIUM

General equilibrium can be characterized by the following variables for each sector: the survival productivity cutoff φ_j^*, the price w_j and supply L_j of the composite input, the mass of entrants M_{Ej}, and aggregate expenditure X_j. To determine this equilibrium vector, we use the model's recursive structure, in which the productivity cutoff φ_j^* can be determined independently of the other equilibrium variables.

4.1. Sectoral Equilibrium

Once again, we drop the sector j subscript to streamline notation, and measure all nominal variables (prices, profits, revenues) relative to the unit cost w in that sector. The zero-profit condition (3) and free entry (4) provide two equations involving only two endogenous variables: the productivity cutoff φ^* and market demand B/w. Combining these two conditions, we obtain a single equation that determines the productivity cutoff:

$$f J(\varphi^*) = f_E, \quad J(\varphi^*) = \int_{\varphi^*}^{\infty} \left[\left(\frac{\varphi}{\varphi^*} \right)^{\sigma-1} - 1 \right] dG(\varphi). \tag{5}$$

Since $J(.)$ is monotonically decreasing with $\lim_{\varphi^* \to 0} J(\varphi^*) = \infty$ and $\lim_{\varphi^* \to \infty} J(\varphi^*) = 0$, the free entry condition (5) identifies a unique equilibrium cutoff φ^*. Market demand is then $B/w = f(\varphi^*)^{1-\sigma}$. Using these two equilibrium variables, we can determine the distribution of all firm performance measures (relative to the input cost w). Productivity φ will be distributed with cumulative distribution function $G(\varphi)/[1 - G(\varphi^*)]$, and the distribution of prices, profits, revenues, output, and employment will be given by the following functions of firm productivity φ and market demand B/w:

$$\frac{p(\varphi)}{w} = \frac{\sigma}{\sigma - 1} \frac{1}{\varphi},$$

$$\frac{\pi(\varphi)}{w} = \frac{B}{w} \varphi^{\sigma-1} - f,$$

$$\frac{r(\varphi)}{w} = \sigma \left[\frac{\pi(\varphi)}{w} + f \right],$$

$$q(\varphi) = \frac{r(\varphi)}{p(\varphi)},$$

$$l(\varphi) = \frac{q(\varphi)}{\varphi} + f.$$

CES preferences and monopolistic competition ensure that sector aggregates such as expenditures and input supply impact neither firm selection φ^* nor the distribution of any of the firm performance measures. Those sector aggregates will only influence the mass of firms. Before deriving this relationship between sector aggregates and the mass of firms, we describe some important properties of the distribution of firm performance measures.

We start by noting that the free entry condition (4) pins down the average profit (and hence the average revenue) of active firms:

$$\frac{\bar{\pi}}{w} = \frac{f_E}{1 - G(\varphi^*)}, \qquad \frac{\bar{r}}{w} = \sigma\left(\frac{\bar{\pi}}{w} + f\right).$$

Let $\tilde{\varphi}$ be the productivity of the firm earning those average profits and revenues. From the free entry condition (4), we can derive $\tilde{\varphi}$ as a function of the cutoff productivity φ^*:

$$\tilde{\varphi}^{\sigma-1} = \int_{\varphi^*}^{\infty} \varphi^{\sigma-1} \frac{dG(\varphi)}{1 - G(\varphi^*)}.$$

$\tilde{\varphi}$ is a harmonic average of firm productivity φ, weighted by relative output shares $q(\varphi)/q(\tilde{\varphi})$. This productivity average also references productivity for the aggregate sector consumption index Q and the price index P in the following sense: a hypothetical monopolistic competition equilibrium with M representative firms sharing a common productivity $\tilde{\varphi}$ would induce the same consumption index $Q = M^{\sigma/(\sigma-1)}q(\tilde{\varphi})$ and price index $P = M^{1/(1-\sigma)}p(\tilde{\varphi})$ as M heterogeneous firms with the equilibrium distribution $G(\varphi)/[1 - G(\varphi^*)]$. We will also show that given the same input supply L and expenditures X for the sector, the hypothetical equilibrium with representative firms would also feature the same mass M of active firms as in our current setup with heterogeneous firms.

In this heterogeneous firm setup, the mass M of active firms represents the portion of the mass M_E of entrants that survive. This portion depends on the survival cutoff φ^*: $M = [1 - G(\varphi^*)]M_E$. The sector's input supply L is used both for production by the M active firms, and to cover the entry cost f_E incurred by all M_E entrants. Since payments to inputs used for production must equal the difference between aggregate sector revenues R and profit Π, we can write the factor market equilibrium condition equating demand and supply for the sector's composite input as:

$$L = \frac{R - \Pi}{w} + M_E f_E.$$

Note that the free entry condition ensures that aggregate profits exactly cover the aggregate entry cost: $\Pi = M\bar{\pi} = wM_E f_E$. Therefore, aggregate sector revenue is determined by the input supply: $R/w = L$. In a closed economy this must also be equal to the sector's expenditures X/w.

Since $L = R/w = X/w$ affects neither firm selection (the cutoff φ^*) nor average firm sales $\bar{r}/w$, changes in this measure of market size must be reflected one-for-one in the mass of both active firms and entrants. This result is analogous to Krugman (1980), where firm size is also independent of market size. In fact, a single-sector version of our model would yield the same sector aggregate variables and firm averages (for the firm with productivity $\tilde{\varphi}$) as in Krugman's (1980) model where all firms share the same productivity level given by $\tilde{\varphi}$. (The key distinction with our heterogeneous firms model is that the reference productivity level $\tilde{\varphi}$ is endogenously determined.) The result that market size affects neither firm selection nor the distribution of firm size is very specific to our assumption of CES preferences. In section 8, we analyze other preferences that feature a link between market size and both firm selection and the distribution of firm performance measures (size, price, mark-ups, profit).

4.2. General Equilibrium

Now that we have characterized equilibrium in each sector j in terms of firm selection (φ_j^*), market demand (B_j/w_j), and the distribution of firm performance measures, we embed the sector in general equilibrium. The simplest way to close the model in general equilibrium is to assume a single factor of production (labor $\bar{L}$) that is mobile across sectors and indexes the size of the economy. Labor mobility ensures that the wage w is the same for all sectors j. If the homogenous numeraire good is produced, we have $w_j = w = 1$. Otherwise, we choose labor as the numeraire so that again $w_j = w = 1$.

With the zero-profit cutoff in each sector (φ_j^*) and the wage (w) already determined, the other elements of the equilibrium vector follow immediately. Aggregate income follows from $Y = w\bar{L}$ and industry revenue and expenditure follow from $R_j = X_j = \beta_j Y = \beta_j w \bar{L}$. The mass of firms in each sector is

$$M_j = \frac{R_j}{\bar{r}_j} = \frac{\beta_j \bar{L}}{\sigma \left[\frac{f_{Ej}}{1 - G(\varphi_j^*)} + f_j \right]}.$$

The results on the efficiency of the market equilibrium from Dixit and Sitlitz (1977) hold in this setting with heterogeneous firms: conditional on an allocation of labor to sector j, the market allocation is constrained efficient. In other words, a social planner using the same entry technology characterized by $G_j(.)$ and f_{Ej} would choose the same mass of entrants M_{Ej} and the same distribution of quantities produced $q_j(\varphi)$ as a function of productivity, including the same productivity cutoff φ_j^* and mass of producing firms M_j with positive quantities.[10] In this multi-sector setting, the allocation of labor across sectors will not be efficient due to differences in mark-ups across sectors (the labor allocation in high mark-up, low elasticity sectors will be inefficiently low). The single-sector version of the model is a special case in which there are no variations in mark-ups and the market equilibrium is therefore efficient.

5. OPEN ECONOMY WITH TRADE COSTS

In the closed economy, sector aggregates such as spending X_j and input supply L_j have no effect on firm selection (the cutoff φ_j^*) and the distribution of firm performance measures

---

[10] See Dhingra and Morrow (unpublished) for a formal analysis of the efficiency of the equilibrium.

within the sector. Since opening the closed economy to costless international trade is the same as increasing aggregate spending and input supply, such a change will have no impact on those firm-level variables. Although this result for costless trade provides a useful benchmark, a large empirical literature finds evidence of substantial trade costs.[11] In this section, we characterize the open economy equilibrium in the presence of costly trade, which yields sharply different predictions for the effects of trade liberalization. We focus on trade costs that use real resources, although we briefly discuss trade policies such as tariffs, which raise revenue that must be taken into account in welfare calculations.

The world economy consists of a number of countries indexed by $i = 1, \ldots, N$. Preferences are identical across countries and given by (1). We assume that each country is endowed with a single homogeneous factor of production (labor) that is in inelastic supply $\bar{L}_i$ and is mobile across sectors.[12] We allow countries to differ in terms of their aggregate labor supply, the productivity distributions in each of the differentiated sectors, and their bilateral trade costs. The open economy equilibrium can be referenced by a zero-profit cutoff for serving each market n from each country i in each sector j (φ_{nij}^*), a wage for each country (w_i), a mass of entrants for each country and sector (M_{Eij}), and industry expenditure for each country and sector (X_{ij}).

For much of our analysis, we assume that the additional homogeneous good (in sector $j = 0$) is produced in all countries. This good is produced with a unit labor requirement, is costlessly traded, and is chosen as our numeraire.[13] In such an incomplete specialization equilibrium, $w_i = w = 1$ for all countries i. Combining this result with our assumption of Cobb-Douglas preferences, consumer expenditure on each sector j in each country i is determined by parameters alone: $X_{ij} = \beta_j L_i$. In some of our analysis below, we consider the case of no outside sector, in which case each country's wage is determined by the equality between its income and world expenditure on its goods.

5.1. Firm Behavior

As in the closed economy, we focus on equilibrium in a given sector and drop the sector subscript. Firm heterogeneity takes the same form in each country. After paying the sunk entry cost in country i (f_{Ei}), a firm draws its productivity φ from the cumulative distribution $G_i(\varphi)$. To serve market n, firms must incur a fixed cost of f_{ni} units of labor in country i and an iceberg variable trade cost such that $\tau_{ni} > 1$ units must be shipped from country i for one unit to arrive in country n.[14] We assume that all production costs (including the fixed exporting costs) are incurred in terms of source country labor.

---

[11] See for example the survey by Anderson and Van Wincoop (2004).

[12] In a later section, we explore the implications of introducing multiple factors of production and Heckscher-Ohlin comparative advantage in the open economy equilibrium.

[13] The assumption that the homogeneous good is produced in all countries will be satisfied if its consumption share and the countries' labor endowments are large enough.

[14] We focus on exporting as the mode for serving foreign markets. For reviews of the literature on Foreign Direct Investment (FDI), see Chapter 2 in this handbook by Antràs and Yeaple and see also Helpman (2006).

The fixed exporting cost captures "market access" costs (e.g. advertising, distribution, and conforming to foreign regulations) that do not vary with exporter scale. With CES preferences, this fixed cost is needed to generate selection into export markets such that only the most productive firms export. Absent this fixed export cost all firms would export.

We denote the fixed costs of serving the domestic market by f_{ii}, which includes both "market access" costs and fixed production costs (whereas the export cost f_{ni} for $n \neq i$ incorporates only the market access cost). Thus, the combined domestic cost f_{ii} need not be lower than the export cost $f_{ni}(n \neq i)$, even if the market access component for the domestic market is always lower than its export market counterpart. When incorporating the fixed production cost into the domestic cost, we are anticipating an equilibrium where all firms serve their domestic market and only a subset of more productive firms export, as in the empirical literature discussed above.[15] Finally, we assume lower variable trade costs for the domestic market, $\tau_{ii} \leq \tau_{ni}$, and set $\tau_{ii} = 1$ and $\tau_{ni} \geq 1$ without loss of generality.

Much of the literature on firm heterogeneity and trade takes these fixed and variable trade costs as exogenously given, although in a later section we discuss the market penetration technology of Arkolakis (2010), in which the fixed costs of serving a market depend on the endogenous fraction of consumers that firms choose to serve. The implications of different microfoundations for trade costs in models of firm heterogeneity remain under-explored, including whether trade costs are sunk, fixed, or variable (e.g. Das et al., 2007), whether variable trade costs are *ad valorem* versus per unit (e.g. Hummels and Skiba, 2004; Irarrazabal et al., unpublished), the role of intermediaries (e.g. Ahn et al., 2011; Antràs and Costinot, 2011; Bernard et al., 2010b), and the role of transport costs versus information, advertising, marketing, and other trade costs (e.g. Allen, unpublished).

If a firm with productivity φ supplies market n from country i, the first-order condition for profit maximization again implies that its equilibrium price is a constant mark-up over its delivered marginal cost in that destination:

$$p_{ni}(\varphi) = \frac{\sigma}{\sigma - 1} \frac{\tau_{ni}}{\varphi}.$$

Revenue and profit earned from sales to that destination are:

$$r_{ni}(\varphi) = A_n p_{ni}(\varphi)^{1-\sigma}, \quad A_n = X_n P_n^{\sigma-1},$$

$$\pi_{ni}(\varphi) = B_n \tau_{ni}^{1-\sigma} \varphi^{\sigma-1} - f_{ni}, \quad B_n = \frac{(\sigma - 1)^{\sigma-1}}{\sigma^\sigma} A_n.$$

As in the closed economy, A_n and B_n are proportional indices of market demand in country n; they are functions of sector spending X_n and the CES price index P_n. Since all

---

[15] With zero domestic market access costs, no firm exports without serving the domestic market, because the fixed cost of production has to be incurred irrespective of whether the domestic market is served and CES preferences imply positive variable profits in the domestic market. In contrast, with positive domestic market access costs, it can be profitable in principle for firms to export but not serve the domestic market (see, for example, Lu, unpublished). Using French export data by firm and destination market, Eaton et al. (2011) find that less than 1% of French firms export without serving the domestic market.

firms serve the domestic market, we account for the fixed production cost in "domestic" profit $\pi_{ii}(\varphi)$.

5.2. Firm Market Entry and Exit

The presence of fixed market access costs implies that there is a zero-profit cutoff for each pair of source country and destination market:

$$\pi_{ni}(\varphi_{ni}^*) = 0,$$

$$\frac{r_{ni}(\varphi_{ni}^*)}{\sigma} = f_{ni} \quad \Longleftrightarrow \quad B_n(\tau_{ni})^{1-\sigma}(\varphi_{ni}^*)^{\sigma-1} = f_{ni}, \tag{6}$$

such that firms from country i with productivity $\varphi < \varphi_{ni}^*$ do not sell in market n and receive $r_{ni}(\varphi) = \pi_{ni}(\varphi) = 0$. Total firm revenue and profit (across destinations) are $r_i(\varphi) = \sum_n r_{ni}(\varphi)$ and $\pi_i(\varphi) = \sum_n \pi_{ni}(\varphi)$. We require restrictions on parameter values that generate selection into export markets and hence $\varphi_{ii}^* \leq \varphi_{ni}^*$ for all $n \neq i$.

Just like the closed economy, the free entry condition for country i equates an entrant's ex-ante expected profits with the sunk entry cost:

$$\int_0^\infty \pi_i(\varphi) dG_i(\varphi) = \sum_n \int_{\varphi_{ni}^*}^\infty \left[B_n \tau_{ni}^{1-\sigma} \varphi^{\sigma-1} - f_{ni} \right] dG_i(\varphi) = f_{Ei}. \tag{7}$$

The zero-profit cutoff (6) and free entry conditions (7) jointly determine all the cutoffs φ_{ni}^* and market demand levels B_n. The domestic cutoffs φ_{nn}^* and market demands B_n can be solved separately using (6) to rewrite the free entry condition (7) as

$$\sum_n f_{ni} J_i(\varphi_{ni}^*) = f_{Ei}, \tag{8}$$

where we use the same definition for $J_i(\varphi^*)$ from (5). We can then use the cutoff condition (6) again to write the cutoffs φ_{ni}^* as either a function of market demands, $\varphi_{ni}^* = (f_{ni}/B_n)^{1/(\sigma-1)}\tau_{ni}$, or as a function of the domestic cutoffs, $\varphi_{ni}^* = (f_{ni}/f_{nn})^{1/(\sigma-1)}\tau_{ni}\varphi_{nn}^*$. Using the former, (8) delivers N equations for the market demands B_n; while the latter delivers N equations for the domestic cutoffs φ_{nn}^*.

The open economy model has a recursive structure that is similar to the closed economy model: the cutoffs and market demands and hence the distribution of all firm performance measures (prices, quantities, sales, profits in all destinations) are independent of the sector aggregates such as sector spending X and sector labor supply L. Thus, only the mass of firms responds to the size of the sectors. We show how the exogenous sector spending $X = \beta \bar{L}$ can be used to solve for these quantities.

5.3. Mass of Firms and Price Index

Given M_{Ei} entrants in country i, a subset $M_{ni} = [1 - G_i(\varphi_{ni}^*)] M_{Ei}$ of these firms sells to destination n. Product variety in that destination then is given by the total mass of sellers

$M_n = \sum_i M_{ni}$. The price index P_n in that destination is the CES aggregate of the prices of all these goods:

$$
P_n^{1-\sigma} = \sum_i \left\{ M_{ni} \int_{\varphi_{ni}^*}^{\infty} p_{ni}(\varphi)^{1-\sigma} \frac{dG_i(\varphi)}{1 - G_i(\varphi_{ni}^*)} \right\}
$$

$$
= \left(\frac{\sigma}{\sigma - 1} \right)^{1-\sigma} \sum_i \left\{ M_{Ei} \tau_{ni}^{1-\sigma} \int_{\varphi_{ni}^*}^{\infty} \varphi^{\sigma-1} dG_i(\varphi) \right\}. \tag{9}
$$

This price index in n is also related to market demand there:

$$
B_n = \frac{(\sigma - 1)^{\sigma-1}}{\sigma^\sigma} X_n P_n^{\sigma-1} \iff P_n^{1-\sigma} = \frac{(\sigma - 1)^{\sigma-1}}{\sigma^\sigma} X_n B_n^{-1}. \tag{10}
$$

Using (9) and (10), we can solve out the price index and obtain

$$
\frac{X_n}{\sigma B_n} = \sum_i M_{Ei} \tau_{ni}^{1-\sigma} \int_{\varphi_{ni}^*}^{\infty} \varphi^{\sigma-1} dG_i(\varphi), \tag{11}
$$

which yields a system of N equations that determines the N entry variables M_{Ei}. (Recall that we have already solved out the left-hand side of those equations.) Using (10) and (6), we can express the price index in destination n as a function of the domestic cutoff only:

$$
P_n = \frac{\sigma}{\sigma - 1} \left(\frac{f_{nn}\sigma}{\beta \bar{L}_n} \right)^{1/(\sigma-1)} \frac{1}{\varphi_{nn}^*}. \tag{12}
$$

5.4. Welfare

This price index summarizes the contribution of each sector to overall welfare. The Cobb-Douglas aggregation of sector-level consumption into utility in (1) implies that welfare per worker in country n (with income $w_n = 1$) is:

$$
\mathbb{U}_n = \prod_{j=0}^{J} P_{nj}^{-\beta_j}, \tag{13}
$$

where the sectoral price index (12) depends solely on the sectoral productivity cutoff φ_{nnj}^*. Therefore, although welfare depends on both the range of varieties available for consumption and their prices (these are the components that enter into the definition of each sector's CES price index in (9)), the domestic productivity cutoffs in each sector are sufficient statistics for welfare. Changes in trade costs will lead to changes in the ranges of imported and domestically produced varieties and their prices. All of these changes have an impact on welfare but their joint impact is summarized by the change in the domestic productivity cutoff. Similarly, the impact of changes in the number of countries or their size on welfare is also summarized by the change in the domestic productivity cutoff.[16]

5.5. Symmetric Trade and Production Costs

To provide further intuition for the mechanisms in the model, we consider the special case of symmetric trade and production costs (across countries):

$$\tau_{ni} = \tau \quad \text{and} \quad f_{ni} = f_X \quad \forall n \neq i,$$
$$f_{ii} = f, \quad \text{and} \quad f_{Ei} = f_E \quad \text{and} \quad G_i(\cdot) = G(\cdot) \quad \forall i.$$

The only difference across countries is country size, indexed by the aggregate (across sectors) labor endowment $\bar{L}_i$. In this special symmetric case, solving the free entry conditions (8) for the market demands B_n using $\varphi_{ni}^* = (f_X/B_n)^{1/(\sigma-1)}\tau$ yields a common market demand $B_n = B$ for all countries. This, in turn, implies that all countries have the same domestic cutoff $\varphi_{ii}^* = \varphi^*$ and that there is a single export cutoff $\varphi_{ni}^* = \varphi_X^*$ for $n \neq i$. These cutoffs are the solutions to the new zero-profit cutoff conditions:

$$\pi_D(\varphi^*) = B(\varphi^*)^{\sigma-1} - f = 0, \tag{14}$$

$$\pi_X(\varphi_X^*) = B\tau^{1-\sigma}(\varphi_X^*)^{\sigma-1} - f_X = 0, \tag{15}$$

and the free entry condition then takes the following form:

$$f J(\varphi^*) + f_X(N-1)J(\varphi_X^*) = f_E. \tag{16}$$

These three conditions (14)–(16) jointly determine the two symmetric cutoffs φ^* and φ_X^* and the symmetric market demand B. Note that the variable trade cost τ does not enter the free entry condition (16). Therefore changes in τ necessarily shift the productivity cutoffs φ^* and φ_X^* in opposite directions.

Under symmetry, the domestic and exporting zero-profit cutoff conditions (14) and (15) imply that the exporting cutoff is a constant proportion of the domestic cutoff:

$$\varphi_X^* = \tau \left(\frac{f_X}{f}\right)^{\frac{1}{\sigma-1}} \varphi^*.$$

Thus selection into export markets ($\varphi_X^* > \varphi^*$) requires strictly positive fixed exporting costs and sufficiently high values of both fixed and variable trade costs: $\tau^{\sigma-1}f_X > f$.

The relationship between profits and productivity is shown graphically in Figure 1.2. Firms drawing a low productivity $\varphi < \varphi^*$ would incur losses if they produced

---

[16] While this expression for welfare in terms of the domestic productivity cutoff holds for a general productivity distribution, it does not extend to observable trade aggregates such as the trade share of a country with itself. Stronger assumptions parameterizing the productivity distribution and eliminating factor movements across sectors are needed to deliver that result, as we discuss in Section 6.

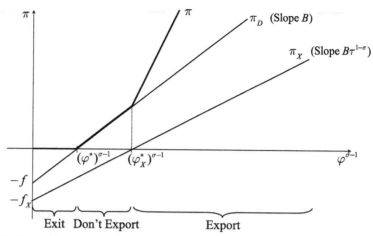

Figure 1.2 Profits and Productivity in the Open Economy

and hence exit immediately. Firms drawing an intermediate productivity $\varphi \in [\varphi^*, \varphi_X^*)$ only serve their domestic market, which generates sufficient revenue to cover fixed costs ($\pi_D(\varphi) \geq 0$). Only firms drawing a high productivity $\varphi \geq \varphi_X^*$ can generate sufficient revenue to cover fixed costs in both the domestic market and every export market. (Recall that each export market has the same level of market demand B; therefore an exporter with productivity φ earns the same export profits $\pi_X(\varphi)$ in each destination.) Export market profits (in each destination) increase less steeply with firm productivity than domestic profits as a result of variable trade costs. The slope of total firm profits $\pi(\varphi) = \pi_D(\varphi) + (N-1)\pi_X(\varphi)$ increases from B to $B(1 + \tau^{1-\sigma}(N-1))$ at the export cutoff φ_X^*, above which higher productivity generates profits from sales to the domestic market and all export markets. While firm profits are continuous in productivity, firm revenue jumps discretely at the export cutoff due to the fixed exporting costs. The model therefore captures empirical findings that exporters are not only more productive than non-exporters but also larger in terms of revenue and employment (e.g. Bernard and Jensen, 1995, 1999).

5.6. Multilateral Trade Liberalization

The impact of multilateral trade liberalization is seen most clearly in the transition between the closed economy and the open economy with symmetric trade and production costs. Comparing the free entry conditions in the open and closed economies (16) and (5) respectively, and noting that $J(.)$ is decreasing, we see that the productivity cutoff in each sector must be strictly higher in the open economy than in the closed economy. From welfare (13), this increase in the zero-profit cutoff productivity in each sector is sufficient to establish welfare gains from trade.

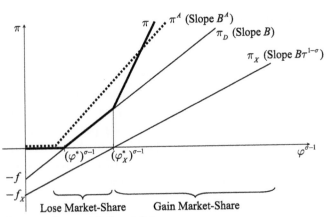

Figure 1.3 Open Economy Symmetric Countries

The effect of opening to trade is illustrated in Figure 1.3. When the economy opens up to trade, the domestic market demand changes from its autarky level B^A to B (symmetric across countries). This new market demand cannot be higher than its autarky level, as this would imply that the total profit curve $\pi(\varphi)$ in the open economy is everywhere above the total profit curve $\pi^A(\varphi)$ in autarky. This would imply a rise in profits for all firms (at all productivity levels) and violates the free entry condition. Therefore, the new market demand B must be strictly below B^A. For the free entry condition to hold in both the closed and open economy equilibria, the total profit curves $\pi(\varphi)$ and $\pi^A(\varphi)$ must intersect. This implies that the combined domestic plus export market demand $B + (N-1)B\tau^{1-\sigma}$ must be strictly higher than the autarky demand level B^A. Thus, the market demands must satisfy $B < B^A < B + (N-1)B\tau^{1-\sigma}$. The first inequality implies that all firms experience a reduction in domestic sales $r(\varphi) = \sigma B\varphi^{\sigma-1}$ (and hence a contraction in total sales for non-exporters); the second inequality implies that exporters more than make up for their contraction in domestic sales with export sales and hence experience an increase in total sales $r(\varphi) = \sigma[B + (N-1)B\tau^{1-\sigma}]\varphi^{\sigma-1}$.[17]

Opening to trade therefore induces a within-industry reallocation of resources between firms. The least productive firms exit with the rise in the domestic cutoff φ^*, the firms with intermediate productivity levels below the export cutoff φ_X^* contract, while the most productive firms with productivity above the export cutoff φ_X^* expand. Each of these responses reallocates resources toward higher productivity firms generating an increase in average industry productivity.[18]

---

[17] Variable profits are proportional to revenues for all firms, but total profits also depend on fixed costs. Total profits move in the same direction as revenues for all firms, except for a subset of the least productive exporters. Although their total revenues increase, they experience a drop in total profit due to the additional fixed cost of exporting.

[18] These reallocations of revenue and profits across firms following trade liberalization can in turn have implications for the political economy of trade protection, as in Bombardini (2008) and Do and Levchenko (2009).

The free entry condition implies that *ex-ante* expected profits in both the open and closed economies are equal to the entry cost f_E. *Ex-post* the average profits of surviving firms $\bar{\pi} = f_E/[1 - G(\varphi^*)]$ will be higher in the open economy due to the higher survival cutoff φ^*. (Recall that this average profit level will not depend on country size.) In both the open and closed economy, average total revenue per firm will be $\bar{r} = \sigma(\bar{\pi} + \bar{f})$, where $\bar{f}$ is the average (post-entry) fixed cost per firm. In the closed economy, $\bar{f} = f$ (the same overhead production cost paid by all firms). In the open economy $\bar{f} = f + f_X[1 - G(\varphi_X^*)]/[1 - G(\varphi^*)]$, which adds the fixed export cost weighted by the proportion of exporting firms. Thus, we see that average firm revenue $\bar{r}$ will be higher in the open economy than the closed economy.

As in the closed economy, differences in country size will be reflected in the mass of entrants in a country. However, in the open economy with trade costs, the relationship between country size and entrants (and hence the mass of producing firms) will no longer be proportional. There will be a home market effect for entry, which responds more than proportionately to increases in country size: solving the system of equations (11) under our symmetry assumptions reveals that $M_{Ei}/M_{Ei'} > \bar{L}_i/\bar{L}_{i'}$ for any two countries i and i'.[19] Differences in the mass of producing firms $M_{ii} = [1 - G(\varphi^*)]M_{Ei}$ will be proportional to entry since all countries have the same survival cutoff under our symmetry assumptions. These differences in the mass of entrants and producing firms across countries also imply disproportionate differences in the allocation of labor to the differentiated sectors across countries. Recall that the free entry condition requires that aggregate sector payments to cover the entry cost, $M_{Ei}f_E$, are equal to aggregate sector profits Π_i (this property must hold for both the open and closed economies). Thus, aggregate sector labor supply L_i must be equal to aggregate sector revenue R_i:[20]

$$L_i = R_i = M_{ii}\bar{r},$$

where average revenue is symmetric across countries. Therefore the disproportionate response of entry M_{Ei} and producing firms M_{ii} is also reflected in a disproportionate response of labor supply L_i in larger countries. Since sector expenditures $X_i = \beta \bar{L}_i$ are proportional to country size, this implies that larger countries run a trade surplus in the differentiated good sectors.

In a single-sector version of our model, trade must be balanced, which implies that labor supply L_i, entry M_{Ei}, and producing firms M_{ii} are proportional to country size $\bar{L}_i$:

$$\frac{L_i}{L_{i'}} = \frac{M_{Ei}}{M_{Ei'}} = \frac{M_{ii}}{M_{i'i'}} = \frac{\bar{L}_i}{\bar{L}_{i'}}.$$

[19] This assumes that there is some available labor in the homogeneous good sector that can be moved to the differentiated good sectors. This would not be possible in the single-sector version of our model. Recall that we are assuming that differences in country size are not so large as to induce specialization away from the homogeneous sector in large countries.

[20] Recall that we assume that all production costs, including the fixed exporting costs f_X, are incurred in terms of labor in the source country.

In this case, opening to trade does not affect the labor supply to the single sector, and would then induce a reduction in the mass of producing firms $M_{ii} = L_i/\bar{r}$ in every country since average revenues are larger in the open economy. Even in this case, the response of product variety in country n, $M_n = \sum_i M_{ni}$ is ambiguous due to the availability of imported varieties. However, even if the mass of varieties available for domestic consumption falls, there are necessarily welfare gains from trade, because the zero-profit cutoff productivity rises and is a sufficient statistic for welfare in (13).[21]

The efficiency properties of the symmetric country open economy equilibrium are the same as in the closed economy: conditional on the allocation of labor across sectors, a world social planner faced with the same entry and export technology (where the trade costs use up real resources) would choose the same distribution of quantities (as a function of firm productivity) and the same mass of producing firms as in the market equilibrium.[22] If trade costs take the form of policy interventions that do not use up real resources and instead raise revenue (e.g. tariffs), national social planners can have an incentive to introduce trade policies to manipulate the terms of trade, as in Demidova and Rodriguez-Clare (2009). In a multi-sector setting with different elasticities of substitution, the allocation of labor across sectors is not efficient, providing a further potential rationale for interventionist trade policies to increase the labor allocation in high mark-up, low elasticity sectors.

Although for simplicity we have concentrated on opening the closed economies to trade, analogous results hold for further multilateral trade liberalization in the open economy equilibrium, where this liberalization again takes the form of an expansion in real trading opportunities. Such multilateral trade liberalization includes (i) an increase in the number of trading partners $(N - 1)$, (ii) a decrease in variable trade costs (τ), and (iii) a decrease in fixed exporting costs (f_X). In each case, increased trade openness raises the zero-profit cutoff productivity and induces exit by the least productive firms, market share reallocations from less to more productive firms, and an increase in welfare.

5.7. Asymmetric Trade Liberalization

While the previous two sections have focused on symmetric trade and production costs, we now examine asymmetric import or export liberalization, where this liberalization again involves a change in the real resource costs of trade. Following Demidova and Rodriguez-Clare (2011), we consider two asymmetric countries (countries 1 and 2) with a single differentiated sector and no outside sector. In this case, the relative wage between the two countries is no longer fixed and is determined by the balanced trade

---

[21] Note the contrast with Krugman (1979), in which the opening of trade increases firm size and reduces the mass of domestically produced varieties, but increases the mass of varieties available for domestic consumption. The underlying mechanism is also quite different: in Krugman (1979) firms are homogeneous and the increase in firm size occurs as a result of a variable elasticity of substitution.

[22] See Dhingra and Morrow (unpublished) for a formal analysis.

condition. We therefore re-introduce the wage w_1 and choose labor in country 2 as the numeraire, so $w_2 = 1$. Re-introducing wages does not change the form of the free entry condition (8), which yields 2 conditions relating the domestic cutoff to the export cutoff for each country. With a slight abuse of notation, we use those conditions to write the domestic cutoffs as functions of the export cutoffs: $\varphi_{22}^* = \varphi_{22}^*(\varphi_{12}^*)$ and $\varphi_{11}^* = \varphi_{11}^*(\varphi_{21}^*)$.[23] The cutoff profit conditions yield:

$$
\begin{aligned}
\varphi_{21}^* &= \tau_{21} \left(\frac{f_{21}}{f_{22}} \right)^{1/(\sigma-1)} (w_1)^{\sigma/(\sigma-1)} \varphi_{22}^*, \\
\varphi_{12}^* &= \tau_{12} \left(\frac{f_{12}}{f_{11}} \right)^{1/(\sigma-1)} (w_1)^{-\sigma/(\sigma-1)} \varphi_{11}^*.
\end{aligned}
\tag{17}
$$

These conditions implicitly define the export cutoffs as functions of the wage w_1 and the domestic cutoff in the other country: $\varphi_{21}^* \equiv h_{21}(w_1, \varphi_{22}^*)$ and $\varphi_{12}^* \equiv h_{12}(w_1, \varphi_{11}^*)$. Combining all these conditions together yields a "competitiveness" condition for the export cutoff in country 1 as a function of the wage w_1:

$$
\varphi_{21}^* = h_{21}\big(w_1, \varphi_{22}^*(\varphi_{12}^*)\big) = h_{21}\left(w_1, \varphi_{22}^*\big(h_{12}(w_1, \varphi_{11}^*(\varphi_{21}^*))\big) \right).
\tag{18}
$$

This competitiveness condition defines an increasing relationship in (w_1, φ_{21}^*) space, as shown in Figure 1.4. Intuitively, a higher wage reduces a country's competitiveness and implies a higher cutoff productivity for exporting.

The "trade balance" condition is derived from labor market clearing, free entry, the zero-profit productivity cutoff conditions, and the requirement that trade is balanced:

$$
\begin{aligned}
M_{E1}&(w_1, \varphi_{21}^*)w_1 f_{21} \left[J_1(\varphi_{21}^*) + 1 - G_1(\varphi_{21}^*) \right] \\
&= M_{E2}(w_1, \varphi_{21}^*) f_{12} \Big[J_2\big(h_{12}(w_1, \varphi_{11}^*(\varphi_{21}^*)) \big) \\
&\quad + 1 - G_2\Big(h_{12}\big(h_{12}(w_1, \varphi_{11}^*(\varphi_{21}^*))\big) \Big) \Big],
\end{aligned}
\tag{19}
$$

which defines a decreasing relationship in (w_1, φ_{21}^*) space, as also shown in Figure 1.4. Intuitively, a higher productivity cutoff for exporting reduces total exports, which induces a trade deficit, and hence requires a reduction in the wage to increase competitiveness and eliminate the trade deficit. Note that since the trade balance condition (19) incorporates the competitiveness condition (18) care must be undertaken in the interpretation of these two relationships.

---

[23] We continue with our notation choice that the first subscript denotes the country of consumption and the second subscript the country of production. The notation in Demidova and Rodriguez-Clare (2011) reverses the order of the subscripts.

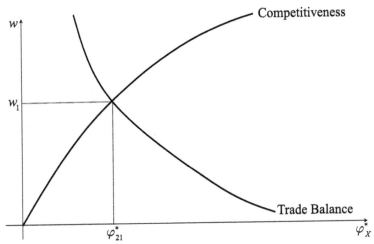

Figure 1.4 Competitiveness and Trade Balance Conditions

The effects of asymmetric trade liberalizations can be characterized most sharply for the case of a small open economy. In the monopolistically competitive environment considered here, country 1 is assumed to be a small open economy if (i) the zero-profit productivity cutoff in country 2 is unaffected by home variables, (ii) the mass of firms in country 2 is unaffected by home variables, and (iii) total expenditure and the price index in country 2 are unaffected by home variables. Nonetheless, the export productivity cutoff in country 2 and the measure of exporters from foreign to home are endogenous and depend on trade costs.

Under these small open economy assumptions, φ_{22}^* is exogenous with respect to country 1 variables and the trade cost between the two countries. In these circumstances, a unilateral trade liberalization by country 1 (a fall in variable trade costs (τ_{12}) and/or fixed exporting costs f_{12}) leaves the competitiveness condition unchanged but shifts the trade balance condition inwards. As a result, w_1 and φ_{21}^* fall, which implies a rise in φ_{11}^* (from the free entry condition). Since the domestic productivity cutoff is a sufficient statistic for welfare in (13), this in turn implies a rise in country 1's welfare. Intuitively, the unilateral domestic trade liberalization reduces the price of foreign goods relative to domestic goods, and requires a fall in the domestic wage to restore the trade balance. This fall in the domestic wage increases export market profits, which induces increased entry and hence tougher selection on the domestic market.

In contrast, a unilateral reduction in variable trade costs by country 2 (a fall in τ_{21}) shifts the competitiveness condition outwards but leaves the trade balance condition unchanged. As a result, w_1 rises and φ_{21}^* again falls, which implies a rise in φ_{11}^*. Thus, once again, welfare in country 1 rises. Intuitively, the fall in foreign variable trade costs increases domestic export market profits, which induces increased entry and tougher selection on the domestic market. The domestic wage rises to restore the trade balance. Reductions in the fixed costs of exporting to country 2 (f_{21}) have more subtle effects, because they shift both the competitiveness and trade balance curves.

The key takeaway from this analysis without an outside sector is that reductions in variable trade costs on either exports or imports raise welfare. In contrast, in the presence of an outside sector, reductions in variable trade costs on imports can be welfare reducing. This negative welfare impact is driven by the home market effect, which relocates production toward the higher trade cost country. Firms can access this market without incurring trade costs and take advantage of the lower variable trade costs on imports in the liberalizing country (see for example Krugman, 1980; Venables, 1987).

6. QUANTITATIVE PREDICTIONS

In order to derive quantitative predictions for trade and welfare, we follow a large part of the literature and assume a Pareto productivity distribution, as in Helpman et al. (2004), Chaney (2008), and Arkolakis et al. (2008, 2012, unpublished). Besides providing a good fit to the observed firm size distribution (see e.g. Axtell, 2001), this assumption yields closed form solutions for the productivity cutoffs and other endogenous variables of the model. For much of the analysis, we maintain our assumption of a composite input supply L_j for each sector j with a unit cost w_j that can vary across sectors. When we solve for factor prices, we restrict our analysis to the case of homogeneous labor with a common wage across sectors. To determine this wage, we dispense with the assumption of an outside sector, and use the equality between country income and expenditure on goods produced in that country.

6.1. Pareto Distribution

We now assume that firm productivity φ is drawn from a Pareto distribution so that

$$g(\varphi) = k\varphi_{\min}^k \varphi^{-(k+1)}, \quad G(\varphi) = 1 - \left(\frac{\varphi_{\min}}{\varphi}\right)^k,$$

where $\varphi_{\min} > 0$ is the lower bound of the support and the shape parameter k indexes dispersion (lower values of k are associated with greater productivity dispersion).[24]

A key feature of a Pareto distributed random variable is that it retains the same distribution and shape parameter k whenever it is truncated from below. Therefore the *ex-post* distribution of firm productivity conditional on survival also has a Pareto distribution. Another key feature of a Pareto distributed random variable is that power functions of this

---

[24] While a common shape parameter k for all countries is an important simplifying assumption, it is straightforward to accommodate cross-country differences in technology in the form of different lower bounds for the support of the productivity distribution $\varphi_{\min}$. For an analysis of the implications of cross-country differences in technology in a heterogeneous firm model with an outside sector, see Demidova (2008).

random variable are themselves Pareto distributed (but with a different shape parameter). Therefore firm size and variable profits are also Pareto distributed with shape parameter $k/(\sigma - 1)$, where we require $k > \sigma - 1$ for average firm size to be finite.[25] With Pareto distributed productivity, $J(\varphi^*)$ is a simple power function of the productivity cutoff φ^*.[26] From this power function, we obtain the following closed form solutions for the survival productivity cutoff in the closed economy:

$$(\varphi^*)^k = \frac{\sigma - 1}{k - (\sigma - 1)} \frac{f}{f_E} \varphi_{min}^k,$$

and in the symmetric country open economy:

$$(\varphi^*)^k = \frac{\sigma - 1}{k - (\sigma - 1)} \left[\frac{f + (N - 1)\tau^{-k} \left(\frac{f_X}{f} \right)^{\frac{-k}{\sigma-1}} f_X}{f_E} \right] \varphi_{min}^k.$$

6.2. Gravity

When firm productivity and hence firm exports to any destination are distributed Pareto, we obtain some very sharp predictions for bilateral trade flows (at the aggregate sector level). Before imposing this distributional assumption, we can write aggregate sector exports from i to n as:

$$X_{ni} = M_{Ei} \int_{\varphi_{ni}^*}^{\infty} r_{ni}(\varphi) dG(\varphi)$$

$$= M_{Ei} \int_{\varphi_{ni}^*}^{\infty} \left(\frac{\varphi}{\varphi_{ni}^*} \right)^{\sigma-1} \sigma w_i f_{ni} dG(\varphi)$$

$$= M_{Ei} \sigma w_i f_{ni} \left[J(\varphi_{ni}^*) + 1 - G(\varphi_{ni}^*) \right].$$

Using the closed form solution for $J(.)$ under Pareto productivity, we can then decompose bilateral aggregate trade into an extensive (mass of exporters) and intensive (average firm exports) margin:

$$X_{ni} = M_{Ei} \underbrace{\left(\frac{\varphi_{min}}{\varphi_{ni}^*} \right)^k}_{\text{mass of exporters}} \underbrace{w_i f_{ni} \frac{\sigma k}{k - \sigma + 1}}_{\text{average firm exports}}. \tag{20}$$

[25] The requirement that $k > \sigma - 1$ is needed given that the support for the Pareto distribution is unbounded from above and the assumption of a continuum of firms. If either of these conditions are relaxed (finite number of firms or a truncated Pareto distribution), then this condition need not be imposed (empirical estimates of the shape parameter $k/(\sigma - 1)$ for the distribution of firm size are below one for some sectors).

[26] In particular, we have:

$$J(\varphi^*) = \frac{\sigma - 1}{k - (\sigma - 1)} \left(\frac{\varphi_{min}}{\varphi^*} \right)^k.$$

Given this distributional assumption, we see that average firm exports are independent of variable trade costs, so that higher variable trade costs reduce bilateral trade solely through the extensive margin of the mass of exporting firms. On one hand, higher variable trade costs reduce firm-level exports for all firms; this reduces average exports per firm. On the other hand, higher variable trade costs also induce low productivity firms to exit the export market; this raises average exports per firm through a composition effect (lower productivity firms have lower exports). With a Pareto productivity distribution these two effects exactly offset one another, so as to leave average firm exports (conditional on exporting) independent of variable trade costs.[27] In contrast, higher fixed costs of exporting (f_{ni}) increase the exporting productivity cutoff (φ_{ni}^*), which reduces the mass of exporting firms and increases average exports conditional on exporting.

This distributional assumption also allows us to write the sector-level bilateral trade flows as a gravity equation that has a very similar structure to gravity equations derived from a variety of other models of trade.[28] Without imposing balanced trade, we can write industry revenue $R_i = \sum_{n=1}^{N} X_{ni}$ and use the export productivity cutoff condition (6) to rewrite bilateral exports from country i to market n in sector j (20) as:

$$
X_{ni} = \frac{R_i}{\Xi_i} \left(\frac{X_n}{P_n^{1-\sigma}} \right)^{k/(\sigma-1)} \tau_{ni}^{-k} f_{ni}^{1-k/(\sigma-1)},
$$

$$
\Xi_i = \sum_n \left(\frac{X_n}{P_n^{1-\sigma}} \right)^{k/(\sigma-1)} \tau_{ni}^{-k} f_{ni}^{1-k/(\sigma-1)}.
$$

(21)

This functional form is very similar to the standard CES gravity equation without firm heterogeneity in Anderson and van Wincoop (2002). Comparing the two expressions, a number of differences are apparent. First, variable trade costs affect aggregate trade flows through both the intensive margin (exports of a given firm) and the extensive margin (the number of exporting firms). However, the exponent on variable trade costs τ_{ni} is the Pareto shape parameter k rather than the elasticity of substitution between varieties, which reflects the invariance of average firm exports with respect to variable trade costs discussed above. Second, fixed exporting costs f_{ni} only affect aggregate trade flows through the extensive margin of the number of exporting firms, and enter with an exponent that depends on both the Pareto shape parameter and the elasticity of substitution. Third, the importer fixed effect in the standard CES formulation ($X_n/P_n^{1-\sigma}$) is amplified under firm heterogeneity by $k/(\sigma - 1) > 1$, which captures the effect of market demand on the extensive margin of exporting firms. Fourth, the exporter fixed effect is the same as in the standard CES formulation (R_i/Ξ_i). This fixed effect combines an exporter's industry revenue (R_i) with its market potential (Ξ_i), where market potential is defined

---

[27] Note the parallel with Eaton and Kortum (2002), in which higher variable trade costs reduce bilateral exports solely through an extensive margin of the fraction of goods exported.

[28] For further discussion of the gravity equation literature, see the Head and Mayer (Chapter 3) in this handbook.

as in Redding and Venables (2004) as the trade cost weighted sum of demand in all markets.

A key implication of the gravity equation (21) is that bilateral trade between countries i and n depends on both bilateral trade costs $\{\tau_{ni}, f_{ni}\}$ and trade costs with all the other partners of each country ("multilateral resistance" as captured in P_n and Ξ_i). This role for multilateral resistance can be further illustrated by solving explicitly for the price indices (P_n), which depend on the mass of entrants (M_{Ei}) across countries. In general, the mass of entrants in country i will depend on both the input supply L_i to the sector as well as the cutoffs φ_{ni}^* to all destinations n, which determine the allocation of inputs between entry and production. However, under Pareto productivity, the dependence of entry on the cutoffs is eliminated and entry only depends on the input supply to the sector (see the web appendix for proof).[29]

$$M_{Ei} = \frac{(\sigma - 1)}{k\sigma} \frac{L_i}{f_{Ei}}. \tag{22}$$

This allows us to write the price index in country n as a function of its own expenditure as well as the input supply and unit cost in all countries:[30]

$$P_n^{-k} = \left[\sum_v (L_v/f_{Ev}) \varphi_{\min}^k \tau_{nv}^{-k} w_v^{-(k\sigma/(\sigma-1)-1)} (f_{nv})^{1-k/(\sigma-1)} \right]$$

$$(X_n)^{-(1-k/(\sigma-1))} \left(\frac{\sigma}{\sigma-1} \right)^{-k} \sigma^{-k/(\sigma-1)} \frac{\sigma-1}{k-\sigma+1}.$$

We can then solve out this price index from the bilateral gravity equation (21) to obtain a trade share that depends only on unit costs (w_i) and input supplies (L_i):

$$\lambda_{ni} \equiv \frac{X_{ni}}{X_n} = \frac{(L_i/f_{Ei}) \tau_{ni}^{-k} w_i^{-(k\sigma/(\sigma-1)-1)} f_{ni}^{1-k/(\sigma-1)}}{\sum_v (L_v/f_{Ev}) \tau_{nv}^{-k} w_v^{-(k\sigma/(\sigma-1)-1)} f_{nv}^{1-k/(\sigma-1)}}. \tag{23}$$

The trade share (23) takes the familiar gravity equation form, as in Eaton and Kortum (2002).[31] The elasticity of trade with respect to variable trade costs again depends on the Pareto shape parameter (k) and there is a unit elasticity on importer expenditure (X_n) for given sectoral input allocations (L_i) and unit costs (w_i) in all countries. One key

---

[29] Instead of using free entry to determine the mass of entrants, Chaney (2008) assumes an exogenous mass of entrants proportional to the input supply L_i. In this case, the marginal entrant makes zero profits, which implies that there are positive expected profits that need to be taken into account in welfare calculations. As apparent from (22), under the assumption of a Pareto productivity distribution, the mass of entrants is proportional to the input supply L_i even under free entry.

[30] Note that the exponent on unit cost differs from the exponent on variable trade costs because of our assumption that fixed exporting costs are incurred in the source country.

[31] This trade share (23) under Pareto productivity can also be used to show that a sufficient condition for the mass of varieties available for domestic consumption to fall following the opening of trade is $w_i f_{ni} > w_n f_{nn}$ for $n \neq i$, as analyzed in Baldwin and Forslid (2010).

difference from Eaton and Kortum (2002) is that the trade share depends directly on the input allocation (L_i), which reflects the presence of an endogenous measure of firm varieties compared to a fixed range of goods.

6.3. Wages and Welfare

We now turn to the general equilibrium across sectors and investigate its welfare properties. To close our model, we again assume that labor is homogeneous, with a fixed supply $\bar{L}_i$ in each country. We dispense with the assumption of an outside sector so that $j = 1, \ldots, J$ and all sectors are differentiated. Sectoral spending is given by $\beta_j w_n \bar{L}_n$, and the country wages (common across sectors j) are determined by the N balanced trade conditions for each country:

$$w_i \bar{L}_i = \sum_{j=1}^{J} \sum_{n=1}^{N} \lambda_{nij} \beta_j w_n \bar{L}_n,$$

where the trade shares λ_{nij} for each sector are determined by (23).

The assumption of Pareto productivity has some strong implications for the functional form of the welfare gains from trade, as analyzed in Arkolakis et al. (2012). Welfare per worker (in country n) takes the same form as in (13), except that wages are no longer unitary: $\mathbb{U}_n = w_n / \left(\prod_{j=1}^{J} P_{nj}^{\beta_j} \right) = \prod_{j=1}^{J} (P_{nj}/w_n)^{-\beta_j}$. The price index for sector j in country n, in turn, can be written as a function of the domestic productivity cutoff in that sector as shown in (12):

$$P_{nj} = \frac{\sigma_j}{\sigma_j - 1} \left(\frac{f_{nnj} \sigma_j}{\beta_j \bar{L}_n} \right)^{1/(\sigma_j - 1)} \frac{w_n}{\varphi_{nnj}^*}. \tag{24}$$

Under the assumption of Pareto productivity, we can write the domestic cutoff in each sector φ_{nj}^* as a function of country n's domestic trade share $\lambda_{nnj} \equiv X_{nnj}/\beta_j w_n \bar{L}_n$ and the mass of entrants M_{Enj} in that sector using (20). From (22), we can write this mass of entrants in terms of the sector's labor supply L_{nj}. This yields the following expression for the domestic cutoff:

$$(\varphi_{nnj}^*)^k = \varphi_{min}^k \frac{\sigma_j - 1}{k_j - (\sigma_j - 1)} \frac{f_{nnj}}{f_{Enj}} \frac{1}{\beta_j \bar{L}_n} \frac{L_{nj}}{\lambda_{nnj}}. \tag{25}$$

By combining (25) and (24), we obtain an expression for welfare that depends only on the endogenous ratio of labor supply to domestic trade shares L_{nj}/λ_{nnj} across sectors. This expression does not contain any per-unit or fixed trade cost measures, τ_{nij} or f_{nij} for $i \neq n$, so the ratios L_{nj}/λ_{nnj} are sufficient statistics that summarize the impact of trade costs on welfare. We can thus summarize the welfare gains from trade, measured as the welfare ratio $\hat{\mathbb{U}}_n \equiv \mathbb{U}_n^{\text{Open}}/\mathbb{U}_n^{\text{Closed}}$ (between the open and closed economies) in terms of a country's domestic trade shares $\lambda_{nnj}^{\text{Open}}$ (the domestic trade shares in the closed economy are fixed at $\lambda_{nnj}^{\text{Closed}} = 1$) and the change in sectoral labor allocations between the open and closed economies ($\hat{L}_{nj} = L_{nj}^{\text{Open}} / L_{nj}^{\text{Closed}}$):

$$\hat{\mathbb{U}}_n = \prod_{j=1}^{J} \left(\frac{\hat{\lambda}_{nnj}}{\hat{L}_{nj}} \right)^{-\frac{\beta_j}{k_j}} = \prod_{j=1}^{J} \left(\lambda_{nnj}^{\text{Open}} \right)^{-\frac{\beta_j}{k_j}} \left(\frac{L_{nj}^{\text{Open}}}{L_{nj}^{\text{Closed}}} \right)^{\frac{\beta_j}{k_j}} .$$

Also, we note that the only relevant parameters for this welfare gain calculation are the expenditure shares (β_j) and trade elasticities (k_j). Lower trade costs have a direct impact on the welfare gains by lowering the domestic trade shares $\lambda_{nnj}^{\text{Open}}$. They also have an indirect effect via the reallocation of labor across sectors. This channel operates through the welfare benefits of higher entry rates (which leads to additional product variety), and is therefore absent in models of trade where the range of consumed goods is constant. To motivate the direction of the welfare gain for this channel, we return to our scenario that adds an additional homogenous good sector $j = 0$ that is produced in every country. In that scenario (with symmetric trade and production costs), we saw that opening to trade would reallocate labor L_{nj}^{Open} to the differentiated sectors $j \geq 1$ for larger countries (larger $\bar{L}_n$). This generates distributional effects for the gains from trade, skewing those gains toward larger markets. (If we break the symmetry assumption for trade costs, then countries with better geography would also increase their relative employment in the differentiated goods sectors, skewing the gains from trade in their favor.) Balistreri et al. (2011) provide a quantitative assessment of the gains from trade liberalization that accounts for these inter-sectoral labor reallocations, based on differences in country size, geography, and comparative advantage.

In the special case where labor allocations across sectors do not change following the opening of trade, the open economy domestic trade shares $\lambda_{nnj}^{\text{Open}}$ provide the single sufficient statistics for the welfare gains from trade.[32] This version of the model falls within a class of models analyzed by Arkolakis et al. (2012). They show that when these models are calibrated to the same empirical trade shares (for the open economy equilibrium), they will all imply the same welfare gains from trade. But note that countries' trade shares with themselves are endogenous variables and can have different determinants in different models. In heterogeneous firm models, the overall welfare gains from trade are composed of both increases in average productivity and changes in variety. In contrast, in homogeneous firm models such as Krugman (1980), they are composed of changes in variety alone. In Melitz and Redding (unpublished), we show that the homogeneous firm model of Krugman (1980) generates different levels of this endogenous trade share than the heterogeneous firm model (given the same exogenous parameters for trade costs and product differentiation). The additional adjustment margin of average productivity

---

[32] This only holds for these specific parametric assumptions on preferences (CES) and productivity (Pareto).

in the heterogeneous firm model implies greater welfare gains from a given reduction in trade costs than in the homogeneous firm benchmark. We also show these differences in welfare gains to be quantitatively substantial.

While our discussion above concentrates on aggregate bilateral trade shares, models of firm heterogeneity in differentiated product markets provide a rationale for the prevalence of zeros in bilateral trade flows. Helpman et al. (2008) develop a multi-country version of the model in Section 3, in which the productivity distribution is a truncated Pareto. In this case, no firm exports from country i to market n if the productivity cutoff (φ_{ni}^*) lies above the upper limit of country i's productivity distribution. Estimating a structural gravity equation, they show that controlling for the non-random selection of positive trade flows and the extensive margin of exporting firms is important for estimates of the trade effects of standard trade frictions.

6.4. Structural Estimation

In addition to shedding new light on aggregate bilateral trade flows, models of firm heterogeneity in differentiated product markets also provide a natural platform for explaining a number of features of disaggregated trade data by firm and destination market. As shown in Eaton et al. (2011), disaggregated French trade data exhibit a number of striking empirical regularities. First, the number of French firms selling to a market (relative to French market share) increases with market size according to an approximately log linear relationship. This pattern of firm export market participation exhibits an imperfect hierarchy, where firms selling to less popular markets are more likely to sell to more popular markets, but do not always do so. Second, export sales distributions are similar across markets of very different size and export propensities by French firms. While the upper tail of these distributions is approximately distributed Pareto, there are departures from a Pareto distribution in the lower tail, where small export shipments are observed. Third, average sales in France are higher for firms selling to less popular foreign markets and for firms selling to more foreign markets.

To account for these features of the data, Eaton et al. (2011) use a version of the model from Section 3 with a Pareto productivity distribution and a fixed measure of potential firms as in Chaney (2008). To explain variation in firm export participation with market size under CES demand, fixed market entry costs are required. But to generate the departures from a Pareto distribution in the lower tail, these fixed market entry costs are allowed to vary endogenously with a firm's choice of the fraction of consumers within a market to serve (e), as in Arkolakis (2010). Finally, to explain imperfect hierarchies of markets, fixed market entry costs are assumed to be subject to an idiosyncratic shock for each firm ω and destination market n ($\varepsilon_{n\omega}$). There is also a common shock for each source country i and destination market n (F_{ni}). Market entry costs are therefore:

$$f_{ni\omega} = \varepsilon_{n\omega} F_{ni} M(e),$$

where the function $M(e)$ determines how market entry costs vary with the fraction of consumers served (e) and takes the following form:

$$M(e) = \frac{1 - (1 - e)^{1 - 1/\lambda}}{1 - 1/\lambda},$$

where $\lambda > 0$ captures the increasing cost of reaching a larger fraction of consumers. Any given consumer is served with probability e, so that each consumer receives the same measure of varieties, but the particular varieties in question can vary across consumers.[33]

To allow for idiosyncratic variation in sales conditional on entering a given export market for firms with a given productivity, demand is also subject to an idiosyncratic shock for each firm ω and destination market n, $\alpha_{n\omega}$:

$$X_{ni\omega} = \alpha_{n\omega} e_{ni\omega} X_n \left(\frac{\tau_{ni} p_{i\omega}}{P_n} \right)^{1-\sigma},$$

where X_n is total expenditure in market n and the presence of $e_{ni\omega}$ reflects the fact that only a fraction of consumers in each market are served. A firm's decision to enter a market depends on the composite shock, $\eta_{n\omega} = \alpha_{n\omega}/\varepsilon_{n\omega}$, but a firm with a given productivity can enter a market because of a low entry shock, $\varepsilon_{n\omega}$, and yet still have low sales in that market because of a low demand shock, $\alpha_{n\omega}$.

Using moments of the French trade data by firm and destination market, Eaton et al. (2011) estimate the model's five key parameters: a composite parameter including the elasticity of substitution and the Pareto shape parameter, the convexity of marketing costs, the variance of demand shocks, the variance of entry shocks, and the correlation between demand and entry shocks. These five parameters are precisely estimated and the estimated model provides a good fit to the data. Firm productivity accounts for around half of the observed variation across firms in export market participation, but explains substantially less of the variation in exports conditional on entering a market.

The estimated model is used to undertake counterfactuals, such as a 10% reduction in bilateral trade barriers for all French firms. In this counterfactual, total sales by French firms rise by around US $16 million, with most of this increase accounted for by a rise in sales of the top decile of firms of around US $23 million. In contrast, every other decile of firms experiences a decline in sales, with around half of the firms in the bottom decile

---

[33] To generate the observed departures from a Pareto distribution in the lower tail of the export sales distribution, one requires $0 < \lambda < 1$, which implies an increasing marginal cost of reaching additional consumers. An alternative potential explanation for the departures from a Pareto distribution in the lower tail is a variable elasticity of substitution. Both endogenous market entry costs and a variable elasticity of substitution provide potential explanations for empirical findings that most of the growth in trade following trade liberalization is in goods previously traded in small amounts, as in Kehoe and Ruhl (2013).

exiting. These results suggest that even empirically reasonable changes in trade frictions can involve substantial intra-industry reallocations.[34]

7. FACTOR ABUNDANCE AND HETEROGENEITY

While models of firm heterogeneity in differentiated product markets emphasize within-industry reallocations, traditional trade theories instead stress between-industry reallocations. Bernard et al. (2007a) combine these two dimensions of reallocation by incorporating the model in Section 3 into the integrated equilibrium framework of neoclassical trade theory. Comparative advantage is introduced by supposing that sectors differ in their relative factor intensity and countries differ in their relative factor abundance. The production technology within each sector is homothetic such that the entry cost and the fixed and variable production costs use the two factors of production with the same intensity. The total cost of producing $q(\varphi)$ units of a variety in sector j in country i is thus:

$$\Gamma_{ij} = \left[f_{ij} + \frac{q_{ij}(\varphi)}{\varphi} \right] (w_{Si})^{\beta_j} (w_{Li})^{1-\beta_j},$$

where w_{Si} is the skilled wage, w_{Li} is the unskilled wage, and β_j indexes the sector's skill intensity.

In the special case in which fixed and variable trade costs are equal to zero, all firms export and the concept of integrated equilibrium from Dixit and Norman (1980) and Helpman and Krugman (1985) can be used to determine the set of factor allocations to the two countries for which trade in goods alone can equalize factor prices. Within this factor price equalization set, the four theorems of the Heckscher-Ohlin model—the Factor Price Equalization, Stolper-Samuelson, Rybczynski, and Heckscher-Ohlin Theorems—continue to hold with firm heterogeneity.

More generally, if fixed and variable trade costs are not equal to zero, factor price equalization breaks down and the opening of trade results in intra-industry reallocations across firms (assuming parameter values that deliver selection into export markets). As these intra-industry reallocations are driven by the differential impact of the opening of trade on exporters and non-exporters, they are stronger in the comparative advantage sector, where export opportunities are relatively more attractive. Although there is a decline in the relative mass of firms in the comparative disadvantage sector, as factors of production are reallocated in accordance with comparative advantage, exit by low productivity firms is strongest in the comparative advantage sector. Thus the opening of trade leads to a larger increase in the zero-profit cutoff and in average productivity in the comparative advantage sector than in the comparative disadvantage sector. This

---

[34] See Corcos et al. (2012) for a quantitative analysis of European integration using a model of firm heterogeneity and trade. See Cherkashin et al. (unpublished) for a quantitative analysis of the Bangladeshi apparel sector.

differential impact of the opening of trade across sectors according to Heckscher-Ohlin-based comparative advantage influences the effect of trade liberalization on welfare and income distribution. In addition to the standard Stolper-Samuelson effects of trade liberalization, the real reward of each factor is influenced by changes in product variety (as in Helpman and Krugman, 1985) and increases with average productivity in each sector. As a result, it becomes possible for trade liberalization to raise rather than reduce the real reward of the scarce factor.

A number of studies have further explored the relationship between within and between-industry reallocations of resources. Fan et al. (unpublished) and Hsieh and Ossa (unpublished) embed firm heterogeneity within a Ricardian model with a continuum of goods. Lu (unpublished) develops a version of the model we have outlined, but specifically considers the case where the domestic market access costs are high enough to generate tougher selection there relative to the export market. In this case, all surviving firms export but only a subset of relatively more productive firms serve the domestic market. She documents that this domestic/export market "reversal" occurs for Chinese firms in sectors where China enjoys a strong comparative advantage relative to its trading partners. Burstein and Vogel (unpublished a) and Harrigan and Reshef (2011) explore complementarities between heterogeneous firm productivity and skill intensity, and how this affects the impact of trade liberalization on wage inequality. Burstein and Vogel (unpublished b) provide general conditions under which changes in the factor content of trade are a sufficient condition for changes in relative factor prices.

8. TRADE AND MARKET SIZE

One limitation of the theoretical framework considered so far is its assumption of constant elasticity of substitution (CES) preferences, which imply constant mark-ups and hence that changes in aggregate demand leave the productivity cutoff for production unchanged. In this section, we extend our analysis of firm heterogeneity to the case of variable mark-ups following Melitz and Ottaviano (2008). Aggregate market conditions are summarized by the "toughness" of competition, which depends on market size in the closed economy and on both market size and trade costs in the open economy. "Tougher" competition in a market is characterized by a larger number of sellers and a lower average price of sellers, which both induce a downward shift in distribution of mark-ups across firms. Differences in competition across markets then feed back and influence firm location and export decisions. Markets that have more attractive fundamentals (for firms) are characterized in equilibrium by "tougher" competition, which implies that it is harder for exporters to break into these markets and harder for domestic firms to survive in these markets.

Consumer preferences are assumed to be quasi-linear between a homogeneous and differentiated sector with quadratic preferences across varieties within the differentiated sector, as in Ottaviano et al. (2002):

$$U_i = q_{0i}^c + \alpha \int_{\omega \in \Omega_i} q_{\omega i}^c d\omega - \frac{1}{2}\gamma \int_{\omega \in \Omega_i} \left(q_{\omega i}^c\right)^2 d\omega - \frac{1}{2}\eta \left(\int_{\omega \in \Omega_i} q_{\omega i}^c d\omega\right)^2,$$

where $q_{\omega i}^c$ and q_{0i}^c denote the representative consumer's consumption of differentiated variety ω and the homogeneous good; Ω_i is the set of varieties available for consumption in country i. Higher α and lower η increase demand for differentiated varieties relative to the numeraire, while higher γ implies greater love of variety, with $\gamma = 0$ corresponding to the special case of perfect substitutes.

Labor is the sole factor of production and each country i is endowed with L_i workers. Total demand for each variety is therefore $L_i q_{\omega i}^c$, where L_i indexes market size. Each country's labor endowment is assumed to be sufficiently large that it both consumes and produces the homogeneous good, which is chosen as the numeraire, so that $p_{0i} = 1$. As long as the homogeneous good is consumed, quasi-linear-quadratic preferences imply that the demand for differentiated varieties can be determined independently of income. Using the first-order conditions for utility maximization, the inverse demand curve for each differentiated variety is:

$$p_{\omega i} = \alpha - \gamma q_{\omega i}^c - \eta Q_i^c, \quad Q_i^c = \int_{\omega \in \Omega_i} q_{\omega i}^c d\omega. \tag{26}$$

Since the marginal utility of consuming a differentiated variety is finite at zero consumption, there is a threshold or choke price above which demand for a variety is zero. Using (26) this threshold can be written:

$$p_{\omega i} \leq \frac{1}{\eta N_i + \gamma}(\gamma \alpha + \eta N_i \bar{p}_i), \tag{27}$$

where N_i is the number of consumed varieties and $\bar{p}_i$ is their average price. This choke price decreases as the number of consumed varieties rises and as their average price falls (tougher competition). Welfare is given by the indirect utility function:

$$U_i = I_i^c + \frac{1}{2}\left(\eta + \frac{\gamma}{N_i}\right)^{-1}(\alpha - \bar{p}_i)^2 + \frac{1}{2}\frac{N_i}{\gamma}\sigma_{pi}^2,$$

where I_i^c is the representative consumer's income; $\bar{p}_i$ and σ_{pi}^2 are the mean and variance of prices. Welfare increases when average prices fall, when the number of varieties increases (consumer love of variety) and when the variance of prices increases (as the variance of prices increases, consumers can substitute toward lower-priced varieties).

The homogeneous good is produced under conditions of perfect competition and constant returns to scale with a unit labor requirement. As long as the homogeneous good is produced, productivity in this sector pins down a unitary wage in each country.

Differentiated varieties are produced under conditions of monopolistic competition and constant returns to scale. To enter the differentiated sector, a firm must incur a sunk entry cost of f_E units of labor, after which its unit labor requirement or cost (c) is drawn from a cumulative distribution function $G(c)$ with support on $[0, c_M]$. This cost draw is the inverse of the productivity draw considered in Section 3. As firms with the same cost (c) behave symmetrically, firms are indexed from now on by c alone. If a firm decides to export, it faces iceberg variable costs of trade, such that $\tau_{ni} > 1$ units of a variety must be exported from country i to country n in order for one unit to arrive.

Since demand exhibits a choke price, firm exit occurs even in the absence of fixed production costs. Firms drawing a marginal cost above the choke price (27) in the domestic market exit, because they cannot generate positive profits from production. In the closed economy, the zero-profit cost cutoff (c_{Di}) is a sufficient statistic that completely summarizes the competitive environment and determines firm outcomes as a function of their cost draw (c):

$$p_i(c) = \frac{1}{2}(c_{Di} + c) \qquad\qquad \text{prices,}$$

$$\mu_i(c) = p_i(c) - c = \frac{1}{2}(c_{Di} - c) \qquad\qquad \text{mark-ups,}$$

$$r_i(c) = \frac{L_i}{4\gamma}\left[(c_{Di})^2 - c^2\right] \qquad\qquad \text{revenues,}$$

$$\pi_i(c) = \frac{L_i}{4\gamma}(c_{Di} - c)^2 \qquad\qquad \text{profits.}$$

As in the model with CES preferences in Section 3, more productive firms (with lower c) have lower prices $(p_i(c))$, higher output and revenue $(r_i(c))$, and higher profits $(\pi_i(c))$. In contrast to the model with CES preferences, more productive firms (with lower c) now also have higher mark-ups $(\mu_i(c))$. Firms with lower marginal cost charge higher mark-ups because their marginal cost intersects marginal revenue at a more inelastic segment of the demand curve. Since more productive firms do not fully pass on their lower marginal costs to consumers, they have higher revenue-based productivity $(r_i(l)/l_i(c))$ even in the absence of fixed production costs.

Under the assumption that productivity $(1/c)$ is Pareto distributed with lower bound $1/c_M$ and shape parameter k, the closed economy cost cutoff is given by:

$$c_{Di} = \left(\frac{\gamma\phi}{L_i}\right)^{\frac{1}{k+2}},$$

where $\phi = 2(k+1)(k+2)c_M^k f_E$. The closed economy cost cutoff falls (higher average productivity) when varieties are closer substitutes (lower γ), when there is a better distribution of cost draws (lower c_M), when sunk costs fall (lower f_E), and in bigger markets (higher L_i). Each of these comparative statics induces an increase in the "toughness of competition" in the form of a larger number of varieties consumed (higher N_i) and lower average prices (lower $\bar{p}_i$).

We now describe the effects of increased market size in further detail. Holding the number of products and their prices fixed, an increase in market size proportionately increases demand for all products. In equilibrium, this generates additional entry. As the number of consumed varieties rises, the new demand curves also shift in. The combination of these two effects generates a rotation of each firm's residual demand curve: demand is lower at higher prices, higher at lower prices, and more elastic at any given price. This induces high cost firms to exit and the remaining firms to set lower mark-ups. Thus, larger markets are characterized by lower prices, both because of higher average productivity (a lower zero-profit cost cutoff c_{Di}) and lower mark-ups for a firm with a given productivity. Average firm size is higher due to the expansion of the low cost firms. Consumers in larger markets also enjoy higher welfare, because of both greater product variety and lower prices. The lower cost cutoff in larger markets reduces the dispersion in productivity, prices, and mark-ups (by compressing the range of firm costs $[0, c_{Di}]$). On the other hand, the dispersion of firm size increases, both in terms of output and revenue. These comparative statics for market size are consistent with the empirical findings in Campbell and Hopenhayn (2005) and Syverson (2004).[35]

In the open economy, markets are assumed to be segmented. Due to the constant returns in production, each firm maximizes independently the profits earned from domestic and export sales.[36] The demand-side choke prices imply that fixed exporting costs are not needed to generate selection into export markets. A firm's marginal costs may lie below the choke price in the domestic market, but may be above the choke price in the foreign market once variable trade costs are taken into account. In this case, the firm serves the domestic market only.

In an open economy equilibrium with symmetric trade costs ($\tau_{ni} = \tau > 1$ for all $n \neq i$, and $\tau_{ii} = 1$), the zero-profit and exporting cost cutoffs are given by:

$$
\begin{aligned}
c_{Di} &= \left\{ \frac{\gamma \phi}{L_i \left[1 + (M-1)\tau^{-k} \right]} \right\}^{\frac{1}{k+2}}, & i &\in \{1, \ldots, M\}, \\
c_{Xni} &= \frac{c_{Dn}}{\tau}, & i, n &\in \{1, \ldots, M\}.
\end{aligned}
\tag{28}
$$

Therefore costly trade does not completely integrate markets and market size differences affect cost cutoffs and have qualitatively similar effects as in the closed economy. Larger markets attract more firms, which implies "tougher" competition in the presence of trade costs, and hence leads to a lower cost cutoff and higher average productivity.

---

[35] See Combes et al. (2012) for evidence on the contributions of agglomeration and selection toward the higher productivity of larger cities.

[36] In equilibrium, prices are such that there are no profitable arbitrage opportunities across markets, because firms absorb a portion of the trade cost difference across markets into lower prices (dumping).

Multilateral trade liberalization (a reduction in the common value of variable trade costs τ) again causes intra-industry reallocation by reducing the zero-profit cost cutoff in (28), which induces low productivity firms to exit and shifts the composition of output toward more productive firms. Similar to the impact of increased market size, multilateral trade liberalization induces more elastic demand for all firms. The surviving firms respond by lowering their mark-ups. Thus, prices fall due to the combined effect of higher average productivity (a lower cost cutoff c_{Di}) and lower mark-ups. This pro-competitive effect is consistent with empirical evidence from trade liberalization episodes (see the empirical studies discussed in Section 2 and the survey by Tybout, 2003) and introduces a new channel for welfare gains from trade (in addition to changes in product variety and average productivity).

Given the presence of an outside sector, the model also features a home market effect, which influences the effects of unilateral and preferential trade liberalization. In the short-run, holding the number of firms in each country fixed, all countries experience welfare gains from unilateral or preferential trade liberalization. This is no longer the case in the long-run, once the number of firms in each country adjusts. If one country unilaterally reduces its import barriers, it can experience welfare losses, as production relocates to other countries to access these markets without trade costs and take advantage of the lower import barriers in the liberalizing country. All of these results relate to the case of variable trade costs that use real resources. If trade barriers instead take the form of tariffs that raise revenue, then this revenue affects the welfare analysis.

While we focus on the quasi-linear-quadratic demand system as a particularly tractable framework to analyze the effects of trade in the presence of firm heterogeneity and variable mark-ups, other research has considered Bertrand competition (Bernard et al., 2003; de Blas and Russ, 2010; Holmes et al., unpublished), Constant Absolute Risk Aversion (CARA) preferences (Behrens and Murata, 2012), translog preferences (Feenstra, 2003), and general additively separable utility (Zhelobodko et al., 2012). Taking a different approach, Edmund et al. (2012) introduce variable mark-ups into a CES demand system by considering the case of a finite number of firms.[37]

9. ENDOGENOUS FIRM PRODUCTIVITY

Up to now, we have assumed that firm productivity is exogenously set at entry and therefore does not respond endogenously to trade liberalization. Recent research has focused on numerous extensions where firms can affect their productivity via decisions regarding

---

[37] In these models of firm heterogeneity with variable mark-ups, the impact of changes in variable trade costs on the distribution of prices and welfare depends critically on the productivity distribution. Under the assumption that productivity is Pareto distributed, Arkolakis et al. (unpublished) show that for a class of preferences featuring variable elasticities of demand and choke prices, the distribution of prices conditional on purchasing a variety is invariant to changes in variable trade costs and the welfare gains from trade can be expressed in terms of a country's trade share with itself and a parametric correction for variable mark-ups.

the range of products produced, innovation and technology adoption, and how production is organized. These decisions, in turn, are affected by the trading environment and the firm's trade participation. This induces a complementarity between choices regarding trade and firm productivity.

In this section, we begin by developing some of these extensions regarding product scope (and the emergence of multi-product firms), innovation, and technology adoption within a static model. Firms make a one-time joint decision regarding this additional characteristic along with the production and trade decisions that we have previously analyzed. This introduces a distinction between a firm's productivity draw upon entry and its measured productivity, which reflects its decisions about product scope, innovation, and technology adoption. We next transition to consider some dynamic models in order to analyze the joint evolution of firm productivity and export market participation over time. In these models, firm productivity can evolve due to exogenous shocks, but also as an outcome of endogenous innovation or technology adoption decisions. These dynamic models capture the complementarity between firm productivity and trade both in the cross-section and time dimensions: the decision to export at one point in time is linked to other decisions regarding innovation or technology adoption at other points in time.

A key feature of all the models covered in this section is that trade liberalization can raise firm-level productivity (as well as generate increases in aggregate productivity via between-firm reallocations of resources as analyzed in previous sections).

9.1. Product Scope Decision and Multi-Product Firms

One of the striking features of international trade is the extent to which it is concentrated in the hands of a relatively small number of firms supplying many products to many destinations. For example, Bernard et al. (2007a) report that US firms exporting more than five ten-digit products to more than five destinations account for only around 12% of exporters but 92% of export value.[38] Motivated by such evidence, a growing body of theoretical and empirical research has sought to model the implications of multi-product, multi-destination firms for understanding aggregate and disaggregate patterns of trade.[39]

The model of firm heterogeneity in differentiated product markets developed in Section 3 admits a natural generalization to incorporate multi-product firms, as explored in Bernard et al. (2011). Suppose that the representative consumer derives utility from the consumption of a continuum of symmetric products h defined on the interval $[0, 1]$:

$$U = \left[\int_0^1 C_h^{\nu} dh \right]^{\frac{1}{\nu}}, \quad 0 < \nu < 1.$$

---

[38] Similar results are found for other countries, as summarized in Mayer and Ottaviano (2007) and World Trade Organization (2008).

[39] While early research on multi-product firms and trade, such as Ottaviano and Thisse (2011) and Allanson and Montagna (2005), modeled firms and products symmetrically, more recent research has emphasized heterogeneity both within and across firms.

Within each product, a continuum of firms supply differentiated varieties of the product. Incurring the sunk entry cost f_E creates a firm brand that can be used to supply one horizontally differentiated variety of each of the continuum of products. Varieties are assumed to be differentiated from one another by their brand, which implies that a given brand cannot be used to supply more than one differentiated variety of each product. After incurring the sunk entry cost, a firm observes realizations of two stochastic shocks to profitability: "ability" $\varphi \in (0, \infty)$, which is common to all products and drawn from a distribution $g(\varphi)$, and "product attributes" $\lambda_h \in (0, \infty)$, which are specific to each product h and possibly to each destination market and drawn from a distribution $z(\lambda)$. A firm in each country i faces a fixed cost of supplying each market n (F_{ni}) and an additional fixed cost of supplying each product to that market (f_{ni}).

Sectoral equilibrium can be determined using a similar approach as in Section 3. There is a product attributes cutoff for each firm ability φ ($\lambda_{ni}^*(\varphi)$) above which a firm can profitably export a product from country i to market n:

$$\pi_{ni}(\varphi, \lambda_{ni}^*(\varphi)) = \frac{r_{ni}(\varphi, \lambda_{ni}^*(\varphi))}{\sigma} - f_{ni} = 0.$$

There is also a firm ability cutoff (φ_{ni}^*) above which a firm can generate enough total variable profits from exporting its range of profitable products from country i to country n to cover the fixed costs of serving market n (F_n):

$$\pi_{ni}(\varphi_{ni}^*) = \int_{\lambda_{ni}^*(\varphi_{ni}^*)}^{\infty} \pi_{ni}(\varphi_{ni}^*, \lambda)z(\lambda)d\lambda - F_{ni} = 0.$$

Higher ability firms can generate sufficient variable profits to cover the product fixed cost at a lower value of product attributes, and therefore supply a wider range of products to each market. For sufficiently low values of firm ability, the excess of variable profits over product fixed costs in the small range of profitable products does not cover the fixed cost of serving the market and therefore the firm does not supply the market. The lowest-ability firms exit, intermediate-ability firms serve only the domestic market, and the highest ability firms export. Within exporters, products with the worst attributes are supplied only to the domestic market, while products with the best attributes are exported to the largest number of markets.

This theoretical framework features selection both within and across firms. Trade liberalization raises average industry productivity not only through the exit of the least productive firms, but also through surviving firms dropping their least-successful products. Consistent with these predictions, Bernard et al. (2011) find that US firms more exposed to tariff reductions under the Canada–US Free Trade Agreement reduce the number of products they produce relative to firms less exposed to these tariff reductions.[40] In this setting with selection within and across firms, reductions in variable trade costs raise aggregate exports through the extensive margins of the number of exporting firms and the number of exported products. In contrast, reductions in variable trade costs have an ambiguous effect on average exports per firm and product. While higher variable trade costs reduce exports for a given firm and product (decreasing average exports), they also change export composition away from firms and products with small export values (increasing average exports). Consistent with these predictions, Bernard et al. (2011) find that the negative effect of distance on aggregate trade flows in the gravity equation is largely accounted for by the extensive margins of firms and products. The effect on the intensive margin (average exports per firm and product) is positive but not statistically significant.

Mayer et al. (forthcoming) introduce multi-product firms into the model of firm heterogeneity with variable mark-ups developed in Section 8. Firms face a product ladder along which productivity/quality declines discretely for each additional variety produced. Differences in the toughness of competition across markets induce changes to both the extensive and intensive product margin within firms. Mayer et al. (forthcoming) focus on the effects of competition on the intensive product margin. Due to the variable price elasticities, firms selling the same set of products in different markets skew their sales toward their best performing products in markets where they face tougher competition (due to the higher price elasticities in those markets). Data on French exporters across export market destinations provides strong empirical confirmation of this competitive effect.[41]

Another source of pro-competitive effects arises when the monopolistic competition assumption is dropped and firms internalize the effects of new products on the sales of their existing products (a cannibalization effect). Eckel and Neary (2010) develop such a model and highlight how this cannibalization effect generates an additional incentive for multi-product firms to drop their worst performing products when faced with increased competition from trade. Thus, trade liberalization generates higher firm productivity and, potentially, lower product variety.[42]

9.2. Innovation

Recent empirical work has consistently found that exporters (relative to non-exporters) are significantly more likely to innovate and adopt new technologies. For example, Verhoogen (2008) reports that Mexican exporters (plants) are more likely to be ISO 9000

---

[40] Evidence of similar product rationalization in Canada is found by Baldwin and Gu (2009). Product adding and dropping is shown to be an important source of aggregate reallocation in Bernard et al. (2010a). Around one half of surviving US firms add and/or drop products from their existing range every five years, and the contribution of these added and dropped products to aggregate output is of around the same magnitude as the contribution of firm entry and exit.

[41] See Arkolakis and Muendler (unpublished) and Nocke and Yeaple (2006) for other monopolistically competitive models of multi-product firms.

[42] See also Feenstra and Ma (2008) and Dhingra (2013) for other models of multi-product firms and trade featuring cannibalization effects.

certified (a proxy for the use of more advanced production techniques); and Bustos (2011) reports that Argentinian exporters (firms) spend more on new technologies (per worker).

As trade liberalization induces firms to start exporting, it is also associated with increased innovation and technology use by those new exporters. Bustos (2011) finds that the Mercosur trade liberalization agreement generated substantial increases in spending on new technologies by new exporters (and some increased spending by existing exporters). Verhoogen (2008) finds that the Mexican peso devaluation in the 1990s induced substantial increases in both plant exports and ISO 9000 certification. Lileeva and Trefler (2010) use econometric techniques to identify the effect of lower US import tariffs on the innovation and technology adoption rates of new Canadian exporters. They find those tariff cuts (part of the CUSFTA trade agreement) induced higher rates of product innovation and the adoption of advanced manufacturing technologies by new Canadian exporters. Those changes, in turn, led to substantial increases in labor productivity for those new exporters: over 15% between 1984 and 1996.

In the following two subsections, we describe two modeling techniques to capture the joint innovation and export decisions by heterogeneous firms. The first technique deals with a binary innovation choice (such as technology adoption) while the latter captures a continuous innovation intensity decision.

9.2.1. A Binary Innovation Choice: Technology Adoption

We briefly sketch how to add a binary technology adoption choice alongside the production and export decisions of heterogeneous firms. Bustos (2011) fully develops this theoretical modeling extension.[43] Every firm with productivity φ has the choice of upgrading to a new technology. This choice involves a tradeoff between an additional fixed cost f_I and a productivity increase to $\iota\varphi$, where the proportional productivity increase $\iota > 1$ is the same for all firms. Just like the export decision, this technology adoption choice involves a tradeoff between a fixed cost and a per-unit profit increase. Therefore technology adoption is characterized by a similar sorting according to firm productivity, such that there is a productivity cutoff φ_I^* above which all firms adopt the new technology.[44] The ranking of the export and innovation cutoffs φ_X^* and φ_I^* (assuming symmetric trade and production costs, so there is a single export cutoff) depends on the innovation parameter values f_I and ι, the trade costs f_X and τ, and the overhead production cost f. Bustos (2011) provides the conditions such that $\varphi_I^* > \varphi_X^*$, which implies that some exporters do not innovate (which is the empirically relevant case for the Argentinian data). In any event,

---

[43] This model extension, in turn, is based on previous work by Yeaple (2005).

[44] Firm profits are supermodular in productivity, technology adoption, and export status, leading to this strict sorting behavior. This is a specific example of the more general case analyzed by Costinot (2009) where firms or factors can sort into multiple different activities (see the working paper version of that paper for a more detailed derivation of the firm-sorting case). Mrazova and Neary (unpublished) also analyze how supermodularity of profits leads to the strict sorting of firm choices.

this modeling framework implies that (a) the most productive firms will choose to both innovate and export, (b) firms of lower productivity only export, (c) firms of still lower productivity choose to do neither, and (d) the least productive firms exit. This framework therefore captures the correlation between trade and innovation that is so prominent empirically in the cross-section of firms.

Several other firm decisions have been modeled in a similar way as involving a tradeoff between a fixed cost and a benefit that scales with firm size. Helpman et al. (2004) consider horizontal foreign direct investment (FDI). Antràs and Helpman (2004) analyze the decision whether to organize production at home or abroad within or beyond the boundaries of the firm. Manova (2013) examines the financing choice of firms and how it interacts with their export decision. Another line of work focuses on the decision to import intermediate inputs, as in Amiti and Davis (2012), Gopinath and Neiman (unpublished), and Goldberg et al. (2010). More generally, other research examines the choice of firm organization and how it interacts with firm productivity and export status; see Caliendo and Rossi-Hansberg (2012).

9.2.2. Innovation Intensity

We now turn to the modeling of innovation intensity allowing for continuous differences in the level of innovation performed by different firms. Following the seminal contributions by Aghion and Howitt (1992), Grossman and Helpman (1991), and Romer (1990), there has been a long literature analyzing how market size and globalization affect the firm innovation intensity choice. Initially, this literature did not focus on cross-sectional differences in innovation intensity across firms; more recently, Atkeson and Burstein (2010) have built a model featuring variation in innovation intensity across firms and over time in response to globalization shocks. We discuss the introduction of firm dynamics in the next section but first sketch out a static version of the innovation intensity decision used by Atkeson and Burstein (2010).

Consider a rescaling of firm productivity $\phi = \varphi^{\sigma-1}$ such that this new productivity measure ϕ is now proportional to firm size.[45] As with the case of the binary innovation choice, we assume that successful innovation increases productivity by a fixed factor $\iota > 1$ (from ϕ to $\iota\phi$). However, the probability of successful innovation is now an endogenous variable α that reflects a firm's innovation intensity choice. The cost of higher innovation intensity is determined by an exogenous convex function $c_I(\alpha) \geq 0$ and scales up proportionally with firm size and productivity ϕ, so the total cost of innovation intensity α is $\phi c_I(\alpha)$. This scaling of innovation cost with firm size is needed in a dynamic setting to deliver the prediction of Gibrat's Law that growth rates for large firms are independent of their size.

---

[45] Since the rescaling involves the demand-side product differentiation parameter σ, caution must be used when interpreting any comparative statics that include this parameter.

We first examine the choice of innovation intensity in a closed economy. Consider a firm with productivity ϕ that is sufficiently high that the firm will produce even if innovation is unsuccessful. This firm will choose innovation intensity α to maximize expected profits

$$E[\pi(\phi)] = [(1 - \alpha) + \alpha \iota] B\phi - \phi c_I(\alpha) - f,$$

where B is the same market demand parameter for the domestic economy as in previous sections. The first-order condition is given by

$$c_I'(\alpha) = (\iota - 1)B. \tag{29}$$

This implies that, in the closed economy, all firms (above a certain productivity threshold satisfying the no exit restriction) will choose the same innovation intensity α. In a dynamic setting, this delivers Gibrat's Law for those firms, and generates an ergodic distribution of firm productivity (hence firm size) that is Pareto in the upper tail independently of the initial distribution of productivity upon entry.[46]

Consider now the innovation intensity choice in an open economy setting with two symmetric countries (and symmetric trade costs) and selection into export markets. The first-order condition for non-exporters will still be given by (29). However, successful innovation is more valuable to exporters because it will generate additional profits from export sales. Their first-order condition is given by:[47]

$$c_I'(\alpha) = (\iota - 1)B(1 + \tau^{1-\sigma}).$$

Thus, exporters will choose a higher innovation intensity than non-exporters. As with non-exporters, all large exporters (firms who will export regardless of the innovation outcome) will choose the same innovation intensity. This modeling of innovation intensity can therefore also replicate the complementarity between innovation and trade. It also offers a particularly tractable way of incorporating endogenous innovation into a dynamic model of trade and innovation, such as the one analyzed by Atkeson and Burstein (2010).

9.3. Dynamics

All the models that we have considered up to now have been static. They contrast an ex-ante period (featuring idiosyncratic firm uncertainty) with a single ex-post period where all uncertainty is realized, firms jointly make all their decisions, and profit is earned. One can also think of this outcome as the stationary equilibrium of a dynamic model where the aggregate conditions remain constant over time. Melitz (2003) describes a simple

---

[46] See the web appendix. The exact shape of the ergodic distribution is sensitive to whether Gibrat's Law holds for all productivities or only for productivities above a certain threshold. See Luttmer (2010) for a review of this literature.

[47] This is the first-order condition for firms who will export regardless of whether innovation is successful. The condition for a firm whose export decision is tied to innovation success would be different.

version of such a stationary equilibrium, where firms face a single additional source of idiosyncratic uncertainty: a death shock that occurs with probability $\delta \in (0, 1)$ and is independent of firm productivity φ. The key free entry and zero cutoff profit conditions that we have previously described are then very similar. In those conditions, firm profit is replaced by firm value, which is just the net present value of the non-fluctuating profits earned in every period (the death shock generates a discount factor for the value computation). As in the static version of the model, the sunk nature of the entry cost f_E is a critical component for delivering ex-post firm heterogeneity. On the other hand, the modeling of the fixed export cost as either sunk or paid in every export period does not affect the stationary equilibrium: there is no uncertainty regarding the export market so firms are indifferent between paying an overhead fixed export cost in every period or its net present value once prior to exporting for the first time. Any uncertainty regarding future export profits will break this equivalence. Sunk export costs then generate hysteresis behavior associated with export market entry and exit.[48]

The combination of sunk entry costs and uncertainty leads to option values associated with entry and exit (manifested by hysteresis). Although there is substantial empirical support for this type of behavior, the modeling of those option values in a dynamic general equilibrium model with heterogeneous firms adds some substantial complexity. As an alternative, significant gains in tractability can be achieved by analyzing dynamic versions of the model that do not feature firm option values. For example, assuming that the fixed export cost is paid per period (and not sunk) will eliminate the option value associated with export market entry/exit. The sunk entry cost f_E must be preserved to generate ex-post heterogeneity; however, if the overhead production cost f is eliminated, then firm exit is exogenously determined by the death shock δ (and not endogenously due to low productivity), and the option value associated with entry/exit is eliminated. Ghironi and Melitz (2005) make these assumptions and then embed the steady-state version of the Melitz (2003) model from Section 3 into a two country dynamic model featuring stochastic fluctuations in aggregate variables (a standard Dynamic Stochastic General Equilibrium (DSGE) open economy model). Ottaviano (2012) incorporates a dynamic version of the Melitz and Ottaviano (2008) model from Section 8 into a business cycle setting.

This type of modeling allows firm productivity to change over time due to changes in aggregate productivity, but the relative productivity of firms remains constant. Other models have incorporated sources of firm-level fluctuations such as idiosyncratic productivity shocks alongside the aggregate fluctuations. Alessandria and Choi (2007) and Ruhl (unpublished) use variants of this type of model to analyze the growth dynamics of exporters in response to changes in trade costs. They characterize both the firm-level

---

[48] See Baldwin (1988) for an early theoretical derivation of this hysteresis effect. Roberts and Tybout (1997) find strong evidence of such behavior for Colombian exporters. Subsequent firm-level empirical work has confirmed this effect for other countries. Das et al. (2007) use the same dataset of Colombian exporters and develop estimation methods to recover the magnitude of the sunk export cost.

responses as well as the aggregate trade response.[49] More recently, the innovation choice decision described in the previous subsection has been incorporated into these dynamic models. There is then both an endogenous (innovation) and exogenous component to the evolution of firm productivity. Aw et al. (2011) estimate this joint model using production, trade, and R&D data for Taiwanese firms. They find that endogenous productivity changes via R&D are needed to explain the joint evolution of productivity and export decisions observed in the data.

Atkeson and Burstein (2010) analyze how modeling endogenous innovations in firm productivity influences the overall welfare gains from trade liberalization. Lower trade barriers boost innovation by current and prospective exporters; however, this also reduces the expected profits of new entrants (who must then compete against much larger and more productive incumbents) and thus reduces entry. Atkeson and Burstein (2010) calibrate their model to US firm-level data and show that these two effects are largely offsetting, so that there is no substantial effect of trade liberalization on the growth rate of welfare—even when innovation is endogenous. Burstein and Melitz (2012) use a very similar model, but focus on the transition paths following trade liberalization. They highlight how firm productivity dynamics and export market selection combine to generate long lasting adjustments to one-time changes in trade costs. Costantini and Melitz (2008) use a binary innovation choice to analyze the timing of the innovation decision relative to the export decision. They show that this relative timing is very sensitive to the timing and anticipation of trade liberalization. Productivity increases following export market entry need not imply a learning by exporting externality, but may rather reflect firms' joint export and innovation decisions. A more general insight is that measured firm productivity is the outcome of a number of endogenous decisions which are taken jointly with trade participation (including both exporting and importing). The contemporaneous relationship between productivity and trade participation therefore reflects complex interactions between these decisions over time and should be interpreted with caution.

Although much of the literature on firm dynamics and trade has been focused on productivity, an emerging literature considers dynamics generated by demand-side considerations. In contrast to productivity shocks—which affect firm profitability in all markets—demand shocks generate market-specific fluctuations in profitability. One strand of research emphasizes learning about uncertain demand in markets as in Albornoz et al. (2012) and Akhmetova (unpublished). Another line of work explores how matches between buyers and sellers evolve over time and across markets, as in Eaton et al. (unpublished) and Chaney (2011). These papers all seek to explain empirical patterns of firm entry and exit across export market destinations and over time. These empirical patterns include high rates of firm exit from new export destinations as well as rapid firm export growth conditional on survival in these destinations.

---

[49] Arkolakis (2011) and Irarrazabal and Opromolla (2008) analyze the stationary equilibrium in similar models. They characterize the steady-state distribution of different types of firms and cohort dynamics in that equilibrium.

10. FACTOR MARKETS

The model of firm heterogeneity in differentiated product markets developed in Section 3 implies that firms are unevenly affected by trade liberalization: low-productivity firms exit, intermediate-productivity domestic firms contract, and high-productivity exporting firms expand. However, workers are symmetrically affected by trade liberalization, because they are identical and the labor market is frictionless, which ensures that all workers are employed for a common wage. These labor market implications contrast with the large empirical literature that finds an employer-size wage premium (see, for example, the survey by Oi and Idson, 1999) and with empirical findings of wage differences between exporters and non-exporters even after conditioning on firm size (see, in particular, Bernard and Jensen, 1995, 1997).

More recent research on firm heterogeneity and trade has highlighted two sets of reasons why wages can differ across firms. One line of research assumes competitive labor markets, so that all workers with the same characteristics are paid the same wage, but wages can differ across firms because of differences in workforce composition (see for example Bustos, unpublished; Sampson, forthcoming; Verhoogen, 2008; Yeaple, 2005). Another line of research introduces labor market frictions, so that workers with the same characteristics can be paid different wages by different firms. One source of such labor market imperfections is search and matching frictions, which can generate variation in wages with firm revenue through bargaining over the surplus from production (see for example Davidson et al., 2008; Davidson and Matusz, 2009; Coşar et al., 2010; Helpman et al., 2010). Another source of labor market imperfections is efficiency or fair wages, which can generate similar wage variation if the wage that induces effort or is perceived to be fair varies with firm revenue (see for example Amiti and Davis, 2012; Davis and Harrigan, 2011; Egger and Kreickemeier, 2009).

This class of theoretical models highlights a new mechanism for trade to affect wage inequality based on wage variation across firms and the selection of firms into international trade. As shown in Helpman et al. (2010), the opening of the closed economy to trade necessarily raises within-industry wage inequality within a class of models satisfying three sufficient conditions: (a) wages and employment are power functions of productivity, (b) only some firms export and exporting raises the wage paid by a firm with a given productivity, and (c) productivity is Pareto distributed. When these three conditions are satisfied, the wage and employment of firms can be expressed in terms of their productivity (φ), a term capturing whether or not a firm exports ($\Upsilon(\varphi)$), the zero-profit cutoff productivity (φ^*), and parameters:

$$l(\varphi) = \Upsilon(\varphi)^{\psi_l} l_d \left(\frac{\varphi}{\varphi^*} \right)^{\zeta_l},$$

$$w(\varphi) = \Upsilon(\varphi)^{\psi_w} w_d \left(\frac{\varphi}{\varphi^*} \right)^{\zeta_w},$$

where l_d and w_d are employment and wage of the least productive firm and:

$$\Upsilon(\varphi) = \begin{cases} \Upsilon_x > 1 & \text{for } \varphi \geq \varphi_X^*, \\ 1 & \text{for } \varphi < \varphi_X^*, \end{cases}$$

where Υ_x is the revenue premium from exporting for a firm of a given productivity. Using the Pareto productivity distribution, the distribution of wages across workers within the industry, $G_w(w)$, can be evaluated as:

$$G_w(w) = \begin{cases} S_{l,d}\,G_{w,d}(w) & \text{for } w_d \leq w \leq w_d(\varphi_x/\varphi_d)^{\zeta_w}, \\ S_{l,d} & \text{for } w_d(\varphi_x/\varphi_d)^{\zeta_w} \leq w \leq w_x, \\ S_{l,d} + (1 - S_{l,d})\,G_{w,x}(w) & \text{for } w \geq w_x, \end{cases}$$

where $w_x = w_d \Upsilon_x^{\psi_w}(\varphi_x/\varphi_d)^{\zeta_w}$ is the wage of the least productive exporter and $S_{l,d}$ is the employment share of domestic firms. The distribution of wages across workers employed by domestic firms, $G_{w,d}(w)$, is a truncated Pareto distribution:

$$G_{w,d}(w) = \frac{1 - \left(\frac{w_d}{w}\right)^{\zeta_g}}{1 - \left(\frac{w_d}{w_x}\right)^{\zeta_g}} \quad \text{for } w_d \leq w \leq w_d(\varphi_x/\varphi_d)^{\zeta_w},$$

while the distribution of wages across workers employed by exporters, $G_{w,x}(w)$, is an un-truncated Pareto distribution:

$$G_{w,x}(w) = 1 - \left(\frac{w_x}{w}\right)^{\zeta_g} \quad \text{for } w \geq w_x.$$

In the class of models satisfying the above three sufficient conditions, Helpman et al. (2010) show that there is strictly greater wage inequality in the open economy when only some firms export than in the closed economy, and there is the same level of wage inequality in the open economy when all firms export as in the closed economy. It follows that wage inequality is at first increasing in trade openness and later decreasing in trade openness. The intuition for these results stems from the increase in firms' wages that occurs at the productivity threshold above which firms export, which is only present when some but not all firms export. When no firm exports, a small *reduction* in trade costs increases wage inequality, because it induces some firms to start exporting and raises the wages paid by these exporting firms relative to domestic firms. When all firms export, a small *rise* in trade costs increases wage inequality, because it induces some firms to stop exporting and reduces the wages paid by these domestic firms relative to exporting firms.

Helpman et al. (2012) provide evidence on the quantitative importance of this new mechanism for understanding the relationship between wage inequality and trade using Brazilian employer-employee and trade transaction data. Consistent with the class of theoretical models discussed above, wage inequality between firms within sector-occupations accounts for a substantial proportion of the level and growth of overall wage inequality, and this between-firm wage inequality remains important after controlling for observable worker characteristics. Estimating an extended version of the structural model discussed above, they find that the model has substantial explanatory power for the distribution of wages across both firms and workers. To the extent that existing empirical studies inspired by neoclassical trade theory focus on changes in relative wages between different sectors and types of workers, they abstract from an important channel through which trade liberalization can affect wage inequality.

Labor market frictions can also generate equilibrium unemployment. In this case, the opening of trade can affect the distribution of income not only through the distribution of wages across employed workers but also through changes in unemployment. Helpman and Itskhoki (2010) develop a heterogeneous firm model in which trade affects unemployment through reallocations of resources across sectors. In contrast, Felbermayr et al. (2011) emphasize the role of the increases in average industry productivity induced by trade liberalization in a heterogeneous firm model in reducing effective search costs. Helpman and Itskhoki (2010) consider a two-country, two-sector model of international trade. One sector is a homogeneous good sector, while the other sector is a differentiated sector with heterogeneous firms. In both sectors, firms face search frictions in the labor market. Differences in labor market institutions across countries and industries provide a source of comparative advantage and shape the impact of trade liberalization on aggregate unemployment.[50] Reductions in a country's labor market frictions in the differentiated sector raise its own welfare, by expanding the size of its differentiated sector and reducing its differentiated-sector price index. This expansion in the differentiated sector in one country intensifies competition in the export market faced by firms in the other country's differentiated sector. As a result, the other country's differentiated sector contracts, which reduces its welfare. In contrast, proportional reductions in labor market frictions in the differentiated sector in both countries raise welfare in each country, by expanding the size of the differentiated sector in each country.

11. CONCLUSION

Motivated by a wealth of evidence from micro data, theoretical research in international trade increasingly focuses on the decisions of heterogeneous firms. This theoretical research rationalizes a number of features of disaggregated trade data (e.g. performance differences between exporters and non-exporters), highlights new mechanisms through which trade affects welfare (e.g. reallocation across firms and within-firm productivity growth), and points to new margins along which economies respond to changes in trade costs (e.g. the extensive margins of the number of exporting firms and exported products).

---

[50] Another setting in which cross-country differences in labor market institutions can provide a source of comparative advantage is where volatility varies across sectors, as in Cuñat and Melitz (2010).

Although the theoretical literature on heterogeneous firms is already quite extensive, there are many open areas for further research. The productivity of the firm remains largely a black box and we still have relatively little understanding of the separate roles played by production technology, management practice, firm organization, and product attributes toward variation in revenues across firms. Most existing research concentrates on heterogeneity in unit costs across firms, whereas firms typically differ along a rich range of dimensions. More broadly, firms are complex organisms and there remains scope for further research on the boundaries of the firm and the determinants of the products, stages of production and workers that are included within a firm's boundaries. Despite some work on dynamics, much of the literature on firm heterogeneity and trade remains static, and we have relatively little understanding of the processes through which large and successful firms emerge and the implications of these processes for the transitional dynamics of the economy's response to trade liberalization. Finally, most extant research assumes that firms are atomistic, whereas in reality large multinational corporations are unlikely to be of measure zero relative to the markets in which they operate. The implications of firm heterogeneity in a world of granular firms is an active area of ongoing research.

REFERENCES

Aghion, P., Howitt, P., 1992. A model of growth through creative destruction. Econometrica 60 (2), 323–351.

Ahn, J.B., Khandelwal, A., Wei, S.J., 2011. The role of intermediaries in facilitating trade. Journal of International Economics 84 (1), 73–85.

Akhmetova, Z., unpublished. Firm Experimentation in New Markets. University of New South Wales.

Albornoz, F., Calvo Pardo, H., Corcos, G., Ornelas, E., 2012. Sequential exporting. Journal of International Economics 88 (1), 17–31.

Alessandria, G., Choi, H., 2007. Do sunk costs of exporting matter for net export dynamics? Quarterly Journal of Economics 122 (1), 289–336.

Allanson, P., Montagna, C., 2005. Multi-product firms and market structure: an explorative application to the product lifecycle. International Journal of Industrial Organization 23, 587–597.

Allen, D., unpublished. Information Frictions in Trade. Northwestern University.

Amiti, M., Davis, D.R., 2012. Trade, firms, and wages: theory and evidence. Review of Economic Studies 79 (1), 1–36.

Anderson, J., van Wincoop, E., 2002. Gravity with gravitas: a solution to the border puzzle. American Economic Review 93 (1), 170–192.

Anderson, J., Van Wincoop, E., 2004. Trade costs. Journal of Economic Literature 42, 691–751.

Antràs, P., Costinot, A., 2011. Intermediated trade. Quarterly Journal of Economics 126 (3), 1319–1374.

Antràs, P., Helpman, E., 2004. Global sourcing. Journal of Political Economy 112 (3), 552–580.

Arkolakis, C., 2010. Market penetration costs and the new consumers margin in international trade. Journal of Political Economy 118 (6), 1151–1199.

Arkolakis, C., unpublished. A Unified Theory of Firm Selection and Growth. Yale University.

Arkolakis, C., Muendler M., unpublished. A Firm-Level Analysis, The Extensive Margin of Exporting Goods (Yale University).

Arkolakis, C., Klenow, P., Demidova, S., Rodriguez-Clare, A., 2008. Endogenous variety and the gains from trade. American Economic Review Papers and Proceedings 98 (2), 444–450.

Arkolakis, C., Costinot, A., Rodriguez-Clare, A., 2012. New trade models, same old gains? American Economic Review 102 (1), 94–130.

Arkolakis, C., Costinot, A., Donaldson, D., Rodriguez-Clare, A., unpublished. The Elusive Pro-Competitive Effects of Trade. MIT.

Atkeson, A., Burstein, A., 2008. Pricing to market, trade costs and international relative prices. American Economic Review 98 (5), 1998–2031.

Atkeson, A., Burstein, A., 2010. Innovation, firm dynamics and international trade. Journal of Political Economy 118 (3), 433–484.

Aw, B.Y., Roberts, M.J., Xu, D.Y., 2011. R&D investment, exporting, and productivity dynamics. American Economic Review 101, 1312–1344.

Axtell, R.L., 2001. Zipf distribution of US firm sizes. Science 293, 1818–1820.

Baldwin, J., Gu, W., 2009. The impact of trade on plant scale, production-run length and diversification. In: Dunne, T., Jensen, J.B., Roberts, M.J. (Eds.), Producer Dynamics: New Evidence from Micro Data. University of Chicago Press, Chicago.

Baldwin, R., 1988. Hysteresis in import prices: the beachhead effect. American Economic Review 78 (4), 773–785.

Baldwin, R.E., Forslid, R., 2010. Trade liberalization with heterogeneous firms. Review of Development Economics 14 (2), 161–176.

Baldwin, R.E., Harrigan, J., 2011. Zeros, quality, and space: trade theory and trade evidence. American Economic Journal: Microeconomics 3 (2), 60–88.

Balistreri, E.J., Hillberry, R.H., Rutherford, T.F., 2011. Structural estimation and solution of international trade models with heterogeneous firms. Journal of International Economics 83 (2), 95–108.

Bartelsman, E.J., Doms, M., 2000. Understanding productivity: lessons from longitudinal microdata. Journal of Economic Literature 38 (3), 569–594.

Behrens, K., Murata, Y., 2012. Trade, competition and efficiency. Journal of International Economics 87 (1), 1–17.

Bernard, A.B., Jensen, J.B., 1995. Exporters, Jobs, and Wages in US Manufacturing: 1976–1987. Brookings Papers on Economic Activity, Microeconomics, pp. 67–112.

Bernard, A.B., Jensen, J.B., 1997. Exporters, skill upgrading and the wage gap. Journal of International Economics 42, 3–31.

Bernard, A.B., Jensen, J.B., 1999. Exceptional exporter performance: cause, effect, or both? Journal of International Economics 47 (1), 1–25.

Bernard, A.B., Eaton, J., Jensen, J.B., Kortum, S.S., 2003. Plants and productivity in international trade. American Economic Review 93 (4), 1268–1290.

Bernard, A.B., Jensen, J.B., Schott, P.K., 2006. Trade costs, firms, and productivity. Journal of Monetary Economics 53 (5), 917–937.

Bernard, A.B., Jensen, J.B., Redding, S.J., Schott, P.K., 2007a. Firms in international trade. Journal of Economic Perspectives 21 (3), 105–30.

Bernard, A.B., Redding, S.J., Schott, P.K., 2007b. Comparative advantage and heterogeneous firms. Review of Economic Studies 74, 31–66.

Bernard, A.B., Jensen, J.B., Schott, P.K., 2009. Importers, exporters, and multinationals: a portrait of firms in the U.S. that trade goods. In: Dunne, T., Jensen, J.B., Roberts, M.J. (Eds.), Producer Dynamics: New Evidence from Micro Data. University of Chicago Press, Chicago.

Bernard, A.B., Redding, S.J., Schott, P.K., 2010a. Multi-product firms and product switching. American Economic Review 100 (1), 70–97.

Bernard, A.B., Jensen, J.B., Redding, S.J., Schott, P.K., 2010b. Wholesalers and retailers in U.S. trade. American Economic Review. Papers and Proceedings 100 (2), 408–413.

Bernard, A.B., Redding, S.J., Schott, P.K., 2011. Multi-product firms and trade liberalization. Quarterly Journal of Economics 126 (3), 1271–1318.

Bernard, A.B., Redding, S.J., Schott, P.K., 2012. The empirics of firm heterogeneity and international trade. Annual Review of Economics 4, 283–313.

Bombardini, K., 2008. Firm heterogeneity and lobby participation. Journal of International Economics 75 (2), 329–348.

Burstein, A., Melitz, M.J., 2012. Trade liberalization and firm dynamics. In: Acemoglu, D., Arellano, M., Deckel, E. (Eds.), Advances in Economics and Econometrics. Cambridge University Press, Cambridge.

Burstein, A., Vogel, J., unpublished a. International Trade, Technology and the Skill Premium. Columbia University.

Burstein, A., Vogel J., unpublished b. Factor Prices and International Trade: A Unifying Perspective (Columbia University).

Bustos, P., 2011. Trade liberalization, exports and technology upgrading: evidence on the impact of MERCOSUR on argentinean firms. American Economic Review 101 (1), 304–340.

Bustos, P., unpublished. The Impact of Technology and Skill Upgrading: Evidence from Argentina. Universitat Pompeu Fabra.

Caliendo, L., Rossi-Hansberg, E., 2012. The impact of trade on organization and productivity. Quarterly Journal of Economics 127 (3), 1393–1467.

Campbell, J., Hopenhayn, H., 2005. Market size matters. Journal of Industrial Economics 53, 1–25.

Chaney, T., 2008. Distorted gravity: the intensive and extensive margins of international trade. American Economic Review 98 (4), 1707–1721.

Chaney, T., 2011. The Network Structure of International Trade. NBER Working Paper No. 16753.

Cherkashin, I., Demidova, S., Kee, H.L., Krishna, K., unpublished. A New Estimation Strategy and Policy Experiments, Firm Heterogeneity and Costly Trade (Penn State University).

Coşar, A.K., Guner, N., Tybout, J., 2010. Firm Dynamics, Job Turnover, and Wage Distributions in an Open Economy. NBER Working Paper No. 16326.

Combes, P., Duranton, G., Gobillon, L., Puga, D., Roux, S., 2012. The productivity advantages of large cities: distinguishing agglomeration from firm selection. Econometrica 80 (6), 2543–2594.

Corcos, G., Del Gatto, M., Mion, G., Ottaviano, G.I.P., 2012. Productivity and firm selection: quantifying the new gains from trade. Economic Journal 122 (561), 754–798.

Costantini, J., Melitz, M.J., 2008. The dynamics of firm-level adjustment to trade liberalization. In: Helpman, E., Marin, D., Verdier, T. (Eds.), The Organization of Firms in a Global Economy, vol. 4. Harvard University Press, Cambridge MA, pp. 107–141.

Costinot, A., 2009. An elementary theory of comparative advantage. Econometrica 77 (4), 1165–1192.

Crozet, M., Head, K., Mayer, T., 2012. Quality sorting and trade: firm-level evidence for French wine. Review of Economic Studies 79 (2), 609–644.

Cuñat, A., Melitz, M.J., 2010. Volatility, labor market flexibility and comparative advantage. Journal of the European Economic Association 10, 225–254.

Das, M., Roberts, M.J., Tybout, J., 2007. Market entry costs. Producer heterogeneity and export dynamics. Econometrica 75 (3), 837–873.

Davidson, C., Matusz, S., 2009. International Trade with Equilibrium Unemployment. Princeton University Press, Princeton NJ, 412.

Davidson, C., Matusz, S., Shevchenko, A., 2008. Globalization and firm-level adjustment with imperfect labor markets. Journal of International Economics 75, 295–309.

Davis, S.J., Haltiwanger, J., 1992. Gross job creation, gross job destruction, and employment reallocation. Quarterly Journal of Economics 107, 819–863.

Davis, D.R., Harrigan, J., 2011. Good jobs, bad jobs, and trade liberalization. Journal of International Economics 84, 26–36.

de Blas, B., Russ, K., 2010. Understanding Markups in the Open Economy under Bertrand Competition, NBER Working Paper No. 16587.

De Loecker, J., Warzynski, F., 2012. Markups and firm-level export status. American Economic Review 102 (6), 2437–2471.

Demidova, S., 2008. Productivity improvements and falling trade costs: boon or bane? International Economic Review 49 (4), 1437–1462.

Demidova, S., Rodriguez-Clare, A., 2009. Trade policy under firm-level heterogeneity in a small open economy. Journal of International Economics 78, 100–112.

Demidova, S., Rodriguez-Clare, A., 2011. The Simple Analytics of the Melitz Model in a Small Open Economy. NBER Working Paper 17521.

Dhingra, S., 2013. Trading away wide brands for cheap brands. American Economic Review 103 (6), 2554–2584.

Dhingra, S., Morrow, J., unpublished. The Impact of Integration on Productivity and Welfare Distortions under Monopolistic Competition. London School of Economics.

di Giovanni, J., Levchenko, A., 2012. Country size, international trade, and aggregate fluctuations in granular economies. Journal of Political Economy 120 (6), 1083–1132.

Dixit, A., Norman, V., 1980. Theory of International Trade: A Dual General Equilibrium Approach. Cambridge University Press, Cambridge UK.

Dixit, A., Sitlitz, J.E., 1977. Monopolistic competition and optimum product diversity. American Economic Review 67 (3), 297–308.

Do, Q., Levchenko, A., 2009. Trade, inequality and the political economy of institutions. Journal of Economic Theory 144, 1489–1520.

Dunne, T., Roberts, M.J., Samuelson, L., 1989. The growth and failure of U.S. manufacturing plants. Quarterly Journal of Economics 104 (4), 671–698.

Eaton, J., Kortum, S.S., 2002. Technology, geography, and trade. Econometrica 70 (5), 1741–1779.

Eaton, J., Kortum, S.S., Kramarz, F., 2004. Dissecting trade: firms, industries and export destinations. American Economic Review 94 (2), 150–154.

Eaton, J., Kortum, S.S., Kramarz, F., 2011. An anatomy of international trade: evidence from French firms. Econometrica 79 (5), 1453–1498.

Eaton, J., Eslava, M., Kugler, M., Tybout, J.R., unpublished. A Search and Learning Model of Export Dynamics. Penn State University.

Eckel, C., Neary, J.P., 2010. Multi-product firms and flexible manufacturing in the global economy. Review of Economic Studies 77 (1), 188–217.

Edmund, C., Midrigin, V., Xu, D.Y., 2012. Competition, Markups, and the Gains from International Trade. NBER Working Paper 18041.

Egger, H., Kreickemeier, U., 2009. Firm heterogeneity and the labour market effects of trade liberalization. International Economic Review 50 (1), 187–216.

Fan, H., Lai, E.L.C., Qi, H., unpublished. A Model of Trade with Ricardian Comparative Advantage and Intrasectoral Firm Heterogeneity. Hong Kong University of Science and Technology.

Feenstra, R.C., 2003. A homothetic utility function for monopolistic competition models without constant price elasticity. Economic Letters 78, 79–86.

Feenstra, R.C., Ma, H., 2008. Optimal choice of product scope for multiproduct firms under monopolistic competition. In: Helpman, E., Marin, D., Verdier, T. (Eds.), The Organization of Firms in a Global Economy, vol. 6. Harvard University Press, Cambridge MA, pp. 356 (173–199).

Felbermayr, G., Prat, J., Schmerer, H., 2011. Globalization and labor market outcomes: wage bargaining, search frictions, and firm heterogeneity. Journal of Economic Theory 146 (1), 39–73.

Fernandes, A., 2007. Trade policy, trade volumes and plant-level productivity in Colombian manufacturing industries. Journal of International Economics 71 (1), 52–71.

Flam, H., Helpman, E., 1987. Industrial policy under monopolistic competition. Journal of International Economics 22, 79–102.

Ghironi, F., Melitz, M.J., 2005. International trade and macroeconomic dynamics with heterogeneous firms. Quarterly Journal of Economics 120, 865–915.

Goldberg, P., Khandelwal, A., Pavcnik, N., Topalova, P., 2010. Imported intermediate inputs and domestic product growth: evidence from India. Quarterly Journal of Economics 125 (4), 1727–1767.

Gopinath, G., Neiman, B., unpublished. Trade Adjustment and Productivity in Large Crises. Harvard University.

Grossman, G.M., Helpman, E., 1991. Innovation and Growth in the Global Economy. MIT Press, Cambridge MA, p. 359.

Harrigan, J., Reshef, A., 2011. Skill-Biased Heterogeneous Firms, Trade Liberalization, and the Skill Premium. NBER Working Paper 17604.

Harrison, A.E., 1994. Productivity, imperfect competition and trade reform. Journal of International Economics 36, 53–73.

Helpman, E., 2006. Trade, FDI, and the organization of firms. Journal of Economic Literature XLIV, 589–630.

Helpman, E., Itskhoki, O., 2010. Labor market rigidities, trade and unemployment. Review of Economic Studies 77 (3), 1100–1137.

Helpman, E., Krugman, P.R., 1985. Market Structure and Foreign Trade. MIT Press, Cambridge MA, p. 271.

Helpman, E., Melitz, M.J., Yeaple, S.R., 2004. Export versus FDI with heterogeneous firms. American Economic Review 94 (1), 300–316.

Helpman, E., Melitz, M.J., Rubinstein, Y., 2008. Estimating trade flows: trading partners and trading volumes. Quarterly Journal of Economics 123 (2), 441–487.

Helpman, E., Itskhoki, O., Redding, S.J., 2010. Inequality and unemployment in a global economy. Econometrica 78 (4), 1239–1283.

Helpman, E., Itskhoki, O., Muendler, M., Redding, S.J., 2012. Trade and Inequality: From Theory to Estimation. NBER Working Paper 17991.

Holmes, T., Hsu, W., Lee, S., unpublished. Allocative Efficiency, Mark-ups, and the Welfare Gains from Trade. University of Minnesota.

Hsieh, C., Ossa, R., unpublished. A Global View of Productivity Growth in China and India. University of Chicago.

Hummels, D.L., Skiba, A., 2004. Shipping the good apples out: an empirical confirmation of the Alchian-Allen conjecture. Journal of Political Economy 112, 1384–1402.

Irarrazabal, A.A., Opromolla, L.D., 2008. A Theory of Entry and Exit into Exports Markets. Working Paper w200820. Banco de Portugal. Economics and Research Department.

Irarrazabal, A.A., Moxnes, A., Opromolla, L.D., unpublished. The Tip of the Iceberg: A Quantitative Framework for Estimating Trade Costs (Dartmouth College).

Johnson, R., 2012. Trade and prices with heterogeneous firms. Journal of International Economics 86 (1), 43–56.

Kehoe, T., Ruhl, K., 2013. How important is the new goods margin in international trade? Journal of Political Economy 121 (2), 358–392.

Khandelwal, A., Topalova, P., 2011. Trade liberalization and firm productivity: the case of India. Review of Economics and Statistics 93 (3), 995–1009.

Krugman, P.R., 1979. Increasing returns, monopolistic competition, and international trade. Journal of International Economics 9, 469–479.

Krugman, P.R., 1980. Scale economies, product differentiation, and the pattern of trade. American Economic Review 70, 950–959.

Kugler, M., Verhoogen, E., 2012. The quality-complementarity hypothesis: theory and evidence from Colombia. Review of Economic Studies 79 (1), 307–339.

Levinsohn, J., 1993. Testing the imports-as-market-discipline hypothesis. Journal of International Economics 35, 1–22.

Lileeva, A., Trefler, D., 2010. Does improved market access raise plant-level productivity. Quarterly Journal of Economics 125 (3), 1051–1099.

Lu, D., unpublished. Exceptional Exporter Performance? Evidence from Chinese Manufacturing Firms. Princeton University.

Luttmer, E.G.J., 2010. Models of growth and firm heterogeneity. Annual Review of Economics 2, 547–576.

Manova, K., 2013. Credit constraints, heterogeneous firms, and international trade. Review of Economic Studies 80, 711–744.

Manova, K., Zhang, Z., 2012. Export prices across firms and destinations. Quarterly Journal of Economics 127, 379–436.

Mayer, T., Ottaviano, G.I.P., 2007. The Happy Few: New Facts on the Internationalisation of European Firms. Bruegel – CEPR EFIM Report. Bruegel Blueprint Series.

Mayer, T., Melitz, M.J., Ottaviano, G., forthcoming. Market size, competition, and the product mix of exporters. American Economic Review.

Melitz, M.J., 2003. The impact of trade on intra-industry reallocations and aggregate industry productivity. Econometrica 71, 1695–725.

Melitz, M.J., Ottaviano, G., 2008. Market size, trade, and productivity. Review of Economic Studies 75 (1), 295–316.

Melitz, M.J., Redding, S., unpublished. New Trade Models, Same Old Gains? Comment. Harvard and Princeton Universities.

Mrazova, M., Neary, J.P., unpublished. Selection Effects with Heterogeneous Firms. University of Oxford.

Neary, J.P., 2010. Two and a half theories of trade. World Economy 33 (1), 1–19.

Nocke, V., Yeaple, S.R., 2006. Globalization and Endogenous Firm Scope. NBER Working Paper 12322.

Oi, W.Y., Idson, T.L., 1999. Firm size and wages. In: Ashenfelter, O., Card, D. (Eds.), Handbook of Labor Economics. Elsevier, Amsterdam, pp. 2939 (33: 2165–214).

Ottaviano, G.I.P., 2012. Firm heterogeneity, endogenous entry, and the business cycle. In: Frankel, J., Pissarides, C. (Eds.), NBER International Seminar on Macroeconomics. University of Chicago Press, Chicago.

Ottaviano, G.I.P., Thisse, J.F., 2011. Monopolistic competition, multiproduct firms and optimum product diversity. Manchester School 79, 938–951.

Ottaviano, G.I.P., Tabuchi, T., Thisse, J.F., 2002. Agglomeration and trade revisited. International Economic Review 43, 409–436.

Pavcnik, N., 2002. Trade liberalization, exit, and productivity improvement: evidence from chilean plants. Review of Economic Studies 69 (1), 245–276.

Redding, S., 2011. Theories of heterogeneous firms and trade. Annual Review of Economics 3, 77–105.

Redding, S., Venables, A.J., 2004. Economic geography and international inequality. Journal of International Economics 62 (1), 53–82.

Roberts, M.J., Tybout, J., 1997. The decision to export in Colombia: an empirical model of entry with sunk costs. American Economic Review 87 (4), 545–564.

Romer, P.M., 1990. Endogenous technological change. Journal of Political Economy 98, S71–S102.

Ruhl, K.J., unpublished. The International Elasticity Puzzle. New York University.

Sampson, T., forthcoming. Selection into trade and wage inequality. American Economic Journal: Microeconomics.

Syverson, C., 2004. Market structure and productivity: a concrete example. Journal of Political Economy 112, 1181–222.

Trefler, D., 2004. The long and short of the Canada-U.S. free trade agreement. American Economic Review 94, 870–895.

Tybout, J.R., 2003. Plant- and firm-level evidence on 'new' trade theories. In: Kwan Choi, E., Harrigan, J. (Eds.), Handbook of International Economics, vol. 13. Basil-Blackwell, Oxford, pp. 435 (388–435).

Venables, A., 1987. Trade and trade policy with differentiated products: a Chamberlinian-Ricardian model. Economic Journal 97 (387), 700–717.

Verhoogen, E., 2008. Trade, quality upgrading and wage inequality in the Mexican manufacturing sector. Quarterly Journal of Economics 123 (2), 489–530.

World Trade Organization, 2008. World Trade Report: Trade in a Globalizing World. World Trade Organization, Geneva.

Yeaple, S.R., 2005. A simple model of firm heterogeneity, international trade, and wages. Journal of International Economics 65, 1–20.

Zhelobodko, E., Kokovin, S., Thisse, J.F., 2012. Monopolistic Competition: Beyond the CES. CEPR Discussion Paper 7947.

CHAPTER 2

Multinational Firms and the Structure of International Trade*

Pol Antràs*,†,‡ and Stephen R. Yeaple†,§

*Harvard University, Cambridge, MA, USA
†National Bureau of Economic Research, Cambridge, MA, USA
‡Centre for Economic Policy Research, London, UK
§Pennsylvania State University, University Park, PA, USA

Abstract

This chapter reviews the state of the international trade literature on multinational firms. This literature addresses three main questions. First, why do some firms operate in more than one country while others do not? Second, what determines in which countries production facilities are located? Finally, why do firms own foreign facilities rather than simply contract with local producers or distributors? We organize our exposition of the trade literature on multinational firms around the workhorse monopolistic competition model with constant-elasticity-of-substitution (CES) preferences. On the theoretical side, we review alternative ways to introduce multinational activity into this unifying framework, illustrating some key mechanisms emphasized in the literature. On the empirical side, we discuss the key studies and provide updated empirical results and further robustness tests using new sources of data.

Keywords

Multinationals, Foreign direct investment, Vertical FDI, Horizontal FDI, Complex FDI, Internalization, Offshoring, Outsourcing, Related party trade, Cross-border acquisitions, Greenfield FDI

JEL classification codes

F23, F12, F2, F1, F61, D21, D23, D22, D2, L2

1. INTRODUCTION

Over the last two decades, international trade theory has undergone a steady transformation that has placed firms rather than countries or industries as the central unit of

* The statistical analysis of firm-level data on U.S. multinational corporations reported in this study was conducted at the U.S. Bureau of Economic Analysis under arrangements that maintained legal confidentiality requirements. Views expressed are those of the authors and do not necessarily reflect those of the Bureau of Economic Analysis. We are grateful to our discussants, John McLaren and Esteban Rossi-Hansberg for their insightful and incisive comments at the handbook conference held in Cambridge in September of 2012. We also benefitted from valuable feedback from the editor, Elhanan Helpman. We also thank Ruiqing Cao and Yang Du for outstanding research assistance, and Davin Chor, Federico Díez, Willi Kohler, Nathan Nunn, Natalia Ramondo, Marcel Smolka, and Dan Trefler for their help with data sources. The Online Appendix mentioned in the text is available in the NBER Working Paper version of this chapter.

55

analysis. This transformation has been fueled by micro-level empirical studies that have shown international activity to be concentrated within a handful of very large firms that produce in multiple countries and multiple industries. In 2000, for instance, the top 1% U.S. exporters accounted for 81% of U.S. exports (Bernard et al., 2009). The involvement of these large firms in the world economy goes well beyond the mere act of selling domestically produced goods to foreign consumers. According to 2009 data from the U.S. Bureau of Economic Analysis, the sales of domestically produced goods to foreign customers account for only 25% of the sales of large American firms. The remaining 75% (nearly U.S. $5 trillion) is accounted for by the sales of foreign affiliates of American multinationals (Yeaple, 2013). Furthermore, data from the U.S. Census Bureau indicates that roughly 90% of U.S. exports and imports flow through multinational firms, with close to one-half of U.S. imports transacted *within* the boundaries of multinational firms rather than across unaffiliated parties (Bernard et al., 2009).

This chapter reviews the state of the international trade literature on multinational firms. Before we begin, a few definitions are in order. In his encyclopedic monograph on the subject, Caves (2007, p. 1) defines a multinational firm as "an enterprise that controls and manages production establishments—plants—located in at least two countries." While the corporate structure of multinational firms can be complicated, it is useful to define two types of entities within a multinational firm, the parent and the affiliate. *Parents* are entities located in one country (the source country) that control productive facilities, while *affiliates* are located in other countries (host countries). The notion of control is a judgmental one but it is often associated with ownership. Such ownership is the result of foreign direct investments, which can alternatively involve the acquisition of a controlling interest in an existing foreign firm (cross-border acquisitions) or the establishment of an entirely new facility in a foreign country (greenfield investment).

The positive theory of the multinational firm revolves around three main questions. First, why do some firms find it optimal to operate in more than one country while others do not? Second, what determines in which countries production facilities are located and in which they are not? Finally, why do firms own foreign facilities rather than simply contract with local producers or distributors?

The modern literature's focus on the firm contrasts sharply with the traditional theory that made little distinction between foreign direct investment and international portfolio investment flows. According to the traditional theory, multinational firms were simply arbitrageurs that moved capital from countries where returns were low to countries where returns were high.[1] The genesis of the modern approach was Hymer's (1960) seminal Ph.D. thesis. Hymer pointed out that the traditional international-finance approach was inconsistent with several features of foreign direct investment (FDI) data. He proposed a new, industrial-organization approach based on the notion that some firms own special assets that confer a strategic advantage over indigenous firms in foreign markets. In some

---

[1] This interpretation is implicit, for instance, in Mundell (1957).

cases, market imperfections preclude the use of these assets by foreign unaffiliated entities, thereby generating the need for a direct involvement of the asset owner. In sum, Hymer envisioned a world in which real (not financial) factors shape the location of multinational activity and financial flows are a mere consequence of the financial structure decisions of multinational firms.

Hymer's approach was later refined by several authors, including Kindleberger (1969), Caves (1971), Buckley and Casson (1976), and Rugman (1981), and culminated with Dunning's (1981) eclectic OLI framework, where OLI is an acronym for Ownership, Location, and Internalization. Put succinctly, the emergence of the multinational firm is explained by an **O**wnership advantage stemming from firm-specific assets that allow firms to compete in unfamiliar environments, a **L**ocation advantage that makes it efficient to exploit the firm assets in production facilities in multiple countries, and an **I**nternalization advantage that makes the within-firm exploitation of assets dominate exploitation at arm's length. The mainstream interpretation of the ownership advantage relates it to a proprietary technology or reputation that provides its owner with some market power or cost advantage over indigenous producers. The location advantage is often associated with the idea that the development of these assets (tangible or intangible) entails significant fixed costs, but these assets can then be used in different locations simultaneously in a nonrival manner. This allows economies of scale to be exploited efficiently within multinational firms, especially when trade frictions inhibit such exploitation via exporting. Another branch of the literature has related location advantages to situations in which production is amenable to geographical fragmentation, thus allowing different parts of the production process to be undertaken in the location where it is most cost-effective to do so. Finally, the internalization advantage is attributed to market failures in the transfer of technology—related to the partial nonexcludable, nonrival, and noncodifiable nature of technology—and to inefficiencies associated with market exchanges of highly customized intermediate inputs.

As insightful as the OLI literature is, it took some time before it was absorbed by international trade theory because a widely accepted general-equilibrium modeling of increasing returns to scale, product differentiation, and imperfect competition did not become available until the late 1970s and early 1980s, and because contract theory was still in its infancy in the 1970s. The modeling of product differentiation and market structure originally developed by Dixit and Stiglitz (1977) and later adopted by Krugman (1979, 1980) served the important role of providing a common language for researchers in the field to communicate among themselves, and opened the door to formally modeling multinational firms within general-equilibrium analysis.[2]

---

[2] Although the heavy use of specific functional forms for preferences and technology was viewed with some reservation by the old guard in the field, the publication of the landmark manuscript by Helpman and Krugman (1985) established the generality of most of the insights from Krugman's work and showed how the new features of New Trade Theory could be embedded into Neoclassical Trade Theory.

Following this tradition, we will organize our exposition of the trade literature on multinational firms around the classical Krugman (1980) model with constant-elasticity-of-substitution (CES) preferences, and the seminal variant of the model incorporating firm heterogeneity developed by Melitz (2003). On the theoretical side, we will review alternative ways to introduce multinational activity into the framework, while trying to illustrate some of the key mechanisms emphasized in the literature, even when these were developed under different modeling assumptions. Although some important papers in the trade literature on multinational firms adopt alternative modeling approaches to imperfect competition (most notably, Markusen, 1984; Horstmann and Markusen, 1987a; Markusen and Venables, 1998) or make less restrictive assumptions on technology and preferences (e.g., Helpman, 1984), we think that the advantage of a common framework outweighs the benefits of comprehensiveness and generality.

Given the space constraint, we will impose several limits on the scope of our review. First, we will not review in great detail certain branches of the literature that, although being associated with aspects of multinational activity, do not model multinational firms explicitly. Second, we will focus almost exclusively on positive issues related to the rationale for multinational activity and will thus not discuss the effects of multinational firms on goods and factor markets or the policy implications of these effects. The only exception to this rule is our brief discussion of the effects of vertical fragmentation on labor markets in Section 5.2. Third, our emphasis will be on qualitative analysis, though we will briefly review recent advances in quantitative analysis in Section 6. Fourth, although we will sometimes refer to the internalization decision of multinational firms as an organizational decision, we will not review the broader literature on the international organization of production, which is concerned not only with multinational firm boundaries, but also with incentive provision, delegation, and hierarchical structure within and across firms in the global economy.[3] Fifth, we will restrict ourselves to discussing the operational decisions of multinational firms (such as those related to employment, production levels, location, and ownership), thus omitting a treatment of the financial aspects of these firms, which are important for understanding the relationship between multinational activity and FDI flows.[4] For more encyclopedic treatments of multinational firms, we refer the reader to the monographs by Caves (2007), Markusen (2002), and Barba-Navaretti and Venables (2004), while an overview of the literature on the international organization of production can be found in Antràs and Rossi-Hansberg (2009).[5]

By limiting our focus, we will be able to take our survey beyond a simple enumeration of the various theoretical and empirical results in the literature. On the theoretical side, we

---

[3] For recent work in this area, see Grossman and Helpman (2004) on incentive provision, Marin and Verdier (2009) and Puga and Trefler (2010) on delegation, and Antràs et al. (2006) and Caliendo and Rossi-Hansberg (2012) on hierarchical structure.

[4] See Klein et al. (2002), Desai et al. (2004), and Antràs et al. (2009) for work on financial aspects of multinational activity.

[5] See Helpman (2006) and Spencer (2005) for recent alternative reviews of this literature.

will explicitly derive a series of analytical results within a unified framework. While most of these results are not new, some had only been illustrated numerically and in somewhat disjointed frameworks. On the empirical side, our review will provide updated empirical results and further robustness tests using new sources of data.

The remainder of this chapter is organized as follows. Section 2 briefly describes the data available to analyze the global operations of multinational firms and provides a list of "stylized" facts about the multinational firm. Section 3 introduces the benchmark model that we will use to guide our overview of the theoretical literature. Sections 4 and 5 focus on the integration of the multinational firms into our benchmark models and cover the relevant empirical literature that both informs the design of these models and tests these models' predictions. Section 6 outlines the approaches taken by a recent literature that explores the global structure of trade in multinational production in multicountry models. The internalization advantage of multinationals is taken as given in Sections 4 through 6, but is explicitly modeled and empirically assessed in Section 7. Section 8 offers concluding remarks.

2. STYLIZED FACTS

In this section, we develop six stylized facts that describe broad features of the structure of multinationals' global operations. We do so using three types of data. First, we use foreign direct investment data from the balance of payments. Foreign direct investment (FDI) occurs when a firm from one country obtains an operating stake (usually 10%) in an enterprise in another country or when a financial flow occurs between parties that are resident in different locations but related by ownership. Second, we use government survey data that distinguish between national firms and the parents and affiliates of multinational firms. We rely particularly on census data on U.S. parents and their foreign affiliates collected by the Bureau of Economic Analysis (BEA) of the United States. Finally, we use U.S. Related Party Trade data collected by the U.S. Bureau of Customs and Border Protection. This source provides data on related and nonrelated party U.S. imports and exports at the six-digit Harmonized System (HS) classification and at the origin/destination country level.[6]

We first document regularities in the countries that are the source of FDI and countries that are the destination of this FDI. FDI flows measure changes in the holdings of controlling interests in equity capital between countries. By aggregating flows over time by country one can obtain crude measures of how important countries are as hosts to parent firm operations (outward stocks) and as hosts to affiliate operations (inward stocks).

---

[6] Related party trade means a minimum ownership stake between trading parties of 6% for imports and 10% for exports.

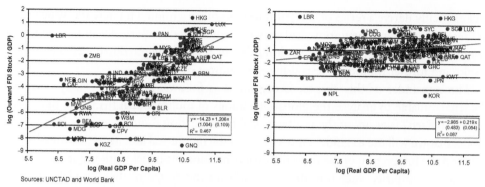

Sources: UNCTAD and World Bank

Figure 2.1 Aggregate FDI Stocks and Development

Figure 2.1 presents outward and inward FDI stocks for a large number of countries. In the left-hand panel, the logarithm of FDI stocks held by the sending country and normalized by the sending country's GDP is plotted against the logarithm of the sending country's GDP per capita. In the right-hand panel the stocks of inward FDI by destination country, normalized by destination country GDP, are plotted against the logarithm of GDP per capita by destination country. In both panels the best linear predictor is displayed as a line with the associated coefficients shown in the bottom right-hand corner.

These data show that developed countries are more engaged in both outward and inward flows than less developed countries, but the positive relationship is much more pronounced for outward flows. The outliers in both figures illustrate some of the deficiencies of FDI data as a measure of real production activity. For instance, Hong Kong, Singapore, Luxembourg, and Liberia have high levels of both inward and outward FDI stocks which reflect in part firms' efforts to park ownership of global assets in low-tax and weak-regulation countries.

Figure 2.1 suggests that there must be substantial two-way flows between countries. The extent of these two-way flows can be measured by Grubel-Lloyd indices

$$GL_{ij} = 100 \times \left(1 - \frac{|S_{ij} - S_{ji}|}{S_{ij} + S_{ji}}\right),$$

where S_{ij} is the stock of foreign direct investment owned by country i firms in country j. This index takes on a value of 100 when $S_{ij} = S_{ji}$ and a value of 0 when the stock is one-way. High values of GL_{ij} are associated with high levels of two-way flows. When computed for OECD data, GL among developed country partners ranges from 45 to 50, indicating a high level of two-way FDI, while the average GL between developed and developing countries tends to be only one-half as large.

The patterns of multinational production revealed by the FDI data can be corroborated by less comprehensive data on real activity from the United States. Most of the sales of

U.S. affiliates are made in developed countries while most of the affiliates active in the United States are owned by parents located in developed countries. Furthermore, U.S. related party trade data reveal that most of the trade between affiliates and their parents into and out of the United States occurs between developed rather than developing countries. We summarize these empirical regularities as the following fact:

> **Fact One:** Multinational activity is primarily concentrated in developed countries where it is mostly two-way. Developing countries are more likely to be the destination of multinational activity than the source.

We now turn from patterns in aggregate multinational activity to patterns across industries. There is substantial variation across industries in the share of real activity contributed by multinational firms. For instance, data from the OECD reveal that foreign affiliates account for approximately a quarter of French manufacturing employment; however, the employment share is well over a third in capital intensive and R&D intensive industries like Chemicals and Machinery, while it is less than one-eighth in labor-intensive Food and Textile industries. This pattern repeats itself across developed countries.

The tendency of multinational activity to be concentrated in certain industries is also evident in the share of international trade that occurs between parties related by ownership. The left panel of Figure 2.2 is constructed using the U.S. related-party data and measures of physical capital intensity from the NBER Manufacturing database. It shows that the share of U.S. imports that occurs within the boundaries of multinational firms is highly correlated with the logarithm of the capital–labor ratio in that industry. Imports of labor-intensive products, such as apparel (North American Industry Classification System (NAICS) 3159) or footwear (NAICS 3162), are transacted mostly at arm's-length, while imports of heavily capital-intensive products, such as motor vehicles (NAICS 3361) and pharmaceuticals (NAICS 3254), are traded within firm boundaries. The right panel of Figure 2.2 depicts a similar strong positive correlation between the share of intrafirm trade and R&D intensity, despite the existence of some notable outliers, such as motor vehicle manufacturing (NAICS 3361).[7]

Another indication of the concentration of FDI in certain industries is the intra-industry nature of the two-way FDI flows observed with aggregate data. When computing Grubel-Lloyd indices of intraindustry FDI into and out of the United States for four-digit U.S. NAICS industries in 2010, one finds indices that generally exceed one-half and are of a similar order of magnitude to those computed with trade data. We summarize the evidence concerning the cross industry structure of the magnitude of FDI as the following fact:

---

[7] R&D intensity is the ratio of R&D expenditures to sales, constructed by Nunn and Trefler (2008) using Orbis data. We exclude from the sample in the right panel those industries for which the ratio of R&D expenditures to sales exceeds one, but the positive and statistically significant correlation with intrafirm trade is robust to their inclusion.

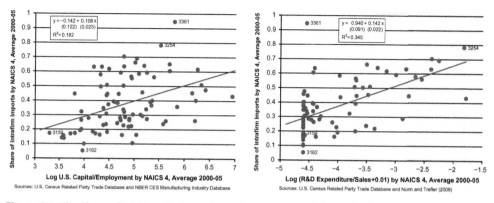

Figure 2.2 The Share of Intrafirm Imports, Capital Intensity, and R&D Intensity

Fact Two: The relative importance of multinationals in economic activity is higher in capital-intensive and R&D intensive goods, and a significant share of two-way FDI flows is intraindustry in nature.

A key issue in international economics is the role of geography in affecting the structure of international commerce. It is well known that a gravity equation fits international trade volumes well. The same is true for many aspects of multinational activity. In serving foreign markets, firms may choose to export their products from their source country s to a destination country d. Let X_{ds} be the aggregate value of exports from s to d. An alternative to exporting their product is to establish a foreign affiliate in country d to serve the local market. Let AS_{ds} be the sales of the affiliates located in country d that are owned by parents in country s. The left-hand panel of Figure 2.3 plots the logarithm of AS_{ds} normalized by source and destination GDP against the logarithm of the distance between s and d, while the right-hand panel plots the logarithm of AS_{ds}/X_{ds} between the two countries against the logarithm of distance.[8]

The left-hand panel shows that a 1% increase in distance is associated with 0.57 fall in affiliate sales. The right-hand panel shows that as distance increases affiliate sales are falling less rapidly than trade volumes, so while gravity holds for affiliate sales, its effect on trade volumes is stronger.

The stronger effect of distance on trade relative to foreign affiliate activity also appears within firms. Parent firms often produce components that are then shipped to foreign affiliates for further processing. According to BEA data, in 2009 the aggregate value added of U.S. manufacturing affiliates was U.S. $474.5 billion while the imports of intermediate inputs by these affiliates from their parents totaled U.S. $104 billion.[9] Figure 2.4 shows

---

[8] Affiliate sales data are from Ramondo (2013). We thank her for sharing her data with us.

[9] According to data highlighted by Ramondo et al. (2012) at the affiliate level much of these imports are highly concentrated in a small number of highly integrated firms.

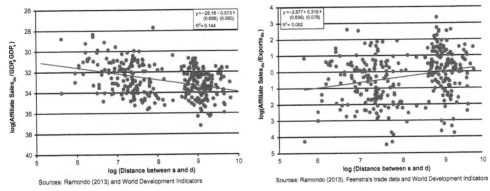

Figure 2.3 Gravity, FDI Sales, and Trade Flows

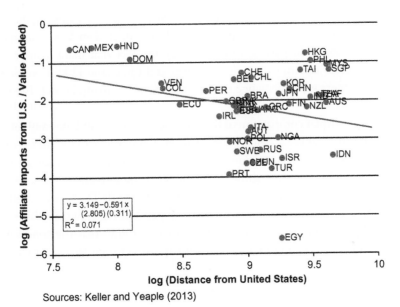

Sources: Keller and Yeaple (2013)

Figure 2.4 Affiliate Imports from U.S. relative to Local Value-Added

that the logarithm of the ratio of the value of imported intermediates to the sum of local value-added plus imported intermediates is declining in the distance between the affiliate and the U.S. parent. This suggests that vertical specialization is harder at long distances, but it is interesting to note that the very open Asian economies of Hong Kong, Malaysia, the Philippines, Singapore, and Taiwan import large amounts of intermediate inputs despite their distance from the United States.

The effect of distance on the structure of international trade and foreign affiliate activity is summarized as the following fact:

Fact Three: The production of the foreign affiliates of multinationals falls off in distance, but at a slower rate than either aggregate exports or parent exports of inputs to their affiliates.

We now compare the performance of multinationals to that of firms that do not own foreign operations. As noted in the introduction there are two distinct entities within multinational firms, the parents and the affiliates. The BEA and the U.S. Census collect a large amount of information about the structure of the operations of U.S.-based firms. From the data it is possible to compare the activities of U.S.-based parents with other firms that are active in the United States. In manufacturing sectors, U.S. parents account for less than one-half of 1% of enterprises but account for over 62% of value-added and 58% of employment (Barefoot and Mataloni, 2011). These numbers imply that labor productivity is higher in multinational parents relative to nonmultinationals. In addition, these parents account for almost three-quarters of private R&D conducted in U.S. manufacturing. This latter observation is in part accounted for by the fact that many parent firms are concentrated in R&D intensive industries. Mayer and Ottaviano (2007) provide similar evidence on the superior performance of parent firms in Germany, France, Belgium, and Norway.

We now make a similar comparison of the activities of foreign affiliates with other firms in their host country. Table 2.1 shows the share of economic activity (rows) of foreign affiliates in their host country (columns) in manufacturing industries for a number of OECD countries. The first row shows that the share of foreign affiliates in the total number of manufacturing enterprises is typically very small. The share of affiliates in manufacturing employment, output, and R&D expenditures, shown in the next three rows, is larger by an order of magnitude. The last line shows that the share of foreign affiliates in total manufacturing exports is even larger than their share in total sales and employment.

Table 2.1 Affiliates Relative to Local Firms (Percentage Accounted for by Affiliates)

	Finland	France	Ireland	Holland	Poland	Sweden
Enterprises	1.6	2.0	13.4	3.4	16.0	2.8
Employment	17.2	26.2	48.0	25.1	28.1	32.4
Sales	16.2	31.8	81.1	41.1	45.2	39.9
R&D Expenditure	13.1	27.4	77.3	35.8	20.9	52.0
Exports	17.5	39.5	92.3	60.0	69.1	45.8

Source: OECD (2007).

Table 2.2 Destination of Affiliate Sales (%) by Industry

	Host Country	Other Foreign	United States
Total manufacturing	55	34	11
Textile and Apparel	45	35	19
Metals and Minerals	60	32	8
Chemicals and Plastics	58	36	6
Machinery	49	36	15
Computers and Electronics	40	43	16
Electronic Equipment	47	40	13
Transport Equipment	47	35	19
Other	66	26	8

Source: 2009 Benchmark Survey of U.S. Direct Investment Abroad, BEA.

These observations lead to the following fact:

Fact Four: Both the parents and the affiliates of multinational firms tend to be larger, more productive, more R&D intensive, and more export oriented than nonmultinational firms.

The large volumes of international trade between parents and affiliates are consistent with vertical specialization across parents and their affiliates. To explore the nature of this specialization we compare the share of U.S. parent firms in the total activity of U.S. multinationals' global operations. In 2009, BEA data reveal that U.S. parents accounted for 65% of total sales, 68% of value-added and employment, and 84% of research and development expenditures. One decade earlier, U.S. parents accounted for 74% of total sales, 78% of value-added, and 87% of R&D expenditures. The high and persistent concentration of R&D services in the parent firm suggests that parents are in the business of creating "ownership advantages."

If parents disproportionately provide R&D services to the multinational firm, what is the role played by the affiliates? This question can be answered in part by observing the destination of affiliate sales. The BEA collects data on how much the foreign affiliates of U.S. parents sell in their host country, how much they export to other foreign countries, and how much they export to the United States. The percentage breakdown of sales by these three categories aggregated across countries by major industry group for 2009 is shown in Table 2.2. The first row shows that 55% of the value of the output of U.S. affiliates stayed in the country of the affiliate, 34% was sold to foreign customers outside the U.S., and 11% was exported back to the United States. Hence, the primary purpose of multinational affiliates is to serve foreign markets rather than to provide inputs or final goods to the source country. However, in industries such as Textiles and Apparel, Machinery, Electronic and Transport Equipment, and especially computers, affiliates are more export oriented.

We summarize this information in the next fact:

Fact Five: Within multinational enterprises, parents are relatively specialized in R&D while affiliates are primarily engaged in selling goods in foreign markets, particularly in their host market.

One last empirical regularity involves the manner in which multinationals obtain foreign production facilities. A firm can obtain production facilities abroad by either opening a new plant (greenfield investment) or by acquiring an existing plant (cross-border merger and acquisition). UNCTAD data show that across all countries in 2007 the value of recorded mergers and acquisitions stood at over 50% of total FDI flows. Furthermore, for developed countries cross-border mergers and acquisitions accounted for 68% of FDI flows while for developing countries the number was only 18%. We summarize this information as the following fact:

Fact Six: Cross-Border Mergers and Acquisitions make up a large fraction of FDI and are a particularly important mode of entry into developed countries.

3. BENCHMARK MODEL: AN EXTENDED KRUGMAN (1980) MODEL

In this section, we describe the framework that we will build on to navigate through the literature. The framework is a strict generalization of the two-country Krugman (1980) model. We depart from Krugman (1980) in allowing for the existence of multiple sectors (including a homogeneous-good sector) and multiple factors of production (for concreteness, capital, and labor) available in fixed supply. Factors of production are internationally immobile but freely mobile across sectors. Our framework is closely related to the one developed by Melitz and Redding in Chapter 1 of this handbook.

The world consists of two countries, H and F, that produce goods in $J + 1$ sectors. One sector produces a homogeneous good z, while the remaining J sectors produce a continuum of differentiated products. Preferences are identical everywhere in the world and given by:

$$U = \beta_z \log z + \sum_{j=1}^{J} \beta_j \log Q_j, \quad \text{with } \beta_z + \sum_{j=1}^{J} \beta_j = 1, \tag{1}$$

and with

$$Q_j = \left(\int_{\omega \in \Omega_j} q_j(\omega)^{(\sigma-1)/\sigma} d\omega \right)^{\sigma/(\sigma-1)}, \quad \sigma > 1.$$

Where desirable, it is straightforward to simplify the product space by setting $\beta_z = 0$ (i.e., dropping the outside good), or by focusing on the case in which there is only one differentiated-good sector (i.e., $J = 1$), as in Krugman (1980). Our interest is on the behavior of firms in a given differentiated goods industry j. Maximizing (1) subject to the budget constraint yields the following demand for variety ω in industry j and country i:

$$q_j^i(\omega) = \frac{\beta_j E^i}{\int_{\omega \in \Omega_j^i} p_j^i(\omega)^{1-\sigma} d\omega} p_j^i(\omega)^{-\sigma} = A_j^i p_j^i(\omega)^{-\sigma}, \quad i = H, F. \tag{2}$$

Good z can be produced in any country under a constant-returns-to-scale technology which combines capital and labor in country i and which we represent by the linearly homogeneous unit cost function $c_z^i = c_z^i(w^i, r^i)$, with $i = H, F$. The unit cost of production can vary across countries due to factor price differences or due to technological differences. This homogeneous-good sector is perfectly competitive and we shall assume throughout that z can be costlessly traded across countries and serves as the numeraire, so that

$$c_z^i(w^i, r^i) \geq 1, z^i > 0, \quad \text{complementary slack, for } i = H, F.$$

Whenever both countries produce good z we thus have $c_z^H(w^H, r^H) = c_z^F(w^F, r^F) = 1$.

Technology in the differentiated-good sectors features increasing returns to scale. As in Krugman (1980) and Helpman and Krugman (1985), the creation and production of differentiated varieties involve a fixed cost and a constant marginal cost in terms of a linearly homogeneous function of capital and labor, which we denote by $c_j^i(w^i, r^i)$. In particular, total costs associated with producing q_j^i units of sector j output in country i are given by

$$C_j^i(w^i, r^i, q_j^i) = \left(f_j + \frac{q_j^i}{\varphi}\right) c_j^i(w^i, r^i). \tag{3}$$

The parameter f_j in (3) captures the extent to which technology features economies of scale, and is assumed common across varieties. As for the marginal cost parameter φ, we will consider the case in which it is also common across firms within an industry, as in Krugman (1980), as well as the case in which it varies across firms within an industry, as in Melitz (2003). In the latter case, we will denote by $G(\varphi)$ the cumulative probability distribution from which firms draw their particular marginal cost parameter. The market structure in all differentiated-good sectors is monopolistic competition. International trade in differentiated goods is costly and entails an iceberg (*ad valorem*) trade cost such that τ_j units of sector j's varieties need to be shipped from one country for 1 unit to reach the other country. Furthermore, in some cases, we also consider the existence of a fixed cost of exporting equal to f_X units of the composite factor represented by the above function $c_j^i(w^i, r^i)$.

It is straightforward to show (see Chapter 1 by Melitz and Redding in this handbook) that this general framework encompasses, under alternative assumptions, the ones in Krugman (1980), Melitz (2003), Chaney (2008), and Bernard et al. (2007).

4. THE PROXIMITY-CONCENTRATION HYPOTHESIS

In the benchmark model above, firms were allowed to serve foreign markets only via exports. The evidence suggests instead that firms frequently choose to service foreign markets through local production by a subsidiary rather than through exporting, thus becoming multinational firms. In this section we focus on models that feature a proximity-concentration tradeoff to explain why multinational firms often replicate the same production activities in multiple countries. In terms of the OLI framework, foreign countries are attractive production locations to serve the local market when shipping costs and tariffs are high. Multiplant operation comes at the cost of failing to fully exploit increasing returns to scale in production. Because these models feature firms that replicate the same activity across countries, they are often referred to as horizontal FDI models.

4.1. Homogeneous Firms

We begin with the case in which firms within an industry are homogeneous and countries are identical to fix ideas with respect to the industry characteristics that affect firm choice of international organization. We then extend the analysis to allow for substantial differences across countries in terms of their endowment. We conclude this subsection with a discussion of evidence concerning the implications of this class of models.

4.1.1. A Symmetric Model

In order to understand the horizontal motive for multinational activity, it is simplest to start with the one-sector ($J = 1$), one-factor model in Krugman (1980), with two symmetric countries each endowed with L units of labor.[10] We drop all subscripts j and set the wage rate to 1 in both countries without loss of generality, so that (3) reduces to

$$C\left(q\right) = f + \frac{q}{\varphi}.$$

For reasons that will become apparent below, we will distinguish two activities that jointly contribute to the fixed cost f. First, the invention or process of differentiation of a variety requires a fixed cost of f_E units of labor: f_E is a measure of economies of scale *at the firm level* and the level of this expenditure is unaffected by the number and location of plants that end up producing the variety (see Markusen, 1984; Helpman, 1984).[11] This fixed cost f_E may include a variety of activities such as R&D expenditures, brand development, accounting, and finance operations. The second component of the fixed cost is denoted by f_D and captures overhead costs necessary for the manufacturing or assembly of the product. Unlike in the case of f_E, the fixed cost f_D needs to be incurred every time

[10] The model in this section is a simplified version of the one in Brainard (1993, 1997).

[11] In the literature, one often encounters more general specifications for the technology representing the process of creation of intangibles. For instance, Helpman (1984) allows for a variable choice of firm intangibles with larger levels of intangibles reducing the marginal cost of downstream activities.

a plant is set up, and thus this parameter captures economies of scale *at the plant level*. Quite naturally, the distinction between f_E and f_D only becomes relevant in multiplant environments, such as the one we are about to consider.

The main innovation relative to Krugman (1980)'s model is that we do not force firms entering one country to service the other country via exporting. Instead, we allow firms to incur the plant-level fixed costs twice and service consumers abroad via local sales, thus avoiding the iceberg-type transportation costs $\tau > 1$. Under which conditions will firms find it optimal to deviate from the "pure-exporting" equilibrium that was the focus of Krugman (1980)? In order to answer this question, we first need to construct such an equilibrium and then explore the circumstances under which our suggested deviation is profitable.

Consider then the problem faced by a firm based in country $i = H, F$ that produces variety ω and services both markets from a plant located in i. Given the isoelastic demand schedule in (2), an exporter from $i = H, F$ will choose a domestic and foreign price that is a constant markup over marginal cost, thus yielding a total profit flow equal to

$$\pi_X^i = \varphi^{\sigma-1} B^i + \varphi^{\sigma-1} \tau^{1-\sigma} B^{-i} - f_E - f_D, \tag{4}$$

where

$$B^i = \frac{1}{\sigma} \left(\frac{\sigma-1}{\sigma} \right)^{\sigma-1} A^i. \tag{5}$$

In the industry equilibrium, free entry ensures that $\pi_X^H = \pi_X^F = 0$ and thus we must have:

$$B^H = B^F = B_X = \frac{f_E + f_D}{\varphi^{\sigma-1} \left(1 + \tau^{1-\sigma} \right)}, \tag{6}$$

from which, using (5) and (2), one can back out the number of entrants in each country.

Having described the equilibrium, we next check whether a firm might have an incentive to deviate from this equilibrium and set up a plant in the foreign country. A potentially deviating firm engaged in FDI would obtain a profit flow equal to

$$\pi_I = \varphi^{\sigma-1} B^H + \varphi^{\sigma-1} B^F - f_E - 2f_D, \tag{7}$$

regardless of where the firm incurred its entry cost. Given the standard continuum assumption in monopolistic competition models, this deviator would have no impact on the demand level in either country and hence, plugging (6) into (7), we find that such deviation will be unprofitable (i.e., $\pi_I^i < 0$) whenever

$$\frac{2f_D}{f_E} > \tau^{\sigma-1} - 1. \tag{8}$$

As long as condition (8) holds, one can thus safely ignore the possibility of multinational activity and focus on equilibria with exporting. It is clear that this is more likely to be the case, the higher are plant-specific economies of scale relative to firm-specific economies of scale (f_D/f_E), the lower are transport costs τ, and the lower is the elasticity of substitution σ. The intuition behind the effects of f_D and τ on the tradeoff between exporting and affiliate sales is rather straightforward. The effects of f_E and σ in (8) are more subtle, and to understand them it is important to bear in mind that from the point of view of a firm, the choice of exporting versus affiliate sales boils down to the choice between a selling strategy associated with low fixed costs but higher marginal costs (exporting) and another one associated with high fixed costs and low marginal cost (affiliate sales). Quite naturally, the latter option might look appealing when the firm expects a large volume of sales abroad and when profits are more sensitive to marginal costs. With that in mind, the positive effect of f_E on the likelihood of a deviation simply reflects the fact that in industries in which the process of innovation is more costly, the industry will end up being populated by a relatively low number of firms, and thus each firm will end up with a higher residual demand level (6). Finally, in industries in which varieties are relatively substitutable with each other, profits will tend to be particularly sensitive to marginal costs, and thus a deviation from a pure exporting equilibrium will be attractive.[12]

Up to now, we have focused on describing the circumstances under which a pure exporting equilibrium of the type studied by Krugman (1980) is robust to the possibility of servicing offshore markets via affiliate sales. A natural question is then: what happens when condition (8) is violated? It is straightforward to show that when the inequality in (8) is reversed then the unique equilibrium will be one with "pure affiliate activity" in the sense that no firm will have an incentive to sell abroad via exporting. This equilibrium features two-way FDI flows between countries that is a key feature of the data as summarized by Stylized Facts One and Two in Section 2. In the knife-edge case in which the left- and right-hand sides of (8) are equal to each other, there might be a coexistence of exporters and multinational firms within an industry, but their relative shares remain indeterminate.[13]

4.1.2. Country Asymmetries

We now consider an extension of the model above that incorporates a role for factor endowment differences to shape trade and multinational enterprise (MNE) activity flows across countries. We build on the work of Markusen and Venables (2000), whose

---

[12] Note that the common market size L does not enter the key condition (8) because, with CES preferences and free entry, the residual demand level faced by firms is independent of market size. With the linear demand system with horizontal product differentiation developed by Ottaviano and Thisse (2002), a symmetric increase in market size would tighten condition (8), thus making an equilibrium with pure exporting less likely. Below, we will illustrate nonneutral effects of *asymmetric* changes in size even in the CES case.

[13] When the number of firms in an industry is fixed (entry is restricted), the share of firms that engage in FDI relative to exports can be determined for a wide range of parameter values as the price index is influenced only by firms' mode choices and not due to a free entry condition.

framework also falls under the umbrella of our benchmark model in Section 3. In particular, they consider a model in which there are two sectors, a homogeneous-good sector ($\beta_z > 0$) and a differentiated-goods one ($J = 1$), and goods are produced using capital and labor, and the endowments of these factors can vary across countries. Their framework abstracts from intraindustry heterogeneity (φ is common for all firms) and trade costs are only variable in nature ($f_X = 0$).[14] We will come back to their two–sector, two–factor model later in the section, but we will first demonstrate that some of their key results continue to apply in a simpler one–sector, one–factor model, with the benefit that these results can be demonstrated analytically.

With that in mind, let us revisit the model developed in the last section, but now let countries differ in their endowment of labor, with $L^H > L^F$ without loss of generality. It is worth emphasizing that one can interpret labor as a composite factor of production and that, given the absence of technology differences across countries, it is advisable to treat L as an efficiency-adjusted endowment of this factor. Thus the larger "size" of Home might reflect both differences in population and differences in the productivity of labor, the latter stemming from technology or from the availability of other factors that are complementary to labor. The key implication of introducing differences in country size is that, with only one sector in the economy, wages across countries will no longer be equalized, and as shown by Krugman (1980), in the absence of MNE activity, it is necessarily the case that the wage rate is higher in the larger country ($w^H > w^F$).

How do these factor price differences (and, indirectly, size differences) affect the likelihood of equilibria with MNE activity? To simplify matters, we follow Markusen and Venables (2000) in assuming that fixed costs of innovation are a function of factor prices in all countries in which production takes place. In the case of exporters, these fixed costs are simply given by $w^i f_E$, where $i = H, F$ is the country where the variety is produced. For multinational firms (i.e., firms with plants in both countries), these costs are given by $\frac{1}{2}\left(w^H + w^F\right) f_E$. The latter assumption implies that fixed costs in terms of labor are evenly split across locations, and thus the model does not allow one to distinguish between the "home" and "host" country of a multinational firm (or between the location of the parent company and that of the affiliate). This is a clear limitation of the analysis but it has the benefit of considerably simplifying the description of the parameter space in which MNE activity will arise in equilibrium. Notice that in the absence of factor price differences and setting labor as the numeraire, the fixed costs of entry for MNEs are equal to f_E, as in the symmetric model above.[15]

---

[14] Strictly speaking, Markusen and Venables (2000) allow for general homothetic preferences over the homogeneous good and the CES aggregator of differentiated varieties, but their results are all numerical in nature and their simulations rely on a Cobb-Douglas aggregator analogous to the one we have imposed in (1).

[15] Markusen and Venables (2000) consider alternative formulations of the fixed costs of entry that allow for substitution between Home and Foreign labor. This does not appear to affect the qualitative nature of the results, but it greatly complicates the analytical derivation of the results below.

We will next describe an equilibrium of the Krugman-type, with single-plant firms in both countries servicing offshore consumers via export sales. After straightforward manipulations analogous to those in the previous section, profits for an exporter from country $i = H, F$ can be expressed as:

$$\pi_X^i = \varphi^{\sigma-1}(w^i)^{1-\sigma}B^i + \varphi^{\sigma-1}(\tau w^i)^{1-\sigma}B^j - w^i\left(f_D + f_E\right),$$

where B^i is defined in (5). If both types of exporters are to break even B^H and B^F must be such that $\pi_X^H = \pi_X^F = 0$. Solving for these equilibrium values for B^H and B^F, and plugging them into the profit function of a potential MNE deviator yields

$$\pi_I = \varphi^{\sigma-1}(w^H)^{1-\sigma}B^H + \varphi^{\sigma-1}(w^F)^{1-\sigma}B^F - \left(w^H + w^F\right)\left(f_D + \frac{1}{2}f_E\right).$$

It thus follows that, for an equilibrium with no MNE activity to exist (i.e., $\pi_I < 0$), it needs to be the case that

$$\frac{\left(\frac{w^H}{w^F}\right)\left(\tau^{\sigma-1} - \left(\frac{w^H}{w^F}\right)^{-\sigma}\right) + \tau^{\sigma-1} - \left(\frac{w^H}{w^F}\right)^{\sigma}}{\left(\frac{w^H}{w^F} + 1\right)\left(\tau^{\sigma-1} - 1\right)} \frac{f_D + f_E}{f_D + \frac{1}{2}f_E} < \frac{\tau^{\sigma-1} + 1}{\tau^{\sigma-1}}. \tag{9}$$

This expression is more cumbersome than the one in (8), but unambiguous comparative statics can still be obtained. First, holding constant the relative wage w^H/w^F, it can be verified that condition (9) is more likely to hold whenever f_D/f_E is high and whenever τ is low. Hence, one can still interpret the choice between exporting and FDI sales as reflecting a proximity-concentration tradeoff even in the presence of country asymmetries. The main novelty relative to the analogous condition (8) in the symmetric case is the fact that the tradeoff now also depends on the ratio of the Home and Foreign wages. Simple (though tedious) differentiation demonstrates that the left-hand-side attains a unique maximum at $w^H/w^F = 1$ (see the Online Appendix). In other words, the incentive for firms to deviate from a pure exporting equilibrium is highest when factor price differences across countries are small. Evaluating (9) at $w^H/w^F = 1$, we find that multinational firms can only arise in equilibrium whenever

$$\tau^{\sigma-1} - 1 > \frac{2f_D}{f_E} \tag{10}$$

just as in the symmetric model. The introduction of size asymmetries implies, however, that even when this inequality holds, as we shall assume for the remainder of this section, the equilibrium may be one with no MNE activity when factor prices are sufficiently dissimilar across countries.

Why do factor price differences favor an equilibrium with pure exporting? Intuitively, whereas exporting firms only use labor from one country, multinational firms use labor from both countries. Thus, the higher are factor price differences, the higher is the cost disadvantage faced by multinational firms relative to exporters from the low-wage country.

We have thus far treated wages as given, but they are naturally pinned down in equilibrium by labor-market clearing. In a Krugman-type equilibrium with no MNEs, the relative wage is implicitly given by

$$L^H \left(\frac{\tau w^F}{w^H} \right)^{\sigma-1} + L^F = \frac{w^H}{w^F} \left(L^H + L^F \left(\frac{\tau w^H}{w^F} \right)^{\sigma-1} \right). \tag{11}$$

As is well known, (11) implies that $w^H > w^F$ whenever $L^H > L^F$. Furthermore, the relative wage w^H/w^F is increasing in the relative size L^H/L^F of the Home country, and converges to $\tau^{(\sigma-1)/\sigma}$ when $L^H/L^F \to \infty$ (this is not proven in Krugman, 1980, but we do so in the Online Appendix).

An implication of this result is that even when (10) holds, the equilibrium will still necessarily only feature exporting when the relative size L^H/L^F of Home becomes sufficiently large.[16] The threshold relative size $\bar{\lambda} > 0$ above which the equilibrium is of the type described in Krugman (1980) is implicitly defined by (11) and by condition (9) when it holds with equality.

What does the equilibrium look like for relative sizes L^H/L^F below the threshold $\bar{\lambda}$ and above 1? Our previous discussion implies that such equilibria will necessarily feature a positive mass of multinational firms as long as (10) holds. In the Online Appendix, we rule out the existence of "pure MNE" equilibria without exporters. Furthermore, numerical simulations suggest that that only two other types of equilibria can arise for $L^H/L^F > 1$. For an interval of relative sizes right below the threshold $\bar{\lambda}$, that is $L^H/L^F \in (\underline{\lambda}, \bar{\lambda})$, the equilibrium is one with MNEs, Home exporters, and Foreign exporters all coexisting. In that interval, the relative wage is implicitly given by (9) holding with equality independently of L^H/L^F, with changes in the relative supply of labor of each country being absorbed via changes in the mix of firms. If the ratio L^H/L^F is even closer to 1 and below a second threshold $\underline{\lambda}$, then the equilibrium is one in which multinational firms and Home exporters coexist, but Foreign exporters cannot profitably operate. Equilibria without exporters from the relatively large country (i.e., Home) do not appear to exist although we have not been able to prove this analytically.

We have focused on the case in which asymmetries arise because Home is larger than Foreign. The case $L^H/L^F < 1$ can be analyzed similarly and delivers analogous results. For a sufficiently small L^H/L^F, we have a pure exporting equilibrium, and the remaining

---

[16] To be precise, when transport costs are so large that $\tau^{\frac{\sigma-1}{\sigma}} - 1 > 2f_D/f_E$, the equilibrium features MNE activity *for all* $L^H/L^F > 0$ (see the Online Appendix). We will abstract from this uninteresting case below.

equilibria feature some MNE activity and some exporting from the larger country, in this case Foreign.

We argued above that one should not interpret variation in L across countries as merely reflecting differences in population, as it might also reflect variation in the availability of factors that are complementary to labor. This brings us precisely to the contribution of Markusen and Venables (2000), who study a two-sector model in which production uses labor and a complementary factor (capital) which, crucially, are combined under different factor intensities in the two sectors, so that L can no longer be treated as a composite factor. In terms of our notation in the benchmark model, the factor cost w^i in the unique differentiated sector is now denoted by $c_1^i = c_1^i \left(w^i, r^i \right)$, while the unit cost of production in the homogeneous-good sector is given by $c_z^i = c_z^i \left(w^i, r^i \right)$. It should be clear that our derivations above regarding the likelihood of an equilibrium with pure exporting remain unaltered, with c_1^i replacing w^i everywhere. Hence, it continues to be the case that the like-lihood of an equilibrium with MNE activity is highest when cost differences are lowest.

Unfortunately, the general equilibrium of this two-sector, two-factor model becomes analytically intractable, so Markusen and Venables (2000) have to resort to numerical analysis from the outset. Their simulations suggest that, in the absence of multinationals, factor price differences across countries appear to be large whenever relative and absolute factor endowment differences across countries are large. This resonates with the effects of absolute differences in L on equilibrium wages in the Krugman (1980) model. When introducing the possibility of MNE activity, Markusen and Venables (2000) graphically illustrate that as long as condition (10) holds, there is a two-dimensional region in the endowment space (which includes the point $L^H = L^F$ and $K^H = K^F$) in which only multinational firms will operate in the differentiated-good sector.[17] Further away from the midpoint of the endowment space, they find that there are two-dimensional regions of the endowment space in which the equilibrium is mixed, with both MNEs and exporting firms being active. Their results also suggest that equilibria with differentiated-good sector exporters from a given country are more likely the larger the size of that country, and in particular the larger that country's endowment of the factor used intensively in the differentiated-good sector. The prediction of the model that FDI is more likely to arise between similarly endowed countries is consistent with the broad facts reported in Section 2.

4.1.3. Evidence

The proximity-concentration tradeoff is intuitive and has a variety of implications for the cross-country and cross-industry structure of trade and FDI, but how well does it explain the data? The most well-known paper assessing the proximity-concentration framework is Brainard (1997) who relates the cross-country and cross-industry structure of trade

---

[17] One way to rationalize the fact that their model is able to feature pure FDI equilibria (and the one-sector, one-factor model above does not) is that the presence of the homogeneous-good sector provides firms with a channel to repatriate profits across asymmetric markets.

and multinational production to proxies for various features of the industry's technology and various features of a country's endowment and policy environment. In this section, we provide estimates of the coefficients of Brainard's econometric model and theory-inspired extensions to that model using more up-to-date data than was available when the original paper was written.

The basic structure of Brainard's econometric model relates the propensity of U.S. firms in industry j to serve country i by exports relative to serving country i via a local affiliate as given by the equation:

$$\log\left(\frac{X_j^i}{X_j^i + S_j^i}\right) = \alpha_0 + \alpha_1 \mathit{Freight}_j^i + \alpha_2 \mathit{Tariff}_j^i + \alpha_3 \mathit{PlantSC}_j + \alpha_4 \mathit{CorpSC}_j + \alpha_5 \mathbf{C}^i + \mu_{ij},$$

where X_j^i is the exports by the United States in industry j to country i and S_j^i is the sales by U.S. affiliates in industry j located in country i. The explanatory variables $\mathit{Freight}_j^i$ and Tariff_j^i are the logarithm of an *ad valorem* measure of shipping costs in industry j from the U.S. to country i and the logarithm of average tariffs facing U.S. firms in industry j and country i. The explanatory variables $\mathit{PlantSC}_j$ and CorpSC_j are logarithms of measures of plant scale economies (number of production workers per representative plant) and corporate scale economies (the number of nonproduction workers per representative firm). Finally, $\mathbf{C}^i$ is a vector of country controls that include a variable GDP/POP^i, which is the logarithm of the absolute difference in GDP per worker in the United States and in country i. This variable controls for factor endowment differences across countries.[18]

The dependent variable here captures the tendency of firms to substitute local production for exports while controlling for industry and country characteristics that jointly explain both the level of trade and the level of affiliate sales. As noted in Section 2, trade and FDI flows are highly correlated both in gross and net terms so these factors that determine both the levels of trade and FDI are in fact important.

Brainard estimates this equation using U.S. trade data and affiliate sales data from the 1989 Benchmark Survey of U.S. Direct Investment Abroad conducted by the Bureau of Economic Analysis (BEA). She finds that α_1, α_2, and α_4 are negative and statistically significant while α_3 is positive and statistically significant. This is the best known evidence in favor of the proximity-concentration framework. She also finds that the coefficient on GDP/POP is positive and statistically significant, which suggests that FDI is primarily directed toward developed countries. If one treats GDP/POP as a proxy for wage differences across countries, the positive coefficient is supportive of our theoretical result above regarding the positive effect of wage differences on the likelihood of an equilibrium with pure exporting.

[18] Other country controls include $TRADE^i$, an index of policy openness to trade, FDI^i, an index of policy openness to foreign direct investment, ADJ^i, a dummy variable for Canada and Mexico, *English*, a dummy variable for English Speaking countries, EC^i, a dummy variable for membership in the European Community, and $PolStab^i$, an index of political stability. See the Online Appendix for more details on these variables.

How well do Brainard's result stand the test of time? To answer this question, we estimate the same equation for both 1989, the year of Brainard's data, and for 2009, the most recent Benchmark Survey that is available from the BEA. Our sample is slightly different from that considered by Brainard. Specifically, we consider only manufacturing industries (excluding several primary-good industries considered by Brainard) and a broader range of countries.[19] Our explanatory variables are also constructed from high-quality data that became available only after Brainard (1997) was written (see our Online Appendix for more information on these data sources).

Our baseline results are shown in columns 1 and 2 of Table 2.3. Column 1 corresponds to the year 1989 while column 2 corresponds to 2009. To conserve space we have suppressed the coefficient estimates for all country controls except for GDP/POP. Comparing the estimates in the two columns, there are not substantial differences across years. As was the case in Brainard (1997), we find that higher trade costs (*Freight* and *Tariffs*) are associated with a statistically significant decrease in exports in favor of affiliate sales while higher plant-level fixed costs (*PlantSC*) and lower corporate fixed costs (*CorpSC*) are also associated with more exports and less affiliate sales. These results support the predictions of the model described in Section 4.1.1. Conversely, the coefficient estimates on GDP/POP are both positive but are not statistically significant in either year. These results call into question the conclusion that income per capita differences (a proxy for wage differences) are associated with less affiliate sales and more exports.[20]

A strong implication of the Markusen and Venables (2000) framework—and of our one-factor version of it—is that relative country sizes play an important role in the structure of bilateral commerce between them. To assess this implication, we added a variable GDP, which is the logarithm of the absolute value of the difference in the GDP of the United States and the GDP of country i. Running this augmented regression on 2009 data, we obtain the coefficient estimates shown in column 3. The positive and (moderately) statistically significant coefficient on GDP suggests that market size does matter: U.S. firms are more likely to export to smaller markets and to engage in foreign direct investment in larger countries.

To further explore the role of relative factor endowment differences, we next replace GDP/POP (GDP per worker differences) with absolute differences in years of schooling (*School*) and capital-labor ratios (*KL*), and estimate the coefficients on the 2009 data. The

---

[19] The countries included in our sample are Argentina, Australia, Austria, Belgium, Brazil, Canada, Chile, China, Colombia, Costa Rica, Denmark, Ecuador, Egypt, Finland, France, Germany, Greece, Hong Kong, India, Indonesia, Ireland, Italy, Israel, Japan, Malaysia, Mexico, Netherlands, New Zealand, Norway, Peru, Philippines, Portugal, Singapore, South Africa, South Korea, Spain, Sweden, Switzerland, Thailand, Turkey, the United Kingdom, and Venezuela.

[20] When the country controls are suppressed, the coefficient on GDP/POP is statistically significant in both years. However, if we limit our sample to the countries considered in Brainard (1997) the coefficient is not statistically significant in either year. Note that although our sample is broader than considered by Brainard, it does not include all countries. It is quite possible that if the least developed countries had been included, the coefficient on GDP/POP might well have been positive.

Table 2.3 Proximity-Concentration Empirics

Dep. Var.: log $\left(\frac{x_j^i}{x_j^i+s_j^i}\right)$	(1)	(2)	(3)	(4)	(5)	(6)
Freight	−0.28**	−0.13**	−0.12**	−0.13**	−0.13*	0.01
	[0.05]	[0.04]	[0.04]	[0.04]	[0.06]	[0.25]
Tariffs	−0.23**	−0.28**	−0.27**	−0.29**	−0.38**	−0.04
	[0.06]	[0.05]	[0.05]	[0.06]	[0.10]	[0.04]
GDP/POP	0.10	0.04	0.06			
	[0.07]	[0.08]	[0.08]			
School				0.07		
				[0.09]		
KL				0.08		
				[0.06]		
GDP			0.32	0.39*		
			[0.17]	[0.17]		
PlantSc	0.09*	0.13*	0.13*	0.14*	0.18	
	[0.04]	[0.05]	[0.05]	[0.05]	[0.15]	
CorpSc	−0.18**	−0.32**	−0.31**	−0.32**	−0.35**	
	[0.03]	[0.04]	[0.04]	[0.04]	[0.14]	
Country Fixed Effects?	No	No	No	No	Yes	Yes
Industry Fixed Effects?	No	No	No	No	No	Yes
Year	1989	2009	2009	2009	2009	2009
Observations	1,762	2,315	2,315	2,315	2,482	2,482
R-Square	0.15	0.09	0.09	0.09	0.16	0.40

Standard errors are in brackets.
*At 1%.
**Significant at 5%.

results, shown in column 4, reveal that neither variable obtains a statistically significant coefficient, which again suggests that there is no role of relative factor endowments in the substitution of affiliate production for exports that is uniform across all industries. We will show in Section 5.4 that to identify the role of comparative advantage requires a model specification that allows the factor abundances of countries to interact with factor intensities of industries.

Finally, we consider the robustness of the proximity-concentration variables to country fixed effects, and country and industry fixed effects. The results are shown in columns (5) and (6). As the estimates in column (5) indicate, the proximity-concentration variables are robust to the inclusion of country fixed effects. However, when both types of fixed effects are included, we obtain the estimates for *Freight* and *Tariff* shown in column (6) that are very close to and statistically indistinguishable from zero. The limits to the robustness of trade cost as a predictor of the export share are not new to our exercise: Brainard (1997) obtained a similar result.

4.2. Firm Heterogeneity

As noted by Fact Four in Section 2, international economic activity is highly concentrated in a handful of very large and productive firms. We now show that explicitly addressing firm heterogeneity in productivity improves the proximity-concentration model by allowing it to be consistent with microlevel facts and by expanding our understanding of the industry characteristics that explain aggregate variables. We do so by considering the framework in Helpman et al. (2004), focusing exclusively on the industry characteristics that drive the proximity-concentration tradeoff.

Consider the simple proximity-concentration model discussed in Section 4.1.1. Again countries are symmetric ($L^H = L^F$) so that we may normalize $w^H = w^F = 1$. For convenience, we limit our attention to a generic industry and suppress industry subscripts for notational simplicity. The key new assumption is that productivity φ varies across producers of differentiated goods. A firm that is contemplating entry does not initially know its productivity φ but knows that it will be drawn from a distribution $G(\varphi)$ that has support on the interval $[\underline{\varphi}, \overline{\varphi})$ where $\overline{\varphi} > \underline{\varphi}$. After paying the industry-specific fixed cost f_E, the firm learns its productivity.

Upon observing its productivity an entrant may open a plant in its home country at an additional fixed cost of f_D or it may exit. If it chooses to produce, it may also choose to sell its variety in the other country, but doing so requires that the firm pay a marketing fixed cost f_X. To serve the foreign market, the firm may export from the plant in its home location and pay an industry-specific *ad valorem* shipping cost τ. Alternatively, the firm may open a foreign affiliate by incurring the marketing fixed cost f_X and an additional plant-level fixed cost f_D.

We now analyze the decisions of a firm that has entered one of the countries and has drawn a productivity of φ. The profit (net of entry cost) earned in the home country market for an active firm of productivity φ is

$$\pi_D(\varphi) = B\varphi^{\sigma-1} - f_D. \tag{12}$$

If the firm were to export its variety to the foreign market, the *additional* profit earned would be

$$\pi_X(\varphi) = B\varphi^{\sigma-1}\tau^{1-\sigma} - f_X, \tag{13}$$

and if it were instead to open an affiliate in the foreign country, its *additional* profit would instead be

$$\pi_I(\varphi) = B\varphi^{\sigma-1} - f_X - f_D. \tag{14}$$

The profit functions in (12), (13), and (14) for a given industry are plotted in Figure 2.5. This figure shows that firms sort into their modes of serving global markets. As in Melitz

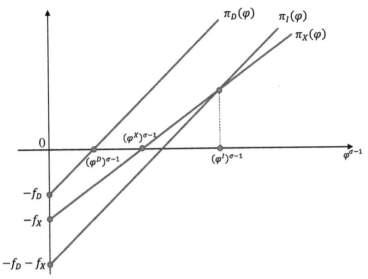

Figure 2.5 Exports, FDI and Heterogeneity

(2003), firms that receive poor draws $\varphi < \varphi^D$ exit. The least productive firms serve only their domestic market $\varphi \in (\varphi^D, \varphi^X)$ while more productive firms also sell their product abroad $(\varphi > \varphi^X)$. Of the firms selling their variety abroad, the most productive do so through a foreign affiliate $(\varphi > \varphi^I)$.[21] This sorting result stems from the supermodularity of the profit function in productivity and in other marginal cost reducing measures: a highly productive firm that sells a lot of units benefits more from a reduction in marginal cost than a firm with lower productivity that sells fewer units.[22]

Unlike the case in models with symmetric firms considered in Section 4.1, firms in a narrowly defined industry organize their international production through different modes and each firm *strictly prefers* its organization strategy to any alternative. The prediction that firms sort on the basis of their productivity has been confirmed in a number of studies. For instance, Girma et al. (2004) and Mayer and Ottaviano (2007) use kernel regression techniques to show that distributions of productivities across firms are consistent with this prediction, with the distribution of firm productivities of multinationals shifted to the right of the distribution of exporters, and even further to the right from the distribution of firms that do not sell their product abroad. Figure 2.6 provides an illustration of this result using 2007 data from the Spanish Encuesta sobre Estrategias Empresariales (ESEE), which also permits reporting the productivity advantage of both

---

[21] Figure 2.5 has been plotted under parameter restrictions that ensure a positive mass of firms engaged in exporting and in FDI. More specifically, this requires $f_X + f_D > (\tau^{ij})^{\sigma-1} f_X > f_D$.

[22] See Mrázová and Neary (2012) for a discussion of the role of supermodularity. Other preference systems can give rise to a profit function in which this feature is absent leading to different sorting implications.

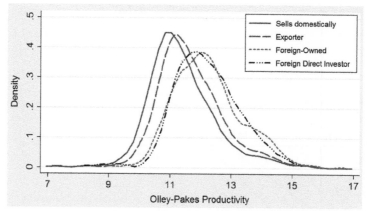

Figure 2.6 Selection into Horizontal FDI in Spain

multinational firms based in Spain as well as of foreign-owned affiliates in Spain relative to domestic producers and exporters. The differences are large and statistically significant.

We now turn to the implications of the model for the aggregate trade and multinational production data that are most widely available. To highlight the substitutability between exports and local affiliate sales (as in Brainard, 1997) we consider the share of sales by industry that are sold via exports relative to those sold through foreign affiliates. First, to fully characterize the equilibrium, we apply the free entry condition, which requires that the *expected* profit from entry is equal to zero. This condition is given by

$$B\left(V(\varphi^D) + \tau^{1-\sigma}\left(V(\varphi^X) - V(\varphi^I)\right) + V(\varphi^I)\right) - (1 - G(\varphi^D))f_D - $$
$$(1 - G(\varphi^I))f_D - (1 - G(\varphi^X))f_X - f_E = 0, \tag{15}$$

where

$$V(\hat{\varphi}) = \int_{\hat{\varphi}}^{\overline{\varphi}} \varphi^{\sigma-1} \, dG(\varphi). \tag{16}$$

Next, integrating over firms' export sales yields aggregate exports of $S^X = \sigma B \tau^{1-\sigma} \left(V(\varphi^X) - V(\varphi^I)\right)$. Repeating this procedure for affiliate sales, we obtain aggregate affiliate sales of $S^I = \sigma B V(\varphi^I)$. The ratio of aggregate exports to aggregate affiliate sales is then

$$\frac{S^X}{S^I} = \tau^{1-\sigma} \left(\frac{V(\varphi^X)}{V(\varphi^I)} - 1\right). \tag{17}$$

It can be established through differentiation of the cutoff conditions, of the free entry condition (15), and of the function (17) that many of the standard proximity-concentration predictions are maintained in the model with heterogeneous firms. In particular S^X/S^I tends to fall as trade costs τ rise (as is also true for the fixed cost of marketing f_X that is new to this section) and tends to rise as plant-level fixed costs f_D

rise. Unlike the case of homogeneous firms as considered in Section 4.1.1, the change is smooth rather than an abrupt shift to a different corner. The effect of a change in corporate fixed costs, f_E, on S^X/S^I is more subtle. An increase in f_E tends to raise the mark-up adjusted demand level B, which in turn causes all cutoffs to fall. As long as $\varphi^I < \overline{\varphi}$ the effect on S^X/S^I depends on the shape of the distribution function G (see equation 16). However, as φ^I is monotonically decreasing in B, for sufficiently small f_E the cutoff φ^I will exceed any finite upper bound $\overline{\varphi}$ and so multinational firms will disappear. In this sense, the effect of f_E on the likelihood of FDI is similar to that in the case of homogeneous firms.

To get further results, Helpman et al. (2004) assume that the upper limit of the support $\overline{\varphi}$ of the distribution G is infinite and that the distribution is Pareto: $G(\varphi) = 1 - \underline{\varphi}^\kappa \varphi^{-\kappa}$. Note that this assumption requires the parameter restriction $\kappa > \sigma - 1$, otherwise the integrals aggregating affiliate sales and profits will not converge. The Pareto assumption has become popular in the literature because it requires few parameters, yields clean analytic solutions, and can be partially justified because it implies (along with the CES preference system) that the size distribution of firm sales is also Pareto, which is a reasonable approximation to the data for the far right tail.

The Pareto assumption means that we can solve the integrals in (17) and then substitute for the cutoffs to obtain the clean expression that relates S^X/S^I to exclusively exogenous parameters:

$$\frac{S^X}{S^I} = \tau^{1-\sigma} \left[\left(\frac{f_D}{f_X} \frac{1}{\tau^{\sigma-1} - 1} \right)^{\frac{\kappa}{\sigma-1} - 1} - 1 \right]. \tag{18}$$

The parameters τ, f_X, and f_D shape the ratio as discussed in the general case above. Interestingly, with the Pareto assumption and the infinite bound on productivity, the corporate fixed cost f_E has no impact on the ratio of exports and FDI sales. Intuitively, an increase in f_E causes both φ^X and φ^I to change by the same proportion and the Pareto distribution ensures that the sales of firms that switch modes as a result of these changes in the cutoff are also in the same proportion, leaving the ratio unchanged.

Note that the distributional parameter κ, working in concert with the elasticity of substitution σ, also has an impact on the composition of commerce. A decrease in this ratio is associated with a decrease in S^X/S^I. It can be shown that if we hold fixed a particular market, the Pareto parameterization (combined with the CES demand system) imply that the standard deviation of the logarithm of sales by all active firms in this market is equal to $(\sigma - 1)/\kappa$. Hence, an increase in the variance of sales across firms within an industry should be associated with a decrease in S^X/S^I. To understand this result consider Figure 2.7, where we plot the Pareto density function for two values of κ. It is clear from the figure that a decrease in κ raises the density of the function at any $\varphi > \varphi^I$—where

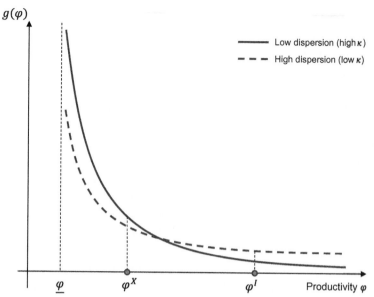

Figure 2.7 Dispersion and the Proximity-Concentration Hypothesis

firms find FDI optimal—relative to the density at any $\varphi \in (\varphi^X, \varphi^I)$—where firms choose exporting.[23]

Helpman et al. (2004) estimate a logarithm linearized version of equation (18) using U.S. data for 1994. They include as regressors country fixed effects, the standard proximity-concentration variables, and a measure of the standard deviation of the logarithm of firm sales by industry as a measure of dispersion.[24] They confirm Brainard's results concerning trade costs and plant-level fixed costs (measured as the average number of nonproduction workers per plant), and they find that an increase in the dispersion measure is associated with a large, statistically significant decrease in S^X/S^I. The extent of firm heterogeneity seems to matter for the aggregates. Their result must be qualified, however, because their estimates of $\frac{\kappa}{\sigma-1}$ for many industries are not consistent with the restriction $\kappa > \sigma - 1$.[25] This means that their results do not have a structural interpretation.[26]

In the working paper version of the paper, Helpman et al. also show that the model can be extended to allow for modestly asymmetric geographies. When trade costs between

---

[23] Note that the mean of the Pareto distribution $G(\varphi) = 1 - \underline{\varphi}^\kappa \varphi^{-\kappa}$ is $\mu = \underline{\varphi}\kappa/(\kappa - 1)$, while the variance is $\varepsilon^2 = \mu^2/(\kappa(\kappa - 2))$. A decrease in κ thus not only increases the variance of the distribution but also its mean. Nevertheless, because S^X/S^I in (18) is independent of the lower bound $\underline{\varphi}$, one can always offset the effect of a lower κ on the mean μ with a reduction in $\underline{\varphi}$, and still raise ε^2. Thus, a mean-preserving spread raises FDI relative to exports.

[24] They also include measures of dispersion estimated from the size distribution of firms with similar results.

[25] The finding that the slope of a linear regression of log rank on log size is less than one is common. The commonly used Pareto approximation only holds for the tail of the distribution.

[26] There is an error in the paper that has been the source of some confusion. On page 307 it is stated that the estimators of dispersion are measuring $\kappa - \sigma + 1$ rather than $\kappa/(\sigma - 1)$.

regions are higher than within regions two tiers of multinationals arise: the most productive firms own affiliates in all countries while the less productive multinationals open a single affiliate that they use to serve the entire region. This yields an additional empirical implication: an increase in firm productivity predicts affiliate entry into a larger number of countries. Yeaple (2009) and Chen and Moore (2010) have shown this prediction to be consistent with the data (for U.S. and European multinationals, respectively).

4.3. Greenfield FDI versus Mergers and Acquisitions

We have modeled the foreign entry decision as a fixed cost of setting up a variety-specific plant in a foreign location. This has the flavor of what is called "greenfield" entry in which a firm builds its foreign production capacity from scratch. However, according to Fact Six in Section 2, in practice most firms that acquire new plants in a foreign location do so by purchasing previously existing plants through cross-border mergers and acquisitions. This fact has resulted in some discussion in the literature as to whether the models that we have described above are consistent with the actual entry modes that firms undertake.

In this section, we extend Helpman et al. (2004) in such a way as to incorporate both greenfield entry and cross-border acquisitions. In this extension, greenfield and cross-border acquisitions coexist and are in fact perfect substitutes from the perspective of the firm (although banning cross-border acquisitions would have consequences in the model). We then discuss the model's implications in light of a small but growing empirical literature. We find that there is evidence that in fact firms do not behave as if cross-border acquisitions and greenfield investment were perfect substitutes. We close this section by describing some theory in which the two entry modes are different.

Going back to the model of Helpman et al. (2004) discussed above, suppose that prior to receiving its productivity draw, an entering firm must pay both f_E and f_D. Thus, the fixed cost of building a plant in the home country market is now sunk. The only other important deviation from the Helpman et al. (2004) model is that a firm may sell its plant to any other entrant on a perfectly competitive merger market. Firms that acquire that plant may now install their own productivity draw φ (replacing the purchased firm's technology) and so avoid paying a fixed cost f_D. As all purchased firms will be homogeneous with respect to purchasers, they will receive the acquisition price in the market of P_A.

A firm will sell itself on the merger market if P_A exceeds the profit that it could generate independently while an acquirer would strictly prefer greenfield if $f_D < P_A$ and cross-border acquisitions otherwise. Hence, in equilibrium it must be that $P_A \leq f_D$ and that all firms with productivity $\varphi \leq \varphi^D$ would sell themselves on the merger market while all foreign firms with $\varphi \geq \varphi^I$ would either engage exclusively in cross-border acquisitions if $P_A < f_D$ or be indifferent between greenfield investment and cross-border acquisition if $P_A = f_D$. The equilibrium we have just constructed is as characterized in the previous section in spirit but we now have a mechanism that gives rise to cross-border acquisitions. Note, however, that cross-border acquisitions do matter in the extension, for if they were not allowed, then weaker firms would have no incentive to exit.

This extension shows that it need not be the case that cross-border acquisitions are fundamentally different from what was modeled in the previous section.[27] It also can be used as a benchmark in interpreting the stylized facts. Let us consider the implication of the model that firms are indifferent between the two entry modes. Nocke and Yeaple (2008) have used data from the Bureau of Economic Analysis to show that parent firms of U.S. multinationals that enter foreign markets appear to sort into their mode of entry: more productive parent firms tend to acquire new plants via greenfield entry rather than cross-border entry. This suggests that the firms do not perceive these modes as perfect substitutes.

Now consider the implication of the extended model that the firms acquired by foreign firms are the least productive in their industries. A number of studies suggest the exact opposite. For instance, Arnold and Javorcik (2009), Guadalupe et al. (2012), and Blonigen et al. (2012) are examples of recent papers that suggest that it is the most productive firms within an industry that tend to be the targets of foreign acquisitions. This again suggests that cross-border acquisitions and greenfield investment are not perfect substitutes.

A number of recent papers develop equilibrium models in which there is sorting of firms into their mode of entry into foreign markets. For instance, Nocke and Yeaple (2007, 2008) develop equilibrium models in which firms are heterogeneous in multiple dimensions that interact in a complementary way to generate profits. The firm heterogeneity is embodied in intangible assets that can be transferred across firms only through ownership and some of these assets are imperfectly mobile across countries (such as relationships with customers and local suppliers, etc.). Equilibrium in a merger market involves improving the assignment of intangible assets to firms to exploit complementarities. Greenfield investment occurs when a firm's relatively immobile asset is so useful that it pays to move it despite high relocation costs. Similar mechanisms appear in models provided by Guadalupe et al. (2012), in which foreign firms possess innovative abilities and access to foreign markets that domestic firms lack and these abilities are best applied to local firms that are already highly productive.

Before leaving the topic of entry mode, it is important to mention that an alternative explanation for cross-border acquisitions is that firms acquire one another in order to reduce competition. The literature exploring this phenomenon develops oligopolist environments and explores the types of acquisitions that might arise whether between or within countries. Examples of such papers are Horn and Persson (2001), Qiu and Zhou (2006), and Neary (2007). An important implication of some of these models is that a

---

[27] Note that firm heterogeneity is important to generate firms that want to sell and firms that want to buy plants.

reduction in trade costs can spur waves of cross-border acquisitions. Breinlich (2008) provides some supportive evidence for this prediction.

5. VERTICAL EXPANSION

Some of the empirical shortcomings of horizontal FDI models are due to the fact that FDI is often motivated by factors other than the mere replication of the production processes in different countries to save on transportation costs or jump over tariffs. In reality, multinational activity might also be motivated by cost differences across countries, which induce some producers to locate different parts of the production process in different countries. Indeed, Fact One, that net FDI flows from developed to developing countries, and Fact Five that R&D expenditures within the multinational firm are concentrated in the parent firm, suggest a need to address international specialization. Further, in all industries there are exports from affiliates to their parent firms that are not easily explained in a purely horizontal setting, and in particular industries the volume of these exports is very large (see Table 2.2).

In this section, we discuss some works that formalize and empirically test these insights, starting with the simplest case of the so-called pure vertical FDI model of Helpman (1984).

5.1. A Factor-Proportions Model of Vertical FDI

Let us now return to the benchmark model in Section 3. In order to shut down the horizontal incentive for multinational activity, let us suppose for now that there are no transport costs so exporting is the dominant strategy in the models in Section 4. For simplicity, consider a two-sector ($\beta_z > 0, J = 1$), two-factor model, in which production uses capital and labor, and capital intensity is higher in the differentiated-good sector than in the traditional-good sector. For the time being, assume also that the distribution of firm productivity is degenerate within sectors and that the cost functions in each sector are identical in both countries, so there are no Ricardian differences in technology. We will relax the latter two assumptions later in this section. So far, the model is essentially a $2 \times 2 \times 2$ Helpman and Krugman (1985) model of international trade, with slightly stronger assumptions on preferences and technology.

The key new feature is that we will now make an explicit distinction between different production stages in the differentiated-good sector and that we will allow for a geographic separation of these stages. More specifically, the total cost function in the differentiated-good sector now follows from the aggregation of the total cost of two distinct production processes: headquarter services provision and manufacturing.

Headquarter services provision entails activities that are typically provided by the production unit from which the ownership advantage originated, i.e., the headquarters. It is useful to think of these as being closely related to our interpretation of the fixed cost of entry in horizontal FDI models, and thus entail R&D expenditures, brand or specialized machine development, financing, etc. This is consistent with our Fact Five in Section 2. These activities have important fixed cost components, but we will also allow their level to affect continuously the marginal product of manufacturing, as in Helpman (1984). In analogy to horizontal FDI models, headquarter services are assumed specialized and are valuable only to the firm incurring them, but within the firm, they are nonrival and can serve many manufacturing plants simultaneously, regardless of where these manufacturing plants are located. Headquarter services are produced with capital and labor according to the total cost function $C_H\left(w^i, r^i, h^i\right)$, where h^i is the number of units of services produced and $C_H\left(\cdot\right)$ is associated with an increasing returns to scale production function.

The manufacturing stage uses capital and labor to convert the available headquarter services into final goods according to an increasing returns to scale technology in which h is essential and which is represented by a cost function $C_M\left(w^i, r^i, \bar{h}, q^i\right)$, where q^i is the amount of output produced and $\bar{h}$ is the aggregate amount of firm-level headquarter services available for production. $C_M\left(\cdot\right)$ is naturally decreasing in $\bar{h}$ and increasing in the other arguments. Following Helpman (1984), we assume that the production of headquarter services is more capital intensive than manufacturing.

Because trade is costless and there are increasing returns associated with each stage, firms will not produce headquarter services or carry out manufacturing in more than one location. When both stages occur in the same country i, the total cost of production will be given by

$$C_1\left(w^i, r^i, q^i\right) = \min_{h^i} \left\{ C_M\left(w^i, r^i, h^i, q^i\right) + C_H\left(w^i, r^i, h^i\right) \right\}. \tag{19}$$

The benchmark model in Section 3 is a particular case of this more general multistage model in which we forced firms to locate all production processes in the same country.[28] The key question that Helpman (1984) posed was then: under which conditions will firms want to deviate from this "Krugman-style" equilibrium and locate headquarter services and manufacturing in different countries, thus becoming multinational firms? An advantage of having related our current model to the benchmark model in Section 3, which in turn is a variant of the canonical $2 \times 2 \times 2$ model studied by Helpman and

---

[28] Strictly speaking, in our benchmark model, we had specified a homothetic total cost function (see equation (3)) involving a fixed cost and a constant marginal cost in terms of a linearly homogeneous function of capital and labor, denoted by $c_1\left(w^i, r^i\right)$. Given our assumptions, nothing ensures that the solution to (19) will indeed give rise to a homothetic cost function of the form in (3). A simple way to make these two formulations consistent with each other (while having headquarter services be more capital intensive than manufacturing) is to assume that: (i) the fixed costs of headquarter services' provision and manufacturing are both linear in $c_1\left(w^i, r^i\right)$; (ii) the marginal cost of headquarter services is a constant amount of capital; (iii) the marginal cost of manufacturing is a constant amount of labor; and (iv) output is a linearly homogeneous function of the level of headquarter services and manufacturing, i.e., $q^i = q\left(h^i, m^i\right)$, where $q\left(h^i, m^i\right)$ is the primal production function associated with the cost function $c_1\left(w^i, r^i\right)$. Naturally, it would be straightforward to relax these conditions to accommodate nonextreme factor intensity in marginal costs.

Krugman (1985), is that we can readily appeal to their results to conclude that multinational activity will be a (weakly) dominated strategy as long as relative factor endowment differences across countries are small. The reason is simple: for sufficiently similar relative factor endowments, factor price equalization (FPE) will attain even in the absence of fragmentation and thus firms based in one country will have no incentive to open subsidiaries (production plants) in the other country.

Outside the traditional FPE set, firms with headquarters in the relatively capital-abundant country would have an incentive to "deviate" from the equilibrium and offshore manufacturing to the relatively labor abundant country simply because wages are lower there in the absence of multinational activity. Helpman (1984) further demonstrated that, outside the traditional FPE set, there exists a set of "not-too-extreme" relative factor endowment differences for which a unique *minimum* measure of multinational firms is sufficient to bring about factor price equalization, thus eliminating the incentive for more firms to fragment production across borders. Importantly, within this set, Helpman (1984) showed that for a constant relative size of the two countries, the minimum measure of multinational firms consistent with equilibrium would be increasing in relative factor endowment differences. Although the model above does not feature intrafirm trade in physical goods, it does feature invisible exports of headquarter services from each headquarter to its subsidiary. Assuming that these services are valued at average cost, Helpman (1984) showed that, for a given relative size of countries, the share of intrafirm trade in the total volume of trade is increasing in relative factor endowment differences.

5.2. Vertical FDI and Wage Inequality

A variant of the Helpman (1984) model in which the two factors of production are interpreted as skilled and unskilled labor sheds light on the effect of vertical FDI (and offshoring, more broadly) on wage inequality in each country. Notice that in the model above, whenever fragmentation brings about factor price equalization, it does so by increasing the relative demand for and remuneration of the relatively abundant factor in each country, thereby increasing wage inequality in the relatively skilled-labor abundant country, while reducing it in the relatively unskilled-labor abundant country. This is essentially the Stolper-Samuelson theorem at work but with the movement in factor prices being shaped by changes in relative input costs rather than in relative final-good prices.

In recent years, there has been an active literature in international trade studying the robustness of this result to alternative and much richer general-equilibrium environments with offshoring. As might have been expected from the well-known limited generality of the Stolper-Samuelson theorem, the effect of fragmentation on relative factor prices and thus wage inequality has been shown to be sensitive to modeling assumptions. A large number of models have been proposed, but we will focus below on outlining two of the most popular ones developed in recent years, the ones in Feenstra and Hanson (1996) and Grossman and Rossi-Hansberg (2008). While both of these models were originally cast in neoclassical environments with homogeneous goods, perfect competition, and constant returns to scale, it is straightforward to embed them in our benchmark model in Section 3.

The main result in Feenstra and Hanson (1996) can be illustrated by considering a variant of our benchmark factor-proportions model of vertical FDI in which, instead of there being two production stages in the differentiated-good sector, there are now a continuum of stages x indexed by $s \in [0, 1]$, and the marginal cost for each activity or input is given by

$$c_x \left(w^i, r^i, s \right) = a_K \left(s \right) r^i + a_L \left(s \right) w^i,$$

where we now use the notation K and r to denote skilled workers (i.e., human capital) and their wages, while L and w are now associated with unskilled workers. This continuum of stages is arranged in increasing order of their skill intensity, so that $a_K \left(s \right) / a_L \left(s \right)$ is increasing in s, and they are combined into final output according to a Cobb-Douglas technology

$$q_1 = \exp \left(\int_0^1 \alpha \left(s \right) \ln x \left(s \right) \, ds \right),$$

where $x \left(s \right)$ is the value of services at stage s. As in our benchmark model, and differently than in the framework in Feenstra and Hanson (1996), we assume that there also exist fixed costs of production at each stage, but we assume that all these are in terms of final-good output, so that the total cost function in the differentiated good, $C_1 \left(r^i, w^i, q_1^i \right)$, remains homothetic. This is isomorphic to assuming that activities or inputs are produced according to a constant-returns-to-scale technology but that there exists a fixed cost (in terms of output) associated with the assembly of intermediate inputs. We finally assume, for simplicity, that the homogeneous final-good sector uses only unskilled labor.

Despite the fact that one of the sectors features product differentiation, increasing returns to scale, and monopolistic competition, the general equilibrium of the model is very similar to that in the continuum version of the Heckscher-Ohlin model in Dornbusch et al. (1980). First, and as in Helpman (1984), if relative factor endowment differences between countries are sufficiently small, the equilibrium features factor price equalization and there is no incentive to fragment production across countries. For slightly higher relative factor endowment differences, fragmentation will occur in equilibrium and will bring about factor price equalization, but unlike in Helpman (1984), the actual pattern of offshoring is indeterminate given the large dimensionality of the commodity space. The most interesting results emerge when relative factor endowment differences are large enough to ensure that factor prices are not equalized even when fragmentation is costless. As in Dornbusch et al. (1980) or Feenstra and Hanson (1996), in such a case, there exists a marginal stage s^* such that the relatively skill-abundant country (call it Home) specializes in the production of stages $s > s^*$, while the unskilled-labor abundant country (call it Foreign) specializes in the stages $s \leq s^*$ and the production of the homogeneous good z. This pattern of production is supported by an unskilled-labor wage which is strictly higher at Home ($w^H > w^F$) and a skilled-labor wage which is strictly higher in Foreign ($r^H < r^F$).

As in Helpman (1984), relative to a world in which fragmentation is not feasible, the factor price equalization set is larger and equilibrium factor price differences are smaller with fragmentation. Nevertheless, within a free trade equilibrium, it is easy to construct comparative static exercises such that increases in offshoring are associated with increased wage inequality *in both countries*. For instance, consider a situation in which relative factor endowment differences are so large that FPE does not attain even with frictionless fragmentation. Consider then a proportional increase in the supply of both factors in Foreign. This will naturally increase the range of tasks produced in (or offshored to) Foreign, and these marginal tasks will feature a higher skill intensity than the tasks previously produced in Foreign. As a result, the relative demand for skilled workers will increase and, in equilibrium, so will the Foreign wage premium (see the Online Appendix for details). Similarly, the relative demand for skills and the wage premium will also increase at Home because these offshored marginal tasks feature a lower skill intensity than the activities that remain at Home. It should be emphasized, however, that relative to a world in which fragmentation is not feasible at all, wage inequality in Foreign is always lower with some offshoring, just as in Helpman (1984).

The above example illustrates that the prediction linking increases in offshoring to reduced wage inequality in less developed countries is not a robust one (see also Zhu and Trefler, 2005; Antràs et al., 2006). We next briefly outline a variant of the framework in Grossman and Rossi-Hansberg (2008) which demonstrates that increases in offshoring might not necessarily be associated with increased wage inequality in skill-abundant countries. To do so, let us first return to our benchmark vertical FDI model with only two inputs, headquarter services and manufacturing, and consider situations in which free trade in these inputs (or what we call above, fragmentation) brings about factor price equalization in that model. To be more specific, we consider a situation in which the unskilled-labor abundant Foreign is "large" and produces the homogeneous good as well as both inputs or stages in the differentiated-good sector, while the skill-abundant Home produces only the two inputs in the differentiated-good sector. Differently than in our benchmark model, we shall assume, however, that the technologies available to firms in both countries are now different and in particular they feature higher productivity at Home than in Foreign. More specifically, productivity levels are $\zeta < 1$ times lower in Foreign than at Home in all sectors and because we are focusing on a situation with *conditional* factor price equalization, factor prices will also be ζ times lower in Foreign than at Home.

Suppose now that each of the two inputs is produced by combining a continuum of measure one of "tasks" involving unskilled labor L and a continuum of measure one of tasks involving skilled workers K. The two inputs continue to vary in terms of the intensity with which these continua of tasks generate value, with headquarters being more skill-intensive than manufacturing. The key innovation relative to our previous model is that we will now allow unskilled-labor tasks to be offshorable, by which we mean that firms at Home can carry them out using Foreign workers while still using the superior Home production technologies. Offshoring is however costly and tasks are ordered according to their degree of offshorability. Producing task s in Foreign inflates unit labor requirements by a multiple $\beta t(s) \geq 1$, where $t'(s) \geq 0$. For simplicity, we assume that skilled-labor tasks are prohibitively costly to offshore.[29]

Given these assumptions, there exists a threshold task s^* such that all unskilled-labor tasks with index $s < s^*$ are offshored to Foreign, while all those with $s > s^*$ remain at Home, with the threshold being implicitly defined by

$$w^H = \beta t(s^*) w^F.$$

The marginal costs of producing headquarter services and of producing final goods are then

$$c_H\left(w^H, w^F, r^H\right) = w^H a_{LH} \Omega\left(s^*\right) + r^H a_{KH} \tag{20}$$

$$c_M\left(w^H, w^F, r^H\right) = w^H a_{LM} \Omega\left(s^*\right) + r^H a_{KM} \tag{21}$$

where

$$\Omega\left(s^*\right) \equiv 1 - s^* + \frac{\int_0^{s^*} t(s)\, di}{t\left(s^*\right)} < 1.$$

Equations (20) and (21) make it clear that offshoring in this framework is isomorphic to unskilled-labor biased technological change. Because Foreign is large and produces both inputs, the marginal costs of each input are pinned down by their Foreign levels.[30] As a result, an increase in the offshorability of tasks, captured by a fall in β, will necessarily increase the unskilled-labor wage w^H commensurately with the fall in $\Omega\left(s^*\right)$, while leaving the skilled-labor wage r^H unaffected. In sum, the offshorability of certain types of tasks leads to a relative increase in the reward of the factor that is used intensively in precisely those tasks. The flip side of this surprising result is another counterintuitive result: increased offshorability leads to an expansion in the share of Home employment devoted to the unskilled-intensive manufacturing at the expense of employment in headquarter services.

5.3. Vertical FDI and Firm Heterogeneity

So far, we have developed vertical FDI models in which firms are homogeneous in productivity. As in the case of horizontal FDI, however, the evidence suggests that aggregate

---

[29] This assumption is relaxed in Grossman and Rossi-Hansberg (2008).

[30] This is true even if headquarter services are firm-specific, given that the location decision precedes production.

vertical MNE activity is accounted for, to a large extent, by a few very large and productive firms. For instance, Ramondo et al. (2012) report that despite the quantitative
significance of the intrafirm component of U.S. trade, the median affiliate reports no
shipments to its U.S. parent. This fact motivates us to introduce firm heterogeneity into
the vertical model developed so far. In order to keep the analysis tractable, however, we
will develop a one-factor (labor) variant of the Helpman (1984) model in which cross-
country differences in factor prices arise due to Ricardian technological differences rather
than due to differences in relative factor endowments.[31]

More specifically, assume that the cost function in the homogeneous-good sector is
$c_z^i(w^i, r^i) = a_z^i w^i$ with $a_z^H < a_z^F$. Assuming further that β_z is large enough to ensure that
both Home and Foreign produce the numeraire good z (i.e., $z^H, z^F > 0$), we necessarily
have $w^H = 1/a_z^H > 1/a_z^F = w^F$, and producers of differentiated goods face a perfectly
elastic supply of labor at those wage rates. In the differentiated-good sector, headquarter
services provision first requires an initial fixed cost of entry or innovation, after which
producers learn their productivity φ which is drawn from $G(\varphi)$. Firms then decide to
exit or stay in the market and produce. In the latter case, headquarters need to incur
an additional fixed cost to be described below. Having incurred this cost, they choose a
variable amount of headquarter services h to combine with manufacturing in production.
Home is assumed to be much more productive than Foreign in innovation/entry and in
the production of headquarter services, so these are always produced at Home. Denote by
f_E the initial fixed cost of entry and by f_D the fixed cost of headquarter services provision,
and assume that units of h can be produced one-to-one with labor. Our assumptions on
technology imply that in equilibrium all these costs are defined in terms of Home labor.
Manufacturing entails no overhead costs and units of m can be produced one-to-one
with labor in both countries. Foreign thus has comparative advantage in manufacturing.
Final-good production combines h and m according to the technology

$$q^i(\varphi) = \varphi \left(\frac{h^i}{\eta}\right)^{\eta} \left(\frac{m^i}{1-\eta}\right)^{1-\eta},$$

where $1 < \eta < 1$ is a sectoral level of headquarter intensity, while φ measures firm-level
productivity.

The lower wage in Foreign makes offshore manufacturing appealing from the point
of view of the firm's headquarter at Home. We shall assume, however, that there are costs
associated with the fragmentation of production. In particular, an additional fixed cost
$f_I - f_D > 0$ is required from the headquarters at Home when h and m are geographically
separated, and such fragmentation also entails an iceberg transportation cost $\tau > 1$,
associated with shipping the manufactured input m back to the Home country (τ could
also reflect communication or coordination costs). Trade in final goods remains free.

---

[31] Factor-proportions models of monopolistic competition with productivity heterogeneity and trade costs are notably
difficult to work with (see Bernard et al., 2007).

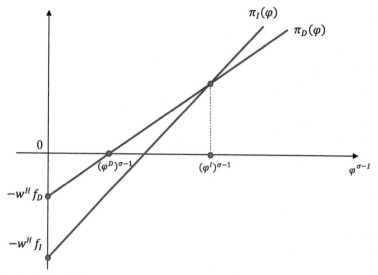

Figure 2.8 Vertical FDI and Heterogeneity

Given the assumptions above, it is straightforward to solve for the operating profits (net of entry costs) associated with domestic sourcing (or no fragmentation)

$$\pi_D\left(\varphi\right) = \varphi^{\sigma-1}\left(B^H + B^F\right)\left(w^H\right)^{1-\sigma} - w^H f_D \tag{22}$$

and those under vertical FDI or offshoring

$$\pi_I\left(\varphi\right) = \varphi^{\sigma-1}\left(B^H + B^F\right)\left(\left(w^H\right)^{\eta}\left(\tau w^F\right)^{1-\eta}\right)^{1-\sigma} - w^H f_I, \tag{23}$$

for a firm with productivity φ, where remember B^i is defined in (5). These profit levels are plotted in Figure 2.8 under the assumption that $w^H > \tau w^F$, so some firms find it optimal to offshore.

As is clear from the figure, the model predicts selection into vertical FDI, in that only the most productive firms within an industry will find it profitable to engage in vertical FDI. This sorting pattern is consistent with the evidence on selection into importing in Bernard et al. (2009) who show that not only U.S. exporting firms but also U.S. importing firms appear to be more productive than purely domestic producers. Figure 2.9 provides further confirmation of this sorting pattern with 2007 data from the Spanish Encuesta sobre Estrategias Empresariales (ESEE). The dataset distinguishes between firms that purchase inputs only from other Spanish producers and firms that purchase inputs from abroad. As is clear from the picture, the distribution of productivity of firms that engage in foreign sourcing is a shift to the right of that of firms that only source locally.[32]

---

[32] Of course, foreign sourcing need not involve vertical FDI, as inputs can be purchased abroad from independent subcontractors. A key feature of the Spanish ESEE data is that it allows one to distinguish between foreign outsourcing

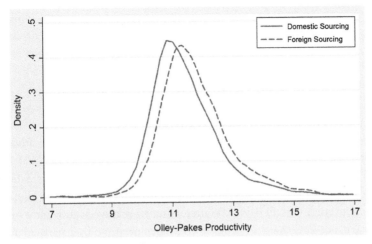

Figure 2.9 Selection into Vertical FDI in Spain

5.4. Vertical FDI: Empirical Evidence

The motives for vertical FDI are intuitive and there are thousands of examples of assembly and parts-producing affiliates in developing countries that fit the description. It is less clear how important vertical FDI is in the aggregates. Consider the facts discussed in Section 2. First, according to Fact One, most of FDI flows not to developing countries but to other developed countries. Second, only a relatively small fraction of affiliate output is exported back to the host country (see Fact Five). Third, as pointed out by Ramondo et al. (2012) very few foreign affiliates are engaged in international trade, selling all of their output in their host country.

A few more facts are worth mentioning before we turn to the econometric evidence. First, exports by U.S.-owned affiliates back to the United States are concentrated in a few countries. The top five affiliate export locations to the United States accounted for 60% of total U.S. affiliate exports to the U.S. while the corresponding number for affiliate sales in their host country is only 43%. This fact is perhaps unsurprising given that the point of vertical FDI is to concentrate production in low cost locations while horizontal FDI is about serial repetition of the same process across countries. Second, the list of countries that are highly engaged in hosting affiliates that export back to the United States features high variation in the level of their development. The top five countries in order of the size of U.S. affiliate exports back to the United States are Canada, Mexico, Ireland, the United Kingdom, and Singapore. This suggests that the treatment of comparative advantage in a two-country, two-factor model may be too simple to be consistent with the richness of the data. Evidently, some U.S. multinationals find Canada, a developed country, to be

and vertical FDI. As we will show later in Figure 2.11, the productivity advantage of firms engaged in vertical FDI is even larger than the one observed in Figure 2.9.

a relatively low cost production location for some production activities while Mexico is relatively low cost for others. The concept of comparative advantage, of course, is that being a low cost location in some activities means being a high cost location in others. Given this observation, it is perhaps not surprising that a regression of a measure of the extent of FDI on country endowments, as was done in Section 4.1.3, yields a coefficient that is not statistically different from zero as the specification did not allow for the effect of endowments to vary across production activities.

Yeaple (2003a) allows for a more flexible treatment of comparative advantage in an effort to better capture vertical FDI in the data. He starts by noting that most of the evidence against vertical FDI comes from econometric studies that use data aggregated across industries to the country level. According to his interpretation, the Helpman (1984) model does *not* predict that FDI will be increasing in relative factor endowment differences. Instead, it predicts that in industries that are intensive in a particular factor, FDI should be flowing to countries that are abundant in that particular factor. In terms of our previous Brainard-style specifications, in which the relative prevalence of FDI is inversely related to the ratio of exports to exports plus the local sales of the affiliates of U.S. firms, Yeaple (2003a) argues that the econometric model should be specified as

$$\log\left(\frac{X_j^i}{X_j^i + S_j^i}\right) = \alpha_0 + \alpha_1 Freight_j^i + \alpha_2 Tariff_j^i + \alpha_3 PlantSC_j + \alpha_4 SkillEnd^i$$

$$+ \alpha_5 SkillInt_j + \alpha_6 SkillEnd^i * SkillInt_j + \alpha_7 \mathbf{C}^i + \mu_{ij}, \qquad (24)$$

where X_j^i is again export sales from the U.S. in industry j to country i and S_j^i are the corresponding affiliate sales. The key changes to the econometric specification relative to that in Section 4.1.3 is the addition of variables $SkillInt_j$, which is the skill intensity of industry j, and $SkillEnd^i * SkillInt_j$, which is the interaction between skill intensity of an industry and $SkillEnd^i$, a measure of the skill-abundance of country i. The relevant coefficient for assessing the vertical motive of FDI is then α_6 rather than α_4, and the predicted sign is negative: skill intensive activities should be done in skill-abundant countries and unskilled-labor intensive industries in unskilled-labor abundant countries.

We follow Yeaple (2003a) and estimate (24) using the most recently available data on U.S. exports and affiliate sales for the year 2009. We include all of the same control variables as in Table 2.3 (coefficients suppressed below for exposition) and measure $SkillEnd^i$ (the logarithm of average human capital per worker) and its interaction with an industry's skill intensity $SkillInt_j$ (more details on the variables and data sources can be found in the Online Appendix). The results are shown in Table 2.4.

The coefficient estimate in the first column confirms that when no interaction terms are included, skill endowments do not predict substitution between trade and affiliate production. Including skill endowments, skill intensity, and the interaction of the two (column 2) leads to coefficient estimates as anticipated: U.S. firms export more to a human capital scarce country in skill-intensive industries and substitute local production

Table 2.4 Skill Interactions

Dep. Var.: log $\left(\frac{x_j^l}{x_j^l+s_j^l}\right)$	(1)	(2)	(3)	(4)
SkillEnd	−0.03	1.57*	1.57*	
	[0.29]	[0.63]	[0.64]	
SkillEnd * SkillInt		−10.5**	−9.83**	−8.77**
		[3.57]	[3.38]	[2.68]
SkillInt		13.7**		
		[2.74]		
Country Fixed Effects?	No	No	No	Yes
Industry Fixed Effects?	No	No	Yes	Yes
Observations	2,315	2,315	2,315	2,482
R-Square	0.17	0.18	0.36	0.40

Standard errors are in brackets.
*At 1%.
**Significant at 5%.

for exports to human capital scarce countries in industries with low skill intensity. Note in columns 3 and 4 that the interaction term is robust to both country and industry fixed effects while the measures of *Freight* and *Tariffs* (not shown but as in Table 2.3) are not.[33]

Vertical production relationships may also be more involved than in the simple model provided above. Many vertical relationships involve a parent firm shipping intermediate inputs to its foreign affiliates for further processing (see Figure 2.4). Rather than focus on factor endowment differences as the motive for this vertical specialization, Keller and Yeaple (2013) consider the input sourcing decisions of foreign assembly plants that sell their output in the host country market. They model the share of imported intermediates in the share of affiliates' total costs as the result of a tradeoff between costly technology transfer on the one hand and costly trade on the other hand. Under the maintained assumption that high R&D industries are the most burdened by technology transfer costs, their mechanism gives rise to gravity in affiliate sales (see Figure 2.3), and the effect of gravity is strongest in high R&D industries. They show that the mechanism is consistent with the data for U.S. multinationals and can explain approximately 30% of the gravity for aggregate affiliate sales that was noted as part of Fact Three.[34]

[33] There are alternative explanations for the interactions. For instance, it could be that skill-intensive products are not consumed much in skill scarce (i.e. poorer) countries.

[34] See also Hanson et al. (2005) and Irrazábal et al. (2013) for additional evidence on the role of gravity. Another approach to thinking about vertical specialization appears in Alfaro and Charlton (2009). They identify vertically specialized affiliates as those that do not share an industry classification with their parent firms. According to this measure, vertical FDI begins to look quite ubiquitous but not necessarily driven by factor endowment differences across countries.

It is important to point out that the vertical model might be highly consistent with the offshoring activities of large internationally engaged firms, but that many of the firms that are engaged in such trade do not own the foreign production facility. As made clear by the OLI framework described in this chapter's Introduction (Section 1), a firm must not only see a benefit of relocating a production process in order for it to be a multinational, but it must also find integration of that facility within the firm as superior to arm's-length contracting. If the activities that are best done in developing countries are best done at arm's-length, then those production networks will not be observed within multinational firms. We will return to this idea in Section 7 below.

6. MULTICOUNTRY MODELS

The two-country models discussed in Sections 4 and 5 isolated trade costs and comparative advantage across stages of production as determinants of multinational production. In this section we consider multicountry models that incorporate both forces. These models address the large share of affiliate sales that are exported to locations other than the source country. The third country sales of multinational affiliates are quantitatively important, accounting for roughly a third of the sales of the affiliates of U.S. multinationals (see Table 2.2). These models also highlight some of the shortcomings of two-country models by showing how the characteristics of a country's neighborhood can affect the structure of its trade and multinational activity.

We consider two approaches. The first builds on the insights of the Eaton and Kortum (2002) model that treats locations as substitutes. In this setting an American firm might choose to serve a country like Germany either by exporting from the United States, producing in Germany, or by exporting from a plant located potentially anywhere. The firm's choice will depend on the cost of production in each country, the size of trade costs between each country and Germany, and possibly the desire to concentrate production for many markets in a single location to conserve on fixed costs of production. The second approach, which is relatively less developed, treats some sets of countries as substitutes for stages of production and other sets as complements along a vertical production chain. In this setting, a firm's decision to engage in horizontal investment in one location takes into account the proximity of that location to sources of low cost intermediates.

6.1. Locations as Substitutes

Historically, the analysis of multilateral trade treated the effects of comparative advantage and trade costs on trade patterns separately because multifactor models quickly become intractable in the absence of factor prices equalization. By modeling comparative advantage as arising from stochastic Ricardian technology shocks rather than as due to relative factor abundances, Eaton and Kortum (2002) made the study of comparative advantage and trade costs in a single multicountry setting relatively tractable. Here we discuss how the insights of the Eaton and Kortum model have been applied with increasing sophistication to the analysis of trade and multinational production in a multicountry setting. As the models discussed in this section require substantial computational analysis, we sketch only their basic features and implications.

Consider a world with N countries, a continuum of industries indexed by j, and a single factor, labor. Perfect competition prevails in all markets. Each potential production location l has a labor productivity associated with production in industry j given by $\varphi_l(j)$ and (endogenous) wage rate of w_l. If the iceberg trade cost between country l and country n is τ_{ln}, then the marginal cost of serving country n from country l is $w_l \tau_{ln}/\varphi_l(j)$.[35] Naturally, each country purchases good j from the lowest cost location and its spending on that good depends on the marginal cost of provision. Because trade costs differ between bilateral pairs, the same good may be produced by multiple countries for different foreign markets.

The key insight of the Eaton and Kortum model is that if productivities across goods and across countries are random and drawn from a particular probability distribution, then aggregate bilateral trade flows between countries can be readily solved in general equilibrium. Moreover, the model relies on a small number of parameters that can be identified from data and equilibrium conditions. Eaton and Kortum parameterize this productivity as Fréchet

$$G_l(\varphi) = \exp\left(-T_l \varphi^{-\theta}\right),$$

where T_l governs the average productivity of country l (absolute advantage) and θ governs the dispersion of productivity across goods (comparative advantage). In the aggregate, this dispersion parameter governs how "substitutable" labor from each country is on the margin. It can then be shown that the probability that country l is the lowest cost supplier of any particular good to country n is

$$\psi_{ln} = \frac{T_l(w_l \tau_{ln})^{-\theta}}{\sum_{k=1}^{N} T_k(w_k \tau_{kn})^{-\theta}}, \tag{25}$$

which is also the share of country n expenditure that is spent on goods from country l. Note the sense in which θ governs the substitutability of labor from country l for labor from competing countries.

Ramondo and Rodríguez-Clare (2013) incorporate multinational production into the Eaton and Kortum model by assuming that each country receives a vector of productivity draws for each good from a multivariate Fréchet distribution where an element of the vector corresponds to a production location. A single parameter, ρ, governs the correlation of productivity draws of country i for a particular j across all possible locations.

---

[35] In the interest of simplicity, we ignore the treatment of intermediate inputs that features prominently in Eaton and Kortum (2002).

To be symmetric with the formulation of international trade costs, the authors assume that technology transfer costs from country i to country l are also iceberg and are denoted γ_{il}. When a productivity draw $\varphi_{il}(j)$ from country i in industry j is used to produce in a country l multinational production has occurred, and when that productivity draw is used to create output consumed in a country $n \neq i, l$ export platform FDI has taken place. In the paper, the authors assume that intermediate inputs from the source country are also an input into final production creating a degree of complementarity between multinational production and trade between the source and host country, while retaining the feature that production locations are substitutes for one another. Multinational production raises global output and welfare by allowing technologies to be used in their most appropriate location and by allowing technologies from productive countries to displace technologies from less technologically capable countries.[36]

Arkolakis et al. (2013) take the insights of Ramondo and Rodríguez-Clare (2013) to a parameterized version of the Melitz model. As this model fits well into the benchmark framework of Section 2, we elaborate a little more on its structure and implications. As in the Melitz model, there is one differentiated-good industry featuring increasing returns to scale ($\beta_z = 0$, and $J = 1$) and labor is the only factor. To sell its variety in a country n the firm must first incur a fixed marketing cost f_X. As in Ramondo and Rodríguez-Clare, there is a full matrix of bilateral trade and technology transfer costs τ and γ.

To develop a new variety a firm must pay a fixed entry cost f_E. Upon paying this fixed cost a firm receives a vector of productivities from a multivariate Pareto distribution where each element corresponds to a productivity in a particular market. This distribution is

$$G_i(\varphi_1, \ldots, \varphi_N) = 1 - T_i^e \left(\sum_{l=1}^{N} \left(T_l^p \varphi_l^{-\theta} \right)^{\frac{1}{1-\rho}} \right)^{1-\rho}, \tag{26}$$

with support $\varphi_l \geq (T_i^e \sum_{l=1}^{N} (T_l^p)^{\frac{1}{1-\rho}})^{1/\theta}$, $\rho \in [0, 1)$, and $\theta > \sigma - 1$. As in the case of Ramondo and Rodríguez-Clare, this distribution has a parameter ρ that governs the correlation across countries in each firm's vector of draws. The parameter T_i^e governs the average quality of draws to entrants in country i, while the parameters T_l^p govern the average quality of draws for country l.

Conditional on selling its variety in country n (i.e., its variable profits justify the fixed marketing cost) it is straightforward to show that the probability that a firm that entered in country i will produce for n in country l is

$$\psi_{iln} = \frac{\left(T_l^p \right)^{\frac{1}{1-\rho}} \left(\gamma_{il} w_l \tau_{ln} \right)^{-\frac{\theta}{1-\rho}}}{\sum_k \left(T_k^p \right)^{\frac{1}{1-\rho}} \left(\gamma_{ik} w_k \tau_{kn} \right)^{-\frac{\theta}{1-\rho}}}. \tag{27}$$

---

[36] Global gains do not ensure that all countries gain as technology transfer has terms of trade effects.

Note how similar this expression is to equation (25), the one that appears in Eaton and Kortum (2002). The numerator of this expression contains the cost components for all firms serving country n from country l ($w_l \tau_{ln}$) adjusted for the bilateral pair-specific cost of technology transfer γ_{il} from country i to country l. The denominator summarizes the common marginal cost components of all potential locations for serving country n. In this sense, geography plays an important role in the manner in which firms choose their production locations. Notice also that the combination of parameters $\frac{\theta}{1-\rho}$ captures the substitutability of each location, and that as $\rho \to 1$ locations become perfect substitutes. Finally, equation (27) summarizes not only the probability that an individual firm uses country l as a production location, but also the share of all spending of country n on goods produced by country i firms (wherever they are located) that is done by affiliates in country l. It is important to note that this is not equal to the share of country n expenditure on goods from country i, which depend on the mass of firms that endogenously *choose* to enter in country i.

By endogenizing the development of new varieties (and their technologies) through free entry, Arkolakis et al. (2013) capture many of the features of the models discussed in earlier sections but now in a multicountry setting. Countries in which entrants receive good productivity draws on average (high T_i^e) will have a comparative advantage in entry (an analog to capital or skill-abundant countries in Section 5). High levels of entry drive up wages and induce firms to produce abroad with the extent of substitution between labor of different countries determined in part by ρ. Higher trade costs discourage trade in favor of multinational production as in Section 4. The combination of fixed costs of entry combined with trade (τ) and technology transfer (γ) costs give rise to home market effects that can work in a number of ways.[37] For instance, when trade costs are large, production is attracted to large countries, thereby driving up the cost of innovation and inducing smaller countries to specialize in entry. When technology transfer costs are high, entry tends to occur in large countries as entrants are attracted by the large labor force. Given the competing forces at work in the model, the relative magnitude of the various effects depends on the model parameters including the full set of bilateral trade and technology transfer costs. The authors assess the model's empirically relevant implications by calibrating it to data on trade flows and multinational production shares across countries.

Arkolakis et al. (2013) achieve tractability by abstracting away from the fixed costs associated with production. In this sense, their model captures a proximity versus comparative advantage tradeoff but contains no fixed cost driven tendency toward concentration.

---

[37] In this respect, the model has implications that are similar to those of the knowledge capital model of Markusen (2002). In that two-country setting, comparative advantage is driven by relative factor abundances and interacts with home-market effects to determine the location of production. As is the case in the models discussed in this section, vertical (comparative-advantage driven) and horizontal (trade-cost driven) investment arise in a single framework depending on the relative size and factor abundances of countries. Finally, the knowledge capital model also delivers the possibility that countries can lose from multinational production.

Fixed costs of opening a foreign affiliate substantially complicate the analysis by making the location decisions to serve each market interdependent. For example, consider a firm that wants to sell its product in Germany and France. Minimizing marginal costs might mean selling to Germany from an Austrian affiliate and selling to France from a Spanish affiliate but the desire to concentrate production in one location that is created by large fixed costs might mean that Belgium is the best location to serve the two markets.

Tintelnot (2012) tackles these issues by further pushing the insights of Eaton and Kortum. In his model, a firm produces a continuum of products. Each time a firm opens an affiliate in a different country by incurring a fixed cost it receives a productivity draw for each of its products in that country. Now, the firm itself becomes a relevant unit of observation as the aggregation across products is at the level of the firm rather than at the level of the country. In this setting an equation of the sort of (27) now applies to the share of a firm from country i's sales to country n that are made via an affiliate in country l given the set of countries in which the firm owns an affiliate. As the firm adds more production locations, it increases its fixed costs and the new production location reduces the share of products produced at its existing affiliates. That is, new production locations are good substitutes for some products in all existing production facilities. The firm will add new production locations until the reduction in the marginal cost of providing its portfolio of products to global markets is balanced by the additional fixed costs that need to be incurred. By pushing the smoothness from the Eaton and Kortum model into the firm, Tintelnot can structurally estimate the distribution of fixed and variable costs of multinational production using firm-level data.[38] He finds that these fixed costs play a large role in the geographic structure of multinational production and are necessary to explain the magnitude of export platform sales in the data.

6.2. Locations as Complements

The previous section discussed multicountry models in which comparative advantage and trade costs were analyzed in an environment in which firms perceived alternative foreign locations as substitutes: an improvement in the attractiveness of one location would tend to induce firms to substitute away from another. This section covers a small literature that demonstrates that in many instances, sets of foreign countries may be complements in multinational production.

Multinational production is motivated by some form of marginal cost reduction relative to purely national firms. By opening a foreign affiliate a firm can avoid transport costs (horizontal or replicating strategies) or reduce the cost of a stage of production by locating near key inputs (vertical or fragmentation strategies). We show how the two types of cost reductions can be complementary: a firm that replicates production of some

---

[38] To make his model tractable, Tintelnot simplifies relative to the Melitz-style models by abstracting from fixed marketing costs in each country and free entry.

activities offshore has a strong incentive to fragment production and vice versa. We refer to firms whose global organization reflects both types of multinational production as following *complex strategies*.

The framework developed here builds on the ideas in Yeaple (2003b) that were developed further in Grossman et al. (2006).[39] We begin with the setting used to illustrate the proximity concentration hypothesis in Section 4.1.1. There are two identical countries, H and F, that are endowed with only labor. There are two goods, one differentiated ($J = 1$) and one that is homogeneous ($\beta_z > 0$). The homogeneous good is freely traded while the differentiated industry faces transport costs $\tau > 1$ in shipping final-good varieties. Now, suppose that there is a third country, which we will refer to as S, that does not consume differentiated varieties. Choosing labor in H and F as the numeraire, we assume that the wage in S, w^S, is strictly less than one because of differences in the productivity in the outside-good sector. Entry of a differentiated-goods producer can only occur in H or F and requires f_E units of labor. Each plant requires a firm to incur fixed cost f_D.

Assume that the production of varieties of the differentiated good can be fragmented into two stages. The first is the intermediate good stage which requires one unit of labor to produce one unit of a firm-specific intermediate. The second stage is assembly that can only be done in H and F. We again choose units such that one unit of labor makes one unit of assembly possible. Building a plant to produce intermediates abroad requires the firm to incur a fixed cost f_I units of labor in its home market. Finally, while the final good is expensive to ship, the intermediate input is not subject to trade costs. The technology for producing a complete final good is such that the marginal cost is equal to $1/\varphi$ when producing both stages locally in a northern country, while it is $c(w^S)/\varphi < 1/\varphi$, when obtaining intermediates from a plant located in S.

Consider a firm from H that will serve both H and F. As in Section 4, the profits from a pure export strategy and a pure replication strategy are

$$\pi_X = \varphi^{\sigma-1} B(1 + \tau^{1-\sigma}) - f_E - f_D, \text{ and}$$
$$\pi_R = 2\varphi^{\sigma-1} B - f_E - 2f_D,$$

respectively. Alternatively, the firm from H can open a plant in S to provide intermediates to its assembly plant located in H. The profits associated with this fragmenting (vertical) strategy are

$$\pi_V = \varphi^{\sigma-1} B(1 + \tau^{1-\sigma}) c(w^S)^{1-\sigma} - f_E - f_D - f_I.$$

Finally, suppose that a firm were to undertake both types of multinational production (complex FDI). In this case, the profits are

$$\pi_{VR} = 2\varphi^{\sigma-1} Bc(w^S)^{1-\sigma} - f_E - 2f_D - f_I.$$

---

[39] Similar issues arise in Ekholm et al. (2007).

It is straightforward to confirm from these equations and the assumptions over the relative costs $(1 > \tau^{1-\sigma}$ and $c(w^S)^{1-\sigma} > 1)$ that the following inequalities must hold:

$$\pi_{VR} - \pi_R > \pi_V - \pi_X \iff \pi_{VR} - \pi_V > \pi_R - \pi_X.$$

The inequalities establish that if a firm has reduced its marginal cost in serving a foreign market through horizontal investment, it will gain more from opening an intermediate producing facility in S than if it had not, and that a firm that has opened an affiliate in S to provide intermediate inputs gains more from opening an assembly plant in the other northern country than had it not opened an intermediate plant. In short, having lowered marginal cost through one type of foreign investment, the firm optimally raises its output and so gains relatively more by lowering its marginal cost through the other type of foreign investment. Grossman et al. (2006) call this mechanism a *unit-cost complementarity*. This complementarity has interesting implications. For instance, an increase in trade costs can raise the relative payoff to horizontal investment and so induce a firm that would otherwise not do any foreign investment to simultaneously invest in F *and* in S as doing so only makes sense if both are done simultaneously. Similarly, although a reduction in f_I has no direct impact on the profitability of replicating strategies relative to national export strategies, it can result in local assembly in F replacing trade with H in final goods.

There have been few empirical studies motivated by models of complex strategies perhaps in part because of the conceptual complications that the models entail. Standard empirical methods treat shocks across countries as independent, but complex models warn us that this may be problematic.[40]

7. MULTINATIONAL FIRM BOUNDARIES

So far we have reviewed theoretical frameworks that illustrate different types of gains associated with firms locating production processes in multiple countries. These models, however, cannot explain why these processes will be offshored within firm boundaries (thus involving FDI sales or foreign insourcing) rather than through arm's-length licensing or subcontracting. As such, and despite the terminology that we have used in the last two sections, these should not be viewed as *complete* theories of the multinational firm, but rather as theories of the *technological* drivers behind the international organization of production.[41] In this section, we will review complete theories of the multinational firm that attempt to also shed light on the crucial internalization decision of multinational firms, and we will also review some empirical work testing these theories.

---

[40] Baldwin and Venables (2010) suggest an even greater complication. They show that the nature of interdependency across countries hinges on the temporal sequence of production stages.

[41] Remember from Caves' (2007) definition in the Introduction (Section 1) that one needs to explain why multinational firms choose to *control* and *manage* their production establishments abroad.

The main unifying theme of the theoretical literature on multinational firm boundaries is the departure from the classical assumption of complete or perfect contracting. After all, and as first pointed out by Coase (1937), firm boundaries are indeterminate and irrelevant in a world in which transactions are governed by comprehensive contracts that specify (in an enforceable way) the course of action to be taken in *any* possible contingency that the contracting parties may encounter. In order to shed light on the internalization decision, this new literature on multinational firms and outsourcing has thus borrowed from the theoretical literature on incomplete contracts (cf., Williamson, 1975, 1985; Grossman and Hart, 1986), and has developed ways to incorporate these contracting frameworks into general equilibrium models. Different contributions emphasize different types of contractual frictions and they also adopt different approaches as to how the internalization of transactions affects these frictions. We will next discuss some of the key ideas and models in this literature.

7.1. Transaction-Cost Approaches

The transaction-cost theory of firm boundaries is based on the premise that firms will internalize particular transactions whenever the *transaction costs* associated with performing these transactions through the market mechanism are greater than within the firm (cf., Coase, 1937). The concept of transaction costs is somewhat vague, but it is often associated with inefficiencies that arise when transactions are not fully governed or secured by comprehensive contracts.[42] We will discuss below two types of inefficiencies that have featured prominently in the literature: rent dissipation and hold up inefficiencies (see Garetto, 2013, for a different perspective).

7.1.1. Licensing versus FDI: Rent Dissipation

We first illustrate the relevance of rent dissipation within the horizontal model of FDI with symmetric firms and countries in Section 4.1.1. Remember that we argued above that the profits obtained by multinational firms were given by

$$\pi_I = \varphi^{\sigma-1} B^H + \varphi^{\sigma-1} B^F - f_E - 2f_D.$$

Implicit in that computation was the notion that Home firms could fully capture the net surplus associated with selling their varieties in the Foreign market, i.e., the amount $\varphi^{\sigma-1} B^F - f_D > 0$. This is a strong assumption when considering FDI transactions, and it is even harder to swallow when modeling market transactions. To be more specific, consider a licensing arrangement. In order to secure a profit flow equal to $\varphi^{\sigma-1} B^F - f_D$, the Home firm would need to be able to costlessly contract with a Foreign licensee that would commit to producing an amount of output optimally dictated by the Home firm,

---

[42] Obviously, not all transaction costs are contractual in nature (take, for instance, the existence of taxes on market transactions).

collecting the sales revenue generated in Foreign, and handing the whole net surplus over to the Home firm, either via ex-ante transfers (before sale revenue is generated) or ex-post payments (after the revenue has been collected).[43]

In practice, various types of contractual imperfections will lead to rent dissipation and the Home firm will end up sharing rents with foreign licensees. A particularly noteworthy source of frictions stems from the (partially) nonexcludable, nonrival, and noncodifiable nature of the technology that the Home firm is attempting to sell to the Foreign firm (see Arrow, 1962; Romer, 1990). The partial nonexcludability of technology generates a risk of intellectual expropriation, which in turn typically limits the ability of the Home firm to appropriate surplus from the Foreign licensee *ex post*. The fact that the firm is selling intellectual property, a noncodifiable and nonrival good, will in turn limit the willingness of the Foreign firm to pay for the technology up-front (i.e., *ex ante*). Even abstracting from the risk of intellectual expropriation, moral hazard and private information constraints will typically also preclude full extraction of rents from licensees.

We next illustrate this rent dissipation phenomenon below with a simple model inspired by the work, among others, of Ethier (1986), Horstmann and Markusen (1987b), and Ethier and Markusen (1996). With that in mind, let us return to the Horizontal FDI model with symmetric countries, but now allow firms the option of servicing the foreign market via licensing. We will emphasize the contractual costs associated with licensing, so it is important to formally introduce the contracting assumptions and the timing of events. There are three relevant periods, $t = 0$, $t = 1$, and $t = 2$.

At $t = 0$, the firm that owns the blueprint for variety ω decides the mode via which it will service the foreign market: exporting, FDI, or licensing. The payoffs associated with exporting and FDI remain identical to those derived in Section 4.1.1, reflecting the notion that these strategies can be performed with no transaction costs.

When licensing is chosen at $t = 0$, the technology owner offers a contract to a licensee abroad which stipulates an initial payment at $t = 1$ (L_1) and a second payment at $t = 2$ (L_2). We allow this initial contract to stipulate the amount of output to be produced by the licensee, but this assumption could be relaxed, thus opening the door for the type of moral hazard effects studied in Horstmann and Markusen (1987b). In order to produce, the licensee needs to incur an overhead cost equal to f_D, just as in our Horizontal FDI model, and we assume that this fixed cost is incurred at $t = 1$. At $t = 2$, the licensee produces the good, generates sale revenue, and uses this revenue to remunerate labor and pay the technology owner the amount L_2. Ex-post payments that exceed the revenues generated at $t = 2$ are not allowed. In order to generate a nontrivial tradeoff between

---

[43] Strictly speaking, the tradeoff between FDI and exports could still be governed by (8), even when the technology owners do not capture the entire surplus, provided that the choice of FDI versus exporting is included in the ex-ante negotiations and that unrestricted ex-ante transfers between the licensee and the technology owner are allowed. As emphasized below, it is important thus to consider limitations on both ex-ante and ex-post transfers of surplus.

licensing and FDI, suppose that the marginal cost of production faced by the licensee is $1/\left(\lambda\varphi\right)$, where $\lambda > 1$.

With no transaction costs, it is clear that the technology owner could easily choose a transfer L_1, or L_2, large enough to appropriate all rents, thus making FDI dominated by this licensing strategy. Suppose, however, that due to the nonexcludable nature of the technology to produce variety ω, the technology owner cannot completely prevent the licensee from using the technology in ways that might prove detrimental to the accrual of cash flows at $t = 2$. To fix ideas, suppose that the licensee can operate the technology "on the side," thereby diverting a share ϕ of revenues. Suppose that this diversion requires a fixed cost equal to f_D associated with setting up production of a competing variety. Then, in order to avoid cash flow diversion (or technology expropriation) on the part of the licensee, the payment L_2 needs to be low enough to satisfy

$$\left(\lambda\varphi\right)^{\sigma-1} B^F - L_2 \geq \left(\sigma\phi - (\sigma - 1)\right)\left(\lambda\varphi\right)^{\sigma-1} B^F - f_D, \qquad (28)$$

where the left-hand side is the ex-post payoff of the licensee under no defection, while the right-hand side is its payoff under defection, assuming that the technology owner captures all nondiverted revenue in that case.[44]

If the above was the only source of transaction costs in the model, then a simple strategy for the technology owner would be to set $L_2 = 0$, thus ensuring that (28) is met, and then setting $L_1 = \left(\lambda\varphi\right)^{\sigma-1} B^F - f_D$, thus extracting all surplus ex ante. Suppose, however, that because of the nonrival nature of technology, the technology owner cannot credibly commit at $t = 1$ to not using his/her own technology to service the foreign market at $t = 2$ via an alternative method. To be more specific, and given our assumption that all plant fixed costs are incurred at $t = 1$, assume that the only feasible alternative method at that point is exporting. This "defection" can have a significant detrimental effect on the sale revenues obtained by the licensee at $t = 2$, particularly when given the noncodifiable dimension of technology and foreseeing a future defection on his/her part, the technology owner might be inclined to transfer an inferior version of the technology to the licensee. For simplicity, we capture this in a stark way by assuming that, by exporting at $t = 2$, the technology owner would drive licensee revenues to 0.

This limited commitment constraint on the part of the technology owner effectively hinders the ability of the technology owner to extract surplus ex ante rather than ex post. More specifically, for the technology owner not to have an incentive to defect at $t = 2$, the ex-post payment L_2 has to be high enough to guarantee that

$$L_2 \geq \tau^{1-\sigma}\varphi^{\sigma-1}B^F, \qquad (29)$$

where the right-hand side corresponds to the ex-post payoff of the technology owner when defecting.

---

[44] Equation (28) assumes that in the absence of expropriation, the choice of output maximizes total revenue net of labor costs, which is consistent with our assumptions above.

Note that both constraints (28) and (29) can only be met whenever

$$fD > \left[\tau^{1-\sigma} - \sigma\left(1 - \phi\right)\lambda^{\sigma-1}\right]\varphi^{\sigma-1}B^F, \tag{30}$$

that is when, for a given residual demand level B^F, transport costs τ are high, the scope of dissipation ϕ is low, the cost advantage λ of the licensee is large, or the defection fixed cost fD is high. Ethier and Markusen (1996) derive similar comparative statics in a far richer framework and interpret a low fD as reflecting an intensive use of knowledge (relative to physical) capital in production.

When condition (30) is satisfied, no defection will occur in equilibrium and the licensing option will necessarily dominate FDI at $t = 0$ since L_1 can be set equal to $\left(\lambda\varphi\right)^{\sigma-1}B^F - L_2 - fD$ thus leaving the technology owner with all the net surplus, which exceeds the same net surplus of FDI because of $\lambda > 1$. Conversely, when condition (30) is not satisfied, licensing will be a (weakly) dominated strategy because, anticipating defection on the part of the technology owner, the licensee will anticipate zero revenue ex post, and thus it will not be willing to pay for the technology upfront, leaving the technology owner with at most its payoff under exporting.

So far we have treated the residual demand term B^F as given. In our model without licensing in Section 4.1.1, we showed that the equilibrium would be one with pervasive FDI and no exporting whenever $2fD/fE < \tau^{\sigma-1}-1$. Plugging the equilibrium value $B^F = \left(fD + \frac{1}{2}fE\right)\varphi^{1-\sigma}$, we find that such an FDI equilibrium will dominate an equilibrium with licensing whenever

$$\frac{2fD}{fE} < \frac{\tau^{\sigma-1}}{\tau^{\sigma-1}\left(1 + \sigma\left(1 - \phi\right)\lambda^{\sigma-1}\right) - 1} - 1.$$

Interestingly, a low ratio of plant-specific economies of scale relative to firm-specific economies of scale (fD/fE) favors FDI not only over exporting, as in Section 4.1.1, but also over licensing. Conversely, the positive effect of trade costs on the likelihood of FDI is now less clear-cut because high trade costs relax the temptation to defect for the technology owner. Notice that when $\tau^{\sigma-1} \to \infty$, the above condition cannot possibly hold and the equilibrium is one with licensing. This provides a potential justification for our stylized Fact Three indicating that *levels* of FDI tend to diminish with distance.

Even when $2fD/fE > \tau^{\sigma-1} - 1$, so FDI is dominated by exporting, licensing can still emerge in equilibrium when (30) holds and provided that λ is high enough. In this case too, licensing becomes more appealing, the higher are trade frictions τ and the cost advantage λ of licensees.[45]

---

[45] The precise condition under which licensing dominates exporting is given by

$$\frac{\lambda^{\sigma-1} - \tau^{1-\sigma}}{\left(1 + \tau^{1-\sigma}\right)}\left(\frac{fE}{fD} + 1\right) < 1.$$

It is worth outlining some additional results that obtain when incorporating country asymmetries and firm heterogeneity in the model above. For the sake of brevity, we will focus only on the choice between FDI and licensing and will treat factor prices and demand levels as given. Consider first the case of wage differences across countries. Denoting by w^H and w^F, the wage at Home and in Foreign, respectively, condition (30) now becomes

$$f_D > \left[\left(\tau w^H \right)^{1-\sigma} - \sigma \left(1 - \phi \right) \lambda^{\sigma-1} \left(w^F \right)^{1-\sigma} \right] \varphi^{\sigma-1} B^F,$$

which preserves the same comparative statics as before, but notice that the right-hand side is now also decreasing in w^H and increasing in w^F. Intuitively, higher Home wages relax the incentive compatibility constraint for the technology owner by making exporting less profitable, while lower Foreign wages relax the licensee's incentive to misbehave by increasing the profitability of cooperating with the technology owner. An implication of this result is that the larger are wage differences across countries, the more likely that licensing will dominate FDI, a result that very much resonates with those obtained by Ethier (1986) and Ethier and Markusen (1996). It thus follows that in horizontal FDI models, both the location and the internalization decisions work against the prevalence of MNEs when relative factor endowment differences are high.

Next consider the choice between FDI and licensing when technology owners within sectors differ in their productivity levels, while sharing a common residual demand level as captured by B^F. Then direct inspection of (30) reveals that there exists a productivity threshold φ^L, such that all firms with productivity φ above φ^L will prefer FDI to licensing, while all firms with productivity below φ^L will prefer licensing to FDI. This result obtains because we have modeled defection as entailing a fixed cost f_D, and thus the no defection constraint will tend to be more binding for large firms than for small firms. Introducing a fixed cost of exporting f_X paid by the technology owner at $t = 2$ upon defecting would generate the same exact sorting of firms between the licensing and FDI modes and would lead to a higher threshold productivity φ^L.[46]

7.1.2. Outsourcing versus FDI: Hold Up Inefficiencies

We next illustrate another source of transaction costs within the Ricardian, one-factor version of Helpman's (1984) vertical FDI model developed in Section 5.3. There we argued a firm may find vertical FDI appealing when its productivity is high and when the Home wage is sufficiently higher than the foreign wage. Vertical FDI yields a profit

---

Note also that when considering licensing as a deviation from an all exporting equilibrium, the equilibrium residual demand term B^F is given in (6), but this has no qualitative effect on how parameters affect the likelihood of licensing dominating FDI.

[46] In fact, the condition becomes identical to (30) except with $f_D + f_X$ on the left-hand side of the inequality.

level (net of entry costs) equal to

$$\pi_I\left(\varphi\right) = \varphi^{\sigma-1}\left(B^H + B^F\right)\left(\left(w^H\right)^{\eta}\left(\tau w^F\right)^{1-\eta}\right)^{1-\sigma} - w^H f_I.$$

For the Home firm to actually appropriate this entire profit flow, however, it is important that an initial contract stipulates precisely the quantity and characteristics (quality, compatibility,...) of the inputs produced in the foreign manufacturing plant, while including payments that transfer all the net surplus to the Home firm. Again, these are strong assumptions in internalized vertical relationships but they are simply untenable in arm's-length vertical transactions. The seminal work of Williamson (1985) has demonstrated that contractual gaps or incompleteness (and the associated renegotiation or "fine-tuning" of contracts) create inefficiencies in situations in which the parties involved in a transaction undertake relationship-specific investments or use relationship-specific assets, a realistic characteristic of offshoring relationships. Intuitively, specificity implies that, at the renegotiation stage, parties cannot costlessly switch to alternative trading partners and are partially locked into a bilateral relationship. Williamson (1985) illustrates how this so-called *fundamental transformation* is a natural source of ex-post inefficiencies (e.g., inefficient termination or execution of the contract) as well as ex-ante or hold-up inefficiencies (e.g., suboptimal provision of relationship-specific investments).

We next develop a simple model, along the lines of Grossman and Helpman (2002), that formalizes some of these insights within the vertical fragmentation model developed in Section 5.3.[47] Consider then the same model as in Section 5.3, but now allow for the possibility that the manufacturing stage of production is outsourced, rather than integrated. The main benefit of outsourcing is that it avoids "governance costs" and thus entails lower costs of production. To be more precise, we assume that marginal costs are lower by a factor $\lambda > 1$ under outsourcing, and that the fixed costs satisfy $f_{DO} < f_{DV}$ and $f_{IO} < f_{IV}$, where the subscripts D and I denote Domestic sourcing and International sourcing, respectively, while the subscripts O and V refer to Outsourcing and Vertical integration, respectively. In Section 5.3, where all transactions were integrated, we used the simpler notation $f_{DV} = f_D$ and $f_{IV} = f_I$.

As in all contracting models, it is important to be explicit about the timing of events and the space of contracts available to agents. The model features two types of agents: headquarters H and operators of manufacturing facilities M. We shall now distinguish between four distinct periods, $t = 0, t = 1, t = 2$, and $t = 3$.

At $t = 0$, the firm observes its productivity φ, decides whether it wants to have the manufacturing part of production be done at Home or in Foreign, and whether to have it done inhouse or at arm's-length. At this stage too, all fixed costs are incurred and headquarter services h are produced. At $t = 0$, H anticipates that domestic vertical

---

[47] Some of the ideas to be formalized were also present in the work of McLaren (2000), but it is harder to map his model to the type of CES frameworks we have been restricting ourselves to in this survey.

integration and foreign vertical integration (or FDI) will be associated with the payoffs derived in Section 5.3 (see equations (22) and (23)), so below we focus on characterizing behavior in stages $t = 1$, $t = 2$, and $t = 3$ for the case of domestic and foreign outsourcing.

Under outsourcing, at $t = 1$, the headquarter H offers an initial (or ex ante) contract to a potential manufacturer for the provision of the input m. The simplest way to illustrate the effects of contractual frictions on outsourcing is to assume that the ex-ante contract is *totally incomplete* in the sense that no aspect of production can be specified in the contract. This is obviously a strong assumption, but it can easily be relaxed. The important thing is that the initial contract cannot fully discipline the behavior of agents during the production stage. The only contractible in the initial contract is a lump-sum transfer between the two agents.

At $t = 2$, M undertakes the investments necessary to produce the manufacturing input m. Because these investments are not disciplined by the initial contract, they will necessarily be set to maximize M's private (ex-post) return from them.

Once the production of m is finalized, H and M sit down at $t = 3$ to (re-)negotiate a transaction price for the manufacturing services provided by M to H. Sale revenue is generated immediately (or shortly) after an agreement between H and M has been reached, and the receipts are divided between the agents according to the negotiated agreement. As is standard in the literature, we characterize this ex-post bargaining, using the symmetric Nash Bargaining solution and assume symmetric information between H and M at this stage. This leaves H and M with their outside options plus a share of the ex-post gains from trade (i.e., the difference between the sum of the agent's payoffs under trade and their sum under no trade). As pointed out by Williamson (1985), the fact that the division of surplus is determined ex post (after investments have been incurred) rather than ex ante becomes significant only when investments are (partly) relationship specific, so that their value inside the relationship is higher than outside of it.

In the global sourcing environments that concern us here, there are two natural sources of "lock in" for manufacturers. First, manufacturing inputs are often customized to their intended buyers and cannot easily be resold at full price to alternative buyers; and second, even in the absence of customization, search frictions typically make separations costly for both H and M. A simple way to capture these considerations in the model above is to assume that if the contractual relationship between the two parties breaks down, (i) H does not have time to turn to an alternative M for the provision of m (and is thus left with nothing), and (ii) M can resort to a secondary market but there he/she would only be able to secure a payoff equal to a share $1 - \phi < 1$ of the revenue generated when combining m with H's headquarter services. The higher is ϕ, the higher the degree of specificity of M's investments.

Solving for the subgame perfect equilibrium of this game under the assumption that arm's-length transactions are "totally incomplete" regardless of the location of M, we have that the profits obtained by H under domestic outsourcing and foreign (or offshore) outsourcing are given by

$$\pi_{DO}\left(\varphi\right) = \varphi^{\sigma-1}\left(B^H + B^F\right)\left(w^H\right)^{1-\sigma}\lambda^{\sigma-1}\Gamma_O - w^H f_{DO}, \qquad (31)$$

and

$$\pi_{IO}\left(\varphi\right) = \varphi^{\sigma-1}\left(B^H + B^F\right)\left(\left(w^H\right)^\eta\left(\tau w^F\right)^{1-\eta}\right)^{1-\sigma}\lambda^{\sigma-1}\Gamma_O - w^H f_{IO}, \qquad (32)$$

respectively, where

$$\Gamma_O = \left(\frac{\sigma - (\sigma-1)\left(1-\frac{1}{2}\phi\right)(1-\eta)}{\sigma - (\sigma-1)(1-\eta)}\right)^{\sigma-(\sigma-1)(1-\eta)}\left(1 - \frac{1}{2}\phi\right)^{(1-\eta)(\sigma-1)} < 1. \quad (33)$$

These expressions are analogous to the insourcing ones in (22) and (23), except for the lower fixed costs, the terms with $\lambda > 1$ capturing the (governance) cost advantage of outsourcing, and the term $\Gamma_O < 1$, which reflects the transaction costs due to incomplete contracting associated with market transactions. Straightforward differentiation indicates that Γ_O is decreasing in the degree of specificity ϕ and reaches a value of 1 when ϕ goes to 0 and there is no specificity. Consequently, outsourcing will tend to dominate integration for low levels of specificity and large values of λ, while integration will instead tend to dominate outsourcing for high values of specificity ϕ and for λ close enough to 1.

Furthermore, cumbersome differentiation (see the Online Appendix) demonstrates that Γ_O in (33) is a strictly increasing function of η, and thus the transaction costs of using the market are particularly high when the input m is relatively important in production. The result is intuitive given that the source of transaction costs is the underinvestment in m, and it suggests a higher relative profitability of outsourcing in headquarter intensive sectors.

So far we have focused on studying how the different parameters of the model shape the profitability of a firm when using alternative organizational models, while treating the equilibrium demand levels B^H and B^F as given. The simplest way to close the model is by assuming that all Home firms have the same productivity level φ and that free entry brings profits down to zero. We will introduce intraindustry heterogeneity in productivity in the next section on property-rights models. With homogeneity, in any generic equilibrium all firms choose the same organizational form. Furthermore, for w^H/w^F sufficiently high, the equilibrium is necessarily one with all firms offshoring in Foreign, with these firms optimally choosing outsourcing whenever

$$\frac{f_{IV}}{f_{IO}}\lambda^{\sigma-1}\Gamma_O > 1,$$

while choosing vertical FDI whenever this inequality is reversed. From our previous discussion it thus follows that the likelihood of *internalized* fragmentation is increasing in the degree of specificity ϕ, and decreasing in the governance costs λ and headquarter intensity η. Introducing intraindustry heterogeneity generates analogous comparative static results regarding the share of offshoring firms and activity associated with vertical FDI, except for a subtle counterbalancing force of headquarter intensity that will be discussed in the next section on property-rights models (see footnote 55).

Although we have drawn inspiration from the work of Grossman and Helpman (2002) in developing the model above, it is important to point out some interesting features of their framework that we have left out.[48] Most notably, key to their analysis are search frictions, which we ruled out above by assuming that when a firm chooses outsourcing instead of integration, it can simply post a contract and pick an operator M from the set of firms applying to fulfill the order. Grossman and Helpman (2002) instead assume that the matching between stand-alone H agents and M operators is random and depends on the relative mass of each type of agent looking for matches. Furthermore, once a match is formed, agents are not allowed to exchange transfers prior to production. Other things equal, it is clear that these features will tend to reduce the attractiveness of outsourcing vis-à-vis integration, even holding constant supplier investments. Intuitively, search frictions and the lack of transfers inhibit the ability of H producers to fully capture the rents generated in production relative to a situation in which they can make take-it-or-leave-it offers to a perfectly elastic supply of M operators. Search frictions can generate much more subtle and interesting results when allowing the matching function governing the search process to feature increasing returns to scale. In such a case, Grossman and Helpman (2002) show that there may exist multiple equilibria with different organizational forms (or industry systems) applying in ex-ante identical countries or industries. Furthermore, the likelihood of an equilibrium with outsourcing is enhanced by an expansion in the market size, which increases the efficiency of matching in the presence of increasing returns to scale in the matching function.

A previous paper by McLaren (2000) also provided an alternative framework in which the organizational decisions of firms within an industry exerted externalities on the decisions of other firms in the industry. Rather than assuming a search/congestion externality, McLaren (2000) focuses on the implications of market thickness on the ex-post determination of the division of surplus between H and M agents. In his framework, the thicker is the market for inputs, the larger is the ex-post payoff obtained by M producers which in turn alleviates hold-up inefficiencies. Crucially, however, the thickness of the market for inputs depends in turn on the extent to which firms rely on outsourcing rather than integration, since only outsourcers enter that market. McLaren (2000) demonstrates too

---

[48] In certain respects, the framework above is much richer than that in Grossman and Helpman (2002), since they focused on a closed-economy model with no producer heterogeneity and with no headquarter investments, or $\eta = 0$ in the model above. The Grossman and Helpman (2002) setup was later extended by the authors to open-economy environments with cross-country variation in the degree of contractibility of inputs in Grossman and Helpman (2003) and Grossman and Helpman, 2005.

the possibility of multiple equilibria and shows that trade opening, by thickening the market for inputs, may lead to a worldwide move toward more disintegrated industrial systems, thus increasing world welfare and leading to gains from trade quite different from those emphasized in traditional trade theory.[49]

7.2. The Property-Rights Approach

The transaction-cost theory of firm boundaries has enhanced our understanding of the sources and nature of inefficiencies that arise when transacting via the market mechanism, but it sheds little light on the limits or costs of vertically or laterally integrated transactions. Transaction-cost models appeal to some vague notion of "governance costs" to deliver a nontrivial tradeoff in internalization decisions, but these governance costs are treated as exogenous parameters and thus orthogonal to the sources of transaction costs in market transactions. The property-rights theory of the firm, as first exposited in Grossman and Hart (1986), and further developed in Hart and Moore (1990) and Hart (1995), has convincingly argued that this approach is unsatisfactory. After all, intrafirm transactions are not secured by all-encompassing contracts and there is no reason to assume that relationship specificity will be any lower in integrated relationships than in nonintegrated ones. For these reasons, opportunistic behavior and incentive provision are arguably just as important in within-firm transactions as they are in market transactions.

If one accepts the notion that within-firm transactions typically entail transaction costs and that the source of these transaction costs is not too distinct from those in market transactions, then a natural question is: what defines then the boundaries of the firm? From a legal perspective, integration is associated with the ownership (via acquisition or creation) of nonhuman assets, such as machines, buildings, inventories, patents, copyrights, etc. The central idea of the property-rights approach of Grossman, Hart, and Moore is that internalization matters because ownership of assets is a source of power when contracts are incomplete. More specifically, when parties encounter contingencies that were not foreseen in an initial contract, the owner of these assets naturally holds *residual* rights of control, and he or she can decide on the use of these assets that maximizes his/her payoff at the possible expense of that of the integrated party. Grossman and Hart (1986) then show that in the presence of relationship-specific investments, these considerations lead to a theory of the boundaries of the firm in which both the benefits and the costs of integration are endogenous. In particular, vertical integration entails endogenous (transactions) costs because it reduces the incentives of the integrated firm to make investments that are partially specific to the integrating firm, and that this underinvestment lowers the overall surplus of the relationship.

---

[49] Another aspect studied by both the McLaren (2000) and Grossman and Helpman (2002) papers but ignored in our discussion above is the choice by M producers of the degree to which they customize their intermediate products to their intended buyers (see also Qiu and Spencer, 2002, and Chen and Feenstra, 2008).

The property-rights theory of the firm has featured prominently in the international trade literature in recent years, starting with the work of Antràs (2003). The vast majority of applications of the property-rights approach have focused on the type of vertical integration decisions inherently associated with vertical FDI models, rather than with lateral integration decisions of the type emphasized in the FDI versus licensing literature (an exception is Chen et al., 2012).

Let us thus go back to our Ricardian, one-factor, vertical FDI model first exposited in Section 5.3. As in Section 7.1.2, we maintain the assumption that when transacting at arm's-length, only "totally incomplete" contracts are available to agents. The key innovation in this section is that integrated transactions also entail transaction costs, and following Grossman and Hart (1986) and Hart and Moore (1990), the source of these costs is related to the fact that intrafirm transactions are also governed by totally incomplete contracts.[50] In particular, we shall assume that when H decides its mode of organization at $t = 0$, it anticipates playing an analogous game with a manufacturing operator M regardless of whether the operator is an employee of H or an independent contractor. Both the "outsourcing" and "integration" branches of the game feature an ex-ante contracting stage ($t = 1$), an investment stage ($t = 2$), and an ex-post bargaining stage ($t = 3$). The only difference between the two branches of the game is at $t = 3$, and more precisely, in the outside options available to H and M at this stage. Remember that in the outsourcing stage we assumed that in the absence of an agreement at $t = 3$, H was left with a zero payoff (since it could not create output without m and there was no time to find an alternative M for the provision of m), while M could sell the input m in a secondary market and obtain a share $1 - \phi < 1$ of the revenue generated when combining m with H's headquarter services. In the case of integration, the above formulation of the outside options is unrealistic. It seems natural to assume instead that H will hold property rights over the input m produced by M, and thus H has the ability to fire a stubborn operator M that has refused to agree on a transfer price (leaving M with nothing), while still being able to capture part, say a fraction $\delta < 1$, of the revenue generated by combining h and m. The fact that $\delta < 1$ reflects the intuitive idea that F cannot use the input m as effectively as it can with the cooperation of its producer, i.e., M.

In the ex-post bargaining, each party will capture their outside option plus an equal share of the ex-post gains from trade. Denote by β_k the share of revenue accruing to H at $t = 3$ under organizational form $k = V, O$. Given our assumptions, we have

$$\beta_V \equiv \frac{1}{2}\left(1 + \delta\right) > \frac{1}{2}\phi \equiv \beta_O,$$

which illustrates the notion that H holds more *power* under integration than under outsourcing.

---

[50] As discussed below, our framework could easily accommodate variation in contractibility across organizational forms but we will refrain from doing so in the spirit of the property-rights approach.

Because we have maintained our assumptions regarding the outsourcing branches of the game, the payoffs associated with domestic and offshore outsourcing are still given by equations (31) and (32), with Γ_O given in (33). Following analogous steps, we can now solve for H's profits under domestic and offshore integration in the presence of within-firm transactions costs. These are given by

$$\pi_{DV}\left(\varphi\right) = \varphi^{\sigma-1}\left(B^H + B^F\right)\left(w^H\right)^{1-\sigma}\Gamma_V - w^H f_{DV} \text{ and} \tag{34}$$

$$\pi_{IV}\left(\varphi\right) = \varphi^{\sigma-1}\left(B^H + B^F\right)\left(\left(w^H\right)^\eta \left(\tau w^F\right)^{1-\eta}\right)^{1-\sigma}\Gamma_V - w^H f_{IV}, \tag{35}$$

respectively, with

$$\Gamma_V = \left(\frac{\sigma - (\sigma-1)\frac{1}{2}(1-\delta)(1-\eta)}{\sigma - (\sigma-1)(1-\eta)}\right)^{\sigma-(\sigma-1)(1-\eta)}\left(\frac{1}{2}(1-\delta)\right)^{(1-\eta)(\sigma-1)} < 1.$$

These expressions are very similar to the outsourcing ones, except for the cost differences in fixed and marginal costs (due to factor prices and exogenous "governance costs") and for the different levels of transaction costs, as captured by the difference between Γ_V and Γ_O. A key object in governing the relative profitability of integration and outsourcing is the ratio Γ_V / Γ_O, which we can reduce to:

$$\frac{\Gamma_O}{\Gamma_V} = \left(\frac{\sigma - (\sigma-1)(1-\beta_O)(1-\eta)}{\sigma - (\sigma-1)(1-\beta_V)(1-\eta)}\right)^{\sigma-(\sigma-1)(1-\eta)}\left(\frac{1-\beta_O}{1-\beta_V}\right)^{(1-\eta)(\sigma-1)}. \tag{36}$$

Differentiating this expression with respect to η, we find that for any $\beta_V > \beta_O$, with $\beta_k \in (0,1)$ for $k = V, O$, this ratio is necessarily decreasing in η (see the Online Appendix). Hence, unlike in the transaction-cost model in Section 7.1.2, low levels of headquarter intensity are now associated with higher (rather than lower) relative profitabilities of outsourcing versus integration. This result resonates with one of the central results in the property-rights theory: with incomplete contracting, ownership rights of assets should be allocated to parties undertaking noncontractible investments that contribute disproportionately to the value of the relationship. The relative importance of the operator M's investment is captured in (36) by the elasticity of output with respect to that agent's investment, i.e., $1 - \eta$, and thus the lower is η, the higher the need for H to give away ownership rights to M by engaging in outsourcing. As argued below, the fact that headquarter intensity shapes the integration decision in opposite ways in transaction-cost and property-rights models opens the door for empirical relative evaluations of the two models.

So far we have only discussed how η affects the relative profitability of integration and outsourcing. A problematic feature of the stylized property-rights model we have developed so far is that because M is the only agent undertaking noncontractible, relationship-specific investments, transaction costs stemming from underinvestment will always be higher under integration than under outsourcing. In terms of our notation, we necessarily have $\Gamma_O > \Gamma_V$. Coupled with the presence of exogenous "governance costs" the model thus predicts that vertical integration of any sort will be a dominated strategy for H. Intuitively, M's underinvestment is minimized by conceding ownership rights to him or her, while H can still capture all the net surplus from production via ex-ante transfers in the initial contract.

In order to generate a nontrivial tradeoff between integration and outsourcing, the literature has followed one of two approaches. A first one consists in allowing some of the investments in headquarter services carried out by H to also be noncontractible. Antràs (2003) and Antràs and Helpman (2004) consider scenarios in which investments in h are completely noncontractible and are carried out at $t = 2$, simultaneously and noncooperatively with the investment in m by the manufacturing plant. Antràs and Helpman (2008) consider a more general framework with partial contractibility of both h and m and show that the ratio Γ_O / Γ_V is necessarily increasing in the relative importance of the *noncontractible* manufacturing investments, and decreasing in the importance of the *noncontractible* headquarter investments. It is then clear that higher headquarter intensity η continues to affect negatively the relative profitability of outsourcing. Importantly, however, for a high enough η, it now becomes possible for transaction costs to be higher under integration than under outsourcing. The reason for which integration is no longer a dominated strategy for H is that incomplete contracting is now generating a *double-sided* holdup problem and thus it is no longer always optimal to allocate as much ex-post bargaining power as possible to M. Even though H can extract rents upfront, it still needs to make sure that it will have high-powered incentives to invest at $t = 2$, when those initial transfers are bygones, and vertical integration provides a way to generate those high-powered incentives.

A second way to generate a nontrivial tradeoff between integration and outsourcing is to introduce restrictions on the ability of the firm to extract rents from M in the ex-ante contract. The literature often motivates these ex-ante constraints by appealing to financial constraints (see Acemoglu et al., 2007; Basco, 2010; Carluccio and Fally, 2012; Antràs and Chor, 2012), but other interpretations are possible.[51] It is intuitively clear that even when headquarter services are fully contractible, H will not necessarily want to maximize the ex-post bargaining power of M if by doing so it reduces the share of surplus it will end up with. Even though "financial constraints" affect the relative transactions costs of integration and outsourcing it can again be shown that the ratio Γ_O / Γ_V continues to be increasing in the relative importance of noncontractible manufacturing investments and decreasing in the relative importance of noncontractible headquarter services (see Antràs, forthcoming).

---

[51] See also Conconi et al. (2012) and Alfaro et al. (2010).

So far we have focused on studying how the different parameters of the model shape the decision of a firm of how to optimally organize production. In practice, and as discussed in more detail below in Section 7.3, these firm decisions are rarely observed by researchers, who instead often work with product-level datasets that aggregate a subset of these firm decisions into a particular observation. With that in mind, we next use the model to integrate over these firm decisions and characterize more formally the relative prevalence of different organizational forms within a sector or industry. The analysis is analogous to that in the vertical FDI model in Section 5.3, although matters are now a bit more involved because H is choosing from four possible organizational modes: domestic outsourcing, domestic integration, foreign outsourcing, and foreign integration.

A first obvious observation, however, is that any form of vertical integration is necessarily a dominated strategy whenever $\lambda^{\sigma-1}\Gamma_O > \Gamma_V$, given the implied efficiency advantage of outsourcing in that case and given the lower fixed costs associated with outsourcing relative to integration. In other words, equilibria with multinational activity are only possible whenever Γ_O is sufficiently low relative to Γ_V, which from our previous discussion requires high levels of headquarter intensity η. When integration is a dominated strategy, the sorting of firms into organizational forms is analogous to that in Figure 2.8 in Section 5.3, but with the most productive firms engaging in foreign outsourcing (rather than vertical FDI) and the least productive firms (among the active ones) relying on domestic outsourcing.

When $\lambda^{\sigma-1}\Gamma_O < \Gamma_V$, much richer sorting patterns can emerge. In particular, the effective marginal cost is now lower under integration than under outsourcing, but outsourcing continues to be a strategy associated with lower fixed costs, and thus a subgroup of relatively unproductive firms might continue to prefer outsourcing to integration. For certain parameter configurations, one can construct an industry equilibrium in which all four organizational forms coexist in equilibrium, as depicted in Figure 2.10. Firms with productivity $\varphi^{\sigma-1}$ below φ^D do not produce, those with $\varphi^{\sigma-1} \in \left(\varphi^D, \varphi^{DV}\right)$ outsource domestically, those with $\varphi^{\sigma-1} \in \left(\varphi^{DV}, \varphi^I\right)$ integrate domestically, those with $\varphi^{\sigma-1} \in \left(\varphi^I, \varphi^{IV}\right)$ outsource abroad, and those with $\varphi^{\sigma-1} > \varphi^{IV}$ integrate abroad, i.e., they engage in foreign direct investment. Naturally, for other configurations of parameter values, we can eliminate one or more of these regimes in equilibrium, but their ranking by productivity will not be affected.

Assuming a Pareto distribution of firm productivity with unbounded support ($G(\varphi) = 1 - \underline{\varphi}^\kappa \varphi^{-\kappa}$ for $\varphi > \underline{\varphi}$), one can explicitly solve for the relative prevalence of different organizational modes within this equilibrium and carry out various comparative statics exercises. To save space, let us focus on the implications of the model for the relative prevalence of vertical FDI versus offshore outsourcing, since this is an object that has featured prominently in the empirical literature (as discussed in Section 7.3 below). There are many ways to measure the relative extent of vertical FDI and offshore outsourcing, but it is simplest to consider the share of offshoring firms (those with $\varphi \geq \varphi^I$) that

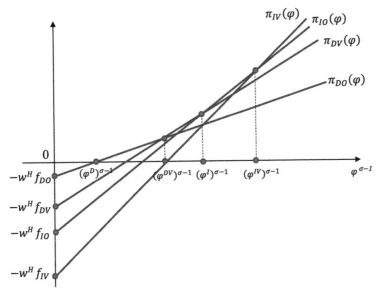

Figure 2.10 Sorting into Organizational Modes

vertically integrate. Analogous results apply when computing, for instance, the share of imports of m that are transacted within multinational firm boundaries, although these formulas become more complicated (see the Online Appendix). Manipulating (32), (34), and (35) to solve for the thresholds φ^I and φ^{IV}, and plugging $G(\varphi)$ we find that the share of offshoring firms that integrate suppliers is given by

$$\frac{N_{IV}}{N_{IV}+N_{IO}} = \frac{1-G\left(\varphi^{IV}\right)}{1-G\left(\varphi^{I}\right)} = \left(\frac{f_{IO}-f_{DV}}{f_{IV}-f_{IO}} \frac{1-\lambda^{\sigma-1}\Gamma_O/\Gamma_V}{\lambda^{\sigma-1}\Gamma_O/\Gamma_V - \left(\frac{w^H}{\tau w^F}\right)^{-(1-\eta)(\sigma-1)}}\right)^{\frac{\kappa}{\sigma-1}-1}.$$

$$(37)$$

Some interesting comparative statics follow from this expression. First, and rather obviously, the prevalence of vertical FDI versus offshore outsourcing is decreasing in λ and Γ_O/Γ_V, because high values of these make arm's-length transacting more appealing. Second, the share $N_{IV}/\left(N_{IV}+N_{IO}\right)$ is increasing in fragmentation barriers $(f_{IO}-f_{DV}$ and $\tau)$ and decreasing in the wage gap (w^H/w^F). This result is more subtle because these parameters do not affect directly the relative marginal efficiency of vertical FDI and foreign outsourcing (compare equations (32) and (35)). Intuitively, an increase in trade barriers or a decrease in the wage gap makes offshoring of any form relatively less productive, and will thus generate an *extensive margin* of trade response by which some firms will switch from foreign to domestic sourcing. Inspection of Figure 2.10 reveals, however, that those switchers are necessarily engaged in foreign outsourcing, thus generating an increase in the relative prevalence of FDI within the set of offshoring firms. Third, and unlike in the transaction-cost model above, the relative prevalence of vertical FDI is increasing in headquarter intensity η. This is for two reasons: because a low headquarter intensity shifts market share from domestic integrating firms to offshore outsourcing firms (the extensive margin of trade effect), and because it also shifts market share from FDI firms to offshore outsourcers (since Γ_O/Γ_V decreases in η). A fourth unambiguous comparative static relates to a positive effect of dispersion (a low κ) on the relative prevalence of integration: the intuition here is analogous to that in Helpman et al. (2004), which was discussed in Section 4.2.

Other contributions to the property-rights approach have suggested and formalized alternative determinants of the organizational form decisions of firms and of the relative prevalence of vertical FDI versus offshore outsourcing. Antràs and Helpman (2008) emphasize the possibility that improvements in the contractibility of manufacturing might increase the relative prevalence of FDI rather than of offshore outsourcing, contrary to what transaction-cost models would predict. Acemoglu et al. (2007) consider an environment in which the headquarters H contract with various suppliers and identify a positive effect of the degree of technological complementarity across inputs on the internalization decision of multinational firms. Antràs and Chor (2012) also consider a multisupplier environment and show that when the production process is sequential in nature, H might have differential incentives to integrate suppliers along the value chain, and thus the "downstreamness" of an input becomes a determinant of the ownership structure decisions related to that input. Basco (2010) and Carluccio and Fally (2012) find that multinationals are more likely to integrate suppliers located in countries with poor financial institutions, and that the effect of financial development should be especially large when trade involves complex goods. The insights of the property-rights theory have also been applied to dynamic, general-equilibrium models of international trade with the goal of understanding how ownership decisions vary along the life-cycle of a product or input (see Antràs, 2005).[52]

7.3. Empirical Evidence

Empirically testing models of the various determinants of the internalization decision of multinational firms poses at least two important challenges. First, data on the internalization decisions of multinational firms are not readily available. The existing datasets on the operations of multinational firms generally contain only limited information on their market transactions, and even less is known about arm's-length exchanges that do not involve multinational firms on either side. A second concern in testing theories of internalization is that the predictions from these theories are associated with subtle features of the environment—such as rent dissipation, relationship-specificity, contractibility, or the

[52] The transaction-cost model has also been applied to dynamic endogenous-growth models of the FDI versus licensing choice. See Glass and Saggi (2002) for a particular example and Saggi (2002) for a broader review of this literature.

relative intensity of distinct noncontractible, and relationship-specific investments—that are generally unobservable in the data (see Whinston, 2003).

The empirical literature on multinational firm boundaries has circumvented the first limitation in two ways. A first approach, featuring prominently in the international business literature, consists in employing unique datasets containing a small sample of internalization decisions of multinational firms in certain industries and countries.[53] A second empirical approach to the study of multinational firm boundaries relies on indirect inference based on official import and export merchandise trade statistics, which in some countries identify whether transactions involve related or nonrelated parties. Although most applications of this second approach rely on product- and country-level tests, some recent contributions have made use of fairly representative firm-level datasets that contain detailed information on the sourcing strategies of firms in different countries. By their nature, the data are better suited to testing models of the FDI versus outsourcing decision underlying vertical models of multinational firms, than to testing "horizontal" models of multinational firm boundaries.

Some of the key contributions to this second approach (see Nunn and Trefler, 2008, 2013; Bernard et al., 2010; Antràs and Chor, 2012) have employed the "U.S. Related Party Trade" data collected by the U.S. Bureau of Customs and Border Protection, and have more specifically studied the determinants of the variation in the share of intrafirm imports in total U.S. imports across products and exporting countries. Underlying these tests is the notion that if goods in a particular product category originating from a particular country tend to be exported to the United States within firm boundaries, then one can infer that U.S. firms in that sector tend to find it optimal to internalize purchases of goods from those countries, or alternatively that firms in the exporting country choose to internalize their sales of those goods to the United States. These tests are well grounded in theory, since the new vintage models of the internalization decision featuring intraindustry heterogeneity deliver predictions about precisely the determinants of the cross-sectional variation in the share of internalized transactions within a sector, as illustrated above in Section 7.2.

Even after accepting that the share of intrafirm imports provides a valid empirical proxy for the relative prevalence of integration and outsourcing in vertical models of internalization, there still remains the issue of how to proxy for the various determinants of this share, as identified by these models. This is the second main challenge facing this line of empirical work, as mentioned above. For instance, one of the central results of the property-rights theory is that the prevalence of integration should be higher in headquarter intensive sectors, that is, in sectors where noncontractible, relationship-specific investments carried out by headquarters are disproportionately more important than

---

[53] For instance, Davidson and McFetridge (1984) studied 1,376 internal and arm's-length transactions involving high-technology products carried out by 32 U.S.-based multinational enterprises between 1945 and 1975. See also Mansfield et al. (1979), Mansfield and Romeo (1980), and Kogut and Zander (1993) for related contributions.

those undertaken by suppliers. A key question is then: how does one measure headquarter intensity in the data? Similar difficulties arise when considering the measurement of parameters governing the degree of relationship-specificity and of contractibility, which were shown above to crucially affect the incentives to integrate suppliers, and in some cases, differently so in transaction-cost and property-rights model.

Following Antràs (2003), a widely used proxy of headquarter intensity is a measure of capital intensity, such as the ratio of physical capital to employment. This approach is justified within Antràs's (2003) stylized model, which features two factors of production, physical capital and labor, and where it is assumed that production of headquarter services is more capital intensive than that of manufacturing, with all investments in his framework being noncontractible and fully relationship-specific. As pointed out by Nunn and Trefler (2013), the latter assumption is unrealistic, since standard measures of capital intensity instead embody several investments that are fairly easy to contract on or that are not particularly relationship-specific. More specifically, one would expect investments in specialized equipment to be much more relevant for the integration decision than investments in structures or in nonspecialized equipment (such as automobiles or computers), which tend to lose little value when used outside the intended production process. Measures of R&D intensity, such as the ratio of R&D expenditures over sales, have also been suggested as appropriate proxies for headquarter intensity (see for instance, Yeaple, 2006, or Nunn and Trefler, 2013), given that these expenditures tend to be carried out by headquarters (see our Fact Five in Section 2) and given that they are hard to contract on. Finally, and for analogous reasons, skill intensity (the ratio of nonproduction worker to production worker employment) is sometimes posited as an alternative proxy for headquarter intensity.

The first three columns of Table 2.5 report the effect of these proxies for headquarter intensity on the share of U.S. intrafirm imports. The trade dataset is disaggregated at the six-digit NAICS level and covers the period 2000–2011. Column 1 reports a positive and highly statistically significant correlation of the intrafirm trade share with R&D intensity and physical capital intensity.[54] Column 2 demonstrates that the physical capital intensity effect is explained by spending on equipment and not structures, while column 3 further disaggregates capital expenditures and shows that the effect of capital equipment is not driven by expenditures on computers and data processing equipment or on automobiles and trucks, consistent with the findings of Nunn and Trefler (2013). In column 4, we further exploit the available variation in the intrafirm import share across source countries and run the same specification as in column 3 but with country-year fixed effects.

Put together, the results in columns 1 through 4 of Table 2.5 demonstrate the existence of a significant and robust positive relationship between the importance of

---

[54] See the Online Appendix for details on the variables used. We add 0.001 to R&D intensity before taking logarithms to avoid throwing away a large number of observations with zero R&D outlays.

Table 2.5 The Determinants of the U.S. Intrafirm Import Share

Dep. Var.: $\frac{\text{Intrafirm Imports}}{\text{Total Imports}}$	(1)	(2)	(3)	(4)	(5)	(6)	(7)	(8)
Log (R&D/Sales + 0.001)	0.33**	0.32**	0.25**	0.09**	0.08**	0.09**	0.07**	0.06*
	[0.05]	[0.05]	[0.06]	[0.02]	[0.02]	[0.02]	[0.02]	[0.03]
Log (Skilled/Unskilled)	0.10	0.16*	0.14	0.07*	0.07*	0.01	0.03	0.03
	[0.07]	[0.07]	[0.11]	[0.029]	[0.029]	[0.02]	[0.03]	[0.03]
Log (Capital/Labor)	0.28**							
	[0.05]							
Log (Buildings/L)		-0.23**	-0.11	-0.14**	-0.14**	-0.08*	-0.10**	-0.05
		[0.10]	[0.09]	[0.03]	[0.03]	[0.03]	[0.04]	[0.04]
Log (Equipment/L)		0.46**						
		[0.09]						
Log (Autos/L)			-0.24**	-0.08**	-0.07**	-0.05**	-0.07**	-0.07**
			[0.06]	[0.02]	[0.02]	[0.01]	[0.02]	[0.02]
Log (Computer/L)			0.12	0.05	0.03	0.06*	0.05	0.02
			[0.10]	[0.03]	[0.03]	[0.03]	[0.03]	[0.04]
Log (Other Eq./L)			0.39**	0.14**	0.17**	0.13**	0.17**	0.13**
			[0.09]	[0.03]	[0.03]	[0.03]	[0.04]	[0.04]
Seller Contractibility					-0.05*	0.05**	0.05**	0.05
					[0.02]	[0.03]	[0.03]	[0.03]
Buyer Contractibility						-0.11**	-0.09**	-0.12**
						[0.02]	[0.03]	[0.03]
Buyer Productivity Dispersion								0.03
								[0.03]
Freight Costs								-0.05**
								[0.01]
Tariffs								-0.02**
								[0.000]
Headquarter controls	Seller	Seller	Seller	Seller	Seller	Buyer	Buyer	Buyer
Restricted Sample	No	No	No	No	No	No	Yes	Yes
Observations	2,888	2,888	2,888	214,694	214,694	227,829	85,691	55,161
R-Squared	0.28	0.30	0.35	0.18	0.18	0.18	0.16	0.20

Standard errors clustered at the industry level are in brackets.
*Significant at 5%
**At 1%.
Columns 1–3 include year fixed effects. Columns 4–8 include country-year fixed effects.

relatively noncontractible investments by headquarters and the prevalence of within-firm import transactions. The literature has generally interpreted this finding as an empirical validation of the property-rights model in Section 7.2, but one should be cautious in interpreting these results since these patterns are not necessarily inconsistent with alternative theories of firm boundaries, such as the transaction-cost model in Section 7.1.2.[55] Similarly, the significance of R&D or skill intensity for the integration decision of multinational firms could be viewed as a validation of transaction-cost theories that emphasize the importance of the nonexcludable nature of knowledge in shaping multinational firm boundaries, with intrafirm trade being simply a manifestation of complex FDI strategies.

A particularly promising way to discriminate between the property-rights theory of the multinational firm and alternative theories of firm boundaries consists in exploiting the implications of the theory for the effect of contractibility on the share of intrafirm trade. In the property-rights model, the effect of contractibility on the prevalence of integration depends crucially on the degree to which contractual incompleteness stems from noncontractibilities in the inputs controlled by the final-good producer or by his or her suppliers. Conversely, in transaction-cost models, any type of improvement in contractibility would be associated with a lower need to integrate and, in industry equilibrium, with a lower share of intrafirm imports.

Column 5 of Table 2.5 indicates that adding this standard measure of contractibility (in particular, one minus the Nunn (2007) measure) to the previous empirical model suggests a negative and statistically significant effect of contractibility on the prevalence of intrafirm trade. Similar results are reported by Bernard et al. (2010) using an alternative measure of contractibility based on the idea that contracting is likely to be easier for products passing through intermediaries such as wholesalers. The observed negative correlation between the share of intrafirm trade and contractibility is intuitively in line with what one would expect from transaction-cost models of firm boundaries.

A caveat of the previous results is that all the industry controls are constructed using data related to the *selling* industry, i.e., of the good or sector being imported into the United States. In assessing the effects of headquarter intensity this may be problematic when the headquarters are based in the U.S. and import intermediate inputs under an industry classification different from their main line of business. In such a case, a more appropriate approach is to construct measures of headquarter intensity of the *buying* industry. Unfortunately, the U.S. Census Related Party data, and publicly available trade statistics more generally, do not contain information on the industry

---

[55] In Section 7.1.2, we emphasized that a higher value of η reduces the level of transaction costs (i.e., increases Γ_O) and thus makes FDI less appealing relative to foreign outsourcing. But with intraindustry heterogeneity, the extensive margin effect illustrated in Figure 2.10 would apply also in a transaction-cost model and a higher η would shrink the set of firms outsourcing abroad, thereby increasing the relative prevalence of FDI on this account. The balance of these two effects is generally ambiguous.

classification of the importer. Antràs and Chor (2012) compute instead measures of head-quarter intensity of the *average buying* industry using interindustry flow data from the U.S. input-output data. The exact same approach can also be used to construct measures of the (Nunn) contractibility of the average buyer of U.S. imports of particular goods. Column 6 of Table 2.5 reports the effects of buyer headquarter intensity as well as buyer and seller contractibility on the share of intrafirm imports. Comparing the results in columns 5 and 6, it is clear that the distinction between buyer versus seller headquarter intensity has little effect on the estimates—only the effect of skill intensity is significantly affected—while the distinction between buyer and seller contractibility turns out to matter much more. In particular, the coefficient estimates imply a negative and statistically significant effect of buyer contractibility and a positive and significant effect of seller contractibility. These results very much resonate with the subtle predictions of the property-rights model of Antràs and Helpman (2008), while they are inconsistent with the unambiguously negative effects of contractibility on integration predicted by transaction-cost models.

Our discussion above regarding the effects of buyer headquarter intensity and buyer versus seller contractibility relied on an interpretation of U.S. intrafirm imports as being associated with U.S. headquarters importing goods from foreign suppliers, integrated or not. An important share of these imports, however, consist of shipments from foreign headquarters to their U.S. affiliates or to U.S. unaffiliated parties, in which case the results in column 6 are harder to interpret. For these reasons, in column 7 we follow Nunn and Trefler (2008) in checking the robustness of our results to a restricted sample that better fits the spirit of the vertical models developed above. More specifically, our restricted sample regressions only include countries from which at least two-thirds of intrafirm U.S. imports reach parent firms in the U.S. (Nunn and Trefler, 2008; Table 2.5), while an industry category is included only if it contains an intermediate input product according to the categorization of Wright (2010). Although these corrections reduce our sample size in column 7 by about 60%, the results are remarkably similar to those in column 6, both qualitatively and quantitatively.

The vertical models of firm boundaries developed above generate further predictions for the relative prevalence of FDI versus foreign outsourcing. For instance, the property-rights models delivered a positive association of the share of intrafirm trade with trade barriers and productivity dispersion, and a negative association with the wage gap (w^H/w^F). Column 8 reports the effect of (buyer) productivity dispersion, freight costs, and U.S. tariffs on the share of intrafirm trade. As is clear, productivity dispersion indeed has a positive effect on the share of intrafirm trade, but the effect is statistically weak. Conversely, we find that trade costs, natural or man-made, have a negative and statistically significant effect on the share of intrafirm trade, a result that is inconsistent with the models developed in this section. Later in this section, we will revisit this issue and will provide a potential explanation for this finding.[56] As for the negative effect of relative wages, the prediction has found some indirect support from regressions that exploit the cross-country variation in the data and have shown a positive effect of a country's aggregate capital-labor ratio on the intrafirm trade share (see Antràs, 2003; Bernard et al., 2010). These cross-country specifications have also unveiled a robust positive effect of the quality of institutions on the share of intrafirm U.S. imports, a counterintuitive result from the point of view of transaction-cost theories. Of course, the standard concerns associated with cross-country regressions (omitted variable bias, endogeneity, etc.) apply here as well, so one should be cautious in interpreting these correlations as necessarily falsifying certain models.

Due to data availability, the bulk of work using product-level data to test the theory of multinational firm boundaries has employed U.S. intrafirm import data. Feenstra and Hanson (2005) and Fernandes and Tang (2010) are two notable exceptions that instead use product-level export data from the Customs General Administration of the People's Republic of China, containing detailed information on whether the exporter is a foreign-owned plant or not.

Recent contributions to the empirical literature on multinational firm boundaries have made use of a few available datasets that include *firm-level* information on the sourcing strategies of firms. Because models of the internalization decision are essentially models of firm behavior, firm-level data are an ideal laboratory to use in testing certain aspects of the models. A notable example of this is the sorting pattern in Figure 2.10, which is key to some of the predictions of these models. There is fairly robust evidence that firms engaging in foreign vertical integration (FDI) appear to be more productive than firms undertaking foreign outsourcing with no FDI (see Tomiura, 2007, for Japan, Corcos et al., 2013, for France, and Kohler and Smolka, 2009, for Spain).[57] An interesting feature of the Spanish ESEE (Encuesta sobre Estrategias Empresariales) database is that it contains information on both the domestic and foreign sourcing strategies of firms in Spain, thus permitting a fuller evaluation of the empirical relevance of the sorting pattern in Figure 2.10, which compares domestic outsourcing, domestic integration, foreign outsourcing, and foreign integration. The probability density functions in Figure 2.11 indicate that, consistently with Figure 2.10, domestic outsourcers are (on average) the least productive firms, while foreign integrators are (on average) the most productive firms. The relative ranking of domestic integrating firms and foreign outsourcing firms is instead inconsistent with the

---

[56] Díez (2010) finds instead a positive correlation between the prevalence of intrafirm trade and U.S. tariffs when working with the more disaggregated six-digit HS data, and when introducing two-digit HS fixed effects into the estimation. He also finds a negative correlation between U.S. intrafirm imports and foreign tariffs and shows that it can be reconciled with a variant of the Antràs and Helpman (2004) framework.

[57] Defever and Toubal (2007) showed that in French data, the productivity advantage of FDI firms over foreign outsourcers in a given market is reversed in some sectors, but their results are based on a sample of multinational firms, and thus selection biases may complicate the interpretation of their results (see Corcos et al., 2013).

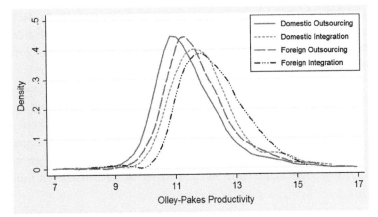

Figure 2.11 Organizational Sorting in Spain

model, and suggests that exploring the implications of a reverse ranking between these two modes is worthwhile, as it may as well help rationalize the negative effects of trade frictions on intrafirm trade shares unveiled by Table 2.5.[58]

Another appealing feature of accessing firm-level data is that they open the door for alternative ways to discriminate between models of the internalization decision by separately identifying the effect of certain variables on the intensive and extensive margin of offshoring (see Corcos et al., 2013, for a recent attempt along these lines).

8. CONCLUSION

This chapter has reviewed the state of the international trade literature on multinational firms. We have addressed to varying degrees the answers that the literature provides to three central questions. Why do some firms become multinational? Where do these firms choose to locate production? And, why do firms own foreign affiliates rather than contract with external providers? In our exposition of the main theoretical contributions of the literature, we have adapted focal models so that they fit within a single organizing framework. It is our hope that the use of consistent tools and notation across models will allow researchers to more easily tease out what is common and, more importantly, what is different about the various approaches. With respect to the empirics, we have re-estimated the econometric models of a few influential papers using the latest available data.

In reviewing a large and diverse literature one is forced to make hard decisions concerning the scope of the coverage. In the case of this chapter, we have faced not only

---

[58] Intuitively, given the sorting pattern suggested in Figure 2.11, a reduction in trade frictions will not only lead some marginal firms to shift to foreign outsourcing, but might also lead some particularly productive domestic integrating firms to switch to vertical FDI, and on that account increasing the share of intrafirm trade.

page constraints, but also constraints imposed by our determination to stick to a single organizational principle. For instance, our decision to focus on monopolistically competitive models has meant that we have entirely abstracted from research on certain strategic aspects of multinational production associated with the oligopolistic nature of certain industries in which multinational firms are pervasive. As another example, because the benchmark framework of Section 3 was built on the assumption of CES preferences, we have omitted promising recent research on the role of nonhomothetic preferences in multinational activity. Finally, we have developed models in which capital is immobile across countries and have thus not explored the interactions between multinational activity and FDI flows, an area of utmost importance that has not been much explored in the literature.

REFERENCES

Acemoglu, D., Antràs, P., Helpman, E., 2007. Contracts and technology adoption. American Economic Review 97 (3), 916–943.

Alfaro, L., Charlton, A., 2009. Intra-industry foreign direct investment. American Economic Review 99 (5), 2096–2119.

Alfaro, L., Conconi, P., Fadinger, H., Newman, A.F., 2010. Trade Policy and Firm Boundaries. NBER Working Paper 16118.

Antràs, P., 2003. Firms, contracts, and trade structure. Quarterly Journal of Economics 118 (4), 1375–1418.

Antràs, P., 2005. Incomplete contracts and the product cycle. American Economic Review 95 (4), 1054–1073.

Antràs, P., forthcoming. Grossman-Hart (1986) goes global: incomplete contracts, property rights, and the international organization of production. Journal of Law, Economics and Organization.

Antràs, P., Chor, D., 2012. Organizing the Global Value Chain. NBER Working Paper 18163, June.

Antràs, P., Helpman, E., 2004. Global sourcing. Journal of Political Economy 112, 552–580.

Antràs, P., Helpman, E., 2008. Contractual frictions and global sourcing. In: Helpman, E., Marin, D., Verdier, T. (Eds.), The Organization of Firms in a Global Economy. Harvard University Press.

Antràs, P., Rossi-Hansberg, E., 2009. Organizations and trade. Annual Review of Economics 1, 43–64.

Antràs, P., Garicano, L., Rossi-Hansberg, E., 2006. Offshoring in a knowledge economy. Quarterly Journal of Economics 121 (1), 31–77.

Antràs, P., Desai, M., Foley, C.F., 2009. Multinational firms, FDI flows and imperfect capital markets. Quarterly Journal of Economics 124 (3), 1171–1219.

Arkolakis, C., Ramondo, N., Rodríguez-Clare, A., Yeaple, S., 2013. Innovation and Production in the Global Economy. Mimeo, Penn State University.

Arnold, F., Javorcik, B., 2009. Gifted kids or pushy parents? Foreign direct investment and plant productivity in Indonesia. Journal of International Economics 79 (1).

Arrow, K., 1962. Economic welfare and the allocation of resources for invention. In: The Rate and Direction of Inventive Activity: Economic and Social Factors. National Bureau of Economic Research, pp. 609–626.

Baldwin, R., Venables, A.J., 2010. Spiders and Snakes: Offshoring and Agglomeration in the Global Economy. CEPR Working Paper 8163.

Barba Navaretti, G., Venables, A.J., 2004. Multinational Firms in the World Economy. Princeton University Press.

Barefoot, K., Mataloni, R., 2011. Operations of U.S. Multinational Companies in the United States and Abroad: Preliminary Results from the 2009 Benchmark. Survey of Current Business, November, 29–48.

Basco, S., 2010. Financial Development and the Product Cycle. Working Paper, Universidad Carlos III.

Bernard, A.B., Redding, S., Schott, P.K., 2007. Comparative advantage and heterogeneous firms. Review of Economic Studies 74 (1), 31–66.

Bernard, A.B., Jensen, J.B., Schott, P.K., 2009. Importers, exporters, and multinationals: a portrait of firms in the U.S. that trade goods. In: Dunne, T., Jenson, J.B., Roberts, M.J. (Eds.), Producer Dynamics: New Evidence from Micro Data. NBER.

Bernard, A.B., Jensen, J.B., Redding, S., Schott, P.K., 2010. Intra-firm trade and product contractibility. American Economic Review Papers and Proceedings 100 (2), 444–448.

Blonigen, B.A., Lionel, F., Nicholas, S., Farid, T., 2012. Cherries for Sale: The Incidence of Cross-Border M&A. Mimeo, University of Oregon.

Brainard, S.L., 1993. A Simple Theory of Multinational Corporations with a Tradeoff between Proximity and Concentration. NBER Working Paper 4269.

Brainard, S.L., 1997. An empirical assessment of the proximity-concentration trade-off between multinational sales and trade. American Economic Review 87(4), 520–544.

Breinlich, H., 2008. Trade liberalization and industrial restructuring through mergers and acquisitions. Journal of International Economics 76 (2), 254–266.

Buckley, P.J., Casson, M., 1976. The Future of the Multinational Enterprise. Holms and Meier, London.

Caliendo, L., Rossi-Hansberg, E., 2012. The Impact of trade on organization and productivity. Quarterly Journal of Economics 127 (3), 1393–1467.

Carluccio, J., Fally, T., 2012. Global sourcing under imperfect capital markets. The Review of Economics and Statistics 94 (3), 740–763.

Caves, R.E., 1971. International corporations: the industrial economics of foreign investment. Economica 38 (149), 1–27.

Caves, R.E., 2007. Multinational Enterprise and Economic Analysis, third ed. Cambridge University Press, Cambridge, UK.

Chaney, T., 2008. Distorted gravity: the intensive and extensive margins of international trade. American Economic Review 98 (4), 1707–1721.

Chen, M.X., Moore, M.O., 2010. Location decision of heterogeneous multinational firms. Journal of International Economics 80 (2), 188–199.

Chen, Y., Feenstra, R.C., 2008. Buyer investment. Export variety and intrafirm trade. European Economic Review 52 (8), 1313–1337.

Chen, Y., Horstmann, I., Markusen, J., 2012. Physical capital, knowledge capital and the choice between FDI and outsourcing. Canadian Journal of Economics 45, 1–15.

Coase, R.H., 1937. The nature of the firm. Economica 4 (16), 386–405.

Conconi, P., Patrick, L., Newman, A.F., 2012. Trade liberalization and organizational change. Journal of International Economics 86 (2), 197–208.

Corcos, G., Irac, D.M., Mion, G., Verdier, T., 2013. The determinants of intra-firm trade. The Review of Economics and Statistics 95 (3), 825–838.

Davidson, W.H., McFetridge, D.G., 1984. International technology transactions and the theory of the firm. Journal of Industrial Economics 32 (3), 253–264.

Defever, F., Toubal, F., 2007. Productivity and the Sourcing Modes of International Firms: Evidence from French Firm-Level Data. CEP Discussion Paper No. 842.

Desai, M., Foley, C.F., Hines, J., 2004. The cost of shared ownership: evidence from international joint ventures. Journal of Financial Economics 73 (2), 323–374.

Díez, F.J., 2010. The Asymmetric Effects of Tariffs on Intra-Firm Trade and Offshoring Decisions, Working Paper No. 10-4, Federal Reserve Bank of Boston.

Dixit, A.K., Stiglitz, J.E., 1977. Monopolistic competition and optimum product diversity. American Economic Review 67, 297–308.

Dornbusch, R., Fischer, S., Samuelson, P.A., 1980. Heckscher-Ohlin trade theory with a continuum of goods. Quarterly Journal of Economics 95 (2), 203–224.

Dunning, J.H., 1981. International Production and the Multinational Enterprise. Allen and Unwin, London.

Eaton, J., Kortum, S., 2002. Technology, geography, and trade. Econometrica 70 (5), 1741–1779.

Ekholm, K., Forslid, R., Markusen, J.R., 2007. Export-platform foreign direct investment. Journal of the European Economic Association 5 (4), 776–795.

Ethier, W., 1986. The multinational firm. Quarterly Journal of Economics 101, 805–833.

Ethier, W., Markusen, J., 1996. Multinational firms, technology diffusion, and trade. Journal of International Economics 41, 1–28.

Feenstra, R.C., Hanson, G.H., 1996. Foreign investment, outsourcing and relative wages. In: Feenstra, R.C., Grossman, G.M., Irwin, D.A. (Eds.), The Political Economy of Trade Policy: Papers in Honor of Jagdish Bhagwati. The MIT Press, Cambridge, MA.

Feenstra, R.C., Hanson, G.H., 2005. Ownership and control in outsourcing to China: estimating the property-rights theory of the firm. Quarterly Journal of Economics 120 (2), 729–761.

Fernandes, A.P., Tang, H., 2010. Determinants of Vertical Integration in Export Processing: Theory and Evidence from China. Working Paper, Tufts University.

Garetto, S., 2013. Input sourcing and multinational production. American Economic Journal: Macroeconomics 5 (2), 118–151.

Girma, S., Gorg, H., Strobl, E., 2004. Exports, international investment, and plant performance: evidence from a non-parametric test. Economic Letters 83 (3), 317–324.

Glass, A.J., Saggi, K., 2002. Licensing versus direct investment: implications for economic growth. Journal of International Economics 56 (1), 131–153.

Grossman, S.J., Hart, O.D., 1986. The costs and benefits of ownership: a theory of vertical and lateral integration. Journal of Political Economy 94 (4), 691–719.

Grossman, G.M., Helpman, E., 2002. Integration versus outsourcing in industry equilibrium. Quarterly Journal Economics 117, 85–120.

Grossman, G.M., Helpman, E., 2003. Outsourcing versus FDI in industry equilibrium. Journal of the European Economic Association 1 (2–3), 317–327.

Grossman, G., Helpman, E., 2004. Managerial incentives and the international organization of production. Journal of International Economics 63 (2).

Grossman, G.M., Helpman, E., 2005. Outsourcing in a global economy. Review of Economic Studies 72 (1), 135–159.

Grossman, G., Helpman, E., Szeidl, A., 2006. Optimal integration strategies for multinational firms. Journal of International Economics 70 (1).

Grossman, G.M., Rossi-Hansberg, E., 2008. Trading tasks: a simple theory of offshoring. American Economic Review 98 (5), 1978–1997.

Guadalupe, M., Olga, K., Catherine, T., 2012. Innovation and foreign ownership. American Economic Review 102 (7), 3594–3627.

Hanson, G., Mataloni, R., Slaughter, M., 2005. Vertical production networks in multinational firms. Review of Economics and Statistics 87 (4), 664–678.

Hart, O., 1995. Firms, Contracts, and Financial Structure. Oxford University Press, New York.

Hart, O., Moore, J., 1990. Property rights and the nature of the firm. Journal of Political Economy 98, 1119–1158.

Helpman, E., 1984. A simple theory of international trade with multinational corporations. Journal of Political Economy 92 (3), 451–471.

Helpman, E., 2006. Trade, FDI and the organization of firms. Journal of Economic Literature 44, 589–630.

Helpman, E., Krugman, P.R., 1985. Market Structure and Foreign Trade. MIT Press, Cambridge, MA (Chapter 12).

Helpman, E., Melitz, M.J., Yeaple, S.R., 2004. Exports versus FDI with heterogenous firms. American Economic Review 94 (1), 300–316.

Horn, H., Persson, L., 2001. The equilibrium ownership of an international oligopoly. Journal of International Economics 53 (2), 307–333.

Horstmann, I.J., Markusen, J.R., 1987a. Strategic investments and the development of multinationals. International Economic Review 28 (1), 109–121.

Horstmann, I.J., Markusen, J.R., 1987b. Licensing versus direct investment: a model of internalization by the multinational enterprise. Canadian Journal of Economics 20, 464–481.

Hymer, S.H., 1960. The International Operations of National Firms: A Study of Direct Foreign Investment. Ph.D. Dissertation. Massachusetts Institute of Technology, Department of Economics. Published Posthumously, 1976. MIT Press, Cambridge, MA.

Irrazábal, A., Moxnes, A., Opromolla, L.D., 2013. The margins of multinational production and the role of intra-firm trade. Journal of Political Economy 121 (1), 74–126.

Keller, W., Yeaple, S., 2013. The gravity of knowledge. American Economic Review 103 (4), 1414–1444.

Kindleberger, C., 1969. American Business Abroad: Six Lectures on Direct Investment. New Haven, London.

Klein, M., Peek, J., Rosengren, E., 2002. Troubled banks, impaired foreign direct investment: the role of relative access to credit. American Economic Review 92 (3), 664–682.

Kogut, B., Zander, U., 1993. Knowledge of the firm and the evolutionary theory of the multinational corporation. Journal of International Business Studies 24 (4), 625–645.

Kohler, W., Smolka, M., 2009. Global Sourcing Decisions and Firm Productivity: Evidence from Spain. CESifo Working Paper No. 2903, CESifo Group, Munich.

Krugman, P.R., 1979. Increasing returns. Monopolistic competition, and international trade. Journal of International Economics 9 (4), 469–479.

Krugman, P.R., 1980. Scale economies. Product differentiation, and the pattern of trade. American Economic Review 70 (5), 950–959.

Mansfield, E., Romeo, A., 1980. Technology transfer to overseas subsidiaries by U.S.-based firms. Quarterly Journal of Economics 95 (4), 737–750.

Mansfield, E., Romeo, A., Wagner, S., 1979. Foreign trade and U.S. research and development. Review of Economics and Statistics 61 (1), 49–57.

Marin, D., Verdier, T., 2009. Power in the multinational corporation in industry equilibrium. Economic Theory 38, 437–464.

Markusen, J., 1984. Multinationals, multi-plant economies, and the gains from trade. Journal of International Economics 16, 205–226.

Markusen, J., 2002. Multinational Firms and the Theory of International Trade. MIT Press, Cambridge, MA.

Markusen, J., Venables, A., 1998. Multinational firms and the new trade theory. Journal of International Economics 46 (2), 183–203.

Markusen, J.R., Venables, A.J., 2000. The theory of endowment. Intra-industry and multinational trade. Journal of International Economics 52, 209–234.

Mayer, T., Ottaviano, G., 2007. The Happy Few: The Internationalisation of European firms. Bruegel Blueprint Series, vol. III.

McLaren, J., 2000. 'Globalization' and vertical structure. American Economic Review 90 (5), 1239–1254.

Melitz, M.J., 2003. The impact of trade on intra-industry reallocations and aggregate industry productivity. Econometrica 71 (6), 1695–1725.

Mrázová, M., Neary, P.J., 2012. Selection Effects with Heterogeneous Firms. Mimeo, University of Oxford.

Mundell, R.A., 1957. International trade and factor mobility. American Economic Review 47 (3), 321–335.

Neary, P.J., 2007. Cross-border mergers as instruments of comparative advantage. Review of Economic Studies 74 (4), 1229–1257.

Nocke, V., Yeaple, S., 2007. Cross-border mergers and acquisitions versus greenfield foreign direct investment: the role of firm heterogeneity. Journal of International Economics 72 (2), 336–365.

Nocke, V., Yeaple, S., 2008. An assignment theory of foreign direct investment. Review of Economic Studies 75 (2), 529–557.

Nunn, N., 2007. Relationship-specificity. Incomplete contracts, and the pattern of trade. Quarterly Journal of Economics 122 (2), 569–600.

Nunn, N., Trefler, D., 2008. The boundaries of the multinational firm: an empirical analysis. In: Helpman, E., Marin, D., Verdier, T. (Eds.), The Organization of Firms in a Global Economy. Harvard University Press, pp. 55–83.

Nunn, N., Trefler, D., 2013. Incomplete contracts and the boundaries of the multinational firm. Journal of Economic Behavior and Organization 94, 330–344.

Ottaviano, T., Thisse, 2002. Agglomeration and trade revisited. International Economic Review 43, 409–436.

Puga, D., Trefler, D., 2010. Wake up and smell the ginseng: the rise of incremental innovation in low-wage countries. Journal of Development Economics 91, 64–76.

Qiu, L.D., Spencer, B., 2002. Keiretsu and relationship-specific investment: implications for market-opening trade policy. Journal of International Economics 58, 49–79.

Qiu, L.D., Zhou, W., 2006. International mergers: incentives and welfare. Journal of International Economics, 68, 38–58.

Ramondo, N., 2013. A Quantitative Approach to Multinational Production. Mimeo, Arizona State University.

Ramondo, N., Rappoport, V., Ruhl, K., 2012. Horizontal vs. Revisiting Evidence from U.S. Multinationals. Mimeo, Arizona State University, Vertical FDI.

Ramondo, N., Rodríguez-Clare, A., 2013. Trade, multinational production, and the gains from openness. Journal of Political Economy 121 (2), 273–322.

Romer, P.M., 1990. Endogenous technological change. Journal of Political Economy 98 (5), S71–S102.

Rugman, A.M., 1981. Inside the Multinationals: The Economics of Internal Markets. Columbia University Press, New York.

Saggi, K., 2002. Trade, foreign direct investment, and international technology transfer: a survey. World Bank Research Observer 17 (2), 191–235.

Spencer, B., 2005. International outsourcing and incomplete contracts. Canadian Journal of Economics 38, 1107–1135.

Tintelnot, F., 2012. Global Production with Export Platforms. Mimeo, Pennsylvania State University.

Tomiura, E., 2007. Foreign outsourcing, exporting, and FDI: a productivity comparison at the firm level. Journal of International Economics 72, 113–127.

Whinston, M.D., 2003. On the transaction cost determinants of vertical integration. Journal of Law, Economics, and Organization 19, 1–23.

Williamson, O.E., 1975. Markets, Hierarchies: Analysis. Antitrust Implications. Free Press, New York.

Williamson, O.E., 1985. The Economic Institutions of Capitalism, Free Press (Chapters 1–3).

Wright, G.C., 2010. Revisiting the Employment Impact of Offshoring. Mimeo, University of Essex.

Yeaple, S., 2003a. The role of skill endowments in the structure of U.S. outward foreign direct investment. Review of Economics and Statistics, 85(3): 726–734.

Yeaple, S., 2003b. The complex integration strategies of multinational firms and cross-country dependencies in the structure of foreign direct investment. Journal of International Economics 60 (2), 293–314.

Yeaple, S., 2006. Foreign direct investment, and the structure of U.S. trade. Journal of the European Economic Association 4, 602–611.

Yeaple, S., 2009. Firm heterogeneity and the structure of U.S. multinational activity: an empirical analysis. Journal of International Economics 78, 206–215.

Yeaple, S., 2013. The multinational firm. Annual Review of Economics 5, 193–217.

Zhu, S.C., Trefler, D., 2005. Trade and inequality in developing countries: a general equilibrium analysis. Journal of International Economics 65 (1), 21–48.

CHAPTER 3

Gravity Equations: Workhorse, Toolkit, and Cookbook*

Keith Head[*,†] and Thierry Mayer[†,‡,§]

[*]Sauder School of Business, University of British Columbia, Canada
[†]Centre for Economic Policy Research, London, UK
[‡]Sciences-Po, Paris, France
[§]Centre d'études prospectives et d'informations internationales, France

Abstract

This chapter focuses on the estimation and interpretation of gravity equations for bilateral trade. This necessarily involves a careful consideration of the theoretical underpinnings since it has become clear that naive approaches to estimation lead to biased and frequently misinterpreted results. There are now several theory-consistent estimation methods and we argue against sole reliance on any one method and instead advocate a toolkit approach. One estimator may be preferred for certain types of data or research questions but more often the methods should be used in concert to establish robustness. In recent years, estimation has become just a first step before a deeper analysis of the implications of the results, notably in terms of welfare. We try to facilitate diffusion of best-practice methods by illustrating their application in a step-by-step cookbook mode of exposition.

Keywords

Bilateral trade, Heterogeneous firms, Distance, Borders, Trade cost elasticity, Poisson

JEL classification codes

F1

* The chapter has a companion website, https://sites.google.com/site/hiegravity/, with an appendix, Stata® code, and related links. We thank Leo Fankhänel and Camilo Umana for outstanding assistance with the programming and meta-analysis in this chapter, Soledad Zignago for great help with providing and understanding subtleties of some of the data used, and Julia Jauer for her update of the gravity data. Scott Baier, Sebastian Sotelo, and João Santos Silva generously provided computer code. Andres Rodríguez-Clare answered many questions we had about welfare calculations but is not responsible, of course, for any mistakes we may have made. Arnaud Costinot, Gilles Duranton, Thibault Fally, Mario Larch, Marc Melitz, Gianmarco Ottaviano, João Santos Silva, and Daniel Trefler made very useful comments on previous drafts. We are especially grateful to Jose de Sousa: his careful reading identified many necessary corrections in an early draft. Participants at presentations at the Hitotsubashi GCOE Conference on International Trade and FDI 2012, National Bank of Belgium, and Clemson University also contributed to improving the draft. Finally, we thank our discussants at the handbook conference, Rob Feenstra and Jim Anderson, for many helpful suggestions. We regret that because of limitations of time and space, we have not been able to fully respond to all of the valuable suggestions we received. This research has received funding from the European Research Council under the European Community's Seventh Framework Programme (FP7/2007-2013) Grant Agreement no. 313522.

1. INTRODUCTION

As the name suggests, gravity equations are a model of bilateral interactions in which size and distance effects enter multiplicatively. They have been used as a workhorse for analyzing the determinants of bilateral trade flows for 50 years since being introduced by Tinbergen (1962). Krugman (1997) referred to gravity equations as examples of "social physics," the relatively few law-like empirical regularities that characterize social inter-actions.[1] Over the last decade, concentrated efforts of trade theorists have established that gravity equations emerge from mainstream modeling frameworks in economics and should no longer be thought of as deriving from some murky analogy with Newtonian physics. Meanwhile empirical work—guided in varying degrees by the new theory—has proceeded to lay down a raft of stylized facts about the determinants of bilateral trade. As a result of recent modeling, we now know that gravity estimates can be combined with trade policy experiments to calculate implied welfare changes.

This chapter focuses on the estimation and interpretation of gravity equations for bilateral trade. This necessarily involves a careful consideration of the theoretical under-pinnings since it has become clear that naive approaches to estimation lead to biased and frequently misinterpreted results. There are now several theory-consistent estimation methods and we argue against sole reliance on any one method and instead advocate a toolkit approach. One estimator may be preferred for certain types of data or research questions but more often the methods should be used in concert to establish robustness. In recent years, estimation has become just a first step before a deeper analysis of the implications of the results, notably in terms of welfare. We try to facilitate diffusion of best-practice methods by illustrating their application in a step-by-step cookbook mode of exposition.

1.1. Gravity Features of Trade Data

Before considering theory, we use graphical displays to lay out the factual basis for taking gravity equations seriously. The first key feature of trade data that mirrors the physi-cal gravity equation is that exports rise proportionately with the economic size of the destination and imports rise in proportion to the size of the origin economy. Using GDP as the economy size measure, we illustrate this proportionality using trade flows between Japan and the European Union. The idea is that the European Union's area is small enough and sufficiently far from Japan that differences in distance to Japan can be ignored. Similarly because the EU is a customs union, each member applies the same trade policies on Japanese imports. Japan does not share a language, religion, currency, or colonial history with any EU members either.

---

[1] Other examples of social physics include power function distributions thought to characterize incomes, firm and city sizes, and network linkages.

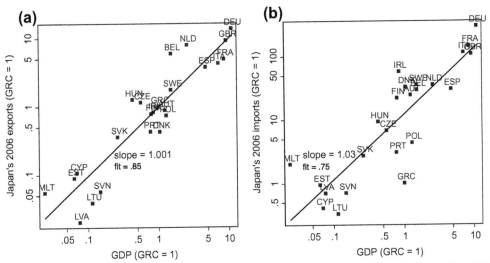

Figure 3.1 Trade is Proportional to Size; (a) Japan's Exports to EU, 2006; (b) Japan's Imports from EU, 2006. GRC: Greece

Figure 3.1(a) shows Japan's bilateral exports on the vertical axis and (b) shows its imports. The horizontal axes of both figures show the GDP (using market exchange rates) of the EU trade partner. The trade flows and GDPs are normalized by dividing by the corresponding value for Greece (a mid-size economy).[2] The lines show the predicted values from a simple regression of log trade flow on log GDP. For Japan's exports, the GDP elasticity is 1.00 and it is 1.03 for Japan's imports. The near unit elasticity is not unique to the 2006 data. Over the decade 2000–2009, the export elasticity averaged 0.98 and its confidence intervals always included 1.0. Import elasticities averaged a somewhat higher 1.11 but the confidence intervals included 1.0 in every year except 2000 (when 10 of the EU25 had yet to join). The gravity equation is sometimes disparaged on the grounds that any model of trade should exhibit size effects for the exporter and importer. What these figures and regression results show is that the size relationship takes a relatively precise form—one that is predicted by most, but not all, models.

Figure 3.2 illustrates the second key empirical relationship embodied in gravity equations—the strong negative relationship between physical distance and trade. Since we have just seen that GDPs enter gravity with a coefficient very close to one, one can pass GDP to the left-handside, and show how bilateral imports or exports as a fraction of GDP varies with distance. Panels (a) and (b) of Figure 3.2 graph recent export and import data from France. These panels show deviations from the distance effect associated

[2] The trade data come from International Monetary Fund (IMF) Direction of Trade Statistics (DOTS) and the GDPs come from World Development Indicators (WDI). The web appendix provides more information on sources of gravity data.

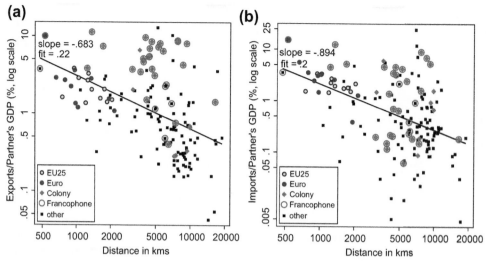

Figure 3.2 Trade is Inversely Proportional to Distance; (a) France's Exports (2006); (b) France's Imports (2006)

with Francophone countries, former colonies, and other members of the EU or of the Eurozone. The graph expresses the "spirit" of gravity: it identifies deviations from a *benchmark* taking into account GDP proportionality and systematic negative distance effects. Those deviations have become the subject of many separate investigations.

This chapter is mainly organized around topics with little attention paid to the chronology of when ideas appeared in the literature. But we do not think the history of idea development should be overlooked entirely. Therefore in the next section we give our account of how gravity equations went from being nearly ignored by trade economists to becoming a focus of research published in the top general interest journals.

1.2. A Brief History of Gravity in Trade

While economists have been estimating gravity equations on bilateral trade data since Tinbergen (1962), this work lay outside of the mainstream of trade research until 1995. One of the barriers to mainstream acceptance was the lingering perception that gravity equations were more physics analogy than economic analysis. In the first volume of this handbook series, Deardorff (1984, p. 503) characterized the "theoretical heritage" of gravity equations as being "dubious." Given the traditional importance of theory in the field of international trade, this was damning criticism. It was not entirely fair to the economists who had begun the work of grounding the gravity equation in theory long before. Savage and Deutsch (1960) contains a multiplicative model of bilateral trade published two years before the empirical work of Tinbergen (1962). Although that model was purely probabilistic, Anderson (1979) set forth a conventional economic model of gravity. The model did not penetrate the consciousness of trade economists. Leamer and Levinsohn (1995, fn. 13), write "An attempt to give a theoretical foundation by Anderson (1979) is formally fruitful but seems too complex to be part of our everyday toolkit."

By contrast with 1995, gravity is now an integral and important part of international trade. We view its recent inclusion as a core element of the field as being articulated in three distinct steps. Firstly, the "admission" wherein researchers realized there was a surprisingly large amount of missing trade, and admitted that gravity was one way to measure and explain it. Then came the "multilateral resistance/fixed effects revolution," a burst of papers that established the relationship between fixed effects in gravity and underlying theories with origins as varied as Ricardo, monopolistic competition, and Armington. The final step was one of "convergence" of the gravity and heterogeneous firms literatures.

Admission (1995): 1995 was a very important year for gravity research. In that year Trefler (1995) introduced the idea of "missing trade." A key empirical problem for the Heckscher-Ohlin-Vanek (HOV) model is that it predicts much higher trade in factor services than is actually observed. Trefler invoked "home bias" rather than distance to explain missing trade but his work pointed to the importance of understanding the impediments to trade. In a *Handbook of International Economics* chapter, Leamer and Levinsohn (1995) pointed out that gravity models "have produced some of the clearest and most robust findings in economics. But paradoxically they have had no effect on the subject of international economics." They asked provocatively, "Why don't trade economists 'admit' the effect of distance into their thinking?" Their explanation was that "human beings are not disposed toward processing numbers, and empirical results will remain unpersuasive if not accompanied by a graph." Their solution was to produce a version of Figure 3.2(a) for Germany.[3] Krugman's (1995) chapter in the same handbook also considers the role of remoteness and intuitively states why bilateral distance cannot be the only thing that matters as in the standard gravity equation (see the end of its Section 3.1.2). Krugman's thought experiment of moving two small countries from the middle of Europe to Mars provides the intuition for why we need the multilateral resistance (MR) terms that Anderson (1979) originated and Anderson and van Wincoop (2003) popularized.

One irony of the history of the gravity equation is that trade economists "discovered" the empirical importance of geographic distance and national border just as some prominent journalists and consultants had dismissed these factors as anachronisms. Thus the business press was proclaiming the "borderless world," "the death of distance," and the "world is flat" while empirical research was categorically demonstrating the opposite. McCallum (1995) used the gravity equation and previously unexploited data on interprovincial trade to decisively refute the notion that national borders had lost their

---

[3] Forty years earlier Isard and Peck (1954) had offered the same graphical device to complain about the lack of consideration for distance (space in general) in international trade theory.

economic relevance. McCallum's article not only showed the usefulness of the gravity equation as a framework for estimating the effects of trade integration policies, but also launched a literature attempting to understand "border effects." While we now think of Anderson and van Wincoop (2003) as being first and foremost a paper about the gravity methodology, it was framed as a resolution to the puzzle McCallum had exposed.

The MR/fixed effects revolution (2002–2004): With the publication of Eaton and Kortum (2002), and Anderson and van Wincoop (2003), the conventional wisdom that gravity equations lacked micro-foundations was finally dismissed. Since neither model relied on imperfect competition or increasing returns, there was no longer a reason to believe that gravity equations should only apply to a subset of countries or industries. Perhaps most importantly, these papers pointed the way toward estimation methods that took into account the structure of the models. In 2004, it became clear, with the chapter by Feenstra (2004) and the article by Redding and Venables (2004), that importer and exporter fixed effects could be used to capture the multilateral resistance terms that emerged in different theoretical models. The combination of being consistent with theory and quite easy to implement (in most cases) leads to rapid adoption in empirical work.

Convergence with the heterogeneous firms literature (2008): 2008 was the third pivotal year for research on gravity as it saw the publication of three papers—Chaney (2008), Helpman et al. (2008), and Melitz and Ottaviano (2008)—that united recent work on heterogeneous firms with the determination of bilateral trade flows. In this final step, the toolkit nature of gravity again appeared as it became a useful tool to measure the new distinction between intensive and extensive margins of adjustment to trade shocks (Bernard et al., 2007; Mayer and Ottaviano, 2007; Chaney, 2008). The "merger" of the two literatures implied changes to the way gravity equations should be estimated and to how the estimated coefficients should be interpreted. It was also a sign of the rising intellectual stature of the gravity equation that the three 2008 papers make a point of showing that their heterogeneous firms models are compatible with gravity.

Clearly, the useful tool of the early 1990s had by then become an object respected by theorists, who even tried to add to the sophistication of it. In a field that has historically been so dominated by pure theory, this sounds like the definitive recognition, which has recently been expanded further, by incorporating gravity as a central component of the theory and measurement of welfare gains from trade (Chapter 4 by Costinot and Rodriguez-Clare in this handbook probably being the best illustration).

Because none of this would probably have happened if the theoretical underpinnings of gravity had not been made clearer, we start with those in Section 2. We then turn in Section 3 to the estimation issues, to cover the many existing practices and give our views on best practice. Section 4 focuses on what has been and probably will remain the main use of gravity: a tool for quantifying the impacts of trade policies. This section focuses particularly on what recent advances mean for the implementation of those evaluations.

We finish with Section 5, covering areas of current, mostly unsettled research and progress: the frontiers of gravity equations, before concluding.

2. MICRO-FOUNDATIONS FOR GRAVITY EQUATIONS

"The equation has...gone from an embarrassing poverty of theoretical foundations to an embarrassment of riches!"

Frankel et al. (1997, p. 53)

As the quote above suggests, the conventional wisdom that gravity equations had no sound theoretical underpinnings has been forcefully dismissed. Indeed, in the 15 years following the Frankel's comment, the "embarrassment of riches" has become substantially more acute. It seems reasonable to credit the empirical success of gravity equations with attracting the attention of theorists. This section of the chapter will proceed by first defining what we mean when we use the term gravity equation and then setting out the theories that conform with the definitions. We close the theory section by summarizing successful efforts to transfer the gravity modeling techniques to interactions beyond trade in goods.

2.1. Three Definitions of the Gravity Equation

While the term gravity equation has been used to refer to a variety of different specifications of the determinants of bilateral trade, we consider three definitions to be particularly useful.

Definition 1.   General gravity comprises the set of models that yield bilateral trade equations that can be expressed as

$$X_{ni} = G S_i M_n \phi_{ni}. \tag{1}$$

The S_i factor represents "capabilities" of exporter i as a supplier to all destinations. M_n captures all characteristics of destination market n that promote imports from all sources. Bilateral accessibility of n to exporter i is captured in $0 \leq \phi_{ni} \leq 1$: it combines trade costs with their respective elasticity to measure the overall impact on trade flows. Lastly, G can be termed the "gravitational constant," although it is only held constant in the cross-section.

Definition 1 has two important features. The most obvious one is the insistence that each term enters multiplicatively. A second important feature is that this definition requires that third–country effects, if there are any, must be mediated via the i and n multilateral terms.[4] The multiplicative form derives from the original analogy with the gravity equation in physics. It is convenient because, after taking logs, equation (1) can be

---

[4] For example, ϕ_{nj} can influence X_{ni} but only by changing S_i or M_n. Thus it would be impossible for a trade agreement between j and n to reduce n's imports from i but leave all its other imports unchanged.

estimated by regressing log exports on exporter and importer fixed effects and a vector of bilateral trade costs variables. However, the multiplicative form is not necessary for estimation. Both the linear demand system used by Ottaviano et al. (2002) or the translog form used by Feenstra (2003) and Novy (2013) are relatively straightforward to estimate despite not being multiplicatively separable in the S_i, M_n, and ϕ_{ni} terms, and therefore not obeying Definition 1.[5] Thus the main reason to insist on the multiplicative form in the definition of gravity is historical usage. It is therefore possible that future work would abandon the multiplicative form and redefine gravity to allow other functional forms.

By imposing a small set of additional conditions, one can express the exporter and importer terms in equation (1)—S and M—as functions of observables, leading to a second way to define the gravity equation.

Definition 2. Structural gravity comprises the subset of general gravity models in which bilateral trade is given by

$$X_{ni} = \underbrace{\frac{Y_i}{\Omega_i}}_{S_i} \underbrace{\frac{X_n}{\Phi_n}}_{M_n} \phi_{ni}, \tag{2}$$

where $Y_i = \sum_n X_{ni}$ is the value of production, $X_n = \sum_i X_{ni}$ is the value of the importer's expenditure on all source countries, and Ω_i and Φ_n are "multilateral resistance" terms defined as

$$\Phi_n = \sum_\ell \frac{\phi_{n\ell} Y_\ell}{\Omega_\ell} \quad \text{and} \quad \Omega_i = \sum_\ell \frac{\phi_{\ell i} X_\ell}{\Phi_\ell}. \tag{3}$$

Definition 2 corresponds, as discussed below, to a surprisingly large set of models. It can be validated against alternatives, by comparing estimated fixed effects to the theoretical counterparts. Because the Φ and Ω terms can be solved for a given set of trade costs, Definition 2 allows for a more complete calculation of the impacts of trade costs changes, something we come back to in Section 4.3.

Structural gravity can be estimated at the aggregate or industry level.[6] At the aggregate level one should measure Y_i as gross production (not value-added) of traded goods (assuming X_{ni} is merchandise trade) and X_n should be apparent consumption of goods (production plus imports minus exports). However, in practice GDP is often used as a proxy for both Y_i and X_n.[7]

Definition 3. Naive gravity equations express bilateral trade as

$$X_{ni} = G Y_i^a Y_n^b \phi_{ni}. \tag{4}$$

---

[5] As we will see later, *heterogeneous firms* versions of the linear and translog models *do* fit equation (1) under Pareto-distributed heterogeneity.

[6] In a series of papers Anderson and Yotov (2010a,b, 2012) estimate structural gravity at the industry level, arguing that this practice reduces aggregation bias.

[7] The web appendix provides details on data sources for aggregate and industry level Y_i and X_n.

Definition 3 is pedagogically useful, was long viewed as empirically successful, and contains the important insight that bilateral trade should be roughly proportional to the product of country sizes. The naive gravity is at once more general and more restrictive than definitions derived from theory. The presence of $a \neq b \neq 1$ is a generalization that has been included in estimation starting with Tinbergen (1962). However, as we shall see, most theories predict unit GDP elasticities and Figures 3.1(a) and (b) suggest the data appear happy to comply (to a reasonable approximation). On the other hand, as pointed out by Krugman (1995), theoretical justifications for Definition 3 impose the implausible restriction that ϕ_{ni} is a constant. This cancels the need for multilateral terms, but cannot be reconciled with the overwhelming evidence that trade costs do vary across bilateral pairs. Baldwin and Taglioni (2007) refer to the omission of $1/(\Omega_i \Phi_n)$ in Definition 3 as the "gold medal mistake" of gravity equations, almost universally characterizing papers appearing before Anderson and van Wincoop (2003).

In the next subsections, we will consider the assumptions underlying structural gravity, before turning to detailed micro-foundations of this relationship. Then we will consider a small number of recent models that fit Definition 1, but violate Definition 2.

2.2. Assumptions Underlying Structural Gravity

Structural gravity relies on two important conditions. The first governs spatial allocation of expenditure for the importer. The second imposes market-clearing for the exporter.

Let i be the origin (exporter) and n be the destination. Importer n's total expenditures, X_n, can be thought of as the "pie" to be allocated. The share of the pie allocated to country i is denoted π_{ni}. As an accounting identity we have

$$X_{ni} = \pi_{ni} X_n,   \tag{5}$$

where $\pi_{ni} \geq 0$ and $\sum_i \pi_{ni} = 1$.

The critical requirement is that π_{ni} can be expressed in the following multiplicatively separable form:

$$\pi_{ni} = \frac{S_i \phi_{ni}}{\Phi_n},   \text{where}   \Phi_n = \sum_\ell S_\ell \phi_{n\ell}.   \tag{6}$$

The definition of Φ_n as the accessibility-weighted sum of the exporter capabilities is required to ensure that the budget allocation shares sum to one. Φ_n therefore measures the set of opportunities of consumers in n or, equivalently, the degree of competition in that market. We will see below that a wide range of different micro-foundations yield equation (6). While (6) might seem an innocuous assumption, it requires that budget shares should be independent of income. This rules out several demand systems, such as quasi-linear models with outside goods. Those models might still fit the conditions of general gravity, as is the case for Melitz and Ottaviano (2008).

A second accounting identity holds that the sum of i's exports to all destinations—including i—equals the total value of i's production, which in aggregate is just Y_i.

$$Y_i = \sum_n X_{ni} = S_i \sum_n \frac{\phi_{ni} X_n}{\Phi_n}. \tag{7}$$

Solving for S_i, one obtains

$$S_i = \frac{Y_i}{\Omega_i}, \quad \text{where} \quad \Omega_i = \sum_\ell \frac{\phi_{\ell i} X_\ell}{\Phi_\ell}. \tag{8}$$

The Ω term is familiar in economic geography as an index of market potential or access (see Redding and Venables, 2004; Head and Mayer, 2004b or Hanson, 2005). Relative access to individual markets is measured as $\phi_{\ell i}/\Phi_\ell$. Hence, Ω_i is an expenditure-weighted average of relative access. Substituting (8) into equation (6) gives

$$\Phi_n = \sum_\ell \frac{\phi_{n\ell} Y_\ell}{\Omega_\ell}, \tag{9}$$

which, once plugged back into (5), provides (2):

$$X_{ni} = \frac{Y_i}{\Omega_i} \frac{X_n}{\Phi_n} \phi_{ni}.$$

Anderson and van Wincoop (2003) assume $X_i = Y_i$ (balanced trade) and $\phi_{ni} = \phi_{in}$ (symmetric trade costs), which implies that $\Phi_i = \Omega_i$. This in turn would imply $S_i = M_i$ in the general gravity equation, leading to a symmetric gravity equation.

2.3. Main Variants of Gravity for Trade

The next step is to show the range of established theories that comply with the structural gravity assumptions. All the specifications we consider specify trade costs (transport for goods, travel for many services, search, and other transaction costs for both goods and services) using the iceberg form. Under this assumption, $\tau_{ni} - 1$ is the *ad valorem* tariff equivalent of all trade costs. Most models work with a single factor of production, denoted L. Factor income is w, and hence GDP is given by $X_n = Y_n = w_n L_n$. Below we specify the different set of assumptions characterizing each of the models, and summarize the theoretical content of S_i, ϕ_{ni}, and M_n in Table 3.1 (see page 149).

We group the models under the category "demand-side" and "supply-side." In the demand-side models the exogenous wage combined with constant returns to scale or constant markups neutralizes the supply side of the model. The models we call supply-side derivations also have demand sides but distributional assumptions used in these models (Fréchet or Pareto) cause the demand-side terms to be eliminated from the final formulation.

2.3.1. Demand-Side Derivations
CES National Product Differentiation (Anderson-Armington)

The earliest "modern" derivation of the gravity equation for trade is Anderson (1979). As in Armington (1969), each country is the unique source of each product (there is National Product Differentiation, NPD). Consumers in country n consume q_{ni} units of the product from country i. Utility exhibits a constant elasticity of substitution (CES), $\sigma > 1$, over all the national products:

$$U_n = \left(\sum_i (A_i q_{ni})^{\frac{\sigma-1}{\sigma}} \right)^{\frac{\sigma}{\sigma-1}}. \tag{10}$$

A_i is a utility shifter that can be thought of as an index of the quality of country i's product.[8] Simple maximization of (10) under budgetary constraint provides optimal demand for each variety. The two terms of equation (6) are then given by $S_i = A_i^{\sigma-1} w_i^{1-\sigma}$, and $\phi_{ni} = \tau_{ni}^{1-\sigma}$.

Following Okawa and Van Wincoop (2010, Section 3.1), we can modify the Armington utility function, adding consumption of a homogeneous "outside" good, here denoted q_n^0, to equation (10). For each differentiated good i has sales of $(w_i/A_i)^{1-\sigma}$. Note that demand for the differentiated goods does not depend on income of country n; all residual income is spent on the homogeneous good. The resulting gravity equation still has $S_i = A_i^{\sigma-1} w_i^{1-\sigma}$, and $\phi_{ni} = \tau_{ni}^{1-\sigma}$ but $M_i = 1$, because $X_n/\Phi_n = 1$ (assuming X_n corresponds to expenditures on the differentiated goods only). Adding an outside good that enters utility linearly therefore leads to a specification that fits the general definition for gravity but not the one we call "structural gravity."[9]

CES Monopolistic Competition (Dixit-Stiglitz-Krugman)

The gravity equation based on standard symmetric Dixit-Stiglitz-Krugman (DSK) monopolistic competition assumptions was derived by multiple authors.[10] It assumes that each country has N_i firms supplying one variety each to the world from a home-country production site. Utility features a constant elasticity of substitution, denoted σ, between all varieties available in the world. Dyadic accessability is given by $\phi_{ni} = \tau_{ni}^{1-\sigma}$. The exporter attribute is given by $S_i = N_i w_i^{1-\sigma}$, where the difference compared to the NPD model is that the N_i term replaces $A_i^{\sigma-1}$. Thus the exporter attribute reflects the monopolistic competition among the symmetric varieties in the DSK model and competitively supplied national varieties in the NPD model. Note that prices are also different

---

[8] Anderson and van Wincoop (2003) use $\beta_i = 1/A_i$ in their formulation. We prefer the one specified above because it allows us to think of A_i as the attractiveness of country i's product, whereas Anderson and van Wincoop's (2003) β_i is an *inverse* measure of quality.

[9] This is an unfortunate aspect of the terminology but we could not find a suitable alternative.

[10] One early derivation based on Krugman (1979) is contained in the unpublished paper of Wei (1996).

since they are a constant positive markup over marginal costs in DSK, and just equal to marginal cost in NPD.

While the Dixit-Stiglitz model is usually interpreted as firms supplying differentiated goods to consumers, the fact that the majority[11] of trade involves intermediates suggests the benefits of generalizing to that case. If we follow Ethier (1982) in assuming that each firm produces a differentiated variety of intermediate input, the S_i, M_n, and ϕ_{ni} terms remain the same.

CES Demand with CET Production

The earliest derivation of a gravity equation using monopolistic competition (MC) of the Dixit-Stiglitz form is Bergstrand (1985). Bergstrand used a more general set of functional forms that were not retained in later work. In particular, he allowed for a nested structure in which domestic varieties are closer substitutes for each other than are foreign varieties. Bergstrand also generalized the production side to allow for the possibility that output might not be transferable to the export sector on a one-for-one basis. Instead he allows for a "constant elasticity of transformation" (CET). The idea is that output to one destination cannot be costlessly transformed into output for a different destination. The elasticity of transformation is denoted γ and ranges from 0, where it is impossible to reallocate output, to infinity, in which case transformation is costless.

Here we follow Baier and Bergstrand (2001) in assuming a finite CET, while retaining the single-layer CES. This specification still yields structural gravity with

$$S_i = L_i w_i^{\frac{\gamma(1-\sigma)}{\sigma+\gamma}} \quad \text{and} \quad \phi_{ni} = \tau_{ni}^{\frac{(1+\gamma)(1-\sigma)}{\sigma+\gamma}}.$$

The model has $M_n = X_n/\Phi_n$ and therefore has a unit income elasticity if X_n is proportional to income.[12] The wage and trade costs elasticities now include the supply-side CET, γ, and the wage elasticity is $\gamma/(1+\gamma)$ times the trade elasticity.

Baier and Bergstrand (2001) motivate the finite CET by arguing that it could reflect distribution costs of entering foreign markets. We believe it is better to think of it as a way of generating upward sloping marginal costs of serving each market. This has the effect of lowering both the wage and trade elasticities. That is, trade is less responsive to wages and trade costs than it would be if only the demand parameter σ mattered.

---

[11] Chen et al. (2005) construct the share of intermediates in total trade for 10 OECD countries using input-output tables in various years between 1968 and 1998. The US share averages 50% while the other countries have higher averages, with Japan above 80% until the 1990s.

[12] Equation (12) of Bergstrand (1985) gives the appearance that the model predicts a less than unit elasticity but this is because it retains the price index. After solving for the price index the elasticity is predicted to be one which implies that the estimated income elasticity cannot be used to back out γ.

Heterogeneous Consumers

The taste for variety present in the CES utility functions may be plausible in some contexts but it does not fit products like laundry detergents or (except for the very rich) passenger cars. In those and many other cases, the natural way to think about consumer choice is that the large variety of products purchased results from consumers making different decisions. If they face the same prices, then the different selections result from a variety of tastes.[13] Anderson et al. (1992) show that two strong functional form assumptions are enough to yield a demand equation that is observationally equivalent to the CES. This equivalence breaks down if there are only a finite number of buyers. In that case the heterogeneous consumer model can account for zeros. This makes it worth laying out rather than just invoking the equivalence result.

Consumers from country n, indexed with $n\ell$, have utility functions defined over the products made by each supplier s in each country i, $u_{n\ell is} = \ln[\psi_{n\ell is}q_{n\ell is}]$, where $q_{n\ell is}$ represents the quantity of products consumed and $\psi_{n\ell is}$ is the idiosyncratic preference shock. The heterogeneity is assumed to be distributed Fréchet with a cumulative distribution function (CDF) of $\exp\{-(\psi/(A_i a_{ni}))^{-\theta}\}$, where θ is an inverse measure of consumer heterogeneity and A_i is a location parameter that is specific to the origin country. In an analogous way to equation (10), an increase in A_i shifts up the utility derived from varieties produced in i, which can be interpreted as an increase in perceived quality. a_{ni} also shifts utility upwards, and is a bilateral preference parameter.

Each of the L_n consumers chooses the product giving highest utility and then spends w_n on it. Hence, individual demand is $q_{n\ell is} = w_n/p_{ni}$ for the selected variety and zero on all other varieties. $p_{ni} = p_i \tau_{ni}$ is the price consumers in country n face for product varieties from country i. On the supply side, we assume constant markups (allowing for competitive pricing $p_i = w_i$). The conditional indirect utility function is given by

$$v_{n\ell is} = \ln w_n - \ln(w_i \tau_{ni}) + \ln \psi_{n\ell is}. \tag{11}$$

The Fréchet form for ψ implies a Gumbel form for $\ln \psi$ and thereby implies multinomial logit forms for the probabilities of choosing one of the N_i varieties produced in country i for consumers in n:

$$\mathbb{P}_{ni} = \frac{w_i^{-\theta} A_i^{\theta} \tau_{ni}^{-\theta} a_{ni}^{\theta}}{\sum_{\ell} w_{\ell}^{-\theta} A_{\ell}^{\theta} \tau_{n\ell}^{-\theta} a_{n\ell}^{\theta}}. \tag{12}$$

This equation has a second interpretation that applies to settings in which products are allocated to consumers via auctions. $\mathbb{P}_{ni}$ becomes the probability that i has the highest valuation and therefore makes the winning bid for a good from n.[14]

---

[13] Income differences would also produce different choices if utility were not homothetic. Fajgelbaum et al. (2011) is a recent combination of the two effects, introducing non-homothetic preferences over quality in a discrete choice logit-type demand system.

[14] Hortaçsu et al. (2009) apply such a model to eBay transactions.

Summing over the set of N_i varieties, $\mathbb{E}[\pi_{ni}] = N_i \mathbb{P}_{ni}$. With a continuum of consumers, the expectation is no longer needed, and $\pi_{ni} = N_i \mathbb{P}_{ni}$. This formulation meets the separability requirement of Definition 2. The exporter attribute and the accessability terms are given by $S_i = N_i w_i^{-\theta} A_i^{\theta}$, and $\phi_{ni} = \tau_{ni}^{-\theta} a_{ni}^{\theta}$. The key difference in this model compared to the first two models lies in the parameter $-\theta$ substituting for $1 - \sigma$ when the demand system is CES. There is a very strong parallel though, since an increase in σ means that products are becoming more homogeneous, and an increase in θ means that consumers are becoming less heterogeneous. Whether consumers are becoming more alike in their tastes, or whether products are becoming more substitutable yields similar aggregate predictions for trade flows, which is quite intuitive.

Note that allowing for the bilateral shock a_{ni} to enter preferences of consumers makes it possible for variables like distance to affect trade not only though freight costs, but also through preferences. Another advantage of this model is that, for finite numbers of consumers in the importing country n, it is possible for imports from i to have realized values of zero, an issue we return to in Section 5.2.

2.3.2. Supply-Side Derivations
Heterogeneous Industries (Ricardian Comparative Advantage)

Eaton and Kortum (2002) derive a gravity equation that departs from the CES-based approaches in almost every respect and yet the results they obtain bear a striking resemblance. In contrast to the CES-NPD approach, each country produces a very large number of goods (modeled as a continuum) that are homogeneous across countries. In contrast to the CES-MC approach, every industry is perfectly competitive.[15] Productivity z is assumed to be distributed Fréchet with a cumulative distribution function (CDF) of $\exp\{-T_i z^{-\theta}\}$, where T_i is a technology parameter that increases the share of goods for which i is the low-cost supplier and θ determines the amount of heterogeneity in the productivity distribution. Note that the θ parameter now corresponds inversely to dispersion in productivity rather than tastes. However, since this parameter plays the same key role in both models, we maintain the notation in order to emphasize the similarity in resulting terms.

Delivered costs of good g from origin i to destination n are $(c_i/z_{ig})\tau_{ni}$, where c_i is an input price index. Consider one of the goods, the probability of buying it from i is

$$\Pr\left[\ln z_{\ell} < \ln z_i + \ln\left(\frac{c_{\ell}\tau_{n\ell}}{c_i\tau_{ni}}\right), \forall h\right]. \tag{13}$$

The Fréchet for z implies Gumbel for $\ln z$, which gives a multinomial logit probability. With a continuum of goods, the share of goods for which consumers in n choose i as

---

[15] Bernard et al. (2003) reformulate the Eaton and Kortum (2002) model to allow for Bertrand competition in each sector but this reformulation does not change the form of the gravity equation.

their supplier is given by

$$\pi_{ni} = \frac{T_i(c_i\tau_{ni})^{-\theta}}{\sum_\ell T_\ell(c_\ell\tau_{n\ell})^{-\theta}}. \tag{14}$$

Total bilateral flow aggregates over each g good and multiplies expenditure on each good by the above probability. With a CES demand structure over goods, countries spread their overall expenditure X_n according to $X_{ng} = X_n \times p_{ng}^{1-\sigma} / \sum_g p_{ng}^{1-\sigma}$, where p_{ng} is the best price available for good g to country n. Total flow is therefore $X_{ni} = \sum_g X_{ng} \times \pi_{ni} = \pi_{ni}X_n$.

Using the Eaton and Kortum (2002) input cost assumption that $c_i = w_i^\beta P_i^{1-\beta}$ where the price index P_i is proportional to $\Phi_i^{-\theta}$ implies that the two structural gravity terms are given by $S_i = T_i w_i^{-\beta\theta} \Phi_i^{(1-\beta)}$, and $\phi_{ni} = \tau_{ni}^{-\theta}$. The trade cost elasticity, $-\theta$, is equal to the input cost elasticity but the wage elasticity will be smaller since $\beta < 1$.

Heterogeneous Firms

Models covered up to this point have allowed consumers to be heterogeneous in their preferences and industries to differ in terms of production costs. The next step is to let each realization of unit input requirement α be unique so that they can be used to identify individual firms. The CDF of unit input requirements is denoted $G(\alpha)$. Suppose there is a mass of active firms in country i given by N_i. A key variable in heterogeneous firms models is the threshold α_{ni}^*, above which firms do not enter a market. It is a dyadic variable since the threshold must depend on trade costs between i and n. We can now use this notation to obtain an expression for the aggregate share of the market. Chaney (2008) and Helpman et al. (2008) embed heterogeneous firms in a Dixit-Stiglitz framework generalizing the Melitz (2003) paper to multiple countries. The pricing equation is now specific to each firm indexed with their α:

$$p_{ni}(\alpha) = \frac{\sigma}{\sigma - 1} w_i \tau_{ni}\alpha. \tag{15}$$

The resulting market share of i firms in n is therefore:

$$\pi_{ni} = \frac{N_i \int_{\underline{\alpha}}^{\alpha_{ni}^*} p_{ni}(\alpha)^{1-\sigma} dG(\alpha)}{\sum_\ell N_\ell \int_{\underline{\alpha}}^{\alpha_{n\ell}^*} p_{n\ell}(\alpha)^{1-\sigma} dG(\alpha)} = \frac{N_i w_i^{1-\sigma} V_{ni}\tau_{ni}^{1-\sigma}}{\sum_\ell N_\ell w_\ell^{1-\sigma} V_{n\ell}\tau_{n\ell}^{1-\sigma}}, \tag{16}$$

where V_{ni} is defined as in Helpman et al. (2008):

$$V_{ni} \equiv \int_{\underline{\alpha}}^{\alpha_{ni}^*} \alpha^{1-\sigma} dG_i(\alpha).$$

When the threshold entry costs, α_{ni}^*, are less than the lower support, $\underline{\alpha}$, then $V_{ni} = 0$ and there will be no exports from i to n. To specify π_{ni}, we need to solve for V_{ni}, and therefore to specify α_{ni}^* and $G_i(\alpha)$.

In this model, the equilibrium threshold α_{ni}^* such that the corresponding firm is the last one to serve market n (zero profit condition with f_{ni} the fixed cost of serving n from i) is

$$\alpha_{ni}^* = \sigma^{\frac{\sigma}{\sigma-1}}(\sigma-1)\left(\frac{X_n}{f_{ni}\Phi_n}\right)^{\frac{1}{\sigma-1}}\frac{1}{w_i\tau_{ni}}. \tag{17}$$

Since α_{ni}^* depends on destination country characteristics X_n and Φ_n, and on i-specific distribution parameters in $G_i(\alpha)$, we generally cannot separate V_{ni} multiplicatively as would be required to obtain the structural form of gravity. The only functional form known to generate a multiplicable closed form for V_{ni} is the Pareto distribution. Hence we follow Helpman et al. (2008) in setting $G_i(\alpha) = (\alpha^\theta - \underline{\alpha}^\theta)/(\bar{\alpha}_i^\theta - \underline{\alpha}^\theta)$, where θ is the shape parameter and the support of input requirements is $\underline{\alpha}, \bar{\alpha}_i$. The lower bound of $\underline{\alpha} > 0$ is the mechanism through which Helpman et al. (2008) generate aggregate bilateral trade flows of zero. However, to obtain the structural gravity form we need to follow Chaney (2008) and Arkolakis et al. (2012b) in making zero the lower bound for α.[16]

Imposing Pareto (with $\underline{\alpha} = 0$ and country-specific $\bar{\alpha}_i$) and solving for V_{ni}, the aggregate market share of i firms in n is

$$\pi_{ni} = \frac{N_i(w_i\bar{\alpha}_i)^{-\theta}\tau_{ni}^{-\theta}f_{ni}^{-\left[\frac{\theta}{\sigma-1}-1\right]}}{\sum_\ell N_\ell(w_\ell\bar{\alpha}_\ell)^{-\theta}\tau_{n\ell}^{-\theta}f_{n\ell}^{-\left[\frac{\theta}{\sigma-1}-1\right]}}. \tag{18}$$

The first point to note, made originally by Chaney (2008), is that the elasticity of trade with respect to trade costs is now $-\theta$ a supply-side parameter, rather than $1-\sigma$, the preference parameter that determines the elasticity of trade for individual firms (and aggregate trade flows in symmetric firms models). Both parameters can be interpreted as inverse measures of heterogeneity. However, while dispersion in the consumer tastes are increasing in $1/(\sigma-1)$, differences in productive efficiency of firms are what rises with $1/\theta$. The disappearance of the demand parameter is purely a consequence of the Pareto assumption, under which the elasticity of V_{ni} with respect to trade costs is given by $-\theta + \sigma - 1$. When adding this elasticity to the intensive margin elasticity, the $1-\sigma$ term drops out.

Equation (18) shows that, in models with an extensive margin of firms' entry, bilateral trade is affected by both variable and fixed trade costs. Eaton et al. (2011a) use $\tilde{\theta}$ to denote $\theta/(\sigma-1)$. Since θ needs to be bigger than $\sigma - 1$ for the integral defined by V_{ni} to be finite, $\tilde{\theta} > 1$. Thus, the elasticity of trade with respect to bilateral fixed costs, $-(\tilde{\theta}-1)$ is negative. The fixed costs of entering markets may involve some costs incurred in the domestic economy, w_i, as well as costs incurred in the destination market, w_n. Following

---

[16] Since α is the inverse of productivity this means that productivity has no upper bound. In that case the continuum assumption implies positive mass of exporters for all country pairs ni.

Arkolakis et al. (2012b), we specify $f_{ni} = \xi_{ni} w_i^{\mu} w_n^{1-\mu}$. Substituting this expression for f_{ni} into (18), we obtain

$$S_i = N_i \bar{\alpha}_i^{-\theta} w_i^{-\theta - \mu\left[\frac{\theta}{\sigma - 1} - 1\right]} \quad \text{and} \quad \phi_{ni} = \tau_{ni}^{-\theta} \xi_{ni}^{-\left[\frac{\theta}{\sigma - 1} - 1\right]}.$$

Many of the underlying determinants of variable trade costs, τ_{ni}, such as distance, common language, and colonial history, can reasonably be expected to also contribute to the determination of ξ_{ni}. Two implications follow from this observation: (i) the elasticity of trade with respect to distance now includes both θ and σ, and (ii) even if one could find a variable determining the fixed costs of entry only, equation (18) reveals that its impact is not confined to the binary observation of whether i and n trade at all. It also enters the equation for the value of aggregate trade, and therefore cannot be validly used as an exclusion restriction in a Heckman-type estimation. Note that the procedure used by Helpman et al. (2008) goes beyond simple Heckman-type estimation, and essentially controls for V_{ni} (which is the only channel through which ξ_{ni} enters bilateral flows) in equation (16).

An important limit of CES monopolistic competition models is their constant markup property. This motivated Melitz and Ottaviano (2008) to propose a model with hetero-geneous firms that could allow for pro-competitive effects on markups. While, when combined with Pareto, their approach maintains tractability for bilateral trade flows, it does require the assumption of an outside good, which as we see below, leads to a departure from our definition of structural gravity.

In Melitz and Ottaviano (2008), the bilateral exporter's cost threshold c_{ni}^* is simply a function of the domestic production threshold c_n^*, such that $c_n^* = c_{ni}^* \tau_{ni}$. With the linear demand structure used

$$p_{ni}(c) = \frac{1}{2}(c_n^* + \tau_{ni} c) \quad \text{and} \quad q_{ni}(c) = \frac{L_n}{2\gamma}(c_n^* - \tau_{ni} c). \tag{19}$$

Integrating over all firms' individual exports $p_{ni}(c) q_{ni}(c)$ and dividing by X_n, one obtains the collective share of the market

$$\pi_{ni} = \frac{N_i \bar{\alpha}_i^{-\theta} w_i^{-\theta} c_n^{*\theta + 2} \tau_{ni}^{-\theta} L_n}{2\gamma(\theta + 2) X_n}. \tag{20}$$

The exporter and bilateral terms of general gravity are given by $S_i = N_i \bar{\alpha}_i^{-\theta} w_i^{-\theta}$ and $\phi_{ni} = \tau_{ni}^{-\theta}$. The importer term is $M_n = L_n c_n^{*\theta + 2}$. Appendix A.2 of Melitz and Ottaviano (2008) shows that the cutoff in country n is a function of its population and of a market access index that sums trade costs over all source countries: $c_n^{*\theta + 2} = \lambda_3 C_n / L_n$, where C_n is a geographical remoteness index (resembling Φ_n of other models) and λ_3 is a constant. After substitution, the importer term in the gravity equation becomes $M_n = \lambda_3 C_n$. Thus, holding the intensity of competition constant in n, M_n is increasing in the *population* of the importing country but not in the per-capita income. This is due to the non-homotheticity of preferences. In the linear-quadratic utility structure, a higher income individual lowers the share of income spent on the traded varieties and spends a higher share on the outside good. However, the competition-increasing effect of L_n in this model exactly offsets the positive demand effect of country size. Note also that in contrast to the version with Dixit-Stiglitz preferences, ϕ_{ni} does not depend on a bilateral fixed export cost. This is because the linear demand system generates zero trade flows through a choke price.

Arkolakis et al. (2012a) investigate a broader class of variable markup demand systems also featuring choke prices. The general demand system they define is

$$\ln q(p_{ni}(j), p_n^*, x_n) = -\beta \ln p_{ni}(j) + \gamma \ln x_n + d(\ln p_{ni}(j) - \ln p_n^*), \qquad (21)$$

for each consumer, where $\gamma \le 1$ is the income elasticity of demand and $\beta \le 1$ is a parameter that enters the price elasticity of demand. The $d()$ function shows what happens to demand as $p(j)$ approaches the choke price, p^*. Arkolakis et al. (2012a) results depend on the assumption that $d''() < 0$. They also assume that if the choke price is exceeded, $d()$ goes to negative infinity. Note that p_n^* is also an aggregator of the prices of all other varieties available in market n. Arkolakis et al. (2012a) show that this demand system encompasses a large set of different preferences that have been used in the literature to generate variable markups (Behrens et al. (2009), Feenstra (2003), and a version of Melitz and Ottaviano (2008) where the outside good is omitted). On the supply side of their economy they maintain the Pareto distribution of the productivity of firms competing under monopolistic competition. The two structural gravity terms are given by $S_i = N_i \bar{\alpha}_i^{-\theta} w_i^{-\theta}$ and $\phi_{ni} = \tau_{ni}^{-\theta}$.

Table 3.1 summarizes the results from nine models that fit Definition 1, seven of which fit the stronger requirements of Definition 2. The final column shows trade elasticities with respect to variable trade costs, ϵ. Note that in most structural gravity models, the elasticity of trade with respect to wages is also given by ϵ. For CES-CET, this occurs in the limit as $\gamma \to \infty$ (reallocation of output across destination is costless), for heterogeneous industries it occurs as $\beta \to 1$ (labor is the only input), and for heterogeneous firms as $\mu \to 0$ (fixed costs are paid in units of foreign labor). In principle, if one had reliable estimates of both wage and trade elasticities, one could infer something about these parameters. An important difficulty is to find good instruments for cross-country variation in wages of the origin country that can be excluded from the trade equation.

2.4. Gravity Models Beyond Trade in Goods

The same modeling tools that yield gravity equations for trade in goods can also be applied to other types of flows and interactions. Head et al. (2009) adapt the Eaton and Kortum (2002) (EK) model to the case of service offshoring. Anderson (2011) presents a migration gravity model drawing on discrete choice techniques. Ahlfeldt et al. (2012) draw on

Table 3.1 Theoretical Content of Monadic, Dyadic Terms, and Elasticities of Gravity

Model:	Term:	S_i Exporter	M_n Importer	ϕ_{ni} Bilateral	ϵ Tr. elas.
			Naive Gravity		
N/A		Y_i^a	Y_n^b	ad hoc	N/A
			Structural Gravity		
CES NPD		$A_i^{-\epsilon} w_i^\epsilon$	X_n/Φ_n	τ_{ni}^ϵ	$1-\sigma$
CES MC (DSK)		$N_i w_i^\epsilon$	X_n/Φ_n	τ_{ni}^ϵ	$1-\sigma$
CES MC CET		$L_i w_i^{\frac{\epsilon\gamma}{1+\gamma}}$	X_n/Φ_n	τ_{ni}^ϵ	$\frac{(1+\gamma)(1-\sigma)}{\sigma+\gamma}$
Heterogeneous consumers		$A_i^{-\epsilon} N_i w_i^\epsilon$	X_n/Φ_n	$\tau_{ni}^\epsilon a_{ni}^{-\epsilon}$	$-\theta$
Het. industries (EK)		$T_i w_i^{\beta\epsilon} \Phi_i^{1-\beta}$	X_n/Φ_n	τ_{ni}^ϵ	$-\theta$
Het. firms (CES)		$N_i \bar\alpha_i^\epsilon w_i^{\epsilon-\mu\left[\frac{\theta}{\sigma-1}-1\right]}$	X_n/Φ_n	$\tau_{ni}^\epsilon \xi_{ni}^{\frac{\theta}{\sigma-1}-1}$	$-\theta$
Het. firms (log-concave)		$N_i \bar\alpha_i^\epsilon w_i^\epsilon$	X_n/Φ_n	τ_{ni}^ϵ	$-\theta$
			General Gravity		
CES NPD (outside good)		$A_i^{-\epsilon} w_i^\epsilon$	1	τ_{ni}^ϵ	$1-\sigma$
Het. firms (linear pref. + outside good)		$N_i \bar\alpha_i^\epsilon w_i^\epsilon$	$L_n c_n^{*\theta+2}$	τ_{ni}^ϵ	$-\theta$

Eaton and Kortum (2002) to specify a commuting gravity model. With a few minor changes, the discrete choice framework can easily produce a gravity equation for tourism.

Portes et al. (2001) and Portes and Rey (2005) establish that gravity equations ("naive" definition) can explain cross border portfolio investment patterns as well as they explain trade flows. Martin and Rey (2004) propose a two-country model that they use to justify a gravity equation for bilateral portfolio investment. Coeurdacier and Martin (2009) generalize the framework to multiple countries and apply it using different types of assets and a fixed effects estimation technology very close to the one used by trade economists. Okawa and van Wincoop (2012) suggest an alternative foundation for gravity in international finance.

Gravity equations have also been shown to do a good job fitting stocks of foreign direct investment (FDI). Head and Ries (2008) consider a model in which FDI takes the form of acquisitions. Using the discrete choice framework in a way that resembles Eaton and Kortum (2002), they develop a gravity equation for FDI which fits the data well. de Sousa and Lochard (2011) extend the model to greenfield investment by imagining that instead of bidding for assets, each corporation selects the best "investment project" across all host countries.

In summary, one of the contributions of the development of micro-foundations for the gravity equation for trade is that they can be applied to a range of other bilateral flows and interactions. The key ingredients tend to be "mass" effects that come from adding up constraints and bilateral and multilateral "resistance" terms. Once these gravity equations are specified, they can usually be estimated using the same techniques that are appropriate for trade flows.

3. THEORY-CONSISTENT ESTIMATION

After having described the different theoretical setups that give rise to the gravity prediction, we turn to estimation methods that are consistent with the theory predictions, in particular because they do account for the multilateral resistance terms that are a key feature of general and structural gravity. Historically, the very first approach was to proxy multilateral resistance with remoteness terms. This approach progressively appeared as too weak once the theoretical modeling of gravity became clearer. Researchers then switched to more structural approaches. Because of the influence of Anderson and van Wincoop (2003) in the literature, we start with a version of their approach (their original approach using non-linear least squares has actually been hardly followed), that applies the full structure of the structural gravity framework. We then describe fixed effects estimation that imposes much less structure, but still complies with general gravity. This method can however encounter computational difficulties when using very large datasets, which is not uncommon in the literature. We therefore turn to alternatives when fixed effects are not feasible, and end with Monte Carlo comparisons of all those methods.

3.1. Proxies for Multilateral Resistance Terms

A few early studies have included variables proxies for $1/\Omega_i$ and $1/\Phi_n$ and referred to them as "remoteness." Wei (1996) used a monopolistic competition model to show the theoretical counterparts of these variables but settled for using "log(GDP)-weighted average distances" in his regressions.[17] This bears little resemblance to its theoretical counterpart. Some other remoteness measures differ from their theoretical counterparts in ways that are even more problematic. For instance, Helliwell (1998) measures remoteness as $\text{REM1}_n = \sum_i \text{Dist}_{ni}/Y_i$. This measure has the feature of giving extraordinary weight to tiny countries: as $Y_i \to 0$, REM1 explodes. A better measure of remoteness is $\text{REM2}_n = (\sum_i Y_i/\text{Dist}_{ni})^{-1}$, that is the inverse of the Harris market potential.[18] Tiny countries have negligible effects on REM2 and the size of very distant countries becomes irrelevant.

---

[17] It is interesting to note that the literature has kept "circling" around those GDP-weighted averages of trade costs as proxies for the MR terms. Baier and Bergstrand (2009), discussed below, can be viewed as the latest approach in that tradition, but one that maintains a clear connection (via approximation) back to the model.

[18] Baldwin and Harrigan (2011) use REM2 to explain the bilateral zero trade flows and Martin et al. (2008) use something close to REM2 as an instrument for trade.

Supposing $\phi_{ni} \sim \text{Dist}_{ni}^{-1}$ and $X_n = Y_n$, the correct Φ_n and Ω_i are $\sum_{\ell}(Y_\ell/\text{Dist}_{n\ell})\Omega_\ell^{-1}$ and $\sum_{\ell}(Y_\ell/\text{Dist}_{\ell i})\Phi_\ell^{-1}$. Thus we see that REM2 is on the right track by summing up GDP to distance ratios but it ends up wide off the mark because it implicitly assumes that Φ_ℓ and Ω_ℓ equal one. This makes no sense when the whole point is to obtain a proxy for those variables. Furthermore, while Dist_{ni}^{-1} is an important factor in determining ϕ_{ni} many other trade costs besides distance ought to be considered. In sum, proxy variables do not take the theory seriously enough, a concern that underlines the need for *gravitas*.

3.2. Iterative Structural Estimation

Our implementation of the Anderson and van Wincoop (2003) method involves assuming initial values of $\Omega_i = 1$ and $\Phi_n = 1$, then estimating the vector of parameters determining ϕ_{ni}, then using a contraction mapping algorithm to find fixed points for Ω_i and Φ_n given those parameters. We then run OLS using $\ln X_{ni} - \ln Y_i - \ln X_n + \ln\hat{\Omega}_i + \ln\hat{\Phi}_{ni}$ as the dependent variable. This gives a new set of ϕ_{ni} parameter estimates. We iterate until the parameter estimates stop changing. This method exploits the structural relationship between Ω_i, Φ_n, and ϕ_{ni}. We therefore call the estimator SILS (structurally iterated least squares). Although it is not identical to the Anderson and van Wincoop (2003) method— which is estimated using a non-linear least squares routine in Gauss—SILS does have the advantage of being available as a Stata® ado file (available on our companion website). On the other hand, while SILS uses OLS only, the iteration is time-consuming. Also, the structural methods require data on trade with self and distance to self, both of which may be problematic.

3.3. Fixed Effects Estimation

Standard estimating procedure involves taking logs of equation (1), obtaining

$$\ln X_{ni} = \ln G + \ln S_i + \ln M_n + \ln \phi_{ni}. \tag{22}$$

The naive form of gravity equations involved using log GDPs (and possibly other variables) as proxies for the $\ln S_i$ and $\ln M_n$ but modern practice has been moving toward using fixed effects for these terms instead (Harrigan (1996) seems to be the first paper to have done so). Note that estimating gravity equations with fixed effects for the importer and exporter, as is now common practice and recommended by major empirical trade economists, does not involve strong structural assumptions on the underlying model. As long as the precise modeling structure yields an equation in multiplicative form such as (1), using fixed effects will yield consistent estimates of the components of ϕ_{ni}, which are usually the items of primary interest.[19]

---

[19] Although the particular model underlying the fixed effects does not matter for the ϕ_{ni} coefficients, it does affect the mapping from the S_i and M_n estimates back to primitives such as technology or demand parameters.

We focus the exposition and our Monte Carlo investigation on cross-sections. However, most current gravity estimations employ datasets that span many years. In such cases the importer and exporter fixed effects should be time-varying as well. The same is true if the data pools over several industries. The S_i and M_n have no reason to be identical across industries since supply capacity of i and total expenditure of n will vary across industries, because of differences in comparative advantages or in consumer's preferences for instance. For panels of trade flows with a large number of years and/or industries, the estimation might run into computational feasibility issues due to the very large number of resulting dummies to be estimated, a challenge that now appears to be solved, as we shall discuss below.

Using country fixed effects has an additional advantage that has nothing to do with being consistent with theory. There can be systematic tendencies of a country to export large amounts relative to its GDP and other observed trade determinants. As an example consider the Netherlands and Belgium. Much of Europe's trade flows through Rotterdam and Antwerp. In principle the production location should be used as the exporting country and the consumption location as the importing country. In practice use of warehouses and other reporting issues makes this difficult so there is reason to expect that trade flows to and from these countries are overstated. Fixed effects can control for this, since they will account for any unobservable that contributes to shift the overall level of exports or imports of a country.

3.4. Ratio-Type Estimation

As mentioned above, the use of fixed effects can sometimes hit a computational constraint imposed upon the number of separate parameters that can be estimated by a statistical package. A solution that has been explored involves using the multiplicative structure of the gravity model to eliminate the monadic terms, S_i and M_n. Head and Mayer (2000) and Eaton and Kortum (2002) normalize bilateral flows X_{ni} by trade with self [20] (X_{nn}) for a given industry/year, delivering a ratio we call the *odds* specification:

$$\frac{X_{ni}}{X_{nn}} = \left(\frac{S_i}{S_n}\right)\left(\frac{\phi_{ni}}{\phi_{nn}}\right). \qquad (23)$$

While this specification simplifies greatly the issue by removing any characteristic of the importer, the origin country term S remains to be measured, presumably with substantial error. A related issue is that constructing S_i requires knowledge of the trade cost elasticity, which is also contained in the ϕ_{ni} to be estimated through (23).

Head and Ries (2001) propose a simple solution to cancel those exporter terms, multiplying (23) by $\frac{X_{in}}{X_{ii}}$. If one is ready to assume symmetry in bilateral trade costs

---

[20] Those manipulations can be done with a reference country other than self. Martin et al. (2008) and Anderson and Marcouiller (2002) use the United States as the reference country.

($\phi_{ni} = \phi_{in}$), and frictionless trade inside countries ($\phi_{nn} = \phi_{ii} = 1$), we end up with a very simple index that Eaton et al. (2011b) call the *Head-Ries Index* (HRI),

$$\hat{\phi}_{ni} = \sqrt{\frac{X_{ni} X_{in}}{X_{nn} X_{ii}}}, \tag{24}$$

and which can be used to assess the *overall* level of trade integration between any two countries.[21]

The problem with the HRI is that it cannot be calculated without a measure of trade *inside* a country (X_{nn}). In principle, it can be proxied using production minus total exports of a country/industry/year combination. Disturbingly, this procedure generates some negative observations, notably for countries like Belgium and the Netherlands, pointing to potential measurement issues related, in particular, to transit shipments, as stated above. Alternative, but related, solutions exist that omit the need for internal trade. Romalis (2007) and Hallak (2006) have used ratios of ratios methods, involving four different international trade flows and thus named the *Tetrads* method by Head et al. (2010). Choosing a reference importer k and a reference exporter ℓ, provides a tetradic term such that

$$\frac{X_{ni}/X_{ki}}{X_{n\ell}/X_{k\ell}} = \frac{\phi_{ni}/\phi_{ki}}{\phi_{n\ell}/\phi_{k\ell}}. \tag{25}$$

The tetradic term can then be used as the LHS to estimate the impact of the usual set of dyadic covariates, with the caveat that all of those covariates need to be "tetrad-ed" as well.[22]

A recent paper that has utilized an alternative trade ratio method is Caliendo and Parro (2012). Their aim is to estimate the trade cost elasticity from tariff data, using asymmetries in protectionism as an identification strategy. Suppose trade costs can be described as $\phi_{ni} = \left[(1 + t_{ni})d_{ni}^{\delta}\right]^{\epsilon}$, where $d_{ni} = d_{in}$ captures all symmetric trade costs (such as distance) in $X_{ni} = GS_i M_n \phi_{ni}$. Introducing a third country h, and multiplying the three ratios X_{ni}/X_{nh}, X_{ih}/X_{hi}, and X_{hn}/X_{in} gives the following estimable equation:

$$\frac{X_{ni} X_{ih} X_{hn}}{X_{nh} X_{hi} X_{in}} = \left(\frac{(1 + t_{ni})(1 + t_{ih})(1 + t_{hn})}{(1 + t_{nh})(1 + t_{hi})(1 + t_{in})}\right)^{\epsilon}. \tag{26}$$

---

[21] Head and Ries (2001) apply it to the US/Canada FTA (free trade agreement), Head and Mayer (2004a) to a comparison of North American and European integration, Jacks et al. (2008) use it to measure trade integration over the very long run using trade data of France, Germany, and the UK from 1870 to 2000, and Eaton et al. (2011b) use it to quantify the effects of the 2008–2009 crisis on trade integration. $\hat{\phi}_{ni}$ can also be used as the left-hand side (LHS) of a regression trying to explain the bilateral determinants of trade integration (Combes et al. (2005) and Chen and Novy (2011) are examples following that path).

[22] A difficulty in implementing Tetrads in practice is the choice of the reference countries, since doing all potential combinations of k and ℓ would drive the number of observations into the billions in most applications. Romalis (2007) focuses on the impact of the North American Free Trade Agreement (NAFTA) where he considers EU12 as a reference importer, and each of the NAFTA countries in turn as a reference exporter. Head et al. (2010) study the erosion of colonial preferences and therefore face a higher dimensional issue. Their preferred specification takes the average of results when reference countries are chosen in turn in the set of the five biggest traders in the world. As shown in the Monte Carlo exercise below, Tetrads yields a very small bias when the share of missing values in the data is minimal.

3.5. Other Methods

The ratios approaches are one way to deal with an exceedingly large number of dummies required by theory. An intuitive alternative is to "double-demean" the gravity dataset, one demeaning for the exporter dimension, one for the importer. However, this solution only yields unbiased estimates if the dataset is completely full, with no missing flows. Another approach is to demean in one dimension only, and use dummies in the other dimension. This hybrid strategy does not require the matrix of trade flows to be full, and divides the computational problem by two, which however might prove insufficient in some cases (with 150 countries and 60 years for instance, 9000 dummies remain to be estimated). Following on the analysis of employer–employee datasets carried out by Abowd et al. (1999), iterative methods have been developed to solve the two-way Fixed Effect (FE) problem with unbalanced data and very large numbers of effects. The command we have employed is **reg2hdfe** by Guimaraes and Portugal (2010) which allows for clustered standard errors.

Another alternative, dubbed Bonus Vetus OLS, has been proposed by Baier and Bergstrand (2009). Define $MRS(\nu_{ni}) = \bar{\nu}_i + \bar{\nu}_n - \bar{\bar{\nu}}$. Similarly let $MRD(\nu_{ni})$ be the GDP-weighted version of these averages. Bonus Vetus adds $MRD(\nu_{ni})$ (or $MRS(\nu_{ni})$ in the unweighted version) for each trade cost variable to the regression and constrains it to have the opposite sign as ν_{ni}. The unweighted version resembles double-demeaning in which one subtracts $MRS(\nu_{ni})$ from the dependent variable as well as all right-hand side (RHS) variables.

3.6. Monte Carlo Study of Alternative Estimators

In order to compare the major set of methods described above, we run a Monte Carlo exercise using structural gravity as a data generating process (DGP). For the determinants of trade, we use actual data for the 170 countries for which we have data on GDP, distance, and the existence of a Regional Trade Agreement (RTA) in 2006. The DGP specifies accessibility as a function of distance and RTA:

$$\phi_{ni} = \exp\left(-\ln \text{Dist}_{ni} + 0.5 \, \text{RTA}_{ni}\right)\eta_{ni},$$

where η_{ni} is a log-normal random term. The η_{ni} is the only stochastic term in the simulation since the GDPs, distances, and RTA relationships are all set by actual data. We calibrate the variance of $\ln \eta_{ni}$ to replicate the root mean squared error (RMSE) of the least squares dummy variables (LSDV) regression on real data. As we will show later, the distance elasticity of -1 and the 0.5 coefficient on the RTA dummy are representative of the literature. Combining this with incomes of exporters and importers, we calculate the multilateral resistance terms, Φ_n and Ω_i using equation (3), which are used in (2) to generate bilateral trade flows.[23]

---

[23] Baier and Bergstrand (2009) adopt the same method to run the Monte Carlo comparison of their Bonus Vetus estimation method with other methods, with one important difference. Rather than including the random term in ϕ_{ni} before calculating the MR index, they introduce the log-normal perturbation just prior to estimation. They therefore adopt a statistical approach, rather than a structural approach to the error term, according to which MR terms should be calculated using the whole of ϕ_{ni} and not only its deterministic part.

Table 3.2 The Estimators Used in this Study

Abbrev.	Description	Introduced by
OLS	Linear-in-logs with GDPs	Tinbergen (1962)
SILS	Structurally Iterated Least Squares	Anderson and van Wincoop (2003)*
LSDV	Least squares w/country dummies	Harrigan (1996)
DDM	Double-Demeaning of LHS & RHS	None
BVU	Bonus Vetus OLS, simple averages	Baier and Bergstrand (2010)
BVW	Bonus Vetus OLS, GDP-weighted	Baier and Bergstrand (2009)
Tetrads	Ratios of reference exporter & importer	Head et al. (2010)

*Section 3.2 explains how SILS differs from the original method.

Since this DGP does not yield missing flows, and such missing flows are a substantial part of the computational issues (due to the problems raised by double-demeaning in unbalanced panels), we propose two ways to generate missing values (which due to the log specification can also be interpreted as zero flows). The first one suppresses $X\%$ of observations randomly, while the second method removes the smallest $X\%$ of the initial set of export flows. The first method can be thought of as representing haphazard data collection and reporting, whereas the second method can be thought of as eliminating exports that are too small to be profitable in the presence of fixed market entry costs. To consider minor, moderate, and major amounts of missing data we set X at 5%, 25%, and 50%.

Table 3.3 presents the results of a simulation of the seven different methods shown in Table 3.2. Each "cell" of the table is a method-sample-regressor combination. The top value in a cell shows the mean estimate over 1000 repetitions, that is the expected value of the estimator. The second value in parentheses is the average standard error and the third, in square brackets, is the standard deviation of the estimate. If the first number is equal to the true values of -1.0 and 0.5 the estimator is unbiased. If the last two values are equal, the estimator also gives unbiased standard errors.

The first point emerging from the simulations reported in Table 3.3 is that *OLS is a poor estimator under the structural gravity DGP*. Its estimates are biased toward zero for both explanatory variables. The method is not robust to deleting the smallest observations. These results validate the decision of Baldwin and Taglioni (2007) to bestow their "gold medal" mistake to gravity regressions that fail to include exporter and importer dummies.

SILS, the structural method we programmed based on Anderson and van Wincoop (2003), gives distance estimates that are close to the assumed true values when there is no missing data. A comparison of the standard deviations of the estimates between SILS and LSDV reveals that LSDV deliver substantially more precise estimates. SILS coefficients are stable in the presence of randomly missing data. With selectively missing data, both

Table 3.3 Monte Carlo Estimates of Distance and RTA Effects

Censoring Estimates	None		Observations Deleted: 5%				Observations Deleted: 25%				Observations Deleted: 50%			
			Random		Smallest Flows		Random		Smallest Flows		Random		Smallest Flows	
	Dist.	RTA	Dist.	RTA	Dist.	RTA	Dist.	RTA	Dist.	RTA	Dist.	RTA	Dist.	RTA
OLS	−0.836 (0.021) [0.051]	0.276 (0.063) [0.114]	−0.836 (0.022) [0.051]	0.277 (0.064) [0.114]	−0.726 (0.021) [0.045]	0.444 (0.062) [0.106]	−0.836 (0.025) [0.052]	0.276 (0.072) [0.118]	−0.578 (0.022) [0.036]	0.485 (0.062) [0.097]	−0.836 (0.030) [0.055]	0.276 (0.089) [0.129]	−0.478 (0.023) [0.031]	0.324 (0.063) [0.089]
SILS	−0.937 (0.021) [0.058]	0.749 (0.060) [0.176]	−0.937 (0.021) [0.058]	0.750 (0.062) [0.176]	−0.833 (0.021) [0.051]	0.666 (0.059) [0.171]	−0.937 (0.024) [0.059]	0.748 (0.069) [0.183]	−0.819 (0.022) [0.046]	0.141 (0.060) [0.161]	−0.937 (0.030) [0.062]	0.752 (0.085) [0.202]	−0.904 (0.024) [0.044]	−0.471 (0.063) [0.146]
LSDV	−1.000 (0.021) [0.021]	0.501 (0.058) [0.059]	−1.000 (0.022) [0.022]	0.501 (0.060) [0.061]	−0.934 (0.021) [0.022]	0.596 (0.058) [0.059]	−1.001 (0.024) [0.026]	0.501 (0.067) [0.069]	−0.799 (0.022) [0.022]	0.651 (0.059) [0.059]	−0.999 (0.030) [0.031]	0.503 (0.083) [0.084]	−0.691 (0.024) [0.024]	0.545 (0.062) [0.062]
DDM	−1.000 (0.021) [0.021]	0.501 (0.058) [0.059]	−0.999 (0.022) [0.022]	0.501 (0.059) [0.061]	−0.920 (0.021) [0.022]	0.624 (0.058) [0.059]	−0.997 (0.024) [0.025]	0.499 (0.067) [0.068]	−0.712 (0.023) [0.022]	0.789 (0.061) [0.061]	−0.988 (0.030) [0.030]	0.497 (0.082) [0.084]	−0.532 (0.026) [0.023]	0.715 (0.065) [0.063]
BVU	−1.000 (0.025) [0.021]	0.501 (0.067) [0.059]	−1.000 (0.025) [0.022]	0.502 (0.069) [0.061]	−0.933 (0.024) [0.022]	0.583 (0.067) [0.060]	−1.000 (0.028) [0.027]	0.501 (0.078) [0.071]	−0.859 (0.026) [0.024]	0.431 (0.069) [0.066]	−1.001 (0.035) [0.032]	0.501 (0.095) [0.088]	−0.839 (0.029) [0.028]	0.060 (0.074) [0.071]
BVW	−0.491 (0.016) [0.093]	0.524 (0.055) [0.157]	−0.491 (0.016) [0.093]	1.230 (0.053) [0.187]	−0.912 (0.021) [0.046]	0.769 (0.054) [0.142]	−0.140 (0.009) [0.048]	1.626 (0.055) [0.154]	−0.616 (0.022) [0.052]	1.233 (0.056) [0.132]	−0.055 (0.006) [0.029]	1.516 (0.063) [0.191]	−0.142 (0.020) [0.052]	1.697 (0.060) [0.122]
Tetrads	−0.998 (0.131) [0.137]	0.509 (0.355) [0.366]	−0.878 (0.160) [0.172]	0.714 (0.413) [0.418]	−0.936 (0.129) [0.134]	0.570 (0.347) [0.358]	−0.530 (0.213) [0.220]	1.258 (0.569) [0.540]	−0.925 (0.131) [0.133]	0.474 (0.338) [0.345]	−0.404 (0.234) [0.252]	1.582 (0.668) [0.645]	−0.962 (0.139) [0.134]	0.294 (0.339) [0.348]

Notes: Top value in each cell is the mean estimate (based on 1000 repetitions). The true parameters are −1 for distance and .5 for RTA. Average standard error in "( )" and standard deviation of estimate in "[ ]". Table 3.2 defines the estimators.

LSDV and SILS estimates deviate notably from the true parameters. We conclude that, even though SILS can be estimated with Stata®, it is not worth the computational effort.

Double-demeaning both log exports and the RHS variables (DDM) and the Bonus Vetus *unweighted* (BVU) approach of double-demeaning just the RHS variables deliver identical results (out to machine precision) when there is no missing data. Unfortunately real gravity data does tend to have missing data. DDM is one of the worst estimators when there are large numbers of non-random missing observations. BVU appears to have better robustness properties. In the worst case scenario with the smallest half of the original data eliminated, BVU gives somewhat better distance elasticities than LSDV but much worse RTA estimates. The GDP-weighted double-demeaning of the RHS variables (BVW) has several disadvantages. Its estimates are not robust to missing data and it is very imprecise as we see in the high standard deviation of the coefficients. Its standard errors appear to be biased downwards.

Tetrads seems to be unbiased except when there are substantial numbers of randomly missing observations. It does quite well with DGPs that eliminate the smallest trade flows. But even there it is imprecise. Fortunately the **cluster2** standard errors we use correctly measure this imprecision. Given the imprecision, the lack of robustness to randomly missing data and sensitivity of results to the choice of reference countries (see Head et al., 2010), the argument for Tetrads hinges on LSDV being computationally infeasible. This is because software such as Stata® cannot handle the large number of dummies needed for panel estimation of time-varying country fixed effects. Fortunately, two-way fixed effects based on the iterative method of Guimaraes and Portugal (2010) yield identical estimates to LSDV (which is why we do not report it separately) and are not subject to arbitrary limits. These 2WFE methods mean that "fixes" like DDM, BVU, and Tetrads are no longer advisable.[24]

These simulations have considered a DGP that follows closely from the major theories that deliver the form we call structural gravity. In this DGP there is a built in relationship between bilateral resistance terms, distance and RTAs, and the multilateral resistance terms. This covariance is sufficient in its own right to cause notably high bias of OLS. Fortunately LSDV solves this problem perfectly so long as there are no other econometric issues. In Section 5 we consider two particularly important additional problems that can undermine the argument for LSDV: heteroskedastic errors and structural zeros.

3.7. Identification and Estimation of Country-Specific Effects

In the presence of importer and exporter fixed effects a variety of potentially interesting trade determinants can no longer be identified in a gravity equation. Notably, (1) anything

---

[24] There is one case where we see Tetrads outperforming LSDV and that is when the smallest 25% of trade flows are selectively removed. In Section 5.2 we point to other methods better suited to such selective censoring of the data.

that affects exporters' propensity to export to all destinations (such has having hosted the Olympics or being an island), (2) variables that affect imports without regard to origin, such as country-level average applied tariff, and (3) sums, averages, and differences of country-specific variables. If any variables of these three forms is added to a trade equation estimated with importer and exporter fixed effects, programs such as Stata® will report estimates with standard errors. However the estimates are meaningless. They are identified by dropping one or more of the country dummies. This is the case for size variables Y_i and Y_n naturally, and country-level institutional variables (e.g. rule of law). Also problematic is the use of exchange rates in this respect. Since (like any relative price) the bilateral value of a currency is defined as a ratio, the fixed effects will swallow each of the price terms after the usual logarithmic transformation of the gravity regression.

To retain monadic variables, authors sometimes resort to creating new dyadic variables using functional form assumptions other than linear relationships. For example, one can create a bilateral institutions variable by multiplying quality of institutions in i times quality of institutions in n. This is identifiable even when having i and n FEs, but this is a sort of constructed identification, with no straightforward interpretation in many cases.[25] A second example is the case of using country-specific average tariff data to try to create a bilateral tariff variable. If one simply averages country i and country n tariffs, the effect is not identified. To get around this, one might take the log of the average tariff. In this case the bilateral tariff effect is identified but only by the choice of functional form: the log of the *product* of i and n tariffs would not work.

While most of the applications are in panel gravity equations, the time dimension clutters notation so we consider the case of a cross-section gravity equation. The underlying estimating equation is

$$\ln X_{ni} = \alpha_i + \beta V_i + \gamma_n + \delta D_{ni} + \varepsilon_{ni}. \tag{27}$$

V_i is a monadic variable of interest. It could be a direct measure of the cost or quality of exports from country i or some geographic or institutional characteristic that underlies cost and quality differences. The D_{ni} are the dyadic controls (e.g. distance, RTAs). The α_i term represents all the other i-level determinants of exports.

There are several possible ways to estimate β and we follow here the treatment of a similar problem in labor economics by Baker and Fortin (2001). The case they consider is the effect of the percent of female workers in an occupation (corresponding to our V_i) on the wages of individuals in that occupation (analogously, our $\ln X_{ni}$). The γ_n destination fixed effect would correspond to an individual worker effect (which Baker and Fortin

---

[25] One good example where the multiplication does seem appropriate is the case of Rauch and Trindade (2002). The idea is that trade is more likely when conducted by an exporting firm who is managed by someone of the same ethnicity as the corresponding importer. The probability that two randomly selected members of each population would encounter each other is given by the product of the ethnicity share in the two counties. Note that the paper itself does not use exporter and importer fixed effects.

do not consider presumably because workers do not move across occupations enough to identify such a term).

Probably the most common approach taken in labor or gravity equations is a one-step estimation. The simplest version combines α_i and ε_{ni} as the error term of equation (27). Even if α_i is uncorrelated with V_i, the error terms for the same exporter will be correlated. This will result in downward biased standard errors of β unless standard errors are clustered by exporter.

A two-step estimator is another way to solve the standard error problem and it has other potential advantages. In the two-step approach, one first estimates the two-way fixed effects version of equation (27) in which exporters fixed effect $\ln S_i$ replaces $\alpha_i + \beta V_i$. The second step is to regress $\widehat{\ln S_i}$ on V_i. Eaton and Kortum (2002) is an early example of the two-step approach in the gravity literature with cross-sectional trade data. Head and Ries (2008) is an example using FDI data.

As pointed out by Baker and Fortin (2001), both methods can be improved by modeling α_i as the sum of the effects of some i-specific controls, C_i, the average characteristics of each exporter, $\bar{D}_i = (\sum_n D_{ni})/N$, and an error term.

$$\alpha_i = \alpha_0 + \alpha_1 C_i + \alpha_2 \bar{D}_i + \psi_i. \tag{28}$$

Substituting this equation into (27) yields a superior version of the one-step equation:

$$\ln X_{ni} = \alpha_0 + \alpha_1 C_i + \beta V_i + \gamma_n + \delta D_{ni} + \alpha_2 \bar{D}_i + (\psi_i + \varepsilon_{ni}). \tag{29}$$

Standard errors should be clustered at the i-level since the presence of ψ_i causes the error to be correlated across n for a given i. This approach looks attractive because it recovers the *within* estimates for the dyadic variables and still allows one-step estimation of the monadic effects. That is, the presence of the $\bar{D}_i$ causes $\hat{\delta}$ to be estimated as if there were i-specific fixed effects. The estimate of β remains vulnerable to correlation between the ψ_i and V_i.

Lastly, we can also consider a two-step version of (29). It first estimates $\widehat{\ln S_i}$ in a fixed effects regression. Recognizing that the fixed effects are estimated with error, denoted ω_i, the estimated i fixed effects are then regressed on all the i-specific variables:

$$\widehat{\ln S_i} = \alpha_0 + \alpha_1 C_i + \alpha_2 \bar{D}_i + \beta V_i + (\psi_i + \omega_i). \tag{30}$$

Since different fixed effects are estimated with differing amounts of precision, the error $\psi_i + \omega_i$ is heteroskedastic. Estimating (30) by generalized least squares gives greater weight to observations with lower standard errors on $\widehat{\ln S_i}$. However, Baker and Fortin (2001) point out that there is no particular reason to expect ψ_i to be heteroskedastic in the same way as ω_i. If ψ_i is homoskedastic and has high variance then more efficient estimation will come from giving equal weight to all observations in the second step. It therefore seems sensible to estimate all three specifications—the one-step equation (29) and the GLS and OLS versions of the two-step equation (30).

Table 3.4 Estimates of Typical Gravity Variables

Estimates:	All Gravity				Structural Gravity			
	Median	Mean	s.d.	#	Median	Mean	s.d.	#
Origin GDP	.97	.98	.42	700	.86	.74	.45	31
Destination GDP	.85	.84	.28	671	.67	.58	.41	29
Distance	−.89	−.93	.4	1835	−1.14	−1.1	.41	328
Contiguity	.49	.53	.57	1066	.52	.66	.65	266
Common language	.49	.54	.44	680	.33	.39	.29	205
Colonial link	.91	.92	.61	147	.84	.75	.49	60
RTA/FTA	.47	.59	.5	257	.28	.36	.42	108
EU	.23	.14	.56	329	.19	.16	.5	26
NAFTA	.39	.43	.67	94	.53	.76	.64	17
Common currency	.87	.79	.48	104	.98	.86	.39	37
Home	1.93	1.96	1.28	279	1.55	1.9	1.68	71

Notes: The number of estimates is 2508, obtained from 159 papers. Structural gravity refers here to some use of country fixed effects or ratio-type method.

4. GRAVITY ESTIMATES OF POLICY IMPACTS

From the first time gravity equations were estimated, one of the main purposes has been to investigate the efficacy of various policies in promoting trade.[26] From this standpoint, production, expenditure, and geography are just controls with the real target being a policy impact coefficient. This section considers the evidence that has been gathered on the policy coefficients and then turns to the harder question of how to move from coefficients to economically meaningful impact measures.

4.1. Meta-Analysis of Policy Dummies

Using Disdier and Head (2008) as a starting point, we have collected a large set of estimates of important trade effects other than distance and extended the sample forward after 2005. The set of new papers augments the Disdier and Head (2008) sample by looking at all papers published in top-5 journals, the *Journal of International Economics* and the *Review of Economics and Statistics* from 2006 to available articles of 2012 issues. A second set of papers were added, specifically interested in estimating the trade costs elasticity. Since those are much less numerous, we tried to include as many as possible based on our knowledge of the literature. A list of included papers is available in the web appendix. The final dataset includes a total of 159 papers, and more than 2500 usable estimates. We provide in Table 3.4 meta-analysis type results for the most frequently used variables in gravity equations, including policy-relevant ones.

---

[26] Tinbergen (1962) found small increases in bilateral trade attributable to Commonwealth preferences ($\approx 5\%$) and the Benelux customs union ($\approx 4\%$).

The table is separated in two groups of four columns: one giving summary statistics of estimates across all papers, and one focusing on structural gravity papers. Here we must have a somewhat looser definition of what structural gravity is, since the use of theory-consistent methods has been quite diverse, and evolving over time. We choose to adopt a rather inclusive definition. For instance many papers include origin and destination country fixed effects, although their data is a panel, and should therefore include country-*year* dummies. We classify as structural the papers that include some form of country dummies or ratio type estimation. We also drop outliers for each of the gravity variables investigated, using a 5% threshold.

The first results are that GDP elasticities are close to unitary as predicted by theory and shown in Figure 3.1 for Japan–EU trade. This is particularly true for origin GDPs (mean of 0.98). The destination GDP elasticity is lower (0.84), a finding that Feenstra et al. (2001) pointed to as evidence of home market effects.

The average distance elasticity of −0.93 is close to the −0.91 reported by Disdier and Head (2008). Thus, the 368 additional estimates we obtained by updating the sample are not out of line with the earlier sample. Consistent with our Monte Carlo results above, we also find that the distance coefficient is biased toward zero empirically when committing the gold medal mistake of not controlling for MR terms. The magnitude of the bias even seems to be quite in line with our Monte Carlo.

Contiguity and common language effects seem to have very comparable effects, with coefficients around 0.5, about half the effects of colonial links. Common language and colonial linkage are frequent proxies for cultural/historical proximity. Those "non-traditional" determinants of economic exchange turn out to be important factors in trade patterns.

The two direct policy relevant variables, RTAs and common currency, have large estimated effects—albeit with large standard deviations. Interestingly, the meta-analysis by Cipollina and Salvatici (2010) on the trade effects of RTAs report a mean effect of 0.59 and median effect of 0.38 for their 1867 estimates. This is quite close to the characteristics of our smaller sample of 257 estimates (mean of 0.59 and median of 0.47). Interestingly, they find that structural gravity yields *stronger* estimates of RTA effects, whereas we find weaker effects (mean of 0.36). Many papers include dummies for RTAs of specific interest, notably the EU and NAFTA which involve some of the largest bilateral trade flows worldwide. Whether looking at the median or mean coefficients, estimated using naive or structural gravity, the North-American agreement seems to be associated with larger amounts of trade creation. Cipollina and Salvatici (2010) also find this pattern, with a mean coefficient for NAFTA (0.90) almost twice as big as the one for EU (0.52).

The trade effects of common currencies have been the subject of controversy. Our mean over 104 estimates is 0.79, which corresponds to a doubling of trade. This is substantially smaller than initial estimates by Rose (2000) who put the currency union coefficient at 1.21, implying more than tripling trade. However, the meta-analysis average is substantially larger than the preferred estimates of some recent work. Baldwin (2006), synthesizing a stream of papers focusing mainly on the Euro, puts the currency effect at about 30%. Santos Silva and Tenreyro (2010) find virtually no effects on trade for the Euro, after taking account of the high level of trade integration of Eurozone members even *before* they formed a common currency. Berthou and Fontagné (2013) use firm-level exports by French firms and find a weakly significant 5% effect, coming mostly from average exports by the most productive firms. Frankel (2010) finds a more optimistic 15% increase of trade that takes about five years to take place, and then stabilizes.[27]

The numbers reported in Table 3.4 establish the *typical* findings but they should not be interpreted as *preferred* estimates of the causal effects of the policy variables. This is because by and large they fail to address the endogeneity related to many of the policy variables and especially to currency unions and RTAs. There are many examples where the countries that sign a trade enhancing agreement already trade a great deal together (NAFTA, EU). Since currency unions economize on transaction costs of converting exchange, they will be greater when there are more transactions, that is when countries trade a lot with each other. Cross-section or pooled panel estimates are therefore not reliable—even if they have country or country-year fixed effects. The textbook solution would be to find instrumental variables but we are not aware of any compelling instruments. Most variables that plausibly cause currency unions or RTAs also "belong" in the trade equation on their own (e.g. distance, colonial history). Lacking plausible instrumental variables (IVs), the most promising approach is to include country-pair fixed effects. This forces identification to come from the *within* dimension of the data. Studies that introduce dyadic fixed effects often obtain dramatically different coefficient estimates from the pooled OLS estimates.[28] Another strategy is to use a natural experiment. In the final part of the paper, Frankel (2010) uses the conversion of the French Franc to the euro in 1999 as an exogenous shock hitting Western African countries that had the CFA Franc (linked to the French Franc) as a currency. The switch to a common currency with members of the Eurozone other than France can reasonably be considered as exogenous for this group of African countries. The trade creating effect seems stronger with this method (around 50%) than with the more classical approach used in the first part of this paper. It also coincides with

[27] Differences might come from different sets of fixed effects, and from different estimators. Baldwin and Taglioni (2007, Table 4) turn the Eurozone coefficient from a significant positive 0.17 with OLS, to a significant −0.09 with the appropriate set of country-year and country-pair fixed effects that account for MR terms, and identify in the within dimension. Santos Silva and Tenreyro (2010) have similar identification strategy and results, with Poisson pseudo-maximum likelihood (PPML) rather than a linear-in-logs estimator. Frankel (2010) regressions have a country pair fixed effect, but not the country-year dummies that would control for MR terms.

[28] For instance, Baier and Bergstrand (2007) find that the RTA estimate is multiplied by more than two, while Glick and Rose (2002) find that the common currency effect is divided by around the same factor. Head et al. (2010) also conduct a dyadic fixed effect specification. Compared to a naive specification, they find a rise in the effect of the General Agreement on Tariffs and Trade (GATT)/World Trade Organization (WTO) (which is also the case in Rose (2004)), and confirm the fall in common currency effects. On RTA they find that the coefficient is halved, in contrast to the results of Baier and Bergstrand (2007).

the switch to the euro, although coefficients puzzlingly lose significance in the two last years of the sample (2005 and 2006).

4.2. The Elasticity of Trade with Respect to Trade Costs

Arkolakis et al. (2012b) show that a gravity equation is all that is needed to calculate welfare gains from trade. Indeed, of the two sufficient statistics required when their macro restrictions hold, one is directly observable (the import ratio), and the other, the trade cost elasticity of trade, can be estimated using a gravity equation for bilateral trade. While relatively few gravity papers estimate trade cost elasticities, we have identified 32 papers that do so, and we summarize their results in Table 3.5. We will refer to those as "gravity-based" estimates. They involve regressing bilateral trade on measures of bilateral trade costs or on exporter "competitiveness" such as wages or productivity.[29] About three quarters of our estimates of ϵ are of the first type, and come from regressions along the lines of

$$\ln X_{ni} = \ln S_i + \ln M_n + \epsilon \ln \tau_{ni}. \tag{31}$$

In many cases, equation (31) is estimated at the industry level. This explains in part the very large variance observed across estimates in the literature, reported in Table 3.5.[30] Most specifications measure $\ln \tau_{ni}$ as the log of one plus the *ad valorem* bilateral tariff rate. In some cases the *ad valorem* freight rates are used instead of or in addition to tariff rates (Hummels (1999) in particular).

We define the gravity-based method broadly enough to encompass estimates derived from regressing bilateral trade on proxies for exporter competitiveness such as wages, exchange rates, and prices. The precise implementation of the competitiveness-based estimate can take two forms: (1) estimate the exporter in a first stage and regress it on wages in a second stage, and (2) directly estimate the bilateral equation using the determinants of S_i, including wages. Eaton and Kortum (2002) is an example of the first approach. They regress exporter fixed effects (derived from a transformed bilateral trade variable) on proxies for technology (R&D expenditures, average years of education) and wages. Instrumenting for wages, they obtain an elasticity of -3.6. As with the trade cost methods, this approach is actually more general than the precise model used by Eaton and Kortum (2002). Indeed, when looking at Table 3.1, we see that the wage in the origin country exhibits an elasticity that is the same or closely related to the elasticity with respect to bilateral trade costs in most foundations of gravity. In Eaton and

---

[29] In addition to the gravity-based estimates included in our meta-analysis, there are two other influential approaches. One method, devised by Feenstra (1994) and applied more broadly by Broda and Weinstein (2006), is to estimate the "Armington" elasticity, σ, using Generalized Method of Moments (GMM) identification via heteroskedasticity. Then $1 - \sigma$ could be used as the estimate of ϵ. A second method originated by Eaton and Kortum (2002) and refined by Simonovska and Waugh (2011), estimates ϵ by relating trade variation to price gaps.

[30] Taking into account this heterogeneity has been shown recently to be particularly important for the estimation of welfare gains from trade, which are larger when ϵ varies across sectors (see Ossa (2012) and Costinot and Rodriguez-Clare (2013) for expositions and estimations of the aggregation bias in welfare gains calculations).

Table 3.5 Descriptive Statistics of Price Elasticities in Gravity Equations

Estimates:	Median	Mean	s.d.	#
Full sample	−3.19	−4.51	8.93	744
Naive gravity	−1.31	−1.35	5.17	122
Structural gravity	−3.78	−5.13	9.37	622
Split structural estimates by:				
Estimation method:				
Country FEs	−3.5	−4.12	8.2	447
Ratios	−4.82	−7.7	11.49	175
Identifying variable:				
Tariffs/Freight rates	−5.03	−6.74	9.3	435
Price/Wage/Exchange rate	−1.12	−1.38	8.46	187

Notes: The number of statistically significant estimates is 744, obtained from 32 papers.

Kortum (2002), the wage elasticity is $-\beta\theta$ whereas the trade elasticity is $-\theta$. Thus, if we know β (the share of wages in the cost function in their model), the effect of wage variation on estimated $\ln \widehat{S_i}$ is an alternative source of identification for the same key parameter.[31] The second approach is chosen by Costinot et al. (2012), who estimate a trade elasticity of -6.5. Their method regresses log corrected exports on log productivity, which they capture based on producer prices data, as their theory is one of perfect Ricardian competition.

Table 3.5 reports the average value and standard deviation of 744 coefficients obtained for the full sample of 32 papers. We then split the sample according to several important characteristics: (1) estimates dealing with the multilateral resistance terms through country fixed effects, ratios or not treating the MR problem, and (2) the variable identifying the price elasticity in the regression (tariffs/freight rates vs exchange rates, relative producer prices, or productivity). This last decomposition is done on the set of estimates that treat the MR problem (structural gravity estimates).

Results in Table 3.5 show that estimates of price elasticities vary immensely with a standard deviation twice as large as the mean. On average the elasticity of trade is -4.51, but when using a median to reduce the influence of outliers, this falls to -3.19. Much of the variance in the estimates can be related to estimation methods: structural gravity (defined the same loose way as in Table 3.4) yields much larger responses of trade flows to price shifters than naive gravity. Also important in the debate between international trade and international macro-economists is the difference between coefficients estimated

---

[31] Since wages are likely to be simultaneously determined with trade patterns, it seems important to instrument for wages, and indeed, the estimated parameter seems to be systematically larger (in absolute value) when instrumenting. It is the case for Eaton and Kortum (2002), Costinot et al. (2012), and Erkel-Rousse and Mirza (2002).

using bilateral tariffs vs exchange rate changes. The latter tend to be much smaller than the former, related to the different usage in the accepted values (for calibrating models in particular) of the two academic populations.[32] Note that the difference between elasticities identified through relative prices or bilateral tariffs holds *within* papers. Studies such as De Sousa et al. (2012) and Fitzgerald and Haller (2012) which estimate the effects of exchange rates and tariffs in the same regressions find comparable differences to ones seen in Table 3.5. Overall, our preferred estimate for ϵ is -5.03, the median coefficient obtained using tariff variation, while controlling for multilateral resistance terms.

Armed with this estimate of the trade elasticity, we can do a simple calculation to determine if estimated RTA effects in Table 3.4 are reasonable. Let ρ be the estimated coefficient on the RTA dummy variable. Since it measures the reduction in trade costs achieved by the RTA, $\rho = \epsilon (\ln \tau_{ni}^{MFN} - \ln \tau_{ni}^{RTA})$, where τ_{ni}^{MFN} is the "most-favored-nation" trade cost factor that n would apply to imports from i were they not in a free trade agreement. Denote as t the Most Favoured Nation (MFN) tariffs that must be removed in the RTA (as per GATT article 24) and let κ capture the *ad valorem* tariff equivalent of all trade barriers that remain in force after the implementation of the RTA. Then $\tau_{ni}^{MFN} = 1 + \kappa + t$ and $\tau_{ni}^{RTA} = 1 + \kappa$. After some algebra, we obtain $t = (1 + \kappa)[\exp(\rho/\epsilon) - 1]$. Martin et al. (2012) estimate $\rho = 0.26$, implicitly assume $\kappa = 0$, and set $\epsilon = 4$ to calculate $t = \exp(0.26/4) = 6.7\%$. With our median structural gravity estimate of $\rho = 0.28$ and tariff-based $\epsilon = -5.03$, assuming $\kappa = 0$ implies $t = 5.7\%$. The problem with this assumption is that "home" (trade with self) coefficients are estimated at 1.55. This implies $\kappa = \exp(1.55/5.03) - 1 = 36\%$. Substituting this value back in yields $t = 7.8\%$. This is considerably higher than the current 3.83% weighted world MFN tariff but lower than the 2000 world simple average MFN tariff of 12.8% (both reported by World Bank WDI database). Thus, our results on border effects, RTA impacts, and trade elasticities are mutually consistent with the proposition that the main channel through which RTAs liberalize trade is the elimination of MFN tariffs. The more general point is that to be in line with actual tariffs, the trade elasticity should be somewhat over 10 times the RTA coefficient; our meta-analysis suggests this is indeed the case.

4.3. Partial vs General Equilibrium Impacts on Trade

The consideration of price index and multilateral resistance terms is not only important from the point of view of estimating the correct β for each of the variables that comprise the trade cost determinants. A second point that Anderson and van Wincoop (2003) emphasize is that the indexes change when trade costs change. Thus, merely exponentiating the coefficients on dummy variables (which we will call the Partial Trade Impact,

---

[32] See Imbs and Méjean (2009) and Feenstra et al. (2010) for recent presentations of the different estimates used by trade and macro economists.

PTI) may not give a reliable estimate of the full impact on trade. Indeed, one of the points emphasized by Anderson and van Wincoop (2003) is that taking into account price index changes leads to substantially smaller trade impacts of borders. The trade impact holding production and expenditure constant but adjusting Φ_n and Ω_i via the contraction mapping does not have an obvious name. It should not really be thought of as a general equilibrium impact because it holds GDP constant and the GDPs depend on factor prices. Anderson (2011) emphasizes the *modular* nature of the structural gravity model: the determination of output and expenditures occurs in a different module from the allocation of bilateral flows. Hence, we will label the trade impact that observes this feature of the model the Modular Trade Impact (MTI). We reserve the title of General Equilibrium Trade Impact (GETI) for the case where wages (and therefore GDPs) also adjust to trade cost changes.

Suppose that B_{ni} is one of the bilateral variables determining τ_{ni}. Further suppose that $\ln \phi_{ni}$ is linear in B_{ni} with coefficient β. We want to see the impact on trade of changing B_{ni} to B'_{ni}. Holding the multilateral terms constant, the ratio of new to original trade is just the ratio of new to original trade freeness. Thus the partial trade impact is given by

$$\text{PTI}_{ni} = \hat{\phi}_{ni} = \phi'_{ni}/\phi_{ni} = \exp[\beta(B'_{ni} - B_{ni})]. \tag{32}$$

Note that $\text{PTI}_{ni} = 0$ for any country pair that does not change bilateral linkages, i.e. $B'_{ni} = B_{ni}$. Thus, the PTI omits third-country effects, which are to be expected because the multilateral resistance terms change whenever other countries change their trade costs.

For any trade equation fitting into structural gravity, the ratio of new bilateral trade, X'_{ni}, to original trade *taking MR changes into account* (but leaving incomes unchanged) is obtained from equation (2) as

$$\text{MTI}_{ni} = \frac{X'_{ni}}{X_{ni}} = \underbrace{\exp[\beta(B'_{ni} - B_{ni})]}_{\text{PTI}} \times \underbrace{\frac{\Omega_i}{\Omega'_i}\frac{\Phi_n}{\Phi'_n}}_{\text{MR adjustment}}. \tag{33}$$

The procedure to implement is therefore to retrieve $\ln \phi_{ni}$, including coefficient β for B_{ni} either using estimates from the literature or estimating ϕ_{ni} through an implementation of equation (22). Then, using ϕ_{ni}, Y_i and X_n in equation (3), a contraction mapping gives us Φ_n and Ω_i. The third step is to do a counterfactual change to B_{ni} (for instance, turn off all RTAs), which results in a new freeness of trade index ϕ'_{ni}. Re-running the contraction mapping provides us with Φ'_n and Ω'_i. We have all the needed elements to calculate X'_{ni}/X_{ni}. Contrary to the PTI approach, a change in a variable specific to a pair of countries using this approach will provide counterfactual changes in trade flows for *all country pairs*.

A growing number of papers, following the initial motivation for structural estimation, do counterfactuals using MTI (although the terminologies vary). Glick and Taylor (2010) is an example where MTI is used to estimate the costs of military conflicts. Anderson and Yotov (2010a) apply this method to assess the impact of an agreement on trade between Canadian provinces that took place in 1995.

An important issue with the MTI is that while (33) does account for changes in MR terms (Φ_n and Ω_i), it assumes constant expenditure (X_n) and output (Y_i) for all countries, which raises a question of interpretation. Recall that $S_i = Y_i/\Omega_i$. Holding Y_i constant, it must be that $S_i' = Y_i/\Omega_i'$. The conceptual problem is that S_i in many models summarized in Table 3.1 depends on wages and exogenous parameters such as quality, A, or technology, T, of all products manufactured in i. Changes in trade costs are not permitted to change wages since that would affect Y_i, but it is peculiar to allow trade costs to change deep parameters.

A second issue is that MTI may omit potentially important effects. For instance, if the thought experiment is the removal of trade costs with a major partner, it is very unlikely that such a drastic change in the trade cost matrix, and therefore in predicted trade flows, would leave incomes unchanged. The MTI remains an interesting entity but we think it also worth calculating the GETI allowing for wage/income changes.

Anderson and van Wincoop (2003) was probably the first paper to calculate the GETI counterfactuals of a removal of national borders, taking into account income changes. Their approach is very related to the "exact hat algebra" methods developed by Dekle et al. (2007) and followers for calculating counterfactual welfare changes. The exact hat algebra approach has a big advantage as a pedagogical tool: it makes it very clear what is the equation driving the wage/income adjustment.[33]

Dekle et al. (2007, 2008) develop a methodology to investigate the consequences in terms of changed wages and welfare of closing trade deficits of all countries. Costinot and Rodriguez-Clare (2013) in this volume show how to adapt the method to determine the welfare impact of trade costs shocks.[34] While the goal of this approach is to provide a quantitative evaluation for welfare, it also yields the GETI as an intermediate step. Here we express the method in terms of our notation and allow for trade deficits (a feature of the data which applications cannot ignore).

The GETI calculation adjusts the income terms Y_i and X_n following the change in trade costs. Denoting $\hat{x} = x'/x$ as the change between new and initial situation of all variables x, the resulting change in bilateral trade is now expressed as

$$\text{GETI}_{ni} = \frac{X_{ni}'}{X_{ni}} = \underbrace{\exp[\beta(B_{ni}' - B_{ni})]}_{\text{PTI}} \times \underbrace{\frac{\Omega_i \Phi_n}{\Omega_i' \Phi_n'}}_{\text{MR adj.}} \times \underbrace{\frac{Y_i' X_n'}{Y_i X_n}}_{\text{GDP adj.}} = \frac{\hat{Y}_i \hat{X}_n}{\hat{\Omega}_i \hat{\Phi}_n} \hat{\phi}_{ni}. \tag{34}$$

To calculate changes in Y, recall that the value of production in the origin country is given by $Y_i = w_i L_i$. Considering the labor endowment as fixed, the change in Y_i will therefore be completely determined by the change in w_i: we have $\hat{w}_i = \hat{Y}_i$. Bilateral trade

---

[33] Egger and Larch (2011) is an example of a set of papers inspired by Anderson and van Wincoop (2003) that calculate trade effects including a GDP updating step. However, as in the inspiring paper, it does not provide a wage updating equation, making it less transparent what are the assumptions that underlie their approach.

[34] Ossa (2011) and Caliendo and Parro (2012) have related implementations.

is a function of the output of the origin country Y_i, but the expenditure at destination X_n also enters. In general, $X_n \neq Y_n$, because of trade deficits, denoted as D_n. There are different ways to handle the presence of trade deficits, which are all ad hoc in the absence of a fully specified intertemporal model. The most straightforward way to incorporate those deficits is to assume that deficit is exogenously given on a per capita basis, that is $D_n = L_n d_n$. With this assumption (which implies that trade deficits are specified in units of labor of country n), $X_n = w_n L_n (1 + d_n)$, so that $\hat{X}_n = \hat{w}_n = \hat{Y}_n$.

At this stage we therefore need to derive the equilibrium change in income, $\hat{Y}$. Note first that market clearing implies that $\hat{Y}_i = Y_i'/Y_i = \frac{1}{Y_i} \sum_n \pi_{ni}' X_n'$. Recall that $\pi_{ni} = X_{ni}/X_n$ is the share of n's expenditure spent on goods from i. In all the models we call structural gravity, changes in π resulting from trade cost shocks take the following form (first demonstrated in Dekle et al. (2007)):

$$\hat{\pi}_{ni} = \frac{(\hat{Y}_i \hat{\tau}_{ni})^\epsilon}{\sum_\ell \pi_{n\ell} (\hat{Y}_\ell \hat{\tau}_{n\ell})^\epsilon}. \tag{35}$$

Plugging this back into the market clearing condition, one can solve for the changes in production of each origin country.

$$\hat{Y}_i = \frac{1}{Y_i} \sum_n \hat{\pi}_{ni} \pi_{ni} \hat{Y}_n X_n = \frac{1}{Y_i} \sum_n \frac{\pi_{ni} \hat{Y}_i^\epsilon \hat{\phi}_{ni}}{\sum_\ell \pi_{n\ell} \hat{Y}_\ell^\epsilon \hat{\phi}_{n\ell}} \hat{Y}_n X_n. \tag{36}$$

The method for calculating the GETI involves four steps.

1. Retrieve β as the coefficient on B_{ni} from a gravity equation in which B_{ni} is a dummy for a trade-cost changing event such as a free trade agreement or a currency union formation (or dissolution). An alternative is to take values of the β vector from the literature. If an *ad valorem* trade cost is included in the study, recover the trade elasticity, ϵ. We use $\epsilon = -5.03$, the median value from our meta-analysis (structural gravity results from tariff rates), which is also the source of each β.
2. The exponential of the coefficient is our estimator of the impact of the trade cost change. That is let $\hat{\phi}_{ni} = \exp(\beta)$ for the ni for whom $B_{ni} = 1$ and $\hat{\phi}_{ni} = 1$ for all other ni pairs.
3. Along with the value of production of each country (Y_i), the original trade share matrix (π_{ni}), plug the estimated $\hat{\phi}_{ni}$ into equation (36), which defines a system of equations determining $\hat{Y}_i$ for each country. Using the estimated value of ϵ, substitute the $\hat{\phi}_{ni}$ and $\hat{Y}_i^\epsilon$ into equation (35) to derive the matrix of trade changes, $\hat{\pi}_{ni}$. Iterate using a dampening factor until $\hat{\pi}_{ni}$ stops changing.[35]
4. The GETI for each country pair is $\hat{\pi}_{ni} \hat{Y}_n$. The welfare change is $\hat{\pi}_{nn}^{1/\epsilon}$.

---

[35] Stata® code is provided online.

We implement the methodologies for PTI, MTI, GETI, and welfare calculations just outlined on a dataset of bilateral trade for 84 countries, and the year 2000. The choice of datasets and sample is dictated by the need to include trade with self X_{ii} in order to calculate meaningful MR terms, needed from MTI to welfare computations. With a few exceptions where "true" internal flows are available (such as trade between and within Canadian provinces), trade with self must be inferred from production and export data as $X_{ii} = Y_i - \sum_{n \neq i} X_{ni}$. Calculating this for total trade is difficult, since the GDP of i includes many service sectors that are hardly traded at all. Furthermore GDP, as a value-added measure, excludes purchases of intermediates, which should be included in trade with self. Data for manufacturing industries is more useful, since comparing the value of production with total exports for the same industry raises less issues. We therefore rely on the CEPII trade and production database, developed for De Sousa et al. (2012), and used in Anderson and Yotov (2010b) and Anderson and Yotov (2012) recently for similar purposes. We take the year 2000 because the production data has a very long lag in release dates, and this makes available a larger set of countries with complete data.[36] We aggregate all 23 industries available in the database to obtain an overall manufacturing sector (with the exception of two sectors—misc. petroleum and other manuf.—which seem to exhibit a large share of negative internal flows, probably due to classification errors).

The results of the trade impacts are displayed in Table 3.6. The two first columns simply gives estimated coefficients and PTIs for the set of variables we want to evaluate: RTAs, Currency Unions, Common Language, Colonial Linkage, and the Border Effect. MTI, GETI, and welfare calculations allow for a separate calculation for members and non-members for each variable. For instance, when evaluating RTAs, the GETI for pairs like the United States and Canada that have an RTA is 1.205 whereas it is 0.96 for pairs like the United States and France which do not have an RTA. Egger et al. (2011) apply a similar methodology to a different dataset and obtain GETIs of 1.39 for members and 0.95 for non-members.

The experiment is to turn off all those dummy variables, in order to calculate the counterfactual trade flows for all pairs, and therefore reveal the amount of trade created by those variables under each methodology. Note first that the MTI is systematically smaller than the PTI. The intuition can be illustrated with RTAs. When signing those, PTI only takes the downward impact on τ_{ni}, when MTI also adjusts the MR terms, in particular Φ_n. Because RTAs make access to n easier, competition is fiercer there, raising Φ_n, and counteracting the direct τ_{ni} effect.

Also note that the difference between MTI and GETI is usually quite small, except for the removal of the effect of national borders, which is a much larger shock. This similarity in the two types of estimates was noted in the original work by Anderson

---

[36] The constraint that internal trade should be available is only binding for the MTI to welfare stages where counterfactual MR and income terms have to be calculated.

Table 3.6 PTI, MTI, GETI, and Welfare Effects of Typical Gravity Variables

Members:	Coeff.	PTI	MTI		GETI		Welfare	
	Yes	Yes	Yes	No	Yes	No	Yes	No
RTA/FTA (all)	.28	1.323	1.129	.946	1.205	.96	1.011	.998
EU	.19	1.209	1.085	1.007	1.136	1.001	1.013	.999
NAFTA	.53	1.699	1.367	1.005	1.443	1	1.048	1
Common currency	.98	2.664	1.749	1.028	2.203	1.003	1.025	.998
Common language	.33	1.391	1.282	.974	1.303	.99	1.005	.999
Colonial link	.84	2.316	2.162	.961	2.251	.984	1.004	.999
Border effect	1.55	4.711	4.647	.938	3.102	.681	.795	n/a

Notes: The MTI, GETI, and welfare are the median values of the real/counterfactual trade ratio for countries relevant in the experiment.

and van Wincoop (2003). Although they only report PTI and GETI, their footnote 26 states that the changes in incomes only affect marginally the outcome (even though their experiment removes the Canada–US border). It is also interesting that the results by Anderson and van Wincoop (2003) from the counterfactual removal of the US–Canada border reveals a steep decline when comparing GETI to PTI (2.43 vs 5.26), a finding we also observe in the last row of Table 3.6 (3.1 vs 4.7), using a quite different dataset.

Looking at welfare effects, it is striking that strong trade impacts may have small welfare consequences. The welfare effects in this class of model are linked to the change in the share of trade that takes place inside a country. Therefore a given variable, colonial link for instance, can turn out to have very large factor effects on the considered flows but very small welfare effects overall, because the initial π_{ni} is very small. Intuitively, because the initial flows are so small, even doubling trade with ex-colonies will result in very tiny changes in the share of expenditure that is spent locally. In contrast, adding even a few percentage points of trade with a major partner will be much more important for welfare.

Finally, it should be kept in mind that the GETI and welfare results shown in Table 3.6 are intended for exposition of the methods, rather than as definitive calculations. There are very important omissions in the analytical framework we used: it lacks sector-level heterogeneity in ϵ, input-output linkages, and other complexities that could alter results in a substantial way. Costinot and Rodriguez-Clare (2013) provide a more complete treatment of the question in their chapter dedicated to welfare effects (see Chapter 4).

4.4. Testing Structural Gravity

The GETI approach to quantifying trade impacts of various policy changes builds a counterfactual world based on a general equilibrium modeling of the economy. Structural gravity is the common core of this modeling. Anderson and van Wincoop (2003) rely on the CES-NPD version of it, Dekle et al. (2007, 2008) or Caliendo and Parro (2012) use the heterogeneous industries version, Bergstrand et al. (2013) and Egger et al. (2011) use the CES-MC view, but all those GETI-related exercises rely on structural gravity, and hence need it to hold empirically. It is also true of Arkolakis et al. (2012b) welfare gains formula, since the assumptions underlying structural gravity overlap to a large degree with the assumptions of that formula. However none of those papers actually test for the empirical relevance of it: the usual approach is to assume it holds, estimate or calibrate a value of ϵ, and then run the counterfactual.

Anderson and Yotov (2010b, 2012) propose that estimated fixed effects can be used to validate the structural gravity model and hence to justify its use for comparative statics. They regress the *estimated* FEs on their counterparts constructed using structural gravity theory and bilateral trade cost estimates. They find very high R^2 and interpret this as confirmation of the theory. One way to think about the issue is that if fixed effects mainly arise due to data issues or unobserved multilateral trade costs, then the estimated fixed effects might be expected to show little relationship to their theoretical determinants. We see some important caveats. The most important is a point raised by Fally (2012). Anderson and Yotov (2012) use Poisson pseudo-maximum likelihood (PML) to estimate the fixed effects and gravity coefficients. Fally (2012) shows that the use of Poisson PML has an unintended consequence: it leads to a perfect fit between the fixed effects and their structural gravity counterparts (the MR terms). To be more precise, if $Y_i = \sum_n X_{ni}$ and $X_n = \sum_n X_{ni}$ as implied by the market clearing and budget allocation assumptions, then $\hat{S}_i = Y_i/\hat{\Omega}_i$ and $\hat{M}_n = X_n/\hat{\Phi}_n$, when using PPML as an estimator for $\hat{S}_i$ and $\hat{M}_n$. The test is therefore bound to succeed perfectly if using this estimation procedure. Even putting that problem on the side, there are important issues to be mentioned with that approach.

First, fit that comes merely from size effects cannot be interpreted as support for the theory. Trade has to go somewhere so larger countries must export and import more as a matter of *accounting* identities, not theory. The real challenge should focus on whether theory-constructed Φ_n and Ω_i are good predictors of the importer and exporter fixed effects after they have been purged by the size effects of X_n and Y_i. In Anderson and Yotov (2010b, 2012), the resistance indexes appear to have much smaller coefficients than the size effects when theory states that they should have the same unit elasticities.

Lai and Trefler (2002) propose a related and potentially devastating critique of structural gravity. Although they specifically address only the CES monopolistic competition model, their results apply to all the models that yield observationally equivalent multilateral resistance terms. The crux of their argument is to show that changes in their constructed price term (a combination of our ϕ_{ni}, Φ_n, and Ω_i) "literally contributes nothing to the analysis of changing trade patterns." They illustrate this finding with a scatter plot showing no relationship between changes in trade and changes in a CES-based computed price index. The price term aggregates tariffs, which Lai and Trefler (2002) established earlier in the paper to have strong effects on bilateral trade.[37] Thus, it is surprising that a tariff-based index term cannot predict trade changes.

Table 3.1 helps to clarify the underlying issue. It shows two versions of the Armington CES model, with and without an outside good. In both cases the fixed effect gravity equation would estimate the same trade elasticity based on bilateral tariffs. However, the "content" of those fixed effects would be very different. With standard CES preferences, the importer term is an index of tariffs. Hence, under the assumptions of that model, changes in that index should lead to changes in trade. On the other hand, with an outside good, the importer fixed effect is just 1 and is obviously not a function of tariffs. We speculate that the absence of tariff-index effects found by Lai and Trefler (2002) does not invalidate CES but rather the homothetic version without an outside good. Nevertheless, the standard CES model is too entrenched—partly because it is so useful!—that it will not be abandoned based on one finding. It seems clear that more research that follows up on Lai and Trefler (2002) is needed to verify just how much violence the structural gravity model does to the data.

5. FRONTIERS OF GRAVITY RESEARCH

This section investigates three areas of ongoing research. The first issue is how to appropriately model the error term in the gravity equation, in particular considering the problem of heteroskedasticity in multiplicative models. The second topic is the appropriate estimation response to large numbers of zero trade flows, a phenomena at odds with a model in which predicted trade is a multiple of strictly positive numbers. The last item covers the rising use of firm-level trade data with its associated set of new issues regarding estimation and interpretation.

5.1. Gravity's Errors

Part of the original attraction of the gravity equation—and of other multiplicative models such as the Cobb-Douglas production function—is that after taking logs they can be estimated with OLS. Santos Silva and Tenreyro (2006) (hereafter SST) brought to the attention of the field that this seemingly innocuous approach involves taking a much stronger stance on the functional form of the error than we do when estimating truly linear models with OLS.

SST frame the problem in terms of heteroskedasticity but this begs the question of which error is not homoskedastic. There are two ways of expressing the error in a gravity equation. Suppose that the exporter and importer fixed effects as well as all determinants of ϕ_{ni} have been combined into a k-length vector $\mathbf{z}_{ni}$ and that the coefficients on these variables are vector ζ. The conventional way to express the error is as the *difference* between

---

[37] Their tightly estimated elasticity of -5 is almost the same mean as found in the Section 4.1 meta-analysis comprising hundreds of estimates.

data and prediction: $\varepsilon_{ni} \equiv X_{ni} - \exp(\mathbf{z}'_{ni}\boldsymbol{\zeta})$. The second way to express the error is as a ratio of data to prediction: $\eta_{ni} \equiv X_{ni}/\exp(\mathbf{z}'_{ni}\boldsymbol{\zeta})$.

After taking logs, the linear regression error term is given by $\ln X_{ni} - \mathbf{z}'_{ni}\boldsymbol{\zeta} = \ln \eta_{ni}$. In standard OLS regressions, heteroskedasticity of $\ln \eta_{ni}$ is a minor concern. The grave concern is whether $\ln \eta_{ni}$ is independent from the $\mathbf{z}_{ni}$. SST point out that if the variance of η depends on $\mathbf{z}_{ni}$ then the log transformation will prevent $\ln \eta_{ni}$ from having a zero conditional expectation and will therefore lead to inconsistent coefficient estimates in linear (in logs) regression.

Should we then try to minimize the sum of the squared residuals, $\hat{\varepsilon}^2_{ni}$, using non-linear least squares? A homoskedastic additive error is an unappealing assumption. It defies common sense to think that deviations of true trade from predicted trade would be of the same order of magnitude for the US and Aruba. Moreover, SST find that non-linear least squares (NLLS) performs very badly in Monte Carlo simulations.

SST argue that Poisson PML is an attractive alternative to linear-in-logs OLS for multiplicative models like the gravity equation. Poisson is not the only PML that could be applied to gravity equations and SST also consider Gamma PML. To understand what each estimator is doing it is useful to compare their first-order conditions side by side.

Actual exports are given by $X_{ni} = \exp(\mathbf{z}'_{ni}\boldsymbol{\zeta})\eta_{ni}$, where η is a multiplicative error term. Using $\sum$ to represent summation over all ni dyads, the moment conditions for the Poisson PML, OLS, and Gamma PML are

$$\underbrace{\sum \mathbf{z}_{ni} \cdot (X_{ni} - \hat{X}_{ni}) = \mathbf{0}}_{\text{Poisson}}, \quad \underbrace{\sum \mathbf{z}_{ni} \cdot (\ln X_{ni} - \ln \hat{X}_{ni}) = \mathbf{0}}_{\text{OLS}}, \quad \underbrace{\sum \mathbf{z}_{ni} \cdot (X_{ni}/\hat{X}_{ni} - 1) = \mathbf{0}}_{\text{Gamma}},$$

$$(37)$$

where $\hat{X}_{ni} \equiv \exp(\mathbf{z}'_{ni}\hat{\boldsymbol{\zeta}})$ denotes the prediction for X_{ni} conditional on the observables. The first set of first-order conditions are the ones used for Poisson "true" maximum likelihood estimator (MLE) on count data. Comparing with the OLS first-order conditions we see that the Poisson involves *level* deviations of X_{ni} from its expected value whereas the OLS involves *log* deviations.[38] The term in parentheses in the Gamma PML first order condition (FOC) is just the percent deviation of actual trade from predicted trade. Since percent deviations are approximately equal to log deviations, the Gamma PML pursues an objective that is very similar to that of OLS shown in equation (37). A useful feature of the two PMLs is that FOC permit the inclusion of zeros, unlike the linear-in-logs form. However, we delay treatment of the zero issue to the following section so as to focus on the role of assumptions about the error term.

Both the Poisson and Gamma PML deliver consistent $\boldsymbol{\zeta}$ estimates regardless of the distribution of η_{ni} so long as $\mathbb{E}[X_{ni} \mid \mathbf{z}_{ni}] = \exp(\mathbf{z}'_{ni}\boldsymbol{\zeta})$. The question of which one is

---

[38] Wooldridge (2010, p. 741) provides further detail on the robustness and efficiency properties of Poisson PML. SST have provided responses to a variety of potential concerns about the Poisson PML estimator on their "log of gravity" page.

more efficient depends on how the variance of X_{ni} relates to its expected value. Consider the following (fairly) general case:

$$\text{Var}[X_{ni} \mid z_{ni}] = h\mathbb{E}[X_{ni} \mid z_{ni}]^{\lambda}. \tag{38}$$

If $\lambda = 1$, a case we will call the Constant Variance to Mean Ratio (CVMR) assumption, then Poisson PML is efficient. The CVMR assumption is a generalization of the Poisson variance assumption in which $h = \lambda = 1$. The Gamma PML is the efficient PML if $\lambda = 2$, that is if the standard deviation is proportional to the mean. We will therefore refer to a DGP that satisfies $\lambda = 2$ as one that adheres to the Constant Coefficient of Variation (CCV) assumption. As the log-normal has a CCV, this provides the intuition for why the Gamma PML estimates tend to be similar to the OLS (on logs), since the latter is the MLE under the assumption of homoskedastic log-normality (which we abbreviate as log-normality). Given that both Poisson and Gamma PML are consistent under the same conditional expectation assumption, their estimates, $\hat{\zeta}$, should be approximately the same if the sample is large enough. Their estimates will only converge on the OLS estimates under log-normality of η_{ni}.

Poisson and Gamma PML remain consistent (and efficient for the corresponding cases for λ) even if $h > 1$, i.e. what is called "over-dispersion." Thus, the finding that variance exceeds the mean does not justify use of estimators such as the negative binomial, suggested by De Benedictis and Taglioni (2011). This estimator is alluring because it has Poisson as a special case but estimates what appears to be more general variance function with a parameter estimating the amount of over-dispersion. We urge researchers to resist the siren song of the Negative Binomial. The most important reason, pointed out by Boulhol and Bosquet (2013), is that Negative Binomial PML estimates depend on the units of measurement for the dependent variable. The web appendix uses actual data to show that measuring trade in thousands of dollars instead of billions not only leads to large changes in the magnitudes of estimated elasticities, it even reverses the signs on some of the indicator variables.[39]

Here we conduct Monte Carlo simulations that re-express some key insights derived from SST. We illustrate attractive robustness features of PML estimators. For each repetition of the simulation we also estimate a test statistic proposed by Manning and Mullahy (2001) to diagnose the error term. This MaMu test—referred to by SST as a "Park-type" test—takes the log of equation (38) and replaces the variance and expected value terms with their sample counterparts to obtain

$$\ln \hat{\varepsilon}_{ni}^2 = \text{constant} + \lambda \ln \hat{X}_{ni}, \tag{39}$$

where $\hat{\varepsilon} = X_{ni} - \exp(z_{ni}'\hat{\zeta})$ and $\ln \hat{X}_{ni} = z_{ni}'\hat{\zeta}$. Equation (39) is estimated using OLS.

[39] Other drawbacks of the negative binomial include: (a) as pointed out in Wooldridge (2010, p. 738), the one-step form of Stata®'s **negbin** command lacks the robustness properties of the other PML, and (b) even the two-step method does not nest the CVMR assumption.

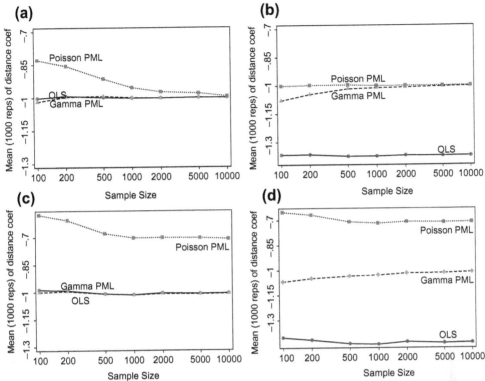

Figure 3.3 Monte Carlo Investigation of PMLs: (a) Log-normal Homoskedastic (CCV); (b) Homoskedastic (CVMR); (c) Model Mis-specification (CCV); (d) Model Mis-specification (CVMR)

In order to focus on issues related to the distribution of the error term, the DGP does not contain i, n, and ni-level components. Rather, as with the Monte Carlos of SST, it is a single-dimensional cross-section. Also following SST, we include a continuous trade determinant, denoted Dist for distance and assumed to be log-normal, as well as a binary variable, called RTA. The results for the binary variable did not offer additional insights but they are available to interested readers by running the program, which is available on the chapter companion website.

Figure 3.3 displays results for four versions of the following data generating process (where u_i denotes a standard normal pseudo-random term):

$$X_i = \exp[\theta_i \ln \text{Dist}_i + 0.5\text{RTA}_i + \sigma_i \times u_i].$$

Versions (a) and (b) have the usual distance elasticity ($\theta_i = -1$) and differ regarding the assumed error term. Case (a) considers log-normal errors with a constant variance parameter $\sigma = 2$. Case (b) departs from log-normal η by assuming a constant mean-variance ratio (CVMR), i.e. heteroskedasticity $á\ la$ Poisson. The σ_i is set to satisfy $\text{Var}[X_i \mid \text{RTA}_i, \text{Dist}_i] = h \times \exp[-1 \ln \text{Dist}_i + 0.5\text{RTA}_i]$. Case (c) reverts to log-normal errors with

$\sigma = 2$ but introduces a mis-specification. True $\theta_i = -0.5$ for $\text{Dist}_i < \overline{\text{Dist}}$ (where we set $\overline{\text{Dist}}$ equal to the median distance) and $\theta_i = -1.5$ for $\text{Dist}_i \geq \overline{\text{Dist}}$. Case (d) uses the same break in the distance elasticity but follows case (b) in using a CVMR error. The regressions in (c) and (d) are mis-specified because they estimate a constant distance elasticity.

The two left panels, (a) and (c), of Figure 3.3 consider the error term structure that is most favorable to OLS and Gamma, that of log-normality with a σ parameter that is constant across all observations. The key result in panel (a) is that Poisson PML underestimates the (absolute) magnitude of the distance effect (and, while not shown, the RTA effect), but the estimates converge on the true value as the sample size rises. The bias exhibited by Poisson PML in panel (a) is increasing in the assumed σ parameter—we have assumed a realistic value of $\sigma = 2$. With $\sigma = 1$, Poisson shows very little bias even in relatively small samples.

Panel (b) of Figure 3.3 replicates the key finding of SST that OLS on log exports becomes an inconsistent estimator in the presence of heteroskedasticity. When the variance of exports is proportional to the mean, OLS overestimates distance and RTA effects. Fortunately, both of the PMLs estimate the effects of distance and RTAs consistently. But now it is the Gamma PML that shows small-sample bias.

Figure 3.3(c) and (d) use a DGP that does not appear in SST, one that features a major error in the specification of the conditional expectation. This DGP features small distance elasticities for flows that travel less than the median distance but much larger (in absolute value) distance elasticities at longer distances. Under such mis-specification, the Poisson and Gamma would be expected to have different probability limits. In the version of this specification with log-normal errors, we find that both OLS and Gamma PML estimate distance elasticities about -1, the average of the short- and long-distance elasticities. In contrast, because Poisson's FOC emphasizes absolute deviations, it puts more emphasis on the high-expected-trade observations, delivering an elasticity, -0.7, that is much closer to the short-distance elasticity. The final simulation shown in Figure 3.3(d) combines the CVMR error with the distance elasticity mis-specification. The two PMLs are hardly changed compared to frame (c), but OLS now estimates the absolute distance elasticity to be over 1.3, as was the case in frame (b).

The Monte Carlo simulations also attest to the usefulness of estimating the MaMu regression. We find that in the log-normal DGP that $\hat{\lambda} \approx 2$. On the other hand, under the CVMR DGP, $\hat{\lambda} \approx 1.6$ with a range of 1.55 to 1.66 if there are 10,000 observations. Even though the MaMu regression does not robustly estimate true λ, it appears to be a reliable method for distinguishing between the two DGPs. Estimates of $\hat{\lambda}$ significantly below two were a near perfect predictor of a CVMR DGP.[40]

Our Monte Carlo results suggest that rather than selecting the Poisson PML as the single "workhorse" estimator of gravity equations, it should be used as part of a robustness-

[40] Specifically under log-normality, in only 6 in 1000 cases with a sample size of 10,000 did the MaMu test find $\lambda < 2$ at the 5% significance. With CVMR errors, the MaMu test rejects $\lambda = 2$ in all repetitions.

exploring ensemble that also includes OLS and Gamma PML. Upon comparing the results of each method, we suggest the following conclusions be drawn.

1. If all three estimates are similar, then we can relax because the model appears to be well specified and η is approximately log-normal with a constant σ parameter.

2. If the Poisson and Gamma PML coefficients are similar to each other and both are distinct from the OLS, then it is reasonable to conclude that heteroskedasticity is a problem and the OLS estimates are unreliable.

3. If the Gamma and OLS coefficients on trade cost proxies are similar and the Poisson coefficients are smaller in absolute magnitude—as occurs in Figure 3.3 (a) and (c)—our simulations suggest two possible interpretations.

    (a) If the root mean squared error is large and sample size is not very large, this pattern might be arising from small-sample bias of the Poisson PML.

    (b) If the sample size is large enough to dismiss small-sample bias, then trade cost elasticities may be falling in absolute value as trade itself rises.

4. More generally, major divergence in large samples between Poisson and Gamma PML—as exhibited in Figure 3.3 (c) and (d)—can signal model mis-specification.

5.2. Causes and Consequences of Zeros

The structural gravity models we have considered in this paper express trade as the multiple of strictly positive variables. Hence, they do not naturally generate zero flows. Most actual trade datasets exhibit substantial fractions of zeros, which become more frequent with disaggregation at the firm or product level. Haveman and Hummels (2004) is an early paper tabulating the frequency of zeros. Even at the country level, Helpman et al. (2008) report that country pairs that do not trade with each other or trade in only one direction account for about half the observations. The high frequency of zeros calls for two things. First, we need to adjust our trade models in order to accommodate zeros since they are an important feature of the data. Second, we need to revise our methods of estimation to allow for consistent estimates in the presence of a dependent variable that takes on zeros frequently.

There a number of possible modifications to the structural gravity model to incorporate zeros. The simplest approach is to assume that zeros are simply a data recording issue, i.e. that there are no "structural zeros" but only "statistical zeros." This would occur due to rounding or declaration thresholds. Structural models of zeros mainly work by adding a fixed cost of exporting a positive amount from i to n. In the Chaney (2008) model, fixed costs are not enough to cause zeros because of the assumption of a continuum of firms with unbounded productivity. Helpman et al. (2008) truncate the productivity distribution and this leads to zeros for some dyads. In contrast, Eaton et al. (2012) generate zeros by abandoning the assumption of a continuum of firms. With a finite number of draws there will be (in realization) a maximum productivity firm even if the productivity distribution has infinite upper support. If the most productive firm from i cannot export profitably to n, then there will be no trade between these countries. Also, as we noted in Section 2.3, with a finite number of consumers, each selecting a single supplier, there will be realizations of the random utility model in which two countries do not trade.

These models all share the feature that zeros are more likely when bilateral trade is expected to be low, i.e. between distant and/or small countries.[41] Unobserved trade costs will endogenously create zeros. When taking logs of the zeros we remove those observations. That leads to the systematic selection bias illustrated in Table 3.3. For this reason, it is important to determine which estimators can deliver good results even when zeros are an endogenous component of the data generating process.

We now proceed to consider several candidate estimating methods prior to judging them using a Monte Carlo simulation. One commonly used method that does not deserve Monte Carlo treatment is the practice of adding one to observed exports and then taking logs. This gives a lower limit of 0 so Tobit is sometimes applied. The method should be avoided because results depend on the units of measurement. Thus, the interpretation of coefficients as elasticities is lost. In the web appendix we show that distance elasticities range from -1.93 to -0.09 as we change the exports units from dollars to billions of dollars. The estimated impact of common currencies switches from negative and significant to positive and significant simply by changing units from millions to billions.

Eaton and Tamura (1994) developed an early solution to incorporate zeros that can be thought of as a model of $\ln(a + X_{ni})$ where instead of arbitrarily setting $a = 1$, it is instead treated as a parameter to be estimated. One could think of a as a fixed amount of trade that "melts" away before the trade flow is measured by government. More formally, the method, which we refer to as ET Tobit, defines a strictly positive latent variable X_{ni}^* and a threshold a such that when $X_{ni}^* > a$ we observe $X_{ni} = X_{ni}^* - a$ and when $X_{ni}^* \leq a$ we observe $X_{ni} = 0$. Unfortunately, $\hat{a}$ lacks a compelling structural interpretation. Another drawback of ET Tobit is that it is not a "canned" program.

Eaton and Kortum (2001) propose another method that has the advantage of being both easier to implement and interpret. Suppose that there is minimum level of trade, a, such that if "ideal" trade, X_{ni}^*, falls below a we observe $X_{ni} = 0$ but otherwise we observe $X_{ni} = X_{ni}^*$. Each a_n is estimated as the minimum X_{ni} for a given n, which we denote as $\underline{X}_{ni}$. To estimate the model, all the observed zeros in X_{ni} are replaced with $\underline{X}_{ni}$ and the new bottom-coded $\ln X_{ni}$ is the dependent variable in a Tobit command that allows for a user-specified lower limit of $\ln \underline{X}_{ni}$. The EK Tobit, as we will refer to this method, has the advantages of (a) not requiring exclusion restrictions and (b) being easily estimable using Stata®'s **intreg** command.

Helpman et al. (2008) take a Heckman-based approach to zeros. This involves first using probit to estimate the probability that n imports a positive amount from i. The second step estimates the gravity equation on the positive-flow observations including a selection correction. A challenge, common to Heckman-based methods, is that it is

---

[41] Baldwin and Harrigan (2011) find this pattern of zeros in the US product-level trade data.

difficult to find an exclusion restriction. Thus, one ideally would like to use a variable in the export status probit that theory tells you can be excluded from the gravity equation. Since both equations have country fixed effects, this variable needs to be dyadic in nature. Helpman et al. (2008) consider overlap in religion and the product of dummies for low entry barriers in countries i and n. While their model deals with zeros, the main focus of their method is to remove the effect of the extensive firm margin so as to estimate intensive margin effects. Thus, they are designed to uncover a different set of parameters than the other approaches which estimate coefficients that combine extensive and intensive margins. Consequently, we omit this method from the Monte Carlo simulations.

In any model that abandons the continuum assumption, the market shares π_{ni} that appear in all structural gravity formulations should be reinterpreted as *expectations*. For a wide class of models featuring finite numbers of buyers and sellers, we conjecture that it is reasonable to stipulate $\mathbb{E}(X_{ni}/X_n) = \pi_{ni}$. In that case, the appropriate estimator is the Multinomial PML, a solution advanced by Eaton et al. (2012) for the case of a finite number of firms. Fortunately, as proven in unpublished notes by Sebastian Sotelo, the Multinomial PML can be estimated by applying the **poisson** command to the market share variable X_{ni}/X_n, along with country-specific fixed effects.[42] By using a dependent variable that divides raw trade by the importing country's total expenditure, the multinomial pseudo-maximum likelihood (MNPML) accords less importance to large levels of trade. This is because the biggest dyadic flows tend to be imported by countries with large aggregate expenditures. Shares prevent this dependent variable from obtaining values over one.[43]

Since one of the original draws of the Poisson PML method was that it allows for easy incorporation of zeros, we will consider the performance of both Poisson and Gamma PML in the Monte Carlo simulation. Previous simulation evidence had produced mixed results. While Poisson PML performs well in Santos Silva and Tenreyro (2006), their simulation uses statistical zeros, obtained via rounding. Santos Silva and Tenreyro (2011) propose a mixture model to generate zeros. Total bilateral exports are given as the product of a random number of exporters and a random level of exports per firm. Santos Silva and Tenreyro (2011) set the share of zeros between 62% and 83% by choosing high variance parameters for the assumed negative binomial count distribution determining the number of exporters. Even with such high zero frequencies, they find both Poisson and Gamma PML outperform alternatives such as linear-in-logs OLS (on the positives), log of one plus exports, and the ET Tobit. These simulations make it clear that the mere presence of large shares of zeros does not undermine the performance of PML estimators such as Poisson and Gamma.

---

[42] The Eaton et al. (2012) specification also includes country dummies interacted with a dummy for trade with self ($n = i$).

[43] The potential drawback is the maintained assumption of an expenditure elasticity of one. In gravity models featuring quasi-linear utility for instance, that elasticity is zero.

The issue left unresolved by Santos Silva and Tenreyro (2011) is whether a DGP that followed modern theory by explicitly featuring fixed costs might be problematic for the PML estimators. In particular, the number of exporting firms should not be purely random but should instead depend on trade costs and market sizes, just as the volume of exports does. Martin and Pham (2011) consider DGPs involving threshold values and find that Tobit and Heckman methods outperform the Poisson PML. However, as noted by Santos Silva and Tenreyro (2011), their DGP is not multiplicative so it does not embed the fundamental problem of linear estimation in the presence of heteroskedasticity.

We consider a DGP that takes as its starting point the structural gravity model. We make a straightforward modification of the heterogeneous firms version of structural gravity seen in Section 2.3.2 so that it can generate zeros. The simple idea is that profits for firm α from i exporting to market n in the CES monopolistic competition model are given by $x_{ni}(\alpha)/\sigma - f_n$. The threshold level of sales at which zero profits would be earned is $x_{ni}^* = \sigma f_n$. Therefore if the initial prediction for aggregate trade X_{ni} falls below σf_n then it would be impossible for any firm to enter and break even. The result would be an observation of $X_{ni} = 0$. Thus this data generating process corresponds to the assumptions of the EK Tobit so long as the disturbances are log-normally distributed.

We do not observe the market-specific entry costs but instead assume that f_n is log-normal, with mean and variance parameters chosen so as to replicate the 25% of zeros in the DOTS data for 2006 that we also used in the first Monte Carlo exercise of Section 3. The procedure is also very much in line with the first Monte Carlo, modified to generate and account for the zeros. The assumed parameters on log distance and RTAs are maintained at -1 and 0.5 respectively, such that $\tau_{ni}^{-\theta} = \exp\left(-\ln \text{Dist}_{ni} + 0.5\text{RTA}_{ni}\right)\eta_{ni}$. As before the model has an error term η_{ni} that is assumed to come from unobserved variable trade costs. We first specify η_{ni} as a homoskedastic log–normal term and then consider a second specification in which η_{ni} is heteroskedastic, such that bilateral trade has a constant variance to mean ratio (CVMR).

The contraction mapping algorithm generating simulated trade flows requires both i and n incomes, combined with bilateral trade freeness, $\phi_{ni} = \tau_{ni}^{-\theta} f_n^{-\left[\frac{\theta}{\sigma-1}-1\right]}$ in this model. Based on our meta-analysis in Section 4.2, we assume $\theta = 5$. Based on Eaton et al. (2011a) we set $\theta/(\sigma - 1) = 2.5$. Combining these assumptions implies $\sigma = 3$. This completes the set of data and parameters needed to generate the predicted aggregate trade X_{ni}, which is cut to zero when falling under σf_n.

Table 3.7 shows the performance of six candidate estimation methods in the presence of zero trade flows. It begins with the most commonly used approach of taking logs and running least squares on the logs of the positive values of bilateral trade. This omits 25% of the sample and does so in a highly selective manner. Under both error DGPs, the coefficients are biased, by about 45%. This result was already anticipated in Table 3.3 in the column where we removed the smallest 25% of the observations and found a 20% bias for distance and a 30% bias for RTA.

Table 3.7 Monte Carlo Results with 25% Structural[a] Zeros

Estimates:	Distance (-1)		RTA (0.5)		Bias[c] (%)	
Error:	Log-normal	CVMR[b]	Log-normal	CVMR	Best	Worst
LSDV on $\ln(X)$ positives	-0.81	-1.07	0.63	0.69	45	46
	[0.02]	[0.01]	[0.06]	[0.03]		
ET Tobit: $\ln[a + X_{ni}]$	-0.94	-1.06	0.53	0.68	12	43
	[0.02]	[0.01]	[0.06]	[0.03]		
EK Tobit: $\ln[X_n^{\min}]$ for 0s	-0.99	-1.23	0.50	0.57	1	36
	[0.02]	[0.01]	[0.06]	[0.03]		
Poisson PML	-0.73	-1.00	0.29	0.50	0	70
	[0.14]	[0.00]	[0.43]	[0.01]		
Gamma PML	-1.05	-1.10	0.41	0.38	23	34
	[0.04]	[0.03]	[0.11]	[0.07]		
Multinomial PML (EKS)	-0.79	-1.00	0.36	0.50	0	49
	[0.06]	[0.02]	[0.15]	[0.03]		

Notes: Mean estimates based on 1000 repetitions. The true parameters are -1 for distance and .5 for RTA. Standard deviation of estimate in "[]". All estimators include exporter and importer fixed effects.
[a]DGP sets trade flows to 0 when $X_{ni} < \sigma f_n$.
[b]CVMR is a Poisson-like error with a constant variance to mean ratio.
[c]"Bias" is the absolute bias in percentage points, with "Best" being the error process that minimizes bias for a given estimator.

The Eaton and Tamura (1994) Tobit-like method estimating $\ln(a+X)$ via MLE works better than LSDV under the maintained assumption of log-normal errors but remains biased. The second Tobit we consider generates better results. Since the EK Tobit is also easier to estimate and has a sound structural interpretation, it dominates the ET Tobit. However, it remains inconsistent under the CVMR assumption. In that case Poisson or Multinomial PMLs are unbiased.

The first and third columns of Table 3.7 reveal that the Poisson PML are biased toward zero under the log-normal DGP. Cameron and Trivedi (1998, Chapter 9, pp. 281–282) prove that Poisson can obtain consistent estimates in panel data even with the number of years fixed and the number of individuals going to infinity. Charbonneau (2012) provides an analytic proof that *with two-way fixed effects*, Poisson PML suffers from an incidental parameters problem. However, we do not think this is the precise problem here. The reason is that the simulation results shown in the second and fourth columns show that Poisson with country effects is unbiased with CVMR errors. Furthermore, the underestimates under log-normality appeared in the previous section even in the absence of fixed effects. We conjecture that asymptotic properties of PPML are not achieved due to the high coefficient of variation in the simulation (calibrated on real data) and the need to estimate $(170 - 1) \times 2 = 338$ importer and exporter effects.

Gamma PML does badly in the presence of the CVMR DGP and is even biased under the log-normal assumption, where it had performed well in the previous simulation.

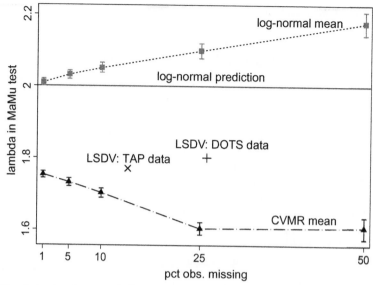

Figure 3.4 Discriminating Between Different DGPs with Structural Zeros

Evidently, the presence of zeros undermines its performance here. The most positive comment on Gamma PML in the presence of structural zeros is that it exhibits the lowest worst-case bias (34%).

The selection of the appropriate estimator therefore appears to be contingent on the process generating the error term. Under the CVMR we would want to use Poisson or Multinomial PML but under log-normality EK Tobit is preferred. This points to the potential of the MaMu test for log-normal errors introduced in the previous subsection. We ran 1000 repetitions of the MaMu test for DGPs featuring varying shares of "structural zeros." We estimated λ by applying OLS to the logged squared residuals from the LSDV model. The results are reported in Figure 3.4.

Since LSDV excludes the zeros, there is reason to be doubtful that a MaMu test based on LSDV errors would be unbiased. Figure 3.4 shows that as the percent of zeros increases, the expected value of $\hat{\lambda}$ under log-normality departs from the true value of two. LSDV estimates give $\hat{\lambda}$ average 2.1 when the DGP is set to reflect the percent of zeros in the DOTS data (25%). Figure 3.4 shows that, when the error term follows the CVMR DGP, $\hat{\lambda}$ is even worse at estimating the true λ, which in that case is one. This is not due to zeros, as we found similar bias in the previous section without zeros. Indeed, raising the share of zeros brings LSDV-based $\hat{\lambda}$ closer to the true value. More importantly, as shown by the 99% confidence intervals on point, there is no overlap in the $\hat{\lambda}$ from the two error structures.

In sum, while the MaMu test delivers biased estimates of λ under both DGPs, it can nevertheless be used to distinguish between log-normal and CVMR with perfect accuracy in 1000 repetitions of each DGP. A finding that $\hat{\lambda} \geq 2$ suggests EK Tobit is the estimator best matched to data where zeros are generated by bilateral fixed entry costs. In contrast a $\hat{\lambda}$ significantly less than 2 militates for Poisson or Multinomial PML, with the preference going to MNPML since its worst-case performance is better than Poisson.

A puzzle illustrated in Figure 3.4 is that the $\hat{\lambda}$ we obtain from regression on real data lie between the simulation predictions. Export data on all goods from the 2006 IMF Direction of Trade Statistics (DOTS) and manufactured goods in 2000 from the Trade and Production (TAP) data yield strikingly similar estimates of 1.77 and 1.79, respectively. This could point to a mixture distribution or to a process, such as the multinomial, that gives intermediate results.

5.3. Firm-Level Gravity, Extensive and Intensive Margins

With the simultaneous emergence of the heterogeneous firms modeling framework and firm-level trade data, questions about the margins of adjustment to trade shocks have become important in the literature. Researchers became interested in whether, after a rise in trade costs, or a fall in final demand for instance, the global trade fall comes from all firms reducing their individual flows, or on the contrary from exit of the smallest exporters. A recent example is Bricongne et al. (2012), who apply this decomposition to the 2008–2009 trade collapse to find that most of the adjustment came from existing firms cutting their shipments rather than from exit. There are however different ways to decompose aggregate exports. To determine the most useful way, we need keep in mind what different models predict.

The first extensive/intensive margin definition was proposed by Eaton et al. (2004), Hillberry and Hummels (2008), and Bernard et al. (2007) and uses the identity that total exports equals the number of active exporters multiplied by average shipments: $X_{ni} = N_{ni}\bar{x}_{ni}$. The total elasticity with respect to trade costs is therefore the sum of the elasticities of these two factors[44]:

$$\frac{\partial \ln X_{ni}}{\partial \ln \tau_{ni}} = \frac{\partial \ln N_{ni}}{\partial \ln \tau_{ni}} + \frac{\partial \ln \bar{x}_{ni}}{\partial \ln \tau_{ni}}. \tag{40}$$

This decomposition respects the traditional use of the extensive margin terminology as being the change in the number of exporters, but the use of the intensive margin is unconventional. It seems more in keeping with traditional usage to limit "intensive margin" changes to the individual responses of firms following the change in trade

---

[44] Bernard et al. (2007), Mayer and Ottaviano (2007), and Bernard et al. (2011) have analyzed finer decompositions, taking into account multiproduct firms. Models of such firms are covered in this handbook by Melitz and Redding (see Chapter 1).

costs. In (40), $\frac{\partial \ln \bar{x}_{ni}}{\partial \ln \tau_{ni}}$ contains this effect, but confounds it with the change in average shipments that comes from the changing composition of exporters. We therefore want to split this term itself into two margins, the intensive and compositional. Using $\bar{x}_{ni} = \frac{1}{G(\alpha_{ni}^*)} \int_0^{\alpha_{ni}^*} x_{ni}(\alpha) g(\alpha) d\alpha$, and using the Leibniz rule as in Chaney (2008), it can be shown that[45]:

$$\frac{\partial \ln X_{ni}}{\partial \ln \tau_{ni}} = \underbrace{\frac{\partial \ln N_{ni}}{\partial \ln \tau_{ni}}}_{\text{ext. margin}}$$

$$+ \underbrace{\frac{1}{\bar{x}_{ni}} \left(\int_0^{\alpha_{ni}^*} \frac{\partial \ln x_{ni}(\alpha)}{\partial \ln \tau_{ni}} x_{ni}(\alpha) \frac{g(\alpha)}{G(\alpha_{ni}^*)} d\alpha \right)}_{\text{int. margin}}$$

$$+ \underbrace{\frac{\partial \ln G(\alpha_{ni}^*)}{\partial \ln \alpha_{ni}^*} \frac{\partial \ln \alpha_{ni}^*}{\partial \ln \tau_{ni}} \left(\frac{x_{ni}(\alpha_{ni}^*)}{\bar{x}_{ni}} - 1 \right)}_{\text{compos. margin}}. \tag{41}$$

This three-way decomposition nests the one proposed by Eaton et al. (2004), Hillberry and Hummels (2008), and Bernard et al. (2007). In their decomposition, they simply add up the intensive and compositional ones and call it intensive. It also nests the alternative decomposition proposed by Chaney (2008), which is obtained when summing up our extensive and compositional and calling it the extensive.[46] The extensive and intensive margins in (41) have the classical respective interpretations. The compositional margin is caused by the fact that new entrants/exitors do not have the same productivity as the existing exporters. This margin is a function of the difference between the marginal firm, with shipments $x_{ni}(\alpha_{ni}^*)$ and the average shipment before the shock, $\bar{x}_{ni}$. This percentage difference is weighted in the overall effect by the change in the distribution of firms associated with changes in trade costs (through changes in the cutoff).

Up to this point, the decomposition is purely definitional and does not depend on specifics of the model nor on the assumed distribution of heterogeneity. Also important is that the two first margins can be measured directly. The extensive margin is the elasticity of the number of exporters (from i to n) with respect to trade costs, and the intensive margin is the elasticity of the *average shipments of the incumbent firms*, that is the firms that

---

[45] The web appendix provides the derivation.

[46] Chaney (2008) starts from aggregate trade $X_{ni} = N_i \int_0^{\alpha_{ni}^*} x_{ni}(\alpha) dG(\alpha)$, and proceeds to decomposing between the elasticity of shipments due to incumbent exporters, and the one caused by entrants/exitors:

$$\frac{\partial \ln X_{ni}}{\partial \ln \tau_{ni}} = \frac{\tau_{ni}}{X_{ni}} \left(N_i \int_0^{\alpha_{ni}^*} \frac{\partial x_{ni}(\alpha)}{\partial \tau_{ni}} dG(\alpha) \right) + \frac{\tau_{ni}}{X_{ni}} \left(N_i x_{ni}(\alpha_{ni}^*) g(\alpha_{ni}^*) \frac{\partial \alpha_{ni}^*}{\partial \tau_{ni}} \right).$$

were exporting before the shock and still do afterwards.[47] One can therefore calculate these two margins and back out the third one as a residual to quantify the share of each. This "margins accounting" can in principle be done independently of the underlying foundation for gravity, or even with models that do not have closed-form solutions for those margins.

What should we expect for the value of the different margin elasticities? This will depend on modeling assumptions naturally. There are two types of such assumptions that are usually made: one has to do with the underlying constant price elasticity (CES + iceberg) modeling, the other imposes the heterogeneity in productivity to be distributed Pareto. Let us proceed by imposing those sequentially, and in that order.

5.3.1. Margins with a CES-Iceberg (Constant Price Elasticity) Model

If the price elasticity is constant, the intensive margin term simplifies to $\frac{\partial \ln x_{ni}(\alpha)}{\partial \ln \tau_{ni}}$ (which factors out of the integral in (41)). In the Melitz/Chaney model of heterogeneous firms exporting to multiple countries, a firm located in i and indexed by its unitary input coefficient α exports the following value to country n:

$$x_{ni}(\alpha) = \left(\frac{\sigma}{\sigma - 1} \right)^{1-\sigma} (\alpha w_i \tau_{ni})^{1-\sigma} \frac{X_n}{\Phi_n}. \tag{42}$$

The intensive margin will therefore be $1 - \sigma$.[48]

To calculate what the theory predicts for the extensive margin, we need to write equilibrium N_{ni}. Since $N_{ni} = G(\alpha_{ni}^*)N_i$,

$$\frac{\partial \ln N_{ni}}{\partial \ln \tau_{ni}} = \frac{\partial \ln G(\alpha_{ni}^*)}{\partial \ln \alpha_{ni}^*} \frac{\partial \ln \alpha_{ni}^*}{\partial \ln \tau_{ni}}. \tag{43}$$

The first elasticity in this product requires an assumption on the distribution of heterogeneity which we will turn to below. As can be seen in (17), the second elasticity is -1 regardless of distributions and follows from the iceberg assumption. Since profits in a given market depend on the product $\alpha w \tau$, to hold profits equal to zero, any increase in τ must be matched by an exactly proportionate decrease in α. Using this result also allows to simplify the compositional margin, such that we have now the following decomposition:

$$\frac{\partial \ln X_{ni}}{\partial \ln \tau_{ni}} = \underbrace{-\frac{\partial \ln G(\alpha_{ni}^*)}{\partial \ln \alpha_{ni}^*}}_{\text{ext. margin}} + \underbrace{1 - \sigma}_{\text{int. margin}} + \underbrace{\frac{\partial \ln G(\alpha_{ni}^*)}{\partial \ln \alpha_{ni}^*} \left(1 - \frac{x_{ni}(\alpha_{ni}^*)}{\bar{x}_{ni}} \right)}_{\text{compos. margin}}. \tag{44}$$

[47] Incumbents is a slight abuse of language here. Strictly speaking, the relevant set of firms in the model is the one of firms that fall below the cost cutoff both before and after the trade cost shock, and therefore is defined in terms of productivity draw, rather than on initial presence in the market.

[48] These elasticities reflect the partial trade impact of a change in trade costs, defined as PTI above, since they hold Φ_n, X_n, and w_i constant when changing τ_{ni}. This is the natural partial effect to consider since fixed effects for each i and n effectively hold those attributes constant.

5.3.2. Margins with a CES-Iceberg Model and Pareto

Any progress on evaluating the expected values of the three elasticities in (44) requires an assumption on $G()$, the distribution of productivity. The literature almost universally uses the Pareto, which offers the very convenient feature of a constant elasticity of the CDF with respect to the cutoff, $\frac{\partial \ln G(\alpha_{ni}^*)}{\partial \ln \alpha_{ni}^*} = \theta$. The web appendix shows that in that case, the deviation of the marginal firms' exports from the average exports is inversely related to θ. The two θ cancel, leaving $\sigma - 1$ as the compositional margin:

$$\frac{\partial \ln X_{ni}}{\partial \ln \tau_{ni}} = \underbrace{-\theta}_{\text{ext. margin}} + \underbrace{1-\sigma}_{\text{int. margin}} + \underbrace{\sigma - 1}_{\text{compos. margin}}. \tag{45}$$

Hence the overall elasticity is $-\theta$, which comes from the fact that the compositional margin exactly compensates the intensive margin, so that the effect of a change in trade costs on average shipments is zero. The intuition is that a rise in trade costs should reduce export flows by all incumbent exporters (the intensive margin), which reduces the average exports. However, the same rise in trade costs causes the weakest firms to exit, which in turn raises average exports (the compositional margin). The fact that the second effect exactly compensates the first is an artifact of the Pareto distribution. We speculate that under other distributions than Pareto, the distributional margin would not be so strong as to compensate fully the intensive margin. We will return to empirical evidence of this below.

Equation (45) also sheds new light on the traditional practice of calculating the margins using (40), i.e. the impact of gravity variables on the number of exporters and the average shipments. Indeed, since this second impact is predicted to be zero in a strict version of the Melitz/Chaney model, one should actually obtain that the extensive margin is systematically 100% of the total effect.

Using data collected in the EU-funded project EFIGE, we have calculated average exports and number of exporters of three origin countries (France, Belgium, and Norway) to each destination country and regress those on the most traditional gravity proxies, GDP and distance to obtain an idea of those margins.[49] Results (available on the chapter companion website) show that the extensive margin is a dominant part of the overall effects in all samples, and for both variables. This is not an isolated finding. Using the same method of decomposition, Bernard et al. (2007), Mayer and Ottaviano (2007), Hillberry and Hummels (2008), and Lawless (2010) all point to the extensive margin accounting for most of the total elasticities of most gravity variables. However it is not 100% as the strict version of the theory would predict. Eaton et al. (2011a) show that under Pareto-heterogeneity, average exports are proportional to fixed cost of market

---

[49] All elasticities with respect to X_n (proxied by GDP) have theoretical predictions that are more complicated than the ones on τ_{ni} (proxied by distance). The main issue is that it is not tenable to use the PTI for those, holding Φ_n constant when changing GDP of n.

entry. Thus, one interpretation of the margins regressions is that such costs are rising in GDP and declining in distance. While plausible for GDP, it would be strange indeed for distance to raise variable trade costs but *lower* fixed entry costs. An alternative inference is that heterogeneity is not Pareto. In that case the intensive margin effects of GDP (positive) and distance (negative) are not completely compensated by opposite effects of the compositional margin. This alternative explanation strikes us to be at least as plausible.

Another advantage of the three-way decomposition (45) over the two-way (40) is that it is more handy if one wants to estimate structural parameters of the model. For instance, with firm-level exports and trade costs data, one can estimate the elasticity of the number of exporters to recover θ. Then change the dependent variable to the average shipments of firms that remain exporters over the whole sample to estimate σ. The two-way decomposition by Chaney (2008) offers the same advantage, and permits the same structural estimations except that one needs to estimate the overall elasticity to recover θ, and aggregate rather than average exports to recover σ.[50] Crozet and Koenig (2010) use firm-level regressions of the same theoretical setup to estimate the structural parameters from the equations for export values, productivity distributions and export probabilities, so as to calculate the Chaney (2008) margins. Interestingly, and in line with the arguments above, Crozet and Koenig (2010) find the share of the extensive margin using Chaney's method to be much smaller than what the literature has found using the first method. Also, they do find a large variance in the shares of the two margins across sectors, a finding hard to reconcile with the decomposition method using (40).

While the intensive margin using the margins decomposition is one method to estimate the parameter σ, there is a more direct way, using firm-level shipments. Firm-level trade data typically takes the form of exports values reported by the national customs administration for each firm over a certain number of years. While it would be very valuable to be able to put together several of those national datasets, confidentiality issues make it very unlikely to happen any time soon. Taking logs of (42), dropping the source country index, and adding a time dimension and a properly behaved error term, one obtains

$$\ln x_{nt}(\alpha) = (1-\sigma)\ln\left(\frac{\sigma}{\sigma-1}\right) + (1-\sigma)\ln(\alpha_t w_t) + (1-\sigma)\ln\tau_{nt} + \ln(X_{nt}/\Phi_{nt}) + \varepsilon_{nt}(\alpha).$$

(46)

The first point to note is that there are two sources of identification for $1-\sigma$: one from the cost component of the firm $(\alpha_t w_t)$, the other one from international price shifters (τ_{nt}). Let us focus on τ_{nt} first. The regression will need to capture both some firm-time level determinant and some destination-time one. It is quite clear from equation (46) that no ideal structure of fixed effects will work, since τ_{nt} and X_{nt}/Φ_{nt} vary along the

---

[50] Berman et al. (2012) use a related approach to evaluate the margins in a model with variable markups where they don't have closed-form solutions for the margins.

same dimensions. One path is to introduce firm-destination effects, that capture the time invariant determinants of αw and X_n/Φ_n, but also any part of $\varepsilon_{nt}(\alpha)$ that does not change over time. The regression can then identify the effect of τ_{nt} from the variation over time (the regression should also include proxies for changes in demand of the destination and efficiency of the firm). Such changes in trade costs can come from trade policy naturally, and there are databases (listed in the web appendix) which can be used to measure changes in applied tariffs by different destination countries. Moreover, any bilateral price shifter would in theory have the same impact: freight rates for instance also reveal the trade cost elasticity. Fitzgerald and Haller (2012) and Berman et al. (2012) estimate this elasticity using firm-level shipments for Irish and French exports respectively. The price shifters in Fitzgerald and Haller (2012) are the real exchange rate, and tariff changes from 2000 to 2004. The impact of tariffs seems to be of the same order of magnitude as the aggregate literature, with an elasticity around −5. Interestingly enough, the coefficient on the exchange rate is much lower, between 0.8 and 1, which is very similar to what Berman et al. (2012) find for French firms. This discrepancy is reminiscent of findings in the aggregate literature.

An interesting case to consider for firm-level exports is when exports of a certain good originate from one country of production only (Scotch whisky would be an example). We can then write

$$x_n(\alpha) = \frac{(\alpha\tau_n)^{1-\sigma}}{N_i \int_0^{\alpha_n^*} (\alpha\tau_n)^{(1-\sigma)} dG(\alpha)} X_n = \frac{\alpha^{1-\sigma}}{N_i V_n} X_n, \quad \text{with} \quad V_n = \int_0^{\alpha_n^*} \alpha^{1-\sigma} dG(\alpha).$$

(47)

The trade costs affects all competitors equally in the destination market, and therefore drops out of the export value equation. In that extreme case the predicted response of trade flows to trade costs is just zero, even though the true price elasticity is $1 - \sigma$. The only case where the trade elasticity of individual exporters with respect to trade costs will be $1 - \sigma$ is when the exporting country considered does not affect Φ_n, and is therefore a marginal player in the considered industry. This is not only true for firm-level exports, but also for industry-level gravity equations. Therefore when trying to estimate the trade elasticity with respect to trade costs, one should be careful about the degree of monopoly that different exporting countries have on world markets. In the limit if a country is the only exporter of a given good, rising tariffs cannot affect its market share. As a consequence, different coefficients on tariffs across industries can be a noisy estimate of different values of σ or θ characterizing the sectors. The difference in coefficients might come from differences in the concentration of supply across industries.

The other source of identification of the trade elasticity is the coefficient on α, the inverse of the firm's productivity. More generally, any cost-shifter in this model is entirely transmitted in the delivered price of the firm, and cuts sales by $1 - \sigma$ percent. Pure cost shifters are however rarely measured at the level of the firm. Let us be as general as possible, and index firms by a "performance" variable s, that shifts utility by a factor γ and raises marginal costs with elasticity λ. Crozet et al. (2012) show that s then impacts individual shipments with elasticity $(\gamma - \lambda)(\sigma - 1)$. The demand parameter σ is now grouped with the quality elasticities. Even estimating the compound parameters poses a challenge because of a selection bias inherent to this whole class of models involving selection into export markets. To see this, we need to add the error term to the estimated model. To simplify exposition, let us continue with firms originating from one country only:

$$\ln x_n(s) = (\gamma - \lambda)(\sigma - 1)\ln s + \ln (X_n/N_i V_n) + \varepsilon_n(s). \tag{48}$$

Crozet et al. (2012) model $\varepsilon_n(s)$ as a firm-destination demand shifter. The econometrician does not observe the quality of the match between a firm's variety and the destination consumer's tastes, which is what $\varepsilon_n(s)$ is capturing. Since only firms with $x_n(s) \geq f_n \sigma$ can enter country n profitably, it is clear from (48) that the firms that are active in n despite a small observed s must have a high $\varepsilon_n(s)$ and vice-versa. This creates a negative correlation between s and $\varepsilon_n(s)$, hence a downward selection bias on s. This issue can be resolved using the EK Tobit method described in Section 5.2. Crozet et al. (2012) show that for the case of exports by Champagne producers, the bias is quite large. They also use Monte Carlo simulations to show that the magnitude of the expected bias is actually very similar when assuming alternative error structures (logistic, gumbel, and exponential) and in line with the bias found in the data.

6. DIRECTIONS FOR FUTURE RESEARCH

Predicting which topics will turn out to be fertile for future research is never easy. However, based on our assessment of the current set of problems and unresolved issues we offer three suggestions.

First, the underlying determinants of trade costs remain poorly understood. We are comfortable with transport costs and tariffs yet we have reason to believe that neither are the most important determinants of trade costs. First, distance effects are too large and have the wrong functional form to be determined by freight costs. Second, border effects are large even along borders where tariffs are very small. Other variables such as language and common currency have impacts on trade that seem very large compared to any reasonable accounting of the costs that different languages or different currencies impose. We believe that authors need to dig deeper to understand what underlies these impacts.

The second topic that is attracting growing interest is the dynamics of trade. All the micro-foundations of gravity that we examined are static models. They provide a derivation for a cross-section but are questionable bases for panel estimation. This raises the econometric problem of how to handle the evolution of trade over time in response to changes in trade costs. More fundamentally, we need to think more about how to incorporate short-run capacity effects, learning, sunk costs, and other dynamic phenomena into the gravity equation framework.

The final topic has been lurking throughout our derivations of the micro-foundations. In every model there came a point where very specific functional forms were imposed in order to maintain tractability. The constant elasticity of substitution model for preferences is nearly ubiquitous. Where it is less important, specific forms for heterogeneity (Fréchet, Pareto) are often essential. Finally theorists have often resorted to modeling firms using a continuum. Given the immense size of firms like Airbus or Boeing, it is an embarrassment to stipulate that all firms have zero mass and act as if they had no influence on the price index. Future research will need to devise ways to investigate the consequences of departing from these assumptions and ways to test whether the data clearly reject the current set of restrictions customarily imposed mainly for tractability rather than realism.

7. CONCLUSION

The use of gravity equations to understand bilateral trade patterns exemplifies the beneficent roles of empirical regularities in guiding theory development and theory in guiding estimation. Our graphic displays of the systematic distance and size effects in trade data show the empirical appeal of the gravity equation. We have cataloged the diverse set of microfoundations that deliver "structural gravity," our label for a formulation that matches stylized facts while calling for a more sophisticated estimation approach than the one initially employed. After a quantitative summary of 1000s of prior estimates, we illustrate the use of the structural form to determine the complete trade and welfare impacts of policy changes. Our selective survey of topics at the frontier of current research suggests that a great deal of interesting work lies ahead.

REFERENCES

Abowd, J., Kramarz, F., Margolis, D., 1999. High wage workers and high wage firms. Econometrica 67 (2), 251–333.

Ahlfeldt, G., Redding, S., Sturm, D., Wolf, N., 2012. The Economics of Density: Evidence from the Berlin Wall, manuscript.

Anderson, J., 1979. A theoretical foundation for the gravity equation. The American Economic Review 69 (1), 106–116.

Anderson, J., 2011. The gravity model. The Annual Review of Economics 3 (1), 133–160.

Anderson, J., Marcouiller, D., 2002. Insecurity and the pattern of trade: an empirical investigation. Review of Economics and Statistics 84 (2), 342–352.

Anderson, J.E., van Wincoop, E., 2003. Gravity with gravitas: a solution to the border puzzle. The American Economic Review 93 (1), 170–192.

Anderson, J., Yotov, Y., 2010a. The changing incidence of geography. American Economic Review 100, 2157–2186.

Anderson, J., Yotov, Y., 2010b. Specialization: Pro-and Anti-Globalizing, 1990–2002. Working Paper 16301, NBER.

Anderson, J.E., Yotov, Y.V., February 2012. Gold Standard Gravity. Working Paper 17835, NBER.

Anderson, S., De Palma, A., Thisse, J., 1992. Discrete Choice Theory of Product Differentiation. MIT Press.

Arkolakis, C., Costinot, A., Donaldson, D., Rodríguez-Clare, A., 2012a. The Elusive Pro-Competitive Effects of Trade, manuscript.

Arkolakis, C., Costinot, A., Rodriguez-Clare, A., 2012b. New trade models, same old gains? American Economic Review 102 (1), 94–130.

Armington, P.S., 1969. A theory of demand for products distinguished by place of production. Staff Papers, International Monetary Fund 16 (1), 159–178.

Baier, S.L., Bergstrand, J.H., 2001. The growth of world trade: tariffs, transport costs, and income similarity. Journal of International Economics 53 (1), 1–27.

Baier, S., Bergstrand, J., 2007. Do free trade agreements actually increase members' international trade? Journal of International Economics 71 (1), 72–95.

Baier, S., Bergstrand, J., 2009. Bonus vetus OLS: a simple method for approximating international trade-cost effects using the gravity equation. Journal of International Economics 77 (1), 77–85.

Baier, S., Bergstrand, J.H., 2010. Approximating general equilibrium impacts of trade liberalizations using the gravity equation. In: Van Bergeijk, P., Brakman, S. (Eds.), The Gravity Model in International Trade: Advances and Applications. Cambridge University Press, pp. 88–134 (Chapter 4).

Baker, M., Fortin, N.M., 2001. Occupational gender composition and wages in Canada, 1987–1988. The Canadian Journal of Economics 34 (2), 345–376.

Baldwin, R., 2006. The Euro's Trade Effects. Technical Report, European Central Bank.

Baldwin, R., Harrigan, J., 2011. Zeros, quality, and space: trade theory and trade evidence. American Economic Journal: Microeconomics 3 (2), 60–88.

Baldwin, R., Taglioni, D., 2007. Trade effects of the euro: a comparison of estimators. Journal of Economic Integration 22 (4), 780–818.

Behrens, K., Mion, G., Murata, Y., Südekum, J., 2009. Trade, Wages, and Productivity. Technical Report 7369, CEPR.

Bergstrand, J., 1985. The gravity equation in international trade: some microeconomic foundations and empirical evidence. The Review of Economics and Statistics 67 (3), 474–481.

Bergstrand, J.H., Egger, P., Larch, M., 2013. Gravity redux: estimation of gravity-equation coefficients, elasticities of substitution, and general equilibrium comparative statics under asymmetric bilateral trade costs. Journal of International Economics 89 (1), 110–121.

Berman, N., Martin, P., Mayer, T., 2012. How do different exporters react to exchange rate changes? The Quarterly Journal of Economics 127 (1), 437–492.

Bernard, A., Eaton, J., Jensen, J., Kortum, S., 2003. Plants and productivity in international trade. American Economic Review 93 (4), 1268–1290.

Bernard, A.B., Jensen, J.B., Redding, S.J., Schott, P.K., 2007. Firms in international trade. Journal of Economic Perspectives 21 (3), 105–130.

Bernard, A.B., Redding, S.J., Schott, P.K., 2011. Multiproduct firms and trade liberalization. The Quarterly Journal of Economics 126 (3), 1271–1318.

Berthou, A., Fontagné, L., 2013. How do multi-product exporters react to a change in trade costs? Scandinavian Journal of Economics 115 (2), 326–353.

Boulhol, H., Bosquet, C., 2013. Applying the GLM variance assumption to overcome the scale-dependence of the Negative Binomial QGPML Estimator. Econometric Reviews, posted online: 14 June 2013.

Bricongne, J.-C., Fontagné, L., Gaulier, G., Taglioni, D., Vicard, V., 2012. Firms and the global crisis: French exports in the turmoil. Journal of International Economics 87 (1), 134–146.

Broda, C., Weinstein, D.E., 2006. Globalization and the gains from variety. Quarterly Journal of Economics 121 (2), 541–585.

Caliendo, L., Parro, F., 2012. Estimates of the Trade and Welfare Effects of NAFTA. Technical Report 18508, NBER.

Cameron, A., Trivedi, P., 1998. Regression Analysis of Count Data. Cambridge University Press.

Chaney, T., 2008. Distorted gravity: the intensive and extensive margins of international trade. American Economic Review 98 (4), 1707–21.

Charbonneau, K.B., 2012. Multiple Fixed Effects in Nonlinear Panel Data Models Theory and Evidence, Princeton mimeo, November.

Chen, H., Kondratowicz, M., Yi, K.-M., 2005. Vertical specialization and three facts about U.S. international trade. The North American Journal of Economics and Finance 16 (1), 35–59.

Chen, N., Novy, D., 2011. Gravity, trade integration, and heterogeneity across industries. Journal of International Economics 85 (2), 206–221.

Cipollina, M., Salvatici, L., 2010. Reciprocal trade agreements in gravity models: a meta-analysis. Review of International Economics 18 (1), 63–80.

Coeurdacier, N., Martin, P., 2009. The geography of asset trade and the euro: insiders and outsiders. Journal of the Japanese and International Economies 23 (2), 90–113.

Combes, P.-P., Lafourcade, M., Mayer, T., 2005. The trade-creating effects of business and social networks: evidence from France. Journal of International Economics 66 (1), 1–29.

Costinot, A., Donaldson, D., Komunjer, I., 2012. What goods do countries trade? A quantitative exploration of Ricardo's ideas. Review of Economic Studies 79 (2), 581–608.

Crozet, M., Koenig, P., 2010. Structural gravity equations with intensive and extensive margins. Canadian Journal of Economics/Revue Canadienne d'Économique 43 (1), 41–62.

Crozet, M., Head, K., Mayer, T., 2012. Quality sorting and trade: firm-level evidence for French wine. Review of Economic Studies 79 (2), 609–644.

Deardorff, A., 1984. Testing trade theories and predicting trade flows. In: Jones, R., Kenen, P.B. (Eds.), Handbook of International Economics, vol. 1. Elsevier, pp. 467–517.

De Benedictis, L., Taglioni, D., 2011. The gravity model in international trade. In: De Benedictis, L., Salvatici, L. (Eds.), The Trade Impact of European Union Preferential Policies: An Analysis Through Gravity Models. Springer, pp. 55–90 (Chapter 4).

Dekle, R., Eaton, J., Kortum, S., 2007. Unbalanced trade. American Economic Review 97 (2), 351–355.

Dekle, R., Eaton, J., Kortum, S., 2008. Global rebalancing with gravity: measuring the burden of adjustment. IMF Staff Papers 55 (3), 511–540.

de Sousa, J., Lochard, J., 2011. Does the single currency affect foreign direct investment? The Scandinavian Journal of Economics 113 (3), 553–578.

De Sousa, J., Mayer, T., Zignago, S., 2012. Market access in global and regional trade. Regional Science and Urban Economics 42 (6), 1037–1052.

Disdier, A.-C., Head, K., 2008. The puzzling persistence of the distance effect on bilateral trade. The Review of Economics and Statistics 90 (1), 37–48.

Eaton, J., Kortum, S., 2001. Trade in capital goods. European Economic Review 45 (7), 1195–1235.

Eaton, J., Kortum, S., 2002. Technology, geography, and trade. Econometrica 70 (5), 1741–1779.

Eaton, J., Tamura, A., 1994. Bilateralism and regionalism in Japanese and U.S. trade and direct foreign investment patterns. Journal of the Japanese and International Economies 8 (4), 478–510.

Eaton, J., Kortum, S., Kramarz, F., 2004. Dissecting trade: firms, industries, and export destinations. The American Economic Review 94 (2), 150–154.

Eaton, J., Kortum, S., Kramarz, F., 2011a. An anatomy of international trade: evidence from French firms. Econometrica 79 (5), 1453–1498.

Eaton, J., Kortum, S., Neiman, B., Romalis, J., 2011b. Trade and the Global Recession. Technical Report, NBER.

Eaton, J., Kortum, S., Sotelo, S., 2012. International Trade: Linking Micro and Macro. Technical Report, NBER.

Egger, P., Larch, M., 2011. An assessment of the Europe agreement's effects on bilateral trade, GDP, and welfare. European Economic Review 55 (2), 263–279.

Egger, P., Larch, M., Staub, K.E., Winkelmann, R., 2011. The trade effects of endogenous preferential trade agreements. American Economic Journal: Economic Policy 3 (3), 113–43.

Erkel-Rousse, H., Mirza, D., 2002. Import price elasticities: reconsidering the evidence. Canadian Journal of Economics 35 (2), 282–306.

Ethier, W.J., 1982. National and international returns to scale in the modern theory of international trade. The American Economic Review 72 (3), 389–405.

Fajgelbaum, P., Grossman, G., Helpman, E., 2011. Income distribution, product quality, and international trade. Journal of Political Economy 119 (4), 721–765.

Fally, T., 2012. Structural Gravity and Fixed Effects. University of Colorado note, June.

Feenstra, R.C., 1994. New product varieties and the measurement of international prices. The American Economic Review 84 (1), 157–177.

Feenstra, R.C., 2003. A homothetic utility function for monopolistic competition models, without constant price elasticity. Economics Letters 78 (1), 79–86.

Feenstra, R.C., 2004. Advanced International Trade: Theory and Evidence. Princeton University Press, Princeton, New Jersey.

Feenstra, R.C., Markusen, J.R., Rose, A.K., 2001. Using the gravity equation to differentiate among alternative theories of trade. Canadian Journal of Economics 34 (2), 430–447.

Feenstra, R., Obstfeld, M., Russ, K., 2010. In Search of the Armington Elasticity. University of California-Davis, mimeo.

Fitzgerald, D., Haller, S., 2012. Exporters and Shocks, manuscript.

Frankel, J., 2010. The estimated trade effects of the euro: why are they below those from historical monetary unions among smaller countries? In: Alesina, A., Giavazzi, F. (Eds.), Europe and the Euro. University of Chicago Press, pp. 169–212 (Chapter 5).

Frankel, J., Stein, E., Wei, S., 1997. Regional Trading Blocs in the World Economic System. Institute for International Economics, Washington, DC.

Glick, R., Rose, A.K., 2002. Does a currency union affect trade? The time-series evidence. European Economic Review 46 (6), 1125–1151.

Glick, R., Taylor, A.M., 2010. Collateral damage: trade disruption and the economic impact of war. Review of Economics and Statistics 92, 102–127.

Guimaraes, P., Portugal, P., 2010. A simple feasible alternative procedure to estimate models with high-dimensional fixed effects. Stata Journal 10 (4), 628–649.

Hallak, J.C., 2006. Product quality and the direction of trade. Journal of International Economics 68 (1), 238–265.

Hanson, G., 2005. Market potential, increasing returns and geographic concentration. Journal of International Economics 67 (1), 1–24.

Harrigan, J., 1996. Openness to trade in manufactures in the OECD. Journal of International Economics 40 (1–2), 23–39.

Haveman, J., Hummels, D., 2004. Alternative hypotheses and the volume of trade: the gravity equation and the extent of specialization. The Canadian Journal of Economics/Revue Canadienne d'Économique 37 (1), 199–218.

Head, K., Mayer, T., 2000. Non-Europe: the magnitude and causes of market fragmentation in the EU. Review of World Economics 136 (2), 284–314.

Head, K., Mayer, T., 2004a. The empirics of agglomeration and trade. Handbook of Regional and Urban Economics 4, 2609–2669.

Head, K., Mayer, T., 2004b. Market potential and the location of Japanese investment in the European Union. Review of Economics and Statistics 86 (4), 959–972.

Head, K., Ries, J., 2001. Increasing returns versus national product differentiation as an explanation for the pattern of US–Canada trade. American Economic Review 91 (4), 858–876.

Head, K., Ries, J., 2008. FDI as an outcome of the market for corporate control: theory and evidence. Journal of International Economics 74 (1), 2–20.

Head, K., Mayer, T., Ries, J., 2009. How remote is the offshoring threat? European Economic Review 53 (4), 429–444.

Head, K., Mayer, T., Ries, J., 2010. The erosion of colonial trade linkages after independence. Journal of International Economics 81 (1), 1–14.

Helliwell, J., 1998. How Much Do National Borders Matter? Brookings Institution Press, Washington, D.C.

Helpman, E., Melitz, M., Rubinstein, Y., 2008. Estimating trade flows: trading partners and trading volumes. Quarterly Journal of Economics 123 (2), 441–487.

Hillberry, R., Hummels, D., 2008. Trade responses to geographic frictions: a decomposition using micro-data. European Economic Review 52 (3), 527–550.

Hortaçsu, A., Martinez-Jerez, F.A., Douglas, J., 2009. The Geography of trade in online transactions: evidence from eBay and Mercado Libre. American Economic Journal: Microeconomics 1 (1), 53–74.

Hummels, D., 1999. Towards a Geography of Trade Costs. Technical Report 17, GTAP Working Paper.

Imbs, J., Méjean, I., 2009. Elasticity Optimism. Technical Report, CEPR.

Isard, W., Peck, M., 1954. Location theory and international and interregional trade theory. The Quarterly Journal of Economics 68 (1), 97–114.

Jacks, D., Meissner, C., Novy, D., 2008. Trade costs, 1870–2000. The American Economic Review 98 (2), 529–534.

Krugman, P., 1979. Increasing returns, monopolistic competition, and international trade. Journal of International Economics 4, 469–479.

Krugman, P., 1995. Increasing returns, imperfect competition and the positive theory of international trade. In: Grossman, G.M., Rogoff, K. (Eds.), Handbook of International Economics, vol. 3. Elsevier, pp. 1243–1277.

Krugman, P., 1997. Development, Geography, and Economic Theory, vol 6. The MIT Press.

Lai, H., Trefler, D., 2002. The Gains from Trade with Monopolistic Competition: Specification, Estimation, and Mis-Specification. Working Paper 9169, NBER, September.

Lawless, M., 2010. Deconstructing gravity: trade costs and extensive and intensive margins. Canadian Journal of Economics/Revue Canadienne d'Économique 43 (4), 1149–1172.

Leamer, E., Levinsohn, J., 1995. International trade theory: the evidence. In: Grossman, G.M., Rogoff, K. (Eds.), Handbook of International Economics, vol. 3. Elsevier, pp. 1339–1394.

Manning, W., Mullahy, J., 2001. Estimating log models: to transform or not to transform? Journal of Health Economics 20 (4), 461–494.

Martin, P., Mayer, T., Thoenig, M., 2008. Make trade not war? Review of Economic Studies 75 (3), 865–900.

Martin, P., Mayer, T., Thoenig, M., 2012. The geography of conflicts and free trade agreements. American Economic Journal: Macroeconomics 4 (4), 1–35.

Martin, W., Pham, C.S., 2011. Estimating the Gravity Model When Zero Trade Flows Are Frequent. Technical Report, World Bank.

Martin, P., Rey, H., 2004. Financial super-markets: size matters for asset trade. Journal of International Economics 64 (2), 335–361.

Mayer, T., Ottaviano, G., 2007. The Happy Few: The Internationalisation of European Firms. Bruegel Blueprint Series.

McCallum, J., 1995. National borders matter: Canada–US regional trade patterns. The American Economic Review 85 (3), 615–623.

Melitz, M.J., 2003. The impact of trade on intra-industry reallocations and aggregate industry productivity. Econometrica 71 (6), 1695–1725.

Melitz, M., Ottaviano, G., 2008. Market size, trade, and productivity. Review of Economic Studies 75 (1), 295–316.

Novy, D., 2013. International trade without CES: estimating translog gravity. Journal of International Economics 89 (2), 271–282.

Okawa, Y., Van Wincoop, E., 2010. Gravity in International Finance. Working Paper 7, Hong Kong Institute for Monetary Research.

Okawa, Y., van Wincoop, E., 2012. Gravity in international finance. Journal of International Economics 87 (2), 205–215.

Ossa, R., 2011. A New trade theory of GATT/WTO negotiations. Journal of Political Economy 119 (1), 122–152.

Ossa, R., 2012. Why Trade Matters After All. Working Paper 18113, NBER.

Ottaviano, G., Tabuchi, T., Thisse, J., 2002. Agglomeration and trade revisited. International Economic Review 43 (2), 409.

Portes, R., Rey, H., 2005. The determinants of cross-border equity flows. Journal of International Economics 65 (2), 269–296.

Portes, R., Rey, H., Oh, Y., 2001. Information and capital flows: the determinants of transactions in financial assets. European Economic Review 45 (4–6), 783–796 (15th Annual Congress of the European Economic Association).

Rauch, J.E., Trindade, V., 2002. Ethnic Chinese networks in international trade. The Review of Economics and Statistics 84 (1), 116–130.

Redding, S., Venables, T., 2004. Economic geography and international inequality. Journal of International Economics 62 (1), 53–82.

Romalis, J., 2007. Nafta's and Cusfta's impact on international trade. Review of Economics and Statistics 89 (3), 416–435.

Rose, A., 2000. One money, one market: the effect of common currencies on trade. Economic policy 15 (30), 7–46.

Rose, A., 2004. Do we really know that the WTO increases trade? The American Economic Review 94 (1), 98–114.

Santos Silva, J., Tenreyro, S., 2006. The log of gravity. The Review of Economics and Statistics 88 (4), 641–658.

Santos Silva, J., Tenreyro, S., 2010. Currency unions in prospect and retrospect. Annual Review of Economics 2, 51–74.

Santos Silva, J., Tenreyro, S., 2011. Further simulation evidence on the performance of the Poisson-PML estimator. Economics Letters 112 (2), 220–222.

Savage, I.R., Deutsch, K.W., 1960. A statistical model of the gross analysis of transaction flows. Econometrica 28 (3), 551–572.

Simonovska, I., Waugh, M.E., 2011. The Elasticity of Trade: Estimates and Evidence. Working Paper 16796, NBER, February.

Tinbergen, J., 1962. Shaping the World Economy: Suggestions for an International Economic Policy. Twentieth Century Fund, New-York.

Trefler, D., December 1995. The case of the missing trade and other mysteries. The American Economic Review 85 (5), 1029–1046.

Wei, S.-J., April 1996. Intra-National versus International Trade: How Stubborn are Nations in Global Integration? Working Paper 5531, NBER.

Wooldridge, J., 2010. Econometric Analysis of Cross Section and Panel Data, second ed. The MIT press.

CHAPTER 4

Trade Theory with Numbers: Quantifying the Consequences of Globalization*

Arnaud Costinot[*,†] and Andrés Rodríguez-Clare[†,‡]

*Massachusetts Institute of Technology, Cambridge, MA, USA
†National Bureau of Economic Research, Cambridge, MA, USA
‡University of California, Berkeley, CA, USA

Abstract

We review a recent body of theoretical work that aims to put numbers on the consequences of globalization. A unifying theme of our survey is methodological. We rely on gravity models and demonstrate how they can be used for counterfactual analysis. We highlight how various economic considerations—market structure, firm-level heterogeneity, multiple sectors, intermediate goods, and multiple factors of production—affect the magnitude of the gains from trade liberalization. We conclude by discussing a number of outstanding issues in the literature as well as alternative approaches for quantifying the consequences of globalization.

Keywords

Quantitative trade theory, Computable general equilibrium, Welfare effects of trade, Trade policy and globalization, Gravity equation

JEL classification codes

F10, F11, F12, F13, F60

1. INTRODUCTION

The theoretical proposition that there are gains from international trade, see Samuelson (1939), is one of the most fundamental results in all of economics. Under perfect competition, opening up to trade acts as an expansion of the production possibility frontier and leads to Pareto superior outcomes. The objective of this chapter is to survey a recent body of theoretical work that aims to put numbers on this and other related comparative static exercises, which we will refer to as globalization.

* We thank Costas Arkolakis, Edward Balistreri, Dave Donaldson, Jonathan Eaton, Keith Head, Elhanan Helpman, Rusell Hillberry, Pete Klenow, Thierry Mayer, Thomas Rutherford, Robert Stern, Dan Trefler, and Jonathan Vogel for helpful discussions and comments. All errors are our own.

197

A unifying theme of our chapter is methodological. Throughout we rely on multi-country gravity models and demonstrate how they can be used for counterfactual analysis. While so-called gravity equations have been estimated since the early sixties, see Tinbergen (1962), the widespread use of structural gravity models in the field of international trade is a fairly recent phenomenon, as also discussed by Head and Mayer in Chapter 3 of this volume. The previous *Handbook of International Economics* (Volume 3, 1995) is a case in point. In his opening chapter, Krugman (1995) notes: "the lack of a good analysis of multilateral trade in the presence of trade costs is a major gap in trade theory." This view is echoed by Leamer and Levinsohn (1995) who argue that: "The gravity models are strictly descriptive. They lack a theoretical underpinning so that once the facts are out, it is not clear what to make of them." But the times they are a-changin'.

The last ten years have seen an explosion of alternative micro-theoretical foundations underlying gravity equations; see Eaton and Kortum (2002), Anderson and Van Wincoop (2003), Bernard et al. (2003), Chaney (2008), and Eaton et al. (2011). While new gravity models encompass a large number of market structures—from perfect competition to monopolistic competition with firm-level heterogeneity à la Melitz (2003)—and a wide range of micro-level predictions, they share the same macro-level predictions regarding the structure of bilateral trade flows as a function of bilateral costs. It is this basic macro structure and its quantitative implications for the consequences of globalization that this chapter will focus on.

Recent quantitative trade models based on the gravity equation share the same primary focus as older Computational General Equilibrium (CGE) models; see Baldwin and Venables (1995) for an overview in the previous handbook. The main goal is to use theory in order to derive numbers—e.g. explore whether particular economic forces appear to be large or small in the data—rather than pure qualitative insights—e.g. study whether the relationship between two economic variables is monotone or not in theory. There are, however, important differences between old and new quantitative work in international trade that we will try to highlight throughout this chapter. First, new quantitative trade models have more appealing micro-theoretical foundations. One does not need to impose the somewhat ad-hoc assumption that each country is exogenously endowed with a distinct good—the so-called "Armington" assumption—to do quantitative work in international trade. Second, recent quantitative papers offer a tighter connection between theory and data. Instead of relying on off-the-shelf elasticities, today's researchers try to use their own model to estimate the key structural parameters necessary for counterfactual analysis. Estimation and computation go hand in hand. Third, new quantitative trade models put more emphasis on transparency and less emphasis on realism. The idea is to construct middle-sized models that are rich enough to speak to first-order features of the data, like the role of country size and geography, yet parsimonious enough so that one can credibly identify its key parameters and understand how their magnitude affects counterfactual analysis.

Section 2 starts by studying the simplest gravity model possible, the Armington model. Building on Arkolakis et al. (2012b), we highlight two basic results. First we show that the changes in welfare associated with globalization, modeled as a change in iceberg trade costs, can be inferred using two variables: (*i*) changes in the share of expenditure on domestic goods; and (*ii*) the elasticity of bilateral imports with respect to variable trade costs, which we refer to as the trade elasticity. Second we show how changes in bilateral trade flows, in general, and the share of domestic expenditure, in particular, can be computed using only information about the trade elasticity and easily accessible macroeconomic data. We refer to this approach popularized by Dekle et al. (2008) as "exact hat algebra."

Armed with these tools, we illustrate how gravity models can be used to quantify the gains from international trade defined as the (absolute value of) the percentage change in real income that would be associated with moving one country from the current, observed trade equilibrium to a counterfactual equilibrium with no trade, i.e. an equilibrium with infinite iceberg trade costs. Since the share of domestic expenditure on domestic goods under autarky is equal to one, the welfare consequences associated with this counterfactual exercise are easy to compute. Although this is obviously an extreme counterfactual scenario that is (hopefully) not seriously considered by policymakers, we view it as a useful benchmark that can shed light on the quantitative importance of the various channels through which globalization affects the welfare of nations.

Section 3 extends the simple Armington model along several directions. First, we relax the assumption that each country is exogenously endowed with a distinct good and provide alternative assumptions on technology and market structure under which the counterfactual predictions derived in Section 2 remain unchanged. Second, we introduce multiple sectors, intermediate goods, and multiple factors of production and discuss how these considerations affect the consequences of globalization. Third, we briefly discuss other extensions including alternative demand systems—that generate variable markups under monopolistic competition—and multinational production. Although one can still use macro-level data and a small number of elasticities to compute the gains from trade in these richer environments, the results of Section 3 illustrate that some realistic departures from the one-sector benchmark, such as the existence of multiple sectors and tradable intermediate goods, tend to increase significantly the magnitude of the gains from trade.

Section 4 focuses on evaluating trade policy. Instead of considering the welfare consequences of a move to autarky, we study counterfactual scenarios in which countries raise their import tariffs, either unilaterally or simultaneously around the world, using the simple Armington model. We then study again how these counterfactual predictions vary across different gravity models. We conclude by discussing how to measure the restrictiveness of trade policy when tariffs are heterogeneous across sectors.

Section 5 reviews a number of outstanding issues in the literature. Since the main output of quantitative trade models are numbers, a fair question is: Are these numbers that we can believe in? To shed light on this question, we first discuss the sensitivity of the predictions of gravity models to auxiliary assumptions on the nature of trade imbalances and the tradability of capital goods. We then turn to the goodness of fit of gravity models in the cross-section and time series. We conclude by discussing how elasticities, i.e., the main inputs of quantitative trade models, are calibrated.

Sections 6 and 7 discuss other approaches to quantifying the consequences of globalization in the literature. Section 6 focuses on recent empirical studies that have used micro-level data, either at the product or firm-level, to estimate gains from new varieties and productivity gains from trade. We discuss how such empirical evidence, i.e., "micro" numbers, relate to the predictions of gravity models reviewed in this chapter, i.e., "macro" numbers. Section 7 turns to structural approaches to quantifying the consequences of globalization that are not based on gravity models. Due to space constraints, we do not review reduced-form evidence on the gains from openness; see e.g. Frankel and Romer (1999), Feyrer (2009a), and Feyrer (2009b). Readers interested in this important topic are referred to the recent survey by Harrison and Rodríguez-Clare (2010).

Section 8 offers some concluding remarks on the current state of the literature and open questions for future research. Additional information about theoretical results and data can be found in the online Appendix on the authors' website.

2. GETTING STARTED

We start this chapter by describing how to perform counterfactual analysis in the simplest quantitative trade model possible: the Armington model. A central aspect of this model is the gravity equation; see e.g. Anderson (1979) and Anderson and Van Wincoop (2003). As we will see in the next section, there exists a variety of micro-theoretical foundations that can give rise to a gravity equation, and in turn, a variety of economic environments in which the simple tools introduced in this section can be applied.

2.1. Armington Model

Consider a world economy comprising $i = 1, \ldots, n$ countries, each endowed with Q_i units of a distinct good $i = 1, \ldots, n$.

Preferences. Each country is populated by a representative agent whose preferences are represented by a Constant Elasticity of Substitution (CES) utility function:

$$C_j = \left(\sum_{i=1}^{n} \psi_{ij}^{(1-\sigma)/\sigma} C_{ij}^{(\sigma-1)/\sigma} \right)^{\sigma/(\sigma-1)}, \tag{1}$$

where C_{ij} is the demand for good i in country j; $\psi_{ij} > 0$ is an exogenous preference parameter; and $\sigma > 1$ is the elasticity of substitution between goods from different countries. The associated consumer price index is given by

$$P_j = \left(\sum_{i=1}^{n} \psi_{ij}^{1-\sigma} P_{ij}^{1-\sigma} \right)^{1/(1-\sigma)}, \tag{2}$$

where P_{ij} is the price of good i in country j.

Trade Costs. International trade between countries is subject to iceberg trade costs. In order to sell one unit of a good in country j, firms from country i must ship $\tau_{ij} \geq 1$ units, with $\tau_{ii} = 1$. For there to be no arbitrage opportunities, the price of good i in country j must be equal to $P_{ij} = \tau_{ij} P_{ii}$. The domestic price P_{ii} of good i, in turn, can be expressed as a function of country i's total income, Y_i, and its endowment: $P_{ii} = Y_i/Q_i$. Combining the two previous expressions we get

$$P_{ij} = Y_i \tau_{ij}/Q_i. \tag{3}$$

Trade Flows. Let X_{ij} denote the total value of country j's imports from country i. Given CES utility, bilateral trade flows satisfy

$$X_{ij} = \left(\frac{\psi_{ij} P_{ij}}{P_j}\right)^{1-\sigma} E_j, \tag{4}$$

where $E_j \equiv \sum_{i=1}^{n} X_{ij}$ is country j's total expenditure. Combining equations (2)–(4), we obtain

$$X_{ij} = \frac{\left(Y_i \tau_{ij}\right)^{1-\sigma} \chi_{ij}}{\sum_{l=1}^{n} \left(Y_l \tau_{lj}\right)^{1-\sigma} \chi_{lj}} E_j,$$

where $\chi_{ij} \equiv (Q_i/\psi_{ij})^{\sigma-1}$. In order to prepare the general analysis of Section 3, we let $\varepsilon \equiv \partial \ln \left(X_{ij}/X_{jj}\right)/\partial \ln \tau_{ij}$ denote the elasticity of imports relative to domestic demand, X_{ij}/X_{jj}, with respect to bilateral trade costs, τ_{ij}, holding income levels fixed. In the rest of this chapter we will refer to ε as the *trade elasticity*. In the Armington model it is simply equal to $\sigma - 1$. Using the previous notation, we can rearrange the expression above as

$$X_{ij} = \frac{\left(Y_i \tau_{ij}\right)^{-\varepsilon} \chi_{ij}}{\sum_{l=1}^{n} \left(Y_l \tau_{lj}\right)^{-\varepsilon} \chi_{lj}} E_j. \tag{5}$$

Equation (5) is what we will refer to as the *gravity equation*.

Competitive Equilibrium. In a competitive equilibrium, budget constraint and goods market clearing imply $Y_i = E_i$ and $Y_i = \sum_{j=1}^{n} X_{ij}$, respectively, for all countries i. Together with equation (5), these two conditions imply

$$Y_i = \sum_{j=1}^{n} \frac{\left(Y_i \tau_{ij}\right)^{-\varepsilon} \chi_{ij}}{\sum_{l=1}^{n} \left(Y_l \tau_{lj}\right)^{-\varepsilon} \chi_{lj}} Y_j. \tag{6}$$

This provides a system of n equations with n unknowns, $\mathbf{Y} \equiv \{Y_i\}$. By Walras's Law, one of these equations is redundant. Thus income levels are only determined up to a constant. Once income levels are known, expenditure levels, $\mathbf{E} \equiv \{E_i\}$, can be computed using budget constraint and bilateral trade flows, $\mathbf{X} \equiv \{X_{ij}\}$, can be computed using the gravity equation. This concludes the description of the Armington model.

2.2. Counterfactual Analysis

We now illustrate how the gravity equation can be used to quantify the welfare conse-
quences of globalization. For simplicity, we focus on a shock to trade costs from $\boldsymbol{\tau} \equiv \{\tau_{ij}\}$
to $\boldsymbol{\tau}' \equiv \{\tau'_{ij}\}$. The same analysis generalizes in a straightforward manner to preference
and endowment shocks. To quantify the welfare consequences of a trade shock in a given
country j, we proceed in two steps. First, we show how changes in real consumption,
$C_j \equiv E_j/P_j$, can be inferred from changes in macro variables, X and Y. Second, we show
how to compute changes in macro variables.

Welfare. In this chapter, whenever we refer to welfare changes in country j, we refer
to percentage changes in real consumption. Such changes correspond to the equivalent
variation associated with a foreign shock (expressed as a share of expenditure before the
shock). Namely, percentage changes in real consumption measures the percentage change
in income that the representative agent would be willing to accept in lieu of the shock
to happen.

   The first result that we establish is that changes in real consumption can be inferred
using only two statistics: (*i*) observed changes in the share of expenditure on domestic
goods, $\lambda_{jj} \equiv X_{jj}/E_j$; and (*ii*) the trade elasticity in the gravity equation, ε.

   Let us start by considering an infinitesimal change in trade costs from $\boldsymbol{\tau}$ to $\boldsymbol{\tau} + d\boldsymbol{\tau}$.
By Shephard's Lemma, we know that

$$d\ln P_j = \sum_{i=1}^{n} \lambda_{ij} d\ln P_{ij},$$

where $\lambda_{ij} \equiv X_{ij}/E_j$ denotes the share of expenditure on goods from country i in country
j. Since consumption is chosen to minimize expenditure, changes in consumption levels,
C_{ij}, only have second-order effects on the consumer price index in country j. Under
the assumption of CES utility, changes in the consumer price index in country j can be
rearranged further into changes into domestic and import prices

$$d\ln P_j = \lambda_{jj} d\ln P_{jj} + \left(1 - \lambda_{jj}\right) d\ln P_j^M,$$

where $P_j^M \equiv \left[\sum_{i \neq j} P_{ij}^{1-\sigma}\right]^{1/(1-\sigma)}$ is the component of the price index associated with
imports. By differentiating equation (4), one can also show that

$$d\ln\left(1 - \lambda_{jj}\right) - d\ln\lambda_{jj} = \left(1 - \sigma\right)\left(d\ln P_j^M - d\ln P_{jj}\right).$$

Combining the fact that $\lambda_{jj} d\ln\lambda_{jj} = -\left(1 - \lambda_{jj}\right) d\ln\left(1 - \lambda_{jj}\right)$ with the two previous
equations, we get

$$d\ln P_j = d\ln P_{jj} - \left(d\ln\lambda_{jj}/\left(1 - \sigma\right)\right). \tag{7}$$

Thus, changes in real consumption, $C_j \equiv E_j/P_j$, in country j are given by

$$d \ln C_j = \left(d \ln E_j - d \ln P_{jj}\right) + \left(d \ln \lambda_{jj}/\left(1-\sigma\right)\right). \tag{8}$$

Since there are no domestic trade costs, $\tau_{jj} = \tau'_{jj} = 1$, and trade is balanced, $Y_j = E_j$, equation (3) implies that the first term is equal to zero. In the simple Armington model, changes in real consumption only depends on the change in the relative price of imported versus domestic goods, P_j^M/P_{jj}, which depends on the share of expenditure on domestic goods, λ_{jj}, and the elasticity of substitution, σ. Using equation (8) and the definition of the trade elasticity $\varepsilon \equiv \sigma - 1$, we get

$$d \ln C_j = -d \ln \lambda_{jj}/\varepsilon.$$

Since the previous expression holds for any infinitesimal shock, the welfare consequences of large changes from τ to τ' can be inferred by integrating the previous formula:

$$\hat{C}_j = \hat{\lambda}_{jj}^{-1/\varepsilon}, \tag{9}$$

where $\hat{v} \equiv v'/v$ denotes the proportional change in any variable v between the initial and counterfactual equilibria. This establishes that for any change in trade costs, two statistics—the trade elasticity, ε, and the changes in the share of expenditure on domestic goods, λ_{jj}—are sufficient to infer welfare changes.[1]

Macroeconomic variables. At this point, we have shown that conditional on the trade elasticity, ε, changes in real consumption are exclusively determined by changes in λ_{jj}. We now describe how one can use gravity models to predict how trade shocks affect trade flows, in general, and the share of expenditure on domestic goods, λ_{jj}, in particular. The approach that we will describe has been popularized recently by Dekle et al. (2008). One can think of this approach as an "exact" version of Jones's hat algebra for reasons that will be clear in a moment.[2]

Let $\lambda_{ij} \equiv X_{ij}/\sum_l X_{lj}$ denote the share of expenditure on goods from country i in country j. Since the gravity equation holds both in the initial and the counterfactual equilibria, we have

$$\hat{\lambda}_{ij} = \frac{\left(\hat{Y}_i \hat{\tau}_{ij}\right)^{-\varepsilon}}{\sum_{l=1}^{n} \lambda_{lj} \left(\hat{Y}_l \hat{\tau}_{lj}\right)^{-\varepsilon}}. \tag{10}$$

In the counterfactual equilibrium, equation (6) further implies

$$Y'_j = \sum_{i=1}^{n} \lambda'_{ji} Y'_i.$$

---

[1] Since the previous result is based on Shepard's Lemma and the fact that domestic prices are unaffected by the shock, $d \ln P_{jj} = 0$, equation (9) would also hold in the case of a shock to foreign preferences or endowments.

[2] Application of this approach can also be found in the older CGE literature; see e.g. Rutherford (2002).

Combining the two previous expressions, we then get

$$\hat{Y}_j Y_j = \sum_{i=1}^{n} \frac{\lambda_{ji} \left(\hat{Y}_j \hat{\tau}_{ji} \right)^{-\varepsilon} \hat{Y}_i Y_i}{\sum_{l=1}^{n} \lambda_{li} \left(\hat{Y}_l \hat{\tau}_{li} \right)^{-\varepsilon}}. \tag{11}$$

Although trade costs, endowments, and preference shifters affect bilateral trade flows, as captured by τ_{ij} and χ_{ij} in equation (5), equation (11) shows that we can compute counterfactual changes in income, $\hat{\mathbf{Y}} \equiv \{\hat{Y}_i\}$, as the solution of a system of non-linear equations without having to estimate any of these parameters. All we need to determine changes in income levels (up to normalization) are the initial expenditure shares, λ_{ij}, the initial income levels, Y_i, and the trade elasticity, ε. Given changes in income levels, changes in the shares of expenditure on goods from different countries, $\hat{\lambda}_{ij}$, and changes in real consumption, $\hat{C}_j$, can then be computed using equations (9) and (10).

2.3. Trade Theory with Numbers: A Preview

In order to illustrate the usefulness of the simple Armington model, we focus on a very particular, but important counterfactual exercise: *moving to autarky*. Formally, we assume that variable trade costs in the new equilibrium are such that $\tau'_{ij} = +\infty$ for any pair of countries $i \neq j$. All other structural parameters are the same as in the initial equilibrium. For this particular shock, we do not need to solve any non-linear system of equations to do counterfactual analysis. Since the share of expenditure on domestic goods must be equal to 1 in the counterfactual equilibrium, $\lambda'_{jj} = 1$, we immediately know that $\hat{\lambda}_{jj} = 1/\lambda_{jj}$.

Throughout this chapter we define the *gains from international trade* in country j, G_j, as the absolute value of the percentage change in real income that would be associated with moving to autarky in country j. Using equation (9) and the fact that $\hat{\lambda}_{jj} = 1/\lambda_{jj}$, we get

$$G_j = 1 - \lambda_{jj}^{1/\varepsilon}. \tag{12}$$

In order to compute G_j we need measures of the trade elasticity, ε, and the share of expenditure on domestic goods, λ_{jj}. There are many econometric issues associated with estimating ε; see e.g. Hummels and Hillberry (2012). A simple way to estimate the trade elasticity ε is to take the log of the gravity equation (5) and run a cross-sectional regression of the following form

$$\ln X_{ij} = \delta_i^X + \delta_j^M - \varepsilon \ln \tau_{ij} + \delta_{ij}, \tag{13}$$

where the first term $\delta_i^X \equiv -\varepsilon \ln Y_i$ is treated as an exporter fixed-effect; the second term $\delta_j^M \equiv \ln Y_j - \ln \left[\sum_{l=1}^{n} \chi_{lj} \left(Y_l \tau_{lj} \right)^{-\varepsilon} \right]$ is treated as an importer fixed-effect; and the third term $\delta_{ij} = \ln \chi_{ij}$ is treated as a preference shock that is orthogonal to $\ln \tau_{ij}$. At this point we set $\varepsilon = 5$, which is a typical value used in the literature; see e.g. Anderson and Van Wincoop (2004) and Head and Mayer (Chapter 3 of this volume). We will come back to the sensitivity of our quantitative results to values of the trade elasticity in Section 5.

In order to measure λ_{jj} in the data, recall that $\lambda_{jj} \equiv X_{jj}/E_j = 1 - \sum_{i \neq j} X_{ij} / \sum_{i=1}^{n} X_{ij}$. We can measure $\sum_{i \neq j} X_{ij}$ as total imports by country j, whereas $\sum_i X_{ij}$ is total expenditure by country j. In this exercise as well as all subsequent exercises, we use data from the World Input-Output Database (WIOD) in 2008. The database covers 27 EU countries and 13 other major countries; see Timmer (2012).[3] The first column of Table 4.1 report the gains from trade G_j for these countries using equation (12). According to the simple Armington model, we see that gains from trade are below 2% for three countries: Brazil (1.5%), Japan (1.7%), and the United States (1.8%). Not surprisingly, gains from trade tend to be larger for smaller countries. The largest predicted gains are for Slovakia (7.6%), Ireland (8.0%), and Hungary (8.1%). Given the strong assumptions that have been imposed in Section 2.1, these numbers, of course, should be taken with more than a grain of salt. We now discuss how richer and more realistic models would affect the magnitude of the gains from trade.

3. BEYOND ARMINGTON

The Armington model is very tractable, which has made it the go-to trade model for quantitative work in policy institutions for more than forty years. This is also a very stylized model, which has led to quite a bit of skepticism about the robustness of its counterfactual predictions in academic circles for about as many years. Fortunately, one can maintain the tractability of the Armington model, without maintaining the somewhat ad-hoc assumption that each country is exogenously endowed with a distinct good. As discussed below, the gravity equation (5), which is the basis for counterfactual analysis in the Armington model, can be shown to hold under various assumptions about technology and market structure. While each gravity model remains special, in the sense that strong functional form assumptions are required for a gravity equation to hold, the ability of these new models to match a large number of micro-level facts, together with the elegance of their micro-theoretical foundations, has led to an explosion of quantitative work in international trade over the last ten years.

In this section we explore how various features of more complex gravity models—market structure, firm-level heterogeneity, multiple sectors, intermediate goods, and multiple factors of production—affect the gains from trade as defined in Section 2.3. Throughout our analysis we calibrate different models to match the same moments in the macro-data, including bilateral trade flows and trade elasticities. Thus different models may lead to different predictions about the magnitude of the gains from trade because

---

[3] The mapping between the simple Armington model presented here and the data is not trivial for two reasons: (*i*) it assumes the share of expenditures on intermediate goods is zero and (*ii*) it assumes that trade is balanced. This implies that GDP is equal to gross output and that total expenditure is equal to GDP. Neither is true in the data. We will deal with intermediate goods and trade imbalances explicitly in Sections 3.4 and 5.1, respectively. Here, as well as in Section 3, we derive and apply our formulas for gains from trade ignoring trade imbalances. If moving to autarky also implies the closing of trade imbalances, our formulas capture the change in real income rather than the change in real expenditure. See online Appendix, Section 4, available on the authors' website for details.

Table 4.1 Welfare Gains from Trade

				G_j Expressed in Percentages Computed Using:				
	One Sector (12)	Multiple Sectors, No Intermediates (23)		Multiple Sectors, with Intermediates (29)				
		Perfect Competition	Monopolistic Competition	Perfect Competition (Data Alphas)	Perfect Competition	Monop. Comp. (Krugman)	Monop. Comp. (Melitz)	
Country	1	2	3	4	5	6	7
AUS	2.3%	8.6%	3.7%	15.8%	15.7%	6.9%	6.8%
AUT	5.7%	30.3%	30.5%	49.5%	49.0%	57.6%	64.3%
BEL	7.5%	32.7%	32.4%	54.6%	54.2%	63.0%	70.9%
BRA	1.5%	3.7%	4.3%	6.3%	6.4%	9.7%	12.7%
CAN	3.8%	17.4%	15.3%	30.2%	29.5%	33.0%	39.8%
CHN	2.6%	4.0%	4.0%	11.5%	11.2%	28.0%	77.9%
CZE	6.0%	16.8%	21.2%	34.0%	37.2%	65.1%	86.7%
DEU	4.5%	12.7%	17.6%	21.3%	22.5%	41.4%	52.9%
DNK	5.8%	30.2%	24.8%	41.4%	45.0%	42.0%	44.8%
ESP	3.1%	9.0%	9.5%	18.3%	17.5%	24.4%	30.5%
FIN	4.4%	11.1%	10.5%	20.2%	20.3%	24.2%	28.0%
FRA	3.0%	9.4%	11.1%	17.2%	16.8%	25.8%	32.1%
GBR	3.2%	12.9%	11.7%	21.6%	22.4%	22.2%	23.5%
GRC	4.2%	16.3%	4.7%	23.7%	24.7%	6.8%	6.1%
HUN	8.1%	29.8%	31.3%	53.5%	55.3%	75.7%	91.0%
IDN	2.9%	5.5%	4.0%	13.1%	11.6%	11.2%	14.6%
IND	2.4%	4.6%	4.3%	9.2%	8.6%	9.5%	11.7%
IRL	8.0%	23.5%	14.2%	37.1%	38.9%	28.1%	29.1%
ITA	2.9%	8.7%	9.2%	16.4%	16.2%	21.7%	26.5%
JPN	1.7%	1.4%	3.7%	4.6%	3.5%	20.7%	32.7%
KOR	4.3%	3.9%	8.6%	12.5%	11.4%	44.1%	70.2%
MEX	3.3%	11.1%	12.1%	18.4%	18.6%	24.3%	28.4%
NLD	6.2%	24.3%	23.1%	40.1%	39.8%	43.4%	47.6%
POL	4.4%	18.4%	19.7%	33.8%	34.5%	46.9%	57.0%
PRT	4.4%	23.8%	20.6%	35.9%	37.4%	36.7%	40.3%
ROM	4.5%	17.7%	12.7%	26.4%	29.2%	20.8%	20.7%
RUS	2.4%	18.0%	0.9%	35.9%	30.7%	−2.1%	−7.1%
SVK	7.6%	22.2%	23.6%	48.3%	50.5%	78.6%	96.4%
SVN	6.8%	39.6%	39.3%	57.8%	61.6%	71.3%	79.7%
SWE	5.1%	12.5%	14.5%	24.4%	23.6%	36.6%	45.8%
TUR	2.9%	11.9%	13.3%	20.0%	20.9%	26.4%	29.5%
TWN	6.1%	9.6%	9.9%	19.9%	19.4%	28.6%	37.8%
USA	1.8%	4.4%	3.8%	8.3%	8.0%	8.6%	10.3%
RoW	5.2%	15.2%	7.3%	33.3%	28.4%	18.1%	21.8%
Average	4.4%	15.3%	14.0%	26.9%	27.1%	32.3%	40.0%

Note: The numbers in parenthesis indicate the equation used for the computation. All data is from WIOD and trade elasticities are from Caliendo and Parro (2010). Perfect competition and monopolistic competition are obtained from the formulas using $\delta_s = 0$ for all s and $\delta_s = 1$ for all s, respectively. Results for the Krugman and Melitz models are obtained setting $\eta_s = 0$ for all s and setting $\eta_s = 0.65$ for all s, respectively.

they predict different counterfactual autarky equilibria, not because they predict different trade volumes in the initial equilibrium. In short, trade volumes are taken as data that discipline the behavior of all models, irrespective of what their particular micro-theoretical foundations may be.[4]

As explained in the Introduction, although a move to autarky is an extreme comparative statics exercise, it should be viewed as a useful benchmark to study the importance, in a well-defined welfare sense, of various economic channels discussed in the literature. We leave the evaluation of trade policy to Section 4 in which we show how to use the exact hat algebra to conduct richer comparative static exercises.

3.1. Many Models, One Equation

The gravity equation (5) has been shown to hold under perfect competition, as in Eaton and Kortum (2002); under Bertrand competition, as in Bernard et al. (2003); under monopolistic competition with homogeneous firms, as in Krugman (1980); and under monopolistic competition with firm-level heterogeneity, as in Chaney (2008), Arkolakis (2010), Arkolakis et al. (2008), and Eaton et al. (2011). Our goal in this subsection is not to describe each of these models in detail, but rather highlight the common features that will lead to a gravity equation as well as the key differences that may affect the magnitude of the gains from trade. Detailed discussions of the microfoundations and functional form assumptions leading to gravity equations can be found in Anderson (2011), Arkolakis et al. (2012b), Head and Mayer (Chapter 3 of this volume), as well as in our online Appendix.

Like the simple Armington model, the alternative gravity models mentioned above assume the existence of a representative agent with CES utility in each country as well as balanced trade, $E_i = Y_i$.[5] The representative agent, however, now has preferences over a continuum of goods or varieties $\omega \in \Omega$:

$$C_j = \left(\int_{\omega \in \Omega} c_j(\omega)^{(\sigma-1)/\sigma} \, d\omega \right)^{\sigma/(\sigma-1)},$$

with $\sigma > 1$. In equilibrium, each good ω is only imported from one country so that equation (1) still holds with the aggregate consumption of goods from country i in country j being given by $C_{ij} = \int_{\omega \in \Omega_{ij}} c_j(\omega)^{(\sigma-1)/\sigma} \, d\omega$, where $\Omega_{ij} \subset \Omega$ denotes the set of goods that country j buys from country i, and $\psi_{ij} = 1$ for all country pairs due to the symmetry across varieties. For the same reason, equation (2) holds as well with the aggregate price of goods from country i in country j being given by $P_{ij} = \left(\int_{\omega \in \Omega_{ij}} p_j(\omega)^{1-\sigma} \, d\omega \right)^{1/(1-\sigma)}$ and $\psi_{ij} = 1$ for all i and j.

[4] In order to match the same cross-section of trade flows, different gravity models may implictly rely on different values of bilateral trade costs as well as other structural parameters.

[5] In recent work, Arkolakis et al. (2012a) have developed a gravity model without CES utility. We discuss the implications of such a model in Section 3.6.

A key difference between the simple Armington model and the alternative gravity models mentioned above is that, due to different assumptions on technology and market structure, Ω_{ij} is no longer exogenously given. In these richer models, firms from country i may now decide to stop producing and selling a subset of goods in country j if it is not profitable for them to do so. Hence changes in prices, P_{ij}, may reflect both: (*i*) changes at the intensive margin, i.e., changes in the price of goods imported in country j, $p_j(\omega)$, and (*ii*) changes at the extensive margin, i.e., changes in the set of goods imported in country j, Ω_{ij}, due either to the selection of a different subset of firms from i in j or the entry of a different set of firms in i. Mathematically, these new economic considerations lead to the following generalization of equation (3):

$$P_{ij} = \underbrace{\tau_{ij}c_i^p}_{\text{Intensive Margin}} \times \underbrace{\left(\left(\frac{E_j}{c_{ij}^x}\right)^{\frac{\delta}{1-\sigma}}\frac{\tau_{ij}c_i^p}{P_j}\right)^{\eta}}_{\text{Extensive Margin: Selection}} \times \underbrace{\left(\frac{R_i}{c_i^e}\right)^{\frac{\delta}{1-\sigma}}}_{\text{Extensive Margin: Entry}} \times \xi_{ij}, \qquad (14)$$

where c_i^p, c_{ij}^x, and c_i^e are endogenous variables that capture how input prices affect variable costs of production, fixed exporting costs, and fixed entry costs, respectively; $E_j \equiv \sum_{i=1}^{n} X_{ij}$ still denotes total expenditure in country j; $R_i \equiv \sum_{j=1}^{n} X_{ij}$ denotes total sales or revenues for producers; and $\xi_{ij} > 0$ is a function of structural parameters distinct from variable trade costs, τ_{ij}, such as endowments or fixed exporting costs. The last two parameters, δ and η, will play a central role in our analysis. The parameter δ is a dummy variable that characterizes the market structure: it is equal to one under monopolistic competition with free entry and zero under perfect or Bertrand competition.[6] The parameter $\eta \geq 0$ is related to the extent of heterogeneity across varieties as we discuss more formally below.

In the rest of this chapter we will use equation (14) to organize the literature and explain how different assumptions about technology and market structure—namely, different assumptions about c_i^p, c_i^e, c_{ij}^x, δ, and η—may lead to different macro-level predictions without getting lost into the algebra through which equation (14) comes about. At this point, it is therefore important to clarify how each term in equation (14) relates to previous work in the literature.

The first term, $\tau_{ij}c_i^p$, captures price changes at the intensive margin. This is the only active margin in the Armington model. In that model, $c_i^p = Y_i$, $\delta = 0$, and $\eta = 0$; see equation (3). This intensive margin will remain active in all models that we study. In most of these models, c_i^p will also remain equal to total income Y_i in country i. This is the case, for instance, if labor is the only factor of production. In this situation, production costs are proportional to wages, which are proportional to countries' total income.

---

[6] For expositional purposes, we often abuse terminology in this chapter and simply refer to the case $\delta = 1$ and $\delta = 0$ as "monopolistic competition" and "perfect competition," respectively.

The second term, $\left(\left(E_j/c_{ij}^x \right)^{\frac{\delta}{1-\sigma}} \tau_{ij} c_i^p / P_j \right)^{\eta}$, captures changes at the extensive margin due to selection effects. If $\eta = 0$, then this term is equal to one and there are no selection effects. This occurs in models of monopolistic competition without firm-level heterogeneity and fixed exporting costs, like Krugman (1980), in which all firms always export. The case $\eta > 0$ captures instead situations in which a subset of firms from country i may start or stop exporting when market conditions change in country j. Specifically, in models of perfect competition, like Eaton and Kortum (2002), Bertrand competition, like Bernard et al. (2003), or monopolistic competition à la Melitz (2003), like Chaney (2008), Arkolakis et al. (2008), Arkolakis (2010), and Eaton et al. (2011), if firms from country i are less competitive relative to other firms serving market j, i.e., $\tau_{ij} c_i^p / P_j$ is high, then less firms from country i will serve this market, which will lead to a decrease in the number of varieties from i available in j and an increase in P_{ij}. In the previous models, the magnitude of selection effects is formally determined by $\eta \equiv \left(\frac{\theta}{\sigma-1} \right) \left(1 + \frac{1-\sigma}{\theta} \right)$, where $\theta > \sigma - 1$ is the shape parameter of the distribution of productivity draws across varieties. Under perfect and Bertrand competition, this distribution is Fréchet. Under monopolistic competition, it is Pareto. In both cases, θ measures the elasticity of the mass of goods produced domestically with respect to their relative cost; $1/\left(1 - \sigma \right)$ measures the elasticity of the price index with respect to new goods; and $\left(1 + \frac{1-\sigma}{\theta} \right)$ corrects for the fact that the marginal variety has a higher price than the average variety. In models of monopolistic competition with firm-level heterogeneity à la Melitz (2003) ($\delta = 1, \eta > 0$), selection also depends on the size of market j relative to the fixed costs of exporting from i to j, which is reflected in $\left(E_j/c_{ij}^x \right)^{\frac{\delta}{1-\sigma}}$. The nature of c_{ij}^x depends on where fixed exporting costs are paid. If they are paid in the exporting country, then c_{ij}^x is proportional to total income, Y_i, in country i. If they are paid in the importing country, then c_{ij}^x is proportional to total income, Y_j, in country j.

The third term, $\left(R_i/c_i^e \right)^{\frac{\delta}{1-\sigma}}$, captures changes at the extensive margin due to entry effects. This last channel is specific to models with monopolistic competition and free entry ($\delta = 1$), whether or not they feature firm-level heterogeneity à la Melitz (2003).[7] In such environments, countries in which entry is more profitable, i.e., R_i/c_i^e is high, export more varieties to all countries, which decreases the price index with an elasticity $1/\left(\sigma - 1 \right)$. If entry costs are paid in terms of labor, as in Krugman (1980) or Melitz (2003), c_i^e is simply proportional to total income Y_i in country i.

To sum up, starting from equation (14), we can turn off and on the selection effects associated with heterogeneity across varieties by setting η to 0 or not. Similarly, we can turn off and on the scale effects associated with monopolistic competition and free entry

---

[7] Without free entry, $\left(R_i/c_i^e \right)^{\frac{\delta}{1-\sigma}}$ would be absent from equation (14) and one would need, in general, to take into account the effect of trade on profits; see e.g. Ossa (2011a). In the one-sector case reviewed in the next subsection, this distinction turns out to be irrelevant, as shown in Arkolakis et al. (2012b). With multiple sectors, however, free entry leads to home market effects, with implications for the magnitude of the gains from trade.

by setting δ to 0 or 1. In the next subsections, we study how much these considerations—as well as the introduction of multiple sectors, tradable intermediate goods, and multiple factors of production—affect the overall magnitude of the gains from trade.

3.2. One Sector

It is standard to interpret models with CES utility, such as those presented in Section 3.1, as one-sector models with a continuum of varieties; see e.g. Helpman and Krugman (1985). Here we focus on such models since they are the closest to the Armington model described in Section 2.1. Later we will consider multi-sector extensions of these models as well as incorporate tradable intermediate goods and multiple factors of production.

In line with the existing literature, we assume that, in addition to equation (14), the two following conditions hold: (*i*) $c_i^p = c_{ii}^x = c_i^e = Y_i$, which reflects the fact that all factors of production are used in the same proportions to produce, export, and develop all varieties; and (*ii*) $R_i = Y_i$, which reflects the fact that trade in goods is balanced.[8] Under these two conditions, equation (14) simplifies into

$$P_{ij} = \tau_{ij} Y_i \left(\left(\frac{E_j}{c_{ij}^x} \right)^{\frac{\delta}{1-\sigma}} \frac{\tau_{ij} Y_i}{P_j} \right)^{\eta} \xi_{ij}. \tag{15}$$

Note that $R_i = Y_i = c_i^e$ implies that, like in the Armington model, there are no entry effects associated with changes in trade costs, even under monopolistic competition. Since equation (1) still holds, bilateral trade flows between country i and country j are still given by equation (4). Combining this observation with equation (15), the gravity equation generalizes to

$$X_{ij} = \frac{\left(Y_i \tau_{ij} \right)^{-\varepsilon} \left(c_{ij}^x \right)^{-\delta\eta} \chi_{ij}}{\sum_{l=1}^{n} \left(Y_l \tau_{lj} \right)^{-\varepsilon} \left(c_{lj}^x \right)^{-\delta\eta} \chi_{lj}} E_j. \tag{16}$$

Compared to the Armington model, here $\varepsilon = (1 + \eta)(\sigma - 1)$ and $\chi_{ij} \equiv \xi_{ij}^{1-\sigma}$. Thus if there are selection effects, i.e., if $\eta \neq 0$, the structural interpretation of the trade elasticity is no longer the same as in the Armington model. This reflects the fact that changes in variable trade costs now affect both the price of existing varieties (intensive margin) and the set of varieties sold from country i to country j (extensive margin). Nevertheless, we can still take the logs of both sides of equation (4) and estimate the trade elasticity ε as we did in Section 2.3. In other words, the mapping between bilateral trade data, **X**, and the trade elasticity, ε, remains unchanged.[9] Finally, we see that changes in the

---

[8] Since some of the models that we consider involve fixed exporting costs paid in the importing country, i.e., trade in exporting services, the assumption that overall trade is balanced, $E_i = Y_i$, is different from the assumption that trade in goods is balanced, $R_i = Y_i$. The latter condition corresponds to the macro-level restriction R1 in Arkolakis et al. (2012b).

[9] This assumes that measures of trade costs are invariant across models. This is a reasonable assumption in the case of import tariffs, but not in the case of price gaps; see Simonovska and Waugh (2012). We come back to the specific issues associated with import tariffs in Section 4.

magnitude of fixed exporting costs, as captured by $(c_{ij}^x)^{-\delta\eta}$, now affect bilateral trade flows under monopolistic competition with firm-level heterogeneity à la Melitz (2003), i.e., if $\delta = 1, \eta > 0$.[10] This extra term—which depends on whether fixed exporting costs are paid in the importing country, the exporting country, or both—opens up the possibility of different predictions across gravity models, as we explain below.

Like in Section 2.2, consider a change in variable trade costs from $\tau \equiv \{\tau_{ij}\}$ to $\tau' \equiv \{\tau'_{ij}\}$, though the same analysis easily extends to shocks to foreign endowments or technology, i.e., changes in $\chi \equiv \{\chi_{ij}\}$. Given CES utility, equation (8) still holds. The key difference compared to our previous analysis is that $d\ln E_j - d\ln P_{jj}$ is no longer equal to zero. Because of selection effects, a change in variable trade costs may lead to a change in the set of goods produced domestically, Ω_{jj}, and so to a change in the aggregate price index associated with these goods, P_{jj}, relative to total expenditure in country j. Specifically, since $E_j = Y_j$ and $c_{jj}^x = Y_j$, equation (15) implies

$$d\ln P_{jj} = \left(1 + \eta\right) d\ln Y_j - \eta d\ln P_j.$$

Using the previous expression with equation (7), which still holds because of CES utility, and the trade balance condition, $E_j = Y_j$, we then get

$$d\ln E_j - d\ln P_{jj} = -\left(\eta/\left(\eta+1\right)\right) \times \left(d\ln\lambda_{jj}/\left(1-\sigma\right)\right). \tag{17}$$

In models featuring selection effects ($\eta > 0$), a positive terms-of-trade shock, $d\ln\lambda_{jj}/(1-\sigma) > 0$, is accompanied by a negative shock to real income in terms of domestic goods, $d\ln E_j - d\ln P_{jj} < 0$. Intuitively, a positive terms-of-trade shock tends to decrease the profitability of domestic firms on the domestic market, which leads to a decrease in the number of goods produced domestically, and, given the love of varieties embedded in CES utility functions, an increase in the aggregate price index associated with these goods.

Together with $\varepsilon = (1+\eta)(\sigma-1)$, equations (8) and (17) imply $d\ln C_j = -d\ln\lambda_{jj}/\varepsilon$. Like in the Armington model, the previous expression can be integrated to get equation (9).[11] Thus, as established in Arkolakis et al. (2012b), changes in the share of expenditure on domestic goods, λ_{jj}, and the trade elasticity, ε, remain two sufficient statistics for welfare analysis. In particular, gains from trade remain given by equation (12). In short, conditional on observed trade flows and the trade elasticity, selection and scale effects have no impact on the overall magnitude of the gains from trade.

The fact that λ_{jj} remains the only macro variable that matters for welfare is intuitive enough. The welfare effect of a trade shock depends on changes in terms of trade and changes in real income measured in terms of domestic goods. Since the latter is in turn

[10] Equation (16) is a special case of the macro-level restriction R3 in Arkolakis et al. (2012b). Compared to Arkolakis et al. (2012b), we no longer need to impose explicitly that profits are proportional to revenues. This restriction is implicit in equation (15).

[11] A more direct, though perhaps less illuminating way of establishing equation (9) consists in computing P_{jj} from equation (15) and substituting for it in $\lambda_{jj} = \left(P_{jj}/P_j\right)^{1-\sigma}$.

determined by changes in terms of trade, it follows that this is all we need to know to measure welfare changes. The fact that the only structural parameter that matters can be recovered as the trade elasticity ε from a gravity equation, by contrast, heavily relies on the fact that selection effects, as captured by η, are identical across countries. It is this assumption that simultaneously generates a gravity equation and guarantees that the trade elasticity in that equation is the relevant elasticity for welfare analysis. It is worth noting that this result does not rely on the fact that new varieties have zero welfare effects. In the models with monopolistic competition considered here, a shock to trade costs, foreign endowments, or foreign technology, may very well increase welfare through its effects at the extensive margin. The point rather is that these effects, no matter how large they are, can always be inferred from changes in aggregate trade flows.

The previous equivalence only establishes that conditional on a change in λ_{jj} and ε, alternative gravity models must predict the same welfare change as the Armington model, but, in principle, they may predict different changes in the share of domestic expenditure for a given trade shock. Under the additional assumption that fixed exporting costs (if any) are paid in the destination country—$c_{ij}^x = c_j^x$, as in Eaton et al. (2011)—one can show a stronger equivalence result. In that case, c_{ij}^x drops out of equation (16). Thus the counterfactual changes in trade flows and income levels associated with changes in variable trade costs can still be computed using the exact hat algebra of Section 2.2, i.e., equations (10) and (11). Given observable macro variables in the initial equilibrium, $\mathbf{X}$ and $\mathbf{Y}$, and a value of the trade elasticity, ε, this implies that counterfactual predictions for macro variables and welfare are exactly the same as in the Armington model.[12] This stronger equivalence result, however, is very sensitive to the assumption that fixed exporting costs are paid in the importing country. If fixed exporting costs are partly paid in the origin country, then one-sector gravity models with monopolistic competition and firm-level heterogeneity à la Melitz (2003) generally predict different changes in relative factor prices, i.e., relative wages if labor is the only factor of production. This leads to different changes in the share of expenditure on domestic goods and, in turn, different welfare changes for a given change in trade costs (moving to autarky being a notable exception).[13]

---

[12] In this special case, one can show that the welfare impact of changes in the number of domestic varieties (if any) exactly compensates the welfare impact of changes in the number of foreign varieties (if any), as emphasized in Feenstra (2010). In general, i.e., if fixed costs are partly paid in the origin country, these exact offsetting effects no longer hold, though the welfare change associated with a shock to variable trade costs remains given by equation (9), as discussed above. Similarly, in the case of shocks to foreign endowments or technology, these exact offsetting effects no longer hold, though welfare changes remain given by equation (9), as shown in Arkolakis et al. (2012b). In short, the main equivalence result in Arkolakis et al. (2012b) does not hinge on these exact offsetting effects.

[13] For finite changes in trade costs, different counterfactual predictions do not arise from selection effects per se, but rather from the fact that fixed exporting costs, if paid at least partly in the origin country, can affect relative demand for factors of production in different countries and so relative factor prices. To see this, note that in a symmetric world economy in which relative factor prices are constant, c_{ij}^x would be constant across countries as well. Thus, in spite of selection effects, c_{ij}^x would again drop out of equation (16), leading to the same counterfactual predictions as in the Armington model.

3.3. Multiple Sectors

Gravity models can be extended to multiple sectors, $s = 1, \ldots, S$, by assuming a two-tier utility function in which the upper-level is Cobb–Douglas and the lower-level is CES; see e.g. Anderson and Yotov (2010), Donaldson (2008), Caliendo and Parro (2010), Costinot et al. (2012), Hsieh and Ossa (2011), Levchenko and Zhang (2011), and Ossa (2012), and Shikher (2012a,b). Formally let us assume that the representative agent in each country aims to maximize

$$C_j = \prod_{s=1}^{S} C_{j,s}^{\beta_{j,s}}, \tag{18}$$

where $\beta_{j,s} \geq 0$ are exogenous preference parameters satisfying $\sum_{s=1}^{S} \beta_{j,s} = 1$ and $C_{j,s}$ is total consumption of the composite good s in country j,

$$C_{j,s} = \left(\int_{\omega \in \Omega} c_{j,s}(\omega)^{(\sigma_s-1)/\sigma_s} d\omega \right)^{\sigma_s/(\sigma_s-1)}, \tag{19}$$

where $\sigma_s > 1$ is the elasticity of substitution between different varieties, which is allowed to vary across sectors. In multi-sector gravity models, each variety remains sourced from only one country so that a sector level version of (1) still holds, $C_{j,s} = \left(\sum_{i=1}^{n} C_{ij,s}^{(\sigma_s-1)/\sigma_s} \right)^{\sigma_s/(\sigma_s-1)}$, with $C_{ij,s} = \int_{\omega \in \Omega_{ij,s}} c_{j,s}(\omega)^{(\sigma_s-1)/\sigma_s} d\omega$. The associated consumer price index is $P_j = \prod_{s=1}^{S} P_{j,s}^{\beta_{j,s}}$, with sector-specific price indices given by a sector level version of (2), $P_{j,s} = \left(\sum_{i=1}^{n} P_{ij,s}^{1-\sigma_s} \right)^{1/(1-\sigma_s)}$, with $P_{ij,s} = \left(\int_{\omega \in \Omega_{ij,s}} p_{j,s}(\omega)^{(1-\sigma_s)} d\omega \right)^{1/(1-\sigma_s)}$.

In line with the literature, we assume that our reduced-form assumption on price indices, equation (14), now holds sector-by-sector; that factors of production are used in the same way across all activities in all sectors, so that $c_{i,s}^p = c_{ii,s}^m = c_{i,s}^e = Y_i$; and that trade in goods is balanced, $R_i = Y_i$.[14] Combining these assumptions, we get

$$P_{ij,s} = \tau_{ij,s} Y_i \left[\left(e_{j,s} \frac{E_j}{c_{ij,s}^x} \right)^{\frac{\delta_s}{1-\sigma_s}} \frac{\tau_{ij,s} Y_i}{P_{j,s}} \right]^{\eta_s} r_{i,s}^{\frac{\delta_s}{1-\sigma_s}} \xi_{ij,s}, \tag{20}$$

where $e_{j,s} \equiv E_{j,s}/E_j$ denotes the share of total expenditure in country j allocated to sector s and $r_{i,s} = R_{i,s}/R_i$ denotes the share of total revenues in country i generated from sector s. All other variables have the same interpretation as in Section 3.1, except that they are now free to vary across sectors. Compared to equation (15), equation (20) allows for scale

---

[14] The assumption, $R_i = Y_i$, is stronger than in the one-sector case. In Section 3.2, it holds in models with monopolistic competition and firm-level heterogeneity independently of where fixed exporting costs are paid, as long as productivity distributions are Pareto. In a multi-sector environment, this may no longer be true even under Pareto if fixed exporting costs are partly paid in the importing country and sectors differ in the share of revenues associated with fixed exporting costs. Such considerations lead to a slight change in the present analysis, which we come back to below.

effects in monopolistically competitive sectors both through selection, $\left(e_{j,s}E_j/c_{ij,s}^x\right)^{\frac{\delta_s}{1-\sigma_s}}$,

and entry, $r_{i,s}^{\frac{\delta_s}{1-\sigma_s}}$. In the one-sector case, the latter effect is necessarily absent because $r_{i,s} = 1$. Here an expansion of production in a monopolistically competitive sector, i.e., a higher value of $r_{i,s}$, leads to entry and gains from new varieties, i.e., a lower value of $P_{ij,s}$, with the standard "love of variety" elasticity of $1/\left(\sigma_s - 1\right)$.[15]

We now focus on the gains from international trade, as defined in Section 2.3, and discuss how they are affected by the introduction of multiple sectors under the assumption that equation (20) holds. Bilateral trade flows at the sector-level satisfy $X_{ij,s} = \left(P_{ij,s}/P_{j,s}\right)^{1-\sigma_s} e_{j,s}E_j$. Together with equation (20), this implies the sector-level gravity equation:

$$X_{ij,s} = \frac{\left(\tau_{ij,s}Y_i\right)^{-\varepsilon_s}\left(c_{ij}^x\right)^{-\delta_s\eta_s} r_{i,s}^{\delta_s}\chi_{ij,s}}{\sum_l \left(\tau_{lj,s}Y_l\right)^{-\varepsilon_s}\left(c_{lj}^x\right)^{-\delta_s\eta_s} r_{l,s}^{\delta_s}\chi_{lj,s}} e_{j,s}E_j, \tag{21}$$

where $\varepsilon_s = \left(1+\eta_s\right)\left(\sigma_s - 1\right)$ and $\chi_{ij,s} \equiv \xi_{ij,s}^{1-\sigma_s}$. As in Section 3.1, one can combine equation (20), equation (21), and the fact that $\lambda_{ij,s} = \left(P_{ij,s}/P_{j,s}\right)^{1-\sigma_s}$ to show that changes in real consumption associated with a trade shock are now given by:

$$\hat{C}_j = \prod_{s=1}^{S} \left(\hat{\lambda}_{jj,s}\left(\hat{e}_{j,s}^{\eta_s}\hat{r}_{j,s}\right)^{-\delta_s}\right)^{-\beta_{j,s}/\varepsilon_s}. \tag{22}$$

Under Cobb-Douglas preferences, we know that $e_{j,s} = e_{j,s}' = \beta_{j,s}$. Thus the previous expression can be simplified further into $\hat{C}_j = \prod_{s=1}^{S}\left(\hat{\lambda}_{jj,s}\hat{r}_{j,s}^{-\delta_s}\right)^{-\beta_{j,s}/\varepsilon_s}$.[16] To compute the gains from trade, we only need to solve for $\hat{r}_{j,s}$ when the counterfactual entails autarky. Since $r_{j,s}' = e_{j,s}'$ under autarky and $e_{j,s} = e_{j,s}' = \beta_{j,s}$, we must have $\hat{r}_{j,s} = e_{j,s}/r_{j,s}$. Using the fact that $\hat{\lambda}_{jj,s} = 1/\lambda_{jj,s}$ for all s, we then get

$$G_j = 1 - \prod_{s=1}^{S}\left(\lambda_{jj,s}\left(\frac{e_{j,s}}{r_{j,s}}\right)^{\delta_s}\right)^{\beta_{j,s}/\varepsilon_s}. \tag{23}$$

Since δ_s appears in equation (23), gains from trade predicted by multi-sector gravity models with monopolistic competition differ from those predicted by models with perfect competition because of scale effects, as discussed in Arkolakis et al. (2012b). In contrast, selection effects still have no impact on the overall magnitude of the gains from trade. Since η_s does not appear in equation (23), conditional on observed trade flows and the trade

---

[15] Similar scale effects can be introduced in the one-sector case by allowing factor supply to be elastic; see Balistreri et al. (2009). The magnitude of such effects then crucially depends on the elasticity of factor supply.

[16] Without balanced trade in goods, $R_j \neq Y_j$, this would generalize to $\hat{C}_j = \prod_{s=1}^{S}\left(\hat{\lambda}_{jj,s}\left(\hat{r}_{j,s}\hat{R}_j/\hat{Y}_j\right)^{-\delta_s}\right)^{-\beta_{j,s}/\varepsilon_s}$.

elasticity, the gains from trade predicted by monopolistically competitive gravity models with and without firm-level heterogeneity are the same, even with multiple sectors.

To compute the gains from trade using equation (23), we need measures of $\lambda_{jj,s}$, $e_{j,s}$, $\beta_{j,s}$ and $r_{j,s}$ as well as sector-level trade elasticities ε_s for $s = 1, \ldots, S$. To compute $\lambda_{jj,s}$, $e_{j,s}$, $\beta_{j,s}$ and $r_{j,s}$, we use data on 31 sectors from the WIOD in 2008, as explained in the online Appendix.[17] Trade elasticities for agriculture and manufacturing sectors are from Caliendo and Parro (2010) while the trade elasticity for service sectors is simply held equal to the aggregate trade elasticity of 5 used in Section 2.3.[18] For the purposes of this chapter, the main advantage of the estimation procedure in Caliendo and Parro (2010) is that it is consistent with all quantitative trade models satisfying the sector-level gravity equation (21).[19]

Columns 2 and 3 in Table 4.1 report the gains from trade G_j for the same set of countries as in Section 2.3, but using equation (23) rather than equation (12). In Column 2, all sectors are assumed to be perfectly competitive, $\delta_s = 0$ for all s, while in Column 3, all agriculture and manufacturing sectors are assumed to be monopolistically competitive. Service sectors are assumed to be perfectly competitive in both cases, an assumption that we maintain throughout this chapter.

Two features of these results stand out. First, even in an environment with active entry effects, such as the one considered here, there are no systematic differences between the gains from trade predicted by multi-sector models with perfect competition, Column 2, and those predicted by models with monopolistic competition, Column 3. For some countries the gains under monopolistic competition are larger than under perfect competition (e.g. gains in Germany increase from 12.7% to 17.6%), while for other countries the opposite holds (e.g. gains for Greece decrease from 16.3% to 4.7%). Second, the gains from trade predicted by multi-sector models under both market structures, Columns 2 and 3, are significantly larger than those predicted by one-sector models, Column 1. For example, moving from Column 1 to Column 2 increases G_j for Belgium from 7.5% to 32.7%, while it increases G_j for Canada from 3.8% to 17.4%. The average among all the countries in Table 4.1 more than triples, increasing from 4.4% (Column 1) to 15.3% (Column 2), a point also emphasized in Ossa (2012).

---

[17] In theory, since the models that we consider do not feature intermediate goods, we have $e_{j,s} = \beta_{j,s}$. In the data, however, gross expenditure shares, $e_{j,s}$, differ from final demand shares, $\beta_{j,s}$. In the analysis that follows we let $\beta_{j,s}$ be different from $e_{j,s}$ when computing gains from trade using equation (23).

[18] Since there is little trade in services, the value of that elasticity has very small effects on our quantitative results.

[19] Caliendo and Parro (2010) use COMTRADE data from 1993. They assume that iceberg trade costs can be decomposed into $\tau_{ij,s} = t_{ij,s} d_{ij,s} \mu_{ij,s}$ where $t_{ij,s}$ is one plus the *ad-valorem* tariff applied by country j on good s imported from i and d_{ni} is a symmetric component of the iceberg-trade cost, i.e., $d_{ij,s} = d_{ji,s}$. Taking a triple log-difference of equation (21) with $\delta_s = 0$ yields

$$\ln \frac{X_{ij,s} X_{jl,s} X_{li,s}}{X_{il,s} X_{lj,s} X_{ji,s}} = \varepsilon_s \ln \frac{t_{ij,s} t_{jl,s} t_{li,s}}{t_{il,s} t_{lj,s} t_{ji,s}} + \mu_{ijl,s},$$

where the error-term $\mu_{ijl,s} = \ln \mu_{ij,s}^{\varepsilon_s} X_{ij,s} + \ln \mu_{jl,s}^{\varepsilon_s} X_{jl,s} + \ln \mu_{li,s}^{\varepsilon_s} X_{li,s} - \ln \mu_{il,s}^{\varepsilon_s} X_{il,s} - \ln \mu_{lj,s}^{\varepsilon_s} X_{lj,s} - \ln \mu_{ji,s}^{\varepsilon_s} X_{ji,s}$. We discuss how we map WIOD and COMTRADE data in the online Appendix.

The fact that models with perfect and monopolistic competition predict, on average, similar gains reflect the opposite consequences of entry effects—$\prod_{s=1}^{S}\left(e_{j,s}/r_{j,s}\right)^{\beta_{j,s}\delta_{s}/\varepsilon_{s}}$ in equation (23)—on countries with a comparative advantage and a comparative disadvantage in sectors with strong scale effects. If $e_{j,s}/r_{j,s}$ is negatively correlated with $\delta_{s}/\varepsilon_{s}$, then country j tends to be a large exporter of goods with strong scale effects. For such a country, the gains from trade tend to be larger than in the absence of scale effects since trade allows specialization in the sectors characterized by strong returns to scale. The converse is true, however, for a country in which $e_{j,s}/r_{j,s}$ is positively correlated with $\delta_{s}/\varepsilon_{s}$, i.e., a country with a comparative disadvantage in sectors with strong scale effects. This is related to Frank Graham's argument for protection; see Ethier (1982a) and Helpman and Krugman (1985) for a general discussion.

Why do multi-sector gravity models predict much larger gains than their one-sector counterparts? Part of the answer is: Cobb-Douglas preferences. This assumption implies that if the price of a single good gets arbitrarily large as a country moves to autarky—because it cannot produce that good—then gains from trade are infinite. According to equation (23), this will happen either if the share of expenditure on domestic goods, $\lambda_{jj,s}$, is close to zero—which implies arbitrarily large costs of production for that good at home—or if the trade elasticity, ε_{s}, is close to zero—which implies that foreign varieties are essential. We come back to this issue when discussing the more general case of nested CES utility functions in Section 5.3.

3.4. Tradable Intermediate Goods

We now enrich the supply-side of gravity models by introducing tradable intermediate goods and input-output linkages as in the early work of Krugman and Venables (1995), Eaton and Kortum (2002), Alvarez and Lucas (2007), and more recently Di Giovanni and Levchenko (2009), Caliendo and Parro (2010), and Balistreri et al. (2011). Formally, we maintain the same preference structure as in the previous section and introduce intermediate goods parsimoniously by assuming that, in each sector s, they are produced in the exact same way as composite goods for final consumption:

$$I_{j,s} = \left(\int_{\omega\in\Omega} i_{j,s}(\omega)^{(\sigma_{s}-1)/\sigma_{s}} d\omega\right)^{\sigma_{s}/(\sigma_{s}-1)}, \tag{24}$$

where $i_{j,s}(\omega)$ denotes the amount of variety ω used in the production of intermediate goods in country j and sector s. Accordingly, the sector-level price index $P_{j,s}$ defined in Section 3.3 now measures the aggregate price of sector s goods in country j for both final consumption and production.

As we did in the previous section, and in line with the existing literature, we assume that sector-level price indices satisfy equation (14) and that trade in goods is balanced so that, together with the overall trade balance, we have total expenditure equals total producer revenues, $E_{i} = R_{i}$, in each country. Compared to Section 3.3, we allow $c_{i,s}^{p}$ to vary across sectors to reflect the differential effect of intermediate goods on unit costs of production in different sectors:

$$c_{i,s}^p = Y_i^{1-\alpha_{i,s}} \prod_{k=1}^{S} P_{i,k}^{\alpha_{i,ks}}, \tag{25}$$

where $\alpha_{i,ks} \geq 0$ are exogenous technology parameters such that $\alpha_{i,s} \equiv \sum_{k=1}^{S} \alpha_{i,ks} \in [0, 1]$. As in the previous section, we assume that all sectors use primary factors in the same way, hence the term Y_i in equation (25). In line with the existing literature, we also assume that entry and exporting activities also use intermediate goods in the same proportion as production, $c_{i,s}^e = c_{ii,s}^x = c_{i,s}^p$.[20]

Under the previous assumptions, equation (14) now implies

$$P_{ij,s} = \tau_{ij,s} c_{i,s} \left[\left(\frac{e_{j,s}}{v_j} \frac{Y_j}{c_{ij,s}^x} \right)^{\frac{\delta_s}{1-\sigma_s}} \frac{\tau_{ij,s} c_{i,s}}{P_{j,s}} \right]^{\eta_s} \left(\frac{r_{i,s}}{v_i} \frac{Y_i}{c_{i,s}} \right)^{\frac{\delta_s}{1-\sigma_s}} \xi_{ij,s}, \tag{26}$$

where $c_{i,s} = c_{i,s}^p$ as given by equation (25); $v_i \equiv Y_i/R_i$ is the ratio of total income to total revenues in country i; and $e_{i,s}$ and $r_{i,s}$ still denote expenditure and revenue shares, the difference being that expenditure and revenue are now "gross," as they include the purchases and sales of both consumption and intermediate goods. In the absence of intermediate goods we have $\alpha_{i,s} = 0$ and $v_i = 1$ for all i and s, so the previous equation reduces to (20).

Bilateral trade flows now include trade in consumption and intermediate goods. But since both are combined using the same CES aggregator, equations (19) and (24), trade flows still satisfy $X_{ij,s} = \left(P_{ij,s}/P_{j,s} \right)^{1-\sigma_s} e_{j,s} E_j$. Together with equation (26), this implies the following sector-level gravity equation:

$$X_{ij,s} = \frac{\left(\tau_{ij,s} c_{i,s} \right)^{-\varepsilon_s} \left(c_{ij,s}^x \right)^{-\delta_s \eta_s} \left(\frac{r_{i,s}}{v_i} \frac{Y_i}{c_{i,s}} \right)^{\delta_s} \chi_{ij,s}}{\sum_{l=1}^{n} \left(\tau_{lj,s} c_{l,s} \right)^{-\varepsilon_s} \left(c_{lj,s}^x \right)^{-\delta_s \eta_s} \left(\frac{r_{l,s}}{v_l} \frac{Y_l}{c_{l,s}} \right)^{\delta_s} \chi_{lj,s}} e_{j,s} E_j, \tag{27}$$

where again $\chi_{ij,s} \equiv \xi_{ij,s}^{1-\sigma_s}$. One can now follow a similar strategy as in previous sections to show that welfare changes associated with a foreign shock are given by

$$\hat{C}_j = \prod_{s,k=1}^{S} \left(\hat{\lambda}_{jj,k} \left(\left(\frac{\hat{e}_{j,k}}{\hat{v}_j} \right)^{\eta_k} \left(\frac{\hat{r}_{j,k}}{\hat{v}_j} \right) \right)^{-\delta_k} \right)^{-\beta_{j,s} \tilde{a}_{j,sk}/\varepsilon_k}, \tag{28}$$

---

[20] Alternatively one could assume that entry and exporting activities only use primary factors of production: $c_{i,s}^e = c_{ii,s}^x = Y_i$. This assumption, however, immediately creates inconsistencies between the predictions of models of monopolistic competition and our dataset. Given our estimates of the trade elasticities ε_s, the factor costs associated with fixed entry and exporting activities is sometimes higher than the total factor costs observed in the data.

where $\widetilde{a}_{j,sk}$ is the elasticity of the price index in sector s with respect to changes in the price index in sector k. These price elasticities are given by the elements of the "adjusted Leontief inverse" of the input-output matrix, i.e., the $(S \times S)$ matrix $(\mathbf{Id} - \widetilde{\mathbf{A}}_j)^{-1}$, with the elements of the $\widetilde{\mathbf{A}}_j$ matrix given by the adjusted technology parameters $\widetilde{\alpha}_{j,sk} \equiv \alpha_{j,sk} (1 + \delta_k (1 + \eta_k) / \varepsilon_k)$. Under perfect competition, $(\mathbf{Id} - \widetilde{\mathbf{A}}_j)^{-1}$ is the standard Leontief inverse matrix, i.e., $(\mathbf{Id} - \widetilde{\mathbf{A}}_j)^{-1} = (\mathbf{Id} - \mathbf{A}_j)^{-1}$ where $\mathbf{A}_j$ is the matrix with typical element $\alpha_{j,sk}$. Under monopolistic competition with intermediate goods used in entry and exporting activities, however, we need to adjust the technology parameters $\alpha_{j,sk}$ by $1 + (1 + \eta_k) / \varepsilon_k = 1 + 1/(\sigma_k - 1)$ to take into account that a decline in the price index of sector s not only decreases the price index of sector k through the standard input-output channels, but also by lowering fixed entry and exporting costs, thereby increasing the number of available varieties.

In addition, intermediate goods affects the results derived in Section 3.3 in two important ways. First, expenditure shares, $e_{j,s}$, are no longer equal to exogenous consumption shares, $\beta_{j,s}$. Hence, $\hat{e}_{j,s}$ may be different from one, which implies that the use of the formula given in equation (28) requires either observing $\hat{e}_{j,s}$, after the shock, or predicting it, before the shock. Second, the scale effect term, $(\hat{e}_{j,k}/\hat{v}_j)^{\eta_k} (\hat{r}_{j,k}/\hat{v}_j)$, now depends on the change in the ratio of value added to gross output, $\hat{v}_j$. Intuitively, under monopolistic competition, welfare depends on entry, which itself depends on the ratio of revenues to factor prices, v_j.

The associated formula for the gains from international trade is obtained from (28) by setting $\hat{\lambda}_{ij,k} = 1/\lambda_{ij,k}$ and by solving for $\left(\frac{\hat{e}_{j,k}}{\hat{v}_j}\right)^{\eta_k} \left(\frac{\hat{r}_{j,k}}{\hat{v}_j}\right)$ as we move to autarky. Since $e_{j,k}$ and $r_{j,k}$ are data while $e_{j,k}^A = r_{j,k}^A$ in autarky, then we just need to solve for $e_{j,k}^A/v_j^A$. In the online Appendix we show that this is given by $e_{j,k}^A/v_j^A = \sum_{l=1}^{S} \beta_{j,l} a_{j,kl}$, where $a_{j,kl}$ are now the elements of the Leontief inverse $(\mathbf{Id} - \mathbf{A}_j)^{-1}$. The gains from trade are then

$$G_j = 1 - \prod_{s,k=1}^{S} \left(\lambda_{ij,k} \left(\left(\frac{e_{j,k}}{b_{j,k}} \right)^{\eta_s} \frac{r_{j,k}}{b_{j,k}} \right)^{-\delta_k} \right)^{\beta_{j,s} \widetilde{a}_{j,sk}/\varepsilon_k}, \tag{29}$$

where $b_{j,k} \equiv v_j \left(\sum_{l=1}^{S} \beta_{j,l} a_{j,kl} \right)$ summarizes how intermediate goods affect the magnitude of scale effects in models with monopolistic competition.

To implement the previous formula using the WIOD data, we compute $\lambda_{jj,s}$, $R_{j,s}$, $E_{j,s}$, $r_{j,s}$, $e_{j,s}$, and $\beta_{j,s}$ in the exact same way as in Section 3.3. In the raw data, we also observe purchases, $X_{ij,ks}$, of intermediate goods from sector k and country i in sector s and country j. Using those, we can then compute shares of intermediate purchases $\alpha_{j,ks} = \sum_i X_{ij,ks}/R_{j,s}$ and value added by sector as $Y_{j,s} = R_{j,s} - \sum_k \sum_i X_{ij,ks}$. In a number of simulations below, we also follow Balistreri et al. (2011) and use an alternative measure of shares of intermediate goods, $\alpha_{j,ks}^* = \left(\sum_k \sum_i X_{ij,ks}/R_{j,s} \right) \times (E_{j,k}/E_j)$, when computing gains from trade using equation (29). Compared to the true share, $\alpha_{j,ks}$, this alternative measure, $\alpha^*_{j,ks}$, counterfactually assumes that firms allocate expenditure on intermediate goods from different sectors in the same proportions, $E_{j,k}/E_j$, though some sectors may have higher shares of intermediate goods, $\sum_k \sum_i X_{ij,ks}/R_{j,s}$. We come back to the benefit of this simplification in a moment.

Columns 4–7 of Table 4.1 report the gains from trade G_j under different market structures using equation (29). Column 4 corresponds to gains from trade under perfect competition, $\delta_s = 0$ for all s, using the true intermediate good shares, $\alpha_{j,ks} = \sum_i X_{ij,ks}/R_{j,s}$. We see that predicted gains from trade are much higher than those predicted by the same models without intermediate goods (Column 2). For example, the gains from trade for the United States and Spain in Column 4 are twice as high as those in Column 2, while for Japan the gains increase by a factor of three. One can think about these results in two ways. First, trade in intermediates leads to a decline in the price of domestic goods, which implies additional welfare gains. If domestic goods are used as inputs in domestic production, this triggers additional rounds of productivity gains, leading to even larger gains; this is the input-output loop often mentioned in the literature.[21] Second, for given data on the share of *expenditure* on domestic goods, $\lambda_{jj,s}$, models featuring intermediate goods necessarily predict more trade relative to total *income*. So, perhaps, it should not be too surprising that the same models predict that real income increases by more because of trade.

Ideally, one would like to study the predictions of models of monopolistic competition using the same data on intermediate good shares, $\alpha_{j,ks}$. Unfortunately, this is not possible in the context of our dataset since it would lead some of the elements of the adjusted Leontief matrix to become negative, in which case gains from trade G_j are not well-defined. To understand why this issue arises, consider a simpler model with monopolistic competition, $\delta_s = 1$, intermediate goods, $\alpha_s > 0$, but only one sector, $S = 1$. In that environment, equation (29) simplifies to $G_j = 1 - \lambda_{jj}^{\tilde{a}_j/\varepsilon}$, where $\tilde{a}_j = \left(1 - \alpha_j \left(1 + \frac{1}{\sigma-1}\right)\right)^{-1}$. As $\alpha_j \left(1 + \frac{1}{\sigma-1}\right)$ gets close to one, $\tilde{a}_j$ goes to infinity and real consumption in autarky goes to zero. If $\alpha_j \geq (\sigma - 1)/\sigma$ then the price index, real consumption, and of course G_j are not well-defined. Intuitively, a given increase in the number of varieties leads to a decline in the price index, which triggers a decline in the cost of entry, which, in turn, leads to a further increase in the number of varieties. We obtain infinite amplification whenever the share of intermediates in production, α_j, is high relative to the love of variety, $1/(\sigma - 1)$. This is precisely what happens when any of the elements of the adjusted Leontief matrix becomes negative.

To get around this issue, Columns 5-7 of Table 4.1 report gains from trade using the alternative measure of intermediate good shares, $\alpha^*_{j,ks}$, as in Balistreri et al. (2011). To

---

[21] A simple way to illustrate this mechanism is to return to the one-sector model. In the case of perfect competition, the formula above becomes $G_j = 1 - (\lambda_{jj})^{1/\varepsilon(1-\alpha)}$; see Eaton and Kortum (2002) and Alvarez and Lucas (2007). Thus a higher share of intermediate goods, α, leads to higher gains from trade.

make sure that the difference between models of perfect and monopolistic competition is not being driven by a different treatment of intermediate goods, Column 5 again reports the gains from trade under perfect competition. The results are very similar whether we use true shares (Column 4) or alternative shares (Column 5). Column 6 reports gains from trade under monopolistic competition without firm-level heterogeneity, $\delta_s = 1$ and $\eta_s = 0$, whereas Column 7 reports gains under monopolistic competition with firm-level heterogeneity, $\delta_s = 1$ and $\eta_s > 0$. Following Balistreri et al. (2011), we set $\eta_s = 0.65$ for all s.[22] In general, gains from trade are slightly higher with monopolistic than perfect competition. For example, the gains for the U.S. increase from 8% to 8.6% as we move from Column 5 to Column 6 in Table 4.1. Across all countries, the average gains increase from 27.1% to 32.3%. The intuition is simple. When entry activities use intermediate goods, trade leads to a decline in the cost of entry and hence to an expansion in the variety of goods produced domestically, bringing about additional welfare gains.

As shown by the results in Column 7, the gains from trade are even higher when we allow for firm-level heterogeneity. To see why, recall that $\varepsilon_s = (\sigma_s - 1)(1 + \eta_s)$, hence if $\varepsilon_s = 3.2$ (as in the Chemicals sector), then $\eta_s = 0.65$ implies $\sigma_s = 2.9$, whereas under the assumption $\eta_s = 0$ we would have concluded $\sigma_s = 4.2$. The difference in the implied elasticity of substitution σ_s between models with and without firm-level heterogeneity leads to large differences in the magnitude of the scale effects arising from love of variety. We come back to this issue in more detail in Section 5.3. For now, we merely want to point out that: (i) welfare calculations are highly sensitive to the value of this parameter; and (ii) the reason behind this sensitivity is that conditional on the value of the trade elasticity ε_s, the value of η_s pins down σ_s and, in turn, the magnitude of scale effects.

In summary, the introduction of tradable intermediate goods dramatically increases the magnitude of the gains from trade, both under perfect and monopolistic competition. Under the latter market structure, the scale effects associated with decreases in the price of intermediate goods are so large that if one were to use the true shares of intermediate purchases across countries and sectors, $\alpha_{j,ks}$, rather than a made-up average, $\alpha^*_{j,ks}$, one would conclude that for all countries in our dataset, gains from trade cannot be finite.

3.5. Multiple Factors of Production

So far, we have restricted ourselves to gravity models featuring only one factor of production, or equivalently multiple factors of production that are used in the same proportions in all sectors. This assumption is formally reflected in the fact that producer prices are proportional to GDP, Y_i, in equations (20) and (25). In this section we introduce differences in factor intensity across sectors, as in the extensions of Eaton and Kortum (2002),

---

[22] Balistreri et al. (2011) use non-linear least squares to estimate the trade elasticity for manufacturing as a whole (as well as other parameters). Their preferred estimate is $\varepsilon = 4.58$. Following Bernard et al. (2003), they set $\sigma = 3.8$. Since $\varepsilon = (\sigma - 1)(1 + \eta)$, these two values imply that $\eta = 0.65$. In Section 5.3 we discuss more direct ways to estimate η_s across sectors using firm-level data.

Bernard et al. (2003), and Melitz (2003) considered by Chor (2010), Burstein and Vogel (2010), and Bernard et al. (2007), respectively.

For expositional purposes, we restrict ourselves to an economic environment in which there are only two factors of production, skilled labor and unskilled labor, and no intermediate goods. Throughout this subsection, we assume that aggregate production functions are CES in all countries and sectors and given by

$$Q_{j,s} = \left[\mu_s^H (H_{j,s})^{(\rho-1)/\rho} + \mu_s^L (L_{j,s})^{(\rho-1)/\rho}\right]^{\rho/(\rho-1)},$$

where $H_{j,s}$ and $L_{j,s}$ denote total employment of skilled and unskilled workers, respectively, in country j and sector s; $\rho > 0$ is the elasticity of substitution between skilled and unskilled labor; and $\mu_j^f > 0$ determines the intensity of factor $f = H, L$ in sector s, with $\mu_{j,s}^H + \mu_{j,s}^F = 1$. In line with the existing literature, we also assume that factors of production have the same share in variable costs of production as in entry and exporting costs (if any): $c_{i,s}^e = c_{ii,s}^m = c_{i,s}^p \equiv c_{i,s}$. Assuming as above that trade in goods is balanced, $Y_i = R_i$, equation (20) then generalizes to

$$P_{ij,s} = \tau_{ij,s} c_{i,s} \left[\left(e_{j,s}\frac{E_j}{c_{ij,s}^x}\right)^{\frac{\delta_s}{1-\sigma_s}} \frac{\tau_{ij,s} c_{i,s}}{P_{j,s}}\right]^{\eta_s} \left(r_{i,s}\frac{Y_i}{c_{i,s}}\right)^{\frac{\delta_s}{1-\sigma_s}} \xi_{ij,s}. \tag{30}$$

All variables have the same interpretation as in previous sections, except for the fact that unit costs are now proportional to

$$c_{i,s} = \left[\left(\mu_s^H\right)^\rho \left(w_i^H\right)^{1-\rho} + \left(\mu_s^L\right)^\rho \left(w_i^L\right)^{1-\rho}\right]^{1/(1-\rho)}, \tag{31}$$

where w_i^H and w_i^L are the wages of skilled and unskilled workers, respectively, in country i.

As in previous sections, if lower-level utility functions are CES, then gravity holds in this environment. Combining equations (19) and (30), we get

$$X_{ij,s} = \frac{\left(\tau_{ij,s} c_{i,s}\right)^{-\varepsilon_s} \left(c_{ij,s}^x\right)^{-\delta_s \eta_s} \left(r_{i,s}\frac{Y_i}{c_{i,s}}\right)^{\delta_s} X_{ij,s}}{\sum_{l=1}^n \left(\tau_{lj,s} c_{l,s}\right)^{-\varepsilon_s} \left(c_{lj,s}^x\right)^{-\delta_s \eta_s} \left(r_{l,s}\frac{Y_l}{c_{l,s}}\right)^{\delta_s} X_{lj,s}} e_{j,s} E_j.$$

For any trade shock, we can normalize factor prices such that $Y_j = Y_j'$. Using this normalization, we can then express welfare changes as

$$\hat{C}_j = \prod_{s=1}^S (\hat{c}_{j,s})^{-\beta_{j,s}} \left(\hat{\lambda}_{jj,s} \left((\hat{c}_{j,s})^{-(1+\eta_s)} \hat{e}_{j,s}^{\eta_s} \hat{r}_{j,s}\right)^{-\delta_s}\right)^{-\beta_{j,s}/\varepsilon_s}.$$

Gains from trade, in turn, are given by

$$G_j = 1 - \prod_{s=1}^S \left(\hat{c}_{j,s}^A\right)^{-\beta_{j,s}} \left(\lambda_{jj,s} \left((\hat{c}_{j,s}^A)^{-(1+\eta_s)} \frac{e_{j,s}}{r_{j,s}}\right)^{\delta_s}\right)^{\beta_{j,s}/\varepsilon_s}, \tag{32}$$

where $\hat{c}_{j,s}^A$ denotes the change in production costs between the initial equilibrium and autarky. Compared to one-factor models, changes in real consumption now also depend on changes in relative factor prices, which affects production costs across sectors, as reflected in $\hat{c}_{j,s}$ and $\hat{c}_{j,s}^A$. Under perfect competition, such changes only affect variable costs of production, whereas under monopolistic competition, they also affect the fixed costs of exporting and entry and so, the number of available varieties in country j and sector s, as reflected in the extra terms $(\hat{c}_{j,s})^{-(1+\eta_s)}$ and $(\hat{c}_{j,s}^A)^{-(1+\eta_s)}$.

In order to compute changes in production costs, one can again use the exact hat algebra introduced in Section 2.2. We illustrate here how this can be done as we move from the initial equilibrium to autarky, though the same methodology can be applied to any shock. Equation (31) implies

$$\hat{c}_{j,s}^A = \left[\varphi_{j,s}^H \left(\hat{w}_i^{A,H} \right)^{1-\rho} + \varphi_{j,s}^L \left(\hat{w}_i^{A,L} \right)^{1-\rho} \right]^{1/(1-\rho)}, \tag{33}$$

where $\varphi_{j,s}^f \equiv \left(\mu_j^f \right)^\rho \left(w_j^f \right)^{1-\rho} / c_{j,s}^{1-\rho}$ is the share of total factor spending going to factor f in country j and sector s in the initial equilibrium. Changes in factor prices, in turn, can be computed by manipulating the two factor-market clearing conditions:

$$\hat{w}_j^{A,H} = \sum_{s=1}^S h_{j,s} \left(\frac{e_{j,s}}{y_{j,s}} \right) \left(\frac{\left(\hat{w}_j^{A,H} \right)^{1-\rho}}{\varphi_{j,s}^H \left(\hat{w}_j^{A,H} \right)^{1-\rho} + \varphi_{j,s}^L \left(\hat{w}_j^{A,L} \right)^{1-\rho}} \right), \tag{34}$$

$$\hat{w}_j^{A,L} = \sum_{k=1}^S l_{j,s} \left(\frac{e_{j,s}}{y_{j,s}} \right) \left(\frac{\left(\hat{w}_j^{A,L} \right)^{1-\rho}}{\varphi_{j,s}^H \left(\hat{w}_j^{A,H} \right)^{1-\rho} + \varphi_{j,s}^L \left(\hat{w}_j^{A,L} \right)^{1-\rho}} \right), \tag{35}$$

where $h_{j,s} \equiv H_{j,s}/H$ and $l_{j,s} \equiv L_{j,s}/L$ denote the share of skilled and unskilled workers, respectively, employed in sector s in country j in the initial equilibrium, and $y_{j,s} \equiv Y_{j,s}/Y_j$ denotes the share of total income earned in sector s in country j. Combining equations (32–35), we can compute the gains from trade in the multi-factor case.

To implement this new formula, we need additional data on the elasticity of substitution between skilled and unskilled workers, ρ, the share of employment of skilled and unskilled workers across sectors, $h_{j,s}$ and $l_{j,s}$, and the factor cost shares, $\varphi_{j,s}^f$. For simplicity, we assume Cobb–Douglas technologies, i.e., $\rho = 1$, and common cost shares across countries, i.e., $\varphi_{j,s}^f = \varphi_s^f$.[23] We compute factor cost shares from the NBER manufacturing database that contains information about employment and average wages for both production and non-production workers in the United States between 1987 and 2005. Following Berman et al. (1994), we treat skilled workers in the model as non-production

---

[23] We have explored the sensitivity of our results to the assumption of Cobb–Douglas technologies for the United States. Following Katz and Murphy (1992), we have set $\rho = 1.4$ rather than $\rho = 1$ and recomputed G_j using equation (32). The results are basically unchanged.

workers in the data and unskilled workers in the model as production workers in the data. Given cost shares, employment shares are computed as $h_{j,s} = \frac{\varphi_s^H \gamma_{j,s}}{\sum_k \varphi_k^H \gamma_{j,k}}$ and $l_{j,s} = \frac{\varphi_s^L \gamma_{j,s}}{\sum_k \varphi_k^L \gamma_{j,k}}$. Since we do not have data on cost shares for sectors outside of manufacturing, we aggregate all non-manufacturing sectors into a single sector which we assume is non-tradable and which has factor cost shares equal to the overall factor cost shares in manufacturing.

When computing the gains from trade using equation (32) under the assumption of perfection competition, $\delta_s = 0$ for all s, we find gains from trade that are virtually the same as those presented in Column 2 of Table 4.1. This reflects the fact that the factor content of trade for skilled and unskilled labor is basically zero in our dataset. In particular, one can check that under the assumption that production functions are Cobb-Douglas ($\rho = 1$), we have $\hat{w}_j^{A,f} = \frac{\sum_s e_{j,s} \mu_s^f}{\sum_s \gamma_{j,s} \mu_s^f} \approx 1$. At this point, thus, it does not appear that, conditional on observed trade flows, allowing for standard Heckscher-Ohlin forces has a large effect on the magnitude of the gains from trade.

An attractive feature of multi-factor gravity models is that they provide a theoretical framework to explore quantitatively the distributional consequences of globalization. Using equations (34) and (35), one could easily compute the change in the skill premium associated with international trade. One caveat, however, is that multi-factor gravity models considered here implicitly rule out differences in factor intensity across firms within the same sector. As discussed in Burstein and Vogel (2010), more productive firms tend to be more skill intensive in practice, which opens up a new channel through which trade liberalization may contribute to an increase in inequality by leading to the exit of the least efficient firms. Burstein and Vogel (2010) find that this "skill-biased" mechanism is quantitatively more important than the Heckscher-Ohlin mechanism. Another caveat is that models in this section abstract from trade in capital goods. Given the existence of capital-skill complementarity, this is another channel through which trade may affect inequality. This issue is explored quantitatively in Burstein et al. (2011) and Parro (2012).

3.6. Other Extensions

Non-CES Utility. Although gravity models reviewed so far differ in terms of their supply-side assumptions, they all share the same demand structure. Starting with the Armington model presented in Section 2, all models feature representative agents with (nested) CES utility. A non-trivial cost of this assumption is that it implies constant markups across firms under monopolistic competition. Hence, the "pro-competitive" effects of trade under this market structure, namely the idea that welfare gains from trade may be larger because of their effects on firm-level markups, are de facto ruled out. In this final subsection, we briefly discuss recent work that has tried to incorporate these considerations into otherwise standard quantitative trade models with monopolistic competition.

The three main alternatives to CES utility in trade models are: (*i*) separable, but non-CES utility functions, as in the pioneering work of Krugman (1979); (*ii*) a quadratic, but non-separable utility function, as in Melitz and Ottaviano (2008); and (*iii*) a translog expenditure function, as in Feenstra (2003). In Arkolakis et al. (2012a), the authors start from a general demand system that encompasses alternatives (i) and (iii), and also (ii) when a homogeneous "outside good" is introduced.

Under the assumptions that there exists a finite reservation price for all varieties; that there are no fixed exporting costs; and that the distribution of firm-level productivity is Pareto, they show that, in spite of variable markups, trade flows satisfy the same gravity equation (16) as in models with CES utility. In this situation, one can use the exact hat algebra to show that the macro-level predictions of non-CES models regarding the consequences of trade liberalization—namely, the predictions regarding the effects of changes in trade costs on wages and trade flows—are the same as in quantitative trade models with CES utility functions discussed in Section 3.1.

Although the predictions regarding trade flows and wages of CES and non-CES models considered in Arkolakis et al. (2012a) are equivalent, their welfare predictions are not. The gains from trade liberalization, in particular, may be larger or smaller depending on whether they trigger factor reallocations towards goods exhibiting larger or smaller markups, respectively.

A potentially fruitful alternative to studying the pro-competitive effects of trade consists in departing from monopolistic competition, while maintaining CES. As already discussed in Section 3.1, the model with Bertrand competition developed by Bernard et al. (2003) leads to the exact same predictions as one-sector gravity models with perfect and monopolistic competition, though alternative assumptions about the distribution of firm-level productivity may lead to different results; see de Blas and Russ (2010) and Holmes et al. (2010). In recent work, Edmond and Midrigan (2011) have used the model with Cournot competition developed by Atkeson and Burstein (2008) to study the magnitude of the gains from trade in economies with variable markups. When calibrating this model using data on manufacturing Taiwanese firms, they find large gains from trade, though the numbers vary depending on assumptions made on the correlation of productivity between Taiwanese and non-Taiwanese firms.

Multinational Production. In all the models reviewed so far, firms serve foreign markets exclusively through exports. In practice, however, a large share of foreign sales are done by foreign affiliates of multinational firms.

Ramondo and Rodríguez-Clare (2013) extend the perfectly competitive framework of Eaton and Kortum (2002) so that the technological know-how from a given country can be used to produce elsewhere, albeit perhaps at a cost. The cost of using local technologies abroad limits the extent of multinational production in the same way as iceberg trade costs limits the extent of international trade in gravity models. They explore how the substitutability and complementarity forces between trade and multinational production affect the magnitude of the gains from trade and the gains from openness more broadly defined. Their calibrated model implies that the gains from trade can be twice as high as the gains calculated in trade-only models.[24]

Arkolakis et al. (2012c) extend the monopolistically competitive framework of Melitz (2003) to allow firms to serve foreign markets by exporting from their home country or by setting up foreign affiliates. In this environment, a gravity equation akin to equation (5) still holds for the sales by firms from a particular origin, i.e., for the sales in country j of goods produced in country i by affiliates of firms from country l. Given data on bilateral trade and multinational production flows (i.e., the value of production by firms from i in country l, independently of where the goods are sold), they show how their model can be used to conduct counterfactual experiments using the exact hat algebra of Section 2.2.

4. EVALUATING TRADE POLICY

In this section we go from changes in iceberg trade costs to changes in trade policy, namely import tariffs. For expositional purposes, we first go back to the simple Armington model presented in Section 2 and describe the welfare implications of tariff changes in that environment. Like in Section 3, we then study how these predictions vary across different gravity models. We conclude by discussing issues of aggregation in the presence of heterogeneous tariffs across sectors. Throughout this section we modify our WIOD data such that, in line with the static models that we study, overall trade is balanced country-by-country; see the online Appendix for details. We tackle the issue of trade imbalances explicitly in Section 5.1.

4.1. Back to Armington

Consider a world economy similar to the one presented in Section 2.1. Compared to our earlier analysis, trade flows may now be subject to import tariffs so that equation (3) generalizes to

$$P_{ij} = Y_i \tau_{ij} \left(1 + t_{ij} \right) / Q_i, \tag{36}$$

where Y_i denotes factor income in country i, i.e., GDP net of tariff revenues, and $t_{ij} \geq 0$ denotes the *ad-valorem* tariff imposed by country j on goods from country i. In the rest of this section, we let $\phi_{ij} \equiv \tau_{ij} \left(1 + t_{ij} \right)$ denote the total trade costs between country i and j. Given CES utility, the value of bilateral trade flows (inclusive of tariffs) are thus given by the following gravity equation:

$$X_{ij} = \frac{\left(Y_i \phi_{ij} \right)^{-\varepsilon} \chi_{ij}}{\sum_{l=1}^{n} \left(Y_l \phi_{lj} \right)^{-\varepsilon} \chi_{lj}} E_j. \tag{37}$$

---

[24] In related work, Ramondo (2012) adapts the framework of Eaton and Kortum (2002) to environments with multinational production but no trade. She derives a gravity equation for multinational production flows and computes the associated gains. Burstein and Monge-Naranjo (2009), Prescott and McGrattan (2010), and Garetto (2012) also quantify the gains from multinational production, albeit in models without a gravity equation for multinational production.

In the presence of import tariffs, budget balance now requires $E_j = Y_j + T_j$, where $T_j \equiv \sum_{i=1}^{n} \frac{t_{ij}}{1+t_{ij}} X_{ij}$ denotes total tariff revenues in country j, whereas the goods market-clearing condition requires $Y_i = \sum_{j=1}^{n} \frac{1}{1+t_{ij}} X_{ij}$. Together with equation (37), these two conditions lead to the following generalization of equation (6):

$$Y_i = \sum_{j=1}^{n} \frac{1}{1+t_{ij}} \frac{\left(Y_i \phi_{ij}\right)^{-\varepsilon} \chi_{ij}}{\sum_{l=1}^{n} \left(Y_l \phi_{lj}\right)^{-\varepsilon} \chi_{lj}} \frac{Y_j}{1-\pi_j}, \tag{38}$$

where $\pi_j \equiv \sum_{i=1}^{n} \frac{t_{ij}}{1+t_{ij}} \frac{\left(Y_i \phi_{ij}\right)^{-\varepsilon} \chi_{ij}}{\sum_{l=1}^{n} \left(Y_l \phi_{lj}\right)^{-\varepsilon} \chi_{lj}} \in (0,1)$ denotes the share of tariff revenues in country j's total expenditure. This completes the description of a competitive equilibrium with import tariffs.

Now consider an arbitrary change in import tariffs from $\mathbf{t} \equiv \{t_{ij}\}$ to $\mathbf{t}' \equiv \{t'_{ij}\}$. To compute proportional changes in factor income, $\hat{\mathbf{Y}} \equiv \{\hat{Y}_i\}$, we can again use the exact hat algebra. Following the same steps as in Section 2.2, we get

$$\hat{Y}_j Y_j = \sum_{i=1}^{n} \frac{1}{1+t'_{ij}} \frac{\lambda_{ji} \left(\hat{Y}_j \hat{\phi}_{ji}\right)^{-\varepsilon}}{\sum_{l=1}^{n} \lambda_{li} \left(\hat{Y}_l \hat{\phi}_{li}\right)^{-\varepsilon}} \frac{\hat{Y}_i Y_i}{1-\pi'_i}, \tag{39}$$

where the share of tariff revenues in the counterfactual equilibrium is itself given by

$$\pi'_i = \sum_{j=1}^{n} \frac{t'_{ji}}{1+t'_{ji}} \frac{\lambda_{ji} \left(\hat{Y}_j \hat{\phi}_{ji}\right)^{-\varepsilon}}{\sum_{l=1}^{n} \lambda_{li} \left(\hat{Y}_l \hat{\phi}_{li}\right)^{-\varepsilon}}. \tag{40}$$

Combining the two previous expressions we can solve for $\hat{\mathbf{Y}} \equiv \{\hat{Y}_i\}$ (up to a normalization). Although the previous system of equations is not quite as compact as equation (11), it still does not depend directly on preference shifters, endowments, or trade costs. All we need to determine changes in factor income levels, $\hat{Y}_i$, are the initial expenditure shares, λ_{ij}, the initial factor income levels, Y_i, and the trade elasticity, ε. Like in Section 2.2, once changes in factor income are known, we can compute changes in expenditure shares using the gravity equation (37),

$$\hat{\lambda}_{ij} = \frac{\left(\hat{Y}_i \hat{\phi}_{ij}\right)^{-\varepsilon}}{\sum_{l=1}^{n} \lambda_{lj} \left(\hat{Y}_l \hat{\phi}_{lj}\right)^{-\varepsilon}}.$$

Finally, to compute the welfare change caused by the change in import tariff, we can start from equation (9). Integrating and taking into account the fact that $E_j = Y_j/(1-\pi_j)$, we obtain

$$\hat{C}_j = \left(\frac{1 - \pi_j}{1 - \pi_j'}\right) \hat{\lambda}_{jj}^{-1/\varepsilon}, \tag{41}$$

where the share of tariff revenues in the initial and counterfactual equilibria are given by $\pi_j = \sum_{i=1}^{n} \frac{t_{ij}}{1+t_{ij}} \lambda_{ij}$ and $\pi_j' = \sum_{i=1}^{n} \frac{t_{ij}'}{1+t_{ij}'} \lambda_{ij} \hat{\lambda}_{ij}$, respectively.[25] Like in Section 2.2, welfare changes can be computed using only a few sufficient statistics. One does not need to estimate all structural parameters of the model to estimate the welfare effect of an arbitrary tariff change.

We start by considering the welfare effects of a change in tariffs imposed by a single country, i.e., a unilateral change in tariffs. For simplicity, we assume that import tariffs are equal to zero in the initial equilibrium, $t_{ij} = 0$ for all i and j. This is not a bad approximation for most OECD countries today, where tariff revenues are a negligible share of GDP.[26] We consider a counterfactual equilibrium in which a single country j imposes a uniform tariff on all its trading partners, i.e., $t_{ij}' = t > 0$ for all $i \neq j$. All other structural parameters are held fixed between the initial equilibrium and the counterfactual equilibrium.

In Figure 4.1, we plot the welfare change associated with a unilateral tariff of $t\%$ for $j = $ United States, France, Portugal, and Ireland under the assumption that the trade elasticity ε is equal to 5. For each counterfactual exercise, we first compute proportional income changes using equations (39) and (40) and then, for each country j, welfare changes using equation (41).

A few features of Figure 4.1 stand out. First, we see that for all countries, the optimal tariff is around 20%. This should not be surprising. In the two-country case, we know from the work of Gros (1987)—see also Helpman and Krugman (1989), Chapter 7—that the optimal tariff in country j is equal to $t_j^* = 1/(\varepsilon\lambda_{jj}^*)$, where λ_{jj}^* denotes the share of expenditure in the rest of the world on goods produced in the rest of the world. For all countries, one should expect λ_{jj}^* to be very close to one in practice. So $1/\varepsilon = 20\%$ provides a good approximation of what the optimal tariff should be; see also Alvarez and Lucas (2007) for a related discussion. Second, we see that the potential gains from trade protection are modest, but non-trivial. At the optimal tariff, they range from 0.3% for the United States to 1.3% for Ireland. To put these numbers in perspective, note that the

---

[25] Equation (41) implies that, with tariffs, the gains from trade are given by $G_j = 1 - (1 - \pi_j)\lambda_{jj}^{1/\varepsilon}$. This generalizes equation (12) to environments in which the share of tariff revenues in total expenditure, π_j, is non-zero. See Felbermayr et al. (2013) for a discussion of the role of tariff revenues on the gains from trade.

[26] For example, in 2005 revenues as a share of GDP were 0.25%, 0.20%, and 0.36% for Canada, the United States, and Mexico, respectively (stats.oecd.org: Public Sector, Taxation and Market Regulation – Taxation, under Revenue Statistics, Customs and Import Duties over GDP). Developed countries in general have tariff revenue shares of 0.2% or less. Tariff revenues are more important for developing countries. For example, they were 1.8% of GDP in India in 2004. Other prominent examples of high tariff revenues are Russia (3.16%) and China (0.84%), both in the year 2000 – before they joined the WTO (Government Finance Statistics, IMF).

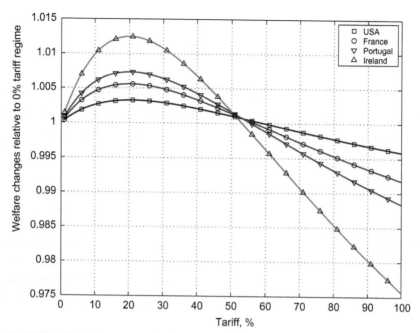

Figure 4.1 Welfare Changes Associated with a Unilateral Tariff in the Country Imposing the Tariff. (Trade elasticity $\varepsilon = 5$. Data are from WIOD in 2008.)

overall gains from trade predicted by the Armington model for these two countries are 1.8% and 8%, respectively; see Table 4.1 Column 1. Third, smaller countries that gain more from trade also gain more from optimal trade protection. Here, although smaller countries have less ability to manipulate their terms–of–trade, they benefit disproportionately more from an improvement in their terms–of–trade.[27] Finally, we see that the range over which trade protection is welfare–improving is large. For all four countries, import tariffs up to 50% are found to increase real consumption relative to free trade.

Up to this point, we have only focused on welfare changes in the country imposing the import tariff. We now turn to the effects on the rest of the world. We restrict ourselves to a counterfactual scenario in which the United States unilaterally imposes an import tariff of 40% on all its trading partners, $t'_{iUS} = 0.4$ for all $i \neq$ United States. This is close to the tariff level observed in the United States in the late 19th and early 20th century; see e.g. Irwin (1998). The welfare changes caused by the 40% tariff in each trading partner of the United States are reported in Column 1 of Table 4.2. The striking feature of these numbers is that in spite of the fact that the United States is the largest country in the

[27] In general, one would expect gains from trade protection to have an inverted-U shape as a function of country size, since gains from applying an optimal tariff must go to zero as countries become either infinitesimally small or infinitely large. Figure 4.1 suggests that countries in our dataset are sufficiently large that they are on the declining segment of this curve.

world (in terms of GDP) and that 40% is a large tariff by historical standards, the impact on the rest of the world is small. On average, real consumption goes down by 0.2%. The only two exceptions are Canada and Mexico, which incur losses of 1.2% and 1.1%, respectively.

The previous counterfactual exercise may mask the true cost of trade protection if other countries retaliate by increasing their own import tariffs. A very crude way to assess the quantitative importance of such a trade war is to consider a counterfactual scenario in which all countries, rather than one, impose a 40% import tariff on all their trading partners. The associated welfare changes are reported in Column 5 of Table 4.2. On average, countries experience losses of 2.3%. The biggest loser is Ireland (-4.4%) while the country that loses the least is the United States (-0.8%). In this particular counterfactual scenario, no country wins the trade war, though the largest country in the world is the one that loses the least.

While the previous numbers are illustrative, a more satisfactory way to study the consequences of trade wars is to solve for the Nash equilibrium of a non-cooperative tariff game. As demonstrated in Ossa (2011b), one can still do so using the exact hat algebra. The only difference between this analysis and the one presented in this section is that proportional changes in trade costs, $\hat{\phi}_{ij}$, are no longer exogenously given, but correspond to the best-response of each country to the vector of import tariffs chosen by its trading partners. Using a multi-sector gravity model with monopolistic competition and estimates of trade elasticities from Broda and Weinstein (2006), Ossa (2011b) finds Nash tariffs around 60% around the world. Ossa finds that the associated welfare loss associated with going from the current, observed equilibrium to the counterfactual Nash equilibrium is equal to 3.5% on average.

4.2. Alternative Gravity Models Revisited

In the previous subsection we have focused on the predictions of a simple Armington model. We now go back to the main gravity models considered in Sections 3.2, 3.3, and 3.4 to see how multiple sectors, intermediate goods, and monopolistic competition affect these predictions. For expositional purposes, we restrict ourselves to counterfactual scenarios in which tariffs are common across sectors. We discuss the specific issues associated with heterogeneity in tariffs in the next subsection.

We start by allowing for multiple sectors and intermediate goods, in the exact same way as in Sections 3.3 and 3.4, while retaining the assumption of perfect competition, $\delta_s = 0$ for all s. As in Section 4.1, we assume that all tariffs are zero in the initial equilibrium. Columns 2 and 4 in Table 4.2 report the welfare effects of a unilateral 40% tariff imposed by the United States on all its trading partners in all sectors. Column 2 corresponds to the predictions of the multi-sector model without intermediate goods, $\alpha_{j,s} = 0$, whereas Column 4 corresponds to the predictions with intermediate goods,

Table 4.2 Welfare Effect of Tariffs Under Perfect Competition

	Unilateral U.S. 40% Tariff				Uniform Worldwide 40% Tariff		
	One Sector	Multiple Sectors			One Sector	Multiple Sectors	
		Without Intermediates	Without Intermediates, With Dispersion	With Intermediates		Without Intermediates	With Intermediates
Country	1	2	3	4	5	6	7
AUS	−0.10%	−0.13%	−0.11%	−0.28%	−1.26%	−1.38%	−2.85%
AUT	−0.09%	−0.06%	−0.05%	−0.13%	−2.97%	−2.04%	−4.31%
BEL	−0.16%	−0.12%	−0.09%	−0.26%	−3.96%	−2.63%	−6.34%
BRA	−0.10%	−0.08%	−0.07%	−0.16%	−0.81%	−0.43%	−0.86%
CAN	−1.20%	−1.16%	−0.96%	−2.28%	−2.06%	−2.14%	−4.16%
CHN	−0.22%	−0.14%	−0.12%	−0.46%	−1.56%	−0.43%	−2.28%
CZE	−0.05%	−0.03%	−0.02%	−0.08%	−3.16%	−1.34%	−4.55%
DEU	−0.16%	−0.10%	−0.08%	−0.20%	−2.48%	−0.74%	−1.83%
DNK	−0.20%	−0.09%	−0.07%	−0.26%	−3.04%	−1.32%	−3.63%
ESP	−0.06%	−0.04%	−0.03%	−0.07%	−1.46%	−0.71%	−1.88%
FIN	−0.09%	−0.04%	−0.03%	−0.10%	−2.36%	−0.94%	−2.82%
FRA	−0.09%	−0.06%	−0.05%	−0.13%	−1.51%	−0.60%	−1.43%
GBR	−0.16%	−0.15%	−0.12%	−0.31%	−1.66%	−1.50%	−3.17%
GRC	−0.08%	−0.02%	−0.01%	−0.06%	−1.84%	−1.65%	−3.03%
HUN	−0.13%	−0.06%	−0.05%	−0.17%	−4.19%	−2.54%	−7.03%
IDN	−0.09%	−0.06%	−0.05%	−0.14%	−1.56%	−0.82%	−2.33%
IND	−0.16%	−0.13%	−0.11%	−0.25%	−1.17%	−0.71%	−1.65%
IRL	−0.91%	−0.56%	−0.47%	−1.58%	−4.41%	−2.17%	−6.65%
ITA	−0.07%	−0.03%	−0.03%	−0.07%	−1.47%	−0.46%	−1.31%
JPN	−0.10%	−0.05%	−0.05%	−0.11%	−0.92%	0.24%	0.04%
KOR	−0.21%	−0.14%	−0.12%	−0.34%	−2.31%	0.22%	−1.06%
MEX	−1.08%	−0.87%	−0.73%	−1.67%	−1.74%	−1.11%	−2.35%
NLD	−0.22%	−0.16%	−0.13%	−0.34%	−3.33%	−1.70%	−4.04%
POL	−0.04%	−0.03%	−0.03%	−0.08%	−2.21%	−1.28%	−3.18%
PRT	−0.06%	−0.05%	−0.04%	−0.09%	−2.12%	−1.85%	−3.67%
ROM	−0.03%	0.00%	0.01%	0.01%	−2.08%	−2.15%	−4.56%
RUS	−0.03%	−0.05%	−0.04%	−0.12%	−1.30%	−2.84%	−4.94%
SVK	−0.05%	−0.01%	−0.01%	−0.04%	−3.97%	−2.51%	−6.22%
SVN	−0.05%	−0.04%	−0.03%	−0.10%	−3.50%	−2.44%	−5.68%
SWE	−0.15%	−0.08%	−0.07%	−0.19%	−2.71%	−1.23%	−3.18%
TUR	−0.03%	−0.01%	−0.01%	−0.02%	−1.34%	−0.45%	−1.24%
TWN	−0.45%	−0.34%	−0.29%	−0.76%	−3.40%	−1.85%	−5.13%
USA	0.21%	0.41%	0.26%	0.63%	−0.80%	−0.44%	−1.00%
RoW	−0.49%	−0.43%	−0.37%	−0.97%	−2.69%	−2.45%	−5.74%
Average	−0.20%	−0.14%	−0.12%	−0.33%	−2.28%	−1.36%	−3.35%

Note: counterfactual results are computed using the exact hat algebra. All data is from WIOD and trade elasticities are from Caliendo and Parro (2010). See the online Appendix for details.

$\alpha_{j,s} > 0.$[28] Columns 6 and 7 show the analogous results when the 40% tariff is imposed uniformly by all countries around the world. For both counterfactual scenarios, welfare changes are computed using the exact hat algebra as we did in the case of the simple Armington model.

Moving from a one-sector to a multi-sector model has ambiguous effects on the welfare losses from a tariff; for many countries we actually see smaller losses. For example, the welfare losses in China from the 40% worldwide tariff fall from 1.6% in the one-sector model (Column 5) to 0.4% in the multi-sector model (Column 6). On average, welfare losses go from 2.3% (Column 5) to 1.4% (Column 6). Although we know from the results of Section 3.3 that a prohibitive tariff should lead to higher welfare losses when there are multiple-sectors, we see that even for tariffs as high as 40% worldwide, this is not the case. Thus one should be careful when extrapolating from the autarky exercises of Section 3 to richer comparative static exercises. Models that point towards larger gains from trade liberalization for one counterfactual scenario may very well lead to smaller gains from trade liberalization for another.

In contrast, allowing for intermediate goods significantly amplifies the losses generated by tariffs for all countries, echoing the results of Section 3.4. Canada now experiences a welfare loss of 2.3% (Column 4) rather than 1.2% (Column 2) as a consequence of the 40% tariff imposed by the United States, while average losses are now 0.33% (Column 4) rather than 0.14% (Column 2). A worldwide tariff of 40% now leads to losses in Belgium of 6.3% (Column 7) rather than 2.6% (Column 6). On average, allowing for intermediate goods leads to welfare losses of 3.4% (Column 7) rather than 1.4% (Column 6).

We next study how market structure affects the welfare effects of a worldwide tariff of 40%. As explained in Section 3, moving from perfect to monopolistic competition introduces scale effects, which complicates the computation of counterfactual equilibria with tariffs. To ease the computational burden, we use a coarser version of our dataset in all the exercises that follow. Specifically, we aggregate the set of countries in the WIOD into 10 regions and 16 sectors: 15 agriculture and manufacturing sectors plus 1 service sector; see the online Appendix for details. Using this coarser dataset, we compare the predictions of gravity models under the assumption of: (*i*) perfect competition; (*ii*) monopolistic competition without firm-level heterogeneity, as in Krugman (1980); and (*iii*) monopolistic competition with firm-level heterogeneity, as in Melitz (2003).[29] In the case of models with monopolistic competition with firm-level heterogeneity, counterfactual predictions depend on whether fixed exporting costs are paid in the importing country or exporting country and whether import tariffs are imposed before or after firm-level markups. In what follows we assume that fixed exporting costs are paid in the

---

[28] In the latter case, shares of intermediate goods are computed as $\alpha^*_{j,ks} = \left(\sum_k \sum_i X_{ij,ks}/R_{j,s} \right) \times \left(E_{j,k}/E_j \right).$

[29] We maintain the assumption that the service sector is perfectly competitive. Formally, in cases (*ii*) and (*iii*) we set $\delta_s = 1$ for all $s \neq 16$ and $\delta_{16} = 0$. The only difference is that in case (*ii*) we set $\eta_s = 0$ for all s whereas in case (*iii*) we set $\eta_s = 0.65$ for all s.

Table 4.3 Welfare Effect of a 40% Worldwide Tariff

	Without Intermediates			With Intermediates		
	Perfect Competition	Monopolistic Competition		Perfect Competition	Monopolistic Competition	
		Krugman	Melitz		Krugman	Melitz
Region	1	2	3	4	5	6
Pacific Ocean	−0.1%	−1.2%	−1.2%	−0.6%	−4.9%	−4.1%
Western Europe	−0.7%	−2.6%	−2.3%	−1.6%	−7.6%	−10.3%
Eastern Europe	−2.2%	−0.8%	−0.3%	−4.4%	−3.6%	−4.5%
Latin America	−0.7%	−1.4%	−1.2%	−1.5%	−3.1%	−3.8%
North America	−0.6%	−0.4%	−0.4%	−1.2%	−1.1%	−1.3%
China	−0.7%	−1.3%	−1.2%	−2.5%	−13.4%	−20.3%
Southern Europe	−0.7%	−1.6%	−1.5%	−1.7%	−4.8%	−6.2%
Northern Europe	−1.6%	−2.0%	−2.0%	−3.2%	−6.0%	−6.5%
Indian Ocean	−0.8%	−0.9%	−0.8%	−1.9%	−3.1%	−5.5%
RoW	−3.1%	−1.4%	−1.0%	−6.4%	−5.0%	−8.0%
Average	−1.1%	−1.4%	−1.2%	−2.5%	−5.3%	−7.0%

Note: counterfactual results are computed using the exact hat algebra. All data is from WIOD and trade elasticities are from Caliendo and Parro (2010). See the online Appendix for details.

exporting country, $c_{ij}^x = Y_i$, and that tariffs are imposed before markups; see the online Appendix for details.[30]

Columns 1–3 of Table 4.3 present results for the model without intermediates, as in Section 3.3, while Columns 4–6 present results for the model with intermediates, as in Section 3.4. Under perfect competition without intermediate goods (Column 1 in Table 4.3), the welfare losses associated with a 40% worldwide tariff are lower than before (Column 6 in Table 4.2). This reflects the fact that, by construction, tariffs are now forced to be zero within regions. Column 2 of Table 4.3 shows the analogous results under monopolistic competition without firm-level heterogeneity. As in Section 3.3, the differences between perfect and monopolistic competition arise because of sector-level scale effects triggered by trade protection. Welfare losses tend to be larger under monopolistic competition than perfect competition, although there are some exceptions, including North America for which losses go from 0.6% to 0.4%. Finally, Column 3 of Table 4.3 shows the results under monopolistic competition with firm-level heterogeneity.

---

[30] When tariffs are imposed before markups, they act as "cost-shifters." Under this assumption, the elasticity of bilateral trade flows with respect to tariffs and iceberg trade costs coincide. When tariffs are imposed after markups, they act as "demand-shifters." Under this assumption, the elasticity with respect to tariffs is equal to $\varepsilon + \eta$ rather than ε; see the online Appendix and Felbermayr et al. (2013). Since there is little empirical evidence to help us discriminate between these two cases, we prefer working under the assumption that there is only one elasticity.

We see that all regions have slightly lower welfare losses than in the absence of firm-level heterogeneity. One potential explanation is that the introduction of tariffs leads to an increase in the ratio of expenditures—which include tariff revenues—to factor prices. This tends to increase the set of varieties available to consumers when a tariff is imposed in models with firm-level heterogeneity through selection effects. Since consumers love variety, this tends to reduce the welfare losses associated with a tariff in such models.

How are the previous results affected by the introduction of intermediate goods? We again find that welfare losses from tariffs tend to be larger in models with monopolistic competition. Moving from Column 4 to Column 5 in Table 4.3, the losses from the tariff for Western Europe and Latin America increase from 1.6% to 7.6% and from 1.5% to 3.1%, respectively. Welfare losses tend to be even larger under firm-level heterogeneity (Column 6 in Table 4.3). The average welfare losses increase from 5.3% to 7.0%. Like in Section 3.4, this reflects stronger scale effects under models of monopolistic competition with firm-level heterogeneity.

In recent work Balistreri et al. (2011) have compared the predictions of a multi-sector Armington model with intermediate goods to those of a multi-sector Melitz (2003) model with intermediate goods. To compare the two models, they first estimate the structural parameters of the Melitz (2003) model using non-linear least squares and investigate the welfare consequences of a 50% reduction in observed tariffs. They then ask what the welfare consequences of the same tariff change would have been in an Armington model calibrated using the same elasticity of substitution between goods (but different trade elasticities) and the same variable trade costs. They find gains from 50% reduction in tariffs that are four times larger according to the Melitz (2003) model and conclude that it is important to add firm-level heterogeneity to standard quantitative trade models.

The similarity between the quantitative results of Balistreri et al. (2011) and those presented in Table 4.3 notwithstanding, there are some important methodological differences. In order to demonstrate the importance of firm-level heterogeneity, Balistreri et al. (2011) compare Armington to Melitz (2003). Here we compare Krugman (1980) to Melitz (2003). To us the latter comparison is preferable to the former since comparing Armington and Melitz (2003) makes it impossible to separate the role of monopolistic competition from the role of firm-level heterogeneity. The results of Table 4.3 illustrate the importance of this distinction both qualitatively and quantitatively. When comparing Columns 1 and 3, one would conclude that gains from trade liberalization are larger in models with firm-level heterogeneity. Yet comparing Columns 2 and 3, we see that the average welfare loss would be even higher in the absence of firm-level heterogeneity. Similarly, when comparing Columns 4 and 6, one would conclude that average welfare losses are almost three times as large. Yet the relevant comparison, Column 5 to Column 6, suggests less dramatic differences, with average welfare losses going from 5.3% to 7.0%.

The more substantial methodological difference comes from how we calibrate the models whose predictions we want to compare. In Balistreri et al. (2011), different models do not match the same set of moments, including the trade elasticity. In this chapter, they do. Our view is that whether or not one wants to "recalibrate" models depends on why one is interested in comparing the predictions of different models in the first place.

The thought experiment that motivates us can be sketched as follows. Consider two trade economists trying to predict the welfare effects of the same tariff change. Both economists have access to the same trade data in 2008, but the first-one has been trained in the 1980s and thinks that Krugman (1980) is a useful approximation of the world economy, whereas the second has been trained in the 2000s and thinks that Melitz (2003) is. We want to know whether *conditional on the same trade data*, the forecasts of the first and second economists would differ. When comparing one model to another, we therefore recalibrate all structural parameters so that each models fits the same cross-section of bilateral trade flows and trade elasticity.

The thought experiment behind the results of Balistreri et al. (2011) is implicitly different. The idea is to start with one economist, trained in the 2000s, ask for his/her forecast of the effects of trade policy in 2008 and then ask whether he/she would have made a different forecast *in a counterfactual world* without firm-level heterogeneity. This is why Balistreri et al. (2011) first structurally estimate a Melitz (2003) model and then "turn off" heterogeneity across firms (among other things).

So which of these two thought experiments is more useful? If the question is how the Melitz (2003) model has changed the evaluation of trade policy, we think that the first thought experiment is the appropriate one and that comparing Column 2 to Column 3 or Column 5 to Column 6 in Table 4.3 is the right way to go. In contrast, if one is interested in decomposing the results of Columns 3 or 6 so that one can quantify the role of heterogeneity for welfare within the Melitz (2003) model, then the second thought experiment is more useful.

4.3. Heterogeneous Tariffs

In practice, tariffs are not uniform across sectors within the same country. This raises a number of questions: Does heterogeneity in tariffs raise the cost of trade protection in the country imposing the tariffs? If so, is this also true in the countries facing the tariffs? In theory, what is the "right" way to measure the restrictiveness of trade policy when trade policy is a multi-dimensional object?

Let us start by focusing on the first two questions. We use the simplest model in which these questions can be addressed: a multi-sector gravity model without intermediate goods and with perfect competition. Thus the assumptions are the same as in Section 3.3 with $\delta_s = 0$ for all s. We again consider the counterfactual scenario in which only one country, the United States, imposes the same tariffs, $t'_{iUS,s} = t_s$, on all its trading partners. But we now allow tariffs to vary across sectors s. Namely, we assume that $t_s = t + \Delta_s$, where $\Delta_s \in \{-a, a\}$ is randomly drawn across sectors. Draws of a and $-a$ have equal probabilities so that the expected value of the tariff is t in each sector. In the simulations below we draw the vector $\Delta \equiv (\Delta_1, \Delta_2, \ldots, \Delta_S)$ one thousand times and report the average results for $\hat{C}_j$ across all these draws.

In Columns 2 and 3 of Table 4.2 we report the welfare change associated with a counterfactual scenario in which $t = 0.4$ and $a = 0$ and $a = 0.2$, respectively. Thus, the expected tariff is 40% in both cases, but there is dispersion in the U.S. tariff across sectors in Column 3 and no dispersion in Column 2. Specifically, in Column 3, some sectors face a 20% import tariff, whereas others face a 60% tariff. Comparing Columns 2 and 3 we see that introducing dispersion leads to a decline in the welfare gain from imposing tariffs in the United States from 0.4% to 0.3%. Although there is no systematic relationship between tariff dispersion and welfare, as discussed in Anderson and Neary (2005), these two numbers resonate well with a simple partial equilibrium intuition. If the welfare distortions associated with a tariff are given by the "triangle" below the import demand curve, then holding the average import tariff fixed, an increase in dispersion should tend to lower welfare, which is what happens in this example. By comparing Columns 2 and 3 in Table 4.2, we also see that other countries are actually better off when the there is dispersion in the U.S. tariff. For example, Canada's welfare loss from the U.S. tariff falls from 1.2% to 1%, while Mexico's losses fall from 0.9% to 0.7%. Intuitively, expenditure functions are concave in prices. So if dispersion in U.S. tariffs also increases dispersion

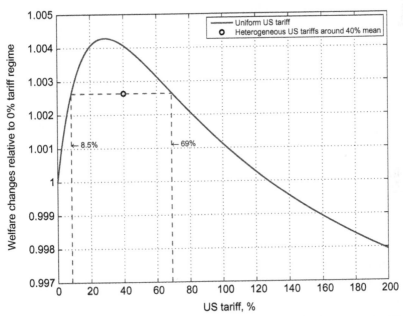

Figure 4.2 Welfare Changes in the United States Associated with a Unilateral U.S. (Tariff with and without dispersion across sectors. $\Delta = 0.4$ in the case with dispersion. Sector-level trade elasticities are from Caliendo and Parro (2010). Data are from WIOD in 2008.)

in the price of U.S. goods abroad, this should tend to reduce expenditure and, in turn, increase welfare abroad.

To conclude, let us go back to the issue of how to measure the restrictiveness of trade policy when trade policy is a multi-dimensional object. Anderson and Neary (2005) propose the following two-step approach. First, ask: What is the welfare loss associated with a vector of heterogeneous tariffs in the country imposing those tariffs? Second, compute the uniform tariff across sectors that would lead to the same welfare loss. This number is what Anderson and Neary (2005) refer to as the Trade Restrictiveness Index (TRI). One way to compute this index is to estimate import demand elasticities and use linear approximations; see e.g. Feenstra (1995) and Kee et al. (2008). An alternative is to use the full structure of the model. We now do so again for the case above with $t = 0.4$ and $a = 0.2$. From Table 4.2 Column 3, we know that the welfare change in the United States is 0.26%. The Trade Restrictiveness Index can then be read off Figure 4.2, which is the counterpart of Figure 4.1 in the multi-sector case. In this particular example, there are two values of the TRI: 8.5% and 69%. The non-uniqueness of the TRI reflects the importance of general equilibrium effects in gravity models.

5. NUMBERS WE CAN BELIEVE IN?

5.1. Sensitivity to Auxiliary Assumptions

In Sections 3 and 4 we have studied how different assumptions about technology and market structure may affect the welfare consequences of trade liberalization. This exercise already gives us a sense of the sensitivity of the counterfactual predictions of gravity models to a set of key economic assumptions. Here we go one step further by exploring how apparently innocuous auxiliary assumptions may also have large implications for counterfactual analysis.

Nature of Trade Imbalances. All models reviewed in this chapter are static models that aim to capture the long-run consequences of trade liberalization. Given their static nature, all these models predict that trade should be balanced country-by-country. In practice, it is not. Volumes of intertemporal trade are substantial: some countries, like the United States, run large current-account deficits, whereas others, like China, run large current-account surpluses. To deal with trade imbalances in the context of a static model, the standard approach consists in modeling trade deficits and surpluses as lump-sum transfers between countries; see e.g. Dekle et al. (2008). Short of a dynamic theory of trade imbalances, in which today's trade deficits are paid back by future trade surpluses, the researcher interested in the effects of a change in trade policy has to assume that these lump-sum transfers remain "unchanged" between the initial and the counterfactual equilibrium.

An obvious question when adopting the previous approach is: "unchanged" compared to what? When thinking about the U.S. deficit, for instance, should one hold its value fixed relative to U.S. GDP or World GDP to mention only two of the most natural alternatives? To get a sense of the importance of these considerations, let us go back to the Armington model with import tariffs considered in Section 4.1. In the presence of trade imbalances across countries, the equilibrium condition (38) generalizes to

$$Y_i = \sum_{j=1}^{n} \frac{1}{1 + t_{ij}} \frac{(Y_i \phi_{ij})^{-\varepsilon} \chi_{ij}}{\sum_{l=1}^{n} (Y_i \phi_{lj})^{-\varepsilon} \chi_{lj}} \frac{Y_j + D_j}{1 - \pi_j}, \tag{42}$$

where $D_j \equiv E_j - (Y_j + T_j)$ denotes the trade deficit in country j. The two assumptions mentioned above about the nature of trade imbalances correspond to $D_j = \varkappa_j Y_j$ and $D_j = \varkappa_j \sum_{i=1}^{n} Y_i$, respectively, where $\varkappa_j$ is treated as an exogenous structural parameter that determines the magnitude of lump–sum transfers across countries.

Starting from equation (42) and some assumption about how trade deficits relate to factor incomes, either $D_j = \varkappa_j Y_j$ or $D_j = \varkappa_j \sum_{i=1}^{n} Y_i$, one can conduct counterfactual analysis using the exact hat algebra, as we did in Section 4.1. In Figure 4.3, we plot the welfare changes associated with 40% import tariffs imposed around the world under the assumption that $D_j = \varkappa_j Y_j$ (x-axis) and $D_j = \varkappa_j \sum_{i=1}^{n} Y_i$ (y-axis). The correlation between the two measures is equal to 0.86. Not surprisingly, the biggest discrepancies

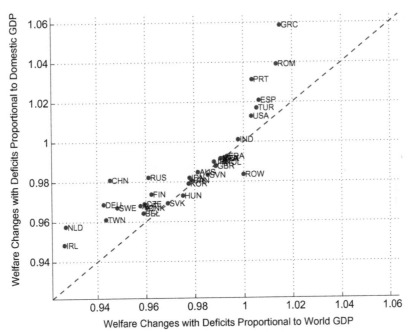

Figure 4.3 Welfare Changes Associated with a 40% Tariff Around the World When Deficits are Proportional to World GDP (x-axis) and Domestic GDP (y-axis). (Trade elasticity $\varepsilon = 5$. Data are from WIOD in 2008).

between the two numbers come from countries running large trade deficits, like Greece or Romania, or large trade surpluses, like Ireland and the Netherlands.[31]

It is worth pointing out, however, that both sets of results differ from the numbers presented in Section 4.1 in which we had removed trade imbalances before analyzing the consequences of a worldwide tariff. The correlation between either one of the two measures presented here and the results of Section 4.1 is 0.57. This discrepancy is caused by larger terms-of-trade improvements for countries that maintain large trade deficits. Intuitively, as tariffs increase, consumers have incentives to substitute away from foreign goods towards domestic goods. Thus, in order to maintain trade deficits "unchanged" in the counterfactual equilibrium, domestic prices must increase relative to the price of foreign goods.

Nature of Physical Capital. In earlier sections we have implicitly treated physical capital as a primary factor of production whose endowment is fixed and unaffected by trade. Alternatively, one could think of physical capital as capital goods that, like other intermediate goods, are traded internationally; see e.g. Eaton and Kortum (2001). To get a sense of how important this assumption on the nature of physical capital could be, we come back to the model of Section 3.4 with multiple sectors, tradable intermediate goods, and perfect competition. Compared to the analysis of Section 3.4, the only difference is that we adjust value-added shares in the data so that the (presumed) one third share of capital in value added is distributed proportionally among intermediate goods from all industries. Formally, we adjust shares by setting $\alpha'_{i,ks} = \alpha_{i,ks}\left(1 + \frac{1}{3}\frac{1-\alpha_{i,s}}{\alpha_{i,s}}\right)$. By construction, the new value added share is therefore two thirds of the one reported in the data: $1 - \alpha'_{i,s} = \frac{2}{3}\left(1 - \alpha_{i,s}\right)$. When physical capital is treated as another tradable intermediate good, the amplification effect from the input-output loop discussed in Section 3.4 is now stronger, and the gains are larger. Using again WIOD data from 2008, we find that average gains from trade are equal to 34.6% compared to 26.9% when physical capital is assumed to be immobile across countries. For example, gains from trade in Canada are now 36.9% rather than 30.2%, and in the United States they are 11.3% rather than 8.3%.

5.2. Goodness of Fit

One way to try to build confidence in the predictions of gravity models is to assess whether they can match cross-sectional or time-series evidence on bilateral trade flows.

Cross-Sectional Evidence. A standard practice in the literature consists in assuming first that iceberg trade costs τ are deterministic functions of various observables such

---

[31] While this example illustrates the potential sensitivity of quantitative predictions to ad-hoc assumptions about the nature of trade imbalances, it should be clear that the importance of these considerations depends, in general, on the variable of interest, the underlying model, and the nature of the counterfactual exercise. For instance, when the counterfactual exercise consists in moving to autarky under perfect competition, changes in real factor income are unaffected by the size and nature of transfers across countries.

as physical distance between country i and country j, whether country i and j share a common border or language, or whether they are part of a regional trade agreement or a monetary union. Once trade cost functions—together with other structural parameters of the model—have been estimated or calibrated, one can assess the goodness of fit of the gravity model by comparing trade flows predicted by the model to those that are observed in the data; see e.g. Di Giovanni and Levchenko (2009), Waugh (2010), and Fieler (2011).

The empirical fit of gravity models tends to be very good; see Anderson (2011). It is not clear, however, whether this should make us very confident in the counterfactual predictions of these models. If iceberg trade costs τ are used as free parameters, then gravity models can replicate any cross-section of bilateral trade flows, $\mathbf{X}$. Thus, one way to interpret the good fit of the gravity models under particular restrictions on the structure of iceberg trade costs is that these restricted trade costs are good proxies of the "wedges" that are necessary for the model to match the data.

An alternative strategy, in the spirit of the test of Heckscher-Ohlin-Theorem in Trefler (1993), is to infer from the trade data the iceberg trade costs such that gravity models fit perfectly and then check whether the inferred iceberg trade costs match observable measures of trade costs such as tariffs and freight costs or price gaps (which should reflect trade costs under perfect competition). An issue with this approach is that one cannot separately identify iceberg trade costs from country-specific biases in preferences in the model. If "wedges" only match observed measures of trade costs very imperfectly, should we conclude that there is a problem with the model or that biases in preferences are important?

In recent work, Anderson and Yotov (2012) propose to test gravity models by focusing on the restrictions that it imposes on the relationship between exporter- and importer-fixed effects in equation (13), whatever the structure of iceberg trade costs may be. Another possible strategy to assess the goodness of fit of quantitative trade models consists in using other, i.e., non-trade, data sources. For instance, since gravity models offer a mapping between trade data and consumer price indices, one could compare the prices predicted by the model to those observed in the data. Waugh (2010) and Fitzgerald (2012) offer two examples of papers exploring the implications of gravity models for prices.

Time-Series Evidence. Perhaps the most direct way to test the predictions of a gravity model is to calibrate the model in a baseline year t, consider a change in trade costs between the baseline year t and some other year t', and report the "distance" between the predictions of the model and the data at date t'.

A natural candidate for large changes in trade costs are regional trade agreements like the North American Free Trade Agreement (NAFTA). Caliendo and Parro (2010) use a multi-sector version of Eaton and Kortum (2002) with intermediate goods calibrated to match trade data from 1993 to study the effects of NAFTA. This model is a special case of the models considered in Section 3.4 in that it does not feature any scale effects: $\delta_s = 0$ for all s. After feeding tariff changes caused by NAFTA between 1993 and 2005, they find that the simulated changes can account for 93% of the observed change in Mexico's total trade over GDP, 58% for Canada, and 55% for the United States.

The relatively good fit of their model contrasts with the fairly poor performance of earlier CGE models reviewed in Kehoe (2005). He evaluates the performances of three of the most prominent multi-sectoral applied general equilibrium models used to predict the impact of NAFTA: the Brown-Deardorff-Stern model of all three North American economies (Brown et al., 1992), the Cox-Harris model of Canada (Cox and Harris, 1992), and the Sobarzo model of Mexico (Sobarzo, 1992). He finds that each of these models drastically underestimated the impact of NAFTA on trade volumes. For instance, the Brown-Deardorff-Stern model predicts changes in exports relative to GDP between 1988 and 1999 equal to 50.8% for Mexico, 4.3% for Canada, and 2.9% for the United States. In the data, these changes are equal 140.6%, 52.9%, and 19.1%, respectively.

It is not entirely clear, however, what accounts for the difference in the performance between more recent and older CGE models. Caliendo and Parro (2010) emphasize the importance of input-output linkages for their results, but such linkages are already present in older CGE models. One economically meaningful difference is that the previous CGE models feature imperfect competition and scale effects, whereas Caliendo and Parro (2010) does not. But there are many other potential sources of discrepancies, from the calibration of the trade elasticities (more on that below) to the choice of the baseline year. Indeed, although the predictions of the models reviewed in Kehoe (2005) are compared with changes in the data over the period 1988-1999, the Brown-Deardorff model was calibrated to a 1976 input-output matrix for Canada, a 1980 input-output matrix for Mexico, and a 1977 input-output matrix for the United States. The good fit of gravity models in the time-series is also called into question by the results of Lai and Trefler (2002) who find that changes in tariffs between 1972 and 1992 fed into a simple model à la Krugman (1980) can explain little of the variation in bilateral trade flows over this time period.

A poor fit of a quantitative trade model may always reflect the fact that the trade shock under study is small compared to other unobserved shocks—e.g. technology, factor endowments—that may have been occurring over the same time period. This generates a tension. One would want to focus on shorter time periods around a particular episode of trade liberalization to exclude other shocks, but quantitative trade models are static models that are better equipped to capture the long-run consequences of trade liberalization than short-term dynamics. In the case of NAFTA, for instance, would quantitative trade models perform better when the final year is 1995, 2000, or 2005?

Donaldson (2008) offers an innovative way to test the predictions of gravity models. He focuses on one of history's great transportation projects: the network of railroads built in colonial India from 1870 to 1930. He first estimates the impact of the railroad on trade costs using information about price gaps across Indian districts. He then feeds the observed changes in trade costs into a multi-sector version of Eaton and Kortum (2002)—a special case of the models considered in Section 3.3 without scale effects: $\delta_s = 0$ for all s—to predict the changes in real income across Indian districts. The test of the model comes from comparing changes in real income predicted by the model to the reduced-form estimates of changes in real income caused by the railroad. He finds that 86% of the total impact of the railroads on real income in an average district can be explained by the model.

5.3. Calibrating Elasticities

The key parameters for counterfactual analysis using gravity models, like other CGE models, are elasticities. We conclude this section by discussing some of the issues arising when calibrating elasticities.

Trade Elasticities. As can already be seen from the counterfactual analysis carried in the context of the Armington model in Section 2, the single most important structural parameter in gravity models is the trade elasticity. Conditional on observed trade shares, it determines both the response of bilateral trade flows and real consumption. In more general environments such as those considered in Section 3, it remains one of the key statistics required to estimate the gains from international trade; see equations (23), (27), and (32). So, how large are trade elasticities?

This question is an old one. It is as important for recent gravity models reviewed in this chapter as for earlier CGE models. The broad consensus in the CGE literature is, in the words of Dawkins et al. (2001), that "the quantity and quality of literature-based elasticity parameters for use in calibrated models is another Achilles' heel of calibration." As John Whalley notes "It is quite extraordinary how little we know about numerical values of elasticities [...] In the international trade area researchers commonly use import price elasticities in the neighborhood of unity, even for small economies, even though elasticity estimates as high as nine appear in the literature." The same pessimism can be found in the review of trade elasticities by McDaniel and Balistreri (2003): "The estimates from the literature provide a wide range of point estimates, and little guidance on correct estimates to apply to a given commodity in a given model for a given regional aggregation. Most of the controversy surrounding the [trade] elasticities reduces to a general structural inconsistency between the econometric models used to measure the response and the simulation models used to evaluate policy."

Part of the success of new quantitative work in international trade lies in the tight connection between the structural estimation of the trade elasticity and the underlying economic model. In their seminal work, Eaton and Kortum (2002) offer multiple ways to estimate structurally the trade elasticity using a gravity equation akin to equation (16). Their estimates range from $\varepsilon = 3.60$ to $\varepsilon = 12.86$ with a preferred value of $\varepsilon = 8.28$ when using price gaps as a measure of trade costs. While the range is wide, it remains in the range of elasticities used in earlier CGE models; see Hertel (1997). In recent work, Simonovska (2011) refines Eaton and Kortum's (2002) preferred estimation strategy to take into account the fact that price gaps are only lower-bounds on trade costs. Simonovska and Waugh (2011) propose a simulated method of moments to correct for the fact that trade elasticities using price gaps tend to overestimate the sensitivity of trade flows to trade costs. Their preferred estimate of ε is 4.12.

The merits of a tight connection between theory and data notwithstanding, the state of affairs remains far from ideal. An issue with simulation using earlier CGE models, such as those used in the evaluation of NAFTA, is that they require a very large number of elasticities. Many recent papers, following Eaton and Kortum (2002), side-step this issue by assuming that all goods enter utility functions through a unique CES aggregator. But empirically, there is ample evidence of significant variation in the trade elasticity across sectors; see e.g. Feenstra (1994), Broda and Weinstein (2006), and Hummels and Hillberry (2012). If so, why should we be more confident in the counterfactual predictions of simpler gravity models that abstract from this heterogeneity? Given the heterogeneity in the trade elasticity across sectors, is the trade elasticity estimated from an aggregate gravity equation like (16) the "right" trade elasticity to calibrate a one-sector model?[32]

A natural way to address the previous concerns is to write down multiple-sector models, such as those considered in Section 3.3, and incorporate formally the heterogeneity in trade elasticities across sectors. But this raises new issues. As the number of elasticities that needs to be estimated increases, the precision with which each of those elasticities is estimated tends to decrease. Accordingly, results become much more sensitive to the presence of outliers. To take a concrete example, the sector-level elasticities from Caliendo and Parro (2010) used in Section 3.3 are around 8 on average. But for some sectors, like automobiles, trade elasticities are not statistically different from zero. An elasticity of zero would imply infinite gains from trade.[33]

Upper-Level Elasticities (I): Substitution Across Sectors. Going from a one-sector to a multi-sector model raises another question: How large is the elasticity of substitution between sectors? All papers referenced in Section 3.3 follow what Dawkins et al. (2001) refer to as the "idiot's law of elasticities": all elasticities are equal to one until shown to be otherwise. How important is the assumption that upper-level utility functions are Cobb-Douglas for the predictions of multi-sector quantitative trade models?

---

[32] Imbs and Mejean (2011) argue that such aggregate trade elasticities suffer from heterogeneity bias and that one should instead use a properly weighted average of sector-level trade elasticities to calibrate one-sector models. Yet if the true model is indeed a multi-sector model, it is not a priori obvious that there exists a single weighted average—independently of how weights are defined—that can be used to predict both changes in trade flows and welfare.

[33] The existing literature rarely reports confidence intervals. Two notable exceptions are Lai and Trefler (2002) and Shapiro (2012) who use the standard errors of the trade elasticities that they have estimated to compute, and report, the standard errors for the gains from trade liberalization.

To shed light on this question, let us make the same assumptions as in Section 3.3, except for the fact the upper-level utility function is now given by

$$C_j = \left(\sum_{s=1}^{S} \beta_{j,s} C_{j,s}^{(\gamma-1)/\gamma} \right)^{\gamma/(\gamma-1)}, \tag{43}$$

where $\gamma > 0$ denotes the upper-level elasticity of substitution between goods from different sectors; $\beta_{j,s} \geq 0$ are exogenous preference parameters, which we normalize such that $\sum_{s=1}^{S} \beta_{j,s} = 1$ for all j; and $C_{j,s}$ still denotes total consumption of the composite good s in country j. The Cobb-Douglas case studied in Section 3.3 corresponds to $\gamma = 1$.

For simplicity let us focus on the case of perfect competition, $\delta_s = 0$ all s. Following a procedure similar to that in Section 3.1, one can show that if sector-level price indices are given by equation (20), then the welfare impact of a shock generalizes to

$$\hat{C}_j = \left(\sum_{s=1}^{S} e_{j,s} \left(\hat{\lambda}_{jj,s}^{-1} \right)^{(\gamma-1)/\varepsilon_s} \right)^{1/(\gamma-1)}. \tag{44}$$

Gains from trade are thus given by

$$G_j = 1 - \left(\sum_{s=1}^{S} e_{j,s} \left(\lambda_{jj,s} \right)^{(\gamma-1)/\varepsilon_s} \right)^{1/(\gamma-1)}. \tag{45}$$

In Section 3.3, we have pointed out that multi-sector models with Cobb-Douglas preferences predict significantly larger gains than one-sector models. Using equation (45), we can now quantify the importance of the Cobb-Douglas assumption for this prediction.

In Figure 4.4 we plot G_j as a function of γ using equation (45) for several countries—the United States, Canada, France, Germany, and Japan—as well as the average G_j for all countries considered in Table 4.1. We see that the value of the upper-level elasticity γ—for which the existing empirical literature provides little guidance—has large effects on the magnitude of the gains from trade. As we go from the Leontief case, $\gamma = 0$, to the Cobb-Douglas case, $\gamma = 1$, to an upper-level elasticity equal to the average of lower-level elasticities, $\gamma = 8$, average gains from trade decrease from 45% to 15% to 3%.[34] The intuition is simple. If the elasticity of substitution between sectors is high, then the consequences of autarky are mitigated by consumers' ability to substitute consumption away from the most affected sectors, i.e., those with lowest values of $\lambda_{jj,s}^{1/\varepsilon_s}$, towards the least affected sectors, i.e., those with highest values of $\lambda_{jj,s}^{1/\varepsilon_s}$. By the same token, however, the gains from further trade liberalization would tend to be higher with a higher γ, since

---

[34] In the particular case in which all lower-level trade elasticities are equal to the upper-level trade elasticity, $\varepsilon_s = \gamma - 1$ for all s, the discrepancy between the predictions of multi-sector and one-sector models disappears: equation (45) reduces to equation (12).

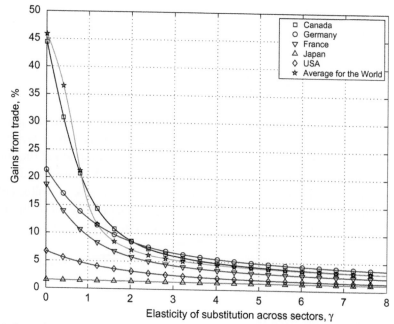

Figure 4.4 Gains from Trade Computed According to Equation (45) for Different Levels of γ. (Sector-level trade elasticities are from Caliendo and Parro (2010). Data are from WIOD in 2008.)

consumers could more easily reallocate their consumption towards goods that experience larger price declines.[35]

Upper-Level Elasticities (II): Domestic versus Foreign. Another, and perhaps deeper issue regarding gravity estimates of the trade elasticity is that they capture the elasticity of substitution between foreign sources of imports. Yet, the elasticity that one needs, for instance, for measuring the gains from trade is the elasticity of substitution between home and import goods. To see this formally, let us go back to the simple Armington model presented in Section 2.1, but let us generalize equation (1) so that

$$C_j = \left[\left(C_{jj} \right)^{(\gamma-1)/\gamma} + \left(C_j^M \right)^{(\gamma-1)/\gamma} \right]^{\gamma/(\gamma-1)},$$

[35] The value of the upper-level elasticity of substitution also has more subtle implications for quantitative trade models with monopolistic competition. Away from Cobb-Douglas preferences, expenditure shares $e_{j,s}$ are no longer constant, which may lead to multiple equilibria. Intuitively, a higher expenditure share in a given sector leads to more entry, which reduces the price index in that sector, thereby leading to a higher expenditure share. Thus, one may obtain different estimates of the gains from trade—or the effect of trade policy—depending on the counterfactual equilibrium one focuses on. Another issue concerns the difference between the predictions of models with firm-level heterogeneity, like Melitz (2003), and those without, like Krugman (1980). In Section 3.3, we have shown that in the Cobb-Douglas case, entry effects lead to a distinction between the predictions of models with perfect and monopolistic competition, but not between models with and without firm-level heterogeneity. This is no longer true in the case of general CES utility functions.

where C_j^M measures total consumption of imported goods,

$$C_j^M = \left(\sum_{i \neq j} \psi_{ij}^{\sigma/(\sigma-1)} C_{ij}^{(\sigma-1)/\sigma} \right)^{\sigma/(\sigma-1)}.$$

The upper-level elasticity $\gamma > 1$ now represents the elasticity of substitution between the domestic good and the composite of the foreign goods, whereas the lower-level elasticity $\sigma > 0$ still represents the elasticity of substitution between foreign goods. The simple Armington model corresponds to the special case, $\gamma = \sigma$. Under this new demand system, bilateral trade flows still satisfy a gravity-like equation:

$$X_{ij} = \left(\frac{P_j^M}{P_j} \right)^{1-\gamma} \left(\frac{P_{ij}}{P_j^M} \right)^{1-\sigma} E_j, \quad \text{for all } i \neq j, \tag{46}$$

where $P_{ij} = \tau_{ij} P_{ii}$ is the price of goods from country i in country j; $P_j^M \equiv (\sum_{i \neq j} \psi_{ij}^{1-\sigma} P_{ij}^{1-\sigma})^{1/(1-\sigma)}$ is the import price index; and $P_j = ((P_{jj})^{1-\gamma} + (P_j^M)^{1-\gamma})^{1/(1-\gamma)}$ is the consumer price index in country j. In this more general environment, one can still rearrange bilateral trade flows as we did in equation (13) and use the cross-sectional variation in trade flows and trade costs to estimate $1 - \sigma$.

Now, like in Section 2.2, consider a small change in trade costs that affects country j. The change in the consumer price index is still given by

$$d \ln P_j = \lambda_{jj} d \ln P_{jj} + (1 - \lambda_{jj}) d \ln P_j^M.$$

But our new demand system now implies

$$d \ln (1 - \lambda_{jj}) - d \ln \lambda_{jj} = (1 - \gamma) \left(d \ln P_j^M - d \ln P_{jj} \right).$$

Following the same strategy as in Section 2.2, one can therefore show that

$$d \ln C_j = d \ln \lambda_{jj} / (1 - \gamma). \tag{47}$$

While gravity estimates can uncover the lower-level elasticity, σ, equation (47) shows that the upper-level elasticity, γ, i.e., the elasticity of substitution between domestic and foreign goods, is the relevant elasticity for welfare analysis.[36]

In standard gravity models, it is only the assumption of symmetric CES utility that allows researchers to go from the commonly estimated elasticity, σ, to the welfare-relevant elasticity, γ. When estimated, does the elasticity of substitution between home and import

---

[36] In more general gravity models, this upper-level elasticity γ would remain a key determinant for welfare analysis, though not the only one.

goods, γ, look similar to the elasticity of substitution between foreign goods, σ? Head and Ries (2001) suggest that the answer is yes. They measure the average of the elasticity of demand for Canadian goods in Canada relative to U.S. goods and the elasticity of demand for U.S. goods in the United States relative to Canadian goods. If all trade was U.S.–Canada trade, their estimate would therefore provide an estimate of γ. They find an average elasticity equal to 7.8, quite in line with previous gravity estimates of σ. Likewise, using the methodology of Feenstra (1994) to estimate both γ and σ, Feenstra et al. (2013) cannot reject the null that γ and σ are equal.

Factor Supply Elasticities. The multi-sector gravity models that we have reviewed assume a perfectly-elastic factor supply to each sector. Thus, except for the case with sector-level differences in factor intensities considered in Section 3.5, the aggregate production possibilities frontier (PPF) is linear. In practice one may expect factors to be imperfect substitutes across sectors. For instance some workers may have a comparative advantage in particular sectors, as in a Roy-type model, or some natural resources may be critical inputs to production in some sectors and not others. Such considerations would lead to more "curvature" in the PPF and, conditional on observed trade flows, larger gains from trade.

To take an extreme example, consider the petroleum sector. The trade elasticity, ε_s, for this sector estimated by Caliendo and Parro (2010) is around 70. The formula presented in Section 3.3 would therefore predict very small gains from trade in this sector. Yet, of course, one would expect many oil importing countries to face enormous losses from moving to autarky. One simple way to capture such considerations would be to go back to the multi-factor model presented in Section 3.5 and assume factors employed in the petroleum sector are specific to that sector, effectively making petroleum an endowment. To explore the quantitative importance of these type of considerations, we have recomputed the gains from trade in the multi-factor model under the assumption that all sectors are perfectly competitive and all factors are sector-specific.[37] In line with the previous discussion, we find larger gains from trade under the assumption that factors are sector-specific, with the cross-country average for G_j going from 15.3% to 17.2%.

Other Elasticities: Love of Variety and Extensive Margin. We conclude by discussing the calibration of the elasticity of substitution, σ, and the extensive margin elasticity, η, introduced in equation (15) and its sector-level counterparts, equations (20), (26), and (30). Given estimates of the trade elasticity, ε, these two elasticities are irrelevant for welfare analysis under perfect competition. Under monopolistic competition, however, we have seen that in the presence of intermediate goods, as in Section 3.4, or in multi-sector models with general CES preferences, as discussed above, the values of σ and η do matter above and beyond the value of the trade elasticity, ε. In these richer environments,

---

[37] Formally, this amounts to using the formula for gains from trade given by equation (32) under the assumption that $\delta_s = 0$ and $\hat{c}_{j,s}^A = e_{j,s}/r_{j,s}$ for all s.

the predictions of models with and without firm-level heterogeneity are different and the magnitude of the difference crucially depends on how σ and η are calibrated.

As shown in Section 3.2, the three elasticities ε, σ, and η are not independent of one another. In gravity models, ε determines the overall response of trade flows to changes in trade costs, whereas $\sigma - 1$ determine their responses at the intensive margin and $\eta = \left(\frac{\varepsilon - (\sigma - 1)}{\sigma - 1}\right)$ determines their response at the extensive margin, $\varepsilon - (\sigma - 1)$, weighted by the love of variety, $\sigma - 1$. Given an estimate of the trade elasticity, ε, one therefore only needs an estimate of σ to compute η and vice versa. The most direct way to estimate σ or η is to use firm-level trade data; see e.g. Crozet and Koenig (2010) and Eaton et al. (2011). When available, they offer a simple way to estimate the intensive margin elasticity, i.e., by how much the sales of a given set of firms respond to changes in trade costs, and the extensive margin elasticity, i.e., by how much the number of firms responds to changes in trade costs.[38] Eaton et al. (2011) estimate a value of 1.5 for η in a one-sector model, whereas Crozet and Koenig (2010) obtain estimates of ε_s and η_s for several sectors. Interestingly, the average η_s across s estimated by Crozet and Koenig (2010) is also 1.5, with little variation across sectors.[39]

Balistreri and Rutherford (2012) nicely illustrate the issues inherent to the calibration of models of monopolistic competition. The authors compare the predictions of a model without firm-heterogeneity, like Krugman (1980), to those of a model with firm-heterogeneity, like Melitz (2003), in a model with identical countries, three sectors, nested CES preferences, but no inter-industry trade, $e_{j,s} = r_{j,s}$. Changes in real consumption are given by equation (22). Using the fact that $\eta_s = \left(\frac{\varepsilon_s - (\sigma_s - 1)}{\sigma_s - 1}\right)$, one can show that the overall scale effects, $\left(\hat{e}_{j,s}^{\eta_s} \hat{r}_{j,s}\right)^{\delta_s/\varepsilon_s}$, are equal to $\left(\hat{r}_{j,s}\right)^{1/(\sigma_s - 1)}$ in the two models. Thus the only difference between the predictions of the two models comes from the different values of σ_s used in the calibration of the two models. In their calibration, Balistreri and Rutherford (2012) assume that ε_s is equal to 4.6 in both models, but that η_s is equal to 0 in the Krugman-version and 0.65 in the Melitz-version. This implies calibrated values of $\sigma_s = \varepsilon_s / (1 + \eta_s) + 1$ equal to 5.6 in the Krugman-version and 3.8 in the Melitz-version. This leads to stronger love of variety and, in turn, larger entry effects and gains from trade liberalization in the latter model. The question, of course, is whether one should take

---

[38] A related, though distinct way to estimate the relative importance of the intensive margin, $\sigma - 1$, consists in using the prevalence of zeros in aggregate trade data; see Helpman et al. (2008). The obvious drawback of this approach is that gravity models, in general, do not allow for zeros, therefore creating a tension between the structural model used for counterfactual analysis and the way its parameters are estimated; see Eaton et al. (2012) for recent work on this topic. Alternatively, one can rely more heavily on the overall structure of the model and use other firm-level measures, like sales and markups, to estimate ε and σ; see e.g. Di Giovanni and Levchenko (2009) and Hsieh and Ossa (2011). Once ε and σ are known, η can then be computed as a residual.

[39] This value is much larger than the value of $\eta_s = 0.65$ used in Section 3.4. If one were to use $\eta_s = 1.5$ rather than 0.65 when computing the gains from trade using equation (29), one would conclude that gains from trade predicted by models of monopolistic competition with firm-level heterogeneity cannot be finite for any country in our dataset.

seriously that love of variety is much stronger than previously thought because the intensive margin is only one particular margin of adjustment of trade flows, $\sigma_s - 1 < \varepsilon_s$, in models with firm-level heterogeneity.

6. "MICRO" VERSUS "MACRO" NUMBERS

Our chapter so far has described what could be referred to as a "macro" approach to quantifying the consequences of globalization. The distinguishing features of this approach can be summarized as follows. First, it aims to study the overall welfare gains from trade. Second, it is based on commonly available aggregate trade data and a few key structural parameters. Third, it tries to remain agnostic about micro-theoretical foundations. These foundations only matter to the extent that they affect "macro" aggregates, as illustrated, for instance, in equations (15) and (16).

A common alternative in the literature consists in following a "micro" approach, more closely related to demand and production function estimation in Industrial Organization. Unlike the "macro" approach described in this chapter, the "micro" approach typically focuses on one particular source of gains from trade using micro-level data, either at the product or firm-level. The two most prominent examples of "new" sources of gains from trade emphasized in this literature are: (*i*) gains from new varieties and (*ii*) productivity gains. The broad objective of this section is to discuss how empirical evidence related to (*i*) and (*ii*), i.e., "micro" numbers, relate to the predictions of quantitative trade models reviewed in this chapter, i.e., "macro" numbers.

6.1. Gains From New Varieties

One of the hallmarks of the "new trade theory" pioneered by Paul Krugman in the early 1980s is that consumers may gain from trade through access to new varieties. These may be direct gains coming from trade in final goods, as in Krugman (1979) and Krugman (1980), or indirect gains coming from trade in intermediate goods, as in Ethier (1982b). An important contribution of the empirical trade literature in the last decade is to put a number on the "new-goods" channel; see e.g. Klenow and Rodríguez-Clare (1997), Broda and Weinstein (2006), Arkolakis et al. (2008), Feenstra and Weinstein (2010), and Goldberg et al. (2009).

In order to illustrate the similarities and differences with the "macro" approach of this chapter, we will focus on the most influential paper in the "micro" approach: Broda and Weinstein (2006). The starting point of this paper is the observation that statistical agencies typically ignore gains from the creation of new varieties (and destruction of old varieties), when computing various components of the Consumer Price Index (CPI), including the Import Price Index. The authors then go on to ask: How different would measured changes in the Import Price Index of the United States be if one were to take into account the creation and destruction of varieties over time?

To answer this question, the authors first need to define what the counterpart of a variety in theory is in the data and then to specify a demand system to evaluate the welfare impact of new varieties. Broda and Weinstein (2006) define a variety as a 10-digit HTS product from a given country, e.g. "Umbrellas and Sun Umbrellas Having a Telescopic Shaft from China," and assume nested CES utility functions like in the present chapter. Given these assumptions, the contribution of appearing and disappearing varieties to the import component of the CES price index, i.e., the expenditure function of a representative U.S. consumer, can then be computed using an estimate of the elasticity of substitution across foreign varieties and measures of the changes in the share of expenditures on continuing varieties as in Feenstra (1994). The main finding of Broda and Weinstein (2006) is that, between 1972 and 2001, the decrease in the Import Price Index associated with the expansion of imported varieties, and omitted by statistical agencies, has led to an additional 2.6% decrease in the U.S. CPI.

It should be clear that in spite of its use of micro-level data, the empirical strategy of Broda and Weinstein (2006) has a lot in common with the approach presented in earlier sections of this chapter. First, the focus is squarely on welfare, i.e., money metric indirect utility function that is constructed by means of the expenditure function. Second, the analysis heavily relies on functional form assumptions, namely CES utility. In particular, the correction term introduced by Feenstra (1994) is closely related to our welfare formula in the simple Armington model; see equation (9). The basic idea is that under CES utility, changes in relative prices can be inferred from changes in relative expenditure modulo the elasticity of substitution. This is true regardless of whether changes in relative prices are due to movements in the price of existing goods or the creation of new goods, a fact that we have exploited more generally in Section 3.1.

There are, however, a number of notable differences. A benefit of the "micro" approach taken by Broda and Weinstein (2006) is that it only requires assumptions on the demand system, which together with data on prices and quantities, are sufficient to compute changes in the Import Price Index of a representative consumer with nested CES utility. These "micro" numbers are independent of technological considerations and market structure. In contrast, the "macro" numbers presented in this chapter do heavily depend on functional form assumptions on the supply-side of the economy, e.g. Fréchet distributions of productivity under perfect competition or Pareto distributions under monopolistic competition.

The previous observation does not imply that technological considerations and market structure are irrelevant for such empirical micro studies. This is best illustrated by the following thought experiment. Suppose first, as Broda and Weinstein (2006) do in the last part of their analysis, that Krugman (1980) is an accurate description of the world. Then changes in the Import Price Index due to new varieties should be reflected one-for-one in the overall CPI. Under this assumption, "micro" numbers indeed measure additional welfare gains. Now suppose instead that Eaton and Kortum (2002) or some other

Ricardian model is an accurate description of the world. There is a priori nothing in the trade data that Broda and Weinstein (2006) look at that would contradict this view of the world. Yet, under this alternative assumption on market structure and technology, changes in the Import Price Index due to the creation of new varieties should be exactly offset by changes in the domestic component of the CPI due to the destruction of old varieties. In this neoclassical world, the set of goods available to consumers is fixed. So the "new-goods" channel is rightly ignored by statistical agencies: in net, it should have no welfare effect. To put it bluntly, "micro" numbers are unaffected by assumptions on technology and market structure, but whether or not one should care about these numbers crucially depend on these assumptions.[40]

Another important difference between the "micro" approach taken by Broda and Weinstein (2006) and the "macro" approach presented in this paper is that, at its core, the "micro" approach is a measurement exercise, not a counterfactual exercise. The goal is to document what actually happened in the data, e.g. in the United States between 1972 and 2001, not what could have happened if China had grown at a different rate or if the United States had chosen different trade policies. To address such counterfactual questions, one again needs the full structure of the model; specifying and estimating a demand system is not enough.

6.2. Productivity Gains

In the canonical model of trade with firm-level heterogeneity developed by Melitz (2003), trade liberalization causes a reallocation of resources from the least to the most productive firms. This theoretical prediction has received considerable support in the data, with many empirical studies finding very large effects of trade on measured productivity. For instance, Trefler (2004) finds that the reallocation of market shares across firms following the Canada–U.S. free trade agreement has caused productivity, measured as real value added per hour worked, to go up by 8.4% in Canadian manufacturing. Using the methodology of Olley and Pakes (1996) to measure productivity at the firm-level, Pavcnik (2002) documents productivity gains of the same order of magnitude following the trade liberalization of the manufacturing sector in Chile.

The goal of this subsection is to clarify the relationship between productivity studies and the body of work reviewed in this chapter. Given space constraints, we will make no attempt at systematically reviewing this large empirical literature; see e.g. Tybout (2001), Melitz and Trefler (2012), as well as Melitz and Redding (Chapter 1 of this volume) for excellent overviews. Here we will focus on the following conceptual issues: What is the difference between productivity and welfare? If welfare and measured productivity simultaneously go up, should we think of productivity gains as a new source of gains from

---

[40] A similar issue arises if one believes that Melitz (2003) rather than Krugman (1980) is an accurate description of the world. In this case, however, changes in the Import Price Index and the domestic component of the CPI due to the creation and destruction of varieties only exactly cancel out under special circumstances, as discussed in footnote 12.

trade? At a qualitative level, should we always expect welfare and measured productivity to go in the same direction? At a quantitative level, can we directly compare the "micro" numbers from productivity studies with the "macro" numbers presented earlier in this chapter?

In theory, productivity measures how much "output" one can produce with a given amount of "input," whereas welfare measures how much "consumption" one can afford. At the macro level, the two concepts are therefore closely related. In a closed economy, the more productive a country is, the more it can produce, and so, the more it consumes. This is why real GDP computed on the revenue and expenditure sides coincide. In an open economy, the two concepts differ because of terms-of-trade effects. Absent any shock to a country's productivity, a country may be able to consume more if it can purchase more imports with the same amount of exports, i.e., if its terms-of-trade improve.

An obvious, but important difference between the results in this chapter and productivity studies therefore lies in the treatment of terms-of-trade effects. They are central to our analysis. In the simple Armington model, like in any neoclassical model, terms-of-trade effects are the only channel through which foreign shocks may affect welfare in another country. One of the main goals of quantitative trade models therefore is to predict the terms-of-trade changes associated with particular shocks. In contrast, terms-of-trade effects play no direct role in productivity studies, whose main goal is to identify the consequences of trade liberalization on productivity at the firm- and industry-level.

For the rest of our discussion, let us set aside the issue of terms-of-trade effects. The exact relationship between measured productivity and welfare depends, of course, on how one measures productivity as well as the model used to compute welfare; see Burstein and Cravino (2011) for a general discussion. For our purposes here, let us simply assume that all firm-level data are consistent with Melitz (2003) and that industry-level measures of productivity (in the data) increase whenever the distribution of firm-level productivity (in the model) shifts to the right.[41] Even under such ideal circumstances, changes in measured productivity caused by reallocations across firms and welfare may be quite different, as we now illustrate through a series of short examples.

Consider first a small decrease in variable trade costs. The decrease in variable trade costs, which can be thought of as an outward shift in the production possibility frontier, will lead to a direct first-order increase in welfare. In addition, there will be a reallocation of resources from the least to the most efficient firms, and this will lead to an increase in measured productivity at the industry level. Since the initial equilibrium is efficient under monopolistic competition with CES utility, see e.g. Dhingra and Morrow (2012), this reallocation of resources is associated with positive, albeit second-order, welfare effects.

---

[41] This assumption is less innocuous than it may appear. For instance, as Burstein and Cravino (2011) demonstrate, if industry productivity is measured as total value added divided by total employment and the underlying model is Melitz with a Pareto distribution of productivity, then measured productivity would be unaffected by the reallocation of resources induced by trade liberalization.

At this point, one might therefore be tempted to conclude that the increase in measured productivity is an additional source of welfare gains. But it should be clear that it is the reallocation rather than the change in productivity per se that has caused the additional welfare gain.

To see this, consider the opposite shock: a small increase in variable trade costs. By the exact same logic, this shock would decrease measured productivity at the industry level through the expansion of the least efficient firms. But as before, the reallocation of resources would remain associated with positive, albeit second-order, welfare effects. That is to say, the first-order welfare loss caused by the increase in trade costs is not as large as it would have been if workers had not been reallocated and measured productivity had remained higher.

A careful reader may have noted that in the two previous examples, there nevertheless exists a perfect correlation between measured productivity and welfare. When trade costs go down, as in our first example, both measured productivity and welfare go up. When trade costs go up, as in our second example, the opposite is true. This is fairly intuitive. Any shock that tends to cause an increase in real wages, i.e., welfare, should also tend to cause the exit of the least profitable firms, and in turn, an increase in measured productivity. This suggests that if one were only interested in qualitative questions—did welfare go up or down?—changes in measured productivity may still be used as a useful proxy for welfare changes. As intuitive as it may sound, the monotonic relationship between measured productivity and welfare does hinge on the nature of the shock being considered. This is illustrated by the results of Demidova and Rodríguez-Clare (2009) and Felbermayr et al. (2011) who study the effects of import tariffs and export subsidies in the Melitz (2003) model. Starting from free trade, they show that an import tariff increases welfare, whereas an export subsidy decreases welfare. Yet, an import tariff leads to labor reallocations from high- to low-productivity firms, whereas an export subsidy leads to a reallocation from low- to high-productivity firms. In this situation, changes in measured productivity at the industry-level and welfare move in opposite directions. The reason is that trade policy not only affects output per variety, but also the set of available varieties, which consumers care about.

The previous discussion illustrates that changes in welfare and changes in measured productivity are, in general, qualitatively different. For the purposes of the present chapter, however, the key question is not a qualitative one—"Are we getting the sign right when focusing on measured productivity rather than welfare?"—but a quantitative one—"Even when changes in welfare and measured productivity are of the same sign, are we getting the order of magnitude right?" The answer to the latter question depends on why firms of different productivity coexist in the economy. To take an extreme example, suppose that firms produce the same homogeneous good under constant returns to scale using labor as their only factor production, but that because of taxes or other distortions, the most efficient firms are prevented from taking over the market. In this hypothetical world, changes in measured productivity are trivially equal to changes in consumption, and hence welfare. In this hypothetical world, "micro" and "macro" numbers should coincide.[42] But this hypothetical world is very different from canonical models of trade with firm-level heterogeneity in which love of variety plays a central role. If one believes such models are a reasonable description of the world we live in, one cannot simply celebrate the death of small firms because they raise measured productivity within an industry. These firms may be less productive, but it is efficient for them to produce differentiated varieties in equilibrium. According to such models, "micro" and "macro" numbers are bound to be different and, according to empirical studies reviewed in Section 6.1, the difference between the two may be quite large.

To sum up: changes in measured productivity do not capture changes in welfare, either qualitatively or quantitatively, except in settings that are very different from canonical trade models.[43] Simply put, "micro" studies estimating the effect of trade shocks on measured productivity and "macro" studies quantifying the effect of trade shocks on welfare are getting at different things. To us, there are costs and benefits in both kinds of studies. Empirical micro studies such as Pavcnik (2002) and Trefler (2004) have the great virtue of letting the data speak. Measured productivity gains are what they are, regardless of what the underlying economic environment may be. However, whether such "gains" are a useful metric for policy evaluation remains open for discussion. In contrast, quantitative macro studies such as those reviewed in this chapter aim to speak directly to welfare considerations, albeit at the cost of stronger assumptions.

7. LIFE WITHOUT GRAVITY

We have described how gravity models can be used for quantitative analysis. We have shown that even richer versions of these models can be calibrated using only a few elasticities. There is, however, a price to parsimony. All gravity models discussed in this chapter rely on strong functional form assumptions. It is those functional form assumptions that allow researchers to estimate trade elasticities from the cross-section—since elasticities are assumed to be constant across countries—and use those to do counterfactual analysis—since elasticities are also assumed to be constant across equilibria. We

---

[42] This equivalence is subject to the caveat that empirical studies typically identify the productivity changes in industries that experience changes in tariffs relative to those that do not; see e.g. Trefler (2004). If industries that do not experience tariff changes are affected by trade liberalization through general equilibrium effects, "micro" numbers estimated using a difference-in-difference approach and "macro" numbers derived using the full structure of the model would still differ.

[43] Although we have focused on Melitz (2003), which is, by far, the most influential trade model featuring firm-level heterogeneity, the caveats illustrated by our simple examples apply more generally. Consider, for instance, the model of monopolistic competition developed by Melitz and Ottaviano (2008). In this model productivity varies across firms because markups vary. Nevertheless, terms-of-trade effects as well as labor reallocations in and out of the outside sector that affect the set of differentiated varieties available to consumers would still introduce a discrepancy between measured productivity and welfare; see Arkolakis et al. (2012a).

conclude by discussing alternative structural approaches to quantifying the consequences of globalization that weaken the need for extrapolation by functional form.

7.1. Sufficient-Statistic Approach

A recent literature in public finance has popularized "the sufficient-statistic approach" to counterfactual and welfare analysis. In the words of Chetty (2009), "the central concept of the sufficient statistic approach is to derive formulas for the welfare consequences of policies that are functions of high-level elasticities rather than deep primitives. Even though there are multiple combinations of primitives that are consistent with the inputs to the formulas, all such combinations have the same welfare implications." While there are some similarities between the approach described in this chapter and the sufficient-statistic approach in the public finance literature—namely, the focus on high-level elasticities rather than the multiple combinations of primitives that are consistent with those—there are also some key differences, which are best illustrated through a simple example.

Consider a small, uniform change in tariffs, $d \ln \left(1 + t_j\right)$, in some country j. The sufficient-statistic approach in the sense of Chetty (2009) consists in using envelope conditions from optimization to reduce the set of parameters that need to be identified. In the case of a small open economy j, the assumptions of (i) utility maximization and (ii) profit maximization under perfect competition imply, without any functional form assumptions, that the welfare changes associated with a change in tariff are given by:

$$d \ln C_j = \left(1 - \lambda_{jj}\right) \times \varepsilon^{SS} \times d \ln \left(1 + t_j\right), \tag{48}$$

where $\varepsilon^{SS} \equiv d \ln M_j / d \ln \left(1 + t_j\right)$ denotes the total elasticity of imports, M_j, with respect to the tariff change. Since country j is a small open-economy, $d \ln C_j$ simply represents the deadweight loss associated with the tariff, i.e., Harberger's triangle. In the international trade literature, the previous formula is the basis of numerous papers evaluating the effects of trade policy; see e.g. Johnson (1960) and Feenstra (1995).

Like in the analysis of the previous sections, equation (48) emphasizes a unique upper-level elasticity. It should be clear, however, that ε^{SS} plays a very different role than the trade elasticity ε in our previous analysis. Here, ε^{SS} is necessary to compute the area of the "triangle" below the demand curve. In Sections 2 and 3, we are interested in "rectangles": $d \ln C_j = \left(1 - \lambda_{jj}\right) d \ln \tau_j$ in the case of changes in iceberg trade costs. In this context, ε is necessary instead to map changes in prices into changes in shares of expenditures. Such changes can then be integrated to compute the gains from trade in a straightforward manner.

The second difference between the two approaches comes from the nature of the upper-level elasticity. ε^{SS} is a total elasticity in the sense that it captures all general equilibrium effects associated with the tariff change. In contrast, ε is a partial elasticity: it captures the impact of changes in trade costs or tariffs on trade flows holding all general equilibrium effects fixed; see Lai and Trefler (2002) and Arkolakis et al. (2012b) for discussions of the distinction between the two. While the recent public finance literature has been very successful in exploiting credible reduced–form estimates of the elasticity of taxable income, credible estimates of the total import elasticity, ε^{SS}, are much more scarce; see Feenstra (1995). In contrast, estimating the trade elasticity ε using a gravity equation is fairly straightforward.

The third difference comes from the importance of price effects. In a closed economy, such as the one considered in Harberger (1964), price changes are a transfer from one group of agents to another. Thus they can be ignored in welfare computations. In an open economy, in contrast, terms–of–trade effects do affect welfare. In the case of a large economy imposing a tariff, equation (48) generalizes to

$$d \ln C_j = \left(1 - \lambda_{jj}\right) \times \left(\varepsilon^{SS} \times d \ln\left(1 + t_j\right) + d \ln P_j^M\right),$$

where $d \ln P_j^M$ is the change in the relative price of imports, i.e., the term-of-trade of country j. To assess the effect of a change in tariff in country j, one therefore either needs to observe price changes after the shock or a model to predict $d \ln P_j^M$ before the shock, as we did in earlier sections. Alternatively, one can ignore terms–of–trade effects by focusing on welfare changes at the world level; see Atkeson and Burstein (2010), Burstein and Cravino (2011), and Fan et al. (2013). In this situation, we are back to the closed economy analysis of Harberger (1964).[44]

7.2. Other Structural Approaches

Another strategy, closely related to the sufficient-statistic approach presented above, consists in using optimality conditions to derive upper-bounds on the gains from trade. This is the approach followed by Bernhofen and Brown (2005). They exploit a unique quasi-natural experiment: the opening up of Japan in 1858. Under perfect competition, one can show that the gains from trade are weakly lower than the difference between the vector of consumption in the trade equilibrium and the vector of consumption in the autarky equilibrium, both evaluated at autarky prices, which is itself lower than the opposite of the vector of net exports in the trade equilibrium, also evaluated at autarky prices. Since Bernhofen and Brown (2005) have direct access to autarky prices in Japan in 1858 as well as net exports in subsequent years, they can compute an upper-bound of the gains from trade by assuming perfect competition, and nothing more. They find upper-bounds between 5.4% and 9.1% of Japan's GDP depending on the trade equilibrium they focus on. Unfortunately, autarky prices are rarely available in practice.[45]

---

[44] Atkeson and Burstein (2010) and Burstein and Cravino (2011) both feature models with monopolistic competition and CES utility. In this case, envelope conditions from optimization can still be invoked since the solution of the planning problem and the decentralized equilibrium coincide; see Dhingra and Morrow (2012).

[45] Irwin (2005) is another exception. He focuses on the Jeffersonian embargo from 1807 to 1809. He finds the cost of autarky, i.e., the gains from trade for the United States over that time period, to be around 5% of GDP.

Costinot and Donaldson (2011) develop a structural approach that tries instead to weaken the need for strong functional form assumptions by focusing on a very particular sector: agriculture. The basic idea is that agriculture is a sector of the economy in which scientific knowledge of how essential inputs such as water, soil and climatic conditions map into outputs is uniquely well understood. As a result, when studying the consequence of restricting trade, one does not need strong functional form assumptions to extrapolate from "factual" productivity levels, that are currently observed, to "counterfactual" productivity levels, that would be observed in economic activities in which production does not currently take place, but would take place in the absence of trade. Agronomists can provide direct information about "counterfactual" productivity levels. Using very detailed micro-level data from the Food and Agriculture Organization's (FAO) Global Agro-Ecological Zones (GAEZ) project, Costinot and Donaldson (2011) are able to construct the Production Possibility Frontiers (PPF) associated with 1,500 U.S. counties and explore the gains from economic integration between these local markets from 1880 to 2002.

8. CONCLUDING REMARKS

The first goal of our chapter was methodological. We have described how to use gravity models to perform welfare and counterfactual analysis. An appealing feature of this approach, which we have referred to as the exact hat algebra, is that the impact of various counterfactual scenarios can be computed without estimating the full structure of the model. All the relevant information about preferences, technology, and trade costs can be inferred directly from the cross-section of bilateral trade flows and estimates of the trade elasticity. This is a flexible approach that requires only commonly available data, that can be applied to answer a wide range of counterfactual questions, and that can be generalized to study a rich set of economic environments.

The second goal of our chapter was to use this methodology to explore quantitatively how various economic considerations—market structure, firm-level heterogeneity, multiple sectors, intermediate goods, and multiple factors of production—affect the magnitude of the gains from trade as well as the effects of trade policy. What are the main lessons?

Out of the various economic channels that we study, multiple sectors and tradable intermediate goods appear to have the largest effects on the magnitude of the gains from trade. For example, the gains from trade for the United States increase from 1.8% to 8.3% simply by moving from the one-sector model to the model with perfect competition with multiple sectors and intermediate goods. Market structure and firm-level heterogeneity also matter, though their implications are more subtle. For instance, in the presence of multiple sectors, gains from trade may be higher or lower under monopolistic competition depending on whether countries specialize in sectors characterized by larger or lower scale effects. Conditional on the same observed trade flows, firm-level heterogeneity may also lead to much larger gains through its indirect implications for the magnitude of scale effects in the presence of intermediate goods. Given the sensitivity of the predictions of gravity models with monopolistic competition to scale effects, more direct evidence on their magnitude would be very valuable.

Regarding the effects of trade policy, gravity models predict welfare gains from unilateral import tariffs over a surprisingly large range. In the one-sector Armington model, the unilaterally optimal tariff is well approximated by the inverse of the trade elasticity. Thus, a trade elasticity of 5 implies optimal tariffs of 20% around the world. In turn, it takes import tariffs to be as high as 50% to get back to the welfare levels observed under free trade. This range gets even larger once we move from a one-sector to a multi-sector model. In addition, the overall welfare effects of large unilateral tariffs on other countries appear to be minimal. Are these numbers we can believe in? Is there something that is present in the data and absent from a baseline gravity model that would dramatically affect these numbers?

The third goal of our chapter was to discuss the costs and benefits of using gravity models to quantify the consequences of globalization. The main benefit of gravity models is parsimony. They rely on a few key structural parameters, first and foremost the trade elasticity, that one can try to estimate credibly in order to make counterfactual and welfare predictions. Parsimony, however, comes at the cost of strong functional form assumptions. How restrictive are those? One would like to see more research regarding the fit of gravity models. The fact these models can perfectly fit any cross-section of bilateral trade flows certainly does not imply that out-of-sample their fit will be perfect as well. What are the dimensions in which gravity models succeed and those in which they fail? How do their predictions compare to reduced-form evidence on the gains from openness? Would alternative models—or alternative ways of estimating the same models—lead to different conclusions? In the short-run, can we think of the consequences of globalization without recognizing that there may be important frictions in factor markets? In the long-run, can we think of the consequences of globalization without knowing how it affects growth? These are all exciting opportunities for future research.

REFERENCES

Alvarez, F., Lucas, R.E., 2007. General equilibrium analysis of the Eaton-Kortum model of international trade. Journal of Monetary Economics 54 (6), 1726–1768.

Anderson, J.E., 1979. A theoretical foundation for the gravity equation. The American Economic Review 69 (1), 106–116.

Anderson, J.E., 2011. The gravity model. Annual Review of Economics 3, 133–160.

Anderson, J.E., Neary, J.P., 2005. Measuring the Restrictiveness of International Trade Policy. MIT Press.

Anderson, J.E., Van Wincoop, E., 2003. Gravity with gravitas: a solution to the border puzzle. The American Economic Review 93 (1), 170–192.

Anderson, J.E., Van Wincoop, E., 2004. Trade costs. Journal of Economic Literature 42 (3), 691–751.

Anderson, J.E., Yotov, Y.V., 2010. The changing incidence of geography. American Economic Review 100 (5), 2157–2186.

Anderson, J.E., Yotov, Y.V., 2012. Gold Standard Gravity. NBER Working Paper.

Arkolakis, C., 2010. Market penetration costs and the new consumers margin in international trade. Journal of Political Economy 118 (6), 1151–1199.

Arkolakis, C., Demidova, S., Klenow, P.J., Rodríguez-Clare, A., 2008. Endogenous variety and the gains from trade. American Economic Review, Papers and Proceedings 98 (4), 444–450.

Arkolakis, C., Costinot, A., Donaldson, D., Rodríguez-Clare, A., 2012a. The Elusive Pro-Competitive Effects of Trade. Mimeo.

Arkolakis, C., Costinot, A., Rodríguez-Clare, A., 2012b. New trade models, same old gains? American Economic Review 102 (1), 94–130.

Arkolakis, C., Ramondo, N., Rodriguez-Clare, A., Yeaple, S., 2012c. Innovation and Production in the Global Economy. Mimeo.

Atkeson, A., Burstein, A., 2008. Pricing to market, trade costs, and international relative prices. American Economic Review 98 (5), 1998–2031.

Atkeson, A., Burstein, A., 2010. Innovation, firm dynamics, and international trade. Journal of Political Economy 118 (3), 433–489.

Baldwin, R.E., Venables, A.J., 1995. Regional economic integration. In: Grossman, G.M., Rogoff, K. (Eds.), Handbook of International Economics, vol. 3. Elsevier.

Balistreri, E., Rutherford, T., 2012. Computing general equilibrium theories of monopolistic competition and heterogeneous firms. In: Dixon, P.B., Jorgenson, D.W. (Eds.), Handbook of Computable General Equilibrium Modeling. Elsevier.

Balistreri, E.J., Hillberry, R.H., Rutherford, T.F., 2009. Trade and welfare: does industrial organization matter. Economics Letters, 109 (2), 85–87. University of Melbourne. Manuscript.

Balistreri, E., Hillberry, R., Rutherford, T., 2011. Structural estimation and solution of international trade model with heterogeneous firms. Journal of International Economics 83 (1), 95–108.

Berman, E., Bound, J., Griliches, Z., 1994. Changes in demand for skilled labor within US manufacturing: evidence from the annual survey of manufactures. Quarterly Journal of Economics 109 (2), 367–397.

Bernard, A.B., Eaton, J., Jensen, J.B., Kortum, S., 2003. Plants and productivity in international trade. American Economic Review 93 (4), 1268–1290.

Bernard, A.B., Redding, S.J., Schott, P., 2007. Comparative advantage and heterogeneous firms. Review of Economic Studies 74 (1), 31–66.

Bernhofen, D.M., Brown, J.C., 2005. An empirical assessment of the comparative advantage gains from trade: evidence from Japan. American Economic Review 95 (1), 208–225.

Broda, C., Weinstein, D., 2006. Globalization and the gains from variety. Quarterly Journal of Economics 121 (2), 541–585.

Brown, D., Deardorff, A., Stern, R., 1992. A North American free trade agreement: analytic issues and a computational assessment. The World Economy 15, 15–29.

Burstein, A., Cravino, J., 2011. Measured Aggregate Gains from International Trade. Mimeo.

Burstein, A., Monge-Naranjo, A., 2009. Foreign know-how, firm control, and the income of developing countries. Quarterly Journal of Economics 124 (1), 149–195.

Burstein, A., Vogel, J., 2010. Globalization, Technology, and the Skill Premium. Columbia University and UCLA, Manuscript.

Burstein, A., Cravino, J., Vogel J., 2011. Importing Skill-Biased Technology. Mimeo.

Caliendo, L., Parro, F., 2010. Estimates of the Trade and Welfare Effects of NAFTA. University of Chicago and Yale University, Manuscript.

Chaney, T., 2008. Distorted gravity: the intensive and extensive margins of international trade. The American Economic Review 98 (4), 1707–1721.

Chetty, R., 2009. Sufficient statistics for welfare analysis: a bridge between structural and reduced-form methods. Annual Review of Economics 1, 451–488.

Chor, D., 2010. Unpacking sources of comparative advantage: a quantitative approach. Journal of International Economics 82 (2), 152–167.

Costinot, A., Donaldson, D., 2011. How Large Are the Gains from Economic Integration? Theory and Evidence from U.S. Agriculture, 1880–2002. Mimeo, MIT.

Costinot, A., Donaldson, D., Komunjer, I., 2012. What goods do countries trade? A quantitative exploration of Ricardo's ideas. Review of Economic Studies 79 (2), 581–608.

Cox, D., Harris, R., 1992. North American free trade and its implications for Canada: results from a CGE model of North American trade. The World Economy 15, 31–44.

Crozet, M., Koenig, P., 2010. Structural gravity equation with extensive and intensive margins. Canadian Journal of Economics 43 (1).

Dawkins, C., Srinivasan, T., Whalley, J., 2001. Calibration. In: Heckman, J.J., Leamer, E. (Eds.), Handbook of Econometrics, vol. 5. Elsevier.

de Blas, B., Russ, K.N., 2010. Teams of Rivals: Endogenous Markups in a Ricardian World. NBER Working Paper, 16587.

Dekle, R., Eaton, J., Kortum, S., 2008. Global rebalancing with gravity: measuring the burden of adjustment. IMF Staff Papers 55 (3), 511–540.

Demidova, S., Rodríguez-Clare, A., 2009. Trade policy under firm-level heterogeneity in a small economy. Journal of International Economics 78 (1), 100–112.

Dhingra, S., Morrow, J., 2012. The Impact of Integration on Productivity and Welfare Distortions Under Monopolistic Competition. Mimeo, LSE.

Di Giovanni, J., Levchenko, A.A., 2009. Firm Entry, Trade, and Welfare in Zipf's World. University of Michigan. Manuscript.

Donaldson, D., 2008. Railroads of the Raj: Estimating the Economic Impact of Transportation Infrastructure. Manuscript, London School of Economics.

Eaton, J., Kortum, S., 2001. Trade in capital goods. European Economic Review 45 (7), 1195–1235.

Eaton, J., Kortum, S., 2002. Technology, geography and trade. Econometrica 70 (5), 1741–1779.

Eaton, J., Kortum, S., Kramarz, F., 2011. An anatomy of international trade: evidence from French firms. Econometrica 79 (5), 1453–1498.

Eaton, J., Kortum, S., Sotelo, S., 2012. International Trade: Linking Micro and Macro. NBER Working Paper 17864.

Edmond, C., Midrigan, V., Xu, D., 2011. Competition, Markups and the Gains from Trade. Mimeo, Duke and NYU.

Ethier, W.J., 1982a. Decreasing costs in international trade and Frank Graham's argument for protection. Econometrica 50 (5), 1243–1268.

Ethier, W.J., 1982b. National and international returns to scale in the modern theory of international trade. American Economic Review 72 (3), 389–405.

Fan, H., Lai, E., Qi, H., 2013. Global Gains from Reduction of Trade Costs. Mimeo.

Feenstra, R.C., 1994. New product varieties and the measurement of international prices. The American Economic Review 84 (1), 157–177.

Feenstra, R.C., 1995. Estimating the effects of trade policy. In: Grossman, G.M., Rogoff, K. (Eds.), Handbook of International Economics, vol. 3. Elsevier.

Feenstra, R.C., 2003. A homothetic utility function for monopolistic competition models, without constant price elasticity. Economics Letters 78 (1), 79–86.

Feenstra, R.C., 2010. Measuring the gains from trade under monopolistic competition. Canadian Journal of Economics 43 (1), 1–28.

Feenstra, R.C., Weinstein, D., 2010. Globalization, Markups, and the U.S. Price Level. NBER Working Paper, 15749.

Feenstra, R.C., Obstfeld, M., Russ K.N., 2013. In Search of the Armington Elasticity. Mimeo.

Felbermayr, G.J., Jung, B., Larch, M., 2011. Optimal Tariffs, Retaliation and the Welfare Loss from Tariff Wars in the Melitz Model. CESifo Working Paper Series.

Felbermayr, G.J., Jung, B., Larch, M., 2013. Icebergs versus Tariffs: A Quantitative Perspective on the Gains from Trade. Mimeo.

Feyrer, J., 2009a. Distance, Trade, and Income—The 1967 to 1975 Closing of the Suez Canal as a Natural Experiment. NBER Working Paper.

Feyrer, J., 2009b. Trade and Income—Exploiting Time Series in Geography. NBER Working Paper, 14910.

Fieler, A.C., 2011. Nonhomotheticity and bilateral trade: evidence and a quantitative explanation. Econometrica 79 (4), 1069–1101.

Fitzgerald, D., 2012. Trade costs, asset market frictions, and risk sharing. American Economic Review 102 (6), 2700–2733.

Frankel, J.A., Romer, D., 1999. Does trade cause growth. The American Economic Review 89 (3), 379–399.

Garetto, S., 2012. Input Sourcing and Multinational Production. Mimeo, Boston University.

Goldberg, P., Khandelwal, A., Pavcnik, N., Topalova, P., 2009. Trade liberalization and new imported inputs. American Economic Review, Papers and Proceedings 99 (2), 494–500.

Gros, D., 1987. A note on the optimal tariff, retaliation and the welfare loss from tariff wars in a framework with intra-industry trade. Journal of International Economics 23, 357–367.

Harberger, A.C., 1964. The measurement of waste. American Economic Review 54 (3), 58–76.

Harrison, A.E., Rodríguez-Clare, A., 2010. Trade, foreign investment, and industrial policy for developing countries. In: Rodrik, D., Rosenzweig, M. (Eds.), Handbook of Development Economics, vol. 5. Elsevier.

Head, K., Ries, J., 2001. Increasing returns versus national product differentiation as an explanation for the pattern of U.S.–Canada trade. American Economic Review 91 (4), 858–876.

Helpman, E., Krugman, P., 1985. Market Structure and Foreign Trade: Increasing Returns, Imperfect Competition, and the International Economy. MIT Press, Cambridge, Massachusetts.

Helpman, E., Krugman, P.R., 1989. Trade Policy and Market Structure. MIT Press, Cambridge, Massachusetts.

Helpman, E., Melitz, M., Rubinstein, Y., 2008. Estimating trade flows: trading partners and trading volumes. Quarterly Journal of Economics 2 (5), 441–487.

Hertel, T., 1997. Global Trade Analysis: Modeling and Applications. Cambridge University Press, Cambridge.

Holmes, T.J., Hsu, W.-T., Lee, S., 2010. Plants and Productivity in Regional Agglomeration. Mimeo, University of Minnesota.

Hsieh, C.-T., Ossa, R., 2011. A Global View of Productivity Growth in China and India. NBER Working Paper.

Hummels, D., Hillberry, R., 2012. Trade elasticity parameters for a CGE model. In: Dixon, P.B., Jorgenson, D.W. (Eds.), Handbook of Computable General Equilibrium Modeling. Elsevier.

Imbs, J., Mejean, I., 2011. Elasticity Optimism. Mimeo.

Irwin, D.A., 1998. Changes in U.S. tariffs: the role of import prices and commercial policies. American Economic Review 88 (4), 1015–1026.

Irwin, D.A., 2005. The welfare costs of Autarky: evidence from the Jeffersonian Embargo, 1807–1809. Review of International Economics 13, 631–645.

Johnson, H., 1960. The cost of protection and the scientific tariff. Journal of Political Economy 68, 327–345.

Katz, L., Murphy, K., 1992. Changes in relative wages, 1963–1987: supply and demand factors. Quarterly Journal of Economics 107 (1), 35–78.

Kee, H.L., Nicita, A., Olarreaga, M., 2008. Import demand elasticities and trade distortions. Review of Economics and Statistics 90 (4), 666–682.

Kehoe, T.J., 2005. An evaluation of the performance of applied general equilibrium models of the impact of NAFTA. In: Kehoe, T.J., Srinivasan, T., Whalley, J. (Eds.), Frontiers in Applied General Equilibrium Modeling. Cambridge University Press, New York, pp. 341–377.

Klenow, P.J., Rodríguez-Clare, A., 1997. Quantifying Variety Gains from Trade Liberalization. University of Chicago. Manuscript.

Krugman, P., 1979. Increasing returns, monopolistic competition and international trade. Journal of International Economics 9 (4), 469–479.

Krugman, P., 1980. Scale economies, product differentiation, and the pattern of trade. The American Economic Review 70 (5), 950–959.

Krugman, P., 1995. Increasing returns, imperfect competition, and the positive theory of international trade. In: Grossman, G.M., Rogoff, K. (Eds.), Handbook of International Economics, vol. 3. Elsevier.

Krugman, P., Venables, A.J., 1995. Globalization and the inequality of nations. Quarterly Journal of Economics 110 (4), 857–880.

Lai, H., Trefler, D., 2002. The Gains from Trade with Monopolistic Competition: Specification, Estimation, and Mis-Specification. NBER Working Paper.

Leamer, E.E., Levinsohn, J.E., 1995. International trade theory: the evidence. In: Grossman, G.M., Rogoff, K. (Eds.), Handbook of International Economics, vol. 3. Elsevier.

Levchenko, A.A., Zhang, J., 2011. The Evolution of Comparative Advantage: Measurement and Welfare Implications. Mimeo, University of Michigan.

McDaniel, C., Balistreri, E.J., 2003. A review of Armington trade substitution elasticities. Integration and Trade 18 (7), 161–173.

Melitz, M.J., 2003. The impact of trade on intra-industry reallocations and aggregate industry productivity. Econometrica 71 (6), 1695–1725.

Melitz, M.J., Ottaviano, G.I.P., 2008. Market size, trade, and productivity. The Review of Economic Studies 75 (1), 295–316.

Melitz, M., Trefler, D., 2012. Gains from trade when firms matter. Journal of Economic Perspectives 26 (2).

Olley, S., Pakes, A., 1996. The dynamics of productivity in the telecommunications equipment industry. Econometrica 64 (6), 1263–1298.

Ossa, R., 2011a. A new trade theory of GATT/WTO negotiations. Journal of Political Economy 119 (1), 112–152.

Ossa, R., 2011b. Trade Wars and Trade Talks with Data. NBER Working Paper.

Ossa, R., 2012. Why Trade Matters After All. Mimeo.

Parro, F., 2012. Capital-Skill Complementarity and the Skill Premium in a Quantitative Model of Trade. Mimeo.

Pavcnik, N., 2002. Trade liberalization, exit, and productivity improvements: evidence from Chilean plants. The Review of Economic Studies 69 (1), 245–276.

Prescott, E.C., McGrattan, E., 2010. Technology capital and the US current account. American Economic Review 100 (4), 1493–1522.

Ramondo, N., 2012. A Quantitative Approach to Multinational Production. Mimeo.

Ramondo, N., Rodríguez-Clare, A., 2013. Trade, multinational production, and the gains from openness. Journal of Political Economy 121 (2), 273–322.

Rutherford, T.F., 2002. Lecture notes on constant elasticity functions. Mimeo, University of Colorado.

Samuelson, P.A., 1939. The gains from international trade. Canadian Journal of Economics 5 (2), 195–205.

Shapiro, J., 2012. Trade, CO2, and the Environment. Mimeo, MIT.

Shikher, S., 2012a. Predicting the effects of NAFTA: now we can do it better! Journal of International and Global Economic Studies 5 (2), 32–59.

Shikher, S., 2012b. Putting industries into the Eaton-Kortum model. Journal of International Trade and Economic Development 21 (6), 807–837.

Simonovska, I., Waugh, M., 2011. The Elasticity of Trade: Estimates and Evidence. Mimeo.

Simonovska, I., Waugh, M., 2012. Different Trade Models, Different Trade Elasticities? Mimeo.

Sobarzo, H., 1992. A general equilibrium analysis of the gains from NAFTA for the Mexican economy. The World Economy 15, 83–100.

Timmer, M., 2012. The World Input-Output Database (WIOD): Contents. Sources and Methods. WIOD Working Paper.

Tinbergen, J., 1962. Shaping the World Economy. The Twentieth Century Fund. New York.

Trefler, D., 1993. International factor price differences: Leontief was right! Journal of Political Economy 101 (6), 961–987.

Trefler, D., 2004. The long and short of the Canada–US free trade agreement. American Economic Review 94 (4), 870–895.

Tybout, J.R., 2001. Plant- and Firm-Level Evidence on New Trade Theories. NBER Working Paper, 8418.

Waugh, M., 2010. International trade and income differences. American Economic Review 100 (5), 2093–2124.

CHAPTER 5

Domestic Institutions as a Source of Comparative Advantage*

Nathan Nunn*,† and Daniel Trefler†,‡

*Harvard University, Cambridge, MA, USA
†National Bureau of Economic Research, Cambridge, MA, USA
‡University of Toronto, Toronto, ON, Canada

Abstract

Domestic institutions can have profound effects on international trade. This chapter reviews the theoretical and empirical underpinnings of this insight. Particular attention is paid to contracting institutions and to comparative advantage, where the bulk of the research has been concentrated. We also consider the reverse causation running from comparative advantage to domestic institutions.

Keywords

International trade, Institutions, Contracts, Property rights

JEL classification codes

D23, F10, F19

1. INTRODUCTION

When Ricardo first presented his theory of comparative advantage, he was preaching to an English audience that was in the midsts of a technological revolution that would transform human history. To Ricardo's cocksure audience, nothing less than divine right dictated that the exporter of the manufactured good should be England, while the exporter of fortified wine should be Portugal, a country whose coast was patrolled to great profit by Her Royal Majesty's loyal navy. It is clear that Portugal would have preferred to be in the midst of an industrial revolution that gave her a comparative advantage in manufacturing, but this was not an option. The question is: Why not?

Today we understand that 19th century English comparative advantage in advanced manufacturing goods can be traced back in no small part to its institutions, institutions that promoted innovation and commercial enterprise. The link between institutions and industrial structure, or between institutions and comparative advantage, has been

* The authors thank Marianna Belloc, Samuel Bowles, Davin Chor, David Donaldson, Andrei Levchenko, Elhanan Helpman, and Thierry Mayer for valuable comments. Trefler gratefully acknowledges the support of the Social Sciences and Humanities Research Council of Canada.

263

discussed for decades by economic historians. However, it is only recently that systematic empirical attempts have been made to assess the importance of this link.

There is, of course, a long history of research on the relationship between levels of development and industrial structure. Rich and poor countries export very different baskets of goods. Our knowledge of the relationship between a country's mix of exports and its income dates back at least to the discussion of ladders of development by Chenery (1960) and Leamer (1984). What has breathed new life into this literature are the insights that come out of the literature on institutions and long-term growth. See Helpman (2004), Acemoglu et al. (2005a), and La Porta et al. (2008) for reviews of this literature. Previous research on comparative advantage and economic development had given pride of place to technology/innovation together with physical and human capital accumulation as the drivers both of growth and, in the tradition of Ricardo and Heckscher-Ohlin, of comparative advantage. We now understand that these proximate drivers of growth are themselves the product of deeper social, political, and economic processes that have come to be gathered under the rubric of "institutions." This insight from the institutions-and-growth literature suggests that we could profitably push beyond these proximate drivers of comparative advantage and dig deeper into the institutional determinants of international trade.

A simple example makes the main point about the role of institutions for comparative advantage. Consider a complex product such as a commercial airliner. Its production requires high levels of innovative effort by all parties involved and this effort is so difficult to verify in a legal setting that only the most incomplete of contracts can be written between these parties. In contrast, more standardized products such as blue jeans do not require any relationship-specific, non-contractable inputs. Thus, a country with good contracting institutions will have relatively low costs of producing airliners and relatively high costs of producing blue jeans. That is, contracting institutions will be a source of comparative advantage. This theme is developed in Section 2.

A skeptic will argue that all this is obvious: Institutions matter for comparative advantage because institutions affect factor accumulation and technological innovation. So to what extent is there anything new in this literature? Has it simply pushed back the determinants of comparative advantage from proximate causes (e.g., endowments) to more fundamental causes (e.g., institutions)? The empirical research to be presented indicates that institutional sources of comparative advantage can and do operate through fundamentally different channels than do traditional sources of comparative advantage such as endowments. Institutions are statistically and economically important determinants of comparative advantage even after controlling for factor endowments. Indeed, there is abundant evidence that institutions are quantitatively as important as these traditional sources.

A skeptic might also argue that contracting institutions are not important because, in their absence, alternative institutions will evolve to deal with underinvestment. There is in fact some evidence of this in the international trade literature. Repeated interactions in long-term relationships, kin- and ethnic-based networks, and vertical integration can all be used as substitutes for weak contracting institutions. Cultural beliefs (e.g., about trust) can also play a similar role. In Section 3 we explore the implications of these alternatives for comparative advantage.

In Section 4, we briefly cast a wider net by considering the indirect impacts of domestic institutions, particularly those working through government policies.

A major obstacle faced by the literature on the impact of domestic institutions on comparative advantage is that of reverse causality: Comparative advantage exerts strong impacts on domestic institutions. The causal mechanism involves power and politics. International trade generates wealth and power and this may be distributed either inclusively or exclusively. To the extent that specialization and trade enriches specific groups in society, it will provide economic power that can translate into political power and affect institutional change. This has been shown historically in studies examining the 17th–19th century Atlantic three-corner trade (Engerman and Sokoloff, 1997; Acemoglu et al., 2005b; Nunn, 2008a; Dippel et al., 2012). The striking lesson from the historical literature is that initial conditions, working through their effect on comparative advantage, are crucially important for whether changes in international trade lead to inclusive or exclusive institutional change. For example, the Atlantic triangle trade enriched a Caribbean plantation elite who then used their riches to exclude workers from political power as well as from education and other public goods. In Europe, the Atlantic triangle trade enriched an emerging merchant class who used their riches to push for growth-enhancing improvements in property-rights institutions. Within Africa, the specialization of production in slaves resulted in a deterioration of domestic institutions and property rights. As we show in Section 5, these heterogeneous institutional responses to changes in international trade patterns are in large part explained by characteristics of the goods initially exported, such as sugar versus manufactures versus slaves. That is, institutional responses to trade depend on initial comparative advantage.

Finally, the reader will have noticed that we have studiously avoided defining institutions. North (1990) famously defines institutions as the "rules of the game"; however, this definition is both narrow and problematic and reviewing alternative definitions would take us too far afield. Deeper thinkers are referred to Greif (2006b, Chapter 1). In a landmark definition of pornography, Supreme Court Justice Stewart states simply: "I know it when I see it." This is a pretty good definition of institutions, too.

2. CONTRACTING AND PROPERTY-RIGHT INSTITUTIONS: IMPACTS ON COMPARATIVE ADVANTAGE

Examples of contracting institutions include laws on the books and contractual flexibility that mitigate contractual incompleteness (La Porta et al., 2008, p. 300). Nunn (2007) was one of the first to empirically examine the impacts of contracting institutions on comparative advantage, focusing specifically on their impacts working through hold-up and underinvestment. Levchenko (2007) examined institutions more broadly defined—contracting institutions, property-rights institutions, etc.—and provided evidence for their impacts on comparative advantage. This set of findings are the subject of Section 2.1.

There are many other institutions that affect comparative advantage, each in its own way. Institutions associated with financial development (e.g., bankruptcy law, securities law, and corporate law) are also a source of comparative advantage: Industries with large fixed costs relative to sales require access to external finance and this external finance comes cheaply when outside investors are protected from the opportunistic behavior of insiders such as CEOs. Beck (2003) and, more persuasively, Manova (2008, 2013) were the first to empirically examine this channel. This is explored in Section 2.3.

A variety of labor-market-related institutions affect comparative advantage. These include institutions that affect the ability of a firm and its workers to enter into contracts that induce high levels of effort (Costinot, 2009), institutions that affect hiring and firing costs (Cunat and Melitz, 2012), and institutions that affect labor market search frictions (Davidson et al., 1999; Helpman and Itskhoki, 2010). These are discussed in Section 2.4.

2.1. Product Markets

In the canonical model of incomplete contracts, an input supplier produces a customized input for a final goods producer. Because the customized input has greater value to the buyer than to other potential buyers, the investments made to produce the input are relationship-specific—i.e., their value is higher within the relationship than outside of it. If contracts are imperfectly enforced, then after the input supplier makes the relationship-specific investments, the purchaser has an incentive to renegotiate the terms of the original agreement. In short, there is a hold-up problem, e.g., Williamson (1985). Anticipating this ex-post renegotiation, the input supplier provides an inefficiently low level of relationship-specific investment and this inefficiency drives up the cost of production. This well-known phenomenon has a striking implication for international trade. Think of contractual incompleteness as an institutional feature that varies across countries and think of the relationship-specific investment as a technological feature that varies across products. Then a country with "good" contracting institutions will suffer less from hold-up and hence be a low-cost producer of goods requiring high levels of relationship-specific investments. In short, good contracting institutions are a source of comparative advantage in industries that intensively use relationship-specific investments.

Levchenko (2007) offers up a formal general equilibrium model of this. Consider first a standard 2×2 Hecksher-Ohlin model with factor price equalization in which one sector only users labor (L with price w) and the other sector only uses capital (K with price r). Factor price equalization pins down w and r. Now introduce a Leontief "middle" sector M that requires one unit each of capital and labor to produce one unit of output. Further, as in Caballero and Hammour (1998), capital is subject to one-sided hold-up. This is captured by assuming that in the M sector labor is able to grab a share

ϕ of the capital. The surplus from the relationship, per unit of input and/or output, is $s \equiv p_M - w - (1 - \phi)r$ where p_M is the price of the final good, w is the outside option of labor (its value in the L-intensive sector), and $(1 - \phi)r$ is the outside option of what remains of the capital (its value in the K-intensive sector). Assuming Nash bargaining over s with equal bargaining weights and equating the returns to capital in the K-intensive and M sectors yields:[1]

$$p_M = w + \phi r + r.$$

Absent hold-up ($\phi = 0$), this is a standard equation relating price to marginal cost. So the key term is ϕr, which captures the hold-up rents received by labor. Neatly, Levchenko has reduced the entire problem of characterizing the equilibrium to the more familiar problem of characterizing the equilibrium of a Heckscher-Ohlin model with a factor-market distortion, and this is a well-understood problem. In particular, while capital receives r in both the K-intensive and M sectors, labor receives w in the L-intensive sector and $w + \phi r$ in the M sector. Since $w + \phi r > w$, there is a distortion.

Levchenko assumes that the hold-up problem is more severe in the North than in the South so that $\phi^N < \phi^S$. When trade opens up, and assuming that factor price equalization holds, the North will be the low-cost producer of M and hence all M production will migrate there. This has two implications. In terms of welfare, if the two countries have identical endowments then opening up to trade raises both r and w. This raises welfare for capital in both countries. It also raises welfare for labor in the L-intensive sectors of both countries. However, labor that was in the Southern M sector migrates to the L-intensive sector and, as a result, it loses its rents ϕr. This may or may not be offset by the rise in w i.e., some Southern labor may not gain from trade.

The second implication of Levchenko's models is that *the country with better institutions will have a comparative advantage in the product whose costs are sensitive to the quality of institutions.* Berkowitz et al. (2006) and Nunn (2007) informally make similar arguments. It is this implication that has been subject to a substantial body of empirical research. A unifying theme of this empirical research is the following estimating equation:

$$y_{gi} = \alpha_g + \alpha_i + \beta(z_g \cdot q_i) + X_{gi}\gamma + \varepsilon_{gi}, \tag{1}$$

where y_{gi} is a measure of country i exports of good g, q_i is a measure of the quality of contracting institutions in country i, and z_g is a measure of the sensitivity of industry g costs to the quality of contracting institutions. α_g and α_i are industry and country fixed effects, respectively, and X_{gi} is a vector of other determinants of comparative advantage. The theory predicts $\beta > 0$, that is, a country with high-quality contracting institutions will export relatively more of those goods whose costs are sensitive to the quality of contracting institutions.

---

[1] To derive this equation, note that Nash bargaining implies that capital in the M sector receives $s/2 + (1 - \phi)r$. Since capital is mobile ex ante, this must equal r, which is what capital receives in the K-intensive sector. The equation follows from manipulating $s/2 + (1 - \phi)r = r$ where $s \equiv p_M - w - (1 - \phi)r$.

The interaction term in equation (1) has a long lineage in international trade, though interest in the equation waned in light of the critique by Leamer and Bowen (1981). Interest was revived for two reasons. The first was the theoretical/structural underpinnings provided by Romalis (2004). The second was the reduced-form difference-in-difference rationale provided by Rajan and Zingales (1998).

The equation (1) prediction that $\beta > 0$ cannot be examined without a credible measure of z_g. By and large, the literature appears to have settled on Nunn's (2007) notion of the "contract intensity" of goods. Nunn starts with Rauch's (1999) three-way classification of goods:

1. Goods that are sold on an organized exchange (e.g., oil);
2. Goods that have a reference price (i.e., they appear in catalogs); and,
3. Differentiated goods (i.e., goods that are neither sold on an organized exchange nor have a reference price).

Nunn interprets a good that is bought and sold on an exchange or that is referenced priced in a trade publication as a good that is traded in a thick market with many buyers and sellers. If there are multiple buyers for an input, then the value of the input outside of the relationship is close to the value within the relationship. Therefore, the investments made to produce the good are not relationship-specific. Put differently, if the buyer were to attempt to renegotiate a lower price ex post, then the seller could simply sell the input to another buyer. On the other hand, if there are only a small number of buyers of a good, then an input produced for a particular buyer has limited value outside of the relationship and the investments undertaken to produce the good are relationship-specific.

Nunn's next step is to calculate, for each output g, the share of its inputs that are not bought and sold on thick markets i.e., whose production involves relationship-specific investments. This information is easily culled from the U.S. input-output Use table. The calculated share is Nunn's measure of the relationship-specific investment intensity of good g. This is a bit of a mouthful so Nunn coins the term "contract intensity" of the good. It enters equation (1) as z_g.

Table 5.1 presents the 20 most and 20 least contract-intensive industries. The ordering of industries he reports is intuitive. For example, the least contract-intensive goods/industries according to his metric are "poultry processing" and "flour milling." For both of these industries, their primary inputs—chickens and wheat—are homogenous and sold on thick markets; therefore, any investments made by wheat and chicken suppliers are not specific to any buyer–seller relationship and hence are not subject to hold-up. Re-stated, if the purchaser were to try and renege on the initially agreed upon contract, the input producers would simply sell their products elsewhere. The most contract-intensive industries include automobile, truck, and aircraft manufacturing. The production of these goods requires the use of customized relationship-specific inputs that are susceptible to hold-up. If the purchaser attempts to renegotiate ex post, the supplier's outside option is limited because he or she will be hard-pressed to find an alternative buyer for these customized inputs.

Table 5.1 Contract Intensity from Nunn (2007)

	Least Contract Intensive		Most Contract Intensive
z_g	*Industry Description*	z_g	*Industry Description*
.024	Poultry processing	.810	Photographic & photocopying equip. manuf.
.024	Flour milling	.819	Air & gas compressor manuf.
.036	Petroleum refineries	.822	Analytical laborator instr. manuf.
.036	Wet corn milling	.824	Other engine equipment manuf.
.053	Aluminum sheet, plate, & foil manuf.	.826	Other electronic component manuf.
.058	Primary aluminum production	.831	Packaging machinery manuf.
.087	Nitrogenous fertilizer manuf.	.840	Book publishers
.099	Rice milling	.851	Breweries
.111	Prim. nonferrous metal, ex. copper, & aluminum	.854	Musical instrument manuf.
.132	Tobacco stemming & redrying	.872	Aircraft engine & engine parts manuf.
.144	Other oilseed processing	.873	Electricity & signal testing instr. manuf.
.171	Oil gas extraction	.880	Telephone apparatus manuf.
.173	Coffee & tea manuf.	.888	Search, detection, & navig. instr. manuf.
.180	Fiber, yarn, & thread mills	.891	Broadcast & wireless comm. equip. manuf.
.184	Synthetic dye & pigment manuf.	.893	Aircraft manuf.
.190	Synthetic rubber manuf.	.901	Other computer peripheral equip. manuf.
.195	Plastics material & resin manuf.	.904	Audio & video equipment manuf.
.196	Phosphatic fertilizer manuf.	.956	Electronic computer manuf.
.200	Ferroalloy & related products manuf.	.977	Heavy duty truck manuf.
.200	Frozen food manuf.	.980	Automobile & light truck manuf.

Notes: Data are from Nunn (2007), Table 2.

In estimating equation (1), Nunn's baseline measure of a country's ability to enforce contracts (q_i in equation (1)) is the country's rule of law from Kaufmann et al. (2003). He also considers objective measures of the quality of the judicial system from World Bank (2004). As is common in this literature, results are not usually sensitive to the measure of q_i. Nunn's dependent variable y_{gi} is the log of country i's total exports of industry g in 1997. His positive estimates of β establish that countries with better contracting institutions export relatively more in contract-intensive industries. Quantitatively, these effects of institutions on comparative advantage are greater than the combined impacts of skill and capital endowments. We discuss magnitudes further below.

In analysis pre-dating Nunn (2007), Berkowitz et al. (2006) consider a variant of equation (1) in which z_g is a dummy variable equal to 1 if the good is differentiated in Rauch's sense and 0 if the good is reference-priced. Goods sold on an organized exchange are deleted from the sample. Their estimate of β is positive, but is huge in that it implies that a one-standard-deviation improvement in the rule of law leads to a 1256% increase in exports.[2] These enormous effects suggest issues of endogeneity: For example, advanced countries have both good institutions and a production structure skewed toward complex goods, which leads to a spurious correlation or bidirectional causality between good institutions and comparative advantage.

The recent analysis by Ma et al. (2010) confirms Nunn's finding at the firm level. Motivated by evidence that domestic institutions vary subnationally (Laeven and Woodruff, 2007; Acemoglu and Dell, 2010), the authors examine perceptions of the quality of the judicial system among approximately 8792 firms in 28 countries, taken from the World Bank's Enterprise Surveys. Although the firm-level variation in judicial quality is surely explained by differences in perception or measurement error, much of the variation is also likely explained by differences in firms' access to the judicial systems because of power or political connections. The authors provide evidence for this by showing that within-country cross-firm differences are correlated with observable characteristics in a sensible manner: For example, state-owned firms report having access to a better judicial system.

Estimating a variant of equation (1) that looks at firm-level exports across a number of countries, Ma et al. find that firms with access to better judicial institutions tend to export more in contract intensive industries, measured using Nunn's (2007) contract-intensity variable. Interestingly, the authors show that this effect is above and beyond the standard comparative advantage effect, which is that firms in *countries* with better judicial quality tend to export more in contract-intensive industries. The authors show that in their data, the standard country-level comparative advantage impacts can be seen. In addition, there also exist subnational comparative advantage effects that work at the firm level.

This firm-level comparative advantage effect has also been confirmed by Li et al. (2012) who look at 77,000 Chinese firms located in the capital of 31 provinces producing in 29 2-digit Chinese Industry Classification (CIC) industries. The authors find that firms located in Chinese regions with better contracting institutions tend to specialize in the production of contract-intensive goods.

Feenstra et al. (2012) also examine cross-province comparative advantage using Nunn's (2007) contract-intensity measure, which they construct using Chinese I-O tables. Their analysis, which looks at variation across 30 provinces, 11 years, and 22 industries, also distinguishes between processing trade and ordinary trade as well as between foreign-owned firms, joint ventures, and domestically owned firms. Consistent with Li et al. (2012), Feenstra et al. (2012) find that provinces with better domestic institutions tend to

---

[2] A subsequent study by Ranjan and Lee (2007), using the same general methodology but different data, roughly confirms the findings from Berkowitz et al. (2006): The impact of better contracting institutions on exports is greater for complex goods than for simple goods (also proxied for using Rauch's measure).

export more in contract-intensive industries. They also show that the impact of domestic institutions on comparative advantage is stronger for foreign-owned firms and for processing trade.

A common characteristic of these papers is that they all examine the impact of contracting institutions on horizontal specialization—i.e., specialization across industries. However, it is also possible that contracting institutions also affect specialization in higher- or lower-quality goods within industries—i.e., vertical specialization. Essaji and Fujiwara (2012) hypothesize that since the production of higher-quality varieties of a good typically requires the use of higher-quality inputs requiring more customization and relationship-specific investments, a country with a better contracting environment will have a comparative advantage in the production of higher-quality varieties of a given good (all else equal). In other words, imperfect contracting institutions and the existence of relationship-specific investments may cause vertical specialization as well as horizontal specialization.

Essaji and Fujiwara (2012) test their hypothesis using data on imports to the United States from 123 exporting countries. The export data, which are measured at the HS 10 product level, report both quantities and prices. Following the empirical strategy of Hallak and Schott (2010) and Khandelwal (2010), the authors infer product quality of exports of all HS 10 products from all countries using unit values and market shares. The authors use Nunn's (2007) contract-intensity measure and show that countries with better contracting institutions (measured by the rule of law) tend to export higher-quality varieties of goods.

Nunn (2007) focuses narrowly on the impact of rule of law on non-contractible relationship-specific investments. However, Levchenko's (2007) theoretical model has a broader interpretation and it is this interpretation that Levchenko takes to the estimation of equation (1). He also undertakes an empirical examination of the importance of institutions for comparative advantage. The main difference from Nunn is in the measure of the sensitivity of a good to the quality of contracting institutions (z_g). Levchenko (2007, page 807) argues theoretically that the larger the number of input suppliers needed to produce a good, the more complex the good is, and therefore the more sensitive it is to imperfect institutions. Empirically, he measures "institutional dependence" as the Herfindahl index of intermediate input use (times minus 1), computed from the U.S. input-output Use table for 1992. For concreteness, suppose that an industry purchases equal amounts of inputs from n sectors. Then each input accounts for a share $1/n$ of all inputs and the Herfindahl index (times minus 1) is $-\sum (1/n)^2 = -n(1/n)^2 = -1/n$. Thus, the more industries that supply inputs, the greater is the measure of institutional dependence. A second motivation for the measure is that every time an intermediate good is purchased, institutions are needed to facilitate the transaction. Therefore, the greater the variety of goods needed for production, the greater the reliance on domestic institutions. The 10 least and 10 most institutionally intensive industries according to Levchenko's (2007) measure are reproduced in Table 5.2.

Table 5.2 Institutional Intensity from Levchenko (2007)

Least Institutionally Intensive		Most Institutionally Intensive	
Code	Industry description	Code	Industry description
2011	Meat packing plants	3728	Aircraft parts and equiment, n.e.c.
2075	Soybean oil mills	3296	Mineral wool
2015	Poultry slaughtering and processing	3842	Surgical appliances and supplies
2429	Special product sawmills, n.e.c.	3565	Packaging machinery
2021	Creamery butter	3644	Noncurrent-carrying wiring devices
2911	Petroleum refining	3643	Current-carrying wiring devices
2026	Fluid milk	3482	Small arms ammunition
2296	Tire cord and fabrics	3999	Manufacturing industries, n.e.c.
2083	Malt	3321	Grey and ductile iron foundries
2652	Setup paperboard boxes	2451	Mobile homes

Notes: Data are from Levchenko (2007), Table 2, Table A1. Industries classified by 4-digit Standard Industry Classification (SIC). Industry codes and descriptions are reported. n.e.c.: not elsewhere classified.

Armed with this institutional-dependence measure of z_g, Levchenko estimates equation (1) using U.S. imports from 116 countries across 389 4-digit SIC industries in 1998. He measures the quality of exporters' domestic institutions (q_i) using the Kaufmann et al. (2003) rule-of-law variable. As predicted by his model, Levchenko estimates a positive β: countries with better rule of law have a comparative advantage in "institutionally dependent" goods. We discuss the magnitude of this estimate below in Section 2.5.

Summarizing, there is now a large body of evidence about the impact of contracting institutions on exports of contract-intensive goods. Empirical evidence strongly confirms that contracting institutions are indeed a source of comparative advantage.

2.2. Methodological Issues

2.2.1. Identification

The interaction term in equation (1) arises because of the complementarity between an industry characteristic and a country characteristic. The nice feature of the interaction term is that it allows one to control directly for country fixed effects and industry fixed effects, resulting in an estimating equation that has the same logic as a standard difference-in-difference equation. However, this also means that as with standard difference-in-difference estimates, the coefficient estimate can only be interpreted as causal given specific assumptions.

The first concern is that of reverse causality. Countries that specialize in the production of contract-intensive or institutional-intensive industries have a greater incentive to develop and maintain good contracting institutions. Not doing so would be very costly.

A few of the papers considered address endogeneity. For example, Nunn (2007) provides instrumental variable (IV) estimates, instrumenting a country's contracting environment with its legal origin.[3] Since legal origin is predetermined and unaffected by current trade flows, it helps to alleviate the concern of reverse causality. However, this IV strategy does raise concerns about whether the exclusion restriction is satisfied; that is, whether legal origin affects the pattern of trade only through contracting institutions. This is particularly true given the large number of studies that have emerged, many since the publication of Nunn (2007), showing that a country's legal origins have wide-ranging impacts on a variety of outcomes including military conscription, labor market regulations, and even economic growth (La Porta et al., 2008).[4]

Recognizing this concern with the IV estimates, Nunn (2007) undertakes an auxiliary procedure to address the issue of causality. He uses propensity-score matching and compares the relative exports of paired British common law and French civil law countries across industries. Matching on per capita GDP, human capital stock, physical capital stock, financial development, and trade openness, Nunn (2007) shows that British common law countries export relatively more in contract-intensive industries relative to (matched) French civil law countries. This same strategy is also employed in subsequent research by Ma et al. (2010) who examine subnational variation in contracting institutions.

One advantage of the matching estimates is that they hold constant a large number of country characteristics in the analysis. Unlike the IV estimates, this can be done without taking a stance on exactly how the country characteristics affect the pattern of trade. In other words, one does not have to take a stance on what the country-industry interactions look like. Since only matched country-pairs (and not all countries) are being compared in the analysis, these country differences, no matter how they affect the pattern of trade, are accounted for.

Another concern is that of omitted-variables bias. As an example, consider the empirical finding from Levchenko (2007) that countries with a better rule of law tend to specialize in goods requiring a broader range of inputs. Producers in an industry that uses a wide variety of inputs may not only produce more complex goods that intensively use institutions, but they may also more intensively use communication, transportation, and distribution infrastructure, because more inputs are being ordered and shipped to the locations of production. The Herfindahl index of input concentration has been proposed by Christopher Clague (1991b), not as a measure of institutional intensity, but as a measure of how "self-contained" an industry is, which affects the extent to which it relies on transportation and communication infrastructure. Given that countries with better institutions

---

[3] See Acemoglu and Johnson (2004) for earlier evidence on the link between legal origin and contract enforcement.

[4] Other studies have employed other instruments to address the issue of reverse causality. For example, Feenstra et al. (2012), who estimate the impacts of provincial-level institutions on comparative advantage within China, use the identity of the colonizer measured in 1953 to address the issue of reverse causality. Essaji and Fujiwara (2012) use a country's population density in 1500, urbanization in 1500, and the European settler mortality measure from Acemoglu et al. (2001).

also have better-developed infrastructure, there is a concern that the estimated interaction between rule of law and Levchenko's measure of institutional dependence may be biased by the fact that countries with better infrastructure specialize in goods whose production relies heavily on this. See Yeaple and Golub (2007) for evidence on the importance of infrastructure.

The primary strategy undertaken by the studies described here is to control for alternative interactions between country and industry characteristics. For example, Levchenko (2007) and Nunn (2007) both control for Heckscher-Ohlin interactions (human capital endowment times skill intensity and capital endowment times capital intensity) in their baseline regressions. As well, Levchenko (2007) recognizes the possibility that his measure of institutional intensity may be correlated with other industry characteristics, including Clague's notion of how self-contained an industry is. To deal with this, Levchenko includes industry fixed effects interacted with a country's real per capita GDP: These interactions control for the possibility that richer countries tend to produce in industries whose characteristics are correlated with his institutional-intensity measure. When these additional interactions are included in his regressions, Levchenko finds that the coefficient on his interaction of interest actually increases.

2.2.2. Benchmarking Bias

A final methodological issue within the literature arises from the fact that all studies rely on an industry measure taken from one country, usually the United States, to approximate the industry characteristic in all countries. In other words, z_g is used rather than z_{gi}. The typical justification for this is that industry characteristics are by-and-large technologically determined and therefore their intensity ordering does not change when moving from one country to another. As an example, although richer countries use more capital than poorer countries this is true across all industries and in a way that preserves the ordering of capital intensity in the different countries. In all countries, construction is relatively capital intensive while services are not, although on average more capital is used in the United States than in Ghana. As an alternative example, consider Levchenko (2007) and Nunn (2007) who both construct their measures using the United States' input-output tables. Their presumption is that no matter where goods are produced they still require the same inputs and in the same proportions. For example, wherever cars are manufactured, they generally still require tires, windshields, textiles for seats, etc.

Ciccone and Papaioannou (2010) derive the properties of OLS estimates when the industry measure from one country is an imperfect proxy for the other countries. They identify two sources of bias. One is standard attenuation bias. If there is random measurement error associated with the industry measure, z_g, then the estimate of β will be biased downwards. However, there is also a second bias that arises if the measure being used z_g is systematically a better proxy for certain countries. They refer to this as amplification bias. As an example, again consider the measure from Levchenko (2007) or Nunn (2007).

If it is the case that countries that are similar to the United States in terms of the rule of law are also similar in terms of input–output production structures, then the industry measure is going to be more accurate for countries with U.S.-like institutions. Ciccone and Papaioannou (2010) show that this results in an estimate of β that is biased away from zero e.g., upwards if $\beta > 0$. The authors suggest a two-step procedure that, under certain conditions, can yield consistent estimates.[5]

2.3. Financial Markets

There are many potential ways that financial development could affect comparative advantage. However, there is no standard model or mechanism for this. Theoretical contributions include Kletzer and Bardhan (1987), Baldwin (1989), Xu (2001), Beck (2002), and Matsuyama (2005). In each of these models, credit market imperfections raise costs in some industries relative to others, thus creating comparative advantage. Beck (2002) was the first to empirically examine the role of financial development for comparative advantage. Following Kletzer and Bardhan (1987), he argues theoretically that manufacturing-sector firms face up-front fixed costs whereas agricultural-sector firms do not. Credit market imperfections make it costly to finance the fixed costs. Since countries with well-developed financial markets have lower finance costs, such countries have a comparative advantage in manufacturing.[6]

Beck (2002) examines the cross-country relationship between manufacturing exports as a share of total exports and measures of financial development. Beck estimates a positive β, which means that more financially developed countries have a comparative advantage in manufacturing. The estimated effect is economically large: A one standard deviation increase in private credit leads to half of a standard deviation increase in manufacturing as a share of total exports. However, he does not control for the endogeneity of financial development.

While Beck's analysis considers just two types of sectors, subsequent research allows for a much richer set of industries. The seminal study by Rajan and Zingales (1998) shows that financially developed countries tend to have higher output in industries that traditionally require large amounts of external finance. They measure *external financial dependence*, e_g, as the fraction of a firm's capital expenditure that is financed from sources

---

[5] Nunn and Trefler (2010) find no evidence of such bias in their work examining the distribution of tariffs across industries. They find very similar results when using factor intensities from countries other than the United States.

[6] There are two types of market frictions in Beck (2002). First, firms have private information about their productivity and hence about their default productivities, information that can only be revealed to financial intermediaries through costly monitoring. Second, savers cannot invest directly in firms but must instead use costly financial intermediation. These costs are proportional to the amount of the investment. (Beck interprets this as costly search, but does not actually model the search.) There are two sectors, one featuring constant returns (agriculture) and one featuring increasing returns (manufacturing) as in Krugman (1980). Because of its fixed costs, manufacturing is relatively more sensitive to intermediation costs than is agriculture. As a result, countries with low costs of financial intermediation have a comparative advantage in manufacturing.

external to the firm. More precisely, it is:

$$e_g \equiv \frac{(\text{capital expenditures}) - (\text{cash flow from operations})}{(\text{capital expenditure})}.$$

The firm-level data are from the United States (COMPUSTAT) and the industry-level data are the external financial dependence of the median firm in each industry. Rajan and Zingales estimate:

$$\Delta VA_{gi} = \alpha_g + \alpha_i + \beta(e_g \cdot f_i) + X_{gi}\gamma + \varepsilon_{gi}, \tag{2}$$

where g indexes 36 International Standard Industrial Classification (ISIC) industries (manufacturing only), i indexes 41 countries, ΔVA_{gi} is the change in real value added between 1980 and 1990, f_i is a measure of financial development, and X_{gi} is a vector of other covariates.[7] β is estimated to be positive, indicating that financially developed countries experienced relatively rapid value-added growth in industries with a high degree of external financial dependence.

This methodology is immediately applicable to studying comparative advantage since all that is needed is to replace the dependent variable in equation (2) with a measure of exports:

$$y_{gi} = \alpha_g + \alpha_i + \beta(e_g \cdot f_i) + X_{gi}\gamma + \varepsilon_{gi}, \tag{3}$$

where y_{gi} is a measure of country i exports of good g. Note that this is simply a variant of equation (1) described above and that this is precisely what Beck (2003) estimates. Measuring y_{ic} as industry-i exports divided by GDP and using a sample of 56 countries and 36 industries averaged over the 1980s, he finds the expected positive estimate of β. However, the magnitude is implausibly large and the sample statistics suggest that there are outliers. Also, as Beck points out, there is an issue of endogeneity, but his method of dealing with it is unsatisfactory.

Svaleryd and Vlachos (2005) consider a variant of equation (3) for 20 OECD countries and 32 4-digit ISIC industries in which the dependent variable is a somewhat unusual measure of competitiveness.[8] Their estimate of β is not statistically significant

---

[7] Rajan and Zingales (1998) provide a large number of empirical measures of financial development at the national level. Many of these are collected in Beck et al. (2010). Studies of financial development as a source of comparative advantage typically report results for several such measures. Rajan and Zingales (1998) prefer to use private credit *plus* stock market capitalization. The correlation between this sum and private credit is 0.67. The seminal cross-country study by King and Levine (1993) considers four measures: (KL 1) The size of the formal financial intermediary sector relative to GDP (specifically, the ratio of liquid liabilities to GDP); (KL 2) The importance of banks relative to the central bank (specifically, deposit money bank domestic credit divided by deposit money bank plus central bank domestic credit); (KL 3) The percentage of credit allocated to private firms (specifically, the ratio of claims on the non-financial private sector to total domestic credit); and, (KL 4) The ratio of credit issued to private firms to GDP (specifically, the ratio of claims on the non-financial private sector to GDP). Rajan and Zingales (1998) consider three measures: (RZ 1) Total capitalization (the ratio of domestic credit plus stock market capitalization to GDP); (RZ 2) Private credit (credit extended to the private sector as a share of GDP); and, (RZ 3) Accounting standards.

[8] The measure is $(C_{gi} + X_{gi} - M_{gi})/C_{gi}$ where C_{gi} is consumption, X_{gi} is exports, and M_{gi} is imports.

when f_i is private credit,[9] but is statistically significant when other measures of f_i are used.[10] The authors do not interpret the magnitude of their estimates. They do, however, attempt to deal with the endogeneity of financial development: A country with industrial structure that is skewed toward sectors with high external financial dependence will have a high demand for financial development. They instrument financial development using a measure of civic engagement from Knack and Keefer (1997). This IV strategy is unfortunately not successful as it produces large standard errors on the estimates of β.

Becker et al. (2012) argue that exporting requires fixed costs and that these fixed costs are higher in financially less-developed countries. Further, fixed costs are higher in industries that are differentiated in the sense of Rauch (1999) or require large sales and R&D outlays. They thus interact private credit f_i with either (a) the average fraction of sales devoted to R&D and advertising by U.S. firms (from COMPUSTAT) or (b) a dummy for being a differentiated product.[11] In a regression similar to equation (3), but with e_g now either the R&D/sales or Rauch variables, the authors estimate a β that is positive. That is, access to lower fixed costs of exporting is a source of comparative advantage.

As discussed, a significant methodological problem with estimating equation (1) or, by symmetry, equation (3) is that there may be omitted country-level factors that interact both with industrial structure and with f_i. This possibility suggests that endogeneity may be a concern. Manova (2008) tackles this in a very neat way. She looks at what happens to the composition of a country's exports as it goes through a period of financial liberalization. Specifically, she starts with:

$$y_{git} = \alpha + \beta(e_g \cdot f_{it}) - \beta'(e_g' \cdot f_{it}) + \varepsilon_{git}, \tag{4}$$

where t indexes years, y_{git} is the log of country i exports of good g, f_{it} is a measure of the degree to which equity markets are liberalized in country i in year t, e_g is external financial dependence in industry g, and e_g' is asset tangibility.[12] Asset tangibility is the share of property, plant, and equipment in total assets (again, for the median firm in the industry). It captures the idea that industries with large fixed assets can use these as collateral for a loan, thus making financial development less important. We have put a minus sign in front of $(f_{it} \cdot e_g')$ so that we expect $\beta' > 0$. Manova estimates β and β' to be positive and statistically significant, as expected. Further, these results hold even when controlling for interactions between country-level factor endowments and industry-level factor intensities.

---

[9] This is defined as the ratio of credit issued to private firms to GDP. ("Private" here means claims on the non-financial private sector.)

[10] Specifically, the size of the stock market relative to GDP (RZ 1 in footnote 7) or accounting standards (RZ 3).

[11] Point (b) is closely related to what Berkowitz et al. (2006) do. See the above discussion.

[12] Manova's data for external financial dependence and asset tangibility are from Braun (2003).

What makes Manova's paper stand out is the treatment of endogeneity. Let d_{it} be a dummy that equals 1 after an equity market liberalization and equals 0 before an equity market liberalization. Then, as in Trefler's (2004) study of the Canada–U.S. trade liberalization, one can estimate a difference-in-difference specification either in levels or in changes:

$$\ln y_{git} = \alpha + \beta(e_g \cdot d_{it}) - \beta'(e'_g \cdot d_{it}) + \varepsilon_{git}, \tag{5}$$

$$\Delta \ln y_{gi} = \alpha + \beta e_g - \beta' e'_g + \varepsilon_{gi}, \tag{6}$$

where $\Delta \ln y_{gi}$ is the log difference of exports before and after liberalization. Manova estimates that β and β' are positive, indicating that financial liberalization leads to a greater comparative advantage in goods that require large levels of external finance and small levels of tangible (collateralizable) assets. While equation (6) does not eliminate endogeneity concerns entirely (the timing of financial liberalization might be endogenous), it is a very large step forward.

The financial crisis of 2008 provides an interesting experiment into the role of financial intermediation. The crisis was more severe in some countries than in others and operated through different mechanisms in different countries. This has allowed researchers to dig deeper into the impacts of short-run financing problems on aggregate trade and comparative advantage. The interested reader is referred to the symposium in the May 2012 (vol. 87, No. 1) issue of the *Journal of International Economics*.

Although this chapter is primarily concerned with comparative advantage across sectors, there have been interesting studies of other outcomes, notably, comparative advantage across firms within a sector and the mode of entry into foreign markets. We start with comparative advantage across firms within a sector. Since the seminal contributions of Bernard et al. (2003) and Melitz (2003), attention has shifted to the role of heterogeneous firms, and in particular, to the role of selection into and out of exporting. Chaney (2005) and Manova (2013) both offer models in which firm heterogeneity interacts with financial constraints. We focus here on Manova's work because it includes a major empirical component. Manova (2013) observes that firms that cannot find financing will be unable to export. This means that in thinking about comparative advantage, it is important to distinguish between the extensive-margin and intensive-margin effects of financial market imperfections. To do this she develops a heterogeneous-firm model (Melitz, 2003) with countries at different levels of financial development and sectors with different levels of tangible assets.

In the model, firms must borrow to cover their fixed costs of exporting. Recognizing that there is default risk, lenders will only lend an amount that is incentive compatible i.e., that will be repaid. This incentive compatible amount will depend on the firm's sales and hence on the firm's productivity. Very productive firms will be able to borrow as much as they need. Very unproductive firms will not export and hence will not need to borrow. Firms with intermediate levels of productivity would borrow and export if credit markets were perfect, but can do neither because they are credit-constrained.[13]

Applying this model to aggregate trade data, Manova (2013) studies the mechanisms through which credit constraints operate and finds that credit constraints substantially reduce exports both at the extensive margin (whether or not to export, how many products to export, and which destinations to enter) and at the intensive margin (how much to export of a product to a destination).

Credit constraints can also have an influence on the mode of entry into foreign markets i.e., on the choice between FDI and outsourcing. This is discussed in Antràs and Foley (2011), Manova et al. (2011), and Shen (2012). Finally, credit constraints can have effects on the size distribution of firms, which has implications for trade via the selection of firms into exporting.

Finally, we have focused here on financial underdevelopment to the exclusion of regulatory barriers to entry. Both of these affect the fixed costs of setting up a business and thus affect the extensive margin of trade. However, as La Porta et al. (2008) point out, financially underdeveloped countries typically have high regulatory barriers to entry. In an influential paper, Helpman et al. (2008) show that regulatory barriers to entry have a major impact on the extensive margin of trade. Thus, more work is needed to sort out the separate roles of regulatory barriers to entry and financial underdevelopment.

2.4. Labor Markets

Research has also explored the importance of other institutions for comparative advantage. Here we consider labor market institutions, starting with Costinot (2009). Costinot emphasizes a trade-off between the costs and benefits of a greater division of labor in production. A good is produced with many tasks, each of which has a fixed training cost so that there are returns to scale at the task level. In a very large market, a firm would like to have each worker learn a single task and specialize in it. This is Adam Smith's observation that specialization is limited by the extent of the market. Against this benefit are the costs of monitoring workers. Each worker exerts non-contractible effort and performs his or her assigned task less than 100% of the time; unfortunately, a good is produced only if all tasks are produced. The greater is the degree of specialization in tasks, the more workers are needed and the lower is the probability that the good will be produced. This trade-off between the productivity gains from task specialization (scale returns) and the productivity costs of task specialization (incomplete contracting/worker monitoring costs) leads to predictions about institutions as a source of comparative advantage. Countries that are effectively able to monitor workers have a comparative advantage in goods that require many tasks i.e., complex goods.

---

[13] In contrast, Chaney (2005) assumes that firms have a randomly drawn, exogenous amount of liquidity which they must use toward the fixed costs of exporting.

To connect the theory with empirics, Costinot shows that in equilibrium there is a one-to-one relationship between the unobservable complexity of a good (i.e., the number of tasks required) and the observable average training costs per worker. Thus, his main result can be stated in terms of observables: Goods with high training costs will locate in countries with better worker monitoring. Costinot creatively measures training costs using responses to the following Panel Study of Income Dynamics (PSID) question: "Suppose someone had the experience and education needed to start working at a job like yours. From that point, how long would it take them to become fully trained and qualified (to do a job like yours)?" Costinot aggregates the individual responses up to 20 2-digit SIC industries.

Costinot first estimates the determinants of bilateral exports across a panel of industries in 1992:

$$\gamma_{gij} = \alpha_{gj} + \alpha_{ij} + \beta_i z_g + \varepsilon_{gij}, \tag{7}$$

where γ_{gij} is a measure of the log of country i's exports to j of good g, α_{gj} and α_{ij} are industry-importer and exporter-importer fixed effects, respectively, and z_g is Costinot's training-cost measure of complexity. Notice that the key term $\beta_i z_g$ is independent of the importer (j) so one can aggregate across importers, which leads to a specification that is very similar to equation (1). The key differences are that the measure of complexity is very different from Levchenko (2007) and Nunn (2007) and β_i flexibly replaces βq_i where q_i is the rule of law. Costinot estimates this model and shows, not surprisingly, that the estimated β_i are positively correlated with the rule of law. More interestingly, Costinot shows that the estimated β_i are positively correlated with an "Ability to Perform" index. This index is calculated from the Business Environment Risk Intelligence (BERI) survey of business persons' views about various country characteristics including: work ethic; availability and quality of trained manpower; class, ethnic and religious factors; attention span and health; and absenteeism. In short, Costinot's result shows that incomplete contracts in labor markets are a source of comparative advantage.[14]

Tang (2012) also studies how a country's labor market institutions, by affecting workers' incentives to acquire skills, can shape export patterns. He develops an open-economy model in which workers undertake non-contractible activities in order to acquire firm-specific skills on the job. In the model, labor market protection raises workers' incentives to acquire firm-specific skills relative to general skills, turning labor laws into a source of comparative advantage. In particular, the model shows that countries with more protective labor laws export relatively more in firm-specific skill-intensive sectors. This is true for both the intensive and extensive margins of exporting.

---

[14] Costinot's analysis is actually more subtle in a very interesting way. His model also predicts an interaction between traditional human capital endowments and a country's ability to monitor workers; specifically, the most complex goods will be produced in the country for which the product of human capital per worker and the effectiveness of worker monitoring is greatest. He is able to show that β_i is correlated with human capital endowments and that the correlation between β_i and ability to perform holds after controlling for human capital.

To test the theoretical predictions, he constructs sector proxies for firm-specific skill intensity and industry-specific skill intensity by estimating the returns to firm tenure and the returns to industry tenure for 63 3-digit U.S. manufacturing industries between 1974 and 1993. Firm-specific skill intensity is measured using firm-tenure returns from a Mincer equation on PSID data. Data on labor regulations (for 84 countries) are taken from the World Bank's *Doing Business Survey* (Botero et al., 2004). Based on countries' legal documents from the late 1990s, Botero et al. quantify the extent to which labor market regulations cover employment, collective relations, and social security. Tang then estimates sector-level gravity equations for 84 countries using the Helpman et al. (2008) framework, and provides evidence that countries with institutions that protect labor have a comparative advantage in goods that are intensive in firm-specific skills.

Cunat and Melitz (2012) explore the impacts of the flexibility of a country's labor market institutions on comparative advantage. They begin by observing that workers change jobs much more flexibly in some countries than in others. For example, gross job flows in manufacturing are twice as high in the United States as in Portugal. Further, workers are much more likely to move jobs in some industries than in others. For example, ranking U.S. manufacturing industries by their gross job flows, the 90th-percentile industry has gross job flows that are twice as high as in the 10th-percentile industry. This suggests that countries with more flexible labor markets will have a comparative advantage in industries that require higher gross job flows.

The precise mechanism that Cunat and Melitz (2012) explore focuses on differences in the volatility of industries—defined as the dispersion of firm-level shocks within an industry—and the extent to which this drives the reallocation of workers across firms within an industry. They conjecture that firms in countries with greater labor market flexibility are better able to respond to firm-specific shocks by hiring and firing workers as necessary. Therefore, countries with more flexible labor market institutions have a comparative advantage in more volatile industries.[15]

Cunat and Melitz (2012) develop a model that illustrates this source of comparative advantage, showing how it manifests itself as a Ricardian technology difference. (See Cunat and Melitz (2010) for a more general version of their model.) Also, a second insight arises from the model when capital is introduced: Their mechanism should be weaker in industries that are more capital intensive. This insight suggests that capital intensity can affect comparative advantage in a manner beyond standard Heckscher-Ohlin effects.[16]

The authors find cross-sectional support for the predictions of their model: Countries with more flexible labor market institutions concentrate their exports in sectors with greater volatility. Also, greater capital intensity reduces this effect. Flexibility of a country's labor market institutions is measured using the 2004 World Bank *Doing Business Survey*

[15] This link between labor market flexibility and specialization of production also appears in Saint-Paul (1997) and Davidson et al. (1999).

[16] Ju and Wei (2011) offer an analysis with a similar flavor that involves financial intermediation.

(see Botero et al., 2004), from which they build an index based on hiring costs, firing costs, and restrictions on changing the number of hours worked. Motivated theoretically, the authors measure a sector's volatility in 2004 as an average of the time-series volatility of each firm within the sector. Their estimating equation is of the form:

$$y_{gi} = \alpha_g + \alpha_i + \beta'(z'_g \cdot q'_i) + \varepsilon_{gi}, \tag{8}$$

where y_{gi} is the log of country i's exports of good g, q'_i is their measure of labor market flexibility, and z'_g is their measure of volatility.[17] The authors find that β' is indeed positive, indicating that flexible labor markets are a source of comparative advantage in volatile industries.

Cunat and Melitz (2012) are clearly concerned with unemployment, but their formal model does not explicitly model the phenomenon. Unemployment varies dramatically across sectors so that unemployment must have important implications for comparative advantage. There are many strands of the literature on trade and unemployment. These include models featuring minimum wages (Brecher, 1974; Davis, 1998), implicit contracts (Matusz, 1986), efficiency wages (Copeland, 1989 and Matusz, 1996 in Heckscher-Ohlin and Ricardian settings, respectively, and Davis and Harrigan, 2011 in a heterogeneous-firms setting), fair wages (Agell and Lundborg, 1995; Kreickemeier and Nelson, 2006; Egger and Kreickemeier, 2009), and unions (Mezzetti and Dinopoulos, 1991; Gaston and Trefler, 1995; Eckel and Egger, 2009; Karasik, 2012). Here we focus on Diamond-Mortensen-Pissarides-type models featuring search and matching in labor markets. We emphasize that our interest here is only in comparative advantage whereas most contributors to the literature are concerned in addition with the impact of trade liberalization on unemployment, income distribution, and welfare.

Consider a world economy with two countries ($i = A, B$), two factors (workers L and firms K), and two identical industries ($g = 0, 1$). In each industry one worker pairs with one firm to produce one unit of output. Suppose that $L > K$ in country A. Because technologies are Leontief and identical across industries there can be no Stolper-Samuelson or Rybczynski effects: $L - K$ workers will be unemployed. In this setting there is unemployment, but no source of comparative advantage and no trade.

Now introduce Diamond-Mortensen-Pissarides search and matching. A worker–firm match produces on unit of output and, since there is a bilateral hold-up problem with zero outside options, each party is assumed to receive a fixed share of the revenue. Workers and firms are in one of two states, matched or unemployed. Unemployed workers and firms choose an industry in which to search—the industry that offers the highest expected future returns—and match probabilistically in the chosen industry. Matched pairs produce, share revenues and then, with probability b_g, the match dissolves and the pair

---

[17] They also include (1) an interaction of sector g's U.S. capital stock times q'_i, (2) g's capital stock times country i's capital endowment, and (3) g's skilled-labor stock times country i's skill endowment. These all perform as expected.

becomes unemployed. All of this happens in continuous time so that $1/b_g$ is the expected duration of a match. The instantaneous probability of matching depends positively on a matching-efficiency parameter m_i.[18] In this setting there are two causes of unemployment: Some matches dissolve and some of the unemployed fail to match. These two causes are controlled by b_g and m_i, respectively.

Consider an unemployed worker's choice of sector. A match has an expected duration of $1/b_g$ so that if a matched worker receives w_{gi} per *period* then he or she receives expected return w_{gi}/b_g per *match*. Suppose $b_1 > b_0$ so that industry 1 has relatively short-lived matches. Then ceteris paribus, w_{1i}/w_{0i} must be high in order to compensate workers for short match durations. Now suppose $m_A > m_B$ so that country A's unemployed workers find new matches relatively fast. This advantage reduces the level of compensation needed by workers in industry 1. That is, $m_A > m_B$ and $b_1 > b_0$ imply $w_{1A}/w_{0A} < w_{1B}/w_{0B}$: Country A has a comparative advantage in industry 1. Empirically, this puts us on familiar ground in that the interaction of a country characteristic m_i with an industry characteristic b_g produces an institutional source of comparative advantage. Since industry 1 has the relatively high rate of unemployment, one may state this result in a more interesting way: *The country with better labor market institutions will have a comparative advantage in the high-unemployment sector.*[19]

This basic argument appears in Davidson et al. (1999, Lemmas 3 and 4). It was first formulated by Davidson et al. (1988) and Hosios (1990), who developed the argument in a Heckscher-Ohlin context. In those earlier models, which use the same production structure as we have used, all adjustment occurs via changes in the pool of unemployed workers and firms. For example, if there is an increase in a country's endowment of workers then the country must expand the sector whose pool of unemployed has relatively more workers than firms. Restated, the Hecksher-Ohlin term "labor intensity of an industry" is now replaced with the term "labor intensity of an industry's pool of unemployed."

There are a number of drawbacks to the above analysis that are elegantly addressed by Helpman and Itskhoki (2010). First, we treated firms as exogenous endowments even though trade economists prefer to allow for the free entry of firms. Second, we assumed that firms are identical even though the importance of productivity heterogeneity for

---

[18] More specifically, the measure of pairs that form instantaneously in industry g in country i is given by the matching function $f(L_{gi}, K_{gi}) = m_i L_{gi}^{\chi} K_{gi}^{1-\chi}$ where L_{gi} and K_{gi} are the measures of workers and firms, respectively, who are searching in sector g in country i.

[19] We said that w_{1i}/w_{0i} must be high *ceteris paribus* and it is useful to explain this. Let p_{gi} be the price of good g in country i. In our simple model, p_{gi} is the per-period surplus of a match so that w_{gi} will be proportional to p_{gi}. If demand outstrips supply for good g then p_{gi} will rise, w_{gi} will rise, and workers will be attracted to the industry. There is thus an upward-sloping industry supply, as is standard in models with industry specificity. As such, w_{1i}/w_{0i} will also depend on demand conditions that influence p_{1i}/p_{0i}. On a separate note, the possibility of a downward-sloping supply schedule is debated by Davidson et al. (1988) and Hosios (1990): The possibility is ruled out if there is efficient matching (the "Hosios Rule").

exporting has been widely acknowledged. Third, we assumed that there is one worker per firm despite overwhelming evidence on heterogeneity in the number of workers per firm. Helpman and Itskhoki address all of these drawbacks by introducing Melitz-style firm heterogeneity. This leads to important insights about the impact of labor market frictions on both firm entry and firm exporting decisions. It also leads to a rich set of predictions about unemployment, income distribution, and the gains from trade that are beyond the scope of this review chapter.

Note that Helpman and Itskhoki (2010) is not a trivial extension of existing work. For example, they address issues with the underlying search-and-matching structure of earlier studies. These studies assume that the key parameter b_g is exogenous. Helpman and Itskhoki address this by eliminating match breakup altogether ($b_g = 0$) and introducing, realistically, costly posting of vacancies by firms. Posting costs v_g together with matching efficiencies m_i generate a source of comparative advantage. Eliminating match breakups also allows Helpman and Itskhoki to move from a complicated dynamic model to a one-period model, which in turn allows them to explore free entry and the extensive margin of trade. Another problem is that when firms choose to hire more than one worker they must engage in multilateral bargaining with these workers. This is elegantly modeled as in Stole and Zwiebel (1996).

The above models do not allow for heterogeneous workers and cannot explain the important fact that large firms pay high wages.[20] Helpman et al. (2010) introduce heterogeneous workers and screening for high-ability workers. This leads to another interesting set of comparative advantage and welfare results, as well as a prediction that large firms and exporters will pay a wage premium. Helpman et al. (2012) show that matched worker-firm data from Brazil is consistent with the predictions of Helpman and Itskhoki (2010) and Helpman et al. (2010). Davidson et al. (2012a,b) also offer a model of two-sided heterogeneity (both workers and firms) and matching. They show empirically that trade liberalization leads to better matching between workers and firms. Clearly, much more empirical work is needed to assess the large class of models featuring unemployment.[21]

---

[20] On the correlation between wages and firm size in an international trade context, see also Davis and Harrigan (2011) and Amiti and Davis (2012). On worker heterogeneity, see also Ohnsorge and Trefler (2007).

[21] Paralleling the literature on labor market frictions is a literature on non-Walrasian product markets. In product markets, buyers and sellers may not be able to identify one another except via costly search and this has a variety of implications. One of these is that specialists in matching buyers and sellers—trade intermediaries—may arise in equilibrium. Antràs and Costinot (2010, 2011) explore the role of intermediaries in reducing matching frictions and draw welfare implications from trade liberalization. Rauch and Watson (2004) explore how costly search affects the evolution of trade networks between developed-country buyers and developing-country suppliers. (See also Rauch (1999, 2001).) A large number of studies have shown that intermediation through wholesalers is empirically important in international trade. See Ahn et al. (2011) for China; Akerman (2010) for Sweden; Basker and Van (2010), Felbermayr and Jung (2011), and Bernard et al. (2010) for the United States; Bernard et al. (2011) for Italy; Bernard et al. (2012) for Belgium; and Blum et al. (2010, 2011) for Chile, Argentina, and Colombia.

2.5. All Together Now

One of the frustrating elements of empirical research in economics (and arguable in all the sciences), is that there are often many statistically significant explanations of a single phenomenon. Often, many studies claim to explain the phenomenon in its entirety, creating an embarrassment of riches. In particular, it is tempting to interpret the above survey as indicating that there are enough institutional explanations of comparative advantage to explain trade patterns many times over. What would happen if all the explanations were examined simultaneously? Would we find that explanatory variables are so highly correlated that none are statistically significant? These questions are answered by Chor (2010).

Chor simultaneously tests five of the comparative advantage mechanisms discussed above. To do this he first constructs the following 2-digit SIC industry measures of z_g in equation (1). These are (1) the average relationship-specificity of inputs (Nunn, 2007); (2) the Herfindahl index of input concentration (Levchenko, 2007); (3) the average complexity of tasks (Costinot, 2009); (4) sales volatility (Cunat and Melitz, 2012); and, (5) external finance dependence (Beck, 2003; Manova, 2013). He also constructs standard Heckscher-Ohlin measures of capital and skill intensity.

The pairwise correlation coefficients of Chor's industry measures are reported in Table 5.3. Coefficients that are statistically significant are in bold. The highest correlation in the matrix is between skill intensity and Costinot's (2009) measure of job complexity. This is intuitive since Costinot's measure is based on the time required to learn the skills of a job, which one would expect to be positively correlated with educational attainment in an industry. The measure of external finance dependence constructed by Chor is also highly correlated with both Levchenko's (2007) input concentration measure and with Costinot's (2009) job complexity measure. For these variables, there is no obvious reason to expect the measures to be correlated.

With these five industry measures of z_g in hand, Chor re-estimates equation (1), but now includes all of the $z_g \cdot q_i$ interactions in a single specification. Letting m index the five models of Nunn, Levchenko, Costinot, Cunat and Melitz, and Manova, Chor estimates

$$y_{gij} = \alpha_i + \alpha_{gj} + \sum_{m=1}^{5} \beta^m \left(z_g^m \cdot q_i^m \right) + X_{ij}\gamma + \varepsilon_{gij}, \tag{9}$$

where y_{gij} is the log of bilateral exports from country i to country j of product g and where $z_g^m \cdot q_i^m$ is the comparative advantage interaction term implied by model m. The regression also includes exporter fixed effects (α_i), industry-importer fixed effects (α_{gj}), and a vector of gravity controls X_{ij} that includes bilateral distance as well as dummies for common language, colony, border, regional trade agreement, and World Trade Organization (WTO) membership. The sample includes 83 countries and 20 SIC 2-digit industries. The coefficients of interest are the $\beta^{m\prime}s$.

Table 5.3 Pairwise Correlation Coefficients Based on Chor (2012)

	Manova (2013): External Finance Dependence	Levchenko (2007): Input Concentration	Nunn (2007): Input Relationship-Specificity	Costinot (2009): Job Complexity	Cunat and Melitz (2012): Sales Volatility	Capital Intensity
Levchenko (2007): Input concentration	**0.628** **(0.00)**					
Nunn (2007): Input relationship-specificity	0.131 (0.58)	**0.551** **(0.01)**				
Costinot (2009): Job complexity	**0.652** **(0.00)**	**0.539** **(0.01)**	0.210 (0.37)			
Cunat & Melitz (2012): Sales volatility	0.382 (0.10)	0.106 (0.66)	−0.200 (0.40)	0.068 (0.78)		
Capital intensity	0.104 (0.66)	−0.344 (0.14)	**−0.536** **(0.01)**	0.191 (0.42)	0.059 (0.80)	
Skill intensity	0.524 (0.02)	**0.465** **(0.04)**	0.088 (0.71)	**0.820** **(0.00)**	−0.085 (0.72)	**0.382** **(0.10)**

Notes: Pairwise correlation coefficients are reported, with *p*-values in parentheses. Coefficients that are statistically significant at the 10% level or lower are reported in bold. Each correlation is across 20 2-digit SIC industries. Authors' calculations based on data from Chor (2010).

Table 5.4 The Significance of Each of the Institutional Determinants of Comparative Advantage (Chor, 2010, Table 1).

	Slope Estimates			Impacts	
	β	Std. Err.	t-stat	Beta Coeff.	75th–25th
	(1)	(2)	(3)	(4)	(5)
Product Market Institutions					
(Relationship-specificity)$_g$ × (Rule of Law)$_i$	9.64	0.86	11.27	0.49	1.6
(Input concentration)$_g$ × (Rule of Law)$_i$	14.31	1.67	8.57	0.65	1.7
(Job complexity)$_g$ × (Rule of Law)$_i$	2.92	0.45	6.52	0.15	1.3
(Job complexity)$_g$ × ln(H/L)$_i$	1.46	0.43	3.41	0.10	1.2
Labor Market Institutions					
(Sales volatility)$_g$ × ln(Flexible lab. markets)$_i$	9.04	2.24	4.04	0.09	1.1
Financial Market Institutions					
(External fin. depend.)$_g$ × (Fin. develop.)$_i$	1.28	0.09	14.37	0.11	1.2
Heckscher-Ohlin	1.25	0.25	4.98	0.17	1.3
ln(H/L)$_g$ × ln(H/L)$_i$					
ln(K/L)$_g$ × ln(K/L)$_i$	0.16	0.02	8.20	0.49	1.6

Notes: The first column reports estimates of equation (9). The dependent variable y_{gij} is the log of bilateral exports from country i to country j for industry g. The trade data are for 1990. Industries are coded at the 2-digit SIC (1987) level so that there are 20 industries. There are 83 countries (accounting for 82% of world trade) and hence 83 × 82 bilateral pairs per good, of which 45,034 (one-third) have positive trade flows. (Zero trade flows are omitted.) The specification also includes a set of regressors that are not reported: (1) the log of distance; (2) indicator variables for common language, colony, border, regional trade agreement, and WTO membership; and, (3) exporter and industry-importer fixed effects.

Table 5.4 reports the results. The first column reports estimates of the β^m in equation (9). The second and third columns report standard errors and t-statistics. Each row reports a single regressor. Row 1 corresponds to Nunn (2007), row 2 to Levchenko (2007), rows 3–4 to Costinot (2009), row 5 to Cunat and Melitz (2012), and row 6 to Manova (2013). The final two rows correspond to traditional Heckscher-Ohlin interactions of industry variables (human- and physical-capital intensity) with country variables (human and physical capital endowments relative to labor). Looking at the t-statistics, the truly remarkable conclusion is that each and every one of the regressors is individually significant.

Chor's findings raise an important question: How is it that all the determinants are significant? The answer lies in the fact that although the determinants considered are each highly significant, the contribution of each to the overall variation in trade patterns is small. For example, Nunn (2007, p. 583) reports that his judicial quality–contract intensity interaction only explains 2.3% of the residual variation in the pattern of trade i.e., variation after controlling for country fixed effects and industry fixed effects. Therefore, the many results from the studies examined here can all be simultaneously true without over-explaining the pattern of trade.

Columns 4–5 examine the economic importance of each factor. Beta coefficients are a standardized measure of in-sample fit: They are the predicted standard deviation change in the dependent variable induced by a one standard deviation change in the independent variable. (Beta coefficients are also proportional to the contribution of the regressor to the R^2.) Chor finds that the most important regressors are those suggested by Levchenko (2007) and Nunn (2007). For example, a one standard deviation change in Nunn's $z_g \cdot q_i$ leads to a 0.49 standard deviation change in log exports. Incredibly, both are at least as important as traditional Heckscher-Ohlin determinants of comparative advantage.

Another economic measure of importance is the OLS estimate of β^m times the interquartile range of the explanatory variable. The latter is the 75th quartile minus the 25th quartile. This measure appears in the last column of Table 5.4. By this economic measure, all of the variables are very important. We conclude from this that each of the many institutional determinants of comparative advantage considered in the literature are important for understanding comparative advantage.

In addition to this remarkable conclusion, another remarkable result has come out of the literature. Institutions matter even after controlling for traditional sources of comparative advantage such as factor endowments. Indeed, institutions matter even after controlling for the interaction of per capita GDP with either Nunn's contract-intensity measure (Nunn, 2007, Table 5) or with industry fixed effects (Levchenko, 2007, Table 3). This is a satisfying conclusion. The obvious interpretation is that institutions affect costs more in some industries than in others and that such relative cost impacts are better captured by institutional variables than by endowments or per capita GDP. Adding Ricardian productivity measures at the country-sector level to the above regressions, something no researcher has done, would help confirm that this interpretation is correct.

3. INFORMAL INSTITUTIONS AND THEIR IMPACTS ON COMPARATIVE ADVANTAGE

It is easy to argue that contracting institutions are not important because, when they are weak, alternative institutions evolve to deal with hold-up problems. In this section we explore the ways in which such alternative institutions have impacted comparative advantage and the extent to which they substitute for formal institutions in the fact of contractual incompleteness.

3.1. Repeated Interactions and Dynamics

As is well known, repeated interactions can facilitate cooperation even in an environment in which contract enforcement is poor. Further, repeated interactions themselves can lead to the creation of networks, especially non-kin-based networks. The standard folk theorem suggests that as long as both parties value the future sufficiently, with repetition full investment can be obtained. Empirically, we do observe many instances in which reputation substitutes for formal contract enforcement. For example, Bigsten et al. (2000) show that for manufacturers in Burundi, Cameroon, Ivory Coast, Kenya, Zambia, and Zimbabwe, repeat relationships are very common and are used as a substitute for legal contract enforcement. In these countries, only the largest firms rely on legal forms of contract enforcement. Further, these reputation-based relationships appear to be one of the most important determinants of success. In addition to providing a form of contract enforcement, the relationship, once formed, is also used to share risk and pool information (Fafchamps and Minten, 1999).

McMillan and Woodruff (1999) study buyer–seller relationships within the Vietnamese context, examining 259 non-state firms between 1995 and 1997. They also find evidence for the importance of repeat relationships. Using the provision of trade credit as a proxy for trust, they show that a seller is more trusting of a buyer the longer is the duration of the relationship.

An important point, however, is that repeat relationships and relational contracting is not without costs. Because well-tested relationships have value, buyers and sellers are likely to stick with existing relationships rather than establishing new, untried ones. This creates barriers to entry and inefficiencies, particularly in dynamic environments, where old partnerships soon become less productive. Johnson et al. (2002) provide evidence for such an effect of relational contracting among countries from the former Soviet Union. They examine 1741 privately owned manufacturing firms from Poland, Slovakia, Romania, Russia, and the Ukraine. They ask firms how likely they would be to switch to a supplier that provided an input at a 10% lower price. They find, consistent with repeat relationships causing barriers to entry, that only 50% of firms in the sample would be willing to switch. They also find that firms that perceive the courts to be more effective are more likely to switch. More generally, they find that the primary impact of courts is to encourage the formation of new buyer–seller relationships.

While the importance of repeat relationships for international trade has received little attention, there are notable contributions. Araujo et al. (2012) develop a model of trade with imperfect contract enforcement. Although the model does not have predictions for comparative advantage per se, it does provide insights into reputation-based trade relationships in an environment with incomplete contracting. The model predicts that trading partners will begin trading small volumes that then grow over time. This dynamic generates a positive relationship between duration and the destruction of trading partnerships. Examining Belgian firm-level data from 1995 to 2008, the authors find support for these patterns, as well as others predicted by their reputation-based trade model. In short, the evidence provided in the study suggests that reputation, not just formal contract enforcement, does play a role in international trade. The findings, however, do not provide evidence for whether reputation and repeat relationships are also important for comparative advantage.

3.2. Networks

Very closely related to the notion of repeat interactions is that of networks, which can also help alleviate contracting issues. While repeat relations—and the accompanying folk theorem—are typically thought about bilaterally, networks can feature a large number of individuals or more complex relationship structures that may or may not feature regular repetition.

If being within the network is valuable to its members, then a credible threat of being expelled can maintain cooperative behavior, such as non-renegotiation, even if the single-period relative payoffs provide an incentive to do so.[22] The value of being within the network could arise for a host of reasons. For example, the network may be a social one that provides direct utility to its members. Alternatively, it could be a business network that provides future benefits.

A second, closely related, reason that networks can help alleviate contractual issues is that information flows are typically higher with networks than without. Therefore the formation of networks may make contracts more complete by reducing the states of the world or contingencies that cannot be contracted upon.

Finally, if networks are kin-based, then participants within the network care about the payoffs of others within the network. In other words, entering into contractual relations among those genetically related kin helps to overcome contracting issues because of altruism within the group. The reason why genetically related organisms care about each other is due to gene-level selection under evolutionary forces.

McMillan and Woodruff's (1999) study of Vietnamese firms in the 1990s provides evidence for the importance of business networks. They distinguish between two benefits of networks: Increased ability to sanction and increased information. They argue that the informational benefit of networks should be decreasing over the life of a buyer–seller relationship. Through increased interactions, the buyer and seller gain information about one another over time. The authors find that in the Vietnamese context, and consistent with the importance of networks, buyers identified by sellers through business networks tended to receive more trade credit. Further, they find that this effect persists over the duration of the buyer–seller relationship, suggesting that it reflects the sanctioning of

---

[22] An important caveat here is that the threat of expulsion must be credible. See Greif (1993, 1994) for an examination of this in an environment of long-distance trade with moral hazard issues.

buyers within the network rather than the increased information about buyers within the network.

The analysis of networks within the international trade literature has focused on the effect that the formation of international buyer–seller networks has on aggregate bilateral trade flows (e.g., Rauch, 1999, 2001; Rauch and Trindade, 2002; Chaney, 2011). Although comparative advantage is not at the core of these studies, some of the findings do have implications for the pattern of trade. For example, Gould (1994) estimates a bilateral gravity equation explaining trade with the United States. He examines the importance of immigrant populations for bilateral trade and shows that the presence of immigrant populations from a particular country is positively correlated with trade with that country. In addition, he finds that the effect is greater for consumer goods than for producer goods. Gould interprets the estimates as reflecting the presence of ethnic networks that facilitate the flow of product information and this increases trade. Gould argues that because consumer goods are more differentiated, information about product characteristics is more important and the effects are stronger for these products relative to producer goods. In a follow-up study, Head and Ries (1998) confirm Gould's findings for immigrant populations in Canada.

Rauch and Trindade (2002) also consider ethnic networks but focus solely on ethnic Chinese networks. They estimate a standard gravity model of countries' bilateral trade and test how the presence of ethnic Chinese populations in the two countries affects bilateral trade flows. (In the gravity equation, Rauch and Trindade include the product of the two shares.) The estimates show that the presence of ethnic Chinese populations in both the importing and exporting countries increases bilateral trade. The authors then disaggregate total trade into goods that are bought and sold on organized exchanges, reference-priced, or differentiated. They find that the impact of ethnic Chinese populations is greatest for differentiated goods, precisely where one might think that informational barriers to trade are most pronounced and hence networks most important.

The studies by Gould (1994) and Rauch and Trindade (2002) provide some evidence that international networks may affect the composition of exports. However, we know little about how the density of domestic networks affects comparative advantage, if at all. One can think about many different reasons that networks would affect production differentially across industries. For example, because resources (e.g., expertise in different fields, entrepreneurship, etc.) within networks tend to be limited—particularly kin-based groups—there are limits to the types of goods that could be produced. It is more difficult to produce more sophisticated goods that require a diversity of skills, expertise, and inputs working solely within a small network. It is possible that higher quality formal contract enforcement (rather than informal networks) enables firms to specialize much more in the production of goods that require expansion beyond the network.

Kolasa (2012) is one of the only studies that provides direct evidence on the importance of informal networks for solving contracting issues. The author examines 10,000 large firms in India from 1998 to 2008. He first shows that firms located in states with better judicial quality tend to capture a greater market share in industries that are contract intensive as defined and measured by Nunn (2007). He then shows that this comparative-advantage effect is much weaker among firms operating within business groups, which are networks of firms with informal connections with one another. It has been argued that these networks, where participants are "linked by relations of interpersonal trust, on the basis of a similar personal, ethnic, or communal background," have emerged in response to institutional failures (Leff, 1978, p. 663). One of the primary benefits of these networks is that they facilitate the purchase and sale of intermediate inputs (Leff, 1978). Therefore, Kolasa's findings suggest that, at least in the Indian context, underinvestment in relationship-specific investments due to imperfect contract enforcement has been partially alleviated by the formation of business groups.

3.3. Cultural Beliefs

The potential importance of cross-country culture differences for determining comparative advantage has received little attention in the literature. There are, however, some important exceptions. Guiso et al. (2009) examine the impact that bilateral trust has on bilateral trade flows. Examining bilateral trade flows among 16 European countries, the authors show that an exporting country's trust of an importing country is strongly correlated with bilateral trade flows even after controlling for importer and exporter fixed effects. The estimated impacts are enormous: A one-standard-deviation increase in bilateral trust is associated with an increase in trade of 1.6 standard deviations. Interestingly, the authors find that the impact of trust only exists for goods classified by Rauch (1999) as differentiated (neither sold on exchanges nor reference priced). Although these results provide some evidence that trust not only affects aggregate trade but also its composition, exactly why differentiated goods are "bilateral-trust-intensive" remains unclear.

Tabellini (2008a) also considers the importance of trust for international trade, but examines the role of trust of citizens within a country rather than trust of those from other countries. He hypothesizes that in contract-intensive industries, trust—in addition to contract enforcement—may be a way to overcome issues related to hold-up. If this is the case, then countries with higher levels of trust should have a comparative advantage in contract-intensive industries.

Tabellini re-estimates the comparative-advantage equations from Nunn (2007)—see equation (1) above—with the addition of an interaction between a country's average level of trust among its citizens and Nunn's contract-intensity measure. Tabellini finds that the trust interaction is highly correlated with trade flows: Countries with more trust tend to specialize in the production of contract-intensive goods. Consistent with the hypothesis that trust can substitute for formal legal enforcement, Tabellini shows that trust only has an impact on the pattern of trade among the countries in the sample with rule of law below the median value.

An important point to bear in mind is that although Tabellini (2008a) and Guiso et al. (2009) both consider trust and trade flows, there is no direct connection between the findings from the two papers. Tabellini considers the level of trust of citizens within a country toward others within the same country. By contrast Guiso et al. do not consider the levels of trust among citizens within a country, but trust between countries. Therefore, it is likely that their analysis has less to do with comparative advantage (as typically understood as being driven by country characteristics), but with frictions between countries and which goods tend to be more sensitive to these distrust-induced trade frictions.

3.4. The Interplay between Culture, Institutions, and International Trade

Belloc and Bowles (2013) study how both culture and institutions can impact comparative advantage. The authors develop a 2-factor, 2-good, and 2-country model in which both preferences (i.e., culture) and contracts (i.e., institutions) are endogenously determined. In the model, production is undertaken by matched employer-employee pairs. Two types of employment contracts are possible: (i) a fixed-wage contract with monitoring and (ii) a partnership where the surplus is split between the employer and the employee.

The cultural trait examined is reciprocity. Employees with reciprocal preferences care about the nature of the contract and their employer's payoff. If the employer implements a fixed-wage monitoring contract the reciprocal worker takes this as a sign of distrust and as a result gets negative utility from the employers' payoff. If the employment contract is a partnership in which the employee's share is judged to be fair, then the employee gets positive utility. Those without the reciprocity trait have conventional self-interested preferences.

The two goods are produced using two types of labor, one that is verifiable and the other that is not. Non-verifiable labor services (e.g., care, creativity, problem-solving) can be provided by the worker in addition to verifiable effort (e.g., time at work, compliance with explicit directions) at a higher cost for him or her. Production requires verifiable aspects of work and productivity is further enhanced by non-verifiable labor services but in different degrees in the two sectors.

Employees in fixed-wage monitoring contracts cannot be forced to provide non-verifiable labor, and they choose not to in equilibrium. By contrast, reciprocal types choose to provide non-verifiable labor under partnership contracts, because in addition to their own return under the share contract, they also place a positive value on the resulting profits of the employer.

In the model, employers' employment contracts (i.e., institutions) and employees' preferences (i.e., culture) evolve over time through a dynamic process based on the relative benefits of each type. The authors show that there are two evolutionarily stable equilibria:

one in which employers choose fixed-wage monitoring contracts and employees do not have reciprocal preferences, and one in which employers choose partnership contracts and employees have reciprocal preferences. Multiple equilibria arise because of the complementarity between partnership contracts and reciprocal preferences. Since reciprocal workers always provide more productive non-verifiable labor services under partnership contracts, countries in the reciprocal preferences, and partnership contracts equilibrium have an absolute advantage in both goods, but also enjoy a comparative advantage in the production of goods intensive in non-verifiable labor investments.

One of the interesting results of the model is that trade liberalization does not support convergence to Pareto-optimal cultural-institutional equilibria configurations, but instead enhances the persistence of existing cultures and institutions, even Pareto-dominated ones.

Tabellini (2008b) provides a theoretical framework for understanding the coevolution of culture and institutions in an environment of international trade. He considers a setting where a continuum of individuals are located on a circle. Individuals are randomly matched and play a prisoner's dilemma game, which can be interpreted as exchange. It is assumed that in addition to material payoffs, individuals obtain utility from cheating on the other trader. The utility from cooperating is decreasing in the distance between the two traders; distance can be interpreted as geographic, cultural, etc. There are two types of cultures in the economy: A "bad" culture characterized by a higher rate of utility decay in distance and a "good" type with a lower rate. This environment results in both types not cheating when matched with less-distant traders and cheating when matched with a trader from a further distance away. The cut-off determining cheating versus cooperation is further away for "good" types than for "bad" types.

In the model, preferences are determined endogenously and are shaped by the effort parents expend instilling values in their children. Parents invest in their children, evaluating their child's expected outcome using their own utility function. "Good" parents make investments to instill "good" values in their children and "bad" parents do not.

The setting is then used to examine the impacts of improved enforcement of cooperation (i.e., better institutions) on the equilibrium prevalence of good types in the economy. Interestingly, the impact of better enforcement institutions depends on whether the enforcement is for less-distant (e.g., domestic) versus more-distant (e.g., international) trades. If enforcement is increased for international trade, then this only affects the good types (since the bad types always cheat in more-distant trades). For the good types, the improved institutions increase the trade distances over which they choose to cooperate. This in turn accentuates the differences in actions between the good and bad types, which causes good parents to invest more in their children, causing an increase in the prevalence of good types in society. In other words, improved enforcement of long-distance trades causes an increase in the prevalence of good types in the economy. Enforcement of close (e.g., domestic) trades impacts bad types, but not good types (since they cooperate at these distances no matter what). Specifically, it increases the length of distances over which bad types continue to cooperate. This in turn decreases the difference between good and bad types making it less important for good parents to invest in instilling good values in their children. Therefore, this form of enforcement decreases the amount of good culture in the economy.

The model highlights an interesting asymmetry in the relationship between institutions and culture in the context of international trade. Better enforcement of domestic trades decreases the prevalence of good culture in the economy. Here, better institutions crowd out good culture. However, better enforcement of international trades increases the prevalence of good culture. Here, better institutions crowd in good culture.

Tabellini (2008b) also allows enforcement of distant trades to be an endogenous outcome of voting. He shows that if the initial prevalence of bad types is large enough, then voting results in weak enforcement (i.e., poor institutions), which in turn maintains a low level of good types in the economy. Here, because of the complementarity between culture and institutions, a society can be stuck in an equilibrium with low levels of successful exchange, poor institutions, and bad culture.

3.5. Vertical Integration, Offshoring, and Outsourcing

Another way for firms to partially overcome underinvestment due to hold-up is through vertical integration. If hold-up is one-sided then underinvestment can be alleviated if the other party purchases and controls the party that underinvests. If hold-up is two-sided, so that both parties underinvest, then the total underinvestment can be reduced by allocating control to one party or the other. If profits are more sensitive to the buyer's underinvestment, then it will be efficient for the buyer to purchase (control) the selling firm. Similarly, if profits are more sensitive to the seller's underinvestment, then it will be efficient for the seller of the product to purchase the buying firm. In short, the possibility of vertical integration provides an additional tool that can be used to help alleviate underinvestment due to hold-up.

The possibility that vertical integration, by affecting the severity of incomplete contracting, has an impact on comparative advantage is noted in Nunn (2007). He reasons that vertical integration as a way to overcome incomplete contracts is more difficult if production requires many different inputs. In this case, a firm has to vertically integrate with many different suppliers to reduce underinvestment. If instead a producer has one important supplier, then underinvestment can be overcome with only one purchase. Consistent with vertical integration being used to alleviate hold-up, he shows that the impact of a country's rule of law on specialization in contract-intensive industries is smaller among the subset of industries that have a large number of inputs (i.e., in which vertical integration is more difficult).

Ferguson and Formai (2011) provide a deeper empirical examination of the interaction between contract enforcement, vertical integration, and comparative advantage.

The authors construct a measure of the ease of vertical integration across industries by looking at the actual prevalence of vertical integration within the United States. The authors re-estimate Nunn's (2007) comparative advantage equations using his measure of contract intensity, but allow for a differential impact of the rule of law on specialization in contract-intensive industries. Consistent with vertical integration providing a way of (at least partially) alleviating contracting issues, they find weaker comparative advantage effects in industries in which vertical integration is easier.

The most progress, on both the theoretical and empirical front, has been on the determinants of vertical integration internationally rather than domestically. A discussion of the determinants of international vertical integration (i.e., FDI versus outsourcing) appears in the Antràs and Yeaple chapter of this handbook volume (see Chapter 2).[23] Although the focus of the literature is on explaining the determinants of the boundaries of the multinational firm, some of the findings provide insights into the determinants of countries' specialization of production. The manner in which contracting institutions affect the way goods are traded (i.e., within or outside of firm boundaries), not just what goods are traded, is also an important impact of institutions for international trade.

Antràs and Helpman (2004) model a headquarter, located in a developed country (North), that chooses to source its products either domestically or from a developing country (South), and either within firm boundaries or at arm's length. The model allows for a headquarter-and-supplier specific (i.e., match-specific) productivity of production. Production is Cobb-Douglas in two inputs: headquarter-provided services and supplier-produced components.

After observing the productivity of the match, the headquarter decides whether to source the product from the North or the South, and whether to vertically integrate or not. The fixed costs associated with each decision satisfy: $f_v^s > f_o^s > f_v^n > f_o^n$, where f_v^s is the fixed cost of vertically integrating production in the South, f_o^s is the fixed cost of sourcing from a stand-alone firm in the South, f_v^n is the fixed cost of vertical integration in the North, and f_o^n is the fixed cost of outsourcing in the North.

As is standard in this literature, it is assumed that contracts are incomplete. Therefore, the headquarter and input supplier bargain over the surplus from the relationship ex post. As in Antràs (2003), the distribution of the surplus is sensitive to the organizational form. When the headquarter owns the input supplier, it is assumed that the headquarter obtains a greater share of the ex-post surplus than when it does not own the firm. Because the ex-post non-contractability affects ex-ante investment, which organizational form is chosen by the headquarter depends on which party's inputs are relatively more important in the production process. If the supplier's investment is most crucial to production, then it is optimal for the headquarter to incentivize the supplier by not vertically integrating. This is the basic insight from Antràs (2003).

---

[23] For earlier reviews of this literature see Spencer (2005), Helpman (2006), and Nunn and Trefler (2008).

Working through the model, Antràs and Helpman (2004) show that the location of production and ownership structure are driven by the relative importance of the headquarter's contribution and the supplier's contribution to production. When the supplier's components are relatively more important, then outsourcing is always preferred to vertical integration. In this environment, the headquarter wants to incentivize the supplier's investment and does this through outsourcing. In addition, the fixed costs of outsourcing are lower than the fixed cost of vertical integration whether the component is produced in the North or the South. Therefore, it is always optimal for the headquarter to purchase the component at arm's length. Further, it is shown that for less productive matches, the component is sourced from the North (which has lower fixed costs but higher wages) and for more productive matches the component is sourced from the South (which has higher fixed costs but lower wages).

When headquarter services are relatively more important, then the headquarter no longer wants to incentivize the supplier (whose investments are less important). Now there is a trade-off since the fixed costs of vertical integration are greater than the fixed cost of outsourcing. The decision of whether to outsource or vertically integrate now depends on the trade-off between higher fixed costs and more efficient production. The benefit depends crucially on the productivity of the match. Intuitively, for more productive matches (with greater production), underinvestment is relatively more important than the one-time fixed costs. This suggests that all else equal more productive matches will vertically integrate.

Antràs and Helpman (2004) fully characterize both the location and integration decision for this scenario. They show that the sourcing strategy of the headquarter depends on the productivity of the match, and the outcome can be characterized by four regions in the productivity space. In the region of the lowest productivity matches, the headquarter chooses to source the component from a stand-alone supplier in the North. In the next more productive region the headquarter vertically integrates with a Northern supplier. Matches of even greater productivity induce the headquarter to source from a stand-alone firm in the South, and the most productive matches result in vertical integration in the South.

Although Antràs and Helpman (2004) do not model a country's contracting environment explicitly, it is reasonable to believe that the average quality of the buyer-supplier match (or their dispersion within industries and countries) may be affected by the quality of domestic institutions. For example, better institutions, all else equal will generate more productive matches. According to their model, this will result in more components being produced in the South, and in a greater prevalence of FDI relative to outsourcing.

Antràs and Helpman (2008) extend the model of Antràs and Helpman (2004) and explicitly model contracting institutions. They do this by allowing for partial contractibility of the inputs provided by the headquarter and of the supplier. It is assumed that a portion μ_h of the headquarter's inputs is contractible and a portion μ_m of the supplier's inputs is contractible. They show that all of the intuition of Antràs and Helpman (2004) continues to hold, with one important exception. Now, when the headquarter engages in its make-or-buy decision, what is important is no longer the relative contribution of the inputs of the headquarter and supplier, but the relative contribution of the *non-contractible* inputs of the headquarter and supplier. This is intuitive, since it is the non-contractible inputs that lead to underinvestment by both parties, which in turn affects the headquarter's make-or-buy decision.

Nunn and Trefler (2013) test the implications of Antràs and Helpman (2008). Specifically, they show that as predicted by the model, when looking across industries, an increase in non-contractible inputs provided by the headquarter is associated with greater FDI and less outsourcing, which they measure at the industry level using the share of U.S. imports that are intra-firm. By contrast, an increase in contractible inputs provided by the headquarter is not associated with a greater share of intra-firm imports. The authors follow Antràs (2003) and assume that capital is an input provided by the headquarter. They further disaggregate capital into buildings, computers, automobiles, and other machinery. They assume that investments in buildings, computers, and automobiles are contractible because they have value outside of the relationship i.e., they are not relationship-specific.

Unfortunately, the model of Antràs and Helpman (2008) does not yield clear predictions for changes in contractibility of the supplier's input. When the headquarter's input is unimportant, an increase in the supplier's contractibility μ_m has no impact on the headquarter's sourcing decision, and when the headquarter's input is important an increase in μ_m increases the share of components sourced from the South, but has an ambiguous impact on the share of these that are through FDI versus outsourcing (i.e., on the share of imports that are intra-firm). The ambiguity arises due to two effects that work in opposite directions. One effect, which Nunn and Trefler (2008) call the "standard effect", is that an improvement in μ_m causes some U.S. production to migrate abroad where it is outsourced, decreasing the share of U.S. imports that are intra-firm. The second effect, which they call the "surprise effect," arises because an improvement in μ_m causes the most productive outsourcing relationships to become vertically integrated, increasing the share of U.S. imports that are intra-firm. In reality, which of the two effects dominates is an empirical question.

Nunn and Trefler (2008) examine data on U.S. intra-firm imports of 5423 products from 210 countries and conclude that improved contracting of the suppliers' inputs increases the share of imports that are intra-firm. They use Nunn's (2007) measure of contract intensity (the share of intermediate inputs that are relationship-specific and susceptible to hold-up problems) to measure the proportion of the supplier's production that is non-contractible. They find that consistent with Antràs and Helpman (2008), for low values of headquarter intensity a change in supplier contractibility μ_m has no impact on the share of imports that are intra-firm. They also find that in headquarter-intensive industries, the surprise effect dominates the standard effect. In other words, an increase in supplier contractibility is associated with an increase in the share of U.S. imports that are intra-firm.

Costinot et al. (2011) propose an alternative measure of contractability based on the extent to which production is composed of predictable and routine tasks, arguing that these can be foreseen and written into contracts. Using information from the U.S. Department of Labor's Dictionary of Occupation Titles (DOT) on the extent to which industries are composed of tasks for which "making decisions and solving problems" are important, the authors construct a measure of routineness that is based on the absence of decisions and problem solving. Their results show that in less routine industries (with worse contractability), a greater share of imports into the United States occurs within firm boundaries.

Their finding is consistent with a Williamsonian theory of firm boundaries, where contracting issues can be overcome through vertical integration. This prediction stands in contrast to a Grossman-Hart-Moore property-rights theory of the firm. Lower contractability of a supplier's product results in a need to incentivize the supplier through independent sourcing rather than vertical integration. Their finding also stands in contrast to Nunn and Trefler (2008) who find that improved contracting is associated with greater vertical integration, not less (at least for the most productive firms).

Overall, the recent literature on the boundaries of the multinational firm show that a country's domestic institutions not only affect what goods a country produces (i.e, its comparative advantage), but they also impact the form that trade takes—namely, whether trade occurs within or outside of firm boundaries. A clear lesson from the literature is that the impacts of institutions on the form of trade are often complex and not obvious ex ante.

4. POLICIES AND THE INDIRECT IMPACTS OF INSTITUTIONS ON COMPARATIVE ADVANTAGE

An important impact of institutions on comparative advantage—and one that we have ignored to this point—arises due to the impact of institutions on intervening factors that in turn affect trade flows. While few papers have examined this indirect relationship directly, there are well-developed literatures showing that: (i) domestic institutions have important and sizeable impacts on many aspects of an economy, such as the accumulation of factors of production and the implementation of economic policies, and (ii) these factors are important for comparative advantage.

Yeaple and Golub (2007) examine the impact of roads, telephone lines, and electrical power generation facilities on comparative advantage and find that roads and electrical power affect comparative advantage, but telecommunications infrastructure does not. These findings complement earlier work by Clague (1991a,b), providing indirect evidence of transportation and communication infrastructure as being important for comparative advantage. In addition, a number of studies (e.g., Romalis, 2004) have shown that a country's stock of physical and human capital are important sources of comparative advantage. Therefore, by affecting the accumulation of infrastructure, education, and capital, domestic institutions also have an indirect impact on comparative advantage.

Institutions not only affect the aggregate endowments of factors in a society, but also their distributions. This is significant since a number of theoretical and empirical papers document the importance of endowment dispersion (inequality) for comparative advantage. These include Grossman and Maggi (2000), Grossman (2004), Ohnsorge and Trefler (2007), and Bombardini et al. (2012). This is another indirect mechanism through which institutions affect comparative advantage.

An additional indirect channel occurs due to the impact of institutions on per capita income. As hypothesized by Linder, per capita income can itself be a source of comparative advantage and affect the pattern of trade. Hallak (2010) provides empirical evidence consistent with income being a source of comparative advantage. Essaji (2008) empirically uncovers another way that underdevelopment may affect comparative advantage. He shows that less-developed countries, with limited human resources and bureaucratic capital, have a comparative disadvantage in the production of products that are heavily exposed to technical regulations. Using data on countries' exports to the United States across 4019 products, he shows that countries with better capacity to meet technical regulations specialize in sectors that have more technical measures.

Turning to policies, Nunn and Trefler (2010) have shown that countries with poor domestic institutions also tend to have tariff structures that are biased toward less skill-intensive industries, which in turn through a dynamic process reduces a country's comparative advantage in skill-intensive industries. Therefore, through endogenous trade policies, domestic institutions can impact comparative advantage.

Once one begins to think about indirect impacts of domestic institutions on the pattern of trade, the potential channels soon become overwhelming. We have simply noted a few here.

5. THE IMPACT OF TRADE AND COMPARATIVE ADVANTAGE ON DOMESTIC INSTITUTIONS

So far we have discussed the impact of institutions on trade and comparative advantage. We have also repeatedly noted a severe endogeneity problem: International trade can have impacts on domestic institutions. Viewed in this way, this reverse causality is nothing more than a nuisance, a detour on the route to understanding the impacts of institutions on comparative advantage. However, it is less widely recognized that the impact of international trade on domestic institutions may be a tremendously important phenomenon. Increasingly, research outside of the mainstream of international economics is providing evidence that international trade has had major impacts on the evolution of domestic institutions. Given that institutions are slow-moving, much of the evidence is from the fields of economic history and economic growth. These studies are reviewed in Section 5.1.

A shortcoming of this literature from our perspective is that it typically focuses on the *volume* of trade rather than on the mix of goods being traded i.e., on comparative advantage. One of the surprising conclusions of this review is that international trade's confusingly varied impacts on domestic institutions can in fact be systematically explained by comparative advantage: The mix of goods that a country exports has a profound impact on the form of the institutions that develop. The example of the Atlantic triangle trade (English manufacturing exports, Caribbean sugar exports, and African slave exports) is one of many illustrative historical examples reviewed in Section 5.2. Contemporary examples are reviewed in Section 5.3.

5.1. International Trade and Domestic Institutional Change

Medieval Europe experienced a massive expansion of long-distance trade during the "Commercial Revolution" of 950–1350 (e.g., de Roover, 1965; Lopez, 1971; North and Thomas, 1973). In response, medieval Europe embarked on a set of major institutional reforms that laid the groundwork for the Rise of the West.

Medieval long-distance trade created a host of commitment problems. Consider a merchant traveling to a distant land. First, the merchant sets out with the capital of his investors, literally carrying the capital over the horizon and out of sight. What real commitment could the merchant give to his investors? Second, the merchant arrives in a foreign land ruled by a powerful monarch who has every short-run incentive to expropriate the merchant's goods. What real commitment could the ruler give to foreign merchants? Third, the merchant contracts with other merchants from other lands who have every short-run incentive to cheat and run. What real commitments could merchants from diverse lands give each other? The Commercial Revolution, by creating the potential for great profits from long-distance trade, was an impetus to institutional innovations that solved these three commitment problems in a way that proved fundamental to Europe's later growth miracle. The innovations included the rapid development of property-right institutions and contracting institutions.

The most discussed innovation is the Law Merchant, which is universally accepted as the foundation of modern commercial law (Berman, 1983). Its very scope—the use of a court of peers to adjudicate commercial disputes between merchants traveling in distant lands—means that the Law Merchant was a direct and immediate response to the needs of long-distance trade (Kadens, 2004). Milgrom et al. (1990) discuss how the Law Merchant was a response to commitment problems. Other examples include property-right protections that committed rulers not to prey on merchants (Greif et al., 1994), the rise of a nascent Western legal system beginning exactly when long-distance trade began to take off (Berman, 1983; Landau, 2004), and the development of many new innovations in contracting institutions (e.g., González de Lara (2008) and additional work by Greif described below). By the early fourteenth century, the latter included: the appearance of rudimentary limited-liability joint stock companies (the *commenda*); thick markets for debt (especially bills of exchange); secondary markets for a wide variety of debt, equity and mortgage instruments; bankruptcy laws that distinguished illiquidity from insolvency; double-entry accounting methods; business education (including the use of algebra for currency conversions); deposit banking; and a reliable medium of exchange. All of these innovations can be related directly back to the demands of long-distance trade. See Puga and Trefler (2012).

The above historical research is pervaded by two themes. First, institutional change does not occur because it is efficient, but because it is advanced by powerful special interests. Second, as trade grows it affects the domestic distribution of income and hence the relative power of competing special interests. It is this change in relative power that drives institutional change.

Puga and Trefler's (2012) analysis of Venice during the Commercial Revolution illustrates these two themes. They show that increases in long-distance trade that were exogenous to Venice enriched a broad-based group of merchants and these merchants then pushed for constraints on the executive i.e., for the end of a *de facto* hereditary Doge in 1032 and for the establishment of a parliament or Great Council in 1172. The merchants also pushed for remarkably modern innovations in contracting institutions (such as the *commenda*) that facilitated large-scale mobilization of capital for risky long-distance trade. The fact that participation in long-distance trade was inclusive and risky (which leads to rapid income churning) led to a society that displayed remarkable economic, political, and social mobility. Over time, a group of extraordinarily rich merchants emerged and in 1323 they were able to erect barriers to political mobility: Participation in parliament became hereditary. These rich merchants then built a coercive state apparatus that was used to suppress opposition. With this state apparatus in place, the rich merchants moved to reduce competition on the most lucrative segments of long-distance trade, especially the state-controlled galley trade. Puga and Trefler document this "oligarchization" using a unique database on the names of 8103 parliamentarians and their families' use of the *commenda*. They show that before 1323 there was tremendous political mobility into and out of parliament and broad-based participation in the *commenda*. After 1323, the oligarchs formed themselves into an exclusive nobility and non–oligarch participation in the *commenda* melted away. In short, long-distance trade first encouraged institutional dynamism and then created powerful forces that blocked social inclusion. These changes operated via the impacts of trade on the distribution of wealth and power.

The role of income distribution as a mediator of the impact of trade on institutions appears elsewhere. Greif and Laitin (2004) and Greif (2006b) study the role of changing income distribution for institutional change in their comparative study of Venice and Genoa. They show that the (endogenous) evolution of income distribution was a decisive force behind Genoa's political instability. Jha (2010) uses detailed data from the English Long Parliament (1640–1660) to examine the formation of a coalition supporting stronger constraints on the Crown. Using data on the investments of about 500 parliamentarians, Jha finds that a financial innovation—shares in overseas companies that allowed broader investor participation—was key in aligning interests against royal discretion over foreign economic affairs.

Jha (2008) provides evidence that in medieval India, overseas trade generated domestic institutions that helped to maintain peace between Hindus and Muslims until this day. Looking across cities within modern India, Jha finds a negative relationship between participation in overseas trade during the medieval period and religious conflict during the late 19th and early 20th centuries. Because Muslims provided access to the markets of the Middle East, in the towns connected to this overseas trade the returns to Hindu–Muslim cooperation were much higher. As a result, institutions that supported exchange and a peaceful coexistence between Hindus and Muslims were developed.

5.2. Heterogeneous Impacts of Trade on Institutions: The Role of Comparative Advantage

The previous subsection dealt with the impacts of rising trade without reference to comparative advantage. From a historical perspective, the rise of the Atlantic three-corner trade following the discovery of the Americas provides a nice case study for examining the impacts of comparative advantage on institutional development. Merchants and entrepreneurs in each of the three corners of the trade—Europe, the Americas, and Africa—specialized in the production and export of very different commodities. While Europe specialized in the production of manufactures such as firearms, gunpowder, copper and iron products, the Americas specialized in the production of raw commodities such as sugar, tobacco, and cotton, while Africa specialized in the export of human beings (slaves). The standard trade circuit saw manufactured items being shipped to Africa for slaves, which were then shipped to the Americas for raw commodities, which were then shipped to Europe where they were used in production (e.g., cotton) or consumption (e.g., sugar).

A number of studies, primarily in the historical development literature, have separately estimated the institutional impacts of specialization in each corner of the trade. For Africa, comparative advantage during the Atlantic trade is equated with the most malign form of resource extraction: the slaving of human beings. Nunn (2008a) shows that the slaving of Africans had very negative effects on post-colonial African growth rates: Growth was slowest in regions whose populations were largely composed of heavily slaved ethnicities. Nunn and Wantchekon (2011) examine the mechanism involved. They document numerous accounts of (supposed) friends, family members, and neighbors tricking, kidnapping, and selling each other into slavery. In the environment of complete insecurity brought on by the slave trade, the temptation to slave or be enslaved proved too much for many. The authors hypothesize that in such an environment, norms of mistrust may have evolved and spread throughout society. Combining individual-level survey data with ethnicity-level slave export estimates (constructed using data sources from Nunn, 2008a), the authors show that individuals belonging to an ethnicity that was more severely affected by the Indian Ocean and trans-Atlantic slave trades exhibit less trust today. This is true for trust in relatives, neighbors, co-ethnics, other ethnicities, and the local government. The authors show that part of this is explained by the fact that the slave trades had a detrimental impact on local institutions that enforce good behavior. Another part is explained by persistent norms of mistrust that evolved over time and persist until today.

The significance of these findings lies in the fact that we now increasingly understand, both theoretically and empirically, that trust is a fundamental determinant of economic development (Fukuyama, 1995; Algan and Cahuc, 2010). Inikori (2003) offers a mechanism consistent with the comparative advantage view in which specialization determines the type of institutions demanded. Inikori points out that Africa was forced to specialize in goods (human slaves) whose production does not require high-quality domestic institutions. To the contrary, the slave trade required *insecurity* of property rights and the *disrespect* of human rights. That is, comparative advantage specialization in slaves created a demand for growth-retarding institutional change.

In Latin America, trade led to specialization in plantation products such as sugar, tobacco, and cotton and in extractive activities such as silver mining. These activities required large landholdings and coercive labor policies that created extreme inequality, with a handful of Europeans garnering vast fortunes. Engerman and Sokoloff (1997, 2000) argue that this comparative advantage specialization and the resulting economic inequality allowed these European elites to dominate politics and shield themselves from economic and social competition. This "shield" involved growth-retarding institutions such as skewed land-tenure rights, abusive labor rights, corporate law, and financial regulation that favored incumbents, and the under-provision of education and other public goods. See also Engerman and Sokoloff (2012).

A particularly careful empirical study of this phenomenon appears in Dell's (2010) fine-grained study of Spanish silver mining in Potosi in modern-day Bolivia. She examines the long-term impacts of the Spanish forced labor system—mining *mita*—that was used to recruit slaves to work in the Potosi silver mines. She finds that the forced labor system had permanent long-term impacts on consumption, education, and public-goods provisions. Naritomi et al. (2012) study the impact of comparative advantage specialization across Brazilian municipalities. They find that colonial specialization in sugar is associated with greater inequality today and that specialization in gold mining is associated with worse governance and property-rights institutions today.

Bruhn and Gallego (2012) extend the Engerman and Sokoloff (1997) thesis in their comparative study of North and South America. The authors construct an impressive dataset of the goods that were initially produced across 345 regions in 17 countries in the Americas. The authors divide the goods into two categories: (i) Those that display economies of scale and were historically produced using coercive methods including slavery e.g., gold, silver, and sugar; and, (ii) Those that display constant returns to scale e.g., subsistence crops, ranching, and manufacturing. The authors show that regions that specialized in increasing-returns goods are less developed today. Further, regions that specialized in constant-returns goods were *not* guaranteed future development because in some of those regions, those with large native populations, constant-returns production may have employed coerced native labor. On a closely related point, Mitchener and McLean (2003) show that the parts of the United States that relied heavily on slave labor in 1860, subsequently had lower levels of labor productivity in manufacturing. Similarly, Nunn (2008b) shows that the historical use of slave labor is associated with long-term underdevelopment both within the United States and across the Americas more broadly.

Europe's experience during the Atlantic trade was very different from the Americas and Africa. Many have argued that the Atlantic trade played an important part in the industrial revolution (e.g., Inikori, 2002). Acemoglu et al. (2005b) empirically examine this assertion, focusing in particular on the institutional impacts of the trade. In Britain and the Netherlands, the Atlantic trade shifted the balance of political power in favor of commercial interests and away from the interests of the royal circle. Since the merchants representing commercial interests were in favor of strong property-rights protections, they used their newfound political muscle to push for reforms that constrained the power of the monarchy. Perhaps the most famous of these is the Glorious Revolution of 1688 which dramatically shifted power from the English Crown to Parliament (Acemoglu and Robinson, 2012, Chapter 7).

To study the links between trade, institutions and economic growth, Acemoglu et al. (2005b) examine variation across countries and cities and show that the rise of Western Europe was due to the economic growth of Atlantic traders—in particular, Britain, the Netherlands, France, Portugal, and Spain. In addition, they also show that the quality of domestic institutions, measured by constraints on the executive, were improved by the Atlantic trade. Perhaps the most interesting part of their analysis is their examination of heterogeneity. They show that among the countries with better initial institutions (measured in 1400 and 1500), the Atlantic trade resulted in greater institutional improvements and greater economic growth. In other words, the impact of international trade on domestic institutions depends critically on initial conditions.

Acemoglu et al.'s finding that the impacts of international trade were dependent on initial conditions has also been shown in other contexts. In particular, in a series of articles Greif (1992, 1993, 1994, 2006a,b) examines how the impacts of medieval trade differed across regions within the Old World. He argues that today's institutions constrain the set of institutions that can develop tomorrow and therefore, trade's impact will depend on initial institutions. While initial property-rights institutions are part of the equation, they need not be the most salient. This is illustrated by Greif's comparative analysis of medieval trade in Western Europe versus the Islamic world (including the Maghreb in North Africa). Comparing initial institutions in Western European versus Islam, one sees individualistic versus kin-based institutions, weak versus strong states, and norms of self-legitimization versus religion-based legitimization. At the start of the medieval period, both regions organized trade in kin-based (and community-based) networks. However, as trade expanded, its volume reached a level that was not supportable by kin-based organizations. The Western European response, as we have seen, was a set of new institutions such as the precursor of the modern corporation. These corporations were collections of non-kin-based individuals and were legitimated by the civil statutes of the cities that flourished under relatively weak Western European monarchs. In contrast, such an institutional response was not possible in Islam. Indeed, one continues to see limited institutional responses to this day, as evidenced for example by the problems with Islamic banking.

Another example of the importance of initial institutions is found in a trio of papers that estimate the impact of terms-of-trade shocks on wages in coercive societies (Bobonis and Morrow, 2010; Dippel et al., 2012; Naidu and Yuchtman, 2013). In neoclassical trade models, favorable term-of-trade shocks translate into positive demand shocks and positive demand shocks translate into higher wages. However, this need not be the case in coercive societies. Dippel et al. (2012) examine the impact of secular movements in sugar prices on wages and coercion in 14 British Caribbean sugar colonies over the period 1838–1914. In a regression of wages on world sugar prices they estimate a zero coefficient on sugar prices. They then argue that this zero effect is caused by an offsetting institutional effect: When sugar prices rise secularly, the plantation elite grows stronger and uses coercion to depress wages. To show this, Dippel et al. first use archival data on the share of sugar in total exports to get a measure of the strength of the plantation economy by colony and year. When this measure is added to their wage regression, the coefficient on sugar becomes very positive (the neoclassical channel) and the coefficient on the strength of the plantation economy becomes very negative (the institutional channel). Dippel et al. (2012) also show that higher sugar prices translate into more coercion as measured by incarceration rates of those of African origin. Finally, Dippel et al. provide a precise mechanism. When the plantation economy is strong, there is no land available for small freeholds so that workers have no choice but to work on the plantation. This makes coercion cheap.[24]

Bobonis and Morrow (2010) examine the impact of world coffee price shocks on labor coercion in 19th century Puerto Rico. Between 1849 and 1874, unskilled workers were forced to work for legally titled landowners. Using variation in labor demand driven by changes in world coffee prices, they show that increased demand for labor increased the coercive measures undertaken by Puerto Rican landowners.

---

[24] Acemoglu and Wolitzky (2011) define coercion as an active attempt to reduce the outside options of workers. As will become apparent, the examples studied in Bobonis and Morrow (2010), Dippel et al. (2012), and Naidu and Yuchtman (2013) are all instances of coercion in this sense.

Finally, Naidu and Yuchtman (2013) examine the impact of labor demand shocks on wages during a coercive period of British labor history. While their paper is not about trade per se, the analysis is of obvious relevance and elegance. The 18th century British Master and Servant Act forced apprentices to sign long-term contracts with their masters. If an apprentice ran away—as was common when positive demand shocks led masters to compete for apprentices—the run-away was criminally prosecuted. Naidu and Yuchtman show that during periods of high demand the Act prevented apprentice wages from rising and led to more incarcerations. Further, when the Act was repealed in 1875, wages became more responsive to demand shocks, especially in those counties with initially high incarceration rates i.e., in those counties that exported textiles, iron, and coal.

5.3. Comparative Advantage and Domestic Institutions: Contemporary Evidence

The insight that international trade can have very different impacts depending on initial conditions and comparative advantage has also been empirically verified using contemporary data. This is most immediately seen in the literature on the "curse of natural resources," which documents a negative relationship between specialization in natural resource production and economic growth. See Ross (1999) for a review of the literature. A number of studies focus on oil production and find that specialization is associated with negative institutional development. An early contributor to this literature is Barro (1999), whose cross-country regression estimates show that oil extraction hinders democracy. Tsui (2011) documents a relationship between oil discoveries and movements of regimes away from democracy and toward autocracy.

The historical evidence examined above suggests that the impact of trade depends on which groups are enriched by changes in the structure of production. According to Acemoglu et al. (2005b), the Atlantic trade empowered merchants that supported pro-business institutions and constraints on the monarchy. In a contemporary context, Braun and Raddatz (2008) test for this same mechanism, but within the context of financial development. A benefit of a more developed financial system is that it facilitates the entry of new firms, thereby increasing competition and reducing the rents of incumbents. The authors use the average price–cost margin of firms in an industry as a measure of the degree of product market competition and profitability of incumbents. They then estimate the relationship between the price–cost margin and a country's level of financial development (measured as private credit to GDP) for 28 3-digit ISIC industries.[25] This generates, for each industry, a measure of the extent to which financial development erodes incumbent profits in the industry. This is then used to group industries into "promoters" and "opponents" of financial development. The "opponents" are defined as the

---

[25] In practice, in a country and industry panel, the price–cost margin is regressed on industry fixed effects, country fixed effects, and country-level financial development interacted with industry fixed effects.

14 industries for which financial development has the most adverse effect on incumbent profitability; the "promoters" are the remaining 14 industries. Braun and Raddatz (2008) then examine the liberalization episodes of 73 countries and show that improvements in financial development following liberalization episodes were greater the greater the economic growth of "promoters" relative to "opponents" of financial development. In other words, if the industries that were strengthened due to trade liberalization were industries that tended to be hurt most by financial development, then financial development tended to be slow after liberalization.

Do and Levchenko (2007) also focus on the relative demand for financial innovation across industries. They start by observing that some industries require more external finance than others. They hypothesize that countries with a comparative advantage in industries that are highly dependent on external finance will have a greater demand for external finance and hence more developed financial markets. To show this empirically, they estimate a cross-section regression in which the dependent variable is private credit as a share of GDP and the key independent variable is the average external-finance intensity of a country's exports. All variables are measured as annual averages from 1970 to 1999. The coefficient estimate is positive, indicating that trade, by raising the demand for external finance, can lead to financial development. To account for potential reverse causality, Do and Levchenko employ an IV strategy that extends the strategy of Frankel and Romer (1999) to a multi-industry setting. In particular, the authors estimate the gravity regressions from Frankel and Romer (1999) sector by sector (across ISIC 3-digit industries) and construct country- and sector-specific measures of predicted exports. They then use this measure of predicted exports to calculate a measure of a country's financial dependence of predicted exports. This is used as an instrument for a country's actual measure of financial dependence of exports.

In subsequent analysis, Levchenko (2013) estimates the relationship between a country's average rule-of-law measure between 1996 and 2000 and its average contract intensity of predicted exports between 1970 and 1999, where predicted exports are constructed as in Do and Levchenko (2007). Levchenko combines the measure of predicted exports with Nunn's (2007) measure of contract intensity. He finds a robust positive relationship between the contract intensity of a country's predicted exports and its rule of law. This is interpreted as evidence that a natural comparative advantage in contract-intensive industries increases the returns to improved institutions and thus causes better institutions in the long run. In other words, trade and comparative advantage shape domestic institutions.

Finally, there is also a literature that examines the potential impacts that international trade has on cultural traits. See for example Olivier et al. (2008), Thoenig et al. (2009), and Atkin (2013).

To conclude, the historical evidence makes clear that international trade has had pronounced impacts on domestic institutions. We noted that for institutions to change, the change must be supported by powerful special interests. Often it is trade itself that makes these groups powerful. Finally, the type of trade (whether or not it involves the production of goods that require good supporting institutions) and the level of coercion trade generates play key roles in whether the institutional change is growth-enhancing or growth-retarding.

6. CONCLUSION

The literature on institutions as a source of comparative advantage has grown rapidly. In this chapter we provided evidence that institutional sources of comparative advantage can and do operate through fundamentally different channels than traditional sources of comparative advantage such as endowments. Indeed, institutional sources of comparative advantage are quantitatively as important as traditional sources. We also reviewed the rapidly growing literature on the impact of international trade on domestic institutions. These impacts are profound, so much so that one is left conjecturing that the impact of international trade on domestic institutions is the single most important source of long-run gains from trade.

REFERENCES

Acemoglu, D., Dell, M., 2010. Productivity differences between and within countries. American Economic Journal: Macroeconomics 2 (1), 169–188.
Acemoglu, D., Johnson, S., 2004. Unbundling institutions. Journal of Political Economy 113, 949–995.
Acemoglu, D., Robinson, J.A., 2012. Why Nations Fail: The Origins of Power, Prosperity, and Poverty. Crown Publishing, New York, NY.
Acemoglu, D., Wolitzky, A., 2011. The economics of labor coercion. Econometrica 79 (2), 555–600.
Acemoglu, D., Johnson, S., Robinson, J.A., 2001. The colonial origins of comparative development: an empirical investigation. American Economic Review 91, 1369–1401.
Acemoglu, D., Johnson, S., Robinson, J.A., 2005a. Institutions as the fundamental cause of long-run growth. In: Aghion, P., Durlauf, S. (Eds.), Handbook of Economic Growth, vol. 1A. North-Holland, London, pp. 386–464.
Acemoglu, D., Johnson, S., Robinson, J.A., 2005b. The rise of Europe: Atlantic trade, institutional change and economic growth. American Economic Review 95, 546–579.
Agell, J., Lundborg, P., 1995. Fair wages in the open economy. Economica 62 (247), 335–351.
Ahn, J., Khandelwal, A.K., Wei, S.J., 2011. The role of intermediaries in facilitating trade. Journal of International Economics 84 (1), 73–85.
Akerman, A., 2010. A Theory on the Role of Wholesalers in International Trade Based on Economies of Scope. Research Papers in Economics 2010:1, Department of Economics, Stockholm University, January.
Algan, Y., Cahuc, P., 2010. Inherited trust and growth. American Economic Review 100 (5), 2060–2092.
Amiti, M., Davis, D.R., 2012. Trade, firms, and wages: theory and evidence. Review of Economic Studies 79 (1), 1–36.
Antràs, P., 2003. Firms, contracts and trade structure. Quarterly Journal of Economics 118, 1375–1418.
Antràs, P., Costinot, A., 2010. Intermediation and economic integration. American Economic Review Papers and Proceedings 100 (2), 424–428.
Antràs, P., Costinot, A., 2011. Intermediated trade. Quarterly Journal of Economics 126 (3), 1319–1374.

Antràs, P., Foley, C.F., 2011. Poultry in Motion: A Study of International Trade Finance Practices. NBER Working Papers 17091, National Bureau of Economic Research, May.

Antràs, P., Helpman, E., 2004. Global sourcing. Journal of Political Economy 112, 552–580.

Antràs, P., Helpman, E., 2008. Contractual frictions and global sourcing. In: Helpman, E., Marin, D., Verdier, T. (Eds.), The Organization of Firms in a Global Economy. Harvard University Press, Cambridge, pp. 9–54.

Araujo, L., Mion, G., Ornelas, E., 2012. Institutions and Export Dynamics. Mimeo, London School of Economics.

Atkin, D., 2013. Trade, tastes and nutrition in India. American Economic Review 103 (5), 1629–1663.

Baldwin, R.E., 1989. Exporting the capital markets: comparative advantage and capital market imperfections. In: Audretsch, D.B., Sleuwaegen, L., Yamawaki, H. (Eds.), The Convergence of International and Domestic Markets. North-Holland, Amsterdam, pp. 135–152.

Barro, R.J., 1999. Determinants of democracy. Journal of Political Economy 107 (6/2), S158–S183.

Basker, E., Van, P.H., 2010. Imports "R" us: retail chains as platforms for developing-country imports. American Economic Review Papers and Proceedings 100 (2), 414–418.

Beck, T., 2002. Financial development and international trade: is there a link? Journal of International Economics 57 (1), 107–131.

Beck, T., 2003. Financial dependence and international trade. Review of International Economics 11, 296–316.

Beck, T., Demirgüç-Kunt, A., Levine, R., 2010. Financial institutions and markets across countries and over time: the updated financial development and structure database. The World Bank Economic Review 24 (1), 77–92.

Becker, B., Chen, J., Greenberg, D., 2012. Financial Development, Fixed Costs and International Trade. Mimeo, Harvard Business School.

Belloc, M., Bowles, S., 2013. Cultural-Institutional Persistence Under Autarchy, International Trade, and Factor Mobility. Santa Fe Working Paper 13–01-003.

Berkowitz, D., Moenius, J., Pistor, K., 2006. Trade, law, and product complexity. Review of Economics and Statistics 88 (2), 363–373.

Berman, H.J., 1983. Law and Revolution: The Formation of the Western Legal Tradition. Harvard University Press, Cambridge, MA.

Bernard, A.B., Eaton, J., Jensen, B., Kortum, S., 2003. Plants and productivity in international trade. American Economic Review 93 (4), 1268–1290.

Bernard, A.B., Jensen, J.B., Redding, S.J., Schott, P.K., 2010. Wholesalers and retailers in U.S. trade. American Economic Review Papers and Proceedings 100 (2), 408–413.

Bernard, A.B., Grazzi, M., Tomasi, C., 2011. Intermediaries in International Trade: Direct Versus Indirect Modes of Export. NBER Working Papers 17711, National Bureau of Economic Research, December.

Bernard, A.B., Blanchard, E.J., Beveren, I.V., Vandenbussche, H.Y., 2012. Carry-Along Trade. NBER Working Papers 18246, National Bureau of Economic Research, July.

Bigsten, A., Collier, P., Dercon, S., Fafchamps, M., Gauthier, B., Gunning, J.W., Oduro, A., Oostendorp, R., Patillo, C., Soderbom, M., Teal, F., Zeufack, A., 2000. Contract flexibility and dispute resolution in African manufacturing. Journal of Development Studies 36 (4), 1–17.

Blum, B.S., Claro, S., Horstmann, I., 2010. Facts and figures on intermediated trade. American Economic Review Papers and Proceedings 100 (2), 419–423.

Blum, B.S., Claro, S., Horstmann, I., 2011. Intermediation and the Nature of Trade Costs: Theory. Mimeo, University of Toronto, June.

Bobonis, G.J., Morrow, P.M., 2010. Labor Coercion and the Accumulation of Human Capital. Mimeo, University of Toronto.

Bombardini, M., Gallipoli, G., Pupato, G., 2012. Skill dispersion and trade flows. American Economic Review 102 (5), 2327–2348.

Botero, J.C., Djankov, S., La Porta, R., de Silanes, F.L., Shleifer, A., 2004. The regulation of labor. Quarterly Journal of Economics 119 (4), 1339–1382.

Braun, M., 2003. Financial Contractibility and Asset Hardness. Mimeo, UCLA.

Braun, M., Raddatz, C., 2008. The politics of financial development: evidence from trade liberalization. Journal of Finance 63 (3), 1469–1508.

Brecher, R.A., 1974. Minimum wage rates and the pure theory of international trade. Quarterly Journal of Economics 88 (1), 98–116.

Bruhn, M., Gallego, F.A., 2012. Good, bad, and ugly colonial activities: do they matter for economic development? Review of Economics and Statistics 94 (2), 433–461.

Caballero, R.J., Hammour, M.L., 1998. The macroeconomics of specificity. Journal of Political Economy 106, 724–767.

Chaney, T., 2005. Liquidity Constrained Exporters. Department of Economics, University of Chicago, Working Papers, July.

Chaney, T., 2011. The Network Structure of International Trade. Working Paper 16753, National Bureau of Economic Research, January.

Chenery, H.B., 1960. Patterns of industrial growth. American Economic Review 50 (4), 624–654.

Chor, D., 2010. Unpacking sources of comparative advantage: a quantitative approach. Journal of International Economics 82 (2), 152–167.

Ciccone, A., Papaioannou, E., 2010. Estimating Cross-Industry Cross-Country Models Using Benchmark Industry Characteristics. Mimeo, Universitat Pompeu Fabra.

Clague, C., 1991a. Factor proportions, relative efficiency and developing countries' trade. Journal of Development Economics 35, 357–380.

Clague, C., 1991b. Relative efficiency, self-containment, and comparative costs of less developed countries. Economic Development and Cultural Change 39, 507–530.

Copeland, B.R., 1989. Efficiency wages in a Ricardian model of international trade. Journal of International Economics 27 (3–4), 221–244.

Costinot, A., 2009. On the origins of comparative advantage. Journal of International Economics 77 (2), 255–264.

Costinot, A., Oldenski, L., Rauch, J., 2011. Adaption and the boundary of multinational firms. Review of Economics and Statistics 93 (1), 298–308.

Cunat, A., Melitz, M.J., 2010. A many-country, many-good model of labor market rigidities as a source of comparative advantage. Journal of the European Economic Association Papers and Proceedings 8 (2–3), 434–441.

Cunat, A., Melitz, M.J., 2012. Volatility, labor market flexibility, and the pattern of comparative advantage. Journal of the European Economic Association 10 (2), 225–254.

Davidson, C., Martin, L., Matusz, S., 1988. The structure of simple general equilibrium models with frictional unemployment. Journal of Political Economy 96 (6), 1267–1293.

Davidson, C., Martin, L., Matusz, S., 1999. Trade and search generated unemployment. Journal of International Economics 48 (2), 271–299.

Davidson, C., Heyman, F., Matusz, S., Sjoholm, F., Zhu, S.C., 2012a. Liberalized trade and worker–firm matching. American Economic Review Papers and Proceedings 102 (3), 429–434.

Davidson, C., Heyman, F., Matusz, S., Sjoholm, F., Zhu, S., 2012b. Globalization and Imperfect Labor Market Sorting. Discussion Papers 10/30, University of Nottingham, GEP.

Davis, D.R., 1998. Does European unemployment prop up American wages? National labor markets and global trade. American Economic Review 88 (3), 478–494.

Davis, D.R., Harrigan, J., 2011. Good jobs, bad jobs, and trade liberalization. Journal of International Economics 84 (1), 26–36.

Dell, M., 2010. The persistent effects of Peru's mining Mita. Econometrica 78 (6), 1863–1903.

de Roover, R., 1965. The organization of trade. In: Postan, M.M., Rich, E.E., Miller, E. (Eds.), The Cambridge economic history of Europe, economic organization and policies in the middle ages, vol. 3. Cambridge University Press, Cambridge, UK, pp. 70–86.

Dippel, C., Greif, A., Trefler, D., 2012. The Rents from Trade and Coercive Labor Markets: Removing the Sugar Coating. University of Toronto and UCLA, Technical Report.

Do, Q.T., Levchenko, A.A., 2007. Comparative advantage, demand for external finance, and financial development. Journal of Financial Economics 86 (3), 796–834.

Eckel, C., Egger, H., 2009. Wage bargaining and multinational firms. Journal of International Economics 77 (2), 206–214.

Egger, H., Kreickemeier, U., 2009. Firm heterogeneity and the labor market effects of trade liberalization. International Economic Review 50 (1), 187–216.

Engerman, S.L., Sokoloff, K.L., 1997. Factor endowments, institutions, and differential paths of growth among new world economies: a view from economic historians of the United States. In: Harber, S. (Ed.), How Latin America Fell Behind. Stanford University Press, Stanford, pp. 260–304.

Engerman, S.L., Sokoloff, K.L., 2000. Institutions, factor endowments, and paths of development in the new world. Journal of Economic Perspectives 14 (3), 217–232.

Engerman, S.L., Sokoloff, K.L., 2012. Economic Development in the Americas since 1500: Endowments and Institutions. Cambridge University Press, Cambridge, MA.

Essaji, A., 2008. Technical regulations and specialization in international trade. Journal of International Economics 76, 166–176.

Essaji, A., Fujiwara, K., 2012. Contracting institutions and product quality. Journal of Comparative Economics 40 (2), 269–278.

Fafchamps, M., Minten, B., August 1999. Relationships and traders in Madagascar. Journal of Development Studies 35 (6), 1–35.

Feenstra, R., Hong, C., Ma, H., Spencer, B.J., 2012. Contractual Versus Non-Contractual Trade: The Role of Institutions in China. NBER Working Paper 17728.

Felbermayr, G., Jung, B., 2011. Trade intermediation and the organization of exporters. Review of International Economics 19 (4), 634–648.

Ferguson, S., Formai, S., 2011. Institution-Driven Comparative Advantage, Complex Goods and Organizational Choice. Mimeo, Stockholm School of Economics.

Frankel, J.A., Romer, D.H., 1999. Does trade cause growth? American Economic Review 89 (3), 379–399.

Fukuyama, F., 1995. Trust: The Social Virtues and the Creation of Prosperity. Free Press Paperbacks, New York.

Gaston, N., Trefler, D., August 1995. Union Wage Sensitivity to Trade and Protection: Theory and Evidence. Journal of International Economics 39 (1–2), 1–25.

González de Lara, Y., 2008. The secret of Venetian success: a public-order, reputation-based institution. European Review of Economic History 12 (3), 247–285.

Gould, D.M., 1994. Immigrant links to the home country: empirical implications for U.S. bilateral trade flows. Review of Economics and Statistics 76 (2), 302–316.

Greif, A., 1992. Institutions and international trade: lessons from the commercial revolution. American Economic Review 82 (2), 128–133.

Greif, A., 1993. Contract enforceability and economic institutions in early trade: the Maghribi traders' coalition. American Economic Review 83 (3), 525–548.

Greif, A., 1994. Cultural beliefs and the organization of society: a historical and theoretical reflection on collectivist and individualist societies. Journal of Political Economy 102 (5), 912–950.

Greif, A., 2006a. The birth of impersonal exchange: the community responsibility system and impartial justice. Journal of Economic Perspectives, 20 (2), 221–236.

Greif, A., 2006b. Institutions and the Path ot the Modern Economy: Lessons from Medieval Trade. Cambridge University Press, New York.

Greif, A., Laitin, D.D., 2004. A theory of endogenous institutional change. American Political Science Review 98 (4), 633–652.

Greif, A., Milgrom, P., Weingast, B.R., 1994. Coordination, commitment, and enforcement: the case of the merchant guild. Journal of Political Economy 102 (4), 745–776.

Grossman, G.M., 2004. The distribution of talent and the pattern and consequences of international trade. Journal of Political Economy 112 (1), 209–239.

Grossman, G.M., Maggi, G., 2000. Diversity and trade. American Economic Review 90 (5), 1255–1275.

Guiso, L., Sapienza, P., Zingales, L., 2009. Cultural biases in economic exchange? Quarterly Journal of Economics 124 (3), 1095–1131.

Hallak, J.C., 2010. A product-quality view of the linder hypothesis. Review of Economics and Statistics 92 (3), 453–466.

Hallak, J.C., Schott, P., 2010. Estimating cross-country differences in product quality. Quarterly Journal of Economics 126 (1), 417–474.

Head, K., Ries, J., 1998. Immigration and trade creation: econometric evidence from Canada. Canadian Journal of Economics 31 (1), 47–62.

Helpman, E., 2004. The Mystery of Economic Growth. Harvard University Press, Cambridge, MA.

Helpman, E., 2006. Trade, FDI, and the organization of firms. Journal of Economic Literature 44 (3), 589–630.

Helpman, E., Itskhoki, O., 2010. Labour market rigidities, trade and unemployment. Review of Economic Studies 77 (3), 1100–1137.

Helpman, E., Melitz, M., Rubinstein, Y., 2008. Estimating trade flows: trading partners and trading volumes. Quarterly Journal of Economics 123, 441–487.

Helpman, E., Itskhoki, O., Redding, S., 2010. Inequality and unemployment in a global economy. Econometrica 78 (4), 1239–1283.

Helpman, E., Oleg, I., Muendler, M.A., Redding, S.J., 2012. Trade and Inequality: From Theory to Estimation. Working Paper No. 17991, National Bureau of Economic Research, April.

Hosios, A.J., 1990. Factor market search and the structure of simple general equilibrium models. Journal of Political Economy 98 (2), 325–355.

Inikori, J.E., 2002. Africans and the Industrial Revolution in England: A Study in International Trade and Economic Development. Cambridge University Press, Cambridge.

Inikori, J.E., 2003. The struggle against the trans-Atlantic slave trade. In: Diouf, A. (Ed.), Fighting the Slave Trade: West African Strategies. Ohio University Press, Athens, Ohio, pp. 170–198.

Jha, S., 2008. Trade, Institutions and Religious Tolerance: Evidence from India. Mimeo, Stanford University.

Jha, S., 2010. Financial Innovations and Political Development: Evidence from Revolutionary England. Research Paper No. 2005, Stanford University Graduate School of Business, August.

Johnson, S., McMillan, J., Woodruff, C., 2002. Courts and relational contracts. Journal of Law, Economics and Organization 18 (1), 221–277.

Ju, J., Wei, S.J., 2011. When is quality of financial system a source of comparative advantage? Journal of International Economics 84 (2), 178–187.

Kadens, E., 2004. Order within law, variety within custom: the character of the medieval merchant law. Chicago Journal of International Law 5 (1), 39–66.

Karasik, L., 2012. The Impact of Labor Market Institutions on Markups and Export Market Performance when Firms and Countries are Heterogeneous. Department of Economics, University of Toronto, Working Paper, April.

Kaufmann, D., Kraay, A., Mastruzzi, M., 2003. Governance Matters III: Governance Indicators for 1996–2002. Working Paper No. 3106, World Bank.

Khandelwal, A., 2010. The long and short (of) quality ladders. Review of Economics and Studies 77 (4), 1450–1476.

King, R.G., Levine, R., 1993. Finance and growth: Schumpeter might be right. Quarterly Journal of Economics 108 (3), 717–737.

Kletzer, K., Bardhan, P., 1987. Credit markets and patterns of international trade. Journal of Development Economics 27 (1–2), 57–70.

Knack, S., Keefer, P., 1997. Does social capital have an economic payoff? A cross-country investigation. Quarterly Journal of Economics 112 (4), 1251–1288.

Kolasa, A., 2012. Business Groups and Contract Enforcement. Mimeo, George Washington University.

Kreickemeier, U., Nelson, D., 2006. Fair wages, unemployment and technological change in a global economy. Journal of International Economics 70 (2), 451–469.

Krugman, P.R., 1980. Scale economies, product differentiation, and the pattern of trade. American Economic Review 70 (5), 950–959.

Laeven, L., Woodruff, C., 2007. The quality of the legal system, firm ownership, and firm size. Review of Economics and Statistics 89 (4), 601–614.

Landau, P., 2004. The Development of law. In: Luscombe, David, Riley-Smith, J. (Eds.), New Cambridge Medieval History, vol. 4. Cambridge University Press, Cambridge, UK, pp. 113–147 (c.1024–c.1198, Part I).

La Porta, R., Lopez-de-Silanes, F., Shleifer, A., 2008. The economic consequences of legal origins. Journal of Economic Literature 46 (2), 285–332.

Leamer, E.E., 1984. Sources of International Comparative Advantage: Theory and Evidence. MIT Press, Cambridge, MA.

Leamer, E.E., Bowen, H.P., 1981. Cross-Section Tests of the Heckscher-Ohlin Theorem: Comment. American Economic Review 71 (5), 1040–1043.

Leff, N.H., 1978. Industrial organization and entrepreneurship in the developing countries: the economic groups. Economic Development and Cultural Change 26 (4), 661–675.

Levchenko, A.A., 2007. Institutional quality and international trade. Review of Economic Studies 74 (3), 791–819.

Levchenko, A.A., 2013. International trade and institutional change. Journal of Law, Economics, and Organization 29 (5), 1145–1181.

Li, K., Wang, Y., Wang, Y., 2012. Judicial Quality, Contract Intensity and Firm Exports: Evidence from China. Mimeo, Nankai University.

Lopez, R.S., 1971. The Commercial Revolution of the Middle Ages, 950–1350. Cambridge University Press, Cambridge, UK.

Ma, Y., Baaozhi, Q., Zhang, Y., 2010. Judicial quality, contract intensity and trade: firm-level evidence from developing and transition countries. Journal of Comparative Economics 38, 146–159.

Manova, K., 2008. Credit constraints, equity market liberalizations and international trade. Journal of International Economics 76 (1), 33–47.

Manova, K., 2013. Credit constraints, heterogeneous firms, and international trade. Review of Economic Studies 80, 711–744.

Manova, K., Wei, S.J., Zhang, Z., 2011. Firm Exports and Multinational Activity under Credit Constraints. NBER Working Papers 16905, National Bureau of Economic Research, March.

Matsuyama, K., 2005. Credit market imperfections and patterns of international trade and capital flows. Journal of the European Economic Association 3 (2–3), 714–723.

Matusz, S.J., 1986. Implicit contracts, unemployment and international trade. Economic Journal 96 (382), 307–322.

Matusz, S.J., 1996. International trade, the division of labor, and unemployment. International Economic Review 37 (1), 71–84.

McMillan, J., Woodruff, C., 1999. Interfirm relationships and informal credit in Vietnam. Quarterly Journal of Economics 114 (4), 1285–1320.

Melitz, M.J., 2003. The impact of trade on intra-industry reallocations and aggregate industry productivity. Econometrica 71 (6), 1695–1725.

Mezzetti, C., Dinopoulos, E., August 1991. Domestic unionization and import competition. Journal of International Economics 31 (1–2), 79–100.

Milgrom, P.R., North, D.C., Weingast, B.R., 1990. The role of institutions in the revival of trade: the law merchant, private judges, and the champagne fairs. Economics and Politics 2 (1), 1–23.

Mitchener, K.J., McLean, I.W., 2003. The productivity of U.S. states since 1880. Journal of Economic Growth 8, 73–114.

Naidu, S., Yuchtman, N., 2013. Coercive contract enforcement: law and the labor Market in 19th century industrial Britain. American Economic Review 103 (1), 107–144.

Naritomi, J., Soares, R.R., Assuncao, J.J., 2012. Institutional development and colonial heritage within Brazil. Journal of Economic History 72 (2), 393–422.

North, D.C., 1990. Institutions, Institutional Change and Economic Performance. Cambridge University Press, New York.

North, D.C., Thomas, R.P., 1973. The Rise of the Western World: A New Economic History. Cambridge University Press, Cambridge, UK.

Nunn, N., 2007. Relationship-specificity, incomplete contracts, and the pattern of trade. Quarterly Journal of Economics 122 (2), 569–600.

Nunn, N., 2008a. The long-term effects of Africa's slave trades. Quarterly Journal of Economics 123 (1), 139–176.

Nunn, N., 2008b. Slavery, inequality, and economic development in the Americas: an examination of the Engerman-Sokoloff hypothesis. In: Helpman, E. (Ed.), Institutions and Economic Performance. Harvard University Press, Cambridge, MA, pp. 148–180.

Nunn, N., Trefler, D., 2008. The boundaries of the multinational firm: an empirical analysis. In: Helpman, E., Marin, D., Verdier, T. (Eds.), The Organization of Firms in a Global Economy. Harvard University Press, Cambridge, MA, pp. 55–83.

Nunn, N., Trefler, D., 2010. The structure of tariffs and long-term growth. American Economic Journal: Macroeconomics 2 (4), 158–194.

Nunn, N., Trefler, D., 2013. Incomplete contracts and the boundaries of the multinational firm. Journal of Economic Behavior and Organization 94 (1), 330–344.

Nunn, N., Wantchekon, L., 2011. The slave trade and the origins of mistrust in Africa. American Economic Review 101 (7), 3221–3252.

Ohnsorge, F., Trefler, D., 2007. Sorting it out: international trade and protection with heterogeneous workers. Journal of Political Economy 115 (5), 868–892.

Olivier, J., Thoenig, M., Verdier, T., 2008. Globalization and the dynamics of cultural diversity. Journal of International Economics 76, 356–370.

Puga, D., Trefler, D., 2012. International Trade and Institutional Change: Medieval Venice's Response to Globalization. Working Paper No. 18288, National Bureau of Economic Research, August.

Rajan, R.G., Zingales, L., 1998. Financial dependence and growth. American Economic Review 88, 559–586.

Ranjan, P., Lee, J.Y., 2007. Contract enforcement and international trade. Economics and Politics 19 (2), 191–218.

Rauch, J.E., 1999. Networks versus markets in international trade. Journal of International Economics 48, 7–35.

Rauch, J.E., 2001. Business and social networks in international trade. Journal of Economic Literature 39 (4), 1177–1203.

Rauch, J.E., Trindade, V., 2002. Ethnic Chinese networks in international trade. Review of Economics and Statistics 84 (1), 116–130.

Rauch, J.E., Watson, J., 2004. Network intermediaries in international trade. Journal of Economics & Management Strategy 13 (1), 69–93.

Romalis, J., 2004. Factor proportions and the structure of commodity trade. American Economic Review 94, 67–97.

Ross, M.L., 1999. The political economy of the resource curse. World Politics 51 (02), 297–322.

Saint-Paul, G., 1997. Is labour rigidity harming Europe's competitiveness? The effect of job protection on the pattern of trade and welfare. European Economic Review 41, 499–506.

Shen, L., 2012. Global Sourcing and Credit Constraints. Mimeo, University of Toronto, April.

Spencer, B.J., 2005. International outsourcing and incomplete contracts. Canadian Journal of Economics 38 (4), 1107–1135.

Stole, L.A., Zwiebel, J., 1996. Organizational design and technology choice under intrafirm bargaining. American Economic Review 86 (1), 195–222.

Svaleryd, H., Vlachos, J., 2005. Financial markets, the pattern of industrial specialization and comparative advantage: evidence from OECD countries. European Economic Review 49, 113–144.

Tabellini, G., 2008a. Institutions and culture. Journal of the European Economic Association 6 (2–3), 255–294.

Tabellini, G., 2008b. The scope of cooperation: values and incentives. Quarterly Journal of Economics 123 (3), 905–950.

Tang, H., 2012. Labor market institutions, firm-specific skills, and trade patterns. Journal of International Economics 87 (2), 337–351.

Thoenig, M., Maystre, N., Olivier, J., Verdier, T., 2009. Product-Based Cultural Change: Is the Village Global? CEPR Discussion Paper No. 7438.

Trefler, D., 2004. The long and short of the Canada–U.S. Free trade agreement. American Economic Review 94 (4), 870–895.

Tsui, K.K., 2011. More oil, less democracy: evidence from worldwide crude oil discoveries. Economic Journal 121, 89–115.

Williamson, O.E., 1985. The Economic Institutions of Capitalism. The Free Press, New York.

World Bank, 2004. Doing Business in 2004: Understanding Regulation. World Bank and Oxford University Press, Washington, D.C.

Xu, B., 2001. Entrepreneurial selection, financial markets, and the patterns of international trade. International Economic Journal 157 (3), 147–167.

Yeaple, S.R., Golub, S.S., 2007. International productivity differences, infrastructure, and comparative advantage. Review of International Economics 15 (2), 223–242.

CHAPTER 6

International Trade Agreements*

Giovanni Maggi
Yale University, New Haven, CT, USA
Graduate School of Economics, Getulio Vargas Foundation, Brasil
National Bureau of Economic Research, Cambridge, MA, USA

Abstract

In this chapter I survey the recent theoretical and empirical advances in the economics of international trade agreements, focusing on three main topics: the motives for trade agreements; the design of rules and institutions for trade policy; and regional trade agreements.

Keywords

International trade agreements

JEL classification codes

F13, F53, K33

1. INTRODUCTION

The starting point for this survey is represented by the two chapters on trade agreements in the previous volume of the *Handbook of International Economics* (1995), namely Robert Staiger's chapter "International Rules and Institutions for Trade Policy" and Richard Baldwin and Anthony Venables' chapter "Regional Economic Integration." For the most part I will focus on the post-1995 advances in the literature on trade agreements; I refer the reader to the previous volume of this handbook for the pre-1995 literature.

Before I plunge into the literature, however, it is useful to start with a quick review of the main developments that have occurred in the real world of international trade agreements since 1995. My aim is not to embark in a comprehensive discussion of these developments, but simply to provide a stylized historical context for the literature that I will survey.

The first major development is that, after the completion of the Uruguay Round in 1995, the General Agreement on Tariffs and Trade (GATT) has been replaced by the World Trade Organization (WTO). The WTO is a considerably more developed

* I am grateful to Bob Staiger and Rachel McCulloch for being my discussants at the handbook conference and providing very detailed and useful comments on an earlier draft, to co-editor Elhanan Helpman for providing an additional set of helpful suggestions, and to Kyle Bagwell, Matthew Grant, Andrés Rodríguez-Clare and participants in the handbook conference for helpful comments and discussions.

international institution than its predecessor, with a broader set of functions that include not only the implementation of the commitments made by member countries in the Uruguay Round, but also a relatively sophisticated judicial system, known as the "Dispute Settlement Procedure."

A second important fact has been the growing role of developing and newly industrialized countries in the WTO and in regional trade agreements. An important milestone in this respect was the 2001 accession of China to the WTO. Another significant manifestation of this trend has been the growing involvement of newly industrialized countries (especially Brazil, India and, after 2001, China) in the WTO dispute settlement system.

The third major development has been a tremendous acceleration in the formation of regional trade agreements. For example, during the first 10 years of the WTO (1995–2005) the number of regional trade agreements in force more than tripled, from 58 to 188. Currently the total number of regional trade agreements in force is about 380, and several potential new ones are currently being negotiated, including one between the US and the EU, which would constitute the largest regional trade agreement in the world.

The fourth and fifth developments are perhaps better described as *non*-developments. After the completion of the Uruguay Round, the WTO member countries embarked in a new major round of multilateral negotiations, the so-called Doha Round. These negotiations started in 2001 but have stalled, and at this point it is safe to say that the Doha Round is effectively dead. Negotiations have stumbled mostly over divisions between developing and developed countries, but there has also been considerable contention between the EU and the US over agricultural subsidies. This lack of progress in multilateral trade liberalization is probably related to both of the developments I mentioned above—the proliferation of regional trade agreements and the growing role of developing countries—but the deep reasons for the failure of the Doha Round are an open question.

The second non-development is—contrary to the one discussed just above—a positive one: the *existing* rules and institutions have held up rather well, even in the face of challenges such as the 2008 Great Recession, which led to a dramatic (though temporary) collapse of trade flows, and the accession of China to the WTO. In particular, the WTO's dispute settlement system has been quite effective. Indeed, many scholars have argued that the enforcement and judicial aspects of the WTO are stronger now than during the GATT years. Furthermore, if judged by the standards of international organizations, it is safe to say that the WTO has established itself as one of the most, if not the most, successful international organization in terms of enforcement and dispute settlement.

This concludes my stylized portrait of the recent developments in trade agreements, and against this backdrop I now turn to my discussion of the recent advances in the academic literature on trade agreements.

Section 2 focuses on theoretical and empirical research investigating the purpose of trade agreements. In the theoretical part, I focus mostly on three theories: the "terms of trade" theory, according to which the purpose of a trade agreement is to prevent governments from manipulating terms of trade; the "domestic commitment" theory, according to which a trade agreement can provide a government with a means to tie its own hands vis-à-vis domestic agents; and the "New Trade" theory, which emphasizes the role that a trade agreement can play in the presence of imperfect competition. The empirical part of the discussion focuses on two sets of contributions: those aimed at testing the predictions of the main theories, and those that study the impacts of trade agreements on trade barriers and trade flows in a more descriptive way.

Section 3 discusses research aimed at understanding the design of trade agreements, with a particular emphasis on the role of transaction costs. In particular, I will focus on two distinct types of transaction cost: *contracting frictions* and *enforcement frictions*. I will argue that taking these transaction costs into account is essential for understanding the design of substantive policy rules (such as tariff ceilings, non-discrimination rules, etc.), enforcement rules (which regulate punishment/retaliation), and dispute settlement procedures.

Section 4 discusses recent research on regional trade agreements. In particular, I will focus on the economic and political determinants of regional trade agreements; on the impacts of such agreements on its members' external trade barriers and on multilateral trade liberalization; and on the design of rules for trade negotiations, that is, on whether the formation of regional trade agreements should be subject to constraints or even prohibited.

Finally, Section 5 offers some concluding remarks and some thoughts about possible avenues for future research.

2. THE MOTIVES FOR TRADE AGREEMENTS

The most basic question regarding trade agreements (TAs) is why countries sign them in the first place. In spite of this being the most fundamental of questions, it is only in the last 15 years or so that the academic literature has made substantial progress in answering it.

Krugman (1997, pp. 113–120) made a famous pessimistic statement: *"Anyone who has tried to make sense of international trade negotiations eventually realizes that they can only be understood by realizing that they are a game scored according to mercantilist rules. (…) The implicit mercantilist theory that underlies trade negotiations does not make sense on any level, indeed is inconsistent with simple adding-up constraints; but it nonetheless governs actual policy (…) the economic theory underlying trade negotiations is nonsense."* The last 15 years of research on TAs are in some way an attempt to prove Krugman wrong, and argue instead that the logic of economics (in a broad sense that includes also the logic of political economy) *can* to a large extent make sense of real-world TAs.

In this section I will offer my critical survey of the main theories for why countries sign TAs and of the small but growing empirical literature on this subject.

Before I proceed, I need to make clear what is the organizing principle of this section. The distinction between analyzing the motives for a TA (which is the subject of this section) and analyzing the design of a TA (which is the subject of the next section) can sometimes be blurred, since the two aspects are obviously inter-related. But I think it is important to keep these two aspects conceptually distinct. In the present section, I abstract from issues of institutional/contract design (which, as I will argue below, are interesting only in the presence of transaction costs) by assuming that governments can negotiate directly and costlessly over all policies (and, in the presence of uncertainty, over all contingencies).

There are two broad stories for why governments sign TAs. The first one is that a TA can provide governments with an escape from an international Prisoners' Dilemma, which is in turn caused by international externalities from trade policy: these include the classic terms-of-trade externalities and the "New Trade" externalities that arise with imperfect competition (such as "delocation" and "profit-shifting" externalities). The second broad story for why governments sign TAs is that these may provide governments with a commitment device vis-à-vis domestic actors, such as industrial lobbies or individuals making investment decisions. I will start by focusing on the classic terms-of-trade story.

2.1. The Terms-of-Trade Theory

The type of international externality from trade policy that has received by far the most attention in the literature (dating back at least to Johnson, 1953) is the terms-of-trade (TOT) externality that arises in a perfectly competitive environment. As it will become clear in Section 2.3, TOT externalities play an important role also with imperfect competition, but their role is clearest in the case of perfect competition, so I will focus on this case here.

I will proceed in two steps. I will first illustrate the TOT theory using a simple "workhorse" model that is very structured and delivers simple formulas and a number of specific predictions. This model is convenient also because it can be used as a basis to illustrate a simple version of the domestic-commitment theory, as I will show in Section 2.2. I will then present a more general version of the TOT theory, which has been developed mostly by Bagwell and Staiger.

2.1.1. A Simple Workhorse Model

My workhorse model is essentially a simplified version of Grossman and Helpman's (1995a) "Trade Wars and Trade Talks" model, where governments may have two motives for unilateral trade policy intervention, namely a terms-of-trade motive and a political-economy motive.

Consider a world with two countries (H and F) and with three sectors, a numeraire sector (0) and two non-numeraire sectors ($j = 1, 2$). All citizens have the same utility function, which takes the form $U = c_0 + \sum_{j=1}^{2} u_j(c_j)$, where each u_j is increasing and concave. The numeraire good is produced one-for-one from labor, so the wage is pinned down to one, while good j is produced from labor and capital according to the constant-returns production function $y_j = F_j(k_j, l_j)$.

Labor is perfectly mobile across sectors. Capital for the moment is assumed to be immobile across sectors (so that it can be effectively viewed as a specific factor); in Section 2.2, where I consider the domestic-commitment theory, I will assume that capital is immobile in the short run but can move across sectors in the long run.

The owners of capital represent a negligible fraction of the total population; this will simplify the political-economy environment. The size of the population is equal to one in each country. Country H is the natural importer of good 1 and country F of good 2.

Assume the numeraire good is freely traded. Each government can choose specific trade taxes/subsidies in the non-numeraire sectors. Later I will consider domestic policies as well.

Next I describe the political-economy environment. In each country, the owners of capital in a given sector may or may not be organized into a lobby. The government's objective is $\Omega^G = aW + C$, where W is aggregate welfare and C denotes total contributions received from lobbies. If sector j is organized, the lobby's objective is $\Omega_j^L = \Pi_j - C_j$, where Π_j denotes returns to capital in sector j. Analogous notation (but with asterisks) will apply to the F country.[1]

Given the quasi-linear preferences, the specific-factor structure, and the wage pinned down at one, this is essentially a partial-equilibrium setting. Defining welfare as aggregate indirect utility, Home welfare can be written (using standard techniques) as $W = Y + S + R$, where Y is total factor income, S is total consumer surplus (summed over the two goods) and R is revenue from trade policy (positive or negative). An analogous expression holds for Foreign welfare.

For each sector j, the demand functions in the two countries are denoted by $d_j(p_j)$ and $d_j^*(p_j^*)$, the supply functions by $y_j(p_j)$ and $y_j^*(p_j^*)$, and the import demand functions by $m_j(p_j)$ and $m_j^*(p_j^*)$.

Let τ_j (τ_j^*) denote the specific trade tax/subsidy chosen by Home (Foreign) in sector j. If good j is imported by Home, τ_j is interpreted as an import tax, and τ_j^* as an export subsidy, and vice-versa if the good is exported by Home. The price arbitrage condition $(p_j = p_j^* + \tau_j - \tau_j^*)$ and the market clearing condition $(m_j(p_j) + m_j^*(p_j^*) = 0)$ together determine equilibrium prices as functions of trade policies: $p_j(\tau_j - \tau_j^*)$ and $p_j^*(\tau_j - \tau_j^*)$. Finally, define the "world price" of good j as $p_j^W = p_j - \tau_j = p_j^* - \tau_j^*$.

I start by focusing on the noncooperative scenario. In each country, assume that government and lobbies choose trade policy (and contributions) by Nash bargaining, taking foreign trade policy as given. Given that bargaining is efficient, trade policy in each country maximizes the joint surplus of government and lobbies given foreign trade policy. Thus Home trade policy maximizes $\Omega \equiv \Omega^G + \sum_{j=1}^2 I_j \Omega_j^L = aW + \sum_{j=1}^2 I_j \Pi_j$,

---

[1] I note here that very little research has been done on the role of *informational* lobbying (as opposed to *quid pro quo* lobbying) in influencing trade negotiations. The only paper of this kind that I am aware of is Milner and Rosendorff (1996). Other papers on this general theme are Tovar (2011) and Ludema et al. (2010), but these papers focus only on unilateral trade policy choices, not trade agreements.

where $I_j = 1$ if sector j is organized and zero otherwise. Similarly, Foreign trade policy maximizes $\Omega^* \equiv a^* W^* + \sum_{j=1}^{2} I_j^* \Pi_j^*$.

As mentioned above, this model can be viewed as a simplified version of Grossman and Helpman (1995a).[2] Note also that this model is equivalent to one where each government maximizes a politically-adjusted welfare function that attaches an extra weight to the organized sectors' rents, as for example in Baldwin (1987).

Maximizing Ω with respect to τ_j and Ω^* with respect to τ_j^* yields the following formulas for τ_j and τ_j^*:

$$\tau_j = \frac{1}{\eta_j^*} + \frac{I_j}{a \cdot \eta_j \cdot \frac{m_j}{y_j}}, \tag{1}$$

$$\tau_j^* = \frac{1}{\eta_j} + \frac{I_j^*}{a^* \cdot \eta_j^* \cdot \frac{m_j^*}{y_j^*}}, \tag{2}$$

where $\eta_j^* \equiv \frac{|m_j^{*\prime}|}{m_j^*}$ and $\eta_j \equiv \frac{|m_j^\prime|}{m_j}$. The first term in each formula is the well-known Johnson's optimum trade tax, which captures the *terms of trade* motive for trade policy; the second part of each formula captures the *political* motive for trade policy. Note that the two motives go in the same direction for organized import-competing industries (both call for a tariff), but are in conflict for organized export sectors (TOT considerations call for an export tax, political considerations call for an export subsidy).

We are now ready to examine the trade policies that are selected if the two countries negotiate a TA. Assuming that the TA maximizes the joint surplus of all governments and lobbies, that is $\Omega + \Omega^*$,[3] we obtain:

$$\tau_j - \tau_j^* = \frac{I_j}{a \cdot \eta_j \cdot \frac{m_j}{y_j}} - \frac{I_j^*}{a^* \cdot \eta_j^* \cdot \frac{m_j^*}{y_j^*}}. \tag{3}$$

Note that for each sector j the optimal agreement pins down only the net trade tax $\tau_j - \tau_j^*$, not the exact levels of τ_j and τ_j^*. To understand intuitively why, consider the case in which governments maximize welfare: $a = a^* = \infty$. Then the formula above yields $\tau_j = \tau_j^*$. A tariff of \$1 and an export subsidy of \$1 on the same good neutralize

---

[2] One simplification relative to Grossman and Helpman (1995a) is that the share of the population represented by lobbies (the α_L parameter) is negligible. Another simplification is that the interaction between government and lobbies is modeled as a Nash bargaining game, whereas in Grossman and Helpman it is modeled as a common-agency game, but in both cases a country's trade taxes maximize the joint surplus of government and lobbies.

[3] This will be the case, for example, if trade negotiations take the form of a Nash bargain that involves the governments and all lobbies and international transfers are available. I note that Grossman and Helpman (1995a) assume a two-stage game where lobbies first offer contribution schedules to their respective governments, and then governments bargain in Rubinstein fashion, but the policy outcome in their model is the same as in the simplified model I consider here. Also note that, even if international transfers are not available, such transfers can be indirectly effected by adjusting import and export tax levels, as I explain below.

each other's effect on domestic prices, and the only effect that remains is a revenue transfer from the exporting country to the importing country; the condition $\tau_j = \tau_j^*$ is the partial-equilibrium analog of the well-known "Mayer curve."[4]

If political motivations are present in the governments' objectives (a and a^* are less than infinity), the efficient policies will reflect only these motivations, and not the TOT motivations: *an efficient agreement simply removes TOT considerations from trade policies.* This in turn suggests that the only source of inefficiency in the noncooperative equilibrium is the governments' temptation to manipulate TOT. Or put another way, even if governments are politically motivated, the reason for signing a TA is inherently economic, not political. As I discuss next, this basic message is further developed and generalized by Bagwell and Staiger.

2.1.2. The Bagwell-Staiger Approach

In an influential series of papers, Bagwell and Staiger have argued that the TOT theory— and in particular the conclusion that the only motive for a TA can be traced to the governments' temptation to manipulate TOT—is considerably more general than previously thought. I refer the reader to Bagwell and Staiger's (2002) book and Bagwell and Staiger's (2010a) survey for more detailed expositions of their work. In this section I will offer a succinct exposition of Bagwell and Staiger's theory under perfect competition; I will discuss their models with imperfect competition in the next section.

Consider a two-country, two-good, perfectly competitive world, with the good exported by Home taken as the numeraire. The production possibility frontier is assumed to be concave, and the goods are assumed to be normal in consumption. The model allows for domestic distortions, such as consumption or production externalities, that call for corrective domestic policies (but monopoly distortions are not allowed).[5] Each government has access to a complete set of (trade and domestic) policy instruments. It is useful to partition policies in two categories: (i) Tax instruments that create wedges between local prices and the world price, or more specifically, trade taxes, production taxes, and consumption taxes. I will refer to these as "wedge policies"[6]; (ii) Other policies (e.g. labor standards) that may affect market conditions but cannot affect price wedges. I will refer to these as "non-wedge policies."

Key to Bagwell and Staiger's approach is the way government objectives are represented. These are represented in reduced form as $\Omega(v, p, q, p^w)$ and $\Omega^*(v^*, p^*, q^*, p^w)$, where p (p^*) is the Home (Foreign) consumer price, q (q^*) the Home (Foreign) producer

[4] See Mayer (1981), who characterizes the locus of efficient tariff combinations in a general equilibrium model with two goods and two countries.

[5] The framework I present here can be seen as combining three variants of the Bagwell-Staiger model: Bagwell and Staiger (1999a), which considers only trade taxes; Bagwell and Staiger (2001), which considers trade taxes and domestic standards; and Bagwell and Staiger (2006), which considers trade taxes and production subsidies.

[6] Of course there is a degree of redundancy in these three taxation instruments, since a trade tax is equivalent to a combination of a production subsidy and a consumption tax.

price, ν (ν^*) the vector of Home (Foreign) non-wedge policies, and p^w the world price. Since wedge policies can be written as price wedges, they need not be included as arguments in the objective functions. Of course, the equilibrium price levels in general will depend on all policies.

A central feature of this setting is that a government's policies affect the other government's payoff through a unique channel: the world price. In other words, the only international externality is the TOT externality. An implicit assumption in this setting is that there are no non-pecuniary international externalities (such as cross-border pollution). But aside from this restriction, the above representation of governments' objectives is general enough to capture the presence of political-economy motives for protection; indeed, Bagwell and Staiger argue that many of the existing political-economy models (including the Grossman-Helpman model presented above) can be represented in this fashion.

The only structure Bagwell and Staiger impose on government preferences is that, for given domestic prices, a government dislikes a worsening of terms of trade: $\frac{\partial\Omega}{\partial p^w} < 0 < \frac{\partial\Omega^*}{\partial p^w}$. This seems like a reasonable restriction, since domestic interest groups care about domestic prices, not directly about world prices. If p^w increases while domestic prices are kept constant, there is simply a transfer of revenue from Home to Foreign (given the assumption of normal goods), so this amounts to assuming that, all else equal, a government values revenue. Finally, the Lerner paradox and the Metzler paradox are assumed away.[7]

As usual, the analysis starts with the noncooperative scenario, that is the Nash equilibrium of the game where governments simultaneously choose policies. Three basic points can be made in this setting.

The first point is that any Nash equilibrium is Pareto-inefficient from the point of view of the governments' objectives. This result is intuitive, since a country's policies exert externalities on the other country through TOT, and hence unilateral policy choices will generically not be efficient.

The second point is that the governments' temptation to manipulate TOT is the only source of inefficiency in the Nash equilibrium, and hence it is the only motive for a TA. Bagwell and Staiger establish this point by considering a diagnostic test to ascertain if TOT manipulation is the only cause of the "disease" in the noncooperative equilibrium. The test is based on the following question: if each government did not value the pure terms-of-trade effects of its policies, would governments make efficient choices? If the test is positive, the diagnosis is that TOT manipulation is the only cause of the disease.

More specifically, Bagwell and Staiger define the *politically optimal* (PO) policies as those that would result if governments did not value changes in p^w. If the PO policies are efficient, then TOT manipulation is deemed to be the only cause of inefficiency in the noncooperative equilibrium. In the setting under consideration, Bagwell and Staiger

[7] The Lerner paradox occurs when an increase in a country's tariff leads to an increase in the world relative price of the imported good; the Metzler paradox occurs when an increase in a country's tariff leads to a decrease in the domestic relative price of the imported good.

show that the PO policies are indeed efficient. A simple intuition for this result can be gained by considering a setting where utility is transferrable, with changes in p^w acting as pure transfers, so that efficient policies must maximize the global payoff $\Omega + \Omega^*$. In this case, at a political optimum, Home's policies maximize Ω given p^w and Foreign policies maximize Ω^* given p^w, therefore the global payoff must be maximum because p^w is a pure transfer.

The third point is that trade volume at the Nash equilibrium is inefficiently low, and a mutually beneficial TA must entail a reciprocal expansion of market access relative to the Nash equilibrium.[8] I will provide a simple local intuition for this result, abstracting from domestic policies for simplicity. Starting from the Nash equilibrium, a small increase in a trade tax has a negative externality on the trading partner. This is not self-evident, since an increase in a country's trade tax could in principle have a positive effect on the trading partner through the latter's local price. But this cannot be the case locally at the Nash equilibrium: the optimality of a country's unilateral policies implies that, at the Nash equilibrium, any effect through the local price cannot outweigh the adverse effect through the world price, so the externality from an increase in the foreign trade tax is negative.[9] Given the negative international externalities from trade taxes, it is intuitive that, starting from the Nash equilibrium, the only way to achieve a Pareto improvement is to decrease both trade taxes, which in turn will expand trade.

In light of the three points highlighted above, Bagwell and Staiger conclude that under the assumptions of their model the only purpose of a TA is to preclude countries from manipulating TOT, and this in turn entails a reciprocal expansion of market access relative to the noncooperative equilibrium. This prediction of the model resonates with the emphasis placed by the GATT-WTO on the exchange of market access between countries.

Next I highlight a prediction that presents a special challenge for the TOT theory, because it is at odds with observed TAs. According to the TOT theory, *a TA should tend to increase export subsidies* relative to the noncooperative equilibrium, whereas in reality export subsidies are typically restricted by TAs. This counterfactual prediction of the TOT

---

[8] Bagwell and Staiger make a distinction between an expansion of "market access" and an expansion of trade volume (see Bagwell and Staiger, 2001, pp. 537–538). The former is a weaker condition than the latter: a policy change is said to expand market access to country A if it shifts out country A's import demand curve for at least *some* world price. As Bagwell and Staiger show, a mutually beneficial trade agreement must entail a reciprocal expansion of market access, but in general it need not entail an expansion of import volumes; it will entail an expansion of import volumes under the additional assumption that any policy change shifts a country's import demand curve in the same direction for all world-price levels. In my intuitive discussion in the text I abstract from domestic policies, so this distinction is not necessary, and a mutually beneficial agreement always entails an expansion of trade volumes.

[9] To see this formally, note first that if only trade taxes are available, we can write Home's payoff as $\Omega(p, p^w)$. Letting τ and τ^* denote trade taxes, we can write the externality of τ^* on Home (with a slight abuse of notation) as $\Omega_{\tau^*} = \Omega_p p_{\tau^*} + \Omega_{p^w} p_{\tau^*}^w = (\Omega_p + \Omega_{p^w}) p_{\tau^*}^w$ (where I used $p_{\tau^*} = p_{\tau^*}^w$). At a Nash equilibrium, the first order condition (FOC) is $\Omega_\tau = \Omega_p p_\tau + \Omega_{p^w} p_\tau^w = 0$, which using $p_\tau = p_\tau^w + 1$ yields $\Omega_p = -\frac{\Omega_{p^w} p_\tau^w}{p_\tau^w + 1}$, which is negative by the no-Lerner-paradox and no-Metzler-paradox assumptions. This in turn implies $\Omega_{\tau^*} < 0$.

model can be illustrated by focusing on a model with two goods. The well-known Lerner symmetry theorem states that an import tax is equivalent to an export tax, thus we can suppose without loss of generality that each government uses only an export tax (or if negative, an export subsidy). In this case, if the noncooperative equilibrium entails export subsidies (which is possible if export interests are politically strong), it is easy to show that a mutually beneficial TA must increase their levels. Intuitively, increasing a country's export subsidy has a positive TOT externality on the other country, so governments "under-subsidize" exports in equilibrium. I will refer to this feature as the *export subsidy puzzle* in the TOT theory. As I discuss below, possible ways to resolve this puzzle include considering domestic-commitment motives and "New Trade" motives for TAs.

Thus far I have focused on a two-country world. Extending the analysis to a multi-country world introduces new considerations. As Bagwell and Staiger (1999a) make clear, when trade policies can discriminate across trading partners, there is no longer a single world price but a whole vector of bilateral world prices, and importantly, international externalities can no longer be viewed as traveling solely through world prices. As a consequence, if trade policies can be discriminatory, the PO policies are inefficient. To understand this point, focus on the impact of foreign trade policies on the Home country. Define the multilateral TOT as an import-weighted average of bilateral world prices. Since the import weights depend on foreign local prices, now international externalities travel not only through world prices but also through foreign local prices. It is then intuitive that the PO policies are not efficient. On the other hand, if governments are constrained by a Most Favored Nation (MFN) rule to choose non-discriminatory trade policies, then Bagwell and Staiger show that all international externalities are channeled through a single world price, and again the PO policies are efficient. To summarize, the PO policies are efficient if and only if trade policies are constrained by the MFN rule.

The result I just highlighted can be interpreted in more than one way. Bagwell and Staiger argue that the result confirms the general point that in a perfectly competitive environment the only purpose of a TA is to prevent the manipulation of TOT. But one could argue that the appropriate thought experiment should diagnose the cause of the disease in a scenario where *no* institutional constraints are in place, not even the MFN rule, in which case PO policies are inefficient and one should conclude that TOT manipulation is not the only motivation for a TA. Thus there is a legitimate question as to which of the two diagnostic tests (with unconstrained policies or with MFN-constrained policies) is more informative about the deep motivation for a TA.

Bagwell and Staiger build on the model outlined above to argue that it can explain some key rules of the GATT-WTO, such as reciprocity, MFN, and the so-called "non violation" rule. I will come back to these themes in the next section, where I focus on the design of TAs, but here I wish to re-iterate a point already mentioned above: in a world without transaction costs, the theory would not be able to explain any such rules, because then governments could simply negotiate directly on the policy levels, and there would be no need for additional rules, so this second part of Bagwell and Staiger's theory implicitly relies on the presence of some kind of transaction costs. As already mentioned, in the present section I am assuming that there are no transaction costs, and hence governments can negotiate directly and costlessly over all policies, so I postpone issues of rules design to the next section.

2.2. The Domestic-Commitment Theory

The TOT theory is by far the one with the deepest roots in the literature, but it is not clear that TOT considerations are the whole story behind TAs, for at least two reasons. First, casual empiricism suggests that small countries (which have negligible influence on world prices) often agree to significant cuts in their trade barriers when they join a TA, an observation that is not easy to reconcile with the TOT theory.[10] And second, as I mentioned above, the TOT theory implies that TAs should tend to increase export subsidies relative to their noncooperative levels, which is a counterfactual prediction. An alternative theory that can explain these observations is based on the idea that a TA can help a government tie its own hands vis-à-vis domestic actors.[11]

There are several models in the literature that fall within the broadly defined domestic-commitment theory. Some are of a purely economic nature, for example Staiger and Tabellini (1987), Tornell (1991), and Lapan (1988), and some are of a political-economy nature, in particular Maggi and Rodriguez-Clare (1998, 2007), Mitra (2002), Brou and Ruta (2009), Limão and Tovar (2011), and Liu and Ornelas (2012). Since the former type of domestic-commitment models was covered by Staiger's (1995a) chapter, I will focus on the latter type, and in particular on the version due to Maggi and Rodriguez-Clare (1998, 2007).

The general idea proposed by Maggi and Rodriguez-Clare is that a TA can serve as a commitment device for a government to close the door to domestic lobbies. It has been argued by a number of scholars and commentators that this type of motivation was central to Mexico's negotiations of the North American Free Trade Agreement (NAFTA). For example, Whalley (1998) argued that Mexican negotiators of NAFTA "were less concerned to secure an exchange of concessions between them and their negotiating partners, and were more concerned to make unilateral concessions to larger negotiating partners with whom they had little negotiating leverage... The idea was clearly

---

[10] The reason I use the expression "casual empiricism" is the following. There is little doubt that at least in *some* cases countries with negligible monopsony power on given goods have agreed to significant tariff cuts on those goods, but I am not aware of any empirical study that investigates whether this is the case more systematically.

[11] Interestingly, in the same 1997 essay where Krugman declared it impossible to understand trade negotiations from a rational perspective, he left a small opening for the domestic-commitment theory of trade agreements, although still with some degree of skepticism. He summarizes this theory as maintaining that "the true purpose of international negotiations is arguably not to protect us from unfair foreign competition, but to protect us from ourselves," then states that "one cannot dismiss such political-economy arguments as foolish," but questions whether in reality international agreements are truly effective in achieving this purpose.

to help lock in domestic policy reform." Similarly, Bajona and Chu (2010) view China's accession to WTO as a way to "... lock-in the agenda for fundamental domestic reforms, which has been difficult to implement by domestic measures alone."

Notice however that, if one considers the typical models of lobbying that have been proposed in the literature, in particular those in the tradition of Grossman and Helpman's (1994) "Protection for Sale," it is not clear why a government would ever want to tie its own hands, since it derives positive rents from the political process.

Maggi and Rodriguez-Clare (1998) provide a theoretical justification for the domestic-commitment argument based on a simple dynamic model. The idea is that a government can derive rents from the interaction with lobbies in the short run, but in the long run this will distort the allocation of resources, and the government is not compensated for this long-run distortion. As a consequence, the government may be better off committing to free trade ex-ante, thereby shutting down the lobbying process.[12]

The basic points can be illustrated within the workhorse model of Section 2.1. Consider the same economic and political structure as in that model, but now suppose that H is a small country, while F is a large "rest of the world." Also assume for simplicity that both sectors 1 and 2 are politically organized.

Consider the following timing: (0) the small-country government chooses whether to commit to free trade; (1) capital is allocated; and (2) given the capital allocation, trade policy and contributions are determined by Nash bargaining between the government and the lobbies (with σ denoting the government's bargaining power). This timing captures the idea that capital is mobile in the long run but not in the short run.

Suppose first that the government does not commit to free trade. Let us proceed by backward induction and find the second-stage equilibrium payoffs given the capital allocation. For the Home country, let K denote the vector of capital allocations and τ the vector of trade policies. Also, let $W(\tau, K)$ and $\Pi(\tau, K)$ denote respectively the levels of general welfare and the aggregate returns to capital in sectors 1 and 2 as functions of trade policies and capital allocations. Given that the government and the lobbies engage in Nash bargaining over policies and contributions, the first step is to derive the status-quo (disagreement) payoffs. In the status quo, lobbies give no contributions and the government chooses the welfare-maximizing policy, which is free trade, hence the government's status-quo payoff is $aW(0, K)$, and the lobbies' total status-quo payoff is $\Pi(0, K)$. The next step is to write down the joint surplus of the government and the lobbies:

$$J(K) = \max_{\tau}[aW(\tau, K) + \Pi(\tau, K)] - [aW(0, K) + \Pi(0, K)].$$

---

[12] I note that, while Maggi and Rodriguez-Clare focus on a setting where a government can be pressured only by its domestic lobbies, similar benefits from committing to free trade may arise if a government can be influenced also by foreign lobbies. For a paper that documents the empirical importance of foreign lobbying, see Gawande et al. (2006).

The government walks away with a share σ of this joint surplus, therefore its payoff in the second stage is given by $aW(0, K) + \sigma J(K)$.

The next step is to derive the equilibrium allocation in the first stage, which I denote $\hat{K}$. The key point is that, if $\sigma < 1$, this will generically be different from the free trade allocation ($\hat{K} \neq K^{FT}$), and hence inefficient, while $\hat{K} = K^{FT}$ if $\sigma = 1$. This is intuitive, because as long as lobbies have any bargaining power ($\sigma < 1$), the presence of lobbying distorts the net returns to capital relative to free trade. If, on the other hand, lobbies have no bargaining power ($\sigma = 1$), they will walk away from the bargain with no surplus, and hence the lobbying process does not affect the returns to capital *net of contributions*, so the equilibrium allocation is efficient. With this in mind, we can write the government's equilibrium payoff in the no-commitment scenario as $G^{NO} = aW(0, \hat{K}) + \sigma J(\hat{K})$.

Now suppose the government commits to free trade. In this case, expecting free trade, capital owners will make efficient allocation decisions: $K = K^{FT}$, and hence the government's payoff in this case is $G^{COMM} = aW(0, K^{FT})$.

The government will commit to free trade if and only if $G^{COMM} > G^{NO}$. Now observe that: (i) if $\sigma = 0$, then $G^{COMM} > G^{NO}$, because $W(0, K^{FT}) > W(0, \hat{K})$; and (ii) if $\sigma = 1$, as I noted above we have $\hat{K} = K^{FT}$, and since $J(K^{FT}) > 0$ then $G^{COMM} < G^{NO}$. We can then conclude that if σ is sufficiently low the government will commit to free trade, and if σ is sufficiently high it will not. Moreover, under some conditions G^{NO} will be increasing in σ, in which case there will be a critical level of σ below which the government commits to free trade and above which it does not. Thus the model yields an interesting prediction: countries whose governments have a weaker bargaining position vis-à-vis domestic lobbies should be more likely to join a TA.

Another prediction generated by the model concerns the impact of the parameter a, the government's valuation of welfare relative to contributions. Provided σ is sufficiently small, the value of commitment ($V = G^{COMM} - G^{NO}$) is non-monotonic in a: it starts negative, then it turns positive, and eventually it approaches zero as $a \to \infty$.[13] This in turn implies that, if there is a small cost of joining the agreement, the government will choose to join if a falls in some intermediate range.

Importantly, note that if export interests are organized the noncooperative equilibrium will entail export subsidies, so in Maggi and Rodriguez-Clare (1998) the government may want to commit to the elimination of export subsidies. Thus the model suggests a possible solution to the "export subsidy puzzle" highlighted above in the context of the TOT theory: if TAs are motivated by domestic-commitment issues, they will reduce export subsidies relative to their noncooperative levels.

---

[13] To see this, note that (i) if $a = 0$, the government does not care about welfare, so clearly $V < 0$; (ii) if $a = \infty$, the government only cares about welfare, so tariffs are zero in the political equilibrium, hence $V = 0$; (iii) that V must be positive for a range of a if σ is sufficiently small follows from the observation made above that, for fixed $a > 0$, if σ is sufficiently small then $V > 0$.

Next I make a point that will be useful to keep in mind when I focus on the implications of incomplete contracting for TAs (Section 3). Recall that in Maggi and Rodriguez-Clare (1998) the inefficiency in the noncooperative equilibrium stems from the government's lack of commitment vis-à-vis domestic agents, and the core of the problem is that the government does not get compensated for the long-run distortions from trade protection. But note that the same problem can be viewed also as a problem of *incomplete contracting* between the government and domestic agents: if the government could sign a long-term contract with all the future beneficiaries of protection, in which it commits to future trade policies and gets compensated for them, the problem would disappear. Of course, if capital is mobile in the long run, this long-term contracting would have to involve all capital owners in the economy, not only those that are currently in the organized sectors, thus it seems reasonable to assume that such long-term contracting is not feasible.

Maggi and Rodriguez-Clare (2007) extends the previous model in four directions. First, it allows for two large countries; thus the model nests two motives for a TA: a domestic-commitment motive and a TOT motive. Second, governments can commit to arbitrary tariff levels (as opposed to free trade or nothing); moreover, they can do so through exact tariff commitments (a complete contract) or through tariff caps (an incomplete contract). Third, specific-factor owners can lobby ex-ante to influence the shape of the agreement, not only ex-post. And fourth, the model allows for different degrees of capital mobility across sectors.

The model considers the following dynamic scenario. The world is sitting at the non-cooperative equilibrium—with its associated allocation distortions—when the opportunity to negotiate an agreement arrives.[14] The agreement maximizes the joint surplus of governments and lobbies. After the agreement is signed, each investor gets a chance to move his or her capital with an (exogenous) probability z. The parameter z thus captures the degree of mobility of capital. After the reallocation of capital has taken place, tariffs are chosen in each country by the government and the lobby subject to the constraints set by the agreement. Of course, this ex-post lobbying process is relevant only if the agreement leaves some discretion, that is, if the TA takes the form of tariff ceilings.

The key results of the model are four. First, the extent of trade liberalization (the tariff cuts enacted by the TA) is increasing in the degree of capital mobility (z). Intuitively, if z is higher, current lobby members care less about future protection, and hence they are less resistant to tariff cuts. This in turn suggests a further prediction, beyond those highlighted above in the context of the small-country model: tariff cuts should be deeper in sectors where capital is more mobile. This prediction seems consistent with the anecdotal

---

[14] In the basic version of the model the opportunity to sign a trade agreement is a surprise to investors, but Maggi and Rodriguez-Clare (2007) also consider a version of the model in which the trade agreement is perfectly anticipated by investors.

observation that in reality trade liberalization has been hard to come by in the agricultural sector, but it would be interesting to test this prediction in a more systematic way.

The second result concerns the impact of "politics"—captured inversely by the governments' valuation of welfare (a)—on the extent of trade liberalization: tariff cuts are deeper when politics are more important, provided the domestic-commitment motive is strong enough (z sufficiently high). This result stands in interesting contrast with the prediction of the pure TOT model, where tariff cuts if anything tend to be *less* deep when a is lower: the reason is that a lower a implies higher noncooperative tariffs, hence a lower trade volume and a weaker TOT externality, and this calls for smaller tariff cuts. Also in Maggi and Rodriguez-Clare (2007), a lower a implies higher noncooperative tariffs, but this in turn implies a bigger allocation distortion, and hence bigger tariff cuts are called for. If z is high, this consideration dominates the previous one.

At a more fundamental level, the divergence in results highlighted above is a manifestation of a key difference between the domestic-commitment theory and the TOT theory. In the domestic-commitment theory, the motive for a TA is inherently political, since the TA is directly aimed at blunting domestic lobbying pressures, thus the TA is *directly* affected by political parameters such as the governments' valuation of welfare; whereas in the TOT theory, the motive for a TA is inherently economic, and hence political forces affect a TA only *indirectly* through economic variables (e.g. outputs and trade volumes).

The third insight is that the presence of a domestic-commitment motive can explain why trade liberalization typically occurs in a gradual manner. In particular, the reduction in tariffs happens in two phases: first, there is an instantaneous drop in tariffs, which reflects the TOT motive for the TA, and subsequently there is a gradual tariff reduction, which reflects the domestic-commitment motive. Intuitively, the allocation distortions caused by protection are more severe in the long run than in the short run, and hence the domestic-commitment motive calls for bigger tariff reductions in the long run than in the short run. Furthermore, the speed of liberalization is increasing in z. The reason is that, if z is lower, the expected length of time for which capital owners are "stuck" in a sector is longer, so the lobby will insist on keeping a high protection level for a longer period of time.

Finally, Maggi and Rodriguez-Clare (2007) show that tariff ceilings are preferred to exact tariff commitments. The intuition is in two steps. First, if one focuses on complete TAs, the optimal exact tariff commitments in general are positive, though lower than the noncooperative levels, and hence induce allocation distortions. Second, consider replacing an optimal exact tariff commitment with a tariff ceiling at the same height: the former shuts down ex-post lobbying and contributions, while the latter leaves some discretion (governments have the *option* of setting tariffs below the ceilings) and hence induces ex-post lobbying and contributions; the latter is preferable because the anticipation of ex-post contributions reduces the expected net returns to capital in organized sectors, and hence mitigates the investment distortion. I will come back to the topic of tariff ceilings and the incompleteness of TAs in Section 3, where I focus on the design of TAs, but here I note that Maggi and Rodriguez-Clare's model can explain why TAs are incomplete contracts without relying on the presence of contracting frictions between governments (although, as I highlighted above, contracting frictions between a government and its domestic actors are key).

Next I briefly discuss other papers that have highlighted domestic-commitment motives for TAs in the presence of lobbying. Mitra (2002) shows that a similar domestic-commitment motive as in Maggi and Rodriguez-Clare (1998) arises also in a setting where there is no long-run distortion in the capital allocation, but there is a resource cost of lobby formation: in this case, if the government does not commit to free trade, the long-run inefficiency generated by the prospect of trade protection (that the government does not get compensated for) is given by the cost of lobby formation. More broadly, Mitra's paper suggests that there may be a domestic-commitment motive for a TA any time the prospect of trade protection leads to a long-run misallocation of resources, whether it is in the form of misallocation of resources between productive activities or waste of resources in unproductive activities.[15] Brou and Ruta (2009) extend Maggi and Rodriguez-Clare's (1998) model by allowing governments to use trade policies and domestic subsidies, and argue that the domestic-commitment theory of TAs can provide a rationale for the WTO's restrictions on the use of production subsidies.

Limão and Tovar (2011) propose a different version of the domestic-commitment argument for TAs. They consider a setting in which a small-country government bargains with a domestic lobby over two policy instruments, a tariff and a non-tariff barrier, where the latter is the less efficient redistributive instrument. In this setting they show that the government may benefit from committing to a tariff reduction because this may improve its bargaining position, and this benefit may outweigh the cost of constraining the more efficient redistributive tool. Finally, Liu and Ornelas (2012) argue that a TA can serve as a commitment device for the purpose of stabilizing a democratic regime. The key idea of this paper is that an incumbent government may value a TA because it leads to the destruction of rents, which in turn reduces the likelihood of a coup by rent-seeking autocratic groups, thereby helping consolidate unstable democracies.[16]

I conclude this section by mentioning another model where a government's lack of commitment vis-à-vis domestic agents has important implications for TAs. McLaren (1997) considers a two-period Ricardian model where a small country (S) negotiates a TA with a large country (L). In the first period, domestic agents commit their resources

---

[15] Krishna and Mitra (2005) explore an interesting consequence of Mitra's argument: if a country liberalizes unilaterally because of a commitment issue as in Mitra (2002), this will have effects on the trade policies chosen by its trading partners. They show that it may induce a trading partner to reduce its own tariffs, because it increases the incentives for the export lobby in the partner country to form and lobby against the import-competing lobby there for lower protection.

[16] This paper focuses on the rationale for joining free trade agreements, but the basic argument applies equally well to the case of a multilateral TA.

to a sector; in the second period, the governments negotiate over a tariff and a transfer through Nash bargaining. Given the resource allocation, the equilibrium TA involves free trade and a transfer from S to L. Ex-ante, anticipating free trade, agents commit resources to the sector where S has a comparative advantage. But this leads L to choose a higher tariff in the Nash equilibrium, which in turn worsens the outside option of country S in the trade negotiation. McLaren shows that this adverse effect of the *anticipation* of a TA on the welfare of the small country may outweigh the standard gains from trade, so this country may be better off by committing ex-ante *not* to sign a TA.

McLaren's point relates in an interesting way to the domestic-commitment theory of TAs. In McLaren's model, the TA can be interpreted as a short-term contract, because it occurs after investment decisions are made. But if the TA were a long-term contract, in the sense of occurring before investment decisions are made, then the hold-up problem highlighted by McLaren would not arise. Thus McLaren's model suggests that TAs can help *only if* they are effective long-run commitments (consistently with the domestic-commitment theory), while they can have perverse effects if they are only short-term commitments.[17]

2.3. New Trade Theories of Trade Agreements

A new and important line of research has emerged recently that explores the implications of imperfect competition for TAs. A central theme in this new area of research is that, in the presence of imperfect competition, TOT externalities are not the only international externalities from trade policy. In particular, three new externalities have been identified and examined: (i) "firm-delocation" externalities in the presence of free entry (Venables, 1985, 1987; Ossa, 2011; Bagwell and Staiger, 2009, 2012b), (ii) "profit-shifting" externalities (Mrazova, 2011; Ossa, 2012; Bagwell and Staiger, 2012a), and (iii) trade-volume externalities when prices are determined by bilateral bargaining (Antras and Staiger, 2012a,b). As I discuss below, these non-TOT externalities *may* be a separate cause of inefficiency in noncooperative policies, hence giving rise to new rationales for TAs, and can have important implications for the design of TAs.

2.3.1. Firm-Delocation and Profit-Shifting Externalities

In this section I focus on the implications of firm-delocation and profit-shifting externalities from trade policy, starting with the former type.

Venables (1985, 1987) was the first to identify the possibility of firm-delocation externalities from trade policies. This type of externality can arise whenever markets are imperfectly competitive and there is free entry. The basic idea is the following: if a

---

[17] In a recent paper, Sovey (2012) develops a model where TAs are motivated by "political hold-up" problems. In her model, if a government makes a public investment in its comparative-advantage sector and hence makes itself more "dependent" on trade, it gives its trading partner an increased ability to extract political concessions in the future. As in McLaren (1997), a political hold-up problem calls for a long-term TA. Sovey then argues that a long-term TA is harder to self-enforce than a short-term one, because of the additional political uncertainty over the longer time horizon, and for this reason a multilateral institution like the WTO, by increasing the severity of punishments, can facilitate self-enforcement.

country imposes a tariff on imports, this will tilt the balance of competition in favor of domestic firms, and this in turn will induce exit of foreign firms and entry of domestic firms. In the presence of transport costs, this effect tends to benefit the country imposing the tariff and hurt the exporting country.

Ossa (2011) has explored the implications of firm-delocation externalities for the purpose and design of TAs. In particular, Ossa considers a Krugman-type model with monopolistic competition, CES preferences over varieties and iceberg transport costs. Governments maximize welfare and can only choose *ad-valorem* import tariffs. In this model, import tariffs have no TOT effects at all. Intuitively, firms apply a constant mark-up over marginal cost, so the incidence of an *ad-valorem* tariff falls entirely on the importing country, and hence ex-factory prices are unaffected.[18] The feature that import tariffs have no TOT effects of course depends on the special model structure, but it serves to isolate the delocation externality, which operates in the following way: an increase in the Home tariff leaves the total number of domestic and foreign firms unchanged, but modifies its composition in favor of domestic firms; because of transport costs, this lowers the Home price index and increases the Foreign price index, thus leading to an increase in Home welfare and a decrease in Foreign welfare.[19]

As a consequence of the negative delocation externality that a tariff exerts on the exporting country, the noncooperative equilibrium entails inefficiently high tariffs, and so there is scope for a TA to reduce tariff levels. Ossa argues that this rationale for TAs resonates with the often-heard informal argument that import protection leads to a loss of manufacturing firms and "good jobs" in the exporting country, and the role of a TA is to prevent governments from engaging in this beggar-thy-neighbor behavior.[20]

Mrazova (2011) and Ossa (2012) focus on the implications of a different type of policy externality that may arise under imperfect competition, namely the *profit-shifting* externality. The profit-shifting effect of trade policies was first studied by Brander and Spencer (1984, 1985) in the context of a Cournot oligopoly with a fixed number of firms. Mrazova (2011) focuses on a setting similar to Brander and Spencer's, while Ossa (2012) focuses on a monopolistic competition model with a fixed number of firms. In

---

[18] Terms of trade in this setting can be defined in two different ways: as the ratio between the ex-factory price of a foreign variety and that of a domestic variety, or as the ratio between the price index for exported varieties and that for imported varieties. Ossa shows that with the first definition tariffs do not affect TOT, and with the second definition a tariff *worsens* the country's TOT. In the text I am implicitly adopting the first of these two definitions. It is also important to point out that, while import tariffs have no TOT effects (according to the first definition above), export taxes would have dollar-for-dollar effects on TOT, as emphasized by Bagwell and Staiger (2009).

[19] There is also a counteracting effect, because the tariff makes foreign products more expensive for consumers, but this effect is shown to be dominated.

[20] Ossa also argues that his model can provide a rationale for GATT's rules of reciprocity and MFN, much in the same way as a TOT model; I will come back to this aspect in Section 3.

both models, governments can only use import tariffs.[21] Just like the TOT externality, the profit-shifting externality from a tariff is negative (holding TOT fixed, an increase in the tariff hurts the exporting country), and as a consequence, a mutually beneficial TA must reduce tariff levels relative to the noncooperative equilibrium. Mrazova (2011) in addition shows that the Bagwell-Staiger "test" fails in her setting (PO tariffs are inefficient), thus the purpose of a TA indeed goes beyond the correction of TOT externalities.

Enter Bagwell and Staiger. In two companion papers (Bagwell and Staiger, 2009, 2012a) they argue that, if import instruments *and* export instruments are available, even in the presence of delocation or profit-shifting externalities the only purpose of a TA remains the correction of TOT externalities. They consider a number of possible market structures, including monopoly, monopolistic competition, and Cournot oligopoly (with or without free entry, and with or without integrated markets), and show that, if countries can use both import and export taxes and there are no income effects (quasi-linear preferences), then PO policies are efficient. On this basis, Bagwell and Staiger conclude that neither delocation nor profit-shifting externalities constitute a "fundamental" rationale for TAs.[22]

I will next try to illuminate the logic of Bagwell and Staiger's argument by considering a slightly more general setting. Focus on a two-country world with any number of goods, and suppose governments can choose specific trade taxes.[23] With a slight abuse of notation, $(\tau, \tau^*, p, p^*, p^w)$ will now denote the *vectors* of trade taxes and prices.

Government objectives can always be expressed in reduced form as functions of trade taxes ($\Omega(\tau, \tau^*)$ and $\Omega^*(\tau, \tau^*)$), and trade taxes in turn can be written as price wedges ($\tau = p - p^w$ and $\tau^* = p^* - p^w$), so government objectives can always be expressed as functions of local, foreign, and world prices ($\tilde{\Omega}(p, p^*, p^w) \equiv \Omega(p - p^w, p^* - p^w)$ and $\tilde{\Omega}^*(p, p^*, p^w) \equiv \Omega^*(p - p^w, p^* - p^w)$), regardless of the nature of the international policy externalities. Importantly, note that this setting allows for virtually any underlying market structure.[24] Note also that a government objective may depend on local prices in both

---

[21] Mrazova justifies the assumption that only tariffs are available by proposing a complementary theory that explains why export subsidies have been banned by the GATT-WTO. I will be more specific on this part of her theory below, where I focus on possible resolutions of the export subsidy puzzle.

[22] Ossa has replied to this criticism by observing that in reality the use of export instruments is severely restricted: (i) export subsidies have been banned by GATT a long time ago, and the subsequent rounds of negotiations have focused mostly on import barriers, and (ii) the US has banned export taxes by constitution. My personal opinion is that Bagwell and Staiger are correct in pointing out that a complete theory should in principle explain, not assume, the pre-existing restrictions on export instruments. However, it is not hard to imagine a model where there are transaction costs or political frictions such that trade negotiations do not address import barriers and export instruments simultaneously in a single round but rather in a sequential manner, or such that the unilateral use of export instruments is subject to frictions. In such a richer model, delocation (or profit-shifting) externalities would indeed be a distinct motive for TAs.

[23] The argument can be easily extended to allow for production and consumption taxes.

[24] Note that I have implicitly made two assumptions for simplicity. The first is that a government can apply different trade taxes for different goods. If goods are differentiated and a government must apply the same trade tax on all the

countries, and this is the new feature relative to the perfect-competition setting described in Section 2.1. This is a key point to keep in mind as we proceed: *non-TOT externalities can always be seen as local-price externalities.*

Assume that there are *no income effects*. Together with the assumption that there are only two countries, this implies that the local price of each good depends only on the *total* trade tax on that good. This feature is the key to Bagwell and Staiger's argument: under the assumptions I just stated, the import tax and the export tax on a given good are perfectly substitutable in affecting local prices.[25]

The PO policies are defined as the ones that would result if governments did not value changes in p^w. Since local prices depend only on total trade taxes (denoted $\bar{\tau} \equiv \tau + \tau^*$), this means that at the political optimum governments are effectively choosing the same variables, $\bar{\tau}$. Since the common choice of $\bar{\tau}$ must maximize both the Home objective and the Foreign objective, and since changes in p^w act as pure transfers, it follows that PO policies are efficient. Formally, PO policies are defined by the first order conditions $\tilde{\Omega}_p p_{\bar{\tau}} + \tilde{\Omega}_{p^*} p_{\bar{\tau}}^* = 0$ and $\tilde{\Omega}_p^* p_{\bar{\tau}} + \tilde{\Omega}_{p^*}^* p_{\bar{\tau}}^* = 0$ (where the notation has the intuitive meaning). Defining global welfare as $\tilde{\Omega} + \tilde{\Omega}^*$, and noting that a change in p^w does not affect global welfare (it is a pure transfer), the FOC for global efficiency is $(\tilde{\Omega}_p + \tilde{\Omega}_p^\tau) p_{\bar{\tau}} + (\tilde{\Omega}_{p^*} + \tilde{\Omega}_{p^*}^*) p_{\bar{\tau}}^* = 0$. Clearly, the PO policies satisfy the FOC for global efficiency.

I summarize this discussion with the following:

Efficiency of Political Optimum (EPO). Assume: (i) there are only two countries; (ii) there are no income effects; and (iii) governments choose only trade taxes. Then PO policies are efficient, even in the presence of local-price externalities.

This result is in a way very general and in a way very special. The sense in which it is very general is that it holds regardless of the nature of international policy externalities. Indeed, it holds even in scenarios where intuition might suggest that there are other motives for a TA beyond the correction of TOT externalities. For example, suppose there are non-pecuniary international externalities, for example because of cross-border pollution: the argument above is still valid, and hence PO policies are efficient. To be more concrete, consider a perfectly-competitive, partial-equilibrium model with a single good, where governments maximize welfare and there is a cross-border pollution externality generated by production in the Foreign country. Let $\Upsilon(x^*)$ denote the environmental damage caused in the Home country by foreign production and $x^*(p^*)$

varieties of that good, the argument must be slightly adapted, but it still goes through. The second assumption is that markets are integrated, so arbitrage implies that there is a single world (offshore) price for each good. If markets are segmented there may be two-way trade in identical commodities, and so there may be two distinct offshore prices for the same good, one for each direction of trade; but again, the argument is easily extended to cover this case.

[25] Intuitively, note first that the wedge between local prices is given by the total trade tax ($p - p^* = \tau + \tau^*$). Next note that changing τ and τ^* in a way that leaves the total trade tax constant causes a transfer of revenue between the countries. If there are no income effects, this transfer of revenue will not affect demand functions, thus only the total trade tax matters for equilibrium local prices, not its composition.

the foreign supply function. If Home welfare net of environmental damage is given by $W(p, p^w) - \Upsilon(x^*(p^*)) \equiv \Omega(p, p^*, p^w)$, and Foreign welfare is defined analogously, then the EPO result above immediately applies.[26]

At the same time, the three assumptions (i)–(iii) are very restrictive, and even though the EPO result only states a sufficient condition, each of the three assumptions plays a key role in delivering the efficiency of the PO policies: when local-price externalities are present, if any of the three assumptions is violated then import-side policies and export-side policies in general are not perfectly substitutable in affecting local prices, and hence PO policies will typically be inefficient.[27]

Before concluding this subsection, I return one last time to the "export subsidy puzzle." In Section 2.2, I discussed how the domestic-commitment theory can provide a possible resolution to this puzzle. As I discuss next, also models with firm-delocation and profit-shifting externalities offer avenues to address the puzzle.

Bagwell and Staiger (2012b) consider a linear Cournot delocation model á la Venables (1985), where two governments choose trade taxes to maximize welfare. First they show that, starting from free trade, a country acting unilaterally can increase its welfare with a small export subsidy (because its beneficial delocation effect outweighs its adverse TOT effect) and with a small import tariff. This suggests that imposing a cap on export subsidies may be jointly beneficial for the two countries. However, it turns out that the Nash equilibrium involves both import taxes and export taxes; what is responsible for this surprising result is the fact that import and export taxes are complementary (increasing the tariff makes an export tax more attractive). Thus, if governments negotiate over import and export instruments starting from the Nash equilibrium, the model is not able to explain why a TA would cap export subsidies. But if negotiations initially focus only on import tariffs, bringing them close enough to zero, in a subsequent phase of negotiation there will be scope for imposing a cap on export subsidies. In a similar vein, DeRemer (2011) considers a monopolistic competition model where governments can choose trade taxes and production subsidies. He argues that capping both export subsidies

---

[26] The EPO result applies also if, in addition to trade taxes, governments can use production taxes, which are the first-best instrument to correct the environmental externality (see footnote 23).

[27] To be clear, there may be special circumstances in which PO policies are efficient even if some of the conditions (i)–(iii) are not satisfied. For example, Bagwell and Staiger (2012a) show that PO policies are efficient in a special three-country setting with competing exporters. And in Antras and Staiger (2012a), as I will mention later, PO policies are efficient in the special case where governments maximize welfare, in spite of there being three countries in their model. But these cases are rather special, and that is why I use the word "typically" in the text. Here I should also highlight the relationship between my EPO result and a result shown by Bagwell and Staiger (2012a): they show that, if conditions (i)–(iii) above are satisfied *and* (iv) government preferences can be represented as functions of world and local prices, then PO policies are efficient. Importantly, they emphasize that condition (iv) can only be assessed given the specific economic structure, and they check that this is the case in a number of imperfect-competition models. The value added of my EPO result is to show that, if conditions (i)–(iii) are satisfied, there is no need to know anything else about the economic structure or the nature of the international externalities to conclude that PO policies are efficient.

and production subsidies may be desirable, but only if import tariffs are sufficiently close to zero, not if they are close to their Nash equilibrium levels.

While the two models mentioned above are broadly suggestive of reasons why the GATT-WTO has banned export subsidies, neither of them can explain an outcome where export subsidies are present in the noncooperative equilibrium *and* a TA bans export subsidies. Mrazova's (2011) model can explain both of these features. Her model allows for political economy considerations, so the Nash equilibrium may entail export subsidies. The basic idea to explain the ban on export subsidies is the following. Recall from Section 2.1.1 that an efficient TA determines only net trade taxes, not the separate import and export tax levels (see equation (3)) so that a given point on the efficiency frontier can be achieved with import instruments alone or with export instruments alone. Assuming a fixed cost of administering each policy instrument, efficiency requires the use of (at most) one policy instrument for each good. Mrazova then considers a repeated-game model of TAs and argues that, due to profit-shifting effects, a tariff-only agreement is more easily self-enforced than a subsidy-only agreement, so an export subsidy ban is desirable.

2.3.2. Trade-Volume Externalities Due to Bilateral Bargaining

When prices of international transactions are determined by bilateral bargaining rather than by market clearing, the international externalities exerted by trade policy are of a different nature than the ones highlighted so far, and have novel implications for the purpose and design of TAs. This is the focus of two recent papers by Antras and Staiger (2012a,b).

It is convenient to start with Antras and Staiger (2012b), which focuses on a simple matching model to highlight some key implications of bilateral bargaining for TAs. More specifically, this paper considers a two-country, partial-equilibrium model where all producers are located in the Foreign country. Each producer is matched with a consumer, and within each match the quantity exchanged and the price are determined by bilateral bargaining. Governments maximize welfare, with the Foreign government choosing an export tax and a domestic input subsidy, and the Home government choosing an import tariff.

In this environment, international policy externalities cannot be viewed as traveling simply through TOT. To understand the key difference between this environment and a setting with market clearing, notice first that in the case of market clearing, Foreign policies can affect the point of Home's offer curve that is selected in equilibrium, but cannot affect Home's offer curve itself; so they can affect world price and trade volume but cannot control them separately; in this sense, there is a single channel of international policy externality, which can be viewed alternatively as a TOT externality or a trade-volume externality. With bilateral bargaining, on the other hand, this link is broken, and Foreign policies can affect TOT and trade volume separately, thus the rationale for a TA is to jointly correct these two separate externalities. Indeed, with bilateral bargaining, PO policies can be shown to be inefficient, so the purpose of a TA goes beyond the correction of TOT externalities.[28]

Pricing by bilateral bargaining is particularly relevant when firms offshore the production of specialized inputs and there is incomplete contracting between downstream and upstream producers. The implications of offshoring for TAs are the focus of Antras and Staiger (2012a). This paper considers an environment with three countries: Home, Foreign, and the rest of the world (ROW). Home is the sole producer of a final good that requires a custom-made intermediate input; Foreign is the sole producer of the intermediate input; and ROW specializes in a plain-vanilla numeraire good. Once a Foreign upstream firm and a Home downstream firm are matched, the former must customize the intermediate input for the latter, and then the price of the input is determined by bilateral bargaining. The customization of the input cannot be contracted upon ex-ante, thus a standard hold-up problem arises. Each government chooses trade taxes to maximize a possibly politically adjusted social welfare function. In this setting, beyond standard TOT externalities, trade policies exert trade-volume externalities of the kind described above, with the additional feature that, by affecting trade volumes, a country's trade policies can affect the severity of the hold-up problem in the other country.

In this environment, Antras and Staiger (2012a) show that PO policies are in general inefficient, except in the special case where governments maximize welfare. Thus, as long as there are political-economy considerations in the governments' objectives, the rationale for TAs goes beyond the correction of TOT externalities.[29]

It is clear that, in this setting, the international externalities from trade policies do not simply travel through TOT. However, as the EPO result of Section 2.3.1 highlights, the presence of non-TOT externalities is not sufficient to conclude that PO policies are inefficient. So why does the EPO result *not* apply here? The key reason is that in this setting there are more than two countries, and as a consequence, export taxes and import taxes are not perfectly substitutable in affecting local prices.[30] To confirm this point, I note that if Antras and Staiger's (2012a) model were played out in a two-country world, then the PO policies would be always efficient, regardless of the government objectives. Thus in

---

[28] The implication that PO policies are inefficient is not highlighted in the paper, but it is easy to show. The paper focuses on a design question, namely whether a "shallow integration" approach can achieve global efficiency, but the paper is relevant also for the question of the purpose of a TA. I will come back to the design question in Section 3. Also, it is interesting to note that the EPO result presented in Section 2.3.1 does *not* apply in Antras and Staiger's (2012b) setting, because trade taxes are not the only policy instruments: Foreign can use also a non-wedge policy, namely an input subsidy, and there is no Home policy that is a perfect substitute for it in affecting local prices.

[29] A second question examined by Antras and Staiger (2012a) concerns the desirability of a "shallow integration" approach. Again, I will focus on this design question in Section 3.

[30] Intuitively, recall that Home is the sole producer of the final good, so the local price of this good in the Home market (say p^H) depends on all three trade taxes on this good, but not through their sum, because Home's export tax has a larger impact on p^H than each of the other countries' import tax. Also note that the reason why the EPO result does not apply in Antras and Staiger (2012a) is different than the one in Antras and Staiger (2012b). As highlighted in footnote 28, in the latter model (which has only two countries) the reason the EPO result does not apply is that trade taxes are not the only policy instruments.

some sense the more surprising aspect of the results in Antras and Staiger (2012a) is not that the PO policies are inefficient in the presence of political-economy considerations, but rather that the PO policies *are* efficient in the case of welfare-maximizing governments.

2.4. The Uncertainty-Managing Motive for a TA

The papers discussed so far abstract from the presence of uncertainty, and highlight the gains that a TA can offer by changing the levels of trade policies relative to the non-cooperative equilibrium. But if the political/economic environment is uncertain, one can distinguish between an "uncertainty managing" motive and a "mean managing" motive for a TA. Suppose that, because of shocks in the political/economic environment, noncooperative trade policies are themselves subject to shocks. We can then ask the following question: can governments achieve mutual gains by changing the degree of uncertainty in trade policies relative to the noncooperative equilibrium, *holding their mean levels constant*? If the answer is yes, we can say that there is an "uncertainty managing" motive for a TA. Limão and Maggi (2013) examine under what conditions there exists an uncertainty-managing motive for a TA, whether it calls for a reduction or an increase in policy uncertainty, and what are the potential gains from a TA that regulates policy uncertainty.[31]

In a standard competitive trade model with risk neutrality, where trade policies exert international externalities only through TOT, Limão and Maggi show that there tends to be an uncertainty-*increasing* motive for a TA, due to the convexity of indirect utility and revenue functions in prices. This model thus seems at odds with the often-heard argument that TAs can provide welfare gains by reducing trade policy uncertainty. When individuals are risk averse, on the other hand, the direction of the uncertainty motive for a TA is determined by a trade-off between risk aversion and flexibility: the degree of risk aversion, in interaction with the degree of openness, favors an uncertainty-reducing motive; while the degree of flexibility of the economy, which is in turn determined by the export supply elasticity and the degree of production diversification, favors an uncertainty-increasing motive. Empirically lower-income countries tend to have lower export supply elasticities and a lower degree of diversification, thus Limão and Maggi's model suggests that the uncertainty-reducing motive might be relatively more important for lower-income countries. Another key result is that, as trade costs decline, the gains from reducing trade policy uncertainty tend to become more important relative to the gains from reducing average trade barriers. A broad implication of this finding is that

---

[31] Policy makers and practitioners often argue that one of the main goals of TAs is to reduce uncertainty in trade policies, and various TAs including the WTO include "mission" statements that can be interpreted along similar lines. For example, the WTO states in its website that "Just as important as freer trade—perhaps more important—are other principles of the WTO system. For example: non-discrimination, and making sure the conditions for trade are stable, predictable and transparent."

uncertainty-reducing motives for TAs are likely to emerge as the world becomes more integrated, and are more likely to be present for countries within a region.[32]

2.5. Empirical Evidence

The empirical literature on TAs is still in its infancy, but it has seen a considerable acceleration in the last decade or so. In this section I discuss some papers that attempt to get at the underlying motives for TAs, and some that examine the impacts of TAs on trade barriers and trade flows in a more descriptive way. I postpone a discussion of the empirical work on regional trade agreements to Section 4.

2.5.1. Tests of the TOT Theory

A number of recent papers have set out to test the predictions of the TOT theory. Four papers stand out in this group. The first one is Broda et al. (2008), who focus on the prediction that, in a noncooperative scenario, tariffs should tend to be higher for countries/goods where market power (the inverse of the export supply elasticity) is higher. Broda et al. consider the tariffs set by 15 non-WTO countries, on the presumption that these countries choose trade policies in a noncooperative manner. They estimate export supply elasticities by country and good—a significant contribution in itself—and find that these elasticities are related with tariffs in the way predicted by the theory, particularly if one focuses on the variation across goods within a country. Next they control for political-economy determinants of tariffs, using a parsimonious specification á la Grossman-Helpman (with the additional assumption that all industries are politically organized), and find that export supply elasticities retain explanatory power even in the extended specification.[33]

Bagwell and Staiger (2011) test the predictions of the TOT model regarding the tariff cuts that a country should make when *acceding* the WTO. Bagwell and Staiger start by showing that, if demand and supply functions are linear, the model predicts that the tariff cut should be deeper, other things equal, when the noncooperative volume of imports is higher. They then test this prediction across six-digit HS level goods and across 16 countries that acceded the WTO between 1995 and 2005, finding a strong positive correlation. The correlation survives also in the presence of country and good

---

[32] Also Handley (2012) and Handley and Limão (2012, 2013) focus on the links between uncertainty and TAs, but from a very different perspective. They examine (theoretically and empirically) the impact that TAs have on trade flows by removing the risk of future increases in protection, taking trade policy (before and after the TA) as exogenous. Handley and Limão do not consider the key questions addressed in Limão and Maggi (2013), namely whether there is "too much" or "too little" uncertainty in the noncooperative trade policies and what are the gains from "correcting" the degree of policy uncertainty through a TA. I will come back to the papers by Handley and Limão in the next section.

[33] However, there is one finding in Broda et al. (2008) that is not easy to reconcile with the TOT theory. According to the theory, a country acting noncooperatively should set discriminatory tariffs, because export supply elasticities vary across exporters, but this almost never happens in the data. The authors argue that the presence of administrative costs can reconcile this observation with the theory, but these costs would have to be very high, because export supply elasticities vary widely across exporters and therefore the potential gains from discrimination are high.

fixed effects, and importantly, it passes the "placebo" test that it should hold only for tariffs on imports from other WTO members, not on imports from non-WTO countries.[34]

The papers discussed above focus on non-WTO countries (Broda et al.) or countries that recently joined the WTO (Bagwell and Staiger), so they leave out the vast majority of current WTO countries. Ludema and Mayda (2010) focus instead on the MFN tariffs of all WTO members. Their test of the TOT theory is based on the following idea: the MFN rule causes a well-known free-rider problem in multilateral negotiations, and for this reason negotiations are only partially successful in removing TOT considerations from tariff levels, therefore the negotiated MFN tariffs should still partially reflect the market power of importing countries. Moreover, the correlation between MFN tariffs and market power should be stronger when exporter concentration (as measured for example by the Herfindahl index) is lower, because in this case the free-rider problem is more severe, thus MFN tariffs should be negatively related to the product of exporter concentration and importer market power. Ludema and Mayda test this prediction on a cross-section of MFN tariffs set by WTO members in the Uruguay Round, finding supportive results.

Finally, Bown and Crowley (2013a) test the predictions of a repeated-game version of the TOT model (namely, Bagwell and Staiger's (1990) model of "managed trade") using data on US temporary tariffs imposed under the US's antidumping and safeguard laws over 1997–2006. The key idea of the model is that, if a TA is to be self-enforcing, it needs to provide for "escape clauses" that allow countries to raise tariffs in periods when the temptation to defect from the agreement is stronger, that is when the incentive to manipulate TOT is stronger, which in turn tends to happen when trade volumes are higher.[35] Thus a key prediction of the model is that temporary tariffs should be observed with higher likelihood when import volumes are higher. Bown and Crowley find strong support for this prediction in the data.

Finally, I should mention that there are a number of empirical studies documenting that a country's tariffs can significantly affect its TOT, which of course is a pre-requisite for the empirical relevance of the TOT theory. Papers in this group include Kreinin (1961), Winters and Chang (2000, 2002), and Bown and Crowley (2006).

2.5.2. Tests of the Domestic-Commitment Theory

As a whole, the studies discussed above are quite supportive of the TOT theory. At the same time, I do not think this body of research has established that the TOT motive is the *only* empirically significant motive for TAs. This leads me to the next question, which is whether other motives for TAs are empirically important. The short answer to this

---

[34] Bagwell and Staiger also consider a more general relationship predicted by TOT theory between tariff cuts, trade elasticities and import volumes, and test this prediction using Broda et al.'s (2008) trade elasticities for the five countries within their sample for which such elasticities are available. Also the results of this test are consistent with the predictions of the theory.

[35] See Section 3.2.1 for further discussion of repeated-game versions of the TOT model.

question is that we do not know yet: domestic-commitment theories and New Trade theories of TAs have thus far received less empirical attention than the TOT theory, and the jury is still out. I will start by focusing on the empirical research on the domestic-commitment theory.

The first paper in this area is by Staiger and Tabellini (1999), who test a prediction of their theoretical model (Staiger and Tabellini, 1987), in which the government is subject to a time-inconsistency problem due to the fact that it chooses trade policy after domestic agents have made their allocation decisions. This model suggests that, if the government commits to a TA to address this time-inconsistency problem, the TA should lead to deeper trade liberalization in sectors where the potential for production distortions from protection is larger. Staiger and Tabellini test this prediction by focusing on the sectoral exclusions chosen by the US government in the Tokyo Round of GATT, using as "control" group the US tariff decisions made under the GATT's escape clause, which arguably were not effectively constrained by GATT. Their findings are broadly supportive of the model's prediction.

Limão and Tovar (2011) test their theoretical model (see Section 2.2) using data on tariffs and non-tariff barriers (NTBs) in Turkey. One key prediction of their model is that a government is more likely to commit to a tariff cap in industries where its bargaining power relative to the lobby is lower, and conditional on committing, the tariff cap should be tighter when the government's bargaining power is lower. A key ingredient in testing this prediction is measuring the government's relative bargaining power industry by industry. To do so, Limão and Tovar posit that the relative bargaining power of the government in a given industry is lower when the rate of firm exit in that industry is lower. The idea is that, if the exit rate is lower, the firms (and the lobby that represents them) discount the future less, while the government's discount rate does not vary across industries, and noncooperative bargaining theory suggests that a player's relative bargaining power is higher when his or her relative patience is higher. Using their estimates of relative bargaining powers, Limão and Tovar find that in the Uruguay Round the Turkish government indeed committed to less stringent tariff bindings in industries where its relative bargaining power was stronger, and did not commit at all if the latter was strong enough.[36] It is interesting to note that this finding is broadly consistent also with the predictions of Maggi and Rodriguez-Clare's (1998, 2007) version of the domestic-commitment theory.[37]

Liu and Ornelas (2012) test their theory that a TA may serve as a commitment device for a fragile democracy to destroy protectionistic rents and hence reduce the likelihood of

[36] Another finding in Limão and Tovar (2011) is that Turkey used NTBs more heavily after the tariff bindings were imposed. This finding as well is consistent with their model, but I note that this kind of policy substitution between tariffs and NTBs is consistent also with a variety of models that do not feature domestic-commitment motives for a TA.

[37] In Maggi and Rodriguez-Clare (1998) the government is more likely to commit to free trade when its bargaining power is lower, and in Maggi and Rodriguez-Clare (2007) tariff caps tend to be tighter when governments have lower bargaining power (see section I.D of that paper).

coups by rent-seeking authoritarian groups (see Section 2.2), by using data on preferential trade agreements for 116 countries over the period 1960–2007. In line with their model's predictions, Liu and Ornelas find that more fragile democracies are indeed more likely to sign preferential TAs, and that signing a preferential TA in turn lowers the likelihood of democratic failure.

I would summarize the thin empirical literature on the domestic-commitment theory of TAs by saying that it has found support for *some* predictions of *some* versions of the theory, but a broad and systematic empirical investigation of this theory is still missing. Ultimately, the hope is to be able to quantify the relative importance of TOT motives and domestic-commitment motives for TAs, but this is certainly no easy task.

2.5.3. Empirical Work on the New Trade Theory

Empirical research focused on New Trade theories of TAs is at the very beginning. I am not aware of any attempts to test these theories with econometric approaches, but a recent paper by Ossa (2013) takes the theory to the data using a calibration approach.

Ossa develops a multi-country model that allows for three drivers of trade protection: TOT effects, profit-shifting effects, and political-economy considerations.[38] The model, which combines elements from Krugman (1980) and Grossman and Helpman (1995a), is calibrated to match observed trade flows and tariffs at the industry level in 2005. Using a technique introduced by Dekle et al. (2007), Ossa performs counterfactual analysis using only estimates of the elasticities of substitution (taken from Broda and Weinstein, 2006), estimates of political-economy weights (taken from Goldberg and Maggi, 1999), and factual levels of trade flows and tariffs. Several interesting findings arise. First, TOT and profit-shifting drivers of protection quantitatively dominate political-economy drivers. Second, a global trade war would lead to tariffs averaging about 60% across industries and countries, and would reduce welfare by about 3.5% relative to the cooperative outcome. Finally, relative to where we are today, the potential gains from further multilateral trade negotiations are negligible.

Whether these are "numbers we can believe in" is not obvious, given the very stylized nature of the model, but this is a thought-provoking paper that points to a promising way forward for addressing important questions such as quantifying the relative importance of different motives for trade protection, the gains achieved by past TAs, and the potential gains from future TAs.

2.5.4. Impacts of the GATT-WTO

In this subsection I briefly discuss a recent wave of papers that have examined the impact of the GATT-WTO on trade barriers and trade flows. This literature was triggered by

---

[38] An earlier attempt at quantifying New Trade motives for protection can be found in Ossa (2011), in the context of a model featuring only firm-delocation effects. In that calibration exercise, Ossa allows each country to set only a single tariff on all imports, and only focuses on noncooperative tariffs.

Rose (2004a), who sent shockwaves through the trade policy community (academic and not) by arguing that the WTO had virtually no impact on trade flows, based on a simple reduced-form regression analysis. In a similar vein, Rose (2004b) argued that the WTO had a negligible effect on the trade policies actually applied by countries.

These papers spawned a number of follow-up studies, most of which qualified Rose's results in significant ways. Subramanian and Wei (2007) show that the impact of WTO has been very uneven across countries and sectors, for example because developing countries enjoyed exemptions from trade liberalization in specific sectors (such as textiles); once these exceptions are accounted for, the WTO is found to significantly promote trade. Tomz et al. (2007) argue that many countries were mistakenly classified as non-members of the GATT, while in reality they were *de facto* members with similar rights and obligations as formal members, and show that this misclassification leads to underestimating the effect of GATT on trade flows. Liu (2009) shows the importance of "zeroes" in bilateral trade flows: if one takes into account that the WTO has lead new country pairs to initiate bilateral trade—the "extensive partner-level margin" of trade—then the WTO is found to have a significant positive effect on trade. Dutt et al. (2011) find that the impact of WTO membership is significant on the extensive product margin of trade, that is, WTO membership leads to an increase in the number of goods traded, but the impact of the WTO is negligible on the intensive margin (the trade volume of already-traded goods).[39]

Next I discuss some recent papers that also examine the effects of TAs on trade flows, but use more structural approaches, and provide some evidence about the mechanisms through which a TA affects trade.

Eicher and Henn (2011) examine the effects of WTO and regional trade agreements on trade flows by considering a panel of 177 countries over 50 years. They start with a reduced-form gravity approach that encompasses the specifications by Rose (2004a), Tomz et al. (2007), and Subramanian and Wei (2007), and find that only regional trade agreements have a significant impact on trade, not the WTO. Then they consider an augmented gravity equation that incorporates a key effect suggested by the TOT theory, namely that countries with more market power should agree to bigger tariff cuts as they join the WTO, and hence their trade volumes should increase by more. When a measure of market power (pre-accession import volumes) is incorporated in the regressions, the WTO is found to have a significant effect for countries with import volumes above the 85th percentile. This finding contributes to reconcile the seemingly contradictory results of reduced-form studies á la Rose (2004a) and theory-driven studies á la Bagwell and Staiger (2010a).

Finally, Handley (2012) and Handley and Limão (2012, 2013) show that the mechanisms through which TAs affect trade flows may be more subtle than just a decrease of tariff *levels*. These papers argue that, when trade policies are subject to shocks, export-

---

[39] Another paper worthy of mention is Tang and Wei (2010), which examines the impact of WTO on GDP growth, finding that WTO membership tends to be associated with higher GDP growth rates for developing countries.

ing firms respond not just to changes in the applied levels of trade barriers, but also to changes in the probability that trade barriers might be raised in the future. Thus, by reducing the risk of future protectionist spikes, a TA may encourage investment in export markets and boost trade volumes even if no change in applied policy levels is observed. Handley (2012) focuses on Australia's accession to WTO, finding evidence that this caused an increase in exports to Australia more because committing to WTO bindings removed the risk of future "bad news" for exporters, than because of actual reductions in Australia's applied tariffs. Handley and Limão (2012) find evidence that Portugal's accession to the EC boosted Portuguese exports to other EC countries in spite of the fact that Portugal already enjoyed free access to those countries before accession, thanks to pre-existing preferences, and estimate that a significant fraction of this effect was due to the fact that accession to the EC eliminated the risk faced by Portuguese exporters of losing pre-existing preferences. Finally, Handley and Limão (2013) estimate that a significant portion of China's rapid increase in exports to the US starting in 2001 is explained by the permanent MFN status gained by China as a consequence of its WTO accession, which removed the US threat of imposing "column 2" tariffs on imports from China.

3. THE DESIGN OF TRADE AGREEMENTS

In a world without transaction costs, the issue of how to design a TA would be rather uninteresting. Imagine for a moment that governments could costlessly write a complete contract that covers all relevant policies and contingencies and can be perfectly enforced. In such a world (which is the world I effectively considered in the previous section) there would be no need to think hard about how to design a TA: governments would be able to achieve a fully efficient outcome by writing a complete contract. Such contract would contain a large amount of detail, but would be conceptually straightforward.

In this section I will discuss the literature on the design of TAs as viewed from the perspective of transaction costs. To be a bit more specific, I will use the expression "transaction costs" as an umbrella term that encompasses two categories of frictions: (1) *contracting frictions*, which include costs of negotiating and writing contracts, imperfect verifiability, and private information, and (2) *imperfect enforcement*, by which I mean the lack of external enforcement power, so that TAs must be self-enforcing contracts.

Note that, while contracting frictions naturally lead to contract incompleteness, meaning that relevant contingencies and/or policies are missing from the contract, enforcement frictions typically do *not* generate contract incompleteness: the presence of self-enforcement constraints *per se* is not a reason for removing contingencies or policies from the contract. In fact, it can have the opposite effect, in the sense of inducing governments to introduce contingencies that otherwise would not be present in the contract. For example, self-enforcement constraints may require the agreement to be contingent on import shocks (escape clauses), whereas a perfectly enforceable agreement would not need to be contingent.[40] For this reason, below I organize my discussion in two parts: first I will focus on the implications of contract incompleteness for TA design, and then I will focus on the implications of imperfect enforcement.

What would we miss if we ignored the presence of transaction costs? Why not stop at the world considered in the previous section, where the only questions concern the motives for a TA and how the efficient policies differ from noncooperative policies? If theory stopped there, it would not be able to explain a number of important features of real-world TAs. For example, it would be hard to explain why the GATT-WTO specifies tariff caps instead of exact tariff commitments; or why many domestic policies such as standards or domestic taxes are left to the governments' discretion; and so on.

Also, if we ignored transaction costs it would be difficult to explain the nature of trade disputes in the WTO and the role of the WTO court, the Dispute Settlement Body (DSB): absent transaction costs the only possible role for a court would be to enforce the obligations specified in the agreement, but in reality trade disputes are more often about the interpretation of vague obligations, or instances for which the agreement is silent, than about the enforcement of clear obligations. Thus a potentially important role of the DSB is to "complete" various dimensions of an incomplete contract, and therefore designing the role of the DSB becomes of key importance.

Before proceeding, it is useful to distinguish between three dimensions of TA design: (1) the design of substantive *policy rules*, that is constraints on governments' policy choices (e.g. tariff ceilings, non-discrimination rules); (2) the design of *enforcement rules* (how should governments behave after a violation of the agreement?); and (3) the design of *procedures*, such as dispute settlement procedures.[41] I will argue that introducing transaction costs in our conceptual frame can take us a long way toward understanding the design of TAs along these three dimensions.

3.1. Contract Incompleteness and Trade Agreements

The overarching theme of this section is that viewing TAs as incomplete contracts can help understand the way TAs are designed. In the models I will discuss below, the incompleteness of the TA is sometimes derived endogenously from contracting frictions, sometimes assumed exogenously, and sometimes left implicit. I would argue that modeling contracting frictions *explicitly* has the advantage of forcing us to think in a disciplined way about the rationale for the rules and procedures we observe in real-world TAs. I am not advocating a dogmatic approach where everything must be explained from "first principles," but I think that too often a theoretical "story" proposed to explain a certain rule

---

[40] This is the case for example in Bagwell and Staiger's (1990) model of "managed trade" (see Section 3.2.1).

[41] Another important type of procedure is the bargaining protocol for trade negotiations. In spite of the obvious importance of negotiation protocols, however, I am not aware of any formal literature addressing this question. On a distinct note, a paper that focuses on questions of procedure but does not fit easily in the taxonomy above is Conconi et al. (2012), which examines how domestic fast-track procedures for congressional approval of trade agreements affect the outcome of trade negotiations.

X has some intuitive appeal, but does not stand up to a more rigorous test, which is the following question: can rule X be part of an optimally designed contract, at least for some plausible contracting environment?

I will organize the discussion below as follows. I will first lay out a simple model of TAs where two distinct forms of contract incompleteness—rigidity and discretion—arise endogenously from contracting frictions, and argue that this model can help explain a number of design features of the observed TAs. I will then discuss other models that have been proposed in the literature to explain specific rules such as tariff caps, reciprocity, MFN, market-access rules, and "liability" vs "property" rules. Finally, I will focus on the design of dispute settlement procedures.

3.1.1. *Contracting costs, rigidity, and discretion*

To lay out some basic concepts I will start by outlining a model by Horn et al. (2010), where the incompleteness of a TA emerges endogenously from the costs of writing a contract. In spite of its simplicity, this form of contracting friction can go surprisingly far in explaining the way TAs are designed.[42]

At the basis of this model is the observation that there are two important sources of complexity in writing a TA: (a) uncertainty about future economic/political conditions, which calls for agreements that are highly contingent, and (b) the wide array of policies (domestic and border measures) that can affect trade, which in turn calls for agreements that are very comprehensive in their policy coverage. For these reasons, writing a complete contract would be very costly, since all contingencies and policies would need to be described ex-ante and verified ex-post.[43] In this context, one can think of two ways to save on writing costs: leaving contingencies out of the contract, which leads to *rigidity*, or leaving policies out of the contract, which amounts to introducing *discretion*.

Real-world TAs exhibit an interesting combination of rigidity and discretion. For example, the GATT-WTO binds trade instruments, but domestic instruments are largely left to discretion, except that (i) the WTO has introduced regulation of domestic subsidies, and (ii) all domestic policies must satisfy the National Treatment rule. Also, constraints on tariffs take the form of ceilings (so governments have downward discretion), and such ceilings are largely rigid, but the contract also provides for "escape clauses" under some contingencies. Horn et al. argue that the presence of contracting costs can help explain these design features.

---

[42] Writing costs can be interpreted more broadly as capturing also the costs of negotiating a TA and the costs of verifying contingencies and policies. I also note here that this approach to modeling endogenous contract incompleteness was first developed, though in a different setting, by Battigalli and Maggi (2002).

[43] Are contracting costs empirically important for an agreement such as the WTO? This is a legitimate question, but given the huge number of products, countries, policy instruments, and contingencies that are involved in the WTO, and the fact that this agreement took eight years of negotiations to complete, contracting costs seem quantitatively important. Many trade-law scholars agree with this view. For example, Schwartz and Sykes (2002) write: "...Many contracts are negotiated under conditions of considerable complexity and uncertainty, and it is not economical for the parties to specify in advance how they ought to behave under every conceivable contingency." (pp. 181–182)

Horn et al. consider a two-country, partial-equilibrium model where markets are perfectly competitive but there may be production and consumption (localized) externalities, so that there is an efficiency rationale for multiple policies, in particular tariffs and production subsidies. There can be uncertainty both in the underlying trade volume and in the externality levels, so that a first-best agreement would need to specify policies in a state-contingent way. At the core of the model is the assumption that the cost of the agreement is increasing in the number of policy instruments and contingencies it specifies.

The analysis focuses on four questions of TA design. The first one is whether it is desirable to leave domestic subsidies to the governments' discretion. Horn et al. find that, for a given level of contracting costs, this is more likely if: (a) trade volumes are low, so that countries gain little from manipulating TOT; or (b) countries have little monopoly power in trade, so that they have little capacity to manipulate TOT; or (c) subsidies are not a good substitute for tariffs as a means of manipulating TOT. The trade-volume effect at point (a) suggests an explanation for why domestic subsidies have been constrained by WTO while they were largely left to discretion under GATT, namely, that a general expansion of trade volumes over time has made it more costly to leave subsidies to discretion. Moreover, the "monopoly power" and "instrument substitutability" effects at points (b) and (c) together suggest a possible explanation for why developing countries have been largely exempted from constraints on subsidies through "special and differential treatment" clauses: developing countries typically do not have strong market power and do not have a broad range of domestic policy instruments that can easily substitute for tariffs.

The second design question is whether and how the TA should be state-contingent. An interesting result in this regard is that, conditional on leaving domestic subsidies to discretion, it can be optimal to specify an escape clause that allows a government to increase its tariff when the level of imports is high, as a way to mitigate the stronger incentives to distort domestic subsidies in periods of high import volume. Thus the model suggests a novel explanation for the desirability of escape clauses in TAs: these can be attractive because they provide an indirect means of managing the distortions associated with leaving domestic policies to discretion.[44]

The third point made by Horn et al. is that the presence of contracting costs can explain why tariffs are constrained by *ceilings* rather than by exact levels. More specifically, the optimal agreement may include *rigid* tariff ceilings. Intuitively, conditional on some contingencies being missing from the agreement, leaving downward discretion in tariffs can only be beneficial, since a government is always tempted to distort tariffs *upwards*, and there may be states of the world where the unilaterally optimal tariff lies below the

---

[44] Note that this explanation for escape clauses is very different from others that have been proposed in the theoretical literature, and in particular those that are based on self-enforcement considerations (e.g. Bagwell and Staiger, 1990, discussed in Section 3.2.1).

ceiling. In Section 3.1.2, I will discuss other possible explanations for the use of tariff ceilings.

Finally, the model by Horn et al. can provide a novel rationale for the National Treatment (NT) rule, showing that such a rule can serve to save on contracting costs. To make this point, Horn et al. extend the basic model outlined above by allowing for consumption taxes on domestically-produced and imported goods, and formalize the NT rule as a constraint that these taxes be equalized. A preliminary observation is that a TA that imposes the NT rule but leaves discretion over the (non-discriminatory) consumption tax can achieve a new form of discretion that cannot be achieved without the NT rule, namely, discretion over the consumer price wedge; indeed, a non-NT agreement can only leave discretion over the producer price wedge.[45] Horn et al. then show that under some conditions the NT rule can indeed be part of an optimal TA. The key observation here is that leaving discretion over the (non-discriminatory) consumption tax may involve a subtle benefit, namely that this tax will be responsive to contingencies, thus this form of discretion is an indirect way to make the TA state-contingent. If specifying contingencies is quite costly and the "indirect state-contingency" effect just highlighted is important, then introducing the NT rule in the TA may be optimal.[46]

Before proceeding, I emphasize that this model focuses on a setting where TAs are motivated by TOT externalities, but an interesting and still unexplored question is the extent to which an incomplete-contracting approach of this kind but applied in the context of the domestic-commitment theory might generate new insights and help interpret features of real-world TAs.

3.1.2. Tariff Caps

As I pointed out in the previous section, tariff restrictions in the GATT-WTO take the form of tariff caps. The rationale for the use of tariff caps has been the subject of several

---

[45] To understand this slightly cryptic statement, focus on the importer country. In the absence of NT, the wedge between consumer price and world price is given by $p - p^w = \tau + t_f$, where τ is the tariff and t_f is the consumption tax on the imported good, while the wedge between producer price and world price is $q - p^w = \tau + t_f + s - t_h$, where s is the production subsidy and t_h the consumption tax on the domestically-produced good. Next focus on the price wedges under the NT rule, which imposes the constraint $t_h = t_f$. Letting t denote the common level of the internal tax, the NT rule transforms the set of policy instruments from (τ, s, t_h, t_f) to (τ, s, t), and the price wedges become $p - p^w = \tau + t$ and $q - p^w = \tau + s$. Now notice that with an NT-based agreement that constrains τ and s and leaves t to discretion, it is possible to tie down the producer price wedge $q - p^w$ while leaving discretion over the consumer price wedge $p - p^w$, whereas this is *not* possible with a non-NT agreement.

[46] The role of the NT rule for domestic taxes has been examined also by Horn (2006). He considers a model where TAs are exogenously incomplete contracts that can include tariff bindings and an NT rule for consumption taxes. Domestic and imported goods are differentiated, so efficiency may call for discriminatory consumption taxes, but Horn shows that, if tariff bindings are set at appropriate levels, including an NT rule always improves global welfare. Saggi and Sara (2008) extend Horn's (2006) analysis by allowing for heterogeneity in product quality and country size. There is also a small literature that examines the role of the NT rule for product standards: see in particular Battigalli and Maggi (2003), Costinot (2008), and Staiger and Sykes (2011).

papers in the literature (in addition to Horn et al., 2010 and Maggi and Rodriguez-Clare, 2007, already discussed above).

Bagwell and Staiger (2005a) consider a model where governments have private information about domestic political-economy shocks, and show that in such a setting tariff caps tend to be preferable to exact tariff commitments. The intuition is similar as in Horn et al. (2010): since the TA cannot be contingent on the political-economy shock, and since a government's temptation is to distort the tariff upward, leaving downward flexibility cannot hurt, and it is strictly preferred if the support of the shock is sufficiently wide. However, just as in Horn et al. (2010), this model can explain only why we do not observe exact tariff commitments, and it stops short of characterizing the *optimal* tariff rule.

Amador and Bagwell (2013) is the first paper that provides a full theoretical explanation of tariff caps, by showing that under some conditions a tariff cap is not only preferable to an exact tariff commitment, but is also the optimal tariff rule. Specifically, Amador and Bagwell consider a partial-equilibrium model where an import tariff is the only available policy instrument, and the importing government has private or non-verifiable information about domestic political pressures. Contingent transfers are not available, thus a TA can only specify a set of permissible tariffs that the importing government may apply. The governments' objective functions are specified in reduced form, say $\Omega(\tau, \gamma)$ for the Home government (where τ is the tariff and γ a political-economy parameter) and $\Omega^*(\tau)$ for the Foreign government.[47] A tariff cap is shown to be optimal if the convexity of the Foreign objective function ($\Omega^*_{\tau\tau}$) is not too pronounced relative to the concavity of the Home objective function ($\Omega_{\tau\tau}$) and the density of γ does not decrease too fast. Amador and Bagwell then examine when these conditions are satisfied in the context of two specific market structures, a perfectly competitive setting and a monopolistic competition setting.

In reality, some governments do exercise the downward discretion afforded by tariff caps and apply tariffs strictly below the cap levels (the so-called "binding overhang"). Empirically there is considerable variation in the extent of binding overhang, as well as in the levels of tariff ceilings, across countries and sectors (see for example Bacchetta and Piermartini, 2011). Beshkar et al. (2011) propose a model that sheds light on one important dimension of this variation. They consider a model where governments have private information about domestic political pressures, and examine how the levels of tariff ceilings and the expected size of the binding overhang depend on countries' market power. Their main result is that, when a country has more market power, the optimal tariff ceiling is lower and the expected binding overhang is smaller. This is a consequence of the fact that when a country has more market power its tariffs exert stronger TOT externalities, so providing flexibility through higher tariff bindings causes greater efficiency

---

[47] I note here that Amador and Bagwell (2013) consider a slightly more general setting than the one described in the text, where the importing government is allowed to "burn" money.

loss. Beshkar et al. then present econometric evidence in support of this prediction, using a dataset on applied and bound tariffs for WTO member countries.[48]

It is useful at this juncture to recall from Section 2.2 that there is another possible explanation for the use of tariff caps, which is not based on frictions in government-to-government contracting, but rather on domestic-commitment issues, as pointed out by Maggi and Rodriguez-Clare (2007). One interesting difference between these two explanations of tariff ceilings—the one based on international contracting frictions and the one based on domestic-commitment issues—is that the former predicts binding overhang with positive probability in equilibrium, whereas the latter predicts no binding overhang in equilibrium. For this reason, while domestic-commitment considerations may be part of the explanation for tariff ceilings, they are probably not the whole story behind them.[49]

One of the challenges of this body of theory is to explain not just why the WTO imposes rule X or why it imposes rule Y, but also why it imposes rules X *and* Y. This is a non-trivial question, since different rules can interact in complex ways, and often it is not easy to rationalize the WTO's joint use of disparate approaches to regulating trade policies. Beshkar and Bond (2012) take a step in this direction by developing a model that can explain why the GATT-WTO combines two different forms of flexibility on tariffs, namely tariff caps and escape clauses. More specifically, the model has a similar structure as Amador and Bagwell (2013), except that a government can produce evidence (at a cost) about the state of its domestic political pressures. Beshkar and Bond show that it may be desirable to combine a tariff cap with an escape clause that allows a government to raise the tariff above the cap if it produces evidence that doing so is politically efficient. They also show that these two forms of flexibility are substitutes, in the sense that the optimal tariff ceiling is lower—and tariff overhang may even disappear—in the presence of the escape clause than in its absence.

3.1.3. "Shallow" vs "Deep" Integration

The GATT agreement was largely based on a "shallow integration" approach, in the sense that the agreement placed direct constraints on border measures (such as trade taxes and quotas), while domestic policies were largely left to discretion, except for the requirement that they not be used to erode the market-access levels previously nego-

---

[48] Amador and Bagwell (2012) also presents an interesting result regarding binding overhang. They consider a variant of Amador and Bagwell (2013) where governments have private information about the value of tariff revenue, a setting that is arguably relevant for developing countries. In a linear-quadratic specification with a uniform type distribution, they show that the optimal tariff cap and the probability of binding overhang are higher when there is greater uncertainty in the type distribution and when the upper bound of the support of the distribution is higher.

[49] It is also relevant to note however that, if tariff ceilings were due solely to the presence of non-contractible contingencies, we would expect that, for a given product in a given country, the applied tariff is sometimes at the bound level and sometimes below it, but it is not clear from existing evidence that this is actually the case in reality.

tiated by governments.[50] Bagwell and Staiger have argued in several papers that the GATT's "non-violation" clause (Art. XXIII.1b) can be interpreted as imposing a kind of "market-access-preservation" constraint on governments. The WTO, on the other hand, has gone beyond a shallow integration approach, by introducing direct restrictions on some domestic policies, notably production subsidies, so in this sense it has moved closer to a "deep integration" approach. What are the relative merits of these two approaches, and why has the approach changed in going from GATT to WTO?

The benchmark paper on this topic is Bagwell and Staiger (2001), which focuses on a standard two-good model with perfect competition and no uncertainty. I will briefly discuss this paper using the notation introduced in Section 2.1.2. The basic idea can be illustrated by supposing that the Foreign government is passive, so its objective can be written simply as $\Omega^*(p^w)$, whereas the Home government can use a tariff τ and a non-wedge policy v (e.g. a labor standard), so that its objective can be written as $\Omega(v,p,p^w)$. Supposing that Home imports the non-numeraire good, let $X^*(p^w)$ be Foreign's export supply for this good and let $p^w(\tau, v)$ be the equilibrium world-price level. In its bare-bone form, a "shallow integration" agreement specifies a reference tariff level τ^A and allows Home to choose its policies (including the tariff) subject to the only constraint that the resulting trade volume be the same as that implied by τ^A and the noncooperative domestic policy level, say v^N. Such a market-access-preservation constraint thus takes the form: $X^*(p^w(\tau, v)) = X^*(p^w(\tau^A, v^N))$.[51]

It is immediate to show that, under perfect competition and in the absence of uncertainty, a shallow-integration agreement is sufficient to achieve global efficiency. The intuition is straightforward: since there is a one-to-one link between trade volume and TOT, a trade-volume-preservation constraint effectively prevents the Home government from manipulating TOT; and since TOT manipulation is the only cause of inefficiency in the Nash equilibrium, this constraint is sufficient to achieve efficiency.[52] This argument can be extended to allow the Foreign government to be policy-active as well.[53]

---

[50] In addition, GATT imposed that certain domestic instruments such as consumption taxes and product standards must satisfy the National Treatment rule, as I discussed in Section 3.1.1.

[51] Note that a simpler but equivalent contract would be one that specifies a trade volume $\bar{X}^*$ that Home is required to deliver, so Home chooses (τ, v) subject to the constraint $X^*(p^w(\tau, v)) = \bar{X}^*$. Clearly this contract is equivalent to the one mentioned in the text, because choosing the baseline tariff level τ^A effectively amounts to choosing the target trade level $\bar{X}^*$.

[52] There is an important caveat to this argument: in GATT-WTO the negotiated tariff levels are not simply reference levels, but tariff *ceilings*. In Bagwell and Staiger's (2001) model, if the contract includes also a tariff ceiling together with the market-access constraint, the inability of a government to raise the tariff above the ceiling may under some conditions lead to inefficient outcomes. This observation leads Bagwell and Staiger to argue that WTO rules could be made more efficient while at the same time affording governments more sovereignty.

[53] See also Bagwell and Staiger (2006), who extend the analysis to a setting where governments can use trade policies and production subsidies. Another related paper is the one by Bajona and Ederington (2012), who argue that, if the TA must be self-enforcing and domestic policies are not observable, the optimal TA may include not only market-access constraints but also tariff bindings.

Bagwell and Staiger's (2001) result represents an important benchmark, but a number of subsequent papers have highlighted reasons why a shallow integration approach may *not* be sufficient to achieve globally efficient outcomes. One reason may be the presence of non-TOT externalities, such as the ones emphasized by the New Trade theories; a second reason may be the presence of domestic-commitment motives for TAs; and a third reason may be the presence of contracting frictions.

A setting with non-TOT externalities where shallow integration is not sufficient to achieve efficiency is the one considered by Antras and Staiger (2012a,b). What is responsible for the insufficiency of shallow integration in that setting is that prices are determined by bilateral bargaining rather than market clearing. This is intuitive in light of the fact that, as discussed in Section 2.3 above, the purpose of a TA in these models goes beyond the correction of TOT externalities.[54] Another example is provided by DeRemer (2011), who argues that shallow integration is not sufficient to achieve efficiency in a monopolistic competition model with delocation externalities, when governments can use trade taxes and production subsidies. Moreover, a natural conjecture is that the same would be true in a Cournot setting with profit-shifting externalities, such as the one in Mrazova (2011) or Bagwell and Staiger (2012a), if domestic policies were allowed in these models.

It should be clear from the discussion above that a shallow integration approach can achieve efficiency only if the international policy externalities travel solely through the TOT channel. It should not come as a surprise, therefore, that if the TA is motivated by domestic-commitment motives then a deep integration approach will be required to achieve efficiency. This point is made in the paper by Brou and Ruta (2009), which I already mentioned in Section 2.2. One important point that emerges clearly from all the papers discussed above is that *the motives for a TA crucially affect the optimal design of a TA.*

As I mentioned earlier, a final reason why a shallow integration approach may not be enough to induce globally efficient outcomes is the presence of contracting frictions. To understand why, let us go back to the Bagwell-Staiger setting considered at the beginning of this section, with perfect competition and a single policy-active country (Home). Suppose that the state of the world is uncertain at the time the TA is negotiated, but Home observes it before choosing its policies. Then, in order for a market-access-preservation rule to induce a globally efficient outcome, such rule would need to be state-contingent. But if some contingencies are not verifiable (or if specifying them in the contract is costly), then a shallow integration approach may not achieve full efficiency. This point is made by Lee (2007, 2011) in the context of a model where governments choose trade taxes and production taxes, and have private information about the level of a domestic externality.

---

[54] However it is important to note that the two questions, "Are the PO policies efficient?" and "Is shallow integration sufficient to achieve efficiency?" do not necessarily yield the same answer. It is possible that PO policies are efficient but shallow integration does not achieve efficiency: in Antras and Staiger (2012a), for example, in the case of welfare-maximizing governments PO policies are efficient but shallow integration does not achieve efficiency.

I now feel the need to take a step back and reflect on the way this design question has been addressed in the literature, and on the way I think it should ideally be framed. The typical approach in the literature (at least implicitly) has been to ask whether a shallow-integration agreement can achieve global efficiency: if the answer is yes, then a shallow-integration agreement is considered preferable to a deep-integration agreement, based on an (implicit or explicit) assumption that "more sovereignty is always better;" and if the answer is no, the conclusion is that a deep-integration agreement is preferable. I find this conceptual approach useful but not entirely satisfactory, for the reasons I explain next.

The argument that it is preferable, other things equal, to give countries sovereignty over domestic policies is presumably based on a notion that relinquishing control over domestic policies entails some cost to a government. This idea has some intuitive appeal, but it is not obvious how it can be given a rational-choice justification. Why would governments not feel similarly about relinquishing control over border measures? Perhaps one way to rationalize the "sovereignty" argument is that domestic policies are needed to address domestic economic or political needs that vary over time, and taking away sovereignty over domestic policies removes a government's flexibility in responding to these varying needs. But this implicitly assumes that the TA constrains domestic policies in a *rigid* way; in the absence of contracting frictions, a TA would constrain these policies in a contingent way, so there would be no shortcoming from a deep-integration approach. Thus one *can* rationalize the idea that giving up sovereignty is costly, but *at the core*, this boils down to an argument that contracting frictions cause rigidity in TAs. For this reason, I think that introducing uncertainty and contracting frictions explicitly in our conceptual framework is important to examine the tradeoff between shallow and deep integration.

The discussion above in turn suggests an alternative, and I think preferable, approach to the comparison between shallow and deep integration. The key question in my opinion should be: what are the transaction costs associated with each of these two approaches, and which one is more efficient when transaction costs are taken into account? The answer to this question is far from obvious: a deep-integration agreement requires specifying all border and domestic policies, and this is likely to involve large transaction costs; a shallow-integration agreement, on the other hand, may save on the costs of contracting over domestic policies, but it will achieve less efficient outcomes (if the environment is uncertain); and if specifying contingencies in the TA is costly, the tradeoff becomes even more complicated. If one takes this explicit transaction costs perspective, then the results of the existing literature appear as a valuable step, but only a first step.

3.1.4. Reciprocity and MFN
The principles of reciprocity and MFN are two major pillars of the GATT-WTO. The role of these principles has been examined by Bagwell and Staiger in a number of writings,

and most notably in the context of the perfect-competition setting of Bagwell and Staiger (1999a). I will start by focusing on the principle of reciprocity in the context of a two-country model (where MFN of course plays no role).

Bagwell and Staiger define a reciprocal change in trade policies as one that leaves world prices unchanged.[55] More specifically, they distinguish between two notions of reciprocity. The first one is a principle guiding tariff *negotiations* starting from the Nash equilibrium: Bagwell and Staiger show that, if tariff negotiations satisfy reciprocity (that is, if they leave world prices unchanged relative to the Nash equilibrium), they will lead to a Pareto-improvement over the Nash equilibrium, although in general they will not lead all the way to the Pareto-efficient frontier.[56] An important note of interpretation is the following: in the GATT-WTO the principle of reciprocity as it applies to tariff negotiations is not a strict rule, but just an informal principle, so Bagwell and Staiger's (1999a) analysis of reciprocity-guided negotiations is best interpreted in normative terms, as highlighting how the negotiation outcome would be affected *if* reciprocity were strictly imposed as a rule.

The second notion of reciprocity considered by Bagwell and Staiger applies to tariff *renegotiations*. Unlike the informal reciprocity principle that applies to negotiations, GATT-WTO does impose a formal rule of reciprocity for tariff renegotiations, specifically in Article XXVIII of GATT. Bagwell and Staiger formalize this rule through a two-stage negotiation game, as follows: (i) in the first stage, governments negotiate a pair of tariffs, with the disagreement point given by the Nash equilibrium tariffs; (ii) in the second stage, governments can renegotiate the tariffs, and if the renegotiation fails, a government can unilaterally change its tariff from the level that was agreed upon in the first stage, but at the condition that the trading partner get compensated through a reciprocal tariff change.

Before proceeding, I make an observation that will be useful later on. Notice the nature of the *disagreement point* for the process of renegotiation under reciprocity: if the renegotiation fails, a government can choose to unilaterally "breach" the contract and compensate the trading partner, with the compensation taking the form of a reciprocal tariff increase by the trading partner. This observation leads me to note that there is a simpler way to interpret such reciprocity rule, which I find more illuminating. Rather than imposing a constraint on renegotiation, this rule can equivalently be modeled as changing the nature of the contract itself, from one that specifies tariff commitments without allowing for "breach" (in law and economics jargon, a "property" contract), to one that allows a government to breach the contract in exchange for a certain amount of "damages" (in law and economics jargon, a "liability" contract). Notice that, if reciprocity is modeled in this way, simply as a liability rule incorporated in the initial contract, then there is no scope for renegotiation in Bagwell and Staiger's setting, and we can simply think

[55] As Bagwell and Staiger show, an equivalent definition is that changes in trade policies are reciprocal if they bring about equal-value changes in each country's volumes of imports and exports when valued at the initial world prices.
[56] The only case in which negotiations according to reciprocity lead to Pareto efficiency is the one where countries are perfectly symmetric.

of governments as negotiating a contract within this particular class (liability contracts with breach damages given by reciprocal tariff changes), ignoring renegotiation.[57]

Bagwell and Staiger's main results regarding the rule of reciprocity are two. The first one is that the only efficient tariff pair that can be implemented under reciprocity (or, adopting my interpretation above, when the contract is restricted to be a liability contract with breach damages given by reciprocal tariff changes) is given by the politically efficient (PO) tariffs. This result is a consequence of the fact that, when viewed in tariff space, each government's iso-payoff curve is tangent to the iso-world-price curve at the PO point, thus starting from this point there is no unilateral incentive for a government to move along the iso-world-price curve. This in turn implies that the reciprocity-constrained Pareto frontier lies inside the unconstrained Pareto frontier, except at the PO point. The second result is that, when governments bargain over the reciprocity-constrained Pareto frontier, the outcome is generically inefficient (it is not the PO point), but it tends to be closer to the PO point as compared with the unrestricted bargaining scenario.[58]

Bagwell and Staiger interpret these results as suggesting that the reciprocity rule induces a rebalancing of power across countries, since it moves the negotiation outcome toward a point that is not affected by bargaining powers (the PO point). This conclusion resonates with the GATT's emphasis on "rules" vs "power," but as remarked above, the rebalancing of power induced by the reciprocity rule in general entails an "efficiency penalty." Bagwell and Staiger then argue informally that reciprocity may provide efficiency gains if it encourages weaker countries to participate in GATT. This idea is based on McLaren's (1997) model: recall from Section 2.2 that in this model a small country trading with a large country may prefer to stay out of a TA to avoid being "held up," and for this reason the large country would like to commit *not* to exploit its bargaining power, in order to encourage the small country to participate in the TA. Thus the broad idea is that, if one thinks of GATT as initially including a set of large/powerful countries, but there is also a set of smaller/weaker countries that may consider accessing GATT at a later stage, the initial members may prefer to commit not to exploit their bargaining power in future negotiations, in order to encourage other countries to seek participation.

I will make two further comments about Bagwell and Staiger's analysis of the reciprocity rule. The first one is a "devil's advocate" comment. Bagwell and Staiger's interpretation of the results outlined above is that reciprocity "works well" when TOT externalities are the only motive for a TA. But one might argue that the model tells the opposite story: reciprocity causes the negotiation outcome to be inside the Pareto frontier, so the world would be more efficient *without* reciprocity. A more cautious interpretation of Bagwell and Staiger's analysis would be that it provides a positive (as opposed to normative)

---

[57] I note that this way of thinking about reciprocity, as a rule specifying breach remedies rather than as a constraint on renegotiation, is close to the way Ossa (2011) formalizes the reciprocity rule in his model.

[58] I say "tends to be closer to the PO point" because this is true only under some conditions, as explained in footnote 25 of Bagwell and Staiger (1999a).

evaluation of the reciprocity rule, highlighting that this rule has a distributional effect (which might be desirable in a richer model that includes participation considerations) and an efficiency cost.

The second comment is that, aside from the participation argument outlined above, Bagwell and Staiger's analysis is suggestive of another potential efficiency benefit of reciprocity. Since, as I argued above, imposing the reciprocity rule is akin to structuring the TA as a (specific type of) "liability" contract, this might be appealing as a way to inject flexibility in the TA when countries are subject to shocks and the TA cannot be fully contingent. But this is just suggestive, since there is no uncertainty or contract incompleteness in the model.[59] This brings me back to one of my overarching points, namely that a better understanding of TA design requires bringing transaction costs explicitly into the picture.

After their analysis of reciprocity within a two-country setting, Bagwell and Staiger (1999a) turn to an examination of the implications of the MFN rule within a multi-country setting. As I mentioned in Section 2.1.2, in a multilateral world where governments can set discriminatory tariffs, there is a whole vector of bilateral offshore prices, which generates a complicated pattern of international policy externalities, but the MFN rule has the effect of channeling all these externalities into a single world-price externality. Building on this observation, Bagwell and Staiger show that the MFN rule, if used in tandem with the reciprocity rule, guides countries toward the PO tariffs (which, recall, are efficient under MFN). The key point here is that the combination of MFN and reciprocity has similar effects in a multi-country world as the reciprocity rule does in a two-country world.

So far I have focused on the implications of reciprocity and MFN within a perfectly competitive environment. It has been argued, however, that reciprocity and MFN can be rationalized also within an imperfectly competitive environment, where the motives for a TA go beyond the correction of TOT externalities. In particular, Ossa (2011) argues that, in a monopolistic-competition setting, reciprocity and MFN can be interpreted as helping countries internalize the production-delocation externalities generated by trade policies.[60]

3.1.5. "Property" vs "Liability" Rules

In the previous section I mentioned the distinction between a "property" contract (one that does not provide for the possibility of breach) and a "liability" contract (one that

---

[59] As I will discuss in the next section, papers by Maggi and Staiger (2012) and Beshkar (2010a,b) have examined this idea more formally in models with non-verifiable or privately observed shocks.

[60] It should be noted however that the implications of reciprocity and MFN in Ossa's model are somewhat different than in Bagwell and Staiger's model. Ossa shows that reciprocity can help countries achieve an efficient outcome if reciprocity is applied to multilateral trade negotiations, and then argues that MFN can serve to multilateralize trade negotiations; Bagwell and Staiger, on the other hand, show that reciprocity and MFN ensure that any bilateral negotiation will lead to an efficient outcome.

gives a government the option to breach-and-compensate). In real-world TAs, there is considerable variation between liability-type rules and property-type rules, both across issues and over time. For example, Pauwelyn (2008) argues that property rules are the "default" approach in the WTO and NAFTA, but for certain issues such as tariff bindings and production subsidies, a liability-rule approach has been taken.[61] Moreover, most legal scholars take the view that the early GATT operated as a system of liability rules, while in more recent times the GATT/WTO has evolved toward a property-rule system (see for example Jackson, 1997).[62]

As mentioned above, a liability approach is appealing in the presence of uncertainty because it can inject flexibility in the TA without the need to specify contingencies explicitly in the contract: intuitively, a liability rule can induce a country to internalize the externalities that its trade policy exerts on its trading partners. However, in the international trade arena, the liability approach has an important shortcoming, namely that government-to-government compensation is inefficient: cash transfers are typically not available, and compensation typically takes the form of "self-help" through tariff retaliation. For this reason, a liability rule can generate deadweight loss, and this gives rise to a non-trivial tradeoff between property and liability rules.[63]

The tradeoff between property and liability rules becomes even more subtle if governments can renegotiate the TA, because in this case a property rule does not necessarily imply inflexible policy outcomes (since it can be renegotiated ex-post), and it can give rise to inefficient compensation in case of renegotiation. Taking renegotiation into account seems important also in light of its empirical importance in the context of GATT-WTO, where renegotiations have taken place in many instances over the years.

The choice between property and liability rules in the presence of renegotiation is analyzed by Maggi and Staiger (2012). In this model, governments negotiate over a binary trade policy (free trade or protection) under uncertainty about the future joint benefits of protection (which can be positive or negative, due to political economy considerations), and can renegotiate the TA after the uncertainty is resolved. A key feature of the model, in line with the discussion above, is that government-to-government compensation entails a deadweight cost.

---

[61] This includes for example the provisions for escape from negotiated tariff bindings (GATT Articles XIX and XXVIII, respectively), the rules on "actionable" production subsidies in WTO, and the provisions to protect investors against expropriation in NAFTA (and in many other bilateral investment treaties).

[62] Here I note that, while the terminology of property and liability rules is more common in the law-and-economics literature, the choice between these two contractual forms is an important topic in the economic literature on optimal contract design, where a liability contract is often referred to as an "option contract," and a property contract is often referred to as a "noncontingent contract," or simply a "property-right" contract (see for example Segal and Whinston, 2002).

[63] The inefficiency of government-to-government compensation is not the only possible shortcoming of a liability approach. Another limitation—which I abstract from here—is that the damage inflicted by trade protection on trading partners is typically non-verifiable, and this makes it impossible to induce a government to perfectly internalize trade policy externalities.

Maggi and Staiger find that a property rule is optimal if uncertainty about the joint benefits of protection is small enough, while a liability rule is optimal when this uncertainty is large. If one interprets uncertainty about the joint benefits of protection as due to political-economy shocks, then this result suggests that liability rules should be more prevalent in issue areas that are more politically sensitive. This prediction seems consistent with the observation that the WTO has taken a liability approach in the areas of import tariffs and production subsidies (which are arguably very sensitive to political-economy shocks) and a property-rule approach in other areas. A further result is that, if a liability rule is optimal, the optimal level of damages falls short of fully compensating the exporter, contrary to the well-known "efficient breach" argument. This result is shown also in a related model by Beshkar (2010a), though in a setting without renegotiation.[64]

The model yields predictions also about the occurrence of renegotiation in equilibrium, and how it correlates with the optimal contract form. I report two findings here. The first is that renegotiation, when it occurs, always entails the exporter agreeing to compensate the importer in exchange for trade liberalization.[65] The second is that an optimal property rule is never renegotiated in equilibrium. This finding may seem counterintuitive, since a property rule is inherently rigid and renegotiation should be useful to mitigate such rigidity, but it turns out that renegotiation can improve the performance of a property rule only if such rule is suboptimally adopted.[66]

3.1.6. Dispute Settlement Procedures and Contract Incompleteness

As I discussed at the beginning of Section 3, the role of the WTO's DSB seems to go well beyond a pure enforcement role, at least judging from casual observations of real-world trade disputes, where the DSB seems to often play an "activist" role by interpreting vague clauses and filling gaps of the agreement. The potential role of the DSB in completing an incomplete agreement is the focus of a paper by Maggi and Staiger (2011).[67]

---

[64] Beshkar (2010b) builds on Beshkar (2010a) by allowing the WTO court (DSB) to observe a noisy signal of the state of the world, and shows that the performance of the contract can be improved by making the remedies for breach (that is, the injured country's retaliatory tariff) contingent on the DSB's signal, which in turn can be accomplished by allowing the injured country to file a complaint that triggers DSB intervention. See also Beshkar (2011), which extends the previous models by allowing for a limited form of renegotiation between governments.

[65] This asymmetry in the predicted direction of renegotiation is a consequence of two features: that the contractual obligation is to liberalize trade, and that it is never optimal to induce renegotiation in states of the world where the threat point is the contractual obligation itself.

[66] In the model just discussed, the court/DSB does not play an active role in equilibrium, so the model is silent about what determines the occurrence of trade *disputes* and their outcomes. In a more recent working paper, Maggi and Staiger (2013) consider a richer model in which trade disputes can occur in equilibrium and can result in a variety of outcomes; in particular, governments may settle early or trigger a DSB ruling, and in the latter case, they may implement the DSB ruling or renegotiate after the ruling. Two new features of the model are responsible for this rich set of possibilities: first, the DSB can observe a noisy signal of the joint benefits of protection (interpreted as the outcome of a DSB investigation), so governments are uncertain about the direction of the DSB ruling; and second, governments have a further opportunity to renegotiate the TA *after* the DSB issues a ruling.

[67] An early attempt to examine the potential role of the DSB in completing an incomplete contract can be found in Battigalli and Maggi (2003), who focus on agreements on product standards. In that model, the TA cannot specify

Maggi and Staiger consider three possible activist roles for the DSB: *interpreting* vaguely stated obligations; *filling gaps* in the agreement; and *modifying* rigid obligations; and for each of these roles, the DSB may or may not have authority to set *precedent* for future rulings. Governments design the institution—that is the combination of contract and DSB mandate—under uncertainty about the future state of the world. The relevant contingencies are assumed to be too costly to describe in a crisp way, so the contract is necessarily incomplete. The model allows for three possible forms of contractual incompleteness: the first two, *rigidity* and *discretion*, are familiar (see Section 3.1.1); the third one, *vagueness*, is novel.[68] There is a natural pairing between these three forms of contractual incompleteness and the three possible activist DSB roles described above: the DSB can interpret a vague contract; it can fill gaps if the contract leaves discretion; and it can grant exceptions if the contract is rigid. Or, the DSB can play a non-activist role and simply enforce clearly stated obligations. Furthermore, for each of the activist roles, the DSB may or may not have precedent-setting authority. A key feature of the model is that invoking the DSB entails two kinds of inefficiency: one is that the governments incur litigation costs, and the other is that DSB rulings are imperfectly accurate.

Maggi and Staiger show that the optimal institutional form depends critically on the degree of DSB accuracy. If the DSB is sufficiently accurate, it is optimal to leave gaps in the contract and give the DSB a mandate to fill those gaps. If the DSB is sufficiently *inaccurate*, it is optimal to write a vague or rigid contract and give a non-activist mandate to the DSB. And if the level of DSB accuracy is intermediate, it is optimal to write a vague contract and allow the DSB to interpret the contract. The "modification" role of the DSB turns out to be always suboptimal.

The model delivers good news and bad news regarding the potential of the DSB to enhance efficiency. The good news is that, if the DSB is sufficiently accurate, the first-best outcome can be achieved, in spite of the incompleteness of the contract, the costs of using the DSB, and the imperfection in DSB rulings. The reason is that the threat of invoking the DSB and the expectation of a not-too-inaccurate DSB ruling are enough to discourage opportunistic behavior by governments. This suggests that an activist DSB can generate substantial efficiency gains even if its information is not perfect. The bad news is that the outcome tends to be efficient only when the DSB is *not* invoked in equilibrium, and disputes are more frequent when the DSB is *less* accurate. Thus, the

---

standards for products that will appear in the future. If a new product appears, governments can negotiate ex-post over the standards for that product, but international transfers are not available ex-post, and as a consequence the ex-post negotiation outcome is ex-ante inefficient. The DSB acts as an "arbitrator" that can be invoked if the ex-post negotiation fails. Battigalli and Maggi show that the DSB can improve ex-ante efficiency by specifying ex-post—if invoked—the standards that should apply to the new product, provided the DSB has sufficiently precise information.

[68] Vagueness is modeled as a language whose meaning is only partially defined. As an example, consider a contract stating that trade protection is allowed only if "there is substantial injury to the domestic industry." The idea is that there are states of the world where the latter sentence is clearly true (e.g. if there is an import surge, the domestic industry shuts down, and the majority of workers in the industry are unemployed), others where it is clearly false (if none of the above events has occurred), and there are "gray area" states where it is not defined whether the sentence is true or false.

efficiency-enhancing effect of the DSB is associated with its *off-equilibrium* impacts. If the DSB is invoked in equilibrium, it is always because one of the governments is being opportunistic: either the importer is protecting when it should not, hoping that the DSB ruling will get it wrong; or the exporter is trying to force free trade by filing a dispute when it should not. A corollary of these observations is that the frequency of DSB use is not a good indicator of the performance of the institution.

The model also has interesting implications regarding the "bias" in observed DSB rulings. Because of selection effects in the filing of disputes, DSB rulings tend to have a pro-trade bias if litigation costs fall more on the exporter government than on the importer government. In reality, it is arguably the case that litigation costs fall more on the exporter government, because the burden of proof falls on the complainant, and the complainant is typically the exporter government. Thus the model suggests a possible explanation for the fact that, both under the GATT and the WTO, complainants have mostly won their cases.

Finally, Maggi and Staiger extend the basic model to a two-period setting in order to examine whether it is desirable to give the DSB precedent-setting authority. This is an important issue of institutional design, and one that is receiving increasing attention from legal scholars.[69] Introducing precedent in this setting is shown to have two opposite effects on efficiency. The beneficial effect of precedent is that it reduces the probability of dispute occurrence *tomorrow*, by clarifying the obligations that will apply should the same state of the world occur again; this leads to a savings in litigation costs. The harmful effect of precedent is that it increases the probability of dispute occurrence *today*; this in turn implies more waste in litigation costs and a less efficient policy outcome (because the DSB ruling is subject to error). Maggi and Staiger show that, as a net result of these effects, precedent is more likely to be beneficial when the accuracy of DSB rulings is lower and when governments care less about the future, or are less likely to interact repeatedly.

3.2. Imperfect Enforcement and Trade Agreements

In this section I will focus on how the presence of enforcement frictions can shape the design of rules and procedures in a TA. More specifically, I will discuss how the presence of self-enforcement constraints affects the design of substantive policy rules, of enforcement rules (i.e. rules that regulate punishments), and of dispute settlement procedures.

In the literature, the dominant approach for modeling a self-enforcing TA has been to consider a game where governments choose trade policies repeatedly and focus on (constrained-)Pareto-efficient equilibria of this game. The implicit assumption in this approach is that governments bargain efficiently over the set of equilibria of the repeated

---

[69] Even at the positive level, the extent to which the WTO-DSB currently operates on a precedent system seems subject to debate. According to Jackson (2006, p. 177), "there is quite a powerful precedent effect in the jurisprudence of the WTO, but ... it is not so powerful as to require panels or the Appellate Body considering new cases to follow prior cases." Jackson concludes that "the 'flavor' of the precedent effect in the WTO is still somewhat fluid."

game. This approach has become fairly standard in the literature and is explained in Staiger's (1995a) chapter, so I will take it for granted and simply provide an informal overview of the contributions in this area after 1995.[70]

3.2.1. Policy Rules

The presence of self-enforcement constraints can have deep implications for the design of policy rules. This point was first made in a pathbreaking paper by Bagwell and Staiger (1990), which showed that, in the presence of (publicly observed) i.i.d. shocks to trade volume, the need to accommodate self-enforcement constraints makes it desirable to include an *escape clause* in the TA. The basic idea is that, in periods of high import volume, a country has a stronger incentive to deviate from its trade policy commitments, so in such periods it may be a good idea to allow a country to escape from its commitments in order to keep cooperation sustainable.[71]

More recently, Bagwell and Staiger (2003) have extended their previous model by allowing for persistent shocks to trade volume as well as an acyclic component of the shock. In this setting, Bagwell and Staiger show that trade protection tends to be countercyclical. The reason is that a boom phase tends to be characterized by fast growth in trade volume, which helps countries sustain lower tariffs than in a recession phase, while acyclic increases in trade volume give rise to increases in tariffs, for a similar reason as in Bagwell and Staiger (1990).[72]

Another group of papers has highlighted that the presence of self-enforcement constraints can help explain why TAs typically take a *gradual* approach to trade liberalization. The first two papers in this group are Staiger (1995b) and Devereux (1997), the former focusing on the implications of sector-specific skills that depreciate when not in use, and the latter on the implications of technological learning-by-doing. Furusawa and Lai (1999) and Chisik (2003) propose two further mechanisms that can generate gradual trade liberalization as part of an optimal self-enforcing TA: Furusawa and Lai focus on the role of adjustment costs in worker reallocation across sectors, and Chisik focuses on the role of irreversible investments in country-specific export capacity. The common theme in all of these papers is the non-stationary nature of the repeated game between governments,

---

[70] Before surveying the relevant literature, I mention briefly four papers that do not focus on issues of rule design, but on a more classic question: what conditions facilitate the self-enforcement of TAs? Furusawa (1999) examines how the sustainability of cooperation is affected by the governments' relative patience and the lag between detection of a violation and retaliation; Park (2000) focuses on a trade agreement between a small country and a large country, and examines how the set of sustainable payoffs is affected by the availability of direct transfers and the presence of sunk investments; Conconi and Sahuguet (2009) explore the impact of policymakers' horizons and alternative electoral regimes on the sustainability of international cooperation; and Conconi and Perroni (2009) examine whether and how the ability of governments to commit to policies in the domestic arena affects the sustainability of international cooperation.

[71] See also Milner and Rosendorff (2001) for a related model of self-enforcing agreements where the presence of uncertainty makes it optimal to introduce escape clauses.

[72] The question of whether or not trade barriers are countercyclical has been the subject of interesting empirical work recently. See in particular Bown and Crowley (2013b) and Rose (2013).

whereby an initial reduction in tariffs leads to a change in some economy-wide state variable (such as the level of physical or human capital allocated to the export sector), which in turn relaxes the self-enforcement constraint and allows governments to sustain further tariff reductions.

One might think that gradual trade liberalization can *only* be explained in a non-stationary trading environment, but Bond and Park (2004) make the surprising point that gradualism can arise even in a stationary economic environment. Specifically, they show that the optimal self-enforcing TA may entail gradual tariff reductions if countries are asymmetric. In this case, it is possible that in the initial phase of the agreement the self-enforcement constraint of only one country is binding, and given this initial asymmetry, the most efficient way to provide incentives to such country is to "backload" its payoff, that is, to promise this country a rising payoff over time.[73]

3.2.2. Enforcement Rules

When countries negotiate a TA, they negotiate not only substantive policy rules, but also rules that regulate punishments for violations of the agreement. I will refer to these as "enforcement rules."

A key consideration for the design of enforcement rules is that they must themselves be self-enforcing, or in other words they must be *credible*: in the language of repeated-game theory, this means that the punishment strategy must be an equilibrium of the continuation game after the initial deviation. In this perspective, the question "What are the optimal enforcement rules?" can be formally phrased as "What is the optimal equilibrium punishment strategy?" It is important to keep in mind that in a repeated game there is a vast multiplicity of equilibrium punishment strategies, just as there is a vast multiplicity of overall equilibria. The implicit assumption in this modeling approach is that, when governments negotiate a TA, they bargain efficiently over policy rules *and* enforcement rules, subject to the constraint that all rules be part of an overall equilibrium of the repeated game.

Maggi (1999) examines the optimal design of enforcement rules in the context of a multilateral trading system. A key question in this context is whether and to what extent punishments should be multilateral rather than bilateral. To be concrete, the question is: if country A cheats on country B, should country C be involved in the punishment? Consider first a benchmark scenario where bilateral trading relationships are symmetric and separable (in the sense that changing a bilateral trade barrier does not affect third countries): in such scenario, Maggi shows that there are no gains from multilateral punishments. The intuition is that, while making punishments multilateral increases the future loss from

---

[73] Another paper that highlights implications of self-enforcement constraints for the design of policy rules is Mrazova (2011). This paper (which I already mentioned in Section 2.3.1) argues that the need to make the TA self-enforcing, in conjunction with the presence of profit-shifting externalities and costs of administering policy instruments, can help explain the WTO ban on export subsidies.

a deviation, it also increases the one-time gain from deviating, because if a country is to deviate it will do so against all trading partners; when bilateral relationships are symmetric and separable these two effects cancel each other out. Next consider a scenario characterized by bilateral imbalances of power, in the sense that different governments stand to lose different amounts from a trade war, with the more "powerful" governments standing to lose less. In this scenario, multilateral punishments *are* desirable because they allow for an exchange of enforcement power that bilateral punishments cannot achieve: more specifically, if punishments are multilateral, each country can offer third-party enforcement in bilateral relationships where it is "strong" in exchange for receiving third-party enforcement from other countries in bilateral relationships where it is "weak."[74]

The next point made by Maggi (1999) is that, even though some third-country punishment is in general desirable, there may be no need to make it very severe. More specifically, increasing the severity of third-country punishments beyond a certain point does not enhance cooperation, so there is no need to make these punishments "maximal." Furthermore, the threat of third-country punishments is necessary only for certain violations, namely those by stronger countries against weaker countries, which are hard to deter with bilateral sanctions alone. The intuition is based on the result I mentioned earlier: if there are no bilateral asymmetries, there is no need for *any* third-country punishments, so it is intuitive that if there is only a limited degree of bilateral asymmetries, a limited amount of third-country punishment will be sufficient. These results seem broadly consistent with the fact that in the GATT-WTO the role of third-country punishments is more subtle and selective than the role of bilateral punishments.[75]

Also Bagwell et al. (2007) focus on the design of enforcement rules in a multilateral world. In particular, this paper examines the desirability of "tradeable" retaliation rights, an idea proposed a few years ago by Mexico in the WTO. The basic idea is that small countries have a limited ability to retaliate against large countries, so allowing small countries to sell their rights of retaliation to third countries might improve the performance of the

---

[74] Gains from multilateral punishments can arise also from non-separabilities across bilateral relationships, which arise if there are trade-diversion effects of bilateral trade barriers. In this case, the benefits from multilateralizing punishments arise from the *aggregation* of enforcement power across trading relationships (see Maggi, 1994). A simple intuition for this effect can be gained by thinking about the effects of trade embargoes: a multilateral embargo inflicts a proportionally more severe punishment than a bilateral embargo, since the latter is partially neutralized by substitution across bilateral trade flows.

[75] There is a legitimate question as to whether third-country punishments play *any* role in the GATT-WTO. Maggi (1999) argues that they do, although in subtle ways. One form of third-country punishment for example may be the withdrawal of some "goodwill" by third countries toward the defecting country, resulting for example in a reluctance to enter new agreements with that country. Also, one should not forget that, as Thomas Schelling made clear, the effectiveness of an army sometimes must be judged by how little it is used: while it is true that full-blown multilateral retaliation has never been observed in the GATT-WTO, it is also true that there have been no cases of blatant and repeated violations of key rules, even by strong countries against vulnerable trading partners. It is reasonable to think that strong countries may have been deterred from abusing weaker partners not by the threat of bilateral retaliation, but by the implicit threat that the whole trading system may unravel as a consequence, that is, by the threat of a multilateral breakdown of cooperation.

system. Bagwell et al. consider a scenario where a violation of the agreement has already occurred and the injured country has been granted the right to retaliate, and examine two mechanisms for selling this right: a "basic" auction, in which the injured country is not allowed to bid to retire the right, and an "extended" auction, where the injured country is allowed to bid as well. Bagwell et al. find that the basic auction may "fail", in the sense that no bids are made despite positive valuation by bidders, while the "extended" auction can never fail, and in such auction the right of retaliation is always retired. The two auction formats are then evaluated from a normative standpoint, and the ranking between them is found to depend critically on the specific normative criterion that one adopts.[76]

Another interesting question of enforcement-rule design arises when countries seek to cooperate over multiple policy areas. In this case, one may ask whether there should be *issue linkage* in the enforcement of the TA, that is, whether violations in one policy area should be met with retaliation in other areas. Two papers that address this question are Ederington (2002) and Limão (2005).

Ederington (2002) considers a repeated-game model where each government can choose a tariff and a domestic policy. In this model markets are competitive, but in each country there is a localized externality which can be corrected by using the domestic policy. First, Ederington shows that domestic policies are always set at their efficient (Pigouvian) levels in the optimal self-enforcing TA, while tariffs are set above their efficient levels to accommodate self-enforcement constraints. The intuition is related to the targeting principle: since the only international externality is a TOT externality, the only reason countries are tempted to deviate from the TA is to manipulate TOT, so raising tariffs is the most efficient way to neutralize this incentive to defect.[77] The second, related result is that issue linkage need not enhance cooperation: in particular, if the punishment strategy takes the form of a permanent reversion to the one-shot Nash equilibrium ("grim-trigger" punishment), then the benefits from issue linkage are nil.

Limão (2005) considers a setting characterized not only by TOT externalities but also by cross-border pollution externalities. Governments choose tariffs and production taxes in repeated-game fashion. In this setting, Limão shows that issue linkage always allows governments to achieve a higher joint welfare relative to a non-linked agreement. This in itself may not be surprising, but a subtle question concerns how linkage affects the level of cooperation on a policy-by-policy basis. The key finding is that, if policies are independent in the governments' objective functions, linkage promotes cooperation

---

[76] Bagwell et al. (2007) are agnostic about the criterion according to which the mechanisms should be evaluated, but I will not be agnostic here. In my view, the natural evaluation criterion is given by the efficiency of the equilibrium of the repeated game that the enforcement mechanism allows to achieve (see my discussion at the beginning of the section). The analysis of Bagwell et al. (2007) is silent about this criterion, simply because they do not model the repeated-game explicitly, but take it as a given that a violation has already occurred and take the amount of permissible retaliation as exogenous.

[77] This result was first derived in Ederington (2001), and then extended by Ederington (2002) to allow for both linked and non-linked agreements, as well as for different types of punishment strategies.

in one policy area at the expense of the other, because linkage effects a reallocation of enforcement power across issues; but if policies are strategic complements, then linkage can lead to more cooperation in both policy areas.[78]

My next theme of discussion is the role of retaliation in the presence of asymmetric information. When governments have private information, for example about domestic political shocks, retaliation can play two distinct roles. First, retaliation can be a "punitive" tool that serves to deter blatant violations of the agreement, along the lines discussed earlier in this section. This type of retaliation is meant to be an off-equilibrium threat, so it need not be observed in equilibrium. Second, retaliation can be used for "screening" (or "truthtelling") purposes, in the sense of inducing governments to increase protection only in states of the world where it is (politically) efficient to do so. Intuitively, retaliation imposes a cost on a government that increases protection, so if the severity of retaliation is appropriately calibrated, it may induce a government to increase protection when—and only when—the political gains from protection are high. Unlike "punitive" retaliation, this latter type of retaliation *is* meant to occur in equilibrium under some contingencies. Some scholars, for example Schwartz and Sykes (2002), have argued that the reciprocity rule in Article XXVIII of GATT—which provides for the "withdrawal of substantially equivalent concessions" in response to a breach of negotiated tariff bindings—can be interpreted as serving a screening function along the lines I just described. What makes this interpretation appealing is that the reciprocity rule provides only for a limited amount of retaliation, which seems consistent with the screening function, whereas the "punitive" function calls for more severe retaliation threats. I also note that the screening role of retaliation is relevant even if the agreement is perfectly enforceable, or if governments are so patient that self-enforcement constraints do not bind. Indeed, some of the papers that consider this role of retaliation, such as Beshkar (2010a,b) or (in a more reduced-form setting) Maggi and Staiger (2012, 2013), assume perfectly enforceable TAs.[79]

In the context of a repeated tariff game with private information, the distinction between the punitive role and the screening role of retaliation can be understood in the following way. Suppose the importing government chooses a tariff and privately observes the value of a political-economy parameter. The agreement can be thought of

---

[78] Here I will also mention a paper by Limão and Saggi (2008) that examines whether it may be desirable to use monetary fines or bonds as part of the enforcement mechanism. Limão and Saggi show that the use of monetary fines does not help if fines must be self-enforcing and hence ultimately supported by the threat of retaliatory tariffs. On the other hand, bonds *can* enhance efficiency if they are posted with a third party prior to trading, and the third party uses the bond to compensate the injured country in case a violation is committed: intuitively, this can relax self-enforcement constraints because it indirectly injects some external enforcement into the agreement.

[79] See Section 3.1.5 for a discussion of these papers. In Maggi and Staiger's models, retaliation is not modeled explicitly, but is captured in reduced form as a deadweight cost associated with government-to-government compensation. I also note that in these models there is no private information, but political-economy shocks are not verifiable by the court/DSB, and this form of information asymmetry has similar implications as private information for the design of incentive contracts.

as specifying a tariff *schedule* that links the tariff to the realization of the political-economy parameter. In order to be self-enforcing, the TA must discourage two types of deviations: (i) "on-schedule" deviations, whereby the government applies a tariff that is meant for another "type"; and (ii) "off-schedule" deviations, whereby the government applies a tariff level that is not meant for any "type". In this context, one can think of the punitive role of retaliation as discouraging off-schedule deviations, while the screening role of retaliation is to discourage on-schedule deviations. A paper that focuses on these themes is Martin and Vergote (2008), which considers a setting where shocks are i.i.d. over time. An interesting finding of this paper is that, even if the TA can specify a "reciprocity" mechanism whereby a government's tariff increase is met with a contemporaneous tariff response by the other government, it is always desirable for the TA to include future retaliation, provided governments are sufficiently patient. Relatedly, Bagwell (2009) considers a setting where political-economy shocks can be persistent over time, and shows that persistence can make enforcement more difficult, because of a "ratchet" effect whereby some government types are more reluctant to reveal themselves today for fear of being perceived as having weak retaliatory power tomorrow. For a broader and informal discussion of these themes, see also the piece by Bagwell (2008).

Finally, it is important to note that retaliation is not the only way to provide "truthtelling" incentives to governments. For example, Bagwell and Staiger (2005a) argue that this can be accomplished by imposing a dynamic constraint on the use of safeguard actions. The nature of this constraint is that, if a government invokes the escape clause today, it has to wait a certain amount of time before invoking it again. Intuitively, this can mitigate governments' temptation to misrepresent their information and over-use the escape clause. A dynamic usage constraint of this kind is contained in the WTO's Safeguard Agreement.[80]

3.2.3. The Enforcement Role of the DSB

An important question concerning the enforcement of TAs is whether and how a judicial system such as the WTO's DSB can assist with the enforcement of the TA. The answer to this question is far from obvious, since in reality TAs must be self-enforcing and international courts have no direct enforcement power. One possible answer to this question is suggested by Maggi's (1999) model, which I briefly discussed in the previous section: the DSB can make multilateral enforcement possible, by disseminating information about violations of the agreement to the whole trading community. To illustrate, suppose that country A commits a violation against country B, and that in the absence of a DSB this violation would be observed only by country B. Then a potential role for the DSB is to

---

[80] Another potential way to induce truthtelling is introducing cross-policy linkages, that is requiring a government to make adjustments in other policies when raising trade protection. This idea plays a key role in the models by Lee (2007, 2011).

verify the violation and bring it to the attention of third countries, thus exposing country A to punishments by third countries.[81]

It is interesting to note that in the context of the WTO institution there exists another procedure that helps disseminate information about trade policies, namely the "Trade Policy Review Mechanism." This mechanism is arguably complementary with the DSB as a way to disseminate information and improve multilateral monitoring: the former is a systematic, periodic, and wide-ranging review, whereas the DSB conducts more thorough and targeted investigations when a country (or a group of countries) files a complaint.

In practice, one important aspect of the WTO's dispute settlement procedure is that it encourages governments to renegotiate, even following clear violations of the agreement. In Section 3.1.5, I pointed out that the renegotiation of trade policy commitments can be beneficial when the TA is an incomplete contract. However, as the repeated game literature has abundantly made clear, the renegotiation of *punishments* can have deleterious effects on cooperation, because it can undermine the credibility of punishments. This is the core of the argument in Ludema (2001), who argues that the WTO's dispute settlement procedure can have adverse effects on cooperation if it encourages the renegotiation of punishments. Interestingly, Watson et al. (2008) make a point that goes in the opposite direction: they argue that, in the absence of a dispute settlement procedure, after a deviation countries would quickly renegotiate, thus undermining the enforcement of the agreement, whereas the presence of a dispute settlement procedure can slow down renegotiation and make it more costly, and this paradoxically can facilitate cooperation.

The above-mentioned papers raise an interesting question concerning the design of dispute settlement procedures: to what extent should they encourage renegotiation and settlement between governments? One clear point that emerges from this literature is that it is critical to distinguish between two kinds of renegotiation, namely the renegotiation of substantive *policy* rules and the renegotiation of *enforcement* rules: the former tends to be desirable, the latter tends to be harmful. But in reality the distinction between these two forms of renegotiation can be blurred, and an interesting research question would be whether and how a dispute settlement procedure can be designed to encourage one form of renegotiation and discourage the other.

4. REGIONAL TRADE AGREEMENTS

In recent years there has been a considerable amount of theoretical and empirical research on regional trade agreements (RTAs), spurred at least in part by the growing role of this

---

[81] Another theoretical paper where the DSB facilitates the self-enforcement of TAs by changing the information structure of the game, but in a two-country setting, is Park (2011). In Park's model, each government privately observes a noisy signal of the other government's trade policy, and the DSB can facilitate cooperation by converting the privately observed signals into public signals. Here I also note that most of the academic research on the enforcement role of the DSB has been theoretical, but there are a few notable empirical papers on this topic, see in particular Bown (2004a), Bown (2004b), Reinhardt (2001), and Busch and Reinhardt (2002).

type of agreement in the real world. In this section I will focus on three topics: (a) the economic and political determinants of RTA formation; (b) the impact of an RTA on its members' external trade barriers and on multilateral trade liberalization; and (c) the design of rules for trade negotiations. The common theme of this section is an emphasis on the endogeneity of trade policies. I will leave aside, on the other hand, the older question of how an exogenously formed RTA affects trade flows and welfare (e.g. through trade-diversion and trade-creation effects), which has been covered extensively in Baldwin and Venables' (1995) handbook chapter.[82]

4.1. Determinants of RTAs

A question of obvious positive and normative relevance concerning RTAs is: in a world where governments are motivated by political economy considerations, under what conditions are RTAs more likely to form? And in particular, is an RTA more likely to form when it is beneficial or detrimental to global welfare? This question is examined by Grossman and Helpman (1995b), who consider a setting similar to Grossman and Helpman (1995a) but with two small economies that can choose whether to form a free trade agreement (FTA). Given the presence of producer lobbies, an FTA is more likely to be adopted when it generates larger rents for the producers of both countries, a situation that Grossman and Helpman label "enhanced protection." In a given sector, enhanced protection can occur under the following circumstances. Suppose that one country has a lower external tariff than the other, and that as a result of the FTA producers from the former country can export all of their output to the latter country without affecting local prices in the latter country. Then producers in the former country get higher rents while producers in the latter country are not affected. If the FTA generates enhanced protection in a sufficient number of sectors and in a relatively balanced way between the countries, then it will be politically viable. But since enhanced protection is more likely when the FTA causes trade diversion, the conclusion is that more trade-diverting FTAs are more likely to be adopted.

A similar question is examined by Krishna (1998), but in the context of an oligopolistic model with segmented markets, where governments care only about the profits of their domestic firms. In such an environment, an FTA is adopted if and only if it increases profits in both countries. This in turn is more likely to happen when the FTA leads to a bigger reduction in the market share of non-member-country firms in the member countries' markets, or in other words, when the FTA induces more trade diversion.

---

[82] The theoretical research on the trade-diversion and trade-creation effects of RTAs was developed mostly before 1995, but there are some notable recent contributions, in particular Panagariya and Krishna (2002), which extends the classic Kemp-Wan result (which applies to customs unions) to the case of free trade agreements, and Freund (2000a), which compares the welfare effects of alternative (exogenous) paths of trade agreements leading to global free trade. In recent years there have been also some interesting empirical studies on the trade-diversion and trade-creation effects of RTAs: some prominent examples are Trefler (2004), Romalis (2007), Magee (2008), and Clausing (2001).

Therefore Krishna's analysis delivers a similarly pessimistic message as Grossman and Helpman (1995b): FTAs are more likely to be adopted when they are more trade-diverting and hence detrimental to welfare.

A counterpoint to the pessimistic message of the two papers discussed above is represented by the well-known argument (made for example by Krugman, 1991) that RTAs are more likely to form among "natural" trading partners, that is countries characterized by especially large gains from mutual trade liberalization (for example because of their geographical proximity or their comparative advantage structure). If this is the case, the argument goes, the RTAs that emerge in equilibrium will be more likely to cause trade creation than trade diversion, and hence more likely to increase welfare.

Given the seemingly contrasting theoretical arguments outlined above, the question of the welfare impact of endogenously formed RTAs is ultimately an empirical one, and indeed this question has been tackled by a number of interesting empirical papers. Krishna (2003) takes a structural approach to this question, estimating a general equilibrium model and using its structural parameters to examine the welfare effects of a number of hypothetical RTAs. Krishna finds that 80% of these hypothetical RTAs would be welfare-improving, but interestingly, he finds that neither geographical variables nor trade volumes are significantly correlated with the welfare gains, thus offering little support for the natural-trading-partners view of the world. Baier and Bergstrand (2004) find that the likelihood of an RTA is higher when countries are closer to each other and are more isolated from the rest of the world, a finding that supports the view that "natural" trading partners are more likely to form RTAs. Baier and Bergstrand (2007) examine the impact of RTAs on trade flows when taking into account the endogeneity of RTA formation. They find that, when this endogeneity is recognized, the trade-creation effects of RTAs appear to be much larger, and in particular, the impact of RTAs on trade flows increases fivefold relative to estimates that take RTA formation as exogenous. Egger and Larch (2008) find results that are consistent with those of the above-mentioned papers using a larger sample, and furthermore find that an RTA is more likely to form when there are pre-existing RTAs involving near-by countries.

Another question that has received some attention in the literature is how the likelihood of RTA formation is affected by multilateral trade liberalization. Freund (2000b) examines this question within a repeated-game model and finds that deeper multilateral trade liberalization leads to more RTAs, for two reasons: it increases the incentives to form an RTA and it increases the likelihood that it is self-enforcing.[83] At the empirical level, Fugazza and Robert-Nicoud (2012) find some evidence that multilateral trade liberalization increases the likelihood of subsequent RTA formation. More specifically, they find that after the Uruguay Round, the US had a higher propensity to liberalize trade on a preferential basis in goods where it had granted the deepest multilateral tariff cuts.

---

[83] See also Ethier (1998) for an examination of the impacts of multilateral trade liberalization on subsequent RTAs.

Finally, an interesting question is: what determines the choice between an FTA and a customs union (CU)? Empirically, most RTAs take the form of FTAs. Facchini et al. (2013) propose a theoretical explanation for stylized fact, based on a three-country political economy model with imperfect competition, where each country elects a representative to choose trade policies. Under a CU, since tariffs are chosen collectively by the member countries, the voters of each country strategically delegate power to a more protectionist representative. Facchini et al. show that, because of this strategic delegation effect, an FTA tends to imply higher welfare for member countries and is more likely to be politically viable than a CU.

4.2. Impacts of RTAs

In this section I will focus on two related themes: the impact of RTAs on member countries' trade barriers against outsiders ("external" trade barriers) and the impact of RTAs on multilateral trade liberalization.

The impact of RTA formation on external trade barriers has been the subject of a sizable theoretical literature. One point that emerges clearly from this literature is that the qualitative impact of RTAs on external tariffs depends crucially on whether the agreement takes the form of an FTA or of a CU. I will focus first on FTAs.

Various papers have pointed out a strong tendency of FTAs to lead to *lower* external trade barriers. This is generally known as the "tariff complementarity" effect, but it is important to point out that such effect can arise from two distinct mechanisms. The first one, highlighted by Richardson (1993), occurs when the FTA leads member countries to compete for tariff revenue, thus inducing them to reduce external tariffs. Interestingly, this mechanism can occur even for small countries that use tariffs only for political-economy reasons and have no TOT power. A second mechanism was pointed out by Bagwell and Staiger (1999b): an FTA leads member countries to import less from non-member countries, and if member countries have TOT power this reduces their incentives to manipulate TOT vis-à-vis non-members, in turn leading to lower external tariffs.[84]

The tariff complementarity effect however is not the only possible effect at play in determining the impact of FTAs on external tariffs, and other effects may arise that mitigate or overturn it. Limão (2007) for example shows that an FTA can lead to higher external tariffs if the FTA serves also non-trade objectives (such as enhancing cooperation on labor standards or security issues). Several real-world FTAs appear to have this feature, with one country (typically the US or the EU) granting tariff preferences, and the other (typically a less developed country) making non-trade concessions. In this type of situation, the country that grants tariff preferences may be better off increasing its external

---

[84] Other papers that have highlighted tariff-complementarity effects in different settings are Bond et al. (2004), Cadot et al. (1999), Bagwell and Staiger (1997a), Ornelas (2005a,c), and Saggi and Yildiz (2010).

tariffs, because this enhances the value of the preferences and hence allows it to extract larger non-trade concessions.[85]

In the case of CUs, tariff-complementarity effects may still be present, but two new forces arise that push in the opposite direction. The first one is known as the "market power" effect: if two member countries import the same good from outsiders, once the CU is formed they *jointly* have more power over TOT, and thus have a stronger incentive to raise tariffs against outsiders. The second effect is known as the "coordination" effect: if country A increases the tariff on imports of a certain good from country B, this has a positive externality on all other countries (both importers and exporters of that good), and a CU allows member countries to internalize this externality, thus leading to higher external tariffs. The first paper in the literature to highlight these two effects was Kennan and Riezman (1990). Note that the coordination effect can arise even in the absence of the market power effect: this is crystal-clear in a setting of "competing exporters," where each country is the sole importer of a given good. Once all the effects are taken into account, a CU can still lead to lower external tariffs, but this is less likely than in the case of an FTA (as shown by Bagwell and Staiger, 1999b).[86]

In a series of papers, Emanuel Ornelas has established a link between the literature on the impacts of RTAs and that on the determinants of RTAs, by showing that taking into account the impact of RTAs on external tariffs has important implications for the likelihood of RTA formation in the first place.

Ornelas (2005a) considers a model similar to Grossman and Helpman (1995b), but in which external tariffs are determined endogenously. Ornelas identifies a "rent destruction" effect of the FTA, which arises from the fact that the rents from external tariff protection spill over to partner countries under the FTA. The rent-destruction effect lowers the incentives of special interest groups to lobby for protection, and this creates a tendency of FTAs to induce reductions in external tariffs. Interestingly, when political-economy motivations are stronger, the drop in external tariffs is larger, thus FTAs are more conducive to multilateral trade liberalization.

The second point made by Ornelas (2005a) is that, since an FTA lowers the total amount of rents that trade protection can generate, this has important implications for the political viability of the FTA. Ornelas starts by considering a situation where there is no ex-ante lobbying (that is, no lobbying to influence directly the decision to join the FTA), and shows that in this case only FTAs that are sufficiently welfare-enhancing can be politically viable: intuitively, a welfare-reducing FTA cannot be attractive to the government, because it reduces both the level of welfare and the available amount of

---

[85] Another effect that may work against the tariff complementarity effect was highlighted by Stoyanov (2009): if foreign lobbying is possible, producers from FTA partners may have stronger incentives to lobby for higher external tariffs once the FTA is formed, since their gains from such external tariffs are higher under the FTA.

[86] The effects of a CU on external tariffs have been examined also by Krugman (1991), Bond and Syropoulos (1996), Bagwell and Staiger (1997b), and Cadot et al. (1999).

rents. Ornelas then allows for ex-ante lobbying, and finds that in this case a welfare-reducing FTA may in some cases be politically viable, but this is made less likely by the rent-destruction effect of the FTA: in particular, a welfare-reducing FTA can be viable only if the governments' valuation of welfare relative to contributions is neither too small nor too large. The bottom line of this paper then is that the rent-destruction effect reduces the political viability of welfare-reducing FTAs.[87]

The impact of RTAs on external trade barriers has also been the subject of recent empirical work. Estevadeordal et al. (2008) focus on the effect of preferential trade liberalization on external tariffs in Latin America from 1990 to 2001. An appealing feature of this dataset is the wide variation in trade preferences across sectors and over time. Employing a rich set of fixed effects, these authors find that preferential tariff reduction induces faster decline in external tariffs. Furthermore, they find that this effect is present only for FTAs, not for CUs, and is stronger in sectors where the potential for trade diversion is larger.[88]

Interestingly, Limão (2006) and Karacaovali and Limão (2008) find results that seemingly diverge from those of Estevadeordal et al. (2008). These two papers examine the impact of preferential trade liberalization by the US and the EU on multilateral trade liberalization, and find that the US and the EU liberalized less during the Uruguay Round in sectors where they had granted tariff preferences, suggesting that preferential liberalization might hinder the cause of global free trade. What can explain the difference in findings between these papers and Estevadeordal et al. (2008)? Theory can help us answer this question. A key difference between the two approaches is that Limão (2006) and Karacaovali and Limão (2008) focus on the US and the EU, whereas Estevadeordal et al. (2008) focus on developing countries. Tariffs are considerably higher in developing countries, so the potential for trade diversion is larger for these countries, and as theory suggests, this implies a stronger tariff complementarity effect. Furthermore, Limão's (2007) theoretical analysis suggests that preferential liberalization may hinder global free trade if RTAs are formed also for non-trade reasons, and this is more often the case for North–South RTAs than for South–South RTAs.[89]

Thus far I have focused on how the formation of an RTA affects its member countries' unilateral choices of external tariffs. Next I focus on the impact of RTAs on the political viability of multilateral trade agreements.

---

[87] Similar results are obtained by Ornelas (2005b,c) in the context of an oligopolistic model similar to Krishna (1998).

[88] Two other papers present findings that are consistent with those of Estevadeordal et al. (2008): Calvo-Pardo et al., (2009) find that the formation of ASEAN led to a reduction in external tariffs by its member countries, and Bohara et al. (2004) find that the increase in preferential imports from Brazil to Argentina that followed the formation of MERCOSUR led to a decrease in Argentina's external tariffs.

[89] Related to this literature is also a recent paper by Baldwin and Jaimovich (2012), which focuses on the impact of RTAs on subsequent RTAs. This paper extends Baldwin's (1995) model of "domino" regionalism and tests its main empirical prediction, namely that the formation of an RTA has a contagion effect and increases the likelihood that further RTAs will be formed. Using a comprehensive panel of FTAs, Baldwin and Jaimovich find support for the contagion prediction.

Levy (1997) considers a model where gains from trade can arise from differences in relative factor endowments and/or from increased product variety, and takes a median-voter approach to the choice of trade policies. He shows that, if the FTA provides a country's median voter with disproportionately large gains, it may raise his or her reservation utility above the level offered by a multilateral agreement, thus undermining political support for the latter. This undermining is more likely to occur in FTAs that involve countries with similar relative factor endowments. For example, suppose Germany joins the EU. Assuming that EU countries have similar relative factor endowments, this will benefit the median voter in Germany mostly through variety gains. In the next stage, Germany considers signing a multilateral agreement. If Germany is relatively rich in capital and its median voter is an unskilled worker, the multilateral agreement is likely to damage the median voter through Stolper-Samuelson effects, without providing much additional variety gains, so he/she will block the multilateral agreement. On the other hand, if the same median voter were asked if he/she supports a multilateral agreement *before* joining the EU, then the answer may be yes, because in this case the variety gains may outweigh the adverse Stolper-Samuelson effects.

The model by Krishna (1998), already mentioned in Section 4.1, leads to a similar result, in spite of the very different structure. Recall that Krishna focuses on a Grossman-Helpman type model with oligopolistic competition. After establishing that politically viable FTAs are more likely to be trade-diverting, Krishna examines how an FTA affects the political viability of a multilateral agreement. The key finding is that the formation of an FTA may increase producers' opposition to a subsequent multilateral agreement, because the latter may reduce or eliminate the rents created by the FTA, and it can even reverse the preferences of producers, from supporting a multilateral agreement to opposing it. Thus, taken together, the papers by Levy (1997) and Krishna (1998) deliver a pessimistic message about the impact of RTAs on the political viability of multilateral agreements.

Finally, Bagwell and Staiger's (1999a) model (already discussed in Sections 2.1 and 3.1.4) also delivers pessimistic implications for the impact of RTAs on multilateral trade agreements, but for a very different reason than the models discussed above. A simple corollary of Bagwell and Staiger's analysis is that the presence of RTAs, by breaking the ability of the MFN rule to channel all international policy externalities into a single world-price externality, undermines the effectiveness of the MFN and reciprocity rules in guiding countries toward an efficient policy outcome.[90]

---

[90] Here I will mention two other strands of literature that are quite interesting but distinct from the ones discussed in the text. The first one examines how RTAs affect the self-enforceability of a multilateral agreement. In particular, Bagwell and Staiger (1997a,b) focus on the transition period during which an RTA is being negotiated, showing that the anticipation of the RTA has an important impact on the sustainability of multilateral tariff cooperation; Saggi (2006) considers the impact of RTAs on the sustainability of a multilateral agreement in an oligopolistic setting, finding that the presence of an RTA undermines multilateral cooperation when countries are symmetric, but not necessarily when countries are asymmetric; finally, Bond et al. (2001) focus on the transition period during which trade barriers within a CU are phased out, and examine how the deepening of intra-CU trade liberalization affects the sustainability

4.3. Rules for Trade Negotiations

In this section I return to my emphasis on the design of rules, but this time I focus on rules that constrain trade negotiations rather than the policy choices of individual governments. A number of papers have been written on the question of what rules (if any) should regulate trade negotiations, but this literature can be hard to tame, as the modeling approach and the exact nature of the question seem to shift from paper to paper. In what follows I propose a simple conceptual framework that might be useful to organize our thinking and define more clearly the relevant questions.

Consider the following senario: imagine that, at some ex-ante stage, all countries involved in the trading system bargain over the rules that regulate future trade negotiations. Also assume that at the ex-ante stage countries cannot write a complete agreement, and in particular they cannot specify actual trade policies, but only negotiation rules (otherwise there would be no reason to set negotiation rules in the first place). One possible reason why negotiation rules might be desirable is that governments may have incentives to sign RTAs that exert negative externalities on non-member countries, in which case the resulting outcome may be globally inefficient.

In the scenario I just described, one can make a distinction between two types of rules constraining trade negotiations: (1) Rules that constrain the nature of the agreement itself. An example of this type of rule is one that prohibits RTAs, or equivalently, a rule requiring that any agreement be approved by all countries. Another example is a rule that prohibits CUs but not FTAs. I refer to these rules (for lack of a better expression) as *rules-to-make-rules;* (2) Rules that constrain the policy content of the agreements. Examples include reciprocity-type rules, which require that tariff reductions be balanced across countries, and non-discrimination rules, such as the MFN rule. These rules do not constrain the type of agreements that countries sign, but do constrain the policies (or policy changes) that countries can agree upon. I refer to these as *policy-content* rules.[91]

Note that the GATT-WTO currently does not impose rules-to-make-rules, but only policy-content rules, and more specifically: (i) GATT Article I imposes the MFN rule,

---

of multilateral agreements. The other line of research I want to mention is the work by Martin et al. (2008, 2012), who explore the two-way relationship between RTAs and military conflicts. At the theoretical level, they argue that RTAs increase the opportunity cost of conflict, thereby reducing the likelihood of war, and conversely, countries with a higher likelihood of conflict are more likely to sign RTAs as a way to promote peace. Furthermore, they argue that this logic does not apply to multilateral trade agreements, because multilateral trade openness decreases bilateral dependence from trade with any given country and hence the cost of a bilateral conflict. At the empirical level, they find support for these predictions using a large dataset of military conflicts during the 1950–2000 period.

[91] In the scenario outlined above I am assuming that at the ex-ante stage countries can only specify rules constraining future negotiations, not rules constraining individual government policies. In reality, of course, even from the very beginning the GATT imposed both types of rules. I am separating the stages at which the two different types of rules are designed for conceptual simplicity. Also, the distinction between policy-content rules and rules-to-make-rules can be subtle but should be conceptually clear. For example, note that imposing the MFN rule does not logically imply prohibiting FTAs, because an FTA in principle need not violate MFN (an FTA eliminates tariffs between its members, but this does not prevent a member from respecting the MFN rule, which it can do by eliminating the relevant tariffs vis-à-vis non-members).

so any negotiated policy changes must be extended in a non-discriminatory way to all member countries; (ii) GATT Article XXIV allows an exception to the MFN rule for the case of an RTA that eliminates substantially all trade barriers among its members, but requires the RTA member countries not to raise their external tariffs above pre-RTA levels;[92] and (iii) GATT requires that negotiations adhere to the principle of reciprocity, although as discussed earlier, this is an informal principle rather than a strict rule.

It is important, however, to consider also the possibility of rules-to-make-rules, both from a positive perspective (why are there no such rules in GATT-WTO?) and from a normative one (should such rules be imposed?). In particular, the simplest such rule—a ban on RTAs—has a special theoretical interest. Indeed, an interesting question can be posed here: if there are no frictions in multilateral bargaining (as assumed in most of the existing models), why would a ban on RTAs *not* be optimal? If governments are forced to choose trade policies at a multilateral bargaining table, why would this not achieve efficiency?[93] I will return to this question at the end of this section, after surveying the recent research in this area.

If one adopts the conceptual framework outlined above, one needs to take a stand on what objective function the rules are supposed to maximize. There are two possible questions that can be asked, each of which is interesting in its own right:

1. What rules maximize the likelihood of reaching global free trade? This is essentially the question raised by Bhagwati (1993): are RTAs "building blocks" or "stumbling blocks" on the path to global free trade?

2. What rules maximize the joint payoff of all governments? This is a more positive question and can lead to different answers than the previous one, if one allows for political motivations in the governments' objectives.

Ideally, a full answer to either question requires comparing the *equilibrium configuration* of trade agreements (or their path, if one takes a dynamic approach) under alternative negotiation rules, of course allowing for RTAs as well as multilateral agreements. Models that focus on the impact of exogenously formed RTAs on multilateral agreements, such as those that I surveyed in the previous section, evidently can only shed partial light on this question.

4.3.1. Policy-Content Rules

As I mentioned earlier, the key policy-content rules that regulate trade negotiations in the GATT-WTO system are the MFN rule and—at a more informal level—the reciprocity principle. In Section 3.1.4, I discussed papers by Bagwell and Staiger (1999a) and

---

[92] Exceptions to MFN are also allowed in a number of extraordinary circumstances, such as national-security or health hazards (GATT Article III).

[93] Of course it is possible that such a rule is not strictly needed, if global efficiency can be achieved also in the absence of any rule on trade negotiations, and in this case a ban on RTAs will only be *weakly* optimal. Indeed, this is the case in some of the models I will survey below.

Ossa (2011) that examine the implications of these rules in the context of multilateral trade negotiations, but these papers do not consider endogenous RTAs.

A paper that does consider the impact of these rules on the endogenous formation of RTAs is Bagwell and Staiger (2005b). This paper considers a two-stage scenario where, in the first stage, countries can sign a multilateral agreement, and in the second stage, pairs of countries can sign bilateral agreements. The first point of the paper is that, if bilateral negotiations are left unrestricted, a problem of "bilateral opportunism" is likely to arise: after multilateral trade concessions have been exchanged, there is an incentive for a pair of countries to take a further step and liberalize trade bilaterally, but this will erode the value of the concessions that the excluded country had obtained in the initial multilateral negotiation, and this in turn makes countries more reluctant to make multilateral trade concessions in the first place. The second point of the paper is that the bilateral opportunism problem described above may be solved if trade negotiations are disciplined by the MFN rule in conjunction with a reciprocity rule. To gain intuition for this result, suppose there are only two goods. Then the MFN rule ensures the existence of a single relative world price (as explained in Section 2.1.2), and reciprocity ensures that this world price is effectively fixed by the initial multilateral agreement; and given that the world price is preserved in subsequent bilateral negotiations, the welfare of countries that do not participate in a bilateral negotiation is preserved as well.

In a related paper, Bagwell and Staiger (2010b) consider a setting in which countries can sequentially sign bilateral agreements in the presence of the MFN rule. Two inefficiencies tend to arise in this setting: the first one is due to the bilateral opportunism problem highlighted above; the second is that, since later negotiating partners can free-ride on the MFN concessions that a country makes to early negotiating partners, a country may be induced to offer too little in the early negotiations ("foot-dragging"). Bagwell and Staiger then argue that these inefficiencies can be removed if two additional rules are imposed, along with MFN: the reciprocity rule and a "non-violation" rule along the lines of GATT Article XXIII.1b. These rules together act as a device to "secure" the concessions received by a country in early negotiations and protect them from potential free riding and bilateral opportunism in the future.[94]

A different argument for the desirability of the MFN rule is proposed by McCalman (2002). This contribution is notable because it is a rare example of a model that explicitly introduces bargaining frictions in multilateral trade negotiations. In this model, a large country negotiates with N small countries over tariffs and transfers, and each small country has private information about its gains from an agreement. McCalman compares two scenarios, one where the large country can make different offers to different countries, and one where the MFN rule constrains the large country to make the same offer to all countries. The large country of course is worse off under the MFN rule, since the

---

[94] This is a good juncture to mention a paper by Ludema and Mayda (2009), which examines empirically the free-rider problem associated with the MFN rule, finding that this problem is indeed of first-order empirical importance.

latter constrains its choice, but global efficiency may be higher under MFN, and this is more likely when N is larger. The reason lies in the fact that bargaining is inefficient, due to private information. If bargaining were frictionless, unconstrained bargaining would always lead to efficiency, and the MFN rule would always be a bad idea. But in the presence of private information, unconstrained bargaining is inefficient, because the large country is not able to appropriate the entire surplus from the negotiations, and as a consequence it is possible that imposing MFN increases the welfare of the N countries more than it reduces the welfare of the large country.[95]

4.3.2. Rules-to-Make-Rules

The simplest rule-to-make-rules, and the one that has received the most attention in the literature, is a rule that prohibits RTAs. Would the world be more efficient if all agreements had to be multilateral in nature? In this section I discuss a number of recent papers that speak to this question.

One of the first papers to examine the desirability of a rule banning RTAs is McLaren (2002), who focuses on the implications of irreversible investments for the formation of trade agreements. McLaren considers a world with three countries: in the first period, individuals choose in what sectors to allocate their resources; in the second period, there is a coalition-formation game among governments, which can yield an FTA, a multilateral free trade agreement, or no agreement at all. Negotiations are costly, and this cost is higher for a multilateral negotiation. This model may have multiple equilibria, including an equilibrium where global free trade arises (and the allocation is efficient), and equilibria where two of the countries form an FTA (and the allocation is inefficient). The latter type of equilibrium is based on a self-fulfilling prophecy. If individuals expect an FTA between countries A and B, they will make investment decisions that make these countries more specialized relative to each other, thus increasing the gains from trade between them. At the same time, countries A and B will become less specialized relative to the outside country, thus decreasing the gains from trade between them and the outside country. As a consequence, ex-post countries A and B will have a strong incentive to sign an FTA, while the benefits from a multilateral agreement will be small. Ex-ante, an FTA equilibrium of this kind may be inefficient if the allocation distortions associated with the FTA outweigh the savings in negotiation costs. Intuitively, then, there is a region of parameters in which an FTA equilibrium exists and is inefficient, and therefore a ban on FTAs is strictly desirable.

---

[95] Another policy-content rule imposed by the GATT-WTO, as I mentioned in the previous section, is contained in GATT Article XXIV. Mrazova et al. (2013) examine the implications of Article XXIV as it applies to CUs, requiring that the common external tariff of the CU must not exceed the average of its members' pre-CU tariffs. Mrazova et al. argue that Article XXIV increases the probability that free trade emerges in equilibrium, but when free trade does not arise in equilibrium, the constraints imposed by this rule may lead to a reduction in world welfare.

Goyal and Joshi (2006) adopt a network-formation approach to study the formation of FTAs, using a particular notion of "stability" to determine the configurations of FTAs that can arise in equilibrium. Focusing on a setting with a homogenous good and symmetric countries, Goyal and Joshi find that the complete FTA network, which yields global free trade, is a stable network, thus suggesting that FTAs are "building blocks" toward global free trade. Another network-theoretic model of FTA formation is Furusawa and Konishi (2007), which differs from Goyal and Joshi (2006) in that it allows for differentiated goods and a richer pattern of asymmetries between countries. Consistently with Goyal and Joshi, this paper finds that when countries are symmetric, the complete FTA network (global free trade) is stable. However, if goods are highly substitutable, there may also be other stable networks that do not yield global free trade. And if countries are asymmetric, the complete FTA network may not be stable. Furusawa and Konishi conclude that FTAs may under some conditions be "stumbling blocks" toward global free trade.[96]

Before moving on, I will make a general observation about the network-theoretic approach to the analysis of RTA formation, of which I just discussed two examples. In these network models, there is no meaningful distinction between a sequence of RTAs that leads to global free trade and a multilateral agreement. Indeed, multilateral agreements *per se* are not considered at all, so these models, though capable of generating interesting insights, are arguably not well equipped to evaluate the desirability of rules-to-make-rules, such as a ban on RTAs. The models that I discuss next, on the other hand, do allow for multilateral agreements as well as RTAs, and hence are better equipped to examine this question.

Seidmann (2009) examines a three-country bargaining model in which countries can negotiate FTAs, CUs, and multilateral agreements. Countries are allowed to continue negotiating after reaching an agreement, and for this reason, an RTA can be used by its member countries to improve their bargaining position for subsequent trade negotiations ("strategic positioning" effect). Two important features of the model are that international transfers are available and that global free trade maximizes the three countries' joint surplus. Seidmann studies the equilibrium configuration of agreements, highlighting for example conditions under which a hub-and-spoke structure emerges. Regarding the question of whether RTAs are building blocks or stumbling blocks toward global free trade, in Seidmann's model global free trade may or may not be reached if RTAs are

---

[96] This is a good juncture to mention a paper by Yi (1996), who takes a coalition-formation approach to study the formation of CUs. Yi compares two possible games: a "unanimous regionalism" game, where a CU forms if and only if all potential members agree to form the CU; and an "open regionalism" game, where each country chooses an "address," and then all the countries that have chosen the same address must be part of the same CU. Yi shows that the grand CU (global free trade) is an equilibrium of the open-regionalism game, but typically is not an equilibrium of the unanimous-regionalism game, and interprets this finding as suggesting that an "open regionalism" rule is desirable. However it is not clear how to interpret Yi's notion of open regionalism in a way that has a meaningful counterpart in the real world: Yi's open-regionalism game implicitly assumes that a country is not free to *leave* a CU (if this were the case then we would be in the unanimous-regionalism game), which seems like a far-fetched idea.

feasible, while global free trade is always reached if RTAs are not feasible, thus a ban on RTAs is always weakly desirable.

Saggi and Yildiz (2010) also consider a three-country bargaining model where governments can negotiate RTAs as well as multilateral agreements. The negotiation game is as follows: governments simultaneously name FTA partners, and an FTA is formed if the announcements agree; if a government names both of the other countries, this is interpreted as a proposal for a multilateral agreement, and if all governments propose a multilateral agreement, it is implemented. A key feature of the model is that international transfers are not available. Saggi and Yildiz examine the implications of a rule banning FTAs, by comparing a game where FTAs are allowed with one where they are not. Focusing on coalition-proof Nash equilibria, they show that when countries are symmetric global free trade is the only stable equilibrium, whether or not FTAs are allowed. But when countries are asymmetric it may happen that global free trade is a stable equilibrium *only if* FTAs are allowed, so a ban on FTAs can make global free trade less likely. To understand this result intuitively, recall that there are no international transfers in the model, so global free trade is not the only Pareto-efficient outcome. Indeed, a ban on FTAs may lead away from global free trade, but *not* away from Pareto-efficiency. If FTAs are banned, it is possible that in equilibrium two countries agree to liberalize trade while the third does not: this outcome is skewed in favor of the country that free rides, but is Pareto efficient. Thus, Saggi and Yildiz's result should be interpreted as suggesting only that FTAs may be needed to achieve global free trade, not that FTAs may be needed to achieve global efficiency.

Saggi et al. (2013) build on Saggi and Yildiz (2010) by considering the case of CUs. The main finding of this paper is that, in contrast with the case of FTAs, in the case of CUs a "stumbling block" scenario is possible, in the sense that the freedom to pursue CUs may prevent the attainment of global free trade. Interestingly, the reason for this difference in results is not that a CU has a more harmful impact on outsiders than an FTA, but rather that it implies a stronger incentive for insiders to deny access to outsiders. Taken together, the two papers just discussed suggest that under some conditions it might be desirable to ban CUs but not FTAs; but this is only suggestive, because in order to make this point rigorously one would need to consider a model where CUs and FTAs are *both* options available to governments, which is not the case in either of the above-mentioned papers.

Aghion et al. (2007) also examine the building-block vs stumbling-block question within a three-country model where countries can negotiate FTAs as well as multilateral agreements, but with some key differences relative to Saggi and Yildiz (2010). In particular, Aghion et al. assume that there is a leading country that chooses whether to engage in sequential bilateral bargains or in a single multilateral bargain, and allow for political economy motivations in the government objectives. In addition, they assume that international transfers are available. Aghion et al. define payoffs to be "grand-coalition superadditive" if the payoff of the grand coalition is larger than the payoff of all countries combined in alternative coalition structures. This property is satisfied for example if free trade is Pareto-efficient and each government maximizes national welfare. A key result of the paper is that, if payoffs are grand-coalition superadditive, then the leading country may prefer sequential bargaining or multilateral bargaining, depending on the nature of coalition externalities, but in either case global free trade must emerge in equilibrium.

Aghion et al. then examine environments where grand-coalition superadditivity fails, which can happen when political-economy motivations are strong. In this case, it is possible that global free trade is attained only if FTAs are permitted (a building-block scenario), and it is also possible that global free trade is attained only if FTAs are banned (a stumbling-block scenario). Note that, as in Saggi and Yildiz (2010), it may happen that a ban on FTAs leads away from global free trade, but not that a ban on FTAs leads away from Pareto-efficiency. However, unlike Saggi-Yildiz, this is not due to the absence of international transfers, but rather to the possibility that governments may not maximize welfare; indeed, a ban on FTAs can lead away from free trade only if governments do not maximize welfare.

A related point is made by Ornelas (2008): if governments do not maximize welfare, it is possible that FTAs have the effect of bringing the world closer to global free trade relative to a multilateral agreement, and hence a ban on RTAs may lead the world away from global free trade. However, this possibility arises in Ornelas (2008) for very different reasons than in the papers mentioned above: here the reasons are that FTAs lead member countries to lower their external tariffs, and that there is a tendency for FTAs to emerge in equilibrium when they are trade-creating rather than trade-diverting.

A common message suggested by the papers discussed above is that, if rules are designed ex-ante when governments are in "constitution-writing" mode and seek to maximize global welfare, but ex-post government objectives may diverge from welfare, then a ban on RTAs may be harmful, because RTAs may lead the world closer to global free trade than a multilateral agreement.

I conclude this section by returning to the question I posed earlier: why has the GATT-WTO *not* banned RTAs? As discussed above, the possible answers suggested by the literature are two: (i) because rules are designed ex-ante when governments are in constitution-writing mode and maximize welfare, whereas ex-post government objectives may diverge from welfare; or (ii) because efficiency might also be achieved by means of other rules, such as MFN and reciprocity. A third, and conceptually simpler, reason why banning RTAs might not be a good idea is the presence of important frictions in multilateral bargaining. This consideration is arguably of first-order empirical importance, but has received little attention in the formal literature.[97] If multilateral bargaining is less efficient than bilateral bargaining, for example because of the complexity of negotiations when a large number of countries is involved, then allowing RTAs may be strictly

---

[97] One notable exception is McLaren (2002), but he models multilateral bargaining frictions in a very reduced-form way, through a parameter that captures the extra cost of multilateral negotiations.

desirable on efficiency grounds. But a more complete understanding of this issue would require introducing bargaining frictions explicitly in our models and examining how they depend on the set of countries and on the set of issues involved in the bargain.

5. CONCLUSION

Coming back to the pessimistic statement made by Krugman (1997) (see beginning of Section 2), one is tempted to ask: have the last 15 years of research proved Krugman wrong? This is a matter of debate, but I think that, at a minimum, the literature has demonstrated that the logic of economics can go a long way toward explaining the purpose and design of trade agreements. As I have argued in this chapter, more progress is needed along several dimensions, but we have made significant advances toward understanding the motivations that drive countries to sign trade agreements and the reasons why trade agreements are designed the way they are, and we are now in a better position to evaluate possible reforms of existing rules from a normative standpoint. Most of the research has been at the theoretical level, but in the last few years there has been an acceleration in empirical research, spurred by the availability of new and better data sets.

What's next for the economics of trade agreements? At a broad level, I think that this research area is ready—both in terms of theoretical tools and data availability—to follow a path that other research areas in international economics have fruitfully taken, namely a tighter integration between theoretical and empirical analysis. Some of the most important questions on the table require counterfactual analysis, and this in turn calls for structural and/or calibration approaches. Some recent papers that I discussed in this chapter have moved in this direction, but we are still at the beginnings.

In terms of substantive questions, I will point to a few directions that seem promising to me. One question that we still know little about is the empirical importance of "New Trade" and domestic-commitment motives for trade agreements. Another important set of open questions concerns multilateral trade negotiations in the presence of bargaining frictions: why has the Doha round failed? Is it because there are no mutual gains left on the table, or because of bargaining frictions due to the large number of countries and issues on the table? If bargaining frictions are part of the problem, can bargaining protocols be designed in a smarter way to facilitate more efficient outcomes?

If history is of any guidance, the release of new important datasets can trigger new waves of empirical and theoretical research. This will hopefully be the case for the recent release by the WTO of an unprecedented dataset that includes extremely detailed information about the bargaining that took place during GATT negotiation rounds. This dataset may help answer new questions, such as those related to the nature of bargaining frictions and the importance of bargaining protocols, as well as old questions, such as the extent to which the MFN rule generates free-rider problems and whether bilateral trade agreements are building blocks or stumbling blocks toward global free trade.

REFERENCES

Aghion, P., Antràs, P., Helpman, E., 2007. Negotiating free trade. Journal of International Economics 73 (1), 1–30.

Amador, M., Bagwell, K., 2013. The theory of optimal delegation with an application to tariff caps. Econometrica 81 (4), 1541–1599.

Amador, M., Bagwell, K., 2012. Tariff revenue and tariff caps. American Economic Review Papers and Proceedings 102 (3), 459–465.

Antras, P., Staiger, R.W., 2012a. Offshoring and the role of trade agreements. American Economic Review 102 (7), 3140–3183.

Antras, P., Staiger, R.W., 2012b. Trade agreements and the nature of international price determination. American Economic Review Papers and Proceedings 102 (3), 470–476.

Bacchetta, M., Piermartini, R., 2011. The Value of Bindings. WTO Staff Working Paper, ERSD-2011-13.

Bagwell, K., 2008. Remedies in the WTO: an economic perspective. In: Janow, M.E., Donaldson, V.J., Yanovich, A. (Eds.), The WTO Governance, Dispute Settlement & Developing Countries. Juris Publishing, pp. 733–770 (Chapter 40).

Bagwell, K., 2009. Self-Enforcing Trade Agreements and Private Information. NBER Working Paper 14812.

Bagwell, K., Staiger, R.W., 1990. A theory of managed trade. The American Economic Review 80, 779–795.

Bagwell, K., Staiger, R.W., 1997a. Multilateral tariff cooperation during the formation of free trade areas. International Economic Review 38, 291–319.

Bagwell, K., Staiger, R.W., 1997b. Multilateral tariff cooperation during the formation of customs unions. Journal of International Economics 42, 91–123.

Bagwell, K., Staiger, R.W., 1999a. An economic theory of GATT. American Economic Review 89 (1), 215–248.

Bagwell, K., Staiger, R.W., 1999b. Regionalism and multilateral tariff cooperation. In: Piggott, J., Woodland, A. (Eds.), International Trade Policy and the Pacific Rim. MacMillan, London, pp. 157–185.

Bagwell, K., Staiger, R.W., 2001. Domestic policies, national sovereignty and international economic institutions. Quarterly Journal of Economics 116 (2), 519–562.

Bagwell, K., Staiger, R.W., 2002. The Economics of the World Trading System. MIT Press, Cambridge, MA.

Bagwell, K., Staiger, R.W., 2003. Protection over the business cycle. Advances in Economic Analysis and Policy 3 (1), 1–43.

Bagwell, K., Staiger, R.W., 2005a. Enforcement, private political pressure, and the GATT/WTO escape clause. Journal of Legal Studies 34 (2), 471–513.

Bagwell, K., Staiger, R.W., 2005b. Multilateral trade negotiations, bilateral opportunism and the rules of GATT/WTO. Journal of International Economics 67, 268–294.

Bagwell, K., Staiger, R.W., 2006. Will international rules on subsidies disrupt the world trading system? American Economic Review 96 (3), 877–895.

Bagwell, K., Staiger, R.W., 2009. Delocation and Trade Agreements in Imperfectly Competitive Markets, Mimeo.

Bagwell, K., Staiger, R.W., 2010a. The WTO: theory and practice. Annual Review of Economics 2, 223–256.

Bagwell, K., Staiger, R.W., 2010b. Backward stealing and forward manipulation in the WTO. Journal of International Economics 82 (1), 49–62.

Bagwell, K., Staiger, R.W., 2011. What do trade negotiators negotiate about? Empirical evidence from the world trade organization. American Economic Review 101 (4), 1238–1273.

Bagwell, K., Staiger, R.W., 2012a. Profit shifting and trade agreements in imperfectly competitive markets. International Economic Review 53 (4), 1067–1104.

Bagwell, K., Staiger, R.W., 2012b. The economics of trade agreements in the linear delocation model. Journal of International Economics 88 (1), 32–46.

Bagwell, K., Mavroidis, P.C., Staiger, R.W., 2007. Auctioning counter-measures in the WTO. Journal of International Economics 73 (2), 309–332.

Baier, S.L., Bergstrand, J.H., 2004. Economic determinants of free trade agreements. Journal of International Economics 64 (1), 29–63.

Baier, S.L., Bergstrand, J.H., 2007. Do free trade agreements actually increase members' international trade? Journal of International Economics 71 (1), 72–95.

Baldwin, R.E., 1987. Politically realistic objective functions and trade policy. Economics Letters 24 (1), 287–290.

Baldwin, R.E., 1995. A domino theory of regionalism. In: Baldwin, R., Haaparanta, P., Kiander, J. (Eds.), Expanding membership of the European Union. Cambridge University Press, pp. 25–53.

Baldwin, R.E., Jaimovich, D., 2012. Are free trade agreements contagious? Journal of International Economics 88 (1), 1–16.

Baldwin, R.E., Venables, A.J., 1995. Regional economic integration. In: Grossman, G., Rogoff, K. (Eds.), Handbook of International Economics, vol. 3. North-Holland, Amsterdam, pp. 1597–1644.

Battigalli, P., Maggi, G., 2002. Rigidity, discretion and the costs of writing contracts. American Economic Review 92 (4), 798–817.

Battigalli, P., Maggi, G., 2003. International Agreements on Product Standards: An Incomplete-Contracting Theory. NBER Working Paper 9533.

Bajona, C., Chu, T., 2010. Reforming state owned enterprises in China: effects of WTO accession. Review of Economic Dynamics 13 (4), 800–823.

Bajona, C., Ederington, J., 2012. Domestic Policies, Hidden Protection and the GATT/WTO, Mimeo.

Beshkar, M., 2010a. Optimal remedies in international trade agreements. European Economic Review 54 (3), 455–466.

Beshkar, M., 2010b. Trade skirmishes and safeguards: a theory of the WTO dispute settlement process. Journal of International Economics 82 (1), 35–48.

Beshkar, M., 2011. Arbitration and Renegotiation in Trade Agreements, Mimeo.

Beshkar, M., Bond, E.W., 2012. Cap and Escape in Trade Agreements, Mimeo.

Beshkar, M., Bond, E.W., Rho, Y., 2011. Tariff Binding and Overhang: Theory and Evidence, Mimeo.

Bhagwati, J., 1993. Regionalism and multilateralism: an overview. In: de Melo, J., Panagariya, A. (Eds.), New Dimensions in Regional Integration. Cambridge University Press, pp. 22–51.

Bohara, A.K., Gawande, K., Sanguinetti, P., 2004. Trade diversion and declining tariffs: evidence from Mercosur. Journal of International Economics 64, 65–88.

Bond, E.W., Park, J.H., 2004. Gradualism in trade agreements with asymmetric countries. Review of Economic Studies 69, 379–406.

Bond, E.W., Syropoulos, C., 1996. The size of trading blocks: market power and world welfare effects. Journal of International Economics 40, 412–437.

Bond, E.W., Syropoulos, C., Winters, L.A., 2001. Deepening of regional integration and multilateral trade agreements. Journal of International Economics 53, 335–362.

Bond, E.W., Riezman, R., Syropoulos, C., 2004. A strategic and welfare theoretic analysis of free trade areas. Journal of International Economics 64, 1–27.

Bown, C., 2004a. On the economic success of GATT/WTO dispute settlement. Review of Economics and Statistics 86, 811–823.

Bown, C., 2004b. Trade disputes and the implementation of protection under the GATT: an empirical assessment. Journal of International Economics 62, 263–294.

Bown, C., Crowley, M.A., 2006. Policy externalities: how US antidumping affects Japanese exports to the EU. European Journal of Political Economy 22, 696–714.

Bown, C.P., Crowley, M.A., 2013a. Self-enforcing trade agreements: evidence from time-varying trade policy. American Economic Review 103 (2), 1071–1090.

Bown, C.P., Crowley, M.A., 2013b. Import protection, business cycles, and exchange rates: evidence from the great recession. Journal of International Economics 90 (1), 50–64.

Brander, J., Spencer, B., 1984. Tariff protection and imperfect competition. In: Kierzkowski, H. (Ed.), Monopolistic Competition and International Trade. Clarendon Press, Oxford.

Brander, J., Spencer, B., 1985. Export subsidies and market share rivalry. Journal of International Economics 18, 83–100.

Broda, C., Weinstein, D., 2006. Globalization and the gains from variety. Quarterly Journal of Economics 121 (2), 541–585.

Broda, C., Limão, N., Weinstein, D.E., 2008. Optimal tariffs and market power: the evidence. American Economic Review 98 (5), 2032–2065.

Brou, D., Ruta, M., 2009. A Commitment Theory of Subsidy Agreements, Mimeo.

Busch, M., Reinhardt, E., 2002. Testing international trade law: empirical studies of GATT/WTO dispute settlement. In: Kennedy, D.L.M., Southwick, J.D. (Eds.), The Political Economy of International Trade Law: Essays in Honor of Robert E. Hudec. Cambridge University Press, pp. 457–481.

Cadot, O., de Melo, J., Olarreaga, M., 1999. Regional integration and lobbying for tariffs against non-members. International Economic Review 40, 635–657.

Calvo-Pardo, H., Freund, C., Ornelas, E., 2009. The ASEAN free trade agreement: impact on trade flows and external trade barriers. In: Barro, R., Lee, J. (Eds.), Costs and Benefits of Regional Economic Integration. Oxford University Press.

Chisik, R., 2003. Gradualism in free trade agreements: a theoretical justification. Journal of International Economics 59 (2), 367–397.

Clausing, K., 2001. Trade creation and trade diversion in the Canada–United States Free Trade Agreement. Canadian Journal of Economics 34, 678–696.

Conconi, P., Perroni, C., 2009. Do credible domestic institutions promote credible international agreements? Journal of International Economics 79, 160–170.

Conconi, P., Sahuguet, N., 2009. Policymakers' horizon and the sustainability of international cooperation. Journal of Public Economics 93, 549–558.

Conconi, P., Facchini, G., Zanardi, M., 2012. Fast-track authority and international trade negotiations. American Economic Journal: Economic Policy 4, 146–189.

Costinot, A., 2008. A comparative institutional analysis of agreements on product standards. Journal of International Economics 75 (1), 197–213.

Dekle, R., Eaton, J., Kortum, S., 2007. Unbalanced trade. American Economic Review Papers and Proceedings 97 (2), 351–355.

DeRemer, D., 2011. The Evolution of International Subsidy Rules, Mimeo.

Devereux, M.B., 1997. Growth, specialization and trade liberalizaton. International Economic Review 38, 565–585.

Dutt, P., Mihov, I., Van Zandt, T., 2011. Does WTO Matter for the Extensive and the Intensive Margins of Trade? Mimeo.

Ederington, J., 2001. International coordination of trade and domestic policies. American Economic Review 91, 1580–1593.

Ederington, J., 2002. Trade and domestic policy linkage in international agreements. International Economic Review 43, 1347–1367.

Egger, P., Larch, M., 2008. Interdependent preferential trade agreement memberships: an empirical analysis. Journal of International Economics 76, 384–399.

Eicher, T.S., Henn, C., 2011. In search of WTO trade effects: preferential trade agreements promote trade strongly, but unevenly. Journal of International Economics, 83 (2), 137–153.

Estevadeordal, A., Freund, C., Ornelas, E., 2008. Does regionalism affect trade liberalization toward non-members? The Quarterly Journal of Economics 123 (4), 1531–1575.

Ethier, W.J., 1998. Regionalism in a multilateral world. Journal of Political Economy 106, 1214–1245.

Facchini, G., Silva, P., Willmann, G., 2013. The customs union issue: why do we observe so few of them? Journal of International Economics 90 (1), 136–147.

Freund, C., 2000a. Different paths to free trade: the gains from regionalism. Quarterly Journal of Economics 115, 1317–1341.

Freund, C., 2000b. Multilateralism and the endogenous formation of preferential trade agreements. Journal of International Economics 52 (2), 359–376.

Furusawa, T., 1999. The Negotiation of sustainable tariffs. Journal of International Economics 48, 321–346.

Furusawa, T., Konishi, H., 2007. Free trade networks. Journal of International Economics 72, 310–335.

Furusawa, T., Lai, E.L.-C., 1999. Adjustment costs and gradual trade libealization. Journal of International Economics 49, 333–361.

Gawande, K., Krishna, P., Robbins, M.J., 2006. Foreign lobbying and US trade policy. The Review of Economics and Statistics 88 (3), 563–571.

Goldberg, P., Maggi, G., 1999. Protection for sale: an empirical investigation. American Economic Review 89 (5), 1135–1155.

Goyal, S., Joshi, S., 2006. Bilateralism and free trade. International Economic Review 47, 749–778.

Grossman, G., Helpman, E., 1994. Protection for sale. American Economic Review 84 (4), 833–850.

Grossman, G., Helpman, E., 1995a. Trade wars and trade talks. Journal of Political Economy 103 (4), 675–708.

Grossman, G., Helpman, E., 1995b. The politics of free-trade agreements. American Economic Review 85, 667–690.

Handley, K., 2012. Exporting Under Trade Policy Uncertainty: Theory and Evidence. Mimeo.

Handley, K., Limão, N., 2012. Trade and Investment under Policy Uncertainty: Theory and Firm Evidence, NBER WP 17790.

Handley, K., Limão, N., 2013. Policy Uncertainty, Trade and Welfare: Theory and Evidence for China, Mimeo.

Horn, H., 2006. National treatment in the GATT. American Economic Review 96 (1), 394–404.

Horn, H., Maggi, G., Staiger, R.W., 2010. Trade agreements as endogenously incomplete contracts. American Economic Review 100 (1), 394–419.

Jackson, J.H., 1997. The WTO dispute settlement understanding–misunderstandings on the nature of legal obligation. American Journal of International Law 91 (1), 60–64.

Jackson, J.H., 2006. Sovereignty, the WTO, and changing fundamentals of international law. Cambridge University Press.

Johnson, H.G., 1953. Optimum tariffs and retaliation. Review of Economic Studies 21 (2), 142–153.

Karacaovali, B., Limão, N., 2008. The clash of liberalizations: preferential vs. multilateral trade liberalization in the European Union. Journal of International Economics 74 (2), 299–327.

Kennan, J., Riezman, R., 1990. Optimal tariff equilibria with customs unions. Canadian Journal of Economics 23, 70–83.

Kreinin, M.E., 1961. Effect of tariff changes on the prices and volume of imports. American Economic Review 51, 310–324.

Krishna, P., 1998. Regionalism and multilateralism: a political economy approach. Quarterly Journal of Economics 113, 227–251.

Krishna, P., 2003. Are regional trading partners natural? Journal of Political Economy 111, 202–226.

Krishna, P., Mitra, D., 2005. Reciprocated unilateralism in trade policy. Journal of International Economics 65 (2), 461–487.

Krugman, P., 1980. Scale economies, product differentiation, and the pattern of trade. The American Economic Review 70 (5), 950–959.

Krugman, P., 1991. Is bilateralism bad? In: Helpman, E, Razin, A. (Eds.), International Trade and Trade Policy. MIT Press, pp. 9–23.

Krugman, P., 1997. What should trade negotiators negotiate about? Journal of Economic Literature 35, 113–120.

Lapan, H.E., 1988. The optimal tariff, production lags, and time consistency. American Economic Review 78 (3), 395–401.

Lee, G.M., 2007. Trade agreements with domestic policies as disguised protection. Journal of International Economics 71 (1), 241–259.

Lee, G.M., 2011. Optimal International Agreement and Treatment of Domestic Subsidy, Mimeo.

Levy, P.I., 1997. A political-economic analysis of free-trade agreements. American Economic Review 87, 506–519.

Limão, N., 2005. Trade policy, cross-border externalities and lobbies: do linked agreements enforce more cooperative outcomes? Journal of International Economics 67 (1), 175–199.

Limão, N., 2006. Preferential trade agreements as stumbling blocks for multilateral trade liberalization: evidence for the US American Economic Review 96, 896–914.

Limão, N., 2007. Are preferential trade agreements with non-trade objectives a stumbling block for multilateral liberalization? Review of Economic Studies 74, 821–855.

Limão, N., Maggi, G., 2013. Uncertainty and Trade Agreements, Mimeo.

Limão, N., Saggi, K., 2008. Tariff retaliation versus financial compensation in the enforcement of international trade agreements. Journal of International Economics 76 (1), 48–60.

Limão, N., Tovar, P., 2011. Policy choice: theory and evidence from commitment via international trade agreements. Journal of International Economics 85 (2), 186–205.

Liu, X., 2009. GATT/WTO promotes trade strongly: sample selection and model specification. Review of International Economics 17 (3), 428–446.

Liu, X., Ornelas, E., 2012. Free Trade Areas and the Consolidation of Democracies, Mimeo.

Ludema, R.D., 2001. Optimal international trade agreements and dispute settlement procedures. European Journal of Political Economy 17 (2), 355–376.

Ludema, R.D., Mayda, A.M., 2009. Do countries free ride on MFN? Journal of International Economics 77, 135–150.

Ludema, R.D., Mayda, A.M., 2010. Do Terms-of-Trade Effects Matter for Trade Agreements? Evidence from WTO Countries, Mimeo.

Ludema R.D., Mayda, A.M., Mishra, P., 2010. Protection for Free: The Political Economy of US Tariff Suspensions, Mimeo.

Magee, C., 2008. New measures of trade creation and trade diversion. Journal of International Economics 75, 340–362.

Maggi, G., 1994. Essays on Trade Policy and International Institutions under Incomplete Information. Ph.D. Dissertation, Stanford University.

Maggi, G., 1999. The role of multilateral institutions in international trade cooperation. American Economic Review 89 (1), 190–214.

Maggi, G., Rodriguez-Clare, A., 1998. The value of trade agreements in the presence of political pressures. Journal of Political Economy 106 (3), 574–601.

Maggi, G., Rodriguez-Clare, A., 2007. A political-economy theory of trade agreements. American Economic Review 97 (4), 1374–1406.

Maggi, G., Staiger, R.W., 2011. The role of dispute settlement procedures in international trade agreements. Quarterly Journal of Economics 126, 475–515.

Maggi, G., Staiger, R.W., 2012. Optimal Design of Trade Agreements in the Presence of Renegotiation, Mimeo.

Maggi, G., Staiger, R.W., 2013. Trade Disputes and Settlement, Mimeo.

Martin, A., Vergote, W., 2008. On the role of retaliation in trade agreements. Journal of International Economics 76 (1), 61–77.

Martin, P., Mayer, T., Thoenig, M., 2008. Make trade not war? Review of Economic Studies 75 (3), 865–900.

Martin, P., Mayer, T., Thoenig, M., 2012. The geography of conflicts and regional trade agreements. American Economic Journal: Macroeconomics 4 (4), 1–35.

Mayer, W., 1981. Theoretical considerations on negotiated tariff adjustments. Oxford Economic Papers 33 (1), 135–153.

McCalman, P., 2002. Multilateral trade negotiations and the most favored nation clause. Journal of International Economics 57 (1), 151–176.

McLaren, J., 1997. Size, sunk costs, and judge Bowker's objection to free trade. American Economic Review 87 (3), 400–420.

McLaren, J., 2002. A theory of insidious regionalism. Quarterly Journal of Economics 117, 571–608.

Milner, H., Rosendorff, P., 1996. Trade negotiations, information and domestic politics: the role of domestic groups. Economics and Politics 8 (2), 145–189.

Milner, H., Rosendorff, P., 2001. The optimal design of international institutions: uncertainty and escape. International Organization 55 (4), 829–857.

Mitra, D., 2002. Endogenous political organization and the value of trade agreements. Journal of International Economics 57 (2), 473–485.

Mrazova, M., 2011. Trade Agreements When Profits Matter, Mimeo.

Mrazova, M., Vines, D., Zissimos, B., 2013. Is the WTO Article XXIV bad? Journal of International Economics 89 (1), 216–232.

Ornelas, E., 2005a. Rent destruction and the political viability of free trade agreements. Quarterly Journal of Economics 120, 1475–1506.

Ornelas, E., 2005b. Endogenous free trade agreements and the multilateral trading system. Journal of International Economics 67, 471–497.

Ornelas, E., 2005c. Trade creating free trade areas and the undermining of multilateralism. European Economic Review 49, 1717–1735.

Ornelas, E., 2008. Feasible multilateralism and the effects of regionalism. Journal of International Economics 74, 202–224.

Ossa, R., 2011. A new trade theory of GATT/WTO negotiations. Journal of Political Economy 119 (1), 122–152.

Ossa, R., 2012. Profits in the new trade approach to trade negotiations. American Economic Review, Papers and Proceedings 102 (3), 466–469.

Ossa, R., 2013. Trade Wars and Trade Talks with Data, Mimeo.

Panagariya, A., Krishna, P., 2002. On necessarily welfare-enhancing free trade areas. Journal of International Economics 57, 353–367.

Park, J.H., 2000. International trade agreements between countries of asymmetric size. Journal of International Economics 50 (2), 473–495.

Park, J.H., 2011. Enforcing international trade agreements with imperfect private monitoring. Review of Economic Studies 78 (3), 1102–1134.

Pauwelyn, J., 2008. Optimal Protection of International Law: Navigating between European Absolutism and American Volunteerism. Cambridge University Press.

Reinhardt, E., 2001. Adjudication without enforcement in GATT disputes. Journal of Conflict Resolution 45 (2), 174–195.

Richardson, M., 1993. Endogenous protection and trade diversion. Journal of International Economics 34 (3–4), 309–324.

Romalis, J., 2007. NAFTA's and CUSFTA's impact on international trade. Review of Economics and Statistics 89, 416–435.

Rose, A., 2004a. Do we really know that the WTO increases trade? American Economic Review 94, 98–114.

Rose, A., 2004b. Do WTO members have more liberal trade policy? Journal of International Economics 63 (2), 209–235.

Rose, A., 2013. The March of an Economic Idea? Protectionism Isn't Counter-Cyclic (Anymore), Mimeo.

Saggi, K., 2006. Preferential trade agreements and multilateral tariff cooperation. International Economic Review 47 (1), 29–57.

Saggi, K., Sara, N., 2008. National treatment at the WTO: the roles of product and country heterogeneity. International Economic Review 49, 1367–1396.

Saggi, K., Yildiz, H.M., 2010. Bilateralism, multilateralism, and the quest for global free trade. Journal of International Economics 81, 26–37.

Saggi, K., Woodland, A., Yildiz, H.M., 2013. On the relationship between preferential and multilateral trade liberalization: the case of customs unions. American Economic Journal: Microeconomics 5 (1), 63–99.

Schwartz, W.F., Sykes, A.O., 2002. The economic structure of renegotiation and dispute resolution in the WTO-GATT system. Journal of Legal Studies 31, 179–204.

Segal, I.R., Whinston, M.D., 2002. The Mirrlees approach to mechanism design with renegotiation. Econometrica 70 (1), 1–45.

Seidmann, D., 2009. Preferential trading arrangements as strategic positioning. Journal of International Economics 79, 143–159.

Sovey, A., 2012. States Held Hostage: Political Hold-Up Problems in International Politics, Mimeo.

Staiger, R.W., 1995a. International rules and institutions for trade policy. In: Grossman, G.M., Rogoff, K. (Eds.), Handbook of International Economics, vol. 3. North-Holland, Amsterdam.

Staiger, R.W., 1995b. A theory of gradual trade liberalization. In: Deardorff, A., Levinsohn, J., Stern, R. (Eds.), New Directions in Trade Theory. University of Michigan Press.

Staiger, R.W., Sykes, A.O., 2011. International Trade, National Treatment and Domestic Regulation. Journal of Legal Studies 40 (1), 149–203.

Staiger, R.W., Tabellini, G., 1987. Discretionary trade policy and excessive protection. American Economic Review 77 (5), 823–837.

Staiger, R.W., Tabellini, G., 1999. Do GATT rules help governments make domestic commitments? Economics and Politics 11 (2), 109–144.

Stoyanov, A., 2009. Trade policy of a free trade agreement in the presence of foreign lobbying. Journal of International Economics 77 (1), 37–49.

Subramanian, A., Wei, S.J., 2007. The WTO promotes trade, strongly but unevenly. Journal of International Economics 72, 151–175.

Tang, M.K., Wei, S.J., 2010. The value of making commitments externally: evidence from WTO accessions. Journal of International Economics 78 (2), 216–229.

Tomz, M., Goldstein, J.L., Rivers, D., 2007. Do we really know that the WTO increases trade? Comment. American Economic Review 97, 2005–2018.

Tornell, A., 1991. Time inconsistency of protectionist programs. Quarterly Journal of Economics 106, 963–974.

Tovar, P., 2011. Lobbying costs and trade policy. Journal of International Economics 83 (2), 126–136.

Trefler, D., 2004. The long and short of the Canada–US free trade agreement. American Economic Review 94, 870–895.

Venables, A.J., 1985. Trade and trade policy with imperfect competition: the case of identical products and free entry. Journal of International Economics 19, 1–20.

Venables, A.J., 1987. Trade and trade policy with differentiated products: a Chamberlinian-Ricardian model. Economic Journal 97, 700–717.

Watson, J., Klimenko, M.M., Ramey, G., 2008. Recurrent trade agreements and the value of external enforcement. Journal of International Economics 74 (2), 475–499.

Whalley, J., 1998. Why do countries seek regional trade agreements? In: Frankel, J. (Ed.), The Regionalization of the World Economy. University of Chicago Press.

Winters, A.L., Chang, W., 2000. Regional integration and the prices of imports: an empirical investigation. Journal of International Economics 51, 363–377.

Winters, A.L., Chang, W., 2002. How regional blocks affect excluded countries: the price effects of Mercusor. American Economic Review 92, 889–904.

Yi, S.S., 1996. Endogenous formation of customs unions under imperfect competition: open regionalism is good. Journal of International Economics 41, 153-177.

CHAPTER 7

International Prices and Exchange Rates*

Ariel Burstein*,† and Gita Gopinath†,‡
*University of California, Los Angeles, CA, USA
†National Bureau of Economic Research, Cambridge, MA, USA
‡Harvard University, Cambridge, MA, USA

Abstract

We survey the recent empirical and theoretical developments in the literature on the relation between prices and exchange rates. After updating some of the major findings in the empirical literature, we present a simple framework to interpret this evidence. We review theoretical models that generate insensitivity of prices to exchange rate changes through variable markups, both under flexible prices and nominal rigidities, first in partial equilibrium and then in general equilibrium.

Keywords

Real exchange rate, Nominal exchange rate, Border prices, Variable markups, Price rigidity, Pass-through, Tradeable goods

JEL classification codes

F3, F4, F15

1. INTRODUCTION

The relation between prices and exchange rates is one of the classic topics studied in international macroeconomics. This relation is of interest both from a positive and normative perspective. One basic hypothesis connecting prices and exchange rates is that of relative purchasing power parity (PPP): changes in prices of goods should be the same across locations when converted into a common currency. Deviations in relative PPP can arise because of differences in the cost of supplying the good to different locations or because firms price discriminate across locations by charging different markups. Since global efficiency requires that as long as changes in the cost of making the good available to each location are the same the change in price should be the same, the sources of

---

* We thank Dennis Kuo and Mikkel Plagborg-Moller for outstanding research assistance. We also thank George Alessandria, Andrew Atkeson, Javier Cravino, Charles Engel, Virgiliu Midrigan, Helene Rey, and Jon Steinsson for detailed comments.

deviations in relative PPP shed light on the efficiency (or lack of it) in the allocation of goods across countries.

In addition to the cross-country comparison of price movements, the magnitude of the response of prices to exchange rates for an individual country, exchange rate pass-through (ERPT), is also of interest to measure the extent of expenditure switching that follows exchange rate changes. This is an important ingredient to understand how a devaluation of the currency can stimulate the domestic economy by inducing substitution from foreign to domestic goods. Milton Friedman made the case for exchange rate flexibility on the grounds that if prices are rigid in the producer's currency, a flexible exchange rate can bring about the same relative price movements as in a world where nominal prices are fully flexible. On the other hand, if prices in the buyer's local currency are insensitive to changes in the exchange rate there are limited expenditure switching effects. The extent of pass-through both in the short and long run is therefore important to understand the impact of exchange rate movements not only on prices but also on quantities and therefore welfare.

The relation between prices and exchange rates also helps shed light on positive issues such as how firms' prices respond to cost shocks. This is informative of the market structure the firm operates in, the nature of the demand it faces, and the extent to which markets are segmented across countries. The gradualness (or lack of it) with which firms respond to cost-shocks, in terms of delayed adjustment, also contributes to our understanding of "real rigidities" (i.e., forces that make firms reluctant to change their price relative to other firms' prices) in the macro economy, which play an important role in propagating money non-neutralities. The advantage of international price data over the price data typically used in industrial organization or in closed economy macro is that exchange rate shocks are arguably exogenous to the firm, are easily measurable, and exhibit considerable time variation.

In this chapter we review both the empirical and theoretical work that sheds light on these positive and normative issues, focusing on developments since the last handbook chapter by Froot and Rogoff (1995) on PPP. We first review and update the major findings in the empirical work. We distinguish between consumer prices (retail prices), producer prices (wholesale prices), and border prices (at the dock). The new developments mainly involve bringing more disaggregated datasets, generating new empirical facts alongside reinforcing several old ones.

After summarizing the empirical evidence we present a simple theoretical framework to help interpret the facts. We first consider the partial equilibrium problem of a firm and the impact of exchange rate movements on the pricing of the firm at the border and at the consumer level. We analyze the case of flexible prices and sticky prices. We then aggregate these prices and study the implications for aggregate price indices. Next we describe developments in the literature that endogenizes variable markups. This work builds on the basic insights of Dornbusch (1987) and Krugman (1987) adding richer details such as firm heterogeneity, consumer search and matching, distribution costs, and inventories.

These can be connected to industry-level data on market structure as well as micro data on firms and plants. Lastly, we describe a workhorse general equilibrium model where exchange rates and wages are determined by monetary shocks and evaluate the success of the model in matching the facts. In the conclusion we discuss what we learn from the literature about the positive and normative issues raised at the start of this introduction.

The chapter is outlined as follows. Section 2 summarizes the empirical evidence, Section 3 presents a simple framework to interpret the empirical evidence, Sections 4 and 5 describe recent theoretical models of variable markups and other mechanisms that generate insensitivity of prices to exchange rate changes. Sections 6 and 7 discuss industry equilibrium and general equilibrium respectively.

2. EMPIRICAL EVIDENCE

In this section we summarize five stylized facts on the relation between international prices and exchange rates. We distinguish between international prices based on consumer prices, producer prices, and border prices and update several findings using recent data (1975–2011 conditional on data availability) for eight major industrial countries (Canada, France, Germany, United Kingdom, Italy, Japan, Switzerland, and the U.S.). The data appendix available online on the authors' websites provide details of data sources and describe how the statistics presented in this section were constructed.

The first finding characterizes the dynamics of consumer price index (CPI)-based real exchange rates (RER), that is the ratio of consumer prices across countries in a common currency, and its relation to nominal exchange rates (NER).

Empirical Finding 1. *Real exchange rates for consumer prices co-move closely with nominal exchange rates at short and medium horizons. The persistence of these RERs is large with long half-lives.*

Define the change in the bilateral CPI-based RER as the log change in the ratio of the CPI in two countries i and n measured in a common currency:

$$\Delta rer_{in,t}^{cpi} = \Delta e_{in,t} + \Delta cpi_{i,t} - \Delta cpi_{n,t}.$$

Here, $\Delta cpi_{i,t}$ represents log changes in the CPI in country i at time t relative to time $t-1$. It is an expenditure-weighted average of the change in retail prices consumers pay for goods and services, including both domestically produced and imported items. $\Delta e_{in,t}$ represents log changes in the NER between countries i and n (units of currency n per unit of currency i). The change in the trade-weighted RER for country n, $\Delta rer_{n,t}^{cpi}$, is defined as a trade-weighted average of bilateral RERs for country n across its trade partners i.

Figure 7.1(a) plots cumulative log changes in the trade-weighted NER and the trade-weighted CPI-based RER for the U.S. between 1975 and 2011. The close co-movement between the NER and the RER and the high persistence of the RER is visually apparent.

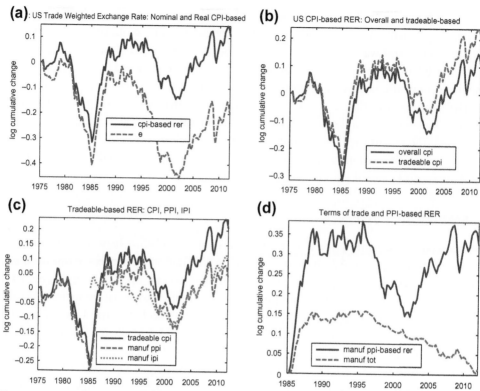

Figure 7.1 Relation between CPI-Based, PPI-Based and Terms of Trade-Based RER and NER

Table 7.1 displays standard deviations and correlations between RER and NER changes for eight major industrialized countries. We report results based on four-quarter logarithmic changes in relative prices, as well as for quarterly deviations from HP trends. The results in this table indicate that changes in NERs and RERs are roughly as large and highly correlated. For the U.S., the standard deviation of changes in the NER relative to those for the RER is 0.92, while the correlation is 0.97.

The persistence of the trade-weighted RER is estimated using an AR(5) with a constant and no time trend as in Steinsson (2008) for the 1975Q1–2011Q4 period.[1] More specifically we estimate,

$$rer_{n,t}^{cpi} = \beta + \alpha_n rer_{n,t-1}^{cpi} + \sum_{k=1}^{4} \psi_k \Delta rer_{n,t-k}^{cpi} + \varepsilon_t. \tag{1}$$

Due to the high persistence of most RER series the grid bootstrap procedure in Hansen (1999) is used to obtain a median unbiased (MU) estimate of α_n, which is the sum of the

---

[1] In calculating these statistics we use the codes from Steinsson (2008).

Table 7.1 Relation Between Nominal ER and CPI-Based RER (1975–2011)

Real vs. Nominal ER	U.S.		Japan		Italy		U.K.		France		Germany		Canada		Switzerland	
	Stdev	Correl	Stdev	Correl	Stdev	Correl	Stdev	Correl	Stdev	Correl	Stdev	Correl	Stdev	Correl	Stdev	Correl
Differences	0.92	0.97	1.03	0.99	0.90	0.82	1.04	0.95	0.87	0.91	0.94	0.90	1.00	0.97	0.95	0.95
HP-filtered	0.92	0.97	1.03	0.99	1.02	0.97	1.07	0.97	0.96	0.98	0.99	0.96	1.01	0.97	0.99	0.99

Table 7.2 Persistence of RER Deviatons (1975–2011)

	U.S.		Japan		Italy		U.K.		France		Germany		Canada		Switzerland	
	Half-Life	Up-Life	Half-Life	Up-Life	Half-Life	Up-Life	Half-Life	Up-Life	Half-Life	Up-Life	Half-Life	Up-Life	Half-Life	Up-Life	Half-Life	Up-Life
Median	6.0	2.4	3.7	1.6	5.60	2.0	2.90	1.3	3.20	1.0	3.7	2.1	8.7	3.4	1.6	1.1
Confidence	2.2	0.5	1.8	0.4	2.0	0.7	1.7	0.3	1.4	0.3	2.0	0.9	2.4	1.0	1.1	0.6
Interval (90%)	Inf	Inf	24.9	6.5	Inf	Inf	10.5	3.0	Inf	Inf	13.4	5.2	Inf	Inf	2.6	1.6

AR coefficients. The other AR parameters are estimated by OLS conditional on the MU estimate of α_n. In Table 7.2 we report estimates and 90% confidence intervals of half-lives defined as the largest time T such that the impulse response function IR satisfies $IR(T-1) \geq 0.5$ and $IR(T) < 0.5$. We also report the up-life that follows a similar definition with 0.5 replaced with 1 and measures the hump-shaped behavior of RER deviations.

The half-life estimate for 7 of the 8 developed countries is in the range of 3–9 years, the exception being Switzerland with a half-life of 1.6 years. These numbers are consistent with the survey in Rogoff (1996) that concludes that the "consensus view" for the average half-life of RER deviations is 3–5 years. Also as documented in Murray and Papell (2002) and Rossi (2005) the confidence intervals on the half-life estimates are very wide. In addition CPI-based RERs exhibit hump-shaped impulse responses as documented in Eichenbaum and Evans (1995), Cheung and Lai (2000), and Steinsson (2008).

The aggregate RER is by construction a composite of more disaggregated sectoral RERs. The literature has used sectoral data to provide alternative measures of aggregate half-lives. Imbs et al. (2005) highlight the potential importance of heterogeneity in sectoral level persistence in impacting measures of aggregate RER persistence. To deal with heterogeneity they estimate the average half-life for a panel of sectoral real exchange rates using the Pesaran Mean Group estimator. This estimator involves calculating (weighted) averages of AR(p) coefficients across a panel of regressions, one for each sector, and then estimating the average half-life using the averaged AR(p) coefficients. They find it to be 11 months, well below the consensus estimates. Chen and Engel (2005) alternatively calculate the average half-life by first estimating half-lives sector by sector and taking a weighted average across these estimates. They show that the average persistence of sectoral RERs is not very different from the consensus estimates.[2]

As a reconciliation Carvalho and Nechio (2011) show that the estimation procedures in Imbs et al. (2005) and Chen and Engel (2005) measure different things. Using a model simulated to generate heterogeneity in persistence of sectoral RERs, owing to heterogeneity in the frequency of price adjustment,[3] they demonstrate that the difference between the average of sectoral half-lives and the aggregate half-life (as in Chen and Engel (2005)) is quite small. On the other hand the Pesaran Mean Group estimator (used in Imbs et al. (2005)) calculates the half-life for the aggregate RER of a counterfactual one-sector economy with a frequency of price adjustment that matches the average frequency of price adjustment of the multi-sector economy. The difference between this estimate and the true estimate of the persistence of the aggregate RER for a multi-sector economy can be quite large in the presence of sectoral heterogeneity.

---

[2] Chen and Engel (2005) and Reidel and Szilagyi (2005) argue that measurement error and small sample bias can impact the estimates of Imbs et al. (2005). Imbs et al. (2004) argue against the importance of these biases.

[3] Kehoe and Midrigan (2007) document that while there is evidence in the data that the stickier the price of the good the more persistent is its RER, the amount of variation is relatively modest.

Micro Data

The fact that there is high co-movement between real and nominal exchange rates has also been established using disaggregated micro-level price data for individual goods. Crucini and Telmer (2012) use annual Economist Intelligence Unit data on retail prices for goods with similar characteristics and show that on average product-level RERs co-move closely with the nominal exchange rates. Gopinath et al. (2011) and Burstein and Jaimovich (2008) find similar evidence of co-movement for the exact same universal product code (UPC) sold in the U.S. and Canada by the same retailer. Broda and Weinstein (2008) find similar patterns using ACNielsen's Homescan^{TM} retail price database of matched goods with a common barcode.

Despite the high co-movement of the product-level RERs and NERs on average, micro-level prices exhibit large idiosyncratic movements. As highlighted in Crucini and Telmer (2012) NERs account for less than 10% of the deviations from relative purchasing power parity (PPP), defined as the time series variation in good-specific law of one price deviations. The importance of the large idiosyncratic component in goods price changes is consistent with the evidence from the closed economy literature as surveyed in Klenow and Malin (2011).[4]

Border Effect

Several studies have also compared the behavior of cross-country RERs to within country RERs, with any differences attributed to the "border effect". Engel and Rogers (1996) is a seminal paper in this literature that documents a sizeable border effect for Canada and the U.S. Identifying the "treatment effect" of the border on prices is difficult because the distribution of prices in the absence of the border is typically not observable. Gorodnichenko and Tesar (2009) highlight that ex-ante differences in countries can be misleadingly attributed to the border.[5] In addition, Gopinath et al. (2011) show that using the information contained in price differences alone is useful only when markets are at least partly integrated. Gopinath et al. (2011) use an alternative approach by studying the response of prices to cost shocks in neighboring markets to compare market segmentation across and within countries.

Using UPC level micro data for the U.S. and Canada, Broda and Weinstein (2008) document as much variation in retail prices across as within countries, while Gopinath et al. (2011) and Burstein and Jaimovich (2008) find evidence of a sizeable border effect for consumer and wholesale prices. While the two datasets are not strictly comparable, one

---

[4] Crucini et al. (2005) investigate the extent of variation in the level of retail prices for similar goods across countries in the European Union. They find significant cross-country dispersion in prices that is centered around zero, and the extent of the dispersion is negatively related to the tradability of the good. In contrast, Cavallo et al. (2012) find that online retail prices of a large number of identical goods sold in the Euro zone display no dispersion across countries.

[5] Relatedly, Burstein and Jaimovich (2008) argue that even if countries are ex-ante symmetric, a border effect can result from region-specific shocks that are more correlated within countries than across countries. For example RERs are more volatile across regions between countries than within countries because NERs are (by construction) less correlated between countries than within countries.

factor that can explain the difference in findings is that the data in Broda and Weinstein (2008) is from multiple retail chains, while the data in Gopinath et al. (2011) and Burstein and Jaimovich (2008) is from the same retail chain.[6]

Empirical Finding 2. *Movements in RERs for tradeable goods are roughly as large as those in overall CPI-based RERs when tradeable goods prices are measured using consumer prices or producer prices, but significantly smaller when measured using border prices.*

The second stylized fact pertains to the importance of movements in relative prices of tradeable goods across countries and movements in the price of non-tradeable goods relative to tradeable goods in accounting for fluctuations in the RER, motivated by the classic Salter-Swan traded/non-traded goods dichotomy. We start by describing the evidence using aggregate price indices.

Engel (1993, 1999) propose an approach to decompose movements in CPI-based RER into two components: movements in the relative price of tradeable goods across countries, and movements in the price of non-tradeable relative to tradeable goods across countries. A standard procedure is to identify non-tradeables with services in the CPI and tradeables with goods in the CPI.[7] While these are aggregate categories, the degree of tradeability varies significantly across individual products. Based on this disaggregation, changes in the CPI-based RER can be decomposed as:

$$\Delta rer_{in,t}^{cpi} = \Delta rer_{in,t}^{tr} + \Delta rer_{in,t}^{ntr},\qquad(2)$$

where

$$\Delta rer_{in,t}^{tr} = \Delta e_{in,t} + \Delta cpi_{i,t}^{tr} - \Delta cpi_{n,t}^{tr},$$
$$\Delta rer_{in,t}^{ntr} = \Delta cpi_{i,t} - \Delta cpi_{i,t}^{tr} - \Delta cpi_{n,t} + \Delta cpi_{n,t}^{tr}.$$

Here, $\Delta cpi_{n,t}^{tr}$ denotes the log changes in the component of the CPI in country n that is categorized as tradeable. The term $\Delta cpi_{n,t} - \Delta cpi_{n,t}^{tr}$ is proportional to the change in the price index of non-tradeable relative to tradeable categories in country n. Hence, Equation (2) serves to quantify the importance of movements in the relative price of non-tradeables to tradeables across countries in accounting for movements in the RER. It is important to note that this decomposition does not provide a causal interpretation or a structural account of the sources of fluctuations in RERs. Moreover, the two terms in Equation (2) are typically not independent, so one can only calculate upper and lower bounds on the importance of each component by attributing the covariance term to one or the other component.

To implement this decomposition one must take a stand on how to measure the price index for tradeable goods. The baseline approach in Engel (1993, 1999) is to measure the

---

[6] The fact that there is large variation across retailers in pricing of the exact same good is consistent with the evidence in Boivin et al. (2012) who compare prices of books from online stores in Canada and the U.S. They also conclude that international markets are segmented.

[7] Non-tradeables categories include education, health, housing, among others. Tradeable categories include non-durables like food and beverages, apparel, and durables like private transportation, household furnishings, among others.

price index for tradeable goods from the CPI, that is based on retail prices. Alternatively, Engel (1999) and Betts and Kehoe (2006) measure changes in the price of tradeable goods using producer price indices (PPI) for manufactured goods or other output price indices. PPIs for manufactured goods differ from CPIs for tradeable goods in three major ways. First, PPIs include investment and intermediate goods, as well as consumption goods. Second, PPIs are constructed using changes in producer and wholesale prices, which on average contain a smaller local distribution margin than retail prices used in the CPI. Third, PPIs tend to exclude changes in prices for imported goods and in some countries include changes in prices for exported goods.

Burstein et al. (2005) and Burstein et al. (2006) measure the price index of tradeable goods using import price indices (IPI). IPIs tend to be constructed using changes in prices of imported goods at the dock (henceforth denominated *border prices*) and hence include a smaller component of local distribution margin in comparison to wholesale and consumer prices. There is large variation across countries in the procedures used to construct these indices, so one must be cautious in interpreting cross-country differences in statistics based on IPIs.[8] In the absence of data on IPIs for certain countries researchers use unit values constructed as the ratio of trade values to trade volumes. Unit values are more likely to be affected by changes in the composition of imports across goods of different price and quality than indices based on actual prices.

Figure 7.1(b) plots cumulative log changes in the overall CPI-based RER and in the CPI-based tradeable RER for the U.S. (trade-weighted), while Figure 7.1(c) adds the other two measures of tradeable RERs: the PPI-based RER using PPIs for manufactured goods and the IPI-based RER using IPIs for manufactured goods (the non-oil IPI in the U.S.). Table 7.3 lists for eight countries in the period 1975–2011 (depending on data availability) relative standard deviations, correlations, and lower and upper bounds of a variance decomposition of quarterly and annual changes in each of the three measures of tradeable RER relative to the overall CPI-based RER.

The central patterns that emerge can be summarized as follows. First, there appears to be little difference in the magnitude of fluctuations in the CPI-based RER for tradeable goods and in the magnitude of fluctuations in the overall CPI-based RER—the relative standard deviation and correlation between these two series is close to 1 in most countries. From expression (2), this implies that movements in the relative price of non-tradeable to tradeable goods measured using consumer prices are not an important source of cyclical RER fluctuations (less than 3% in the U.S.). While we focus on quarterly fluctuations, Engel (1999) shows that this observation holds both at short- and medium- term horizons. Second, tradeable RERs computed using PPIs are on average only slightly less volatile (and less correlated) than CPI-based RERs for tradeable goods. Third, movements in tradeable RERs computed using IPIs tend to be smaller (especially in U.S., Japan, and

---

[8] For example, Statistics Canada proxies import prices for some goods using prices from foreign sources.

Table 7.3 Relation between Tradeable RER and Overall CPI-Based RER (1975 (or Higher)–2011)

Relative to Overall CPI-Based RER	U.S.		Japan		Italy		U.K.		France		Germany		Canada		Switzerland	
	Stdev	Correl	Stdev	Correl	Stdev	Correl	Stdev	Correl	Stdev	Correl	Stdev	Correl	Stdev	Correl	Stdev	Correl
Tradeable CPI Annual diff.	0.96	0.99	0.98	0.99	1.08	0.99	0.99	0.99	0.94	0.94	1.01	1.00	0.95	0.97	0.94	0.94
HP-filtered quart.	1.01	0.99	0.98	1.00	0.98	0.94	0.99	0.98	0.93	0.95	0.98	0.98	0.95	0.97	0.94	0.93
Manuf PPI Annual diff.	0.93	0.97	0.95	0.99	0.91	0.98	0.88	0.97	1.05	0.89	1.09	0.96	0.77	0.91	1.01	0.97
HP-filtered quart.	0.98	0.97	0.95	0.99	0.95	0.98	0.85	0.97	0.96	0.87	1.08	0.96	0.80	0.90	1.02	0.97
Manuf IPI Annual diff.	0.51	0.58	0.33	0.56	0.69	0.55	0.52	0.65	0.98	0.83	0.75	0.82	0.74	0.23	0.85	0.91
HP-filtered quart.	0.48	0.51	0.33	0.49	0.71	0.55	0.47	0.60	0.93	0.85	0.76	0.82	0.83	0.29	0.85	0.91

Contribution of Tradeable RER	Lower	Upper	Lower	Upper	Lower	Upper	Lower	Upper	Lower	Upper	Lower	Upper	Lower	Upper	Lower	Upper
Tradeable CPI Annual diff.	0.92	0.97	0.97	0.99	0.98	1.16	0.98	0.99	0.89	0.89	0.99	1.01	0.91	0.94	0.88	0.89
Manuf PPI Annual diff.	0.86	0.94	0.91	0.98	0.82	0.95	0.77	0.94	0.78	1.11	0.90	1.19	0.60	0.81	0.93	1.02
Manuf IPI Annual diff.	0.26	0.33	0.11	0.26	0.28	0.48	0.27	0.40	0.67	0.95	0.57	0.67	−0.21	0.55	0.72	0.82

Note: See online data appendix for series description. Coverage is as follows. U.S.: CPIT and PPI (1975–2011), IPI (1985–2011); Japan: CPIT, PPI, IPI (1975–2011); Italy: CPIT (1996–2011), PPI (1981–2011), IPI (1975–2011); U.K.: CPIT (1988–2011), PPI and IPI (1975–2011); France: CPIT (1975–2011), PPI (1980–2011), IPI (1981–2011); Germany: CPIT (1996–2011), PPI and IPI (1975–2011); Canada: CPIT, PPI, and IPI (1975–2011); Switzerland: CPIT and PPI (1975–2011), IPI (1990–2011).

U.K.) than the other two measures. In the U.S., in the period 1985–2011 the IPI-based RER is roughly half as volatile as the overall CPI-based RERs, the correlation is roughly 0.5, and the upper bound of its importance in the variance decomposition is 30%.

Taken together, these observations show that a large fraction of RER fluctuations can be accounted for by movements in the relative price of tradeable goods across countries, but the extent of cyclical movements in the relative price of tradeable to non-tradeable goods depends on the price measure for tradeable goods—movements in the RER for tradeable goods tend to be smaller and movements in the relative price of tradeable to non-tradeable goods tend to be larger, when tradeable price indices are constructed using border prices than when constructed using consumer prices.

The observation that movements in consumer and wholesale price-based RERs for tradeable goods are large and highly correlated with movements in NERs has also been established using goods level data (see e.g., Crucini and Telmer (2012), Gopinath et al. (2011), and Broda and Weinstein (2008)). Crucini and Landry (2012) show that goods with a smaller non-tradeable distribution component exhibit smaller movements in RERs. This is consistent with the observation that tradeable RERs are less volatile using import prices (that contain a small non-tradeable component) than using consumer prices (that contain a larger non-tradeable component).

The fact that relative prices at the consumer level co-move more closely with the NER and are more volatile than when using border relative prices is consistent with the next empirical finding on exchange rate pass-through.

Empirical Finding 3.   *ERPT into consumer prices is lower than into border prices. ERPT into border prices is typically incomplete in the long run, displays dynamics, and varies considerably across countries.*

Pass-through regressions estimate the sensitivity of prices in a given location to exchange rates, controlling for other variables relevant for pricing. Several studies estimate dynamic lag regressions of the kind:

$$\Delta p_{in,t} = \alpha_{in} + \sum_{k=0}^{T} \beta_{in,k}\Delta e_{in,t-k} + \gamma_{in}X_{in,t} + \varepsilon_{in,t}, \tag{3}$$

where $\Delta p_{in,t}$ represents either log changes in prices, price indices, or log changes in unit values for goods imported in country n from country i, expressed in country n's currency. $k > 0$ allows for lags in the pass-through of exchange rates into prices and t refers to months/quarters/years. $X_{in,t}$ represents a vector of controls (including lags), besides the nominal exchange rate and typically includes a measure of the cost of production in country i, such as wages or producer prices.[9] $\beta_{in,0}$ measures short-run pass-through (SRPT) and long-run pass-through (LRPT) is estimated as $\sum_{k=0}^{T} \beta_k$ where T is typically set at 2 years.

[9] In certain cases a measure of prices of competitors in country n, such as producer prices in country n and controls for local demand conditions such as local GDP are also included.

Table 7.4 Short-Run and Long-Run ERPT Using Aggregate Indices

BIS Narrow NER		U.S.		Japan		Italy		U.K.		France		Germany		Canada		Switzerland	
		ERPT	SE	ERPT	SE	ERPT	SE	ERPT	SE	ERPT	SE	ERPT	SE	ERPT	SE	ERPT	SE
Import Price Index Dynamic Lag																	
Short run	Narrow NER	0.20	0.05	0.75	0.07	0.53	0.05	0.37	0.04	0.40	0.09	0.43	0.05	0.75	0.05	0.13	0.03
	Broad NER	0.20	0.04														
Long run	Narrow NER	0.51	0.08	0.71	0.12	0.53	0.16	0.87	0.08	0.97	0.13	0.64	0.10	0.80	0.12	0.47	0.09
	Broad NER	0.27	0.11														
Tradeable CPI Dynamic Lag																	
Short run	Narrow NER	0.06	0.02	−0.04	0.02	−0.03	0.19	0.02	0.05	0.04	0.05	−0.01	0.04	0.02	0.05	0.11	0.05
	Broad NER	0.09	0.03														
Long run	Narrow NER	0.17	0.04	0.10	0.04	0.01	0.11	0.14	0.07	0.36	0.11	−0.01	0.05	0.14	0.19	0.29	0.10
	Broad NER	0.14	0.08														

Note: Standard errors (SE) are calculated using the Newey–West (1987) HAC estimator with a bandwidth of 8. See online data appendix for series description. Coverage is U.S.: CPIT (1975–2011); IPI (1985–2011); Japan: CPIT, IPI (1975–2011); Italy: CPIT (1996–2011); IPI (1975–2011); U.K.: CPIT (1988–2011), IPI (1975–2011); France: CPIT (1975–2011), IPI (1981–2011); Germany: CPIT, IPI (1975–2011), IPI (1975–2011); Canada: CPIT, IPI (1975–2011); Switzerland: CPIT (1975–2011), IPI (1990–2011).

In Table 7.4 we report estimates from a quarterly regression of the log import price index (in domestic currency) on lags 0–8 of the log trade-weighted nominal exchange rate (in units of domestic per foreign currency) and lags 0–8 of log trade-weighted foreign PPI (in foreign currency). The contemporaneous pass-through is given by the lag-0 coefficient on the NER, while the long-run pass-through is given by the sum of the nine coefficients on lags of the NER.

As is evident the pass-through into consumer prices is uniformly low and well below pass-through into border prices for each country. For the U.S. both SRPT and LRPT are at least twice as high into border prices as it is into retail prices. A similar finding is documented for other countries. There is also large variation in ERPT into border prices across countries with countries like Japan, Canada, U.K., France, and Germany having high LRPT while the U.S., Italy, and Switzerland have low LRPT. The estimates of ERPT for border prices update the findings in Campa and Goldberg (2005) who provide cross-sectional and time-series estimates of ERPT for import prices.

We reiterate that unlike consumer prices, import price indices are constructed differently across countries. The large variation in ERPT estimates can also be attributed to the differing composition of import bundles since ERPT estimates differ a great deal across goods.

In the case when IPIs, NERs, and producer prices are cointegrated, dynamic lag regressions (3) are misspecified. To allow for cointegration a vector error correction model (VECM) is estimated.

$$\Delta y_t = A\left(B y_{t-1} + \alpha\right) + \sum_{k=0}^{n} \Delta y_{t-k} + \delta + \epsilon_t, \tag{4}$$

where y is a three-dimensional VECM in the log import price index, the log NER, and the log foreign PPI, and B is the vector of coefficients in the cointegrating relationship.[10] If the data points toward a cointegration rank of 1, the VECM is estimated by maximum likelihood. The long-run exchange rate pass-through is given by (negative) the coefficient on the exchange rate in the estimated cointegrating vector (the coefficient on import prices is normalized to 1). For four (Japan, Italy, Canada, and Switzerland) of the eight countries we cannot reject the null that the log import price index, the log of the NER, and the log of foreign PPI are not cointegrated, that is for these countries the dynamic lag regression provides consistent estimates. When the log tradeable CPI is used in place of the log IPI the number of countries for which the null cannot be rejected increases to five (the previous four plus France). In general we find that the standard errors are quite large and the estimates are highly unstable in the VECM specification depending on the sample period chosen. Accordingly we decided not to report any numbers.

---

[10] The lag length n is determined by the Akaike information criteria and the cointegration rank is estimated by the Johansen trace statistic using a significance level of 95%. Standard errors are based on the usual asymptotic normal approximation.

Large Devaluation Episodes

The ranking in ERPT across consumer and border prices is also evident in the episodes of large exchange rate devaluations. These episodes provide a particularly useful lens to study the impact of changes in exchange rates on prices.[11] Burstein et al. (2005) use basic accounting to provide a breakdown of the impact of large devaluations on border and consumer prices. Table 7.5 summarizes the results, reporting changes in aggregate prices for the large devaluations in Argentina 2001, Brazil 1998, Korea 1997, Mexico 1994, Thailand 1997, the European devaluations in Finland, Italy, Sweden, and the U.K. in 1992, and the recent large depreciation of the Icelandic Krona between 2007 and 2009. Burstein et al. (2005) also present some evidence on prices for Indonesia 1997, Malaysia 1997, Philippines 1997, and Uruguay 2002.

The central patterns of prices in the aftermath of these devaluation episodes can be summarized as follows. The increase in prices of non-tradeable goods and services tends to be low relative to the large exchange rate depreciation. The increase in prices of tradeable goods is higher, with the extent of the increase depending critically on whether prices are measured at the retail level (CPI) or at the border (IPI). In particular, the rise in prices of imports at the dock is significantly higher than the increase of tradeable consumer prices. In Argentina, Brazil, and Mexico, ERPT for the IPI in the first year is close to complete. In the European devaluations of 1992, ERPT for import prices is lower than in the other countries, but significantly higher than ERPT for consumer prices of tradeable goods. Note that, consistent with the importance of distribution costs, consumer prices of imported goods in Argentina rise by far less than import prices at the dock (130% compared to 204% in the first year after the 244% NER devaluation).

Based on the RER decomposition in expression (2), Burstein et al. (2005) show that for all devaluation episodes, movements in tradeable RERs are much larger measured using consumer prices than measured using import prices. In many episodes, movements across countries in the price of non-tradeable goods relative to border prices of tradeable goods comprise the most important source of RER movements.

Empirical Finding 4. *Border prices, in whatever currency they are set in, respond partially to exchange rate shocks at most empirically estimated horizons.*

Incompleteness in ERPT can arise because prices are completely rigid for a period of time in the local currency and/or because when prices change they respond only partially to exchange rate changes. Aggregate pass-through regressions of the kind described above are a combination of the two phenomenons. Gopinath and Rigobon (2008) and Gopinath et al. (2010) use the micro price data underlying the construction of U.S. import and

---

[11] Unlike episodes of regular-sized exchange rate movements, large devaluations tend to be associated with large declines in output, consumption, and imports. Those factors inducing contractions in economic activity before or after large devaluations can play an important role in shaping the small observed increase in wages and prices of non-tradeable goods, as discussed in e.g., Burstein et al. (2007) and Kehoe and Ruhl (2009). For a survey of the literature on currency and financial crises we refer the reader to the chapter by Guido Lorenzoni (Chapter 12) in this handbook.

Table 7.5 Prices and Exchange Rates in Large Devaluations

	Cumulative Percentage Change Since Pre-Devaluation Month											
	Argentina – Dec. 2001		Brazil – Dec. 1998		Korea – Sept. 1997		Mexico – Dec. 1994		Thailand – June 1997		Iceland – Nov. 2007	
	12 months	24 months	12 months	24 months	12 months	24 months	12 months	24 months	12 months	24 months	12 months	24 months
U.S. dollar NER	243.7	192.8	52.9	62.8	50.9	31.8	122.5	130.0	64.3	43.0	122.6	103.6
Trade-weighted NER	202.2	195.5	48.6	50.7	45.3	36.1	123.3	129.1	43.1	33.2	94.4	100.3
Import prices (at the dock)	204.4	169.9	53.9	64.1	24.0	21.8	131.6	138.5	49.8	22.6		
Consumer price index	41.0	46.1	8.9	15.4	6.9	7.7	48.5	64.0	10.6	9.3	17.2	27.3
Non-tradeable prices	13.8	20.1	5.2	10.2	5.2	4.9	37.2	53.6			11.5	20.3
Retail price of tradeables	67.4	71.3	12.0	18.3	8.6	10.7	57.8	105.6			20.9	38.8
Import prices	129.8										27.0	49.0

	Finland – August 1992		Italy – August 1992		Sweden – Sept. 1992		U.K. – August 1992	
	12 months	24 months	12 months	24 months	12 months	24 months	12 months	24 months
U.S. dollar NER	46.6	29.2	45.6	43.5	49.5	40.5	30.0	25.7
Trade-weighted NER	19.7	11.4	23.5	30.2	32.2	30.3	12.0	14.4
Import prices (at the dock)	13.8	13.2	13.4	19.0	17.7	23.0	13.7	20.3
Consumer price index	2.1	4.0	4.5	8.5	4.2	6.9	1.7	4.2
Non-tradeable prices	1.1	3.0	4.4	8.1	4.4	7.6	4.9	8.3
Retail price of tradeables	5.0	7.3	5.3	9.8	6.4	8.9	1.8	3.1
Import prices								

For data description see Burstein et al. (2005), Iceland data source: Statistics Iceland.

export price indices to document the extent of price rigidity and pass-through conditional on price change of actual traded goods.[12] Fitzgerald and Haller (2012) provide evidence using data for Irish producers. We describe below the findings on the frequency of price adjustment in the invoicing currency and pass-through conditional on a price change.[13]

2.1. Frequency

Gopinath and Rigobon (2008) document that the weighted median duration of border prices in their currency of pricing is 11 months for U.S. imports and 13 months for U.S. exports. Fitzgerald and Haller (2012) find that for Irish exporters the weighted mean duration is 6.2 months.

The higher degree of stickiness in border prices in comparison to consumer prices is consistent with evidence on prices in the PPI as documented in Nakamura and Steinsson (2008) for the U.S. and Gautier et al. (2007) for six European countries.[14] Eichenbaum et al. (2011) estimate reference price durations for wholesale prices from a retail chain that are similar to that found from border prices for comparable categories of goods.[15]

Conditional on Price Change

A "medium-run pass-through" (MRPT) regression takes the form

$$\Delta p_{in,t} = \alpha_{in} + \beta \Delta_c e_{in,t} + \gamma X_{in,t} + \varepsilon_{in,t}.$$

$\Delta p_{in,t}$ is the change in the log price (in local currency) of the good imported in country n from country i, where the sample is restricted to those observations that have a non-zero price change in their currency of pricing. $\Delta_c e_{in,t}$ is the cumulative change in the bilateral nominal exchange rate over the duration for which the previous price was in effect. $X_{in,t}$ are controls that include the cumulative change in the foreign consumer/producer price level. Gopinath et al. (2010) also provide estimates of "life-long pass-through" (LLPT) that involves cumulating price changes and exchange rate changes over the entire life of the good in the sample. We report in Table 7.6 estimates from medium-run and life-long pass-through regressions for U.S. import prices by country of origin of goods. These numbers update the results in Gopinath et al. (2010) and Gopinath and Rigobon (2008) to cover the period 1994–2009. Overall, MRPT is 20% and LLPT is 28%.

---

[12] These findings are further explored in Gopinath and Itskhoki (2010a,b).

[13] Given limited data availability of actual traded goods prices there is limited country coverage for the facts on frequency and conditional pass-through.

[14] One has to be cautious in comparing measures of price stickiness across producer/border goods and consumer goods. First, the coverage of goods is very different with the former including intermediate and capital goods that are not included in the CPI bundle. Second, producer/border prices include many business-to-business transactions and contracts that may incorporate non-price features, while goods consumer prices cover mostly list (spot) prices. Friberg and Wilander (2008) use survey data for Swedish exporters and find that even for exporters that list a price the median price adjustment is once per year.

[15] Gagnon (2009), Gagnon et al. (2012a), and Alvarez et al. (2011) document the state contingent behavior of pricing with sharp increases in the frequency of price adjustment of consumer prices during episodes of high inflation and large devaluations.

Table 7.6 ERPT into Border Prices Using Micro Data (1994–2009): Medium-Run PT (MRPT) and Life-Long PT (LLPT)

	MRPT		LLPT		MRPT			
					Dollar		Non-dollar	
	ERPT	SE	ERPT	SE	ERPT	SE	ERPT	SE
All	0.20	0.01	0.28	0.04	0.16	0.01	0.80	0.04
Japan	0.24	0.02	0.32	0.03	0.17	0.02	0.84	0.06
France	0.24	0.05	0.36	0.11	0.18	0.06	0.81	0.10
Germany	0.41	0.04	0.51	0.08	0.22	0.04	0.84	0.08
Canada	0.27	0.07	0.51	0.09	0.25	0.07	0.60	0.45

Conditional on changing, prices in their currency of pricing respond only partially to exchange rate shocks. This is why MRPT of dollar priced goods is low at 16% while that of non-dollar priced goods is high at 80%. Further there are dynamics in pass-through estimates with life-long pass-through significantly exceeding MRPT for dollar priced goods.[16]

As one would expect ERPT in the short-run is higher for goods with a higher frequency of price change, but Gopinath and Itskhoki (2010a) document that this correlation is evident even for the longer-run based on LLPT estimates.

Finding 4 offers one potential explanation for Finding 3 regarding the large dispersion in estimates of border ERPT across countries. In a pure accounting sense the observation that ERPT to border prices for developing countries is high is consistent with the fact that the vast majority of imports into these countries is priced in foreign currencies. Similarly ERPT into import prices for the U.S. is one of the lowest across countries because 92% of U.S. imports are priced in dollars.[17]

Empirical Finding 5. *There are large deviations from relative PPP for traded goods produced in a common location and sold in multiple locations. On average, these deviations co-move with exchange rates across locations.*

---

[16] The average size of price adjustment conditional on a change is large, consistent with the importance of idiosyncratic factors in pricing. Gopinath and Rigobon (2008) document that the weighted median absolute size of price change is 8.2% for U.S. imports and 7.9% for U.S. exports.

[17] An argument in favor of using micro price data as opposed to aggregate price indices is that one can condition on an observable price change. As pointed out in Gopinath et al. (2010) and Nakamura and Steinsson (2012) in the Bureau of Labor Statistics (BLS) import/export series for the U.S. there are several goods that exit the BLS sample without a single price change, either because of product substitution or resampling or lack of reporting and consequently estimates of long-run pass-through using aggregate indices will be biased. Nakamura and Steinsson (2012) provides a bias correction factor for such index-based numbers under certain assumptions and claim that it is large. Gagnon et al. (2012b) under alternative assumptions claim that the correction factor is small.

Findings 1 and 2 summarized the evidence on deviations from relative PPP across countries (i.e., movements in product-level RERs) for tradeable goods, without distinguishing whether goods are produced in a common location or not. Finding 5 summarizes the evidence on deviations from relative PPP for actual traded goods that are produced in one location and sold in multiple locations. Under the assumption that changes in marginal costs for individual goods produced in a common location are independent of the destination to which the good is shipped, this evidence can be used to quantify the extent of the practice of *pricing-to-market* by exporters through which they vary markups systematically across destinations. This evidence is mostly based on producer and wholesale prices, which in principle contain a smaller local cost component than retail prices.

To quantify deviations from relative PPP for traded goods, researchers have used price data that differs in the degree of disaggregation. Consider first the use of aggregate price data (see e.g., Atkeson and Burstein (2008) and Drozd and Nosal (2012b)). Applied to aggregate price data, the hypothesis of relative PPP implies that import prices that consumers in one country pay for another country's goods should move one-for-one with the producer prices for goods in those countries that are the sources of those imports, when all of these prices are expressed in a common currency. Likewise, a country's export prices should move one-for-one with that country's producer prices. Relative PPP thus implies that the terms of trade (the ratio of export and import at-the-dock prices for a country relative to its trading partners) should be as volatile as the PPI-based RER, as can be seen in the following accounting identity:

$$\Delta rer_{in,t}^{ppi} = \left(\Delta ipi_{in,t} - \Delta epi_{ni,t}\right) + \left(\Delta ppi_{i,t} + \Delta e_{in,t} - \Delta ipi_{in,t}\right) + \left(\Delta epi_{ni,t} - \Delta ppi_{nt}\right). \quad (5)$$

Here, $\Delta epi_{in,t}$ denotes the log change in the export price index (EPI) for goods produced in country i and sold in country n measured in country i's currency, $\Delta ipi_{in,t} = \Delta epi_{in,t} + \Delta e_{in,t}$ denotes the import price index (IPI) in country n for goods imported from country i, and $\left(\Delta ipi_{in,t} - \Delta epi_{ni,t}\right)$ denotes the bilateral terms of trade between these two countries. Relative PPP applied to aggregate price data implies that the second term and third terms should be zero, so that the bilateral terms of trade moves one-to-one with the bilateral PPI-based RER. Averaging over country i's trade partners, expression (5) implies that the overall terms of trade for this country should move one-to-one with its trade-weighted PPI-based RER.

Data on international relative price fluctuations for major industrialized countries reveal that the terms of trade for manufactured goods are substantially less volatile than the corresponding PPI-based RER for manufactured goods, as can be see in Figure 7.1(d) for the U.S., and Table 7.7 for our set of industrialized countries. In the U.S., the standard deviation of annual changes in the manufacturing terms of trade is half as large as that of the manufacturing PPI-based RER. This observation arises because, at the aggregate level, changes in export and import price indices deviate systematically from changes in source country producer prices. In particular, an increase in home producer

Table 7.7 Terms of Trade and PPI-Based RER

Relative to Manuf. PPI-Based RER		U.S.		Japan		Italy		U.K.		France		Germany		Canada		Switzerland	
		Stdev	Correl	Stdev	Correl	Stdev	Correl	Stdev	Correl	Stdev	Correl	Stdev	Correl	Stdev	Correl	Stdev	Correl
IPI − EPI	Annual differences	0.40	0.53	0.51	0.65	0.58	0.47	0.36	0.56	0.87	0.19	0.60	0.74	0.55	0.61		
	HP-filtered quart.	0.32	0.57	0.51	0.72	0.58	0.52	0.39	0.52	0.89	0.20	0.59	0.78	0.55	0.56		
EPI − PPI	Annual differences	0.32	0.44	0.48	0.82	0.50	0.66	0.55	0.61	1.09	0.17	0.16	0.00	0.89	0.69		
	HP-filtered quart.	0.30	0.43	0.45	0.83	0.58	0.52	0.57	0.65	1.07	0.16	0.16	−0.13	0.86	0.69		
Foreign PPI + e − IPI	Annual Differences	0.81	0.80	0.44	0.63	0.65	0.61	0.62	0.75	0.80	0.81	0.68	0.82	0.74	0.07	0.94	0.84
	HP-filtered quart.	0.73	0.73	0.43	0.61	0.64	0.62	0.57	0.74	0.83	0.77	0.67	0.84	0.72	0.14	0.92	0.86

Note: See online data appendix for series description. Coverage is as follows. U.S.: 1985–2011; Japan: 1975–2011; Italy: 1981–2011; U.K.: 1975–2011; France: 1981–2011; Germany: 1975–2011; Canada: 1975–2011; Switzerland: 1990–2011.

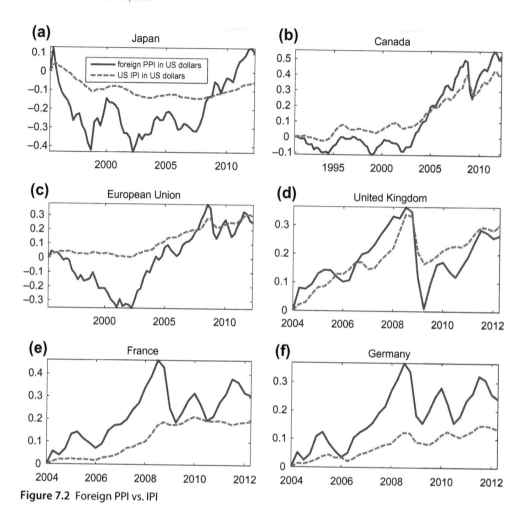

Figure 7.2 Foreign PPI vs. IPI

prices relative to foreign producer prices is typically associated with an increase in home producer prices relative to export prices, and an increase in home import prices relative to foreign producer prices. In other words, all three components in the identity (5) tend to be positively correlated, as shown in Table 7.7.

Figure 7.2 illustrates these aggregate deviations from relative PPP using U.S. manufacturing import price data by source country. Between the years 2006 and 2008, the appreciation of the Euro against the U.S. dollar resulted in an increase of Germany's manufacturing PPI measured in U.S. dollars ($\Delta ppi_{i,t} + \Delta e_{in,t}$) of more than 0.3 log points. Import prices in the U.S. for manufactured goods from Germany ($\Delta ipi_{in,t}$) rose by less than 0.1 log points. The extent of aggregate deviations from relative PPP displayed in Figure 7.2 varies by source country.

Other studies use data on unit values (ratios of export or import values to export or import volumes evaluated at border prices) at the level of goods categories or industries to quantify the extent of deviations from relative PPP, see e.g., the survey in Goldberg and Knetter (1997). The typical regression is of the form

$$\Delta p_{in,t} = \lambda_t + \theta_n + \beta_n \Delta e_{in,t} + \varepsilon_{in,t},$$

where $\Delta p_{in,t}$ is the log change in the export unit value of a good produced in country i and sold in destination n. If changes in unit values (measured in country i's currency) are uncorrelated with changes in the nominal exchange rate across destination countries, then $\beta = 0$. The typical finding in the literature, as surveyed in Goldberg and Knetter (1997), is that β is significantly negative, meaning that an appreciation of the Euro (country i) against the U.S. dollar (country n), $\Delta e_{in,t} > 0$, results in a decline in the export price of a German firm in the U.S. relative to the price in other destinations. There is substantial variation in β across industries and across exporting countries. Knetter (1989, 1993) use this type of regression to show that pricing-to-market by U.S. exporters is less prevalent than pricing-to-market by exporters from other major industrialized countries.

In order to infer deviations from relative PPP for individual goods from aggregate price indices or unit values, one has to worry that movements in international relative aggregate prices can result from differences in the product and quality composition of the indices, and not from changes in relative price across locations for common goods. To address this concern, recent work measure deviations from relative PPP using relative price movements for individual products sold in multiple locations.

Burstein and Jaimovich (2008) and Fitzgerald and Haller (2012) focus on products produced in a common location and sold in multiple destinations to identify the extent of pricing-to-market. Fitzgerald and Haller (2012) use domestic and export prices at the plant level from Ireland's PPI monthly survey. Burstein and Jaimovich (2008) use wholesale prices of individual products produced in a common location and purchased by a large retailer in Canada and the U.S. Both papers find that, on average, export prices relative to domestic prices (measured in the same currency) follow closely movements in the bilateral exchange rate.

In Fitzgerald and Haller (2012), a 10% appreciation of the Pound Sterling against the Euro results in a roughly 10% increase in the price charged by Irish exporters in the U.K. relative to the domestic price. In Burstein and Jaimovich (2008), a 10% appreciation of the Canadian dollar against the U.S. dollar results in a roughly 8% increase in prices charged by exporters in Canada relative to the price charged in the U.S. Both papers find that these large movements in relative prices are also observed conditional on nominal price adjustment. Burstein and Jaimovich (2008) show that, while on average movements in product-level RERs for traded goods produced in a common location track changes in nominal exchange rates, there are large idiosyncratic movements in product-level

RERs: movements in international product-level RERs are three to four times as large as movements in the Canada–U.S. nominal exchange rate.

3. A SIMPLE FRAMEWORK TO INTERPRET EMPIRICAL FINDINGS

The facts in the empirical section provide a model-free description of the data. However, understanding what might be generating these facts and their implications for how firms price requires the use of models. In this section we use a simple model to interpret the evidence. This model, as well as those presented in Sections 4–6 are in partial equilibrium in that wages and exchange rates are taken as given. The general equilibrium model in Section 7 endogenizes wages and exchange rates.

Let p_{in} represents the log border price and p_{in}^r the log retail (consumer) price of a good exported from country i (Germany) to country n (U.S.), where all prices are expressed in the buyer's local currency (dollars). To sell the good, a retailer combines the physical good with local distribution services according to some constant returns to scale technology, and then adds a markup. For simplicity, we lump together wholesale and retail costs and markups. Up to a first-order approximation, the log change in the consumer price, Δp_{in}^r, is given by

$$\Delta p_{in}^r = \left(1 - s_{in}^d\right) \Delta p_{in} + s_{in}^d \Delta p_n^d + \Delta \mu_{in}^r, \tag{6}$$

where Δp_n^d denotes the log change in the price of distribution services in country n, $\Delta \mu_{in}^r$ denotes the log change in the gross retail markup, and s_{in}^d denotes the share of distribution costs in the pre-markup retail price, $s_{in}^d = 1 - \exp\left(p_{in} + \mu_{in}^r - p_{in}^r\right)$.

A number of papers have measured the "distribution wedge" as the difference between producer and retail prices as a fraction of retail prices, $1 - \exp\left(p_{in} - p_{in}^r\right)$, or similarly, the sum of wholesale and retail gross margins relative to retail sales.[18] In our specification, the distribution wedge is equal to $s_{in}^d + \left(1 - s_{in}^d\right) \left(\exp\left(\mu_{in}^r\right) - 1\right) / \exp\left(\mu_{in}^r\right)$, and hence combines distribution costs and retail markups. Burstein et al. (2003) and Campa and Goldberg (2010) calculate the distribution wedge for consumer goods in the U.S. and other OECD countries using Input-Output tables, while Berger et al. (2009) use matched micro price data in the U.S. This distribution wedge is found to be large ranging between 40% and 70% across tradeable goods (i.e., not including services) and is quite stable over time.

Aggregating changes in consumer prices across all tradeable goods consumed in country n (domestically produced and imported) in two consecutive time periods, we obtain the log change in the tradeables CPI:

$$\Delta cpi_n^{tr} = \left(1 - s_n^d\right)\left(1 - s_n^m\right) \Delta ppi_{nn} + \left(1 - s_n^d\right) s_n^m \Delta ipi_n + s_n^d \Delta p_n^d + \Delta \mu_n^r, \tag{7}$$

where s_n^m denotes the share of expenditures (exclusive of distribution costs) on imported goods in country n, s_n^d denotes the aggregate share of distribution costs in country n, Δipi_n

---

[18] The distribution wedge can also be calculated as the gap between total goods consumption at purchaser prices (from NIPA) and goods production attributed to consumption, at producer prices, as reported in Input-Output tables.

is a weighted average of import border prices, Δppi_{nn} denotes the log change in the producer price index in country n including only goods sold domestically (we do not use ppi_n for this since the PPI in some countries include prices of exported goods), and $\Delta\mu_n^r$ denotes the average change in retail markups in country n. The change in the CPI-based RER for tradeable goods for two ex-ante symmetric countries, country 1 and country 2 can be expressed as:

$$\Delta rer_{12}^{tr} = \left(1 - s^d\right)\left(1 - 2s^m\right)\left(\Delta ppi_{11} + \Delta e_{12} - \Delta ppi_{22}\right)$$
$$+ s^d\left(\Delta p_1^d + \Delta e_{12} - \Delta p_2^d\right)$$
$$+ \left(1 - s^d\right)s^m\left(\Delta epi_2 - \Delta ppi_2 - \Delta epi_1 + \Delta ppi_1\right). \tag{8}$$

We can use Equations (6)–(8) to interpret Findings 1–3 and 5. Consider first ERPT for goods imported in country n from country i. The fact that for imported goods, ERPT for consumer prices is lower than for border prices (Finding 3) can be the result of two forces as seen from equation (6). First, for a given ERPT into border prices, wholesale and retail markups may fall in response to an exchange rate shock, $\Delta\mu_{in}^r / \Delta e_{in} < 0$. Second, the price of local distribution services, p_n^d, may respond partially (less than border prices) to exchange rate movements.

While there is ample evidence of high distribution wedges, measures of changes in the price of local distribution services and measures of changes in retail and wholesale markups are less readily available. This has led to an active literature quantifying the role of local distribution costs and variable wholesale and retail markup, using different approaches. Berger et al. (2009) find that changes in distribution wedges are not correlated with exchange rate changes, which from our expression above is consistent with constant distribution cost shares s_{in}^d and constant markups μ_{in}^r. Gopinath et al. (2011) show using Canada–U.S. scanner data from a large retail chain that changes in retail markups have low correlation with changes in the Canada–U.S. exchange rate.[19] Goldberg and Hellerstein (2006) estimate a structural industrial organization (IO) model featuring local distribution costs, variable wholesale and retail markups, and menu costs, using U.S. data on the beer industry. They show through counterfactuals that, because retail markups do not vary much with exchange rate changes, local costs must be insensitive to exchange rate movements and play a significant role in generating incomplete pass-through to consumer prices.[20] Alessandria et al. (2010) consider the role of inventory management frictions of retailers as an important ingredient of retail distribution costs. We discuss this model in Section 4.

To sum up, lower ERPT for consumer prices than for border prices of imported goods can be mechanically explained by the presence of significant local costs that are insensitive

[19] Eichenbaum et al. (2011) also find, using the same data, that on average retail markups are quite insensitive over time exclusive of temporary sales.

[20] Nakamura and Zerom (2010) consider a similar exercise for the case of the coffee market in the U.S. in response to changes in the world price of coffee grain and find rapid pass-through of changes in producer prices to consumer prices.

to exchange-rate movements. There is less support for the role of variable retail markups in inducing low ERPT for consumer prices. Given this conclusion, for the remainder of the chapter we assume that retail markups are constant, $\Delta \mu_{in}^r = 0$.

Finding 3 that ERPT is low for consumer prices of tradeable goods (which include domestic and imported goods) can be understood using (7). If tradeable consumption includes a large portion of domestically produced goods and services (stemming from a combination of $s_m < 0.5$ and $s^d > 0$) and prices of domestically produced goods and services are not very sensitive to exchange rates, then ERPT for the tradeable CPI is low even if ERPT at the border is high. The high share of domestically produced goods in the tradeable CPI can also explain, using equation (8), Finding 2 that movements in the CPI-based RER for tradeable goods are almost as large as the relative price of domestically produced goods (the PPI-based RER) and as large as movements in the overall CPI-based RER (which combines the CPI-based RER for tradeable goods and non-tradeable services)[21,22]. Moreover, based on Finding 5, firms price-to-market. In response to an exchange rate depreciation in country 1, relative prices for traded goods tend to increase in country 2 relative to country 1 : $\Delta ppi_2 > \Delta epi_2$, and $\Delta epi_1 > \Delta ppi_1$—both of which imply that the terms of trade move less than the PPI-based RER. Deviations from relative PPP for traded goods, the third term in the expression on the right-hand side of equation (8), therefore contribute to larger movements in rer_{12}^{tr}. In sum, the evidence points to all three terms on the right-hand side of the equality in equation (8) co-moving with the exchange rate and are contributing factors that explain Finding 2 that the CPI-based RER for tradeable goods is roughly as volatile as the RER for domestically produced goods. Given the evidence on large home bias and important distribution shares the volatility of rer_{12}^{tr} appears to be driven mainly by the first two terms, with the third term playing a smaller role.

Finding 2, that for many countries the RER for tradeable goods constructed using import price indices move less closely with nominal exchange rates than the RER for tradeables constructed using consumer price indices, can be understood by the higher share of distribution costs and local goods in the CPI than in the IPI.[23]

---

[21] Burstein et al. (2005) and Fitzgerald (2008) perform accounting exercises of this form to explain the link between exchange rates and CPI and CPI-based RER for a number of countries, using measures of trade shares in consumption. Hau (2002) shows that more open economies tend to display less volatile RERs.

[22] Here we are abstracting from changes in the relative price between domestically produced tradeable goods and domestically produced services. These are potentially important to understand lower frequency trends in relative prices (see e.g., Asea and Mendoza (1994)) and movements in RERs in certain episodes such as exchange-rate-based stabilizations (see e.g., Rebelo and Vegh (1995)).

[23] Note that if countries import different sets of commodities, we should *not* expect the RER constructed using IPIs to be constant over time even if relative PPP holds for each commodity (in a two-country world, for example, the IPI-based RER is equal to the terms of trade). Similarly, even if relative PPP holds for each commodity, we should *not* expect the RER constructed using PPIs to be constant over time if countries specialize in the production of a different set of commodities. In contrast, in the absence of home bias in consumption and if relative PPP holds for each good, it follows from Equation (8) that the RER constructed using tradeable CPIs should be constant over time because the set of tradeable goods consumed in each country is identical.

Throughout this discussion, we have taken as given the fact that prices of domestically produced goods and services are not very sensitive to NERs. If the share of these domestically produced goods and services in the CPI is high, then Finding 1 that movements in the overall CPI-based RER co-move closely with nominal exchange rates follows. This begs the question, why are prices of domestically produced goods and services so insensitive to NERs? We discuss this further in the general equilibrium Section 7.

We now consider the pricing of goods at the border (at the dock). We first consider an environment with flexible prices and then allow for nominal rigidities in pricing. We use the model with nominal rigidities to interpret Finding 4.

3.1. Flexible Prices

Suppose that firms face segmented markets in each country so that they can charge a different price by destination. The optimal flexible log border price can be expressed as the sum of the log marginal cost and gross markup:

$$p_{in} = \mu_{in} + mc_{in}. \tag{9}$$

We assume that the mark-up depends on the price charged by the exporting (German) firm relative to the (log) aggregate industry price level in the destination country n (U.S.), p_n. That is, $\mu_{in} = \mu_{in}(p_{in} - p_n)$. We describe in Section 4 a number of models that produce this reduced-form relationship between markups and relative price, where the exact specification of $\mu_{in}(.)$ as well as the definition of the relevant aggregate industry price index p_n depends on model. The dollar marginal cost is given by $mc_{in} = mc_{in}(q_{in}, w_i, e_{in})$, where q_{in} is the quantity sold by the German firm in the U.S. markets and w_i summarizes those variables that impact the costs of production incurred by the German firm that are local to Germany such as German wages in Euros and total factor productivity.

Log-differentiating (9), we have that the log change in price, Δp_{in}, can be approximated as

$$\Delta p_{in} = -\Gamma_{in} \left(\Delta p_{in} - \Delta p_n \right) + mc_q \Delta q_{in} + \Delta w_i + \alpha_{in} \Delta e_{in},$$

where $\Gamma_{in} \equiv -\frac{\partial \mu_{in}(.)}{\partial (p_{in} - p_n)}$ is the elasticity of the markup with respect to the relative price, $mc_q \equiv \frac{\partial mc_{in}(.....)}{\partial q}$ is the elasticity of marginal cost with respect to output (which we assume is common across firms), and $\alpha_{in} \equiv \frac{\partial mc_{in}(.....)}{\partial e_{in}}$ is the partial-elasticity of the marginal cost (expressed in the destination country's currency) to the exchange rate. Note that we have assumed, without loss of generality, that $\frac{\partial mc_{in}(.....)}{\partial w_i} = 1$. In the case of constant markups, $\Gamma_{in} = 0$. When the production technology is constant returns to scale then $mc_q = 0$, with decreasing returns to scale $mc_q > 0$. When all production costs for a German firm are in Euros $\alpha_{in} = 1$.

Log demand is given by $q_{in} = \mathbf{q}\left(p_{in} - p_n\right) + q_n$ where q_n denotes the log of aggregate quantities/demand in country n. Log-differentiating,

$$\Delta q_{in} = -\varepsilon_{in}\left(\Delta p_{in} - \Delta p_n\right) + \Delta q_n,$$

where $\varepsilon_{in} \equiv -\frac{\partial \mathbf{q}(.)}{\partial p_{in}} > 0$ is the price elasticity of demand. Combining these two equations and collecting terms we obtain:

$$\Delta p_{in} = \frac{1}{1 + \Gamma_{in} + \Phi_{in}}\left[\Delta w_i + \alpha_{in}\Delta e_{in} + \left(\Gamma_{in} + \Phi_{in}\right)\Delta p_n + mc_q\Delta q_n\right], \qquad (10)$$

where $\Phi_{in} = mc_q\varepsilon_{in} \geq 0$ is the partial elasticity of marginal cost with respect to the relative price.

Consider a change in the bilateral exchange rate, Δe_{in}, assuming for now that $\Delta w_i = 0$. The resulting change in the price charged by firm i in country n implied by expression (10) can be decomposed into a direct effect at fixed aggregate prices and quantities in country n (i.e., $\Delta p_n = \Delta q_n = 0$), and an indirect effect induced by changes in aggregate prices and quantities in country n. The direct effect can be thought of as the overall effect when country i is very small relative to country n in that changes in the bilateral exchange rate do not affect aggregate outcomes in country n. The following proposition characterizes the direct component of exchange rate pass-through.

Proposition 1. *Exchange rate pass-through, when $\Delta w_i = \Delta p_n = \Delta q_n = 0$, is given by*

$$\frac{\Delta p_{in}}{\Delta e_{in}} = \frac{\alpha_{in}}{1 + \Gamma_{in} + \Phi_{in}}.$$

If $\Gamma_{in} = 0$, $\Phi_{in} = 0$, and $\alpha_{in} = 1$, then ERPT is 1.

Intuitively, when the dollar depreciates relative to the Euro this raises the dollar marginal costs of the German firm, all else equal. The sensitivity of dollar marginal costs to the exchange rate movement depends on α_{in}. Suppose the German firm sources some of its production inputs globally and these inputs are priced in dollars, whose dollar price is unaffected by the exchange rate movement. In this case, only a fraction of the firm's marginal cost is affected, so $\alpha_{in} < 1$ and ERPT is less than 1. In response to the rise in dollar marginal cost, the firm considers raising the dollar export price. The increase in the profit-maximizing price depends on two factors.

The first factor is the degree to which marginal costs increase in the firm's scale of production. If $mc_q > 0$, as the firm raises its prices the quantity sold declines, this reduces the marginal cost of the firm and dampens the initial desire to raise prices. The extent to which this happens depends not only on the extent of decreasing returns to scale, but also on the elasticity of demand the firm faces ε_{in}, since that determines the magnitude of the quantity response. A higher value of $\Phi_{in} = mc_q\varepsilon_{in}$ works to reduce ERPT below 1.

The second factor determining ERPT is the degree to which desired markups depend on a firm's price relative to the aggregate price. Suppose that desired markups are decreasing in the relative price set by the firm, $\Gamma_{in} > 0$. As the price of the German firm relative to the aggregate industry price in the U.S. increases, that reduces its desired markup, another reason to dampen price increase and reduce pass-through.

Proposition 1 displays the direct effect on German prices in the U.S. resulting from a change in the Euro/dollar exchange rate when aggregate industry prices and quantities in the U.S. remain unchanged to this exchange rate movement (i.e., $\Delta p_n = \Delta q_n = 0$). In practice, however, changes in the Euro/dollar bilateral exchange rate may be associated with changes in U.S. aggregate prices and quantities, which give rise to additional indirect effects from exchange rate changes on German prices in the U.S. At this point we do not discuss what generates this association and take it as given.

Proposition 2.   *ERPT including both direct and indirect effects, when $\Delta w_i = 0$, is given by*

$$\frac{\Delta p_{in}}{\Delta e_{in}} = \frac{\alpha_{in}}{1 + \Gamma_{in} + \Phi_{in}} + \frac{\Gamma_{in} + \Phi_{in}}{1 + \Gamma_{in} + \Phi_{in}} \frac{\Delta p_n}{\Delta e_{in}} + \frac{mc_q}{1 + \Gamma_{in} + \Phi_{in}} \frac{\Delta q_n}{\Delta e_{in}}.$$

The indirect effects of changes in aggregate prices and quantities in country n on country i's prices charged in country n can be understood as follows. An increase in the U.S. aggregate industry price, $\Delta p_n > 0$, increases the price charged by German firms if $\Gamma_{in} + \Phi_{in} > 0$. Intuitively, an increase in the U.S. aggregate price increases the German firm's desired markup (when $\Gamma_{in} > 0$) and increases quantity sold and marginal cost (when $\Phi_{in} > 0$), both of which result in a higher price. Moreover, an increase in U.S. aggregate quantities, $\Delta q_n > 0$, increases the German firm's demand and marginal cost (when $mc_q > 0$), resulting in an increase in the German firm's price. These results imply that, unless markups are independent of relative prices ($\Gamma_{in} = 0$) and marginal costs are independent of quantities ($mc_q = 0$), the overall degree of ERPT depends crucially on the details of how aggregate prices and quantities respond to exchange rate movements.

Interpretation of Results of ERPT Regressions

The ERPT regressions reported under the empirical Finding 3 provide a useful way of summarizing the response of border prices to movements in exchange rates. Here we discuss to what extent ERPT estimates can be used to shed light on the underlying forces that shape ERPT in our model. Propositions 1 and 2 point out that incompleteness of ERPT into border prices can arise either because of the lack of sensitivity of the exporter's cost to the exchange rate shocks, variability of markups or decreasing returns to scale. ERPT also depends on the specifics of the regression being estimated, whether direct and indirect effects are considered.

The direct effects reported in Proposition 1 can be viewed as the estimated ERPT assuming that changes in other components of marginal cost, aggregate quantities, and aggregate prices can be "controlled for" in those regressions. Shocks that affect the exchange rate can simultaneously induce movements in marginal cost components (such as foreign wages or global commodity prices) that impact pricing. If these costs are not well measured then the ERPT estimate includes the effect of these omitted variables on prices.[24] The precise definitions of marginal cost and the aggregate price index depend on model details. For example, in the CES model with a finite number of firms per sector described below, the price index p_n only includes the subset of prices of firms in the sector that directly compete with firm i. Empirical work trying to estimate the degree of ERPT typically lacks data on prices of a firm's direct competitors.[25] Using the PPI as a proxy for this price index may be highly imperfect. Given the difficulties in measuring p_n, ERTP regressions may be effectively estimating the "uncontrolled" degree of ERPT (which include both the direct and the indirect effects).

The sensitivity of p_n to the exchange rate, which determines the indirect effect of ERPT, depends on important details such as the source of the shock to the exchange rate (which shapes the response of e.g., costs and prices of domestic producers competing with foreign exporters). It also depends on whether the exchange rate shock being considered is idiosyncratic to the bilateral country pair or is a common shock, for instance where the dollar simultaneously depreciates relative to the currencies of all its trading partners. In the latter case the movement in p_n will tend to be larger and the estimated ERPT will be large. Consistent with this implication, Gopinath and Itskhoki (2010b) document that for the U.S. ERPT for border prices is higher when the trade-weighted NER is used compared to when the bilateral NER is used. Auer and Schoenle (2012) and Pennings (2012) document a similar finding at the sectoral level using the same micro price data. Note that α_{in} is also sensitive to the scope of the exchange rate shock. If the shock is common across countries and the German firm uses inputs from other countries affected by the shock then α_{in} can be higher.

To re-emphasize, while measures of ERPT provide a simple reduced form way of summarizing the response of prices to exchange rates, there is no single measure of ERPT that is independent of model details and driving shocks. One needs to be cautious when comparing estimates across studies, countries, and time periods and drawing implications for model parameters of pricing models, without knowledge of details of the environment.

Pricing to Market

Next, consider the evidence summarized in Finding 5 on deviations from relative PPP for individual goods produced in a common location and sold in multiple destinations. The change in the relative price of a good produced in country i and sold in countries n

---

[24] Corsetti et al. (2008) use a general equilibrium (GE) model to investigate possible biases from omitted variables and measurement error in ERPT regressions.

[25] There are exceptions, such as Auer and Schoenle (2012), that construct structural measures of competitors' price indices using micro price data.

and m, both expressed in the same currency, is given by

$$\left(\Delta p_{in} + \Delta e_{ni}\right) - \left(\Delta p_{im} + \Delta e_{mi}\right) = \left(\Delta mc_{in} + \Delta e_{ni} - \Delta mc_{im} - \Delta e_{mi}\right) + \left(\Delta \mu_{in} - \Delta \mu_{im}\right).$$

If the change in marginal cost is independent of where the good is sold, then changes in relative prices across countries are given by $\left(\Delta \mu_{in} - \Delta \mu_{im}\right)$. Note that to obtain pricing to market one requires not just variable markups but the response of markups should vary across locations. Therefore, incomplete pass-through arising from variable markups in and of itself is not sufficient to generate pricing-to-market.

Data on deviations from relative PPP for individual goods without information on the country of production of individual goods and based on retail prices that have a substantial local cost component are not informative enough to separate movements in relative markups from movements in relative marginal costs across locations. The evidence summarized in Finding 5, based on producer and wholesale prices for goods produced in a common location for sales in multiple destinations, suggests a substantial role for variable markups in generating deviations from relative PPP.[26] The fact that relative markups move even conditional on price adjustment, as documented in Fitzgerald and Haller (2012), suggest that movements in markups are not purely driven, mechanically, by sticky prices in the buyer's local currency.

What determines how markups for goods produced in a common location change across destinations in the model considered above? To ensure that changes in marginal costs are the same across destinations, we assume $mc_q = 0$ and $\alpha_{ij} = 1$. The following proposition derives the change in relative prices (and relative markups) under the assumption that the markup elasticity for this good is equal in the two destinations.

Proposition 3.   *If $\Gamma_{in} = \Gamma_{im}$, then the change in the markup across destinations for a good produced in country i is given by*

$$\Delta \mu_{in} - \Delta \mu_{im} = \frac{\Gamma_{in}}{1 + \Gamma_{in}} \left[\left(\Delta p_n + \Delta e_{ni}\right) - \left(\Delta p_m + \Delta e_{mi}\right)\right]. \tag{11}$$

According to expression (11), the change in the relative markup set by a country i firm in countries n and m is proportional to the change in the aggregate (industry-wide) real-exchange rate between these two countries. In response to a change in marginal cost of production faced by the German exporter that does not affect the Germany–U.S. industry-wide real exchange rate, relative markups between Germany and the U.S. are unchanged, even if $\Gamma_{in} > 0$ (in which case ERPT is incomplete). On the other hand, if the aggregate industry price level in the U.S. rises relative to that in Canada (both prices measured in a common currency), then a German exporter will increase the markup it charges in the U.S. relative to that in Canada. The relative markup more closely tracks

---

[26] While Burstein and Jaimovich (2008) use wholesale prices, which are not free of local distribution costs, they report that the average gross margin as a percentage of wholesale sales for groceries and related products in the U.S. is only 16%.

the aggregate real exchange rate, the higher is the elasticity of markup with respect to the relative price Γ_{in}. More generally, if the markup elasticity Γ_{in} varies across destination markets, then the size and direction of pricing-to-market depends on the specific shape of Γ_{in}, which is determined by model details.

We now consider the environment when prices adjust infrequently consistent with the evidence surveyed in Finding 4.

3.2. Nominal Rigidities in Pricing

When prices are sticky the sensitivity of prices to exchange rate changes depends on the currency in which prices are rigid and pass-through of shocks display dynamics over time. Infrequent price adjustments can be modeled in different ways, under the assumption of Calvo pricing (Calvo, 1983), using menu costs and state contingent pricing or with imperfect information and rational inattention.[27] To present some insights we use the Calvo environment that lends itself to analytical characterizations using first-order approximations. Given that this pricing model is dynamic, we must re-introduce time notation.

Once again consider a German firm i selling in the country n, the U.S. For now let us assume that firm i prices in currency n, that is it follows local currency pricing and prices in U.S. dollars when selling in the U.S. Define the desired (or flexible) price of firm i, $\tilde{p}_{in,t}$, as the logarithm of the price it would set if it could flexibly adjust its price in every state, that is,

$$\tilde{p}_{in,t} = \arg\max_{p_{in}} \Pi(p_{in}|s_t), \tag{12}$$

where s_t summarizes the firm's relevant state at time t. The logarithm of the reset price by a firm from country i selling in country n is denoted by $\bar{p}_{in,t}$. The observed price is $p_{in,t} = \bar{p}_{in,t}$ when prices change and $p_{in,t} = p_{in,t-1}$ when it does not. The optimal reset price in a Calvo environment is determined by the first-order condition

$$\sum_{\ell=0}^{\infty} \kappa^{\ell} \mathbb{E}_t \Theta_{t+\ell} \Pi_p\left(\bar{p}_{in,t}|s_{t+l}\right) = 0 \tag{13}$$

where κ is the constant probability of non-adjustment at each date, Π_p denotes the partial derivative of the profit function with respect to p, and $\Theta_{t+\ell}$ represents the stochastic discount factor. In steady state with zero inflation, $\Theta_{t+\ell} = \beta^l$, where $\beta < 1$ is the discount factor. Log-linearizing equation (13) around the flexible price first-order condition, as shown in Gopinath et al. (2010), the optimal reset price can be approximated as:

$$\bar{p}_{in,t} = (1 - \beta\kappa) \sum_{\ell=0}^{\infty} (\beta\kappa)^{\ell} \mathbb{E}_t \tilde{p}_{in,t+\ell}. \tag{14}$$

That is, the reset price $\bar{p}_{in,t}$ can be expressed as a weighted average of expected desired prices where the weights depend on the probability of non-adjustment and the discount factor.

[27] See e.g., Midrigan (2007) for a menu cost model of international relative price fluctuations, and see e.g., Crucini et al. (2010) for a model with imperfect information.

We now derive the reset price under the assumptions of Section 3.1 and, for expositional simplicity, constant returns to scale in production, $mc_q = \Phi = 0$. Starting from equation (9) and approximating the level of the markup and the marginal cost around their steady-state levels, the desired price is, up to a first-order approximation:

$$\tilde{p}_{in,t+\ell} = \frac{1}{1+\Gamma_{in}} \left[w_{i,t+\ell} + \alpha_{in} e_{in,t+\ell} + \Gamma_{in} p_{n,t+\ell} + const_{in} \right], \tag{15}$$

where $const_{in}$ contains steady-state values. Combining (14) and (15), the reset price is, up to a first-order approximation:

$$\bar{p}_{in,t} = \frac{(1-\beta\kappa)}{1+\Gamma_{in}} \sum_{\ell=0}^{\infty} (\beta\kappa)^\ell \mathbb{E}_t \left[w_{i,t+\ell} + \alpha_{in} e_{in,t+\ell} + \Gamma_{in} p_{n,t+\ell} + const_{in} \right]. \tag{16}$$

In the instances when the German firm i does not change its dollar price then clearly ERPT is 0. When it does adjust, ERPT is determined by the change in the reset price. The following proposition derives ERPT conditional on price adjustment when the exchange rate follows an AR(1) process and aggregate prices are constant.

Proposition 4.   *If the exchange rate follows an AR(1) with persistence parameter $0 \leq \rho_e \leq 1$ and $w_{i,t}$ and $p_{n,t}$ are constant for all t, ERPT for a firm, conditional on changing price (MRPT) equals:*

$$\frac{\Delta p_{in,t}}{\Delta_e e_{in,t}} = \frac{(1-\beta\kappa)}{(1-\beta\kappa\rho_e)} \frac{\alpha_{in}}{1+\Gamma_{in}}, \tag{17}$$

where we use the same notation as in the empirical section. Expression (17) follows immediately from equation (16) and the assumption that the NER follows an AR(1) process.[28] When $\rho_e = 1$, that is the NER follows a random walk, then ERPT conditional on price change is the same as that in the static section. With $\rho_e < 1$, ERPT is less than 1 even conditional on a price change, and even if flexible price ERPT is complete (i.e., $\alpha_{in} = 1$, $\Gamma_{in} = \Phi_{in} = 0$). When the NER change is not expected to last firms choose to adjust only partially since they will be stuck with the new price for a period of time within which the NER can revert back to its original value.

In the case when p_n is impacted by the exchange rate change and Γ_{in} is non-zero, ERPT depends on the response of the aggregate price index p_n to the exchange rate change. As long as there is staggered price adjustment, the aggregate price index will

---

[28] The proof is as follows: for a good that changes prices at time t and time $t-j$, $\frac{\Delta p_{in,t}}{\Delta_e e_{in,t}} = \frac{\bar{p}_{in,t} - \bar{p}_{in,t-j}}{e_{in,t} - e_{in,t-j}}$. Equation (16) implies

$$\bar{p}_{in,t} - \bar{p}_{in,t-j} = (1-\beta\kappa)\frac{\alpha_{in}}{1+\Gamma_{in}} \left[\mathbb{E}_t \sum_{\ell=0}^{\infty} (\beta\kappa)^\ell e_{in,t+\ell} - \mathbb{E}_{t-j} \sum_{\ell=0}^{\infty} (\beta\kappa)^\ell e_{in,t-j+\ell} \right].$$

Using $\mathbb{E}_t e_{in,t+\ell} = \rho_e^\ell e_{in,t}$ we obtain the equation in (17).

depend on lagged exchange rate shocks even prior to the last round of price adjustment. This implies that, if Γ_{in} is non-zero, $\frac{\Delta p_{in,t}}{\Delta_c e_{in,t}}$ will depend on lagged exchange rates prior to the last round of price adjustment, in contrast to the result in Proposition 4. There will be dynamics in pass-through with one price adjustment being insufficient to attain long-run pass-through.[29]

We now calculate the change in the aggregate price in country n for goods imported from country i, i.e., the import price index Δipi_{int}, assuming that all firms from country i selling in country n are symmetric except for the timing of price adjustment. Since a random fraction $(1 - \kappa)$ of firms change prices and they all choose the same price (given symmetry), the change in the import price index is given by:

$$\Delta ipi_{in,t} = (1 - \kappa)(\bar{p}_{in,t} - ipi_{in,t-1}).$$

Short-run pass-through into the import price index is a combination of the fraction of firms changing prices and desired pass-through.

In the next sub-section we explore the role of the currency in which prices are set on ERPT.

3.2.1. Currency of Pricing and Exchange Rate Pass-through

Most countries import goods that are priced in multiple currencies. Let $\bar{p}_{in}^{j}$ represent the reset price of imports into country n from country i priced in the currency of country $j \in (n, i)$. Suppose a fraction $(1 - \vartheta)$ of firms from Germany price in Euros (i) and ϑ in U.S. dollars (n), and that the frequency of price adjustment $(1 - \kappa)$ is equal for both groups of firms. Assuming symmetry across all firms within a particular currency pricing category, the change in the aggregate import price index (in dollars) is given by:

$$\Delta ipi_{in,t} = (1 - \kappa)\left[\vartheta\,(\bar{p}_{in,t}^{n} - ipi_{in,t-1}^{n}) + (1 - \vartheta)\,(\bar{p}_{in,t}^{i} - ipi_{in,t-1}^{i} + \Delta e_{in,t})\right]$$
$$+\kappa(1 - \vartheta)\Delta e_{in,t},$$

where $ipi_{in,t}^{j}$ denotes the import price index for goods priced in the currency of country j. By construction, ERPT for firms that do not adjust price is zero for dollar pricing firms and is 1 for Euro pricing firms. The following proposition characterizes short-run ERPT into the import price index.

Proposition 5.   *Short-run ERPT into the aggregate import price index is given by:*

$$\frac{\Delta ipi_{in,t}}{\Delta e_{in,t}} = (1 - \vartheta) + (1 - \kappa)\left[\vartheta\frac{\Delta \bar{p}_{in,t}^{n}}{\Delta e_{in,t}} + (1 - \vartheta)\frac{\Delta \bar{p}_{in,t}^{i}}{\Delta e_{in,t}}\right] \tag{18}$$

assuming symmetry across all firms within a particular currency pricing category.

---

[29] Note that when p_n changes over time in response to the shock, controlling only for the contemporaneous effect on p_n will not suffice to arrive at the direct component of ERPT, unlike the case of flexible prices. This is because lags of changes in p_n will impact ERPT in addition to the direct effect, derived in Proposition 4.

The first term on the right-hand side of equation (18) indicates that the larger the fraction of goods priced in Euros, $(1 - \vartheta)$, the higher the short-run pass-through. The second term captures price changes in the currency of invoicing.

The dollar reset price $\bar{p}^n_{in,t}$ is given by equation (14) replacing for notation sake $\tilde{p}_{in,t+\ell}$ with $\tilde{p}^i_{in,t+\ell}$ to represent desired prices in dollars. A similar derivation gives the Euro reset price $\bar{p}^i_{in,t}$ as:

$$\bar{p}^i_{in,t} = (1 - \beta\kappa) \sum_{\ell=0}^{\infty} (\beta\kappa)^{\ell} \mathbb{E}_t \tilde{p}^i_{in,t+\ell},$$

where $\tilde{p}^i_{in,t+\ell}$ is the desired price in Euros. In the case when flexible desired prices are the same regardless of currency of invoicing, that is $\tilde{p}^i_{in,t+\ell} + e_{in,t} = \tilde{p}^n_{in,t+\ell}$, we obtain the following proposition linking the two reset prices, as derived in Gopinath et al. (2010).

Proposition 6.   *If the NER follows a random walk and flexible desired prices are the same across firms regardless of the currency of pricing, then the reset price and ERPT conditional on changing price is equal across firms, up to the first order:*

$$\bar{p}^n_{in,t} = \bar{p}^i_{in,t} + e_{in,t},$$

$$\frac{\Delta p^n_{in,t}}{\Delta_c e_{in,t}} = \frac{\Delta p^i_{in,t}}{\Delta_c e_{in,t}} + 1.$$

That is, the law of one price holds for the reset price if the fundamentals are the same. Note that ERPT conditional on price change is the same across firms including both the direct and indirect effects as well as any other change in costs.

We now discuss the findings in the empirical section in the context of the current framework. In the absence of micro price data pass-through estimates using import price indices typically combine the effect of sticky prices and pass-through conditional on a price change as discussed earlier. Proposition 4 discusses the conditions under which pass-through conditional on a price change (MRPT) as estimated in the empirical section for Finding 4 is a measure of life-long pass-through (LLPT). It requires $\rho_e = 1$ and $\Gamma_{in} = 0$. In the case when $\Gamma_{in} \neq 0$, the indirect effects of ERPT arising from changes in the aggregate price level show up dynamically over time and one would require multiple rounds of price adjustment to arrive at LLPT. As documented in Gopinath et al. (2010), the fact that MRPT is lower than LLPT is consistent with an important role for $\Gamma_{in} \neq 0$.

The combination of the fact that prices adjust infrequently in the currency in which they are priced in, and that even conditional on a price change they respond only partially to the NER, as documented in Finding 4, implies that aggregate pass-through estimates are heavily determined by the currency composition of the import bundle, in the short and medium run. This is evident from the expression in Proposition 5.

As demonstrated in Proposition 6, if firm fundamentals (that is, desired flexible prices) are the same and the NER follows a random walk, MRPT should be the same conditional on a price change regardless of the currency in which goods are priced. As documented in Finding 4 this is not the case in the data. Pass-through of dollar priced imports into the U.S. is significantly lower than for non-dollar priced imports even conditional on a price change. As demonstrated in Engel (2006) (for one period ahead price stickiness) and Gopinath et al. (2010) (for Calvo pricing) this is consistent with a model where firms optimally choose what currency to set their prices in. If prices adjust every period, currency choice is irrelevant. However when prices are sticky, the firm can choose its currency to keep its preset price closer to its desired price.

We present the argument in a one period ahead sticky price environment as in Engel (2006). A risk neutral firm chooses to price in the local (n) currency as opposed to the producer (i) currency if $\mathbb{E}_{t-1}\Pi(\bar{p}^n_{in,t}) > \mathbb{E}_{t-1}\Pi(\bar{p}^i_{in,t})$.[30] Taking a second-order approximation to the profit function around the flexible price at date t we have that,

$$\mathbb{E}_{t-1}\left[\Pi(\bar{p}^n_{in,t}) - \Pi(\bar{p}^i_{in,t})\right] \approx \mathbb{E}_{t-1}\frac{1}{2}\tilde{\Pi}_{pp}\left[(\bar{p}^n_{in,t} - \tilde{p}^n_{in,t})^2 - (\bar{p}^i_{in,t} + e_{in,t} - \tilde{p}^n_{in,t})^2\right], \quad (19)$$

where $\tilde{\Pi}_{pp} < 0$ is the second derivative of the profit function evaluated at the date $t-1$ price. Here we have used the fact that flexible price profits are the same regardless of currency, that $\tilde{p}^n_{in,t} = \tilde{p}^i_{in,t} + e_{in,t}$, and that the first derivative of the profit function equals zero when evaluated at the flexible price. Expanding the right-hand side of (19) and taking the expectation we have:[31]

$$\mathbb{E}_{t-1}\left[\Pi(\bar{p}^n_{in,t}) - \Pi(\bar{p}^i_{in,t})\right] \approx \frac{1}{2}\tilde{\Pi}_{pp}Cov_{t-1}(-e_{in,t}, e_{in,t} - 2\tilde{p}^n_{in,t}). \quad (20)$$

The firm will therefore choose local currency pricing if:

$$\frac{Cov_{t-1}(\tilde{p}^n_{in,t}, e_{in,t})}{Var_{t-1}(e_{in,t})} < \frac{1}{2}, \quad (21)$$

that is if its desired pass-through is low enough. The cut-off of 0.5 follows from the second-order approximation. Intuitively, if a firm desires low exchange rate pass-through in the short-run before it has a chance to adjust prices, the firm is better off choosing local

[30] The result is unchanged if the firm is risk averse as long as the discount factor is exogenous to the decisions of the firm as pointed out by Engel (2006).

[31] To derive Equation (20), the right-hand side of (19) can be expressed as:

$$\mathbb{E}_{t-1}\frac{1}{2}\tilde{\Pi}_{pp}\left[(\bar{p}^n_{in,t} - \bar{p}^i_{in,t} - e_{in,t})(\bar{p}^n_{in,t} + \bar{p}^i_{in,t} + e_{in,t} - 2\tilde{p}^n_{in,t})\right]$$

$$= \mathbb{E}_{t-1}\frac{1}{2}\tilde{\Pi}_{pp}\left[(\mathbb{E}_{t-1}e_{in,t} - e_{in,t})(\bar{p}^n_{in,t} + \bar{p}^i_{in,t} + e_{in,t} - 2\tilde{p}^n_{in,t})\right].$$

The equality follows because $\bar{p}^n_{in,t} = \bar{p}^i_{in,t} + \mathbb{E}_{t-1}e_{in,t}$ up to the first order. Using the definition of the covariance and the fact that $\mathbb{E}_{t-1}(\mathbb{E}_{t-1}e_{in,t} - e_{in,t}) = 0$ we arrive at the cut-off rule (21).

currency pricing that results in 0% pass-through in the short-run. Conversely, if short-run desired pass-through is high, the firm should choose producer currency pricing that results in complete (100%) pass-through prior to price adjustment.

A number of papers in the literature fit into this simple framework. Devereux et al. (2004) consider an environment with one period ahead price stickiness, constant markups, and constant returns to scale. They show that an exporter will price in local currency if $Cov_{t-1}(w_{i,t} + e_{in,t}, e_{in,t})/Var_{t-1}(e_{in,t}) < 0.5$. It follows from Equation (15), that if $\Gamma = 0$, $\Phi = 0$, and $\alpha = 1$ then $Cov_{t-1}(w_{i,t} + e_{in,t}, e_{in,t}) = Cov_{t-1}(\tilde{p}_{in,t}^n, e_{in,t})$. The cut-off rule is the same as (21). Bacchetta and van Wincoop (2005) assume constant markups ($\Gamma = 0$) and decreasing returns to scale ($\Phi > 0$). They show that all else equal a marginal exporter selling to a country where all local firms price in the local currency will choose to price in local currency the higher the elasticity of demand it faces. This again fits into condition (21). To see this, recall that $\Phi = mc_q\varepsilon$, therefore for a given mc_q the higher is the elasticity of demand ε, the larger is Φ, and the lower is desired pass-through.

In the case of Calvo pricing, as derived in Gopinath et al. (2010), the currency choice rule depends on the average desired pass-through over the period of non-adjustment. This depends both on the dynamic path of desired pass-through and the duration of non-adjustment.[32] Gopinath et al. (2010) also show that MRPT, that is pass-through conditional on the first adjustment to the exchange rate shock, as estimated in the empirical section, is a good measure of this average desired pass-through.

In terms of empirical evidence linking currency choice to primitives of desired pass-through, Goldberg and Tille (2008) find evidence in support of the role of strategic complementarities in pricing in the currency decision using data on currency invoicing of international trade for 24 countries. Consistent with Gopinath et al. (2010) they find that more homogenous goods are priced in U.S. dollars, given the predominance of the dollar in trade transactions. Goldberg and Tille (2009) use disaggregated data for Canadian imports and find that exporters tend to use the currency of the country that dominates their industry. In addition they find that the Canadian dollar is used more for larger shipments into Canada.[33]

Lastly, Bacchetta and van Wincoop (2005), Devereux et al. (2004), and Gopinath et al. (2010) highlight the potential for multiple equilibria in the currency choice decision. Consider an environment where firms have an incentive to keep their price relative to their competitors' prices stable (high Γ). The currency choice decision depends on the currency of choice of the other firms. So for instance if the marginal firm selling to the U.S. competes with firms that price in dollars, then in response to movements in the U.S.

---

[32] An implication of this point is that currency choice cannot be predicted solely by long-run pass-through or desired pass-through on impact of the exchange rate shock. A firm, for instance, with a high flexible price (long-run) pass-through can well choose local currency pricing if desired pass-through is low in the medium-run.

[33] To explain this finding Goldberg and Tille (2008) build a pricing and currency choice model based on bargaining between the exporter and an importer that gets higher utility when facing stable prices in local currency.

NER its desired pass-through in dollars is low and it will choose to price in dollars. If on the other hand its competitors all price in Euros then its desired pass-through in dollars will be high and it will choose to price in Euros.

4. MODELS WITH DESIRED VARIABLE MARKUPS

We now illustrate a number of alternative models that have been used in the literature on international pricing in macroeconomic models that produce a negative relationship between markups and relative price $p_{in} - p_n$, so that $\Gamma_{in} > 0$ in the model presented in the previous section.

To start, as a benchmark, we briefly describe the case of monopolistic competition and CES demand. A continuum of intermediate goods, that in an abuse of notation we index by i, are combined in country n in amounts Q_{in} to produce a final good Q_n (or utility) according to the constant returns to scale technology

$$Q_n = \left[\int_{\Omega_n} A_{in}^{\frac{1}{\theta}} Q_{in}^{\frac{\theta-1}{\theta}} \, di \right]^{\frac{\theta}{\theta-1}}, \quad \theta > 1,$$

where Ω_n denotes the set of available varieties in country n, and A_{in} denotes a taste parameter for good i in country n. We introduce these taste parameters to allow for home bias in consumption if $A_{in} < A_{nn}$ for $i \neq n$. Cost minimization by the final good producer (or, equivalently, utility maximization by households) gives rise to the demand for variety i of the form $Q_{in} = A_{in} \left(\frac{P_{in}}{P_n} \right)^{-\theta} Q_n$, where P_{in} is the price of variety i in country n, and P_n is the cost-minimizing aggregate price index in country n given by $P_n = \left[\int_{\Omega_n} A_{in} \left(P_{in} \right)^{1-\theta} di \right]^{\frac{1}{1-\theta}}$. The demand elasticity is $\varepsilon_{in} = \theta$. Profit maximization by a monopolistic producer i gives rise to a simple pricing rule with a constant markup given by

$$\mu_{in} = \log \left(\frac{\varepsilon_{in}}{\varepsilon_{in} - 1} \right) = \log \left(\frac{\theta}{\theta - 1} \right).$$

Given that markups are constant, $\Gamma_{in} = 0$.

4.1. Non-CES Demand

Kimball (1995) introduces a simple departure from CES using a homothetic aggregator over individual varieties implicitly defined by:

$$\frac{1}{|\Omega_n|} \int_{\Omega_n} A_{in} \Upsilon \left(\frac{|\Omega_n| \, Q_{in}}{A_{in} Q_n} \right) di = 1.$$

The function Υ satisfies the constraints $\Upsilon(1) = 1$, $\Upsilon'(.) > 0$ and $\Upsilon''(.) < 0$. Under CES, $\Upsilon \left(\frac{|\Omega_n| Q_{in}}{A_{in} Q_n} \right) = \left(\frac{Q_{in}}{A_{in} Q_n} \right)^{\frac{\theta-1}{\theta}}$. Cost minimization (or utility maximization) gives rise to the following first-order condition:

$$P_{in} = \Upsilon' \left(\frac{|\Omega_n| \, Q_{in}}{A_{in} Q_n} \right) \frac{\lambda_n}{Q_n},$$

where λ_n denotes the Lagrange multiplier. Expenditures over all varieties are given by

$$P_n Q_n = \int_{\Omega_n} Q_{in} P_{in} di = \lambda_n D_n,$$

where P_n is the price index and $D_n \equiv \int_{\Omega_n} \Upsilon' \left(\frac{|\Omega_n| Q_{in}}{A_{in} Q_n} \right) \frac{Q_{in}}{Q_n} di$. Hence, the inverse demand function for variety i in country n is

$$\Upsilon' \left(\frac{|\Omega_n| \, Q_{in}}{A_{in} Q_n} \right) = D_n \frac{P_{in}}{P_n},$$

which can be inverted to obtain

$$Q_{in} = A_{in} \psi \left(D_n \frac{P_{in}}{P_n} \right) Q_n,$$

where $\psi \, (.) = \Upsilon'^{-1} (.) / |\Omega| > 0$ and $\psi' \, (.) < 0$ applying the inverse derivative theorem and $\Upsilon'' (.) < 0$. In logs,

$$q_{in} = a_{in} + \log \left(\psi \left(\exp \left(x_{in} \right) \right) \right) + q_n,$$

where $x_{in} = \log \left(D_n \right) + p_{in} - p_n$ and $a_{in} = \log \left(A_{in} \right)$. The demand elasticity is:

$$\varepsilon_{in} = - \frac{\psi' \, (.)}{\psi \, (.)} \frac{D_n P_{in}}{P_n},$$

which can vary across firms depending on the shape of $\psi \, (.)$. Note that a_{in} does not directly affect the demand elasticity.[34]

To put more structure on the dependence of ε_{in} on the relative price, Klenow and Willis (2006) choose a specification Υ that results in a demand function:

$$\log \left(\psi \left(x \right) \right) = \frac{\theta}{\eta} \log \left[1 - \eta x \right].$$

The limit of $\log \left(\psi x \right)$ as $\eta \longrightarrow 0$ is $-\theta x$ as under CES. The demand elasticity is

$$\varepsilon_{in} = - \frac{\partial \log \psi \, (x)}{\partial x} = \frac{\theta}{1 - \eta x_{in}},$$

---

[34] Starting around an equilibrium in which ε_{in} is equal across all firms selling in country n, it is straightforward to show that $dD_n = 0$ up to a first-order approximation.

which is constant when $\eta = 0$ and increasing in x when $\eta > 0$. The log markup is

$$\mu_{in} = \log\left(\frac{\theta}{\theta - 1 + \eta x_{in}}\right),$$

and the elasticity of the markup with respect to the relative price is

$$\Gamma_{in} = \frac{\eta}{\theta - 1 + \eta x_{in}}.$$

Hence, when $\eta > 0$ markups are decreasing in the relative price. Note that the elasticity of the markup with respect to relative price, Γ_{in}, varies systematically across firms. Specifically, markups are more sensitive to relative prices $p_{in} - p_n$ (i.e., Γ_{in} is higher) the lower is a firm's relative price.

A similar relationship between markups and relative prices is implied by other commonly used non-CES utility functions over a continuum of products such as quadratic (e.g., Melitz and Ottaviano (2008)) or translog utility (e.g., Bergin and Feenstra (2001)).[35]

4.2. Strategic Complementarities in Pricing with CES Demand

We now describe a setting with CES demand and a discrete number of products which gives rise to variable markups of the form assumed above. This setting was originally studied in Dornbusch (1987) and more recently in Atkeson and Burstein (2008).

Final sector output is modeled as a CES of the output of a continuum of sectors with elasticity of substitution η and sector output is CES over a *finite* number of differentiated products with elasticity θ, where $1 \leq \eta \leq \theta$. Firms own single products within each sector and compete in prices (Bertrand). Taking as given prices of other firms in its sector, the elasticity of demand for good i selling in country n in any given sector is

$$\varepsilon_{in} = \eta s_{in} + \theta \left(1 - s_{in}\right),$$

where $s_{in} = \exp\left(a_{in} + \left(1 - \theta\right)\left(p_{in} - p_n\right)\right)$ represents the expenditure share of product i with taste parameter a_{in} in that sector and $p_n = \frac{1}{1-\theta}\log\left(\sum_i a_{in} + \left(1 - \theta\right)\left(p_{in} - p_n\right)\right)$ is the log of the aggregate sector price. Note that, if $\eta < \theta$, ε_{in} is decreasing in the expenditure share of the firm in that sector. A firm with a small share assigns a larger weight to competitors in its same sector (high elasticity of substitution) than to competitors in other sectors (low elasticity of substitution). A firm with a higher share assigns a larger weight to firms in other sectors whose products are less substitutable, thus facing a lower price-elasticity of demand.

---

[35] For other models of non-CES demand over a continuum of products, see e.g., Simonovska (2010) and Gust et al. (2010). Arkolakis et al. (2012) consider the effects of international trade on markups in a general class of models featuring a decreasing relationship between markups and relative prices.

The optimal markup (obtained by choosing price to maximize profits taking prices of other firms in the sector as given) is

$$\mu_{in} = \log \left(\frac{\eta s_{in} + \theta \left(1 - s_{in}\right)}{\eta s_{in} + \theta \left(1 - s_{in}\right) - 1} \right),$$

which is increasing in s_{in} (and decreasing in $p_{in} - p_n$ for a fixed a_{in}) if $\theta > \eta$.[36] The elasticity of the markup with respect to relative price is

$$\Gamma_{in} = \left(\theta - \eta\right) \left(\theta - 1\right) \frac{s_{in}}{\left[\eta s_{in} + \theta \left(1 - s_{in}\right)\right] \left[\eta s_{in} + \theta \left(1 - s_{in}\right) - 1\right]}, \qquad (22)$$

which is positive if $\eta < \theta$. That is firms with lower relative price, $p_{in} - p_n$, and higher expenditure share, s_{in}, set higher markups. Markups are more sensitive to relative prices $p_{in} - p_n$ the higher is a firm's market share s_{in}. These results are qualitatively unchanged if firms compete in quantities (Cournot).[37] Finally, note that with a finite number of positive-mass firms per sector, any change in a product's price p_{in} has a non-zero effect on the aggregate sector price p_n, so that in expression (24) Δp_n directly depends on Δp_{in}. Taking into account this effect, equation (10) becomes (assuming constant returns to scale)

$$\Delta p_{in} = \frac{1}{1 + \left(1 - s_{in}\right) \Gamma_{in}} \left[\Delta w_i + \alpha_{in} \Delta e_{in} + \left(1 - s_{in}\right) \Gamma_{in} \Delta p_{-in}\right],$$

where Δp_{-in} is an expenditure-weighted average of price changes in the sector exclusive of firm or product i (in models with a continuum of firms, $s_{in} = 0$). Markups are constant if $s_{in} = 0$ or if $s_{in} = 1$. Hence, ERPT (both the direct effect and the sum of the direct and indirect effects) is non-monotonic in size.

4.3. Distribution Costs

We now consider a simple model of pricing with CES demand and additive distribution costs which gives rise to variable markups of the form assumed above. This setting was originally explored in Corsetti and Dedola (2005).

When country i firms sell to country n there is a retail (and wholesale) sector that bundles the imported good with distribution services to bring it to the final consumer. Assuming that the retail sector is competitive and combines the good and distribution services at fixed proportions, the retail price (in levels) P_{in}^r is given by:

$$P_{in}^r = P_{in} + \eta_{in} P_n^d,$$

---

[36] See de Blas and Russ (2012) for an analytical characterization of the distribution of markups as a function of primitives in a related model.

[37] Under Cournot competition, $\varepsilon_{in} = \left(\frac{s_{in}}{\eta} + \frac{1 - s_{in}}{\theta}\right)^{-1}$ and $\Gamma_{in} = \left(\theta - 1\right) \left(\frac{1}{\eta} - \frac{1}{\theta}\right) \mu_{in} s_{in}$, where s_{in} and p_n are given by the same expressions as under Bertrand competition, and $\mu_{in} = \varepsilon_{in} / \left(\varepsilon_{in} - 1\right)$. Once again, Γ_{in} is decreasing in $p_{in} - p_n$ and increasing in s_{in}.

where η_{in} denotes the fixed distribution cost per good. We assume that production of one unit of distribution services uses one unit of the industry bundle, which implies $P_n^d = P_n$.[38]

In this setup, the presence of local distribution services immediately implies that retail prices move less than one-to-one with changes in producer prices. Corsetti and Dedola (2005) show that the presence of additive distribution costs can lead to variable markups at the producer level. To see this, consider a CES demand at the retail level with elasticity of substitution θ : $Q_{in} = A_{in} \left(\frac{P_{in}^r}{P_n} \right)^{-\theta} Q_n$, where P_n denotes the aggregate CES price inclusive of distribution costs. The elasticity of demand country i firm faces when selling in country n is

$$\varepsilon_{in} = -\frac{\partial \log Q_{in}}{\partial \log P_{in}} = \theta \left(1 - s_{in}^d \right),$$

where $s_{in}^d = \frac{\eta_{in} P_n}{P_{in} + \eta_{in} P_n}$ denotes the share of distribution services in the retail price. The distribution share and the elasticity of demand are both decreasing in the ratio of the firm's producer price to the local cost component P_{in}/P_n. The optimal markup for a monopolistic price-setter is:

$$\mu_{in} = \log \left[\frac{\theta \left(1 - s_{in}^d \right)}{\theta \left(1 - s_{in}^d \right) - 1} \right] = \log \left[\frac{\theta}{\theta - 1 - \eta_{in} \exp \left(- \left(p_{in} - p_n \right) \right)} \right].$$

The elasticity of the markup with respect to the relative price $p_{in} - p_n$ is

$$\Gamma_{in} = \frac{1}{\frac{\theta - 1}{\eta_{in} \exp\left(-(p_{in} - p_n) \right)} - 1} = \frac{1}{(\theta - 1) \frac{1 - s_{in}^d}{s_{in}^d} - 1}. \tag{23}$$

Clearly $\Gamma_{in} = 0$ if $s_{in}^d = 0$ and $\Gamma_{in} > 0$ if $s_{in}^d > 0$. Intuitively, as the firm raises its relative price, that raises the elasticity of demand it faces and reduces its desired markup.[39]

Note from expression (23) that the elasticity of the markup with respect to relative price, Γ_{in}, varies systematically across firms. Specifically, markups of firms with lower relative price $p_{in} - p_n$ (or higher distribution share s_{in}^d) are more sensitive to relative price.

The specific models discussed above produce systematic differences in the elasticity of markup to relative price Γ_{in} across firms from country i selling in country n. To recap, in the first model (non-CES demand), the markup elasticity is higher for low relative price firms. In the second model (CES demand with a finite number of firms), the markup elasticity is higher for higher market share firms. In the third model (distribution costs),

---

[38] An alternative, standard assumption is that distribution services are produced using local labor instead of the industry bundle. In such case, the markup is a decreasing function of the price relative to the wage, $p_{in} - w_n$, instead of $p_{in} - p_n$. Markups in this case respond to changes in local wages and not directly to changes in the local aggregate price. If there are positive trade costs or home bias in preferences (so that relative aggregate prices across countries co-move relative wages), the two models behave similarly.

[39] A necessary condition for $\Gamma_{in} > 0$ in this model is that the elasticity of substitution in the retail technology between the good and distribution services be less than one. In the Cobb-Douglas case, $\Gamma_{in} = 0$.

the markup elasticity is higher for firms with higher distribution share. In all of these models, everything else the same, more productive firms have a lower relative price, a higher expenditure share, and a higher markup elasticity.

What are the implied differences in the degree of ERPT across firms? From expression in Proposition 2, we can see that, ceteris paribus, firms with higher markup elasticity, Γ_{in}, have a smaller ERPT stemming from direct effects (changes in exchange rate at fixed aggregate prices and quantities) but higher ERPT stemming from indirect effects (from changes in the aggregate prices and quantities in the destination country). The net effect of a higher Γ_{in} on ERPT is ambiguous.[40] If firms have a non-trivial effect on the industry aggregate price (as in the CES model with a finite number of firms), there is an additional source of non-monotonicity of ERPT across firms described above.

These model implications for how ERPT varies across heterogeneous firms have recently motivated empirical work using detailed micro data that merges measures of ERPT and firm characteristics. Berman et al. (2012) find evidence that higher productivity firms in France have lower ERPT than low productivity firms.[41] Similarly, Amiti et al. (2012) find evidence that Belgian exporters with higher expenditure shares in the destination market have lower ERPT. This is both because of the markup channel (i.e., Γ_{in}) and because larger exporters import a larger fraction of intermediate inputs that in turn lowers their sensitivity to bilateral exchange rate shocks, that is they have a lower α_{in}.

Goldberg and Hellerstein (2006), Hellerstein (2008), Goldberg and Verboven (2001), and Nakamura and Zerom (2010) develop structural models of international pricing featuring heterogeneous consumer choosing among horizontally differentiated varieties that better suit their preferences. These models, which give rise to richer and more flexible demand systems, are simulated and estimated using detailed micro data and econometric methods that are standard in the field of industrial organization. Goldberg and Hellerstein (2008) provide a recent survey of this work. These flexible demand models typically do not generate simple closed form solutions for Γ_{in} or ε_{in} and, in contrast to the models presented in this section, are less tractable to embed in general equilibrium setups like the one presented in Section 7. Consumer heterogeneity gives rise to a potentially important effect that is not present in the models described in this section. Specifically, when prices increase, consumers with high demand elasticity exit the market causing average demand elasticity to fall and markups to rise. Hence, pass-through can be larger than 100%.

5. OTHER MODELS OF INCOMPLETE PASS-THROUGH

We now discuss a number of alternative models of incomplete pass-through considered in the literature that do not directly fit into the framework used above.

---

[40] Auer and Chaney (2009) present a model of pricing-to-market under perfect competition that features consumers with heterogeneous preferences for quality. In equilibrium, ERPT is lower for high quality goods.

[41] Chatterjee et al. (2012), using Brazilian data, find similar results on ERPT across individual products exported by multi-product firms.

5.1. Consumer Search

Search models, as formulated by Burdett and Judd (1983) in a closed-economy context and by Alessandria (2009) in an international context, provide an alternative approach to obtaining variable markups of a similar form of those in the framework above. Consumer-search limits consumer arbitrage and can hence provide one rationalization for the observed dispersion of prices across locations for identical products at a point of time.

In the model of Alessandria (2009), firms from each country produce a single good at a constant, common marginal cost. Search is a costly activity that buyers in each country undertake to reduce the expected cost of purchasing the good from each source country. In equilibrium, for every good there is a distribution of prices in each country. Firms are indifferent between charging different prices in the distribution: a higher price entails a higher markup but a lower expected quantity sold. Alessandria (2009) shows that the average price posted by country i producers in country n is

$$P_{in} = MC_{in} + \eta P_n^s,$$

where MC_{in} denotes the marginal cost of all country i producers for sales to country n (expressed in the currency of country n), P_n^s denotes the cost of a unit of search effort for a country n consumer, and η is a parameter shaped by the search technology parameters.[42] The higher is the consumer's cost of search effort, ηP_n^s, the higher is the average markup. The logarithm of the average markup for country i producers selling to country n can be represented in terms of the notation used above as

$$\mu_{in} = \log\left(\frac{P_{in}}{MC_{in}}\right) = \log\left(1 + \eta \frac{1}{1 - \exp\left(p_n^s - p_{in}\right)}\right).$$

If the cost of search effort is in terms of the aggregate good in each country (so that $p_n^s = p_n$) we obtain a negative relationship between the average markup and the average price of country i producers in country n relative to the aggregate price in country n, as in the previous models.[43] Note that, since firms are indifferent between charging different markups in the distribution, the markup elasticity Γ_{in} is not uniquely determined for each individual firm.[44]

5.2. Customer Accumulation

Incomplete pass-through from costs to prices may arise if firms face adjustment costs to expand sales in any destination market. These adjustment costs may arise from invest-ments in distribution infrastructure, marketing, or other costs to the firm of expanding

[42] A similar relation holds for the average transacted prices, with a different mapping between parameters and η.

[43] If the search effort is in terms of time, then the negative relationship is between the average markup and the price–wage ratio.

[44] Alessandria and Kaboski (2011) argue that the search mechanism can partly account for differences in price levels between rich and poor countries.

its customer base. In response to a depreciation of the Euro against the U.S. dollar, a German exporter to the U.S. will not find it optimal to fully reduce its dollar price if there is no capacity to meet additional demand. This insight was initially developed in Krugman (1987) and later embedded in dynamic general equilibrium models by Kasa (1992) and Lapham (1995).

More recently, Drozd and Nosal (2012b) build an international business cycle model in which producers face costs to match with additional retailers in each market, while retailers search in an undirected way for domestic and foreign producers. Once matched, Nash bargaining between producers and retailers result in a producer price given by

$$P_{in} = (1 - \eta) MC_{in} + \eta P_{in}^r,$$

where MC_{in} denotes the marginal of production expressed in country n's currency, P_{in}^r the retail price, and $0 < \eta < 1$ the bargaining power of retailers. That is, as in previous models, there is an additive local component (P_{in}^r) that disconnects prices from costs. An appreciation of the Euro that increases marginal costs of a German exporter in U.S. dollars relative to the retail price in the U.S., results in incomplete ERPT into border prices. Deviations from relative PPP for German goods sold in Germany and the U.S. occur if retail prices P_{in}^r change across countries when measured in a common currency. Drozd and Nosal (2012b) show that changes in relative retail prices across countries arise from two forces. First, from changes across countries in the local cost of increasing the number of matches (this destination-specific cost component operates similarly to distribution costs described above). Second, from adjustment costs to the accumulation of matches. Intuitively, if adjustment costs are large, retail quantities do not change much in the short-run, and neither do retail prices. Over time, as quantities adjust, deviations from relative PPP become smaller. Drozd and Nosal (2012b) discipline the degree of adjustment costs to account for the observed differences between (low) short-run and (high) long-run price elasticity of international trade flows (see e.g., Ruhl (2008)).

Relatedly, and building on the partial equilibrium models of pricing-to-market with consumer switching costs developed in Froot and Klemperer (1989), Ravn et al. (2007) present a dynamic model of pricing-to-market stemming from preferences with habit formation at the level of individual varieties. In particular, preferences are given by

$$Q_{n,t} = \left[\int_{\Omega_n} \left(Q_{in,t} - \eta \overline{Q}_{in,t-1} \right)_{in,t}^{\frac{\theta-1}{\theta}} di \right]^{\frac{\theta}{\theta-1}},$$

where $\overline{Q}_{in,t} = \rho \overline{Q}_{in,t-1} + (1 - \rho) \tilde{Q}_{in,t}$ denotes the stock of habit for good i in country n, and $\tilde{Q}_{in,t}$ denotes average consumption of this good (which each consumer takes parametrically and equals $Q_{in,t}$ in a symmetric equilibrium). Utility maximization results in demand for good i in country n at time t of the form

$$Q_{in,t} = \left(\frac{P_{in,t}}{P_{n,t}} \right)^{-\theta} Q_{n,t} + \eta \overline{Q}_{in,t-1}.$$

The price-elasticity ε_{in} is a weighted average of θ and 0, where the weight on θ is increasing in expected future sales. When the present value of future sales rises in a country, firms selling there have incentives to invest in market share by lowering current markups. Any shock that increases the present value of sales in the U.S. relative to Germany reduces markups in the U.S. relative to Germany for any traded good. Ravn et al. (2006) show that, in response to an increase in government spending in the U.S., the CPI-based RER depreciates in the U.S., and prices for any traded good rise in Germany relative to the U.S., consistent with the correlations summarized in Finding 5. Drozd and Nosal (2012a) show, however, that the ability of this model to reproduce the correlations in Finding 5 are sensitive to the source of aggregate shocks.[45]

5.3. Inventories

Alessandria et al. (2010), as discussed previously, show that in the case of goods that are storable the retail or wholesale price of imported goods can be disconnected from the border price. Pass-through from changes in import prices into retail or wholesale prices can be incomplete even with CES preferences that in the baseline model without inventories generate full pass-through. Specifically, when a good is storable and firms face shipping lags and fixed costs of importing, they choose to import infrequently and hold inventories. These frictions are carefully documented in Alessandria et al. (2010). Holding inventories is not costless because goods depreciate if not sold. As derived in Alessandria et al. (2010) the retail or wholesale price charged by a monopolist is given by

$$ p_{in}^r = \frac{\theta}{\theta - 1} V_s(s), $$

where V_s is the value of an additional increment of stock of inventories. Therefore, prices in general depend on the firm's current stock of inventories. When the firm decides to import goods to add to inventories, then $V_s = p_{in}$, where p_{in} is the marginal cost of importing another unit. In this case there is 100% pass-through from changes in border prices into wholesale or retail prices. When the level of inventories is high, that is $V_s < p_{in}$, the firm will choose to price at lower than the replacement cost because its inventories are too high. In response to an increase in the border price p_{in}, a firm may find itself with too much inventories, in which case $V_s < p_{in}$ and pass-through is incomplete. Note that in response to a decline in the border prices, pass-through will be complete if firms choose to sell more or to replenish their inventories. Hence, this model generates an asymmetry in the extent of pass-through to increases and decreases in the border price p_{in}.

Thus far we have mainly focused on the partial equilibrium problem of a firm from country i selling in country n. We now examine the industry equilibrium and a general equilibrium environment.

[45] Dynamics models of incomplete pass-through have implications in terms of how the degree of pricing-to-market varies with the permanence of movements in exchange rates.

6. INDUSTRY EQUILIBRIUM

How does the aggregate industry price respond to exchange rate movements? We calculate the log change in the aggregate price index in country n, Δp_n, as an expenditure-weighted average of changes in all prices of goods sold in country n. This definition corresponds to the change in the CPI for an industry calculated at producer prices, as well as the change in the aggregate industry price, up to a first-order approximation, in the type of models described in Section 4.

To calculate the first-order change in the aggregate price index, we make some simplifying assumptions: there are constant returns to scale ($mc_q = 0$) and in the initial equilibrium all firms within each country are homogeneous so that Γ_{in} is equal across all producers from country i selling in country n and $\alpha_{in} = \alpha_{ni} = 1$. The following proposition presents the change in the aggregate price when prices are flexible:

Proposition 7.   *If all firms within each country are homogeneous and $mc_q = 0$, then the log change in the aggregate price, when prices are flexible, is*

$$\Delta p_n = \left[\sum_j \frac{s_{jn}}{1 + \Gamma_{jn}} \right]^{-1} \sum_i \frac{s_{in}}{1 + \Gamma_{in}} \left(\Delta w_i + \Delta e_{in} \right), \tag{24}$$

and the change in quantity sold from country i to country n is

$$\Delta q_{in} = \frac{\varepsilon_{in}}{1 + \Gamma_{in}} \left(\Delta w_i + \Delta e_{in} - \Delta p_n \right) + \Delta q_n, \tag{25}$$

where s_{in} denotes the total expenditure share of country i producers selling in country n. From expression (24) we can observe that an increase in the marginal cost (in U.S. dollars) affecting a larger expenditure share of firms selling into the U.S. results in a larger increase in the aggregate price and, through the indirect effects on ERPT, a higher increase in any country j's prices into country n.

If markets in countries m and n are not segmented in the sense that $s_{jn} = s_{jm}$, $\Gamma_{jn} = \Gamma_{jm}$ for all j, then the industry aggregate RER is constant, $\Delta p_m + \Delta e_{mn} - \Delta p_n = 0$. According to expression (11), relative markups between these two countries are constant for any traded good, even if $\Gamma_{in} > 0$. Hence, trade costs or home bias in preferences that segment markets across countries are essential to obtain pricing-to-market, as discussed in Atkeson and Burstein (2008).

From expression (24) we can also observe that if $\Gamma_{jn} = \Gamma_n$, then for given changes in wages and exchange rates, the change in the aggregate price is independent of Γ_n and hence is the same as if markups are constant, $\Gamma_n = 0$. To understand why Γ_n does not affect the change in aggregate prices, suppose that country n's currency depreciates against country i's currency, $\Delta e_{in} > 0$, while $\Delta w_j = 0$. The higher is Γ_n, the lower is ERPT in country n for imports from country i, but the higher is the increase in prices by all other producers selling to country n.

This result can be related to expression (8) for movements in CPI-based RERs for tradeable goods. A higher markup elasticity Γ_n increases the movements in export prices relative to producer prices, $\Delta epi_n - \Delta ppi_n$, contributing to larger movements in rer_{in}^{tr}, but also reduces movements in PPI's across countries, $\Delta ppi_{ii} + \Delta e_{in} - \Delta ppi_{nn}$, contributing to smaller movements in rer_{in}^{tr}. When $\Gamma_{jn} = \Gamma_n$, these effects exactly offset each other and movements in rer_{in}^{tr} are not affected by the markup elasticity for given changes in wages and exchange rates.

While the markup elasticity does not affect the response in aggregate prices to given changes in wages and exchange rates across countries, it does affect the response of quantities as can be seen in expression (25). In particular, a higher markup elasticity Γ_{in} reduces the effects of a change in exchange rates on relative quantities in the same way as a reduction in the price elasticity of demand, ε_{in}, does.

The irrelevance of Γ_{in} for aggregate price movements is an outcome of flexible prices. When prices adjust infrequently, as in the data, Γ_{in} affects the price response. Assume that there are only two countries i and n. Reset prices are given by (16). The aggregate price in country n is given by:

$$p_{n,t} = \kappa p_{n,t-1} + (1 - \kappa)\bar{p}_{n,t}, \tag{26}$$

where

$$\bar{p}_{n,t} = s^m \bar{p}_{in,t} + (1 - s^m)\bar{p}_{nn,t}, \tag{27}$$

and s^m represents the import share of spending in each country ($s^m = s_{21}$ in country 1 and $s^m = s_{12}$ in country 2). Assuming that countries are symmetric, $s^m = s_{21} = s_{12}$, $\Gamma_{in} = \Gamma_{nn} = \Gamma_{ni} = \Gamma$, after some algebraic manipulation (derived in the appendix, see Section 9) we arrive at the following expressions for the evolution of producer price inflation in country n:[46]

$$\Delta p_{n,t} - \beta \mathbb{E}_t \Delta p_{n,t+1} = \frac{(1 - \kappa)(1 - \beta\kappa)}{\kappa(1 + \Gamma)} \left[s^m (w_{i,t} + e_{in,t}) + (1 - s^m)w_{n,t} - p_{n,t} \right]. \tag{28}$$

Using the definition of the real exchange rate, $rer_{in,t} = e_{in,t} + p_{i,t} - p_{n,t}$ and combining the previous two expressions we arrive at the following expression for the evolution of the real exchange rate:

$$\Delta\, rer_{in,t} - \beta\mathbb{E}_t \Delta\, rer_{in,t+1} = \Delta\, e_{in,t} - \beta\mathbb{E}_t \Delta\, e_{in,t+1} \tag{29}$$
$$+ \frac{(1 - \kappa)(1 - \beta\kappa)}{\kappa(1 + \Gamma)} \left[(1 - 2s^m)(w_{i,t} + e_{in,t} - w_{n,t}) - rer_{in,t}\right]$$

For given paths of wages and exchange rates, a higher Γ works the same way as a higher κ, as it reduces the response of the firm changing prices to the exchange rate shock.

---

[46] These assumptions allow for home bias in consumption stemming from differences in preference parameters, $A_{in} < A_{nn}$.

7. GENERAL EQUILIBRIUM

In the previous sections we described mechanisms through which prices adjust incompletely and gradually to exchange rate shocks and generate relative price movements for the same good across different markets. We adopted a partial equilibrium approach, focusing on the problem of a firm and solving for industry equilibrium. We modeled the cost components of the firm including the exchange rate shock and wages as exogenous variables. In this section we describe one standard form of closing the model to endogenize wages and exchange rates. Movements in real and nominal exchange rates are driven by monetary shocks, motivated by the evidence presented in Mussa (1986). This is the approach adopted in Chari et al. (2002), Kehoe and Midrigan (2007), and Carvalho and Nechio (2011), among others.

Here we sketch the main features of the general equilibrium model and spell out more details in the appendix (see Section 9). There are two ex-ante symmetric countries. Households in each country derive utility from leisure and consumption of tradeable and non-tradeable goods, and have access to a complete set of state-contingent assets. To sell tradeable goods, a competitive distribution sector combines them with non-tradeable goods. Tradeable and non-tradeable consumption goods are each composed of a continuum of differentiated goods according to a non-CES aggregator of the form described in Section 4.1. Differentiated goods are produced using a symmetric technology that is linear in labor so that marginal cost is $(w_i + e_{in})$. We consider two alternative assumptions on price and wage rigidity. In Section 7.1 we consider the case of flexible wages and price rigidity in local currency and in Section 7.2 we present the case of rigid wages and flexible prices.

7.1. Local Currency Pricing

Monopolistically competitive firms set prices in each country that are sticky in the currency of the buyer. For a given path of wages and exchange rates, the dynamics of prices and RER for tradeable (at the producer level) and non-tradeable goods is represented by Equations (28) and (29), where $s^m = 0$ for non-tradeable goods.

Labor supply is determined by the consumers' intra-temporal labor-leisure decisions, which under a utility function of the form $U(C, N) = \frac{C_i^{1-\sigma}}{1-\sigma} - \frac{L_i^{1+\gamma}}{1+\gamma}$ is given by

$$\sigma c_{i,t} + \gamma l_{i,t} = w_{i,t} - p_{i,t}^c, \tag{30}$$

where $1/\gamma$ is the Frisch elasticity of labor supply, and $p_{i,t}^c$ is the aggregate consumer price in country i (including tradeable and non-tradeable goods). Up to a first-order approximation, $\Delta p_{i,t}^c = \Delta cpi_{i,t}$.

With complete asset markets, risk sharing implies

$$\sigma \left(c_{n,t} - c_{i,t} \right) = e_{in,t} + p_{i,t}^c - p_{n,t}^c = rer_{in,t}, \tag{31}$$

where $rer_{in,t}$ is the consumer-price-based RER. Combining risk sharing and labor supply, we obtain:

$$w_{i,t} + e_{in,t} - w_{n,t} = \gamma \left(l_{i,t} - l_{n,t} \right). \tag{32}$$

The nominal side of the economy is modeled using a money growth ($\Delta m_{i,t}$) rule and a cash-in-advance constraint:

$$\Delta m_{i,t} = \rho_m \Delta m_{i,t-1} + \sigma_{\epsilon_m} \epsilon_{i,t},$$

where $\varepsilon_{i,t}$ are *iid* shocks. The cash in advance constraint is given by,

$$p_{i,t}^c + c_{i,t} = m_{i,t}. \tag{33}$$

The following proposition, derived in Carvalho and Nechio (2011), analytically characterizes the first-order dynamics of RERs (taking into account the endogenous determination of wages and exchange rates) under certain parameter restrictions.[47]

Proposition 8.   *When $\sigma = 1$, $\gamma = 0$, $\alpha_{in} = \alpha_{ni} = 1$ and $\Gamma = 0$, the real exchange rate is given by*

$$(1 - \rho_m L)(1 - \kappa L) rer_{in,t} = \left(\kappa - (1 - \kappa) \frac{\rho_m \beta \kappa}{1 - \rho_m \beta \kappa} \right) u_{in,t},$$

and the nominal exchange rate follows

$$\Delta e_{in,t} = \rho_m \Delta e_{in,t-1} + u_{in,t},$$

where $u_{in,t} \equiv \sigma_{\epsilon_m} (\epsilon_{n,t} - \epsilon_{i,t})$.

One measure of the persistence of the real exchange rate is given by the sum of autoregressive roots: $\mathcal{P} = 1 - (1 - \rho_m)(1 - \kappa)$. The persistence of the RER is increasing in the persistence of the money growth rate and in the frequency of non-adjustment κ.[48] When $\rho_m = 0$ there is a one-to-one mapping between the RER persistence and the frequency κ. Kehoe and Midrigan (2007) find a positive but weak relationship between these two statistics using data for a number of developed countries. However, as is evident in the case when ρ_m is high the effect of variations in κ can be small.

More generally, when $\Gamma \neq 0$ and $\gamma \neq 0$ there is no simple closed form solution for the real exchange rate that evolves according to (29). In Figure 7.3 we graph the half-life (in quarters) for the RER as a function of Γ.[49] As expected, the higher is Γ the longer is the half-life.

[47] Kehoe and Midrigan (2007) derive a similar expression for the case when $\rho_m = 0$.

[48] Carvalho and Nechio (2011) show that a multi-sector model with sectoral heterogeneity in the frequency of price adjustment will tend to generate larger aggregate RER persistence than a one-sector model with the average sectoral frequency of price adjustment.

[49] For this figure, we assume $\kappa = 0.75$, $\rho_m = 0.5$, $\beta = 0.99$, $\sigma = 1$, and $\gamma = 0$. Given that with $\sigma = 1$ and $\gamma = 0$ the price dynamics are equal for tradeables and non-tradeables, the share of non-tradeables in consumption, the share of distribution costs, and the elasticity of substitution between tradeable and non-tradeable goods do not affect these results.

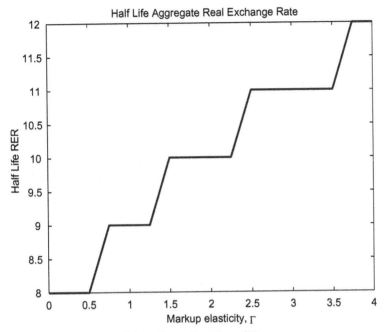

Figure 7.3 Half-Lives (in Quarters) of the RER as a Function of Γ

With only price rigidity and with flexible wages this model implies a close tie between exchange rates and relative wages at high frequencies. According to (32), if the Frisch elasticity is infinite, relative wages (measured in a common currency) are constant, independent of the source of the shock. If the Frisch elasticity is finite, countries that expand experience an increase in relative wages. It is difficult to reconcile these movements (or lack of) in relative wages with Findings 1–3 that relied on the disconnect between non-traded prices (and hence wages) and exchange rates. In addition, with sticky local currency prices a devaluation leads to an increase in export prices relative to import prices and the real trade balance deteriorates in the case when prices are rigid in the local currency and wages are flexible.

The impulse responses to a money growth shock that induces a depreciation of the nominal exchange rate in country 1 are depicted in Figure 7.4. While the model can generate a persistent, hump-shaped response of the RER, it does not reproduce the rankings of ERPT and movements in tradeable RER (based on consumer, producer, and border prices) reviewed in Findings 2 and 3, or the relative movements of the terms of trade and PPI-based RER reviewed in Finding 5. This is because relative costs (and hence the relative price of domestically produced goods) remain constant across countries.

One standard way of disconnecting wages and non-traded good prices from exchange rates in the short-run is to allow for sticky wages. We describe this extension in the next subsection.

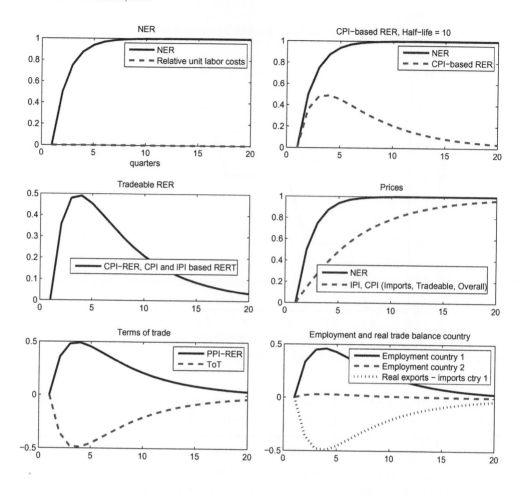

Figure 7.4 Impulse Responses to Money Growth Shock: Sticky Local Currency Prices, Flexible Wages

7.2. Wage Rigidity

A textbook treatment of this extension can be found in Galí (2008). Each household is assumed to supply a differentiated variety of labor and there is monopolistic competition among the various types of labor. The aggregate labor composite is

$$L_{i,t} = \left[\int_0^1 L_{i,t}(h)^{\frac{\eta-1}{\eta}} \, dh \right]^{\frac{\eta}{\eta-1}},$$

where η is the elasticity of substitution across labor varieties. Firm's demand for each variety is then given by:

$$L_{i,t}(h) = \left(\frac{W_{i,t}(h)}{W_{i,t}} \right)^{-\eta} L_{i,t} \tag{34}$$

$$W_{i,t} = \left[\int_0^1 W_{i,t}(h)^{1-\eta} dh \right]^{\frac{1}{1-\eta}}.$$

The staggered wage setting problem of household h is to maximize

$$\mathbb{E}_t \left\{ \sum_{l=0}^{\infty} (\beta \kappa_w)^l U(C_{i,t+l}(h), L_{i,t+l}(h)) \right\}$$

subject to labor demand (34) and its budget constraint. Following standard steps as in Galí (2008) we have the optimal reset wage for each household (given symmetry we drop h) given by

$$\bar{w}_{i,t} = (1 - \beta \kappa_w) \sum_{l=0}^{\infty} (\beta \kappa_w)^l \mathbb{E}_t \left\{ mrs_{i,t+l} + p^c_{i,t+l} \right\},$$

where mrs is the log of the marginal rate of substitution between consumption and labor supply. We solve for the dynamics of the wage following similar steps as in the derivation of (28).

Figure 7.5 depicts impulse responses for the case when wages are rigid and prices are flexible.[50] In response to a depreciation of the currency in country 1, the wage falls in country 1 relative to country 2, and so does the price of domestically produced goods. The model reproduces the rankings of ERPT and movements in tradeable RER constructed (based on consumer prices, producer prices, and border prices) reviewed in Findings 2 and 3, as well as the relative movements of the terms of trade and PPI-based RER reviewed in Finding 5. Clearly, matching all the findings described in the empirical section including infrequent price adjustment in the local currency requires a combination of both price and wage rigidity.

The literature has pointed out a number of important limitations of this model in terms of its implications on the relation between exchange rates and other macro variables. First, equation (31) implies a perfect correlation between RERs and relative consumption, while in the data it is much closer to zero (see e.g., Backus and Smith (1993))[51]. Second, the model implies a relation between exchange rates and interest rates across countries that satisfies uncovered interest parity, which does not appear to hold in the data (see e.g., Fama (1984)). Third, and more generally, this model implies a counterfactually strong relation between exchange rates and macro variables at short and medium horizons, which is referred to as the "exchange rate disconnect" puzzle (see e.g., Baxter and Stockman (1989) and Obstfeld and Rogoff (2000)). The model abstracts from non-monetary shocks, real, financial, expectation, and information-based, etc. that may be

---

[50] For this figure, we assume $\kappa = 0$, $\kappa_w = 0.75$, $\rho_m = 0.5$, $\beta = 0.99$, $\sigma = 1$, $\gamma = 0$, price elasticity (elasticity between domestic and foreign goods) $\varepsilon = 1.5$, import share in tradeables (exlusive of distribution) $s^m = 0.25$, distribution share in tradeables $s^d = 0.5$, and expenditure share of tradeables in total consumption $s^{tr} = 0.5$.

[51] Corsetti et al. (2008) show that this correlation can be matched to the data in a model with incomplete markets and a very low elasticity of substitution between home and foreign goods.

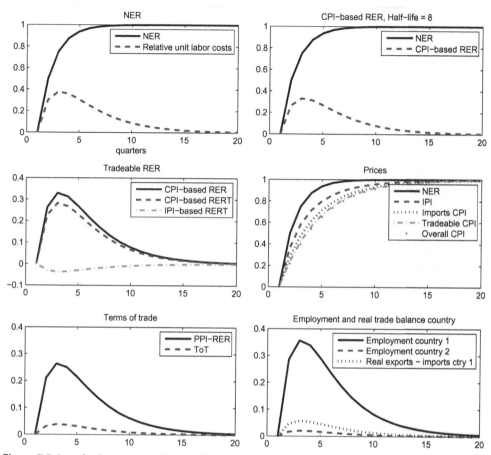

Figure 7.5 Impulse Responses to Money Growth Shock: Sticky Wages, Flexible Prices

important drivers of nominal exchange rates. For a broad survey of the literature on exchange rate determination and fundamentals we refer the reader to the chapter by Charles Engel in this handbook (Chapter 8) and to the book by Evans (2011). Overall, the general equilibrium literature in open economy macro has yet to deliver theoretical models that generate predictions consistent with the empirical findings while matching the exchange rate disconnect phenomenon.

8. CONCLUSION

What does the literature teach us about the positive and normative issues raised in the introduction? On the question of deviations from relative PPP the takeaway is that for retail prices this has much less to do with inefficient relative price movements of the exact same good across locations. It has more to do with the fact that a large fraction of prices are of non-tradeable goods or only locally consumed tradeable goods. At the same time for developed countries for the subset of goods that are actually traded, there is evidence that firms do price-to-market by charging (inefficiently) different markups, despite costs being the same. It is yet to be determined how large the aggregate welfare impact of these inefficient relative price movements is given the relatively small share of the pure traded goods component in total consumption.

As for the question of ERPT and expenditure switching, once again retail prices are not very sensitive to exchange rate movements. For border prices there is higher pass-through and the fact that it takes multiple rounds of price adjustment for ERPT to attain its long-run value suggests an important role for real rigidities in pricing. The magnitude of ERPT also depends on whether the country's currency is used in trade transactions. Since most developing countries trade in a currency that is not their own, ERPT in these countries tends to be higher than for developed countries like the U.S. for which 90% of its imports are priced in dollars.

Given local currency price stability for retail prices the ability of flexible exchange rates to generate large expenditure switching at the consumer level is limited for small to moderate exchange rate movements. It is possibly higher for intermediate inputs at the producer level or for large devaluations that coincide with large contractions in economic activity. To provide a more definite conclusion on the extent of expenditure switching it is important to address the relationships between prices and quantities in the data.[52]

As for the debate on fixed vs. floating exchange rates, the fact that firms mimic the short-run flexible price benchmark by choosing their border pricing currency optimally may reduce the welfare gap between floating exchange rates and pegs.

9. APPENDIX

9.1. Industry and General Equilibrium with Nominal Rigidities

In this appendix we provide additional details on the aggregate industry model of Section 6 and on the general equilibrium model of Section 7. We present log-linear approximations (around the non-stochastic steady state) of the equations that determine the model dynamics. We first consider the one-sector model of Section 6 under the general equilibrium assumptions of Section 7. Next, we consider a two-sector (trade-ables and non-tradeables) version of this model that we relate to the empirical findings. Throughout this appendix we assume that countries are symmetric so that in the initial steady state, the elasticity, the markup, and the markup elasticity are equal across countries and producers selling in each country: $\varepsilon_{in} = \varepsilon$, $\mu_{in} = \mu$, and $\Gamma_{in} = \Gamma$.

---

[52] Cravino (2012) uses detailed Chilean exports to measure the response of prices and quantities to exchange rate movements for goods priced in different currencies and sold in a given destination. Even though exchange rate movements induce large changes in relative prices between goods priced in different currencies, expenditure switching is on average quite limited.

9.1.1. One-Sector Model

We first embed the one-sector model of Section 6 in general equilibrium. For a given path of wages and exchange rates, the dynamics of the reset price for producers from each country is given, up to a first-order approximation, by expression (16), which can be re-written as

$$\bar{p}_{in,t} = \left(1 - \beta\kappa\right)\frac{\left(w_{i,t} + e_{in,t} + \Gamma p_{n,t} + const_{in}\right)}{1 + \Gamma} + \beta\kappa\mathbb{E}_t\bar{p}_{in,t+1}. \tag{35}$$

Aggregate source-country specific prices (or import price indices $ipi_{in,t}$) follow the law-of-motion

$$p_{in,t} = \kappa p_{in,t-1} + (1 - \kappa)\bar{p}_{in,t}. \tag{36}$$

The aggregate producer price with two-symmetric countries n is

$$p_{n,t} = s_m p_{in,t} + (1 - s_m)p_{nn,t}. \tag{37}$$

Expression (28) is obtained as follows. Combining (35) and (37), we have

$$\bar{p}_{n,t} = \frac{\left(1 - \beta\kappa\right)}{1 + \Gamma}\left(\hat{p}_{n,t} + \Gamma p_{n,t}\right) + \beta\kappa\mathbb{E}_t\bar{p}_{n,t+1}, \tag{38}$$

where

$$\hat{p}_{n,t} = s^m e_{in,t} + \left(1 - s^m\right)w_{n,t} + s^m w_{i,t} + constant, \text{ for } i \neq n.$$

Using equation (36),

$$p_{n,t} - p_{n,t-1} = \left(1 - \kappa\right)\left(\bar{p}_{n,t} - p_{n,t-1}\right)$$

$$= \left(1 - \kappa\right)\left(\frac{\left(1 - \beta\kappa\right)}{1 + \Gamma}\left(\hat{p}_{n,t} + \Gamma p_{n,t}\right) + \beta\kappa\left(\mathbb{E}_t\bar{p}_{n,t+1} - p_{n,t}\right)\right.$$

$$\left. + \beta\kappa p_{n,t} - p_{n,t-1}\right)$$

$$= \left(1 - \kappa\right)\left(\frac{\left(1 - \beta\kappa\right)}{1 + \Gamma}\left(\hat{p}_{n,t} + \Gamma p_{n,t}\right) + \beta\kappa\left(\frac{\mathbb{E}_t p_{n,t+1} - \kappa p_{n,t}}{1 - \kappa} - p_{n,t}\right)\right.$$

$$\left. + \beta\kappa p_{n,t} - p_{n,t-1}\right)$$

$$= \left(1 - \kappa\right)\left(\frac{\left(1 - \beta\kappa\right)}{1 + \Gamma}\left(\hat{p}_{n,t} - p_{n,t}\right) + p_{n,t} - p_{n,t-1}\right) + \beta\kappa\left(\mathbb{E}_t p_{n,t+1} - p_{n,t}\right),$$

and combining terms we obtain expression (28):

$$\Delta p_{n,t} - \beta \mathbb{E}_t \Delta p_{n,t+1} = \frac{(1-\kappa)(1-\beta\kappa)}{\kappa(1+\Gamma)} (\hat{p}_{n,t} - p_{n,t}). \tag{39}$$

Consumption of any good (domestic or foreign) requires distribution costs in terms of the final good. At this point we only assume that consumption and distribution costs are combined through some constant returns to scale technology. Under these assumptions, the price and quantity of final consumption are proportional to the price and quantity of production of the final good,

$$c_{n,t} = q_{n,t} + \text{constant},$$
$$p^c_{n,t} = p_{n,t} + \text{constant}. \tag{40}$$

Aggregate consumption, given money supply and the aggregate price level, is determined from the cash in advance constraint (33). Given aggregate prices and consumption, aggregate quantities of country i goods sold in country n are given, to a first-order approximation, by

$$q_{in,t} = -\varepsilon(p_{in,t} - p_{n,t}) + q_{n,t}. \tag{41}$$

Labor-market clearing requires that labor used for domestic production and for exporting must equal total labor $l_{n,t}$. The condition for labor market clearing in country n can be expressed, up to a first-order approximation (ignoring higher-order productivity losses from price dispersion), as

$$l_{n,t} = (1 - s^m) q_{nn,t} + s^m q_{ni,t}. \tag{42}$$

To close the model, wages in each country must be consistent with labor supply (30) and the nominal exchange rate with the risk sharing condition (31).[53]

This finishes the description of the equations that are required to solve for all endogenous variables in the model. Equations (35) and (36) conform a second-order difference equation that must be solved using standard methods.

Note that in this one-sector general equilibrium model we have not specified the details that give rise to variable markups. Given other parameters (including the elasticity ε), variable markups only matter through the markup elasticity Γ in Equation (35).

Proof of Proposition 8

The proof here follows Carvalho and Nechio (2011) closely. When $\sigma = 1$ and $\gamma = 0$ it follows from equations (30)–(33) that $w_{i,t} + e_{in,t} = w_{n,t}$ and $w_{i,t} = m_{i,t}$ in both

---

[53] Assuming instead financial autarky (trade balance equal to zero) instead of complete asset markets, expression (31) is substituted by $e_{in,t} + p_{in,t} + q_{in,t} = p_{ni,t} + q_{ni,t}$.

countries. The assumption that money growth follows an AR(1) process implies $\mathbb{E}_t \Delta m_{i,t+\ell} = \rho_e^\ell \Delta m_{i,t}$. Using these results, equation (16) can be written as

$$\bar{p}_{in,t} = \bar{p}_{nn,t} = \bar{p}_{n,t} = m_{n,t} + \frac{\rho_m \beta \kappa}{1 - \rho_m \beta \kappa}(m_{n,t} - m_{n,t-1}).$$

The aggregate price index in country n is

$$p_{n,t} = \kappa p_{n,t-1} + (1 - \kappa)\bar{p}_{n,t}$$

$$= \kappa p_{n,t-1} + (1 - \kappa)\left(m_{n,t} + \frac{\rho_m \beta \kappa}{1 - \rho_m \beta \kappa}(m_{n,t} - m_{n,t-1})\right).$$

The real exchange rate can be expressed, using the equivalence between producer and consumer prices in equation (40), as

$$rer_{in,t} = p_{i,t}^c + e_{in,t} - p_{n,t}^c$$

$$= \kappa \cdot rer_{in,t-1} + \left(\kappa - (1 - \kappa)\frac{\rho_m \beta \kappa}{1 - \rho_m \beta \kappa}\right)\Delta e_{in,t}.$$

Given that $e_{in,t} = m_{n,t} - m_{i,t}$, we have $\Delta e_{in,t} = \rho_m \Delta e_{in,t-1} + u_{in,t}$ where $u_{in,t} \equiv \sigma_{\epsilon_m}(\epsilon_{n,t} - \epsilon_{i,t})$. Using the lag operator notation $\Delta e_{in,t} = \frac{u_{in,t}}{1 - \rho_m L}$ and $rer_{in,t} - \kappa rer_{in,t-1} = (1 - \kappa L)rer_{in,t}$ and substituting into the previous equation we arrive at the main expression in the proposition.

9.1.2. Two-Sector Model

We introduce a non-tradeable final good because, as discussed under empirical Finding 2, movements in the price of traded goods (at border prices) relative to non-traded goods account for a non-trivial share of overal RER movements. Final consumption in country n is a Cobb-Douglas composite of consumption of the tradeable and non-tradeable final good,

$$c_{n,t} = s^{tr}c_{n,t}^{tr} + \left(1 - s^{tr}\right)c_{n,t}^{ntr}.$$

The final good price is a composite of the retail tradeable price index and the non-tradeable price index:

$$p_{n,t}^c = s^{tr}p_{n,t}^r + \left(1 - s^{tr}\right)p_{n,t}^{ntr}.$$

We assume that each unit of final tradeable consumption requires a fixed number of units of distribution costs in the form of the final non-traded good. The retail tradeable price index is, up to a first-order approximation

$$p_{n,t}^r = \left(1 - s^d\right)p_{n,t}^{tr} + s^d p_{n,t}^{ntr}.$$

Given prices and consumption, tradeable and non-tradeable consumption are given by

$$c_{n,t}^{ntr} = p_{n,t}^c + c_{n,t} - p_{n,t}^{ntr},$$
$$c_{n,t}^{tr} = p_{n,t}^c + c_{n,t} - p_{n,t}^r.$$

With two sectors, we have a reset price and an aggregate price for each sector. That is, equations (35)–(37) apply separately for tradeables and non-tradeables, where $s^m = 0$ for non-tradeables. Note that, in equation (35) the term $\Gamma p_{n,t}$ indicates that markups depend on a firm's price relative to the aggregate price index in its sector. This formulation depends on the particular specification of variable markups. It is consistent with non-CES demand such as the Kimball aggregator described in Section 4.1. On the other hand, in the model of variable markups with distribution costs in Section 4.3, the price index multiplying Γ in expression (35) would be $p_{n,t}^{ntr}$ if distribution costs use non-tradeable goods. Hence, in using equation (35) with the term $\Gamma p_{n,t}$, we are assuming that variable markups result from a non-CES aggregator as in Section 4.1, and that distribution costs do not affect markups because they apply to the final tradeable good.

Labor-market clearing requires that labor used for domestic production of tradeable goods, exports, and production of non-tradeable goods (including non-tradeable consumption and distribution costs which are proportional to tradeable consumption) must equal total labor $l_{n,t}$. This condition can be expressed as:

$$l_{n,t} = s^{tr}(1 - s^d)\left[(1 - s^m)\, q_{nn,t} + s^m q_{in,t}\right] + s^{tr} s^d c_{n,t}^{tr} + \left(1 - s^{tr}\right) c_{n,t}^{ntr},$$

where $q_{in,t}$ denotes the aggregate quantity of country i tradeable goods sold in country n, given by

$$q_{in} = -\varepsilon\left(p_{in,t}^{tr} - p_{n,t}^{tr}\right) + c_n^{tr}.$$

Other market clearing conditions that determine wages and exchange rates are the same as in the one-sector model.

Recall that if $\sigma = 1$ and $\gamma = 0$ (as in Proposition 8), relative wages between countries are constant. In this case it is straightforward to show that in response to a monetary shock as the one considered in Section 7, the aggregate price of tradeable and non-tradeable goods change by the same amount. This explains the price patterns in Figure 7.4: the rise in prices is equal for tradeable prices at the border $p_{in,t}^{tr}$, tradeable prices at the consumer level $p_{in,t}^r$, as well as the overall consumer price $p_{n,t}^c$.

REFERENCES

Alessandria, G., 2009. Consumer search, price dispersion and international relative price volatility. International Economic Review 50 (3), 803–829.

Alessandria, G., Kaboski, J.P., 2011. Pricing-to-market and the failure of absolute PPP. American Economic Journal: Macroeconomics 3 (1), 91–127.

Alessandria, G., Kaboski, J.P., Midrigan, V., 2010. Inventories, lumpy trade, and large devaluations. American Economic Review 100 (5), 2304–2339.

Alvarez, F., Neumeyer, A., Gonzalez-Rozada, M., Beraja, M., 2011. From Hyperinflation to Stable Prices: Argentina's Evidence on Menu Cost Models. Working Paper.

Amiti, M., Itskhoki, O., Konings, J., 2012. Importers, Exporters and Exchange Rate Disconnect. Working Paper.

Arkolakis, C., Costinot, A., Donaldson, D., Rodriguez-Clare, A., 2012. The Elusive Pro-competitive Effects of Trade. Working Paper, MIT.

Asea, P.K., Mendoza, E.G., 1994. The Balassa–Samuelson model: a general-equilibrium appraisal. Review of International Economics 2 (3), 244–267.

Atkeson, A., Burstein, A., 2008. Trade costs, pricing-to-market, and international relative prices. American Economic Review 98 (5), 1998–2031.

Auer, R., Chaney, T., 2009. Exchange rate pass-through in a competitive model of pricing-to-market. Journal of Money, Credit and Banking 41(s1), 151–175.

Auer, R., Schoenle, R., 2012. Market Structure and Exchange Rate Pass-through. Working Paper.

Bacchetta, P., van Wincoop, E., 2005. A Theory of the Currency Denomination of International Trade. Journal of International Economics 67 (2), 295–319.

Backus, D.K., Smith, G.W., 1993. Consumption and real exchange rates in dynamic economies with non-traded goods. Journal of International Economics 35 (3–4), 297–316.

Baxter, M., Stockman, A.C., 1989. Business cycles and the exchange-rate regime: some international evidence. Journal of Monetary Economics 23 (3), 377–400.

Berger, D., Faust, J., Rogers, J.H., Steverson, K., 2009. Border Prices and Retail Prices. Board of Governors of the Federal Reserve, International Finance Discussion Paper No. 972.

Bergin, P., Feenstra, R., 2001. Pricing to market, staggered contracts and real exchange rate persistence. Journal of International Economics 54 (2), 333–359.

Berman, N., Martin, P., Mayer, T., 2012. How do different exporters react to exchange rate changes? Theory, empirics and aggregate implications. Quarterly Journal of Economics 127 (1), 437–492.

Betts, C., Kehoe, T., 2006. U.S. real exchange rate fluctuations and relative price fluctuations. Journal of Monetary Economics 153, 1297–1326.

Boivin, J., Clark, R., Vincent, N., 2012. Virtual borders. Journal of International Economics 86 (2), 327–335.

Broda, C. Weinstein, D. 2008. Understanding International Price Differences Using Barcode Data. NBER Working Paper 14017.

Burdett, K., Judd, K., 1983. Equilibrium price dispersion. Econometrica 51 (4), 955–969.

Burstein, A., Jaimovich, N., 2008. Understanding Movements in Aggregate and Product-level Real Exchange Rates. UCLA Working Paper.

Burstein, A., Neves, J., Rebelo, S., 2003. Distribution costs and real exchange dynamics during exchange-rate-based stabilizations. Journal of Monetary Economics 50 (6), 1189–1214.

Burstein, A., Eichenbaum, M., Rebelo, S., 2005. Large devaluations and the real exchange rate. Journal of Political Economy 113 (4), 742–784.

Burstein, A., Eichenbaum, M., Rebelo, S., 2006. The importance of the nontradable goods' prices in cyclical real exchange rate fluctuations. Japan and the World Economy 18 (3), 247–253.

Burstein, A., Eichenbaum, M., Rebelo, S., 2007. Modeling exchange rate passthrough after large devaluations. Journal of Monetary Economics 54 (2), 346–368.

Calvo, G., 1983. Staggered prices in a utility-maximizing framework. Journal of Monetary Economics 12 (3), 383–398.

Campa, J., Goldberg, L., 2005. Exchange rate pass through into import prices. Review of Economics and Statistics 87 (4), 679–690.

Campa, J., Goldberg, L., 2010. The sensitivity of the CPI to exchange rates: distribution margins, imported inputs, and trade exposure. Review of Economics and Statistics 92 (2), 392–407.

Carvalho, C., Nechio, F., 2011. Aggregation and the PPP puzzle in a sticky-price model. American Economic Review 101 (6), 2391–2424.

Cavallo, A., Neiman, B., Rigobon, R., 2012. Product Introductions, Currency Unions, and the Real Exchange Rate. Working Paper.

Chari, V., Kehoe, P., McGrattan, E., 2002. Can sticky price models generate volatile and persistent exchange rates? Review of Economic Studies 69 (3), 533–563.

Chatterjee, A., Carneiro, R.D., Vichyanond, J., 2012. Multi-product firms and exchange rate fluctuations. American Economic Journal, Economic Policy 5 (2), 77–110.

Chen, S.-S. Engel, C. 2005. Does 'aggregation bias' explain the PPP puzzle? Pacific Economic Review 10 (1), 49–72.

Cheung, Y.-W., Lai, K.S., 2000. On the purchasing power parity puzzle. Journal of International Economics 52 (2), 321–330.

Corsetti, G., Dedola, L., 2005. A macroeconomic model of international price discrimination. Journal of International Economics 67 (1), 129–155.

Corsetti, G., Dedola, L., Leduc, S., 2008. High exchange-rate volatility and low pass-through. Journal of Monetary Economics 55 (6), 1113–1128.

Cravino, J., 2012. Exchange Rates, Aggregate Productivity and the Currency of Invoicing of International Trade. Working Paper.

Crucini, M. Landry, A. 2012. Accounting for Real Exchange Rates Using Micro Data. NBER Working Paper No. 17812.

Crucini, M., Telmer, C., 2012. Microeconomic Sources of Real Exchange Rate Variability. Working Paper.

Crucini, M., Telmer, C., Zachariadis, M., 2005. Understanding European real exchange rates. American Economic Review 95 (23), 724–738.

Crucini, M.J., Shintani, M., Tsuruga, T., 2010. Accounting for persistence and volatility of good-level real exchange rates: the role of sticky information. Journal of International Economics 81 (1), 48–60.

de Blas, B., Russ, K., 2012. Understanding Markups in the Open Economy. Working Paper.

Devereux, M.B., Engel, C., Storgaard, P.E., 2004. Endogenous exchange rate pass-through when nominal prices are set in advance. Journal of International Economics 63 (2), 263–291.

Dornbusch, R., 1987. Exchange rate and prices. American Economic Review 77 (1), 93–106.

Drozd, L., Nosal, J., 2012a. Pricing to Market in Business Cycle Models. Working Paper, Columbia University.

Drozd, L., Nosal, J., 2012b. Understanding international prices: customers as capital. American Economic Review 102 (1), 364–395.

Eichenbaum, M., Evans, C., 1995. Some empirical evidence on the effects of shocks to monetary policy on exchange rates. Quarterly Journal of Economics 110 (4), 975–1009.

Eichenbaum, M., Jaimovich, N., Rebelo, S., 2011. Reference prices, costs, and nominal rigidities. American Economic Review 101 (1), 234–262.

Engel, C., 1993. Real exchange rates and relative prices: an empirical investigation. Journal of Monetary Economics 32 (1), 35–50.

Engel, C., 1999. Accounting for U.S. real exchange rate changes. Journal of Political Economy 107 (3), 507–538.

Engel, C., 2006. Equivalence results for optimal pass-through, optimal indexing to exchange rates, and optimal choice of currency for export pricing. Journal of European Economic Association 4 (6), 1249–1260.

Engel, C. Rogers, J. 1996. How wide is the border? American Economic Review 86 (5), 1112–1125.

Evans, M., 2011. Exchange-Rate Dynamics. Princeton University Press, NJ, USA.

Fama, E.F., 1984. Forward and spot exchange rates. Journal of Monetary Economics 14 (3), 319–338.

Fitzgerald, D., 2008. Can trade costs explain why exchange rate volatility does not feed into consumer prices? Journal of Monetary Economics 55 (3), 606–628.

Fitzgerald, D., Haller, S., 2012. Exchange Rates and Producer Prices: Evidence from Micro Data. Stanford University, Working Paper.

Friberg, R., Wilander, F., 2008. The currency denomination of exports – a questionnaire study. Journal of International Economics 75 (1), 54–69.

Froot, K., Rogoff, K., 1995. Perspectives on PPP and long-run real exchange rates. In: Grossman, G., Rogoff, K. (Eds.), Handbook of International Economics, vol. 3. Elsevier.

Froot, K.A., Klemperer, P.D., 1989. Exchange rate pass-through when market share matters. American Economic Review 79 (4), 637–654.

Gagnon, E., 2009. Price setting during low and high inflation: evidence from Mexico. The Quarterly Journal of Economics 124 (3), 1221–1263.

Gagnon, E., Lopez-Salido, D., Vincent, N., 2012a. Individual price adjustment along the extensive margin. In: NBER Macroeconomics Annual, vol. 27. National Bureau of Economic Research Inc.

Gagnon, E., Mandel, B., Vigfusson, R., 2012b. Missing Import Price Changes and Low Exchange Rate Pass-through. International Finance Discussion Papers 1040, Board of Governors of the Federal Reserve, System (U.S.).

Galí, J., 2008. Monetary Policy, Inflation and the Business Cycle. An Introduction to the New Keynesian Framework. Princeton University Press.

Gautier, E., Hernando, I.,Vermeulen, P., Dias, D., Dossche, M., Sabbatini, R., Stahl, H., 2007. Price Setting in the Euro Area: Some Stylised Facts from Individual Producer Price Data (February 2007). ECB Working Paper No. 727.

Goldberg, L.S.,Tille, C., 2008.Vehicle currency use in international trade. Journal of International Economics 76 (2), 177–192.

Goldberg, L.S.,Tille, C., 2009. Micro, Macro, and Strategic Forces in International Trade Invoicing. Working Paper.

Goldberg, P., Hellerstein, R., 2006. A Framework for Identifying the Sources of Local-currency Price Stability with an Empirical Application. Federal Reserve Bank of New York, Working Paper.

Goldberg, P., Knetter, M., 1997. Goods prices and exchange rates: what have we learned? Journal of Economic Literature 35 (3), 1243–1272.

Goldberg, P.,Verboven, F., 2001. The evolution of price dispersion in the European car market. Review of Economic Studies 68 (4), 811–848.

Goldberg, P.K., Hellerstein, R., 2008. A structural approach to explaining incomplete exchange-rate pass-through and pricing-to-market. American Economic Review 98 (2), 423–429.

Gopinath, G., Itskhoki, O., 2010a. Frequency of price adjustment and pass-through. Quarterly Journal of Economics 125 (2), 675–727.

Gopinath, G., Itskhoki, O., 2010b. In search of real rigidities. In:Acemoglu, D.,Woodford, M. (Eds.), NBER Macroeconomics Annual, vol. 25. University of Chicago Press.

Gopinath, G., Rigobon, R., 2008. Sticky borders. Quarterly Journal of Economics 123 (2), 531–575.

Gopinath, G., Itskhoki, O., Rigobon, R., 2010. Currency choice and exchange rate pass-through. American Economic Review 100 (1), 306–336.

Gopinath, G., Gourinchas, P.-O., Hsieh, C.-T., Li, N., 2011. International Prices, Costs and Markup Differences. NBER Working Paper No. 14938.

Gorodnichenko,Y.,Tesar, L., 2009. Border effect or country effect? Seattle may not be so far from Vancouver after all. American Economic Journal: Macroeconomics 1 (1), 219–241.

Gust, C., Leduc, S.,Vigfusson, R., 2010. Trade integration, competition, and the decline in exchange-rate pass-through. Journal of Monetary Economics 57 (3), 309–324.

Hansen, B., 1999. The grid bootstrap and autoregressive model. Review of Economics and Statistics 81 (4), 594–607.

Hau, H., 2002. Real exchange rate volatility and economic openness: theory and evidence. Journal of Money, Credit and Banking 34 (3), 611–630.

Hellerstein, R., 2008. Who bears the cost of a change in the exchange rate? Journal of International Economics 76, 14–32.

Imbs, J., Mumtaz, H., Ravn, M., Rey, H., 2004. Aggregation Bias Does Explain the PPP Puzzle. Working Paper.

Imbs, J., Mumtaz, H., Ravn, M., Rey, H., 2005. PPP strikes back: aggregation bias and the real exchange rate. Quarterly Journal of Economics 120 (1), 1–43.

Kasa, K., 1992. Adjustment costs and pricing-to-market theory and evidence. Journal of International Economics 32 (1–2), 1–30.

Kehoe, P., Midrigan,V., 2007. Sticky Prices and Real Exchange Rates in the Cross-section. Working Paper, NYU.

Kehoe, T.J., Ruhl, K.J., 2009. Sudden stops, sectoral reallocations, and the real exchange rate. Journal of Development Economics 89 (2), 235–249.

Kimball, M., 1995. The quantitative analytics of the basic neomonetarist model. Journal of Money, Credit and Banking 27, 1241–1277.

Klenow, P.,Willis, J., 2006. Real Rigidities and Nominal Price Changes. Stanford Working Paper.

Klenow, P.J., Malin, B., 2011. Microeconomic evidence on price-setting. In: Friedman, B.,Woodford, M. (Eds.), Handbook of Monetary Economics. North-Holland.

Knetter, M., 1989. Price discrimination by U.S. and German exporters. American Economic Review 79 (1), 198–210.

Knetter, M., 1993. International comparison of price-to-market behavior. American Economic Review 83 (3), 473–486.

Krugman, P., 1987. Pricing to market when the exchange rate changes. In: Arndt, S., Richardson, J. (Eds.), Real Financial Linkages Among Open Economies. MIT Press, Cambridge, pp. 49–70.

Lapham, B.J., 1995. A dynamic general equilibrium analysis of deviations from the laws of one price. Journal of Economic Dynamics and Control 19 (8), 1355–1389.

Melitz, M.J., Ottaviano, G.I.P., 2008. Market size, trade, and productivity. Review of Economic Studies 75 (1), 295–316.

Midrigan, V., 2007. International price dispersion in state-dependent pricing models. Journal of Monetary Economics 54 (8), 2231–2250.

Murray, C.J., Papell, D.H., 2002. The purchasing power parity persistence paradigm. Journal of International Economics 56 (1), 1–19.

Mussa, M., 1986. Nominal exchange rate regimes and the behavior of real exchange rates: evidence and implications. Public Policy, Carnegie Rochester Conference Series 25.

Nakamura, E., Steinsson, J., 2008. Five facts about prices: a re-evaluation of menu cost models. Quarterly Journal of Economics 123 (4), 1415–1464.

Nakamura, E., Steinsson, J., 2012. Lost in transit: product replacement bias and pricing to market. American Economic Review 102 (7), 3277–3316.

Nakamura, E., Zerom, D., 2010. Accounting for incomplete pass-through. Review of Economic Studies 77 (3), 1192–1230.

Obstfeld, M., Rogoff, K., 2000. The six major puzzles in international macroeconomics: is there a common cause? NBER Macroeconomics Annual 2000 (15), 339–412.

Pennings, S., 2012. Pass-through of Competitors Exchange Rates. Mimeo, New York University.

Ravn, M., Schmitt-Grohe, S., Uribe, M., 2006. Deep habits. Review of Economic Studies 73 (1), 195–218.

Ravn, M.O., Schmitt-Groh, S., Uribe, M., 2007. Pricing to habits and the law of one price. American Economic Review 97 (2), 232–238.

Rebelo, S., Vegh, C.A., 1995. Real effects of exchange rate-based stabilization: an analysis of competing theories. NBER Working Paper 5197.

Reidel, D., Szilagyi, I., 2005. A Biased View of PPP. Mimeo, Harvard University.

Rogoff, K., 1996. The purchasing power parity puzzle. Journal of Economic Literature 34, 647–668.

Rossi, B., 2005. Confidence intervals for half-life deviations from purchasing power parity. Journal of Business and Economic Statistics 23 (4), 432–442.

Ruhl, K.J., 2008. The International Elasticity Puzzle. Working Paper.

Simonovska, I., 2010. Income Differences and Prices of Tradables. Working Paper, UC Davis.

Steinsson, J., 2008. The dynamic behavior of the real exchange rate in sticky price models. American Economic Review 98 (1), 519–533.

CHAPTER 8

Exchange Rates and Interest Parity*

Charles Engel
University of Wisconsin, Madison, WI, USA
National Bureau of Economic Research, Cambridge, MA, USA

Abstract

This chapter surveys recent theoretical and empirical contributions on foreign exchange rate determination. The chapter first examines monetary models under uncovered interest parity and rational expectations, and then considers deviations from UIP/rational expectations: foreign exchange risk premium, private information, near-rational expectations, and peso problems.

Keywords

Exchange rates, Uncovered interest parity, Foreign exchange risk premium

JEL classification codes

F31, F41

1. EXCHANGE RATES AND INTEREST PARITY

This chapter surveys empirical and theoretical research since 1995 (the publication date of the previous volume of the *Handbook of International Economics*) on the determination of nominal exchange rates. This research includes innovations to modeling based on new insights about monetary policymaking and macroeconomics. While much work has been undertaken that extends the analysis of the effects of traditional macroeconomic fundamentals on exchange rates, there have also been important developments that examine the role of non-traditional determinants such as a foreign exchange risk premium or market dynamics.

This chapter follows the convention that the exchange rate of a country is the price of the foreign currency in units of the domestic currency, so an increase in the exchange rate is a depreciation in the home currency. S_t denotes the nominal spot exchange rate, and $s_t \equiv \log(S_t)$.

A useful organizing feature for this chapter is the definition of λ_t:

$$\lambda_t \equiv i_t^* + E_t s_{t+1} - s_t - i_t. \tag{1}$$

In this notation, i_t is the nominal interest rate on a riskless deposit held in domestic currency between periods t and $t + 1$, while i_t^* is the equivalent interest rates for

* I thank Philippe Bacchetta and Fabio Ghironi, as well as Gita Gopinath and Ken Rogoff for helpful comments.

453

foreign-currency deposits.[1] $E_t s_{t+1}$ is the rational expectation of s_{t+1}: the mean of the probability distribution of s_{t+1}, conditional on all information available to the market at time t. λ_t is the difference between (approximately) the expected return on the foreign-currency deposit expressed in units of the domestic currency, $i_t^* + E_t s_{t+1} - s_t$, and i_t. It can be called the deviation from uncovered interest parity,[2] the expected excess return, or less generally, the foreign exchange risk premium. Rearrange equation (1) to get:

$$s_t \equiv -(i_t - i_t^*) - \lambda_t + E_t s_{t+1}. \tag{2}$$

An increase in the domestic to foreign short-term interest differential, $i_t - i_t^*$, *ceteris paribus* is associated with an appreciation. An increase in the expected excess return on the foreign deposit, λ_t, is also associated, *ceteris paribus*, with an appreciation. Holding interest rates and λ_t constant, a higher expected future exchange rate implies a depreciation.

Models of the exchange rate for the past 40 years have often focused on the case in which $\lambda_t = 0$. Let q_t be the log of the real exchange rate (the relative foreign to domestic consumer price levels, expressed in common units, where p_t is the log of the domestic consumer price index (CPI), and p_t^* is the log of the foreign CPI in foreign-currency units), so $q_t = s_t + p_t^* - p_t$, and set $\lambda_t = 0$. Equation (2) can be written as:

$$s_t \equiv -(i_t - i_t^*) + E_t \pi_{t+1} - E_t \pi_{t+1}^* + p_t - p_t^* + E_t q_{t+1} = -(r_t - r_t^*) + p_t - p_t^* + E_t q_{t+1}, \tag{3}$$

where $\pi_{t+1} \equiv p_{t+1} - p_t$ is approximately the domestic inflation rate and $r_t \equiv i_t - E_t \pi_{t+1}$ is approximately the domestic ex ante real interest rate (with analogous definitions for the foreign variables). Iterate equation (3) forward to get:

$$s_t \equiv -\sum_{j=0}^{\infty} E_t(i_{t+j} - i_{t+j}^*) + \lim_{j \to \infty} E_t s_{t+j+1}$$

$$= -\sum_{j=0}^{\infty} E_t(i_{t+j} - i_{t+j}^*) + \sum_{j=0}^{\infty} E_t(\pi_{t+j+1} - \pi_{t+j+1}^*) + p_t - p_t^* + \lim_{j \to \infty} E_t q_{t+j+1}$$

$$= -\sum_{j=0}^{\infty} E_t(r_{t+j} - r_{t+j}^*) + p_t - p_t^* + \lim_{j \to \infty} E_t q_{t+j+1}. \tag{4}$$

This equation summarizes the concerns of the literature that sets $\lambda_t = 0$, and helps to demarcate the scope of this chapter. Monetary models of exchange rates have focused on the role of monetary policy in setting interest rates and determining inflation. These models have also emphasized the macroeconomic forces that determine expected future interest rates, real and nominal, and expected future inflation. We will survey recent developments in this line of research.

---

[1] Generally, a superscript * in the chapter refers to a foreign-country variable.
[2] This is a version of uncovered interest parity that assumes rational expectations.

The term $\lim\limits_{j\to\infty} E_t q_{t+j+1}$ can be thought of as the long-run real exchange rate. This survey will not attempt to encompass the large literature that examines the neoclassical determinants of equilibrium real exchange rates. The chapter is about nominal exchange rates, but economists, policymakers, and individuals are concerned about nominal exchange rates mostly because they believe that their fluctuations matter for real exchange rates and other relative prices such as the terms of trade, so we focus on models in which the determination of real prices depends integrally on the nominal exchange rate level.

We are also not concerned with the $p_t - p_t^*$ term. This term is of course important in nailing down the level of nominal exchange rates—it helps to answer the question of why a dollar buys 80 yen instead of 8 yen. It also is important in high-inflation countries for understanding shocks to the nominal exchange rate, $s_t - E_{t-1}(s_t)$. Here we stipulate that in these high-inflation countries, monetary growth is most influential in determining the variance of $p_t - E_{t-1}(p_t)$. There is little need to go further than that for high-inflation countries; and for low-inflation countries, the behavior of $p_t - E_{t-1}(p_t)$ contributes little to our understanding of nominal exchange rate shocks, so we set it aside.

Much recent theorizing about exchange rate determination focuses on λ_t. There are a number of reasons why λ_t may not equal zero. If agents require a higher expected return on foreign compared to domestic deposits, because of a foreign exchange risk premium or some sort of liquidity premium, then $\lambda_t \neq 0$. The definition of λ_t uses rational expectations, but participants in the market may form expectations using some other algorithm. There might be private information relevant for the demand for foreign and home deposits, so even if agents all form their expectations rationally on the basis of their own information, the market equilibrium condition might not aggregate to $i_t^* + E_t s_{t+1} - s_t = i_t$. Individuals might have "rational inattention," so that they do not act continuously on publicly available information. The market microstructure—how foreign-currency demand and supply gets translated into a price for foreign exchange—might affect the market equilibrium. The modern "asset-market" approach is built off the assumption that capital flows freely between markets, but capital controls or other transactions costs can upset the asset-market equilibrium, as could other limits to arbitrage such as collateral constraints. Equation (4) can be generalized to:

$$s_t \equiv -\sum_{j=0}^{\infty} E_t(i_{t+j} - i_{t+j}^*) - \sum_{j=0}^{\infty} E_t \lambda_{t+j} + \lim_{j\to\infty} E_t s_{t+j+1}$$

$$= -\sum_{j=0}^{\infty} E_t(i_{t+j} - i_{t+j}^*) + \sum_{j=0}^{\infty} E_t(\pi_{t+j+1} - \pi_{t+j+1}^*)$$

$$-\sum_{j=0}^{\infty} E_t \lambda_{t+j} + p_t - p_t^* + \lim_{j\to\infty} E_t q_{t+j+1}$$

$$= -\sum_{j=0}^{\infty} E_t(r_{t+j} - r_{t+j}^*) - \sum_{j=0}^{\infty} E_t\lambda_{t+j} + p_t - p_t^* + \lim_{j\to\infty} E_t q_{t+j+1}, \qquad (5)$$

which demonstrates that it is not only current but also expected future values of λ_t that matter for the exchange rate.

Of special interest are the theories of λ_t that might account for the *uncovered interest parity puzzle*. This is the empirical puzzle that finds over many time periods for many currency pairs the slope coefficient in the regression:

$$s_{t+1} - s_t = a + b(i_t - i_t^*) + u_{t+1} \qquad (6)$$

is less than one and often negative. Under the null hypothesis that $\lambda_t = 0$ in equation (1), the regression coefficients should be $a = 0$ and $b = 1$. This survey will draw the link between models that are derived to explain the empirical findings concerning regression (6) and the implications of the implied behavior of λ_t for the exchange rate. In addition to the theoretical reasons noted in the previous paragraph for why we might have $\lambda_t \neq 0$, the literature has also raised the possibility that empirical work mismeasures $E_t s_{t+1}$ (the "peso problem"), or that econometric issues lead to spurious rejection of the null hypothesis.

The plan of the chapter is to consider first the "traditional" asset market approach, in which $\lambda_t = 0$. We survey how the New Keynesian literature has given theoretical and empirical insights into nominal exchange rate behavior. We consider exchange rate dynamics and volatility, and whether models are useful for forecasting exchange rate changes.

Then we consider different exchange-rate regimes and survey the large empirical literature on sterilized foreign exchange market intervention in floating-exchange rate countries.

The last part of the survey turns to models of λ_t. We take up the literature that has modeled foreign exchange risk premiums, and approaches that allow for violations of the representative-agent rational-expectations framework. Both have implications for the determination of exchange rates and the resolution of the uncovered interest parity puzzle.

2. MONETARY STICKY-PRICE MODELS OF EXCHANGE RATES

2.1. New Keynesian Monetary Models

In this section, we ignore deviations from uncovered interest parity, $\lambda_t = 0$, and we give scant attention to determinants of the equilibrium long-run level, $\lim_{j\to\infty} E_t(q_{t+j+1})$.

Equation (4) shows that q_t in this case depends only on the behavior of current and expected future real interest rates in the domestic and foreign countries. In sticky-price monetary models, the proximate determinant of ex ante real interest rates is monetary policy. A tight monetary policy increases the real interest rate, and an easy monetary policy lowers it. If real interest rates are positively serially correlated, expected future real interest rates tend to move in the same direction as the current real interest rate. Then a monetary contraction leads to a real appreciation, and monetary easing to a real depreciation.

This is the conclusion reached in the textbook Mundell-Fleming model, in Dornbusch's (1976) classic contribution to the asset-market approach to exchange rates, and in modern New Keynesian models, but this description only presents part of the picture. Real exchange rates and real interest rates are endogenous macroeconomic variables. Their dynamic path, and the determination of expected future real interest rates, depend on the structure of the macroeconomy. There are differences in the structure of the models and in the dynamics of real exchange rates in Dornbusch's approach versus the standard New Keynesian model. The New Keynesian models are derived from optimizing behavior by households and firms under uncertainty, while Dornbusch's model is behavioral and derived under perfect foresight with no shocks except an initial monetary policy surprise. If firms are slow to adjust prices, they must have enough power in the market to set their own prices. They cannot be perfectly competitive price takers. New Keynesian models posit that firms are monopolistic, with the economy populated by many such firms whose products are imperfect substitutes for each other. The models assume that not all firms are able to adjust nominal prices every period. Because firms are monopolists, when they are able to set prices, they set them above average and marginal costs, and earn profits. When the firm subsequently cannot change its price, it is willing to sell the amount demanded (for small enough changes in demand) because the firm makes a profit on each unit sold.

In Dornbusch, the money supply is the instrument of monetary policy, and the price level is determined in the long-run independently of initial prices. In many New Keynesian models, the interest rate is the instrument of monetary policy. Inflation rates are determined in the model, but the price level even in the long-run depends on past prices. Finally, monetary policy is exogenous in the Dornbusch model—it is determined as an exogenous path for the money supply. In many New Keynesian models, the interest rate is set according to a policy rule, where the interest rate reacts to inflation, the output gap and possibly other variables.

We consider here a simple New Keynesian two-country model (the countries are designated Home and Foreign). It assumes uncovered interest parity holds. In terms of equation (1), $\lambda_t = 0$:

$$i_t = i_t^* + E_t s_{t+1} - s_t. \tag{7}$$

Monetary policy sets the interest rate endogenously. A simple Taylor rule for the Home country takes the form:

$$i_t = \tilde{r}_t + \sigma \pi_t + \alpha(i_{t-1} - \tilde{r}_{t-1}) + \varepsilon_t, \quad \sigma + \alpha > 1, \quad 0 \leq \alpha < 1. \tag{8}$$

The Home country policymaker tightens monetary conditions by increasing the nominal short-term interest rate, but it practices interest-rate smoothing so that the current interest rate depends on the previous period's rate. $\tilde{r}_t$ is the "Wicksellian" real interest rate—here it is the real interest rate that would prevail if prices fully adjusted instantaneously. In other words, if the central bank hit its target of zero inflation at all times, and $\varepsilon_t = 0$, it would want i_t to equal $\tilde{r}_t$. ε_t accounts for other influences in setting the interest rate, so that higher values of ε_t mean tighter money. Taking into account the gradual adjustment of the interest rate, the ultimate effect of an increase in inflation on the nominal interest rate is, *ceteris paribus*, equal to $\sigma/(1-\alpha)$. The condition $\sigma + \alpha > 1$ amounts to a condition that an increase in inflation leads policymakers eventually to increase the nominal interest rate more than one for one.

The aggregate relationships in New Keynesian models are derived from the underlying decisions of households and firms. Each country produces a range of products, with each good being produced by a monopolist. In this model, labor markets are competitive and workers are mobile between sectors within an economy.

We assume that the two countries are symmetric, and to keep with a simple example, that they have identical preferences so there is no "home bias" in consumption. π_t is the consumer price index inflation rate, which is the simple average of the inflation rates in the Home country of the goods produced in each country.

We assume the Foreign policymaker follows a rule similar to (8), with the same parameters. Foreign monetary policy targets the Foreign inflation rate, π_t^*, and includes other exogenous factors, ε_t^*. The Foreign policy rule is given by:

$$i_t^* = \tilde{r}_t^* + \sigma \pi_t^* + \alpha(i_{t-1}^* - \tilde{r}_{t-1}^*) + \varepsilon_t^*. \tag{9}$$

Since Home and Foreign consumers have identical preferences, if faced with the same price they would consume the same basket, and purchasing power parity (PPP) would hold all the time. However, we can assume that there is pricing to market that arises from a particular type of nominal price stickiness. Assume that firms set different prices for their goods sold in each country, and each of those prices is sticky in the currency in which it is set—"local-currency pricing" or LCP. This contrasts to the New Keynesian models of Obstfeld and Rogoff (1995a) and Clarida et al. (2002) that assume producers set nominal prices in their own currency, and the law of one price holds. The price of imported goods for consumers then fluctuates with the exchange rate. That type of price stickiness is known as "producer-currency pricing" or PCP.

We assume Calvo price setting. Under this price-setting mechanism, any given firm has a constant hazard rate of changing its two prices in a given period. The firm cannot adjust prices at all during a given period unless it receives a signal that it "won the lottery" and is allowed to change prices in the period. Because preferences are identical, the only source of movements in the real exchange rate is attributable to the LCP price stickiness, which engenders deviations from the law of one price as the nominal exchange rate fluctuates. These deviations are expected to converge toward zero, so long-run purchasing power parity holds.

Consider the evolution of the price for Home firms' goods for sale in the Home market. The log of the aggregate price of these goods is given by

$$p_{Ht} = (1 - \theta)\tilde{p}_{Ht} + \theta p_{Ht-1}. \tag{10}$$

$\tilde{p}_{Ht}$ is the log of the price of firms that reset their price in period t. A fraction $1 - \theta$ reset their price, so equation (10) describes the evolution of the aggregate price of Home goods at Home.

Firms produce output using only labor, so $w_t - a_t$ is the log of the unit cost. w_t is the log of the nominal wage, and a_t is the log of labor productivity. If prices were completely flexible, p_{Ht} would be set equal to $w_t - a_t$ (plus a constant mark-up). With a discount factor of β and a probability θ that the price will not change, the firms that reset prices in time t set them to maximize the expected present discounted value of profits, which implies that (to a log-linear approximation) the optimal price satisfies the recursion:

$$\tilde{p}_{Ht} = (1 - \theta\beta)(w_t - a_t) + \theta\beta E_t \tilde{p}_{Ht+1}. \tag{11}$$

With a bit of manipulation, equations (10) and (11) give us:

$$\pi_{Ht} = \delta(w_t - a_t - p_{Ht}) + \beta E_t \pi_{Ht+1}, \quad \delta \equiv (1 - \theta)(1 - \theta\beta)/\theta, \tag{12}$$

where $\pi_{Ht} \equiv p_{Ht} - p_{Ht-1}$. The larger the probability that a firm will be able to adjust its price, the larger is δ.

The cost per unit in Foreign-currency terms of the Home good is $w_t - s_t - a_t$. Following similar steps as in the derivation of (12), we can find an equation for the evolution of prices of Home goods sold in the Foreign country, priced in Foreign currency, p^*_{Ht}:

$$\pi^*_{Ht} = \delta(w_t - a_t - s_t - p^*_{Ht}) + \beta E_t \pi^*_{Ht+1}, \tag{13}$$

where $\pi^*_{Ht} \equiv p^*_{Ht} - p^*_{Ht-1}$. Then (12) and (13) give us:

$$\pi_{Ht} - \pi^*_{Ht} = \delta(s_t + p^*_{Ht} - p_{Ht}) + \beta E_t(\pi_{Ht+1} - \pi^*_{Ht+1}). \tag{14}$$

In a symmetric model, the deviations from the law of one price are equal for Home- and Foreign-produced goods:

$$p_{Ht} - s_t - p^*_{Ht} = p_{Ft} - s_t - p^*_{Ft}, \tag{15}$$

which also implies

$$p_{Ft} - p_{Ht} = p^*_{Ft} - p^*_{Ht}. \tag{16}$$

Under the assumption of identical preferences, $p_t = (p_{Ht} + p_{Ft})/2$, and $p^*_t = (p^*_{Ht} + p^*_{Ft})/2$. In this case, $\pi_{Ht} - \pi^*_{Ht} = \pi_{Ft} - \pi^*_{Ft} = \pi_t - \pi^*_t$. Also, $q_t \equiv s_t + p^*_t - p_t = s_t + p^*_{Ht} - p_{Ht} = s_t + p^*_{Ft} - p_{Ft}$. We can then derive the relationship:

$$\pi_t - \pi^*_t = \delta q_t + \beta E_t(\pi_{t+1} - \pi^*_{t+1}). \tag{17}$$

Uncovered interest parity, equation (7), along with the Taylor rule, (8), and its Foreign equivalent, (9), and the price adjustment equation (17), allow us to derive a three-equation dynamic system for the real exchange rate, and Home relative to Foreign inflation:[3]

$$E_t z_{t+1} = B z_t + w_t, \tag{18}$$

---

[3] In this derivation, we have used the fact that $\tilde{r}^*_t - \tilde{r}_t = 0$. The difference in the Wicksellian real interest rates equals the expected change in the real exchange rate under flexible prices, which here is zero given identical preferences.

$$\text{where } z_t = \begin{bmatrix} \pi_t - \pi_t^* \\ q_t \\ i_{t-1} - i_{t-1}^* \end{bmatrix}, \ w_t = \begin{bmatrix} 0 \\ \varepsilon_t - \varepsilon_t^* \\ \varepsilon_t - \varepsilon_t^* \end{bmatrix}, \ B = \begin{bmatrix} 1/\beta & -\delta/\beta & 0 \\ (\sigma\beta - 1)/\beta & (\beta + \delta)/\beta & \alpha \\ \sigma & 0 & \alpha \end{bmatrix}.$$

At time t, only one element of z_t is predetermined. Both $\pi_t - \pi_t^*$ and q_t may jump in response to contemporaneous Home or Foreign monetary shocks. Algebraically, for the dynamic system (18) to have a unique stable solution, two roots of the matrix B must be greater than one, which requires $\sigma + \alpha > 1$.[4] This is the familiar "Taylor condition" where the central banks ultimately raise nominal interest rates more than one-for-one with an increase in inflation.

The solution to equation (18) in general is somewhat complicated. We will consider some special cases. In the first case, we will assume that the errors to the monetary policy rules are i.i.d. random variables that have mean-zero; i.e., $E_t\varepsilon_{t+j} = E_t\varepsilon_{t+j}^* = 0$ for $j > 0$. We will also make the following assumption on the parameters: $\sigma + \alpha = 1/\beta$. We make this assumption only because it allows for a simpler algebraic solution, but make two observations. First, this assumption on the parameters does satisfy the condition for a stable unique solution. Second, the equations in (18) can be rewritten under this assumption to give us:

$$i_t - E_t\pi_{t+1} - \left(i_t^* - E_t\pi_{t+1}^*\right) = \left(\frac{\delta}{\beta}\right)q_t + \alpha\left[i_{t-1} - \pi_t - \left(i_{t-1}^* - \pi_t^*\right)\right] + \varepsilon_t - \varepsilon_t^*. \quad (19)$$

We can interpret this equation as saying that the Home less the Foreign real interest rate is set by policymakers to rise when there is a home real depreciation (an increase in q_t). There is real interest-rate smoothing in which the ex ante real interest rate at time t responds to the lagged ex post real interest rate. Under this assumption on parameters, the eigenvalues of the matrix B in equation (18) are given by $1/\beta$, μ_1, and μ_2, where

$$\mu_1 = \frac{1}{2}\left(1 + \alpha + \delta/\beta + \sqrt{(1 + \alpha + \delta/\beta)^2 - 4\alpha}\right) > 1,$$

and $\mu_2 = \alpha/\mu_1 < 1$.

The solution for the real exchange rate in this case is given by:

$$q_t = \mu_2 q_{t-1} + \frac{(1 - \beta)(1 - \alpha\beta) - \delta}{(1 - \alpha\beta)\left[(1 - \beta)(\alpha - \mu_1) + \delta\mu_1\right]}(\varepsilon_t - \varepsilon_t^*). \quad (20)$$

With some labor, it can be shown that the coefficient in front of the monetary shocks is negative. This means that a Home monetary policy contraction (or a Foreign monetary expansion) leads to a Home real appreciation.

The expected rate of convergence of the real exchange rate toward purchasing power parity is determined by the eigenvalue μ_2. We see from (20) that $E_t q_{t+1} = \mu_2 q_t$. Since $\mu_2 = \alpha/\mu_1 < 1$, we have that $\mu_2 \le \alpha$. The real exchange rate can be no more persistent

---

[4] See Blanchard and Kahn (1980) for the method of solving a system of rational expectations difference equations such as (18).

than the degree of interest-rate smoothing. If there is no interest-rate smoothing, the real exchange rate adjusts immediately to its purchasing power parity level even when prices are sticky through movements in the nominal exchange rate. Benigno (2004) first pointed out how real exchange rate persistence might be independent of the sluggishness of price adjustment in a New Keynesian model, and illustrated the role of interest-rate smoothing. We have assumed that the frequency of price adjustment for home and foreign goods is identical. Benigno shows that when the speed of adjustment is different, then relative prices and hence real exchange rates adjust more slowly.

It is also the case that $\mu_2 \leq \theta$, where θ is the probability that a firm's price will not change during the period. In other words, an upper limit for the persistence of the real exchange is given by the persistence of nominal price stickiness. Rogoff (1996) coined the phrase the "purchasing power parity puzzle" to refer to the fact that real exchange rates in advanced countries converge very slowly (an estimated half-life of 3–5 years) yet are very volatile. As we will see, potentially monetary sticky-price models can account for the volatility of the real exchange rate, but the implication of many models is that real exchange rate adjustment should be no more sluggish than nominal price adjustment. It is not plausible that nominal prices have a half-life of 3–5 years, so the models seem incapable of accounting for real exchange rate persistence. One extension of the model is to allow for different preferences in the Home and Foreign countries, allowing the possibility that even in the long-run purchasing power parity does not hold. Let $u_t = \lim_{j \to \infty} E_t(q_{t+j+1})$ be the long-run equilibrium real exchange rate. We can write

$$q_t = (q_t - u_t) + u_t.$$

In the model we have considered so far, $u_t = 0$, but more generally nominal price adjustment may explain persistence in $q_t - u_t$. The overall slow convergence of the real exchange rate might be governed by the persistence of the equilibrium real exchange rate, u_t, so a resolution to the purchasing power parity puzzle may require a fleshed-out model of equilibrium deviations from purchasing power parity.[5]

We move on to another special case of (18). We will allow for persistence in the monetary policy errors, but will now assume there is no interest-rate smoothing, so $\alpha = 0$. In this case, the system (18) reduces to two equations. The inflation differential, $\pi_t - \pi_t^*$ and the real exchange rate, q_t, have forward-looking solutions. Each can be expressed as the sum of two infinite sums. Each infinite sum can be interpreted as a present discounted value of current and expected future exogenous variables, $\varepsilon_t - \varepsilon_t^*$ (the relative errors in the Taylor rules), with the discount factors being the inverses of the two eigenvalues of B. Because the solutions are entirely forward-looking, as we noted above, there is no "endogenous persistence" in the real exchange rate. It will only be persistent if $\varepsilon_t - \varepsilon_t^*$ is persistent.

---

[5] Engel (2000), however, argues that in practice the variance of u_t is so small relative to the variance of $q_t - u_t$ that it cannot plausibly account for the measured persistence of the real exchange rate.

A special case helps to illustrate this point. We can express the solution for q_t very simply in the case in which $\sigma\beta = 1$, the special case of our assumption above that $\sigma + \alpha = 1/\beta$, when $\alpha = 0$:

$$q_t = \frac{-\beta}{\delta+\beta} \sum_{j=0}^{\infty} \left(\frac{\beta}{\delta+\beta}\right)^j E_t(\varepsilon_{t+j} - \varepsilon_{t+j}^*). \qquad (21)$$

The dynamics of q_t are determined by the dynamics of $\varepsilon_t - \varepsilon_t^*$. For example, suppose $\varepsilon_t - \varepsilon_t^*$ follows a first-autocorrelation, with an autocorrelation coefficient of ρ_ε, (and $0 < \rho_\varepsilon < 1$). The solution for the real exchange rate is given by:

$$q_t = -\frac{\beta}{\delta+(1-\rho_\varepsilon)\beta}(\varepsilon_t - \varepsilon_t^*). \qquad (22)$$

In this relationship, q_t follows a first-order autoregression, and its persistence is determined by the persistence of $\varepsilon_t - \varepsilon_t^*$.

The sluggishness of prices does not affect the persistence of the real exchange rate in this New Keynesian model, but stickier prices do lead to a more volatile exchange rate. A smaller value of δ indicates less frequent price adjustment. From equation (22), we can see that smaller δ leads to a higher variance of q_t. A smaller δ in equation (21) increases the weight on expected future fundamentals in the discounted sum, which magnifies the effect of a change in those fundamentals on the real exchange rate.

We must find a solution for $\pi_t - \pi_t^*$ to get a solution for the nominal exchange rate. Keeping with the case of $\sigma\beta = 1$, we find:

$$\pi_t - \pi_t^* = \delta E_t \sum_{j=0}^{\infty} \beta^j q_{t+j}. \qquad (23)$$

When $\varepsilon_t - \varepsilon_t^*$ follows a first-order auto regression, we have:

$$\pi_t - \pi_t^* = -\left(\frac{\delta\beta}{\delta+\beta(1-\rho_\varepsilon)}\right)\left(\frac{1}{1-\beta\rho_\varepsilon}\right)(\varepsilon_t - \varepsilon_t^*). \qquad (24)$$

We see from (22) and (24) that the real exchange rate and the relative inflation rates are stationary when the exogenous variables are first-order autoregressions.[6] The relative consumer price level, $p_t - p_t^*$, clearly has a unit root. This implies that the nominal exchange rate also has a unit root:

$$s_t = q_t + \pi_t - \pi_t^* + p_{t-1} - p_{t-1}^*. \qquad (25)$$

Combining equation (25) with the solutions for the real exchange rate in (22) and the relative inflation rate in (24) gives a full solution for the nominal exchange rate in terms of the current values of exogenous variables $(\varepsilon_t - \varepsilon_t^*)$ and the lagged endogenous variable, $p_{t-1} - p_{t-1}^*$.

[6] And, more generally, when they are stationary.

While there are many variants of open-economy New Keynesian models, most have not focused on the implications of the model for exchange rate dynamics.[7] Benigno and Benigno (2008) examine the dynamics of the nominal exchange rate in a PCP model similar to the one considered here. They show that when not targeted by monetary policy, the nominal exchange rate will have a unit root. If monetary policy targets a particular level for the nominal exchange rate, it will be stationary. Policy rules that target the real exchange rate or the terms of trade (perhaps indirectly, by targeting output gaps that depend on these variables) will influence the volatility and persistence of those variables.

Betts and Devereux (1996, 2000) examine the implications of LCP for nominal exchange rate behavior. Because prices are set in the buyers' currencies, they are not as sensitive to nominal exchange rates as they are under PCP. As a result, nominal exchange rates have a small effect in the short-run on relative prices faced by consumers. The expenditure-switching effect of exchange rates on demand is diminished. There still may be wealth effects on consumer demand—for example, the profits of Home firms (owned by households) increase in Home currency terms with a depreciation of the Home currency. Or there may be wealth effects operating through the effects of exchange rates on the value of securities that are denominated in either the Home or Foreign currency. Overall, however, the equilibrating role of the exchange rate appears to be smaller under LCP, which in turn means that larger exchange rate changes are required to bring markets into equilibrium. Betts and Devereux find that nominal exchange rates may be substantially more volatile under LCP.[8] Devereux and Engel (2002) push this idea farther by minimizing or eliminating wealth effects through various assumptions. Then they show that the exchange-rate volatility can be unboundedly high, because in the limit the exchange rate is "disconnected" from the real economy.

Obstfeld and Rogoff (2001) coin the term "exchange-rate disconnect" to encapsulate two puzzles. On the one hand, as in the context above, changes in the exchange rate seem to have only small effects on the real economy. Even very large swings in nominal exchange rates in advanced countries seem to have quite small effects on output, inflation, unemployment, and even the trade balance. On the other hand, there seems to be very little evidence that the supposed determinants of exchange rates—monetary policy and the determinants of real income and inflation—can explain exchange rate movements. This is true in two senses: the correlation of the exchange rate with the economic fundamentals is low, and the economic models are not very useful for forecasting changes in the exchange rate. We will return to the latter problem below. As to the contemporaneous

---

[7] Note, however, that the first of the open-economy New Keynesian models, Obstfeld and Rogoff (1995a), emphasizes the comparison of exchange rate dynamics in their model to the Dornbusch model. Kollmann (2001) examines exchange rate dynamics in a model with Calvo price setting. Hau (2000) and Dotsey and Duarte (2008) show how the presence of non-traded goods influences exchange rate dynamics in New Keynesian models. Landry (2009) considers a two-country model with state-dependent pricing, and demonstrates the effects of monetary shocks on exchange rates.

[8] The benchmark is the PCP model of Obstfeld and Rogoff (1995a), which is the original open-economy New Keynesian model.

correlation between exchange rates and fundamentals, some insight can be gotten by considering the solution for the real exchange rate in equation (21). As above, assume that the relative monetary shocks follow a first-order autoregression (define $\varepsilon_t^R \equiv \varepsilon_t - \varepsilon_t^*$):

$$\varepsilon_t^R = \rho_\varepsilon \varepsilon_{t-1}^R + \omega_t, \quad 0 < \rho_\varepsilon < 1. \tag{26}$$

In the solution (22), we assumed in effect that $E_t \omega_{t+j} = 0$ for all $j > 0$, but now we assume that potentially there is a signal at time t of future monetary policy shocks. We assume the signals are uncorrelated with the current and past values of ε_t^R. We find:

$$q_t = -\left(\frac{\beta}{\delta + \beta(1 - \rho_\varepsilon)}\right)\left[\varepsilon_t^R + N_t\right], \quad \text{where} \quad N_t \equiv E_t \sum_{j=1}^{\infty} \left(\frac{\beta}{\delta + \beta}\right)^j \omega_{t+j}. \tag{27}$$

N_t is the component of the real exchange rate that incorporates news about the future. Let q_t^N represent the solution for the real exchange rate when there is news, as in equation (27) and q_t^{NN} be the solution when there is no signal about the future, as in equation (22). Since N_t is uncorrelated with ε_t^R, then clearly

$$\text{var}(q_t^N) > \text{var}(q_t^{NN}). \tag{28}$$

When markets have sources of news beyond the current realization of the economic fundamentals, the variance of the real exchange rate increases. It is also less correlated with the current fundamentals, which follows from the fact that $\text{cov}(q_t^N, \varepsilon_t^R) = \text{cov}(q_t^{NN}, \varepsilon_t^R)$, but $\text{var}(q_t^N) > \text{var}(q_t^{NN})$. Potentially, news plays an important role in accounting for the lack of correlation between the current values of economic fundamentals and the real exchange rate, as with any asset price that is forward-looking.

News may play a smaller role in accounting for real exchange-rate volatility. Equation (28) is an example of the general result (extending Shiller, 1981) that when an asset price is given by a present value of expected fundamentals that are stationary, the variance of the asset price increases when the market has more information about the future. However, West (1988) shows that the variance of innovations (unexpected changes) in the asset price fall when there is more information, a result that does not depend on stationarity of the fundamentals. Maybe even more surprisingly, Engel (2005) shows that the variance of changes in the asset price falls with more information, so that, if the fundamentals are stationary or have a unit root:

$$\text{var}(q_t^N - q_{t-1}^N) < \text{var}(q_t^{NN} - q_{t-1}^{NN}).$$

That is, news can account for a high variance in the real exchange rate, but not for a high variance in the change in the real exchange rate.

In sum, because asset prices (such as exchange rates) are forward-looking, their correlation with the current fundamentals may be low because there is a news component driving the asset price. This same news component can account for a high unconditional variance of the real exchange rate, but not for a high variance in the change in the real exchange rate.

An alternative view of the exchange-rate disconnect puzzle is that exchange rates are driven by noise—something other than the economic fundamentals. Jeanne and Rose (2002) and Devereux and Engel (2002) examine models in which a small amount of noise trading can lead to a sizeable component of exchange rate movements that is unrelated to fundamentals. A related literature examines how order flow aggregates information of different traders. In the models of Evans and Lyons (2002a, 2008), Evans (2002, 2010), and Bacchetta and van Wincoop (2006), this imperfect knowledge, not only of the economic fundamentals but also imperfect knowledge by one agent of another's expectations, leads to fluctuations in exchange rates that are greater than those predicted from simple models based on economic fundamentals.

2.2. Current Account Balances and Exchange Rates

In policy-related work and in older descriptive models, the current account balance is often identified as an important determinant of exchange rates. From a general equilibrium viewpoint, this is difficult to interpret—current account balances and exchange rates are both determined in the macroeconomic system as a whole, and are functions ultimately of exogenous variables. However, there are intuitive links between the two variables that suggest that there might be dynamic relationships between them. As exchange rates change, when goods prices are sticky, relative international costs and prices change, which in turn might influence import demand and export supply. In reverse, to unwind a current account imbalance, some exchange rate adjustment might be required. In addition, current account imbalances lead to changes in wealth in one country relative to another, which might have feedback effects on exchange rates.

A simple generalization to the model presented in the previous section illustrates how these forces might work. Allow "home bias" in consumption—each country's households put a relatively higher weight on consumption of the good produced within their own country:

$$p_t = v p_{Ht} + (1 - v) p_{Ft}, \ p_t^* = v p_{Ft}^* + (1 - v) p_{Ht}^*. \tag{29}$$

Under home bias, $v > 1/2$. Expressing things in terms of inflation:

$$\pi_t = v \pi_{Ht} + (1 - v) \pi_{Ft}, \ \pi_t^* = v \pi_{Ft}^* + (1 - v) \pi_{Ht}^*. \tag{30}$$

Using equations (12) and (13) and their counterparts for pricing of Foreign goods, we obtain:

$$\pi_t - \pi_t^* = \delta(2v - 1)(w_t - s_t - w_t^*) + \delta(q_t - u_t) + \beta E_t(\pi_{t+1} - \pi_{t+1}^*). \tag{31}$$

As in Section 2.1, u_t is the level the real exchange rate would take on if prices were flexible. In this case, $u_t = (2v-1)(a_t-a_t^*)$. Under flexible prices, an increase in Home productivity relative to Foreign reduces the price of Home goods, $p_{Ht} - p_{Ft}$, proportionately. Under home bias, this reduces the relative price of Home's consumption basket, implying an increase in u_t.

Suppose in each country, the utility each period is a power function of consumption, and linear in labor input. In the Home country, for example, this is given by

$$\frac{1}{1-\sigma} C_t^{1-\sigma} - L_t, \quad \sigma > 0,$$

where C_t is consumption and L_t is labor supply. The first-order condition that sets the marginal rate of substitution between consumption and leisure to the real wage is, in logs,

$$w_t = p_t + \sigma c_t. \tag{32}$$

We can now define:

$$\vartheta_t \equiv w_t - s_t - w_t^* = \sigma(c_t - c_t^*) - q_t. \tag{33}$$

The log of the purchasing power of a unit of Home currency is given by $-p_t$, so the log of the marginal utility of consumption of a unit of Home currency for Home consumers is $-\sigma c_t - p_t$. The log of the marginal utility of a unit of Home currency for Foreign consumers is $-\sigma c_t^* - s_t - p_t^*$. So $\sigma(c_t - c_t^*) - q_t$ is the log of the ratio of the marginal utility of consumption of a unit of Home currency for Foreign consumers relative to Home consumers. Similarly, $w_t - s_t - w_t^*$ is the log of the marginal utility of leisure that can be bought for a unit of Home currency, in the Foreign country relative to the Home country. If financial markets are complete, so there is a nominal contingent claim traded for each state of the world, ϑ_t is a constant (set equal to zero when countries have equal wealth). Equation (18) still completely describes the dynamics of the economy when markets are complete, except that q_t in (18) is replaced with $q_t - u_t$. (The relative monetary policy rules in this case are given by $i_t - i_t^* = \tilde{r}_t - \tilde{r}_t^* + \sigma(\pi_t - \pi_t^*)$, where the relative Wicksellian real interest rates equal the expected change in the expected Wicksellian real exchange rate by interest parity: $\tilde{r}_t - \tilde{r}_t^* = E_t u_{t+1} - u_t$.)

When markets are incomplete, ϑ_t, varies over time. ϑ_t is the marginal utility of an additional unit of wealth for Foreign relative to Home households, so it rises when Home wealth rises relative to Foreign wealth. There is a role for current account imbalances to influence the macroeconomy in general, and the exchange rate in particular, because when a country runs a current account imbalance, its net claims on the rest of the world change. *Ceteris paribus*, if Home has a current account surplus at time t, its wealth increases between t and $t+1$, so $\vartheta_{t+1} - \vartheta_t$ will be positive. In the New Keynesian model, higher relative wealth in the Home country is associated with higher relative wages in Home (by equation (33)). An increase in wealth changes the marginal rate of substitution between consumption and leisure, tending to raise consumption and reduce labor supply. This leads to higher relative inflation in the prices of Home-produced goods, which in turn implies higher relative consumer price inflation in the Home country (equation (31)) under home bias. Monetary policymakers react to higher inflation by raising nominal interest rates, which will appreciate the currency. There is a self-equilibrating mechanism at work here. If some exogenous shock depreciates Home's currency in real terms, the current account of Home will rise and it will accumulate claims on the Foreign country. We have described how that real depreciation is reversed as wealth accumulates.

The particular way in which current account balances correlate with exchange rates depends on the specifics of the model—the structure of asset markets and goods markets. The channel through which the current account affects the economy is somewhat different than in the descriptive models of the 1970s. Some models posited a portfolio balance channel—changes in relative wealth affected relative demands for risky assets—but that link is not present under our uncovered interest parity assumption.[9] Another channel in the 1970s models was a link from wealth to money demand. If the money demand includes a wealth term, then current account balances may affect money demand. In contrast, in the New Keynesian model, an increase in wealth affects the marginal utility of leisure. Under our utility specification, the wage is driven up, which increases the relative cost of producing goods in the Home country.

Cavallo and Ghironi (2002) investigate the properties of exchange rates in a New Keynesian model in which asset markets are incomplete in that only nominal non-state-contingent bonds are traded.[10] The set-up of the model is similar to the one described here, except that there is population growth in an overlapping-generations framework as new households are born into the economy. Households maximize utility that depends on consumption of Home and Foreign goods, and there is home bias in preferences. Cavallo and Ghironi assume that the law of one price holds for all goods: goods prices are set in the currency of the producer. There is a quadratic cost to adjusting prices which results in aggregate price dynamics that are identical to those under Calvo pricing. The accumulation of claims on foreigners affects exchange rates through a channel similar to the one described above. However, different assumptions on preferences and monetary policy imply that an accumulation of claims on the Foreign country leads to a Home real depreciation. Cavallo and Ghironi assume identical Home and Foreign preferences, so purchasing power parity holds at all times. However, monetary policy targets domestic output. When wealth increases, labor supply falls, leading to lower Home output and therefore a drop in the Home interest rate, which in turn causes a depreciation.

Ganelli (2005) examines a similar model to trace the effects of fiscal policy on exchange rates. One important difference between Ganelli's model and the New Keynesian models such as Cavallo and Ghironi is that Ganelli assumes that the money supply is the instrument of monetary policy, and that money supply growth is exogenous. Money demand depends on home consumption and the home interest rate. The effects of a fiscal expansion, however, work through familiar channels. A tax cut, for example, leads

---

[9] Blanchard et al. (2005) use such a model to analyze the dynamics of the needed U.S. dollar exchange rate change that might facilitate adjustment of the U.S. current account deficit.

[10] See also Ghironi (2008).

to an expansion in Home demand. Home households expand demand in an overlapping generations framework because they will not bear the full burden of future taxes that must be raised to pay off government debt. The increase in home consumption results in an increase in money demand. For a given Home money supply, interest rates must increase, which leads to a Home currency appreciation.

In a representative agent two-country New Keynesian model with imperfect capital markets, Benigno and Thoenissen (2003) examine the effects of productivity shocks on exchange rates. In this model, there are three factors that influence the behavior of real and nominal exchange rates. First, there are non-traded goods. In the long-run, an increase in productivity in the traded sector leads to a real appreciation through the traditional Balassa-Samuelson effects. Second, there is home bias in preferences. This channel tends to promote a real depreciation in the long-run in response to Home productivity shocks in the traded sector. As supply of the Home good increases, its price relative to Foreign traded goods falls. This reduces the aggregate consumer price level in the Home country relative to the Foreign because Home goods are weighted more heavily in the Home consumption basket (the home bias assumption). These two channels work in opposite directions for the long-run determination of real exchange rates. Third, in the short-run, firms set prices in the currency of consumers. A Home productivity increase leads to higher potential Home output. As potential output rises, inflationary pressures decline, which in turn leads policymakers to reduce interest rates. This reduction in interest rates contributes to a short-run real and nominal Home currency depreciation.

An important related contribution is Gourinchas and Rey (2007). They begin with the accounting identity:

$$NA_{t+1} = R_{t+1}(NA_t + NX_t), \tag{34}$$

where NA_t is the country's net foreign assets, and NX_t refers to net exports. R_{t+1} is the gross return on the country's portfolio of net foreign assets. Imposing a no-Ponzi condition, Gourinchas and Rey then derive an approximation around values in a deterministic economy in which variables may be trending:

$$nxa_t \approx -\sum_{j=1}^{\infty} \rho^j E_t(r_{t+j} + \Delta nx_{t+j}). \tag{35}$$

The specifics of the approximation are complex, but we can think of nxa_t as a weighted sum of the log of foreign assets and the log of exports less a weighted sum of the log of foreign liabilities and the log of imports. Gourinchas and Rey call this the "cyclical external imbalance." Equation (35) tells us that, subject to approximation error, nxa_t should predict perfectly the discounted sum of $r_{t+j} + \Delta nx_{t+j}$, where r_{t+j} is a measure of the return on foreign assets. Equation (35) is derived only from the budget identity (34), and so must hold up to the approximation error.

The equation has the following interpretation. Suppose a country has a negative value for its cyclical external imbalance, perhaps because it is a net debtor. There are two possible sources of adjustment toward cyclical balance. On the one hand, the country could run trade surpluses in the future, which Gourinchas and Rey call the "trade channel." Alternatively, the country may adjust through the "valuation channel": returns on net foreign assets may be higher than average. An important possible avenue for higher expected returns is through currency depreciation.

Equation (35) shows that nxa_t is the market's best forecast of $-\sum_{j=1}^{\infty} \rho^j (r_{t+j} + \Delta nx_{t+j})$. Gourinchas and Rey are particularly interested in the hypothesis that the predictability of this sum arises because of predictability of future returns. Especially relevant for our purposes is the possibility that a particular component of the returns, the currency depreciation, may be predictable. Gourinchas and Rey present several types of empirical evidence that support this hypothesis using data on nxa_t constructed for the U.S., quarterly, 1952:I–2004:I.

Using the methods of Campbell and Shiller (1988), Gourinchas and Rey find that they cannot reject the intertemporal restrictions implied by equation (35). In a sense, this is a test of whether a budget constraint holds (along with the approximations used to derive equation (35)), so perhaps this finding is not surprising. But Gourinchas and Rey go further, to test whether nxa_t can forecast returns and exchange rate changes. Consider their findings for an FDI-weighted U.S. exchange rate. There is evidence of in-sample predictability derived from regressing $s_{t+1} - s_t$ on nxa_t and other controls over the sample, with a finding of a statistically significant coefficient on nxa_t. This predictability remains even over longer horizons. That is, nxa_t is a significant (in-sample) predictor of exchange rate changes over horizons as long as 24 quarters. Moreover, as we will discuss in the next section, they find that nxa_t is able to forecast the change in this dollar exchange rate out of sample.

We next turn to a more comprehensive survey of recent empirical work on exchange rates.

3. EMPIRICAL STUDIES OF EXCHANGE RATES

Much of the earliest empirical work on testing models of exchange rates evaluated models by their in-sample fit. While this work continues to be valuable, ever since the seminal paper of Meese and Rogoff (1983) the "gold standard" for evaluation of exchange-rate models has been their usefulness in predicting exchange rates. We first survey recent in-sample evaluation of exchange-rate models before turning to the out-of-sample exercises.

3.1. In-Sample Exchange-Rate Model Evaluation

We can further divide the within-sample evaluations into methods that rely on single-equation methods (such as in the early work of Frankel, 1979); methods that use VARs (vector autoregressions) or evaluate general equilibrium models; and the approach of using the model's implications about the response of exchange rates to market news.

3.1.1. Single-Equation Empirical Models

Most empirical work on exchange-rate models has focused on finding better tests for uncovering the link, if any, between the monetary fundamentals and exchange rates outlined in the models of Section 2. Few recent papers have looked for new economic variables that are important in accounting for exchange rate movements. As has been noted already, Gourinchas and Rey (2007) have explored the role that external imbalances play in driving exchange rates. Another line of research has related exchange rates for commodity-exporting countries to prices of those commodities. Chen and Rogoff (2003) uncover empirical links between the real exchange rates of Canada, Australia, and New Zealand, and the real prices of commodities that they export (measured as weighted averages of the world prices of commodities, with weights determined by their shares in each country's total commodity exports). Chen et al. (2010) extend this finding with evidence that exchange rates have forecasting power for commodity prices at short horizons in these countries.

A literature has developed that asks whether nominal exchange rates are related in the long-run to the monetary and real variables that the models say are supposed to drive them. Since exchange rates and the fundamentals are non-stationary unit root (I (1)) random variables, the research question has been posed: are exchange rates and the fundamentals cointegrated? A key contribution in this area is Groen (2000). Using a panel of quarterly data for fourteen major currencies from 1973:I to 1994:I with the U.S. dollar, and alternatively the German mark, as numeraire, Groen rejects the null hypothesis that the exchange rate is not cointegrated with relative log money supplies and relative log GDPs. Mark and Sul (2001) use quarterly data for a panel of nineteen countries from 1973:I to 1997:I, and test the null hypothesis that $s_t - (m_t - m_t^*) + (y_t - y_t^*)$ contains a unit root. They consider the U.S., Switzerland, and Japan as numeraire countries, and they strongly reject the null of no cointegration. Rapach and Wohar (2002) find cointegration between U.S. dollar exchange rates and these economic fundamentals using annual data for fourteen countries with samples of over 100 years.[11] Cerra and Saxena (2010) extend the analysis to an unbalanced panel of 98 developing and developed countries with annual data from 1960 to 2004. They find strong evidence for cointegration in their entire sample, as well as sub-samples consisting only of developing and of developed countries.

Tests for cointegration assume a linear process for the adjustment of exchange rates and the economic fundamentals. Several papers have found evidence of nonlinear adjustment—specifically, when the exchange rate is far out of line with its "fundamental value," the exchange rate and fundamentals converge more quickly. Suppose $s_t - f_t$ is stationary, where f_t is a linear combination of economic variables that determine the

---

[11] However, in country by country tests, this paper finds the exchange rate is not cointegrated with fundamentals for Australia, Canada, Denmark, Norway, Sweden, and the U.K.

exchange rate in the long-run. When the absolute value of $s_t - f_t$ is large, the convergence between s_t and f_t may be faster then when $s_t - f_t$ is much smaller. Taylor and Peel (2000), and others, find nonlinear relationships between the exchange rate and $(m_t - m_t^*) - (y_t - y_t^*)$ using various nonlinear models and exchange rates. Taylor and Peel, for example, estimate models for the dollar/pound and dollar/mark exchange rates using quarterly data from 1973:I to 1996:IV. They find evidence to support an exponential smoothed-transition autoregression (ESTAR) specification. Under this specification, the speed of adjustment declines smoothly as $s_t - f_t$ declines to zero.

So far, the discussion has been about the empirical fit of the monetary model. The implication is that monetary policy exogenously sets money supply growth, and the exchange rate is ultimately determined by monetary growth and output growth in one country relative to another. Monetary policy research in the last twenty years has conformed more to the reality that central banks use the interest rate as the policy instrument rather than money supply growth, and that monetary policy is endogenous. The interest rate is set to react to inflation, the output gap, and potentially other important economic variables. The New Keynesian models have developed to analyze open economies under such monetary regimes. Engel and West (2006) and Mark (2009) present similar empirical models based on Taylor rules such as (8) and uncovered interest parity. Both papers emphasize the forward-looking nature of the determinants of exchange rates. Engel and West specify a more sophisticated monetary policy rule than (8), with monetary policy-makers setting interest rates to react to expected inflation, rather than current inflation, in their own countries. In addition to consumer price inflation, central banks in the Home and Foreign country are each concerned about the output gap ($\tilde{y}_t$ and $\tilde{y}_t^*$) in their respective countries. Also they assume at least one of the countries reacts to exchange-rate misalignments, and that purchasing power parity holds in the long-run equilibrium, so that the interest rate responds to movements in the real exchange rate. Then we can specify the Home relative to Foreign monetary policy rules as:

$$i_t - i_t^* = \gamma_q q_t + \gamma_\pi E_t(\pi_{t+1} - \pi_{t+1}^*) + \gamma_y(\tilde{y}_t - \tilde{y}_t^*) + \varepsilon_t. \quad \gamma_q > 0, \gamma_\pi > 1, \gamma_y > 0. \quad (36)$$

By adding and subtracting Home relative to Foreign inflation, uncovered interest parity can be expressed as:

$$i_t - i_t^* = E_t q_{t+1} - q_t + E_t(\pi_{t+1} - \pi_{t+1}^*). \quad (37)$$

Equations (36) and (37) can be two equations in a general equilibrium New Keynesian model. We discuss estimation of general equilibrium models below. To close the system, we would need to add price adjustment equations in each country and equations relating the output gap to the real exchange rate in each country.

Instead, Engel and West substitute (37) into (36) and rearrange to obtain

$$q_t = \frac{1}{1 + \gamma_q} E_t q_{t+1} - \frac{(\gamma_\pi - 1)}{1 + \gamma_q} E_t(\pi_{t+1} - \pi_{t+1}^*) - \frac{\gamma_y}{1 + \gamma_q}(\tilde{y}_t - \tilde{y}_t^*) - \frac{1}{1 + \gamma_q}\varepsilon_t. \quad (38)$$

Then, solving the model forward, we obtain an expression for the real exchange rate in terms of present values of current and expected future relative inflation rates and output gaps (here, assuming ε_t is mean-zero, i.i.d.):

$$
q_t = -\sum_{j=0}^{\infty} \left(\frac{1}{1+\gamma_q}\right)^j E_t \left\{ \frac{(\gamma_\pi - 1)}{1+\gamma_q}(\pi_{t+j+1} - \pi_{t+j+1}^*) + \frac{\gamma_y}{1+\gamma_q}(\tilde{y}_{t+j} - \tilde{y}_{t+j}^*) \right\}
$$

$$
- \frac{1}{1+\gamma_q}\varepsilon_t. \tag{39}
$$

This equation shows that the real exchange rate is determined as a discounted present value of current and expected future output gaps and inflation rates (Home relative to Foreign in both cases). The equation delivers an interesting message: expected higher Home inflation (or expected higher Home output gaps) leads to a Home real appreciation. This surprising relationship holds because of the endogeneity of monetary policy. When expected inflation or the output gap is higher, the central bank raises the interest rate. When the stability condition, $\gamma_\pi > 1$, holds, the interest rate rises sufficiently to increase real interest rates, precipitating a real appreciation.

Engel and West estimate the present value from a VAR that contains relative inflation rates, relative output gaps, and interest rate differentials. Using standard VAR forecasting equations, the forecasted discounted sum is constructed at each point in time. The paper uses monthly data for the U.S. and Germany from 1979:10 to 1998:12. The present value is estimated over this period, then compared with the actual dollar/deutschemark real exchange rate. That paper finds mildly positive support for the model: the model's implied real exchange rate has a correlation of 0.32 with the actual real exchange rate, though the correlation of changes in the model's implied real exchange rate with the actual real exchange rate is only 0.09. Mark's (2009) study uses similar techniques, though the details differ, producing a model real exchange rate for U.S./Germany, quarterly from 1976:I to 2007:III. A key innovation in Mark's study is to allow for a changing monetary policy rule, which the public learns about only over time by observing outcomes of economic variables. While the correlation of the model's implied real exchange rate with the actual real exchange rate is similar to Engel and West's in levels and slightly worse for short-horizon changes, it vastly improves on their fit in two ways. First, the model real exchange rate fit by Mark has volatility that is similar to that of the actual real exchange rate, while Engel and West's implied real exchange rate is much less volatile. Second, Mark's implied real exchange rate has relatively high correlation for long-horizon changes, in the range of 0.40.

3.1.2. VARs and Structural Macroeconomic Models

An important strand of the empirical literature has attempted to measure the effects of monetary shocks on exchange rates in "structural" vector autoregressions (VARs).

The seminal paper in this literature is Eichenbaum and Evans (1995), which considers a five variable VAR on U.S. data, containing a measure of output, inflation, nonborrowed reserves (assumed to be the policy instrument), U.S. relative to foreign interest rates, and the CPI real exchange rate. For various advanced countries relative to the U.S., Evans and Eichenbaum find that a U.S. monetary contraction leads to higher U.S. interest rates in the short-run. The dollar appreciates in the short-run. The key finding is that the maximum appreciation of the dollar does not occur immediately following the monetary policy shock. Depending on the currency, the maximum real appreciation occurs 24–39 months after the shock.[12]

As Eichenbaum and Evans note, this behavior of exchange rates is not consistent with uncovered interest parity. According to interest parity, if $i_t - i_t^*$ increases, then $E_t s_{t+1} - s_t$ should rise. If all other sources of interest rate variation are held constant and only monetary shocks lead to the increase in $i_t - i_t^*$, then the impulse response of the exchange rate to that shock should show a depreciation of the currency between period t and period $t + 1$. But Eichenbaum and Evans' empirical finding is that the currency continues to appreciate after the initial monetary contraction, contradicting the implications of uncovered interest parity. This phenomenon has been dubbed "delayed overshooting."

Delayed overshooting could potentially account for the empirical puzzle noted at the outset of this chapter, that the slope coefficient in equation (6) is generally estimated to be negative, implying $\mathrm{cov}(E_t s_{t+1} - s_t, i_t - i_t^*) < 0$. The intuition of this line of reasoning is clear: when $i_t - i_t^*$ rise from a monetary shock, if s_t falls and then s_{t+1} falls even more, there is a drop in $s_{t+1} - s_t$ associated with the positive shock to $i_t - i_t^*$. However, it is important to note two caveats. First, monetary shocks are not the only determinant of interest rate and exchange rate movements. Even if monetary shocks tend to lead to a negative correlation of $i_t - i_t^*$ with $s_{t+1} - s_t$, there may be other forces that are important in driving these variables. The second caveat is that, even if monetary shocks are the most important or even the sole driver of exchange rates and interest rates, the logic of the dynamics we have described refers to innovations in $i_t - i_t^*$ and $s_{t+1} - s_t$. Even if innovations in $i_t - i_t^*$ and $s_{t+1} - s_t$ are negatively correlated, we may not have $\mathrm{cov}(E_t s_{t+1} - s_t, i_t - i_t^*) < 0$.

Faust and Rogers (2003) cast doubt on the robustness of the delayed overshooting finding. They argue that there are a large number of plausible assumptions on the structure of VARs that can be used to identify monetary policy shocks. Considering various plausible identification assumptions, and taking into account parameter uncertainty, Faust and Rogers find no robust evidence to support delayed overshooting. Moreover, they conclude that it is unlikely that monetary policy shocks account for very much of the variance of the dollar exchange rate against the U.K. pound or German mark in the 1974:1–1997:12 period.

---

[12] However, Kim and Roubini (2000), using a different identification scheme, find that the maximum appreciation occurs within a few months of the monetary policy shock.

There continues to be a dispute in the literature over whether delayed overshooting is a robust feature of the data. Scholl and Uhlig (2008) use a sign restriction identification scheme and consider a VAR with the same variables as in Eichenbaum and Evans' study. They identify a U.S. monetary contraction by making the following assumptions on the first twelve impulse responses: the impulse response function of nonborrowed reserves (relative to borrowed reserves) is negative; U.S. interest rates relative to foreign interest rates are positive; and, prices are negative. They estimate the model with monthly data over the original Eichenbaum-Evans sample period, as well as a sample that is updated through 2002. In both samples, they find significant delays in the maximal response of the exchange rate, though the maximum delay is somewhat shorter in the longer sample compared to the original sample.

Bjørnland (2009) instead uses long-run restrictions to identify monetary policy shocks. The assumption here is that monetary shocks have no effect on the long-run real exchange rate. Then, in VARs using quarterly data from 1983:I to 2004:IV for four small countries (Australia, Canada, New Zealand, and Sweden), Bjørnland finds that the maximum appreciation in response to a monetary shock occurs within one or two quarters.

The structural VARs are not fully specified dynamic models, in contrast to the general equilibrium New Keynesian models discussed in previous sections. Unfortunately, the New Keynesian models do not seem capable of explaining exchange rate movements. Calibrated versions of the model fail to match the volatility of exchange rates. For example, see Chari et al. (2002) or Jung (2007). Models which include an exogenous (not modeled) shock to the uncovered interest parity relationship, such as Kollmann (2001), Bergin (2006), Adolfson et al. (2007), are more successful in accounting for exchange-rate volatility.

Bergin (2006) performs structural estimation of New Keynesian models using maximum likelihood techniques, while Lubik and Schorfheide (2006) and Adolfson et al. (2007) use Bayesian estimation methods. Both papers find some success with the models in accounting for exchange rate movements. Bergin in particular finds that the model fits the data better than a random-walk model for exchange rates, in the sense that the in-sample one-period ahead forecast of the exchange rate outperforms the random-walk forecast of no change. Moreover, it is not the case that the interest parity shocks are the primary drives of the exchange rate. More than half of the variance in exchange rates in the estimated model is due to monetary shocks. Lubik and Schorfheide (2006) find less encouraging results for the exchange rate, but their model does not allow for endogenous deviations from purchasing power parity. The estimated model of Adolfson et al. (2008) is able to match the persistence and volatility of real exchange rates by allowing time-varying pricing to market.

It is probably a fair assessment that rarely have estimated open-economy New Keynesian models been put to very rigorous tests of their ability to match the data. For example, none of these papers have reported the correlation of the implied model exchange rate with the actual exchange rate. More rigorous tests would include investigation of whether the model can capture the dynamic relationship between exchange rates and other macroeconomic variables, and whether the model is useful in producing forecasts of exchange rates. There are exceptions to this statement, however. Adolfson et al. (2008) considers the ability of a New Keynesian model to forecast real exchange rates compared to several alternative statistical models. It finds the estimated New Keynesian structural model provides the best out-of-sample forecasts (as measured by lowest root mean-squared-error) at horizons of 1–8 quarters.

Juvenal (2011) presents an interesting hybrid between the structural VAR analysis and full model estimation. That paper builds a fully specified New Keynesian model with multiple sources of shocks. Then, Juvenal simulates the model to derive the response of endogenous variables to exogenous shocks. The dynamics of the responses then are used to impose sign restrictions as in the approach of Scholl and Uhlig (2008). Juvenal finds that in fact monetary shocks account for a very small fraction of the variance of real exchange rates, while preference shocks (to the utility discount factor) account for a large fraction. A very similar approach is taken by Enders et al. (2011). The primary focus of the paper is to investigate the effects of government spending and technology shocks on real exchange rates. They find that shocks to government spending lead to a real depreciation while a positive productivity shock in the trade sector leads to a real appreciation. Note that these reactions contrast to the predictions of the models of Ganelli (2005) and Benigno and Thoenissen (2003) discussed above. The reversal in sign of the response is possible within the New Keynesian model when the elasticity of substitution between Home and Foreign goods is sufficiently low and there is home bias in preferences, as in Corsetti et al. (2008). In that case, for example, in the long-run a Home productivity shock must lead to an increase in the price of the Home traded good. This leads to an increase in Home's wealth, which allows them to absorb the increased production of Home goods.

3.1.3. Response to News

The exchange rate is determined in general equilibrium and macroeconomic aggregates such as interest rates and output are not exogenous with respect to the exchange rate. The empirical work of the previous section is all aimed at identifying exogenous shocks—to monetary policy, exchange rates, technology—and tracing the effects of these shocks on exchange rates.

The literature that looks at the effects of news announcements on exchange rates takes another approach to finding exogenous variation. This literature examines exchange rate changes over very short time intervals at the time of news announcements. Over these intervals, the economic fundamentals that drive exchange rates are not likely to have changed much or at all, so that the primary driver of the exchange rate change is the news itself. Take the change in the exchange rate between time $t - \Delta$ and $t + \Delta$ from the Taylor rule model of Engel and West (2006), equation (39). A time period is one month in their model, while Δ is a fraction of an hour. We can write approximately

$$s_{t+\Delta} - s_{t-\Delta} \approx -\sum_{j=1}^{\infty} \left(\frac{1}{1+\gamma_q}\right)^j (E_{t+\Delta} - E_{t-\Delta})$$

$$\times \left\{ \frac{(\gamma_\pi - 1)}{1+\gamma_q}(\pi_{t+j+1} - \pi_{t+j+1}^*) + \frac{\gamma_y}{1+\gamma_q}(\tilde{y}_{t+j} - \tilde{y}_{t+j}^*) \right\}. \quad (40)$$

Because prices of consumer goods do not adjust over very short intervals, the change in the real exchange rate comes exclusively from changes in the nominal exchange rate, so comparing this equation to equation (39), on the left-hand side, the change in q_t is taken to be $s_{t+\Delta} - s_{t-\Delta}$. On the right-hand side, we have assumed that u_t, $\pi_t - \pi_t^*$, and $\tilde{y}_t - \tilde{y}_t^*$ do not change between $t - \Delta$ and $t + \Delta$. The notation $(E_{t+\Delta} - E_{t-\Delta})z_{t+j}$ for any variable z means $E_{t+\Delta}z_{t+j} - E_{t-\Delta}z_{t+j}$. According to (40), the change in the exchange rate over the very short interval is driven only by changes in expectations of future relative inflation rates and output gaps.

As noted above, the Taylor rule model has the implication that higher expected inflation or a higher output gap in the Home country leads to a Home real appreciation, assuming that the central bank follows a sufficiently stabilizing monetary policy ($\gamma_q > 0$, $\gamma_\pi > 1$, $\gamma_y > 0$). This prediction of the Taylor rule model tends to be borne out in empirical work on the impact of news.

The methods of studies of news announcements are all similar. Let x_t be an announcement at time t. Some measure of the expected value of x_t is required in order to measure the news content of the announcement. Typically studies use surveys that ask traders what they expect the announcement to be. Suppose x_t is the announcement in July of the U.S. unemployment rate in June. x_t^e is a survey measure of what traders expect the announced June unemployment number to be. Usually the survey is completed a few days before the announcement. The studies then examine the change in the exchange rate from immediately before to immediately after the announcement, by regressing $s_{t+\Delta} - s_{t-\Delta}$ on $x_t - x_t^e$. This regression is not looking at the change in the June unemployment rate on the exchange rate. Instead, it is looking at the impact effects on the exchange rate of news about unemployment that is contained in the announcement (which comes in July) of the unemployment rate that prevailed the previous month. x_t^e is not a measure of the market's expectation of some future unemployment rate. It is the market's expectation of the announcement of a past unemployment rate.

Andersen et al. (2003) use exchange rate data recorded in five-minute intervals for the U.S. dollar against five major currencies, in the period January, 1992 to December, 1998. They take announcements of 28 American economic variables data on GDP, employment, consumer prices, etc. In addition, they consider the effects on the dollar/deutschemark exchange rate of 13 German economic variables. They measure expectations of the U.S. variables from a survey of 40 money managers, conducted by International Money

Market Services (MMS). Not surprisingly, news that the Federal Reserve has raised its target interest rate above expectations leads to a dollar appreciation within five-minutes of the announcement. But also, any U.S. news that might be interpreted as the economy being stronger than expected, or inflationary pressures greater than expected, also leads to a dollar appreciation. On the other hand, news of greater than expected activity in Germany leads to an immediate dollar depreciation. Andersen et al. (2007) confirm these findings in an extended sample that runs through the end of 2002.

Faust et al. (2007) consider five-minute windows around the announcements of ten U.S. economic variables. They examine the response of dollar exchange rates and interest rates, and use MMS to measure x_t^e. Their data run from January 1987 to December 2002. In all of the statistically significant cases, news that the economy is stronger than expected leads to a dollar appreciation, and an increase in expected future interest rates as captured by the yield curve.

Ehrmann and Fratzscher (2005) make similar findings, for data covering January 1993 to Feburary 2003. They look at the daily changes in the exchange rate, measured at 6 p.m. New York time. They also use MMS to measure x_t^e. In general, they find that good news for the U.S. economy appreciates the dollar, while good news for the German economy appreciates the German currency.

Clarida and Waldman (2008) compare the response of exchange rates to news about inflation rates in countries that explicitly follow inflation-targeting monetary policy to countries that do not. While they find that news of higher than expected inflation tends to appreciate the currency in all countries, the effect is stronger and more statistically significant in the inflation-targeting countries. Moreover, the effect was small and insignificant in two countries (the U.K. and Norway) before they adopted inflation-targeting but became large and significant when the policy regime changed.

Fatum and Scholnick (2006) take a similar approach to these papers, but they do not use MMS to measure the expectation of the markets. Instead, they look at the Fed Funds futures rate as a measure of the expected interest rate. They then look at how day-to-day changes in the exchange rate relate to changes in the Fed Funds futures rate on days in which the actual Fed Funds rate stays constant. The change in the exchange rate might be attributed to changes in expectations of monetary policy. The paper controls for six U.S. economic news announcements, changes in interest rates in other countries, and foreign exchange intervention by foreign central banks. The study looks at the U.S. dollar relative to the yen, pound, and deutschemark from March 1989 to April 2001.[13] The paper finds strong evidence that changes in expectations of future monetary policy affect exchange rates. When the market increases its expectations of the Fed Funds rate, the dollar appreciates.

[13] The end date for the deutschemark is December 1998.

3.2. Out-of-Sample Forecasting

With a few exceptions, the studies surveyed above evaluate the in-sample fit of exchange-rate models. In recent years, tests of the out-of-sample forecasting power of exchange-rate models have become the gold standard for model assessment. The predecessor of this approach is the famous Meese and Rogoff (1983) paper, though that paper actually tested the out-of-sample fit of the models, rather than their forecasting ability. Mark (1995) is the progenitor of the more recent forecasting literature.

3.2.1. Empirical Studies

Mark (1995) hypothesizes that an equation of the form:

$$s_{t+k} - s_t = \alpha_k + \beta_k (f_t - s_t) + u_{k,t+k} \tag{41}$$

will be useful in forecasting the exchange rate at a k-period horizon. f_t is measured as some "fundamental" value of the nominal exchange rate. Mark considers two different candidates for f_t. One is the purchasing power parity value for the exchange rate, $p_t - p_t^*$. The other is taken from the monetary model, assuming money demand has a unitary income elasticity: $m_t - y_t - (m_t^* - y_t^*)$. Equation (41) is not derived from the dynamics of any specific exchange-rate model. Instead, Mark makes the intuitive assumption that f_t represents the long-run equilibrium value for the exchange rate. Equation (41) has the interpretation that, for some unmodeled reasons, the exchange rate is not always equal to its equilibrium value, and between periods t and $t + k$ the log change in the exchange rate will be linearly related to the gap between the exchange rate and its fundamental value at time t. $u_{k,t+k}$ is the error for the kth horizon regression. Equation (41) is a simple equation that can be estimated within a sample, and used to forecast outside the sample.

Mark (1995) makes two uses of the equation. First, the study estimates (41) over the entire sample (quarterly observations from 1973:II to 1993:IV for the U.S., Canada, Germany, Japan, and Switzerland) and tests the null that $\beta_k = 0$. It is the second exercise that has sired the literature on out-of-sample forecasts as a tool for model evaluation. Mark estimates equation (41) for horizons of 1, 4, 8, 12, and 16 quarters, using only the data through 1981:III. The estimated model is then used to construct forecasts of exchange rates, which are compared to the actual exchange rates in the remainder of the sample. Mark calculates the root-mean-squared error (RMSE) of the model forecast compared to the random-walk forecast (of no change in the exchange rate). He finds that for the U.S. dollar exchange rate relative to Germany, Japan, and Switzerland, the forecasting model has lower RMSE at many horizons, and always at the longer horizons (12 and 16 quarters). The model does not beat a random walk for the Canadian dollar exchange rate. Mark evaluates the significance of the forecasting power using Diebold and Mariano (1995) statistics, and bootstrapped statistics, concluding that there is significant evidence of forecasting power.

Mark's (1995) finding that equation (41) can be used to forecast exchange rates, currency-by-currency, out of sample did not hold up well to subsequent investigations.

Kilian (1999) finds that Mark's results are not robust when the sample is extended, and when an error in Mark's bootstrap for the significance of the out-of-sample forecasts is corrected. Faust et al. (2003) re-examined Mark's forecasting model making two changes. First, they introduced the use of "real time" data. Even though Mark estimated the model using data only through 1981:III, and tested the model's ability to forecast exchange rate changes in subsequent periods, Faust et. al. point out that some of the data used by Mark was revised by statistical agencies after the end of the estimation window. That is, the data would not have been available to forecasters in 1981:III. So Faust et. al. use archives of data published in previous years to construct real-time data that would have been available to forecasters. They find that using the real-time data actually tends to produce better forecasts (lower RMSE) than using the revised data. Second, they find that the usefulness of equation (41) for forecasting exchange rates is very sensitive to the time period being examined. The equation loses forecasting power in most time periods except those around the time that Mark's study used.

Cheung et al. (2005) casts further doubt on the forecasts generated by estimation of equation (41) currency-by-currency. In fact, Cheung et. al. consider not only the two measures of f_t that Mark examines, but also measures that include interest rate differentials, trade balances, inflation differentials, and productivity differentials between countries. These other variables are included in various combinations to match single-equation models of the exchange rate that had been proposed in earlier literature. The models do not perform well in out-of-sample RMSE comparisons to the random-walk forecast. While Mark's models of f_t do not require any parameter estimation, Cheung et. al. use rolling sample estimation of the parameters of the models. They consider forecasts at horizons of 1, 4, and 20 quarters, using the same currencies as Mark (1995), using data over the period 1973:II–2000:IV. They look at forecast windows of 1987:II–2000:IV and 1983:II–2000:IV. In general, Cheung et. al. find little consistent evidence of forecasting power of the models. For some models, and some currencies, over some windows, the RMSE of the models' forecasts are lower than the random walk, but there is no consistent evidence that any model can outforecast the random walk consistently for any currency or horizon.[14]

Mark and Sul (2001) find better success using eighteen exchange rates and panel methods to estimate equation (41). In particular, their method forces the slope coefficient in equation (41) to be the same for all exchange rates in the panel, and allows for a common time effect, but allows the intercepts to be different currency-by-currency. Mark and Sul estimate the model for both the monetary and the PPP measures of f_t, allowing alternatively the U.S. dollar, Japanese yen, and Swiss franc to be the numeraire currency. The model is estimated on data from 1973:I to 1983:I, and then used to construct forecasts that can be compared to actual exchange rate data that run through 1997:I. They again compare the RMSE of the model to the RMSE of the random–walk forecast for each

---

[14] See Abhyankar et al. (2005), who use an alternative measure of forecasting performance to find support for the monetary model over a random walk.

exchange rate, and construct bootstrap tests of significance. They find strong forecasting power both at the 1-quarter ahead and 16-quarter ahead horizon, for both models of fundamentals. However, the results are especially favorable for the monetary model, and especially at the longer horizon. At the 16-quarter horizon, the monetary model produces a lower RMSE for seventeen of the eighteen dollar exchange rates, and the improvement over the random walk is significant in fifteen of those cases.

Groen (2005) considers a small panel of exchange rates, involving the euro exchange rates of the yen, Canadian dollar, and U.S. dollar, using data from 1975:I to 2000:IV.[15] Rolling estimates of the model are used to produce forecasts beginning in 1989:I.[16] In comparison with the random walk, the monetary model generally produces forecasts with lower RMSE at horizons of 12–16 months. Groen produces bootstrapped tests of significance that find the model significantly outforecasts the random walk at the 16-month horizon for most currencies.

McCracken and Sapp (2005) employ a test statistic that takes into account the fact that the forecasts generated by equation (41) require estimation of parameters, while the random-walk forecast does not. The parameter uncertainty will tend to increase the RMSE of the model's forecast if the model is true, thus biasing results against the model in comparisons with the random walk. Clark and West (2006) propose a simple test statistic to deal with this bias that has become popular in subsequent papers that test the power of models to beat the random walk in out-of-sample forecasting exercises. McCracken and Sapp find that the corrected statistics offer more power to reject the random walk, using the same sample and bootstrap procedure as Kilian (1999).

Cerra and Saxena (2010) find strong evidence of out-of-sample forecasting power in their panel of 98 countries. Using annual data to estimate the model initially over the 1960–1983 period, and then updating estimates using a rolling window, they find that the monetary model has strong forecasting power at 1- and 5-year horizons. They find that the RMSE of the monetary model is significantly lower (using the Clark-West test) than that of the random walk at both horizons when the model is estimated and tested on the entire panel of countries. Moreover, that forecasting power does not come just from a small subset of countries. The model has forecasting power when fit over different geographical regions, or when countries are grouped together by income levels. The forecasting power holds for both high-inflation and low-inflation subsets of countries.

Engel et al. (2008) update the panel estimates of Mark and Sul (2001) for the monetary and PPP models for U.S. dollar exchange rates against the eighteen countries in the original panel. They also use a model based on Taylor rules, as in Engel and West (2006). They begin by noting that uncovered interest parity says that the interest differential

---

[15] Groen constructs a synthetic euro for the pre-1999 data, and constructs weighted-average money supplies and income levels to use as European fundamentals, although Groen also uses the German variables as an alternative measure in the pre-1999 era.

[16] Groen's model is a vector error-correction model with a slightly different specification than Mark and Sul (2001).

should be an unbiased predictor of exchange rates: $E_t s_{t+1} - s_t = i_t - i_t^*$. In the context of equation (41), this implies that when the forecast horizon is $k = 1$, that $i_t - i_t^* + s_t$ (which is approximately the log of the one-period ahead forward exchange rate) is a candidate for the economic fundamental, f_t. But rather than use the actual interest rate differential, Engel et. al. assume the interest rates are set by Taylor rules as in (36), but replacing expected inflation differentials between t and $t + 1$ with the actual inflation differential between $t - 1$ and t. They set $\gamma_q = 0.1$, $\gamma_y = 0.1$, and $\gamma_\pi = 1.5$, based on Taylor-rule estimates from the literature, implying $f_t = 0.1 q_t + 1.5 E_t(\pi_{t+1} - \pi_{t+1}^*) + 0.1(\tilde{y}_t - \tilde{y}_t^*) + s_t$. They use quarterly data beginning in 1973:I. The models are estimated in-sample, then used to produce 1-quarter and 16-quarter ahead forecasts. The estimation sample is updated recursively to produce forecasts for 1983:I–2005:IV. As in previous studies, the monetary model and PPP model produce significantly better out-of-sample forecasts (using the Clark-West statistic) at the 16-quarter horizon than either the driftless random walk or a random walk with drift (where the estimate of the drift is updated recursively). The Taylor rule model also beats the random walk with drift at the 16-quarter horizon, but not the driftless random walk.

Molodtsova and Papell (2009) use the Taylor rule model to forecast exchange rates one month ahead. However, unlike Engel et al. (2008), Molodtsova and Papell do not impose the coefficients of the Taylor rule. Instead, they estimate a model of the form:

$$s_{t+1} - s_t = \alpha_0 + \alpha_1 \pi_t + \alpha_2 \pi_t^* + \alpha_3 \tilde{y}_t + \alpha_4 \tilde{y}_t^* + \alpha_5 q_t + \alpha_6 i_{t-1} + \alpha_7 i_{t-1}^* + u_t, \qquad (42)$$

with the coefficients unrestricted. In particular, they do not impose any sign restrictions in the model. They argue that since in fact uncovered interest parity does not hold in the data, and many empirical studies find that $s_{t+1} - s_t$ is negatively correlated with $i_t - i_t^*$, we should not impose the signs of the parameters a priori. Equation (42) is estimated over the March 1973–December 1998 period, then used to produce 1-month ahead forecasts for the dollar against twelve different currencies from January 1999 to June 2006. The model is estimated using several different specifications, and using different methods of producing a measure of the output gap in each country. The version of the model that performs best in out-of-sample forecasts produces a significantly lower RMSE than the random walk for nine of the twelve exchange rates. Related papers by Molodtsova et al. (2008, 2011) find the Taylor rule model can forecast the dollar/deutschemark exchange rate in the pre-euro era and dollar/euro exchange rate, using real-time data. Also, Wang and Wu (2012) develop evidence based on forecast intervals that is favorable toward the Taylor rule model.

Gourinchas and Rey (2007) find the approximate measure of the net foreign asset position, nxa_t, from equation (35) can be used to forecast exchange rate changes out of sample. They construct nxa_t beginning with the period 1952:I–1978:I, and use the variable to forecast exchange rate changes from 1 to 16 quarters ahead (for weighted-average dollar exchange rates). They then update the estimate of nxa_t using rolling windows, and construct forecasts for the period up until 2004:I. They find, using the Clark-West statistic, that forecasts based on nxa_t have significantly lower RMSE than the random-walk forecast at all horizons.

3.2.2. Exchange-Rate Forecastability

Is out-of-sample forecasting power a valid way to test exchange-rate models? Engel and West (2005) show that even if the model is true, under some circumstances exchange rates cannot be forecast.

To motivate the class of models they consider, consider a standard monetary model (such as Frankel, 1979) in which money demand equations with identical parameters hold in both the Home and Foreign countries, so we have:

$$m_t - m_t^* - (p_t - p_t^*) = -\gamma(i_t - i_t^*) + v_t - v_t^*. \tag{43}$$

Now take the definition of ex ante excess returns given in equation (1), $\lambda_t \equiv i_t^* + E_t(s_{t+1}) - s_t - i_t$, and assume purchasing power parity holds $(s_t = p_t - p_t^*)$ to arrive at:

$$s_t = (1 - b)(m_t - m_t^* - (v_t - v_t^*)) - b\lambda_t + bE_t s_{t+1}, \quad b \equiv \gamma/(1+\gamma). \tag{44}$$

This model is an example of a typical model in which the exchange rate is determined by some current economic fundamentals $(m_t, m_t^*, v_t, v_t^*, \lambda_t)$ and the expected future exchange rate. The future expected exchange rate is "discounted" by the factor b, where $0 < b < 1$. Some of the fundamental economic variables are multiplied by $1 - b$, but the risk premium is multiplied by b.

The general class of models considered by Engel and West (2005) takes the form:[17]

$$s_t = (1 - b)f_{1t} + bf_{2t} + bE_t s_{t+1}, \quad 0 < b < 1 \tag{45}$$

where f_{1t} and f_{2t} are linear combinations of "fundamental" economic variables that determine the exchange rate. In the example of equation (44), $f_{1t} = m_t - m_t^* - (v_t - v_t^*)$ and $f_{2t} = -\lambda_t$. Engel and West note that many variants of the monetary model, as well as models in which the interest rate is the instrument of monetary policy, take on the form of equation (45). Engel and West assume the solution for the exchange rate in this model is the forward-looking, no-bubbles solution that expresses the exchange rate as a present discounted value (with discount factor b) of current and expected future values of the fundamentals.

Engel and West show that under some circumstances, as the discount factor gets large, the exchange rate approaches a random walk. Formally, they show that $\lim_{b \to 1}(s_{t+1} - s_t)$ is an i.i.d. random variable. There are two possible conditions under which this result holds: (1) $f_{2t} = 0$, and f_{1t} has a unit root (is I (1)); or, (2) $f_{2t} \neq 0$, f_{2t} has a unit root (with no restriction on f_{1t}). The exchange rate will nearly follow a random walk when either there are no f_{2t} variables and the other economic fundamentals have a unit root, or f_{2t} has

---

[17] Constant terms are suppressed in this discussion for simplicity.

a unit root. f_{2t} may include a risk premium, or the error in a Taylor rule equation, such as ε_t in equation (36).

The conditions of the theorem do not require that f_{1t} or f_{2t} themselves be random walks, but only that they have a permanent component. The intuition of the theorem can be gleaned by recognizing that any I (1) random variable can be written as the sum of a pure random walk (call it x_t) and a stationary, I (0), component (call it y_t). Since the exchange rate is the present discounted sum of I (1) fundamentals, it is a present discounted sum of x_t plus y_t. When the discount factor is close to one, expected values of the fundamentals far into the future matter for the exchange rate. $E_t x_{t+j}$ is a random variable even as the horizon j goes to infinity, but $E_t y_{t+j}$ converges to a constant. More and more of the variance of the expected fundamentals in the future is attributable to the random-walk component as the horizon increases. As the discount factor goes to one, the random-walk term dominates the variance of the present value, so the exchange rate approaches the behavior of a variable that is determined simply as the infinite discounted sum of pure random-walk fundamentals—which would behave as a random walk.

The practical question is whether the models actually do imply that the exchange rate is so close to being a random walk that the change in the exchange rate cannot be forecast. If the discount factor is very close to one, or if the fundamentals themselves are very close to being pure random walks, the exchange rate will look very unforecastable. Engel and West turn to implied estimates of the discount factor in various models, and estimates of the serial correlation of the changes in the fundamentals. They show that even with relatively low values for the discount factor and high values for serial correlation of the changes in fundamentals, the change in the exchange rate will exhibit very low serial correlation and low correlation with lagged fundamentals. They also show that even if the fundamentals are I (0), not I (1), the exchange rate will look nearly like a random walk if the largest root driving the fundamental is close to one.

An example in which the fundamentals obey the assumptions of the Engel-West theorem is:

$$f_{1t} - f_{1t-1} = \phi(f_{1t-1} - f_{1t-2}) + \varepsilon_t, \quad 0 < \phi < 1, \tag{46}$$

$$f_{2t} - f_{2t-1} = \eta(f_{2t-1} - f_{2t-2}) + u_t \quad 0 < \eta < 1,$$

where ε_t and u_t are mean-zero, i.i.d. random variables. The solution to the model given in (45) is:

$$s_t - s_{t-1} = \frac{(1-b)\phi}{1-b\phi}(f_{1t-1} - f_{1t-2}) + \frac{1}{1-b\phi}\varepsilon_t$$

$$+ \frac{b\eta}{1-b\eta}(f_{2t-1} - f_{2t-2}) + \frac{b}{(1-b)(1-b\eta)}u_t. \tag{47}$$

In the case in which $f_{2t} = 0$, we can see that as $b \to 1$, $s_t - s_{t-1} \to \frac{1}{1-\phi}\varepsilon_t$. For values of b close to, but not equal to one, $s_t - s_{t-1}$ can be forecast using $f_{1t-1} - f_{1t-2}$, but the forecasting power will be low. When $f_{2t} \neq 0$, as $b \to 1$ the variance of the innovation in $s_t - s_{t-1}$ goes to infinity. For values of b that are nearly equal to one, the term multiplying u_t is very large, so the forecastable component of $s_t - s_{t-1}$ has a very small variance relative to the unforecastable component. It is also clear from this example that the further f_{1t} and f_{2t} are from being random walks—i.e., the larger are ϕ and η—the more forecastable is $s_t - s_{t-1}$ for a given value of b.

Suppose the assumptions on the stochastic processes for the fundamentals in this example apply to the model in equation (44), with $f_{1t} = m_t - m_t^* - (v_t - v_t^*)$, and $f_{2t} = -\lambda_t$. This model assumes that the change in the exchange rate is predictable, because one of the building blocks of the model is $E_t(s_{t+1}) - s_t = i_t - i_t^* + \lambda_t$. Both $i_t - i_t^*$ and λ_t should be useful in forecasting $s_{t+1} - s_t$, so why does the Engel-West theorem tell us the exchange rate is nearly a random walk? We can solve to find:

$$i_t - i_t^* = \frac{(1-b)\phi}{1-b\phi}(f_{1t} - f_{1t-1}) + \frac{1}{1-b\eta}f_{2t} - \frac{b\eta}{1-b\eta}f_{2t-1}, \quad \lambda_t = -f_{2t}.$$

The forecast error is given by

$$s_{t+1} - E_t s_{t+1} = \frac{1}{1-b\phi}\varepsilon_{t+1} + \frac{b}{(1-b)(1-b\eta)}u_{t+1}.$$

In the case of no risk premium ($f_{2t} = 0$), as b approaches one in value, the variance of the forecastable part of $s_{t+1} - s_t$, $\frac{(1-b)\phi}{1-b\phi}(f_{1t} - f_{1t-1})$, relative to the variance of the unforecastable component, $\frac{1}{1-b\phi}\varepsilon_{t+1}$, goes to zero. So even if uncovered interest parity holds, a regression of $s_{t+1} - s_t$ on $i_t - i_t^*$ has a very low R-squared. In fact, West (2012) argues that the estimator of the regression coefficient in this classic regression is inconsistent as $b \to 1$. Even if $f_{2t} \neq 0$, and even if the econometrician could observe the risk premium, the variance of the predictable component of $s_{t+1} - s_t$ relative to the variance of the forecast error goes to zero as $b \to 1$.

Suppose f_{2t} is stationary, but has a root that is close to one in absolute value. For example, replace the stochastic process in the example above with:

$$f_{2t} - \alpha f_{2t-1} = \eta(f_{2t-1} - \alpha f_{2t-2}) + u_t \quad 0 < \eta < 1, \quad 0 < \alpha < 1. \tag{48}$$

Then we find:

$$s_t - s_{t-1} = \frac{(1-b)\phi}{1-b\phi}(f_{1t-1} - f_{1t-2}) + \frac{1}{1-b\phi}\varepsilon_t + \frac{b(\alpha - 1 + \eta(1-b\alpha))}{(1-b\alpha)(1-b\eta)}f_{2t-1}$$

$$- \frac{b(1-b)\alpha\eta}{(1-b\alpha)(1-b\eta)}f_{2t-2} + \frac{b}{(1-b\alpha)(1-b\eta)}u_t. \tag{49}$$

We have that $\lim_{b\to 1}\left(\lim_{\alpha\to 1}(s_{t+1} - s_t)\right)$ is the same as $\lim_{b\to 1}(s_{t+1} - s_t)$ in equation (47). For large enough values of α and b, $s_t - s_{t-1}$ will be approximately i.i.d.

Engel and West suggest an alternative means of assessing the models, instead of the out-of-sample forecasting power. Equation (45) has the forward-looking solution:

$$s_t = (1 - b) \sum_{j=0}^{\infty} b^j (E_t f_{1t+j}) + b \sum_{j=0}^{\infty} b^j (E_t f_{2t+j}). \tag{50}$$

If all of the economic fundamentals, f_{1t} and f_{2t} were observable to the econometrician, the exchange rate itself should provide an optimal forecast of the discounted sum of ex post fundamentals in equation (50). If the data generating processes for the fundamentals can be represented by linear processes, then the method of Campbell and Shiller (1988) can be used to test the model directly. However, Engel and West argue that in the case of exchange-rate models, many of the fundamentals are not measurable, so the Campbell-Shiller method cannot be applied directly. Nonetheless, it might be reasonable to conclude that the exchange rate contains information that is useful in forecasting the observable economic fundamentals. So one testable implication turns the forecastability question on its head—are economic fundamentals forecastable using the exchange rate? Engel and West find some weakly favorable evidence using Granger-causality tests.

In light of the Engel-West theorem, how do we interpret the evidence summarized above that we can use the models to forecast exchange rates at long horizons? Does that mean the models are not true? Or perhaps the conditions of the Engel-West theorem are not satisfied, but then why do the models have success only at long horizons and not short horizons? One answer to these questions is that even the evidence of long-horizon predictability is not unshakeable. As Cheung et al. (2005) demonstrate, it may appear that the exchange rate change is forecastable over some periods, but that outcome may simply be luck. The current evidence of long-run forecastability might be overturned.

Another answer arises from the possibility that there is a driving variable for exchange rates—possibly the ex ante excess return, λ_t—for which the econometrician does not have a measure. If λ_t is persistent but stationary, the change in the exchange rate may be nearly unforecastable in the short-run, but there may be more forecasting power over longer horizons.

If the conditions of the Engel-West theorem are satisfied, there is no reason to expect that long-horizon predictability will be greater than short-horizon. That theorem simply states that $\lim_{b \to 1} (s_{t+1} - s_t)$ is an i.i.d. random variable, which would mean that the change in the exchange rate is unpredictable at all horizons. On the other hand, suppose f_{2t} is a stationary variable. Then from equation (45), we can conclude that s_t and f_{1t} are cointegrated, and that $s_t - f_{1t}$ is stationary. This means that $s_{t+k} - f_{1t+k}$ is predictable at time t, $E_t(s_{t+k} - f_{1t+k})$ converges to a constant. If f_{1t} is an exogenous random variable, then the predictability of $s_{t+k} - f_{1t+k}$ must arise out of our ability to forecast the exchange rate. In other words, if $s_t - f_{1t}$ deviates from its unconditional mean, we can predict that s_t will converge toward the sum of f_{1t} and the unconditional mean of $s_t - f_{1t}$. At very short horizons, the change in the exchange rate may still be nearly unpredictable if f_{2t} is stationary, as example (49) shows. At longer horizons, $s_{t+k} - s_t$ may be predictable because of the convergence of $s_{t+k} - f_{1t+k}$. At the longest horizons, we know $s_{t+k} - s_t$ will be unpredictable because the exchange rate has a unit root.

This logic suggests that if the econometrician observes f_{1t} but not f_{2t}, and estimates Mark's regression (41) using f_{1t} as the measure of the fundamental, a plot of the R-squareds against the horizon k will be hump-shaped. At the shortest and longest horizons, the change in the exchange rate should be almost unpredictable, but at some intermediate horizons there may be some forecasting power. Engel et al. (2008) consider the example in which f_{1t} is a pure random walk, so $\phi = 0$ in equation (46), and f_{2t} follows an AR (1) with serial correlation α, so $\eta = 0$ in equation (48). We can solve to find:

$$s_t = f_{1t} + \frac{b}{1 - b\alpha} f_{2t}. \tag{51}$$

Then we can see that the error-correction term from Mark's regression (41), $f_{1t} - s_t$ is proportional to the unobserved fundamental $f_{2t} : f_{1t} - s_t = \frac{-b}{1-b\alpha} f_{2t}$.

The k-period change in the exchange rate is given by:

$$s_{t+k} - s_t = (1 - \alpha^k)(f_{1t} - s_t) + \sum_{i=1}^{k} \varepsilon_{t+i} + \frac{b}{1 - b\alpha} \sum_{j=1}^{k} \alpha^{k-j} u_{t+j}. \tag{52}$$

The R-squared for the k-horizon regression of $s_{t+k} - s_t$ on $f_{1t} - s_t$ is given by:

$$R_k^2 = \frac{(1 - \alpha^k)^2 \text{var}(u_t)}{2(1 - \alpha^k)\text{var}(u_t) + [k(1 - \alpha^2)(1 - b\alpha)^2/b^2]\text{var}(\varepsilon_t)}. \tag{53}$$

When b and α are large, R_1^2 may be quite small, but R_k^2 may rise to fairly large values before ultimately converging toward zero as $k \to \infty$. For example, if we set $\text{var}(u_t) = \text{var}(\varepsilon_t) = 1$, and set $\alpha = b = 0.95$, we find $R_1^2 \approx 0.025$, so the short-run forecasting power of $f_{1t} - s_t$ is low. At a horizon of 25 periods, the forecasting power has increased to $R_{25}^2 \approx 0.35$. Ultimately a maximum R-squared is reached at the 92-period horizon, $R_{92}^2 \approx 0.473$, and then the forecasting power declines slowly toward zero.

A possible explanation for the finding of low forecasting power at short horizons and higher power at long horizons is a stationary λ_t. Section 4 examines the evidence on the failure of uncovered interest parity empirically, and the theoretical literature that has been built to account for it. As equation (5) shows, λ_t is potentially an important determinant of exchange rates. Before turning to the literature on uncovered interest parity, we turn to the empirical evidence on foreign-exchange market intervention, and exchange-rate regimes. From a theoretical perspective, understanding the factors behind λ_t may be important in understanding channels through which sterilized foreign-exchange intervention can be effective.

3.3. Exchange-Rate Regimes and Exchange-Rate Intervention

The preceding analysis has assumed that exchange rates are floating and determined by market forces. There are many real-world alternatives to fully flexible exchange rates— "hard pegs," monetary union, dollarization, crawling pegs, managed floating, etc.[18]

Both in academic studies and in policymaking circles in the past twenty years, there has been increasing recognition that monetary policy can and perhaps should be defined by the targets of policy. Many central banks have adopted inflation-targeting regimes, in which central banks explicitly announce desired level of inflation that monetary policy tries to achieve. Sometimes central banks implicitly or explicitly adopt "flexible inflation targeting." For example, the inflation rate is targeted but allowed to deviate from the target under exceptional circumstances such as a financial crisis. Other central banks may trade off different goals. For example, the Federal Reserve has a dual mandate to keep inflation low and employment high. In this context, targeting the exchange rate can be seen as one form of flexible inflation targeting. A managed float is simply a form of a monetary policy rule in which an exchange rate target is included.

If sterilized intervention can be used to stabilize exchange rates, policymakers have the luxury of using an instrument separate from monetary policy to achieve their exchange-rate goals. Sterilized intervention may only be available as an independent tool when a country has capital controls in place. In fact, Eichengreen and Razo-Garcia (2006) argue that control of the exchange rate and control of capital flows are ineluctably linked. On the one hand, when capital flows freely between a pair of countries, the well-known "trilemma" tells us that the countries must either have monetary policy that is tightly linked or there must be flexibility in the exchange rate. Eichengreen and Razo-Garcia further argue that it is difficult to maintain floating exchange rates when capital controls are in place. A country that introduces floating exchange rates must cope with currency volatility. Firms with foreign-currency exposure will want to be able to buy financial instruments that hedge their risk. There must be a banking system in place that can provide the forward cover to firms. None of this is very feasible in a country that maintains tight capital controls.

3.3.1. Classification of Exchange-Rate Regimes

The International Monetary Fund (IMF) has maintained an "official" classification of exchange-rate regimes since the breakdown of the Bretton Woods system. It is official in the sense that countries report their exchange-rate regime to the IMF. Since 1999 that classification scheme has included eight categories: no separate legal tender; currency board arrangements; other conventional fixed pegs; horizontal bands; crawling pegs; crawling bands; managed floating with no preannounced path for the exchange

---

[18] See Tavlas et al. (2008) for a discussion of types of exchange-rate regimes, and a survey of the literature on exchange-rate regime classification.

rate; and, independently floating.[19] But the adequacy of the IMF classification scheme has long been questioned. On the one hand, Obstfeld and Rogoff (1995b) noted that countries that are classified as having fixed exchange rates very rarely maintain the same exchange rate peg for as long as five consecutive years. On the other hand, Calvo and Reinhart (2002) find that many countries that claim to have floating exchange rates in fact do not. They often use foreign exchange reserves or interest rates to target exchange rate movements.

These observations have led to some attempts to provide "de facto" (as opposed to "de jure") classification schemes in which the exchange-rate regime is determined by the actual behavior of the policymakers rather than what they claim.

Reinhart and Rogoff (2004) make several adjustments to the official classification of regimes based on the actual performance of exchange rates. One important distinction they make is between the behavior of the official exchange rate and the exchange rate that prevails on black markets. They note that these dual or parallel market rates are much more prevalent than had previously been acknowledged over some periods. In the 1940s and 1950s, they were prevalent in industrialized countries, and they have remained important in developing countries until the present. They also introduce a new category of exchange rates, "freely falling." In countries that have very high inflation, the currency depreciates at a very rapid rate. It is misleading to lump such countries in with those that have stable monetary policy and freely floating rates. For example, if we were interested in assessing the economic performance of countries with different types of exchange-rate regimes, the freely falling group would clearly be outperformed by the stable floaters on many dimensions. They find that the true exchange-rate regime of countries changes frequently. Their basic classification is finer than the IMF official scheme, allowing for fourteen categories: no separate legal tender; preannounced peg or currency board arrangement; preannounced narrow ($\pm 2\%$) horizontal band; de facto peg; preannounced crawling peg; preannounced narrow crawling band; de facto crawling peg; de facto narrow crawling band; preannounced wide crawling band; wider de facto crawling band; narrow non-crawling band; managed floating; freely floating; freely falling.

Shambaugh (2004) goes the other direction from Reinhart and Rogoff, in a sense, by classifying countries either as having pegged exchange rates or being non-peggers. He first determines the base currency against which a country has set its peg, which is where there is a role for judgment. Then a country is classified as a pegger during any given year if its official exchange rate stays within a $\pm 2\%$ band against the base currency. For Shambaugh's set of 155 countries from 1973 to 2000, there are 4388 country/year observations, of which 2220 are coded as pegged.

Levy-Yeyati and Sturzenegger (2003) classify exchange rates into floats, fixed and intermediate regimes for each year from 1974 to 2000 for 183 countries. They first

---

[19] See Hagen and Zhou (2007) for a discussion.

calculate measures of exchange rate movements—the average absolute monthly percentage change over the year and the standard deviation of the monthly percentage change. They also calculate a measure of the volatility of the country's foreign exchange reserves. Then countries are grouped together using a statistical tool called cluster analysis. They form three groupings—ones with high exchange-rate volatility and low reserve volatility, which are classified as floaters; ones with low exchange-rate volatility and high reserve volatility, which are the fixers. Ones with moderate levels of both measures are classified as the intermediate regimes, and ones with low values for all three measures are left unclassified.[20]

These classification schemes have been used to assess economic performance under various exchange-rate regimes. For example,Reinhart and Rogoff (2004) measure how output growth, inflation, and volume of trade (relative to GDP) are influenced by the choice of regime. Levy-Yeyati and Sturzenegger (2003) and Dubas et al. (2010) investigate the effects of exchange-rate regime on growth performance. Shambaugh (2004) and Frankel et al. (2004) consider how the independence of monetary policy is influenced by the regime. Husain et al. (2005) evaluate regimes according to their inflation performance, levels and volatility of output growth, and the probability of banking and currency crises.

3.3.2. Empirical Studies of Sterilized Intervention

Sterilized intervention in foreign exchange markets by central banks or other government agencies presents an empirical and theoretical challenge. Traditionally sterilized intervention is defined as buying and selling of currencies by central banks, with offsetting operations to leave the money supply unchanged. For example, if Bank of Japan buys U.S. dollars with Japanese yen, it sterilizes the foreign exchange operation by selling some of its holdings of Japanese government bonds.[21] Some central banks sell "sterilization bonds," an action that reduces the money supply just as would selling government bonds.

Most central banks no longer target monetary aggregates, so instead, sterilized intervention can be thought of as foreign exchange market activity by the central bank that does not change its target interest rate. The theoretical question that has occupied the literature concerns how sterilized intervention can affect exchange rates if it does not change the interest rate. Consider the first line of equation (5). If the current interest differential, $i_t - i_t^*$, is held constant, there are still three other channels through which intervention might affect the exchange rate: expected future values of the interest differential; current and expected future values of the ex ante excess return, λ_t; and, the long-run expected future exchange rate. We focus on the first two as channels through which sterilized intervention may affect the spot exchange rate.

---

[20] See also Dubas et al. (2010), who use a statistical method for classifying regimes.

[21] The amount of U.S. money in circulation also is ultimately unaffected because the Bank of Japan takes the dollars it has purchased and buys U.S. government bonds.

One hypothesis that has been advanced is that sterilized intervention works by signaling to markets the intention of central banks to change monetary policy in the future, so the intervention changes expected future interest rates.[22] However, to quote Neely (2011), "The literature on intervention has not been kind to the signaling hypothesis. Lewis (1995) and Kaminsky and Lewis (1996) found that intervention generated perverse impacts on monetary policy in their sample. Fatum and Hutchison (1999) found that intervention had no impact on federal funds futures rates."

This leaves changes in current λ_t or $E_t\lambda_{t+j}$ as channels through which intervention can affect foreign exchange rates. We have taken so far a very broad view of the determinants of λ_t, and Section 4 surveys some recent models of the determinants. Here we will briefly consider how intervention could work through three possible determinants of λ_t: a foreign exchange risk premium; imperfections in capital markets; and deviations from the strictest meaning of rational expectations.[23]

The "portfolio balance" channel is one possible way in which intervention could affect λ_t. In this case, λ_t is interpreted as a risk premium rewarded for holding foreign bonds. Intervention changes the supply of assets denominated in different currencies, and so changes their risk characteristics. Imagine again that the Bank of Japan undertakes sterilized intervention that effectively increases the amount of Japanese government bonds and reduces the amount of U.S. government bonds held by the public. In order to induce the public to hold a greater share of their portfolio of assets in the form of Japanese government bonds relative to U.S. bonds, the expected return on Japanese bonds must increase. Investors are rewarded with a risk premium for holding Japanese government bonds.[24]

From a theoretical perspective, generating a portfolio balance effect requires some sophistication in model building. A model with an infinitely lived representative agent that has rational expectations will not allow a role for intervention to affect exchange rates through this channel. In that type of model, the central bank is effectively owned by households—the balance sheet of the central bank is incorporated in the household balance sheet. Consider again the example in which the Bank of Japan sells Japanese government bonds to the public and buys U.S. government bonds. On the one hand, the portfolio held directly by the public becomes more tilted toward Japanese government bonds. On the other hand, the portfolio held by the Bank of Japan has become more tilted toward dollar denominated assets. A dollar depreciation has a smaller effect now on the yen value of assets held by the public, but a larger effect on the yen value of the Bank of Japan's portfolio. If the Bank of Japan suffers a capital loss from dollar depreciation, the loss is ultimately passed onto Japanese taxpayers because the Japanese government must rely more heavily on taxes and less on profits from the central bank to finance expenditures.

---

[22] See Vitale (2003) for a model that explains why a central bank would use foreign exchange intervention to signal future monetary policy.

[23] See Ho (2004) and Pasquariello (2010) for models in which intervention can affect λ_t via a liquidity effect.

[24] See, for example, Dominguez and Frankel (1993).

So while directly households may find their portfolios less exposed to foreign exchange risk, indirectly through the central bank their portfolios are more exposed. On net, Japanese investors with rational expectations will recognize the indirect exposure they have through the central bank, so sterilized intervention will not influence the equilibrium risk premium. This neutrality result can be broken if there is heterogeneity in households, so that the households that bear the ultimate tax burden are in some ways different than investors on average. For example, in a framework of overlapping generations of unrelated households, the burden of taxes is borne by generations that are not yet born and therefore not currently players in international financial markets.[25] From a practical standpoint, it seems unlikely that sterilized intervention could have a large impact on foreign exchange risk premiums for large financially developed economies. The size of sterilized interventions is small compared to the size of outstanding government bonds.[26]

Another possible reason for a wedge between expected returns on Home and Foreign assets is the presence of capital market imperfections. For example, it is widely acknowledged that China can successfully implement sterilized intervention because China has strong controls on both inflows and outflows of capital. Many emerging markets also employ sterilized foreign exchange intervention as a policy tool. Its effectiveness might depend on the presence of capital controls, or on underdevelopment of financial markets. When markets are thin, speculative forces might not strongly move to push expected returns on Home and Foreign assets into equality even if investors are not very averse to foreign exchange risk. If markets are not very liquid, the size of central bank intervention may be large relative to typical market turnover, and therefore have at least a temporary effect on exchange rates. Unfortunately, there is a relative scarcity of studies of foreign exchange intervention in developing countries, primarily because of a lack of data on official intervention. Disyatat and Galati (2007) survey empirical studies of sterilized intervention in emerging markets. They find that in general, foreign exchange intervention has been found to have some weak influence on exchange rates, and that influence is stronger when capital controls are present and markets are thin. In some cases, the intervention also seems to be more effective when there is communication concerning the intervention.

Our definition of λ_t includes a role for deviations of expectations held by the market of the interest rate differentials, $i_{t+j} - i_{t+j}^*$, from the "rational expectation," $E_t(i_{t+j} - i_{t+j}^*)$. In the latter, the expectation is assumed to be the mathematical expectation conditional on all publicly available information. However, expectations of agents in the market might differ from these rational expectations. Perhaps market participants follow rules of thumb in forming expectations, or suffer from overconfidence or other biases. We explore models

---

[25] On the other hand, see Kumhof (2010) for a model in which fiscal policy is influenced by foreign exchange intervention through the effects of exchange rates on government liabilities.

[26] However, see Ito (2003) on the massive interventions by the Bank of Japan in the 1990s. See also Dominguez and Frankel (1993) and Fatum (2010).

based on these deviations from rationality in Section 4.4. Alternatively, there is a large recent literature that considers models in which the market equilibrium exchange rate depends not only on expectations based on publicly available information but also on the aggregation of differential private information. Of particular note in this regard are the studies of Evans and Lyons (2002a, 2008), Evans (2002, 2010), and Bacchetta and van Wincoop (2006, 2010).

Sarno and Taylor (2001) propose a "coordination channel" through which sterilized intervention can affect exchange rates. As in Bacchetta and van Wincoop (2006), agents in financial markets might have imperfect private information about the economic fundamentals. According to the coordination channel model, the central bank undertakes sterilized intervention as a way to coordinate expectations. This channel is then similar to the signaling channel, in that the intervention works through its effects on expectations of future interest rates. Reitz and Taylor (2008) develop a model in which there are "uninformed" traders whose flow demand for foreign exchange depends on a simple rule of thumb, while "informed traders" have a flow demand that depends on their expectations of the current level of the fundamentals. Informed traders do not observe the actual current fundamentals, and become increasingly less confident of their beliefs about the fundamentals the further the exchange rate is from its fundamental value. Intervention can increase the confidence of the fundamentals traders in their information, and therefore lead to greater demand from the informed traders that pushes the exchange rate toward its fundamental value. This type of model explicitly gives a role to flow demand for foreign exchange, rather than asset market equilibrium, in determining exchange rates.[27]

There is a burgeoning literature on central bank communication that examines the contrary idea that the central bank would like to inform the market about the fundamental value of the exchange rate. Jansen and de Haan (2005) conclude that statements by European Central Bank officials have at most a small effect on the mean level of the exchange rate, but have increased its volatility. In contrast, Fratzscher (2006) examines the effects of statements regarding the exchange rate by officials in the U.S., Japan, and the euro area from 1990 to 2003. That study finds that communication does have a small but significant effect in the desired direction on exchange rates. Using impulse response functions, the effect appears to be short-lived. However, the reaction of forward exchange rates suggests that the influence of the communications may be longer-lived, perhaps up to six months. In addition, verbal interventions work to reduce volatility significantly.[28]

Beine et al. (2009) find that actual foreign exchange market interventions are more effective when accompanied by communication. Official statements either confirming or commenting on intervention tend to lead to more significant changes in exchange rates in the desired direction, and to reduce the volatility of exchange rates. This finding

---

[27] See also Dominguez (2003, 2006) for a discussion of the role of foreign exchange intervention in influencing expectations of agents with different information sets.

[28] See also Fratzscher (2008, 2009), which bolster these findings.

is confirmed in studies of dollar/yen interventions (1991–2003), and euro area/yen interventions (1989–2002).

Empirical studies of actual interventions, as well as verbal interventions, are hampered by the simultaneous causality problem. Interventions do not occur randomly, but instead always in reaction to conditions in the foreign exchange market. It is generally believed (see, for example, Sarno and Taylor, 2001) that this simultaneity problem biases studies against finding an effect on exchange rates of intervention. That conclusion makes sense when intervention leans against the wind. That is, when markets are bidding up the value of a currency, any central bank intervention to weaken the currency might only slow down the market tide. After the intervention, the currency might continue to strengthen, but at a slower rate if the intervention is successful. The problem for the econometrician is in determining what would have happened in the absence of the intervention. If the null is that the exchange rate is not expected to change, then in the leaning-against-the-wind scenario, the intervention might appear to have little or no effect on exchange rates when in fact it stifled the market trend. On the other hand, suppose intervention occurs when policymakers believe the currency is misaligned. Then the intervention might appear to be effective when in fact the exchange rate may be returning to its equilibrium because of market forces that are independent of the intervention. In this case, the econometric analysis would tend to overstate the effects of intervention.

It is difficult to find a valid instrument to deal with this simultaneity problem. Almost any variable that is correlated with the intervention is also correlated with the economic factors that drive the exchange rate.[29] One way the literature has attempted to reduce the simultaneity problem is to look at very narrow windows around the time of the intervention. The notion is that within the narrow time period, the direct effects of the intervention are likely to be the most important determinants of the exchange rate movements, and dominate any changes being driven by other market forces. That conclusion is especially tenuous during times of foreign exchange market volatility, when trading activity might be high, but those are exactly the times when intervention is likely to occur. In addition, this approach limits our ability to trace out longer-run effects of foreign exchange intervention. Very few studies have found significant evidence of a sustained effect of sterilized intervention on the level of the exchange rate.

The literature is filled with dozens of recent studies on the effectiveness of intervention. Sarno and Taylor (2001) and Neely (2005) provide surveys of the empirical work. Most of the studies use very short-term data to investigate the effectiveness of intervention. There is almost always evidence that sterilized intervention is effective in changing exchange rates. However, given that the window investigated is very small, it is essentially impossible to ascertain how permanent the effect of intervention is. Typically these studies report that $s_{t+\Delta} - s_t$ responds in the desired direction of the intervention, where

[29] See Kearns and Rigobon (2005) who identify the effects of foreign exchange intervention by claiming that there was an exogenous change in the size of interventions undertaken by many central banks.

Δ is a very small time interval after the intervention. Changes over subsequent short time intervals are generally found to be insignificantly affected. These tests cannot tell us whether the exchange rate is different one week from the time of intervention than it would have been without the intervention. Because of the econometric difficulties of separating out the effects of intervention from other forces driving exchange rates, the empirical studies are not able to provide evidence on whether the policymakers can influence exchange rates over a week, a month, or a quarter with sterilized intervention. Some studies also find that volatility increases at times of intervention. In some cases, the volatility appears to increase prior to the intervention. However, again, simultaneity problems prevail. Does the volatility precipitate the action by the policymaker, so that intervention occurs when markets are volatile? Or does the intervention lead to more volatility, and in some cases cause volatility in anticipation of the intervention?

Despite many empirical studies, it is not clear yet whether sterilized intervention meets the same criteria that regulators use to decide whether to approve a cancer drug—that it is safe and effective.

4. EX ANTE EXCESS RETURNS AND THE UNCOVERED INTEREST PARITY PUZZLE

We have so far focused attention on models of exchange rates in which uncovered interest parity holds. However, we have noted that there are some reasons to suspect that these models are not adequate. First, there is a weak relationship between exchange rates and the economic fundamentals that are supposed to explain them. In a model with uncovered interest parity, exchange rates are related not only to current economic fundamentals but news about future fundamentals, so there may be "disconnect."[30] We have also seen that models based on fundamentals are not able to forecast exchange rates out of sample, although the Engel and West (2005) theorem states that in fact under plausible assumptions if uncovered interest parity holds, the models imply that the exchange rate is nearly unforecastable.[31] However, there is some evidence that exchange rate changes can be forecast at long horizons. One possible way to reconcile the fact that exchange rates are nearly unforecastable at shorter horizons with the long-horizon evidence, is to introduce a stationary but persistent deviation from uncovered interest parity.[32]

4.1. Recent Empirical Evidence

Exchange-rate models that incorporate uncovered interest parity have difficulty accounting for the high volatility of exchange rates across high-income countries. For example, the calibrated variance of the nominal exchange rates in some sticky-price dynamic

---

[30] See the discussion in Section 2.1, concerning equation (27).
[31] See the discussion in Section 3.2
[32] See the discussion in Section 3.2, concerning equations (52) and (53).

stochastic general equilibrium models is too low if the model assumes interest parity. Many models simply assume an exogenous stochastic process for λ_t in equation (1) in order to account for the high volatility.[33] Duarte and Stockman (2005), develop a model in which news drives exchange rates. As in the example given in equation (27), the news leads to a disconnect between the exchange rate and the economic fundamentals. But in their model, the news concerns the foreign exchange risk premium. Their model allows for disconnect to occur because the econometrician does not observe the risk premium, which in turn is time varying because it is driven by news.

One reason the literature has focused on the foreign exchange risk premium is to explain exchange-rate volatility and exchange-rate disconnect.[34] A second reason is the uncovered interest parity puzzle. Equation (6), repeated here for convenience, is the regression estimated by Bilson (1981) and Fama (1984) that tests uncovered interest parity

$$s_{t+1} - s_t = a + b(i_t - i_t^*) + u_{t+1}. \tag{54}$$

Under the null, the regression coefficients should be $a = 0$ and $b = 1$. However, a long history of empirical work has found the estimated value of b to be less than one, and usually less than zero. Hodrick (1987), Froot and Thaler (2001), and Engel (1996) are older surveys of the empirical work, but the puzzle is still present in more recent studies. For example, Burnside et al. (2006) estimate equation (54) for nine currencies against the U.K. pound using monthly data from January 1976 to December 2005. In all cases, the estimated slope coefficient is negative. It is always found to be significantly less than one (at the 5% level of significance), and usually significantly less than zero.[35]

Several recent studies have measured the economic return to taking positions based on the deviation from uncovered interest parity implied by the empirical findings of regression (54). One investment rule is the "carry trade," under which the investor simply takes a long position in the currency with the higher interest rate. Suppose that interest parity does not hold, but that the only time t information that is useful in forecasting the exchange rate is the interest differential, $i_t - i_t^*$. Suppose further that the intercept term in (54) is zero: $a = 0$. Then

$$\lambda_t = i_t^* + E_t s_{t+1} - s_t - i_t = (1 - b)(i_t^* - i_t). \tag{55}$$

As long as $b < 1$, the ex ante excess return on the Foreign bond, λ_t, is positive precisely when $i_t^* > i_t$. If the Foreign interest rate is higher than the Home interest rate, the Foreign deposit has a higher expected return than the Home deposit, and vice versa.

Burnside et al. (2008, 2011c) consider the payoffs to holding portfolios of short-term bonds based on the carry trade. They assess the return to holding an equal-weighted

---

[33] See for example, Kollmann (2004), Adolfson et al. (2007), and Wang (2010).

[34] For example, that is the motivation for Bacchetta and van Wincoop (2006). See also Engel and West (2004) for evidence that observed economic fundamentals can only account for a fraction of the variance of the innovation in exchange rates.

[35] Bekaert and Hodrick (2001) also find evidence of b less than one, but note that statistical problems imply that the confidence interval is wider than generally reported.

portfolio of 23 currencies. The strategy is to borrow in the foreign country and invest in the U.S. when the U.S. interest rate is above the interest rate in each of these countries. When the U.S. interest rate is below the interest rate of the other country, the position is reversed. Burnside et al. (2008) consider monthly returns from January 1976 to June 2007, as well as sub-samples. The mean annualized return on this portfolio is 5.4%, with a Sharpe ratio (the ratio of the average return to the standard deviation of the return) of 0.83. Burnside et al. (2011c) extend the sample period through 2010, and find an average payoff of 4.6%, with a Sharpe ratio of 0.89. Both studies find that the volatility of the return on the carry trade is substantially reduced by holding the portfolio (compared to the average Sharpe ratio for the carry trade for individual currencies).

Lustig and Verdelhan (2007), Brunnermeier et al. (2009), and Lustig et al. (2011) all consider returns to a carry-trade portfolio in which assets are grouped. For example, Lustig and Verdelhan (2007) use exchange rate data and interest rate data for 81 countries to construct portfolios, and measure returns in the 1953–2002 period and the subperiod of 1971–2002. At the beginning of each month, they group the countries into eight equal-sized portfolios, ranked by their interest rate in the previous month relative to the U.S. interest rate, and rebalance the portfolio each month. Then they measure the average ex post annualized returns on a long position in each portfolio. The portfolio with the lowest interest rate (portfolio 1) has an average return of −2.99% in the 1971–2002 period, while the portfolios with the highest (portfolio 8) and next-highest interest rates (portfolio 7) have average returns of 1.48 and 3.94%, respectively. The Sharpe ratios for these three portfolios are −0.38, 0.10, and 0.39. Because the highest interest rate portfolio generally contains some very high-inflation countries, the most interesting comparison might be between the returns on portfolio 7 and portfolio 1. Clearly there is a high return and low standard deviation to the strategy of going long in high-interest rate countries and short in low-interest rate countries.

Jordà and Taylor (2012) suggest augmenting the carry-trade strategy by including economic fundamentals. They argue that the profits from the standard carry-trade strategy (using an equal-weighted portfolio of nine currencies relative to the U.S. dollar) disappeared for many currencies, and were even reversed, in the 2007–2008 period as low-interest rate currencies appreciated strongly. However, a strategy that takes into account not only the interest rate differential but also the deviation of the exchange rate from its "fundamental" level remained profitable over that time span. The fundamental value of the currency is measured as the long-run mean real exchange rate. The trading strategy that appears to be most robust across periods is a threshold one in which trades are only made when the absolute values of the interest differential and the deviation of the real exchange rate exceed certain amounts.

An alternative trading strategy that has been examined is a momentum strategy. Under this strategy, if returns on, say, the Foreign bond were positive in the previous period: $i^*_{t-1} + s_t - s_{t-1} - i_{t-1} > 0$, then the investor should go long in the Foreign asset and short the Home bond. Menkhoff et al. (2012b) and Burnside et al. (2011c) calculate the profits from following this rule. The former paper considers one-month returns for 48 countries relative to the U.S. dollar from January 1976 to January 2010. They report a return on the portfolio of around 10%, and a Sharpe ratio of around 0.95. The latter paper reports somewhat lower expected returns and Sharpe ratios, but ones that are still impressively high.

Burnside et al. (2006, 2011c), and Menkhoff et al. (2012b) investigate whether the excess returns on carry trade or momentum strategies can be explained by traditional risk factors such as the growth rate of real consumption, the market return, the term structure spread, the spread between LIBOR and Treasury rates, etc. None of these factors are correlated with the excess returns from either strategy in foreign exchange markets. On the other hand, Menkhoff et al. (2012a) do find that the returns to the carry trade are correlated with volatility of exchange rates. Sorting currencies into five portfolios as in Lustig and Verdelhan (2007), they find a high average return to the carry trade. They further find that ex post returns for high-interest rate currencies are low during times of high volatility. They interpret this to mean that high-interest rate currencies are risky because they have poor payoffs when a measure of global volatility is high.

Clarida et al. (2009) find regularities similar to those in Menkhoff et al. (2012a). They examine weekly returns of G10 currencies relative to the dollar. They construct carry-trade portfolios that put the investor long in the n currencies with the highest interest rate relative to the U.S. and short in the n lowest return currencies, $n = 1, 2, 3, 4, 5$. They divide their sample into periods of high, medium, and low return volatility for each portfolio using both measures of ex post volatility and volatility implied in options. They find that in the periods of lowest volatility, the slope coefficient in regression (54) is negative, but in the periods of highest volatility, the slope coefficient is positive. High-interest rate currencies pay a low return in volatile times, but a high return during less volatile times. These results also coincide with the conclusions of Brunnermeier et al. (2009) that the gains from the carry-trade unwind during times of "currency crashes," when there are dramatic depreciations of the high-interest rate currencies.

There are some circumstances under which regression (54) does not provide much evidence of deviations from uncovered interest parity. Bansal and Dahlquist (2000) and Frankel and Poonawala (2010) find that the slope coefficient in that regression is much closer to 1 for emerging market currencies relative to the U.S. dollar. Another circumstance in which there is some evidence that uncovered interest parity holds is at longer horizons. Alexius (2001), Chinn and Meredith (2004), and Chinn (2006) all report a regression of long-term changes in exchange rates on long-term interest rate differentials. For example, Chinn (2006) considers a regression of the 10-year change in the log of the exchange rate on the difference in 10-year yields to maturity on quarterly data for Japan, Germany, the U.K., and Canada relative to the U.S. from 1983:I to 2004:IV. The equation is estimated as a panel, imposing the same slope coefficient across currencies. Chinn finds an estimated slope coefficient of 0.708, and cannot reject the null that the slope coefficient equals one. Similar results are found in currency-by-currency regressions, and regressions using 5-year yields.[36]

At the other end of the time spectrum, Chaboud and Wright (2005) find that uncovered interest parity holds well over very short horizons. Specifically, they take into account the fact that a position held during the day does not pay interest, but overnight balances do. A position is deemed to be overnight if it is held past 5 p.m. New York time. So any interest received on a deposit held at 5 p.m. is the same whether the position was held all day or just for a few minutes. The change in the exchange rate from right before until right after 5 p.m. is expected (before 5 p.m.) to equal the interest differential if uncovered interest parity holds. Using data on the Swiss franc, euro, U.K. pound, and yen relative to the dollar, Chaboud and Wright estimate regression (54) for very short time periods that span 5 p.m. New York time. They find that the slope coefficient is nearly one when the time interval is only an hour or two, but as the time interval increases toward six hours and more, the estimated slope coefficient turns negative.

4.2. Risk Premium Models

The most direct explanation for the presence of ex ante expected returns is a risk premium. In this case, the risk is from foreign exchange fluctuations. From the outset, we can recognize that there is something different about the logic of foreign exchange risk premiums from the standard intuition about risk premiums. Consider a two-country framework. For Home agents, the Home short-term bond is riskless, and for the Foreign agent, the Foreign short-term bond is riskless. The Home agent bears foreign exchange risk by holding Foreign bonds, and vice versa. Who should be compensated for bearing foreign exchange risk if all agents can avoid bearing that risk by only holding bonds from their own country?

A key assumption of a useful international model of asset pricing is that different agents get different returns on a given asset. Home agents evaluate nominal returns in units of the Home currency or real returns in units of the Home consumption basket, but Foreign agents evaluate nominal (real) returns in terms of the Foreign currency (consumption basket). This chapter does not allow space for a detailed examination of foreign-exchange risk, and only can touch on the basics that are relevant for understanding the recent economic literature. We briefly review the basic theory of foreign exchange risk premiums and relate the factors driving the risk premium to the state variables driving stochastic discount factors. See, for example, Backus et al. (2001) or Brandt et al. (2006).

Define $D_{t+1} \equiv Q_{t+1}/Q_t$ (and Q_t is the level of the real exchange rate given by $Q_t \equiv \exp(q_t)$), and let $d_{t+1} \equiv q_{t+1} - q_t$. For simplicity, we will assume in this section that inflation rates are zero, so there is no difference between real and nominal returns in each country. We will assume exchange rates are lognormally distributed.

---

[36] In contrast, Bekaert et al. (2007) find no evidence to support the claim that long-horizon uncovered interest parity holds better than short horizon. A related paper is Clarida et al. (2003), which develops evidence that term structure spreads are useful in forecasting short-run changes in exchange rates.

λ_t as defined in equation (1) is technically not the ex ante excess return for any investor. For Home agents, who evaluate returns in Home currency, the expected return on Home bonds compared to Foreign bonds is given by $\lambda_t^H \equiv r_t^* - r_t + E_t d_{t+1} + \frac{1}{2}\text{var}_t d_{t+1}$. Notice that $\lambda_t^H \neq \lambda_t$ because of the convexity term, $\frac{1}{2}\text{var}_t d_{t+1}$. For Foreign investors, the difference between the expected return on Foreign bonds and Home bonds is given by $-\lambda_t^F \equiv r_t^* - r_t + E_t d_{t+1} - \frac{1}{2}\text{var}_t d_{t+1}$. Given the sign convention adopted here, λ_t^F is the risk premium earned by Foreign investors on Home bonds. Under these definitions

$$\lambda_t^H - \frac{1}{2}\text{var}_t d_{t+1} = \lambda_t = -\lambda_t^F + \frac{1}{2}\text{var}_t d_{t+1}. \tag{56}$$

It is possible, in other words, for Home investors to expect a premium for holding Foreign bonds and Foreign investors to expect a premium for holding Home bonds because $\lambda_t^H = \lambda_t + \frac{1}{2}\text{var}_t d_{t+1}$ and $\lambda_t^F = -\lambda_t + \frac{1}{2}\text{var}_t d_{t+1}$. Note that λ_t is the simple average of λ_t^H and $-\lambda_t^F$, so it is the average ex ante risk premium on Foreign bonds.

One of the most famous theorems in asset pricing states that in the absence of opportunities for arbitrage, there exists a stochastic discount factor, M_{t+1} such that the returns on any asset j denominated in units of Home consumption satisfy $1 = E_t(M_{t+1}e^{r_{j,t+1}})$.[37] This condition may look familiar as the first-order condition for an agent that is maximizing intertemporal expected utility. M_{t+1} is the agent's intertemporal marginal rate of substitution. But the theorem is much more general than this setting. It says that in the absence of arbitrage, we can always find a strictly positive random variable M_{t+1} that satisfies this condition. Even if agents are not rational, even if there are plenty of market imperfections, as long as pure arbitrage opportunities do not exist, this condition holds. However, as we shall see, the application of this condition in economic models has indeed been to a setting in which agents maximize utility, and in fact generally one in which there are no market imperfections so that markets are complete.

The models we examine assume that in each country there is a short-term bond whose return is riskless in real terms. Applying this relationship to returns on Home and Foreign riskless real bonds, expressing returns in units of Home consumption, we have:

$$1 = e^{r_t} E_t M_{t+1}, \quad \text{and} \tag{57}$$

$$1 = e^{r_t^*} E_t M_{t+1} D_{t+1}. \tag{58}$$

Under log normality, we can derive from these equations:

$$r_t = -E_t m_{t+1} - \frac{1}{2}\text{var}_t m_{t+1}, \tag{59}$$

$$r_t^* = -E_t m_{t+1} - E_t d_{t+1} - \frac{1}{2}\text{var}_t m_{t+1} - \frac{1}{2}\text{var}_t d_{t+1} - \text{cov}_t(m_{t+1}, d_{t+1}). \tag{60}$$

[37] See Cochrane (2005), for example.

Taking differences, we get

$$\lambda_t = r_t^* - r_t + E_t d_{t+1} = -\frac{1}{2} \mathrm{var}_t d_{t+1} - \mathrm{cov}_t(m_{t+1}, d_{t+1}). \tag{61}$$

For returns expressed in units of the Foreign consumption basket, there exists a stochastic discount factor M_{t+1}^* that satisfies

$$1 = e^{r_t^*} E_t M_{t+1}^*, \tag{62}$$

$$1 = e^{r_t} E_t M_{t+1}^* D_{t+1}^{-1}. \tag{63}$$

Clearly for any M_{t+1} that satisfies (58), there must be an M_{t+1}^* that satisfies (62) defined by $M_{t+1}^* = M_{t+1} D_{t+1}$. Or,

$$d_{t+1} = m_{t+1}^* - m_{t+1}. \tag{64}$$

In general, there is not a unique stochastic discount factor that satisfies equations (57) and (58) for returns in Home units, or (62) and (63) for returns in Foreign units. However, it can be shown that the discount factor is unique when markets are complete. The models we consider in the rest of this subsection assume complete markets.

From the equations above, $\lambda_t^H = -\mathrm{cov}_t(m_{t+1}, d_{t+1})$ and $\lambda_t^F = -\mathrm{cov}_t(m_{t+1}^*, -d_{t+1})$. As with any asset, the excess return is determined by the covariance of the return with the stochastic discount factor. If the foreign exchange return, d_{t+1} is negatively correlated with the Home discount factor, m_{t+1}, Home investors require a compensation for risk so the Foreign security has an excess return relative to the Home bond. For Foreign investors, the foreign exchange return on a Home bond is $-d_{t+1}$. If $-d_{t+1}$ is negatively correlated with the Foreign discount factor, m_{t+1}^*, the Home asset is relatively risky for the Foreign investor. Standard empirical methods do not measure λ_t^H or λ_t^F but instead give us more direct evidence on λ_t.

$$\lambda_t = \frac{\lambda_t^H - \lambda_t^F}{2} = -\mathrm{cov}_t\left(\frac{m_{t+1} + m_{t+1}^*}{2}, d_{t+1}\right). \tag{65}$$

From equation (64), we have

$$E_t d_{t+1} = E_t(m_{t+1}^* - m_{t+1}), \tag{66}$$

and from (65) we find

$$\lambda_t = \frac{1}{2}(\mathrm{var}_t(m_{t+1}) - \mathrm{var}_t(m_{t+1}^*)). \tag{67}$$

From equation (67), it is apparent that if the high–interest rate currency has the riskier bonds, we must have $\mathrm{cov}(r_t - r_t^*, \mathrm{var}_t(m_{t+1}) - \mathrm{var}_t(m_{t+1}^*)) < 0$. A model with this property requires that the variances of the stochastic discount factors be random variables. In the general equilibrium models we discuss, m_t, for example, is related to moments of Home consumption, and so $\text{var}_t(m_{t+1})$ is driven by volatility in the Home country consumption. When $\text{var}_t(m_{t+1}) - \text{var}_t(m^*_{t+1})$ is high, in essence the model must incorporate a precautionary saving effect on interest rates, so that $r_t - r^*_t$ tends to be low.

The no-arbitrage conditions, equations (57)–(58) and (62)–(63) hold under very general conditions, but do not by themselves give us much insight into the economic determinants of the risk premium. We will next turn to two models built on utility-maximizing representative agents with rational expectations in the Home and Foreign countries. In these models, M_{t+1} and M^*_{t+1} are the intertemporal marginal rate of substitutions for Home and Foreign agents, respectively.

Generally, models with standard utility functions are not able to account for the uncovered interest parity puzzle.[38] Some recent papers have employed the representative agent framework, but introduced non-standard preferences. Verdelhan (2010) builds a model based on the Campbell and Cochrane (1999) specification of external habit persistence to explain the familiar uncovered interest parity puzzle. In Verdelhan (2010) there are two symmetric countries. The objective of Home household i is to maximize

$$E_t \sum_{j=0}^{\infty} \beta^j (C_{i,t+j} - H_{t+j})^{1-\gamma}/(1-\gamma), \tag{68}$$

where γ is the coefficient of relative risk aversion, and H_t represents an external habit. H_t is defined implicitly by defining the "surplus," $s_t \equiv \ln\left((C_t - H_t)/C_t\right)$, where C_t is aggregate consumption, and s_t is assumed to follow the stochastic process:

$$s_{t+1} = (1-\phi)\bar{s} + \phi s_t + \mu(s_t)(c_{t+1} - c_t - g), \quad 0 < \phi < 1. \tag{69}$$

Here, ϕ and $\bar{s}$ are parameters, and $c_t \equiv \ln(C_t)$ is assumed to follow a simple random walk with drift, g:

$$c_{t+1} = g + c_t + u_{t+1}, \quad \text{where } u_{t+1} \sim i.i.d.N(0, \sigma^2). \tag{70}$$

$\mu(s_t)$ represents the sensitivity of the surplus to consumption growth, and is given by:

$$\mu(s_t) \equiv \frac{1}{\bar{S}}\sqrt{1 - 2(s_t - \bar{s})} - 1, \quad \text{when } s_t \leq s_{\max}, \quad 0 \text{ elsewhere.} \tag{71}$$

$\bar{S}$ is the steady-state surplus–consumption ratio, and $s_{\max} \equiv \bar{s} + (1 - \bar{S}^2)/2$ is an upper bound on the ratio. The log of the stochastic discount factor is given by:

$$m_{t+1} = \ln(\beta) - \gamma\left[g + (\phi - 1)(s_t - \bar{s}) + (1 + \mu(s_t))(c_{t+1} - c_t - g)\right]. \tag{72}$$

When the parameters $\bar{S}$ and $s_{\max}$ are suitably normalized, Verdelhan shows we can write the expected rate of depreciation as:

$$E_t d_{t+1} = -\gamma(1 - \phi)(s_t - s^*_t), \tag{73}$$

[38] See Bekaert et al. (1997) on this point.

where s_t^* is the Foreign surplus. The excess return is given by:

$$\lambda_t = -(\gamma^2 \sigma^2 / \bar{S}^2)(s_t - s_t^*). \tag{74}$$

From the definition of λ_t, we have $r_t - r_t^* = E_t d_{t+1} - \lambda_t$. Although the empirical evidence that we survey establishes $\text{cov}(s_{t+1} - s_t, i_t - i_t^*) < 0$, a relationship for nominal returns, the theoretical literature is largely built to explain real returns. But it is well known that in advanced low-inflation countries, nominal and real exchange rate changes are highly correlated. To a lesser extent, it is agreed that most of the variation in nominal interest differentials can be attributed to variation in real interest differentials. So the literature builds models to deliver $\text{cov}(d_{t+1}, r_t - r_t^*) < 0$.

Under the assumption of Verdelhan (2010) that $\gamma \left(1 - \phi\right) < \gamma^2 \sigma^2 / \bar{S}^2$, this model can account for the finding that $\text{cov}(d_{t+1}, r_t - r_t^*) < 0$. The key to this assumption is that it delivers $\text{var}(\lambda_t) > \text{var}(E_t d_{t+1})$, which Fama (1984) showed is a necessary condition to account for the uncovered interest parity puzzle. In this model, $E_t d_{t+1}$ and λ_t must be positively correlated, and under the appropriate assumptions λ_t is more volatile than $E_t d_{t+1}$, so the interest differential and $E_t d_{t+1}$ move in opposite directions since $r_t - r_t^* = E_t d_{t+1} - \lambda_t$.[39]

We next turn attention to models based on Epstein and Zin (1989) preferences. Colacito and Croce (2011) have recently applied the model to understand several properties of equity returns, real exchange rates, and consumption. Bansal and Shaliastovich (2012) and Backus et al. (2013) demonstrate how models based on Epstein–Zin preferences can account for the interest-parity anomaly, by delivering $\text{var}(\lambda_t) > \text{var}(E_t d_{t+1})$.

We consider a simplified example based on Bansal and Shaliastovich (2012). In each country, households are assumed to have Epstein–Zin (1989) preferences. The Home agent's utility is defined by the recursive relationship:

$$U_t = \left\{ (1 - \beta) C_t^\rho + \beta \left[E_t \left(U_{t+1}^\alpha \right)^{\rho/\alpha} \right] \right\}^{1/\rho}. \tag{75}$$

In this relationship, β measures the patience of the consumer, $1 - \alpha$ is the degree of relative risk aversion, and $1/(1 - \rho)$ is the intertemporal elasticity of substitution.

Assume an exogenous path for consumption in each country. In the Home country (with $c_t \equiv \ln(C_t)$):

$$c_{t+1} - c_t = \mu + \sqrt{u_t^h} \varepsilon_{t+1}^x. \tag{76}$$

In the Foreign country, we have:

$$c_{t+1}^* - c_t^* = \mu^* + l_t^* + \sqrt{u_t^f} \varepsilon_{t+1}^{*x}. \tag{77}$$

---

[39] Moore and Roche (2002, 2010) also develop a model based on Campbell-Cochrane preferences.

The innovation, ε_{t+1}^x, is distributed *i.i.d.* $N(0, 1)$, but may be correlated with ε_{t+1}^{*x}. Conditional variances are stochastic and follow first-order autoregressive processes:

$$u_{t+1}^i = (1 - \varphi_u^i)\theta_u^i + \varphi_u^i u_t^i + \sigma_u^i \varepsilon_{t+1}^{iu}, \quad i = h, f. \tag{78}$$

Assume for now that the innovations, ε_{t+1}^{iu}, are uncorrelated, distributed *i.i.d.* with mean-zero and unit variance.

We can log-linearize the first-order conditions as in Backus et al. (2013). We will ignore terms that are not time-varying or that do not affect both the conditional means and variances of the stochastic discount factors, lumping those variables into the catchall terms Ξ_t and Ξ_t^*.

The Home discount factor is given by:

$$-m_{t+1} = \gamma_u^r u_t^h + \lambda_x^r \sqrt{u_t^h} \varepsilon_{t+1}^x + \Xi_t. \tag{79}$$

The Foreign discount factor is given by:

$$-m_{t+1}^* = \gamma_u^{*r} u_t^f + \lambda_x^{*r} \sqrt{u_t^f} \varepsilon_{t+1}^{*x} + \Xi_t^*. \tag{80}$$

The parameters in these log-linearizations are:

$$\gamma_u^r = \alpha(\alpha - \rho)/2 \quad \gamma_u^{*r} = \alpha^*(\alpha^* - \rho^*)/2 \quad \lambda_x^r = 1 - \alpha \quad \lambda_x^{*r} = 1 - \alpha^*.$$

Bansal and Shaliastovich (2012) and Backus et al. (2013) assume agents have a preference for "early resolution of risk" in the sense described by Epstein and Zin, so $\alpha < \rho$. They also assume that the intertemporal elasticity of substitution is greater than one, which requires $0 < \rho < 1$. As Bansal and Shaliastovich (2012) explain, these parameter choices are needed in order for this model to account for various asset pricing facts, such as the term structure of interest rates. Further, they assume $\alpha < 0$, in which case the model can generate $\text{cov}(E_t d_{t+1}, r_t - r_t^*) < 0$.

Bansal and Shaliastovich assume identical parameters for Home and Foreign household preferences, and assume identical parameters in the stochastic processes for consumption growth. In this case, we find:

$$E_t d_{t+1} = \gamma_u^r (u_t^h - u_t^f), \tag{81}$$

$$\lambda_t = \frac{1}{2}(\lambda_x^r)^2(u_t^h - u_t^f). \tag{82}$$

Assuming $\alpha < 0$ and $0 < \rho < 1$ as above, we find $\text{cov}(E_t d_{t+1}, r_t - r_t^*) < 0$.

Lustig et al. (2011) consider a version of this model in which idiosyncratic shocks do not play a key role. Instead, it is asymmetric preferences, which imply different loadings on the common factors that deliver the result that $\text{cov}(E_t d_{t+1}, r_t - r_t^*) < 0$. Assume now that u_t^h and u_t^f are common to the Home and Foreign countries, and relabel them u_t^c to indicate a common shock to the variance of output growth. Then

$$E_t d_{t+1} = (\gamma_u^r - \gamma_u^{*r})u_t^c, \tag{83}$$

$$\lambda_t = \frac{1}{2}((\lambda_x^r)^2 - (\lambda_x^{*r})^2)u_t^c. \tag{84}$$

This model can account for $\mathrm{cov}(E_t d_{t+1}, r_t - r_t^*) < 0$ if we assume there is asymmetry in the degree of risk aversion, $\alpha \neq \alpha^*$, but assume $\rho = \rho^*$ and, as above, that $\alpha, \alpha^* < 0$ and $0 < \rho < 1$.

Recent sophisticated extensions of the model with Epstein–Zin preferences are Gourio et al. (2013), Colacito and Croce (2013), and Benigno et al. (2012). The first extends the model by allowing output to be produced using capital and labor, so that agents get utility over both consumption and leisure. They incorporate the possibility of a "disaster"—a very bad outcome for output in both countries. An important assumption in their model is that the two countries have different exposures to the disaster shock, and that the probability of the disaster is time varying. The model is able to account for some of the important empirical regularities, such as a time-varying risk premium, though it does have the implication (counter to the interpretation of the interest parity puzzle) that low-interest rate currencies are riskier.

In all of the general equilibrium models discussed so far, there is no actual trade in output. Home consumers, for example, get utility only from home goods. This greatly simplifies the solution for equilibrium consumption since it must equal equilibrium output (less investment). Colacito and Croce (2013) solve a simple two-country endowment model, in which households in each country consume products produced in both countries, though with a home bias in consumption, putting more weight in utility on goods produced in their own country. They show that the uncovered interest parity puzzle and other real exchange rate anomalies can be reconciled when agents have Epstein–Zin preferences and there is a risky persistent component to output growth. Benigno et al. (2012) also consider a two-country model with home bias in preferences, and, on the production side, a standard New Keynesian model in which a continuum of monopolistic firms produce goods that are imperfect substitutes for other goods produced in the same country. Output is produced using labor, and households get utility from not working. They consider both a neoclassical version of the model with flexible nominal prices and a sticky-price version with Calvo-price setting with firms setting prices in the currency of the country in which they produce. Monetary policy is determined by a simple Taylor rule. There are shocks to productivity and to monetary policy which drive the uncertainty in the economy. They solve the model via an approximation method, and find that under certain parameter assumptions, the model can account for some of the empirical stylized facts. For example, a monetary policy contraction will lead to the delayed overshooting found in Eichenbaum and Evans (1995), and can reproduce the negative correlation of exchange rate changes and interest rate differentials that defines the interest parity puzzle.[40] The model can also reproduce the high volatility of real exchange rates we see in the data, and the model draws a link between volatility and the levels of real exchange rates.

Lustig and Verdelhan (2007) implement a test of the model of Epstein–Zin preferences. Theirs is not a test of the general equilibrium models described above, but, in essence a test of whether expected returns are consistent with the Euler equation for U.S. investors. They consider an extended version of the preferences given in equation (75), where C_t can be interpreted as an aggregate over consumption of nondurable goods, N_t, and durable consumption flows, K_t:

$$C_t = \left[(1 - \varepsilon)N_t^\phi + \varepsilon K_t^\phi\right]^{1/\phi}. \tag{85}$$

They show that the expected excess return for any asset j (the expected return minus the U.S. real interest rate) can be written as:

$$E_t(r_{t+1}^j - r_{t+1}) = b'\Sigma_{fj}. \tag{86}$$

Here, b is a vector of parameters derived from the model. Σ_{fj} is the 3x1 vector of covariances between the "factors," $f_t' = \left[n_t - n_{t-1}, k_t - k_{t-1}, r_t^W\right]$, and $r_t^j - r_t$, where $n_t = \ln(N_t)$, $k_t = \ln(K_t)$, and r_t^W is the log of the U.S. market return. We can rewrite (86) as:

$$E_t(r_{t+1}^j - r_{t+1}) = x'\beta_j, \tag{87}$$

where $x = \Sigma_{ff}b$, $\beta_j = \Sigma_{ff}^{-1}\Sigma_{fj}$, and Σ_{ff} is the variance-covariance matrix of f_t. Lustig and Verdelhan (2007) then follow the standard two-step procedure from the finance literature. We can see from the definition of β_j that it can be estimated by a regression of $r_t^j - r_t$ on f_t, for the time-series of each asset j. They estimate the "factor prices," the elements of x, by doing a cross-section regression of the mean of $r_{t+1}^j - r_{t+1}$ on the "betas" (the estimated β_j) across the carry-trade portfolios described in Section 4.1 above. They find that these betas can explain 87% of the cross-section variation in the average annual return on their eight portfolios.[41]

Alvarez et al. (2009) do assume standard constant relative risk aversion preferences but do not assume a representative agent in each country. Instead, there is a cost to accessing asset markets which varies across individuals in the economy. Agents earn money in the goods market, but must pay a time-varying fixed cost to enter the asset market. Suppose the Home country has an increase in money growth. This leads to inflation, which increases the costs of not participating in the financial market, so more agents enter the financial market. They show that as money growth increases, the variance of the pricing

---

[40] See the discussion in Section 3.1.
[41] However, Burnside (2011) disputes the statistical significance of their estimates, to which Lustig and Verdelhan (2011) reply.

kernel for the agents participating in the market falls. Nominal interest rates rise, thus leading to the conclusion that the foreign exchange risk premium is negatively correlated with the Home less Foreign nominal interest differential.

In the next section, we examine a literature in which agents are heterogeneous in a different way—they have access to different information, and so expectations are not homogenous across all agents.

4.3. Models of Market Dynamics and Market Microstructure

All of the models that we have considered up until this point have assumed a strict form of rational expectations, which includes the assumption that there is a publicly available set of information shared by all agents and no private information. However, a large literature examines cases in which market participants have different sets of information and how that may impact exchange rate dynamics. One important strand of that literature has developed models based on the "microstructure" of foreign exchange markets, highlighting the important role for foreign exchange dealers in aggregating private information.[42] These models show that in an environment in which the exchange rate is determined by orders submitted to traders who then clear the market, order flow—the demand coming from individuals for foreign exchange—will help determine the exchange rate, because the order flow embodies information. Even when underlying demands are determined by portfolio balance, the flows of foreign exchange into and out of markets can play an important role because of their information content. This approach has received empirical support in a number of studies.[43] This literature is large and too complex to survey satisfactorily in a small space. Fortunately, Evans (2011) provides a comprehensive synthesis of this literature.

In this section, we briefly touch on two models of heterogeneous information that can be placed easily into the context of the previous rational expectations models discussed in Section 2. Bacchetta and van Wincoop (2006) consider a monetary model in which agents have symmetric, private information. This model sheds some light on the exchange-rate disconnect puzzle mentioned in Section 2.2.[44] Bacchetta and van Wincoop (2010) build a model in which there are dynamics to information aggregation, which can account for the uncovered interest parity puzzle.[45]

To get some intuition of how private information affects the exchange rate, we work through the simple example in Bacchetta and van Wincoop (2006). Suppose the exchange

---

[42] See the seminal contributions by Evans and Lyons (2002a,b), Evans (2002, 2010), Jeanne and Rose (2002), and Bacchetta and van Wincoop (2006). Also see Devereux and Engel (2002) and Breedon and Vitale (2010).

[43] See, for example, Evans and Lyons (2002a,b, 2005, 2008), Evans (2002, 2010), Froot and Ramadorai (2005), Berger et al. (2008), Breedon and Vitale (2010), Chinn and Moore (2011), and Rime et al. (2010).

[44] See also Bacchetta and van Wincoop (2013) for a model in which there is private information and model uncertainty, which can lead to an unstable relationship between exchange rates and economic fundamentals.

[45] See Bacchetta and van Wincoop (2012) for a survey of these and related papers.

rate is determined by the model in equation (45), repeated here for convenience:

$$s_t = (1 - b)f_{1t} + bf_{2t} + bE_t s_{t+1}. \tag{88}$$

Assume that the first fundamental follows a random walk: $f_{1t+1} = f_{1t} + \varepsilon_{1t+1}$. We will assume ε_{1t} is a $N(0, \sigma_1^2)$, i.i.d. random variable. Assume f_{2t} is simply a $N(0, \sigma_2^2)$, i.i.d. random variable. Clearly the solution for the exchange rate under rational expectations is:

$$s_t = f_{1t} + bf_{2t}. \tag{89}$$

Now suppose there is a public signal (a signal that all agents receive) about $f_{1t+1} : v_t = f_{1t+1} + \varepsilon_{vt}$, where ε_{vt} is a $N(0, \sigma_v^2)$, i.i.d. random variable. In that case, agents in essence have two independent signals about f_{1t+1}. There is v_t, and, assuming they observe f_{1t}, it is an unbiased signal since $f_{1t} = f_{1t+1} - \varepsilon_{1t}$. Given that the signals are independent, $E_t f_{1t+1}$ is a weighted average of the two signals, with the weight on each signal proportional to the inverse of its variance:

$$E_t f_{t+1} = af_{1t} + (1 - a)v_t, \tag{90}$$

where $a = \sigma_1^{-2}/(\sigma_1^{-2} + \sigma_v^{-2})$. From equation (88) iterated one period forward, and taking expectations, we have $E_t s_{t+1} = (1 - b)E_t f_{1t+1} + bE_t f_{2t+1} + bE_t s_{t+2}$. Since markets have no signal about the second fundamental, $E_t f_{2t+1} = 0$. Markets do not have any news about future fundamentals past period $t + 1$, so $E_t f_{t+j} = E_t f_{t+1}$ for $j \geq 1$, which implies that $E_t s_{t+2} = E_t s_{t+1}$ given that f_{1t} follows a random walk. Hence $E_t s_{t+1} = E_t f_{1t+1}$. Using (88) and (90), we find:

$$s_t = (1 - b(1 - a))f_{1t} + b(1 - a)v_t + bf_{2t}. \tag{91}$$

We compare (91) to (89) in a moment, after we derive the equilibrium exchange rate under the assumption of heterogeneous signals. We will use the label "Model 1" to refer to the model with no signal, and "Model 2" to the case of a public signal.

Bacchetta and van Wincoop (2006) build a model in which agents receive a private signal about the future value of the first fundamental: agent i receives the signal $v_t^i = f_{1t+1} + \varepsilon_{vt}^i$, where ε_{vt}^i is a $N(0, \sigma_v^2)$, i.i.d. random variable. We call this "Model 3." In their model, agents are symmetric, so the equilibrium exchange rate is determined by the average expectation of the future exchange rate, $\bar{E}_t s_{t+1}$. Equation (88) is replaced by:

$$s_t = (1 - b)f_{1t} + bf_{2t} + b\bar{E}_t s_{t+1}. \tag{92}$$

Agents in the model are assumed not to observe f_{2t}. In their model, f_{2t} is interpreted as an equilibrium risk premium. The risk premium comes from idiosyncratic "hedging" demands by each agent, but agents receive no signal on the aggregate hedge component.

We can conjecture that the solution to this model is similar to (91). The exchange rate will be a function in equilibrium of f_{1t}, f_{2t} and the average signal, which Bacchetta and van Wincoop assume is equal to the true future value of the first fundamental, $\bar{v}_t = f_{1t+1}$. We can write this in undetermined coefficients form as: $s_t = c_1 f_{1t} + c_2 f_{2t} + c_3 f_{1t+1}$. In this case, the exchange rate itself will provide information about the future fundamentals. Define $g_t \equiv (s_t - c_1 f_{1t})/c_3$.

Then from the undetermined coefficients solution, we see $f_{1t+1} = g_t + \varepsilon_{gt}$, where $\varepsilon_{gt} \equiv -c_2 f_{2t}/c_3$. Here, ε_{gt} is a $N(0, \sigma_g^2)$, i.i.d. random variable, where $\sigma_g^2 = (c_2/c_3)^2 \sigma_2^2$. Each individual has three independent signals about f_{1t+1} : f_{1t}, v_t^i, and g_t. We can write agent i's expectation about f_{1t+1} as a weighted average of those signals, with the weight on each proportional to the inverse of its variance:

$$E_t^i f_{t+1} = a_1 f_{1t} + a_v v_t^i + a_g g_t, \tag{93}$$

where $a_j = \sigma_j^{-2}/(\sigma_1^{-2} + \sigma_v^{-2} + \sigma_g^{-2}), j = 1, v, g$. Averaging across all agents, we get:

$$\bar{E}_t f_{1t+1} = a_1 f_{1t} + a_v f_{1t+1} + a_g g_t. \tag{94}$$

Using the same logic as in the case of a public signal, we can conclude $\bar{E}_t s_{t+1} = \bar{E}_t f_{1t+1}$. Then substituting from (94) into (92), we find:

$$s_t = (1 - b(1 - a_1))f_{1t} + b(1 - a_1)f_{1t+1} + b(1 + (a_g/a_v))f_{2t}. \tag{95}$$

Compare equation (95) to the solution when there is a public signal of f_{1t+1}, given in equation (91). If the public signal were perfect, so that $v_t = f_{1t+1}$, the solutions are almost the same, except that under heterogeneous private information, the weight on f_{2t} is greater. That is because in the private signal case, agents individually do not actually know f_{1t+1}. They try to infer f_{1t+1} based on their information, but they cannot separate out the effects of others' expectations of f_{1t+1} on the exchange rate from the effect of f_{2t}. So when f_{2t} rises, which causes s_t to rise, they attribute some possibility that there has been a permanent increase in f_{1t+1}. Because a permanent increase in the first fundamental has a larger effect on the exchange rate than a transitory increase in the second fundamental in Model 1, this "rational confusion" tends to magnify the effect of an increase in f_{2t} on the exchange rate.

Bacchetta and van Wincoop (2006) use this model to help account for the "disconnect" between exchange rates and fundamentals. This refers to the lack of a relationship that econometricians find between the exchange rate and the economic fundamentals that are supposed to drive the exchange rate according to models. The success of the econometric enterprise depends on the information that is used to explain exchange rates. Define Ω_t to be the econometrician's information set used to explain s_t and let $\sigma^2 \equiv \text{var}(s_t - E(s_t|\Omega_t))$, so that σ^2 is the unexplained exchange-rate variance. We will assume that the econometrician is not able to observe f_{2t}, perhaps because it is an unmeasurable risk premium or other unmeasurable economic fundamental.

First compare Model 1 to Model 2. In Model 1, if f_{2t} is not in Ω_t, $\sigma^2 = b^2 \sigma_2^2$. In Model 2, if f_{2t} is not in Ω_t but f_{1t} and v_t are, then $\sigma^2 = b^2 \sigma_2^2$, just as in Model 1 when

f_{2t} is not observed by the econometrician. However, it is likely that the econometrician will not measure all of the public signals that the market uses, so v_t is also not in Ω_t. Recognizing that $v_t = f_{1t} + \varepsilon_{1t+1} + \varepsilon_{vt}$, we can rewrite (91) as:

$$s_t = f_{1t} + b(1 - a)(\varepsilon_{1t+1} + \varepsilon_{vt}) + bf_{2t}. \tag{96}$$

Then when Ω_t contains only f_{1t}, we find

$$\sigma^2 = b^2 \left[(1 - a)^2(\sigma_1^2 + \sigma_v^2) + \sigma_2^2\right] = b^2 \left[\frac{\sigma_1^4}{\sigma_1^2 + \sigma_v^2} + \sigma_2^2\right]. \tag{97}$$

We see that the more precise the signal about f_{1t+1}, which means smaller σ_v^2, the greater the disconnect for the econometrician. That is because the stronger the signal the market has about f_{1t+1}, the more important is ε_{1t+1} in driving the exchange rate.

Now consider the private information model. If only f_{2t} is excluded from Ω_t, we find that the variance of the econometrician's fit is given by $b^2(1 + (a_g/a_v))^2\sigma_2^2$. This is a larger variance than in Model 1 or Model 2 in the case when only f_{2t} is excluded from Ω_t, and this arises from the fact that the rational confusion causes an excess response of the exchange rate to the unobserved variable f_{2t} in Model 3. Now consider the plausible case in which the econometrician only includes f_{1t} in Ω_t. We can rewrite the solution (54) as

$$s_t = f_{1t} + b(1 - a_1)\varepsilon_{1t+1} + b(1 + (a_g/a_v))f_{2t}. \tag{98}$$

In this case

$$\sigma^2 = b^2 \left[(1 - a_1)^2\sigma_1^2 + (1 + (a_g/a_v))^2\sigma_2^2\right]. \tag{99}$$

With some effort, it can be shown that the variance in expression (99) is larger than the variance in (97)—that is, when signals are private, the variance of the exchange rate that is unexplained by the econometrician is even larger than when signals are public.

A different sort of information heterogeneity arises in Bacchetta and van Wincoop's (2010) model of the uncovered interest parity puzzle. Their model formalizes an idea raised in Froot and Thaler (2001) and developed informally in Eichenbaum and Evans (1995). The notion is that investors may react slowly to changes in financial markets because it is costly to evaluate new information and costly to adjust portfolios continuously.

Suppose, as in Bacchetta and van Wincoop (2010), the short-term interest rate is controlled by monetary policymakers, and follows a simple autoregressive process:

$$i_t - i_t^* = \rho(i_{t-1} - i_{t-1}^*) + u_t, \qquad 0 < \rho < 1. \tag{100}$$

Agents hold portfolios of Home and Foreign bonds, which are imperfect substitutes because of foreign exchange risk. Suppose that the Foreign interest rate rises. *Ceteris paribus*, this leads to an increase in demand for Foreign bonds, which causes the Foreign currency to appreciate. Only some agents, however, enter the market and purchase more Foreign bonds because of the costs of adjustment. The agents that act first will earn an excess return on their Foreign bonds. As time passes, other agents reassess their portfolios and buy foreign bonds, leading to a further appreciation. So, after the initial increase in the Foreign interest rate, the currency appreciates initially but continues to appreciate for some time as the whole market gradually adjusts its portfolio. The early movers might earn a high excess return, but the expected return differential will die out over time. For example, suppose the expected excess return on the Foreign bond has a persistence given by δ:

$$\lambda_t = \delta\lambda_{t-1} - \gamma u_t, \qquad 0 < \delta < 1. \tag{101}$$

Assume u_t has unit variance, and using the fact that $i_t - i_t^* = E_t s_{t+1} - s_t - \lambda_t$, it is straightforward to calculate $\text{cov}(E_t s_{t+1} - s_t, i_t - i_t^*) = \frac{-\gamma}{1-\rho\delta} + \frac{1}{1-\rho^2}$. This will be negative if $\gamma > \frac{1-\rho\delta}{1-\rho^2}$. If the initial reaction of λ_t is large enough, and λ_t is sufficiently persistent relative to the interest differential, the model can deliver the negative correlation of the interest differential with the change in the exchange rate.

If some investors are buying Foreign bonds, who is selling them? Bacchetta and van Wincoop assume that the inactive investors maintain the shares of their wealth invested in Home and Foreign bonds constant in between periods of portfolio rebalancing. Since the Foreign currency has appreciated, the value of Foreign bonds increases for these inactive investors, so they must sell some of those bonds in order to maintain the constant share. The infrequent adjustment of portfolios can be optimal because of the cost of reassessing the optimal portfolio and rebalancing.

4.4. Deviations from Rational Expectations

Perhaps a simpler explanation of the uncovered interest parity puzzle is that even with no private information, agents do not form expectations rationally. It is obvious that one could "hardwire" a model of expectations formation that can account for the empirical failure of uncovered interest parity from regression (54). There are no explicit ground rules for building models of expectations that deviate from rational expectations. Implicitly, the literature has applied two criteria: that the model of expectations is somehow intuitively plausible, and/or that it has other support in the data beyond its ability to account for the interest parity puzzle.

In the spirit of McCallum (1994), we can modify the New Keynesian model of Section 2.2, but assume that the market's expectation of the currency depreciation differs from the rational expectation by a mean-zero, i.i.d. random variable, u_t:

$$\hat{E}_t(s_{t+1} - s_t) = E_t(s_{t+1} - s_t) + u_t, \tag{102}$$

where $\hat{E}_t$ refers to the market's expectation, rather than the rational expectation. This model of expectations has a ring of plausibility. Perhaps agents in the market do not make the effort to calculate the fully rational expectations, so that each period they make an error in expectations formation that has a mean of zero and is not persistent, so the deviation from rational expectations is not systematic.

We can combine this assumption with the price adjustment equation and the monetary policy rule of the New Keynesian model of Section 2.1. We summarize those equations here:

$$\pi_t - \pi_t^* = \delta q_t + \beta E_t(\pi_{t+1} - \pi_{t+1}^*) \tag{103}$$

$$i_t - i_t^* = \sigma(\pi_t - \pi_t^*) + \varepsilon_t - \varepsilon_t^*. \tag{104}$$

Assume uncovered interest parity holds, but using market expectations, so

$$\hat{E}_t(s_{t+1} - s_t) = i_t - i_t^*. \tag{105}$$

Eliminating the interest differential, the system comprised of (102)–(105) can be written

$$E_t z_{t+1} = B z_t + w_t, \tag{106}$$

where $z_t = \begin{bmatrix} \pi_t - \pi_t^* \\ q_t \end{bmatrix}$, $w_t = \begin{bmatrix} 0 \\ \varepsilon_t - \varepsilon_t^* - u_t \end{bmatrix}$, $B = \begin{bmatrix} 1/\beta & -\delta/\beta \\ (\sigma\beta - 1)/\beta & (\beta + \delta)/\beta \end{bmatrix}$.

This system is identical to that of the New Keynesian model, (18), except that $\varepsilon_t - \varepsilon_t^* - u_t$ replaces $\varepsilon_t - \varepsilon_t^*$ in the second element in the w_t vector, and there is no interest-rate smoothing. As in Section 2.1, assume (for purposes of making the solution simpler) that $\sigma\beta = 1$. Also assume ε_t and ε_t^* are serially uncorrelated (so ρ_ε from Section 2.1 equals zero). The solution to (106) is the same as the solution to (18), but replacing $\varepsilon_t - \varepsilon_t^*$ with $\varepsilon_t - \varepsilon_t^* - u_t$. From (24) we have

$$\pi_t - \pi_t^* = -\frac{\delta\beta}{\delta + \beta}(\varepsilon_t - \varepsilon_t^* - u_t). \tag{107}$$

Then from (104) we can solve for the interest differential,

$$i_t - i_t^* = \frac{\delta + \beta - \sigma\delta\beta}{\delta + \beta}(\varepsilon_t - \varepsilon_t^*) + \frac{\sigma\delta\beta}{\delta + \beta}u_t. \tag{108}$$

From (108) as well as (102) and (105), we find

$$E_t s_{t+1} - s_t = \frac{\delta + \beta - \sigma\delta\beta}{\delta + \beta}(\varepsilon_t - \varepsilon_t^* - u_t). \tag{109}$$

Comparing (108) and (109), we see immediately that $E_t(s_{t+1} - s_t) = i_t - i_t^*$ if there are no expectational errors ($u_t = 0$). However, if $\delta + \beta - \sigma\delta\beta > 0$, it is evident that the expectational shock imparts a force that drives $E_t(s_{t+1} - s_t)$ and $i_t - i_t^*$ in opposite directions. If the variance of u_t is sufficiently large relative to the variance of ε_t, this model can even deliver a negative slope coefficient in the familiar interest parity regression, (6).

Even though the deviations from rational expectations in equation (102) are white noise, these errors induce a correlation between the expected change in the exchange rate and the interest differential. Since $E_t(s_{t+1} - s_t) = i_t - i_t^* - u_t$, holding interest rates constant, a positive realization of u_t implies the Home currency is expected (rationally) to appreciate between t and $t + 1$. That is, $E_t(s_{t+1} - s_t)$ falls. In this sticky-price framework, and given the stationarity of the real exchange rate, there must be a real Home depreciation at time t in order to generate the expectation of the appreciation. The Home real depreciation raises Home inflation relative to Foreign inflation, inducing a reaction by policymakers in both countries so that $i_t - i_t^*$ rises, which implies a negative correlation between $E_t(s_{t+1} - s_t)$ and $i_t - i_t^*$.

Burnside et al. (2011b) generate a negative correlation between $E_t(s_{t+1} - s_t)$ and $i_t - i_t^*$ in a monetary model in which agents receive a signal about future growth of the monetary fundamental. The expectational error that agents make is putting too much weight on the signal they receive. Their signal, in other words, is actually less informative than agents believe. This assumption not only sounds plausible, but, as the paper notes, has empirical support in two forms. First, surveys and experimental data tend to confirm traders overweight their private signals. Second, the model of overconfidence is helpful in explaining anomalies in stock and bond markets.

Begin with a present-value model of the type we have discussed in Section 3:

$$s_t = (1 - \beta)f_t + \beta \hat{E}_t s_{t+1}, \quad 0 < \beta < 1, \tag{110}$$

where f_t is the economic fundamental that drives the exchange rate. $\hat{E}_t s_{t+1}$ refers to agents' expectation of s_{t+1}, which does not equal the rational expectation, $E_t s_{t+1}$, in this model. Assume the fundamental evolves according to:

$$f_{t+1} - f_t = u_{t+1}, \tag{111}$$

where $u_{t+1} \sim i.i.d., N(0, \sigma_u^2)$. Agents receive a signal, v_t at time t that conveys some information about u_{t+1}, but does not reveal u_{t+1} perfectly.

In a present-value model, when the expected growth in the fundamental increases holding f_t constant, there is both an increase in the expected value of $s_{t+1} - s_t$, and a jump up in s_t. The latter implication can be seen by rewriting (110) as $s_t = f_t + \beta(\hat{E}_t s_{t+1} - s_t)/(1 - \beta)$. When agents overweight their signal, a positive realization of v_t leads them to increase their expectation of $f_{t+1} - f_t$ too much. As a result, $\hat{E}_t s_{t+1} - s_t$ rises too much compared to the rationally expected depreciation, so the increase in $i_t - i_t^*$ is excessive. Also, s_t increases more than it would under rational expectations. When the actual value of f_{t+1} is realized in period $t + 1$, on average $f_{t+1} - f_t$ is less than $E_t f_{t+1} - f_t$ conditional on a positive realization of the signal v_t. Then on average $s_{t+1} - s_t$ rises less than $E_t s_{t+1} - s_t$, while $i_t - i_t^*$ has risen more than under rational expectations. This accounts for the downward bias, and possibly even negative coefficient, in the regression of $s_{t+1} - s_t$ on $i_t - i_t^*$.

Gourinchas and Tornell (2004) provide another avenue for deviations from rational expectations. They note that evidence from the term structure can be interpreted as markets underestimating the persistence of short-run nominal interest rate changes. Suppose $i_t - i_t^*$ rises, but the market believes the increase is transitory. In period $t + 1$, the interest differential, $i_{t+1} - i_{t+1}^*$ on average turns out to be greater than the market expected. In the model of Gourinchas and Tornell, an increase in $i_t - i_t^*$ is associated with a Home currency appreciation—a decline in s_t—as in the models of Section 2. In their model, equation (105) holds, so an increase in $i_t - i_t^*$ also leads to an expected depreciation—that is the currency appreciates at time t but is expected to depreciate between t and $t + 1$ so that $\hat{E}_t s_{t+1} - s_t$ exactly equals $i_t - i_t^*$. At time $t + 1$ investors are surprised (on average) to find that $i_{t+1} - i_{t+1}^*$ is higher than they expected, so it is as if there is a positive surprise in $i_{t+1} - i_{t+1}^*$ at time $t + 1$. On average, the currency appreciates relative to $\hat{E}_t s_{t+1}$. So, while $i_t - i_t^*$ equals $\hat{E}_t s_{t+1} - s_t$, the average change in $s_{t+1} - s_t$ is smaller than the change in $i_t - i_t^*$, which can account for the empirical findings of the uncovered interest parity puzzle. Indeed the correlation between $s_{t+1} - s_t$ and $i_t - i_t^*$ can be negative if the average (absolute value of the) mistake in the forecast of $i_{t+1} - i_{t+1}^*$ is large enough.

Ilut (2012) develops a model of ambiguity aversion that can be seen as providing a foundation for the assumption that agents underestimate the persistence of the interest-rate differential, as in Gourinchas and Tornell (2004). In Ilut's model, agents exhibit ambiguity aversion, which implies that they tend to overweight possible bad outcomes in forming their expectations. In the model, investors seek profit when there is an interest differential. The profit is smaller when the interest differential is less persistent, an outcome which the investors believe is more probable than would be inferred under rational expectations.

4.5. Peso Problems

Several recent papers have suggested that the uncovered interest parity puzzle is a mirage—that, in essence, the standard errors of the estimated slope coefficient in regression (54) are much larger than are generally reported, so that we really cannot reject the null hypothesis of uncovered interest parity.[46]

The "peso problem" is not a statistical bias per se, but a problem that arises when the econometrician's sample is biased. The name arises from the situation that occurred in the 1970s, when the Mexican peso exchange rate was fixed to the dollar, but markets anticipated the devaluation that eventually occurred in 1976. The market's expectation was embodied in forward exchange rates, but any sample of the forward premium that ends before the actual devaluation would find the peso price of a dollar on forward markets persistently larger than the fixed spot rate. Without further information, there is an unexplained bias in the forward rate. The term is used more generally to describe a situation in which there is a large event that may occur but with a small probability, so that a given sample has either no examples of the event or the event occurs less frequently in the sample than its true probability.

[46] See for example, Baillie and Bollerslev (2000), Zivot (2000), Bekaert and Hodrick (2001), and West (2012).

Some recent literature[47] has proposed that the apparent risk-adjusted profitability of the carry trade is really an artifact of the peso problem. Suppose an investor in the Home country follows the strategy of investing $k(i_t^* - i_t - \bar{i})$ of the Home currency in the Foreign short-term bond in period t, financed by borrowing in the Home currency.[48] The profits one period later per unit of investment are

$$\varphi_{t+1} \equiv (S_{t+1}/S_t)(1 + i_t^*) - (1 + i_t)$$

given in Home currency units. This strategy is on average profitable if

$$E(\varphi_{t+1}(i_t^* - i_t - \bar{r})) = \text{cov}(\varphi_{t+1}, i_t^* - i_t) > 0,$$

which is approximately equivalent to the condition that the slope coefficient in regression (54) is less than one.

Suppose there are two states of the world, state 1 and 2. Conditional on state 1, the profits from this carry-trade strategy are expected to be positive, which we denote as $E_1(\varphi_{t+1}(i_t^* - i_t - \bar{i})) > 0$. State 2 is a state which occurs infrequently, and is one of a "currency crash."[49] In state 2, $E_2(\varphi_{t+1}(i_t^* - i_t - \bar{i})) < 0$. If state 2 occurs with probability π, then the true expected profit per unit of investment from the carry trade is:

$$(1 - \pi)E_1(\varphi_{t+1}(i_t^* - i_t - \bar{i})) + \pi E_2(\varphi_{t+1}(i_t^* - i_t - \bar{i})). \tag{112}$$

Now suppose in the econometrician's data set, the currency crash state is observed with frequency π', which is smaller than the true probability, $\pi' < \pi$. The econometrician's measured expected profit is

$$(1 - \pi')E_1(\varphi_{t+1}(r_t^* - r_t - \bar{r})) + \pi' E_2(\varphi_{t+1}(r_t^* - r_t - \bar{r})),$$

which is greater than the true expected profit given by equation (112).

Can a peso problem of this type account for the finding of a slope coefficient less than one in the Fama regression, (54)? That is, does it mean that the apparent profitability of the carry trade is just an illusion because the currency crash state has been observed less frequently in the data than its true likelihood of occurring? Burnside et al. (2006, 2011a,c) use data on foreign exchange options that allow an investor to hedge their carry-trade portfolio against large losses in the case of a rare event that has a large negative payoff. They find that the profit from the hedged carry trade is not too different from the unhedged carry trade, suggesting that the potential losses in the currency crash state are not large enough to account for the apparent profitability of the carry trade.

However, when investors are risk averse, profits in all states are discounted by the stochastic discount factor, as in the no-arbitrage condition discussed above equation (57).

---

[47] See Brunnermeier et al. (2009), Burnside et al. (2011a,c), Farhi et al. (2013), Farhi and Gabaix (2011), Gourio et al. (2013).

[48] $\bar{i}$ is the mean of $i_t^* - i_t$ in this example.

[49] This is the term introduced by Brunnermeier et al. (2009).

In this case, we can write the no-arbitrage condition as:

$$(1 - \pi)E_1(M_{t+1}\varphi_{t+1}(i_t^* - i_t - \bar{i})) + \pi E_2(M_{t+1}\varphi_{t+1}(i_t^* - i_t - \bar{i})) = 0,$$

where M_{t+1} is the discount factor for nominal returns. It may appear to an econometrician that plausible values of the stochastic discount factor still imply a violation of the no-arbitrage condition:

$$(1 - \pi')E_1(M_{t+1}\varphi_{t+1}(i_t^* - i_t - \bar{i})) + \pi'E_2(M_{t+1}\varphi_{t+1}(i_t^* - i_t - \bar{i})) > 0.$$

But Burnside et al. (2011a,c) make the case that if the frequency of state 2 is sufficiently underestimated, the stochastic discount factor in state 2 (when there are losses, and the marginal utility of investors is relatively high) could be high enough to account for the apparent failure of the no-arbitrage condition. They conclude that we cannot reject the hypothesis that the risk-adjusted return from the carry trade is expected to be zero, taking into account the peso problem and the variation in the discount factor.

5. CONCLUSIONS

Although this survey has suggested many different models, it is questionable that the models allow us to explain, even after the fact, the movements in major currency rates. The U.S. dollar/euro market is by far the most heavily traded, and that exchange rate is in many ways the most important. Consider the following swings in the dollar price of a euro:

1. November 2005–July 2008: The price of a euro rises from $1.17 to $1.59.
2. July 2008–November 2008: The price of a euro falls from $1.59 to $1.25.
3. November 2008–November 2009: The price of a euro rises from $1.25 to $1.50.
4. November 2009–May 2010: The price of a euro falls from $1.50 to $1.19.
5. May 2010–April 2011: The price of a euro rises from $1.19 to $1.48.
6. April 2011–July 2012: The price of a euro falls from $1.48 to $1.22.

Clearly the post-2007 era has been one of great financial market volatility and stress. That period perhaps presents a laboratory to test and refine theories of the exchange rate. At this stage, we do not have adequate explanations for these exchange-rate swings:

- Was the depreciation of the dollar in the first period associated with the property and equity market boom in the U.S., or does it foretell its bust? What is the mechanism to relate booms and busts to the currency value? Or is the change related to monetary policy?
- Why did the dollar appreciate sharply in the second period, which was the apex of the global financial crisis? Was the dollar a "safe haven"? What does that mean?
- Did the appreciation of the euro in the third period represent a return to normality—a reversal of the safe haven motive?
- What accounts for the fall of the euro in the fourth period and rise in the fifth period? Was it comparative ease of monetary policy in the U.S. versus the eurozone?

- The euro's fall in the final period is attributed usually to fears of sovereign default in the eurozone. What mechanism links default risk with currency value?

Answering these questions should provide international economists with plenty of work in the years to come. Currencies are a country's only true national asset (or, in the case of the eurozone, the only asset of the entire currency union). Understanding their movements surely will shed light on broader asset pricing and macroeconomic questions. While the work of the past fifteen years that is surveyed here has broadened and deepened our understanding of the factors that influence exchange rates, we still are not at the stage where we can provide a convincing explanation for the actual movements in currency values.

REFERENCES

Abhyankar, A., Sarno, L., Valente, G., 2005. Exchange rates and fundamentals: evidence on the economic value of predictability. Journal of International Economics 66, 325–348.

Adolfson, M., Laséen, S., Lindé, J., Villani, M., 2007. Bayesian estimation of an open economy DSGE model with incomplete pass-through. Journal of International Economics 72, 481–511.

Adolfson, M., Laséen, S., Lindé, J., Villani, M., 2008. Evaluating an estimated New Keynesian small open economy model. Journal of Economic Dynamics and Control 32, 2690–2721.

Alexius, A., 2001. Uncovered interest parity revisited. Review of International Economics 9, 505–517.

Alvarez, F., Atkeson, A., Kehoe, P., 2009. Time-varying risk, interest rates and exchange rates in general equilibrium. Review of Economic Studies 76, 851–878.

Andersen, T.G., Bollerslev, T., Diebold, F.X., Vega, C., 2003. Micro effects of macro announcements: real-time price discovery in foreign exchange. The American Economic Review 93, 38–62.

Andersen, T.G., Bollerslev, T., Diebold, F.X., Vega, C., 2007. Real time price discovery in global stock, bond, and foreign exchange markets. Journal of International Economics 73, 251–277.

Bacchetta, P., van Wincoop, E., 2006. Can information heterogeneity explain the exchange rate determination puzzle? The American Economic Review 96, 552–576.

Bacchetta, P., van Wincoop, E., 2010. Infrequent portfolio decisions: a solution to the forward discount puzzle. The American Economic Review 100, 870–904.

Bacchetta, P., van Wincoop, E., 2012. Modeling exchange rates with incomplete information. In: James, J., Marsh, I., Sarno, L. (Eds.), Handbook of Exchange Rates. Wiley.

Bacchetta, P., van Wincoop, E., 2013. On the unstable relationship between exchange rates and macroeconomic fundamentals. Journal of International Economics 91, 18–26.

Backus, D.K., Foresi, S., Telmer, C.I., 2001. Affine term structure models and the forward premium anomaly. The Journal of Finance 56, 279–304.

Backus, D.K., Gavazzoni, F., Telmer, C., Zin, S.E., 2013. Monetary Policy and the Uncovered Interest Parity Puzzle. Working Paper, Stern School of Business, New York University.

Baillie, R.T., Bollerslev, T., 2000. The forward premium anomaly is not as bad as you think. Journal of International Money and Finance 19, 471–488.

Bansal, R., Dahlquist, M., 2000. The forward premium puzzle: different tales from developed and emerging economies. Journal of International Economics 51, 115–144.

Bansal, R., Shaliastovich, I., 2012. A Long-Run Risks Explanation of Predictability Puzzles in Bond and Currency Markets. Unpublished Working Paper, Duke University and Wharton Business School

Beine, M., Janssen, G., Lecourt, C., 2009. Should central bankers talk to the foreign exchange markets? Journal of International Money and Finance 28, 776–803.

Bekaert, G., Hodrick, R.J., 2001. Expectations hypotheses tests. The Journal of Finance 56, 1357–1394.

Bekaert, G., Hodrick. R.J., Marshall, D.A., 1997. The implications of first-order risk aversion for asset market risk premiums. Journal of Monetary Economics 40, 3–39.

Bekaert, G., Wei, M., Xing, Y., 2007. Uncovered interest rate parity and the term structure. Journal of International Money and Finance 26, 1038–1069.

Benigno, G., 2004. Real exchange rate persistence and monetary policy rules. Journal of Monetary Economics 51, 473–502.

Benigno, G., Benigno, P., 2008. Exchange rate determination under interest rate rules. Journal of International Money and Finance 27, 971–993.

Benigno, G., Thoenissen, C., 2003. Equilibrium exchange rates and supply-side performance. The Economic Journal 113, 103–124.

Benigno, G., Benigno, P., Nisticò, S., 2012. Risk, monetary policy and the exchange rate. NBER Macroeconomics Annual 2011, 247–309.

Berger, D.W., Chaboud, A.P., Chernenko, S.V., Howorka, E., Wright, J.H., 2008. Order flow and exchange rate dynamics in electronic brokerage system data. Journal of International Economics 75, 93–109.

Bergin, P.R., 2006. How well can the new open economy macroeconomics explain the exchange rate and current account? Journal of International Money and Finance 25, 675–701.

Betts, C., Devereux, M.B., 1996. The exchange rate in a model of pricing-to-market. European Economic Review 40, 1007–1021.

Betts, C., Devereux, M.B., 2000. Exchange rate dynamics in a model of pricing-to-market. Journal of International Economics 50, 215–244.

Bilson, J.F.O., 1981. The 'speculative efficiency' hypothesis. Journal of Business 54, 435–451.

Bjørnland, H.C., 2009. Monetary policy and exchange rate overshooting: Dornbusch was right after all. Journal of International Economics 79, 64–77.

Blanchard, O.J., Kahn, C.M., 1980. The solution of linear difference models under rational expectations. Econometrica 48, 1305–1311.

Blanchard, O., Giavazzi, F., Sa, F., 2005. International investors, the U.S. current account, and the dollar. Brookings Papers on Economic Activity 1, 1–49.

Brandt, M.W., Cochrane, J.H., Santa-Clara, P., 2006. International risk sharing is better than you think, or exchange rates are too smooth. Journal of Monetary Economics 53, 671–698.

Breedon, F., Vitale, P., 2010. An empirical study of portfolio-balance and information effects of order flow on exchange rates. Journal of International Money and Finance 29, 504–524.

Brunnermeier, M.K., Nagel, S., Pedersen, L., 2009. Carry trades and currency crashes. NBER Macroeconomics Annual 2008, 313–347.

Burnside, C., 2011. The cross section of foreign currency risk premia and consumption growth risk: comment. The American Economic Review 101, 3456–3476.

Burnside, C., Eichenbaum, M., Kleshchelski, I., Rebelo, S., 2006. The Returns to Currency Speculation. National Bureau of Economic Research, Working Paper No. 12489.

Burnside, C., Eichenbaum, M., Rebelo, S., 2008. Carry trade: the gains of diversification. Journal of the European Economic Association 6, 581–588.

Burnside, C., Eichenbaum, M., Kleshchelski, I., Rebelo, S., 2011a. Do peso problems explain the returns to the carry trade? Review of Financial Studies. 24, 853–891.

Burnside, C., Han, B., Hirshleifer, D., Wang, T.Y., 2011b. Investor overconfidence and the forward premium puzzle. Review of Economic Studies 78, 523–558.

Burnside, C., Eichenbaum, M., Rebelo, S., 2011c. Carry trade and momentum in currency markets. Annual Review of Financial Economics 3, 511–535.

Calvo, G.A., Reinhart, C.M., 2002. Fear of floating. Quarterly Journal of Economics 117, 379–408.

Campbell, J.Y., Cochrane, J.H., 1999. By force of habit: a consumption-based explanation of aggregate stock market behavior. Journal of Political Economy 107, 205–251.

Campbell, J.Y., Shiller, R.J., 1988. The dividend-price ratio and expectations of future dividends and discount factors. Review of Financial Studies 1, 195–228.

Cavallo, M., Ghironi, F., 2002. Net foreign assets and the exchange rate: redux revived. Journal of Monetary Economics 49, 1057–1097.

Cerra, V., Saxena, S.C., 2010. The monetary model strikes back: evidence from the world. Journal of International Economics 81, 184–196.

Chaboud, A.P., Wright, J.H., 2005. Uncovered interest parity: it works, but not for long. Journal of International Economics 66, 349–362.

Chari, V.V., Kehoe, P.J., McGrattan, E.R., 2002. Can sticky price models generate volatile and persistent real exchange rates? The Review of Economic Studies 69, 533–563.

Chen, Y.-C., Rogoff, K., 2003. Commodity currencies. Journal of International Economics 60, 133–160.

Chen, Y.-C., Rogoff, K.S., Rossi, B., 2010. Can exchange rates forecast commodity prices? Quarterly Journal of Economics 125, 1145–1194.

Cheung, Y.-W., Chinn, M.D., Garcia Pascual, A., 2005. Empirical exchange rate models of the nineties: are any fit to survive? Journal of International Money and Finance 24, 1150–1175.

Chinn, M.D., 2006. The partial rehabilitation of interest rate parity in the floating rate era: longer horizons, alternative expectations, and emerging markets. Journal of International Money and Finance 25, 7–21.

Chinn, M.D., Meredith, G., 2004. Monetary policy and long-horizon uncovered interest parity. IMF Staff Papers 51, 409–430.

Chinn, M.D., Moore, M.J., 2011. Order flow and the monetary model of exchange rates: evidence from a novel data set. Journal of Money, Credit and Banking 43, 1599–1624.

Clarida, R.H., Waldman, D., 2008. Is bad news about inflation good news for the exchange rate? And if so, can that tell us anything about the conduct of monetary policy? In Asset Prices and Monetary Policy (NBER) 371–396.

Clarida, R., Galí, J., Gertler, M., 2002. A simple framework for international monetary policy analysis. Journal of Monetary Economics 49, 879–904.

Clarida, R.H., Sarno, L., Taylor, M.P., Valente, G., 2003. The out-of-sample success of term structure models as exchange rate predictors: a step beyond. Journal of International Economics 60, 61–83.

Clarida, R., Davis, J., Pedersen, N., 2009. Currency carry trade regimes: beyond the Fama regression. Journal of International Money and Finance 28, 1375–1389.

Clark, T.E., West, K.D., 2006. Using out-of-sample mean squared prediction errors to test the martingale difference hypothesis. Journal of Econometrics 135, 155–186.

Cochrane, J.H., 2005. Asset Pricing: Revised Edition. Princeton University Press, Princeton.

Colacito, R., Croce, M.M., 2011. Risks for the long-run and the real exchange rate. Journal of Political Economy 119, 153–181.

Colacito, R., Croce, M.M., 2013. International asset pricing with recursive preferences. Journal of Finance 68, 2651–2686.

Corsetti, G., Dedola, L., Leduc, S., 2008. International risk sharing and the transmission of productivity shocks. Review of Economic Studies 75, 443–473.

Devereux, M.B., Engel, C., 2002. Exchange rate pass-through, exchange rate volatility, and exchange rate disconnect. Journal of Monetary Economics 49, 913–940.

Diebold, F.X., Mariano, R.S., 1995. Comparing predictive accuracy. Journal of Business and Economic Statistics 13, 253–263.

Disyatat, P., Galati, G., 2007. The effectiveness of foreign exchange intervention in emerging market countries: evidence from the Czech koruna. Journal of International Money and Finance 26, 383–402.

Dominguez, K.M.E., 2003. The market microstructure of central bank intervention. Journal of International Economics 59, 25–45.

Dominguez, K.M.E., 2006. When do central bank interventions influence intra-daily and longer-term exchange rate movements? Journal of International Money and Finance 25, 1051–1071.

Dominguez, K.M., Frankel, J., 1993. Does foreign exchange intervention matter? The portfolio effect. The American Economic Review 83, 1356–1369.

Dornbusch, R., 1976. Expectations and exchange rate dynamics. Journal of Political Economy 84, 1161–1176.

Dotsey, M., Duarte, M., 2008. Nontraded goods, market segmentation, and exchange rates. Journal of Monetary Economics 55, 1129–1142.

Duarte, M., Stockman, A.C., 2005. Rational speculation and exchange rates. Journal of Monetary Economics 52, 3–29.

Dubas, J.M., Lee, B.-J. Mark, N.C., 2010. A multinomial logit approach to exchange rate policy classification with an application to growth. Journal of International Money and Finance 29, 1438–1462.

Ehrmann, M., Fratzscher, M., 2005. Exchange rates and fundamentals: new evidence from real-time data. Journal of International Money and Finance 24, 317–341.

Eichenbaum, M., Evans, C.L., 1995. Some empirical evidence on the effects of shocks to monetary policy on exchange rates. Quarterly Journal of Economics 110, 975–1009.

Eichengreen, B., Razo-Garcia, R., 2006. The international monetary system in the last and next 20 years. Economic Policy 21, 393–442.

Enders, Z., Müller, G.J., Scholl, A., 2011. How do fiscal and technology shocks affect real exchange rates? New evidence for the United States. Journal of International Economics 83, 53–69.

Engel, C., 1996. The forward discount anomaly and the risk premium: a survey of recent evidence. Journal of Empirical Finance 3, 123–192.

Engel, C., 2000. Long-run PPP may not hold after all. Journal of International Economics 51, 243–273.

Engel, C., 2005. Some new variance bounds for asset prices. Journal of Money, Credit and Banking 37, 949–955.

Engel, C., West, K.D., 2004. Accounting for exchange rate variability in present value models when the discount factor is near one. The American Economic Review, Papers and Proceedings 94, 119–125.

Engel, C., West, K.D., 2005. Exchange rates and fundamentals. Journal of Political Economy 113, 485–517.

Engel, C., West, K.D., 2006. Taylor rules and the deutschemark-dollar real exchange rate. Journal of Money, Credit and Banking 38, 1175–1194.

Engel, C., Mark, N.C., West, K.D., 2008. Exchange rate models are not as bad as you think. NBER Macroeconomics Annual 2007, 381–441.

Epstein, L.G., Zin, S.E., 1989. Substitution, risk aversion, and the temporal behavior of consumption and asset returns: a theoretical framework. Econometrica 57, 937–969.

Evans, M.D.D., 2002. FX trading and exchange rate dynamics. Journal of Finance 57, 2405–2447.

Evans, M.D.D., 2010. Order flows and the exchange rate disconnect puzzle. Journal of International Economics 80, 58–71.

Evans, M.D.D., 2011. Exchange Rate Dynamics. Princeton University Press, Princeton.

Evans, M.D.D., Lyons, R.K., 2002a. Order flow and exchange rate dynamics. Journal of Political Economy 110, 170–180.

Evans, M.D.D., Lyons, R.K., 2002b. Informational integration and FX trading. Journal of International Money and Finance 21, 807–831.

Evans, M.D.D., Lyons, R.K., 2005. Do currency markets absorb news quickly? Journal of International Money and Finance 24, 197–217.

Evans, M.D.D., Lyons, R.K., 2008. How is macro news transmitted to exchange rates? Journal of Financial Economics 88, 26–50.

Fama, E.F., 1984. Forward and spot exchange rates. Journal of Monetary Economics 14, 319–338.

Farhi, E., Gabaix, X., 2011. Rare Disasters and Exchange Rates. Working Paper. Harvard University.

Farhi, E., Fraiberger, S.P., Gabaix, X., Ranciere, R., Verdelhan, A., 2013. Crash Risk in currency markets. Working Paper, Harvard University.

Fatum, R., 2010. Foreign Exchange Intervention When Interest Rates Are Zero: Does the Portfolio Balance Channel Matter after All? Federal Reserve Bank of Dallas, Globalization and Monetary Policy Institute Working Paper, No. 57.

Fatum, R., Hutchison, M., 1999. Is intervention a signal of future monetary policy? Evidence from the federal funds futures market. Journal of Money, Credit and Banking 31, 54–69.

Fatum, R., Scholnick, B., 2006. Do exchange rates respond to day-to-day changes in monetary policy expectations when no monetary policy changes occur? Journal of Money, Credit and Banking 38, 1641–1657.

Faust, J., Rogers, J.H., 2003. Monetary policy's role in exchange rate behavior. Journal of Monetary Economics 50, 1403–1424.

Faust, J., Rogers, J.H., Wright, J.H., 2003. Exchange rate forecasting: the errors we've really made. Journal of International Economics 60, 35–59.

Faust, J., Rogers, J.H., Wang, S.-Y.B., Wright, J.H., 2007. The high-frequency response of exchange rates and interest rates to macroeconomic announcements. Journal of Monetary Economics 54, 1051–1068.

Frankel, J.A., 1979. On the mark: a theory of floating exchange rates based on real interest differentials. The American Economic Review 69, 610–622.

Frankel, J., Poonawala, J., 2010. The forward market in emerging currencies: less biased than in major currencies. Journal of International Money and Finance 29, 585–598.

Frankel, J., Schmukler, S.L., Servén, L., 2004. Global transmission of interest rates: monetary independence and currency regime. Journal of International Money and Finance 23, 701–733.

Fratzscher, M., 2006. On the long-term effectiveness of exchange rate communication and interventions. Journal of International Money and Finance 25, 146–167.

Fratzscher, M., 2008. Oral interventions versus actual interventions in FX markets—an event-study approach. The Economic Journal 118, 1079–1106.

Fratzscher, M., 2009. How successful is the G7 in managing exchange rates? Journal of International Economics 79, 78–88.

Froot, K.A., Ramadorai, T., 2005. Currency returns, intrinsic value and institutional-investor flows. Journal of Finance 60, 1535–1566.

Froot, K., Thaler, R.H., 2001. Anomalies: foreign exchange. Journal of Economic Perspectives 4, 179–192.

Ganelli, G., 2005. The new open economy macroeconomics of government debt. Journal of International Economics 65, 167–184.

Ghironi, F., 2008. The role of net foreign assets in a New Keynesian small open economy model. Journal of Economic Dynamics and Control 32, 1780–1811.

Gourinchas, P.-O., Rey, H., 2007. International financial adjustment. Journal of Political Economy 115, 665–773.

Gourinchas, P.-O., Tornell, A., 2004. Exchange rate puzzles and distorted beliefs. Journal of International Economics 64, 303–333.

Gourio, F., Siemer, M., Verdelhan A., 2013. International risk cycles. Journal of International Economics 89, 471–484.

Groen, J.J.J., 2000. The monetary exchange rate model as a long-run phenomenon. Journal of International Economics 52, 299–319.

Groen, J.J.J., 2005. Exchange rate predictability and monetary fundamentals in a small multi-country panel. Journal of Money, Credit and Banking 37, 495–516.

Hagen, J., Zhou, J., 2007. The choice of exchange rate regimes in developing countries: a multinomial panel analysis. Journal of International Money and Finance 26, 1071–1094.

Hau, H., 2000. Exchange rate determination: the role of factor price rigidities and nontradeables. Journal of International Economics 50, 421–447.

Ho, W.-M., 2004. The liquidity effects of foreign exchange intervention. Journal of International Economics 63, 179–208.

Hodrick, R., 1987. The Empirical Evidence on the Efficiency of Forward and Futures Foreign Exchange Markets. Harwood, Chur.

Husain, A.M., Mody, A., Rogoff, K.S., 2005. Exchange rate regime durability and performance in developing versus advanced economies. Journal of Monetary Economics 52, 35–64.

Ilut, C., 2012. Ambiguity aversion: implications for the uncovered interest parity puzzle. American Economic Journal: Macroeconomics 4, 33–65.

Ito, T., 2003. Is foreign exchange intervention effective? The Japanese experience in the 1990s. In: Mitzen, P. (Ed.), Monetary History, Exchange Rates and Financial Markets, Essays in Honour of Charles Goodhart 2. Edward Elgar, U.K.

Jansen, D.-J., de Haan, J., 2005. Talking heads: the effects of ECB statements on the euro–dollar exchange rate. Journal of International Money and Finance 24, 343–361.

Jeanne, O., Rose, A.K., 2002. Noise trading and exchange rate regimes. Quarterly Journal of Economics 117, 537–569.

Jordà, Ò., Taylor, A.M., 2012. The carry trade and fundamentals: nothing to fear but FEER itself. Journal of International Economics 88, 74–90.

Jung, Y., 2007. Can the new open economy macroeconomic model explain exchange rate fluctuations? Journal of International Economics 72, 381–408.

Juvenal, L., 2011. Sources of exchange rate fluctuations: are they real or nominal? Journal of International Money and Finance 30, 849–876.

Kaminsky, G.L., Lewis, K.K., 1996. Does foreign exchange intervention signal future monetary policy? Journal of Monetary Economics 37, 285–312.

Kearns, J., Rigobon, R., 2005. Identifying the efficacy of central bank interventions: evidence from Australia and Japan. Journal of International Economics 66, 31–48.

Kilian, L., 1999. Exchange rates and monetary fundamentals: what do we learn from long-horizon regressions? Journal of Applied Econometrics 14, 491–510.

Kim, S., Roubini, N., 2000. Exchange rate anomalies in the industrial countries: a solution with a structural VAR approach. Journal of Monetary Economics 45, 561–586.

Kollmann, R., 2001. The exchange rate in a dynamic-optimizing business cycle model with nominal rigidities: a quantitative investigation. Journal of International Economics 55, 243–262.

Kollmann, R., 2004. Welfare effects of a monetary union: the role of trade openness. Journal of the European Economic Association 2, 289–301.

Kumhof, M., 2010. On the theory of sterilized foreign exchange intervention. Journal of Economic Dynamics and Control 34, 1403–1420.

Landry, A., 2009. Expectations and exchange rate dynamics: a state-dependent pricing approach. Journal of International Economics 78, 60–71.

Levy-Yeyati, E., Sturzenegger, F., 2003. To float or to fix: evidence on the impact of exchange rate regimes on growth. The American Economic Review 93, 1173–1193.

Lewis, K.K., 1995. Are foreign exchange intervention and monetary policy related and does it really matter? Journal of Business 68, 185–214.

Lubik, T.A., Schorfheide, F., 2006. A Bayesian look at new open economy macroeconomics. NBER Macroeconomics Annual 2005, 313–366.

Lustig, H., Verdelhan, A., 2007. The cross section of foreign currency risk premia and consumption growth risk. The American Economic Review 97, 89–117.

Lustig, H., Verdelhan, A., 2011. The cross section of foreign currency risk premia and consumption growth risk: reply. The American Economic Review 101, 3477–3500.

Lustig, H., Roussanov, N., Verdelhan, A., 2011. Common risk factors in currency markets. Review of Financial Studies 24, 3731–3777.

Mark, N.C., 1995. Exchange rates and fundamentals: evidence on long-horizon predictability. The American Economic Review 85, 201–218.

Mark, N.C., 2009. Changing monetary policy rules, learning, and real exchange rate dynamics. Journal of Money, Credit and Banking 41, 1047–1070.

Mark, N.C., Sul, D., 2001. Nominal exchange rates and monetary fundamentals: evidence from a small post-Bretton Woods panel. Journal of International Economics 53, 29–52.

McCallum, B., 1994. A reconsideration of the uncovered interest parity relationship. Journal of Monetary Economics 33, 105–132.

McCracken, M.W., Sapp, S.G., 2005. Evaluating the predictability of exchange rates using long-horizon regressions: mind your p's and q's! Journal of Money, Credit and Banking 37, 473–494.

Meese, R.A., Rogoff, K., 1983. Empirical exchange rate models of the seventies: do they fit out of sample? Journal of International Economics 14, 3–24.

Menkhoff, L., Sarno, L., Schmeling, M., Schrimpf, A., 2012a. Carry trades and global foreign exchange volatility. Journal of Finance 67, 681–718.

Menkhoff, L., Sarno, L., Schmeling, M., Schrimpf, A., 2012b. Currency momentum strategies. Journal of Financial Economics 106, 660–684.

Molodtsova, T., Papell, D.H., 2009. Out-of-sample exchange rate predictability with Taylor rule fundamentals. Journal of International Economics 77, 167–180.

Molodtsova, T., Nikolsko-Rzhevskyy, A., Papell, D.H., 2008. Taylor rules with real-time data: a tale of two countries and one exchange rate. Journal of Monetary Economics 55, S63–S79.

Molodtsova, T., Nikolsko-Rzhevskyy, A., Papell, D.H., 2011. Taylor rules and the euro. Journal of Money, Credit and Banking 43, 535–552.

Moore, M.J., Roche, M.J., 2002. Less of a puzzle: a new look at the forward forex market. Journal of International Economics 58, 387–411.

Moore, M.J., Roche, M.J., 2010. Solving exchange rate puzzles with neither sticky prices nor trade costs. Journal of International Money and Finance 29, 1151–1170.

Neely, C.J., 2005. An analysis of recent studies of the effect of foreign exchange intervention. Federal Reserve Bank of St. Review 87, 685–717.

Neely, C.J., 2011. A foreign exchange intervention in an era of restraint. Federal Reserve Bank of St. Louis Review 93, 303–324.

Obstfeld, M., Rogoff, K., 1995a. Exchange rate dynamics redux. Journal of Political Economy 103, 624–660.

Obstfeld, M., Rogoff, K., 1995b. The mirage of fixed exchange rates. Journal of Economic Perspectives 9, 73–96.

Obstfeld, M., Rogoff, K., 2001. The six major puzzles in international macroeconomics: is there a common cause? NBER Macroeconomics Annual 2000, 339–390.

Pasquariello, P., 2010. Central bank intervention and the intraday process of price formation in the currency markets. Journal of International Money and Finance 29, 1045–1061.

Rapach, D.E., Wohar, M.E., 2002. Testing the monetary model of exchange rate determination: new evidence from a century of data. Journal of International Economics 58, 359–385.

Reinhart, C.M., Rogoff, K.S., 2004. The modern history of exchange rate arrangements: a reinterpretation. Quarterly Journal of Economics 119, 1–48.

Reitz, S., Taylor, M.P., 2008. The coordination channel of foreign exchange intervention: a nonlinear microstructural analysis. European Economic Review 52, 55–76.

Rime, D., Sarno, L., Sojli, E., 2010. Exchange rate forecasting, order flow and macroeconomic information. Journal of International Economics 80, 72–88.

Rogoff, K., 1996. The purchasing power parity puzzle. Journal of Economic Literature 34, 647–668.

Sarno, L., Taylor, M.P., 2001. Official intervention in the foreign exchange market: is it effective and, if so, how does it work? Journal of Economic Literature 39, 839–868.

Scholl, A., Uhlig, H., 2008. New evidence on the puzzles: results from agnostic identification on monetary policy and exchange rates. Journal of International Economics 76, 1–13.

Shambaugh, J.C., 2004. The effect of fixed exchange rates on monetary policy. The Quarterly Journal of Economics 119, 301–352.

Shiller, R.J., 1981. Do stock prices move too much to be justified by subsequent changes in dividends? The American Economic Review 71, 421–436.

Tavlas, G., Dellas, H., Stockman, A.C., 2008. The classification and performance of alternative exchange-rate systems. European Economic Review 52, 941–963.

Taylor, M.P., Peel, D.A., 2000. Nonlinear adjustment, long-run equilibrium and exchange rate fundamentals. Journal of International Money and Finance 19, 33–53.

Verdelhan, A., 2010. A habit-based explanation of the exchange rate risk premium. Journal of Finance 65, 123–146.

Vitale, P., 2003. Foreign exchange intervention: how to signal policy objectives and stabilise the economy. Journal of Monetary Economics 50, 841–870.

Wang, J., 2010. Home bias, exchange rate disconnect, and optimal exchange rate policy. Journal of International Money and Finance 29, 55–78.

Wang, J., Wu, J.J., 2012. The Taylor rule and forecast intervals for exchange rates. Journal of Money, Credit and Banking 44, 103–144.

West, K.D., 1988. Dividend innovations and stock price volatility. Econometrica 56, 37–61.

West, K.D., 2012. Econometric analysis of present value models when the discount factor is near one. Journal of Econometrics 171, 86–97.

Zivot, E., 2000. Cointegration and forward and spot exchange rate regressions. Journal of International Money and Finance 19, 785–812.

CHAPTER 9

Assessing International Efficiency*

Jonathan Heathcote[*,†] and Fabrizio Perri[*,†,‡]

*Federal Reserve Bank of Minneapolis, Minneapolis, MN, USA
†Centre for Economic Policy Research, London, UK
‡National Bureau of Economic Research, Cambridge, MA, USA

Abstract

This chapter is structured in three parts. The first part outlines the methodological steps, involving both theoretical and empirical work, for assessing whether an observed allocation of resources across countries is efficient. The second part applies the methodology to the long-run allocation of capital and consumption in a large cross section of countries. We find that countries that grow faster in the long run also tend to save more both domestically and internationally. These facts suggest that either the long-run allocation of resources across countries is inefficient, or that there is a systematic relation between fast growth and preference for delayed consumption. The third part applies the methodology to the allocation of resources across developed countries at the business cycle frequency. Here we discuss how evidence on international quantity comovement, exchange rates, asset prices, and international portfolio holdings can be used to assess efficiency. Overall, quantities and portfolios appear consistent with efficiency, while evidence from prices is difficult to interpret using standard models. The welfare costs associated with an inefficient allocation of resources over the business cycle can be significant if shocks to relative country permanent income are large. In those cases partial financial liberalization can lower welfare.

Keywords

International risk sharing, Long-run risk, Long-run growth, International business cycles, Real exchange rate

JEL classification codes

F21, F32, F36, F41, F43, F44

1. INTRODUCTION

Is the observed allocation of resources across residents in different countries Pareto efficient? Or is it possible for a single government or an international organization to devise a mechanism (for example, a tax/subsidy system or the introduction of a new asset) so

* We thank the editors Gita Gopinath and Ken Rogoff for their suggestions and their patience, Karen Lewis and Maury Obstfeld for insightful discussions, Alberto Polo for outstanding research assistance, and seminar participants at the handbook conference in Cambridge for great comments. Perri thanks the ERC for financial support. The datasets and computer codes used in the chapter are available on request. The views expressed herein are those of the authors and not necessarily those of the Federal Reserve Bank of Minneapolis or the Federal Reserve System.

523

as to achieve a different allocation of resources that improves the welfare of residents in all countries? If observed allocations are inefficient, how large are the potential welfare gains from improving efficiency?

These questions cannot be answered by using theory alone, as our interest is in the efficiency of allocations we observe in the data, in a given set of countries and in a given time frame. At the same time, they cannot be answered with data alone, since the same data are in principle consistent with either efficiency or inefficiency depending on the underlying model of preferences, technologies, and frictions.

Researchers have attempted to answer these questions in two popular strands of literatures in international macroeconomics. The first is the international consumption risk-sharing literature (see, for example, the seminal work of Cole and Obstfeld, 1991) that deals with the allocation of consumption across countries and states of the world, taking as given the distribution of output. The second is the literature on the efficient distribution of productive assets across countries (see, for example, the work on capital by Lucas, 1990, and the work on labor by Hamilton and Whalley, 1984). The issue in this strand is whether world output and welfare can be increased by reallocating factors of production across countries.

The main objective of this chapter is to provide a simple but integrated methodological framework that lays down precisely the issues involved in combining data and theory to assess international efficiency along both of these dimensions.

The first part of the chapter (Section 2) describes in a general form the methodological steps that are needed to assess the efficiency of a given allocation of resources, and highlights the potential problems associated with each of these steps. The second part of the chapter (Sections 3 and 4) discusses two applications of the general methodology. These applications are closely related to various influential articles in the international macro literature, and our discussion of these applications within a single framework will highlight new connections and complementarities among these papers. Section 3 analyzes the long-run allocation of consumption and investment in a large cross section of countries. Section 4 deals with the allocation of consumption and investment in developed countries over the business cycle. Section 5 concludes, attempting an answer to the efficiency questions posed at the beginning and pointing to future interesting research directions.

The main limitation of our survey is that we follow the traditional approach in international macro and assume an efficient distribution of resources within a country (i.e., the existence of a representative agent/firm within a country). We will not discuss recent and interesting research (e.g., Kocherlakota and Pistaferri, 2007; Mendoza et al., 2009) that studies the international allocation of resources in a world where the intranational distribution of resources is not efficient.

2. A METHODOLOGY FOR ASSESSING INTERNATIONAL EFFICIENCY

In this section we outline the general methodological steps that are needed to assess the efficiency of a given allocation.

2.1. Specifying Preferences, Technologies, and Frictions

The first necessary step in assessing whether various features of the data (e.g., the international comovement of consumption, capital flows between countries) are consistent with efficiency is to specify a model economy, i.e., preferences, technologies, and frictions. The model economy can then be used to generate theoretical counterparts to the empirical variables of interest.

2.1.1. Preferences

This step is essential as preferences ultimately determine the value of transferring resources across countries. Absent restrictions on preferences, it is impossible to determine whether allocations are efficient and to quantify the welfare costs of any inefficiencies. To see this, consider the following example. Suppose that during a global recession, we observe country A reducing consumption by more than country B. In some models—with symmetric preferences—this observation would be interpreted as a lack of consumption risk sharing and hence inefficiency. In alternative models—with asymmetric preferences—this same allocation can be efficient. For example, if country A is more risk tolerant than country B, then it is efficient for country A to take on a bigger share of global risk and hence reduce consumption more in a global recession (for a model of this type, see Gourinchas et al., 2010).

As another example, consider a model in which the efficient consumption allocation is the one that equalizes consumption growth rates across different countries, and suppose that a researcher is interested in assessing the gains of moving from the observed consumption allocations (in which growth rates are not equalized) to the efficient allocation. Different assumptions about preferences can make the gains from risk-sharing arbitrarily large (for example, if agents are extremely risk averse) or arbitrarily small (if preferences are close to linear).

As is well known (see Stigler and Becker, 1977), the preference problem is endemic in economics; here we just want to stress that it is of first order-importance in international efficiency problems. Ideally, researchers should justify assumptions about preferences, preference heterogeneity, and/or preference shocks using observables (e.g., asset price data, long-run trends, trade flows).

2.1.2. Technologies

The specification of technology concerns the primitive (i.e., taken as given by the researcher) distribution of resources across countries/agents, time, and states of the world in the economy. Examples include the endowments of goods, labor, capital, total factor productivity, or productive opportunities. As with preferences, the distribution of resources should be pinned down by observables, but, unlike preferences, the connection between model and observables is usually more direct. Consider, for example, the issue of specifying a process of endowments of consumption goods in each country in the classic international consumption risk-sharing problem. In this case, a researcher can identify these endowments simply by constructing time series of the production of tradable consumption goods in each country, using national accounts data.

In many international business cycles studies, the primitive resource that is assumed to differ across countries is total factor productivity (TFP). A researcher can construct time series for TFP across countries using data from national accounts plus assumptions on the production functions.

An important remark is that observables are sometimes not sufficient to distinguish whether differences in resources among countries are due to *ex post* risk or *ex ante* heterogeneity, but this distinction has important implications for efficiency. Consider, for example, two poor countries and assume at some point that we observe one of the countries extracting a lot of oil. If the presence of oil was not known to residents in the two countries at the beginning of time, it would be (*ex ante*) efficient for them to share this resource risk, and efficient allocations would all involve substantial transfers from the lucky country to the unlucky. If, on the other hand, this difference was known to the residents at date zero, allocations that do not involve any transfer can also be efficient.

2.1.3. Frictions

Frictions are constraints that all market allocations (efficient or not) have to satisfy because of some physical or technological features of the environment. A classical example of a friction in international macro is limited tradability of goods: it is often assumed that a fraction of resources in a given country cannot be shipped to other countries. To see why frictions matter for assessing efficiency, consider the extreme example (borrowed from Brandt et al., 2006) of Earth and Mars. Suppose both planets face income risk, but shipping any goods between them is impossible. In this case, the resulting market allocation is that in each planet consumption is equal to income. This allocation of resources is efficient because no other allocation satisfies the physical no-trade constraint (the friction) and yields higher welfare to residents. A very influential paper by Obstfeld and Rogoff (2001) argues that many aspects of international macro data that suggest inefficiency no longer do so once they are analyzed within a model that features limited tradability.

Another friction often introduced in international macro models is the assumption of a limited enforcement technology on international contracts. In particular, it is assumed that if countries default on international obligations, the harshest punishment that can be imposed on them is exclusion from future trade (autarky). This friction implies that any market allocation has to yield, in each date and in each state, expected welfare to any country at least as high as the expected welfare under autarky (see, for example, Kehoe and Perri, 2002). This typically rules out allocations that involve large intertemporal transfers between countries, which reduces the set of allocations that can be achieved by a world planner/policymaker. If there is no Pareto-improving reallocation of resources that preserves incentives to repay debts or report truthfully in environments with enforcement or information frictions, allocations are labeled "constrained efficient."

2.2. Efficient Allocations and Market Allocations

Once the fundamentals of the economy are described, a researcher can first characterize (analytically or numerically) the set of efficient allocations, which is usually done by solving a (constrained) planning problem. These efficient allocations are a natural baseline to compare with data.

However, which features of efficient allocations are hallmarks of international efficiency will not always be obvious. For this reason a useful step is to compute the theoretical predictions of alternative models in which there is no world social planner, and in which allocations are determined in a competitive equilibrium in which agents trade an exogenously limited set of assets internationally. Examples of commonly assumed market structures are autarky (no markets across countries), financial autarky (no intertemporal markets between countries), limited asset trade between countries (e.g., a single non-contingent bond), and complete markets within and between countries. Before turning to the data, an instructive approach will be to compare and contrast the predictions of alternative market structures alongside the constrained-efficient baseline, in order to learn which features of the data are more or less sensitive to the scope for international asset trade, and—relatedly—which moments offer the sharpest tests of international efficiency. It will also be useful to learn when and whether trade in a limited set of assets can perfectly decentralize constrained-efficient allocations.

2.3. Comparing Models and Data

This step involves the comparison of several model allocations with data, to get a sense of which setup can better account for the data. Obviously, there are many dimensions along which one can perform this comparison. Many authors have focused on the international correlations of quantities such as GDP, consumption, and investment at a business cycle frequency (see, for example Baxter and Crucini, 1995), since in some models efficient and inefficient allocations yield very different correlations of these quantities. Another commonly used statistic involves comovement between consumption ratios and real exchange rates (Backus and Smith, 1993). More recently some authors have also suggested using asset prices (Brandt et al., 2006), portfolios (Heathcote and Perri, forthcoming), or capital flows (Gourinchas and Jeanne, 2013) as additional pieces of evidence against which researchers should benchmark models. Other authors have used seminatural experiments, such as financial liberalizations, to assess whether responses to these observed changes suggested efficient, or inefficient allocations of resources across countries (e.g., Kose et al., 2009).

Ideally, one should use as much relevant empirical evidence as possible to discriminate between different models, because bringing in more data gives the researcher more confidence in evaluating whether an observed allocation is efficient. However, when considering any particular dimension of the data, it is important that at least one theoretical allocation (efficient or inefficient) comes close to replicating the empirical moments of interest. If none of the models on the table can account for certain features of the data, then the combination of those models and those moments is not useful for learning about efficiency. An example of this issue, which we will discuss in detail, is that it is difficult to use moments involving the real exchange rate to assess efficiency in the context of models that cannot replicate basic properties of real exchange rate dynamics.

2.4. Assessing Welfare Gains and Designing Policy Interventions

Once we have established that a model and an associated market structure offers a reasonable account of several dimensions of relevant data, we can use the model to assess efficiency and answer additional questions. The first is simply to ask, in case the allocations resulting from the model that best fits the data are not efficient, how big are the welfare gains of moving from the observed allocation to an allocation within the set of efficient allocations. This is a number in which many researchers have been interested (see, for example, Cole and Obstfeld, 1991, or Gourinchas and Jeanne, 2006) and a number that, unfortunately, differs widely across different studies. A second question is why, within the context of the model, efficiency is not achieved, and whether instruments are available to a policymaker that could improve welfare while still respecting the frictions in the environment.

We will now proceed to illustrate all of these steps in concrete applications.

3. ASSESSING LONG-RUN EFFICIENCY

We now follow the steps described above to assess the efficiency of long-run allocations of consumption and capital across a large cross section of countries, specifically the set of countries in the Penn World Tables, which have continuous data for the period 1960–2010.

3.1. Preferences, Technologies, and Frictions

We will think about each country in the data as being small relative to a fictional "world economy." The role of the world economy is to pin down the world interest rate. There is one tradable good used for consumption and investment (later we will discuss introducing a nontradable sector). A representative agent in each small country i has preferences

$$\sum_{t=0}^{\infty} \beta^t u\left(C_{it}, \phi_{it}\right),$$

where

$$u\left(C_{it}, \phi_{it}\right) = \phi_{it} \frac{C_{it}^{1-\sigma}}{1-\sigma}$$

and ϕ_{it} is a country and date-specific preference shifter.

The production technology in country i is

$$Y_{it} = F(K_{it}, A_{it}) = K_{it}^{\alpha} A_{it}^{1-\alpha},$$

where K_{it} and A_{it} denote, respectively, capital and labor productivity (hours worked are assumed constant and normalized to one). At date zero, per-capita capital and productivity in each country i are assumed identical to those in the world economy: $K_{i0} = K_0$ and $A_{i0} = A_0$.

The representative agent in the world economy has a similar utility function, absent the preference shifters. World productivity grows at a constant rate $A_{t+1}/A_t = \gamma$. Thus, the world economy features a balanced growth path along which output, consumption and investment all grow at rate γ. The constant gross interest rate along this balanced growth path is given by $R = \gamma^{\sigma}/\beta$.

The risk each small country i faces is growth rate risk. Country i will experience a country-specific growth rate for labor productivity, $A_{i,t+1}/A_{i,t} = \gamma_i$ for all $t \geq 0$. We consider two alternative models for how information about γ_i is revealed. In the first model, which we label "perfect foresight," we assume that γ_i is revealed at date 0, and from that date onward agents are perfectly informed about productivity at each future date. Thus, for example, this model presumes that in 1960 everyone knew that Korea would subsequently grow quickly while Argentina would grow slowly.

In the second model, which we label "repeated surprises," we make the opposite assumption and assume that at each date t, agents assign probability 1 to the event $A_{i,\tau+1}/A_{i,\tau} = \gamma$ for all $\tau \geq t$. Subsequently, they are repeatedly surprised to observe realized growth $A_{i,\tau+1}/A_{i,\tau} = \gamma_i$.

3.2. Efficient Allocations

Allocations $\{C_{it}, K_{i,t+1}\}$ in country i are efficient if they solve the following two planner problems:

1. The time path for consumption $\{C_{it}\}$ solves

$$\max_{\{C_{it}\}_{t=0}^{\infty}} \sum_{t=0}^{\infty} \beta^t u\left(C_{it}, \phi_{it}\right),$$

subject to

$$\sum_{t=0}^{\infty} \frac{C_{it}}{R^t} \leq B_{i0},$$

for some present value of consumption $B_{i0} > 0$ allocated to country i.

2. The time path for capital $\{K_{i,t+1}\}$ solves the following series of problems:

$$\max_{K_{i,t+1}} \left\{E_t\left[F(K_{i,t+1}, A_{i,t+1})\right] + (1-\delta)K_{i,t+1} - RK_{i,t+1}\right\} \qquad \forall t,$$

where the expectation is over possible values for $A_{i,t+1}$ and is conditional on the sequence $\{A_{i\tau}\}_{\tau=0}^{t}$. Under the information structures described above, agents (and the planner) assign probability 1 to the value $A_{i,t+1} = \gamma_i A_{it}$ in the perfect foresight model, and assign probability 1 to $A_{i,t+1} = \gamma A_{it}$ in the repeated surprises model.

Allocations for consumption that solve the first problem satisfy consumption efficiency. The first-order conditions with respect to C_{it} and $C_{i,t+1}$ imply

$$\frac{\phi_{it}}{\beta \phi_{i,t+1}} \left(\frac{C_{it}}{C_{i,t+1}} \right)^{-\sigma} = R \qquad \forall t. \tag{1}$$

Thus, the intertemporal marginal rate of substitution of consumption in each country i is equated to the world gross return to capital. Different choices for B_{i0} correspond to different levels for country i's consumption, each of which corresponds to a different point on the Pareto frontier.

Allocations for capital that solve the second problem satisfy production efficiency. The first-order condition with respect to $K_{i,t+1}$ is

$$E_t \left[\alpha \left(\frac{K_{i,t+1}}{A_{i,t+1}} \right)^{\alpha-1} \right] + (1 - \delta) = R \qquad \forall t. \tag{2}$$

Thus, the expected marginal product of capital is equal to that in the world economy for all $t \geq 1$.

Note that consumption efficiency (equation (1)) is a difficult equation to test empirically, absent knowledge of the preference shifters ϕ_{it}. Production efficiency (equation (2)) is in principle easier to test because it does not involve preferences.[1]

Suppose we assume common preferences across countries (i.e., $\phi_{it} = 1$ for all i and for all t). This will be our baseline assumption. Then the consumption efficiency condition 1 simplifies to

$$\frac{1}{\beta} \left(\frac{C_{i,t+1}}{C_{it}} \right)^{\sigma} = R \qquad \forall t,$$

which implies that all countries share the same consumption growth rate.

3.3. Market Allocations

Now that we have characterized efficient allocations, we will consider decentralized competitive equilibria under alternative explicit market structures, to investigate when and where deviations from efficiency arise.

---

[1] However, note that since capital must be put in place one period in advance, if the realized value for $A_{i,t+1}$ differs from the expected value, the realized marginal product of capital will differ from the world interest rate. Still, given those expectations, the allocation of capital is efficient *ex ante*. There is no expectation sign in the consumption efficiency condition, because consumption can be instantaneously reallocated across countries.

Financial Autarky. Here we assume no asset trade between countries. The absence of asset trade means that each country's net exports must be zero at each date, because there is no way to import the tradable good in return for a contractual promise to export the tradable good at a future date. The resource constraint is

$$C_{it} + K_{i,t+1} = F(K_{it}, A_{it}) + (1 - \delta)K_{it} \qquad \forall t.$$

Under financial autarky, we can envision allocations in each country being determined by a country-specific planner who maximizes expected lifetime utility subject to the resource constraint. The first-order condition for capital accumulation is

$$\phi_{it} C_{it}^{-\sigma} = \beta E_t \left[\phi_{i,t+1} C_{i,t+1}^{-\sigma} \left(1 + \alpha \left(\frac{K_{i,t+1}}{A_{i,t+1}} \right)^{\alpha-1} - \delta \right) \right].$$

The previous equation indicates that agents will choose to equate the expected marginal rate of substitution to the expected marginal rate of transformation. However, absent international asset trade, the marginal rate of substitution will not in general be equalized across countries. In contrast, equilibrium consumption growth rates will be country specific and mirror country-specific productivity growth rates. Given differential consumption growth, countries will optimally choose country-specific marginal products of capital. This teaches us something useful about the two efficiency conditions described above, namely, that efficiency requires that both hold jointly. In the financial autarky economy, when missing asset markets lead to a deviation from consumption efficiency, it is not optimal to equate the marginal product of capital across countries, and so the production efficiency condition is not satisfied either.

Bond Economy. Under this market structure, agents in country i can borrow and lend from the world economy by trading an international one period bond whose price is R^{-1}. We assume that residents in country i hold all the domestic capital and finance all domestic investment. At each date, country i faces a budget constraint of the form

$$C_{it} + K_{i,t+1} + \frac{B_{i,t+1}}{R} = F(K_{it}, A_{it}) + (1 - \delta)K_{it} + B_{it} \qquad \forall t,$$

where $B_{i0} = 0$.[2]

Whether efficiency is achieved in the bond economy model depends on the model for expectations. Given perfect foresight, trade in a bond delivers efficiency. To understand this result, consider the capital and bond accumulation choices for the representative agent in country i. Given perfect foresight, the two corresponding intertemporal first-order conditions deliver the two hallmark conditions for efficiency described above: the

---

[2] An alternative would be to assume that agents hold all their wealth in the international bond and that foreigners own all domestic capital. Given perfect foresight about productivity growth, these two alternative assumptions on portfolios would be identical, since returns will be equalized across countries. In the repeated surprises model, expected returns will be equated, but the assumption about who owns domestic capital will have a minor impact on *ex post* returns.

intertemporal marginal rate of substitution is equalized across countries, and the marginal product of capital is equalized across countries. Note that asset trade is crucial to delivering this outcome. In particular, bond trade equates the marginal rate of substitution across countries, since the bond offers countries a common rate at which to exchange current for future consumption. Then arbitrage within each country leads to investment choices that equate the expected (country-specific) marginal product of capital to the (common global) interest rate.

Things are slightly different in the repeated surprise version of the bond economy. The expected marginal rate of substitution is again equalized across countries and equal to the world interest rate. Arbitrage again equates the expected marginal product of capital across countries to the world interest rate, thereby achieving productive efficiency. However, consumption efficiency is not achieved. Although the *expected* marginal rate of substitution is equated, *ex post* fast-growing countries will enjoy faster consumption growth than slow-growing countries. Given common preferences, this is inefficient.

Complete Markets. In this economy, people trade a full set of state-contingent claims at each date.[3]

In the complete markets model, allocations are always efficient. Each country invests to equate the expected return to capital to the world interest rate. Trade in contingent claims ensures that the marginal utility of consumption in each country i grows at the same rate as in the world economy. Absent preference shifters (i.e., assuming $\phi_{it} = 1$), the level of consumption is equal to that in the world economy at each date, $C_{it} = C_t$.

Although allocations in the complete markets and bond economy models are both efficient under perfect foresight, the two market structures pick out different points on the Pareto frontier. With complete markets, insurance in the initial period translates into growth-rate-specific initial transfers that equate the present value of consumption across countries. With only a bond, in contrast, the present value of each country's consumption reflects the present value of country-specific net output, corresponding to the planner's problem defining efficient allocations with $B_{i0} = 0$. In this case (assuming common preferences), countries with faster productivity growth will enjoy higher consumption at each date.

3.4. Comparing Models and Data

We start the section by first describing some general features of the data we are going to use to assess efficiency.

---

[3] In the perfect foresight version of the model, an alternative way to complete markets is to assume that agents initially trade Arrow securities contingent on the realization of the vector $\{\gamma_i\}$. After the vector $\{\gamma_i\}$ is realized, the securities pay out. Then, and in every subsequent period, the market structure corresponds to that in the bond economy model, where the starting bond position B_{i0} is the payoff from initial trade in Arrow securities.

3.4.1. Data

In Figures 9.1–9.3 we describe some details of the growth experiences of all the 112 countries that have continuous data in the Penn World Tables over the period 1960–2010. First consider in Figure 9.1 the plot of consumption growth against output growth. Growth rates show dramatic variation, ranging from some African countries, where output grew as many as 4 percentage points per year slower than the world average, to China, where output grew 4 percentage points faster. In terms of corresponding growth in consumption, countries almost line up along the 45 degree line. However, the least squares regression line suggests that faster output growth does not translate quite one-for-one into faster consumption growth: if one country's output grows 1 percentage point per year faster than another's, the faster-growing country on average enjoys a 0.86 percentage point faster growth rate for consumption.

Next, Figure 9.2 plots the relationship between output growth on the one hand and the growth of investment on the other. Notice that once again, countries tend to line up along the 45 degree line. However, the least squares regression line suggests that faster output growth translates more than one-for-one into faster investment growth. If one country's output grows 1 percentage point per year faster than another's, the faster growing country experiences a 1.07 percentage point faster growth rate for investment.

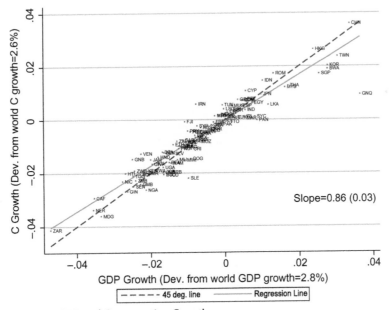

Figure 9.1 Long-Run GDP and Consumption Growth

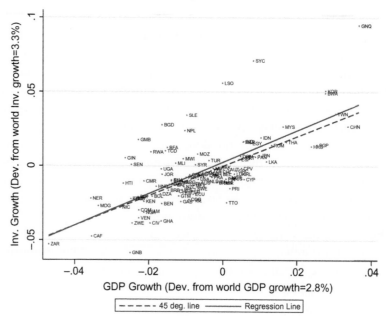

Figure 9.2 Long-Run GDP and Investment Growth

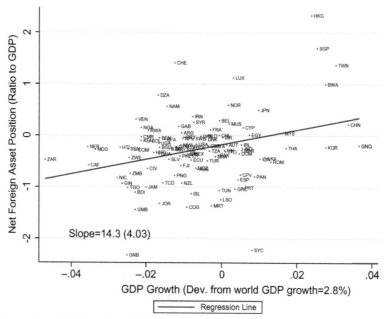

Figure 9.3 Long-Run GDP Growth and Net Foreign Asset Positions

Finally, in Figure 9.3 we plot the relationship between output growth and the end of sample net foreign asset (NFA) position.[4] Here we note that there is not much evidence of a systematic relationship between the two variables: the set of country points form something of a cloud. To the extent that there is a relationship, it is positive, as Gourinchas and Jeanne (2013) originally emphasized for the set of developing countries. Faster-growing countries (like Singapore or China) tend to have accumulated positive NFA positions, whereas slow-growing countries (like Niger or Nicaragua) have accumulated negative positions. Alfaro et al. (2011) argue that once one strips official sovereign flows out of international capital flows, fast growers on average are net recipients of private international capital flows, though the relationship remains noisy. Finally, note that most countries' absolute NFA positions are smaller than 50 percent of their GDP.

3.4.2. The Perfect Foresight Model: Predictions

We now quantitatively compare the predictions of the three market structures with the data. We set the preference parameters β and σ to relatively standard values of 0.97 and 2. We set the technology parameters α and δ to 0.36 and 0.06. We set the growth rate of labor productivity in the world economy γ so that aggregate consumption at each date is equal to average consumption across a set of bond economies, where the distribution of country productivity growth rates in the set corresponds to the distribution of output growth in our Penn World Table sample. The implied growth rate for world productivity is 2.46% per year, so $\gamma = 1.0246$. Our choices for γ, σ, and β translate into a constant world interest rate of 8.2%.[5]

We then consider a range of constant country-specific growth rates from 4% slower to 4% faster than the world growth rate, which covers the range of country experiences in our data. Thus, $\gamma_i \in [1.0246 - 0.04, 1.0246 + 0.04]$.[6]

---

[4] Net foreign asset position data are from Lane and Milesi-Ferretti (2007) and refer to the end of 2007. The number of countries represented in Figure 9.3 is slightly smaller than the number in Figures 9.1 and 9.2 (108 vs. 112), since NFA data are not available for all countries in the Penn World Tables.

[5] This interest rate is high relative to most empirical estimates. It is high because this is a model with growth. Setting $\beta = 1$ would reduce R to 5.0%, but would be less appealing from the standpoint of the welfare calculations presented later. An alternative approach would be to use non-time-separable preferences à la Epstein and Zin (1989).

[6] Characterizing equilibria for these economies is fairly straightforward. Given a fixed and exogenous world interest rate, the bond economy model is analytically tractable. At each date, consumption is set such that the expected present value of current and future consumption equals the expected present value of current and future labor earnings plus the gross return on initial wealth. For example, date 0 consumption in the perfect foresight version of the bond model is given by

$$\frac{C_{i0}}{1 - \frac{\gamma}{R}} = \frac{(1 - \alpha)K_{i0}^{\alpha}A_{i0}^{1-\alpha}}{1 - \frac{\gamma_i}{R}} + RK_{i0},$$

where the left-hand side defines the present value of consumption (which grows at rate γ), and the right-hand side captures the expected present value of lifetime earnings (which grows at rate γ_i), plus the gross return on initial wealth. Allocations in the autarky model must be characterized numerically. We guess an initial value for consumption and then use the intertemporal first-order condition for investment alongside the resource constraint to iterate forward and verify convergence to the balanced growth path.

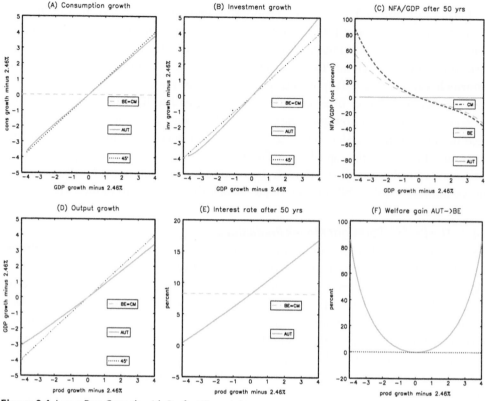

Figure 9.4 Long-Run Growth with Perfect Foresight

Figure 9.4 plots the model predictions for each market structure, assuming perfect foresight about country-specific productivity growth. Panels A and B plot average consumption and investment growth against average output growth. Panel C plots the ratio of net foreign assets to output in year 50—a value of one means that holdings of the international bond are equal to output. Panel D plots average annual output growth over a 50-year period relative to annual labor productivity growth γ_i. Panel E plots the net interest rate in year 50. Finally, Panel F shows the welfare gain of being able to trade the international bond relative to autarky, measured as the constant percentage increase in autarky consumption required to deliver equal lifetime utility to that achieved in the bond economy.

First consider autarky. Here, because net exports are zero at each date, the net foreign asset position remains constant at zero. Faster productivity growth translates into faster output growth (Panel D), and because there is no scope for international borrowing and lending, faster output growth translates into faster consumption growth (Panel A). Indeed, if countries have time-invariant preferences, then in the limit as $t \to \infty$, each country i

will converge to a country-specific balanced growth path, in which capital, output, and consumption will all grow at the country-specific growth rate for labor productivity γ_i. Differentials in consumption growth translate into interest rate differentials, with faster-growing countries having higher interest rates (Panel E). These interest rate differentials are very large: at a 5% growth rate, the balanced growth path interest rate is $1.05^2/0.97 = 13.7\%$ whereas at a 0% growth rate, the interest rate is $1/0.97 = 3.1\%$.

A couple of details are worth noting about the autarky economy. First, for slow-growing countries, because the domestic balanced growth path interest rate is lower than for the world economy, capital must grow more rapidly than productivity during transition. Thus, in slow-growing countries, output growth exceeds productivity growth (Panel D). Second, in slow-growing countries, consumption growth tends to exceed output growth, whereas investment grows more slowly than output (Panels A and B). Again, this is because slow-growing countries divert a relatively large share of output to investment rather than consumption early in the transition.

Now look at the bond economy and the complete markets economy. The first thing to note is that the implications of these two economies are quite similar. First, consumption efficiency (equation (1)) implies that country consumption growth is divorced from country output growth. Production efficiency (equation (2)) implies that interest rates and the marginal product of capital are equated across countries (Panel E), and the growth rates of country output and investment are therefore identical to the growth rate of country productivity (Panels B and D). With common preferences across countries, as in this example, consumption growth is equated across countries (Panel A).

Although the paths for capital and output in the complete markets and bond economy models are identical, the levels of country-specific consumption paths, as well as the dynamics for net exports and net foreign asset positions, differ slightly across the two market structures. In both cases, however, fast-growing countries have accumulated large negative net foreign asset positions after 50 years of fast growth. For example, in the bond economy model, a country growing consistently 1 percentage point faster than the world economy has a negative net foreign asset position exceeding 600% of GDP. The logic is simply that a country that knows it will grow fast and thus has high permanent income relative to current income at date 0 sets initial consumption equal to permanent income and finances the gap between permanent and current income by borrowing from abroad. Net foreign asset positions are even larger in the complete markets economy, since countries that draw fast growth rates must make large initial transfers, and thus begin the transition with large negative net foreign asset positions.

3.4.3. The Perfect Foresight Model: Comparing with Data
Which market structure predicts outcomes that most closely approximate the historical experiences of actual economies as described above?

At first glance, the implications of the bond and complete markets models appear grossly counterfactual. First, consumption growth closely tracks output growth in our sample of countries. Countries that have enjoyed relatively fast economic growth (like Korea) now enjoy higher consumption levels than countries that have not (like Argentina). This stands in stark contrast to the complete markets and bond economy models, in which—given perfect foresight—consumption should grow at the same rate in all countries.

However, it is important to note that ours is a model in which all output is tradable. Suppose a fraction of output actually comprises nontradable goods. Nontradable consumption will—by definition—track nontradable output. If countries with faster growth in aggregate output also enjoy faster growth in nontradable output, then aggregate consumption will tend to track aggregate output, even if asset markets are complete. The quantitative predictions of such a model for growth in aggregate output and consumption will depend on the details of how nontradables are introduced. With separable preferences over tradable and nontradable consumption, as well as an endowment process for nontradable output, all the pictures plotted in Figure 9.4 still apply, except that now they should be interpreted as applying to the tradable sector only. How would the predictions for aggregate consumption and output change? To develop one concrete example, suppose that preferences over tradables c_t^T and nontradables c_t^N take the form

$$u(c_t^T, c_t^N) = \alpha \log c_t^T + (1 - \alpha) \log c_t^N.$$

Suppose in addition that the nontradable endowment grows at rate γ_i, the growth rate of labor productivity in the tradable sector. In such a model, aggregate consumption in country i will grow at gross rate $\gamma^\alpha \gamma_i^{(1-\alpha)}$. The growth rate of aggregate output will vary over time, but at the date when tradable consumption equals tradable output, output will be growing at rate γ_i. Thus, the larger is nontradables share in consumption $(1 - \alpha)$, the closer will be the growth rate of consumption to the growth rate of output. In the data, the slope of a regression of consumption growth on output growth is 0.86 over the period 1960–2010, which the model can replicate given a nontradable share of $(1 - \alpha) = 0.86$. This exceeds all reasonable estimates of the fraction of output that is nontradable, indicating that while introducing nontradables can account for some of the comovement between output and consumption in our cross section of countries, it cannot explain all of it: comovement remains between growth in output of tradables and growth in consumption of tradables.

A second problem with the complete markets and bond economy models is that they predict enormous net foreign asset positions, with fast-growing countries accumulating large negative net foreign asset positions. Introducing a nontradable sector in the model would imply smaller net foreign asset positions. For example, suppose for a country with a particular growth rate γ_i, tradable output was 50% of total output after 50 years. Then the net foreign asset position relative to total output would be half as large as the one suggested by Panel C of Figure 9.4. However, such positions would still be much larger than those observed in the data. Moreover, the systematic theoretical link between faster growth and more negative NFA positions is absent in the data, where the correlation between past growth and the current NFA position is positive.

That seems to leave the financial autarky model as the most plausible baseline market structure. Indeed, in some respects the autarky model offers a reasonable account of the nature of growth across fast- versus slow-growing countries. As noted above, the autarky model replicates the fact that consumption (investment) growth in relatively slow-growing countries tends to be faster (slower) than output growth. However, the financial autarky model faces some challenges of its own. In particular, that model implies very large differences in the marginal product of capital across countries, whereas in practice the marginal product of capital appears to be roughly equalized (see Caselli and Feyrer, 2007). Relatedly, the model is also inconsistent with Kaldor's (1957) economic growth facts, since the capital-to-output ratio rises over time in slow-growing countries and falls in fast-growing countries.

3.4.4. Alternative Model 1: Repeated Surprises

A key challenge to the models presented thus far is that it is difficult to reconcile cross-country differences in expected consumption growth rates with common-across-countries returns to capital. The autarky model generates differences in long-term expected growth rates but also implies country-specific returns, whereas conversely asset trade ensures a common world interest but seems to dictate equalization of expected growth rates.

One way to reconcile the two facts is to postulate that fast-growing countries never expected such rapid growth, and that slow-growing countries never expected to stagnate relative to the rest of the world. If all countries expect identical future productivity growth, then trade in a bond will equate expected consumption growth rates (and expected returns to capital) but will not equate realized consumption growth if some countries consistently enjoy faster productivity growth than others. Figure 9.5 describes the growth dynamics under the "repeated surprises" scenario, in which agents always expect country productivity to grow at a 2.46% rate.[7]

Here, the plots for complete markets and autarky look very similar to those for the perfect foresight model. Under complete markets, consumption is again equalized across countries. Because agents underestimate growth in fast-growing countries, and installed capital cannot be instantly reallocated, the complete markets model now delivers small differences in returns to capital across countries, with slightly higher returns in fast-growing

---

[7] This model is slightly more complicated to solve. In autarky, at each date t, we solve for consumption such that given expected future productivity growth at rate γ, the economy converges to the world economy balanced growth path. This value for consumption determines the capital-to-output ratio in $t + 1$. When $\gamma_i \neq \gamma$, this ratio is not the one expected at date t, and thus a new transition path must be computed to determine consumption at $t + 1$.

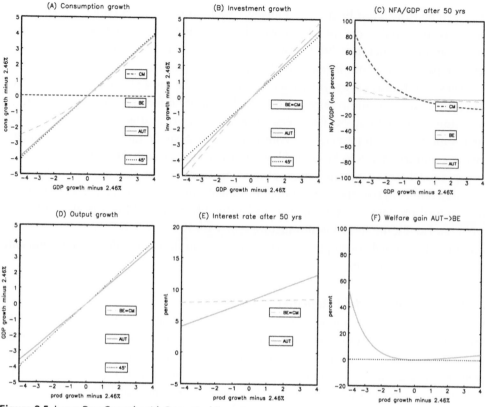

Figure 9.5 Long-Run Growth with Repeated Surprises

countries. The autarky model now generates smaller interest rate differentials across countries relative to the perfect foresight model. The logic is that fast-growing countries now (mistakenly) expect slower consumption growth, and thus a lower interest rate leaves them indifferent on the margin between consuming and investing.

The economy that looks most different relative to the perfect foresight specification is the bond economy. In the repeated surprise version of this economy, consumption growth broadly follows output growth. Thus, the allocation of consumption is no longer efficient. However, consumption growth exceeds output growth for slow-growing countries, whereas consumption growth is weaker than output growth for fast-growing countries, so some consumption smoothing is achieved. Slow-growing countries still accumulate large positive NFA positions relative to output, whereas fast-growing countries accumulate large deficits. The logic for these patterns is that at each date during transition, a slow-growing country sees current income turn out lower than expected and revises downward expected permanent income. Relative to actual income, wealth is higher than expected. But the slow-growing country does not want to reduce savings, because the representative agent is a permanent income consumer. Rather, the slow-growing country invests its excess wealth abroad, and the NFA position rises. Consumption growth for the slow-growing country is faster than output growth because as the NFA position rises, an ever-increasing share of consumption comes from interest income out of saving, and thus the consumption-to-output ratio rises.

Overall, with the repeated-surprise model for expectations, the bond economy offers a more reasonable account of the data. The key strength of the model is that it can deliver an equilibrium outcome in which realized long-run consumption growth rates differ across countries, while returns to capital are roughly equalized. The one dimension along which the model remains most at odds with the data is the dynamics of capital flows. For example, a country that grows (unexpectedly) 1 percentage point faster than the rest of the world for 50 years should end up with a negative net foreign asset position approaching 100% of GDP, whereas a country that grows 1 percentage point slower should end up with a positive position of around 150% of GDP. These numbers are very large relative to the actual variation in the NFA position across countries (see Figure 9.3). As in the perfect foresight version of the model, introducing a nontradable sector would imply smaller NFA positions.

An alternative or complementary explanation for the relatively small net foreign asset positions observed in the data is that countries differ with respect to preferences, and that preferences vary systematically with productivity growth such that fast-growing countries also tend to be more patient. We will explore this possibility in the next section.

3.4.5. Alternative Model 2: Preference Variation

Suppose that in the data we observe cross-country equality in marginal products of capital (as argued by Caselli and Feyrer, 2007) but cross-country variation in consumption growth. In the context of a model with asset trade, this can only be explained by country variation in preferences. Moreover, if one assumes that countries can trade a bond freely, then the first-order condition for bonds can be used to identify preference shocks from data on consumption and interest rates. For example, if $\frac{\phi_{i,t+1}}{\phi_{it}} = \frac{\beta_i}{\beta}$, so that countries differ with respect to their rates of time preference, then the constant expected consumption growth rate for country i will be given by

$$\frac{E\left[C_{i,t+1}\right]}{C_{it}} = \left(\beta_i R\right)^{\frac{1}{\sigma}}.$$

The identification of preference shocks is important since it affects the calculation of the welfare gains from alternative market structures and the assessment of whether allocations are efficient. To see this, consider the allocation for capital and consumption along the equilibrium path of the bond economy model under the baseline calibration in which $\phi_{it} = 1$ for all t. Denote this allocation $\{K_{it}^{BE}, C_{it}^{BE}\}$. One can then construct an alternative time-varying path $\{\tilde{\phi}_{it}\}$ such that given $\{\tilde{\phi}_{it}\}$, the equilibrium in the bond economy model features exactly the same path $\{K_{it}^{BE}\}$ but where the path for consumption $\{\tilde{C}_{it}\}$ is different and such that there is no bond trade. In particular, this path $\{\tilde{\phi}_{it}\}$ can be reverse engineered from the intertemporal first-order condition, by setting consumption equal to the difference between domestic output and domestic investment at each date t and computing the value for $\tilde{\phi}_{i,t+1}$ such that the first-order condition is satisfied:

$$\tilde{\phi}_{i,t+1} = \frac{\tilde{\phi}_{it}\tilde{C}_{it}^{-\sigma}}{\beta R \tilde{\phi}_{i,t+1} E_t \left[\tilde{C}_{i,t+1}^{-\sigma} \right]},$$

where

$$\tilde{C}_{it} = \left(K_{it}^{BE} \right)^\alpha A_{it}^{1-\alpha} - K_{i,t+1}^{BE} + (1-\delta)K_{it}^{BE}$$

and $\tilde{\phi}_{i0} = 1$. Note that because the time path for capital is identical to that in the original bond economy model, expected returns are equal to the world interest rate at each date. At this common world interest rate, given preferences described by $\{\tilde{\phi}_{it}\}$, agents have no incentives to trade bonds, and thus allocations with a bond market are identical to those under financial autarky.[8] It follows that if preferences were truly described by $\{\tilde{\phi}_{it}\}$, then the welfare gains of moving from financial autarky to a bond economy market structure would be zero. Moreover, given perfect foresight, allocations under financial autarky would be efficient.

What do the paths $\{\tilde{\phi}_{it}\}$ look like for the countries with the sorts of growth experiences in our Penn World Tables sample? It turns out that under both models for expectations, the required growth rate for $\tilde{\phi}_{it}$ is constant after the initial period. Thus, we can express preference differences across countries in terms of differences in the rate of time preference. Given perfect foresight, the mapping from γ_i to β_i such that the bond economy and autarky allocations coincide is defined by $\frac{\beta_i}{\gamma_i^\sigma} = \frac{\beta}{\gamma^\sigma} = R$. The mapping is more involved in the repeated surprises model. We plot both mappings in Figure 9.6.

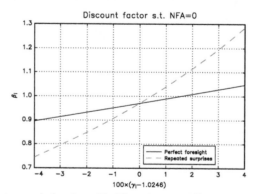

Figure 9.6 Discount Factors such that Autarkic Allocations are Efficient

---

[8] Bond economy allocations are identical to those under financial autarky given the preference path $\{\tilde{\phi}_{it}\}$. They are not identical to allocations under financial autarky assuming $\phi_{it} = 1$ for all t.

Note that much larger cross-country variation in the rate of time preference is required to generate an absence of asset trade in the repeated surprises model. The logic is that in that model, in each period a slow-growing country finds itself with too much capital relative to productivity. To be willing to immediately consume all this excess capital (rather than invest in the bond), the slow-growing country must be very impatient.

From a positive perspective, the models with preference heterogeneity seem to offer a reasonable approximation to the experiences of fast- versus slow-growing economies. Consumption growth tends to track output growth, and fast-growing countries are not net foreign savers. At the same time, interest rates are equated across countries. However, before concluding that cross-country heterogeneity in preferences accounts for cross-country heterogeneity in savings rates, it would be nice to see some independent evidence (besides the differences in savings rates) that preferences really do differ across countries.

In this light, one leading candidate explanation for observed "global imbalances" (see Chapter 10 by Gourinchas and Rey in this volume) is that countries in which idiosyncratic household-level risk is larger and/or less well insured have a stronger precautionary motive to save. In practice, a stronger precautionary motive will deliver very similar aggregate predictions to a higher discount factor. In particular, following international capital market liberalization, those countries with a stronger precautionary motive will reduce current consumption and lend to the rest of the world (see Mendoza et al., 2009).

Although differences in idiosyncratic risk are an appealing potential justification for differences in patience it is not obvious why greater idiosyncratic risk should be systematically connected to faster growth. Some recent research develops models in which, because of domestic financial frictions, reforms which fuel growth simultaneously generate an increase in saving with the rest of the world. A common feature of those models is that the determinant of external saving is not the marginal rate of substitution (MRS) of the representative agent (i.e., aggregate consumption growth), but rather the MRS of a subset of agents in the country which has a stronger desire to save. This can be either because the savers face entrepreneurial risk (Sandri, 2010), because the savers are not the ones benefitting from faster growth (Song et al., 2011), or because fast growth implies rising wages and thus declining income for employers (Buera and Shin, 2011). It remains an open quantitative question whether these mechanisms can generate strong enough incentives for external saving to dominate the standard intertemporal motives that link relatively fast growth to capital inflows in the simple models we have worked through in this section. An alternative way to connect patience and growth that does not rely on financial frictions is to posit that patience drives growth, because more patient countries are more likely to devote current resources toward investments that are conducive to long-run growth (for more on this see Doepke and Zilibotti, 2006).

3.4.6. Comparing All Models

Table 9.1 summarizes various features of the data for our sample of countries and for the various models we have considered.

Table 9.1 Long-Run Growth Patterns in the Data and in Theory

	DATA			MODELS						
				Perfect Foresight			Repeated Surprises			Alt.Prefs Foresight
	(1)	(2)	(3)	(4)	(5)	(6)	(7)	(8)	(9)	(10)
Dep. Variable	1960–2010	60–85	86–10	AUT	BE	CM	AUT	BE	CM	BE = AUT
(1) Cons. Growth	0.86	0.88	0.70	0.94	0.00*	0.00*	0.97	0.78	0.00*	1.00*
	(0.03)	(0.036)	(0.038)	(0.00)	(0.00)	(0.00)	(0.00)	(0.01)	(0.00)	(0.00)
(2) Inv. Growth	1.07	1.04	1.39	1.21	1.00*	1.00*	1.11	1.29*	1.25*	1.00*
	(0.11)	(0.13)	(0.12)	(0.00)	(0.00)	(0.00)	(0.00)	(0.00)	(0.00)	(0.00)
(3) ΔNFA/GDP	14.3	7.75	3.82	0.00	−865*	−1196*	0.00	−174	−947*	0.00*
	(4.03)	(2.81)	(2.79)		(24.9)	(48.0)		(10.2)	(55.0)	

Notes: The labels AUT, BE, and CM denote, respectively, the financial autarky, bond economy, and complete markets models. * next to a coefficient denotes that the allocation for the dependent variable is efficient. Each coefficient corresponds to the OLS coefficient on average annual growth in GDP per capita (standard errors are in parentheses). The dependent variables are: (1) growth in consumption per capita, (2) growth in investment per capita, and (3) the sample period change in the ratio of net foreign assets to GDP. Each regression includes a constant. We assume that NFA/GDP $_{1960} = 0$. The sample of countries for regressions (1) and (2) is the set of 112 countries in the Penn World Tables with data over the entire 1960–2010 period. The sample for the regressions in row (3) is the set of 108 countries with NFA position data in the IMF International Financial Statistics.

Column (1) simply reports the least squares slope coefficients plotted in Figures 9.1, 9.2, and 9.3. Columns (2) and (3) present results from splitting the sample into two equal length subperiods, one from 1960 to 1985, and a second from 1986 to 2010. Because of greater international financial integration in the second subperiod, one might expect to find more evidence of international risk sharing. Indeed it appears that country consumption growth has become less tightly linked to country output growth over time, suggesting movement toward a more efficient cross-country allocation of consumption. Comparing the empirical consumption regression coefficients with the ones for various models reported in columns (4)–(10), one interpretation of this reduced sensitivity is that autarky was a reasonable approximation to the world economy in the first half of the sample period, whereas in the second part the bond economy under the repeated surprises model for expectations looks like a reasonable candidate model. However, note that the allocation of consumption is not efficient under either of these models.

In addition, capital flows in the wrong direction relative to all the theoretical models in columns (5), (6), (8), and (9). The models predict that fast-growing countries should be using international financial markets to fund high investment rates and (in the foresight models) to increase consumption in line with high expected future income. Instead, fast-growing countries have on average been exporting savings and increasing their net foreign asset positions over time. Comparing row (3) columns (2) and (3) indicates no evidence of a change in the direction of capital flows over time.

Since none of the models offers a compelling positive theory of capital flows, it is difficult to interpret what the capital flow evidence has to say about risk sharing. In addition, although it seems that we can reject consumption efficiency, recall that our simple models abstract from nontradables. Conceivably, if nontradables are very important, one might be able to reconcile the second-period consumption regression coefficient with efficiency. To bring some more evidence to bear on these issues, we now assess how the three indicators of efficiency developed above vary with two popular measures of openness. The first is the *de jure* index of capital market openness developed by Chinn and Ito (2008). The second is simple trade openness. In Table 9.2 we report regression coefficients analogous to those in Table 9.1 for four subgroups of our 1986–2010 sample: countries with Chinn-Ito index values above the sample median (Capital Open) and below the sample median (Capital Closed), and countries with trade (imports plus exports) over GDP above the sample median (Trade Open) and below the sample median (Trade Closed).

Surprisingly, countries with more open capital markets seem to enjoy less risk sharing according to all three measures. In particular, within the set of financially open countries, consumption and investment track output quite closely, and capital flows out of rather than into relatively fast-growing countries. One interpretation of this evidence is that actual international capital flows typically work against risk sharing and that financially closed economies achieve more efficient allocations than financially open ones (we will develop a simple model with this feature in Section 4.4.2). An alternative interpretation

Table 9.2 Efficiency and Openness

| | Sample: 1986–2010 | | | |
Dependent variable:	(1) Capital Open	(2) Capital Closed	(3) Trade Open	(4) Trade Closed
(1) Cons. Growth	0.80	0.65	0.61	0.83
	(0.06)	(0.05)	(0.06)	(0.05)
(2) Inv. Growth	0.95	1.55	1.56	1.16
	(0.24)	(0.15)	(0.17)	(0.18)
(3)ΔNFA/GDP	14.8	0.68	6.17	−2.50
	(6.8)	(2.8)	(4.20)	(3.61)

Note: Each number is the OLS coefficient on average annual growth in GDP per capita (standard errors in parentheses).

is that the model in which countries differ only with respect to productivity growth is the wrong model for understanding international capital flows. In the spirit of the example economy with preference heterogeneity and/or differential precautionary saving motives described above, perhaps fast-growing countries are effectively so much more patient than slow-growing countries that, given the chance, they would choose to lend to their slow-growing neighbors rather than borrow from them.

Greater trade openness translates into better risk sharing, according to the consumption risk-sharing indicator. One possible interpretation of this finding is that nontradables account for a larger fraction of output in countries that trade relatively little, leading to a stronger tendency for consumption growth to track income growth. If a country trades relatively little because it faces relatively high transportation costs, relatively strong comovement between output and consumption is efficient.

3.5. Welfare

In our numerical example, we can compare welfare across alternative market structures. Panel *F* in Figures 9.4 and 9.5 shows the permanent percentage increase in consumption under autarky that delivers equal welfare to the bond economy, conditional on the country growth rate being γ_i. Given perfect foresight about productivity growth, expected welfare *ex ante* and realized welfare *ex post* are the same. In the repeated surprise model, the two welfare measures are different. We focus on realized welfare.

In the perfect foresight economy, welfare gains are U-shaped and approximately symmetrical. If $\gamma_i = \gamma$, so that country productivity growth is identical to that in the world economy, then there are no welfare gains from being able to trade a bond: autarkic allocations are efficient. As the absolute difference between γ_i and γ increases, the welfare gains from bond trade increase and become very large. For countries growing

4 percentage points faster or slower than the world economy, the welfare gains reach 100% of consumption. One might wonder whether welfare gains would be larger or smaller in an endowment economy version of the model. In fact, in an endowment economy, one can solve for the welfare gain in closed form.[9] Quantitatively, welfare gains turn out to be similar in the endowment and production economy versions of the model.

Now look at the corresponding plot for the repeated surprise economy (Panel F, Figure 9.5). Welfare gains from being able to trade a bond are smaller here. The reason is that fast-growing countries do not anticipate fast growth and therefore do not borrow so much early in transition. However, even in this case the welfare gains from trade in a bond are nontrivial. The reason is that bond trade gives access to foreign capital to fast-growing (high autarkic interest rate) countries that are net foreign borrowers, and gives higher returns on saving to slow-growing (low autarkic interest rate) countries that are net foreign lenders.

Suppose we were to extend the model to include a nontradable sector as discussed above. How would that change the welfare results? The answer, assuming tradables and nontradables enter preferences separably, is that the welfare gains of introducing bond trade will be exactly those plotted, except that now they should be interpreted as measuring the percentage increase in tradable consumption required to leave the agent indifferent between the two market structures (given the same nontradable consumption in both cases).

We now estimate the average welfare gain of moving from autarky to free bond trade in our panel of countries in the Penn World Tables. More precisely, we ask what is the permanent percentage increase in consumption under autarky that would leave an individual indifferent between being allocated a nationality at random in 1960, knowing that each country will remain permanently in autarky, versus experiencing the same lottery given free bond trade between countries at the world risk-free rate?[10] We also compute the analogous welfare gain associated with moving from autarky to complete markets. We then redo both experiments assuming that the lottery is between the bond economy on the one hand versus autarky or complete markets on the other.[11] Table 9.3 shows the results, under both models for expectations.

---

[9] The expression for the welfare gain is $100 \times \left(\left(\frac{\gamma^\sigma - \beta\gamma}{\gamma^\sigma - \beta\gamma_i} \right) \left(\frac{1 - \beta\gamma_i^{1-\sigma}}{1 - \beta\gamma^{1-\sigma}} \right)^{\frac{1}{1-\sigma}} - 1 \right)$, where γ_i and γ now denote the growth rates of the endowment in country i and in the world economy.

[10] Note that this thought experiment abstracts from inequality in initial conditions in 1960, since we assume all countries share the same initial capital and productivity, irrespective of market structure. By assuming that agents assign the same probability to drawing China's growth rate as Iceland's, the calculation also abstracts from heterogeneity in country size.

[11] For the purposes of these calculations, we take the distribution of γ_i to be the set of annual output per capita growth rates in our Penn World Tables sample over the period 1960–2010, since country output and country productivity grow at the same rate in the bond economy given perfect foresight. Since aggregate consumption grows at the same rate in the (perfect foresight) bond and complete markets models, the welfare gains associated with moving from a bond economy to complete markets come solely from equalizing the distribution of consumption.

Table 9.3 Welfare Gains of Moving from Market Structure *A* to *B*

Structure *A*	Structure *B*	Gain (% of Cons.) Perfect Foresight	Gain (% of Cons.) Repeated Surprises
AUT	*BOND*	9.6	4.8
AUT	*CM*	16.0	16.8
BOND	*AUT*	−8.8	−4.6
BOND	*CM*	5.9	11.4

The welfare gain from being able to trade a bond is equivalent to a 9.6% increase in consumption in financial autarky, assuming perfect foresight about future productivity growth. Given access to a bond, the additional gain from being able to insure against growth rate risk is worth 5.9% of consumption. Recall that bond trade in our example offers no insurance, in the sense that bond markets open only after γ_i is drawn, after which point each country's destiny is known. Rather, bond trade just allows countries to allocate capital and consumption more efficiently across countries. It is perhaps surprising that the welfare gains from achieving efficient intertemporal allocations within countries exceed the additional potential gains from being able to insure *ex ante* against the draw for γ_i and equating the level of consumption across countries. Note also that these welfare gains are extremely large relative to Lucas's (1987) estimates of the welfare costs of business cycles (0.008%). The reason they are so much larger is simply that here we are evaluating the cost of lack of insurance against different long-run growth outcomes as opposed to the cost of lack of insurance against transitory business cycle fluctuations. In other words, we are looking at big shocks, whereas Lucas focused on small shocks.

How do these welfare numbers change when differences in growth rates come as a surprise? Now, as expected, the gains from bond trade are smaller, because trade in a bond is no longer sufficient to deliver an efficient intertemporal allocation of consumption. The counterpart to that result is that the gains from being able to explicitly insure against growth rate risk are larger.

The welfare gains of moving to complete markets are of theoretical interest, but it is hard to imagine what sorts of markets or institutions might provide insurance against long-run growth rate risk. Suppose we take autarky under the repeated surprise model for expectations as the closest theoretical approximation to the actual global economy over the past 50 years. We would then conclude that an expected welfare gain worth 4.8% of consumption would be an upper bound for the potential welfare gains from countries having access to a globally integrated bond market over this period. It is an upper bound for three reasons. First, as discussed above, this gain should more properly be viewed as being expressed as a percentage of tradable consumption rather than total consumption. Second, realizing these gains would have required especially fast-growing countries to accumulate very large negative net foreign asset positions—positions that would presumably be difficult to sustain in practice given difficulties in enforcing repayment of international debts. Third, these welfare calculations were computed assuming no preference asymmetries across countries. In the example economy described in Section 3.4.5, preferences differ systematically across countries in such a way that allocations and welfare are identical under the autarkic and bond economy market structures.

3.6. Summary

Our overall assessment of the evidence in Tables 9.2 and 9.3 and in Figures 9.1 through 9.5 is that the long-run allocations of consumption across countries are inefficient. With sufficient creativity, one can conjure up cross-country variation in preferences and technologies such that observed allocations are efficient, but in our view those models require implausibly large nontradable sectors, and an implausible pattern of covariation between growth rates and rates of time preference across countries. The fraction of output devoted to domestic consumption varies little across countries of very different income levels, which is another way of saying that countries that have experienced fast output growth have experienced similarly rapid consumption growth. The simplest and most compelling explanation for this fact in our view is that there is limited consumption insurance against long-run risk. Put differently, the long-run welfare of a country's citizens is much more tightly linked to the performance of their home country than to that of the world economy.

On the other hand, productive efficiency is harder to reject. Caselli and Feyrer (2007) have argued that marginal products of capital are roughly equated across countries, which suggests a high degree of international capital mobility. One way to reconcile small cross-country differences in returns on the one hand with large cross-country differences in consumption growth rates on the other is to postulate that differences in expected consumption growth rates across countries are small, even though differences in realized growth rates are large. The repeated surprises model for expectations we outlined has that feature, and that model offers a reasonable account of the data in those dimensions. However, recall that although capital is allocated efficiently in that model, consumption is not.

Finally, we note once again that explaining the observed dynamics of capital flows remains an open challenge. All the models with asset trade we have considered predict a strong negative correlation between long-run growth and the net foreign asset position, while in practice cross-country NFA variation is modest (relative to the theory) and is positively (though not closely) related to output growth. As more satisfactory positive theories of global imbalances develop, we expect the question of long-run efficiency to be revisited.

4. ASSESSING EFFICIENCY IN INTERNATIONAL BUSINESS CYCLES

The seminal contribution of Backus et al. (1992) has started a very active research line that has tried to assess whether the international allocation of resources across developed economies over the business cycle is efficient. In this section, we use the methodological framework described above to organize and describe the main contributions of this literature, to summarize its main findings so far, and to suggest future research directions. To stay in close contact with the literature, the theoretical framework we use in this example is the two-country, two-good international business cycle model developed in Backus et al. (1994). The key difference between this model and the one used in the previous section is that in this model countries produce different goods that are imperfect substitutes. In response to country-specific shocks, this imperfect substitutability will give rise to changes in relative prices. It is plausible that domestic and foreign goods are less substitutable in the short run than in the long run, when production processes and supply chains can be adjusted in response to changes in international relative prices (see, for example, Ruhl, 2008).

4.1. Preferences, Technologies, and Frictions

The economy is composed of two countries, indexed $i = 1$ and $i = 2$, each populated by mass one of identical, infinitely lived households. In each period t, the economy experiences one event $s_t \in S$. We denote by s^t the history of events up to and including date t. The probability at date 0 of any particular history s^t is given by $\pi(s^t)$.

Each household derives utility from consumption, $c_i(s^t)$, and disutility from labor supply, $n_i(s^t)$. Preferences are given by

$$\sum_{t=0}^{\infty} \beta^t \sum_{s^t}^{\infty} \pi(s^t) U\left(c_i(s^t), n_i(s^t)\right), \tag{3}$$

where the parameter β captures the rate of time preference and the period utility function is $U\left(c_i, n_i\right) = \left(c_i^{\mu}\left(1 - n_i\right)^{1-\mu}\right)^{1-\gamma} / (1 - \gamma)$.

Capital in place $k_i(s^{t-1})$ (chosen in the previous period) and labor are combined to produce two country-specific intermediate goods. These are the only tradable goods in the economy. The intermediate good produced in country 1 is labeled a, and the good produced in country 2 is labeled b. The intermediate goods production functions are Cobb-Douglas:

$$F_i\left(z_i(s^t), k_i(s^{t-1}), n_i(s^t)\right) = \exp\left(z_i(s^t)\right)\left(k_i(s^{t-1})\right)^{\theta}\left(n_i(s^t)\right)^{1-\theta}, \tag{4}$$

where $z_i(s^t)$ is an exogenous productivity shock that follows a symmetric autoregressive process:

$$\begin{bmatrix} z_1(s^t) \\ z_2(s^t) \end{bmatrix} = \begin{pmatrix} \rho & \psi \\ \psi & \rho \end{pmatrix} \begin{bmatrix} z_1(s^{t-1}) \\ z_2(s^{t-1}) \end{bmatrix} + \begin{bmatrix} \varepsilon_1(s^t) \\ \varepsilon_2(s^t) \end{bmatrix},$$

$$\begin{bmatrix} \varepsilon_1(s^t) \\ \varepsilon_2(s^t) \end{bmatrix} \sim N\left(\begin{pmatrix} 0 \\ 0 \end{pmatrix}, \sigma_\varepsilon^2 \begin{pmatrix} 1 & Corr_{\varepsilon_1,\varepsilon_2} \\ Corr_{\varepsilon_1,\varepsilon_2} & 1 \end{pmatrix}\right).$$

Within each country, the intermediate goods a and b are combined to produce country-specific nontradable final consumption and investment goods according to the following constant returns to scale technology:

$$G_i\left(a_i(s^t), b_i(s^t)\right) = \begin{cases} \left[\omega a_i(s^t)^{\frac{\sigma-1}{\sigma}} + (1-\omega)b_i(s^t)^{\frac{\sigma-1}{\sigma}}\right]^{\frac{\sigma}{\sigma-1}}, & i = 1 \\ \left[(1-\omega)a_i(s^t)^{\frac{\sigma-1}{\sigma}} + \omega b_i(s^t)^{\frac{\sigma-1}{\sigma}}\right]^{\frac{\sigma}{\sigma-1}}, & i = 2, \end{cases} \tag{5}$$

where $a_i(s^t)$ and $b_i(s^t)$ denote the quantities of intermediate goods a and b used in country i as inputs, σ is the elasticity of substitution between domestic and foreign-produced inputs, and ω determines the extent to which there is a home or foreign bias in the composition of domestically produced final goods. This bias allows the model to replicate empirical measures for the volume of trade relative to GDP.

Investment augments the capital stock in the standard way:

$$k_i(s^t) = (1-\delta)k_i(s^{t-1}) + x_i(s^t), \tag{6}$$

where δ is the depreciation rate and $x_i(s^t)$ is the amount of the final good devoted to investment in country i.

The resource constraints for this economy are

$$a_1(s^t) + a_2(s^t) = F\left(z_1(s^t), k_1(s^{t-1}), n_1(s^t)\right), \tag{7}$$

$$b_1(s^t) + b_2(s^t) = F\left(z_2(s^t), k_2(s^{t-1}), n_2(s^t)\right), \tag{8}$$

and

$$c_i(s^t) + x_i(s^t) = G_i\left(a_i(s^t), b_i(s^t)\right), \qquad i = 1, 2. \tag{9}$$

We will consider two alternative measures of output in this economy. The first, following Backus et al. (1994), is the physical quantity of intermediate goods produced, which we denote $y_i(s^t) = F_i\left(z_i(s^t), k_i(s^{t-1}), n_i(s^t)\right)$. The second values intermediate goods output in country i in units of i's final consumption-investment good. We denote this alternative $y_1^f(s^t) = G_{a1}(s^t)y_1(s^t)$ and $y_2^f(s^t) = G_{b2}(s^t)y_2(s^t)$, where G_{ai} and G_{bi} denote the marginal products of intermediates a and b in country i's final goods production. The value of country 1's net exports, in units of the domestic final good, is $nx_1(s^t) = G_{a1}(s^t)a_2(s^t) - G_{b1}(s^t)b_1(s^t)$. Note that when each component of GDP is measured in units of the final good, the national income accounting identity is preserved: $y_i^f(s^t) = c_i(s^t) + x_i(s^t) + nx_i(s^t)$.

4.2. Efficient Allocations

Efficient allocations in this framework are easily computed using a planning problem that maximizes a weighted average of the welfare of the representative agents in the two countries. Let κ denote the relative weight on country 1. The key first-order conditions defining efficiency are

$$\kappa U_{c1}(s^t)G_{a1}(s^t) = (1 - \kappa)U_{c2}(s^t)G_{a2}(s^t),$$
$$\kappa U_{c1}(s^t)G_{b1}(s^t) = (1 - \kappa)U_{c2}(s^t)G_{b2}(s^t),$$ (10)

$$U_{c1}(s^t)G_{a1}(s^t)F_{n1}(s^t) = -U_{n1}(s^t),$$
$$U_{c2}(s^t)G_{b2}(s^t)F_{n2}(s^t) = -U_{n2}(s^t),$$ (11)

$$U_{c1}(s^t) = \beta E_{s^t}\left[U_{c1}(s^{t+1})\left[G_{a1}(s^{t+1})F_{k1}(s^{t+1}) + (1 - \delta)\right]\right],$$ (12)

$$U_{c2}(s^t) = \beta E_{s^t}\left[U_{c2}(s^{t+1})\left[G_{b2}(s^{t+1})F_{k2}(s^{t+1}) + (1 - \delta)\right]\right],$$ (13)

where U_{ci}, U_{ni}, F_{ki}, and F_{ni} denote, respectively, marginal utilities from consumption and hours and the marginal products of capital and labor in intermediate goods production.

The first pair of equations (equation (10)) defines an efficient division of tradable goods across countries. This is the generalization of the consumption-risk-sharing condition from the one-good model to a two-good world. It is efficient to divide good a such that the marginal value to the planner from putting an additional unit in either country is the same. One interpretation of these conditions is that the planner equates the marginal rate at which it is willing to substitute domestic for foreign consumption, $(1 - \kappa)U_{c2}(s^t)/\kappa U_{c1}(s^t)$, to the marginal rate at which it is able to transform domestic into foreign consumption by reallocating intermediates across countries, $G_{a1}(s^t)/G_{a2}(s^t) = G_{b1}(s^t)/G_{b2}(s^t)$.

Since the relative weight κ is constant, the intertemporal marginal rate of substitution for intermediate goods is equated state-by-state across countries:

$$\frac{U_{c1}(s^{t+1})G_{a1}(s^{t+1})}{U_{c1}(s^t)G_{a1}(s^t)} = \frac{U_{c2}(s^{t+1})G_{a2}(s^{t+1})}{U_{c2}(s^t)G_{a2}(s^t)} = Q(s^t, s^{t+1}) \qquad \forall s^t, s^{t+1}.$$

The second two pairs of efficiency conditions define efficient allocations of labor and capital. These conditions are standard. Note that the second intertemporal efficiency condition 13 can alternatively be written as

$$\frac{G_{b1}(s^t)}{G_{b2}(s^t)}U_{c1}(s^t) = \beta E_{s^t}\left[\frac{G_{b1}(s^{t+1})}{G_{b2}(s^{t+1})}U_{c1}(s^{t+1})\left[G_{b2}(s^{t+1})F_{k2}(s^{t+1}) + (1 - \delta)\right]\right].$$

Comparing this equation to equation (12) reveals an analog to the result from the one-good model that efficiency dictates equating the marginal product of capital across countries (equation (2)). In this economy, capital in country 1 and capital in country 2 are different goods. Productive efficiency here requires equating the expected returns to investing in the two countries, given that the "prices" of capital in country 2 today and tomorrow relative to corresponding capital in country 1 are $G_{b1}(s^t)/G_{b2}(s^t)$ and $G_{b1}(s^{t+1})/G_{b2}(s^{t+1})$, respectively.

4.2.1. Efficiency in Endowment Economy Example

Before exploring this model's predictions for productive efficiency, it will be useful to consider a simpler version of the model (Pakko, 1997) in which labor supply and capital are both fixed and equal to one, so that

$$y_i(s^t) = z_i(s^t) \tag{14}$$

and $U(c_i) = c_i^{(1-\gamma)}/(1-\gamma)$.

In this simpler problem, the planner's only choice is how to allocate intermediate endowments across countries, and an efficient consumption allocation is defined by equations (7), (10), and (14). Although this model is very simple, it clarifies the characterization of efficient consumption allocations in two-good models. The richer business cycle model will endogenize output, but the consumption efficiency condition (equation (10)) is the same, and thus much of the intuition that can be gleaned from the simpler model will carry over.

To warm up, consider a one-good model, or equivalently the special case of the model described in which $\omega = 1/2$ and $\sigma \to \infty$. In a one-good model, the marginal rate of transformation between domestic and foreign consumption is one, and thus efficiency simply dictates equating planner-weighted marginal utilities of consumption. Each country i receives a fixed fraction of the world endowment: the fraction for country 1 is $\kappa^{\frac{1}{\gamma}}/\left(\kappa^{\frac{1}{\gamma}} + (1-\kappa)^{\frac{1}{\gamma}}\right)$. Thus, consumption comoves perfectly across countries, while the correlation of output is just dictated by the correlation of the exogenous productivity shocks. If country 1 has a relatively favorable productivity shock, it should increase exports to country 2. Thus, net exports should be procyclical.

These stark predictions are the starting point for a large fraction of the empirical work on international consumption risk sharing. As we will report below, in the data movements in consumption are typically less strongly positively correlated across countries than output, contrary to efficiency in the one-good model. In addition, net exports are typically counter- rather than procyclical, again in apparent contradiction to efficiency.

The characterization of efficient consumption sharing is less stark in the two-good model with σ finite. Suppose country 1 enjoys a positive productivity shock and therefore produces more of good a. The first difference with respect to the one-good model is that the productivity (shadow price) of good a will now fall relative to good b. Thus, output in country 1 valued in terms of the final good will increase by less than the increase in the endowment, and output in country 2 will rise, even though productivity there did not move. Thus the cross-country correlation between y_1^f and y_2^f will tend to be larger than the correlation between z_1 and z_2. The second difference relative to the one-good model is that with two goods the planner faces a trade-off in deciding where to allocate the extra good a that is produced. On the one hand, the incentive to equalize consumption will push the planner toward exporting a good chunk of it abroad. On the other hand, imperfect substitutability between intermediate goods in producing the final consumption good, coupled with the bias in preferences toward the locally produced intermediate ($\omega > 0.5$), will push the planner toward devoting more of the extra good a to country 1.

We now show that for certain combinations of parameter values, the business cycle properties of efficient allocations in the two-good model differ sharply from those familiar from one-good models. In particular, efficient allocations can feature countercyclical net exports and a cross-country output correlation exceeding the cross-country consumption. A critical locus dividing the parameter space into regions in which business cycle properties differ qualitatively between the two- and one-good models is

$$\tilde{\sigma}(s, \gamma) = \frac{1}{\gamma} - \frac{(1 - \gamma)}{2s\gamma},$$

where $s = (1 - \omega)^{-\sigma} / \left((1 - \omega)^{-\sigma} + \omega^{-\sigma}\right)$ is the steady-state fraction of the domestic intermediate allocated to producing the domestic final good (in the case $\sigma = 1$, $s = \omega$).

Proposition 1.   Efficient allocations have the following properties if and only if $\sigma < \tilde{\sigma}(s, \gamma)$:

1. Pass-through from relative output to relative consumption is larger than one.
2. Net exports are countercyclical.
3. The cross-country output correlation exceeds the cross-country consumption correlation.

Proof.   See Section 6, the Appendix. The characterization in Proposition 1 is based on a log-linearization of equations (7), (10), and (14). We then solve in closed form for the solutions to this log-linear system. Note that Proposition 1 states results for output measured in units of the final good (y_i^f). Pakko (1997) explored the same model but measured output in units of the intermediate good (y_i). The analogous condition for properties 1 and 3 when output is defined that way is $\sigma < (2s - 1)/2s\gamma$.

The three properties listed in the proposition are obviously closely interrelated, and they all run counter to the conventional wisdom about efficiency derived from one-good models. The intuition centers on the trade-off sketched above between minimizing fluctuations in consumption mix within a country versus minimizing fluctuations in total consumption across countries. Consider a concrete example, with country 1 producing apples and country 2 producing bananas. Suppose country 1 has a particularly good harvest. If apples and bananas are poor substitutes, and if residents in country 1 have a preference bias toward apples, concentrating fruit consumption in country 1 will be efficient. In that case, the relative value of country 1's consumption will increase even more than the value of their output (property 1), net exports will fall (property 2), and consumption will end up comoving less strongly than output across countries (property 3).

Panel A of Figure 9.7 plots the locus $\tilde{\sigma}(s, \gamma)$ below for $s = 0.85$, corresponding to an import share of 15%. The locus goes through the point $\sigma = \gamma = 1$, indicating that with (i) a unitary elasticity of substitution between domestic and foreign goods and

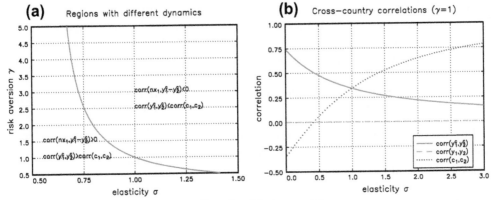

Figure 9.7 Business Cycle Dynamics in a Two-Good Endowment Economy

(ii) logarithmic utility over consumption, net exports are always exactly zero, and the cross-country consumption correlation is identical to the cross-country output correlation. Higher risk aversion strengthens the planner's incentive to equalize consumption across countries, and thus a stronger incentive to maintain the steady-state mix of goods in consumption (a lower value for σ) is required to prevent the planner from wanting the more productive country to run a trade surplus.

A large part of the literature on international risk sharing investigates whether country-specific output growth helps predict country-specific consumption growth (see, for example, Lewis, 1996). If it does, that is taken as evidence against efficiency. However, property 1 indicates that even a large positive relationship between the two is not necessarily indicative of inefficiency.

With respect to property 2, Cole and Obstfeld (1991) were the first to emphasize that at certain parameter configurations, allocations are efficient absent any intertemporal borrowing and lending. We will revisit their paper when discussing evidence on efficiency from international portfolios.

Panel B of Figure 9.7 plots consumption and output correlations in this model as functions of σ, for $s = 0.85$, $\gamma = 1$, and uncorrelated endowment shocks. As $\sigma \to \infty$, so that the model collapses to a one-good model, the consumption correlation tends to 1, while the output correlation (in units of the final good) tends to 0.

4.3. Market Allocations

We now turn to the version of the economy with production. Here the literature has explored a variety of alternative market structures. Our baseline will be an economy where a full set of Arrow securities is traded internationally (complete markets). We will also consider economies where a limited set of assets is traded internationally: only stocks (as in Heathcote and Perri, forthcoming), only a bond (Arvanitis and Mikkola, 1996), or no assets at all (Heathcote and Perri, 2002).

In all market economies households rent labor to competitive intermediate goods-producing firms at wage $w_i(s^t)$ (measured in units of the final good). They also trade intermediate goods at prices $q_i^a(s^t)$, $q_i^b(s^t)$. Final goods-producing firms purchase the intermediate inputs and produce the final consumption/investment good, solving

$$\max_{a_i(s^t),b_i(s^t)} \left\{ G_i(a_i(s^t), b_i(s^t)) - q_i^a(s^t)a_i(s^t) - q_i^b(s^t)b_i(s^t) \right\}. \tag{15}$$

Intermediate goods-producing firms hold capital and make investment decisions. The intermediate goods firm's maximization problem in country i is to choose $k_i(s^t)$, $n_i(s^t)$ for all s^t and for all $t \geq 0$ to maximize

$$\sum_{t=0}^{\infty} \sum_{s^t} Q_i(s^t) d_i(s^t),$$

taking as given $k_i(s^{-1})$, where $Q_i(s^t)$ is the price the firm uses to value dividends at s^t relative to consumption at date 0, and dividends (in units of the final good) are given by

$$d_1(s^t) = q_1^a(s^t)\gamma_1(s^t) - w_1(s^t)n_1(s^t) - x_1(s^t), \tag{16}$$

$$d_2(s^t) = q_2^b(s^t)\gamma_2(s^t) - w_2(s^t)n_2(s^t) - x_2(s^t). \tag{17}$$

The state-contingent consumption prices $Q_i(s^t)$ play a role in intermediate goods firms' state-contingent decisions regarding how to divide earnings between investment and dividend payments. We assume that firms use the discount factor of the representative local household to price the marginal cost of forgoing current dividends in favor of extra investment:

$$Q_i(s^t) = \frac{\pi(s^t)\beta^t U_{ci}(s^t)}{U_{ci}(s^0)}. \tag{18}$$

We now describe how the representative households' budget constraints differ across the different market structures.

4.3.1. Complete markets
Without loss of generality, we can assume that a complete set of Arrow securities is denominated in units of good a. Let $B_i(s^t, s_{t+1})$ be the quantity of the security purchased by households in country i after history s^t that pays one unit of good a in period $t+1$ if and only if the state of the economy is s_{t+1}. Let $Q(s^t, s_{t+1})$ be the price in units of good a of this security. The budget constraint for the representative household in country i is

$$c_i(s^t) + q_i^a(s^t)\sum_{s_{t+1}} Q(s^t, s_{t+1})B_i(s^t, s_{t+1}) = w_i(s^t)n_i(s^t) + d_i(s^t) + q_i^a(s^t)B_i(s^{t-1}, s_t). \tag{19}$$

4.3.2. Stock Economy

In this economy, agents trade internationally equity of the intermediate goods-producing firms. Let $P^a(s^t)$ and $P^b(s^t)$ denote the price of shares in the representative firms in countries 1 and 2, in units of those countries' respective consumptions. Let $\lambda_i^a(s^t)$ and $\lambda_i^b(s^t)$ denote the shares of country 1 and 2 stocks purchased by agents in country i. The budget constraint for the representative household in country 1 (country 2 is analogous) is

$$c_1(s^t) + P^a(s^t)\lambda_1^a(s^t) + e(s^t)P^b(s^t)\lambda_1^b(s^t)$$
$$= w_1(s^t)n_1(s^t) + \lambda_1^a(s^{t-1})\left[P^a(s^t) + d_1(s^t)\right] + \lambda_1^b(s^{t-1})e(s^t)\left[P^b(s^t) + d_2(s^t)\right], \quad (20)$$

where $e(s^t)$ is the real exchange rate.

4.3.3. Bond Economy

In this model, only a single noncontingent bond is traded. Let $B_i(s^t)$ denote the quantity and $P(s^t)$ the price (in units of good a) of bonds bought by households in country i after history s^t. The bond pays one unit of good a in period $t+1$ irrespective of the state in $t+1$. The budget constraint for the representative household in country i is

$$c_i(s^t) + q_i^a(s^t)P(s^t)B_i(s^t) = w_i(s^t)n_i(s^t) + d_i(s^t) + q_i^a(s^t)B_i(s^{t-1}). \quad (21)$$

4.3.4. Financial Autarky

In the financial autarky model, no assets are traded internationally; hence, the budget constraint for the representative household in country i is given by

$$c_i(s^t) = w_i(s^t)n_i(s^t) + d_i(s^t). \quad (22)$$

4.3.5. Households' Problems

Households choose $c_i(s^t) \geq 0$, $n_i(s^t) \in [0, 1]$ and asset purchases (if assets are traded) for all s^t and for all $t \geq 0$ to maximize (3) subject to the appropriate sequence of budget constraints given by equation (19), (20), (21), or (22), taking as given initial productivity shocks, initial capital stocks and, if assets are traded internationally, the initial distribution of wealth.

4.3.6. Definition of Equilibrium

An equilibrium is a set of prices for all s^t and for all $t \geq 0$ such that when households solve their problems taking these prices as given, all markets clear. The goods market-clearing conditions are (7) and (9). The asset market conditions for the complete markets, stock and bond economies are, respectively,

$$B_1(s^t, s_{t+1}) + B_2(s^t, s_{t+1}) = 0, \qquad \forall s_{t+1} \in S. \quad (23)$$
$$\lambda_1^a(s^t) + \lambda_2^a(s^t) = 1,$$
$$\lambda_1^b(s^t) + \lambda_2^b(s^t) = 1.$$
$$B_1(s^t) + B_2(s^t) = 0. \quad (24)$$

4.4. Comparing Models and Data

We now compare allocations (efficient and market) in the setup described above with the data in order to assess international efficiency over the business cycle. In the following four subsections, we explore comparisons for four different sorts of observables that have been used in the literature: (1) standard macroeconomic quantities, (2) the real exchange rate, (3) asset prices, and (4) international portfolio diversification.

4.4.1. Assessing Efficiency Using Quantities

Our first comparison is based on international comovement of macro quantities and international flows of resources (i.e., net exports) at business cycle frequencies. In order to obtain predictions for business cycle dynamics in the various setups described above, we first calibrate the parameters of the model and the productivity process. We then numerically solve the models using standard linearization techniques. Finally, we simulate the models to compute statistics that can be compared with data. The first row of Table 9.4 reports our main statistics for quantities: international correlations of macro aggregates between the United States and the G6 (an aggregate of Canada, France, Germany, Italy, Japan, and the U.K.), the standard deviation of GDP (as a measure of business cycle risk), and the standard deviation and cyclicality of net exports (as a fraction of GDP).[12] Following most of the literature since Backus et al. (1994), we focus on output measured in units of intermediate goods, $y_i(s^t)$.

The key features of the data can be summarized as follows:

1. Output, investment, and employment comove positively and strongly across countries.
2. The cross-country correlation of consumption is positive but smaller than the correlation of output.
3. Net exports are not very volatile (their standard deviation is about one-third that of GDP) and are strongly countercyclical.

These features have been documented in many business cycle studies, and they are typical of many developed countries in different periods of time (see, for example, Backus and Kehoe, 1992). The first question we ask is whether a reasonably calibrated version of the model described above can generate efficient allocations with these features. The first to address this question were Backus et al. (1992 and 1994, hereafter BKK). They concluded that features (1) and (2) of the data appear inconsistent with efficiency, naming this inconsistency the "quantity anomaly." Here we first revisit the anomaly using the same calibration as in BKK, reported in Table 9.5.[13] The second row of Table 9.4 reports the statistics for efficient allocations in the complete markets BKK economy. The

---

[12] We focus here on correlations and standard deviations at business cycle frequencies. Statistics at other frequencies might also be informative about risk sharing. See, for example, Baxter, 2012, Pakko, 2004, and Rabanal and Rubio-Ramirez, 2010.

[13] The only difference between our calibration and BKK's is that we set the standard deviation and correlation of the productivity innovations to match the standard deviation of U.S. GDP and the correlation between U.S. GDP and G6 GDP in our sample.

Table 9.4 Assessing Efficiency Using Quantities

	International Correlations				Domestic Statistics		
	(y_1, y_2)	(c_1, c_2)	(x_1, x_2)	(n_1, n_2)	% sd y	% sd $\frac{nx}{y}$	corr$(\frac{nx}{y}, y)$
1. Data	0.55	0.31	0.51	0.57	1.54	0.44	−0.51
Complete markets models							
2. BKK (see Table 9.5)	0.55	0.93	−0.07	−0.01	1.54	0.23	−0.43
3. No spillovers: $\rho = 0.91$, $\psi = 0$	0.55	0.71	0.35	0.56	1.54	0.19	−0.40
4. Separable utility: $\gamma = 1$	0.55	0.94	0.02	0.15	1.54	0.23	−0.43
5. Low elasticity: $\sigma = 0.6$	0.55	0.88	−0.08	0.10	1.54	0.28	−0.47
6. All: $\rho = 0.91$, $\psi = 0$, $\gamma = 1$, $\sigma = 0.6$	0.55	0.35	0.39	0.71	1.54	0.47	−0.46
Bond economy model							
7. BC: $\rho = 1$, $\psi = 0$, $\sigma = 5$	0.55	0.29	−0.39	0.92	1.54	0.82	−0.39

Notes: All data are from the OECD Quarterly National Accounts (GDP and components) and Main Economic Indicators (employment). The sample for the data statistics is 1960.1–2012.2. The variable y denotes real GDP, c denotes real consumption (both private and public), n denotes civilian employment, x denotes real gross fixed capital formation, and nx/y denotes net exports over GDP (all nominal). All variables except net exports are in logs. All variables are HP filtered with a smoothing parameter of 1600. Statistics from the model are produced by simulating the model for the same numbers of periods as the data and taking averages over 20 simulations. In lines 2 through 7 the standard deviation and correlation of shock innovations are calibrated to replicate the standard deviation of output and the international correlation of GDP. BKK: Backus et al. (1994); BC: Baxter and Crucini (1995).

Table 9.5 Baseline Parameter Values (From Backus et al., 1994)

Preferences

	Discount factor	$\beta = 0.99$
	Weight on consumption	$\mu = 0.34$
	Curvature	$\gamma = 2$
Technology		
	Capital's share	$\theta = 0.36$
	Depreciation rate	$\delta = 0.025$
	Elasticity of substitution	$\sigma = 1.5$
	Import share	$1 - s = 0.15$
Productivity process		
	Persistence and spillover	$\rho = 0.906$
		$\psi = 0.088$
	Variance and correlation	$\sigma_\varepsilon^2 = 0.0097$
		$\eta = 0.65$

cross-country correlation of consumption (0.93) exceeds the corresponding correlation of output (0.55), contrary to the data. This discrepancy was also present in the endowment version of the model with relatively high elasticities of substitution between goods ($\sigma = 1.5$ in the BKK calibration).[14]

The version of the economy with production introduces additional implications for investment and employment. As long as goods are not too complementary, it is efficient to increase labor supply and to invest more in the country where productivity is relatively high, that is, to "make hay where the sun shines." This implies that efficient allocations feature low cross-country correlations of investment (-0.07) and employment (-0.05), again at odds with the data. One dimension along which the production economy does much better than the endowment model is the dynamics of net exports, which are now countercyclical in line with data. Efficient allocations predict countercyclical net exports because of the incentive to invest in good times, which makes domestic absorption more procyclical (relative to the endowment case) and hence net exports more countercyclical. Overall, though, a comparison of lines (1) and (2) in Table 9.4 seems to point strongly against efficiency. Before we consider alternative market structures, however, we will show that alternative reasonable parameterizations make the efficient complete markets model allocation consistent with the three quantity facts described earlier.

Three important elements of the BKK calibration account for the large differences between the quantity dynamics observed in the data versus those predicted by the model.

[14] Defining output in units of the consumption good slightly increases the model output correlation, to 0.60.

The first element is the estimation of the productivity process, which includes a positive spillover term ψ (see Table 9.5). Because a positive productivity shock in one country signals high future productivity in the other, it is efficient for both countries to increase current consumption. Thus, consumption comovement ends up exceeding output comovement. Empirical work (see, for example, Baxter and Crucini, 1995, or Heathcote and Perri, 2004) has shown that precisely estimating spillovers is difficult, and that estimates are sensitive to the details of whether and how productivity series are detrended prior to estimating the transmission coefficients ρ and ψ.

The second element is the nonseparability between consumption and leisure in the utility function used by BKK. This feature makes it difficult to resolve the quantity anomaly, because it ties together comovement in labor and consumption. In their calibration, if both countries work more in response to a shock, the marginal utility of consumption in both countries will rise, which is a force toward equalizing consumption.

The third element is the relatively high value for the elasticity of substitution between foreign and domestic goods assumed by BKK which, as discussed in Section 4.2.1, implies strong cross-country comovement in consumption as a feature of efficient allocations.

In lines (3), (4), and (5) of Table 9.4 we modify the BKK parameterization by changing these elements one at a time. In line (3) we consider a process for productivity with no spillovers ($\psi = 0$), as estimated by Heathcote and Perri (2004). In line (4) we consider log-separable preferences ($\gamma = 1$). In line (5) we consider a low elasticity of substitution ($\sigma = 0.6$). Comparing lines (3), (4), and (5) with the data (1), we see that each change in the parameterization moves the model closer to the data, but none of the changes alone can solve the quantity anomaly. In line (6) we introduce all three changes simultaneously. Comparing lines (1) and (6) shows that a reasonable calibration of the complete markets model generates fluctuations in quantities that are very similar to those observed in the data.[15]

The next question is whether these fluctuations could also be replicated by a (non-efficient) market economy with limited asset trade. In particular, Baxter and Crucini (1995) argue that a bond economy (as described in Section 4.3) can generate international comovement of consumption that is lower than the correlation of GDP. In line (7) of Table 9.4, we reproduce the Baxter and Crucini (BC) finding, using a special case of our general setup. In particular, we consider the BC process for productivity (unit roots with no spillovers), and, since theirs is a one-good setup, we set elasticity of substitution between goods to a high value ($\sigma = 5$). Line (7) shows that this model does indeed generate a consumption correlation lower than the output correlation. The economic mechanism through which the model delivers this is completely different from the one discussed in the two-good model. It does not hinge on imperfect substitutabilty of goods but rather on changes in the international interest rate.

---

[15] In this calibration, the cross-country correlation of output measured in units of consumption is 0.63.

Suppose country 1 experiences a positive productivity shock. Its demand for international loans increases strongly for two reasons. The first is that because markets are incomplete, risks are not shared and residents in country 1 are the sole beneficiaries of the increase in productivity. The second is that shocks are permanent, so residents in country 1 want to increase both consumption and investment. The strong demand for funds on the international market causes an increase in the world interest rate, which in turn induces residents in country 2 to supply more labor, to save more in international bonds and less in domestic capital, and to consume less. The result is an international consumption correlation that is below the output correlation, but also counterfactually negative international comovement in investment (-0.39 in the model versus 0.51 in the data).

To summarize, many authors have interpreted the quantity anomaly as evidence against international efficiency and have considered variants of the one-good international business cycle model in which observed international comovement can be explained by frictions that preclude efficient allocations across countries. Here we have shown that international comovement of quantities is perhaps better captured by assuming complete financial markets in the context of a two-good model with a low elasticity of substitution.[16] Thus, the international comovement of quantities is not necessarily inconsistent with international efficiency.[17]

4.4.2. Assessing Efficiency Using Real Exchange Rates

In the setup described above a direct implication of efficiency is that the ratio of marginal utilities across countries should be proportional to the rate at which foreign consumption can be transformed into domestic consumption by reallocating intermediate goods (see equation (10)). In our decentralized economies the marginal products of intermediate goods are their respective prices (relative to final goods), so that the ratio of the marginal products across countries $(G_{a1}(s^t)/G_{a2}(s^t) = G_{b1}(s^t)/G_{b2}(s^t))$ is the price of foreign consumption relative to domestic consumption, i.e., the real exchange rate, hereafter denoted $e(s^t)$. Thus, efficiency implies perfect comovement between the ratio of marginal utility in country 2 to marginal utility in country 1 and the real exchange rate. Intuitively, an increase in marginal utility in, say, country 2 relative to country 1 is compatible with efficiency only if resources consumed by country 2 become more expensive relative to

---

[16] See also Viani, 2011, for a conclusion in this spirit.

[17] Fitzgerald (2012) uses a different model and a different quantity-based moment to assess efficiency, but comes to a similar conclusion. Her framework is a multicountry model, in which each country produces a country-specific intermediate good. All countries have identical symmetric preferences over a composite of all country varieties, but country-pair-specific transportation costs generate differences in final consumption prices P_i across countries. Fitzgerald notes that the quantity of imports into country i from country k (relative to the size of the two economies) should be systematically linked to P_i, to a "multilateral resistance" term for country k (capturing its distance from other potential trading partners) and to trade costs between i and k. With perfect risk sharing, P_i can be mapped directly into consumption for country i. She tests this specification for the import equation against an alternative in which P_i is treated as a time dummy, and finds that for developed countries the risk-sharing specification is not rejected.

those consumed by country 1. If one assumes that the utility function is separable between consumption and leisure, with exponent $(1 - \gamma)$ on the consumption component, this implies a perfect linear relationship (and hence a correlation of 1) between the ratio of domestic to foreign log consumption and the log real exchange rate:

$$\log \frac{1 - \kappa}{\kappa} + \gamma \log \left(\frac{c_1(s^t)}{c_2(s^t)} \right) = \log e(s^t). \tag{25}$$

In an influential paper, Backus and Smith (1993) show that for various pairs of developed countries, this correlation is actually close to zero or even negative. Moreover, equation (25) implies a relationship between the volatilities of relative log consumption and the log real exchange rate: with logarithmic preferences $(\gamma = 1)$ the two should be equally volatile. In the data, however, the real exchange rate is typically much more volatile than relative consumption. In the first row of Table 9.6, we report the standard deviations of the real exchange rate and relative consumption for the United States versus the G6, as well as the correlation between the two variables. In the second row, we report the predictions for these variables in the BKK model assuming complete markets (we use the parameterization of the model in line 6 of Table 9.4 that resolves the quantity anomaly). Comparing lines 1 and 2 suggests a sharp rejection of efficiency, because efficient model allocations feature a real exchange rate that is both not very volatile and at the same time perfectly correlated with relative consumption.

Can alternative market structures with limited scope for international asset trade account for the observed features of the real exchange rate? If they can, that would be evidence against efficiency. If they cannot, we would instead conclude that the BKK framework does not offer a satisfactory theory of real exchange rates and that its implications for exchange rates should not be used to assess efficiency. Before we address this question (in the next subsection), a useful step is to first relate the exchange rate e (price of foreign consumption relative to domestic) to the terms of trade p (price of foreign intermediate b relative to domestic intermediate a). Since consumption in both countries is a mix of domestic and foreign intermediates for which the law of one price holds, movements in the real exchange rate are mechanically related to changes in the terms of trade. Indeed, a log-linear approximation gives

$$\widehat{e} = (2s - 1)\,\widehat{p}, \tag{26}$$

where $\widehat{e}$ and $\widehat{p}$ denote log deviations from the steady state. Note that when both countries consume the same bundle of intermediate goods $(s = 0.5)$, the real exchange rate is constant. If each country consumes only its own intermediate goods $(s = 1)$, the real exchange rate and the terms of trade are the same variable. Also, as long as the trade share is less than 50%, $(s > 1/2)$, the model predicts that the real exchange rate and the terms of trade should move together.

Table 9.6 Assessing Efficiency Using Real Exchange Rates

	% sd e	% sd $\frac{c_1}{c_2}$	corr$(\frac{c_1}{c_2}, e)$
1. Data	6.39	0.97	−0.21
Baseline parameters: $\rho = 0.91, \psi = 0, \gamma = 1, \sigma = 0.6$			
2. Efficient allocations	0.47	0.47	1
3. Bond Economy	0.73	0.36	0.99
4. Financial Autarky	3.15	0.02	0.79
Very low elasticity: $\rho = 0.91, \psi = 0, \gamma = 1, \sigma = 0.38$			
5. Efficient allocations	0.54	0.54	1
6. Bond Economy	2.88	0.15	−0.17
High elasticity and pers. shocks: $\rho = 1, \psi = 0, \gamma = 1, \sigma = 5$			
7. Efficient allocations	0.14	0.14	1
8. Bond Economy	0.23	1.28	−0.69

Notes: Real exchange rate data and relative consumption refer to U.S. v/s G6. Real exchange rate between the U.S. and the G6 is computed as the ratio between a weighted average of consumption deflators (all converted into dollars) in the G6 countries and the U.S. consumption deflator. Weights are proportional to GDP over the sample. Consumption and consumption deflators are from the OECD Quarterly National Accounts while nominal exchange rates are from the IMF International Financial Statistics. The sample for the data statistics is 1960.1–2012.2. In each parameterization, the standard deviation and correlation of innovations of productivity shocks are set so that the model reproduces the standard deviation of GDP in the U.S. and international correlation of GDP between the U.S. and the G6.

Are real exchange rates informative about efficiency? The literature to date disagrees on the answer to this question. Chari et al. (2002) have argued that when allocations are not efficient, the BKK setup can generate a more volatile exchange rate but cannot account for the low correlation between the exchange rate and relative consumption (even considering variants with nominal rigidities). To see why incomplete markets can generate more volatility, consider a positive productivity shock in country 1 that increases the supply of good a and thus pushes up the terms of trade and (by (26)) depreciates the real exchange rate. As discussed in Section 4.2.1, when goods are imperfect substitutes, efficiency calls for consumption of country 1, which is intensive in good a, to go up. This increase in "demand" for good a mitigates its fall in price because of higher relative productivity, reducing the size of the real exchange rate depreciation. When markets are incomplete, the increase in consumption in country 1 is smaller, the demand effect is weaker, and the exchange rate depreciates more, implying more volatility. Notice, though, that the Backus-Smith puzzle is not really solved: lines 2, 3, and 4 of Table 9.6 show that going from efficient to incomplete markets (inefficient) allocations increases exchange rate volatility, but the real exchange rate remains strongly positively correlated with relative consumption.

In contrast, Corsetti et al. (2008) have argued that inefficiency can, in two different parameterizations of this setup, solve the Backus-Smith puzzle. The first case is a very low elasticity of substitution between intermediates. In this case, in response to a positive productivity shock in country 1, the relative price of good *a* must actually increase, implying a real exchange rate appreciation. This perverse dynamic arises because with a very low elasticity, the only way to generate additional demand for good *a* is to increase its relative price and thereby the income and purchasing power of residents of country 1, who are the main customers for good *a*. This is the case considered in lines 5 and 6 of Table 9.6, where we set the elasticity of substitution to 0.38. Notice that in this case the inefficient allocations in the bond economy generate both a fairly volatile real exchange rate and a negative correlation between the real exchange rate and relative consumption.[18]

The second case considered by Corsetti et al. (2008) is one of a very high elasticity of substitution and very persistent shocks. The intuition here is similar to the one discussed in the previous section, describing the Baxter and Crucini (1995) model. When markets are incomplete, a very persistent shock in country 1 makes residents want to increase both consumption and investment. Demand for good *a* is so strong that the exchange rate appreciates.[19] In lines 7 and 8 of Table 9.6 we contrast efficient and inefficient allocations in this case. Note that although the bond economy generates exchange rates that are negatively correlated with consumption, the exchange rate remains much less volatile than in the data.

We conclude that within this framework it is possible to account for real exchange rate fluctuations, but doing so requires a very low—and arguably implausible—elasticity of substitution between imported and domestically produced goods. It is also important to note that this setup (along with many variants, including versions with nontradable goods) has the feature that real exchange rates are driven by fundamentals. Unfortunately, however, a solid link between exchange rates and fundamentals has not yet been established, for two related reasons.

First, at least since Mussa (1986), it has been well known that real exchange rates are much more volatile between pairs of countries with flexible exchange rates as compared with pairs of countries with fixed nominal exchange rates or a common currency. This suggests that a satisfactory theory of real exchange rate dynamics requires a theory of nominal exchange rates, and that even if the BKK model can be parameterized to generate realistic volatility, the fact that it is purely a real model suggests that it might not do so for the right reasons. From the perspective of using real exchange moments to assess efficiency, Hadzi-Vaskov (2008), Hess and Shin (2010), and Devereux and Hnatkovska (2011), report a particularly telling fact: the correlation between exchange rates and relative consumption is negative only for country pairs with flexible exchange rates, whereas for countries or regions sharing a fixed exchange rate, the correlation is mostly positive.

---

[18] Although this setup can account for the Backus-Smith puzzle, it can do so only for a very narrow range of elasticities of substitution.

[19] Another way to obtain this mechanism would be to introduce trend shocks as in Aguiar and Gopinath, 2007.

Once again, it appears that a theory of nominal exchange rates is needed to make inferences about risk sharing. However, a satisfactory theory of nominal exchanges rates remains work in progress. Engel concludes his chapter (Chapter 8) in this handbook as follows: "Although this survey has suggested many different models, it is questionable that the models allow us to explain, even after the fact, the movements in major currency rates."

A second challenge when trying to connect the exchange rate to fundamentals is that empirical evidence suggests that a large share of real exchange rate movements in the data reflect changes in the relative price of traded goods (Engel, 1999) and that in accounting for changes in the relative price of traded goods, deviations from the law of one price and pricing to market play an important role (see Chapter 7 by Burstein and Gopinath in this volume). The efficient ratio of foreign to domestic consumption should respond to changes in the real exchange rate that reflect changes in fundamental preferences or technologies, but not to changes that simply reflect changes in cross-country price differentials for the same goods. Berka et al. (2012) sketch a model in which a large share of real exchange rate movements reflect nominal shocks that move the nominal exchange rate and which are not offset by changes in relative pricing thanks to assumptions of infrequent price adjustment and local currency pricing. Thus, the real exchange rate moves in line with the nominal rate. These real exchange rate movements lead to fluctuations in real allocations that are inefficient.

This discussion highlights that evidence on efficiency from exchange rates (or asset price data) is indirect. Allocations are efficient if they satisfy a planner's problem and the planner's problem does not have any prices in it. Exchange rate data are informative about international efficiency only to the extent that exchange rates are informative about preferences or technologies (fundamentals). To make this point as sharply as possible, in the next subsection we compare and contrast two simple alternative exchange rate models. In one of these models, exchange rate movements are informative about changes in the underlying technology, and efficient allocations feature a systematic relationship between the exchange rate and relative consumption. In the second model, exchange rate movements are disconnected from fundamentals, in the spirit of Berka et al., and the efficient allocation of consumption is in turn disconnected from the exchange rate.

As work on decomposing the fundamental sources of exchange rate movements progresses, it should become easier to disentangle the fundamental-driven component of exchange rate movements from exchange rate movements that do not reflect changes in preferences and technologies. In the meantime, we put little weight on moments involving the real exchange rate, such as the Backus-Smith correlation, when assessing international efficiency.

Exchange rates and efficiency: a simple example. Consider the following static (repeated) two-country, two-good economy. The representative agent in country 1 receives one unit of good a, while the representative agent in country 2 receives one unit of good b. Goods a and b are freely tradable. Agents in country 1 derive utility from consuming good a, while those in country 2 derive utility from consuming good b. The period utility function is $u_i(c_i) = c_i^{(1-\gamma)}/(1 - \gamma)$.

The only source of uncertainty is the real exchange rate e, defined as the price of a unit of good b in units of good a. We will consider two different theories for the exchange rate.

In the first model, a linear technology can convert 1 unit of good b into e units of good a, or 1 unit of good a into $1/e$ units of good b. Thus, in this model e is the stochastic production price of b in units of a.

In the second model, the technology is constant: goods a and b can always be transformed one into the other at a rate of one-for-one. Exchange rate fluctuations are driven by non–fundamental stochastic tariffs. Country 1 imposes a stochastic import tax/subsidy $\tau^{im} = 1 - e$ on imports of good b and an export tax/subsidy of $\tau^{ex} = 1 - \frac{1}{e}$ on exports of good a. Thus, to receive 1 unit of b in 1 (which can be transformed into 1 unit of a and consumed) requires buying $(1 - \tau^{im})^{-1} = e^{-1}$ units of good b in 2, while receiving 1 unit of a in 2 requires buying $(1 - \tau^{ex})^{-1} = e$ units of a in 1. From the perspective of agents, who care only about after-tax prices, in both countries the price of b relative to a is e, just as in the first model. Revenues from these taxes are rebated lump-sum to residents of country 2.

Let $e \in E = \{e_1, e_2, \ldots, e_N\}$ and let $\pi(e_j)$ denote the probability of drawing e_j. We assume the same support and probability distribution for e across both models for the exchange rate.

We consider two alternative financial market structures. The first is financial autarky, under which agents can only barter good a in exchange for good b. Note, though, that there will be no barter in equilibrium, since after the exchange rate e is realized, there are no gains from trade.

The second market structure is complete markets. We assume that each period, before the shock e is realized, agents can trade state-contingent contracts that deliver a unit of good a in country 1 in a particular state e_j. Let $b_i(e_j)$ denote the number of units of the contract purchased by the representative agent in country i contingent on the exchange rate being e_j, and let $q(e_j)$ be the corresponding price. Market clearing requires $b_1(e_j) + b_2(e_j) = 0$ for all $e_j \in E$.

We will compare allocations and welfare in autarky and under complete markets, and contrast the welfare gains from financial integration under the two alternative models for the exchange rate.

Under financial autarky, allocations are simply given by $c_i(e_j) = 1$, for $i = 1, 2$ and $\forall e_j \in E$. Since relative consumption is constant in autarky, there is zero correlation between relative consumption and the real exchange rate, and thus the autarkic version of this model will replicate the low correlation between the real exchange rate and relative consumption that Backus and Smith document in the data.

Under complete markets, the problems agents face are formally similar across the two alternative exchange rate models. In both cases, the respective problems for agents in countries 1 and 2 are

$$\max_{\{b_1(e_j)\}} \sum_{e_j \in E} \pi(e_j) u(c_1(e_j))$$

$$\text{s.t.} \sum_{e_j \in E} q(e_j) b_1(e_j) = 0$$

$$c_1(e_j) = b_1(e_j) + 1$$

and

$$\max_{\{b_2(e_j)\}} \sum_{e_j \in E} \pi(e_j) u(c_2(e_j))$$

$$\text{s.t.} \sum_{e_j \in E} q(e_j) b_2(e_j) = 0$$

$$c_2(e_j) = \frac{b_2(e_j)}{e_j} + 1 + T(e_j).$$

Note that if agents in country 2 have bought $b_2(e_j)$ units of a claim to good a in state e_j and that state is realized, they will be able to exchange the payoff into an additional $b_2(e_j)/e_j$ units of good b, which is the good they consume. $T(e_j)$ denotes the lump-sum rebate of tax revenue. This term is zero in the first exchange rate model.

By taking first-order conditions to these problems, it is straightforward to show that the equilibrium ratio of consumption across countries has the familiar form from complete markets models:

$$\left(\frac{c_1(e_j)}{c_2(e_j)}\right)^\gamma = e_j \qquad \forall e_j \in E. \tag{27}$$

Thus, agents use financial markets to divide aggregate world resources in the way that seems optimal given the price e.

Note that this relationship holds under both of the alternative exchange rate theories. The key difference between the two theories is as follows. In the first model, the exchange rate e is truly the marginal rate of transformation between a and b, so the price e is sending the correct signal about the relative costs of delivering consumption to the two representative agents. In the second model, in contrast, the true technology for transforming one good into the other never changes, so the price e is sending a false signal about the relative costs of producing consumption. In this model, the efficient allocation is characterized by a constant (e-invariant) consumption ratio across countries.

This difference between the two exchange rate models shows up in their respective world resource constraints. In the first model, this constraint (expressed in units of good a) is

$$c_1(e_j) + e_j c_2(e_j) = 1 + e_j,$$

whereas in the second model it is

$$c_1(e_j) + c_2(e_j) = 2.$$

Combining the consumption-sharing rule (27) with these two resource constraints allows us to solve for equilibrium consumption in the two models.

In the first,

$$c_1(e) = e^{\frac{1}{\gamma}} \frac{1+e}{e^{\frac{1}{\gamma}}+e}, \qquad c_2(e) = \frac{1+e}{e^{\frac{1}{\gamma}}+e}.$$

In the second,

$$c_1(e) = e^{\frac{1}{\gamma}} \frac{2}{e^{\frac{1}{\gamma}}+1}, \qquad c_2(e) = \frac{2}{e^{\frac{1}{\gamma}}+1}.$$

We now compare welfare across market structures. For this purpose, we suppose $E = \{1/\chi, \chi\}$ and that $\pi(e_1) = \pi(e_2) = 0.5$, so that the mean log exchange rate is zero and the standard deviation is $\ln \chi$. The standard deviation of the real exchange rate reported in Table 9.6 is 0.0639. Thus we set $\chi = \exp(0.0639) = 1.066$.

Expected utility under autarky is simply $U^{AUT} = (1-\gamma)^{-1}$. Expected utility under complete markets is $U_i^{CM} = 0.5u(c_i(1/\chi)) + 0.5u(c_i(\chi))$. In both exchange rate models, $U_1^{CM} = U_2^{CM}$. We define the welfare gain of moving from autarky to complete markets as the value for η that solves

$$(1+\eta)^{1-\gamma} U^{AUT} = U^{CM}.$$

Figure 9.8 plots η for a range of values for risk aversion γ.

Focus first on the fundamentals-driven model for the exchange rate. For this model, the welfare gains of moving from autarky to an efficient allocation are small but nontrivial. For $\gamma = 1$ (log preferences) the gain is 0.051% of consumption, which is much larger than Lucas's (1987) estimate of the welfare cost of business cycles of 0.008%. One reason gains are larger is that the real exchange rate is much more volatile than consumption at business cycle frequencies. Welfare gains are declining in risk aversion. The logic is that the less tolerant are agents of fluctuations in consumption, the smaller are the gains to diverting resources to the country in which consumption is cheapest. In the limit as $\gamma \to \infty$, $\eta \to 0$. As $\gamma \to 0$, $\eta \to (\chi - 1)/2 = 3.3\%$.

Now look at the second tariff-driven model for the exchange rate. In this model, autarky is efficient, and introducing complete markets reduces welfare. In fact, the welfare plot is the mirror image of that for the fundamentals-driven exchange rate model!

The key message to take away from this example is that identifying the source of exchange rate variation is critical for interpreting exchange-rate-based measures of efficiency. When the exchange rate is driven by fundamental technology shocks, autarky is inefficient, and there are welfare gains from introducing asset trade. The Backus–Smith

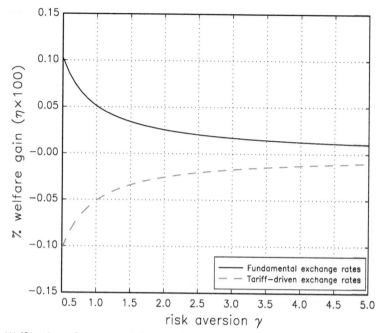

Figure 9.8 Welfare Gains from Financial Integration

correlation is a useful diagnostic for this inefficiency. In autarky the correlation is zero, and in complete markets (when allocations are efficient) it is one.

When the exchange rate is driven by random tariffs and disconnected from preferences and technologies, everything is reversed. Autarky is efficient, and there are welfare losses from introducing asset trade. The Backus–Smith correlation is a completely misleading diagnostic tool. In autarky (when allocations are efficient) the correlation is zero, whereas in complete markets (when allocations are inefficient), it is one.

A second message from the example is that in a distorted economy, financial liberalization can be welfare reducing. In particular, in our second example distortionary tariffs lead to an inefficient allocation of resources when international financial markets are complete. One remedy is to eliminate the tariffs. An alternative is to prevent agents from acting on the resulting distorted price signals by ruling out international asset trade.

4.4.3. Assessing Efficiency Using Asset Prices

Taking first differences of the consumption efficiency condition (equation (10)) gives

$$\log e(s^{t+1}) - \log e(s^t) = \log m_2(s^{t+1}) - \log m_1(s^{t+1}), \qquad (28)$$

where the left-hand side is the log change in the real exchange rate, and the right-hand side is the difference between the growth rate of the marginal utility of consumption in country 2 and the corresponding growth rate in country 1. In finance, these growth rates are called stochastic discount factors (SDFs) because they define the appropriate way to discount payoffs when pricing assets. In particular, any asset j traded in country i with payoffs $x^j(s^{t+1})$ in state s^{t+1} has price $p^j(s^t)$ given by

$$p^j(s^t) = E_{s^t}\left[m_i(s^{t+1})x^j(s^{t+1})\right].$$

As noted before, growth rates of marginal utility (SDFs) are not observed directly. The standard macroeconomic approach that we have followed up to now has been to make assumptions on preferences (time separability and the absence of any preference shocks) such that the stochastic discount factor is proportional to consumption growth, which can be measured directly. However, these assumptions are quite restrictive.

An alternative approach is to note that although the SDF is not directly observable, we can learn something about its statistical properties by looking at asset prices. The fact that there is a substantial excess return to stocks over bonds indicates that there must be a large negative covariance between $m_i(s^{t+1})$ and stock returns, which in turn requires that $m_i(s^{t+1})$ must be very volatile.

Brandt et al. (2006) start with equation (28). They then note that the variance of the left-hand side (the variance of real exchange rate changes) must be equal to the variance of the right-hand side. The variance of the right-hand side is the sum of the variances of the two SDFs, minus twice the covariance between them. They plug in empirical values for the variance of exchange rate changes and (high) variances for SDFs consistent with equity premium evidence and conclude that the covariance between SDFs must be positive and large. They conclude that "international risk sharing is better than you think."

At this point, it is important to emphasize that the Brandt et al. (2006) notion of risk sharing is quite different from our notion of efficiency. We have defined allocations to be efficient if no Pareto-improving reallocation of resources is possible, taking as given physical transportation frictions and taking as given differences in preferences across countries. Brandt et al. define perfect risk sharing as being achieved when all restrictions on goods trade as well as all restrictions on asset trade are removed. They write, "Risk sharing requires frictionless goods markets. The container ship is a risk sharing innovation as important as 24 hour trading." In their view, real exchange rate volatility itself is a direct measure of (lack of) risk sharing. If all costs of trading goods and assets could be eliminated, SDFs would comove perfectly across countries, and the real exchange rate would not move at all. Because the real exchange rate already moves so little (relative to SDFs) Brandt et al. conclude that risk sharing in this broad sense is already very good.

Colacito and Croce (2011) take inspiration from the Brandt et al. paper. They set themselves the task of trying to construct a model in which SDFs comove strongly, even though measured consumption growth does not. Their answer is that such a scenario is perfectly possible in a world with non-time-separable preferences (à la Epstein and Zin, 1989) and long run risks (à la Bansal and Yaron, 2004). The idea is that the cross-country correlation of SDFs is driven primarily by highly correlated long-run risks, whereas the cross-country correlation of consumption growth (in the short run) is driven by weakly correlated transitory shocks. In the Colacito and Croce environment, there is full home bias in preferences, so agents in each country only want to consume their local endowment. Thus, equilibrium allocations are efficient (by our definition) for any asset market structure, including autarky. This highlights an undesirable feature of the Brandt et al. (2006) measure of risk sharing: in the context of the Colacito and Croce model, nothing can be learned about risk sharing by examining the covariance between SDFs across countries or the volatility of the real exchange rate.

Colacito and Croce (2010) explore the welfare gains generated by moving from financial autarky to complete markets in a similar environment to their (2011) paper. One important extension relative to their previous paper is that they do not impose perfect home bias in preferences, so the welfare gains from increasing financial integration are not zero by construction. They find that the potential welfare gains in moving from autarkic to efficient allocations are potentially very large when (i) there is intermediate home bias in preferences, (ii) risk aversion is high, and (iii) there is substantial long-run risk that is not strongly correlated across countries. Lewis and Liu (2012) conduct a similar exercise, using a different strategy for identifying the critical persistent risk correlation that does not rely on assuming complete financial markets but only exploits standard asset pricing equations.

These papers connect the assessment of insurance against long-run risk (Section 3) and the assessment of insurance against business cycle risk (Section 4). In particular, both papers conclude that little is at stake when it comes to insuring transitory business cycle shocks, whereas the potential welfare costs from inefficient allocations are much larger when shocks are very persistent. However, it remains an open question how well these long-run risks are actually insured. Colacito and Croce (2010) and Lewis and Liu (2012) argue that long-run shocks are either highly correlated or well insured across countries. Is this conclusion consistent with the substantial cross-country variation in long-run consumption growth described in Section 3? Nakamura et al. (2012) present some new empirical evidence that can potentially be used to address this question.

4.4.4. Assessing Efficiency Using International Portfolios
The most obvious mechanism via which agents can hedge country-specific risk is by holding foreign assets that increase agents' exposure to shocks in other countries and appropriately reduce exposure to domestic shocks. Within the context of a specific model, one can ask what portfolios (if any) deliver an efficient cross-country allocation of consumption and capital. One can then compare those portfolios to the ones observed in the data. If one has confidence in the model, then the distance between observed and efficient portfolios can be used to gauge efficiency.

A very simple model is a symmetric two-country world in which two trees (one in each country) produce stochastic dividends of apples in each period (see Lucas, 1982).

Agents in the two countries enjoy apples equally. An efficient allocation involves agents in each country consuming fixed fractions of the world apple endowment in each period. Now consider a decentralized environment. Absent any opportunities for international asset trade, consumption in each country would equal the country-specific dividend. This allocation is inefficient. If stock markets are introduced that allow agents to freely trade shares in trees, then in equilibrium the representative agent in each country will choose to hold half the shares in each tree. This equilibrium is efficient because each representative agent receives and consumes half of the world apple endowment in each period.

It is well known that in practice portfolios tend to be heavily biased toward domestic assets. Thus, for example, Americans mostly hold stocks in U.S. companies and U.S. government or corporate bonds. Relative to the simple model outlined above, these portfolio choices would appear to be inefficient. But this setup is obviously too simple. One important respect in which it is too simple is that it assumes that asset income is the agents' only source of income. In practice, most of household income comes from labor income, which is inherently almost impossible to diversify (short of working in multiple countries). Baxter and Jermann (1997) emphasize that introducing nondiversifiable labor income increases the gap between portfolios predicted by theory versus those observed in the data. In the context of our apple tree example, suppose that domestic agents receive half of their domestic tree's apple endowment, as compensation for the work of picking the apples. Stock owners have the rights to the remaining half. Now equilibrium portfolios will be 100% foreign biased: domestic agents will buy all the shares in the foreign tree and vice versa. With those portfolios, agents will again end up consuming half the world endowment of apples in each period. Thus, introducing labor income seems to make the international diversification puzzle worse, as Baxter and Jermann emphasized.

The simple model we started with is unrealistic along another dimension: it is a one-good model. Consider the simple two-good endowment economy described in Section 4.2.1. Suppose that the tree in the domestic country produces apples and the foreign tree produces bananas, and that fruit can be freely traded between countries. Now if the domestic tree has a particularly good year and produces lots of apples, the world relative price of apples will fall and the price of bananas will rise. This relative price movement provides automatic insurance against country-specific shocks. In fact, as Cole and Obstfeld (1991) showed, given a unitary elasticity of substitution in preferences between fruit, the terms of trade will move one-for-one with the relative fruit endowment. In that case, irrespective of the portfolio mix between shares in domestic and foreign trees, income will automatically be equated across countries. Thus, if domestic and foreign agents have identical preferences, any portfolio will deliver the same efficient allocation. In that special case, even complete home bias is efficient.

Heathcote and Perri (forthcoming) explore equilibrium portfolio choice in the stock economy model described in Section (4.3.2) above. That is a natural environment for studying portfolio diversification, since it is the same model that has been widely used to study other dimensions of risk sharing, notably cross-country correlations of consumption, output, and investment, as well as comovement between relative consumption and the real exchange rate. The model features both labor income, as emphasized by Baxter and Jermann (1997), and the relative price effects emphasized by Cole and Obstfeld (1991). Recall that agents trade shares in representative domestic and foreign firms, which pay dividends equal to revenue less wage payments and investment spending. It turns out that the portfolios implied by a calibrated version of that model feature domestic-foreign compositions that are quantitatively similar to those observed in the data. Moreover, given (i) logarithmic utility over the consumption composite ($\gamma = 1$) and (ii) a unitary elasticity of substitution between domestic and foreign intermediates in producing the final good (so that $G_1(a_1, b_1) = a_1^\omega b_1^{1-\omega}$), it is possible to characterize the equilibrium fraction of wealth invested in foreign stocks in closed form. Heathcote and Perri (Proposition 1) show that this share is constant and given by

$$1 - \lambda = \left(\frac{1 - \theta}{1 - \omega} + 2\theta \right)^{-1}. \tag{29}$$

They also show that allocations in this equilibrium are efficient. Note that diversification is increasing in the steady-state trade share in the model, $1 - \omega$. In addition, assuming $1 - \omega < 0.5$, diversification is decreasing in labor's share $1 - \theta$, contrary to the Baxter and Jermann result.

How do the (efficient) portfolio predictions of this model compare with the data? To answer that question, Heathcote and Perri (forthcoming) assemble data on diversification $(1 - \lambda)$ and trade shares $(1 - \omega)$ for OECD economies over the period 1990–2007 (they assume a common-across-countries share for capital income $\theta = 0.36$). Figure 9.9 plots diversification against the trade share as predicted by equation (29) (the solid line) alongside an analogous scatter plot for their sample of countries. Most country points are close to the line, and thus observed portfolios are close to the ones that in theory are consistent with efficiency.[20]

How is it possible that home-biased portfolios allow for perfect pooling of country-specific risk, even though agents are already heavily exposed to domestic risk, thanks to nondiversifiable labor income? Perfect risk sharing in this environment requires that the ratio of marginal utilities of consumption across countries should be equal to the real exchange rate (which is the marginal rate of transformation between domestic and foreign consumption). Given logarithmic utility over consumption, this implies that the value of consumption should be equated across countries. A positive domestic shock raises the relative present value of domestic labor earnings. To equate the relative value of permanent income across countries, it is clear that the return on domestic agents' portfolios must decline relative to the return on foreign agents' portfolios. In the model,

---

[20] Great Britain is an exception, but high observed diversification there reflects the country's special position as an international financial center.

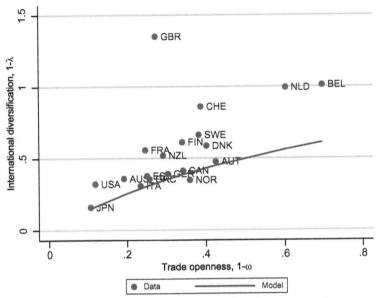

Figure 9.9 Portfolio Diversification in the Heathcote-Perri Model and in the Data

the relative return to domestic stocks falls following a positive domestic shock because the real exchange rate depreciates, reducing the relative value of domestic capital. Thus, a portfolio biased toward domestic assets offers a hedge against nondiversifiable labor income risk.

For risk aversion above one, efficient relative consumption becomes less sensitive to the real exchange rate than in the logarithmic example described above. In decentralized environments, the covariance between relative equity returns and the real exchange rate then becomes an additional driver of portfolio choice, since agents have an incentive to bias portfolios toward assets that offer relatively high returns in states in which the real exchange rate appreciates and the relative price of domestic consumption is high (see Van Wincoop and Warnock, 2010). Coeurdacier (2009) explores how introducing trade costs in goods affects the covariation between relative equity returns and the real exchange rate, and thus how trade costs impact portfolio composition. He finds that the theoretical pattern of covariation and thus the direction of portfolio bias depends on the level of trade costs: moderate costs imply a foreign bias, whereas high costs imply home bias.

The literature on international portfolio choice continues to grow. One lesson from this literature to date is that the extent of diversification predicted by theory is quite sensitive to model details, and new insights continue to emerge as richer models are built featuring more general preferences, alternative sources of risk, and more refined asset market structures. Engel and Matsumoto (2009) explore diversification in an environment with nominal frictions and find that the level of diversification that delivers efficient allocations (taking the frictions as given) depends on the degree of price stickiness. Coeurdacier and Gourinchas (2011) explore diversfication in bonds and equities separately and find that bonds are well suited to hedging exchange rate risk, whereas equities are good for hedging nontradable (e.g., labor income) risk. Berriel and Bhattarai (2013) argue that domestic nominal bonds are a natural hedge for domestic agents against price level risk: if policy generates a surprise increase in the price level, the real return on domestic bonds will go down at the same time that the real value of debt and thus the present value of future taxes on domestic agents is reduced. Coeurdacier and Rey (2013) offer a much more comprehensive survey of the rapidly growing literature on this topic than we have provided here.

4.5. Welfare and Policies

One lesson that could be drawn from the analysis in this section is that the international allocation of resources across the business cycle is not necessarily inconsistent with efficiency. If that is the case it is interesting to ask what would be the welfare costs of shutting down the international financial markets that generate efficient allocations in our models. In Table 9.7 we report the welfare changes (in percentages of lifetime consumption) of going from complete markets to restricted asset market structures.[21] In particular we report the value of η that solves the following equation

$$\sum_{t=0}^{\infty}\sum_{s^t}\beta^t\pi(s^t)U\left((1+\eta)c_i^{CM}(s^t), n_i^{CM}(s^t)\right) = \sum_{t=0}^{\infty}\sum_{s^t}\beta^t\pi(s^t)U(c_i^{MKT}(s^t), n_i^{MKT}(s^t)),$$

where initial conditions $k_i(s_0)$, $z_i(s_0)$, $i = 1, 2$ are set to their nonstochastic steady state values, and where a CM superscript denotes complete markets allocations, while an MKT superscript denotes a given market allocation. In particular, we focus on the market structures where only a bond is traded and on financial autarky.[22] Line 1 of the table reports these numbers for the parameters used in row 6 of Table 9.4 (i.e., those which deliver international correlations close to the data). At business cycle frequencies the efficiency gains associated with complete markets are not worth much in welfare terms. For example, going from complete markets to financial autarky is equivalent to a loss of lifetime consumption of around 0.02%. In line 2 we report welfare numbers for the economy described in Section 4.2.1 in which the two intermediate goods are received as endowments rather than being produced.[23]

---

[21] We compute welfare using second order approximations of the model since first order approximations yield inaccurate welfare results (see Kim and Kim, 2003).

[22] We do not report the welfare losses of going to a stock economy, as in this simple setup an economy where two stocks are traded always yields welfare extremely close to complete markets (welfare is identical in the case discussed in Section 4.4.4).

[23] The process for endowments is again chosen to match the standard deviation and international correlation of GDP in the data.

Table 9.7 The Value of International Financial Markets ($100 \times \eta$)

	Bond	Fin. Aut.
	(% of cons.)	
1. Baseline $\rho = 0.91, \psi = 0, \gamma = 1, \sigma = 0.6$ $\sigma_\varepsilon = 0.0082, corr(\varepsilon_1, \varepsilon_2) = 0.435$	−0.013	−0.021
2. Endowment	−0.003	−0.009
3. High Volatility, $\sigma_\varepsilon = 0.016$	−0.051	−0.086
4. Unit Elasticity, $\sigma = 1$	−0.003	−0.001
5. High Elasticity, $\sigma = 5$	−0.007	−0.004
Persistent shocks		
6. $\beta = 0.8, \rho = 0.91$	−0.132	−0.015
7. $\beta = 0.8, \rho = 0.91, \sigma = 5$	−0.054	−0.012
8. $\beta = 0.99, \rho = 0.999$	−0.409	−0.378

In this case the value of international financial markets is even lower, and the numbers are in line with the similar exercise performed by Cole and Obstfeld (1991). The reason is that in the endowment case financial markets cannot affect productive efficiency and only serve to keep marginal utilities aligned across countries (consumption efficiency). In the production economy, in contrast, financial markets also equalize the expected returns to investment across countries, thereby raising world productivity and allowing agents to enjoy higher average levels of consumption.

Are there plausible parameter values that deliver larger estimates for the value of international financial markets? In line 3 we consider a case in which the standard deviation of innovations to productivity is twice as large as the one needed to replicate the volatility of U.S. GDP. This value is consistent with the volatility of business cycles observed in emerging economies (see Neumeyer and Perri, 2005). Now the welfare benefits of financial markets are larger (about 4 times as large as in the baseline case). Lines 4 and 5 consider two different values for the elasticity of substitution, σ. Note that the welfare value of financial markets is non-monotone in this parameter. When the elasticity is close to one, the value of financial markets is minimal because relative price movements provide a lot of insurance against idiosyncratic productivity shocks (recall that autarky is efficient given $\sigma = 1$ in the endowment version of the model).

In all the cases considered so far, welfare in the bond economy is higher than in financial autarky, suggesting that financial liberalization is always welfare-improving. The last three cases considered in Table 9.7 paint a rather different picture. In these cases parameters are chosen so that shocks generate large differences between the permanent incomes of the two countries. In order to generate such differences productivity shocks have to be persistent relative to individual discounting: ρ must be large relative to β.

In lines 6, 7, and 8 we consider three parameterizations with this property, the first two with a low discount factor and baseline persistence, the last with the baseline discount factor and higher persistence. Two aspects of the results are remarkable. The first is that the welfare value of financial markets can be an order of magnitude larger than in the cases previously considered. The second is that the welfare ordering is reversed: welfare is higher under financial autarky than in the bond economy.

It is not surprising that the costs of eliminating all financial markets are larger the more persistent are relative shocks, because more persistent shocks mean larger gains from mutual insurance. Bonds (being noncontingent) are not able to deliver this insurance. Welfare can actually be higher in financial autarky than in the bond economy because of the presence of pecuniary externalities, i.e., general equilibrium price effects.[24] As an illustration of these effects consider the response to a productivity shock in country 1 in the high elasticity parameterization (line 7). The symmetric efficient allocation involves consumption increasing almost identically in both countries (consumption efficiency) while investment (not plotted) and labor rise by more in country 1 than in country 2 (productive efficiency). These responses are displayed in Panel A of Figure 9.10.

In the incomplete markets models (Panels B and C) allocations are not efficient. Country 1 is the prime beneficiary of its higher productivity (because insurance markets do not exist) and thus residents of that country permanently increase consumption sharply relative to residents of country 2. The shock to relative wealth also shows up in labor supply: relative to the efficient allocation, agents in country 1 work too little, while those in country 2 work too much.

Now consider the differences between the financial autarky and bond economy models. In financial autarky, country 1's desire to save (given its temporarily high income) translates into a large fall in the equilibrium interest rate (Panel D), and an associated sharply declining consumption profile during most of transition. When countries can trade a bond, country 1 is able to achieve a smoother consumption profile by saving in country 2, and as savings flow abroad there is less downward pressure on the domestic interest rate. Thus, relative to financial autarky, the equilibrium interest rate declines by less in country 1, and declines by more in country 2. Higher interest rates are beneficial for country 1, which is a net saver. In country 2 it is in each atomistic agent's best interests to borrow from country 1. But in aggregate, their borrowing raises interest rates, which hurts all borrowers in country 2. Thus, introducing trade in a bond changes interest rates in a way that effectively amplifies the differential impact of the initial shock across countries, reduces effective insurance, and moves equilibrium allocations further away from the efficient ones.[25]

---

[24] For a discussion of these effects in this class of models see also Corsetti et al., 2012.

[25] In general it also changes the terms of trade, which can be important. Here we isolate the role of general equilibrium interest rate movements by considering a high elasticity parameterization in which the terms of trade moves little.

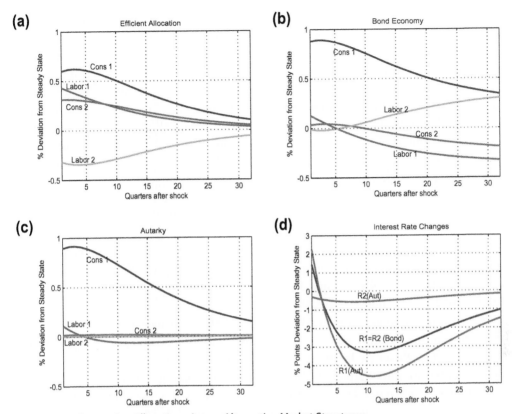

Figure 9.10 Comparing Allocations Across Alternative Market Structures

This finding is intriguing from a policy point of view because it suggests that it might be desirable for two countries that can only trade a noncontingent bond to close international financial markets altogether. Interestingly, the model suggests that this situation is more likely in exactly those cases where welfare differs significantly across market structures. Thus, welfare effects of going from a bond economy to financial autarky might be both positive and economically significant (in the example considered in line 6 of Table 9.7, the gain exceeds 0.1 percent of consumption).

5. CONCLUSION

The conclusions we take from this paper are simple. First, over the long run alloca-tions appear inefficient. In particular, there is little evidence that consumption responds efficiently to persistent cross-country differentials in output growth. This is important, because the potential welfare gains from achieving more efficient allocations in the long run are large. In contrast, it is difficult to reject the hypothesis that allocations respond efficiently to business cycle frequency fluctuations. Patterns of cross-country comovement in macro aggregates are consistent with efficiency, as are observed levels of portfolio diversification. It is difficult to reconcile observed exchange rate dynamics with efficiency, but it is also difficult to reconcile them with alternative decentralized asset market structures that explicitly limit international risk sharing. Thus we view evidence on efficiency from prices as inconclusive, pending better theories of nominal exchange rate dynamics. Future work should also focus on connecting evidence on risk-sharing from asset prices to evidence from quantities. To date, the macroeconomic literature has largely neglected asset price evidence, while the finance literature has typically treated the process for consumption as exogenous.

One important area for future research that we have largely neglected in this survey is the interaction between risk sharing against idiosyncratic shocks within a country versus risk sharing against country-level shocks between countries. In environments with idiosyncratic risk the extent of openness to international financial flows can interact with information or enforcement frictions that preclude a first best allocation of resources within a country (see, for example, Broer, 2010, Broner and Ventura, 2010, Martin and Taddei, 2012, and Mendoza et al., 2009).

Given our assessment that actual international allocations are inefficient, at least in the long run, an obvious next step is to consider whether specific policy interventions might increase efficiency. In many instances, if country-specific risks are not pooled because of frictions in international financial markets, working to remove these frictions should increase efficiency. However, we have discussed two examples in which financial liberalization can be welfare reducing. First, in Section 4.5 we discussed an example in which complete markets guarantee efficiency, but partial liberalization—introducing international bond trade relative to financial autarky—reduces welfare. Second, in Section 4.4.2 we discussed an example in which the source of inefficiency is nonfundamental-driven fluctuations in the exchange rate. In that context, closing international financial markets is a way to insulate the economy from these otherwise distortionary shocks.

6. APPENDIX: PROOF OF PROPOSITION 1

For any variable x, let $\hat{x}(s^t) = \log x(s^t) - \log \bar{x}$, where $\bar{x}$ is the nonstochastic steady-state value for x.

Efficient allocations are defined by values for (a_1, a_2, b_1, b_2) that satisfy the resource constraints and the consumption efficiency conditions.

The log-linearized versions of these equations are

$$s\hat{a}_1 + (1-s)\hat{a}_2 = \hat{z}_1,$$
$$(1-s)\hat{b}_1 + s\hat{b}_2 = \hat{z}_2,$$

$$\left(-\gamma + \frac{1}{\sigma}\right)\left(s\hat{a}_1 + (1-s)\hat{b}_1\right) - \frac{1}{\sigma}\hat{a}_1 = \left(-\gamma + \frac{1}{\sigma}\right)\left(s\hat{b}_2 + (1-s)\hat{a}_2\right) - \frac{1}{\sigma}\hat{a}_2,$$

$$\left(-\gamma + \frac{1}{\sigma}\right)\left(s\hat{a}_1 + (1-s)\hat{b}_1\right) - \frac{1}{\sigma}\hat{b}_1 = \left(-\gamma + \frac{1}{\sigma}\right)\left(s\hat{b}_2 + (1-s)\hat{a}_2\right) - \frac{1}{\sigma}\hat{b}_2.$$

The solutions are

$$\hat{a}_1 - \hat{z}_1 = (1-s)\Omega(\hat{z}_1 - \hat{z}_2),$$
$$\hat{a}_2 - \hat{z}_1 = -s\Omega(\hat{z}_1 - \hat{z}_2),$$
$$\hat{b}_2 - \hat{z}_2 = -(1-s)\Omega(\hat{z}_1 - \hat{z}_2),$$
$$\hat{b}_1 - \hat{z}_2 = s\Omega(\hat{z}_1 - \hat{z}_2),$$

where

$$\Omega = \frac{(1 - \sigma\gamma)(1 - 2s)}{4s(1 - \sigma\gamma)(1 - s) - 1}.$$

Consumption and output (measured in units of the final consumption good) deviations are given by

$$\hat{c}_1 = s\hat{a}_1 + (1-s)\hat{b}_1,$$
$$\hat{c}_2 = (1-s)\hat{a}_2 + s\hat{b}_2,$$
$$\hat{\gamma}_1^c = \frac{1}{\sigma}\hat{c}_1 - \frac{1}{\sigma}\hat{a}_1 + \hat{z}_1,$$
$$\hat{\gamma}_2^c = \frac{1}{\sigma}\hat{c}_2 - \frac{1}{\sigma}\hat{b}_2 + \hat{z}_2.$$

1. The pass–through coefficient from changes in relative output to relative consumption is given by

$$(\hat{c}_1 - \hat{c}_2) = \frac{(2s - 1)}{2\gamma(s - 1) + 4s(\sigma\gamma - 1)(1 - s) + 1}(\hat{\gamma}_1^c - \hat{\gamma}_2^c).$$

2. Net exports are given by

$$(\hat{\gamma}_1^c - \hat{c}_1) = \frac{2s(1 - \sigma\gamma) - (1 - \gamma)}{2\gamma + 4s(1 - \sigma\gamma) - \frac{1}{1-s}}(\hat{\gamma}_1^c - \hat{\gamma}_2^c).$$

3. The cross-country consumption and output correlations are

$$corr(\hat{c}_1, \hat{c}_2) = \frac{K_c + (1 - K_c)\rho}{(1 - K_c) + K_c\rho},$$

$$corr(\hat{\gamma}_1^c, \hat{\gamma}_2^c) = \frac{K_y + (1 - K_y)\rho}{(1 - K_y) + K_y\rho},$$

where ρ is the correlation of productivity shocks, and if and only if

$$K_c = 2s(1-s)\left(\frac{2\left(1-\sigma\gamma\right)\left(1-s\right)-1}{4s\left(1-\sigma\gamma\right)\left(1-s\right)-1}\right)\left(1-2s\frac{\left(1-\sigma\gamma\right)\left(1-2s\right)}{4s\left(1-\sigma\gamma\right)\left(1-s\right)-1}\right)$$

$$K_\gamma = 2\frac{\gamma(1-s)}{4s\left(\sigma\gamma-1\right)\left(1-s\right)+1}\left(1-\frac{\gamma(1-s)}{4s\left(\sigma\gamma-1\right)\left(1-s\right)+1}\right).$$

Given these expressions, it is straightforward to verify that if and only if $\sigma < \tilde{\sigma}(s,\gamma)$,

$$\frac{\hat{c}_1 - \hat{c}_2}{\hat{\gamma}_1^c - \hat{\gamma}_2^c} > 1$$
$$corr(\hat{\gamma}_1^c - \hat{c}_1, \hat{\gamma}_1^c - \hat{\gamma}_2^c) < 0$$
$$corr(\hat{\gamma}_1^c, \hat{\gamma}_2^c) > corr(\hat{c}_1, \hat{c}_2).$$

REFERENCES

Aguiar, M., Gopinath, G., 2007. Emerging market business cycles: the cycle is the trend. Journal of Political Economy 115 (1), 69–102.

Alfaro, L., Kalemli-Ozcan, S., Volosovych, V., 2011. Sovereigns, Upstream Capital Flows and Global Imbalances, NBER Working Paper No 17396.

Arvanitis, A.V., Mikkola, A., 1996. Asset-market structure and international trade dynamics. American Economic Review 86 (2), 67–70.

Backus, D.K., Kehoe, P.J., 1992. International evidence on the historical properties of business cycles. American Economic Review 82 (4), 864–888.

Backus, D.K., Smith, G.W., 1993. Consumption and real exchange rates in dynamic economies with non-traded goods. Journal of International Economics 35 (3–4), 297–316.

Backus, D.K., Kehoe, P.J., Kydland, F.E., 1992. International real business cycles. Journal of Political Economy 100 (4), 745–775.

Backus, D.K., Kehoe, P.J., Kydland, F.E., 1994. Dynamics of the trade balance and the terms of trade: the J-Curve? American Economic Review 84 (1), 84–103.

Bansal, R., Yaron, A., 2004. Risks for the long run: a potential resolution of asset pricing puzzles. Journal of Finance 59 (4), 1481–1509.

Baxter, M., 2012. International risk-sharing in the short run and in the long run. Canadian Journal of Economics 45 (2), 376–393.

Baxter, M., Crucini, M.J., 1995. Business cycles and the asset structure of foreign trade. International Economic Review 36 (4), 821–854.

Baxter, M., Jermann, U., 1997. The international diversification puzzle is worse than you think. American Economic Review 87 (1), 170–180.

Berka, M., Devereux, M.B., Engel, C., 2012. Real exchange rate adjustment in and out of the Eurozone. American Economic Review 102 (3), 179–185.

Berriel, T.C., Bhattarai, S., 2013. Hedging against the government: a solution to the home asset bias puzzle. American Economic Journal: Macroeconomics 5 (1), 102–134.

Brandt, M.W., Cochrane, J.H., Santa-Clara, P., 2006. International risk sharing is better than you think, or exchange rates are too smooth. Journal of Monetary Economics 53 (4), 671–698.

Broer, T., 2010. Domestic or Global Imbalances? Rising Inequality and the Fall in the U.S. Current Account, Working Paper, Institute for International Economic Studies, Stockholm.

Broner, F.A., Ventura, J., 2010. Rethinking the Effects of Financial Liberalization, NBER Working Paper No. 16640.

Buera, P.J., Shin, Y., 2011. Productivity Growth and Capital Flows: The Dynamics of Reforms, Working Paper, University of California at Los Angeles.

Caselli, F., Feyrer, J., 2007. The marginal product of capital. Quarterly Journal of Economics 122 (2), 535–568.

Chari, V.V., Kehoe, P.J., McGrattan, E.R., 2002. Can sticky price models generate volatile and persistent real exchange rates? Review of Economic Studies 69 (3), 533–563.

Chinn, M.D., Ito, H., 2008. A new measure of financial openness. Journal of Comparative Policy Analysis 10 (3), 309–322.

Coeurdacier, N., 2009. Do trade costs in goods markets lead to home bias in equities? Journal of International Economics 77 (1), 86–100.

Coeurdacier, N., Gourinchas, P.-O., 2011. When Bonds Matter: Home Bias in Goods and Assets, NBER Working Paper No. 17560.

Coeurdacier, N., Rey, H., 2013. Home bias in open economy financial macroeconomics. Journal of Economic Literature 51 (1), 63–115.

Colacito, R., Croce, M.M., 2010. The short and long run benefits of financial integation. American Economic Review 100 (2), 527–531.

Colacito, R., Croce, M.M., 2011. Risks for the long run and the real exchange rate. Journal of Political Economy 119 (1), 153–181.

Cole, H.L., Obstfeld, M., 1991. Commodity trade and international risk sharing: how much do financial markets matter? Journal of Monetary Economics 28 (1), 3–24.

Corsetti, G., Dedola, L., Leduc, S., 2008. International risk sharing and the transmission of productivity shocks. Review of Economic Studies 75 (2), 443–473.

Corsetti, G., Dedola, L., Leduc, S., 2012. Demand Imbalances. Exchange-Rate Misalignment and Monetary Policy, Working Paper, European Central Bank.

Devereux, M.B., Hnatkovska, V., 2011. Consumption Risk-Sharing and the Real Exchange Rate: Why Does the Nominal Exchange Rate Make Such a Difference? NBER Working Paper No. 17288.

Doepke, M., Zilibotti, F., 2006. Occupational choice and the spirit of capitalism. Quarterly Journal of Economics 123 (2), 747–793.

Engel, C., 1999. Accounting for U.S. real exchange rate changes. Journal of Political Economy 107 (3), 507–538.

Engel, C., Matsumoto, A., 2009. The international diversification puzzle when goods prices are sticky: it's really about exchange-rate hedging, not equity portfolios. American Economic Journal: Macroeconomics 1 (2), 155–188.

Epstein, L.G., Zin, S.E., 1989. Substitution, risk aversion, and the temporal behavior of consumption and asset returns: a theoretical framework. Econometrica 57 (4), 937–969.

Fitzgerald, D., 2012. Trade costs, asset market frictions, and risk sharing. American Economic Review 102 (6), 2700–2733.

Gourinchas, P.-O., Jeanne, O., 2006. The elusive gains from international financial integration. Review of Economic Studies 73 (3), 715–741.

Gourinchas, P.-O., Jeanne, O., 2013. Capital flows to developing countries: the allocation puzzle. Review of Economic Studies 80 (4), 1484–1515.

Gourinchas, P.-O., Rey, H., Govillot, N., 2010. Exorbitant Privilege and Exorbitant Duty, IMES Discussion Paper Series 10-E-20, Bank of Japan.

Hadzi-Vaskov, M., 2008. Does the Nominal Exchange Rate Explain the Backus-Smith Puzzle? Evidence from the Eurozone, Discussion Paper 07–32. Utrecht School of Economics.

Hamilton, B., Whalley, J., 1984. Efficiency and distributional implications of global restrictions on labor mobility: calculations and policy implications. Journal of Development Economics 14 (1–2), 61–75.

Heathcote, J., Perri, F., 2002. Financial autarky and international business cycles. Journal of Monetary Economics 49 (3), 601–627.

Heathcote, J., Perri, F., 2004. Financial globalization and real regionalization. Journal of Economic Theory 119 (1), 207–243.

Heathcote, J., Perri, F., forthcoming. The international diversification puzzle is not as bad as you think. Journal of Political Economy.

Hess, G., Shin, K., 2010. Understanding the Backus-Smith puzzle: it's the (nominal) exchange rate, stupid. Journal of International Money and Finance 29 (1), 169–180.

Kaldor, N., 1957. A model of economic growth. Economic Journal 67 (268), 591–624.

Kehoe, P.J., Perri, F., 2002. International business cycles with endogenous incomplete markets. Econometrica 70 (3), 907–928.

Kim, J., Kim, S.H., 2003. Spurious welfare reversals in international business cycle models. Journal of International Economics 60 (2), 471–500.

Kocherlakota, N.R., Pistaferri, L., 2007. Household heterogeneity and real exchange rates. Economic Journal 117 (519), C1–C25.

Kose, A., Prasad, E., Rogoff, K., Wei, S.J., 2009. Financial globalization: a reappraisal. IMF Staff Papers 59, 8–62.

Lane, P.R., Milesi-Ferretti, G.M., 2007. The external wealth of nations mark II: revised and extended estimates of foreign assets and liabilities, 1970–2004. Journal of International Economics 73 (2), 223–250.

Lewis, K.K., 1996. What can explain the apparent lack of international consumption risk sharing? Journal of Political Economy 104 (2), 267–297.

Lewis, K.K., Liu, E.X., 2012. International Consumption Risk Is Shared After All: An Asset Return View, NBER Working Paper No. 17872.

Lucas, R.E., 1982. Interest rates and currency prices in a two-country world. Journal of Monetary Economics 10, 335–359.

Lucas, R.E., 1987. Models of Business Cycles. Basil Blackwell, Oxford.

Lucas, R.E., 1990. Why doesn't capital flow from rich to poor countries? American Economic Review 80 (2), 92–96.

Martin, A. Taddei, F., 2012. International capital flows and credit market imperfections: a tale of two frictions. Journal of International Economics 89 (2), 441–452.

Mendoza, E.G., Quadrini, V., Rios-Rull, J.V., 2009. Financial integration, financial development, and global imbalances. Journal of Political Economy 117 (3), 371–416.

Mussa, M., 1986. Nominal exchange rate regimes and the behavior of real exchange rates: evidence and implications. Carnegie-Rochester Conference Series on Public Policy 25 (1), 117–213.

Nakamura, E., Sergeyev, D., Steinsson, J., 2012. Growth-Rate and Uncertainty Shocks in Consumption: Cross-Country Evidence, NBER Working Paper No. 18128.

Neumeyer, P.A., Perri, F., 2005. Business cycles in emerging economies: the role of interest rates. Journal of Monetary Economics 52, 345–380.

Obstfeld, M., Rogoff, K., 2001. The six major puzzles in international macroeconomics: is there a common cause? In: Bernanke, B., Rogoff, K., (Eds.), NBER Macroeconomics Annual 2000, vol. 15. MIT Press, pp. 339–412.

Pakko, M.R., 1997. International risk sharing and low cross-country consumption correlations: are they really inconsistent? Review of International Economics 5 (3), 386–400.

Pakko, M.R., 2004. A spectral analysis of the cross-country consumption correlation puzzle. Economics Letters 84 (3), 341–347.

Rabanal, P., Rubio-Ramirez, J.F., 2010. Can International Macroeconomic Models Explain Low-Frequency Movements of Real Exchange Rates? Duke University, Working Paper.

Ruhl, K.J., 2008. The International Elasticity Puzzle, Working Paper 08–30, New York University. Leonard N. Stern School of Business, Department of Economics.

Sandri, D., 2010. Growth and Capital Flows with Risky Entrepreneurship, IMF Working Paper 10/37.

Song, Z., Storesletten, K., Zilibotti, F., 2011. Growing like China. American Economic Review 101 (1), 196–233.

Stigler, G.J., Becker, G.S., 1977. De Gustibus Non Est Disputandum. American Economic Review 67 (2), 76–90.

Van Wincoop, E., Warnock, F., 2010. Can trade costs in goods explain home bias in assets? Journal of International Money and Finance 29 (6), 1108–1123.

Viani, F., 2011. International Financial Flows, Real Exchange Rates and Cross-Border Insurance, Banco de Espana Working Paper 1038. Banco de Espana.

CHAPTER 10

External Adjustment, Global Imbalances, Valuation Effects*

Pierre-Olivier Gourinchas[*,†,‡] and Hélène Rey[†,‡,§]

[*]University of California, Berkeley, CA, USA
[†]National Bureau of Economic Research, Cambridge, MA, USA
[‡]Centre for Economic Policy Research, London, UK
[§]London Business School, London, UK

Abstract

We provide an overview of the recent developments of the literature on the determinants of long-term capital flows, global imbalances, and valuation effects. We present the main stylized facts of the new international financial landscape in which external balance sheets of countries have grown in size and discuss implications for the international monetary and financial system.

Keywords

Exchange rates, Current account, International capital flows, International monetary system

JEL classification codes

F21, F3, F33, F36, F4, F41, G01, G15

1. INTRODUCTION

The question of external adjustment is a central issue in international macroeconomics. Early approaches such as Hume's (1752) price specie flow mechanism emphasized the self-regulating nature of international exchanges through settlements in hard currency. Following the disruptions of the interwar period, the early Keynesian analyses of Machlup (1943), Meade (1951), or Metzler (1960) focused instead on the role of monetary and fiscal policy in achieving a desired level of internal and external balance. These static models focused on nominal price and wage rigidity and did not feature any self-correcting force that would ensure long-term stability. When Mundell (1968) asked "To what extent

* Comments on an earlier draft of this chapter are gratefully acknowledged. Thanks to Evgenia Passari and Nicolas Govillot for their help with the U.S. data. Thanks to Gian Maria Milesi-Ferretti and Philip Lane for providing us with the 2010 update of their dataset. Thanks to the editors and discussants Vincenzo Quadrini and Paolo Pesenti as well as to Maury Obstfeld for detailed comments. Rey gratefully acknowledges support from ERC grant 210584. This chapter was written while Pierre-Olivier Gourinchas was visiting professor at SciencesPo, Paris, France, whose hospitality is gratefully acknowledged.

585

should surplus countries expand; to what extent should deficit countries contract?" the debate was about the relative merits of expenditure-switching and expenditure-reducing policies, that is, policies that would alter the composition of demand between domestic and foreign goods, versus policies that would directly affect patterns of aggregate demand. Subsequent research, started by Hamada (1969) and Bruno (1970) and summarized in Obstfeld and Rogoff (1995) borrowed from the optimal growth theory of Ramsey (1928), Cass (1965), and Koopmans (1965). Since the current account measures the difference between national saving and domestic investment, both forward-looking decisions, proper modeling of the external adjustment requires an explicit theory of economic agents' consumption/saving and investment decisions. The resulting synthesis, in the form of the "intertemporal approach to the current account" characterized the dynamics of the current account as the result of forward-looking decisions by households and investment decisions by firms, set in market structures of varying degrees of complexity. This was the focus of Obstfeld and Rogoff (1995) in the previous volume of the handbook, and constitutes a natural starting point for this chapter. Conceptually, the intertemporal approach ascribes movements in a country's current account to the difference between the current situation of a country, and its long run circumstances. Formally, it states that countries should borrow whenever their current income is below their permanent income, or whenever the return to domestic capital is higher than the cost of borrowing. The precise amount of borrowing is then pinned down by the requirement that debts be repaid, and returns to capital be equated across locations.[2]

From a conceptual point of view, this approach constitutes a giant leap forward. From an empirical perspective, however, the theory has yielded mixed results and its key empirical predictions have often been rejected by the data, a point already noted by Obstfeld and Rogoff (1995).[3] We emphasize here two particularly relevant empirical shortcomings, which we document in Section 2: first, the model performs particularly poorly in explaining the empirical pattern of *net* long-term capital movements, both between developing and mature economies and across developing countries. Second, the model does not take into account that the current account represents an increasingly imperfect measure of the change in a country's net foreign asset position since the latter also reflects changes in the market value of cross-border claims and liabilities. The relative importance of these *"valuation effects"* is particularly high for advanced economies, but increasingly

---

[2] This chapter does not deal with situations where countries may decide not to repay their debts. For a discussion of the specific issue of sovereign debt, see Chapter 11 by Mark Aguiar and Manuel Amador in this handbook.

[3] For instance, Nason and Rogers (2006) found that the present-value-model of the current account was soundly rejected for Canada over the post-war period. In general, the current account balances ascribed by the theory tend to be much smaller and less variable than their empirical counterpart. Put another way, output fluctuations appear much more persistent to the econometrician's eyes than actual current account movements suggest. There are some important exceptions. For instance, Aguiar et al. (2007) find that the current account fluctuations of small emerging economies are consistent with the theory precisely once one takes into account that productivity shocks appear much more persistent in emerging economies. Obstfeld and Rogoff (2000) show that introducing transportation costs in an otherwise standard model helps understanding Feldstein and Horioka's (1980) puzzle of small current account imbalances and allows to make progress on other important international macroeconomics puzzles.

so too for emerging ones. The growing empirical importance of these valuation effects requires that we look more closely at the determinants of international portfolios.

We explore these two dimensions in turn. Understanding the source of "global imbalances"—deficits in advanced countries, surpluses in rapidly growing emerging ones—constitutes the principal objective of Sections 3 and 4. Section 3 lays out a simple model of long-term capital flows. The starting point is the neoclassical growth model in continuous time under perfect foresight, a standard framework which allows us to derive many key results without having to spend too much time on the necessary machinery. The model's predictions regarding capital flows rest on two key elements. First, capital will tend to flow from countries with low autarky returns to countries with high autarky returns. Second, the model identifies two key determinants of a country's autarky returns: capital scarcity and long run growth prospects both taken as exogenous and country-specific. Putting both things together, the theory unambiguously points to advanced economies as countries with low autarky interest rates, and emerging ones as countries with high autarky interest rates. Hence capital should flow "downstream" from rich to poor countries.

Existing attempts to explain the observed pattern of global imbalances introduce additional determinants of autarky interest rates. The various models put forward in the literature, surveyed in Section 4, all share the feature that advanced economies—chiefly the U.S.—can exhibit *higher* autarky real returns than the rest of the world, especially emerging economies. Equivalently, these countries have high *desired* saving (or low *desired* investment) relative to the U.S. Hence, these theories predict that capital should flow from South to North, as observed in the data. Most of these theories rely on asymmetries between financial and economic development in advanced and emerging countries. Caballero et al. (2008a), for instance, assume that developing countries face a shortage of stores of value. This shortage depresses the autarky rates of returns of these countries, and rapid growth in this part of the world can exacerbate global imbalances. Other theories, such as Mendoza et al. (2009) or Angeletos and Panousi (2011), emphasize cross-country differences in the ability to insure away idiosyncratic risk. In a Bewley-type model, these differences translate into different strength of the precautionary saving motive. Less financially developed countries, faced with higher residual levels of idiosyncratic risk will save more, depressing autarky rates of return. Yet other theories, such as Antràs and Caballero (2009), emphasize the interactions between financial frictions and international trade.

Most of these models do not feature aggregate uncertainty and do not have an international diversification motive. They make predictions about *net* capital flows, that is, about the intertemporal transfer of resources across countries. Section 5 follows a different track. It starts by observing that the current account does not, in general, coincide with the change in a country's net foreign asset position. The latter also reflects changes in the *market value* of claims and liabilities underlying a country's net position, including exchange rate movements. As documented in Section 2 and by Lane and Milesi-Ferretti (2001) these *valuation changes*, ignored in much of the earlier literature, have grown tremendously in importance since the 1980s, to the point where over a given period, their fluctuations can easily dominate the current account balance. Obtaining precise estimates of these valuation changes is not an easy task, and we discuss the empirical methodological advances that have allowed researchers to make progress on that front. Valuation changes would not matter much for the underlying process of external adjustment if they were purely unexpected and random. We present a simple framework to analyze the structure of total external returns and their predictability. We discuss how such returns can be constructed from the underlying balance sheet position, with a particular attention to the relevant empirical caveats that are involved in any exercise of this nature. Section 5 also focuses more specifically on the U.S. external balance sheet and presents updated estimates of the excess return the U.S. enjoys on its external balance sheet. We discuss the origin of what has sometimes been called an "exorbitant privilege." We show how the predictable component of this excess return contributes to relaxing the external constraint of the United States. A legitimate question to ask then is to what extent existing theories and in particular to what extent the new stream of literature featuring dynamic stochastic general equilibrium models can accommodate the valuation channel of adjustment in their dynamics of the net foreign asset positions.

Finally, our discussion on the structure of external balance sheets of countries has a bearing on the functioning of the International Monetary and Financial System which we take up in Section 6. Traditionally the country at the center of the system—the U.K. in the 19th century and before the First World War or the U.S. after the Second World War—has been described as a global liquidity provider. The center country issues the currency used in most international exchanges whether on goods markets or on financial markets. By emphasizing the heterogeneity in risk profiles of the different countries, the role of the center country can be reinterpreted as one not only of a liquidity provider but also one of a global insurer. After all, the U.S. dollar is not merely a very liquid international mean of exchange but it is also the currency denomination of U.S. Treasuries, which are held as reserve assets all over the globe. We discuss how the endogenous structures of portfolios of countries affects net returns on the external asset position and leads to potentially very large wealth transfers in crisis times.

We conclude with a review of intriguing research questions left open by the literature.

2. STYLIZED FACTS

We begin by highlighting some important stylized facts characterizing recent developments in international capital markets.

2.1. Global Imbalances, World Interest Rates, and Allocation Puzzle

Over the last twenty years capital has flown from South to North, and especially toward the United States, arguably among the most advanced economies in the world. The large current account deficits of the United States have started to expand after the

% of World GDP

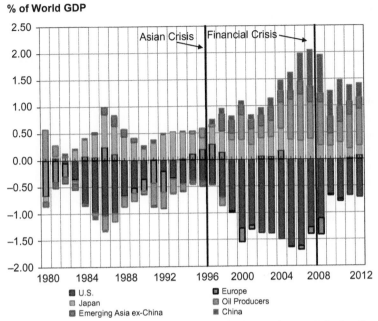

Figure 10.1 Global Imbalances: Current Accounts. *Notes:* Oil Producers: Bahrein, Canada, Kuwait, Iran, Libya, Nigeria, Norway, Mexico, Oman, Russia, Venezuela, Saudi Arabia. Emerging Asia ex-China: Indonesia, Korea, Malaysia, Philippines, Singapore, Taiwan, Thailand. Europe: European Union. *Data Source:* IMF World Economic Outlook Database, Various Issues

Asian Crisis to reach 5.3% of U.S. GDP in 2004, 5.8% in 2005, and about 6% in 2006. Figure 10.1 illustrates this pattern by reporting the current account balances of various groups of countries, as a fraction of world output between 1980 and 2012. Table 10.1 reports average ratios of current accounts to world output for three periods: between 1980 and 1996 (before the Asian financial crisis); from 1997 to 2006 (between the Asian and global financial crises); and since 2007.[4] U.S. current account deficits have been financed by a broad array of creditors, mostly Japan in the 1980s and early 1990s, oil producing economies and emerging Asia since 1996, and especially China over the recent period.[5] These massive net capital flows into the world's dominant capital market have been referred to as "global imbalances."

Figure 10.2 reports the world real interest rate over the same period.[6] We observe a dramatic decline in the world real interest rate, from 5% to 6% at the beginning of the 1980s, to −2% by the end of 2011. As Bernanke (2005) observed in his early and

---

[4] Current account balances in Table 10.1 do not sum to zero because of the discrepancy between global saving and investment. The missing surplus (or deficit in recent years) averages about 0.5% of world output.

[5] See Blanchard and Milesi-Ferretti (2009) for a detailed account of the evolution of global external deficits.

[6] The world real interest rate is defined as the GDP-weighted average of 3-months nominal interest rates minus realized inflation, for the countries of the G-7. The figure also reports two measures of ex-ante long-term U.S. rates.

Table 10.1 Current Account Balances, Fraction of World GDP

Region	Period		
	1980–1996	1997–2006	2007–2012
United States	−0.44	−1.17	−0.86
Japan	0.32	0.36	0.26
European Union	−0.10	0.04	−0.07
Oil producers	−0.06	0.28	0.57
China	0.01	0.15	0.49
Emerging Asia ex-China	−0.01	0.19	0.26
Latin American and Caribbean	−0.13	−0.10	−0.07
Rest of the World	−0.08	−0.02	−0.14

Source: IMF World Economic Outlook, April 2012. Oil producers consist of Canada, Norway, Mexico, Russia, Venezuela, Saudi Arabia, Iran, Kuwait, Libya, Oman, and Bahrein. Emerging Asia ex-China consists of Taiwan, Korea, Malaysia, Indonesia, Philippines, Singapore, and Thailand.

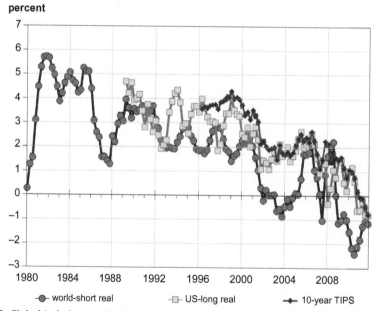

Figure 10.2 Global Imbalances: World Interest Rates. *Notes:* world-short real: ex-post 3-month real interest rate for the G-7 countries (GDP weighted). U.S.-long real: 10-year yield on U.S. Treasuries minus 10-year expected inflation. 10-year TIPS: yield on inflation indexed 10-year Treasuries. *Source:* Global Financial Database, IMF International Statistics, OECD Economic Outlook, Survey of Professional Forecasters

influential piece on the "savings glut," any account for the pattern of global imbalances needs also to be consistent with the evidence on real interest rates.

Stylized Fact 1 (Global Imbalances). *The largest and arguably most advanced world economy, the United States, has been a net capital importer since 1982 and has been increasingly financed*

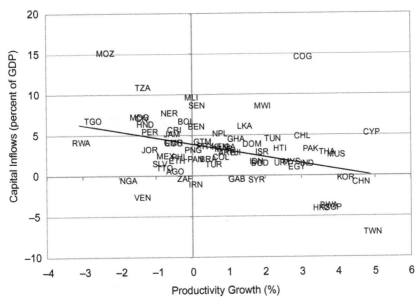

Figure 10.3 Average Productivity Growth and Capital Inflows Between 1980 and 2000. *Note*: Sample of 68 developing economies. *Source:* Gourinchas and Jeanne (2013)

by fast-growing emerging economies. The absolute value of world current account balances scaled by world GDP, the "global imbalances," have been increasing starting in 1996—with a short dip at the time of the 2001–2002 recession and a more sustained one since 2008. The emergence of these global imbalances coincides with a general decline in world real interest rates.

Moreover, the pattern of *total* net capital inflows to developing countries stands also in contradiction with the basic theory. Figure 10.3, reproduced from Gourinchas and Jeanne (2013), plots average productivity growth between 1980 and 2000 (horizontal axis) against the average net capital inflows relative to GDP. According to the theory, the relationship should be strongly positive. Instead, the figure exhibits a strong negative correlation, which the authors label the "allocation puzzle." Gourinchas and Jeanne (2013), Aguiar and Manuel (2011), and Alfaro et al. (2011) find that this negative correlation between growth and capital flows is mostly driven by public flows, while private capital inflows appear positively correlated with productivity fundamentals.

Stylized Fact 2 (Allocation Puzzle).   *Aggregate net capital inflows tend to be negatively correlated with productivity growth across developing countries. This pattern is largely driven by public sector capital flows.*

2.2. The Growth of Cross-Border Gross Positions

Another key stylized fact in international economics since the 1990s has been the massive increase in *gross* capital flows. As capital controls were taken down, as financial regulation and transaction costs decreased, the gross external asset positions of countries underwent a remarkable surge. At the beginning of the 21st century, some small open economies invested abroad and/or owed to foreigners several times their level of annual output. The example of Iceland, which in 2007 owned about 524% of its annual GDP in external assets while owing foreigners 636% of its annual GDP, is particularly striking but not isolated: for instance, in 2010, the gross external assets of the U.K. were 488% and 507% of annual output respectively.[7]

In pioneering work, Lane and Milesi-Ferretti (2001, 2007a) constructed an annual panel of cross-border assets and liabilities for a large number of countries. A simple and widely used measure of *de facto* financial integration is the sum of cross-border financial claims (A) and liabilities (L), scaled by annual GDP: $(A + L)/Y$.[8] As reported in Lane (2012), this measure of financial integration has risen from 68.4% in 1980 to 438.2% in 2007 for advanced economies.[9] Meanwhile, the same measure for emerging market economies increased from 34.9% in 1980 to 73.3% in 2007. Financial integration has therefore been a general phenomenon. But unlike trade globalization, which was mostly driven by emerging markets, financial integration has been more pronounced so far for advanced economies. Using the latest update of the Lane and Milesi-Ferretti (2007a) dataset with data up to 2010, Figure 10.4 reports the sum of gross external assets and liabilities, scaled by world GDP for the G-7 economies as well as for four large and fast-growing emerging economies—the so-called BRICs (Brazil, Russia, India, China). The magnitude of financial globalization for G-7 economies increased sharply from 75% of world output in 1990s to 210% at its peak in 2007. For the BRIC economies, it increased tenfold, from 2% in 1990 to 20% in 2010.

Stylized Fact 3 (Increase in Cross-Border Gross Flows and Positions). *Cross-border gross asset and liability positions have massively increased since the 1980s and especially in the 1990s and 2000s. This increase has been particularly pronounced for advanced economies.*

Furthermore, the type of cross-border positions taken by different economies, i.e. the *composition* of the balance sheets, is very heterogeneous across countries. While it is relatively common to find that "risky" assets (portfolio equity or direct investment assets) account on average for a large share of the asset side of the balance sheet of advanced economies (49% for the United States, 50% for Canada, 26% for the U.K., 31% for France), emerging markets' external portfolios have a lower weight on risky assets (India

---

[7] Source: Lane and Milesi-Ferretti (2007a) updated until 2010. We report gross external assets and liabilities excluding financial derivatives. Data on financial derivatives are available toward the end of the sample for most countries. For the United States, they are available since 2005. At that date they amounted to $1.2 trillion on the asset side and to $1.1 trillion on the liability side. In 2010 derivatives had grown to represent $3.6 trillion on the asset side (i.e. 18% of gross assets) and $3.5 trillion on the liability side (i.e. 16% of gross liabilities).

[8] There are also *de jure* measures of financial integration based on the institutional framework as described in the IMF Annual Report on Exchange Arrangements and Exchange Restrictions and refined in Quinn (1997), Quinn and Toyoda (2008), or Chinn and Ito (2008). Other *de facto* measures are based on convergence in asset prices, rather than quantities traded. All these measures indicate increased financial integration since 1970, especially so for advanced economies.

[9] These numbers exclude countries with annual GDP smaller than 10 billion U.S. dollars.

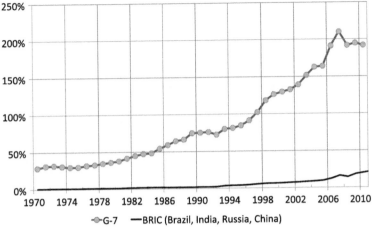

Figure 10.4 G-7 and BRIC Cross-Border Assets and Liabilities (Percent of World GDP). Cross-Border Assets and Liabilities Defined as the Sum of Gross External Assets and Liabilities. *Source:* Lane and Milesi-Ferretti (2007a) updated to 2010

5%, Indonesia 5%, Russia 18%, China 9%, Brazil 21%), as these economies tend to invest in safer securities such as government bonds.[10] Interestingly, and in particular since the 1990s, the BRICs (Brazil, Russia, India, China) have taken increasingly net short positions in risky assets while the G-7 economies, which often double up as important financial centers (the U.S., the U.K., large euro area countries) are increasingly long in risky assets.[11] Figure 10.5 reports the net risky position of these two groups of countries as a fraction of the groups' annual GDP. Starting in the 1990s, the expansion of the external balance sheet of countries has been accompanied by a marked heterogeneity in their structure across countries, with advanced economies increasingly involved in international maturity and liquidity transformation.

Stylized Fact 4 (Heterogeneity in Gross Flows and Positions). *The asset composition of the external balance sheet of countries is heterogeneous with advanced economies tending to be long in risky assets and emerging markets short in risky assets.*

[10] The share of risky assets is calculated as the sum of FDI assets and equity assets as a ratio of total assets. The average is taken between 1970 and 2010 except for Russia (1993–2010) and China (1981–2010).

[11] The net risky position is defined as the difference between portfolio equity and direct investment assets and liabilities. Other components of the external balance sheet also include risky assets: portfolio debt includes long-term corporate and sovereign bonds. Cross-border banking positions also involves long-term syndicated loans. However, these asset categories also include shorter-term or safer fixed-income assets, such as official reserves, government securities or short-term loans. It is possible that some of the asymmetries we now observe *across* asset categories were present in the past *within* asset categories. For instance, Despres et al. (1966) argue that the United States was providing liquidity to the rest of the world by lending long term and borrowing short term, transactions that would both be recorded in the "other" categories of the international investment position. The observed asymmetry coupled with the increase in the size of the external balance sheet leaves little doubt that these activities have, if anything, increased over time.

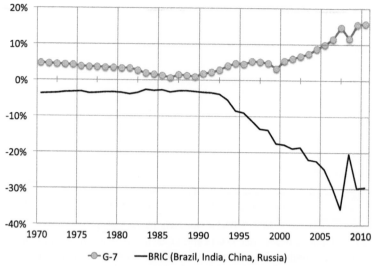

Figure 10.5 Net Risky Position Defined as Equity and Direct Investment Assets, Minus Equity and Direct Investment Liabilities. *Source:* Lane and Milesi-Ferretti (2007a) updated to 2010

2.3. The Importance of Valuations for the External Balance Sheet

Large and heterogeneous leveraged portfolios open the door to potentially important wealth transfers across countries when asset prices and exchange rate fluctuate. In turn, these capital gains and losses are bound to affect the external asset positions of countries. To illustrate, Figures 10.6 and 10.7 compare Lane and Milesi-Ferretti's (2007a) measure of a country's net external position with a measure obtained simply by cumulating current account balances for a group of advanced economies (Figure 10.6) and a group of emerging ones (Figure 10.7). Since the current account does not—by definition—incorporate fluctuations in the value of existing assets and liabilities, the two measures differ from one another in theory by the cumulated value of capital gains and losses on the country's external position.[12] As Figure 10.6(a) shows for the United States, simply cumulating the balance on the U.S. current account since 1970 would lead to a severe underestimate of the U.S. external position, by about 36% of U.S. GDP in 2010. *A contrario*, this suggests that the U.S. has enjoyed important net capital gains on its net external asset positions over this period. These *valuation effects* are economically quite sizable: they represent the equivalent of an additional surplus of the U.S. current account of about 2% of output, for every year between 1970 and 2010. Figures 10.6(b) and (d) show smaller cumulated

---

[12] In practice, data discrepancies between the Balance of Payments and the International Position surveys can also account for the gap between the two series. We revisit this issue at length in Section 5.

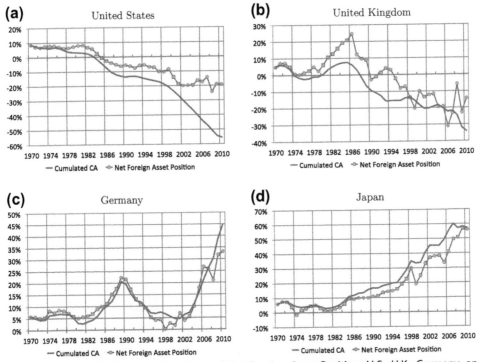

Figure 10.6 Cumulated Current Account and Net Foreign Asset Position: U.S., U.K., Germany, and Japan, 1970–2010. Percent of GDP. *Source:* Lane and Milesi-Ferretti (2007a) updated to 2010.

valuation gains for the other advanced economies we consider.[13] Figure 10.7 shows that the BRIC economies tended to experience significant cumulated valuation losses since 2000, between 10% of output for China and 40% for Russia. Figures 10.6 and 10.7 illustrate the asymmetry between the U.S. (large positive valuation gains) and emerging economies (large valuation losses). By contrast, Figures 10.6(b) and (d) show that cumulated current accounts provide a roughly accurate guide to the low frequency movements in the net external position of other advanced economies, although the valuation component can be large in any given year. Table 10.2 documents the average magnitude of absolute valuation effects (as a percentage of GDP), as well as the average of the absolute value of current accounts of a number of countries over four periods.[14] For most countries, including emerging economies, the importance of valuation effects has been increasing

---

[13] The U.K. external position is underestimated by about 20% of GDP in 2010 while the German and Japanese positions are overestimated by 11% and 1.5% of GDP, respectively.

[14] Specifically, we calculate $\bar{VA} = 1/T \sum_t \left| \frac{NA_t - NA_{t-1} - CA_t}{GDP_t} \right|$ and $\bar{CA} = 1/T \sum_t \left| \frac{CA_t}{GDP_t} \right|$ over the four periods 1971–1980, 1981–1990, 1991–2000, and 2001–2010 where NA_t denotes the net foreign asset position and CA_t the current account.

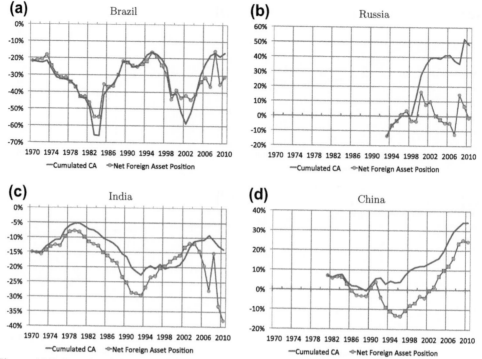

Figure 10.7 Cumulated Current Account and Net Foreign Asset Position: Brazil, Russia, India, and China, 1970–2010. Percent of GDP. *Source:* Lane and Milesi-Ferretti (2007a) updated to 2010.

over time. For economies very open to cross-border investments, such as Ireland, the average valuation change per annum reaches more than 13% of GDP in the most recent period (it reaches 11.8% for Switzerland). The absolute value of current accounts has also increased over these four periods for all the countries considered. Except for Germany, Japan, and to a lesser extent China, the average magnitude of the current accounts, though rising over time, tends to be dominated by the average magnitude of valuation effects.

Stylized Fact 5 (The Growing Importance of Valuation Effects).   *Valuation effects, which are capital gains and losses on gross external assets and liabilities, account for an important and increasing part of the dynamics of the net foreign asset positions of countries. For the U.S., valuation effects have tended to be positive and economically large.*

3. LONG-TERM CAPITAL FLOWS IN THE NEOCLASSICAL GROWTH MODEL

This section presents the prototype neoclassical model of long-term capital flows. We begin with a riskless infinite-horizon model in continuous time, that corresponds to the open economy version of the Ramsey (1928), Cass (1965), and Koopmans (1965) model.

Table 10.2 Valuations and Current Accounts (Average p.a., % GDP)

Period	U.S. (%)	U.K. (%)	Ireland (%)	Germany (%)	Japan (%)	Brazil (%)	Russia (%)	China (%)	India (%)	Switzerland (%)
Valuations										
1971–1980	0.84	1.29	3.12	0.67	1.3	0.97	N/A	0.00	0.44	10.74
1981–1990	0.93	3.59	3.73	0.75	0.83	2.02	N/A	1.47	0.98	9.76
1991–2000	1.79	4.71	18.67	1.42	2.03	2.11	4.26	2.95	1.16	9.39
2001–2010	4.75	7.57	13.29	3.91	2.67	8.38	13.71	2.22	6.08	11.84
Current accounts										
1971–1980	0.40	1.16	5.75	1.00	1.15	5.74	N/A	0.00	0.82	2.16
1981–1990	1.95	2.16	4.23	2.71	2.32	2.32	N/A	1.52	1.68	3.72
1991–2000	2.12	2.21	0.48	1.48	2.26	2.05	9.02	1.94	1.13	8.55
2001–2010	4.56	2.24	2.37	4.50	3.39	1.67	7.94	5.43	1.41	10.96

The table reports the average valuation and current account components, as a share of GDP, for each sub period, where the average valuation and current account components are defined as $VA = 1/T \sum_t \left| \frac{NA_t - NA_{t-1} - CA_t}{GDP_t} \right|$ and $CA = 1/T \sum_t \left| \frac{CA_t}{GDP_t} \right|$.

We assume that the reader has enough familiarity with the details of this model and skip many intermediate derivations in the interest of conserving space.[15]

3.1. The Set-Up

Time is continuous and there is no uncertainty, aggregate, or otherwise. Consider a country with one homogeneous good and a population N_t that grows at a constant rate $n = \dot{N}_t / N_t$. The population can be viewed as a large family that maximizes the integral utility

$$U_t = \int_t^\infty e^{-\rho(s-t)} N_s u\left(c_s\right) ds, \tag{1}$$

where $\rho > 0$ is the rate of time preference, c_t denotes consumption per capita, and $u(c) = c^{1-\gamma}/(1-\gamma)$ is an isoelastic instantaneous utility function with an intertemporal elasticity of substitution $1/\gamma$. Since there is no disutility of labor, labor is supplied inelastically and the labor force equals the population, N_t. Output is produced with physical capital and labor, according to a Cobb-Douglas production function:

$$Y_t = K_t^\alpha \left(\xi_t N_t\right)^{1-\alpha}, \tag{2}$$

where $0 \le \alpha \le 1$ represents the share of capital income and ξ_t is an exogenous labor-augmenting productivity term that grows at a constant rate $g = \dot{\xi}_t / \xi_t$.

Output can be consumed, or invested:

$$Y_t = C_t + I_t, \tag{3}$$

where $C_t = c_t N_t$ denotes aggregate consumption and I_t aggregate gross investment. For simplicity, we assume away capital adjustment costs, so that capital accumulates according to[16]:

$$\dot{K}_t = I_t - \delta_k K_t, \tag{4}$$

where δ_k is the constant rate of depreciation of physical capital. Given some initial conditions $K_0, \xi_0, N_0 > 0$, the set-up is complete.

3.2. Financial Autarky

Consider, to begin with, the case where the country is in financial autarky. With a single good, and no possibility of intertemporal trade, this corresponds to the textbook closed economy neoclassical growth model. Following standard steps, it is immediate to show that optimal consumption/saving and investment decisions by the representative household yield a consumption path that satisfies the usual Euler equation:

$$\frac{d \ln c_t}{dt} = \frac{1}{\gamma}\left(\alpha \tilde{k}_t^{\alpha-1} - \delta_k - \rho\right), \tag{5}$$

---

[15] A full detailed treatment can be found in Blanchard and Fischer (1989, Chapter 2)
[16] Adjustment costs to capital are relatively unimportant for the model's predictions regarding long-term capital flows.

where "tilde" denotes variables expressed in efficient units per capita: $\tilde{x} = X/(\xi N)$. Equation (5) states that consumption per capita grows if the *autarky real interest rate* $r_t^a = \alpha \tilde{k}_t^{\alpha-1} - \delta_k$ exceeds the rate of time preference ρ. In that case, along the optimal plan, the representative household prefers to reduce consumption in order to benefit from the high return delivered by the additional unit of saving. The strength of that effect on consumption growth is controlled by the willingness of the household to shift consumption across periods, that is, by the elasticity of intertemporal substitution $1/\gamma$.[17]

Different countries with the same technology parameters α and δ_k will face different autarky interest rates only to the extent that they have different *levels* of capital per efficient unit. That is, if we consider two countries i and j: $r_t^{a,i} > r_t^{a,j}$ if and only if $\tilde{k}_t^i < \tilde{k}_t^j$: autarky rates are high if countries are *capital-scarce*.

3.2.1. Relation to the Lucas Puzzle

This argument forms the basis for the well-known Lucas (1990) puzzle. Lucas observed that if countries had access to the same technology α and ξ, then the ratio of their marginal product of capital $MP_k = \alpha \tilde{k}^{\alpha-1}$ can be expressed simply as a function of relative output per worker: $MP_k^i / MP_k^j = \left(y^i/y^j\right)^{1-1/\alpha}$.

Applying this calculation to India and the U.S., where Lucas estimated a 15-fold difference in output-per-worker and assuming $\alpha = 0.4$, the ratio of marginal products equals a whopping $(1/15)^{1-1/0.4} = 58$! Of course, the assumption that technology ξ is the same in India and the U.S. is a strong one, and a "trivial" way to solve the Lucas puzzle is to allow for differences in productivity levels.[18] There is no puzzle if differences in productivity entirely offset differences in output per worker: $\xi^i/\xi^j = y^i/y^j$. Indeed, the literature on development accounting has found significant differences in productivity or social infrastructure across countries. For instance, Gourinchas and Jeanne (2006) using data for 1995, estimate an average sixfold difference in labor-augmenting productivity for 65 non–OECD economies relative to the U.S.[19] Clearly, cross-country differences in productivity levels are important.

Other factors can also account for the Lucas puzzle. Most prominently, Caselli and Feyrer (2007) find that, despite large differences in capital-output, marginal products of capital $MP_k = \alpha Y/K$ are remarkably close across countries, after properly adjusting the effective share of capital α for differences in the share of reproducible capital and the

---

[17] The rate of growth of population n does not affect consumption growth under our choice of preferences. With faster population growth, a unit of output saved today yields fewer units of consumption per capita tomorrow. But because flow utility is scaled by population, future consumption per capita is also valued more and the two effects cancel exactly.

[18] One of Lucas's proposed explanations for the puzzle was to take into account how external effects of human capital accumulation translate into differences in productivity.

[19] Gourinchas and Jeanne (2006, Table 9 p.736) report a development accounting gap of 0.11 and a contribution of 0.58 and 0.2, respectively for exogenous labor-augmenting productivity and human capital (in log-share). We obtain the number reported in the text as $\exp(-(0.58 + 0.2)\ln(0.11))$. Hall and Jones (1999) and Caselli (2005) document similar results. Alfaro et al. (2008) also confirm that controlling for institutional quality differences removes the puzzle for direct and portfolio equity investments.

relative price of investment to output across countries.[20] An alternative approach is to note that countries may face domestic capital market distortions. Suppose that the *private* return to capital is $r = (1 - \tau)(MP_k - \delta_k)$ where τ denotes a wedge between social and private returns. This wedge is a shorthand for all the distortions that potentially affect the return to capital: credit market imperfections, taxation, expropriation, bribery, and corruption… With open capital markets, we would expect private returns to be equated, and differences in capital-output ratio to reflect differences in capital wedges. This approach is followed empirically in Gourinchas and Jeanne (2013). Calibrating the capital wedge in each country to match the long run investment rate, the measured private rates of returns r are remarkably similar across countries.

To sum up, the evidence indicates that private returns to capital are fairly well equated across countries, either because of differences in productivity, in the share or price of reproducible capital, or because of country-specific wedges between the private and the social return to capital. This is an important observation since it indicates that international financial frictions are likely to be small, and that direct observation of *realized* rates of return provides little if any information about the *autarky* rates that determine the direction of capital flows.

3.2.2. Steady-State Autarky Rates

We now focus on the *long run* interest rate that obtains once the economy has settled into its steady state. It is easy to verify that the steady state is characterized by constant levels of capital and consumption per efficient units, $\tilde{k}_{ss}$ and $\tilde{c}_{ss}$. This implies that consumption per capita grows at the same rate as technology $d \ln c_t / dt = g$. Substituting into the Euler equation, we obtain:

$$\tilde{k}_{ss} = \left(\frac{\alpha}{\rho + \gamma g + \delta_k}\right)^{1/(1-\alpha)} \quad ; \quad r_{ss}^a = \rho + \gamma g. \tag{6}$$

This expression tells us that, once initial capital scarcities are eliminated (the gap between $\tilde{k}$ and $\tilde{k}_{ss}$), differences in autarky interest rates across countries with similar preferences are driven by differences in productivity growth: $r_{ss}^{a,i} > r_{ss}^{a,j}$ if and only if $g^i > g^j$.

3.3. Open Economy and the Direction of Capital Flows
3.3.1. Small Open Economy

Consider now the case of a small open economy that opens its financial account at time $t = 0$ and faces a constant world real interest rate r at which it can borrow or lend. Optimal investment requires that the marginal return to capital equals the world interest rate:

$$\alpha \tilde{k}_t^{\alpha-1} - \delta_k = r. \tag{7}$$

---

[20] Since the price of investment relative to output is high in poor countries, this tends to depress the marginal return to capital in these countries.

This pins down the stock of capital per efficient units at $\tilde{k}(r) = \left(\alpha / \left(r + \delta_k\right)\right)^{1/(1-\alpha)}$, a decreasing function of the world interest rate. Denote the financial wealth of the country by $W = K + B$ where B represents net foreign claims. Along the optimal plan, consumption and wealth evolve according to:

$$\frac{d \ln c_t}{dt} = \frac{1}{\gamma}\left(r - \rho\right); \quad \frac{d\tilde{w}_t}{dt} = \left(r - n - g\right)\tilde{w}_t + \left(1 - \alpha\right)\tilde{y}\left(r\right) - \tilde{c}_t, \tag{8}$$

where $\tilde{y}(r) = \tilde{k}(r)^\alpha$ represents the constant level of output and $(1-\alpha)\tilde{y}(r)$ represents the part of output that is not paid out as capital income. According to (8), the growth rate of consumption per capita is constant and equal to:

$$g_c = \frac{1}{\gamma}\left(r - \rho - \gamma g\right) + g = \frac{1}{\gamma}\left(r - r_{ss}^a\right) + g. \tag{9}$$

Consumption per capita grows faster (respectively slower) than the rate of domestic productivity growth if the world interest rate is higher (resp. lower) than the autarky interest rate.

To fix ideas further, we can think of the rest of the world as a closed economy that has reached its steady state. In that case, the world interest rate r satisfies $r = \rho + \gamma \bar{g}$, where $\bar{g}$ is the growth rate of world productivity. Substituting into equation (9), we obtain $g_c = \bar{g}$: the rate of growth of consumption per capita equals the world's growth rate of productivity, regardless of domestic output growth per capita g.

Under the assumption that $r > n + \max\langle g, \bar{g}\rangle$ and after a few tedious but elementary steps of algebra, we can substitute back into the dynamic budget constraint (8) and integrate to obtain:

$$\tilde{c}_t = \left(r - n - \bar{g}\right)\left[\tilde{w}_t + \frac{\left(1 - \alpha\right)\tilde{y}\left(r\right)}{r - n - g}\right]. \tag{10}$$

The consumption rule is linear in total wealth with a propensity to consume equal to the interest rate minus the growth rate of aggregate consumption $n + \bar{g}$. Total wealth consists of financial wealth $\tilde{w}_t$ and the present value of labor income $(1-\alpha)\tilde{y}(r)/(r-n-g)$. After a few extra steps, one can also solve for the path of external wealth and the current account (noting that $CA_t = \dot{B}_t$)[21]:

$$\tilde{b}_t = \left(\tilde{w}_0 + \frac{\left(1 - \alpha\right)\tilde{y}\left(r\right)}{r - n - g}\right)e^{(r - r_{ss}^a)t/\gamma} - \frac{\left(1 - \alpha\right)\tilde{y}\left(r\right)}{r - n - g} - \tilde{k}\left(r\right). \tag{11a}$$

---

[21] In this expression, $\tilde{w}_0 = \tilde{k}_{0-} + \tilde{b}_{0-} = \tilde{b}_0 + \tilde{k}(r)$, where $\tilde{k}_{0-}$ and $\tilde{b}_{0-}$ denote the stock of capital and the net external position immediately before the financial account opening at time $t = 0$. At the time of the opening, initial external debt positions are rolled over and the country finances any capital shortfall through external borrowing: $\tilde{b}_0 = \tilde{b}_{0-} + \tilde{k}_{0-} - \tilde{k}\left(r\right)$.

$$\tilde{ca}_t = \left(n + \bar{g}\right)\left(\tilde{w}_0 + \frac{(1-\alpha)\,\tilde{\gamma}\,(r)}{r - n - g}\right) e^{(r - r_{ss}^a)t/\gamma}$$

$$- (n+g)\left(\frac{(1-\alpha)\,\tilde{\gamma}\,(r)}{r - n - g} + \tilde{k}\,(r)\right). \tag{11b}$$

Inspection of these expressions reveals that the long-term external position depends on the gap between the world and autarky interest rates $r - r_{ss}^a$, proportional to the gap between world and country productivity growth, $\bar{g} - g$. We can distinguish three cases:

- Case 1: $r_{ss}^a < r$. From the preceding discussion, this occurs when $g < \bar{g}$. The first term in the expression for $\tilde{ca}_t$ and $\tilde{b}_t$ asymptotically dominates the dynamics. Eventually the country runs a *current account surplus* and holds a positive net foreign position. Because optimal consumption grows at a higher rate than output, the country needs to accumulate growing claims against the rest of the world.[22]
- Case 2: $r_{ss}^a = r$. In that case $g = \bar{g}$ and the current account and net foreign asset positions are driven by initial capital scarcity and external claims: $\tilde{ca}_t = (g+n)(\tilde{w}_0 - \tilde{k}_{ss})$ and $\tilde{b}_t = \tilde{w}_0 - \tilde{k}_{ss}$. The country runs a permanent current account deficit if it is initially capital scarce or has initial external liabilities. If initial capital scarcities and external claims are small, so that $\tilde{w}_0 \approx \tilde{k}_{ss}$, then $\tilde{ca} = \tilde{b} = 0$.
- Case 3: $r < r_{ss}^a$. From the preceding discussion, this corresponds to $\bar{g} < g$. The first term in (11a) and (11b) disappear asymptotically and the economy becomes a *net borrower* and runs a *current account deficit*. Since the country's output grows faster than the rest of the world, foreigners want to invest domestically.[23]

The preceding analysis reveals that countries export (resp. import) capital when the autarky interest rate is below (resp. above) the world interest rate. The determinants of *intertemporal* trade are thus similar to those of *intratemporal* trade and dictated by the principles of comparative advantage: just as countries export goods that are relatively abundant (i.e. with low autarky prices), countries export capital when capital is relatively abundant, i.e. when autarky real interest rates are relatively low.[24]

3.3.2. Large Open Economy

Consider now the case of two economies (home and foreign), not necessarily small, with open financial accounts. One can characterize the pattern of capital flows and net foreign positions by following the same steps as above, now with the condition that $B_t + B_t^* = 0$ at any instant where $*$ denotes foreign variables. Assuming that the technology parameters

---

[22] Expressed in *world* efficient units, B stabilizes at $B/\bar{\xi}N = \tilde{w}_0 + (1-\alpha)\tilde{\gamma}(r)/(r-n-g) \geq 0$.

[23] In that case, the country will not permanently remain small relative to the rest of the world. Eventually, the world interest rate will have to converge to the domestic autarky rate r_{ss}^a. The country will still run a current account deficit $\tilde{ca}_{ss} = (n+g)\tilde{b}_{ss}$ since it will have accumulated large net foreign liabilities $\tilde{b}_{ss} < 0$ along the way to the steady state.

[24] Obstfeld and Rogoff (1996, Chapter 2) present a similar analysis in a two-period model.

δ_k and α are the same in both countries, free capital mobility ensures that $\tilde{k}_t = \tilde{k}_t^*$, so that the world interest rate satisfies $r_t = \alpha \tilde{k}_t^{\alpha-1} - \delta_k$. Faced with a common real return to capital, optimal consumption plans in both countries satisfy:

$$\gamma \frac{d \ln c_t}{dt} + \rho = \gamma^* \frac{d \ln c_t^*}{dt} + \rho^* = r_t, \tag{12}$$

so that with common preferences (γ and ρ) the rate of growth of consumption per capita g_c is the same in both countries and $r = \rho + \gamma g_c$.

Without lack of generality, assume that home has a higher growth rate of productivity than foreign: $g > g^*$. Equation (6) then implies that home has a higher autarky interest rate: $r_{ss}^a > r_{ss}^{a*}$. Assume further that there are no initial capital scarcities, so that we focus on differences in productivity growth. It is easy (but tedious) to show that the world interest rate r is located somewhere between home and foreign interest rates: $r_{ss}^{a*} \leq r \leq r_{ss}^a$. Since $r = \rho + \gamma g_c$, one can equivalently show that the growth rate of consumption per capita is located between the domestic and foreign productivity growth rates $g^* \leq g_c \leq g$. Countries with an autarky interest rate above the equilibrium world interest rate will experience capital inflows; those with autarky interest rates below the world interest rate will experience capital outflows.[25]

3.4. Current Account Movements and Productivity Differentials

For the preceding theory to account for the empirical evidence on capital flows from emerging economies to advanced ones, two conditions need to be met. First, initial capital scarcities must not be too large for the developing world: $\tilde{k}_0 \approx \tilde{k}_{ss}$. This will be the case if productivity levels are lower or if capital market distortions (τ) are higher in poorer countries. Second, productivity growth must be higher in advanced economies than in developing ones.

This interpretation of the theory would be relatively bad news for developing countries: the direction of capital flows would simply reflect a broader pattern of economic *divergence* that would see advanced economies pulling further and further away from developing ones.[26] Fortunately, it does not survive careful empirical scrutiny. Instead, the empirical evidence indicates that it is precisely the (developing) countries with the strongest productivity growth that also experienced the strongest capital *outflows* (stylized Fact 2).

Large net capital inflows in the eurozone's periphery (Blanchard and Giavazzi, 2002) or in Eastern European economies (Alfaro et al., 2011) in the early 2000s were held as strong examples of the validity of the neoclassical theory. However, given the ongoing eurozone crisis, the deep structural adjustment in many Eastern European economies, and

---

[25] A source of global imbalances in that model arises from differences in impatience ρ. More patient countries will have lower autarky rates, and run current account surpluses. See Ghironi et al. (2008) for a model along these lines.

[26] Although, under financial integration and common preferences, the rate of growth of consumption per capita would remain equal in advanced and developing economies. See equation (12).

the fact that many of these capital inflows appear to have fueled ultimately unsustainable residential housing and financial booms, the argument that net capital flows in both regions were triggered by strong productivity growth as predicted by the neoclassical growth model is not so clear cut anymore.

If differences in productivity growth are not the main driver of capital flows over long periods of time, what is? The next section of this chapter reviews recent theoretical advances that help us understand the pattern of "global imbalances" (stylized Facts 1 and 2).

4. MODELS OF GLOBAL IMBALANCES

The previous section established two results. First, capital flows to countries with high autarky returns to capital, until returns are equalized. Second, productivity growth is one of the main determinants of autarky returns in the neoclassical growth model. Existing attempts to explain the pattern of observed external imbalances maintain the first element but relax the second. They all share the feature that some other ingredient depresses autarky interest rates in emerging economies relative to advanced ones. Equivalently, these countries feature a high *desired* saving (or low *desired* investment) relative to the U.S. As first analyzed by Bernanke (2005), this can account simultaneously for the external deficits of the U.S. and the observed low world real interest rates (stylized Fact 1). Bernanke identified a number of potential culprits for the increase in global desired savings: the increased savings and reserve accumulation in emerging economies following the East Asian financial crisis of 1997–1998; the rapidly aging population in many advanced economies (and some emerging ones), requiring additional saving to provide for an increasingly large retired population; and the sharp increases in oil prices and the corresponding swing toward current account surpluses of oil exporting economies (see Figure 10.1). Contemporaneously, Dooley et al. (2004a,b) emphasized the role of export-led growth development strategies in developing Asia, with an undervalued currency and the accumulation of official claims on the center country.

We begin with a review of theories relying on asymmetries in financial development between countries at different stages of development. The form that these financial frictions takes does matter. For instance, consider the capital wedge τ introduced in Section 3.2.1. In the steady state of the neoclassical model, this capital wedge does not affect the private rate of return to capital, still equal to $\rho + \gamma g$: the effect of the financial friction τ falls entirely on the marginal product of capital, $MP_k = (\rho + \gamma g)/(1 - \tau) + \delta_k$. Instead, we emphasize below financial frictions that also influence the autarky interest rate. In the model we consider, these financial frictions simultaneously drive up the equilibrium marginal product of capital and drive down the autarky risk-free rate. The first such model argues that developing countries suffer from a shortage of "stores of value." This shortage tends to drive up the price of financial assets, that is, to drive down the equilibrium interest rate. We use that framework to also explore the role of demographic factors, in particular population aging, and the interaction between demographic forces and financial frictions. The second model borrows from Bewley (1987) and Aiyagari (1994) and emphasizes the general equilibrium effects of precautionary saving. In that model, agents try to self insure against idiosyncratic risk. In equilibrium this depresses autarky interest rates below the riskless rates of the neoclassical model. The stronger the precautionary saving motive, the lower the autarky interest rate. Differences in idiosyncratic risk then translate into differences in autarky interest rates. The third class of models focuses on the interaction between financial frictions and international trade. Lastly, we discuss the role of public vs. private capital flows and reserve accumulation.

4.1. Asset Shortages

We begin with a model of asset shortage. The model captures the notion that financial markets in many emerging economies are not sufficiently developed and that these countries suffer from a shortage in stores of value. It generalizes Caballero et al. (2008a) to a production economy with overlapping generations. In the model, the demand for stores of value arises from the asynchronicity between income and consumption decisions.[27] That idea is implemented in a perpetual youth model à la Blanchard (1985) and Weil (1987). The model exhibits an essential *non-Ricardian* feature: households currently alive are unable to trade in claims on the resources of yet unborn generations. The lower the share of total income that accrues to the financial assets, the more acute is the resulting *shortage of stores of value*. Under financial autarky, this depresses equilibrium real interest rates. The model provides a link between levels of financial development, measured by the capacity of a country's financial system to capitalize streams of future income into real assets, and global imbalances.

4.1.1. The Individual Problem and Aggregate Dynamics

At every instant, households face an i.i.d instantaneous probability of dying θ. Since θ is common to all households, it represents the fraction of the population that dies every instant. A fraction θ of the population is also born every instant, so that total population remains constant, normalized to 1.[28] Since mortality risk is idiosyncratic, it is perfectly insurable: a competitive market for life-insurance will offer a rate of return θ per unit of wealth, in exchange for a claim on the household's estate when it dies.[29] Denote by

---

[27] The focus on consumption-saving decisions is done mostly for modeling simplicity. One could equivalently focus on the asynchronicity between sales and investment decisions in a production economy, or on a precautionary motive due to liquidity shocks.

[28] It is straightforward to introduce population growth. One could simply assume that the fraction of the population that is born every instant is $n + \theta$. Alternatively, one could follow Weil (1987) and assume that each cohort is an infinitely lived dynasty, but new cohorts are born every period.

[29] The life-insurance company breaks even under this scheme. If assets under management are W_t, it pays out θW_t per unit of time, and receives θW_t from households that just died.

$c(s, t)$, $w(s, t)$, $z(s, t)$ the consumption, financial assets, and non-financial income at time t of an individual born at time $s \leq t$. As of time t, the household maximizes

$$U_t = E_t \left[\int_t^\infty e^{-\rho(u-t)} u(c(s, u)) du \right] = \int_t^\infty e^{-(\rho+\theta)(u-t)} u(c(s, u)) du, \quad (13)$$

where the expectation is taken over the (random) time of death. The second equality uses the fact that life expectancy is exponentially distributed. Mortality risk makes households more impatient: they discount future flow utility at rate $\rho + \theta$ instead of ρ.

The budget constraint is

$$\frac{dw(s, t)}{dt} = (r_t + \theta)w(s, t) - c(s, t) + z(s, t), \quad (14)$$

where r_t is the risk-free interest rate, and we used the fact that the life-insurance company pays a premium $\theta w(s, t)$. Following standard steps, the optimal consumption plan of a household with iso-elastic utility $u(c) = c^{1-\gamma}/(1-\gamma)$ satisfies the following Euler condition:

$$\gamma \frac{d \ln c(s, t)}{dt} = r_t - \rho. \quad (15)$$

This is the same Euler equation as in the infinite-horizon model (see equation (5)). The intuition is simple: mortality risk makes the household more impatient. But the household also receives a premium θw that exactly offsets this effect. From now on, we limit the analysis to the case $\gamma = 1$ (logarithmic preferences).[30] Following standard (and tedious) steps, the consumption function takes a simple form:

$$c(s, t) = (\rho + \theta)[w(s, t) + h(s, t)]. \quad (16)$$

It is linear in the household's total wealth, defined as the sum of financial holdings $w(s, t)$ and non-financial wealth $h(s, t) = \int_t^\infty z(s, u) \exp\left(-\int_t^u (r_v + \theta) dv\right) du$ equal to the expected present discounted value of future non-financial income over the household's expected lifespan.

We can now derive aggregate variables by summing across existing cohorts. With obvious notation, the aggregate value X_t of a variable $x(s, t)$ is defined as:

$$X_t = \int_{-\infty}^t x(s, t)\theta e^{-\theta(t-s)} ds \quad (17)$$

since the size of a cohort born at time s as of time $t \geq s$ is $\theta e^{-\theta(t-s)}$. With linear budget constraints (14) and consumption rules (16), aggregate consumption and wealth follow:

$$C_t = (\rho + \theta)[W_t + H_t], \quad \dot{W}_t = r_t W_t + Z_t - C_t. \quad (18)$$

[30] With logarithmic preferences, income and substitution cancel out and the marginal propensity to consume does not depend upon the interest rate. The model can be solved in the general iso-elastic case, but the increased complexity does not deliver deep additional insights.

In this expression H_t represents the present discounted value of non-financial income of all *currently alive* cohorts, but does not include the present discounted value of non-financial income accruing to yet unborn cohorts. This *non-Ricardian* feature is essential for the results.[31]

To fix ideas, assume, as in Blanchard (1985) that cross-section income profiles decrease with age:

$$z\left(s, t\right) = \frac{\phi + \theta}{\theta} Z_t e^{-\phi(t-s)}, \quad \phi \geq 0. \tag{19}$$

Equation (19) states that, at any given time t, older workers (lower s) receive lower income with a slope controlled by ϕ. In the limit of $\phi \to \infty$, all non-financial income is received by the newborn generation: $z(t, t) = Z_t$, $z(s, t) = 0$ for $s < t$, and $H_t = 0$. This case maximizes the asynchronicity between income and consumption decisions since all income is received at birth, but consumption decisions need to be sequenced over a (random) lifetime. Conversely, when $\phi = 0$, all households receive the same income, regardless of age, which mitigates the need for saving. Under assumption (19), H_t satisfies:

$$\dot{H}_t = \left(r_t + \theta + \phi\right) H_t - Z_t. \tag{20}$$

4.1.2. Financial Autarky

We close the model by specifying the market structure and technology available to the household. As in the previous section, suppose that output is produced with the aggregate production function $Y_t = K_t^{\alpha} \left(\xi_t N_t\right)^{1-\alpha}$, where $\dot{\xi}_t/\xi_t = g$. Under financial autarky, physical capital K is the only asset available, so $W_t = K_t$. We make two simplifying assumptions. First, we assume that there is no depreciation of capital: $\delta_k = 0$.[32] Second, we assume that the share of aggregate non-financial income in total income is constant: $Z_t = (1 - \delta) Y_t$. δ is a key parameter, it controls the *supply of stores of value*. To see this, observe that the payments to capital rK equal δY since there is no depreciation. It follows trivially that the value of the capital-output ratio is:

$$K/Y = \delta/r. \tag{21}$$

For a given interest rate r, the market value of the capital stock (the supply of stores of value under financial autarky) varies one-to-one with δ.[33] Under these two assumptions, it is simple but tedious to combine (18) and the equilibrium condition $W_t = K_t$ to show that the steady-state autarky interest rate satisfies:

$$\left[r_{ss}^a - \delta\left(g + \rho + \theta\right)\right]\left(r_{ss}^a + \theta + \phi - g\right) = \left(1 - \delta\right) r_{ss}^a \left(\rho + \theta\right). \tag{22}$$

---

[31] If we define $\bar{H}_t = \int_t^\infty Z_u \exp\left(-\int_t^u r_v dv\right) du$ as the non-financial wealth of current and future generations, where Z_t denotes aggregate non-financial income. It is easy to check that $H_t \leq \bar{H}_t$ with equality when $\theta = 0$.

[32] This assumption is innocuous but simplifies the algebra.

[33] One can also verify that δ maps directly into the capital wedge τ introduced at the beginning of Section 4: $\delta = \alpha\left(1 - \tau\right)$.

A few cases are worth exploring:

- When $\phi = \theta = 0$, the model collapses to the neoclassical benchmark of the previous section and $r^a_{ss} = g + \rho$ (recall that $\gamma = 1$ with logarithmic preferences).[34]
- In the polar case where $\phi \to \infty$, we obtain instead:

$$r^a_{ss} = \delta \left(g + \rho + \theta \right). \tag{23}$$

Compared to the neoclassical model, two parameters influence the autarky rate. First, the interest rate increases because the mortality risk θ makes agents more impatient, which reduces saving. Second, the interest rate decreases because only a share $\delta \leq 1$ of income is paid out as financial income. This second effect is due to the *scarcity of stores of value* in the non–Ricardian economy. When $\delta < (g + \rho)/(g + \rho + \theta)$, the second effect dominates and the interest rate falls below the autarky rate of the benchmark model. Economies with distorted domestic capital markets (low δ or high τ) are more likely to have lower autarky interest rate.

- In the general case where $\phi, \theta > 0$, one can check that the autarky interest rate lies in the interval $[\rho + g - \phi, \rho + g + \theta]$. The shortage of assets dominates if $\delta(\theta + \rho + g + \theta(\rho + \theta)/\phi) \leq \rho + g$. In that case the autarky interest rate decreases below the neoclassical benchmark: $r^a_{ss} < \rho + g$.

The main implication of the model is that low levels of financial development, associated with sufficiently low δ, can depress autarky interest rates. It is then possible for a country to have a low autarky rate, despite a high growth rate of productivity g. When $\phi \to \infty$, the marginal product of capital remains constant and equal to: $MP_k = \alpha Y/K = \alpha(g + \rho + \theta)$, regardless of δ. In that case, we obtain the opposite result from the neoclassical benchmark model: variations in τ (or δ) are fully reflected in r^a_{ss}, and not in the marginal product of capital or the capital-output ratio. For the general case where $\phi, \theta > 0$, one can show that the marginal product of capital increases with $\tau = 1 - \delta/\alpha$, while the autarky interest rate decreases. Hence the model provides simultaneously a rationale for high marginal product of capital and low autarky rates in countries with low levels of financial development.

4.1.3. Open Economy and the Direction of Capital Flows

Small Open Economy. Following the steps described in the previous section, consider now the case of a small open economy facing a constant real interest rate r. For simplicity, we limit ourselves to the case where $\phi \to \infty$. With a constant interest rate r, it is easy to check that the following equations hold[35]:

$$\frac{W_t}{Y_t} = \frac{1 - \delta}{g + \rho + \theta - r}; \quad \frac{K_t}{Y_t} = \frac{\delta}{r}. \tag{24}$$

[34] There is another solution with $r^a_{ss} = \delta g$. However, that solution is not valid since it implies a negative value of human wealth.

[35] We assume in what follows that $r < g + \rho + \theta$ so that domestic wealth is well defined.

The first equation expresses domestic wealth, i.e. the domestic *demand for stores of value* per unit of output, W/Y, as a function of the world interest rate. A higher interest rate increases the demand for stores of value since wealth accumulates at a higher rate. The second equation expresses the *domestic supply of stores of value* (here capital) as a function of the interest rate. A higher interest rate depresses the present discounted value of the payments to capital δY, which lowers the equilibrium capital–output ratio. The difference between W and K represents the net foreign asset position of the country, B. With some simple manipulations, it is easy to express the net foreign asset position and the current account as a function of the autarky and world interest rates, as in the preceding section[36]:

$$\frac{B_t}{Y_t} = \frac{W_t - K_t}{Y_t} = \frac{\delta \left(r - r_{ss}^a\right)}{r \left(r_{ss}^a - \delta r\right)}; \qquad \frac{CA_t}{Y_t} = g \frac{\delta \left(r - r_{ss}^a\right)}{r \left(r_{ss}^a - \delta r\right)}. \tag{25}$$

This expression makes clear that the net foreign asset position is positive (resp. negative) depending on whether the world interest rate is higher (resp. lower) than the autarky interest rate. From the previous discussion, we infer that it is now possible for capital to flow out of emerging countries, provided that they have a sufficiently low autarky interest rate, i.e. a sufficiently low supply of stores of value.

Asymptotic Metzler Diagram. The previous results can be summarized in a version of the celebrated Metzler (1960) diagram. The vertical axis in Figure 10.8 reports the real interest rate while the horizontal axis reports either the long run domestic financial wealth

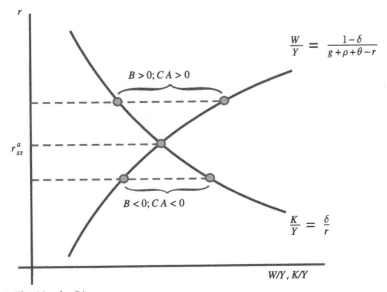

Figure 10.8 The Metzler Diagram

[36] The current account satisfies $N\dot{A}_t = CA_t$.

W or the value of domestic assets K, scaled by output Y. By construction, the difference between domestic financial wealth and the value of domestic assets equals the country's long run net foreign asset position: $B = W - K$. From the previous discussion, the value of domestic assets decreases with the real interest rate, while the value of domestic wealth increases with the real interest rate. Financial autarky corresponds to the situation where $W = K$. This pins down the autarky real interest rate r_{ss}^a. When $r > r_{ss}^a$, the small open economy runs an asymptotic current account surplus and is a net foreign creditor. Conversely, when $r < r_{ss}^a$ the country runs an asymptotic current account deficit and is a net foreign borrower.

World Economy. Consider now a world economy composed of two countries, a and b. The two countries are identical, except in terms of their level of financial development, captured by δ. Assume that $\delta^a > \delta^b$. It follows that country a will have a higher autarky interest rate than country b. Each country satisfies equations (18) and (21). Combining these equations, and denoting $\omega^a = Y^a / (Y^a + Y^b)$ the share of country a in global output, the steady-state world interest rate r_{ss}^a is a weighted average of the autarky interest rate in both countries:

$$r_{ss}^a = \omega^a r_{ss}^{a,a} + \left(1 - \omega^a\right) r_{ss}^{a,b} = \bar{\delta}\left(g + \rho + \theta\right). \tag{26}$$

r_{ss}^a depends on the output-weighted level of financial development $\bar{\delta} := \omega^a \delta^a + \left(1 - \omega^a\right) \delta^b$. Since $r_{ss}^{a,b} < r_{ss}^a < r_{ss}^{a,a}$, following a financial liberalization, capital will flow from b to a, and a will run an asymptotic negative net foreign asset position given by:

$$\frac{B^a}{Y^a} \to \frac{\left(1 - \omega^a\right)}{r_{ss}^a\left(1 - \bar{\delta}\right)}\left[\delta^b - \delta^a\right] < 0; \qquad \frac{CA^a}{Y^a} \to \frac{g\left(1 - \omega^a\right)}{r_{ss}^a\left(1 - \bar{\delta}\right)}\left[\delta^b - \delta^a\right] < 0. \tag{27}$$

According to the model, a simultaneous decline in world interest rates and the emergence of global imbalances (stylized Fact 1) can be the result of the integration of countries with low financial development—low δ— into the world economy (e.g. China after 1980), or the decline in the *market perception* of financial development in some countries (e.g. emerging Asia after the Asian financial crisis of 1997).

Assessing the Model. We can think of a variety of reasons why countries may be unable to pledge a high share of future output. Government, managers, or insiders can dilute and divert a substantial share of profits. δ can thus capture a number of capital market frictions, from explicit taxation, lack of enforcement of property rights, corruption, or rent-seeking, etc. Many of these features tend to be associated with developing economies, as measured by indicators of social infrastructure. A small set of papers in the empirical literature have explored the reduced-form link between indicators of financial development and global imbalances, following the popular panel-regression approach of Chinn and Prasad (2003), with somewhat mixed results (Chinn and Ito, 2007; Gruber and Kamin, 2009). For instance, Gruber and Kamin (2009) find that quantity measures of financial development, such as the ratio of credit to GDP, do not systematically predict larger current account deficits. One issue is whether quantity measures such as credit to GDP accurately capture the level of a country's financial development when some countries' financial systems are bank-based, while others are market based. Gruber and Kamin (2009) also find that real long-term interest rates are similar in the U.S. and other industrial countries. But the model predicts that under integration the risk-free rates should be equalized, so differences in observed long-term interest rates should simply reflect risk characteristics, and not differences in autarky interest rates. A deeper question is why excess savings from emerging markets should flow disproportionately toward the United States, and not other industrial countries. One answer is that external balances worsened in other industrial economies too, such as the United Kingdom and Australia, or many peripheral eurozone economies such as Spain, Ireland, or Portugal. But this was offset by growing current account surpluses in Germany and Japan. Another possible answer is that even if the U.S. offers similar levels of financial development (high δ) as other industrialized economies as a whole, it experiences more robust growth (high g) and therefore should have higher autarky interest rates.[37] Another part of the answer, to which we return later in this chapter, is that the U.S. dollar remains the leading international reserve currency.

4.1.4. Productivity and Financial Frictions

In the model of the previous section, external imbalances arising from differences in levels of financial development, as measured by δ, are amplified by differences in productivity growth. To see why, consider the two-country model from the previous section, but now suppose country b grows faster: $g^b > g^a$. The world interest rate is still the output weighted average of the two autarky rates: $r_{ss,t}^a = \omega_t^a r_{ss}^{a,a} + (1 - \omega_t^a) r_{ss}^{a,b}$. The difference is that ω_t^a tends to zero so the world interest rate converges to $r_{ss}^{a,b}$. As long as g^b is not too high, so that $r_{ss}^{a,b} < r_{ss}^{a,a}$, this leads to *larger* capital flows from b to a, unlike the neoclassical growth model where $g^b > g^a$ leads to capital flows from a to b. A similar mechanism is at work in Buera and Shin (2009). That paper models an emerging economy that experiences a growth acceleration. In the model individuals choose between supplying labor (worker) or becoming entrepreneurs. In an efficient allocation, low productivity individuals choose to become workers and high productivity ones become entrepreneurs. The economy, however, suffers from two frictions: idiosyncratic wedges that distort the allocation of factors away from efficiency, and financial frictions. Both frictions lower total factor productivity (TFP). The paper then considers the effect of a program of structural reforms that increases TFP, while keeping the financial friction unchanged. This is similar to an increase in g while keeping δ low in our model. Initially, this reform lowers investment and increases savings. Investment decreases due to the exit of low-productivity firms, while

---

[37] Engel and Rogers (2006) argue along those lines that the U.S. current account deficit can be explained by the country's higher growth relative to other industrial countries.

high productivity ones are constrained by the financial friction. The response of aggregate saving is more complex. Workers face an upward wage profile due to the rise in TFP. This tends to decrease savings. On the other hand, incumbent entrepreneurs experience temporarily high profits, since wages are initially low. In addition, individuals with high productivity but little wealth will choose a high saving rate to overcome the financial frictions. The net effect is an increase in saving, and net capital outflows. Song et al. (2011) present a similar model tailored specifically to the experience of China after the economic reforms of 1978. At the beginning of the reform process, the economy features high productivity private firms with limited access to credit markets, and inefficient state owned firms with better access to credit. The paper shows that the financial frictions slow down the reallocation of factors toward efficient private firms, while sustaining high returns to capital during the transition. It can also lead high productivity firms to specialize initially in labor intensive activities, where the financial frictions are less relevant. In these papers, it is the *interaction* between financial friction and productivity growth that triggers external surpluses in emerging economies.

4.2. Demographics and Global Imbalances

As noted by Bernanke (2005), demographic characteristics can also explain global imbalances. In general, demographics can have complex effects on net savings. A faster rate of population growth increases investment as a larger workforce increases the marginal return to capital, increasing autarky rates. Faster population growth also increases the fraction of young (savers) relative to old (dissavers), increasing aggregate saving and reducing the autarky rate.[38] In general, the impact of demographic factors on the autarky rate and capital flows depends on the age-structure of the working age population and the age-profile of income. Aging countries should save more to provide sufficient resources in retirement for the increasing number of retirees per worker. Lane and Milesi-Ferretti (2001) find strong empirical support for this claim when studying the determinants of net foreign asset position, with a negative impact of the share of younger age cohorts and a positive effect of the share of workers near retirement. Domeij and Flodén (2006), in a calibrated overlapping generation model, find that demographic variables account for a small but significant fraction of capital flows for OECD countries between 1960 and 2002. Ferrero (2010) explores the effect of population aging in a two-country extension of Gertler's (1999) model of "perpetual youth and perpetual retirement," calibrated to the U.S. and the G-6. The model allows for differences in fiscal policy, as well as productivity growth and finds that the more pronounced aging of the population in the G-6 (relative to the U.S.) accounts for a significant share of the deterioration in the U.S. trade balance and the decline in global real interest rates. We illustrate the basic mechanism with a simple extension of our model. Households evolve through two distinct stages

---

[38] See Obstfeld and Rogoff (1996).

of life: work and retirement. While working, households earn labor income. With some instantaneous probability λ, i.i.d. across workers, they retire. Once in retirement, they do not earn income any longer and die with instantaneous probability θ, as before. We maintain total population constant, so that the dependency ratio—the ratio of retirees to workers—is equal to λ/θ. A decline in mortality rate (a decline in θ) will increase the dependency ratio for a given length of the working life (equal to $1/\lambda$). To simplify further the analysis, suppose that households only consume when they are about to die. Aggregate consumption must then equal θW_t^r where W_t^r denotes the aggregate financial wealth of retirees. Since aggregate output is given by Y_t, this pins down the aggregate wealth of retirees: $W_t^r = Y_t/\theta$. Consider now the wealth accumulation dynamics of retirees and workers respectively:

$$\dot{W}_t^r = r_t W_t^r - \theta W_t^r + \lambda W_t^w. \tag{28a}$$

$$\dot{W}_t^w = r_t W_t^w + (1 - \delta) Y_t - \lambda W_t^w. \tag{28b}$$

Equation (28a) states that the retirees' wealth increases with the interest rate r_t, decreases with consumption, and increases with the arrival of newly retired workers. Equation (28b) states that the aggregate wealth of workers W_t^w increases with savings (equal to non-financial income) and decreases when workers retire. In steady state, the aggregate wealth of both groups must increase at rate g. Substituting the expression for W^r and W^w, it follows that the autarky interest rate satisfies:

$$(1 - \delta) \lambda \theta = (g + \theta - r_{ss}^a)(g + \lambda - r_{ss}^a). \tag{29}$$

It is easy to verify that $r_{ss}^a < g + \delta\lambda < g + \lambda$ and that $\partial r_{ss}^a/\partial\theta > 0$: population aging lowers the autarky interest rate. This result allows us to understand why economies with rapidly aging populations, such as Germany, Japan, or China, run sizable external surpluses.[39]

In a recent paper, Coeurdacier et al. (2012) explore further the interaction of demographic characteristic and financial frictions for an emerging economy such as China. In their three-period overlapping generation models, young workers in emerging economies (the South) face tighter credit constraints, preventing them from borrowing against their middle-age income. As a result, autarky interest rates are lower and following financial integration, capital flows to industrial countries (the North). The model also features higher growth in the South, so that the world interest rate declines over time—a consequence of the rising share of the South in global output, as discussed above. The model can explain why a decline in global interest rates leads to a decrease in saving rates in the North and an increase in the South. The reason is twofold. First, the substitution effect

[39] According to United Nations projections, the dependency ratio, defined as the ratio of population aged 65 or over to population aged 20–64, was 21.8% in the U.S. in 2010. For Germany, Japan, and China, the corresponding numbers are 33.4%, 38.3%, and 12.7%. By 2050, the dependency ratio will have increased to 39.5% for the U.S., and 62%, 76.4%, and 45.4% for Germany, Japan, and China, respectively.

dominates for younger workers in the South: they would like to borrow more but are prevented from doing so by the financial friction. Second, the income effect dominates for middle-aged workers in the South: they want to save more, since they have fewer debts to repay. The paper documents through a careful analysis of cohort-level saving in the U.S. and China that the savings of the young decreased more in the U.S. than in China, while the savings of middle-aged workers increased more in China than in the U.S. One simple way to re-interpret their model is to observe that tighter borrowing constraints on young workers is equivalent to a more steeply declining age–income profile, a higher ϕ in equation (19). A larger ϕ causes more asynchronicity between income and consumption decisions, increasing saving and depressing the autarky interest rate.[40]

4.3. Bewley Models and Precautionary Savings

The previous section showed how lack of financial development can simultaneously depress real autarky interest rates and generate global imbalances (stylized Fact 1) in a model without risk. We now consider a complementary explanation, based on idiosyncratic risk and precautionary saving in a Bewley (1987)-type economy. In this class of models, agents face uninsurable idiosyncratic risk. Yet, because risk is purely idiosyncratic, there is no aggregate uncertainty.[41] Idiosyncratic risk triggers a precautionary saving motive. The strength of this precautionary term depends on the households' level of prudence and the volatility of the uninsurable idiosyncratic shocks. Under financial autarky, the additional demand for saving depresses the equilibrium interest rate. This is the central result of Aiyagari (1994). Willen (2004), Mendoza et al. (2009), and well before them Clarida (1990) were the first to consider the implications in an open economy. In Mendoza et al. (2009), differences in levels of financial development imply that some countries can better insure against idiosyncratic shocks. Hence countries face different autarky interest rates and capital will tend to flow from countries with higher levels of residual uninsurable idiosyncratic risk (i.e. less financially developed) to countries with lower levels of risk (i.e. more advanced financial systems).

Unlike Caballero et al. (2008a), it is not differences in the ability to supply *riskless* stores of value, i.e. the pledgeability of future income, that matters but the ability to supply *contingent* assets, i.e. differences in the degree of risk sharing. These differences in risk sharing translate into differences in the demand for stores of value, thus affecting equilibrium interest rates. A similar mechanism is at work in Sandri (2010).[42] Our presentation

---

[40] From equation (22), one can check that $\partial r_{ss}^a / \partial \phi < 0$.

[41] This greatly simplifies the analysis since the distribution of wealth becomes time-invariant in the steady state. Models that allow for idiosyncratic and aggregate risk need to keep track of the dynamics of the wealth distribution.

[42] In addition, in that model entrepreneurs need to accumulate wealth to relax their borrowing constraint, as in Buera and Shin (2009) and Song et al. (2011).

follows Angeletos and Panousi (2011) which allows for investment risk in a continuous time setting similar to that of the previous section.[43]

4.3.1. The Set-Up

Consider a country populated with a continuum of infinitely lived households uniformly distributed over [0, 1]. Each household supplies one unit of labor inelastically to a competitive labor market, so that the aggregate labor supply is constant and equal to 1. In addition, each household runs a "privately-held" firm. This firm operates with capital k_{it} and labor n_{it} and produces $y_{it} = k_{it}^{\alpha} (\xi_t n_{it})^{1-\alpha}$, where productivity ξ_t is common to all firms and grows at a constant rate g. In addition to capital invested in their own firm, households can trade a riskless bond in zero net supply. Denote $w_{it} = k_{it} + b_{it}$ the domestic financial wealth of household i, composed of holdings of physical capital k_{it}, and bond holdings b_{it}. The budget constraint for household i is:

$$dw_{it} = d\pi_{it} + [r_t b_{it} + z_t - c_{it}] \, dt, \tag{30}$$

where z_t denotes labor income, equal to the wage since each household supplies one unit of labor, r_t is the equilibrium risk-free rate, and $d\pi_{it}$ denotes the household's capital income. Labor income and the interest rate are deterministic due to the absence of aggregate risk. Household capital income $d\pi_{it}$ is subject to idiosyncratic and uninsurable risk:

$$d\pi_{it} = [y_{it} - z_t n_{it} - \delta_k k_{it}] \, dt + \sigma k_{it} d\omega_{it}. \tag{31}$$

The first term in brackets represents the deterministic part of the capital income, equal to output minus labor costs and depreciation. The second part represents the stochastic component. $d\omega_{it}$ is a standard Wiener process, i.i.d. across agents and time, akin to an obsolescence shock. Importantly, while the shock is idiosyncratic—and therefore perfectly insurable with complete markets—we assume that markets remain incomplete. More specifically, σ measures the *residual idiosyncratic risk* faced by households, after all available formal and informal domestic risk sharing opportunities have been exhausted. The case of complete markets then corresponds to $\sigma = 0$. A country with a higher level of financial development—and therefore more opportunities to diversify risk domestically—will have a lower σ.[44]

---

[43] See also Corneli (2009). Mendoza et al. (2009) allow for both investment and income risk. The case with investment risk only is more tractable and delivers as an additional result that the capital-output ratio is low (and hence the marginal product of capital is high) when the level of financial development is low. Instead, in the Aiyagari (1994) set-up with labor income risk, there is no risk premium and precautionary saving increases the capital stock above its complete market level. This would imply the counterfactual result that capital-output is high (and marginal product of capital low) in less financially developed countries.

[44] Of course, this interpretation may not be warranted. For instance, one could imagine situations where higher levels of financial sophistication allow for better sharing of idiosyncratic risk, at the expense of a higher exposure to aggregate risk. Since the model does not feature aggregate risk, this is not a feature we explore here.

4.3.2. Individual Consumption and Portfolio Decisions

Assume that labor demand decisions are taken *after* the realization of the idiosyncratic shock. Since production exhibits constant returns to scale, this implies that employment and capital income will be proportional to capital with $n_{it} = \bar{n}_t k_{it}/\xi_t$, where $\bar{n}_t = ((1-\alpha)\xi_t/z_t)^{1/\alpha}$, and $d\pi_{it} = \bar{r}_t k_{it}\,dt + \sigma k_{it}\,d\omega_{it}$, where $\bar{r}_t = \alpha\bar{n}_t^{1-\alpha} - \delta_k$ represents the expected return to capital, common to all firms, and therefore also the average expected return to capital in the economy.

The linearity of the budget constraint in capital implies that the problem is a simple variant of the standard Samuelson (1969) and Merton (1971) optimal consumption and portfolio problem. Define h_t the present discounted value of current and future non-financial income, which is common across households since labor supply and the wage are identical: $h_t = \int_t^\infty e^{-\int_t^s r_v\,dv} z_s\,ds$. Define also total wealth $x_{it} = w_{it} + h_t$ as the sum of financial and human wealth.

One can then show that optimal consumption and investment plans are linear and independent of the household, with[45]:

$$c_{it} = m_t x_{it}; \quad \frac{\dot{m}_t}{m_t} = m_t + \frac{(1-\gamma)\hat{\rho}_t - \rho}{\gamma}, \tag{32a}$$

$$\phi_t := \frac{k_{it}}{x_{it}} = \frac{\bar{r}_t - r_t}{\gamma\sigma^2}, \tag{32b}$$

where $\hat{\rho}_t = r_t + (\bar{r}_t - r_t)^2 / (2\gamma\sigma^2)$ is the risk-adjusted return on the portfolio. The first equation states that consumption is linear in total wealth and characterizes the evolution of the marginal propensity to consume m_t, common to all households. In the case of logarithmic preferences ($\gamma = 1$), m_t is constant and equal to ρ. The second equation shows that the share of investment in the domestic physical capital stock ϕ_t satisfies the familiar formula: it increases with expected excess return $\bar{r}_t - r_t$ and decreases with idiosyncratic risk σ and risk aversion γ.

With linear consumption and investment rules, the model aggregates very easily. Observe that equilibrium on the labor market requires $\int n_{it}\,di = 1$ from which we can recover the aggregate wage as a function of the aggregate stock of capital: $z_t = \xi_t(1-\alpha)(K_t/\xi_t)^\alpha$ with the obvious notation for aggregate capital: $K_t = \int k_{it}\,di$. Substituting into the expression for $\bar{r}_t$, one obtains the familiar expression for the expected return to capital: $\bar{r}_t = \alpha(K_t/\xi_t)^{\alpha-1} - \delta_k$.

4.3.3. Financial Autarky

Consider the case of financial autarky: $B_t = 0$, or $W_t = K_t$. In steady state, all aggregate variables grow at the same rate: $d\ln C_t/dt = d\ln K_t/dt = d\ln Y_t/dt = d\ln H_t/dt = g$.

---

[45] See the appendix available on the authors' websites for detailed derivations.

Solving the aggregate Euler equation for the risk-adjusted return $\hat{\rho}$, one obtains:

$$r = \hat{\rho} - \frac{\gamma}{2}\phi^2\sigma^2 \leq \hat{\rho} = \rho + \gamma g - \frac{\gamma^2}{2}\phi^2\sigma^2 \leq \rho + \gamma g. \tag{33}$$

This condition states that in equilibrium the precautionary motive depresses both the riskless rate r and the risk-adjusted return $\hat{\rho}$ below the benchmark return in the riskless economy, $\rho + \gamma g$. Investing in capital is risky, so the precautionary motive increases the demand for riskless bonds. In equilibrium these bonds are in zero net supply so the risk-free rate has to decrease up to the point where households decide not to hold them. This is the same logic as in Aiyagari (1994). The precautionary motive also tends to depress the demand for capital, since it is the source of risk. Therefore, capital has to offer a premium in equilibrium. Substituting the definition of $\hat{\rho}$ and ϕ, and after simple manipulations, we obtain[46]:

$$\phi(r) = \left(\frac{2\left(\rho + \gamma g - r\right)}{\gamma\sigma^2\left(1 + \gamma\right)}\right)^{1/2}. \tag{34a}$$

$$\bar{r} = \alpha\tilde{k}^{\alpha-1} - \delta_k = r + \gamma\sigma^2\phi(r) \geq r. \tag{34b}$$

The first equation expresses the share of wealth invested in the risky asset as a function of the riskless rate r. The second equation expresses the expected return to capital as a function of the riskless rate. It is immediate that in the riskless case $\sigma^2 = 0, \bar{r} = r$. It can be solved implicitly for the level of capital as a function of the riskless rate: $\tilde{k}(r)$. As Angeletos and Panousi (2011) show, $\tilde{k}(r)$ is not monotonously decreasing with the interest rate. Instead, it is U-shaped, decreasing only if $r \leq \underline{r} \equiv \rho + \gamma g - (\gamma/(1+\gamma))\sigma^2/2$. The intuition is that a higher interest rate allows households to accumulate more wealth, making them more willing to take risks, and reducing the risk premium required by households to hold capital. It follows that for $r > \underline{r}$, an *increase* in the riskless rate is associated with a *decrease* in the marginal product of capital as the decline in the risk premium more than offsets the increase in the riskless rate.

One solves for the autarky interest rate by substituting $\tilde{k}(r)$ into the asset market equilibrium condition: $\phi(\tilde{k}(r) + \tilde{h}(r)) = \tilde{k}(r)$ where $\tilde{h}(r) = (1 - \alpha)\tilde{k}(r)^\alpha/(r - g)$. This yields the implicit expression:

$$1 = \phi\left(r_{ss}^a\right)\left(1 + \frac{\left(1 - \alpha\right)\tilde{k}\left(r_{ss}^a\right)^{\alpha-1}}{r_{ss}^a - g}\right). \tag{35}$$

It is immediate to check that $r_{ss}^a = \rho + \gamma g$ when $\sigma = 0$, and that $\partial r_{ss}^a/\partial\sigma < 0$: more uninsurable idiosyncratic risk depresses autarky rates.

---

[46] Where we use our notation $\tilde{x} = X/(\xi N)$.

4.3.4. Open Economy

Small Open Economy. Consider now the case of a small open economy facing a constant riskless interest rate r. From the previous derivations, the domestic capital stock (per efficient unit) will be given by $\tilde{k}(r)$ that solves (34b) while the portfolio share will be $\phi(r)$ that solves (34a). The demand for stores of value is $\tilde{w}(r) = \tilde{k}(r)/\phi(r) - \tilde{h}(r)$. The supply is $\tilde{k}(r)$, and the difference between the two determines the net foreign asset position $\tilde{b}(r) = \tilde{w}(r) - \tilde{k}(r)$. One can check that $\tilde{b}(r)/\tilde{k}(r)$ is always *increasing* with the interest rate: as the interest rate increases, the propensity to save in the riskless bond increases, relative to saving in the risky capital. If $r > r_{ss}^a$ (resp. $r < r_{ss}^a$), the small open economy is a net creditor (resp. borrower).

Following Kraay and Ventura (2000), we can use the model to ask how the current account should respond to transitory income shocks. To do so, rewrite equations (34) as:

$$\frac{\tilde{k}}{\tilde{x}} = \frac{\alpha\tilde{k}^{\alpha-1} - \delta_k - r}{\gamma\sigma^2} \tag{36}$$

and solve for the response of domestic capital $\tilde{k}$ to a change in domestic wealth $\tilde{x}$:

$$\frac{\partial\tilde{k}}{\partial\tilde{x}} = \frac{\gamma\sigma^2}{\gamma\sigma^2 + \alpha(1-\alpha)\tilde{k}^{\alpha-2}\tilde{x}}\frac{\tilde{k}}{\tilde{x}} \geq 0. \tag{37}$$

When σ^2 is close to 0 (full risk sharing), the marginal increase in domestic wealth is invested in international riskless bonds ($\partial\tilde{k}/\partial\tilde{x} \approx 0$). In this case, countries run current account surpluses in response to transitory positive shocks. Conversely, when $\alpha \approx 1$, so that $\partial\tilde{k}/\partial\tilde{x} \approx \tilde{k}/(\tilde{k}+\tilde{b})$, the marginal increase in wealth is invested like the average unit.[47] The implication is that net creditor countries (for which $\tilde{b} > 0$) run current account surpluses in response to a transitory positive income shock, while net debtor countries (for which $\tilde{b} < 0$) run current account deficits. In a panel of 13 industrial countries between 1973 and 1995, Kraay and Ventura (2000) find that the interaction term between the share of gross national saving in GDP and the ratio of foreign assets to total assets is highly significant, with an $R2$ of 0.37.

Large Open Economy. Following the now familiar steps, suppose a world economy is composed of two otherwise identical countries facing different levels of residual uninsurable risks with $0 < \sigma < \sigma^*$ where $*$ denotes the foreign, less financially developed, economy. Assuming that the conditions are satisfied for $r_{ss}^{a,i} \geq \underline{r}^i$ in each country i, the equilibrium satisfies:

$$r_{ss}^a \leq r \leq r_{ss}^{a*} < \rho + \gamma g. \tag{38a}$$

$$\tilde{k}(r_{ss}^{a*}) < \tilde{k}^* < \tilde{k} < \tilde{k}(r_{ss}^a). \tag{38b}$$

$$\tilde{b} < 0 < \tilde{b}^*. \tag{38c}$$

[47] We use the fact that $\tilde{h} \approx 0$ when $\alpha \approx 1$.

The integrated risk-free rate settles somewhere between the two autarky rates, as usual. Moreover, the capital stock in the riskier economy is lower than in the safer one. This is because the risk premium effect dominates. This has two interesting implications. First, the capital stock increases in the less developed economy upon financial integration: $\tilde{k}(r_{ss}^a) < \tilde{k}(r)$, the increase in interest rates in the less financially developed economy makes them richer and willing to take more risk. Second, the marginal product of capital is higher—and the capital-output ratio is lower—in less financially developed economies, something that accords well with the empirical evidence.

Cross-Border Flows as Safe Asset Flows. Finally, this model predicts that the advanced economy is a net borrower while the less financially developed economy is a net creditor: $\tilde{b} < 0 < \tilde{b}^*$. In the model, all cross-border flows take the form of *riskless loans*: there is no cross-border investment in risky projects. This provides a way to re-interpret the results: faced with larger uninsurable risks, households in the foreign country want to invest in *safe assets*. The domestic country faces lower uninsurable risks, so it has less need for insurance and is willing to *supply* these safe assets to foreigners. Stated differently, the domestic economy has a *comparative advantage* in supplying safe assets. In turn, it earns a premium that allows it to consume more than it produces along the transition to the new steady state (i.e. it runs a trade deficit). This result parallels Gourinchas et al. (2010) whom we will discuss later in this chapter.[48]

4.3.5. Aggregate Uncertainty

The models considered so far only feature idiosyncratic uncertainty. Some recent models consider instead the impact of aggregate uncertainty.[49] In a business cycle framework, Fogli and Perri (2006) consider the effect of the Great Moderation (the decline in the volatility of the U.S. business cycle between the mid-1980s and the onset of the 2007 financial crisis). Faced with a decline in aggregate volatility, the U.S. representative household would reduce its precautionary holdings. This would result in a deterioration of the U.S. external balance. In a calibration of their model, they find that the Great Moderation can account for around 20% of the U.S. external imbalance. Note however, that the decline in precautionary saving would be associated with an *increase* in global interest rates, in contradiction with stylized Fact 1. In a recent paper, Coeurdacier et al. (2013) study jointly the gains from capital accumulation and risk sharing in a model with aggregate uncertainty. Using global numerical methods they study the dynamics of the model along the transition path from autarky to financial integration. They find that aggregate uncertainty interacts with the classical determinants of capital flows explored in Section 3 and that the precautionary motive can overturn the direction of net capital flows as in the models explored in this section.

---

[48] Mendoza et al. (2009) also allow for investment risk. In their model, agents can invest in risky assets in foreign countries. As a result, in equilibrium, the financially developed country still runs a negative net foreign position, but holds a long position in foreign risky assets and earns excess returns on its external portfolio.

[49] These models abstract from idiosyncratic uncertainty. As mentioned earlier, in models with both idiosyncratic and aggregate uncertainty the wealth distribution varies over time and becomes a state variable.

4.4. Financial Frictions and International Trade

Two recent papers focus on the interaction between trade flows and capital flows. Jin (2012) presents a stochastic two-country overlapping generations model with production and capital accumulation in which factor intensities are (exogenously) different across countries. The paper combines insights from the factor proportions trade literature with those of the standard neoclassical open economy growth model. In her model, there is both an intertemporal motive for capital flows and an intratemporal motive since capital will tend to flow to countries that are more specialized in capital intensive industries. Hence two competing effects determine the direction of net capital flows: the composition effect (linked to asymmetries in specialization across countries) and the standard efficiency effect (stemming from capital scarcity). A country hit by a positive productivity shock, or experiencing a relative increase in its labor force—as was the case for many emerging economies since 1990—can nevertheless become a capital exporters if it specializes in labor intensive industries. Hence specialization is the key mechanism through which Jin (2012) may account for global imbalances.

Antràs and Caballero (2009) present a model where financial frictions determine patterns of capital flows and trade flows. Countries are heterogeneous in terms of financial development and sectors differ in their degree of financial dependence. They feature a two-country (North and South, where South is financially underdeveloped), two-factor (capital and labor), two-sector general equilibrium model where a homogeneous good is internationally traded. Under trade *and* financial autarky, South invests disproportionately in the sector without financial frictions. This depresses wages and rental rates of capital. If capital is now allowed to move freely, but international trade in goods remains restricted, capital will flow out of the financially underdeveloped economy toward the financially developed one, as in the models presented in this section. By contrast, if international trade in goods is *also* liberalized, countries will specialize along the lines of comparative advantage: the financially underdeveloped South specializes (incompletely) in the sector unaffected by the financial friction. This raises the rental rate of capital in the South because of good price equalization, while domestic wages remain depressed, and this can reverse the direction of capital flows. Hence it is the difference in production structures due to the pattern of specialization induced by comparative advantage that interacts with financial liberalization to shape the direction of net capital flows. The pattern of specialization is thus endogenously determined by cross-country differences in financial development, echoing the main theme of this section.

4.5. Global Imbalances and Financial Fragility

An important theme developed in Bernanke (2005) is that other asset prices may adjust beside the global interest rates to a shortage of stores of value. In Caballero et al. (2008b), the decline in world interest rates can be so strong as to make the economy dynamically inefficient, opening the door to rational bubbles. While the financial bubble increases asset supply endogenously, it is also prone to crashes. More generally, low world interest rates can fuel search for yield, or inefficient investments (e.g. Rajan, 2005). A number of observers noted the close connection between current account deficits and housing booms (Bernanke, 2010; Ferrero, 2012). Lower global interest rates, and in particular mortgage rates, can account for part of the increase in housing prices. As Ferrero (2012) observes, a gradual relaxation of borrowing constraints for households, or a favorable change in property taxes would lead to a simultaneous current account deficit and housing boom, as observed in the data, but would also lead to an increase in interest rates. In the same vein, Adam et al. (2011) use a small open economy model with endogenous housing and learning. In their model, bullish agents about the housing market respond strongly to a decline in world interest rates, triggering a housing boom and a current account deficit.

4.6. Private Flows, Public Flows, and Reserve Accumulation

A number of papers have pointed out that private and public flows behave quite differently, and that most of the net accumulation of foreign assets by emerging economies is in the form of public flows, especially through official reserve accumulation by central banks (see Aguiar and Manuel, 2011; Gourinchas and Jeanne, 2013; Alfaro et al., 2011). Indeed, a large share of emerging markets' gross external asset holdings takes the form of central bank reserves or other official holdings. The distinction between private and public capital flows becomes relevant once we depart from the—admittedly extreme—case of full Ricardian equivalence. In that class of models, any change in public flows is offset one-for-one by a corresponding change in private sector capital flows so the model pins down total net capital flows but not their composition. It is quite reasonable to depart from full Ricardian equivalence and the stringent assumptions it requires (non-distortionary taxation, perfect capital markets, infinitely lived dynasties). But the precise channels by which models depart from Ricardian equivalence matters greatly for the predictions of the model about the *joint fluctuations* in private and public flows. It is not in general a good idea to simply assume private flows behave as if there were *no* public flows. Spelling out the right model of public and private flows is an active area of ongoing research. At one extreme, some models assume that there are no private capital flows and governments provide the only form of intermediation of domestic resources into foreign stores of value (semi-open economy). For instance, one may see governments as financial intermediaries for the domestic private sector, intermediating domestic savings into global uses, as pointed out by Song et al. (2011). Similarly, in Aguiar and Manuel (2011) a government that has access to international capital markets faces a commitment problem. It accumulates international reserves as a way to post collateral, and limit the temptation to expropriate investors in the future. In Jeanne and Rancière (2011), the domestic government faces instead the possibility of a sudden loss of access to external credit and accumulates reserves for precautionary reasons.[50] Bacchetta et al. (2012) present a model where households face borrowing constraints and where the planner may choose to impose capital controls and accumulate reserves. In steady state, when financial constraints don't bind, it is optimal to replicate the open economy, and the central bank is simply a shell for international financial intermediation. Along the transition, binding financial constraints may lead the planner to choose an interest rate different from the world interest rate, through reserve accumulation and capital control policy, as in Jeanne (2012). Many of these models emphasize the strong demand from emerging market economies for liquid and safe global assets. Indeed, as Bernanke (2011) show, surplus emerging market economies concentrated their reserve accumulation on the safest U.S. securities: U.S. Treasuries and agency debt. To understand this pattern, one needs to go beyond models with no aggregate risk and no diversification motive.

5. EXTERNAL BALANCE SHEETS, VALUATION EFFECTS, AND ADJUSTMENT

Many of the models of the previous section, with no aggregate uncertainty or no diversification motive, make predictions about *net* capital flows, that is, about the intertemporal transfer of resources across countries. However, as emphasized in Section 2, one key stylized facts in international economics since the 1990s has been the massive increase in gross capital flows. The properties of the international balance sheet of countries determine how different shocks propagate across countries and how countries adjust to their long run solvency constraint.

5.1. International Adjustment

This section highlights the quantitative importance of valuation effects and the financial channel of external adjustment. To do so, we explore the implications of the external solvency constraint. Unlike Sections 3 and 4, we present derivations in discrete time for two reasons. First, it allows for an easier mapping between the theoretical objects of analysis and their empirical counterpart. Second, many of the issues discussed in this section have a business cycle dimension, for which a discrete time set-up is better adapted.

5.1.1. External Solvency Constraint

We begin by writing down the external budget constraint of a country and deriving some implications for the process of international adjustment. Define $NA_t = A_t - L_t$ as the net foreign asset position (at market value) of a country at the end of period t, where A_t and

---

[50] Bacchetta and Benhima (2012) present a model where the demand for precautionary liquid reserves arises from the corporate sector. In the model, credit-constrained firms face liquidity shocks and their demand for liquid assets (foreign bonds) increases with investment. Therefore, a more rapidly growing economy will invest more and demand more foreign bonds.

L_t denote respectively gross external assets and liabilities.[51] The change in net foreign asset position from one period to the next is given by the following accumulation equation:

$$NA_t = R_t NA_{t-1} + NX_t, \tag{39}$$

where $NX_t = X_t - M_t$ denotes the balance on goods, services, and net transfers during period t, and R_t represents the gross portfolio return on the net foreign portfolio between the end of period $t-1$ and the end of period t. Adding and subtracting the net investment income balance NI_t, we can write:

$$NA_t - NA_{t-1} = \left[(R_t - 1) NA_{t-1} - NI_t \right] + CA_t = VA_t + CA_t \tag{40}$$

using the definition of the current account as the sum of the trade balance NX_t and the net factor payment: $CA_t = NX_t + NI_t$. The change in the net foreign position equals the current account, CA_t, plus the valuation adjustment VA_t. This valuation adjustment equals the *capital gain* on the net foreign asset portfolio, i.e. the net return $(R_t - 1)$ minus income, dividends, and earnings distributed.[52] Traditionally, this valuation term has been omitted and the net external position of a country has been calculated as the cumulated sum of past current accounts. This is in keeping with the National Income and Product Accounts (NIPA) and the Balance of Payments methodology that focuses on produced transactions and ignores capital gains and losses. But cumulated current accounts will give a very approximate and potentially misleading reflection of a country's net foreign asset position—the object of interest in most of our economic models—unless the cumulated valuation gain is correspondingly small. While this assumption may have been reasonably accurate in eras of limited levels of financial integration, it is not one we can maintain in the face of large cross-border gross positions, as seen in stylized Fact 5. We now turn to the empirical methodology allowing us to value assets and liabilities at market prices.

5.1.2. Valuation Effects: Empirical Methodology

Obtaining precise estimates of these valuation changes is not an easy task. We start with a discussion of the empirical methodological advances that have allowed researchers to focus on valuation changes with a particular attention to the relevant empirical caveats that are involved in any exercise of this nature.

---

[51] Note that this definition of the net foreign asset position coincides with the one presented in the previous section since domestic wealth W consists of domestic holdings of domestic assets V^d and gross external claims A, while domestic assets V can be held either by domestic residents (V^d) or by foreigners in the form of gross external liabilities $(V^f = L)$. It follows that $NA = A - L = (W - V^d) - (V - V^d) = W - V$.

[52] To be complete, the accumulation equation should also include the capital account KA_t, unilateral transfers UT_t, and the statistical discrepancy SD_t. We abstract from these components in this discussion and will bring them back when necessary. For many countries, especially industrialized ones, capital account transactions and unilateral transfers are typically small. Errors and omissions are also excluded from the financial account in the U.S. Bureau of Economic Analysis estimates of the U.S. international investment position.

Stocks and Flows. The relatively recent availability of periodic surveys of cross-border assets and liabilities has it made possible to investigate empirically the channels of adjustments of a country's external balance sheet.[53] Constructing external balance sheets of countries *at market value* involves reconciling data on stocks and balance of payment data on flows.[54]

For each asset class, we can write a general law of motion as follows:

$$PX^i_{t+1} = PX^i_t + FX^i_{t+1} + VX^i_{t+1} + OX^i_{t+1}, \tag{41}$$

where PX^i_t represents the position at the *end of period t* for asset class i reported in the disaggregated net international investment position for gross claims ($X = A$) or gross liabilities ($X = L$), FX^i_t denotes the corresponding flow during period t as recorded in the balance of payments, VX^i_t is the valuation gain that can be attributed to currency and asset price movements, while OX^i_t ("other changes") represents an error term due to changes in coverage or mismeasurements of various kinds. Summing across all the series and using a simplified version of the balance of payment identity $FA_t = CA_t + SD_t$, where SD_t denotes the statistical discrepancy of the balance of payment, we obtain the international investment position at the end of period $t + 1$[55]:

$$NA_{t+1} = NA_t + CA_{t+1} + VAL_{t+1} + OC_{t+1} + SD_{t+1}, \tag{42}$$

where $VAL_t = \sum_j VA^j_t - \sum_i VL^i_t$, is the sum of the valuation effects across asset classes, and $OC_t = \sum_j OA^j_t - \sum_i OL^i_t$ is the corresponding sum of the "other changes."

These simple accounting relations allow in principle researchers to construct time series of estimates of cross-border positions at market values which are consistent with flow data and with the periodic surveys. In practice, of course, the exercise is rarely straightforward and a number of assumptions are needed to ensure everything "adds up."

Lane and Milesi-Ferretti (2001, 2007a) in pioneering work constructed and updated annual estimates of external assets and liabilities for over 178 countries and the euro area over the period 1970–2007 (data release August 2009). Gourinchas and Rey (2007a) and Gourinchas et al. (2010) focused on the United States and provided quarterly estimates for the period 1952–2010. Bertaut and Tryon (2007), building on Thomas et al. (2004) perform a number of refinements to the data and provide monthly estimates of U.S. cross-border securities positions from 1994. Stoffels and Tille (2009) constructed data on

[53] For example, the Coordinated Portfolio Investment Surveys of the IMF, covering external holdings of securities of 73 countries (in 2010) started in 1997 and became annual from 2001. The CPIS surveys are complemented by the surveys on Securities Held as Foreign Exchange Reserves (SEFER), and Securities Held by International Organizations (SSIO). The Coordinated Direct Investment Survey (CDIS) of the IMF covering 97 countries started in 2009. The U.S. Treasury has performed very occasional surveys of external assets or liabilities since at least the Second World War but has done so on a more regular (annual) basis only since 2002 for the liability side and 2003 for the claim side.

[54] In the case of the U.S., data on stocks comes from surveys performed infrequently by the Treasury and reported by the Bureau of Economic Analysis.

[55] As before, we ignore the capital account and unilateral transfers in this derivation.

the Swiss external investment position. In more conjectural work given the data limitations, Kubelec and Sá (1980) provide estimates of *bilateral* holdings among 18 advanced economies and emerging markets, Milesi-Ferretti et al. (2010) estimated a snapshot of bilateral holdings in a sample of 70 countries at end year 2007 while Gourinchas et al. (2012) extended this sample to 2009. Lane and Shambaugh (2010) present *currency compositions* of external claims and liabilities for a large panel of countries over 1990–2004. Finally, exploiting a unique Swiss database, Zucman (2013) shows that non recorded assets held in offshore accounts can explain the discrepancy between assets and liabilities at the world level.

5.1.3. The Case of the United States

A World's Banker Balance Sheet. The case of the United States is particularly interesting. We have already noted the very sizeable gap between the reported U.S. net international position and cumulated current account deficits (stylized Fact 5). This suggests possible important roles played by valuation effects in the dynamics of the net foreign asset position of the U.S. Along the same line, Tille (2008) observed the potential important stabilizing effects of a dollar depreciation on the external balance sheet of the United States due to a large asymmetry in currency composition between liabilities (all in dollars) and assets (mostly in foreign currency): when the dollar depreciates, the value of liabilities in dollars is unchanged while the value of external claims goes up.

As a number of papers noted, the structure of the U.S. external balance sheet is also asymmetric in other ways. Writing in the 1960s while the U.S. was the center country of the Bretton Wood system of fixed exchange rates, Kindleberger (1965) and Despres et al. (1966) observed that the U.S. was the "Banker of the World," lending mostly at long and intermediate terms, and borrowing short, thereby supplying loans and investment funds to foreign enterprises and liquidity to foreign asset holders. Figure 10.9 presents the decomposition of the U.S. external accounts by asset classes (FDI, bank—which includes trade credits, debt, equity). In the wake of the Second World War, the United States was a creditor country, with a positive Net International Investment Position (NIIP) of about 12% of U.S. output. More importantly, U.S. gross external claims and liabilities were small, reflecting the large direct and indirect costs of cross-border financial transactions. Most of the external claims of the U.S. were direct investment or bank loans, while a sizeable share of its external liabilities were foreign holdings of U.S. government securities. Fast forward to the beginning of the 21st century, after an unprecedented period of deregulation of cross-border financial flows. By then, the U.S. has become a sizeable debtor country, with a negative NIIP of about 22% of output in 2010. More dramatically, gross external claims and liabilities soared, to more than 100% of output in recent years. Figure 10.10 presents the evolution of net portfolio equity and FDI position of the U.S. (its risky asset position) and its net debt and bank asset position (as a proxy for its safe asset position). The risky position skyrocketed upwards in the run up to the crisis while the U.S. was increasingly

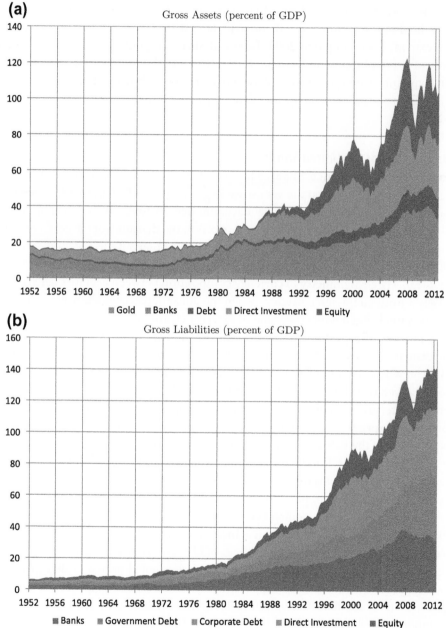

Figure 10.9 U.S. Gross Asset and Liabilities, by Asset Class, 1952–2012. *Source:* Gourinchas et al. (2010)

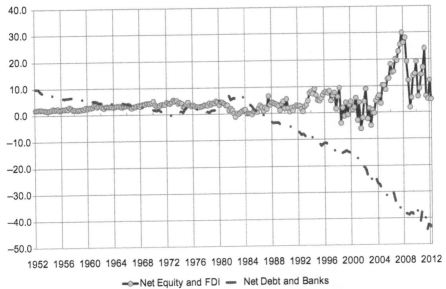

Figure 10.10 U.S. Net Portfolio Equity and Direct Investment (Percent of GDP) and Net Portfolio Debt and Other Assets (Percent GDP). *Source:* Gourinchas et al. (2010) Updated to 2012

short in safe and liquid assets: as noted by Gourinchas and Rey (2007a), the U.S. became an increasingly leveraged global financial intermediary. The pattern of *liquidity and maturity transformation* already noted by observers in the 1960s is still a characteristic of the U.S. balance sheet. This is all the more surprising if one puts this stylized fact in parallel with the evolution of the banking sector in recent years. In a series of thought provoking papers, Shin argues that European global banks have become intermediaries for U.S. savings, financing themselves in the United States, in particular via the wholesale market (money market funds) and channeling the liquidity worldwide including back into the U.S. markets (see for example Shin, 2012). Shin points out that U.S.-dollar denominated assets of banks outside the United States amounted to about $10 trillion prior to the 2007 crisis. This pattern of banking investment flows whereby global banks are liquidity providers to the United States goes against the previously described role of the U.S. as a World Banker. In the aggregate balance sheet of the country though, it is still dominated by the overall pattern of *liquidity and maturity transformation* performed by the United States as a whole.

Computing Returns on the U.S. External Asset Position. The particular structure of the external balance sheet of the United States has been shown to generate an "Exorbitant Privilege": the United States is able to earn higher returns on its external assets than on its external liabilities (see Gourinchas and Rey, 2007a).[56] This French claim has been under intense scrutiny in the literature, igniting a lively debate, which we now briefly summarize.

From equation (42), the formula linking the change in net foreign asset position and the return is:

$$NA_{t+1} = R_{t+1}NA_t + NX_{t+1} + SD_{t+1} + OC_{t+1}. \tag{43}$$

When computing the returns on the net foreign asset position of a country, the researcher is immediately faced with a problem: where should OC_{t+1}, the residual term whose raison d'être is to reconcile stock and flow data coming from different sources be allocated?[57] Different authors have taken different (time varying) views on this question and obtained estimates of external returns on samples of different lengths, resulting in a debate which may look confusing for the lay person. But the underlying issue is quite simple and easy to summarize: as a residual item, OC_{t+1} can only represent mismeasured valuations, mismeasured flows, mismeasured initial positions, or some combination of the three. Let's consider each possibility in turn.

- OC_{t+1} represents mismeasured capital gains. This is a plausible assumption for some asset categories, such as direct investment, where capital gains are notoriously hard to measure. This was the assumption adopted in the first wave of papers of the literature. In that case, the total return is given by $(R_{t+1} - 1) NA_t = NI_{t+1} + VAL_{t+1} + OC_{t+1}$. This set of papers tends to find that the U.S. enjoys a strong excess returns on its overall external position. Gourinchas and Rey (2007a) report a real excess return of 2.1% per year on the 1952–2004 period; Lane and Milesi-Ferretti (2007b) report 3.9% per year for the shorter 1980–2004 period; similarly Obstfeld and Rogoff (2005) find a 3.1% per year excess return for 1983–2003; and Meissner and Taylor (2008) 3.7% per year on 1981–2003.

- OC_{t+1} represents mismeasured financial flows as pointed out in a second wave of papers (Curcuru et al., 2008b; Lane and Milesi-Ferretti, 2009).[58] In that case, the dynamics of net assets is given by $NA_{t+1} = NA_t + \hat{FA}_{t+1} + VAL_{t+1}$ with the "corrected" flow term defined as $\hat{FA}_t = FA_t + OC_t$. Such an adjustment must have a counterpart in the Balance of Payments identity $\hat{FA}_t = CA_t + KA_t + SD_t - OC_t = 0$. By definition, if $\hat{FA}$ measures the correct financial flows, then the residual term $SD - OC$ must correspond to mismeasured current account transactions:

[56] Giscard d'Estaing (February 16, 1965), then finance Minister of President Charles De Gaulle coined the term "exorbitant privilege."

[57] OC_{t+1} can also reflect some reclassification. For example when a portfolio investor has a position in a firm and then acquires more equity such that total holdings exceed 10%, his/her entire holdings are classified as direct investment, including those that were held prior to meeting the 10% threshold. This results in OC for both portfolio and FDI. A similar reclassification occurs when a U.S. firm reincorporates offshore or onshore.

[58] Their argument relies on the difference in revision policies between the stock and the flow data for equity and bond portfolio investment.

$C\hat{A}_t = CA_t + (SD_t - OC_t)$.[59] Hence, if flow adjustments are large, this implies that trade flows are also *de facto* grossly misrecorded for the United States, especially in the recent period (for a discussion on the implications for the balance of payments see Lane and Milesi-Ferretti (2009) and Curcuru et al. (2008a)). Adding residuals to flows, Curcuru et al. (2008b) find *no* excess returns on the portfolio component nor on the overall net foreign asset position of the U.S. for the 1990–2005 period.[60] Forbes (2010) implements the Curcuru et al. (2008b) methodology and, in contrast, estimates very large excess returns of about 6.9% per year during 2002–2006.[61] Curcuru et al. (2013) find excess returns of 1.9% on the total net foreign asset position of the U.S. for the 1990–2011 period and show that direct investment yield differentials play an important role in their sample.

- OC_{t+1} represents mismeasured positions as advocated by Lane and Milesi-Ferretti (2009) for non-portfolio positions of banks and non-banks. For these categories covering bank loans, deposits, short-term paper and trade credits, capital gains are unlikely to be large. However the scope of the surveys has progressively expanded over time and the methodology has improved making it plausible that initial positions were mismeasured.

Lane and Milesi-Ferretti (2009) offer a detailed and careful discussion of these different options, indicating where mismeasurements are likely to be more severe. They end up recommending that for portfolio assets and liabilities, the residual be partly reallocated to financial flows; for FDI that it be reallocated to capital gains; and for non-portfolio positions of banks and non-banks that it be reallocated to mismeasured initial positions.

How Large is the "Exorbitant Privilege"? We follow an agnostic approach and allocate the residual term in different ways to assess quantitatively whether the results change substantially. As pointed out already by Lane and Milesi-Ferretti (2009) allocating the residual term to valuations increases the excess returns on the net foreign asset position, while allocating it to flows decreases it. Table 10.3 presents in (a) the most conservative results regarding the excess returns (following Curcuru et al. (2008b)—whose own estimates are presented in row (e) for the shorter period analyzed in their paper—we allocate *all* the residuals to flows); in (b) we allocate all the residuals to flows except for FDI where they are allocated to valuations as argued by Lane and Milesi-Ferretti (2009); in (c) we present an upper bound for the excess returns as all the other changes are allocated to valuations. In rows (d)–(h) we present earlier estimates of the literature pertaining to

---

[59] Capital account transactions are well measured if they correspond mostly to official aid and grants. However, we note that the capital account also includes transactions in non-produced, non-financial assets, such as patents and trademarks which should be included in direct investment returns and are unlikely to be measured with great precision.

[60] For the return on the overall position, they use BEA original data releases instead of revised data to compute their estimates, arguing this corrects the problem of disparate revision policies between stocks and flows.

[61] As we show below, the difference in estimates comes from the short sample period and volatility of underlying returns.

Table 10.3 Various Estimates of the Excess Returns, $r^a - r^l$ (%), on the U.S. Net Foreign Asset Position

	Period		
	1952:1–2011:4	1952:1–1972:4	1973:1–2011:4
(a) OC_{t+1} allocated to flows	1.6	0.8	2.0
(b) OC_{t+1} allocated to flows (except for FDI)	2.1	0.8	2.8
(c) OC_{t+1} allocated to valuations	2.7	0.8	3.8
Previous estimates			
(d) Initial Gourinchas and Rey (2007a) on 1952–2004	2.1		
(e) Curcuru et al. (2008b) on 1994–2005	0.72		
(f) Forbes (2010) on 2002–2008	6.9		
(g) Lane and Milesi-Ferretti (2009) on 1980–2004	3.9		
(h) Obstfeld and Rogoff (2005) on 1983–2003	3.1		

various sample lengths and estimation methods. Estimates (d), (g), and (h) allocate all residuals to valuations; estimates (e) and (f) allocate residuals to flows. In all cases we find evidence of an "exorbitant privilege" ranging on the whole 1952:1–2011:4 period from 1.6% to 2.7% depending on the assumptions. This is far from being negligible.

The key lessons of this robustness exercise are (i) that the sample length is important (see the very different results obtained by Curcuru et al. (2008b) and Forbes (2010) who use the same methodology). This is to be expected given the large volatility of the excess returns; (ii) that the refinements on construction of positions data (Bertaut and Tryon, 2007) while undoubtedly improving the quality of the data, do not make much of a quantitative difference; (iii) that the allocation of the residuals does not alter the substance of the results if the sample is long enough.

The most natural interpretation of the results is that this positive excess return may come from a composition effect. The composition effect is positive if, just like a bank or a venture capitalist, U.S. claims on foreigners are weighted toward riskier asset classes with higher average returns and liabilities are safer and more liquid. In addition, there may be excess returns within asset classes, for example because U.S. government bonds earn a liquidity discount compared to foreign bonds or because of tax asymmetries in the realm of direct investment. More research is doubtlessly needed to understand the underlying determinants of these excess returns.

5.1.4. Intertemporal Approach to the Current Account

We now go back to the external solvency constraint (39), and iterate it forward, imposing a no-Ponzi condition and taking conditional expectations[62]:

$$NA_t = -E_t \left[\sum_{i=1}^{+\infty} \left[\prod_{j=1}^{i} R_{t+j} \right]^{-1} NX_{t+i} \right]. \tag{44}$$

This expression states that the net foreign asset position of a country should equal the (opposite of) the expected present discounted value of future trade balances, discounted at the cumulated return on the net foreign asset position. Hence the current value of a country's net foreign asset position reflects both the expected future path of net exports and of returns on the net foreign asset position. Equation (44) is very generic: it has to hold, regardless of the details of the economic model, provided Ponzi schemes are ruled out. To illustrate the economic intuition behind this intertemporal constraint, imagine that some news leads agents to update upwards their estimates of future next exports. That same news would either decrease the value of current net foreign assets (either by movements in the exchange rate or by increasing consumption and current indebtedness for example) or would affect expectations of future returns on the net foreign asset position (or both).

In a world where internationally traded assets consist only in riskless government bonds whose gross rates of returns are R_t^f, the rate of return on the net foreign asset positions R_t simplifies to R^f. In such a world, which may not be so different from the pre-1980s international capital markets, equation (44) takes the familiar form $NA_t = -E_t \sum_{i=1}^{+\infty} (1+r)^{-i} NX_{t+i}$ where we also assumed that $R_t^f = (1+r)$ is constant. Hence in this "relatively non-financially globalized world", any movements in the net foreign asset position has to be made up in the future by net exports. The international adjustment process of countries relies exclusively on *quantity* adjustments through the classical *trade channel*.[63] Furthermore, since there are no capital gains or losses on net riskless bond positions, it is immediate from (40) that there is no valuation effect either and the change in the net foreign asset position $NA_{t+1} - NA_t$ coincides with the current account CA_t. From there, the simplest version of the *intertemporal approach to the current account* assumes an infinite-horizon certainty-equivalent representative consumer, with a

---

[62] The no-Ponzi condition is: $\lim_{k \to \infty} \left(\prod_{j=1}^{k} R_{t+j} \right) NA_{t+k} = 0$.

[63] Whether this adjustment requires movements in the real exchange rate and/or the terms of trade, is a debated issue. Obstfeld and Rogoff (2005) present estimates of the adjustment in relative prices needed to close the U.S. current account. Corsetti et al. (2013) argue that some of the adjustment can come from adjustments at the extensive margin, i.e. through the export/import of new varieties, without much adjustment in terms of trade. Faruqee et al. (2007) present a richer simulation based on four regional blocs.

rate of time preference equal to interest rate, to obtain[64]:

$$CA_t = Q_t - \hat{Q}_t = \sum_{s=t+1}^{\infty} (1+r)^{-(s-t)} E_t (Q_s - Q_{s-1}),\qquad(45)$$

where Q_t denotes net output, i.e. output minus government expenditures and domestic investment and a "hat" denotes the permanent value of a variable.[65]

This expression makes particularly transparent some of the main lessons of the intertemporal approach to the current account: movements in the current account in a world where riskless bonds with constant rate of returns r are the only assets traded internationally, are driven by temporary deviations of macroeconomics quantities from their permanent levels. A U.S. external deficit reflects a combination of a temporary shortfall in U.S. output or an investment level or government spending temporarily above trends. It leads to an accumulation of U.S. riskless debt by foreign countries on which the U.S. pays a constant interest rate r.[66] As discussed above, the new international financial landscape characterized by large cross-border holdings of a myriad of different assets denominated in different currencies cannot be forced into that mold. The empirical failure of the intertemporal approach to the current account underlines this discrepancy between the simple market structure of the models and the real world. We therefore go back to equation (39) to derive a more general characterization of the dynamics of the net foreign asset position that is the core of the empirical analysis of Gourinchas and Rey (2007b).

5.1.5. Trade and Valuation Channels of International Adjustment

Gourinchas and Rey (2007b) start with the external constraint identity (39), with a slightly altered timing (for notational convenience)[67]:

$$NA_{t+1} \equiv R_{t+1} (NA_t + NX_t).\qquad(46)$$

As above, NX_t represents net exports during period t, defined as the difference between exports X_t and imports M_t of goods and services. NA_t represents net foreign assets, defined as the difference between gross external assets A_t and gross external liabilities L_t measured in the domestic currency, while R_{t+1} denotes the (gross) return on the net foreign asset portfolio. A first step consists in loglinearizing equation (46). But while in most theories the ratios of exports, imports, external assets and liabilities to wealth are all statistically

---

[64] See Obstfeld and Rogoff (1995) in the previous handbook.

[65] Formally, $\hat{Q}_t = rE_t \left[\sum_{t+1}^{\infty} (1+r)^{-(s-t+1)} Q_s \right]$.

[66] For a richer model with non-traded and traded goods where stochastic movements in real interest rate plays a role, see Bergin and Sheffrin (2000).

[67] In equation (46), net foreign assets are measured at the beginning of the period. This timing assumption is innocuous. One could instead define NA'_t as the stock of net foreign assets at the end of period t, i.e. $NA_{t+1} = R_{t+1} NA'_t$. The accumulation equation becomes: $NA'_{t+1} = R_{t+1} NA'_t + NX_{t+1}$ which brings us back to the notation of the previous section.

stationary along a balanced-growth path, even a cursory look at the data shows in contrast, that the stock of gross assets and gross liabilities, exports and imports are on a transition path. Looking at international financial integration from a historical perspective (see for example Obstfeld and Taylor, 2004), capital mobility increased between 1880 and 1914, decreased between the First World War and the end of the Second World War, and has been increasing until the advent of the global financial crisis. Many of these long run structural shifts are driven by exogenous forces, chief among them technological innovations in the shipping and communication industries. Hence a natural approach consists in modeling the world economy as a stochastic economy around a slow-moving deterministic trend. The variables of interest are the fluctuations of the net asset, and net export variables *in deviation from these trends*.[68] The derivation of the loglinearized solvency constraint requires several steps and some ancillary assumptions, which are relegated to the appendix available on the authors' websites. Denote by nxa_t a linear combination of the stationary components of exports, imports, assets and liabilities (the weights are constant given by the loglinearization). The loglinearized approximation of (46) takes the following form:

$$nxa_{t+1} \approx \frac{1}{\rho} nxa_t + r_{t+1} + \Delta nx_{t+1}, \tag{47}$$

where r_t are the loglinearized returns on the net foreign asset position, the variable nxa_t is a measure of *cyclical external imbalances*, and Δnx_{t+1} measures the cyclical net export growth. Unlike the current account, this expression incorporates information both from the trade balance (the flow) and the foreign asset position (the stock). It increases with assets and exports and decreases with imports and liabilities. Finally, the constant ρ equals the ratio of the long-term growth rate of the economy to the long-term gross return on the net foreign asset position, assuming the economy eventually settles in a balanced-growth path. Assuming a no-Ponzi condition and taking expectations, one obtains:

$$nxa_t \approx -E_t \sum_{j=1}^{+\infty} \rho^j \left[r_{t+j} + \Delta nx_{t+j} \right], \tag{48}$$

where we assume $\rho < 1$, i.e. that the long-term growth rate of the economy is lower than the steady-state rate of return, a plausible restriction.[69]

Equation (48), which is the loglinearized equivalent of (44), is central to the analysis of external adjustment dynamics in a world of integrated financial markets. It shows that movements in net exports and the net foreign asset position must forecast either future

---

[68] In that sense the exercise is similar to the one performed in the business cycle literature, which separates trend growth from medium frequency fluctuations and focuses exclusively on the latter. It differs from it though, in that the trends considered here have considerably lower frequency. Evans (2012) proposes a variation that keeps the trend component. It requires that the ratio of gross assets to gross liabilities be stationary.

[69] This also implies that the steady-state mean ratio of net exports to net foreign assets NX/NA satisfies $NX/NA = \rho - 1 < 0$. In other words, countries with long run creditor positions ($NA > 0$) should run trade deficits ($NX < 0$) while countries with steady-state debtor positions ($NA < 0$) should run trade surpluses ($NX > 0$).

portfolio returns, or future net export growth, or both. Consider the case of a country with a negative value for *nxa*, either because of a deficit in the cyclical component of the trade balance, or a cyclical net debt position, or both. If returns on net foreign assets are expected to be constant: $E_t r_{t+j} = r$. In that case, equation (48) implies that any adjustment *must* come through future increases in net exports: $E_t \Delta nx_{t+j} > 0$. As above, this is the standard implication of the intertemporal approach to the current account, where adjustment is done by quantities. This is the *trade channel of adjustment*.

But instead, the adjustment may also come from high *expected* net foreign portfolio returns: $E_t r_{t+j} > 0$. This is the *valuation channel of adjustment*. Such movements in predictable returns can occur via a depreciation of the domestic currency which induces a predictable wealth transfer from foreigners to domestic residents. The role of the exchange rate can be illustrated by considering the case—relevant for the U.S., the U.K., and generally advanced economies—where foreign liabilities are mostly denominated in domestic currency while foreign assets are mostly denominated in foreign currency. Holding local currency returns constant, a currency depreciation helps stabilize the net external asset position as it increases the domestic return on foreign assets, an effect that can be magnified by the degree of leverage of the net foreign asset portfolio. If we consider emerging markets, external liabilities are likely to be at least partly denominated in foreign currency (U.S. dollar or euro). A domestic currency depreciation might then lead to sizable losses on the net foreign asset position for these countries and be destabilizing, as in the Asian financial crisis of 1997–1998.[70]

Quantifying the Trade and the Valuation Channels of Adjustment. It is possible that some of today's fluctuations in the cyclical net foreign asset position come from *unexpected* changes in asset prices or net exports. These unexpected changes would be reflected simultaneously in the left- and right-hand side of equation (48). If valuation changes were mostly unexpected and had a white noise structure, they would not matter much for the underlying process of external adjustment. If, on the contrary, they had a predictable component they would be potentially an important component of the process of international adjustment, just like the trade channel.

We can decompose the cyclical imbalance nxa_t into a valuation and a net export component $nxa_t = nxa_t^r + nxa_t^{\Delta nx}$ where nxa_t^r is the component of nxa_t that forecasts future returns, while $nxa_t^{\Delta nx}$ is the component that forecasts future net exports growth. We construct empirical estimates of nxa_t^r and $nxa_t^{\Delta nx}$ using a VAR formulation. Specifically consider the VAR (p) representation for the vector $\left(r_{t+1}, \Delta nx_{t+1}, nxa_t\right)'$. Appropriately stacked, this VAR has a first order companion representation: $z_{t+1} = Az_t + \epsilon_{t+1}$. We construct nxa_t^r and $nxa_t^{\Delta nx}$ as:

$$nxa_t^r = \beta e_r' A \left(I - \rho A\right)^{-1} z_t; \quad nxa_t^{\Delta nx} = -e_{\Delta nx}' A \left(I - \rho A\right)^{-1} z_t,$$

where e_r' $(e_{\Delta nx}')$ defines a vector such that $e_r' z_t = r_t'$ (resp. $e_{\Delta nx}' z_t = \Delta nx_t'$).

---

[70] Corsetti and Konstantinou (2012) use a similar approach to show that transitory shocks are important drivers of gross asset and liability positions while variations in aggregate consumption are dominated by permanent shocks.

We can also compute the unconditional decomposition of the variance of nxa_t:

$$1 = -\frac{\text{cov}\left(\sum_{j=1}^{+\infty} \rho^j r_{t+j}, nxa_t\right)}{\text{var}\left(nxa_t\right)} - \frac{\text{cov}\left(\sum_{j=1}^{+\infty} \rho^j \Delta nx_{t+j}, nxa_t\right)}{\text{var}\left(nxa_t\right)} \equiv \beta_r + \beta_{nx}.$$

The empirical study of the measure of cyclical imbalances of the United States nxa_t uncovers the following stylized facts:

1. The valuation channel has historically accounted for roughly 30% of the process of adjustment of the United States toward its long run solvency constraint. The results are similar for the conditional decomposition and the unconditional variance decomposition (β_r).
2. The capital gains on the net foreign asset position are positively correlated with net exports for the United States.
3. Current imbalances help predict net exports (especially in the medium to long run), returns in the net foreign asset position (in the short to medium run), and the exchange rate from one quarter onwards, both in and out of sample.

Writing models compatible with these facts has proved to be a challenging task, as discussed in the next section.

5.2. Theoretical Models and Valuation Effects

5.2.1. Expected and Unexpected Valuation Effects

Valuation effects come in two flavors: unpredictable and predictable. The first variety does not create any particular difficulty for standard models of international finance: while we may argue over what model best characterizes international portfolio holdings, most models from our toolbox would incorporate in one form or another something akin to a parity condition. Conceptually, perhaps the simplest way to understand unpredictable valuation terms is by reference to a standard complete market model. In such a set-up, one can interpret unexpected valuation effects as the record-keeping of future payments on the contingent claims held by domestic and foreign investors, payments that implement full risk sharing. Interpreted in this light, the volatility generated by valuation adjustments could be interpreted as "good volatility" insofar as it reduces the volatility of marginal utility of consumption and improves welfare.

Consider for example a symmetric two-country, two-good endowment economy in complete markets. Imagine the domestic economy is hit by a positive output shock. As is well known (see for example Chapter 5 of Obstfeld and Rogoff (1995)), when current realization of domestic output is high compared to foreign's, the domestic economy is running a trade surplus, while the real exchange rate is depreciating due to the relative abundance of the domestic good. In complete markets, the home country becomes a net debtor as foreigners hold claims on current and future domestic output and domestic asset is worth more relative to foreign's. Hence foreigners realize an (unexpected) capital gain on their net asset position. So when its trade balance is in surplus, the domestic economy experiences a valuation loss on its net external asset position. This is the desired outcome from an efficient risk sharing point of view and these valuation gains and losses tend to stabilize the external debt dynamics. External liabilities will tend to disappear over time so that the relative wealth distribution remains stationary. Hence, in that standard set-up, there are potentially strong valuation effects but these are unexpected capital gains and losses on the net foreign asset position. As such, they do not contribute to the adjustment process described in equation (48) which is driven by *expected* gains and losses. This is not to say that it would be impossible to get expected valuation effects in models with complete markets, but for this to happen, one would need, for example, models with time variation in the risk premia, such as external habits models (see Campbell and Cochrane, 1999).

Conversely, models with incomplete markets do not necessarily generate expected valuation effects. Pavlova and Rigobon (2012) present a continuous time two-country pure exchange model with incomplete markets in which stocks and a bond are traded and in which valuation effects are non-existent. There are supply shocks in both countries as well as preference shocks for the home country good. By assuming logutility, Pavlova and Rigobon (2012) are able to elegantly obtain closed form solutions and to gain a number of important insights. Interestingly, in their model, preference shifts can introduce enough heterogeneity to generate non-zero bond holdings in equilibrium. They show that in the absence of intertemporal hedging –which comes from the log preference specification, the net foreign asset position is exactly equal to the present value of future trade deficit. This result reflects the absence of time varying risk premia in their incomplete asset market model. In loglinearized models with more general utility specifications and incomplete markets such as for example Tille and van Wincoop (2010) or Evans and Hnatkovska (2012), similar results have been obtained as a first order approximation around the deterministic steady state. More generally, as long as the Euler condition of the model implies expected returns are equalized at the first order around the non-stochastic steady state, expected valuation effects can only be of second or higher order, a point noted by Devereux and Sutherland (2010). Expected valuation effects will therefore generally not be quantitatively large in this class of models, as they can only reflect changes in second or higher order moments. As a result, and despite significant methodological advances made by Devereux and Sutherland (2011) and Tille and van Wincoop (2010), the recent microfounded literature on optimal portfolios in Dynamic Stochastic General Equilibrium (DSGE) models of the open economy surveyed in Coeurdacier and Rey (2013) has not, so far, led to frameworks in which expected gains and losses on net foreign asset positions can be substantial.

5.2.2. Modeling Expected Valuation Effects

By contrast, the predictable valuation effects that are relevant for the U.S. adjustment along its long run solvency constraint require large deviations from standard arbitrage conditions. Some limited progress has been made toward modeling predictable valuation effects with a revival of the older portfolio-balance literature associated with the work of Dale Henderson, Pentti Kouri, or the late Bill Branson. Blanchard et al. (2005) provide a very elegant presentation of the Kouri portfolio balance model and explore its implications for the joint dynamics of the U.S. current account and the dollar. In this literature, a key assumption is imperfect asset substitutability. A negative shock to the trade balance of the United States leads to a depreciation of the U.S. dollar. But this immediate unexpected depreciation does not fully offset the shock. If it did, there would be excess demand for U.S. assets since the supply of assets is assumed inelastic and in dollar terms the value of the rest of the world's wealth rises. Instead, there is a less than offsetting drop in the dollar and foreigner's demand for U.S. assets is kept in check by a further *expected* depreciation of the dollar toward its long run steady-state value. The U.S. keeps on accumulating more debt along the depreciation path so that the long run level of the dollar will be below that which would have been needed to offset the negative shock at once. If in contrast assets were perfect substitutes then the exchange rate would have immediately jumped to offset the negative shock fully. The imperfect substitutability of assets implies a slow adjustment of the portfolios together with expected exchange rate changes. Very interestingly the model does therefore predict that foreigners will be purchasing U.S. dollar assets while expecting a dollar depreciation. The model however has the drawback of assuming exogenous interest rates and ad hoc demand functions for financial assets. Microfoundations and general equilibrium effects tend to mute portfolio balance effects. For example, Backus and Kehoe (1989) have shown in the context of sterilized interventions on foreign exchange markets that if a general equilibrium setting is adopted, portfolio balance effects are not present any longer. Changes in the relative supplies of bonds do not matter if one takes into account the ensuing changes in monetary and fiscal variables. As Woodford (2012) recently remarked in his Jackson Hole address assessing the effectiveness of open market purchases, in most of our microfounded general equilibrium models, a Modigliani-Miller irrelevance result holds (see Wallace, 1981). When assets are valued "only for their pecuniary returns" (they may not be perfect substitutes from the standpoint of investors, owing to different risk characteristics, but not for any other reason) and when there are no limits to arbitrage, one of the core predictions of portfolio balance models, which is that changing the relative supply of assets has an effect on prices, goes away. This is because the market price of any asset is taken to be the present value of returns. Since changing the relative supplies of assets should not change the real quantity of resources available for consumption in each state of the world, the representative household's marginal utility of income in different states of the world should not change. Hence the pricing kernel should not change, and the market price of a given asset should not change either (see Woodford, 2012, p. 61).

The open economy literature has so far not managed to come up with a new generation of portfolio balance models microfounded and embedded in a general equilibrium set-up. In the context of closed economies some recent papers have introduced strong frictions on asset markets in order to rationalize the effect of net supply changes on prices.

Greenwood and Vayanos (2008) for example build on the idea of "preferred habitat" for bond market investors, a very strong form of non-substitutability of assets, to study the effect of open market interventions. A similar research agenda could be pursued in the open economy.

6. THE INTERNATIONAL MONETARY AND FINANCIAL SYSTEM

The world banker balance sheet of the U.S. generates excess returns in normal times. But, as explained in Gourinchas et al. (2010), this "exorbitant privilege" has a counterparty in times of financial turmoil. The U.S. as the center country of the international monetary system provides insurance to the rest of the world. During a global crisis, there is a massive wealth transfer from the U.S. to the rest of the world. This insurance transfer occurs at a time where the marginal utility of consumption is high. This is the "exorbitant duty." It is implemented very naturally by a portfolio long in risky assets—whose value goes down dramatically in crisis times—and short on government debt—whose value remains relatively stable in crisis times. This is precisely the external portfolio of the U.S., issuer of the safe asset, the reserve currency, which is held in large quantities abroad. Hence Gourinchas et al. (2010) argue that the U.S. plays the role of a *global insurer*. This interpretation of the role of the center country in the international monetary system is new. Traditional views have focused on the network externality in the use of the center country's currency as a medium of exchange: the dollar is used in international transactions because the sheer size of the U.S. economy in the world makes it more likely that other agents use it and therefore dollar transaction costs are low (see for example Krugman, 1980).

The economic intuition of the global insurance role of the U.S. can be simply captured within a CCAPM framework.[71] If we denote the net foreign asset position of the U.S. as $NA_t = A_t - L_t$, the external solvency constraint (in a world with no government consumption nor investment) is given by $NA_{t+1} = \left(1 + r_{t+1}^a\right) A_t - (1 + r_{t+1}^l) L_t + Y_t - C_t$, where r_{t+1}^a and r_{t+1}^l are the returns on gross external assets and liabilities.

Let us call r_t the risk-free rate of interest, we can then use the no arbitrage condition of a representative consumer model to get

$$\left(1 + r_t\right) E_t \left(\frac{\beta u'\left(C_{t+1}\right)}{u'\left(C_t\right)}\right) = E_t \left(\frac{\beta u'\left(C_{t+1}\right)}{u'\left(C_t\right)} \left(1 + r_t^a\right)\right) = E_t \left(\frac{\beta u'\left(C_{t+1}\right)}{u'\left(C_t\right)} \left(1 + r_t^l\right)\right) = 1.$$

Multiplying the external constraint through by the pricing kernel and taking expectation:

$$E_t \left[\frac{\beta u'\left(C_{t+1}\right)}{u'\left(C_t\right)} NA_{t+1}\right] = A_t - L_t + \frac{Y_t - C_t}{1 + r_t},$$

[71] We are very grateful to Maury Obstfeld for this insight.

which is equivalent to

$$E_t\left(NA_{t+1}\right) = \left(1 + r_t\right) NA_t + Y_t - C_t - \left(1 + r_t\right) cov_t \left[\frac{\beta u'\left(C_{t+1}\right)}{u'\left(C_t\right)}, NA_{t+1}\right].$$

Hence, by having a net external position which comoves negatively with the stochastic discount factor (i.e. which decreases when the marginal utility of consumption is high), the U.S. is able to increase the expected return on its net foreign asset position (this is the "exorbitant privilege"). As a mirror image, the rest of the world sees its return on its net foreign asset position decreased due to the hedge provided by the center country. Indeed during the 2007–2009 global financial crisis, the U.S. wealth transfer to the rest of the world amounted to about $2 trillion. Gourinchas et al. (2012) present some empirical evidence on the geographical distribution of gains and losses. Interestingly during that period, some regional insurers such as Switzerland and the euro area also provided wealth transfers to the rest of the world alongside the U.S., albeit on a much smaller scale.

Gourinchas et al. (2010) provide a theoretical model of the role of the U.S. as the global insurer. The model features both business cycle and global risk. The U.S. portfolio, endogenously determined, is long equity and short in safe assets. This portfolio reflects an assumed asymmetry in risk aversion between the U.S. and the Rest of the World (more risk averse).[72] One way of microfounding this asymmetry in risk aversion is provided by Maggiori (2011) who models a world in which financial development is unequal. The country whose financial intermediaries are less constrained will behave in the aggregate as if it were less risk averse. Another possible microfoundation can be found in Mendoza et al. (2009), where it is a better ability to share idiosyncratic risk within the U.S., which enables the U.S. to be long in risky assets internationally. Focusing on international bond markets, Hassan (forthcoming) emphasizes differences in country sizes to explain differences in real rates of returns. In his model, bonds of larger economies (in particular the U.S.) are better hedges because they insure against shocks that affect a larger fraction of the world economy.

This interpretation of the workings of the International Monetary System, where the U.S. is a global insurer, puts center stage the ability of the U.S. to issue safe assets (government bonds). Those are backed by the *fiscal capacity* of the United States. During times of global crisis, U.S. government bonds are the only assets able to provide insurance on a massive scale (the Swiss bond market can also be considered a safe haven but its sheer size precludes it from being the world insurer). This in turn suggests the emergence of a modern version of the Triffin dilemma. In the 1960s, Robert Triffin identified a fundamental weakness in the Bretton Woods institutions. Under that system, the currencies of member countries could be exchanged at a fixed rate against the dollar while the value of

---

[72] Stepanchuk and Tsyrennikov (2011) also model the U.S. as a less risk averse economy and use global solution methods to solve for optimal portfolios under incomplete markets.

the dollar was fixed against gold at $35/oz. Triffin observed that global liquidity demand grows with the global economy. As the rest of the world grew, so did the stock of dollars held abroad. In the meantime, however, the United States' gold stocks (backing the dollars held abroad) remained more or less constant. Maintaining the gold value of the dollar had to become increasingly difficult, and the crisis of the dollar unavoidable. Ten years before the end of the Bretton Woods system, Triffin had thus predicted its collapse. The gold value of the dollar is no longer fixed, but we still live in a Triffin style world. There is a growing asymmetry between the fiscal capacity of the United States (the "backing" of U.S. Treasury bills) and the stock of reserve assets held abroad, in other words, the U.S.'s external debt, thus threatening the ability of the U.S. to act as a world insurer (see Farhi et al., 2011; Obstfeld, 2011).

7. CONCLUSION

The consequences of these dramatic changes in the landscape of international finance have only started to be investigated recently. A large part of the economics profession, as well as international organizations (see for example Fischer, 1997) often see financial integration as an ideal toward which economies should aspire. The belief was that by moving toward a more integrated world, the international economy would reap many of the benefits from better risk sharing. The recent crisis however, having shaken advanced economies' financial systems more deeply than emerging markets', has altered this view and put at the forefront the dangers of contagion inherent to large cross-border holdings. It has become more obvious that current accounts deficits or surpluses, linked to net capital flows, miss important dimensions of the process of international adjustment of countries and of their financial fragility in crisis times.[73] After all, the euro area was running a balanced current account vis-à-vis the U.S. and yet it was deeply affected by the U.S. financial crisis of 2007–2008. The properties of the international balance sheet of countries determine how different shocks propagate across countries and how countries adjust. There is a clear need for a deeper analysis of the international financial landscape.

REFERENCES

Adam, K., Kuang, P., Marcet, A., 2011. House price booms and the current account. In: NBER Macroeconomics Annual 2011, vol. 26, National Bureau of Economic Research, pp. 77–122.
Aguiar, M., Amador, M., 2011. Growth in the shadow of expropriation. The Quarterly Journal of Economics 126 (2), 651–697.
Aguiar, M., Gopinath, G., 2007. Emerging market business cycles: the cycle is the trend. Journal of Political Economy 115 (1), 69–102.
Aiyagari, R., 1994. Uninsured idiosyncratic risk and aggregate savings. Quarterly Journal of Economics 109, 659–684.

---

[73] See Obstfeld (2012) for a recent careful and nuanced discussion of the role of current accounts.

Alfaro, L., Kalemli-Ozcan, S., Volosovych, V., 2008. Why doesn't capital flow from rich to poor countries? An empirical investigation. The Review of Economics and Statistics 90 (2), 347–368.

Alfaro, L., Kalemli-Ozcan, S., Volosovych, V., 2011. Sovereigns, Upstream Capital Flows and Global Imbalances. NBER Working Papers 17396, August.

Angeletos, G.-M., Panousi, V., 2011. Financial integration, entrepreneurial risk and global dynamics. Journal of Economic Theory 146 (3), 863–896.

Antràs, P., Caballero, R.J., 2009. Trade and capital flows: a financial frictions perspective. Journal of Political Economy 117 (4), 701–744.

Bacchetta, P., Benhima, K., 2012. The Demand for Liquid Assets, Corporate Saving, and Global Imbalances. Working Paper University of Lausanne, December.

Bacchetta, P., Kalantzis, Y., 2012. Capital Controls with International Reserve Accumulation: Can this Be Optimal? CEPR Discussion Papers 8753.

Backus, D.K., Kehoe, P.J., 1989. On the denomination of government debt: a critique of the portfolio balance approach. Journal of Monetary Economics 23 (3), 359–376.

Bergin, P., Sheffrin, S., 2000. Interest rates, exchange rates and present value models of the current account. Economic Journal 110, 535–558.

Bernanke, B., 2005. The Global Saving Glut and the U.S. Current Account Deficit. Sandridge Lecture. Virginia Association of Economics, Richmond, Virginia, Federal Reserve Board, March.

Bernanke, B., 2010. Monetary Policy and the Housing Bubble. Annual Meeting of the American Economic Association, Atlanta, GA, Federal Reserve Board, January.

Bernanke, B., 2011. International capital flows and the returns to safe assets in the United States 2003–2007. Revue de la Stabilité Financière, Banque de France (15), 15–30.

Bertaut, C.C., Tryon, R.W., 2007. Monthly Estimates of U.S. Cross-Border Securities Positions. International Finance Discussion Papers 910, Board of Governors of the Federal Reserve System (U.S.).

Bewley, T., 1987. Stationary monetary equilibrium with a continuum of independently fluctuating consumers. In: Hildenbrand, W., Mas-Colell, A. (Eds.), Contributions to Mathematical Economics in Honor of Gerard Debreu. North-Holland, pp. 79–102.

Blanchard, O.J., 1985. Debt, deficits, and finite horizons. Journal of Political Economy 93, 223–247.

Blanchard, O.J., Fischer, S., 1989. Lectures on Macroeconomics. The MIT Press.

Blanchard, O.J., Giavazzi, F., 2002. Current account deficits in the euro area: the end of the Feldstein Horioka puzzle? Brookings Papers on Economic Activity 33 (2), 147–210.

Blanchard, O.J., Milesi-Ferretti, G.M., 2009. Global Imbalances: In Midstream? Staff Position Note 2009/29, International Monetary Fund.

Blanchard, O.J., Giavazzi, F., Sá, F., 2005. International investors, the U.S. current account, and the dollar. Brookings Papers on Economic Activity, Spring, pp. 1–65.

Bruno, M., 1970. Trade, Growth and Capital. Working Papers 65. Department of Economics. Massachusetts Institute of Technology (MIT), November.

Buera, F.J., Shin, Y., 2009. Productivity Growth and Capital Flows: The Dynamics of Reforms. NBER Working Papers 15268. National Bureau of Economic Research, Inc.

Caballero, R.J., Farhi, E., Gourinchas, P.-O., 2008a. An equilibrium model of global imbalances and low interest rates. American Economic Review 98 (1), 358–393.

Caballero, R.J., Farhi, E., Gourinchas, P.-O., 2008b. Financial crash, commodity prices and global imbalances. Brookings Papers on Economic Activity 2, 1–55.

Campbell, J., Cochrane, J., 1999. By force of habit: a consumption-based explanation of aggregate stock market behavior. Journal of Political Economy 107 (2), 205–251.

Caselli, F., 2005. Accounting for cross-country income differences. In: Aghion, P., Durlauf, S. (Eds.), Handbook of Economic Growth, first ed. vol. 1, Part A. Elsevier, pp. 679–741 (Chapter 9).

Caselli, F., Feyrer, J., 2007. The marginal product of capital. Quarterly Journal of Economics 122 (2), 535–568.

Cass, D., 1965. Optimum growth in an aggregative model of capital accumulation. The Review of Economic Studies 32 (3), 233–240.

Chinn, M.D., Ito, H., 2007. Current account balances, financial development and institutions: assaying the world 'saving glut'. Journal of International Money and Finance 26 (4), 546–569.

Chinn, M.D., Ito, H., 2008. A new measure of financial openness. Journal of Comparative Policy Analysis 10 (3), 309–322.

Chinn, M.D., Prasad, E.S., 2003. Medium-term determinants of current accounts in industrial and developing countries: an empirical exploration. Journal of International Economics 59 (1), 47–76.

Clarida, R. H., 1990. International lending and borrowing in a stochastic, stationary equilibrium. International Economic Review 31 (3), 543–558.

Coeurdacier, N., Rey, H., 2013. Home bias in open economy financial macroeconomics. The Journal of Economic Literature 51 (1), 63–115.

Coeurdacier, N., Guibaud, S., Jin, K., 2012. Credit Constraints and Growth in a Global Economy, July. Mimeo, SciencesPo.

Coeurdacier, N., Rey, H., Winant, P., 2013. Financial Integration in a Risky World. Technical Report, December. Mimeo, SciencesPo.

Corneli, F., 2009. The Saving Glut Explanation of Global Imbalances: The Role of Underinvestment. Economics Working Papers ECO2009/41, European University Institute.

Corsetti, G., Konstantinou, P.T., 2012. What drives US foreign borrowing? Evidence on the external adjustment to transitory and permanent shocks. American Economic Review 102 (2), 1062–1092.

Corsetti, G., Martin, P., Pesenti, P., 2013. Varieties and the transfer problem. Journal of International Economics 89 (1), 1–12.

Curcuru, S.E., Thomas, C.P., Warnock, F.E., 2008a. Current account sustainability and relative reliability. NBER International Seminar on Macroeconomics 5 (1), 67–109.

Curcuru, S.E., Dvorak, T., Warnock, F.E., 2008b. Cross-border returns differentials. Quarterly Journal of Economics 123 (4), 1495–1530.

Curcuru, S.E., Thomas, C.P., Warnock, F.E., 2013. On returns differentials. Journal of International Money and Finance 36, 1–25.

Despres, E., Kindleberger, C., Salant, W., 1966. The dollar and world liquidity: a minority view. The Economist 218 (5).

Devereux, M.B., Sutherland, A., 2010. Valuation effects and the dynamics of net external assets. Journal of International Economics 80 (1), 129–143.

Devereux, M.B., Sutherland, A., 2011. Country portfolios in open economy macro models. Journal of the European Economic Association 9 (2), 337–369.

Domeij, D., Flodén, M., 2006. Population aging and international capital flows. International Economic Review 47 (3), 1013–1032.

Dooley, M., Folkerts-Landau, D., Garber, P.M., 2004a. The revived Bretton Woods system. International Journal of Finance & Economics 9 (4), 307–313.

Dooley, M., Folkerts-Landau, D., Garber, P.M., 2004b. The Revived Bretton Woods System: The Effects of Periphery Intervention and Reserve Management on Interest Rates and Exchange Rates in Center Countries. NBER Working Papers 10332, National Bureau of Economic Research.

Engel, C., Rogers, J., 2006. The U.S. current account deficit and the expected share of world output. Journal of Monetary Economics 53, 1063–1093.

Evans, M.D.D., 2012. International Capital Flows and Debt Dynamics. IMF Working Papers 12/175, International Monetary Fund.

Evans, M.D.D., Hnatkovska, V., 2012. A method for solving general equilibrium models with incomplete markets and many financial assets. Journal of Economic Dynamics and Control 36 (12), 1909–1930.

Farhi, E., Gourinchas, P.-O., Rey, H., 2011. Reforming the International Monetary System. CEPR.

Faruqee, H., Laxton, D., Muir, D., Pesenti, P., 2007. Smooth landing or crash? Model-based scenarios of global current account rebalancing. In: Clarida, R. (Ed.), G-7 Current Account Imbalances: Sustainability and Adjustment. University of Chicago Press, Chicago, pp. 377–456.

Feldstein, M., Horioka, C., 1980. Domestic saving and international capital flows. Economic Journal 90 (358), 314–329.

Ferrero, A., 2010. A structural decomposition of the U.S. trade balance: productivity, demographics and fiscal policy. Journal of Monetary Economics 57 (4), 478–490.

Ferrero, A., 2012. House price booms, current account deficits, and low interest rates. Staff Reports 541, Federal Reserve Bank of New York.

Fischer, S., 1997. Capital Account Liberalization and the Role of the IMF. Presented at the Seminar "Asia and the IMF", Hong-Kong, China, September 19, IMF.

Fogli, A., Perri, F., 2006. The great moderation and the U.S. external imbalance. Monetary and Economic Studies 24 (S1), 209–225.

Forbes, K.J., 2010. Why do foreigners invest in the United States? Journal of International Economics 80 (1), 3–21.

Gertler, M., 1999. Government debt and social security in a life-cycle economy. Carnegie-Rochester Conference Series on Public Policy 50 (1), 61–110.

Ghironi, F., Iscan, T.B., Rebucci, A., 2008. Net foreign asset positions and consumption dynamics in the international economy. Journal of International Money and Finance 27 (8), 1337–1359.

Giscard d'Estaing, V., 1965. Le Figaro [cited by Raymond Aron]. Les Articles du Figaro, February 16, pp. 1475.

Gourinchas, P.-O., Jeanne, O., 2006. The elusive gains from international financial integration. Review of Economic Studies 73 (3), 715–741.

Gourinchas, P.-O., Jeanne, O., 2013. Capital flows to developing countries: the allocation puzzle. The Review of Economic Studies 80 (4), 1484–1515.

Gourinchas, P.-O., Rey, H., 2007a. From world banker to world venture capitalist: US external adjustment and the exorbitant privilege. In: Clarida, R. (Ed.), G-7 Current Account Imbalances: Sustainability and Adjustment. University of Chicago Press, Chicago, pp. 11–55.

Gourinchas, P.-O., Rey, H., 2007b. International financial adjustment. Journal of Political Economy 115 (4), 665–703.

Gourinchas, P.-O., Rey, H., Govillot, N., 2010. Exorbitant Privilege and Exorbitant Duty. Mimeo, UC Berkeley.

Gourinchas, P.-O., Rey, H., Truempler, K., 2012. The financial crisis and the geography of wealth transfers. Journal of International Economics 88 (2), 266–283.

Greenwood, R., Vayanos, D., 2008. Bond Supply and Excess Bond Returns, NBER Working Papers 13806. National Bureau of Economic Research, Inc., February.

Gruber, J.W., Kamin, S.B., 2009. Do differences in financial development explain the global pattern of current account imbalances? Review of International Economics 17 (4), 667–688.

Hall, R., Jones, C., 1999. Why do some countries produce so much more output per worker than others? Quarterly Journal of Economics 114 (1), 83–116.

Hamada, K., 1969. Optimal capital accumulation by an economy facing an international capital market. Journal of Political Economy 77 (4), 684–697.

Hassan, T.A., forthcoming. Country size, currency unions, and international asset returns. Journal of Finance.

Hume, D., 1752. Political discourses. Printed by R. Fleming, for A. Kincaid and A. Donaldson, Edinburgh.

Jeanne, O., 2012. Capital account policies and the real exchange rate. In: NBER International Seminar on Macroeconomics 2012. National Bureau of Economic Research, March.

Jeanne, O., Rancière, R., 2011. The optimal level of international reserves for emerging market countries: a new formula and some applications. Economic Journal 121 (555), 905–930.

Jin, K., 2012. Industrial structure and capital flows. American Economic Review 102 (5), 2111–2146.

Kindleberger, C., 1965. Balance of payments deficits and the international market for liquidity. Essays International Finance 46, May.

Koopmans, T., 1965. On the concept of optimal economic growth. In: (Study Week on the) Econometric Approach to Development Planning. North-Holland Publishing Co., Amsterdam, pp. 225–287.

Kraay, A., Ventura, J., 2000. Current accounts in debtor and creditor countries. Quarterly Journal of Economics 115 (4), 1137–1166.

Krugman, P., 1980. Vehicle currencies and the structure of international exchange. Journal of Money, Credit and Banking 12 (3), 513–526.

Kubelec, C., Sá, F., 2010. The Geographical Composition of National External Balance Sheets: 1980–2005. Working Papers 384, Bank of England.

Lane, P.R., 2012. Financial Globalisation and the Crisis. BIS Working Papers 397, Bank for International Settlements, December.

Lane, P.R., Milesi-Ferretti, G.M., 2001. The external wealth of nations: measures of foreign assets and liabilities for industrial and developing countries. Journal of International Economics 55, 263–294.

Lane, P.R., Milesi-Ferretti, G.M., 2007a. The external wealth of nations mark II: revised and extended estimates of foreign assets and liabilities, 1970–2004. Journal of International Economics 73 (2), 223–250.

Lane, P.R., Milesi-Ferretti, G.M., 2007b. A global perspective on external positions. In: Clarida, R. (Ed.), G-7 Current Account Imbalances: Sustainability and Adjustment. University of Chicago Press, Chicago.

Lane, P.R., Milesi-Ferretti, G.M., 2009. Where did all the borrowing go? A forensic analysis of the U.S. external position. Journal of the Japanese and International Economies 23 (2), 177–199.

Lane, P.R., Shambaugh, J.C., 2010. Financial exchange rates and international currency exposures. American Economic Review 100 (1), 518–540.

Lucas Jr., R.E., 1990. Why doesn't capital flow from rich to poor countries? American Economic Review 80, 92–96.

Machlup, F., 1943. International Trade and the National Income Multiplier. Blakiston.

Maggiori, M., 2011. Financial Intermediation, International Risk Sharing and Reserve Currencies. Mimeo, Haas School of Business, November.

Meade, J.E., 1951. The Theory of International Economic Policy – The Balance of Payments. Oxford University Press.

Meissner, C.M., Taylor, A.M., 2008. Losing our marbles in the new century? The great rebalancing in historical perspective. In: Global Imbalances and the Evolving World Economy. Federal Reserve Bank of Boston, J.S. Little Boston, Mass.

Mendoza, E.G., Quadrini, V., Ríos-Rull, J.-V., 2009. Financial integration, financial development, and global imbalances. Journal of Political Economy 117 (3), 371–416.

Merton, R., 1971. Optimum consumption and portfolio rules in a continuous time model. Journal of Economic Theory 3, 373–413 and erratum. Journal of Economic Theory 6, 213–214.

Metzler, L.A., 1960. The process of international adjustment under conditions of full employment. A keynesian view. In: Caves, R., Johnson, H.G. (Eds.), Readings in International Economics. Richard D. Irwin, Homewood, IL, pp. 465–486.

Milesi-Ferretti, G.M., Strobbe, F., Tamirisa, N., 2010. Bilateral Financial Linkages and Global Imbalances: A View on The Eve of the Financial Crisis. Discussion Paper 8173, CEPR.

Mundell, R.A., 1968. International Economics. Macmillan Company, New York.

Nason, J.M., Rogers, J.H., 2006. The present-value model of the current account has been rejected: round up the usual suspects. Journal of International Economics 68, 159–187.

Obstfeld, M., 2011. International Liquidity: The Fiscal Dimension. Bank of Japan Lecture, Monetary and Economic Studies, November.

Obstfeld, M., 2012. Does the current account still matter? American Economic Review: Papers and Proceedings 102 (3), 1–23 (Richard T. Ely Lecture).

Obstfeld, M., Rogoff, K., 1995. The intertemporal approach to the current account. In: Grossman, G.M., Rogoff, K. (Eds.), Handbook of International Economics. North-Holland, Amsterdam, pp. 1731–1799.

Obstfeld, M., Rogoff, K., 1996. Foundations of International Macroeconomics. MIT Press, Cambridge.

Obstfeld, M., Rogoff, K., 2000. The six major puzzles in international macroeconomics: is there a common cause? In: Bernanke, B., Rogoff, K. (Eds.), N.B.E.R. Macroeconomics Annual. MIT Press, Cambridge, MA, pp. 73–103.

Obstfeld, M., Rogoff, K., 2005. Global current account imbalances and exchange rate adjustments. Brookings Papers on Economic Activity 36 (1), 67–123.

Obstfeld, M., Taylor, A., 2004. Global Capital Markets: Integration, Crisis, and Growth. Cambridge University Press, UK.

Pavlova, A., Rigobon, R., 2012. Equilibrium Portfolios and External Adjustment under Incomplete Markets. Mimeo, London Business School, March.

Quinn, D.P., 1997. The correlates of change in international financial regulation. American Political Science Review 91, 531–551.

Quinn, D.P., Toyoda, A.M., 2008. Does capital account liberalization lead to growth? Review of Financial Studies 21 (3), 1403–1449.

Rajan, R.G., 2005. Has financial development made the world riskier? In: Federal Reserve Bank of Kansas City Proceedings, August, pp. 313–369.

Ramsey, F., 1928. A mathematical theory of saving. The Economic Journal 38 (152), 543–559.

Samuelson, P.A., 1969. Lifetime portfolio selection by dynamic stochastic programming. The Review of Economics and Statistics 51 (3), 239–246.

Sandri, D., 2010. Growth and Capital Flows with Risky Entrepreneurship. IMF Working Papers 10/37, International Monetary Fund.

Shin, H.S., 2012. Global banking glut and loan risk premium. IMF Economic Review 60 (4), 155–192. Mundell Fleming Lecture.

Song, Z., Storesletten, K., Zilibotti, F., 2011. Growing like China. American Economic Review 101 (1), 196–233.

Stepanchuk, S., Tsyrennikov, V., 2011. International Portfolios: An Incomplete Markets General Equilibrium Approach. Mimeo, Cornell University, August.

Stoffels, N., Tille, C., 2009. Where Have the Savings Gone To? Assessing the Return on Switzerland's External Assets. Working Paper, Graduate Institute for International and Development Studies.

Thomas, C.P., Warnock, F.E., Wongswan, J., 2004. The Performance of International Portfolios. International Finance Discussion Papers 817, Board of Governors of the Federal Reserve System (U.S.).

Tille, C., 2008. Financial integration and the wealth effect of exchange rate fluctuations. Journal of International Economics 75 (2), 283–294.

Tille, C., van Wincoop, E., 2010. International capital flows. Journal of International Economics 80 (2), 157–175.

Wallace, N., 1981. A Modigliani-Miller theorem for open-market operations. American Economic Review 71 (3), 267–274.

Weil, P., 1987. Overlapping families of infinitely-lived agents. Journal of Public Economics 38 (2), 183–198.

Willen, P., 2004. Incomplete Markets and Trade. Working Papers 04–8, Federal Reserve Bank of Boston.

Woodford, M., 2012. Methods of policy accommodation at the interest-rate lower bound. Presented at the 2012 Jackson Hole Symposium, August.

Zucman, G., 2013. The missing wealth of nations: are Europe and the U.S. net debtors or net creditors? The Quarterly Journal of Economics 128 (3), 1321–1364.

CHAPTER 11

Sovereign Debt*

Mark Aguiar* and **Manuel Amador†**

*Princeton University, Princeton, NJ, USA
†Federal Reserve Bank of Minneapolis, Minneapolis, MN, USA

Abstract

In this chapter, we use a benchmark limited-commitment model to explore key issues in the economics of sovereign debt. After highlighting conceptual issues that distinguish sovereign debt as well as reviewing a number of empirical facts, we use the model to discuss debt overhang, risk-sharing, and capital flows in an environment of limited enforcement. We also discuss recent progress on default and renegotiation; self-fulfilling debt crises; and incomplete markets and their quantitative implications. We conclude with a brief assessment of the current state of the literature and highlight some directions for future research.

Keywords

Sovereign debt, Debt overhang, Default

JEL classification codes

F34, F32, F21, F41, E62

1. INTRODUCTION: CONCEPTUAL ISSUES

The defining feature of sovereign debt is the limited mechanisms for enforcement. This distinguishes sovereign debt from private debt, whether domestic or international.[1] A private agent or corporation, at least technically, is always subject to a legal authority. Sovereign nations are not. International bonds and bank loans are typically issued or contracted in a major financial center, such as New York or London. As such, they are subject to the legal jurisdiction of the place of issue. If a sovereign debtor fails to make a contracted payment, creditors have limited legal recourse, relying only on overseas legal instruments and reputational considerations. The mechanisms by which countries are induced to follow the terms of contracts, and the implications of limited enforcement for risk–sharing, growth, and other macroeconomic outcomes, is a major theme developed in

---

* We thank Mark Wright and the editors for very detailed and useful suggestions on an initial draft. We also thank Klaus Adam, Satyajit Chatterjee, Enrique Mendoza, and Vivian Yue for helpful comments.

[1] Nevertheless, the lessons derived from the study of sovereign debt are often applicable to other contexts, such as private credit markets in which enforcement is imperfect.

---

this chapter. This introductory section lays out some of the conceptual issues that underlie the economics of sovereign debt.

In practice, the standard sovereign debt contract is typically non-contingent.[2] That is, the contract specifies a pre-determined, non-state-contingent sequence of payments in a defined currency due at defined points in time. This notional non-contingency obscures a richer contracting space that comes about through maturity structure, renegotiation, rescheduling, and "haircuts." The question of state contingency is an important theme discussed in this chapter. In addition to limited enforcement, the lack of contingency may reflect asymmetric information. To the extent the government can manipulate the actual or reported behavior of macroeconomic aggregates, contracts with state-contingent payoffs may be prone to moral hazard. Even if the government cannot affect the outcome of the economy, the true state of the economy may not be verifiable to creditors.

The contract (or the legal jurisdiction in which the bond is issued) will detail how the terms can be changed at some future point. For example, collective-action clauses will establish what fraction of bond holders must agree to change the terms of the initial debt contract. There are several conceptual issues involved with renegotiation. One was mentioned in the previous paragraph; namely, renegotiation can allow for ex post state contingency. Another is the normative question of which type of collective-action clauses are best. A third is that in practice, renegotiation is a lengthy and seemingly costly process. This raises the positive question of why this is so. Finally, the fact that debt may be renegotiated or rescheduled makes the definition of default rather subjective. One strict definition of default is failure to make the specified payment at the required date. However, often such payments are renegotiated under the threat of default, with creditors accepting less in place of none.

As a rule, there is no strict seniority in sovereign debt issues (with a few "de facto" exceptions, like credit extended by the IMF). This opens the possibility that existing creditors may see their debt "diluted" by subsequent new bond issuances. This makes long-term sovereign debt vulnerable to capital losses. Moreover, this incentive to dilute has implications for the payoff to voluntary "debt buybacks," (Bulow and Rogoff, 1991), which, as we will discuss, can be considered a reverse dilution of existing bondholders. The lack of strict seniority also raises the question of whether a defaulting government can treat certain creditors preferentially, for example domestic holders of sovereign debt. The extent to which internationally issued bonds are held by domestic residents may influence the net payoff to default (Broner et al., 2010).

In this chapter, we will take up the above themes. There are corollary issues related to sovereign debt we will discuss as well. For example, given a particular contracting space, there may be multiple equilibria, which raises the possibility of self-fulfilling debt

---

[2] There are a few exceptions, including some of the Brady bond restructurings in the early 1990s and recent bonds issued by Argentina and Greece. Such state-contingent "macro assets" have been advocated by Shiller (1993) and others, although such markets face challenges due to asymmetric information and limited verifiability.

crises. The issue of enforcement quickly leads to the role of reputation, both in regard to debt repayment and spill-overs to other economic activities. One important question is whether default affects private agents' beliefs about property rights more generally and the returns on private investment. Also it is important to consider the preferences of the decision maker, which may be different from a benevolent planner. We will discuss these issues more formally using a basic conceptual framework introduced in Section 3, which is then extended and modified in subsequent sections. Before introducing the framework, we first review several key empirical facts regarding sovereign debt.

2. EMPIRICAL FACTS

In this section we briefly summarize recent empirical research on default and its consequences, the macroeconomic consequences of sovereign debt overhang, and empirical facts regarding bond prices. There has been a recent boom in the collection and analysis of historical data on default. This work has generated novel facts as well as guided the theoretical approach to sovereign debt discussed in the subsequent sections (see Tomz and Wright, 2013, for a recent survey). We list several key findings. The first four concern default and its aftermath. The fifth finding concerns recent evidence on bond spreads. The sixth finding concerns the fact that successful growth episodes are associated with low and declining levels of foreign indebtedness.

1. **Default happens with regularity throughout history:** As an empirical event, default is typically defined as a failure of a government to meet a principal or interest payment on time and/or a rescheduling of debt on terms less favorable to the creditors. Reinhart and Rogoff (2009) emphasize that most countries that are able to raise funds internationally have had one or several default episodes in their history, including major European economies such as England, France, and Germany, and "graduation" to non-default status is extremely rare, even among high-income countries. Moreover, countries rarely default just once; serial default is the norm rather than the exception. Reinhart and Rogoff also emphasize that defaults happen in waves, with many countries being in default simultaneously. Recent episodes of multi-country debt crises include the Great Depression, the Latin American crisis of the 1980s, and the ongoing European debt crisis.

2. **Default often occurs in bad times, but with exceptions:** The fact that default happens most often when output is low provides a natural starting point for thinking about default. Using a newly constructed historical data set, Tomz and Wright (2007) conclude that defaults are more common in bad times than in good, but they also document that there are many exceptions. Specifically, Tomz and Wright document that in their sample of 175 countries, output is on average 1.6 percentage points below trend at the start of a default episode. Nevertheless, more than one-third of their 169

default episodes began when income was at or above trend, and countries frequently fall below trend without defaulting, indicating that a recession is neither necessary nor sufficient for default. Reinhart and Rogoff (2009) document that default crises frequently coincide with major financial crises. The pressure from bank failures and recession on a government's fiscal situation combined with the fact that many financial institutions hold government debt on their balance sheets makes the two types of crises intertwined. From a historical perspective, the fact that the 2008 financial crisis accompanied a sovereign debt crisis in multiple countries is no outlier. In addition to financial crises, default often precedes a large drop in trade (Rose, 2005; Martinez and Sandleris, 2011), and current account reversals/capital flight (Mendoza and Yue, 2012).

3. **Defaults involve a heterogeneous pattern of "haircuts":** Sturzenegger and Zettelmeyer (2008) review debt restructuring episodes from the 1990s and 2000s in six countries and across a number of debt instruments. The defaults in the 1990s and 2000s frequently involved bonds, and therefore differed from the primarily bank-debt crisis of the 1980s. Bond restructurings typically include a public offer of exchange, allowing researchers to compute the implied losses. Sturzenegger and Zettelmeyer (2008) compute the difference in promised payments between the old and new bond offerings in each exchange. A main finding is that these losses varied considerably over the sample. Relative to the face value of outstanding debt, the restructured bonds implied losses ranging from roughly 30% in Uruguay to over 60% for some bond series in Argentina and Russia. The Sturzenegger and Zettelmeyer (2008) sample is relatively small; however, Benjamin and Wright (2008) and Cruces and Trebesch (2011) explore a number of additional restructurings and alternative methodologies and find investor losses of roughly 30–40% on average, and again with considerable heterogeneity across individual default episodes.

4. **Default generates a period of lengthy renegotiation:** Benjamin and Wright (2008) study a large sample of bank-debt and bond renegotiations ranging from 1989 through 2005 involving seventy-three countries and ninety default episodes. In addition to the large and heterogeneous losses discussed above, they document that restructurings are a time-consuming process, taking eight years on average. Moreover, they find that the longer the negotiations, the larger the losses associated with the restructuring. The renegotiation process appears to be sensitive to the behavior of output, with large recessions generating somewhat longer restructurings and final settlement typically occurring when output has returned to trend. Benjamin and Wright (2008) also find that the median country exits restructuring carrying 5% higher debt-to-GDP loads then at the time of default.

5. **Sovereign bond spreads:** Broner et al. (2013) use a sample of emerging market bond yields from 1990 to 2009 to document several facts regarding bond yields and maturities. Specifically, they show that on average spreads over US bonds are higher

for longer maturity bonds, and while all spreads increase during crises, the short-term bond spread increases relatively more so that the yield curve "inverts" during periods of very high average spreads. The authors also document that the maturity of newly issued bonds shorten during crises, as the issuance of debt with more than three-year maturity declines when spreads are high.[3] A standard assumption in the theoretical literature on emerging markets is that foreign investors can hedge idiosyncratic country risk. However, emerging market bond yields exhibit significant co-movement, much more so than the often weak correlation for output. Longstaff et al. (2011) and Borri and Verdelhan (2011) document that global factors, like the return to the U.S. stock market, U.S. corporate bond market, or change in the VIX volatility index explain a large fraction of the common variation in spreads. This evidence suggests that holders of sovereign bonds are being compensated for taking on aggregate risk in addition to idiosyncratic default risk. This is not to say that bond spreads are not correlated with domestic output. Neumeyer and Perri (2005) and Uribe and Yue (2006) document that spreads are strongly countercyclical in emerging markets (see also Edwards, 1984).

6. **Debt overhang and growth:** The standard open-economy growth model predicts that a country with above average growth prospects should attract capital for both investment and consumption smoothing. The empirical pattern, at least for emerging markets since the opening of capital accounts in the 1970s and 1980s, is the opposite. Gourinchas and Jeanne (2007) document what they term the "allocation puzzle"; namely, that countries with above average growth rates are net exporters of capital on average. Aguiar and Amador (2011) show that this pattern is driven by government net foreign assets. In particular, they show that governments of high-growth economies increase net public assets held abroad (foreign reserves minus sovereign debt), while under-performing economies increase their public indebtedness. Moreover, this is not simply high-growth countries paying down a relatively large initial stock of debt nor is it consumption-smoothing at business cycle frequencies. On the other hand, Aguiar and Amador (2011) show that private capital flows accord with the standard intuition; that is, growth is accompanied by an increase in private net foreign liabilities. Alfaro et al. (2011) show that emerging market governments are contracting with other sovereigns, so the allocation puzzle involves governments on both sides of the transactions. Reinhart et al. (2012) document a negative correlation in advanced economies between debt-to-GDP ratios and growth. In sum, the evidence indicates that successful long-term development is not financed through sovereign debt, but rather is associated with a government paying down debt and/or accumulating net foreign assets.

---

[3] Arellano and Ramanarayanan (2012) confirm these results for a subset of the considered countries using data until 2011.

3. A BENCHMARK FRAMEWORK

In this section we introduce a benchmark limited-commitment environment. The analysis generates a rich set of implications, many of which carry over to the environments considered in subsequent sections. The benchmark framework was initially explored in the closed-economy models of Thomas and Worrall (1988) and Kehoe and Levine (1993). Key conceptual elements can be found in the seminal sovereign debt paper by Eaton and Gersovitz (1982).

Consider a small open economy populated by a representative agent and a government. Time runs discretely and is indexed $t = 0, 1, \ldots$ The economy is subject to exogenous shocks to output, which can be considered endowment or productivity shocks, depending on the context. To set notation regarding shocks and histories, let $s_t \in S$ denote the current state, which follows a finite-state Markov chain starting from some initial state s_0. Let $s^t = (s_0, s_1, \ldots, s_t) \in S^t$ denote a history truncated at time t. Let $\pi(s^t)$ denote the unconditional probability of history s^t, where $\pi(s^{t+j}|s^t)$ denotes the probability conditional on history s^t, $j \geq 0$. The notation $s^{t+j}|s^t$ indicates histories through $t + j \geq t$ that contain s^t, and $s^{t-j} \in s^t$ indicates history s^t truncated at $t - j \leq t$. Similarly, $\pi(s_{t+1}|s^t) = \pi(s^{t+1} = (s^t, s_{t+1})|s^t)$ denotes the probability period $t + 1$'s state is s_{t+1} conditional on history s^t. Finally, we let $\sum_{t \geq 0, s^t}$ denote the summation over all $t \geq 0$ and histories $s^t \in S^t$, $\sum_{s^j \in s^t}$ denote the sum over all truncated histories contained in s^t, and $\sum_{\tau \geq t, s^\tau | s^t}$ denote the sum over all infinite histories following s^t. For an allocation series $x = $ consumption, capital, debt, etc., we let $x(s^t)$ denote the allocation at a particular node s^t, and $\mathbf{x} \equiv \{x(s^t)\}_{t \geq 0, s^t} = (x(s^0), x(s^1), \ldots)$ denote the allocation over the infinite history.

There is an international financial market where the final good can be traded intertemporally using a full set of state-contingent assets. Let $Q^*(s^t) = \pi(s^t)/R^t$ denote the international price of a unit of consumption delivered at history s^t in units of period-zero consumption units, where $R = 1 + r$ is the gross interest rate in the international financial markets. When the economy is small and its shocks are uncorrelated with the rest of the world's consumption, standard diversification arguments imply risk-neutral pricing. We also assume that international asset markets have full commitment to financial contracts.

Let $c(s^t)$ denote consumption of the representative agent in history s^t. The government's preferences are

$$U(\mathbf{c}) = \sum_{t \geq 0, s^t} \pi(s^t) \beta^t u(c(s^t)), \tag{1}$$

where $u : \mathbb{R}_+ \to \mathbb{R}$ is a standard utility function, strictly increasing, concave and satisfying Inada conditions. We assume that the government has sufficient instruments to control the representative agent's decisions, subject to the resource constraints. We postpone discussion of alternative objective functions and how to decentralize the resulting allocation as a competitive equilibrium. The representative agent is endowed with a unit of labor, which it supplies inelastically. To ensure the small open economy's assets remain bounded, we assume $\beta R \leq 1$.

The timing of investment and production is as follows. The economy enters period t with installed capital $k(s^{t-1})$ and a portfolio of state-contingent liabilities $\sum_{s_t} b((s^{t-1}, s_t))$. We use the notation $k(s^{t-1})$ for period-t's capital as it is invested before s_t is realized, with $k(s^{-1})$ standing for the initial period capital stock. Once s_t is realized, the economy hires labor $n(s^t)$ and operates a neoclassical production function $F(s^t, k(s^{t-1}), n(s^t))$. Given that labor supply is inelastic, an endowment economy is nested in this formulation by dropping k as an argument. For simplicity, we drop the labor argument in the production function when convenient. The government then decides the consumption of the representative agent $c(s^t)$, pays liability $b(s^t)$, issues next period's portfolio of state-contingent liabilities, and makes net investment $k(s^t) - (1 - \delta)k(s^{t-1})$, where δ is the depreciation rate.

Assuming that the value of production at international prices is finite, the resource constraint of the small open economy can be written as:

$$b_0 \leq \sum_{t \geq 0, s^t} Q^*(s^t)(F(s^t, k(s^{t-1})) - c(s^t) - k(s^t) + (1 - \delta)k(s^{t-1})), \qquad \text{(RC)}$$

where $b_0 \equiv b(s^0)$ is the initial net foreign liability position. The elements of the sum on the right-hand side are net exports at each history, and balance of payments accounting requires that initial net foreign liabilities equals the discounted sum of net exports.

At the end of the period in history s^t, we can define

$$\tilde{b}(s^t) \equiv b(s^t) - Rk(s^{t-1})$$

as the economy's total liability position inclusive of domestically held wealth, where previous period's investment is carried forward at the world interest rate. This is the relevant wealth position at the time decisions regarding consumption, investment, and financial trades are made. There are no inter-temporal adjustment costs to capital, so financial assets and capital can be exchanged at the end of a period before the next shock is realized (but once invested, capital remains in place for a full period). As financial assets span the payouts on physical capital, physical and financial capital are perfect substitutes at the time financial claims are settled and new investment is made, hence we can collapse the two into a single state variable. Therefore, the relevant state variable for the economy is foreign liabilities less installed capital, which is the negative of total wealth held both abroad and at home.

From the above discussion, we can start the economy before initial capital is installed, so that b_0 and $k(s^{-1})$ are chosen simultaneously subject to $\tilde{b}_0 \geq b(s^0) - Rk(s^{-1})$. This exploits the small open-economy assumption to collapse debt and capital into a single state variable. Using $\tilde{b}_0$ as the economy's initial state, we can rewrite (RC) as

$$\tilde{b}_0 \leq \sum_{t \geq 0, s^t} Q^*(s^t)\Big(F(s^t, k(s^{t-1})) - c(s^t) - k(s^t) + (1-\delta)k(s^{t-1})\Big) - Rk(s^{-1})$$

$$= \sum_{t \geq 0, s^t} Q^*(s^t)(F(s^t, k(s^{t-1})) - c(s^t) - (r+\delta)k(s^{t-1})), \tag{RC'}$$

where the second line is a rearranged version of the first.[4]

The critical assumption is that the government has limited commitment: that is, at any point in time, the government can decide to change its policy. In this simple set up, this means that the government can decide not to repay its debt to foreigners and/or expropriate foreign-owned capital invested domestically. We will refer to this as "deviation," rather than "default" to avoid confusion when discussing the empirical implications of the model. In particular, we discuss below interpretations of state-contingent debt as default with partial forgiveness or default with renegotiation. This is distinct from deviation, which as we shall see happens off the equilibrium path.[5]

We let $\underline{V}(s^t, k(s^{t-1}))$ summarize the value of deviation to the government at history s^t with installed capital $k(s^{t-1})$. The fact that capital is a state variable for deviation utility reflects that it cannot be removed within the period. We will sometimes refer to the deviation value using the more evocative terminology of "punishment." The nature of this value will be a key object of interest across different environments. The cases we consider require that the punishment utility is independent of outstanding debt at the time of deviation, and depends on previous equilibrium choices only through the existing capital stock. We further assume that $\underline{V}(s^t, k(s^{t-1}))$ is weakly increasing in $k(s^{t-1})$.

For an allocation to be compatible with the government's ability to deviate, it must deliver present value utility at least as great as $\underline{V}(s^t, k(s^{t-1}))$:

$$\sum_{\tau \geq t, s^\tau | s^t} \pi(s^\tau | s^t)\beta^{\tau-t}u(c(s^\tau)) \geq \underline{V}(s^t, k(s^{t-1})) \quad \text{for all } t, s^t. \tag{PC}$$

---

[4] To obtain this, we can use the fact that for a given t,

$$\sum_{s^t \in S^t} Q^*(s^t)k(s^{t-1}) = R^{-t} \sum_{s^{t-1} \in S^{t-1}} \sum_{s_t \in S} \pi((s^{t-1}, s_t))k(s^{t-1})$$

$$= R^{-t} \sum_{s^{t-1} \in S^{t-1}} \pi(s^{t-1})k(s^{t-1})$$

$$= R^{-1} \sum_{s^{t-1} \in S^{t-1}} Q^*(s^{t-1})k(s^{t-1}).$$

Using this equivalence in (RC) and rearranging, we have (RC').

[5] Some authors use the term repudiation or "inexcusable" default rather than deviation, which is entirely consistent, while others use the empirically suggestive term default, which can lead to confusion.

This constraint is commonly referred to as the "participation constraint" or "debt constraint." An allocation that satisfies the sequence of participation constraints ensures that the government would never prefer to deviate. As noted below, this can be construed as a borrowing limit, as the international loan market recognizes that additional debt will not be repaid.

Definition 1. A government-controlled allocation conditional on $\tilde{b}_0$, is defined to be non-negative consumption and capital allocations, $\{\mathbf{c}, \mathbf{k}\}$, that solve the following problem

$$V(\tilde{b}_0) = \max_{\{\mathbf{c}, \mathbf{k}\}} \sum_{t \geq 0, s^t} \pi(s^t) \beta^t u(c(s^t)) \quad \text{subject to (RC') and (PC).} \qquad \text{(P)}$$

Note that the solution to Problem (**P**) corresponds to a "self-enforcing" equilibrium in the game between the government, owners of physical capital, and international lenders, or, in the terminology of Chari and Kehoe (1990), a "sustainable plan."

The resource constraint (RC') implies that V is a strictly decreasing function, assuming we remain in the interior of the constraint set. Viewed recursively, the left-hand side of (PC) can be viewed as the value function conditional on outstanding liabilities at history s^t. The fact that this value is monotonic in $\tilde{b}$, which recall is the sum of net foreign liabilities minus installed capital, implies that the constraint can be viewed as an upper bound on net foreign liabilities (conditional on installed capital) at each history. Conversely, conditional on net foreign liabilities, the constraint implies an upper bound on domestic capital, a point that will feature prominently in our discussion of debt overhang below.

Before studying this problem in detail, we briefly summarize the full-commitment solution. That is, if the government could commit to all financial contracts, the allocation would feature:

(i) Complete risk-sharing, such that $c(s^t) = c_t$ is constant across states at a point in time, and satisfies $\beta R u'(c_t) = u'(c_{t-1})$ inter-temporally; and
(ii) First-best investment, such that $\sum_{s_t \in S} \pi(s_t | s^{t-1}) F_k((s_t, s^{t-1}), k(s^{t-1})) = r + \delta$.

The corresponding level of initial consumption can be recovered from the resource constraint (RC') given the sequence of first-best capital stocks.

3.1. An Endowment Economy

To focus on how limited commitment impedes risk-sharing, let us assume, as a starting point, an endowment economy. That is, there is no capital, and $F(s^t) = y(s^t) = y_t$, where y_t follows a stationary, first-order Markov process that takes discrete values $0 < y^1 < y^2 < \cdots < y^N$. To make the problem more concrete, we specify $\underline{V}(s^t)$. Specifically, we assume that deviation results in total exclusion from international asset markets. If the economy could not trade financial assets at all (autarky), the utility of the representative agent would be:

$$\underline{V}(\gamma) = V^{Aut}(\gamma) \equiv u(\gamma) + \sum_{j=1}^{\infty} \sum_{k=1}^{N} \beta^j \pi (\gamma_{t+j} = \gamma^k | \gamma_t = \gamma) u(\gamma^k). \tag{2}$$

Autarky, as defined above, is the canonical punishment for deviation in the sovereign debt literature (the classic reference is Eaton and Gersovitz (1982)). This punishment is often interpreted as the loss of a country's reputation in international financial markets due to a deviation.

In the environment under consideration, in which the government makes decisions on behalf of a representative agent, the autarky value represents the lowest utility for the government that can be sustained as a self-enforcing equilibrium. Or, as noted above, the autarky value defines a state-contingent upper bound on the economy's liabilities (which, in the endowment economy, equals outstanding sovereign debt). The fact that a self-enforcing equilibrium at the borrowing limit delivers the utility associated with permanent exclusion makes the autarky value (but not the autarkic allocation) a re-negotiation proof punishment.[6]

There are some important caveats associated with autarky as a punishment value. If we take the reputational interpretation literally, there remains a question of why the loss of reputation prevents the government from continuing to save in world financial markets. In a seminal paper, Bulow and Rogoff (1989b) build on this insight to construct a celebrated critique of reputational models of debt. In particular, Bulow and Rogoff propose an alternative deviation equilibrium from autarky, one in which countries can never borrow again, but are able to save. That is, they can buy (a sequence of) cash-in-advance insurance contracts in which they pay upfront and are not obligated to pay out in any state the following period. With such contracts available, an economy that has reached its upper bound on liabilities can choose not to repay this debt, but rather use the scheduled payments to buy cash-in-advance contracts. Bulow and Rogoff (1989b) show that this is feasible and generates higher utility, as long as the upper bound on debt is strictly positive. Thus the equilibrium places an upper bound of debt of zero.

This insight has spawned a large literature. We briefly summarize some of the main themes. A straightforward response is to rule out cash-in-advance contracts by appealing to legal enforcement mechanisms in the international financial markets. That is, an unpaid creditor can sue to seize the debtor's overseas assets or exports. In this environment, the legal enforcement implicit in the foreign market's ability to commit to cash-in-advance contracts can also be used to enforce the punishment. In practice, this is reflected in the heavy role of courts, lawyers, and legal contracts involved in adjudicating sovereign debt claims. Direct sanctions under the auspices of a foreign legal authority is the environment favored by Bulow and Rogoff themselves in motivating the re-contracting model

---

[6] See Wright (2002) and Kletzer and Wright (2000) for the case of one- and two-sided limited commitment, respectively.

discussed below (Bulow and Rogoff, 1989a). However, there is mixed empirical evidence regarding the effect of trade sanctions as an enforcement mechanism (Rose, 2005; Martinez and Sandleris, 2011).[7]

Kletzer and Wright (2000) drop the commitment assumption for foreign creditors and show that debt can be sustained in "anarchy," as in the absence of any legal enforcement there is no mechanism to ensure that foreign commitments implicit in cash-in-advance contracts are honored. Imperfect enforcement of foreign savings vehicles is not necessary, however. Wright (2002) develops an environment in which a limited number of foreign banks can commit (that is, the one-sided limited commitment of our benchmark), but choose not to offer cash-in-advance contracts that disrupt established lending relationships. Others have also appealed to non-legal mechanisms to sustain debt. One prominent theme is that a loss of reputation in debt markets spills over to other economic spheres, depressing trade, output, or investment, without the need for creditor-country courts per se (e.g., Cole and Kehoe, 1998).[8] Relatedly, Amador (2012) argues that, if the government decisions are the result of a political game among distinct agents, then a tragedy of the commons may occur which renders the strategy of using cash-in-advance contracts after a deviation unsustainable, restoring the sustainability of sovereign debt.

While Bulow and Rogoff argued that complete financial autarky may be unrealistic as a punishment without additional legal enforcement to prevent savings, Broner and Ventura (2011) and Broner et al. (2010) argue that autarky may deliver a utility payoff even worse than the one modeled above. Broner and Ventura (2011) note that the failure to enforce international obligations may be associated with a failure to enforce domestic contracts, if the residency of the contracting parties cannot be ascertained. Similarly, domestic residents may hold the government's debt, leading to a potentially damaging redistribution of wealth across domestic agents in the event of a deviation (Broner et al., 2010). This may be particularly severe if domestic banks hold government bonds as assets and face net worth constraints in lending (Gennaioli et al., 2010). Thus, deviation may be associated with a breakdown in domestic risk-sharing that makes the value defined in (2) an upper bound.

That said, the key implications of the benchmark endowment model are robust to alternative enforcement mechanisms. Under standard monotonicity assumptions on the Markov process, $\underline{V}(y)$ in (2) is increasing in y. That is, a high current endowment makes deviation relatively attractive. Moreover, the deviation utility is independent of equilibrium allocations; in particular, it does not depend on the amount of debt outstanding at the time of deviation. As long as $\underline{V}(s^t)$ has these properties, the main implications derived below are robust to alternative punishments. The details of enforcement, and in particular

[7] For an interesting discussion on the role of sanctions versus reputation in sustaining sovereign debt in Spain under Philip II, see Conklin (1998) and Drelichman and Voth (2011).
[8] See Fuentes and Saravia (2010) for evidence with regard to falls in FDI after default.

the severity of the punishment, will determine the level of $\underline{V}$, which in turn determines the equilibrium limits to debt and risk sharing.

We now characterize the constrained-optimal allocation using Lagrangian techniques.[9] Let μ denote the multiplier on the resource constraint (RC), and $\lambda(s^t)\pi(s^t)\beta^t$ denote the sequence of multipliers on the participation constraints. We scale each participation multiplier by a strictly positive number for notational convenience. Note that in the endowment economy case, the problem stated in (**P**) has an objective function that is strictly concave and the constraints are convex. The first-order condition for consumption in state s^t is:

$$\beta^t \left(\pi(s^t) + \sum_{s^j \in s^t} \pi(s^t|s^j)\pi(s^j)\lambda(s^j) \right) u'(c(s^t)) = \mu Q^*(s^t).$$

Note that $\pi(s^t|s^j)\pi(s^j) = \pi(s^t)$ if $s^j \in s^t$, that is, if s^j precedes history s^t. We can use $Q^*(s^t) = \pi(s^t)/R^t$ to simplify this first-order condition:

$$\beta^t R^t \left(1 + \sum_{s^j \in s^t} \lambda(s^j) \right) u'(c(s^t)) = \mu. \tag{3}$$

The right-hand side of (3) is the marginal value of initial assets. If the participation constraints are always slack ($\lambda(s^t) = 0$, $\forall t$), then $\beta^t R^t u'(c(s^t))$ is a constant. This is the full risk-sharing allocation, in which consumption is not state dependent and varies over time only to the extent that the agent is impatient relative to the world interest rate. However, when $\lambda(s^t) > 0$, the participation constraint is binding[10] and full risk-sharing is not compatible with limited commitment. It can be shown that across states when the constraint binds, consumption is strictly increasing in the current endowment, highlighting the limits to risk sharing imposed by limited commitment. Moreover, the summation on the left-hand side of (3) is non-decreasing, and strictly increasing whenever $\lambda(s^t) > 0$. As the

---

[9] There are many technical assumptions that lie behind the validity of Lagrangian techniques in infinite-dimensional spaces. Given the infinite sequence of participation constraints, a natural environment is to assume that the set of participation constraints maps allocations into the space of bounded sequences (ℓ_∞). This requires that utility is bounded over the set of feasible allocations (where the difficulty usually lies in ensuring utility is bounded below at zero, as zero consumption is typically feasible). The natural space for multipliers is the space of summable sequences, ℓ_1. However, the dual of ℓ_∞ is larger than ℓ_1. Fortunately, for many environments of economic interest, it can be shown that the Lagrange multipliers are indeed elements of ℓ_1. See Dechert (1982) and Rustichini (1998) for details. A final requirement is that the participation constraint set includes an interior feasible allocation (if the constraint set is convex and we are characterizing a global optimum), or satisfies a local regularity condition (similar to the full-rank Jacobian condition in finite dimensions) if necessary conditions for an interior optimum are the object of interest. The standard reference is Luenberger (1969). Throughout the chapter, we assume the existence of an interior optimum and the validity of Lagrangian techniques without further comment.

[10] We use the term "binding" to indicate the constraint's multiplier is strictly positive, which, from complementary slackness, requires the constraint is satisfied with equality. With this usage, the constraint is not considered "binding" if the constraint is satisfied with equality but the multiplier is zero.

right-hand side is constant, this implies that the marginal utility of consumption is falling over time faster than βR. In particular, when $\beta R = 1$, consumption is non-decreasing, and strictly increasing whenever the participation constraint binds.

Another view of this implication comes from the Euler equation. Consider $s^{t+1} = (s^t, s_{t+1})$ and evaluate (3) at s^t and s^{t+1} to obtain:

$$\beta R \left(1 + \frac{\lambda(s^t, s_{t+1})}{\Lambda(s^t)}\right) u'(c(s^t, s_{t+1})) = u'(c(s^t)), \tag{4}$$

where $\Lambda(s^t) \equiv 1 + \sum_{s^j \in s^t} \lambda(s^j)$. If the participation constraint is slack at s_{t+1}, then $\beta R u'(c(s^t, s_{t+1})) = u'(c(s^t))$, which is the full-commitment Euler equation from state s^t to state s^{t+1}. When the participation constraint binds, $\lambda(s^{t+1}) > 0$, and marginal utility in s^{t+1} is distorted down relative to s^t (and consumption is distorted up). This captures that limited participation provides an incentive for consumption to grow over time. This feature of the optimal allocation is often referred to as "back loading," as consumption is higher in the later periods.

The intuition for back loading is as follows. The country always has the option of deviating and enjoying $\underline{V}(y_t)$. To ensure continued participation, the allocation at each history must deliver at least this utility, which requires a certain stream of consumption. Additional consumption in a particular period helps satisfy this requirement. Moreover, it also helps satisfy the requirement in all previous periods as well. This is because the left-hand side of the constraint (PC) is forward looking; it is the discounted sum of all future utility. At the margin, therefore, consumption in the future is preferable as it relaxes all preceding participation constraints. The math of the first-order condition (3) reflects this feature by including the cumulative sums of Lagrange multipliers from all previous periods.

This is perhaps a sophisticated way of saying that limited commitment provides an incentive to save. However, it also says more. When $\beta R = 1$, we see that consumption never declines, regardless of the state of nature. That is, current consumption always provides a floor for future consumption. Moreover, the fact that μ is finite implies the expression on the left-hand side of (3) converges. For $\beta R = 1$, this implies that $\lim_{t \to \infty} \lambda(s^t) = 0$, and $c(s^t)$ converges to a constant. In the limit, therefore, the economy achieves perfect risk sharing (see Ray, 2002), for a general statement of this result). Along the transition, consumption increases at each node at which the participation constraint binds. As $\underline{V}(y)$ is increasing in y, it reaches a maximum at $y = y^N$. Once the highest endowment is realized, consumption is constant thereafter and full risk-sharing is attained (Worrall, 1990).

This last result requires $\beta R = 1$. When $\beta R < 1$, we have that $\lim_{t \to \infty} \beta^t R^t = 0$, and from equation (3), we see that the cumulative sum therefore must diverge, that is, $\lambda(s^t)$ is strictly positive infinitely often. In particular, whenever the participation constraint is slack, consumption is below the previous period's due to impatience as shown by (4). However, consumption cannot fall indefinitely, as this will eventually violate the participation constraint. When the constraint binds, consumption's fall is mitigated, or even reversed if the current endowment realization is high enough. Moreover, as (PC) holds with equality when $\lambda(s^t) > 0$, we see that continuation utility is state dependent (as $\underline{V}(\gamma_t)$ is state dependent). The combination of front loading due to impatience and back loading due to limited commitment implies consumption will converge to an ergodic distribution, which in general will be non-degenerate.

The model predicts that large debt positions impede risk-sharing. The resource constraint at any history requires that the present discounted value of net exports equals outstanding debt. Heuristically, a large stock of outstanding debt lowers the present value of consumption, making the participation constraint relevant in more states. This generates the empirical prediction that, all else equal, a large stock of outstanding debt is associated with more volatile consumption. If a country is patient, it will respond to this by saving. This is a general implication of many limited-commitment environments—the presence of a borrowing constraint provides an incentive to save. Placed in an international general equilibrium, this effect can be used to micro-found $\beta R < 1$. Perhaps more important for the discussion of risk-sharing, we see that borrowing today not only requires repayment in the future (as in the full-commitment environment), it may also generate more volatile consumption going forward due to impaired risk-sharing, a form of "debt overhang" onto consumption volatility.

The participation constraint is also informative about net payments (the trade balance). In particular, suppose the constraint is binding at a particular point in time, t. Rearranging (PC), this implies:

$$u(\gamma_t) - u(c(s^t)) = \sum_{\tau \geq t+1, s^\tau | s^t} \pi(s^\tau | s^t) \beta^{\tau - t} \left[u(c(s^\tau)) - u(\gamma_\tau) \right].$$

Note that the right-hand side must be greater than or equal to zero to satisfy the participation constraint in every state at $t + 1$. This implies that $\gamma_t \geq c(s^t)$. That is, the country does not receive net inflows when its constraint is binding. Or, perhaps more intuitively, the constraint only binds if the country is expected to make a non-negative payment—the country is never tempted to renege when it is due payments from the rest of the world.

This plus risk-sharing considerations imply that the participation constraint tends to bind when the endowment is relatively high. Or, more precisely, fix a history through $t - 1$ and consider two endowment realizations $\gamma^j < \gamma^k$ at time t. If the participation constraint binds for γ^j, then it also binds for γ^k. This reflects the fact that a high endowment makes deviation attractive, plus the risk-sharing requirement that a high-endowment state is the time to repay creditors (given state-contingent asset markets). While intuitive, this implication has often led to the confusing and incorrect statement that the model predicts that "default happens in high-endowment states." The incentive to deviate in a high-endowment state is met, in equilibrium, with a reduction in the amount of net exports required in those states, ensuring continued participation. From the budget constraint, this must be balanced with lower net imports in other states. In particular, a binding participation constraint in high-endowment states reduces the amount of transfers the country receives in low-endowment states. That is, it acts as a constraint on borrowing in bad times, a natural and general implication of limited commitment.

To summarize the results so far, we see that limited commitment impedes risk-sharing, and does so particularly severely when the country is heavily indebted. The natural response to the lack of commitment is to save, which, if the country has sufficient patience, will ultimately lead to first-best risk-sharing; otherwise, consumption fluctuates with output indefinitely. When the country's participation constraint binds, net exports are non-negative, implying that borrowing is limited in other states of the world. The limited risk-sharing, volatility of consumption, and the negative consequences of indebtedness are all implications with clear counterparts in the data.

A natural question is whether these allocations can be implemented with realistic financial contracts and how to interpret empirical "default" episodes. The environment admits alternative interpretations of state-contingent contracts and default episodes. Grossman and Van Huyck (1988) argue that the state-contingent assets can be interpreted as partial defaults that are excused. That is, the lenders can observe the state and forgive a certain portion of the outstanding debt conditional on the state. A similar point is made by Bulow and Rogoff (1989a), who argue that sovereign debt can be renegotiated ex post under the threat of legal sanctions. This makes debt payments de facto state contingent, although the participation constraint is based on an explicit bargaining protocol rather than the reputational autarky value introduced above. They point out that the face value of debt can be set to match the highest possible payment, and lower payments are decentralized as default and renegotiation.[11]

While these interpretations are consistent with the fact that observed defaults are not punished severely (e.g., sovereign foreign assets are protected and economies regain access to financial markets), they suggest that some element of default is a high-frequency occurrence. At the other extreme, a narrow notion of default focuses on the model's prediction for a binding participation constraint in the lowest endowment state. If the constraint binds in the lowest state, it also binds for all continuation values. From the participation constraint, we then have that net exports are zero. This implies that the country is in autarky for that one period. Moreover, as pointed out above, the country will not exit this autarkic state until it makes a payment. While it refuses to make the payment, it continues to be denied net inflows and remains at the autarky value. This pattern predicts a punishment phase followed by partial repayment. However, the punishment phase lasts only until an endowment above the lowest state occurs, making it relatively short-lived, depending on the persistence of the endowment process. Another difficulty with this interpretation

---

[11] In both Grossman and Van Huyck (1988) and Bulow and Rogoff (1989a) renegotiation is either not time-consuming, or, via backwards induction, prolonged renegotiation takes place off the equilibrium path. We discuss other bargaining outcomes in Section 4.

of default is that if the country is relatively patient (i.e., $\beta R = 1$), a binding constraint with $y_t = y^1$ can only occur in the initial period(s), after which, savings (and state-contingent assets) will prevent the constraint from ever binding again in the low-endowment state. If the economy is impatient (βR is less than one), the economy may revisit this worst-outcome value due to borrowing and repeated low-endowment realizations.

3.2. Debt Overhang in a Production Economy

The preceding analysis concerned an endowment economy, and it contained one example of "debt overhang"; namely, risk-sharing is impeded by a large stock of outstanding debt. In a production economy, limited commitment predicts that output and growth is also adversely affected by debt. We should note at the start that in this subsection we consider allocations that are on the constrained Pareto frontier between investors/lenders and the domestic government. There is an early literature on sovereign debt overhang, such as Sachs (1989) and Krugman (1988), that explores Pareto inefficiencies that arise due to debt overhang. In these models, debt is assumed to be exogenous, and debt relief is shown to enhance investment and in some cases generate a Pareto improvement. In the analysis that follows, debt overhang arises in a model of endogenous debt dynamics due to the limited ability of the government to commit. The "ex post" constrained efficiency of the equilibrium allocation implies that a Pareto improvement cannot be engineered through debt forgiveness.

In this subsection, we assume that the economy operates the neoclassical production function $F(s^t, k(s^{t-1}), n(s^t))$, using the notation introduced at the beginning of this section. Recall as well that capital is a state variable in the deviation utility $\underline{V}(s^t, k(s^{t-1}))$. This allows the government to expropriate and redistribute capital following a deviation. That is, limited commitment extends to the protection of property located within the country. A natural benchmark for $\underline{V}(s^t, k(s^{t-1}))$ is the closed-economy neoclassical growth model. Specifically, following a deviation on promises to creditors or investors, the economy reverts to autarky but continues with the existing capital stock and technology. This is the deviation considered in Marcet and Marimon (1992). A harsher alternative is that some of the expropriated capital is rendered unusable without foreign involvement and/or the production function is operated with less efficiency. A perhaps even tougher environment can be constructed assuming that private (domestic) entrepreneurs are required to operate capital and can invest abroad following a deviation. In this case, the combination of capital flight and a government without commitment on capital taxation prevents the economy from accumulating domestic capital. Several of these alternatives are explored numerically in Aguiar and Amador (2011). While the precise modeling of the deviation value matters quantitatively, the conceptual points developed below rest on the assumption that $\underline{V}$ is strictly increasing in the domestic capital stock and is independent of equilibrium debt.

We consider the government-controlled allocation. The government's problem is given by (**P**) subject to (RC′) and (PC). We are confronted with a non-convex participation constraint due to the presence of a choice variable $k(s^t)$ on the right-hand side of (PC). In this case, there is not a general method for addressing this issue. Thomas and Worrall (1994) and Aguiar et al. (2009) provide some restrictions on the relative concavity of u and F that ensure the constraint is globally convex. Nevertheless, we can gain important insights by characterizing necessary conditions for an interior optimum without verifying their sufficiency.

As in the endowment economy, we use Lagrangian techniques. We continue to let μ denote the multiplier on the resource constraint (RC′) and $\lambda(s^t)\pi(s^t)\beta^t$ denote the multipliers on the participation constraints (PC). The first-order condition for consumption is the same as in the endowment economy (equation 3). The first-order condition for $k(s^t)$ is

$$\mu \sum_{s^{t+1}|s^t} Q^*(s^{t+1}) \left(F_k(s^{t+1}, k(s^t)) - r - \delta\right) = \sum_{s^{t+1}|s^t} \beta^{t+1}\pi(s^{t+1})\lambda(s^{t+1})\underline{V}_k(s^{t+1}, k(s^t)).$$

Dividing through by $\pi(s^t)$ and using the definition of $Q^*(s^{t+1})$, we have

$$\mu \sum_{s_{t+1}} \pi(s_{t+1}|s^t) \left(F_k(s^{t+1}, k(s^t)) - r - \delta\right) = \sum_{s_{t+1}} \beta^{t+1}R^{t+1}\pi(s_{t+1}|s^t)\lambda(s^{t+1})\underline{V}_k(s^{t+1}, k(s^t)).$$

The left-hand side is the expected marginal product of capital minus its opportunity cost, scaled by the marginal value of period-0 resources. In a world of full commitment, this will equal zero. The right-hand side reflects the distortions of limited commitment. In particular, if $\lambda(s^{t+1}) > 0$ in period $t + 1$, then investment in period t is distorted. As $\underline{V}_k > 0$, we have that $\lambda(s^{t+1}) > 0$ implies that the expected marginal product of capital across states in period $t + 1$ is strictly greater than the opportunity cost of capital; that is, investment is distorted down today if the participation constraint binds in any state tomorrow. The intuition is that a large capital stock raises the value of deviation ($\underline{V}_k > 0$), providing an increased incentive for the government to renege on debt promises. To relax the participation constraint, the government underinvests. This can be decentralized by a higher tax on capital income (Aguiar et al., 2009; Aguiar and Amador, 2011), where "taxes" may take the form of statutory taxes as well as bribes, permits and red tape, or *anticipated* ex post expropriations of capital income by politicians. Another direct implication of the non-negativity of the right-hand side is that capital is never greater than the first-best level; that is, over investment in this environment never enhances commitment.

The fact that the constraint in $t + 1$ matters for period t investment provides a link between borrowing and investment volatility. Aguiar et al. (2009) explore this link in detail, and we briefly summarize their results. Consider two alternative histories in period t, s_1^t and s_2^t, with output higher in s_1^t, and identical initial wealth positions so resources are greater in s_1^t. To make the point in its simplest form, assume *iid* shocks so that the first-best investment level is independent of histories. In the low-output state s_2^t, the government would like to smooth the consumption by borrowing against high states in the future. Conversely, the government in state s_1^t would like to borrow less, or even use the extra output to pay down debt, raising consumption and risk-sharing opportunities going forward. In order to relax the borrowing constraint in the former case, the government invests less in s_2^t. That is, low output leads to low investment, indicating that limited commitment can prolong the impact of a transitory shock.

Moreover, this effect is most severe when the economy is heavily indebted. In particular, an economy can avoid distorted investment by maintaining a sufficiently low level of outstanding debt. For example, take the case of $\beta R = 1$. As in the endowment case, the first-order condition for consumption implies that the economy eventually saves to a point where the participation constraint no longer binds. In the production economy, this implies that investment ultimately achieves the first-best level, but only when debt is low enough. If $\beta R < 1$, then the economy converges to an ergodic distribution in which investment cycles indefinitely at a level always strictly below the first best. The implication that high levels of sovereign debt enhances the cyclicality and reduces the level of investment is consistent with the empirical results on the poor macroeconomic performance of heavily indebted economies. A particularly striking case study is Argentina's debt crisis of 2001, which coincided with the start of a sequence of government expropriations of private capital income.[12]

The analysis thus far highlights the deleterious implications of debt overhang in a world of limited commitment. The efficient allocation, when the country's government is sufficiently patient, addresses this by paying down debt. This begs the question of why so many countries stagnate in a heavily indebted state. One explanation is that some countries, due perhaps to demographics or mortality, discount at a relatively high rate. As we saw, if $\beta R < 1$, the efficient allocation does not achieve a debt level low enough to support first-best investment or risk-sharing. However, assuming $\beta R < 1$ is not completely satisfactory as an explanation. For example, many countries eventually do pay down their debt, but do so over a very long period of time. In the terminology of Reinhart and Rogoff, countries do "graduate" from debt overhang, but the process is a prolonged one. Note that a low value of β does not necessarily imply slow convergence to the steady-state or ergodic distribution; that is, even though a low value of β implies that saving is depressed, this is balanced by a reduction in the level of steady-state capital.

Aguiar and Amador (2011) provide an alternative explanation for the fact that successful countries reduce net foreign liabilities, but the speed at which this occurs may vary across economies. Specifically, they propose a model of political turnover in which political actors rotate in and out of power according to a Markov process. Motivated by the work of Persson and Svensson (1989) and Alesina and Tabellini (1990), participants in the political process are assumed to prefer consumption during their incumbency. Specifically, an incumbent places a premium $\tilde{\theta} > 1$ on consumption while in power. Aguiar and Amador consider an environment in which output is deterministic, but political turnover

---

[12] Restrepo-Echavarria (2013) explores the ability of the model to explain Latin America's "lost decade" following the 1980s debt crisis.

is stochastic, isolating the frictions due to political uncertainty. Let $p_{t,t+j}$ denote the probability that the incumbent in period t is also in power in $t + j$. The preferences of the incumbent at period t are:

$$\tilde{W}_t = \tilde{\theta} u(c_t) + \sum_{\tau > t} \beta^{\tau - t} \left(p_{t,\tau} \tilde{\theta} + 1 - p_{t,\tau} \right) u(c_\tau).$$

Considering the simplest case in which the political turnover process is *iid* across political participants (i.e., $p_{t,t+j} = p, \forall j > 0$), incumbent utility becomes:

$$W_t \equiv \frac{\tilde{W}_t}{p\tilde{\theta} + 1 - p} = \theta u(c_t) + \sum_{\tau > t} \beta^{\tau - t} u(c_\tau)$$

$$= \theta u(c_t) + \beta V_{t+1},$$

where $\theta = \frac{\tilde{\theta}}{p\tilde{\theta} + 1 - p}$, and we have renormalized the incumbent utility. Note that V_{t+1} is the utility of private agents in the economy.

In this environment, the current incumbent discounts between today and tomorrow at the rate $\beta/\theta < \beta$, but discounts across future periods at the geometric rate β. In this sense, the incumbent has hyperbolic or quasi-geometric preferences in the spirit of Laibson (1994). The fact that the current incumbent discounts in a non-geometric fashion is a natural consequence of stochastic political turnover; for the incumbent, the current period is special because it is in power with probability one. Any future period must be down-weighted by the probability that the current incumbent will lose office in the interim, but also reflect the fact that it may return to power as well. The *iid* environment implies that the conditional probability of incumbency is the same across any two future periods, and therefore those are weighted equally using the undistorted discount factor β. Aguiar and Amador (2011) show how to generalize this to persistent political processes. Political economy distortions are captured by θ, with $\theta = 1$ reflecting a benevolent government and $\theta > 1$ reflecting an incumbent who strictly favors front-loading consumption.

If the incumbent makes decisions regarding debt repayment or capital taxation, the relevant participation constraint is

$$W_t \geq \underline{W}(k_{t-1}), \tag{5}$$

where $\underline{W}(k_{t-1})$ is the deviation utility of the current incumbent given invested capital k_{t-1}. This utility incorporates any punishment the political process may impose on deviation, as well as the consequences of financial autarky. We continue to assume that $\underline{W}'(k_t) > 0$, so that additional capital makes deviation less costly.[13] An efficient allocation

---

[13] We also implicitly use the concavity assumption that $(F'(k) - r - d)/\underline{W}'(k)$ is declining in k. This is satisfied, for example, by a broad class of deviation value functions in the neighborhood of the first-best capital.

in this environment is to maximize (**P**) subject to (RC′) and the sequence of incumbent participation constraints (5).

The first-order condition for consumption is:

$$\beta^t R^t \left(1 + \sum_{j=0}^{t} \lambda_j + (\theta - 1)\lambda_t \right) u'(c_t) = \mu, \tag{6}$$

where λ_t denotes the scaled multiplier on incumbent t's participation constraint and μ denotes the multiplier on the resource constraint. This condition is similar to (3), the first-order condition absent political economy frictions, save for the presence of $(\theta - 1)\lambda_t$ on the left-hand side of (6). This additional term reflects that for the incumbent political party, current consumption is particularly valued. This additional term does not overturn the implication that if $\beta R = 1$, then $\lim_{t \to \infty} \lambda_t = 0$, as the cumulative sum continues to imply back loading of consumption. However, the presence of the additional term does influence dynamics. To see this transparently, consider the case of $\beta R = 1$ and assume risk neutral preferences: $u'(c) = 1$. (Aguiar and Amador, 2011, show how the results extend to the general environment with $\beta R \leq 1$ and concave utility). In this case, the cumulating sum on the left-hand side of (6) is constant over time, implying the following first-order dynamics:

$$\lambda_{t+1} = \left(1 - \frac{1}{\theta} \right) \lambda_t, \tag{7}$$

with $\lambda_0 = \frac{\mu - 1}{\theta} \geq 0$. This implies that λ_t converges to zero at a rate $1/\theta$, so convergence is governed by the extent of political distortions reflected in θ.

As in the benchmark case, the participation-constraint multiplier λ determines the distortions in investment, as the first-order condition for capital takes the same form (absent productivity shocks):

$$F'(k_t) - (r + \delta) = \lambda_{t+1} \underline{W}'(k_t). \tag{8}$$

Therefore the magnitude of political economy distortions also governs the convergence of capital to the first-best level. That is, a more politically distorted economy grows at a slower rate. The environment exhibits the standard implication of limited commitment that the participation constraint is relaxed as the sovereign accumulates wealth. Aguiar and Amador (2011) use this insight to generate an environment where growth occurs by reducing the government's net foreign liabilities, consistent with the "allocation puzzle" empirical facts discussed in Section 2. However, countries experience differential growth rates depending on the extent of political economy distortions. This is consistent with the fact that some countries experience long periods of stagnation in which debt is high and growth is low, while other countries exhibit extremely high levels of growth all the while serving as net exporters of capital. The model suggests that political economy distortions do not preclude an economy from eventually achieving high-income status, but does suggest that the process will be a long one. Moreover, Aguiar and Amador (2011) show that the more distorted economy must achieve a lower level of steady-state debt to support the same level of capital as a less distorted economy, consistent with the "debt intolerance" pattern documented by Reinhart et al. (2003) in which less-developed economies encounter macroeconomic difficulties at lower levels of external debt than high-income economies.

We conclude our discussion of the benchmark economy with a few comments on how to decentralize the constrained-efficient allocation as a competitive equilibrium. In regard to investment, the previous discussion highlights that the stock of physical capital may influence the government's incentive to renege on debt and tax promises. This can be decentralized with a tax on the returns to investment, as discussed in Kehoe and Perri (2004) in a two-country general equilibrium model and Aguiar et al. (2009) in a small-open-economy environment. Equation (8) directly implies that the returns to capital must be distorted relative to the opportunity cost if the participation constraint is strictly binding (whether the government is benevolent or not), and a tax on capital income is a natural decentralization of this wedge.

The decentralization of the endowment economy of Section 3.1 has been studied by Jeske (2006) and Wright (2006) in an environment in which heterogeneous private agents insure endowment risk with each other and with foreign financial markets. These authors assume complete enforcement of financial contracts signed by two domestic agents, but limited enforcement of private international contracts. If a private agent defaults on a foreign debt commitment, the agent retains access to domestic financial markets. This is a weak punishment, as the agent can use other domestic agents (and their continued access to foreign financial markets) to insure its endowment shocks, and in this sense the incentives to deviate are greater for an individual agent than they are for a benevolent government that is punished by aggregate financial autarky. Jeske (2006) shows that the undistorted competitive equilibrium is not efficient. Wright (2006) shows that a subsidy to foreign borrowing can be used to decentralize the constrained efficient allocation. The need for a subsidy reflects the fact that the competitive equilibrium's inefficiency stems from debt constraints that are too tight. By making repayment less burdensome, a subsidy to foreign debt allows the individual to increase its borrowing from abroad. This, plus complete and fully enforced domestic asset markets, allows the individuals to achieve the constrained efficient allocation in a competitive equilibrium.

4. RICHER NOTIONS OF "DEFAULT"

A drawback of the benchmark model is the modeling of "default." In fact, there are two concepts in the model that could be interpreted as default. In the terminology of Grossman and Van Huyck (1988), there is excusable default as well as repudiation (or inexcusable default). Repudiation is what occurs off the equilibrium path and delivers utility $\underline{V}(s')$. Excusable default is when a state-contingent payment is made, which Grossman and Van Huyck (1988) interpret as a partial default and state-contingent haircut. In this section, we enrich both concepts. In regard to inexcusable default, we can observe a severing of the creditor–debtor relationship in equilibrium by introducing unobservable shocks to the outside option $\underline{V}$. Regarding the notion of excusable default and haircuts, a literature is developing on generating haircuts endogenously after a non-trivial bargaining problem. We review some of the key concepts in Section 4.2.

4.1. Equilibrium Default

In the benchmark model, insurance contracts are rich enough that there is never a severing of a risk-sharing relationship in equilibrium. In practice, we do see periods of limited access to international financial markets after a failure to make a scheduled payment. As noted above, one interpretation of the fully contingent set of contracts is a reduced form of incomplete contracts combined with state-contingent renegotiation. In the next subsection, we take up renegotiation more formally. In this subsection, we consider an environment where markets are incomplete because some shocks are not observable, which can generate an endogenous separation between creditors and debtors.

Specifically, assume that there are unobservable (to lenders) shocks that enter as arguments to the outside option $\underline{V}$. Such an environment has been explored in the corporate context by Cooley et al. (2004) and in a general setting in Hopenhayn and Werning (2008). Let s_t denote the shock to productivity as before, and introduce z_t as a shock to the deviation utility that is not observable by foreign creditors. The unobserved shock could represent the economy's vulnerability to direct sanctions or financial autarky (e.g., the vulnerability of the domestic banking system to sovereign default), which is known to the government but not to lenders, or the political consequences the incumbent faces in deciding whether to repay or deviate (e.g., the political consequences of the wealth transfers stemming from default). In this subsection, we use the term default to be synonymous with opting for the deviation utility $\underline{V}$ to highlight the precise notion of default we have in mind.

The environment follows that of the benchmark endowment economy. Let s_t index the endowment, which for simplicity we assume to be *iid* and drawn from a discrete set S. Let z denote an *iid* continuous random variable that is independent of s and has support Z. Let $\underline{V} : Z \times S \rightarrow \mathbb{R}$ denote the value of deviation as a function of the outside option shock and the endowment shock, which we assume is strictly increasing in both arguments. Conditional on s, the variable z indexes the government's outside option for default. Inverting this mapping, let $F_s(v) = \Pr\{\underline{V}(z, s) \leq v | s\}$ denote the probability that the realized z is such that $\underline{V}(z, s) \leq v$ conditional on s, and let $f_s(v) = F'_s(v)$. This problem is relatively tractable given that z affects the outside option only and therefore is not something that can be credibly revealed absent separation. The problem of unobserved shocks that directly influence payoffs within the creditor–debtor relationship is treated, for example, by Atkeson (1991), Tsyrennikov (2012), and Dovis (2012) in the sovereign debt context, and by Clementi and Hopenhayn (2006), DeMarzo and Fishman (2007), and Quadrini (2004) in the corporate bond context.

We write the problem recursively, letting the utility of the representative foreign creditor be the objective function and the utility of the debtor be the state variable. In particular, let $B(v)$ denote the expected net present value of payments to the creditor(s) conditional on the debtor enjoying utility greater than or equal to v, prior to the realization of today's shocks. This "inverts" the government's strictly decreasing value function that maps promised debt payments into discounted utility. We assume that $\beta R = 1$. The timing of default is that the decision is made after observing s and z, but before receiving transfers from financial markets:

$$B(v) = \max_{\{v(s),c(s),w(s)\}} \sum_s \pi(s) F_s(v(s)) \Big(y(s) - c(s) + \beta B(w(s)) \Big)$$

subject to:

$$\sum_s \pi(s) \left(F_s(v(s)) v(s) + \int_{v(s)}^{\infty} \tilde{v} dF_s(\tilde{v}) \right) = v, \tag{9}$$

$$u(c(s)) + \beta w(s) = v(s). \tag{10}$$

Equation (9) is a "promise keeping" constraint that ensures that the debtor receives v in expectation. Equation (10) reflects that we have broken up the problem into choosing state-contingent utility $v(s)$, and then allocating that utility over consumption today $c(s)$ and future promises $w(s)$ for notational convenience. Note the creditor receives net payments $y(s) - c(s)$ only if the government decides not to default in that state, and receives zero otherwise. Therefore payments are discounted by $F_s(v(s))$ in each state. Note also that the concavity of the problem is not guaranteed without suitable assumptions on $F_s(v)$.

Let us assume the support Z is such that $\underline{V}(z, s) \le u(y(s)) + \beta \sum_{s'} \pi(s') u(y(s')) / (1 - \beta)$ for all z, s.[14] Under this assumption, in an efficient allocation, if $y(s) - c(s) + \beta B(w(s)) \le 0$, then $F_s(v(s)) = 1$: that is, if the country in state s expects to receive a positive net present value from abroad, then it will not default, independent of the realization of the shock z.

We proceed now under the premise that $B(v)$ is differentiable and the optimum is characterized by first-order conditions. Let μ denote the multiplier on the promise-keeping constraint and $\pi(s)\gamma(s)$ on the $v(s)$ constraints.[15] The first-order conditions for

---

[14] This assumption can be interpreted as stating that the variation in the outside option is due to a random non-negative cost of default in addition to financial autarky.

[15] In the present context, promise keeping can be written as an inequality constraint, as the creditor can always choose to deliver more without violating the other aspects of the problem. This ensures the multipliers are non-negative.

$v(s)$, $c(s)$, and $w(s)$, considering the cases where $F_s(v(s)) \in (0, 1)$, are:

$$f_s(v(s))\Big(\gamma(s) - c(s) + \beta B(w(s))\Big) = -F_s(v(s))\mu + \gamma(s)$$

$$F_s(v(s)) = u'(c(s))\gamma(s)$$

$$-F_s(v(s))B'(w(s)) = \gamma(s).$$

The envelope condition is $B'(v) = -\mu$. Combining conditions and rearranging gives:

$$\frac{1}{u'(c(s^{t-1}, s))} - \frac{1}{u'(c(s^{t-1}))} = \frac{f_s(v(s^{t-1}, s))}{F_s(v(s^{t-1}, s))}\Big(\gamma(s^{t-1}, s) - c(s^{t-1}, s) + \beta B(w(s^{t-1}, s))\Big),$$

(11)

for all states s and all histories s^{t-1}. In the equation above, we have used the condition that $-B'(w(s)) = 1/u'(c(s))$ in period t and $t-1$. The left-hand side is the distortion to consumption smoothing; absent distortions from limited commitment, this should be zero as $\beta R = 1$. On the right-hand side is the benefit from reducing the probability of default at the margin. The first term is the elasticity of the probability of default with respect to promised utility, and this is multiplied by discounted net payments promised to creditors. In states in which this term is positive (that is, states s in which the country is a debtor and defaults with positive probability), there is an incentive to have $c(s^{t-1}, s) > c(s^{t-1})$. That is, there is an incentive to distort consumption to reduce default at the margin, and in particular to shift consumption toward states when the probability of default is particularly elastic and net repayments are particularly large. Note that in states where the country is a saver, then, as discussed above, the country does not default for any z, and thus consumption is constant: $c(s^{t-1}, s) = c(s^{t-1})$. The resulting pattern of increasing consumption is similar to the benchmark model: the economy has an incentive to pay down its debt and increase consumption over time. Moreover, the option to default distorts risk-sharing across endowment states. In contrast to the benchmark model, there will be default with positive probability and the probability of default is greater when debt is high. While under suitable assumptions it is the case that default is more likely when $\gamma(s)$ is particularly low,[16] the independent shock z weakens the correlation between output and default, consistent with the empirical facts that default is more likely in recessions, but occurs with some probability in booms as well.

4.2. Renegotiation

One of the drawbacks of the benchmark model is the treatment of the default *process*. As noted above, several papers have motivated a complete-markets asset structure with

---

[16] For example, assume $\underline{V}(z, s)$ depends only on z and $f(v)/F(v)$ is weakly decreasing in v. Assuming $B(v)$ is concave, differentiation of (11) implies that $v(s)$ is increasing in $\gamma(s)$, or that $F(v(s))$ is decreasing in $\gamma(s)$. The assumption that the outside option is independent of $\gamma(s)$ is extreme, but the intuition that imperfect risk-sharing combined with incomplete markets generates default in bad states will reappear in the quantitative models discussed in Section 6.

default and partial repayment, as in the papers of Grossman and Van Huyck (1988) and Bulow and Rogoff (1989a). While useful as foundations for rich risk-sharing possibilities implemented with non-contingent contracts, they do not speak to the delays observed in actual default episodes. The bargaining models of Fernandez and Rosenthal (1990) and Yue (2010), while generating many useful insights in regard to risk sharing and debt dynamics, have limited implications for endogenous delay in equilibrium. As noted in the empirical review (Section 2), the average default episode lasts eight years, calling for a richer model of debt renegotiation.

We briefly review some of the recent contributions in regard to sovereign debt renegotiation. The models of Bi (2008a) and Benjamin and Wright (2008) share the emphasis on limited commitment that we emphasized in the benchmark model, but also emphasize the role of incomplete markets. In their framework, the creditor and debtor bargain over the surplus of the relationship. As in our benchmark environment, limited commitment prevents the debtor from fully pledging future income. However, in the benchmark, the debtor could make state-contingent promises that were self enforcing, allowing it to credibly pledge more in high states. In a state-contingent world, there is no incentive to delay negotiation until after output shocks are realized, as all payments can be made contingent on the histories of shocks. In the absence of state-contingent assets, the debtor can only pledge a non-contingent amount. In an incomplete-markets environment, there is therefore an incentive to delay. In particular, the parties would like to delay until expectations of future output are high in order to credibly pledge these endowment streams.[17,18]

Sovereign debt typically involves multiple creditors, and particularly so when debt takes the form of bonds rather than bank loans, which is the recent trend. Renegotiation of debt therefore requires some level of coordination among creditors. The difficulty involved with coordination may raise the costs of renegotiation and prolong debt restructuring. Pitchford and Wright (2012) show that there is an incentive to hold out in debt negotiations, as the last to agree to a settlement has disproportionately large bargaining power due to its ability to veto the entire settlement. Limited commitment plays a role here as well, as the borrower cannot commit to treat hold outs more harshly than those that settle early. Pitchford and Wright (2012) argue that this incentive to hold out can create delays in debt restructuring. One proposed solution to such hold outs is collective-action

---

[17] Both Bi (2008a) and Benjamin and Wright (2008) have a rich model of the bargaining process, including stochastic variation in bargaining power, and both papers include a quantitative evaluation of the respective model's ability to match key empirical facts. The Benjamin and Wright (2008) model also predicts the evolution of debt during the restructuring process.

[18] An additional explanation for why debt renegotiations or default durations are prolonged is that the parties have asymmetric information. Two recent papers in this regard are D'Erasmo (2011) and Bai and Zhang (2012). Cole et al. (1995) present a model in which the government's type is not observable and varies over time; to signal a switch to a relatively patient government, a payment is made and the country exits default. A similar spirit but a different application than renegotiation underlies Sandleris (2008), in which the decision not to default is a signal regarding the government's private information on the health of the economy.

clauses (CAC's), in which restructuring can be implemented by a sub-set of bondholders (usually a super-majority). Pitchford and Wright (2012) show somewhat paradoxically that this may serve to increase delay, as negotiation is costly and with only a subset of bondholders required for settlement, there is an incentive to free ride on negotiation costs.

Bolton and Jeanne (2007) and Bolton and Jeanne (2009) analyze CAC's with an eye toward ex ante efficiency. Making settlement more costly raises ex post restructuring costs, but may ease ex ante incentive problems. In particular, difficult restructuring may induce a borrower to repay when it otherwise would default. Thus an ex post inefficient restructuring process may ease the fundamental inefficiency due to limited commitment. However, Bolton and Jeanne show that this mechanism must be used with care as it may be taken one step too far. In particular, there is an individual incentive for one or a group of creditors to make their bonds relatively hard to restructure; this is particularly relevant in a dynamic setting as the government is tempted to dilute existing bondholders by issuing harder-to-restructure new bonds. This could make some bonds de facto senior to other issues, as bonds that are more difficult to restructure have a greater chance for repayment. In equilibrium, this externality generates bond issues that are excessively difficult to renegotiate, potentially lowering ex ante welfare.

5. SELF-FULFILLING DEBT CRISES

In the benchmark model of Section 3 we characterized efficient equilibria; that is, we solved a planning problem subject to a break-even constraint for creditors and capital owners. However, that model often admits other equilibria which are not on the constrained Pareto frontier. The multiplicity of equilibria raises the possibility of self-fulfilling debt crises in which agents "switch" to a Pareto-inferior equilibrium.

We illustrate the possibility of self-fulfilling crises in a simple, two-period model and then discuss extensions to a dynamic setting. Consider a small open economy with constant tradable output endowment y. There are two periods $t = 1, 2$, with preferences given by $u(c_1) + \beta u(c_2)$. Let $\beta = R^{-1}$, so that the government discounts at the world interest rate.

The country begins period one with outstanding liabilities b. The timing is as follows[19]: the government begins the first period by issuing new bonds b' to competitive bondholders with discount factor $\beta = R^{-1}$, given an equilibrium price schedule $q : \mathbb{R} \to \mathbb{R}_+$. While the government takes the schedule q as given, it chooses new debt issuances b' internalizing the shape of the price schedule. After selling the newly issued bonds, the

---

[19] We have followed the timing introduced by Cole and Kehoe (2000), which is different from the timing usually assumed in the quantitative literature discussed in Section 6. In Cole and Kehoe, the price schedule is offered before the government makes its default decision, while the typical assumption in the quantitative literature is that the price schedule is offered after the government makes its within-period default decision. The key distinction is whether the price schedule (that is, the price as a function of newly issued debt, b') is conditional or unconditional on non-default within the period.

country decides to repay or not the legacy debt b. Failure to pay the legacy debt sends the country into financial autarky, where it faces a reduction in endowment of amount τ every period. In particular, default in period one yields value:

$$\underline{V}(q(b')b') = u(y - \tau + q(b')b') + \beta u(y - \tau).$$

Note that the timing assumption implies that the government retains the money raised by new bond issues $q(b')b'$ whether or not it defaults in the first period. In the second period, if the government has previously defaulted it simply consumes $y - \tau$. If the country did not default in the first period, it decides whether to repay b'; that is, it chooses the maximum of repayment consumption $y - b'$ and default consumption $y - \tau$.

To summarize the optimal default decision let $D_2 : \mathbb{R} \to \{0, 1\}$ be the policy function for default in period 2. Specifically, $D_2(b') = 1$ if $b' > \tau$, and equals 0 otherwise. Let $D_1 : \mathbb{R} \times \mathbb{R} \times Q \to \{0, 1\}$ be the policy function for default in period 1 conditional on new debt b', legacy debt b, and the equilibrium price schedule $q \in Q$, where Q is the set of functions mapping $\mathbb{R}$ into $\mathbb{R}_+$[20]:

$$D_1(b'; b, q) = \begin{cases} 1 \text{ if } u(y + q(b')b' - b) + \beta u \left(y - (1 - D_2(b'))b' - D_2(b')\tau \right) < \underline{V}(q(b')b') \\ 0 \text{ otherwise.} \end{cases}$$

We define equilibrium as follows:

Definition 2. An equilibrium given initial debt b is a price schedule, q, default policy functions D_1 and D_2, and a debt choice b^* such that:

(i) Given b and q, D_1 and D_2 are defined by the government's optimal default decision for each b';

(ii) Given b and q and the optimal default policies, the government chooses new debt optimally:

$$b^* = \underset{b'}{\operatorname{argmax}} \left\{ (1 - D_1(b'; b, q))u(y + q(b')b' - b) + D_1(b'; b, q)u(y + q(b')b' - \tau) \right.$$
$$\left. + \beta(1 - D_1(b'; b, q)D_2(b'))u(y - b') + \beta D_1(b'; q, b)D_2(b')u(y - \tau) \right\};$$

(iii) Given D_1 and D_2, q satisfies $q(b') = \beta(1 - D(b'; b, q))$ for all b', where $D \equiv D_1 \times D_2$.

The first condition of equilibrium states that the government makes its default decision in order to maximize utility, whether default occurs in the first period or second, and this decision is made after new debt issuances b'. The second condition states that the government chooses new debt optimally. Note that at the time it issues new debt in the

---

[20] To streamline the exposition, we do not formally limit the debt domain to ensure consumption is non-negative (that is, $b' \le y$ and $b - q(b')b' \le y$). It should be understood that default will be chosen over negative consumption. This decision may be relevant in equilibrium if $b > y$ and the government cannot issue new debt at a positive price, making default its only feasible option.

first period, the government cannot commit to a default decision for that period, and so recognizes that default will be chosen optimally ex post. The third condition states that investors break even for any bond issuance b'. The fact that condition three holds for all b' implies equilibrium satisfies a perfection requirement; that is, even if the government chose a sub-optimal level of debt, investors break even.

The following proposition states that the model can have multiple equilibria:

Proposition 1 (Self-Fulfilling Debt Crises). *Let $\underline{b}$ be the unique value such that $u(y - \underline{b}) + \beta u(y) = (1 + \beta)u(y - \tau)$. Let $\bar{b}$ be the unique value such that*

$$(1 + \beta)u\left(y - \frac{\bar{b}}{1 + \beta}\right) = u\left(y - \tau + \frac{\beta \bar{b}}{1 + \beta}\right) + \beta u(y - \tau).$$

If $b \in (\underline{b}, \bar{b}]$, then there exists at least two equilibria, one of them with $q(b') = 0$ for all b', and another one with an equilibrium schedule such that $q(b/(1 + \beta)) = \beta$.

This proposition captures the concept of a self-fulfilling debt crisis. A price schedule $q(b') = 0$ for all b' is one in which lenders are unwilling to purchase bonds of any amount. That is, the government is unable to issue new bonds and existing bond holders demand immediate repayment. For $b > \underline{b}$, we have that $u(y - b) + \beta u(y) < (1 + \beta)u(y - \tau)$, and so the government's best response to such a roll-over crisis is to default (for any b'), and this confirms the zero price. On the other hand, there is an equilibrium which supports positive lending up to $\bar{b}$. In particular, if lenders were willing to buy new bonds and $b \leq \bar{b} < \tau(1 + \beta)$, then the government would prefer to issue new bonds and then repay outstanding debt as long as it can issue $b' = b/(1 + \beta)$ at the price $q(b') = \beta$ and outstanding debt is below $\bar{b}$. Issuing $b' = b/(1 + \beta)$ at a price of β implements the full-commitment solution and delivers a utility that favors repayment over default. Hence, the solution in part (iii) would be $b^\star = b/(1 + \beta)$. The price schedule q can be extended to off-equilibrium debt issuances such that equilibrium conditions (i) and (ii) hold.

In this manner, we can construct two equilibria with distinct price schedules and that generate distinct equilibrium allocations, as long as initial debt $b \in (\underline{b}, \bar{b}]$. In particular, one equilibrium features an inability to roll-over debt and an immediate default, while the other features the ability to issue new bonds and avoid default. In this range of initial debt, the government is vulnerable to self-fulfilling expectations about its willingness to repay. Proposition 1 does not guarantee that $\underline{b} < \bar{b}$, so the relevant region for multiple equilibria may not always exist. However, there exists a $\tau^* < y$ such that if $\tau \in (\tau^*, y)$, then $\underline{b} < \bar{b}$.[21]

An important point is that while the government is vulnerable for $b > \underline{b}$, a price schedule of zero is not an equilibrium if $b \leq \underline{b}$. That is, if initial debt is low enough, the government is not subject to self-fulfilling crises. While b is a primitive in the two-period

---

[21] To see this, note that $\bar{b} < \tau(1 + \beta)$ and that $\bar{b}$ is increasing in $\tau \in [0, y)$, which can be seen from the definition of $\bar{b}$. Note also that $\underline{b} \leq y$. Define τ^* so that $\underline{b} = y$, which from the definition of $\underline{b}$ must be strictly less than y. Therefore, for $\tau \in (\tau^*, y)$ we have $\bar{b} > y > \underline{b}$.

model, in a fully dynamic model debt levels are endogenous state variables. Cole and Kehoe (2000) build a dynamic equilibrium model that embeds the above analysis. One important modeling device is that as long as the government's liability position lies in the range where a self-fulling crisis is possible, then there exists a constant and strictly positive probability that such a crisis occurs. A main result of their analysis is that the government has an incentive to save its way out of the crisis zone $(\underline{b}, \overline{b}]$. That is, the government responds to the vulnerability to self-fulfilling debt crises by reducing its debt.[22]

A number of extensions to the Cole and Kehoe model have been made in the recent literature. Consea and Kehoe (2011) allow shocks to income. In particular, they suppose the economy is in recession and faces a constant hazard of recovery. In this case, saving exacerbates the consumption impact of the recession and the government may opt to remain in the crisis zone hoping that a recovery occurs before a debt crisis. They refer to this as "gambling for redemption."

A second extension concerns nominal bonds. The option to inflate away the real value of nominal debt provides an alternative to outright default in the event of a debt crisis. Aguiar et al. (2012) show that issuing nominal bonds has an ambiguous effect on vulnerability to a self-fulfilling debt crisis. Specifically, if the government's commitment to low inflation is high absent a crisis, then nominal bonds have a desirable state-contingent feature; in good times, the real return is high, while in the event of a crisis, the government inflates away part of the real value of the bonds. As creditors prefer partial repayment to outright default, the ability to respond with inflation generates a superior outcome to real bonds. However, if the commitment to low inflation is weak even in good times, the government loses the state-contingency potentially allowed by nominal bonds. In particular, the government has a temptation to inflate ex post even in normal times, and this will be reflected in lower bond prices (or higher interest rates) ex ante, making repayment that much more burdensome. This effect may be large enough to dominate, generating a larger crisis zone for nominal bonds. Aguiar et al. (2012) use this fact to rationalize why many emerging markets with weak inflationary regimes issue bonds in foreign currency, while economies like the U.S., the U.K., and Japan issue large amounts of domestic currency bonds at low nominal interest rates and seemingly without risk of self-fulfilling crises.

Chatterjee and Eyigungor (2012b) quantitatively explore the benefit of long-maturity bonds in an environment prone to self-fulfilling crises. The paper contrasts the temptation to dilute existing bond holders in an incomplete-markets setting (a point discussed in detail in the next section) with the protection long-maturity bonds provide from rollover crises. The calibrated model of Chatterjee and Eyigungor (2012b) indicates that even a small likelihood of a rollover crisis implies that a country would seek to limit its short-term debt to the point where the probability of a rollover crisis is endogenously reduced

---

[22] The one caveat to this result is if initial debt is so large that the transition to $\underline{b}$ may be long enough that the government is better off remaining in the crisis zone indefinitely.

to a small value. Moreover, the use of long-maturity bonds, despite the costs rising from debt dilution, reduces the reliance of debt reduction as the optimal response to potential rollover crises.

6. INCOMPLETE-MARKET MODELS AND THEIR QUANTITATIVE IMPLEMENTATION

In this section, we discuss how well models of sovereign debt perform quantitatively as well as some additional conceptual issues that arise in models of incomplete markets. The primary paradigm for quantitative analysis is the model of Eaton and Gersovitz (1982). In particular, a small open-economy trades a non-contingent bond in order to insure itself against endowment or productivity shocks. The only state contingency spanned by the asset markets is through the option to default.

We first introduce a simple version of the model and then discuss some of the extensions in the literature. The model follows early quantitative versions of the Eaton-Gersovitz model explored by Aguiar and Gopinath (2006), Arellano (2008), and Hamann (2002).

Consider a small open economy that has a stochastic endowment stream y_t, which follows a Markov process. The government has preferences given by (1) and trades a one-period bond with risk neutral investors. Time is discrete and the timing within a period is as follows. At the start of period t, the government has outstanding liabilities b_t. It observes the endowment shock y_t and then decides whether to repay b_t or default. If it defaults, it enjoys deviation utility $\underline{V}(y_t)$ to be defined below. If it repays, it issues new bonds b_{t+1} at price $q(b_{t+1}, y_t)$. The price of a bond is a stationary function of outstanding debt and the current endowment shock. As discussed in Section 5, the literature has different timing conventions regarding whether new bonds are auctioned before or after the current period default decision is made. The standard assumption in the quantitative debt literature is that the bond price schedule is contingent on no default in the current period.

Let $V^{ND}(b, y)$ denote the value of choosing to repay its debts when it starts the period with an amount of debt b and an income y:

$$V^{ND}(b, y) = \max_{b'} \left\{ u(y + q(b')b' - b) + \beta \mathbb{E}[V(b', y')|y] \right\} \tag{12}$$

and $b'(b, y)$ denotes an associated optimal debt-issuance policy.

Let $\underline{V}(y)$ be the value of default, conditional of the current income value y:

$$\underline{V}(y) = u((1 - \tau)y) + (1 - \lambda)\beta\mathbb{E}[\underline{V}(y')|y] + \lambda\beta\mathbb{E}[V(0, y')|y]. \tag{13}$$

Then, $V(b, y)$, the government's value function at the start of the period conditional on outstanding debt due b and current endowment shock y, is the maximum of $V^{ND}(b, y)$

and the default value $\underline{V}(y)$:

$$V(b, y) = \max_{D \in [0,1]} \{(1 - D)V^{ND}(b, y) + D \times \underline{V}(y)\} \tag{14}$$

and $D(b, y)$ denotes an associated optimal default policy. Note that neither $b'(b, y)$ nor $D(b, y)$ may be uniquely defined.

A few things to note in the definition of $\underline{V}$. First, the economy is excluded from asset markets in the period of default and suffers a loss in output τy. This is designed to capture direct sanctions and other output consequences from default. In equation (13), the loss is proportional to output, which is the formulation used by Aguiar and Gopinath (2006). Arellano (2008) allows τ to vary with the level of the endowment according to a function $\tau(y)$. A second feature of equation (13) is that with probability $\lambda \in [0, 1)$, the country can regain access to financial markets, starting anew with a clean credit rating and zero debt. This is a reduced form for the default process discussed in Section 4. In the simplest quantitative models, the haircut is set at one hundred percent so the country emerges with zero debt.

A few further remarks on the direct costs τ are in order. At a conceptual level, debt can be sustained in equilibrium through financial exclusion alone, as shown by Eaton and Gersovitz (1982). As a quantitative matter, the amount of debt that can be supported by the threat of financial autarky is relatively small in this benchmark economy. This is related to the fact that in a closed-economy representative-agent model, aggregate consumption fluctuations at business cycle frequencies have relatively small welfare implications, a point made using a simple numerical example by Lucas (1987). Aguiar and Gopinath (2006) extend the Lucas example to show that financial autarky is not a harsh punishment in a small open endowment economy, and thus very little debt is sustainable in equilibrium. A second point is that the output costs of default may depend on the level of output. This is the formulation proposed by Arellano (2008). While default provides a crude form of state contingency, as described in previous sections there is a fair amount of contingency built into the renegotiation process. A simple way to incorporate this into an otherwise incomplete-markets environment is to assume that default is punished (disproportionately) less severely if it occurs in low-output states. Finally, a recent paper by Mendoza and Yue (2012) endogenizes the link between the state-contingent output costs of default and the reputational costs of financial autarky using a model of trade credit.

The break-even constraint for risk neutral lenders is

$$q(b', y) = \frac{\mathbb{E}[1 - D(b', y')|y]}{R}. \tag{15}$$

Let us define an equilibrium:

Definition 3. A recursive equilibrium is a price schedule $q(b', y)$, value functions $V(b, y)$, $V^{ND}(b, y)$, and $\underline{V}(y)$, and policy functions $b'(b, y)$ and $D(b, y)$ such that: (i) the government optimizes given the price schedule, that is $\underline{V}(y)$, $V(b, y)$, $V^{ND}(b, y)$ solve equations (12), (13), and (14) and b' and D are the resulting policy functions; and (ii) creditors earn R in expectation given the government's equilibrium policy functions, that is, equation (15) holds.

The quantitative literature typically computes an equilibrium as follows. For clarity, assume that $\lambda = 0$, so that default leads to permanent financial autarky. Note that the value function $V^{ND}(b, y)$ depends on the bond-price schedule q via the budget constraint. In fact, V^{ND} is weakly increasing in q for all b and y. When $\lambda = 0$, $\underline{V}(y)$ is independent of q. Therefore, $V^{ND}(b, y) - \underline{V}$ is weakly increasing in q. We can construct an equilibrium by iterating on the following operator. Let $B = [\underline{b}, \overline{b}]$ denote the state space of debt and Y the state space of y. Define the operator T on the space of functions that map $B \times Y \to [0, R^{-1}]$ by:

$$Tq = \frac{\mathbb{E}_y \left(1 - \chi_{\{V^{ND}(b, y; q) < \underline{V}(y)\}}\right)}{R}, \tag{16}$$

where we make the dependence of V^{ND} on q explicit. As the indicator function $\chi_{\{V^{ND}(b, y; q) < \underline{V}(y)\}}$ is weakly decreasing in q, if $q \geq q'$ then $Tq \geq Tq'$. Thus the operator is monotone. As $q \leq \frac{1}{1+r^*}$, the typical algorithm starts with this upper bound and iterates on the operator until convergence to a fixed point.[23] If $\lambda > 0$, then the analysis is complicated by the fact that $\underline{V}(b)$ depends on q through the re-entry value function V. As a computational matter, the algorithm can still be used to search for a solution, although the monotonicity of the operator is not guaranteed.

While straightforward to compute, the model yields few analytical insights without further restrictions. The value function V is the maximum of two other value functions and in general is not concave or differentiable. However, some intuition for the quantitative results can be obtained by stripping the model down to a two-period decision problem. In particular, assume the country owes b and has endowment y in the current period, and chooses b' to be repaid in the second period. Let $F(y')$ denote the cdf of next period's endowment conditional on y, which takes values in $[\underline{y}, \overline{y}]$. In the second period, the government can repay the debt and enjoy utility $u(y' - b')$, or default and enjoy utility $u((1 - \tau)y')$. The country will default if $b' > \tau y$.

The government's problem in the first period is:

$$\max_{b'} u(y + q(b')b' - b) + \beta \int_{\underline{y}}^{\frac{b'}{\tau}} u((1 - \tau)y')dF(y') + \beta \int_{\frac{b'}{\tau}}^{\overline{y}} u(y' - b')dF(y'). \tag{17}$$

The first-order condition is:

$$u'(c) \left(q(b') + q'(b')b'\right) = \beta \int_{\frac{b'}{\tau}}^{\overline{y}} u'(y' - b')dF(y'), \tag{18}$$

---

[23] For more on computational algorithms, see Hatchondo et al. (2010).

where $c = y + q(b')b' - b$. The default decision implies an equilibrium price schedule:

$$q(b') = \frac{1 - F\left(\frac{b'}{\tau}\right)}{R}. \tag{19}$$

Using this and rearranging the government's first-order condition gives:

$$u'(c) \left(1 + \frac{q'(b')b'}{q(b')}\right) = \beta R \mathbb{E}\left\{u'(y' - b')dF(y')|b' \leq \tau y\right\}, \tag{20}$$

where the expectation is conditional on not defaulting. The right-hand side is the expected marginal cost of repaying the debt conditional on repayment, discounted by relative impatience. The left-hand side is the marginal value of an additional unit of debt inclusive of the price effect; that is, the marginal utility of consumption times one plus the elasticity of the bond-price schedule with respect to new debt. The elasticity of the bond price reflects that the government internalizes the effect of new debt issues on the price it faces. This elasticity is non-positive, and the greater in magnitude the less the government is willing to borrow at the margin.

If the bond-price schedule is very elastic, the government has a strong desire to save (or not borrow). This is the same effect discussed in Section 5 to describe why the government saves its way out of the crisis zone in a model of self-fulfilling debt crises. While in the current context we consider a single equilibrium price schedule, the fact that this schedule may be elastic provides the same incentive to save.

To replicate debt levels high enough to induce frequent default in this basic framework, calibration typically involves βR significantly below one. This counters the incentive to save in response to limited commitment and generates realistic debt levels. A motivation for this assumption is that the governmental decision maker is relatively impatient due to political turnover.

Moreover, the elasticity is sensitive to the "marginal" probability of default as well as the "average." In particular, the elasticity of the price schedule can be written

$$\frac{q'(b')b'}{q(b')} = \frac{-f\left(\frac{b'}{\tau}\right)\frac{b'}{\tau}}{1 - F\left(\frac{b'}{\tau}\right)}, \tag{21}$$

where $f(y') = F'(y')$. A high probability of default implies a small denominator, reflecting a large average probability of default $F(b'/\tau)$. The numerator reflects the pdf at the debt level under consideration. If the variance of y' is relatively high (or the pdf has a fat lower tail), there is substantial mass below the key threshold, lowering the ratio of marginal to average. Therefore, volatility generates more frequent default. Aguiar and Gopinath (2006) build on the empirical work of Aguiar and Gopinath (2007) to argue that emerging markets have large shocks to the trend growth rates, which raises the probability of default in equilibrium. This rationalizes why volatility in trend growth and frequency of default occur together in an economy.

As noted above, Arellano (2008) generates plausible default probabilities by introducing state-contingent punishments; that is, having τ depend on the realization of y'. This makes default more responsive to output shocks and therefore relatively less responsive to outstanding debt, lowering the elasticity of the bond-price schedule as well as making non-contingent debt more attractive as an insurance option. Such a nonlinear output cost has been derived endogenously by Mendoza and Yue (2012).

An important property of the bond-price elasticity in the benchmark dynamic setting with persistent shocks is that it may vary with the output shock. In particular, the quantitative models of Aguiar and Gopinath (2006) and Arellano (2008) generate a counter-cyclical net export process. That is, when endowment is low and absent default, the economy is a net saver on average. This undermines risk-sharing, which in an endowment economy calls for net inflows in low-income states. The reason this occurs is that the costs of borrowing on average (q) and at the margin ($|q'|$) are counter-cyclical, providing a relatively strong incentive to reduce debt in low-endowment states.

Note that the above example implied default in the final period if $b' > \tau y$; that is, the government defaults in low endowment states conditional on debt. It may be tempting to conclude that the fully dynamic quantitative models generate default in bad states solely due to the fact that the output cost is increasing in endowment. Although this is true in the final-period default decision in our example (and is an important contributing mechanism in the quantitative models), the loss of access to credit markets is also relevant in dynamic quantitative models. In particular, concavity of u implies that the marginal burden of net repayment of debt is higher the smaller the current endowment, all else equal. Arellano (2008) uses this insight in an infinite horizon environment with *iid* shocks to show that if default is optimal for an endowment y, it will also be optimal for $y' < y$, holding debt constant. Note that default occurs only if the country cannot generate a net inflow by borrowing (otherwise, it could consume more by borrowing, and then default the next period), and it is the burden of net repayment that is more costly in low endowment states. The fact that a country may be required to make a net payment even in the lowest endowment states reflects the incompleteness of the asset markets. Conversely, for a high-endowment shock, the desire to smooth consumption by paying down debt (or increasing assets) makes default less attractive, as default prevents carrying the high endowment into the future via asset markets. The implications under persistent shocks are muddied by the fact that the endowment realization also influences the bond prices going forward; nevertheless, in the calibrated models popular in the literature, the consistent prediction is that conditional on b there is a threshold endowment above which the country repays and below which the country defaults.

While the calibrated models of Aguiar and Gopinath (2006) and Arellano (2008) provide quantitative insights regarding which economies may be prone to default and why, the simplicity of the models cannot address many of the facts discussed in Section 2. Filling these gaps is an active area of current research. We briefly summarize several innovations. Yue (2010) quantifies a model of one-shot renegotiation, capturing the fact that default begins a bargaining process that leads to partial repayment. Benjamin and Wright (2008) calibrate the dynamic bargaining model discussed in Section 4, matching the key empirical relationships between length of default and subsequent repayment.

The single shock model cannot explain why default may occur in relatively good times (*conditional* on debt levels), as it sometimes does in practice. Cuadra and Sapriza (2008) and Hatchondo et al. (2009) introduce political uncertainty with heterogeneous potential incumbents as an additional source of volatility, similar in spirit to the model of Cole et al. (1995). A hybrid of the Cole et al. model and the Grossman and Van Huyck (1988) complete-markets model is quantified in Alfaro and Kanczuk (2005). The additional shocks, particular to the discount factor, generate a more empirically plausible level of debt and default, highlighting the tension between political economy distortions and the incentive to save in response to limited commitment.

A series of recent papers have relaxed the one-period bond assumption by considering instead bonds with longer maturities, and have shown that the introduction of longer maturities significantly improves the quantitative properties of the models. Hatchondo and Martinez (2009) and Chatterjee and Eyigungor (2012b) replace single-period bonds with bonds of longer duration in a tractable manner.[24] In particular, Hatchondo and Martinez (2009) assume bonds pay a geometrically declining sequence of coupons $(1, \delta, \delta^2, \dots)$ indefinitely, while Chatterjee and Eyigungor (2012b) adapt a "perpetual youth" framework to bonds, assuming that a bond matures next period with constant hazard $\lambda = 1 - \delta$. A law of large numbers assumption generates a predictable stream of aggregate payments given the stock of outstanding bonds. The parameters δ and λ are primitives of the environment and do not vary over time. Either modeling approach renders bond maturity a stationary variable, allowing for longer durations without having bonds issued in different periods carrying heterogeneous maturities.

The equilibrium bond-price schedule in this framework is no longer characterized by the simple operator (16). In particular, the return to a bond depends on whether the government defaults, as in (16), but in addition depends on the price of bonds next period absent default. This reflects the capital gain or loss a bond holder experiences over the life span of the bond. Chatterjee and Eyigungor (2012b) discuss issues related to existence and computability of an equilibrium in this environment.[25]

A key element of the long-maturity framework is that non-maturing bonds that were issued in previous periods are subject to dilution. That is, existing bond holders will take a capital loss on their bonds if the government's subsequent decisions raise the probability

---

[24] For an earlier quantitative model of maturities see Bi (2008b).

[25] For an alternative approach at dealing with the computational issues that arise in sovereign debt models, see Pouzo and Presno (2012).

of future default. The government lacks commitment regarding future bond issuance and bond holders are assumed to lack a mechanism with which to punish dilutions; in particular, the models do not consider trigger strategies or direct sanctions regarding bond dilutions, distinguishing them from outright default. Moreover, mirroring actual practice, bonds issued at an earlier period are not senior to subsequently issued bonds. That is, otherwise identical bonds issued at different dates have the same legal standing in the event of default, reflecting the *pari passu* clause that is standard in sovereign bond contracts.[26]

As a capital loss for existing bond holders is an implicit transfer to the government (abstracting from any deadweight loss of default costs), there is an incentive for the government to issue new bonds to dilute the existing bonds. This point was highlighted by Bulow and Rogoff (1991) in reverse; namely, Bulow and Rogoff argued it is sub-optimal for a sovereign to repurchase its own debt on secondary markets. A repurchase generates a capital gain for existing bond holders, which is an implicit transfer from the government to bond holders. This insight has gained renewed attention as the Greek government bought back outstanding debt at a premium (relative to initial market prices) in 2012.

Long-term bonds and the associated movements in price over the life of the bond implies the bonds have different hedging properties than short-term debt. Arellano and Ramanarayanan (2012) propose a quantitative model with both short-term and long-term debt. Having both bonds available allows richer insurance possibilities than in a one-bond model. Moreover, a portfolio of bonds of different maturities allows a richer enforcement mechanism. Recall that the benchmark model of Section 3 allowed punishment of any deviation from the equilibrium allocation. Deviations (depending on the decentralization) could involve failure to pay debt, as in the current environment, but it could also take the form of not "saving" in anticipation of future liabilities that may come due. In the current incomplete-markets environment, the government is only punished if it fails to make a debt payment. A combination of short-term and long-term debt can replicate a pattern of near-term and long-term payments to financial markets, better mimicking the complete-markets allocation.[27]

Arellano and Ramanarayanan (2012) exploit the spanning and incentive-provision possibilities of multiple-maturity bonds to rationalize the fact that countries shorten maturities when a debt crisis is likely. The advantages of short-term debt are greatest when default is likely in the short-run, generating an increase reliance on short-term debt for new issues, consistent with the empirical evidence of Broner et al. (2013) and Arellano and Ramanarayanan (2012). Broner et al. (2013) take a different view,

[26] Chatterjee and Eyigungor (2012a) explore the benefits of allowing seniority to be enforced in the environment of Chatterjee and Eyigungor (2012b), documenting that enforceable seniority would substantially reduce default and increase equilibrium borrowing and welfare.

[27] Alfaro and Kanczuk (2009) discuss a similar point while introducing reserves into the model and studying the resulting portfolio problem. Interestingly, Alfaro and Kanczuk (2009) found that the standard quantitative model with reserves could not account for the significant amount of reserves that countries hold in the data. More recently, Bianchi et al. (2012) have shown that introducing long-maturity bonds also helps improve the ability of the model in this dimension.

arguing that this pattern reflects changing risk premia on the part of the lenders, rather than hedging motives on the part of the borrower. Both of these papers highlight the result that *temporary* increases in the probability of default during a time of crisis can account for the inversion of the yield curve observed in the data.

Quantitative models of sovereign debt is an active area of research and has already generated a number of important insights. We conclude with a few caveats on this literature, which can also serve as an indicator of where future research is warranted. The quantitative models often lack microfoundations for key assumptions. In particular, the limitations on financial contracts are typically taken as primitives. There is a parallel literature on optimal contracting subject to frictions such as limited enforcement and asymmetric information, as discussed in previous sections. These models are often qualitative, and have proven difficult to map into the data and quantify, although some attempts have been made (for example, Tsyrennikov, 2012). Bridging this gap is an important open question in the sovereign debt literature. Secondly, while the quantitative models are designed with empirical targets in mind, it is often not clear how to interpret the data through the lens of the model. For example, Dias et al. (2011) highlight that the data on debt stocks is a mixture of face values and market values, with different maturities, durations, and coupon payments, that are difficult to aggregate into a parsimonious set of state variables that appear in a quantitative model. More generally, when comparing the quantitative predictions of sovereign debt models to the data, it is important that we are comparing conceptually similar objects.

7. CONCLUDING REMARKS

This chapter has provided an overview of the economics of sovereign debt, with a particular emphasis on the implications of limited enforcement that distinguishes this market. The set of models reviewed offer important insights into a variety of phenomena, including: the role of reputations versus legal enforcement mechanisms; the implication that limited commitment generates debt overhang onto macroeconomic outcomes such as investment, growth, and volatility; the often slow process of graduation to non-frequent-defaulter status and the associated role played by debt overhang and political economy frictions; the possibility of unobserved or unverifiable shocks in limiting risk-sharing; the vulnerability to self-fulfilling debt crises; the difficulties in renegotiating debt in a timely and efficient manner; and the ability of theoretical models to quantitatively match key empirical patterns. The recent literature has generated a substantial number of important insights along these dimensions. That said, more progress is needed on mapping the theoretical models to the data. This includes exploring decentralizations that rely on realistic assets, legal mechanisms, and reputational concerns, combined with a coherent theory of equilibrium selection as many models in the literature support multiple equilibria. Any such decentralization has implications for prices that can be compared to the growing empirical literature on bond spreads. This process will provide the microfoundations for the growing quantitative literature that has begun to match empirical prices and quantities, but often relying on ad hoc assumptions that restrict equilibrium objects such as financial contracts and the output costs of default. As noted at the end of the previous section, the counterpart to this agenda of bringing theory to data is ensuring the measured quantities from the data are the conceptually appropriate counterparts to the model's equilibrium objects.

REFERENCES

Aguiar, M., Amador, M., 2011. Growth in the shadow of expropriation. Quarterly Journal of Economics 126, 651–697.

Aguiar, M., Gopinath, G., 2006. Defaultable debt, interest rates, and the current account. Journal of International Economics 69 (1), 64–83.

Aguiar, M., Gopinath, G., 2007. Emerging market business cycles: the cycle is the trend. Journal of Political Economy 115 (1), 69–102.

Aguiar, M., Amador, M., Gopinath, G., 2009. Investment cycles and sovereign debt overhang. Review of Economic Studies 76 (1), 1–31.

Aguiar, M., Amador, M., Farhi, E., Gopinath, G., 2012. Crisis and Commitment: Inflation Credibility and the Vulnerability to Sovereign Debt Crises. Working Paper.

Alesina, A., Tabellini, G., 1990. A positive theory of fiscal deficits and government debt in a democracy. Review of Economic Studies 57, 403–414.

Alfaro, L., Kanczuk, F., 2005. Sovereign debt as a contingent claim: a quantitative approach. Journal of International Economics 65 (2), 297–314.

Alfaro, L., Kanczuk, F., 2009. Optimal reserve management and sovereign debt. Journal of International Economics 77 (1), 23–36.

Alfaro, L., Kalemli-Ozcan, S., Volosovych, V., 2011. Sovereigns, Upstream Capital Flows and Global Imbalances. NBER Working Paper 17396.

Amador, M., 2012. Sovereign Debt and the Tragedy of the Commons. Working Paper.

Arellano, C., 2008. Default risk and income fluctuations in emerging economies. American Economic Review 98 (3), 690–712.

Arellano, C., Ramanarayanan, A., 2012. Default and the Maturity Structure in Sovereign Bonds. Journal of Political Economy 120 (2), 187–232.

Atkeson, A., 1991. International borrowing with moral hazard and risk of repudiation. Econometrica 59, 1069–1089.

Bai, Y., Zhang, J., 2012. Duration of sovereign debt renegotiation. Journal of International Economics 86, 252–268.

Benjamin, D., Wright, M., 2008. Recovery Before Redemption: A Model of Delays in Sovereign Debt Renegotiations. UCLA Working Paper.

Bi, R., 2008a. "Beneficial" Delays in Debt Restructuring Negotiations. IMF Working Paper WP/08/38.

Bi, R., 2008b. Debt Dilution and the Maturity Structure of Sovereign Debt. PhD Dissertation, University of Maryland.

Bianchi, J., Hatchondo, J.C., Martinez, L., 2012. International Reserves and Rollover Risk. Working Paper.

Bolton, P., Jeanne, O., 2007. Structuring and restructuring sovereign debt: the role of a bankruptcy regime. Journal of Political Economy 6, 901–924.

Bolton, P., Jeanne, O., 2009. Structuring and restructuring sovereign debt: the role of seniority. Review of Economic Studies, 76 (3), 879–902.

Borri, N., Verdelhan, A., 2011. Sovereign Risk Premia. MIT Sloan Working Paper.

Broner, F., Ventura, J., 2011. Globalization and risk sharing. Review of Economic Studies 78, 49–82.

Broner, F., Martin, A., Ventura, J., 2010. Sovereign risk and secondary markets. American Economic Review 100, 1523–1555.

Broner, F., Lorenzoni, G., Schmukler, S., 2013. Why do emerging economies borrow short term? Journal of the European Economics Association 11, 67–100.

Bulow, J., Rogoff, K., 1989a. A constant recontracting model of sovereign debt. Journal of Political Economy 97, 155–178.

Bulow, J., Rogoff, K., 1989b. Sovereign debt: is to forgive to forget? American Economic Review 79, 43–50.

Bulow, J., Rogoff, K., 1991. Sovereign debt repurchases: no cure for overhang. The Quarterly Journal of Economics 106 (4), 1219–1235.

Chari, V.V., Kehoe, P., 1990. Sustainable plans. Journal of Political Economy 98, 783–802.

Chatterjee, S., Eyigungor, B., 2012a. Debt dilution and seniority in a model of defaultable sovereign debt. Federal Reserve Bank of Philadelphia Working Paper 12–14.

Chatterjee, S., Eyigungor, B., 2012b. Maturity, indebtedness, and default risk. American Economic Review 102, 2674–2699.

Clementi, G., Hopenhayn, H., 2006. A theory of financing constraints and firm dynamics. Quarterly Journal of Economics 121, 229–265.

Cole, H., Kehoe, P., 1998. Models of sovereign debt: partial versus general reputations. International Economic Review 39, 55–70.

Cole, H., Kehoe, T., 2000. Self-fulfilling debt crises. The Review of Economic Studies 67, 91–116.

Cole, H., Dow, J., English, W., 1995. Default, settlement, and signaling: lending resumption in a reputational model of sovereign debt. International Economic Review 36, 365–385.

Conesa, J.C., Kehoe, T., 2011. Gambling for Redemption and Self-Fulfilling Debt Crises. Working Paper.

Conklin, J., 1998. The theory of sovereign debt and Spain under Philip II. Journal of Political Economy 106 (3), 483–513.

Cooley, T., Marimon, R., Quadrini, V., 2004. Aggregate consequences of limited contract enforceability. Journal of Political Economy 112, 817–847.

Cruces, J., Trebesch, C., 2011. Sovereign Defaults: The Price of Haircuts. CESIFO Working Paper 3604.

Cuadra, G., Sapriza, H., 2008. Sovereign default, interest rates and political uncertainty in emerging markets. Journal of International Economics 76, 78–88.

Dechert, W.D., 1982. Lagrange multipliers in infinite horizon discrete time optimal control models. Journal of Mathematical Economics 9, 285–301.

DeMarzo, P., Fishman, M., 2007. Optimal long-term financial contracting. Review of Financial Studies 20, 2079–2128.

D'Erasmo, P., 2011. Government Reputation and Debt Repayment in Emerging Economies. University of Maryland Working Paper.

Dias, D., Richmond, C., Wright, M., 2011. The Stock of External Debt: Can We Take the Data At 'Face Value'? NBER Working Paper 17551.

Dovis, A., 2012. Efficient Sovereign Default. Working Paper.

Drelichman, M., Voth, H.-J., 2011. Lending to the borrower from hell: debt and default in the age of Philip II. The Economic Journal 121 (557), 1205–1227.

Eaton, J., Gersovitz, M., 1982. Debt with potential repudiation: theoretical and empirical analysis. The Review of Economic Studies 48 (2), 289–309.

Edwards, S., 1984. LDC foreign borrowing and default risk: an empirical investigation, 1976–1980. American Economic Review 74, 726–734.

Fernandez, R., Rosenthal, R., 1990. Strategic models of sovereign-debt renegotiations. The Review of Economic Studies 57, 331–349.

Fuentes, M., Saravia, D., March 2010. Sovereign defaulters: do international capital markets punish them? Journal of Development Economics 91 (2), 336–347.

Gennaioli, N., Martin, A., Rossi, S., 2010. Sovereign Default, Domestic Banks and Financial Institutions. Working Paper.

Gourinchas, P.-O., Olivier J., 2007. Capital Flows to Developing Countries: The Allocation Puzzle. NBER Working Paper 13602.

Grossman, H., Van Huyck, J.B., 1988. Sovereign debt as a contingent claim: excusable default, repudiation, and reputation. American Economic Review 78 (5), 1088–1097.

Hamann, F., 2002. Sovereign Risk and Macroeconomic Fluctuations. Banco de la Republica de Colombia Working Paper 225.

Hatchondo, J.C., Martinez, L., 2009. Long-duration bonds and sovereign defaults. Journal of International Economics 79, 117–125.

Hatchondo, J.C., Martinez, L., Sapriza, H., 2009. Heterogeneous borrowers in quantitative models of sovereign default. International Economic Review 50, 1129–1151.

Hatchondo, J.C., Martinez, L., Sapriza, H., 2010. Quantitative properties of sovereign default models: solution methods matter. Review of Economic Dynamics 13, 919–933.

Hopenhayn, H., Werning, I., 2008. Equilibrium Default. MIT Working Paper.

Jeske, K., 2006. Private international debt with risk of repudiation. Journal of Political Economy 114, 576–593

Kehoe, P.J., Perri, F., 2004. Competitive equilibria with limited enforcement. Journal of Economic Theory 119 (1), 184–206.

Kehoe, T., Levine, D., 1993. Debt-constrained asset markets. The Review of Economic Studies 60, 865–888.

Kletzer, K., Wright, B., 2000. Sovereign debt as intertemporal barter. American Economic Review 90, 621–639.

Krugman, P., 1988. Financing vs. forgiving a debt overhang. Journal of Development Economics 29, 253–268.

Laibson, D., 1994. Hyperbolic Discounting and Consumption. PhD Dissertation, MIT.

Longstaff, F., Pan, J., Pedersen, L., Singleton, K., 2011. How sovereign is sovereign credit risk? American Economic Journal: Macroeconomics 43, 75–103.

Lucas, R., 1987. Models of Business Cycles. Blackwell.

Luenberger, D.G., 1969. Optimization by Vector Space Methods. John Wiley and Sons Inc.

Marcet, A., Marimon, R., 1992. Communication, commitment, and growth. Journal of Economic Theory 58, 219–249.

Martinez, J.V., Sandleris, G., 2011. Is it punishment? Sovereign defaults and the declines in trade. Journal of International Money and Finance 30, 909–930.

Mendoza, E., Yue, V., 2012. A general equilibrium model of sovereign default and business cycles. Quarterly Journal of Economics 127, 889–946.

Neumeyer, P., Perri, F., 2005. Business cycles in emerging economies: the role of interest rates. Journal of Monetary Economics 52, 345–380.

Persson, T., Svensson, L., 1989. Why a stubborn conservative would run a deficit: policy with time-inconsistent preferences. Quarterly Journal of Economics 104, 325–345.

Pitchford, R., Wright, M., 2012. Holdouts in sovereign debt restructuring: a theory of negotiation in a weak contractual environment. Review of Economic Studies 79 (2), 812–837.

Pouzo, D., Presno, I., 2012. Sovereign Default Risk and Uncertainty Premia. Working Paper.

Quadrini, V., 2004. Investment and liquidation in renegotiation-proof contracts with moral hazard. Journal of Monetary Economics 51 (4), 713–751.

Ray, D., 2002. The time structure of self-enforcing agreements. Econometrica 70 (2), 547–582.

Reinhart, C., Rogoff, K., 2009. This Time is Different: Eight Centuries of Financial Folly. Princeton Univeristy Press.

Reinhart, C., Rogoff, K., Savastano, M., 2003. Debt intolerance. Brookings Papers on Economic Activity 34 (1), 1–74.

Reinhart, C., Reinhart, V., Rogoff, K., 2012. Public debt overhangs: advanced-economy episodes since 1800. Journal of Economic Perspectives 26, 69–86.

Restrepo-Echavarria, P., 2013. Endogenous Borrowing Constraints and Stagnation in Latin America. Working Paper.

Rose, A.K., 2005, One reason countries pay their debts: renegotiation and international trade. Journal of Development Economics 77 (1), 189–206.

Rustichini, A., 1998. Lagrange multipliers in incentive-constrained problems. Journal of Mathematical Economics 29, 365–380.

Sachs, J., 1989. The debt overhang of developing countries. In: Calvo, G., Findlay, R., Kouri, P., De Macedo, J. (Eds.), Debt, Stabilization, and Development: Essays in Memory of Carlos Dias-Alejandro. Blackwell, Oxford, pp. 81–102.

Sandleris, G., 2008. Sovereign defaults: information, investment and credit. Journal of International Economics 76, 267–275.

Shiller, R., 1993. Macro Markets: Creating Institutions for Managing Society's Largest Economic Risks. Oxford University Press.

Sturzenegger, F., Zettelmeyer, J., 2008. Haircuts: estimating investor losses in sovereign debt restructurings, 1998–2005. Journal of International Money and Finance 27, 780–805.

Thomas, J., Worrall, T., 1988. Self-enforcing wage contracts. Review of Economic Studies 55, 541–53.

Thomas, J., Worrall, T., 1994. Foreign direct investment and the risk of expropriation. Review of Economic Studies 61 (1), 81–108.

Tomz, M., Wright, M., 2007. Do countries default in bad times? Journal of the European Economics Association 5, 352–360.

Tomz, M., Wright, M., 2013. Empirical research on sovereign debt and default. Annual Review of Economics, Annual Reviews 5 (1), 247–272.

Tsyrennikov, V., 2012. Capital Flows Under Moral Hazard. Working Paper.

Uribe, M., Yue, V., 2006. Country spreads and emerging countries: who drives whom? Journal of International Economics 69, 6–36.

Worrall, T., 1990. Debt with Potential Repudiation. European Economic Review 34, 1099–1109.

Wright, M., 2002. Reputations and Sovereign Debt. Working Paper.

Wright, M., 2006. Private capital flows, capital controls, and default risk. Journal of International Economics 69, 120–149.

Yue, V., 2010. Sovereign default and debt renegotiation. Journal of International Economics 80, 176–187.

CHAPTER *12*

International Financial Crises*

Guido Lorenzoni

Northwestern University, Evanston, IL, USA
National Bureau of Economic Research, Cambridge, MA, USA

Abstract

This chapter surveys recent research on international financial crises. A financial crisis is characterized by a sudden, dramatic outflow of financial resources from an economy with an open capital account. This outflow may be primarily driven by the expectation of a large nominal devaluation, in a situation in which the domestic monetary-fiscal regime appears inconsistent with a fixed exchange rate. Or the outflow may be driven by a reallocation of funds by foreign and domestic investors, due to a changed perception in the country's growth prospects, to an increase in the risk of domestic default, or to a shift in investors' attitudes toward risk. Often times, monetary and financial elements are combined. A drop in domestic asset prices and in the real exchange rate can act as powerful amplifiers of the real effects of the crisis, through adverse balance-sheet adjustments. The chapter surveys research that looks both at the monetary and at the financial side of crises, also discussing work that investigates the accumulation of imbalances preceding the crisis and the scope for preventive policies.

Keywords

Currency crisis, Current account reversal, Sudden stop, Sovereign debt crisis

JEL classification codes

F32, F34, F41, G15

1. INTRODUCTION

This chapter surveys the recent literature on international financial crises. I define international financial crises broadly as episodes of financial turbulence in which the international dimension plays an important role. The typical immediate manifestation of an international financial crisis is a large capital flight from the country affected, in which both foreign investors and domestic residents sell domestic assets and buy foreign assets. The associated pressure on the currency market leads to a depreciation of the domestic currency. If the central bank is pursuing a pegged exchange rate, the capital flight pushes the central bank to abandon the peg and devalue. While these elements are common to different episodes, the underlying causes and imbalances behind the crisis can be very different, depending on what triggered the capital flight in the first place. In particular, a

* I thank for useful comments Fernando Broner, Gita Gopinath, Olivier Jeanne, and Ken Rogoff. Dan Reese and Dejanir Silva provided excellent research assistance.

capital flight can be triggered by concerns with the country's monetary or fiscal outlook, by bad news about the country's growth prospects, by concerns with the ability to repay of some domestic sector that accumulated debt in the past, or by a generalized flight to safety in international capital markets. Often these different elements come combined. Moreover, crises can have very different consequences on the country affected depending on the monetary regime in place, the balance sheets of banks and firms, and so on. In this chapter, I will present and discuss models that have been used to interpret different types of crises, both in terms of the different underlying causes and in terms of the different transmission channels.

From an empirical point of view, we distinguish international crises in terms of their immediate measurable effects. In particular, a common distinction is between a *currency crisis*, defined as an episode in which the nominal exchange rate drops by more than a certain amount and/or in which the central bank experiences reserve losses larger than some threshold, and a *current account reversal*, defined as a sharp reversal from a large current account deficit into a much smaller deficit or a small surplus. Many researchers have also emphasized the connections between external crises and domestic banking crises, defined as episodes in which a large number of bank failures occurs and large scale public sector intervention in the banking sector takes place (Kaminsky and Reinhart, 1999). This leads to identify a peculiar type of crisis, a *twin crisis* in which balance of payment and domestic banking trouble coexist.

I will use the empirical distinction between currency crises and current account reversals as a way of organizing the presentation. I begin with models that focus on the currency crisis dimension, starting with the classic contributions of Krugman (1979) and Obstfeld (1994a), covered in Sections 2 and 3. These models focus on the nominal exchange rate as a monetary phenomenon and on the sustainability of fixed exchange rate regimes. Under a fixed exchange rate regime, free capital mobility imposes constraints on monetary policy. A crisis is a situation in which these constraints are put to the test and a capital flight occurs when monetary and fiscal policy are perceived to be inconsistent with the fixed exchange rate regime.

In the following sections, I turn to current account reversals, presenting models that put more emphasis on financial flows. In particular, I look at so-called *sudden stops* in capital flows, i.e., a sudden loss of access to international borrowing which forces a country to drastically reduce its current account deficit, a notion introduced by Dornbusch et al. (1995) and Calvo (1998). In Section 4, I look at models that take the sudden stop as an exogenous event and analyze its effects on the exchange rate and real activity. In the dynamics of a sudden stop an important amplifying mechanism comes from the presence of external liabilities denominated in foreign currency. Therefore, my treatment of sudden stops will be integrated with the treatment of the balance sheet effects due to currency mismatch.

Next, I will look at models that try to explain the sources of sudden stops, rather than taking them as exogenous events. A first step in this direction is to take as given some initial conditions, in particular some accumulated stock of debt coming from the past, and to investigate the mechanisms by which international investors may suddenly turn away from a borrowing country. In Section 5, I do so focusing on models with defaultable debt, in which the fear of default can trigger self-fulfilling capital flights. In that section, I also discuss the role of debt maturity in exposing a country to self-fulfilling liquidity crises.

The next step is to go further back and investigate the root causes of a crisis: Why do countries accumulate external debt? Why does the real exchange rate become overvalued? Why do borrowing countries choose short-term and/or foreign-currency-denominated liabilities? What is the role of international banking in the buildup of imbalances? Here I will discuss different ways of approaching these hard questions and discuss the potential for preventive policies that limit the exposure of a country to crises.

This organization of the material roughly reflects a timeline of the evolution of the literature over the last thirty years or so, which, in turns, was stimulated by major developments in international capital markets. In the exposition, I discuss how some notable crisis episodes have shaped the debate and prompted the construction of new models. However, I will avoid the common labels of "first, second, and third generation" models. This is because I prefer to distinguish the various models discussed here in terms of the mechanisms they emphasize, rather than in some overall philosophy of what causes a crisis and whether crises are caused by fundamentals or sunspots.

The chapter focuses on models and mechanisms and so I cover only a small part of the enormous empirical literature on the subject. Also, I do not hope to be exhaustive in covering all the theoretical work in the area, but rather to give a guide to some useful tools that have been developed to interpret different facets of actual crises.

2. FISCAL-MONETARY IMBALANCES

In this section and the next I focus on currency crises. When a country chooses to peg its exchange rate, in a regime of capital mobility, it loses the independent use of monetary policy. The central bank commits to conduct a monetary policy consistent with maintaining the peg. However, different pressures can induce the central bank to abandon this commitment. Two pressures explored here are the pressure to monetize government debt, in this section, and the pressure to respond to a recession, in the next section.

In the 1970s and 1980s, many emerging economies facing high inflation tried to use a fixed exchange rate as a nominal anchor for the purpose of inflation stabilization. Sometimes these experiments succeeded, but in a number of cases they failed. Many saw at the roots of this failure the presence of persistent fiscal deficits combined with a lack of central bank independence. This combination makes the low inflation regime not credible, as the public expects the central bank to eventually cave in to pressures to monetize government debt, leading to inflation and devaluation. However, the process by which the exchange rate was abandoned was typically characterized by a sudden, dramatic capital flight, leading to large losses of reserves by the central bank trying to defend the peg and eventually by devaluation. These crisis dynamics were often interpreted as the outcome of an irrational swing in the moods of currency markets. The classic Krugman (1979) model of currency crises shows instead that a discontinuous process of adjustment can be the outcome of rational behavior. Facing an unsustainable policy regime, forward-looking investors can trigger a sudden adjustment that anticipates the "day of reckoning." Let me illustrate these ideas using a simple version of the model, which builds on expositions in Flood and Garber (1984) and Obstfeld (1994).

2.1. Model

The model is a small open economy model set in continuous time. The first ingredient of the model is the domestic money demand equation

$$\frac{M}{P} = f(i)Y, \tag{1}$$

where M is the stock of money, P is the price level, i is the domestic interest rate, and f is a decreasing function. We consider an endowment economy and take the output level Y as a fixed constant, normalized to $Y = 1$. The second ingredient is the assumption that there is a single good in the world and that the law of one price holds. This implies that the domestic price level is equal to the foreign price level P^* converted in domestic currency at the nominal exchange rate $\mathcal{E}$, that is, we have the purchasing power parity (PPP) assumption

$$P = \mathcal{E}P^*.$$

We assume that the foreign price level is constant at $P^* = 1$, another convenient normalization. Next, we have the uncovered interest parity (UIP) condition

$$i = i^* + \dot{\mathcal{E}}/\mathcal{E},$$

where i^* is the foreign interest rate. Combining PPP and UIP implies that the real interest rate $r = i - \pi$ is given and equal to i^* (π denotes price inflation).

The last ingredient is the government budget constraint, which is really the consolidated budget constraint of the government and of the central bank,

$$\dot{D} - \mathcal{E}\dot{R} + \dot{M} = PH + iD - i^*\mathcal{E}R, \tag{2}$$

where D is government debt, H is the real primary deficit, and R are foreign currency reserves held by the central bank. I assume that foreign reserves earn the foreign interest rate i^*.

To complete the description of the model we need to specify the way in which monetary and fiscal policy are conducted. The assumption here is that fiscal policy is non-Ricardian, meaning that the government sets a path for the primary deficit H and the central bank needs to choose a path for money supply that ensures that the net liabilities of the government satisfies the no-Ponzi condition. To see how this constrains the choice of monetary policy, it is useful to derive the government intertemporal budget constraint, integrating (2). Define the net real liabilities of the government as

$$N \equiv \frac{D+M}{P} - \frac{\mathcal{E}}{P}R.$$

Differentiating this equation and using PPP yields

$$\dot{N} = \frac{\dot{D}+\dot{M}}{P} - \frac{\dot{P}}{P}\frac{D+M}{P} - \dot{R}.$$

Substituting (2) on the right-hand side and using $i^* = r$, we get

$$\dot{N} = rN + H - i\frac{M}{P}.$$

Finally, we can integrate, substitute the money demand (1), and use the no-Ponzi condition $\lim_{t\to\infty} e^{-rt}N(t) = 0$ to obtain the intertemporal budget constraint

$$N(0) = \int_0^\infty e^{-rt}\left[i(t)\frac{M(t)}{P(t)} - H(t)\right] dt. \tag{3}$$

The initial stocks of money, bonds, and reserves are inherited from the past. With a pegged exchange rate at date 0, we have $P(0) = \mathcal{E}(0) = 1$. Therefore, $N(0)$ is given and equal to $D(0) + M(0) - R(0)$. The intertemporal constraint (3), together with the money demand equation (1), give us a menu of paths for $i(t)$ consistent with the intertemporal budget constraint. The idea is that if the government is not going to adjust the path for the primary deficit $H(t)$, the central bank cannot at the same time sustain the peg at date 0 *and* choose its desired path for the nominal rate $i(t)$. Rather, the interest rate path needs to adjust at some point in the future to deliver inflation tax revenues consistent with the repayment of the initial debt.

Now assume the government fixes a constant level for the deficit $\bar{H}$ and keeps government debt fixed at the level $D(0) = \bar{D}$ and assume the initial conditions are such that $rN(0) > rf(r) - \bar{H}$ and $R(0) > f(r) - f(r + \mu)$. Suppose the central bank's only objective is to keep the currency pegged at $\mathcal{E} = 1$ for as long as possible. How long can the peg last? The central bank uses its foreign currency reserves to back up its commitment to a stable exchange rate. Basically, the central bank stands ready to exchange foreign for domestic money one for one, so the peg can survive as long as there are reserves to satisfy the demand for foreign currency. The problem is that the central bank is also under pressure to satisfy the government budget constraint. The central bank does not want to use money creation to finance the deficit, as it would create inflation and undermine the peg, so its only alternative is to run down its reserves to finance the government deficit. This leads reserves to fall at the following rate:

$$\dot{R} = -\bar{H} - r(\bar{D} - R). \tag{4}$$

An equivalent way to tell the same story is that the central bank uses money creation to finance the deficit, but its commitment to the peg implies that the private sector immediately converts the newly printed money into foreign currency, so the money creation is undone at every instant. The final result is the same: the money supply remains constant and the central bank loses reserves at the rate shown in equation (4).

It would seem natural at this point to conjecture that the central bank will lose reserves gradually, as in (4), and the peg will last until the time T when the central bank hits $R(T) = 0$. At this point, the central bank will abandon the peg and start printing money so as to generate seignorage revenue sufficient to cover the deficit, i.e., at the rate μ that satisfies[1]

$$\mu f\left(r + \mu\right) = \bar{H} + r\bar{D}. \tag{5}$$

This conjecture is, however, incorrect. The problem is that the demand for foreign currency reserves is affected by the agents' forward-looking behavior. As long as the peg holds, UIP is satisfied and investors (domestic and international) have an infinitely elastic demand for foreign currency reserves, so they are happy to absorb the amount of reserves that the central bank is selling to plug the fiscal deficit. However, a moment before time T the UIP fails to hold. To see why this is the case, notice that along the conjectured path the money supply is continuous at T while real money balances need to jump from $f(r)$ to $f(r+\mu)$. This requires a discrete increase in the price level from 1 to $f(r)/f(r+\mu) > 1$. By PPP, the exchange rate needs to increase discretely by the same amount. But a discrete increase in the exchange rate is incompatible with UIP as long as the nominal interest rate is finite. Therefore, the conjectured path is not an equilibrium path.

To solve for the correct equilibrium dynamics, we need to find a path in which the price level and the exchange rate change continuously at the time when the peg is abandoned, so that UIP is satisfied. This requires a discrete jump in M. Namely, at time T^* investors (domestic and foreign) will suddenly absorb all the reserves still in the hand of the central bank, so reserves will move discontinuously from a positive level $R(T^*_-) > 0$ immediately before T^* to zero at time T^*.[2] The reserve outflow will be exactly matched

---

[1] This equation can be derived by writing the intertemporal budget constraint (3) at time T, and noticing from then on we will have constant real money balances, inflation equal to the rate of money growth, and a constant nominal interest rate $i = r + \mu$. Notice, that if $\bar{D}$ and $\bar{B}$ are too large there may be no value of μ that satisfies this equation. In that case, seignorage is insufficient to plug the fiscal deficit and the government will have either to adjust the deficit or default.

[2] The reserve path is continuous for $t < T^*$ and $R(T^*_-)$ denotes the limit $\lim_{t \to T^*_-} R(t)$.

by an equivalent discontinuous reduction in money supply. From T^* onwards, the central bank will finance the deficit with money creation, according to equation (5). Therefore, money supply has to drop by the amount $\Delta M = f(r) - f(r + \mu)$. To find the time T^* when the peg collapses we then need to solve the differential equation (4) with the terminal condition $R(T^*_-) = \Delta M$. Since $\Delta M > 0$ the time T^* at which the peg collapses arrives earlier than the time T we derived under our initial, incorrect conjecture.

A crucial observation here is that reserve losses can suddenly accelerate when a crisis approaches: the fact that the central bank is losing reserves at a relatively slow pace today cannot be taken as a sign that the same pace will continue into the future. As investors start anticipating the risk that the peg will be abandoned, they start buying reserves at a faster rate, so that the defenses of the central bank that seemed sufficient to defend the peg for months can be exhausted in a matter of days.

2.2. Discussion

There are two main messages here. First, unsustainable policies can lead to a possibly discontinuous adjustment process. The discontinuity is due to the fact that forward-looking agents anticipate a regime change and adjust their behavior accordingly. Notice that in the original model the discontinuity concerns the dynamics of the stock of reserves but not of the exchange rate. Broner (2008) shows that enriching the model's informational structure introduces the possibility of discrete jumps in the exchange rate in equilibrium. Also, one may wonder whether the discontinuity is driven by the way the behavior of the policy-maker is formulated. Rebelo and Végh (2008) study what happens when policy is the result of explicit optimizing behavior by a monetary authority who is trying to avoid a devaluation.

The second message is that the conduct of fiscal policy can be a source of exchange rate instability. As long as agents entertain the possibility that monetary policy will lose its independence at some point in the future, this will affect their behavior today. This message is closely linked to the idea that monetary policy and fiscal stability are linked by the government intertemporal budget constraint (Sargent and Wallace, 1981), a linkage captured here by equation (3). An important observation that follows is that current deficits are not necessary to put a fixed exchange regime under stress, as long as the public foresees the risk of high deficits in the future. In the East Asian crisis of 1997 the countries involved did not display high fiscal deficits in the years preceding the crisis.[3] Corsetti et al. (1999) and Burnside et al. (2006) notice that, however, the crisis had a large impact on the banking sector in these countries and that there were strong ties between the banking sector and the government. This combination meant that investors expected the government to step in and spend substantial fiscal resources to bail out banks. The

---

[3] See Table 8 in Radelet and Sachs (2000).

prospective deficits associated to future bail-outs can then be used to interpret also the East Asian crisis as a fiscal-monetary phenomenon.[4]

An important observation that follows the analysis above is that a successful fixed exchange rate regime requires both central bank independence and some form of commitment to fiscal discipline. This idea is at the root of the institutional design of the European currency union. Both the budgetary rules in the Maastricht treaty of 1992 and the rules governing the European Central Bank were explicitly designed to minimize the risk of debt monetization. These rules are being put to the test in the current euro crisis. However, a big difference between a fixed exchange rate regime and a currency union is that in a currency union there is a single central bank. The situation in a currency union is equivalent to a fixed exchange regime in which national central banks are bound to provide each other unlimited reserves to defend the peg. In the context of the euro area, such an arrangement is made explicit in the functioning of the payment system, the so-called TARGET2 system, as discussed in Garber (1999). There is currently a heated debate on what are the fiscal implications of such an arrangement.[5] But the size of the balances accumulated by deficit nations suggests that, absent this regime, the euro system would have already succumbed to speculative attacks.

The simple model above does not capture another important feature of the euro crisis, namely the possibility that an unsustainable fiscal regime is not resolved by inflation, but by outright default. The role of default and risk premia in financial crises will be discussed in Section 5. Uribe (2006), Jeanne (2011), and Aguiar et al. (2012) explore the interaction between monetary and fiscal policy in models where government default is possible.

3. OVERVALUATION, UNEMPLOYMENT, AND MULTIPLE EQUILIBRIA

The model in the previous section focused on fiscal-monetary issues and abstracted, for simplicity, from the effects of currency dynamics on relative prices. Under the assumption of PPP holding at all times, a devaluation was simply the international manifestation of an inflationary event.

In this section, I use an open economy new Keynesian model in which movements in the nominal exchange rate have real effects in the short run. This model allows us to consider episodes in which a nominal depreciation leads to a real depreciation. More generally, the model allows us to explore the effects of currency crises on real activity and the options faced by the central bank in these episodes. In particular, I use the model to discuss the possibility of multiple equilibria à la Obstfeld (1994a), in which lack of

---

[4] A fact that is harder to square with this interpretation of the East Asian crisis is that, after devaluing, these countries did not experience high inflation and the nominal devaluation was associated to a real devaluation. I will return below to these issues and to alternative interpretation of the East Asian crisis.

[5] See Buiter and Rahbar (2012).

credibility of the central bank commitment to a peg is self-fulfilling, as it leads to a recessionary shock that pushes the central bank to choose a devaluation.

3.1. A Small Open Economy New Keynesian Model

The model is a general equilibrium open economy model with nominal rigidities in the tradition of Obstfeld and Rogoff (1995) and Corsetti and Pesenti (2001). In particular, I consider the case of a small open economy, as in Galí and Monacelli (2005). I simplify the environment relative to standard treatments. In particular, I focus on a perfect foresight equilibrium with no shocks and only look at the effect of one-time unexpected shocks. At the same time, I avoid log-linearization, which allows me to capture some interesting non-linearities in later sections.[6]

Consider a small country, populated by infinitely lived consumers with utility function

$$\sum_{t=0}^{\infty} \beta^t \left(\frac{1}{1-\sigma} C_t^{1-\sigma} - \frac{\psi}{1+\phi} N_t^{1+\phi} \right).$$

Consumption C_t is a Cobb-Douglas aggregate of a home good C_{ht} and a foreign good C_{ft}:

$$C_t = \xi C_{ht}^{\omega} C_{ft}^{1-\omega},$$

with $\xi = \omega^{-\omega}(1-\omega)^{-(1-\omega)}$. The home good is a CES aggregate of a continuum of varieties $j \in [0, 1]$ produced by monopolistic competitive firms à la Dixit-Stiglitz, owned by the representative consumer. Using $Y_t(j)$ to denote the production of variety j, the total production of the home good is

$$Y_t = \left(\int_0^1 Y_t(j)^{\frac{\varepsilon-1}{\varepsilon}} dj \right)^{\frac{\varepsilon}{\varepsilon-1}},$$

and its price index is

$$P_{ht} = \left(\int_0^1 P_{ht}(j)^{1-\varepsilon} dj \right)^{\frac{1}{1-\varepsilon}}.$$

Each firm j uses the linear technology $Y_t(j) = N_t(j)$. The foreign good is in perfectly elastic supply at the price $P_{ft} = 1$ in foreign currency. The nominal exchange rate is $\mathcal{E}_t$, so the price of the foreign good in domestic currency is $\mathcal{E}_t$.

Since the representative consumer receives the entire domestic income $P_{ht} Y_t$, in the form of wages or profits, his/her budget constraint is

$$\sum_{t=0}^{\infty} Q_{t|0} \left(P_t C_t - P_{ht} Y_t \right) = \mathcal{E}_0 B_0,$$

---

[6] See, in particular, Section 4.

where B_0 is the country's initial asset position in foreign currency and $Q_{t|0}$ is the price of a unit of domestic currency at time t in terms of date 0 domestic currency.

Consumer optimality implies that the domestic demand for the home good is

$$C_{ht} = \omega \left(\frac{P_{ht}}{P_t} \right)^{-1} C_t, \tag{6}$$

where the domestic consumer price index P_t includes the price of the home and foreign good and is

$$P_t = P_{ht}^{\omega} \mathcal{E}_t^{1-\omega}. \tag{7}$$

The demand of home goods by the rest of the world is given by

$$C_{ht}^* = \zeta \left(\frac{P_{ht}}{\mathcal{E}_t} \right)^{-\rho}. \tag{8}$$

This demand function captures two assumptions: (i) we are in a small open economy, so consumption of home goods is a negligible fraction of spending in the rest of the world, and (ii) the foreign consumption level and the foreign CPI are constant and are captured by the parameter ζ. Also the foreign interest rate i^* is constant and equal to $1/\beta - 1$. There is perfect capital mobility and the UIP condition is

$$1 + i_t = \frac{\mathcal{E}_{t+1}}{\mathcal{E}_t} \left(1 + i^* \right). \tag{9}$$

For simplicity, I assume we are in a cashless world, where the domestic central bank directly controls the nominal interest rate i_t. When prices are flexible, the choice of the nominal interest rate will only have nominal effects and monetary policy will be completely neutral. Not so with nominal rigidities.

Consumer optimality implies the consumer Euler equation:

$$C_t^{-\sigma} = \beta \left(1 + i_t \right) \frac{P_t}{P_{t+1}} C_{t+1}^{-\sigma}, \tag{10}$$

and the optimal labor supply condition:

$$\frac{W_t}{P_t} C^{-\sigma} = \psi N_t^{\phi}. \tag{11}$$

For simplicity, I will abstract from wage rigidities and assume the nominal wage W_t is flexible.

Prices are sticky. In period 0, a fraction α of firms cannot adjust their price and keep it at the level $\bar{P}_h$ inherited from the past, a fraction $1 - \alpha$ of firms are free to adjust their price. To simplify the analysis, we assume that from time $t = 1$ onwards all prices can be freely adjusted. Optimal price setting implies that firms that are allowed to adjust their price, set it as a constant markup over marginal costs,

$$P_{ht}(j) = \frac{\varepsilon}{\varepsilon - 1} W_t. \tag{12}$$

For the rest of the analysis, it is useful to define the relative price of the home good in terms of foreign goods

$$p_{ht} \equiv \frac{P_{ht}}{\mathcal{E}_t},$$

and to express the relative prices of the home and foreign good in terms of domestic consumption as

$$P_{ht}/P_t = p_{ht}^{1-\omega},$$
$$\mathcal{E}_t/P_t = p_{ht}^{-\omega}.$$

3.2. Equilibrium

We solve the model backward. In periods $t = 1, 2, \ldots$ the economy reaches a flexible price steady state equilibrium. So we first characterize prices and quantities in steady state and then go back to period $t = 0$ and complete our characterization.

Steady state variables are denoted by an asterisk. The steady state is characterized by a constant net foreign asset position $B_t = B^*$, constant consumption and output, $C_t = C^*$ and $Y_t = Y^*$, and a constant relative price $p_{ht} = p_h^*$. Given B^*, which is inherited from period 0, the equilibrium values of C^*, Y^*, and p_h^* are found solving the equations

$$C^* = \left(p_h^*\right)^{1-\omega} Y^* + (1 - \beta) \left(p_h^*\right)^{-\omega} B^*, \tag{13}$$

$$\left(p_h^*\right)^{1-\omega} \left(C^*\right)^{-\sigma} = \frac{\varepsilon}{\varepsilon - 1} \psi \left(Y^*\right)^{\phi}, \tag{14}$$

$$Y^* = \omega \left(p_h^*\right)^{-(1-\omega)} C^* + \zeta \left(p_h^*\right)^{-\rho}. \tag{15}$$

The first equation comes from the budget constraint, the second from combining optimal price setting and optimal labor supply, and the third from market clearing in the domestic good market.

I make the following assumptions

$$\frac{\varepsilon}{\varepsilon - 1} \psi = 1, \tag{16}$$

$$\omega + \zeta = 1, \tag{17}$$

which imply that if the steady state net foreign asset position B^* is zero, all quantities and relative prices are equal to 1 in steady state.

Let us go back to time $t = 0$. To simplify notation, I drop the time subscript for time zero variables. The equilibrium is determined by combining forward-looking spending decisions by consumers with equilibrium in the home good market. Combining the consumer's Euler equation with the UIP, and using the fact that the foreign interest rate is $1/\beta - 1$, we have

$$C^{-\sigma} = \left(\frac{p_h}{p_h^*}\right)^{\omega} \left(C^*\right)^{-\sigma}. \tag{18}$$

Equilibrium in the domestic good market requires

$$Y = \omega p_h^{-(1-\omega)} C + \zeta p_h^{-\rho}. \tag{19}$$

The consumer flow budget constraint gives

$$\beta B^* = p_h Y - p_h^{\omega} C + B. \tag{20}$$

Finally, I assume that the central bank successfully targets an inflation rate of π so the UIP condition becomes

$$1 + i_0 = \left(\frac{p_h}{p_h^*}\right)^{\omega} \left(1 + i^*\right) \left(1 + \pi\right). \tag{21}$$

Given that prices are sticky in period 0, monetary policy has real effects: the central bank is free to choose the value of i_0 and the quantities and prices C, Y, p_h, C^*, Y^*, p_h^*, B^* are then determined by equations (13)–(15) and (18)–(21).

To complete the equilibrium characterization, we need to solve for employment N, for the price of flexible price goods, denoted by $\hat{P}_h$, and for the price indexes P_h and P. These variables are found solving the equations

$$N = JY, \tag{22}$$

$$\hat{P}_h = PC^{\sigma} N^{\phi}, \tag{23}$$

$$P_h = \left(\alpha \bar{P}_h^{1-\varepsilon} + \left(1 - \alpha\right) \hat{P}_h^{1-\varepsilon}\right)^{\frac{1}{1-\varepsilon}}, \tag{24}$$

$$P = p_h^{-(1-\omega)} P_h, \tag{25}$$

where

$$J = \alpha \left(\frac{\bar{P}_h}{P_h}\right)^{-\varepsilon} + \left(1 - \alpha\right) \left(\frac{\hat{P}_h}{P_h}\right)^{-\varepsilon}. \tag{26}$$

Equation (22) comes from labor market clearing, after summing the demand of goods (and hence of labor) of flexible price and fixed price firms. Equation (23) combines optimal price setting for flexible price firms with optimal labor supply. The following equations simply follow from the price index for home goods and the definition of p_h. The factor J captures the inefficiency associated to price dispersion, commonly found in sticky price environments, and is useful in the welfare derivations below.

3.3. A Policy Game

Suppose the central bank is committed to keep the nominal exchange rate pegged at $\mathcal{E} = 1$. Suppose also that we are coming from a period of real appreciation, so $\bar{P}_h > 1$. In the following sections, I will look more into the roots of a currency crisis and show that a real appreciation can be the by-product of boom–bust dynamics in capital flows. For now, I just take $\bar{P}_h > 1$ as an initial condition.

Given initial conditions, we analyze a game between price setters and the central bank, with the following timing:

1. the $1 - \alpha$ flexible price firms set the price $\hat{P}_h$, this determines the prices P_h and P;
2. the central bank sets the nominal interest rate i_0, this determines the consumption C, the exchange rate $\mathcal{E}$ and all remaining prices and quantities.

The central bank is benevolent and its objective is to maximize domestic consumers' welfare.

For the purpose of this section, I make some additional simplifying assumptions. First, I assume that the initial asset position B_0 is zero. Second, I assume that consumers have log utility, $\sigma = 1$, and that foreign demand for domestic good is unit elastic, $\rho = 1$. Third, I assume that $\omega = \psi$, which simplifies the analysis of optimal monetary policy.

Under our additional assumptions, the domestic economy maintains a zero net foreign asset position in all periods, independently of monetary policy.[7] In particular, consumption and output in period 0 simplify to

$$C = p_h^{-\omega}, \tag{27}$$

$$Y = 1/p_h, \tag{28}$$

and the current account $P_h Y - PC$ is zero, for any value of p_h.[8] This means that the steady state allocation and welfare from period $t = 1$ onward are independent of what happens in period 0. Therefore, the central bank monetary decisions in period 0 only affect utility in period 0. Using (27) and (28), we can express period 0 utility in terms of current output, defining the function

$$W\left(Y, J\right) \equiv \omega \log Y - \frac{\psi}{1 + \phi}\left(JY\right)^{1+\phi}. \tag{29}$$

I further assume that there is a fixed long-run welfare cost $\kappa > 0$ from abandoning the peg. This welfare cost could be microfounded in a richer, repeated game model in which inflation is costly, the central bank has a positive inflation bias, and a pegged exchange

---

[7] This result is a version of a result of Cole and Obstfeld (1991).

[8] Guess that the foreign asset position is $B^* = 0$. This implies that all steady state quantities and prices are equal to 1. Equation (18) then simplifies to (27). Substituting for C in (19) and using the assumption $\omega + \zeta = 1$ then yields (28). The current account in terms of foreign goods can then be written as $p_h Y - p_h^\omega C$, which equals zero since both terms are equal to 1. Since $B_0 = 0$, equation (20) then confirms the conjecture $B^* = 0$.

rate is a way to commit to a low inflation equilibrium. In such a model, abandoning the peg would trigger a Nash punishment phase with higher inflation. Here, to simplify the analysis, I just introduce an exogenous fixed cost.

We can now analyze our policy game formally. First, flexible price setters maximize expected profits and set prices according to

$$\hat{P}_h = \tilde{P}\tilde{C}\tilde{N}^\phi, \tag{30}$$

where the tilde denotes price setters' expectations.[9] The choice of $\hat{P}_h$ by price setters determines P_h and J through equations (24) and (26). Next, given J, the central bank chooses either to defend the peg or to abandon it. If the central bank defends the peg, the relative price p_h is equal to P_h and the value of i_0 needed to defend the peg can be derived from the UIP equation (21) (with $p_h^* = 1$). If instead the central bank decides to abandon the peg, it then chooses i_0 to maximize $W(Y, J)$. In this case, the choice of i_0 determines p_h through the UIP equation (21). In both cases, given the relative price p_h consumption, output, employment, and the consumption price index are determined, respectively, by equations (27), (28), (22), and (25). In the case of floating, the nominal exchange rate can be derived from $\mathcal{E} = p_h^{-\omega}P$. To have a Nash equilibrium, we need to check that the values of P, N, and C associated to the optimal choice of i_0 by the central bank are equal to the price setters' expectations $\tilde{P}, \tilde{N}$, and $\tilde{C}$.

3.4. Multiple Equilibria

We are now ready to derive the main result of this section, showing that, under some parameter configurations, the game above has multiple equilibria. In particular, there can be a "good" equilibrium in which price setters are confident in the peg and the central bank is able to maintain it, and a "bad" equilibrium in which price setters lose confidence in the peg and the central bank abandons it. The crucial step of the argument is to show that the beliefs of the price setters affect the short–run cost of defending the peg.

Consider first a good equilibrium. In a good equilibrium, price setters expect the peg to survive. In this case the relative price p_h is equal to the domestic price index P_h and the equilibrium price for flexible price firms $\hat{P}_h$ is the solution to the equation[10]

$$\hat{P}_h = \left(\frac{\alpha \bar{P}_h^{-\varepsilon} + (1-\alpha)\,\hat{P}_h^{-\varepsilon}}{\alpha \bar{P}_h^{1-\varepsilon} + (1-\alpha)\,\hat{P}_h^{1-\varepsilon}} \right)^\phi. \tag{31}$$

---

[9] Given that flexible price setters set prices before the central bank moves and are not allowed to change it afterwards, "flexible" is a bit of a misnomer here, but it is useful to distinguish them from the price setters that keep their price at $\bar{P}_h$. Allowing for a third group of price setters that act after the central bank sets i_0 would complicate the algebra, but not alter the results.

[10] Substituting $p_h = P_h$ and equating P, C, N with their expectations, yields

$$\hat{P}_h = PCN^\phi = P_h^\omega P_h^{-\omega} (J/P_h)^\phi.$$

Substituting (23) and (26) and rearranging gives the desired expression.

We can then use (23) and (26) to compute J. Two results are useful here: first, the domestic price level in equilibrium must satisfy

$$1 < P_h < \bar{P}_h; \tag{32}$$

second, since there is price dispersion, $J > 1$.[11] We can then turn to the central bank's behavior. If the central bank sticks to the peg, the nominal exchange rate is fixed at 1 and output is given by

$$Y^{peg,good} = 1/P_h < 1,$$

where the inequality follows from (32). Since we are coming from a period of over-valuation, if the nominal exchange rate is kept fixed, output is depressed relative to its flexible price level, which is 1. If the central bank decides to float, it can freely choose the nominal interest rate and thus determine the exchange rate and the level of output. A good equilibrium exists if the short-run gains from floating are less than the long-run costs, that is, if

$$\Delta W^{good} \equiv \max_Y \left\{ W\left(Y,J\right) - W\left(Y^{peg,good},J\right)\right\} < \kappa. \tag{33}$$

Consider next a bad equilibrium. We guess and verify that an equilibrium exists in which flexible price firms expect the central bank to float and all set their price equal to the price of fixed price firms, so that

$$P_h = \hat{P}_h = \bar{P}_h.$$

Since all firms set the same price we have $J = 1$. If the central bank decides to float, it then chooses output to maximize $W(Y, 1)$. Given the definition of the function W, in (29), and given the assumption $\omega = \psi$, the optimal level of output is $Y = 1$. From (28) this requires an exchange rate equal to

$$\mathcal{E} = P_h > 1.$$

The quantities in the floating equilibrium are then equal to their flexible price level, that is,

$$C = Y = N = 1.$$

Given these prices, if instead the central bank decides to deviate and defend the peg $\mathcal{E} = 1$, we have

$$Y^{peg,bad} = 1/\bar{P}_h < Y^{peg,good} < 1. \tag{34}$$

[11] The first result can be proved using the right-hand side of (31) to construct a fixed point mapping for $\hat{P}_h$ and arguing that the fixed point must be in between the value that yields $P_h = 1$ and the value $\bar{P}_h$. The second result can be proved using a Jensen's inequality argument.

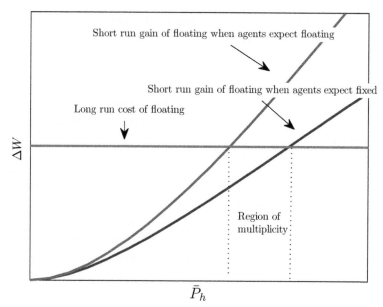

Figure 12.1 Initial Overvaluation and Multiple Equilibria

A bad equilibrium exists if the short-run gains from floating are larger than the long-run costs, that is, if

$$\Delta W^{bad} \equiv \max_{Y} \left\{ W\left(Y, 1\right) - W\left(Y^{peg,bad}, 1\right) \right\} > \kappa. \tag{35}$$

Both the good and the bad equilibrium exist if both (33) and (35) are satisfied. To understand why multiple equilibria are possible it is useful to start from interpreting inequality (34). If price setters expect the central bank to defend the peg, they lower their prices to a value lower than $\bar{P}_h$, as per equation (32). In this case, the real exchange rate is overvalued (and output is depressed), but at least the country achieves some amount of real exchange rate devaluation via domestic deflation. If instead price setters expect the central bank to float they keep the price level at $\bar{P}_h > 1$. If then the central bank decides to defend the peg, the real exchange rate is more overvalued and domestic output is more depressed than in the case of optimistic expectations. Therefore, when price setters expect the peg to be abandoned, their pricing decisions make it more costly for the central bank to defend the peg.[12]

The possibility of multiple equilibria is illustrated in Figure 12.1. The figure shows a numerical example in which ΔW^{bad} and ΔW^{good} are computed for different values

---

[12] The presence of the term $J > 1$ in (33) reinforces this argument, as the distortion due to price dispersion also reduces the benefits from increasing output under optimistic expectations.

of the initial price level $\bar{P}_h$. Both gains coincide and are equal to 0 when $\bar{P}_h = 1$, since then the optimal policy after floating is to leave the exchange rate unchanged. As $\bar{P}_h$ increases, the gain from floating increases both under "good" and "bad" expectations, but it increases more under bad expectations. The figure shows that when $\bar{P}_h$ is large enough we have $\Delta W^{bad} > \kappa$ and $\Delta W^{good} < \kappa$ so both equilibria are possible. In other words, the possibility of multiple equilibria depends on the initial degree of overvaluation. When $\bar{P}_h$ is sufficiently large the good equilibrium disappear and the unique equilibrium involves a certain abandonment of the peg.

There are two main reasons why a country may find itself with an overvalued exchange rate. A first case, is a country that is using a fixed exchange rate to anchor inflation expectations. If the inflation stabilization program is not fully credible, inflation will adjust downward gradually. As the exchange rate is pegged, the domestic currency will then gradually appreciate. These dynamics were the subject of a rich literature in the 1980s, that aimed to explain the difficult experiences of many countries that attempted exchange-rate-based stabilizations.[13] A second case, is a country that experiences positive capital flows that go to finance a boom in domestic spending. The boom will lead to a domestic appreciation, both due to an increase in the price of non-tradables and to an increase in the price of domestically produced tradables (due to home bias in spending). If the capital flow slows down, or worse, is reversed, the country will find itself with an overvalued exchange rate. These capital flow reversals are the subject of Section 4. Of course, these two elements may go hand in hand, and indeed several countries have experienced domestic consumption booms associated to exchange-rate-based stabilizations.

The exposition above emphasizes overvaluation as the original imbalance tilting the incentives of the central bank in favor of abandoning the peg. Other shocks may push the economy in a region where the peg may be abandoned in equilibrium. In particular, Obstfeld (1994a) aimed to develop a model to describe the currency attacks of 1992–1993 leading to sharp devaluations in Britain, Italy, Spain, and Sweden. The countries attacked did not fit the model of fiscal-monetary imbalances of Section 2. Some displayed an overvalued real exchange rate. But the common element was that they were all facing recessionary shocks that made a defense of the peg especially costly.[14] It is easy to adapt the model above to introduce these types of recessionary shocks and to show that a large enough shock can push the economy in the multiple-equilibria region.[15]

---

[13] See Calvo and Végh (1999) for a comprehensive review of the literature on inflation stabilizations and balance of payment crises.

[14] A common shock was an increase in interest rates in Germany, in response to the expansionary fiscal policies enacted following Germany's reunification. Sweden was also facing the contractionary effects of a banking crisis.

[15] Notice also that multiple equilibria are also possible in models that emphasize fiscal-monetary interactions as the one examined in Section 2. In fact, the seminal Obstfeld (1986) article first discusses the possibility of multiple equilibria in currency crises in the context of a similar model.

A feature of the Obstfeld (1994a) model is that the cost of defending the peg arises because people expected in the past that the exchange rate will be devalued today. In the model above, this was captured in the timing: first flexible firms were choosing prices, then the central bank was choosing the nominal rate. Krugman (1996) notices that an alternative modeling approach is to assume that the fixed rate is costly to defend, because agents expect now that the peg will be devalued in the future. By UIP, a higher expected nominal exchange rate in the future requires a higher nominal interest rate today, if the nominal exchange rate today is to remain fixed. But increasing the nominal exchange rate today leads to output losses. So a large expected devaluation may push the central bank to abandon the peg. This alternative modeling approach seems to capture well the dynamics of the devaluation of the Swedish krona 1992, in which the central bank abandoned the peg after attempting a defense with sharp increases in the nominal interest rate. Extending the new Keynesian model to capture this forward-looking channel seems a promising avenue to explore.

3.5. A Detour: Multiple Equilibria and Global Games

The model above displays multiple equilibria. Models with multiple equilibria capture well situations in which a change in sentiment can trigger a sudden, dramatic change in economic outcomes. In some crises, market participants seem to be unaware of any looming problem until some critical moment in which prices and financial flows take a sharp turn following no apparent shock to fundamentals. For example, Radelet and Sachs (1998) make a compelling case that in the case of the East Asian crisis of 1997 there were very few warning signs and the crisis was mostly unexpected. In other crises, the critical point is reached after a gradual and inexorable process of deterioration, so that market participants are hardly taken by surprise, as for example in the case of Argentina's default in 2001. The first type of episodes are usually taken as natural candidates for multiple-equilibria stories. In this chapter, I use multiple equilibria as a useful device to identify feedback effects. In practice these effects may not be strong enough to generate multiplicity, but still be powerful sources of amplification.

The literature has sometimes overly emphasized the distance between multiple-equilibria models and models driven by fundamentals. As shown in Figure 12.1, the possibility of a bad equilibrium is not independent of fundamentals, as multiple equilibria are only possible when the currency is sufficiently overvalued and if it is too overvalued a devaluation is the unique outcome. Still, if we are in the region of multiplicity, the model's predictions are not tight: we know that a devaluation is possible, but the probability of a devaluation is not monotonically related to the degree of overvaluation and indeed the relation between the two can be completely arbitrary.

A large theoretical literature, starting from Carlsson and Van Damme (1993) and Morris and Shin (1998), has used a so-called "global games" approach to reduce the distance between multiple equilibrium models and models with a unique equilibrium.

The idea of these models is not to ignore the strength of amplification effects or the possibility of discrete jumps between different outcomes, but to obtain sharper predictions on the occurrence of crises, speculative attacks, devaluations, and so on. These tighter predictions should make both empirical testing and policy analysis easier to conduct.[16] While this approach has been applied to a variety of applied contexts, currency crises have been prominent examples, as in the benchmark model used by Morris and Shin (1998).

The starting point of Morris and Shin (1998) is a simple game-theoretic model, with a single unobservable state, call it θ, which captures some aggregate fundamental. The central bank is facing a continuum of speculators, who have a binary choice: attack the currency or not. The central bank prefers to defend the peg if θ is high enough *and* not too many speculators are attacking. On the other hand, the speculators' gain from attacking is positive only if the central bank abandons the peg and devalues. Since the central bank moves after the speculators make their decision, we can solve for the central bank's best response and analyze the game just as a coordination game among the speculators. This game displays strategic complementarity: more speculators attacking increases the benefits of attacking for any individual speculator, because it increases the chances that the central bank will devalue. Under perfect information, this coordination game admits two equilibria if the parameter θ is in some region $\left[\underline{\theta}, \overline{\theta}\right]$. In this region, a speculative attack is a purely self-fulfilling event.

The novelty of Morris and Shin (1998) is to add a small amount of imperfect information in the game above. The speculators, instead of observing θ exactly, observe it perturbed by noise, namely they observe $\theta + \epsilon_i$, where ϵ_i is an agent-specific idiosyncratic shock. Morris and Shin (1998) show that with this modification the model delivers a unique equilibrium and that this uniqueness survives even as we make the noise vanishingly small. The idea of the uniqueness argument is that coordination failures require a high degree of coordination in expectations. If agents are uncertain about other agents' beliefs on the country's fundamental, they will take into account that some other agents may get a sufficiently positive signal that they will decide to not attack the currency irrespective of the behavior of others, or that they may get a sufficiently negative signal that they will decide to attack irrespective of the behavior of others. If this is not a situation they are contemplating, they may still contemplate the possibility that other agents may contemplate this situation, or the possibility that other agents are contemplating this possibility, and so forth. Once this uncertainty is made explicit into the model it is possible to prove uniqueness, using an argument based on iterated deletion of dominated strategies.[17]

For the purpose of deriving uniqueness results and of understanding their logic, it is useful to send the noise in private signals to zero. However, from the point of view of

---

[16] The econometrics of multiple equilibria is growing, but there are few applications to the case of currency crises. An exception is Jeanne (1997).

[17] See Proposition 2.1 in Morris and Shin (2001a).

applications, models with non–negligible amounts of private noise have nice properties. In particular, if we also enrich the information structure by letting all speculators observe a public signal $y = \theta + \eta$, we get a model in which, when y is in some range, the probability of a currency attack is in between zero and one, and is monotonically increasing in y. That is, we have a model in which there is a self-fulfilling element to a crisis, in the sense that a bad outcome is triggered by enough agents having pessimistic expectations, and, at the same time, there are tight predictions about the stochastic process generated by the model.[18]

The role of policy in the Morris and Shin (1998) game is fairly limited, as the central bank responds mechanically to the actions of the speculators. Things get more interesting on the policy front if we consider the possibility of policy intervening before speculators act—for example, by trying to defend the peg with domestic interest rate increases—and if we consider the possibility that the policy-maker has privileged access to information on the country's fundamentals (which include parameters in the policy-maker objective function). Then, the actions of the policy-maker can be interpreted in different ways by market participants, leading to very different outcomes. For example, a central bank may signal its determination to defend the peg by raising interest rates sharply, but the same intervention may also signal its desperation and thus accelerate an attack. The concern with how policy interventions will be interpreted by the markets is always present in policy discussions preceding crises. Angeletos et al. (2006) explore this question in a currency attack model similar to that used in Morris and Shin (1998). They show that the endogeneity of policy can undermine the uniqueness result and that multiple regimes are possible in which the same actions of the central bank can be interpreted in different ways. Moreover, they show that preventive policy interventions arise only when fundamentals are in an intermediate range, which means that, for example, if the policy-maker knows fundamentals are weak but not too weak, the signaling cost of intervening outweighs the benefit of the intervention itself. The paper also emphasizes that the market expectations about policy actions can impair the effectiveness of policy. This idea of "policy traps," may be useful to capture the difficulty facing emerging economies who, in the language of Qian et al. (2010), try to "graduate" from a pattern of recurrent crises.

Morris and Shin (2001a) notice that the presence of sufficiently informative public signals can undermine the uniqueness result. In market interactions, asset prices typically provide endogenous sources of public information. Therefore, an important question is whether the information in asset prices is sufficiently strong to generate multiplicity. Angeletos and Werning (2006) and Hellwig et al. (2006) address this question and, at the same time, provide useful tools to develop rational expectations equilibria with partially revealing prices in crisis settings.

---

[18] See Morris and Shin (2001b).

4. FINANCIAL FLOWS, SUDDEN STOPS, AND BALANCE SHEET EFFECTS

In the models seen so far, financial flows do not play a prominent role. Capital mobility of course places a constraint on the conduct of monetary policy and this is captured by the UIP condition. This means that there is an off-the-equilibrium-path threat of an unbounded capital flight if the domestic interest rate ever deviates from UIP. But since the UIP is satisfied in equilibrium, equilibrium capital flows do not play much of a role. In the one good economy of Section 2, capital flows are indeterminate, while in the two goods economy of Section 3 we made simplifying assumptions that implied a zero current account balance in all periods.

In this section, I turn to models where financial flows play a more direct role in the story. As more countries liberalized their capital accounts through the 1980s and 1990s, we have witnessed an increasing number of episodes of capital flow reversals. A country is running a persistent current account deficit, which may go to finance the government deficit or a consumption or investment boom in the private sector. At some point a domestic or external shock hits and the country loses the ability to raise external finance, leading to a sudden contraction in the current account deficit. The adjustment following these episodes typically involves a recession and a sharp exchange rate depreciation. If the country is pegging its currency, the peg is typically abandoned. This type of event has been dubbed a sudden stop by Dornbusch et al. (1995) and Calvo (1998). In this section, I discuss macroeconomic adjustment following a sudden stop, taking the event as purely exogenous. In the following sections, I will discuss possible reasons behind the stop and possible interpretations of the boom–bust dynamics leading to it.

The main stylized facts on sudden stop events were first documented in Reinhart and Calvo (2000) and Ferretti and Razin (2000). Mendoza (2010) offers a recent update looking at 33 episodes identified by Calvo et al. (2006): in the median episode, net exports to GDP go from −2% to a positive 1% in the year of the sudden stop, so the median current account reversal is about 3%, this is associated to a severe recession, with GDP going from 3% above trend to 4% below trend, consumption going from 4% above trend to 4% below trend, and investment going from about 12% above trend to about 20% below trend. Other regularities include a sharp depreciation of the real exchange, a sharp fall in the domestic stock market and in credit conditions (Calvo et al., 2004; Calvo et al, 2006).

Many pointers suggest that domestic fiscal conditions are not always the main culprit in these episodes and that a crisis may be purely triggered by a cutback in financial flows driven by external factors. First, there are episodes in which public debt clearly plays a minor role and in which most of the capital flows preceding the crisis were going to the private sector. For example, at the inception of the 1997 crisis, Korea's public debt hovered around only 10% of GDP. Second, there are "contagious" episodes, in which a generalized retreat of international investors from risky assets hits several countries unrelated by geography, trade, or institutions. An outstanding example is given by the events following the Russian August 1998 crisis, in which virtually all emerging markets suffered serious sudden stops and increases in country risk premia.

It is possible to interpret a sudden stop episode as driven purely by news about the growth prospect of the domestic economy. A standard permanent-income argument implies that a country facing a reduction in growth prospects will cut back on consumption. This adjustment can lead to a reversal in capital flows if the reduction in permanent income is larger than the reduction in current income. Standard business cycle models that focus on transitory deviations of income from a deterministic trend cannot generate this outcome. However, Aguiar and Gopinath (2007) show that enriching an open economy Real Business Cycle model with shocks to the growth rate of TFP can generate current account reversals and they offer a calibrated interpretation of Mexico's 1994 crisis along these lines. However, the bulk of the literature on sudden stops has put financial constraints at the center of the story, assuming that the domestic economy has imperfect access to international capital markets and that this access is restricted in a sudden stop episode (either for domestic or external reasons).[19]

It will be useful to explore a sudden stop in the context of a model in which external debt is denominated in foreign currency, since this opens the door to valuation effects that make the adjustment especially painful. The role of foreign-denominated debt was highlighted by several researchers following the Asian crisis of 1997–1998, in particular by Krugman (1998) and Aghion et al. (2000).

Consider the economy introduced in Section 3.1 and suppose the economy is coming from a period of current account deficits and has accumulated a stock of debt D, denominated in foreign currency. The initial net foreign asset position in domestic currency is thus $B_0 = -D$. Suppose the economy has reached a steady state at date 0—characterized by equations (13), (14), and (15)—and is keeping its foreign debt constant at D and paying interests on it each period. A shock hits which makes foreign investors concerned about the country's ability or willingness to repay in the future. Following this shock, foreign investors are willing only to finance a maximum stock of debt $\bar{D} < D$ in all future dates.[20] This implies that the country has to make a sharp correction in the current account, which needs to go from zero—since we start from a steady state with constant debt—to a temporary surplus in the adjustment period. After the adjustment period, the country goes back to a different steady state, in which it repays only the interest on $\bar{D}$. This tightening of the borrowing limit is a simple form of sudden stop.[21]

---

[19] Clearly, shocks to the country's growth prospects can be an important driver of the domestic country's access to external finance. In fact, Aguiar and Gopinath (2006) first introduced growth-rate shocks in the context of a model in which the country has imperfect access to domestic capital markets due to domestic default risk.

[20] The model does not explicitly allow for default, so here I am just giving an informal story for the capital flight. Models with default will be discussed in the next sections.

[21] Starting the economy in a steady state with zero current account is a convenient simplification. The results are similar if we use as a term of comparison not a steady state with zero current account but a period of current account deficit.

Since the country faces a binding financial constraint and has to make a large repayment in the first period, the Euler equation becomes an inequality and C is determined by the flow budget constraint

$$C = \frac{p_h Y - \Delta}{p_h^\omega}, \tag{36}$$

where $\Delta = D - \beta \bar{D}$ is the trade balance needed to reach the new debt level. Substituting for C in the goods market equilibrium condition (19) we then obtain

$$Y = \omega \frac{p_h Y - \Delta}{p_h} + \zeta p_h^{-\rho}. \tag{37}$$

4.1. Adjustment with Flexible Prices

Consider first the case in which prices are flexible. In this case, combining optimal price setting with labor market equilibrium we obtain a relation analogous to (14). After substituting (36) and rearranging yields the following relation between the relative price p_h and output,

$$p_h^{1-\omega+\sigma\omega} = \left(p_h Y - \Delta\right)^\sigma Y^\phi. \tag{38}$$

Under flexible prices the equilibrium values of Y and p_h are then found solving equations (37) and (38). Monetary policy can affect the nominal exchange rate, but has no effects on the real allocation and on relative prices. In particular, if the nominal exchange rate $\mathcal{E}_0$ is fixed, the price P_{h0} adjusts to ensure that (37) and (38) are satisfied. The flexible price benchmark provides useful insights about the problems facing a country that needs to quickly repay external debt denominated in foreign currency.

Leaving aside our dynamic setup for a moment, we can look at equations (37) and (38) as two standard demand and supply equations in a static Walrasian economy, except that the domestic consumer holds a "negative endowment" of the foreign good $-\Delta$. Then we can make the following observations:

- the demand of domestic consumers in (37) is increasing in p_h due to an income effect and to the foreign denomination of domestic debt: as the relative price of the domestic good increases it gets less costly to repay debt, boosting domestic demand;
- the demand of foreign consumers in (37) is decreasing in p_h due to a substitution effect, since the economy is small there are no income effects on foreign consumers;
- the supply of domestic goods in (38) may be increasing or decreasing in p_h depending on the relative strength of the income and substitution effect for domestic workers and the presence of Δ tends to reinforce the income effect.

Figure 12.2 illustrates a numerical example, comparing the equilibrium in the original steady state (which is given by the same equations with $\Delta = 0$) and after a sudden stop. Let us focus first on the non-monotone demand curve. A lower relative price of domestic goods means that the real burden of debt repayment is large. This impoverishes domestic

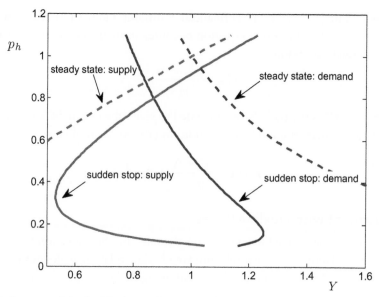

Figure 12.2 Output and the Real Exchange Rate in a Sudden Stop

consumers and depresses domestic demand. Due to the depreciated real exchange rate, higher foreign demand can make up for the drop in domestic demand. However, if foreign demand is not sufficiently elastic, it is possible that a large depreciation ends up having a stronger depressing effect on domestic demand—through the balance sheet channel— than the expansionary effect through the external channel. In the figure, for example, this happens for a real exchange rate lower than 0.2. The general point here is that balance sheet effects can make aggregate demand for domestic output relatively unresponsive to a domestic depreciation. This leads to a sharper contraction in output and to a sharper devaluation.

The mechanism at work here goes back to the so-called "transfer problem" of Keynes (1929): as the country needs to make a transfer to the rest of the world, the relative demand for domestic goods is depressed, making it harder for the country to repay. The problem is especially bad for a small open economy, as the transfer Δ received by foreign consumers has no expansionary effect on foreign spending on domestic goods, as only an infinitesimal fraction of foreign spending goes toward goods produced in the home economy.

The non-monotonicity of the demand curve implies that multiple equilibria are possible, as illustrated in the figure.[22] Here, I focus on the equilibrium with the higher

---

[22] In the figure we only see two equilibria, while in general equilibrium we are used to finding an odd number of equilibria (and to rule out unstable ones). The problem here is the presence of a region in which the price is so low that consumption would be negative. To resolve the issue we can assume that when the burden of debt repayment gets

exchange rate, but the presence of multiplicity emphasizes the power of the feedback effect at work. The general point is that if a country is forced to make a large payment in foreign goods in a short period of time, the general equilibrium effects on the real exchange rate can make the burden of repayment very costly.

Turning to the supply side, notice that the need to repay Δ shifts the supply curve to the right. In the example illustrated in Figure 12.2, this effect is not too strong and in equilibrium the demand shift dominates, leading to a reduction in equilibrium output. However, under different parameterizations it is possible to obtain the opposite result, leading to a sharp depreciation with a domestic boom in output. The observation that a sudden stop can generate a domestic output boom through income effects was recently made by Chari et al. (2005).[23]

Martin and Rey (2006) is a recent paper that emphasizes the role of the feedback between domestic demand and relative prices in a stochastic two–country, two–period model that focuses on investment and asset pricing. Domestic firms have to make an initial investment to produce domestic goods. If they choose to invest, domestic wealth is higher and demand for domestic goods is higher. Due to home bias in consumption, this generates strategic complementarity in investment decisions, which yields multiple equilibria, one with a positive amount of domestic investment and one with zero domestic investment. Interestingly, this multiplicity arises when financial markets are at an intermediate level of integration. If trading assets across borders is very costly, domestic savers have no option but to invest in domestic firms, which rules out a bad equilibrium with zero domestic investment. If trading assets across borders is very easy, domestic savers can perfectly diversify, breaking the link between the profits of domestic firms and the wealth of domestic consumers.[24]

4.2. A Monetary Policy Dilemma

Now let us go back to the model with nominal rigidities as in Section 3.2. To simplify things, suppose that all producers have pre-set prices at $t = 0$ (that is, $\alpha = 1$). Then, equation (38) drops from the system and the determination of output and the real exchange rate depends on monetary policy. In other words, by choosing the nominal interest rate, the central bank chooses a point on the demand curve (37).

Now we must distinguish what happens under different exchange rate regimes. If the exchange rate is fixed and the central bank decides to defend the peg, the real exchange rate remains at its steady state level of 1 and the drop in output can be read directly from the shift in the demand curve at $p_h = 1$ in Figure 12.2. In other words, we are

---

too large, the country renegotiates debt repayments to reach some minimum consumption level $\underline{C}$. This makes the demand curve downward sloping for low levels of p_h yielding a third equilibrium.

[23] In particular, if we assume $\sigma = 1$ and so have preferences consistent with balanced growth, the response of output is always positive.

[24] A paper that also exploits a home-bias feedback, to capture the possibility of inefficient diversification, albeit not in an explicit international context, is DeMarzo et al. (2005).

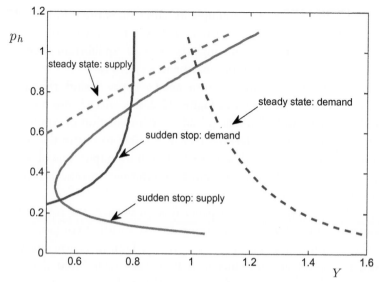

Figure 12.3 Output and the Real Exchange Rate in a Sudden Stop: The Case of a Contractionary Devaluation

in a situation in which, at the goods prices inherited from the past, the real exchange rate is overvalued relative to the level that would deliver the "natural" level of output. In other words, to sustain the peg the central bank has to be ready to accept a deep recession. Notice that this is a situation very much like the one analyzed in Section 3, where an overvalued exchange rate was taken as a primitive. Now we made some progress in explaining what can be the shock that puts a country in the position of suffering a currency attack. A sudden stop in capital flows can make the real exchange rate inherited from the past too high. If the central bank had committed to a peg, a sudden stop can make the commitment especially costly and create a situation in which a self-fulfilling shift in expectations may produce a currency crisis. This relation between sudden stops and currency crises was first emphasized in Calvo (1998). The empirical literature has noticed that not all current account reversals are associated to currency crises, but that the presence of a current account reversal increases the probability of a currency crisis (Hutchison and Noy, 2006). This discussion points out that the notion of an "overvalued" exchange rate shouldn't be an absolute notion based on some deviation from trend, but rather it should be based on the ability of a country to reach its potential output, given the capital flows it is able to attract at a given point in time.

Consider next what happens if we are in a flexible exchange rate regime or if we are in a fixed exchange rate regime and the central bank decides to abandon the peg. Now the central bank faces a potential dilemma. Letting the exchange rate depreciate can stimulate external demand, but, through the valuation channel, it can depress domestic demand even more. The non-monotonicity of the demand curve in Figure 12.2 captures this dilemma. In Figure 12.3, I show an example in which a devaluation would be counterproductive. Of course, in reality there is considerable uncertainty on the shape of the demand curve and on its slope at different levels of the domestic interest rate, making it hard to assess the potential benefits of a devaluation. The observation that valuation channels can generate non-monotone responses of domestic demand to the exchange rate was made by DeLong (2001) in the context of a standard IS-LM model.

4.3. Financial Frictions

In the model presented here I have emphasized a simple aggregate financial friction, modeling the domestic economy as a representative agent that faces an aggregate borrowing limit and using a model with no investment. In practice, domestic financial markets are at least partially segmented, and, in a crisis, a cutback in foreign lending may hit with different force different domestic agents. Moreover, loss of access to external financing for domestic firms and banks will also have depressing effects on investment spending. The role of segmented domestic financial markets has been explored in Caballero and Krishnamurthy (2001), who have emphasized how loss of access to foreign financing for some agents can lead to higher financing premia in domestic financial markets. The role of a tightening financial constraint on investment and the role of firms' balance sheets are analyzed in Aghion et al. (2004).

In the model presented, I have emphasized the idea that financing restrictions and balance sheet effects bite on the demand side. However, once we introduce the possibility that firms are financially constrained, it is possible that the availability of outside finance affects firms' ability to hire workers, either because hiring is a form of investment or through some working-capital constraint. Then a sudden stop can also lead to a depressed labor demand, and thus to a leftward shift of the supply curve. The model presented also abstracts from asset prices. Domestic asset prices can drop dramatically in a sudden stop and this drop can have real effects, through credit availability and collateral constraints. These additional ingredients have been explored in the large literature on the role of financial frictions in open economies. A partial list of papers that have developed small scale dynamic models to analyze sudden stops includes Mendoza (2002), Christiano et al. (2004), Cook and Devereux (2006), Cúrdia (2007), Gertler et al. (2007), Braggion et al. (2009), Mendoza (2010). These papers incorporate some version of a collateral constraint in the spirit of Kiyotaki and Moore (1997) and Bernanke et al. (1999), where the value of collateral responds to asset prices and to the real exchange rate. In some of these papers outside finance is required to pay wages, with a working-capital constraint of the type introduced in Neumeyer and Perri (2005). This type of constraint introduces the possibility of a contractionary supply side effect of a devaluation. Christiano et al. (2004) focus on the effects of monetary policy and show the possibility of a contractionary effect of lower nominal interest rates, where the contractionary effect is due to the associated real devaluation, as in the simple case illustrated in Figure 12.3.[25] Mendoza (2010) argues that the presence of endogenous asset prices plays an important role in the quantitative performance of this class of models. He also argues that for the sudden stop to have large effects it must hit an economy that has accumulated sufficient leverage, so that an asset price correction has an amplified effect on net worth. We return to these issues in Section 6.

5. SPREAD SPIRALS AND ROLLOVER CRISES

In this section, we explore some ways in which a country can lose access to international credit, focusing on the possibility that international investors get concerned about the country's ability to repay. This requires modeling explicitly the possibility of default. There is a huge literature that studies international borrowing with the possibility of default (see Chapter 11 by Aguiar and Amador in this handbook). Given that the focus of this chapter is crisis episodes, here I focus on the risk of default as a potential source of instability, focusing on two mechanisms that seem especially important in international debt crises.

The first mechanism focuses on the equilibrium determination of the sovereign spread, the difference between the interest rate at which a country can borrow and a benchmark risk-free world interest rate. If international investors lose confidence in a government's ability to repay its debt, they demand higher rates of return, to be compensated for the possibility of default. These higher rates of return imply that, for a given level of the primary deficit, the stock of debt accumulates faster. Over time, the stock of debt will then reach a level that triggers a default episode, thus validating the concerns of international investors. This narrative has been recently used in the context of the recent crisis in the euro area, to interpret the sudden increase in sovereign spreads on government debt issued by Italy and Spain in the Summer of 2011. The change did not seem triggered by any specific exogenous event and has been interpreted as the possible result of a self-fulfilling switch to pessimistic expectations in international capital markets. As in the case of instability and multiple equilibria associated to a real exchange rate overvaluation, the country's initial conditions—in particular, the initial stock of debt—are crucial for the possibility of a self-fulfilling crisis in sovereign spreads.

A related source of fragility/multiplicity, also relevant in sovereign debt crises, is the possibility of lack of coordination between creditors in a situation in which the government needs to roll over a sizable amount of debt. At some point, international investors may lose faith in the ability of a sovereign to successfully roll over its debt. This implies that the government may have trouble placing new bond issues in auctions or borrowing

---

[25] An important difference with the model developed here is that real exchange rate movements in their model, and in most of the papers discussed, are driven by the relative price of tradables vs non-tradables, rather than by the relative price of home vs foreign goods. This rules out the "transfer" problem channel emphasized above, given that, by definition, net trade of non-tradables with the rest of the world is zero.

from foreign banks. Given the lack of liquidity, the government may find the only way out in some form of default or restructuring. Therefore, the initial change of sentiment of the investors can be self-fulfilling.

In this section, I present a simple model that captures these two mechanisms—the feedback between spreads and debt-accumulation and coordination failures in debt rollovers. I will first show how both forms of fragility can arise. Then, I will show that assumptions about timing and about the size of the investors are crucial in determining the possibility of multiplicity.

5.1. A Model of Debt Dynamics and Default

The possibility of self-fulfilling crises due to some form of government's repudiation on its debt obligations goes back at least to Calvo (1988). The main model in Calvo (1988) considers the case in which debt is denominated in domestic currency and default is achieved via inflation, which reduces the real value of a given stock of nominal debt. Here I present a dynamic variant that focuses on outright default, based on Lorenzoni and Werning (2013). Early papers that focus on explicit default are Alesina et al. (1990) and Giavazzi and Pagano (1990). Unlike in most of the recent literature, I do not microfound the government's behavior and assume it follows an exogenous rule, so I can focus on the coordination problem among investors. A similar approach is taken in Ghosh et al. (2011). Time is infinite and discrete. A government starts at $t = 0$ with a stock D_0 of one-period bonds to repay. At the beginning of each period t the government stock of debt is D_t and the government runs a primary fiscal surplus S_t, which is used to repay debt. The difference between debt repayments D_t and the surplus S_t is covered by new issuances of one-period bonds, at the price Q_t. So the government's budget constraint, if default does not occur, is

$$Q_t D_{t+1} = D_t - S_t. \tag{39}$$

We assume that S_t is an exogenous i.i.d. random variable with c.d.f. F, and that the government's behavior is completely mechanical: as long as it can, the government rolls over its debt. Government debt is held by risk neutral investors that discount the future at rate β and, for simplicity, I assume investors receive nothing in the event of default. So the equilibrium bond price must satisfy the rational expectation condition

$$Q_t = \beta \Pr [\text{Repayment at time } t + 1].$$

We now look for equilibria in which default depends only on the current net financing need $N_t = D_t - S_t$. More precisely, we look for Markov equilibria in which N_t is the relevant state variable and the bond price satisfies these properties:

- when N_t exceeds some threshold $\overline{N} > 0$, the bond price Q_t jumps to zero, the government is unable to rollover its bonds, and we have default;
- when N_t is below some threshold $\underline{N}$, the probability of default is zero and the bond price Q_t is equal to the investors' discount factor β;

- when N_t is in the intermediate range $(\underline{N}, \overline{N})$, there is no default today but a positive probability of default in the next period and the bond price is $Q_t \in (0, \beta)$.

From the point of view of time t, the probability of default at $t + 1$ is $F(D_{t+1} - \overline{N})$, since the government will repay if $D_{t+1} - S_{t+1} \leq \overline{N}$. Combining rational expectations and the government budget constraint, we then have the condition

$$Q_t = \beta \left(1 - F \left(\frac{D_t - S_t}{Q_t} - \overline{N} \right) \right). \tag{40}$$

Depending on the distribution F and on the value of the financing need $D_t - S_t$, there can be multiple positive values of Q_t that solve this equation. This possibility is illustrated in Figure 12.4, for an example in which the distribution F is log-normal. The three curves correspond to the expression on the right-hand side of (40), for three different values of $D_t - S_t$. An equilibrium price corresponds to a value of Q_t for which these curves cross the 45° line.

Let us analyze now each of the three configurations in Figure 12.4. The topmost curve corresponds to a low value of $D_t - S_t$. In this case, the only positive Q_t that satisfies (40) is β. In this case, the country's financing needs are low enough that the investors expect the country to repay for sure in the next period. The bottom curve, on the other hand, corresponds to a value of $D_t - S_t$ high enough that the only positive Q_t that satisfies (40) is smaller than β. In this case, the country's financing needs are high enough that

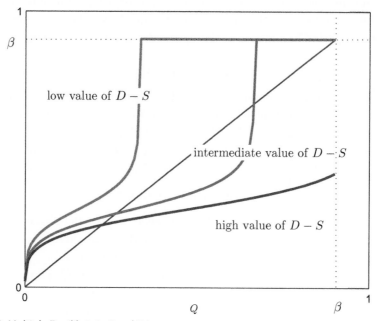

Figure 12.4 Multiple Equilibria in Bond Prices

the investors expect the country to default with positive probability in the next period. The most interesting case is the intermediate curve. In this case, there are two possible positive equilibrium values of Q_t, one smaller and one equal to β.[26] If international investors expect the country to repay for sure next period, they demand a low interest rate, i.e., they are willing to pay a high price for the bond. The country then accumulates debt more slowly (remember that debt next period is $(D_t - S_t)/Q_t$) and this implies that the country won't be forced into default next period for any realization of S_{t+1}. If instead international investors expect the country to default with some probability, they demand a high interest rate, i.e., they offer a low bond price. The country accumulates debt faster and so it enters the default region with positive probability next period.

The multiplicity illustrated in Figure 12.4 captures the feedback between cost of borrowing and debt accumulation. Notice that the dynamics of the model also capture well the cumulative nature of the process: if the bad equilibrium is played in one period, debt accumulates faster. So, in the following period, if default does not take place, the country is more likely to remain in the multiple equilibrium region. An important observation is that the initial stock of debt is crucial in determining whether a country can enter the multiplicity region in which market sentiment can set in motion a cumulative process leading to default.

The model also captures the second form of multiplicity discussed above, which here is captured by the possibility of switching to the "very bad" equilibrium with $Q_t = 0$. That equilibrium reflects a situation in which creditors coordinate on expecting instantaneous default and, indeed, default occurs. In the construction above, I assumed that this possibility only materializes when $D_t - S_t > \overline{N}$, but that was just a way of constructing a possible equilibrium. Notice also that the construction above leaves to some extent indeterminate the choice of the cutoff $\overline{N}$ itself.

Both forms of multiplicity stem from a coordination problem among lenders at time t. However, they differ in the nature of the problem. In the first case, miscoordination does not cause a liquidity crisis right away, but it leads the country to accumulate debt at a faster rate and, thus, to a higher probability of a future crisis. In the second case, miscoordination leads to an instantaneous lack of funding. In the first case, lenders are worried that the bidding behavior of other lenders in the bond market will make debt accumulate faster and thus increase the probability of default. In the second case, lenders are worried that the government will simply be unable to raise the needed funds today.

I have illustrated the logic of both types of multiplicity in the context of a standard model based on a mechanical use of the dynamic budget constraint (39). The advantage of this approach is that it is only a step away from so-called "debt sustainability" exercises, which are used in practice to evaluate the repayment prospects of governments and countries. The model here shows that once we endogenize bond prices and default

---

[26] There is a third equilibrium with $Q_t > 0$, which we can rule out based on a usual stability argument. The same argument can be used to rule out the equilibrium at $Q_t = 0$ which always exists as long as $D_t > S_t$.

events, the model can display multiple equilibria, making debt dynamics especially hard to forecast. A natural next step is to enrich the model by letting the fiscal surplus S_t respond to the debt stock and to the cost of borrowing. Lorenzoni and Werning (2013) follow this route and explore how different fiscal rules can help rule out bad equilibria. The following step is to fully endogenize both the decision to adjust S_t and the decision to default, by specifying an objective function for the government and solving for its optimal behavior. There is a large recent literature on sovereign debt that follows this approach and is reviewed extensively by Aguiar and Amador in Chapter 11 of this handbook. A subset of this literature explores the possibility of multiple equilibria. In particular, I will discuss Cole and Kehoe (2000) below.

5.2. Timing and Coordination Issues, Liquidity Crises

While the simple model just developed captures nicely our two sources of instability in debt accumulation, it is sensitive to the assumptions made on the timing of the game between the government and the investors. If we change a bit our assumptions the multiplicity identified in Figure 12.4 disappears. In the model above, we assumed that the investors have to bid for the bonds issued by the country *before* the country announces the amount of bonds it is issuing. That is, Q_t is determined before the government gets to choose D_{t+1}. An alternative timing assumption is that the government first announces the amount D_{t+1} it plans to issue (say in an auction) and then the investors bid for it, determining Q_t. This timing assumption has become the dominant approach in the recent literature on sovereign borrowing. This approach requires us to specify the equilibrium price schedule $Q_t(D_{t+1})$. When issuing debt D_{t+1} the government forms rational beliefs on the price that investors will bid for any potential value of D_{t+1}, and these beliefs are captured by $Q_t(D_{t+1})$. Let us go through our analysis again, with this alternative timing assumption.

Focusing attention on Markov equilibria and exploiting the i.i.d. assumption for S_t, we have a price schedule $Q(.)$ that is constant over time. Then we can derive the maximum amount of resources that can be raised by the government on the bond market solving[27]

$$\max_D Q(D)D.$$

Let $\overline{N}$ be the maximum of this problem. We can then find an equilibrium in which the borrower repays if $D_t - S_t \leq \overline{N}$, by choosing the smallest D_{t+1} that satisfies $Q(D_{t+1}) D_{t+1} = D_t - S_t$, and defaults if $D_t - S_t > \overline{N}$, because in that case, by construction, no amount of debt issued is sufficient to cover the government's current financing needs. The price of debt is then given by

$$Q\left(D_{t+1}\right) = \beta \Pr\left[D_{t+1} - S_{t+1} \leq \overline{N}\right], \tag{41}$$

---

[27] I am assuming for now that the function $Q(.)$ is continuous and that this problem is well defined, a conjecture that will be verified later.

and the value of $\overline{N}$ can be found solving the following fixed point problem:

$$\overline{N} = \max_{D} \beta \left(1 - F\left(D - \overline{N}\right)\right) D. \tag{42}$$

An envelope argument can be used to show that there is a unique fixed point and so there is a unique equilibrium of this type.[28] This means that the first type of multiplicity identified in the previous section disappears when we adopt the new timing and look for an equilibrium price schedule $Q(D)$. We'll return to the second type of multiplicity below.

The logic that rules out the first type of multiplicity is the following. If we are in a "bad" equilibrium in Figure 12.4, with a high interest rate, it means that the government is issuing a large amount of debt—in terms of face value—which the market is pricing at a low Q_t since it is expecting repayment with low probability. However, the presence of a "good" equilibrium means that the government can achieve the same amount of resources today by offering a lower face value tomorrow. Faced with this lower issuance the market will price the debt at a higher Q_t. So in case of multiplicity the government can always choose the equilibrium with the lower promised repayment and lower probability of default.

Which timing assumption is more plausible? On the face of it, one would favor the timing in which the government chooses D_{t+1} first, since it seems to capture better the way treasury auctions work in reality. However, this timing assumption hides an assumption of commitment. Suppose we are in a case where multiple equilibria are possible, under the timing assumption of Section 5.1. What happens if the government announces it is issuing the amount D_{t+1} corresponding to the good equilibrium and investors decide to bid the price that corresponds to the bad equilibrium? The government will not be able to raise enough resources to cover its current financing needs and plausibly will have to resort to an additional issuance. But then, as long as the markets insist on paying the bad equilibrium price, the total amount of bonds issued will eventually be the bad equilibrium level of D_{t+1}, thus validating the market's expectations. This argument is proposed and formally analyzed in Lorenzoni and Werning (2013). This discussion suggests that there are arguments in favor of both ways of modeling the game between the government and the investors and that the ability of the government to commit to a certain path of debt issuances, even in the short run, can have important consequences. Of course, matters get more complicated once, as it is natural, we extend the model to allow the government some leeway in the choice of the primary surplus. The take away from the analysis above is that if our objective is to study spread spirals it may be useful to

---

[28] The first-order condition for the maximization problem implies $f\left(D - \overline{N}\right) D = 1 - F\left(D - \overline{N}\right)$. The envelope theorem implies that the derivative of the expression on the right-hand side of (42) with respect to $\overline{N}$ is equal to $\beta f\left(D - \overline{N}\right) D$, which is then equal to $\beta\left(1 - F\left(D - \overline{N}\right)\right) < 1$ for any $\overline{N}$. Therefore, this function of $\overline{N}$ has a unique fixed point.

rethink the common approach of modeling the game by letting the government choose D_{t+1} before the market opens.[29]

Notice that the analysis above also rules out the second type of multiplicity and pins down a unique Markov equilibrium, with a unique level of $\overline{N}$. When we assume that there is a risk neutral international investor, we can interpret the model as featuring a certain number of risk neutral investors, each with a large endowment. With this interpretation, a single investor can buy all the debt issued by the government. Then the price of the bond issued is given by (41) and there is no coordination problem between lenders. However, it is easy to change the interpretation of the model and assume that there is a continuum of small investors, each with an endowment that is infinitesimal relative to the bonds issued by the borrowing country. With this interpretation, coordination problems are back, since the borrower can only successfully rollover if all lenders are willing to lend.

Cole and Kehoe (2000) is an example of a paper where the second type of coordination problem arises, while the first does not. Using the notation above, their approach is to assume that the government faces a bond schedule $Q(D_{t+1}, D_t, S_t, \omega_t)$ where ω_t is a sunspot variable drawn from a uniform distribution on $[0, 1]$. If $D_t - S_t \leq 0$ the sunspot has no effect, but when $D_t - S_t > 0$ and the sunspot is below some threshold $\hat{\omega}$ we have a coordination failure, $Q(D_{t+1}, D_t, S_t, \omega_t)$ is identically equal to zero for all values of D_{t+1} and the government is forced into default.

The fundamental ingredient of a debt panic is the presence of sufficiently strong strategic complementarity among the decisions of lenders to supply funding to the borrowers in a country. In particular, the decision of a large number of lenders not to provide funds must have the effect of reducing the expected return for a lender who decides to lend.

While many researchers agree that panic elements are present in some debt crises, the specific channels of complementarity are different in different models and the question is still open on which of these channels are most relevant in international crises. In the simple model above, the complementarity was generated by the default decision of the borrowing government. If enough lenders bid a zero price for the bonds issued today, the government is forced to default. An important assumption we made above is that once default occurs at date t, the government will not repay in future dates. However, there are other potential channels by which the refusal to rollover by a given creditor can lead to a loss for creditors that continue lending. Chang and Velasco (1999) use a modeling approach similar to the classic Diamond and Dybvig (1983) paper on bank runs. In that context, creditors that refuse to rollover short-term loans to banks located in the borrowing country trigger a liquidation of domestic assets. In this case it is the liquidation of domestic assets that lowers the payoffs of the creditors that continue lending to the country. Therefore, this class of models emphasizes complementarities that arise due to the real effects of a default event. A default event may be self-fulfilling because it

---

[29] Chamon (2007) is a recent paper that explores how different auction protocols can eliminate multiple equilibria.

harms capital accumulation and growth in the home country, thus reducing the country's ability to pay in the future. The financial sector is clearly the place where the potential for liquidity crises is higher, due to the nature of banks' liabilities. We will return to this topic in Section 6.1.

6. SOURCES OF FRAGILITY

Summing up different remarks made in previous sections, currency crises and current account reversals are typically preceded by one or more different symptoms of fragility: budget deficits, current account deficits, an overvalued real exchange rate, large stocks of public or private debt, especially if short-term and foreign-currency denominated. These symptoms are not unrelated, as, for example, current account deficits driven by a capital inflow can be the underlying cause of the overvaluation. A vast empirical literature has explored the role of these variables in forecasting financial crises (e.g., Eichengreen et al., 1995). But while these symptoms capture well the proximate causes of a crisis, a harder question is what are the underlying sources of fragility. In this section, I discuss different ways of approaching this question.

6.1. Boom-Bust Cycles and Banking

A narrative that goes back at least to Diaz-Alejandro (1985) is that of a country that opens up its capital markets and starts borrowing from abroad. The inflow of foreign funds contributes to fuel a domestic credit boom and an expansion in domestic demand. This leads both to the accumulation of debtor positions and to an appreciation of the exchange rate. This sets the stage for a potential reversal of capital flows, with the consequences discussed in Section 4. Recent papers that document the dynamics of credit booms and busts in developed and emerging economies are Gourinchas et al. (2001) and Mendoza and Terrones (2008).

In the classic intertemporal approach to the current account, a simple way to interpret a boom-bust episode is to imagine that when the country opens up its capital markets, this is associated to optimistic growth expectations as the country can increase domestic investment by borrowing abroad. So the country's borrowing in the boom phase is justified by the anticipation of higher domestic income in the future. The bust can then be interpreted as a negative shock, that disappoints the ex ante optimistic growth expectations. This is the interpretation that, for example, Blanchard and Giavazzi (2002) and Blanchard (2007) hold of the experience of Portugal after entering the euro area.

However, when one develops this idea in the context of models with reasonable degrees of risk aversion, it is hard to replicate observed crises, because domestic borrowers in the model prefer to accumulate precautionary assets to be protected in the event of a crisis. Models with occasionally binding financial constraints can partly address this issue. Mendoza (2010) shows a model that can generate severe crises, which occur with non-negligible frequency, and are typically preceded by a credit-financed expansion. The crucial state variable in the model is the leverage of the domestic economy, that is the ratio of domestic capital to external debt. A sequence of good shocks leads the economy to finance domestic investment with foreign borrowing, leading to high leverage. However, when leverage is high the economy becomes very sensitive to negative shocks, because of a binding financial constraint. This is why a boom can be followed by a severe crisis, generating a boom-bust cycle. The further development of non-linear models that capture these dynamics is certainly a promising area for future research.

While the standard intertemporal approach emphasizes net borrowing and lending positions that arise out of differences in growth profiles, the current account literature has recently shifted toward paying more attention to gross financial flows. That is, to the combination of debt, equity, and direct investments that are driven by the portfolio choice of a set of domestic and foreign actors. The current account is then the flow variable that results from the simultaneous adjustment of these gross positions.[30] Two recent papers that document the patterns of gross flows that generate net flows along the business cycle and during crises are Forbes and Warnock (2012) and Broner et al. (2013a). The latter paper, in particular, shows that a reduction in net flows during a crisis is associated to a reduction in foreign holdings of domestic assets and, more surprisingly, to a reduction in domestic holdings of foreign assets. A possible interpretation of this finding is that during crises domestic assets are reallocated from foreign to domestic agents, and domestic agents liquidate their foreign positions to finance this reallocation. This interpretation leads to favor models in which during a crisis the foreign demand for domestic assets contracts more dramatically than the domestic demand.[31]

Another recent literature has emphasized the importance of disaggregating the domestic economy and looking separately at the foreign exposures of financial firms. The idea is that financial institutions hold much more leveraged positions, compared to the whole country. So looking at the balance sheet of these agents is important to understand the dramatic reversals of financial flows associated to leveraging and de-leveraging. Many recent episodes, in which financial turbulence has been transmitted from country to country, point to the important role of gross flows and banking. For example, the transmission of the 2007 crisis from the U.S. to Germany traveled through the gross positions taken by German banks in the U.S. market for mortgage backed securities. In the years preceding the crisis, German banks had financed these investments by borrowing dollars short-term. So German banks were at the same time increasing their foreign assets and their foreign liabilities. These changes in gross positions were not associated to an overall increase in the net debtor position of Germany vs the U.S. In fact, Germany was running a current account surplus in the years before the crisis. However, the gross positions made

---

[30] See Obstfeld (2012) for an overall evaluation of the relation between gross financial flows and the current account.

[31] A different but related interpretation is offered in Bianchi et al. (2013), who focus on the different role of long-maturity government debt and foreign reserve accumulation for liquidity purposes.

the German banking system vulnerable to a crash in the MBS market in the U.S. Acharya and Schnabl (2010) provide a detailed analysis of this mechanism. Bruno and Shin (2012) is a recent paper that models banks' leverage as a source of transmission of financial crises across countries and documents the importance of cross-country exposures.

Understanding better the role of financial intermediaries seems important also to understand the sources of financial contagion and the transmission of shocks across countries. Pavlova and Rigobon (2008) solve a three countries portfolio model, with two periphery countries—representing emerging markets—and a center country—representing an international banking center. They then introduce portfolio constraints and show how they can lead to a stronger transmission of shocks across countries. A novel feature of their approach is that they distinguish home goods and foreign goods and allow for home bias in consumption. This implies that shocks to the wealth distribution can be amplified through the response of relative prices, through a "transfer" mechanism similar to that discussed Section 4. Combining portfolio choice in multi-good, multi-country models, will most likely continue to be a challenging and open line of research. Recognizing the presence of constraints and limits to arbitrage in international capital markets can also contribute to our understanding of the choice of short-term borrowing for emerging economies. Broner et al. (2013b) show that the risk premia on long-term lending increase dramatically in periods of financial turbulence. This increased risk premia are not a reflection of higher probabilities of default at longer horizons, but instead capture a decrease in the willingness of international investors to absorb the higher price risk of long-term bonds.

It is important to remark that while gross positions are crucial to evaluate the fragility of a given configuration of financial flows, net flows are still important for their macroeconomic implications. For example, if banks in a given country accumulate financial exposures to some other country, but the net result is not a current account deficit, the country will not experience a real appreciation and will be less at risk of a currency crisis of the type discussed in Section 3. A recent example of the fact that current account deficits still contain important information is in Shambaugh (2012), who shows that current account deficits in the years before the crisis are very effective at predicting the severity of the sovereign debt crisis across European countries (measured by sovereign spreads during the crisis).

The interest toward international banking has also grown due to the special nature of banks' liabilities and the fact that they may be subject to panics. We already touched on the subject of liquidity crises in Section 5.2. There is a vast banking literature that capture mechanisms that are important for the transmission of international crises across borders. Allen and Gale (2000) show how contagion can take place when banks hold claims on each other and withdrawals in some region can trigger a chain of withdrawals across banks. Recent work on the sensitivity of debt capacity to asset values with short-term debt financing by Acharya et al. (2011) and on the dynamics of debt panics by

He and Xiong (2009) can provide useful lessons to understand rollover crises in international debt markets. Liquidity considerations are also important in understanding the effects of increased financial integration. Traditional models of risk-sharing emphasize the idea that increased integration leads to diversification and reduced volatility, as in Obstfeld (1994b). Castiglionesi et al. (2010) develop a model with assets of different liquidity and show that increased financial integration can lead to lower liquidity ratios and deeper crises.

Finally, the recent euro-zone crisis has fueled a growing interest in the interplay between sovereign risk and banking stability. Research following the 1997 Asian crisis by Corsetti et al. (1999) and Burnside et al. (2006) did emphasize one side of the interaction between the banks' and the government's budget constraints. Trouble in the banking sector can result in severe fiscal costs, when the government intervenes to bail out financial institutions. Recent research points attention to the reverse channel. Fiscal trouble and the risk of sovereign default can hurt the banking sector if domestic banks are overly exposed to domestic government debt. Basu (2010) and Gennaioli et al. (2012) argue that the distress caused to the banking sector by a sovereign default can be an important channel making defaults more costly. Gennaioli et al. (2012) show that in a panel of countries, larger holdings of domestic government bonds by domestic banks are indeed associated to larger declines in credit in the event of a default and to less frequent defaults.

6.2. Fragility and Moral Hazard

As noticed above, some forms of borrowing make a country especially exposed to a crisis. In particular, debt financing makes domestic firms' obligations less sensitive to domestic conditions relative to equity financing, short-term borrowing increases the probability of debt runs, and foreign-currency-denominated debt opens the possibility of a feedback between the exchange rate and domestic borrowers' balance sheets. An important open question is why private and public borrowers choose these forms of borrowing. More generally, one can ask why borrowers do not try to make their future repayments state contingent, so as to reduce the debt burden following negative aggregate shocks. If we endogenize the choice of loans in the type of models presented so far, the domestic borrowers would prefer long-term, domestic-currency-denominated debt, and, if possible, they would prefer to use equity financing or some form of state-contingent debt.

The literature has explored this question in different ways. First, a group of papers have emphasized the idea that exposure to international crises can be useful from an ex ante point of view. The idea is that the possibility of a crisis acts as a discipline device that helps induce the country's government to implement some costly reform effort or not to be tempted by the opportunity to expropriate foreign investors. Other papers have looked at the problem from a different perspective, looking at the accumulation of fragile debt as an inefficient outcome that is the result of various forms of externalities. Let me start by looking at two models that capture the first idea of *ex ante efficient crises*. In the next two subsections, I will look at models that explore the idea of externalities causing *ex ante inefficient crises*.

Consider a two-period model of a country that is receiving an exogenous income stream y_1 in the first period and a random income stream y_2 in the second period. In particular, let y_2 be a discrete random variable with probability distribution $\pi(y_2)$. Suppose the government is benevolent and maximizes the utility of a representative consumer with utility function:

$$u(c_1) + E[u(c_2)]. \tag{43}$$

The country faces risk neutral international investors with zero discount factor and can issue fully state-contingent bonds, that is, it can issue claims that promise repayment contingent on the realization of y_2. The country has the option to default, in which case it loses a fraction θ of its output, so we have the limited enforcement constraint

$$c_2 \geq (1 - \theta) y_2. \tag{44}$$

We then can set up the problem of the domestic government as maximizing (43) subject to the limited enforcement constraint (44) and the budget constraint

$$c_1 + E[c_1] \leq y_1 + E[y_2]. \tag{45}$$

The optimality condition takes the form

$$\pi(y_2) u'(c_2(y_2)) + v(y_2) = \lambda \pi(y_2),$$

where λ is the Lagrange multiplier on the budget constraint and $v(y_2)$ is the Lagrange multiplier on the limited enforcement constraint. It is possible to show that the optimal contract involves a constant c_2 for y_2 below some cutoff $\hat{y}_2$ and $c_2 = (1 - \theta)y_2$ for y_2 above the cutoff $\hat{y}_2$.

This simple model shows in a nutshell why it is hard to generate crisis episodes in models with fully state-contingent borrowing and default. If in equilibrium the country is borrowing in period 1, then it must be the case that $E[c_2] < E[y_2]$, so that c_2 must be lower than y_2 in some state of the world. However, given the optimal shape of $c_2(y_2)$, this means that the country will tend to repay more in *good states* of the world. In other words, this model cannot be used to deliver a situation in which the country is hit by a bad shock—i.e., a low realization of y_2—and experiences larger than usual capital outflows—i.e., a larger value of $y_2 - c_2$.

The observation above was the motivation behind the seminal paper by Atkeson (1991).[32] The solution offered by Atkeson (1991) is to introduce a form of moral hazard.

---

[32] Atkeson (1991) is also a seminal paper in developing recursive-contract methods to analyze dynamic models of international borrowing. Here, I use a simple two-period version to focus on its interpretation of crises.

Suppose that the country can use the funds received in period 1 for two purposes: to consume or to invest. Investment k affects the country's ability to produce output in the second period and, for simplicity, can only take two values $\underline{k}$ and $\bar{k}$, with $\underline{k} < \bar{k}$. The probability distribution of second-period output is now given by $\pi\left(y_2|k\right)$. The crucial assumption is that investment is unobservable. That is, the foreign country observes the difference between the endowment y_1 and total domestic spending $c_1 + k$, but does not observe the composition of domestic spending. Then, in order to induce the country to choose $k = \bar{k}$ the country consumption profile has to satisfy the incentive compatibility constraint

$$u\left(c_1\right) + E\left[u\left(c_2\right)|\bar{k}\right] \geq u\left(c_1 + \bar{k} - \underline{k}\right) + E\left[u\left(c_2\right)|\underline{k}\right]. \tag{46}$$

Suppose now that it is part of an optimal plan to implement the high investment level $\bar{k}$, then the optimal consumption profile can be derived choosing c_1, $c_2(y_2)$ that maximize expected utility of the borrowing country subject to the limited enforcement constraint (44), the incentive compatibility constraint (46), and the budget constraint

$$c_1 + \bar{k} + E\left[c_1|\bar{k}\right] \leq y_1 + E\left[y_2|\bar{k}\right].$$

The first-order condition for $c_2(y_2)$ can be rearranged to yield, for the states in which the limited enforcement constraint is not binding,

$$\frac{u'\left(c_2\left(y_2\right)\right) - \lambda}{u'\left(c_2\left(y_2\right)\right)} = \mu\left[1 - \frac{\pi\left(y_2|\underline{k}\right)}{\pi\left(y_2|\bar{k}\right)}\right],$$

where μ is the Lagrange multiplier on the incentive compatibility constraint. A standard result in the moral-hazard literature is that a monotone likelihood ratio $\pi\left(y_2|\bar{k}\right)/\pi\left(y_2|\underline{k}\right)$ implies that the consumption profile $c_2(y_2)$ is increasing. It is then possible to construct examples in which this effect is so strong (i.e., the signal y_2 is so informative about the unobservable "effort" level k) that the difference $c_2(y_2) - y_2$ is also increasing. In such examples, a bad realization of the endowment y_2 is associated to a reduction in capital inflows.

These type of examples show that it may be optimal for a country to expose itself to capital flow reversals that hurt exactly when things get worse. The idea is that this exposure is efficient from an ex ante perspective, because it induces the country to make the best use of the resources it's receiving from international investors. The model here is very stylized, but it may be used to capture not just the effects of capital accumulation but also the effects of various market-oriented reforms which may be costly in the short run but increase the country growth prospects in the future. The idea is that international financial crises are a useful discipline device that punishes countries exactly when they are sending negative signals.

The model here takes the point of view of a benevolent domestic social planner who can directly control the state-contingent financial flows between the country and the rest of the world. Let me now look at a model that contains a similar message, but that makes an explicit distinction between private financing decisions and policy choices made by the government. This extension is important because of the role that private capital flows play in many actual crisis episodes. The model is a simplified version of Tirole (2003).

The model is a two-period model and features three groups of agents: domestic entrepreneurs, domestic investors, and foreign investors. They are all risk neutral and only consume in the second period. Entrepreneurs hold some initial wealth A and choose how much to invest I in a risky project. The amount $I - A$ they raise from domestic and foreign investors, in exchange for promises of repayment in period 2. The project payoff is $R^S I$ in the event of success and $R^F I$ in the event of failure. However, there is an upper bound on how much entrepreneurs can promise to repay. This upper bound is $r^S I$ in the event of success, with $r^S < R^S$, and $r^F I$ in the event of failure, with $r^F = R^F < r^S$.[33] The probability of success is p and is taken as given by entrepreneurs and investors. For simplicity, assume success is perfectly correlated across entrepreneurs. Finally, there is a domestic government, whose objective is to maximize the sum of the utilities of domestic entrepreneurs and domestic investors. The government can increase the probability of success p of all the domestic entrepreneurial projects, through reform efforts or other forms of public investment. The social cost associated to the probability p is given by the increasing, convex function $\gamma(p)$. An important timing assumption is that the government choice of p happens after financial contracts have been written and the investment I has taken place, and that the government cannot commit.

A financial contract is given by an investment level I and two levels of promise repayments: D^S, in the event of success, and D^F, in the event of failure. We assume that entrepreneurs make a take-it-or-leave-it offer to investors. Then, given that domestic and foreign investors are risk neutral, the optimal contract optimal between lenders and entrepreneur comes from the solution of the maximization problem:

$$\max_{I,D} \quad p\left(R^S I - D^S\right) + \left(1 - p\right)\left(R^F I - D^F\right)$$
$$s.t. \quad D^j \le r^j I, \quad \text{for } j = S, F$$
$$pD^S + \left(1 - p\right)D^F + A = I.$$

Assuming $pR^S + (1-p)R^F > 1$ and $pr^S + (1-p)r^F < 1$ the problem is well defined and the solution is to choose maximum leverage, setting investment equal to

$$I = \frac{1}{1 - pr^S - \left(1 - p\right)r^F} A. \tag{47}$$

Suppose the optimal contract is implemented by issuing two types of securities: safe debt claims that repay $R^F I$ and equity claims that repay $\left(r^S - R^F\right)I$ only in the event of

---

[33] See Tirole (2005) for microfoundations of this type of pledgeability constraint.

success. Since domestic and foreign investors are both risk neutral, how these securities are allocated is, to some extent, indeterminate. Assume that domestic investors have a limited endowment $\bar{I}_d$ in period 1. Then, as long as $\bar{I}_d < I$, the domestic entrepreneurs must sell securities valued $I - \bar{I}_d$ to foreign investors. Using α^D and α^E to denote the fraction of debt and equity claims sold to foreigners, any pair α^D, α^E is fine as long as

$$I - \bar{I}_d = \alpha^D R^F I + \alpha^E p \left(r^S - R^F \right) I. \tag{48}$$

The sum of the expected payoffs of domestic entrepreneurs and domestic investors is then given by the total payoff of the investment projects minus the payments made to foreign investors:

$$p \left[\left(R^S - R^F \right) - \alpha^E \left(r^S - R^F \right) \right] I + \left(1 - \alpha^D \right) R^F I.$$

The government payoff is given by the last expression minus the cost of reform $\gamma(p)I$. This implies that the government's best response is given by the first-order condition

$$\left(R^S - R^F \right) - \alpha^E \left(r^S - R^F \right) = \gamma'(p). \tag{49}$$

An equilibrium of the model is then given by four values I, p, α^D, α^E that satisfy the three equations (47)–(49). Since there are only three equations, the model admits equilibria for α^E in some interval. From equation (49) we see that equilibria with lower values of α^E correspond to higher values of p. It is easy to show that higher values of p are Pareto superior, since in equilibrium there is, in general, under-provision of reform effort. Notice that equilibria with lower values of α^E display more financial fragility, in the sense that they display more volatile domestic consumption. In other words, international financial flows provide less insurance against the "failure" shock hitting the domestic economy.

The conclusions we want to draw from the model are: (1) that there are many equilibria associated with different levels of fragility; (2) the equilibria which display more fragility are Pareto superior. The paper thus questions the wisdom of policy proposals oriented at reducing fragility, by noticing that it is this very fragility which provides incentives for reform. The presence of indeterminacy in the model is not crucial for the argument, but it helps present it in a stark form, because it implies that adding a small incentive in favor of equity or debt financing in international capital markets can tilt the economy toward very different equilibria, and that the optimal policy in this case is to subsidize debt financing.

While here I have exposed models that focus on abstract state-contingent contracts, it is clear that the logic of these models extends to specific forms of fragility. For example, Missale and Blanchard (1994) and Jeanne (2000) focus on the discipline benefits of short-term borrowing using a similar logic.

Both the Atkeson (1991) model and the Tirole (2005) model emphasize the ex ante efficiency properties of crises from a normative point of view. When applying these models as positive models, one is faced with delicate issues of decentralization and implementation. Since crises are aggregate events, their incentive benefits must show up for some agent who internalizes the effects of his actions on the probability of a crisis. Tirole (2005) emphasizes the distinction between the large agent in the model (the government) who can affect the probability p and the small agents who take it as given and yet determine the structure of the country's liabilities. The decentralized nature of the financing decisions imply that in equilibrium there is too little fragility and too little crises. Therefore, to employ these models as positive models of why crises occur, one needs to spell out what kind of policies are present to induce private agents, who have an incentive to protect themselves against crises, to take less protection so as to give the right reform incentives to the central government.[34]

6.3. Bailouts and Policy-Induced Externalities

We now take a different view and look at a country's exposure to international crises not as the efficient response to an incentive problem but as a symptom of inefficiency not internalized by private contracts.

A first source of inefficiency may come from policy. In particular, after the East Asian crisis of 1997, a number of observers have pointed out the close ties between banks and political power in the countries affected and noticed that bailout expectations can lead to asset overvaluation and excessive borrowing (McKinnon and Pill, 1996; Krugman, 1998). If a bank is borrowing money abroad to finance investment, say, in domestic real estate, the bank (and its foreign creditor) will be less concerned about downside risks if they expect the government to step in. This will lead both to excess borrowing and to capital misallocation, as investment is distorted in favor of risky projects that benefit more from the bailout option. Another channel of misallocation arises in general equilibrium as financial institutions with bailout guarantees will bid up asset prices discouraging investment by other firms.

Schneider and Tornell (2004) show that the combination of bailout guarantees and binding financing constraints in the event of a crisis can lead to an inefficient boom-bust episode. An important observation they make is that the presence of *systemic* bailout guarantees tends to lead to taking correlated risks. If the government is expected to step in and bailout financial firms only if a sufficient fraction of them is in trouble, then in

---

[34] In the Atkeson (1991) model one could interpret the investment decision k as the aggregate of private investment decisions of a large number of agents. However, if one goes that route and one models k as affecting the pdf of the endowment at date 2 agent by agent, the issue is not easily resolved. In that kind of model, it is typically optimal to do relative performance evaluation and not punish or reward the individual in response to aggregate shocks. So country-level crises would be perfectly insured.

equilibrium firms will tend to be exposed to correlated risk as each single firm prefers to face trouble when other firms do, so as to receive assistance. Schneider and Tornell (2004) use this idea to explain the preference for foreign-currency-denominated debt, since the burden of this debt increases precisely at times of economy-wide trouble. Farhi and Tirole (2012) further develop this idea in a model in which bailout policies are endogenous and welfare maximizing, thus emphasizing the fact that these distortions do not need to arise from "crony capitalism" but can also arise with a benevolent policy-maker that cannot commit.

6.4. Pecuniary and Aggregate Demand Externalities

I will now go back to the simple model introduced in Section 3.1 and use it to discuss two other forms of externality that can produce excess fragility. Consider a time prior to $t = 0$, say time $t = -1$, in which the country is running a current account deficit and suppose the current account deficit is driven by private sector borrowing. At that time, the decisions of individual borrowers are determining the level of debt D that will have to be repaid at $t = 0$. Domestic borrowers may be accumulating debt for consumption-smoothing reasons, as they expect future productivity growth, or because they are facing high expected returns to investment and are borrowing to finance an investment boom. For our purposes here, all that matters is that the accumulation of debt D is the result of optimal borrowing decisions of domestic private borrowers. The question is, will private borrowers choose a socially efficient level of D, from an ex ante point of view? Or is the domestic credit boom inefficient?

Consider first the flexible price environment discussed in Section 4.1. To simplify the analysis, I slightly modify the model, assuming that the domestic good is sold on a competitive market, so I can abstract from the distortion due to monopolistic competition. If we replace the assumptions of monopolistic competition and $\psi \varepsilon / (\varepsilon - 1) = 1$ with the assumptions of competitive markets and $\psi = 1$, the equilibrium conditions (37) and (38) still characterize the equilibrium and the rest of the analysis is unchanged, except that the level of output is socially efficient in equilibrium.

Consider now a private borrower who is considering a marginal increase in borrowing at $t = -1$. The private marginal cost of increasing D is

$$\frac{\mathcal{E}}{P} C^{-\sigma},$$

because, by promising to repay a unit of foreign currency at date 0, the consumer is foregoing $\mathcal{E}/P$ units of consumption and $C^{-\sigma}$ is his/her marginal utility of consumption. However increasing D also affects the equilibrium real exchange rate p_h, as we saw in

Figure 12.2, so if *all* domestic borrowers increase D the total effect on their welfare is[35]

$$\frac{\mathcal{E}}{P} C^{-\sigma} \left[1 + (Y - C_h) \frac{dp_h}{dD} \right], \tag{50}$$

where dp_h/dD denotes the equilibrium response of the real exchange rate to the debt level D. The second term in square brackets is present because when the relative price of the domestic good increases, domestic consumers benefit as they are net sellers of the domestic good on the world market, and their utility gain is proportional to their net sales of domestic goods $Y - C_h$.

The presence of the additional term in expression (50) captures a pecuniary externality by which increasing borrowing ex ante makes domestic consumers worse off ex post, given that $dp_h/dD < 0$. The presence of this pecuniary externality is not sufficient, per se, to make the equilibrium ex ante Pareto inefficient. While domestic consumers are losing ex post due to the real depreciation, foreign consumers are gaining as they are buying domestic goods at a lower price. But the pecuniary externality does lead to an inefficiency result if we embed this analysis in a stochastic model, in which the sudden stop event occurs at date 0 with probability smaller than one and in which borrowing is not state contingent. In that model, due to incomplete markets, the marginal utilities of the domestic consumer and of the foreign consumer are not equalized across states of the world, and, in particular, the domestic marginal utility is relatively higher in the sudden stop event. In a model with these features, an ex ante coordinated reduction in D, together with an ex ante transfer from domestic consumers to foreign consumers can make everyone better off. This observation goes back to the result of inefficiency of competitive equilibria with incomplete markets of Geanakoplos and Polemarchakis (1986). In this case, the credit boom preceding the sudden stop event is constrained inefficient, and policies aimed at curbing borrowing at $t = -1$ may be welfare improving.

In the context of international financial crises, welfare-reducing pecuniary externalities have been explored in a number of recent papers, that have emphasized different channels by which borrowing ex ante can lead to adverse relative price changes ex post. Bianchi (2011) and Korinek (2011) explore the real exchange rate channel, along the lines

---

[35] To derive this expression notice that the indirect utility of the domestic consumer at date 0, under perfect competition, is

$$V(D, p_h) = \max_{C, C_h, C_f, N} \left\{ \left(\frac{C^{1-\sigma}}{1-\sigma} - \psi \frac{N^{1+\phi}}{1+\phi} \right), \text{ s.t. } C = \xi C_h^\omega C_f^{1-\omega}, p_h C_h + C_f = p_h Y + \beta \bar{D} - D \right\}.$$

Letting λ denote the Lagrange multiplier on the budget constraint and using the envelope theorem and the first-order condition with respect to C_h, we have

$$\frac{\partial V}{\partial p_h} = \lambda (Y - C_h) = \frac{1}{p_h} C^{-\sigma} \omega \frac{C}{C_h} (Y - C_h) = \frac{\mathcal{E}}{P} C^{-\sigma} (Y - C_h).$$

The last equality follows from $P_h C_h = \omega P C$ and $p_h = P_h / \mathcal{E}$.

of the model presented here. The main difference is that real exchange rate movements in their model are driven by changes in the relative price of tradables vs non-tradables. Since net trade of non-tradables is zero, by definition, the pecuniary externality in (50) is thus absent in their model. However, a different pecuniary externality arises because the relative price of non-tradables appears in the financial constraint faced by domestic agents.[36] Caballero and Krishnamurthy (2001, 2003) study pecuniary externalities associated to the determination of the spread charged on domestic financial markets, in models in which financial markets are segmented and only some domestic firms have access to foreign borrowing. In their model, firms with international collateral help to keep domestic interest rate low in the domestic credit market in the event of a crisis. A pecuniary externality arises because the benefit of low interest rates accrues partly to firms with no access to foreign lending. So firms with access do not fully internalize the social benefit of holding international collateral and hold too little of it in equilibrium. Caballero and Lorenzoni (2007) explore a pecuniary externality that works through the dynamics of the export sector. Domestic exporters are hurt by an exchange rate appreciation in the boom phase of a boom-bust cycle in foreign borrowing, and this can lead to a slow recovery in the bust phase, with depressed real wages. Reducing borrowing ex ante may be beneficial for the consumers as it props up real wages in bust. Jeanne and Korinek (2010) focus on the effect of excessive borrowing on asset prices.[37]

A different form of externality arises when we introduce nominal rigidities. Going back to our small open economy of Section 3.1, consider what happens when prices are sticky. In particular, consider the case in which no firm can adjust its price in $t = 0$, as in Section 4.2. Now the model implications differ depending on the response of monetary policy after the shock. Suppose we are in a fixed exchange rate regime and the central bank is keeping the nominal exchange rate fixed at $\mathcal{E} = 1$. In period $t = 0$, home good prices are pre-set at their steady state level $\bar{P}_h = p_h^*$.[38] From equation (37) we then get output in period 0,

$$Y = \frac{\zeta \left(p_h^* \right)^{-\rho} - \omega \Delta / p_h^*}{1 - \omega}.$$

As we did in the flexible price case, consider the marginal effect of increasing D (and thus Δ). The effect on output is

$$\frac{dY}{d\Delta} = -\frac{\omega / p_h^*}{1 - \omega} < 0,$$

---

[36] This goes back to the general observation that in models with optimal contracting, pecuniary externalities arise when relative prices appear in some incentive constraint. See Arnott et al. (1994).

[37] This links the international literature to a growing literature on over-borrowing and asset price volatility in financial markets and in closed economies, e.g., Gromb and Vayanos (2002), Lorenzoni (2008), Bianchi and Mendoza (2011), Jeanne and Korinek (2013).

[38] In the initial steady state discussed in Section 4, p_h^* is not equal to 1, because in steady state the country is making the interest payment $(1 - \beta) D$ each period.

and the effect on consumption, from (36), is

$$\frac{dC}{d\Delta} = \left(p_h^*\right)^{-\omega}\left(p_h^*\frac{dY}{d\Delta} - 1\right) < 0. \tag{51}$$

When individual borrowers choose D optimally they only internalize the second term in parenthesis in (51). The remaining effects on C and Y capture an aggregate demand externality. As consumers are more indebted, they need to cut back on consumption. Since monetary policy cannot respond, under a fixed exchange rate, the reduction in consumption leads to a reduction in output. As consumers are against their borrowing constraints, the reduction in domestic output further depresses domestic consumption through a standard Keynesian multiplier effect. The welfare effect of this aggregate demand externality is

$$\left[\left(p_h^*\right)^{1-\omega} C^{-\sigma} - \psi N^{\phi}\right]\frac{dY}{d\Delta} < 0.$$

This inequality follows because the term in square brackets is positive. This follows from two considerations: first, there is a monopolistic distortion which is present also in the steady state (see equation (14)); second, C and N are below their steady state value in a sudden stop with a fixed exchange rate.

Notice that the relative price of domestic goods remains unchanged. So if we model the foreign lenders as having linear intertemporal preferences, we can construct simple non-stochastic examples in which foreign lenders' welfare is unaffected by changes in D, so that the aggregate demand externality leads immediately to Pareto inefficient over-borrowing ex ante. Recent papers that have introduced this notion of aggregate demand externality are Farhi and Werning (2012) and Schmitt-Grohe and Uribe (2012). The magnitude of the effects found in these studies suggest that aggregate demand externalities will be an active area of research in coming years.

In the example above, the presence of aggregate demand externalities is due to inefficient monetary policy ex post. If monetary policy was not constrained by the fixed exchange rate regime, it could replicate a flexible price equilibrium in which the only remaining externality is the pecuniary externality discussed above. Clearly, given that externality, replicating the flexible price equilibrium may not be the optimal policy. This brings us to a broader question: if the government has access to instruments that mitigate the effects of a crisis ex post, how should they optimally be combined with ex ante preventive policies? This is an open research question and the answer surely depends on the power of the ex post tools available and on the potential problems associated to time consistency. For example, Benigno et al. (2013) show that in a model similar to Bianchi (2011), if the government has sufficient tools to prevent a sharp real depreciation ex post, then the welfare benefit of ex ante interventions is smaller.

7. CONCLUDING REMARKS

This paper has surveyed a number of mechanisms that can be at work during episodes of capital flights and currency crises. To conclude, let me go over some of the open questions that have been identified as potential areas of future research. On the interaction between fiscal and monetary policy discussed in Section 2, the recent crisis in the euro zone has pointed to a number of open questions: What kind of fiscal commitment is needed to sustain an exchange rate peg? If a country is part of a monetary union, what kind of fiscal integration is needed to stave off speculative capital flights driven by the expectation of default of a single country? Much work also remains to be done on how the expectation of a devaluation can lead to a capital flight, forcing the central bank to tighten domestic policy and thus to a domestic recession, a mechanism explored in Section 3. The mechanism seems to be at work also in flexible exchange rate regimes, as long as the central bank tries to dampen the effects of swings in expectations on the current exchange rate. These swings in expectations seem to be a major reason why monetary authorities are concerned about a pure floating regime. Where do these swings in expectations come from? How should we update our models of the currency market to capture this form of financial volatility and its real consequences?

The model of capital flows used in Section 4 to explore the effects of capital flights was in the tradition of the intertemporal approach to the current account, in which capital flows are simply the outcome of net lending or borrowing by the country as a whole. As mentioned in Section 6, there is a growing interest toward models of gross flows, that disintiguish different asset classes and different groups of agents inside each country to reach implications about the financial flows at the macro level from the aggregation of portfolio adjustments by each group. In particular, models that explicitly account for financial intermediation and for the cross-border activities of banks are likely to play an important role for our understanding of capital account crises.

REFERENCES

Acharya, V., Schnabl, P., 2010. Do global banks spread global imbalances? Asset-backed commercial paper during the financial crisis of 2007–09. IMF Economic Review 58 (1), 37–73.

Acharya, V., Gale, D., Yorulmazer, T., 2011. Rollover risk and market freezes. Journal of Finance 66 (4), 1177–1209.

Aghion, P., Bacchetta, P., Banerjee, A., 2000. A simple model of monetary policy and currency crises. European Economic Review 44 (4), 728–738.

Aghion, P., Bacchetta, P., Banerjee, A., 2004. A corporate balance-sheet approach to currency crises. Journal of Economic Theory 119 (1), 6–30.

Aguiar, M., Gopinath, G., 2006. Defaultable debt, interest rates and the current account. Journal of International Economics 69, 64–83.

Aguiar, M., Gopinath, G., 2007. Emerging market business cycles: the cycle is the trend. Journal of Political Economy 115 (1).

Aguiar, M., Amador, M., Farhi, E., Gopinath, G., 2012. Crisis and Commitment: Inflation Credibility and the Vulnerability to Sovereign Debt Crises. Discussion Paper, Mimeo.

Alesina, A., Prati, A., Tabellini, G., 1990. Public confidence and debt management: a model and a case study of Italy. In: Dornbush, R., Draghi, M., (Eds.), Public Debt Management: Theory and History. Cambridge University Press, p. 94.

Allen, F., Gale, D., 2000. Financial contagion. Journal of Political Economy 108 (1), 1–33.

Angeletos, G., Werning, I., 2006. Crises and prices: information aggregation, multiplicity, and volatility. American Economic Review 96 (5), 1720–1736.

Angeletos, G., Hellwig, C., Pavan, A., 2006. Signaling in a global game: coordination and policy traps. Journal of Political Economy 114 (3), 452–484.

Arnott, R., Greenwald, B., Stiglitz, J., 1994. Information and economic efficiency. Information Economics and Policy 6 (1), 77–82.

Atkeson, A., 1991. International lending with moral hazard and risk of repudiation. Econometrica 59 (4), 1069–1089.

Basu, S.S., 2010. Sovereign Debt and Domestic Economic Fragility. Mimeo, MIT.

Benigno, G., Chen, H., Otrok, C., Rebucci, A., Young E., 2013. Financial crises and macro-prudential policies. Journal of International Economics 89 (2), 453–470.

Bernanke, B., Gertler, M., Gilchrist, S., 1999. The financial accelerator in a quantitative business cycle framework. In: Taylor, J.B., Woodford, M., Handbook of Macroeconomics, vol. 1. Elsevier, pp. 1341–1393.

Bianchi, J., 2011. Overborrowing and systemic externalities in the business cycle. American Economic Review 101 (7), 3400–3426.

Bianchi, J., Mendoza, E., 2011. Overborrowing, Financial Crises and Macro-Prudential Policy? Discussion Paper, International Monetary Fund Washington, DC.

Bianchi, J., Hatchondo, J., Martinez, L., 2013. International Reserves and Rollover Risk. IMF Working Paper 13/33.

Blanchard, O.J., 2007. Adjustment within the euro. The difficult case of Portugal. Portuguese Economic Journal 6 (1), 1–21.

Blanchard, O.J., Giavazzi, F., 2002. Current account deficits in the euro area. The end of the Feldstein-Horioka puzzle? Brooking Papers on Economic Activity 2, 147–209.

Braggion, F., Christiano, L., Roldos, J., 2009. Optimal monetary policy in a 'sudden stop'. Journal of Monetary Economics 56 (4), 582–595.

Broner, F., 2008. Discrete devaluations and multiple equilibria in a first generation model of currency crises. Journal of Monetary Economics 55, 592–605.

Broner, F., Didier, T., Erce, A., Schmukler, S.L., 2013a. Gross capital flows: dynamics and crises. Journal of Monetary Economics 60, 113–133.

Broner, F., Lorenzoni, G., Schmukler, S., 2013b. Why do emerging economies borrow short term? Journal of the European Economic Association 11, 67–100.

Bruno, V., Shin, H.S., 2012. Capital Flows, Cross-Border Banking and Global Liquidity. Mimeo, Princeton University.

Buiter, W.H., Rahbar, E., 2012. Target2 Redux. CEPR Discussion Paper 9211.

Burnside, C., Eichenbaum, M., Rebelo, S., 2006. Government finance in the wake of currency crises. Journal of Monetary Economics 53 (3), 401–440.

Caballero, R., Krishnamurthy, A., 2001. International and domestic collateral constraints in a model of emerging market crises. Journal of monetary Economics 48 (3), 513–548.

Caballero, R., Krishnamurthy, A., 2003. Excessive dollar debt: financial development and underinsurance. Journal of Finance 58 (2), 867–894.

Caballero, R.J., Lorenzoni, G., 2007. Persistent Appreciations and Overshooting: A Normative Analysis. Discussion Paper, NBER Working Papers.

Calvo, G., 1988. Servicing the public debt: the role of expectations. American Economic Review 78 (4), 647–661.

Calvo, G.A., 1998. Capital flows and capital market crises: the simple analytics of sudden stops. Journal of Applied Economics 1, 35–54.

Calvo, G.A., Végh, C.A., 1999. Inflation stabilization and BOP crises in developing countries. In: Taylor, J.B., Woodford, M. (Eds.), Handbook of Macroeconomics, vol. 1. Elsevier, pp. 1531–1614 (Chapter 24).

Calvo, G., Izquierdo, A., Mejia, L., 2004. On the Empirics of Sudden Stops: The Relevance of Balance-Sheet Effects. Discussion Paper, National Bureau of Economic Research.

Calvo, G., Izquierdo, A., Talvi, E., 2006. Phoenix Miracles in Emerging Markets: Recovering Without Credit from Systemic Financial Crises. Discussion Paper, National Bureau of Economic Research.

Carlsson, H., Van Damme, E., 1993. Global games and equilibrium selection. Econometrica: Journal of the Econometric Society 61 (5), 989–1018.

Castiglionesi, F., Feriozzi, F., Lorenzoni, G., 2010. Financial Integration and Liquidity Crises. Mineo, Tilburg University.

Chamon, M., 2007. Can debt crises be self-fulfilling? Journal of Development Economics 82 (1), 234–244.

Chang, R., Velasco, A., 1999. Liquidity crises in emerging markets: theoy and policy. In: Bernanke, B., Rotemberg, J. (Eds.), NBER Macroeconomics Annual 1999, MIT Press, pp. 11–58.

Chari, V., Kehoe, P., McGrattan, E., 2005. Sudden stops and output drops. American Economic Review 95 (2), 381–387.

Christiano, L., Gust, C., Roldos, J., 2004. Monetary policy in a financial crisis. Journal of Economic Theory 119 (1), 64–103.

Cole, H., Kehoe, T., 2000. Self-fulfilling debt crises. Review of Economic Studies 67 (1), 91–116.

Cole, H., Obstfeld, M., 1991. Commodity trade and international risk sharing: how much do financial markets matter? Journal of Monetary Economics 28 (1), 3–24.

Cook, D., Devereux, M., 2006. Accounting for the East Asian crisis: a quantitative model of capital outflows in small open economies. Journal of Money, Credit, and Banking 38 (3), 721–749.

Corsetti, G., Pesenti, P., 2001. Welfare and macroeconomic interdependence. Quarterly Journal of Economics 116 (2), 421–445.

Corsetti, G., Pesenti, P., Roubini, N., 1999. Paper tigers? A model of the Asian crisis. European Economic Review 43 (7), 1211–1236.

Cúrdia, V., 2007. Optimal Monetary Policy Under Sudden Stops. FRB of New York Staff, Report No. 278.

DeLong, J.B., 2001. International Financial Crises in the 1990s: The Analytics. Mimeo, Berkeley.

DeMarzo, P., Kaniel, R., Kremer, I., 2005. Diversification as a public good: community effects in portfolio choice. The Journal of Finance 59 (4), 1677–1716.

Diamond, D., Dybvig, P., 1983. Bank runs, deposit insurance, and liquidity. The Journal of Political Economy 91 (3), 401–419.

Diaz-Alejandro, C., 1985. Good-bye financial repression, hello financial crash. Journal of Development Economics 19 (1–2), 1–24.

Dornbusch, R., Goldfajn, I., Valdés, R.O., 1995. Currency crises and collapses. Brookings Papers on Economic Activity 2, 219–293.

Eichengreen, B., Rose, A., Wyplosz, 1995. Exchange market mayhem: the antecedents and aftermath of speculative attacks. Economic Policy 21, 249–312.

Farhi, E., Tirole, J., 2012. Collective moral hazard, maturity mismatch and systemic bailouts. American Economic Review 102, 60–93.

Farhi, E., Werning, I., 2012. Fiscal Unions. Mimeo, Harvard.

Ferretti, G., Razin, A., 2000. Current account reversals and currency crises, empirical regularities. In: Krugman, P. (Ed.), Currency Crises. University of Chicago Press, pp. 295–323.

Flood, R.P., Garber, P.M., 1984. Collapsing exchange-rate regimes: some linear examples. Journal of International Economics 17 (1–2), 1–13.

Forbes, K.J., Warnock, F.E., 2012. Capital flow waves: surges, stops, flight, and retrenchment. Journal of International Economics 88 (2), 235–251.

Galí, J., Monacelli, T., 2005. Monetary policy and exchange rate volatility in a small open economy. Review of Economic Studies 72 (3), 707–734.

Garber, P., 1999. The target mechanism: will it propagate or stifle a stage III crisis? In: Carnegie-Rochester Conference Series on Public Policy, vol. 51. Elsevier, pp. 195–220.

Geanakoplos, J., Polemarchakis, H., 1986. Existence, regularity and constrained suboptimality of competitive allocations when the asset market is incomplete. Uncertainty, Information and Communication: Essays in Honor of KJ Arrow 3, 65–96.

Gennaioli, N., Martin, A., Rossi, S., 2012. Sovereign Default, Domestic Banks, and Financial Institutions. Mimeo, CREI.

Gertler, M., Gilchrist, S., Natalucci, F., 2007. External constraints on monetary policy and the financial accelerator. Journal of Money, Credit and Banking 39 (2–3), 295–330.

Ghosh, A., Kim, J., Mendoza, E., Ostry, J., Qureshi, M., 2011. Fiscal Fatigue, Fiscal Space and Debt Sustainability in Advanced Economies. Discussion Paper, National Bureau of Economic Research.

Giavazzi, F., Pagano, M., 1990. Confidence crises and public debt management. In: Dornbush, R., Draghi, M. (Eds.), Public Debt Management: Theory and History. Cambridge University Press.

Gourinchas, P., Valdés, R., Landerretche, O., 2001. Lending booms: Latin America and the world. Economía 1 (2), 47–89.

Gromb, D., Vayanos, D., 2002. Equilibrium and welfare in markets with financially constrained arbitrageurs. Journal of Financial Economics 66 (2), 361–407.

He, Z., Xiong, W., 2009. Dynamic Debt Runs. Discussion Paper, National Bureau of Economic Research.

Hellwig, C., Mukherji, A., Tsyvinski, A., 2006. Self-fulfilling currency crises: the role of interest rates. American Economic Review 96 (5), 1769–1787.

Hutchison, M., Noy, I., 2006. Sudden stops and the Mexican wave: currency crises, capital flow reversals and output loss in emerging markets. Journal of Development Economics 79 (1), 225–248.

Jeanne, O., 1997. Are currency crises self-fulfilling? A test. Journal of International Economics 43 (3–4), 263–286.

Jeanne, O., 2000. Foreign currency debt and the global financial architecture. European Economic Review 44 (4), 719–727.

Jeanne, O., 2011. Capital Account Policies and the Real Exchange Rate. Mimeo, Johns Hopkins University.

Jeanne, O., Korinek, A., 2010. Excessive volatility in capital flows: a Pigouvian taxation approach. American Economic Review 100 (2), 403–407.

Jeanne, O., Korinek, A., 2013. Macroprudential Regulation versus Mopping Up After the Crash. Discussion Paper 18675, NBER.

Kaminsky, G.L., Reinhart, C.M., 1999. The twin crises: the causes of banking and balance-of-payments problems. American Economic Review 89 (3), 473–500.

Keynes, J., 1929. The German transfer problem. Economic Journal 39 (153), 1–7.

Kiyotaki, N., Moore, J., 1997. Credit cycles. Journal of Political Economy 105 (2), 211–248.

Korinek, A., 2011. Excessive Dollar Borrowing in Emerging Markets: Balance Sheet Effects and Macroeconomic Externalities. Mimeo, Maryland.

Krugman, P., 1979. A model of balance-of-payments crises. Journal of Money, Credit and Banking 11 (3), 311–325.

Krugman, P., 1996. Are currency crises self-fulfilling? In: Bernanke, B., Rotembers, J. (Eds.), NBER Macroeconomics Annual 1996, vol. 11. MIT Press, pp. 345–407.

Krugman, P., 1998. What Happened to Asia. Mimeo, MIT.

Lorenzoni, G., 2008. Inefficient credit booms. The Review of Economic Studies 75 (3), 809–833.

Lorenzoni, G., Werning, I., 2013. Slow Moving Debt Crises. Mimeo.

Martin, P., Rey, H., 2006. Globalization and emerging markets: with or without crash? American Economic Review 96 (5), 1631–1651.

McKinnon, R., Pill, H., 1996. Credible liberalizations and international capital flows: the overborrowing syndrome. In: Ito, T., Krueger, A. (Eds.), Financial Deregulation and Integration in East Asia. University of Chicago Press, pp. 7–50.

Mendoza, E., 2002. Credit, prices, and crashes: business cycles with a sudden stop. In: Preventing Currency Crises in Emerging Markets. University of Chicago Press, pp. 335–392.

Mendoza, E., 2010. Sudden stops, financial crises, and leverage. American Economic Review 100 (5), 1941–1966.

Mendoza, E., Terrones, M., 2008. An Anatomy of Credit Booms: Evidence from Macro Aggregates and Micro Data. NBER Working Paper Series 14049.

Missale, A., Blanchard, O., 1994. The debt burden and debt maturity. American Economic Review 84 (1), 309–319.

Morris, S., Shin, H., 1998. Unique equilibrium in a model of self-fulfilling currency attacks. American Economic Review 88 (3), 587–597.

Morris, S., Shin, H., 2001a. Global Games: Theory and Applications. Discussion Paper.

Morris, S., Shin, H., 2001b. Rethinking multiple equilibria in macroeconomic modeling. In: NBER Macroeconomics Annual 2000, vol. 15. MIT Press, pp. 139–182.

Neumeyer, P., Perri, F., 2005. Business cycles in emerging economies: the role of interest rates. Journal of Monetary Economics 52 (2), 345–380.

Obstfeld, M., 1986. Rational and self-fulfilling balance-of-payments crises. American Economic Review 76 (1), 72–81.

Obstfeld, M., 1994a. The Logic of Currency Crises. NBER Working Paper 4640.

Obstfeld, M., 1994b. Risk-taking, global diversification, and growth. American Economic Review 84 (5), 1310–1329.

Obstfeld, M., 2012. Does the Current Account Still Matter? National Bureau of Economic Research Inc., Discussion Paper.

Obstfeld, M., Rogoff, K., 1995. Exchange rate dynamics redux. Journal of Political Economy 103 (3), 624–660.

Pavlova, A., Rigobon, R., 2008. The role of portfolio constraints in the international propagation of shocks. Review of Economic Studies 75 (4), 1215–1256.

Qian, R., Reinhart, C., Rogoff, K., 2010. On Graduation from Default, Inflation and Banking Crisis: Elusive or Illusion? Discussion Paper, National Bureau of Economic Research.

Radelet, S., Sachs, J., 1998. The East Asian financial crisis: diagnosis, remedies, prospects. Brookings Papers on Economic Activity 1998 (1), 1–90.

Radelet, S., Sachs, J., 2000. The onset of the East Asian financial crisis. In: Currency Crises. University of Chicago Press, pp. 105–162.

Rebelo, S., Végh, C., 2008. When is it optimal to abandon a fixed exchange rate? 1. Review of Economic Studies 75 (3), 929–955.

Reinhart, C., Calvo, G., 2000. When capital inflows come to a sudden stop: consequences and policy options. In: Kenen, P.B., Swoboda, A.K. (Eds.), Reforming the International Monetary and Financial System. International Monetary Fund, Washington, DC, pp. 175–201.

Sargent, T., Wallace, N., 1981. Some unpleasant monetarist arithmetic. Federal Reserve Bank of Minneapolis Quarterly Review 5 (3), 1–17.

Schmitt-Grohe, S., Uribe, M., 2012. Prudential Policy for Peggers. Discussion Paper, Mimeo, Columbia.

Schneider, M., Tornell, A., 2004. Balance sheet effects, bailout guarantees and financial crises. Review of Economic Studies 71 (3), 883–913.

Shambaugh, J., 2012. The euro's three crises. Brookings Papers on Economic Activity 44 (1), 157–231.

Tirole, J., 2003. Inefficient foreign borrowing: a dual- and common-agency perspective. American Economic Review 93 (5), 1678–1702.

Tirole, J., 2005. The Theory of Corporate Finance. Princeton University Press.

Uribe, M., 2006. A fiscal theory of Sovereign risk. Journal of Monetary Economics 53 (8), 1857–1875.

CPI Antony Rowe
Eastbourne, UK
September 15, 2022